ARTIFICIAL INTELLIGENCE, MEDICAL ENGINEERING AND EDUCATION

Advances in Transdisciplinary Engineering

Transdisciplinary engineering is the exchange of knowledge about product, process, organization, or social environment in the context of innovation. The ATDE book series aims to explore the evolution of engineering, and promote transdisciplinary practices, in which the exchange of different types of knowledge from a diverse range of disciplines is fundamental. The series focuses on international collaboration and providing high-level contributions to the internationally available literature on the theme of the conference.

Volume 48

Recently published in this series

ISSN 2352-751X (print)
ISSN 2352-7528 (online)

Artificial Intelligence, Medical Engineering and Education

Proceedings of the 7th International Conference (AIMEE 2023),
Guangzhou, China, 9–10 November 2023

Edited by

Zhengbing Hu

National Technical University of Ukraine "Igor Sikorsky Kyiv Polytechnic Institute", Kyiv, Ukraine

Qingying Zhang

Wuhan University of Technology, Wuhan, China

Matthew He

Nova Southeastern University, Fort Lauderdale, USA

and

Felix Yanovsky

Delft University of Technology, Delft, The Netherlands

IOS Press

Amsterdam • Berlin • Washington, DC

ISBN 978-1-64368-490-1 (print)
ISBN 978-1-64368-491-8 (online)
Library of Congress Control Number: 2024931373
doi: 10.3233/ATDE48

Publisher
IOS Press BV
Nieuwe Hemweg 6B
1013 BG Amsterdam
Netherlands
e-mail: order@iospress.nl

For book sales in the USA and Canada:
IOS Press, Inc.
6751 Tepper Drive
Clifton, VA 20124
USA
Tel.: +1 703 830 6300
Fax: +1 703 830 2300
sales@iospress.com

Preface

The 7th International Conference of Artificial Intelligence, Medical Engineering, Education (AIMEE2023) was held in Guangzhou, China on November 9–10, 2023. This conference was jointly organized by Wuhan University of Technology, Hubei University of Technology, the International Center of Informatics and Computer Science, and the International Research Association of Modern Education and Computer Science.

This volume encompasses three sections: 1) Artificial Intelligence and Scientific Methodology; 2) Systems Engineering and Analysis: Concepts, Methods, and Applications; 3) Education Reform and Innovation. A total of 238 submissions were received by AIMEE2023, with 89 papers selected for presentation and publication after a rigorous international peer-review process. These papers put forth novel concepts and methodologies that may pave the way for further research across diverse populations.

We hope this volume will contribute to the rapid evolution of artificial intelligence and its applications by facilitating collaboration and knowledge sharing among the growing interdisciplinary workforce in this exciting field. We extend our gratitude to all those who helped make this conference a success. We thank our keynote speakers (Prof. IEEE Fellow, Felix Yanovsky, Delft University of Technology, Delft, Netherlands; Prof. Harrison Hao Yang, Distinguished Teaching Professor, State University of New York at Oswego, USA) for sharing their invaluable insights and setting the stage for thought-provoking discussions. We are grateful to the program committee members for their diligent efforts in reviewing submissions and assembling an outstanding technical program. We also thank all the authors for contributing their innovative research results, as well as the attendees for joining us and making the conference a vibrant forum for learning and connecting.

Finally, our sincere appreciation goes to the publisher, IOS Press, for preparing and publishing this volume.

Conference Chairs
Prof. Felix Yanovsky, Delft University of Technology, Delft, Netherlands
Prof. Z.W. Ye, Hubei University of Technology, China
November 2023

About the Conference

Peer Review Statement
Papers submitted: 238
Papers accepted: 89

Conference Chairs
Prof. Felix Yanovsky, Delft University of Technology, Delft, The Netherlands
Prof. Z.W. Ye, Hubei University of Technology, China

General Co-Chairs
Prof. Q.Y. Zhang, Wuhan University of Technology, China
Prof. Matthew He, Nova Southeastern University, Fort Lauderdale, USA
Prof. Yuriy Ushenko, Chernivtsi National University, Chernivtsi, Ukraine

Program Committee Members
Prof. Anatoliy Sachenko, Kazimierz Pułaski University of Technology and Humanities
   in Radom, Poland
Prof. G. Liu, Hubei University, China
Prof. Sergiy Gnatyuk, National Aviation University, Ukraine
Prof. H.F. Yang, Waseda University, Shinjuku City, Japan
Ph.D. G. Darvas, Institute Symmetrion, Hungary
Prof. X. Jiang, East China Normal University, China
Dr. Q.L. Zhou, Shizuoka University, Japan
Prof. Y. Gu, Wuhan University of Technology, China
Dr. Harrison Hao Yang, State University of New York at Oswego, USA
Prof. M. Wang, Wuhan Technology and Business University, China
Dr. L.J. Du, Wuhan University of Technology, China
Dr. Oleksii K. Tyshchenko, University of Ostrava, Czech Republic
Dr. W.H. Yue, Henan University of Technology, China
Dr. Rabah Shboul, Al-albayt University, Jordan
Prof. M.Y. Zhang, Wuhan University of Technology, China
Prof. E. Fimmel, Mannheim University of Applied Sciences, Germany
Prof. L. Cao, Wuhan Technology and Business University, China
Prof. S.S. Ge, National University of Singapore, Singapore
Prof. X.J. Wei, Wuhan Technology and Business University, China
Prof. M. He, Nova Southeastern University, Fort Lauderdale, USA
Prof. H.J. Xu, Xinjiang University, Urumqi, China
Dr. X.J. Ma, Huazhong University of Science and Technology, China
Prof. Y.C. Zhang, Business School of Hubei University, China
Dr. Essa Alghannam, Tishreen University, Syria
Prof. Z. Wei, South China Normal University, China
Prof. Roman Kochan, University of Bielsko-Biała, Bielsko-Biala, Poland
Prof. H.B. Xie, Fujian Normal University, China
Prof. A.U. Igamberdiev, Memorial University of Newfoundland, Canada

Prof. Z.W. Ye, Hubei University of Technology, China
Prof. W.H. Peng, Central China Normal University, China
Prof. J.S. Dai, National University of Singapore, Singapore
Prof. S.C. Qu, Central China Normal University, China
Prof. Q. Z. Qiu, Wuhan University of Technology, China
Dr. P.L. Simeonov, Institute of Pathology, Berlin, Germany
Dr. C. Chen, Wuhan Business University, China
Dr. Solomiia Fedushko, Lviv Polytechnic National University, Lviv, Ukraine
Prof. D.W. Zhang, Guangdong University of Petrochemical Technology, China
Prof. Vitaly Deibuk, Chernivtsi National University, Chernivtsi, Ukraine
Dr. Feng Liu, Huazhong Agricultural University, China
Prof. Sergey Petoukhov, MERI RAS, Moscow, Russia

Steering Chairs
Prof. M. Wang, Wuhan Technology and Business University, China
Dr. J. Su, Hubei University of Technology, China

Local Organizing Committee Members
Ms. Z.R. Hu, President of Guangdong Sanshe Human Capital Management Co., Ltd.,
    China
Prof. Z.P. Liu, Wuhan University of Technology, China
Prof. Y. Wang, Wuhan Technology and Business University, China
Prof. H.L. Zhong, South China University of Technology, China
Prof. G.E. Zhang, Nanning University, China
Prof. W.J. Xiong, Wuhan Business University, China
Prof. X.J. Zhou, Wuhan Textile University, China
Prof. G.B. Gao, Yangzhou University, China
Prof. H.M. Gao, Tianjin Agricultural University, China

Scientific Secretary
Dr. Y. Gu, Wuhan University of Technology, Wuhan, China
Dr. C. Chen, Wuhan Business University, China
Prof. V.E. Mukhin, National Technical University of Ukraine "Igor Sikorsky Kyiv
    Polytechnic Institute", Kyiv, Ukraine

Contents

**Part 2. Systems Engineering and Analysis: Concepts, Methods, and
Applications**

Part 3. Education Reform and Innovation

Part 1

Artificial Intelligence and Scientific Methodology

Part I

Artificial Intelligence and Scientific Methodology

Artificial Intelligence, Medical Engineering and Education
Z.B. Hu et al. (Eds.)
© *2024 The Authors.*
This article is published online with Open Access by IOS Press and distributed under the terms
of the Creative Commons Attribution Non-Commercial License 4.0 (CC BY-NC 4.0).
doi:10.3233/ATDE231310

Neural Networks for Environmental Monitoring: A Web Application for Image Recognition

Nataliya BERNATSKA[a], Elvira DZHUMELIA[b], Iryna TYPILO[a], Orest KOCHAN[c d][1], Ivan SALAMON[e]

[a] *Department of Physical, Analytical and General Chemistry, Institute of Chemistry and Chemical Technologies, Lviv Polytechnic National University, Lviv, 79000, Ukraine*
[b] *Software Department, Institute of Computer Science and Information Technologies, Lviv Polytechnic National University, Lviv, 79000, Ukraine*
[c] *Department of Information-Measuring Technologies, Institute of Computer Technologies, Automation and Metrology, Lviv Polytechnic National University, Lviv, 79000, Ukraine*
[d] *School of Computer Science, Hubei University of Technology, Wuhan 430068, China*
[e] *Department of Ecology, Faculty of Humanities and Natural Sciences, University of Presov, Presov, 080 01, Slovakia*

ORCiD ID: Nataliya BERNATSKA https://orcid.org/0000-0002-6062-1971
Elvira DZHUMELIA https://orcid.org/0000-0003-3146-8725
Orest KOCHAN https://orcid.org/0000-0002-3164-3821
Ivan SALAMON https://orcid.org/0000-0001-5379-3989

Abstract. Environmental monitoring is increasingly reliant on image recognition through neural networks, automating the identification and classification of environmental threats. This automation optimizes resource allocation, enhances monitoring accuracy, and empowers researchers to address climate-related challenges. In response to this, we present a web application built using React.js and TensorFlow.js, which enables real-time image recognition. This application facilitates tasks ranging from climate analysis to disaster response and wildlife conservation, offering valuable insights into environmental trends. Moreover, it engages the public, promotes awareness, and contributes to conservation efforts, making it a versatile and cost-effective tool for environmental monitoring. The application leverages advancements in image recognition technology, availability of datasets, open-source frameworks, and cloud computing infrastructure. It supports a wide range of applications, promotes global collaboration, and ensures data security. While challenges exist, the potential of neural networks in environmental monitoring is promising. The web application combines the power of React.js and artificial neural networks, enhancing environmental monitoring efficacy and fostering sustainable practices on a global scale. Ongoing research and standardization efforts are essential for refining and expanding this approach.

Keywords. Environmental Monitoring, React.js, Tensorflow.js, Machine Learning, Image Recognition

---

[1] Corresponding Author: Orest KOCHAN, orest.v.kochan@lpnu.ua.

1. Introduction

Image recognition using artificial neural networks (ANNs) is becoming increasingly important in environmental monitoring due to their ability to process large amounts of data, detect patterns, and extract meaningful information from images. The use of neural networks automates the analysis of huge amounts of image data, reducing the need for manual inspection. ANNs help analyse images related to climate change, including monitoring glacial retreat, sea ice changes, and changes in vegetation patterns. This helps climate researchers to understand and overcome the effects of climate change.

Image recognition helps in predicting and responding to natural disasters. ANNs can analyse satellite or drone imagery to identify potential risk factors, assess the extent of damage during and after natural disasters, and facilitate timely and effective response.

ANNs contribute to the monitoring of protected areas by analysing images for signs of illegal activity, encroachment, or violations. This strengthens conservation efforts and helps protect biodiversity in environmentally sensitive regions.

Image recognition based on ANNs can be integrated into educational tools and public engagement initiatives. Access to interactive applications allows the public to engage in environmental monitoring, increasing awareness and participation in conservation.

2. Literature Review

Developing a web application for image recognition in environmental monitoring is important for several reasons:

- real-time monitoring: a web application allows you to analyse environmental data in real time using image recognition [1, 2]. This capability allows for timely detection and response to changes in environmental conditions, such as deforestation, pollution, or natural disasters [3, 4];

- data accessibility: the web-based platform makes environmental data available to a wider audience. Researchers, policy makers, and the general public can access and interpret image-based information, contributing to greater awareness and understanding of environmental issues [5-7];

- early detection of environmental changes: Image recognition can help in the early detection of environmental changes, allowing proactive measures to be taken to mitigate the impact of factors such as deforestation, habitat loss or climate-related events [8];

- species monitoring and conservation: the use of image recognition to monitor wildlife and plant species supports conservation efforts. It helps to track population trends, identify endangered species, and evaluate the effectiveness of conservation initiatives [9, 10];

- efficient resource management: image recognition can help in the effective management of natural resources. For example, it can be used to monitor agricultural practices, assess land use changes, and optimize resource allocation for sustainable development [11];

- improved decision-making: access to accurate and up-to-date environmental data enables decision makers to make informed choices. This is especially important for policy makers, land managers, and environmentalists who need reliable information for effective environmental planning and management [12, 13];

- public engagement and education: web applications with image recognition can engage the public in environmental monitoring. Visualizing environmental data through user-friendly interfaces encourages public participation, citizen science initiatives, and environmental education [14, 12];

- cost-effective surveillance: web-based image recognition systems can offer a cost-effective alternative to traditional surveillance methods. Automated analysis of large data sets can replace manual monitoring, reducing costs and increasing the efficiency of monitoring programs [15, 16];

- global collaboration: Web-based applications facilitate global collaboration in environmental monitoring. Researchers and organizations from around the world can share and access data, collaborate on projects, and contribute to a more complete understanding of global environmental trends [17-19].

The development of a web application for image recognition in environmental monitoring has great potential for solving various environmental problems. Here are some key considerations that emphasize its feasibility [18]:

1) Development of image recognition technology:
- Image recognition technology, especially in the field of machine and deep learning, has made significant progress. Algorithms such as Convolutional Neural Networks (CNNs) are excellent at image analysis tasks, making them suitable for environmental monitoring applications [20].

2) Availability of datasets:
- Datasets for environmental imagery, such as satellite imagery, drone footage, or ground-based camera data, are becoming increasingly available. These datasets can be used to train and tune machine learning models, improving the accuracy of image recognition [21, 22].

3) Open source tools and frameworks:
- Numerous open-source tools and frameworks, such as TensorFlow and PyTorch, facilitate the development and deployment of machine learning models for image recognition. These tools provide a solid foundation for building web applications with powerful image analysis capabilities [23, 24].

4) Cloud computing infrastructure:
- Cloud computing services such as AWS, Google Cloud, and Azure offer a scalable and cost-effective infrastructure for hosting web applications with image recognition capabilities. Using these services can make it easier to deploy and maintain your environmental monitoring application [25].

5) Potential use cases:
- Image recognition in environmental monitoring can be applied to a variety of use cases, including deforestation detection, wildlife tracking, pollution monitoring, and land cover analysis. The diverse range of applications demonstrates the versatility of the technology.

6) Real-time monitoring [25, 26]:
- Web-based applications can provide real-time monitoring capabilities, allowing users to get instant information about changes in the environment. This is crucial for timely decision-making and intervention in response to emerging environmental issues [27].

7) User-friendly interface:
- A well-designed web interface can make the application user-friendly, allowing non-specialists to access and interpret environmental data. This democratization of information helps to raise public awareness and engage the public in environmental conservation efforts [22, 28, 29].

8) Integration with IoT devices:

- The web application can be integrated with Internet of Things devices such as sensors and cameras to expand data collection capabilities. This integration provides a more comprehensive approach to environmental monitoring.

9) Security and privacy:
- Given the sensitivity of environmental data, it is important to prioritize security and privacy. Implementing robust security measures and adhering to data protection regulations will help increase the credibility of the app [15].

Neural networks have a number of advantages over traditional methods of environmental monitoring [30, 31]:
- High accuracy: neural networks can be trained on large data sets, which allows them to achieve high accuracy in classification and forecasting tasks;
- speed: neural networks can process large amounts of data quickly and efficiently;
- flexibility: neural networks can be adapted to various environmental monitoring tasks. However, there are also some challenges associated with using neural networks for environmental monitoring [12-15]:
- Data requirements: neural networks require large data sets to train.
- Overtraining: neural networks can be prone to overtraining, which can lead to reduced accuracy.
- Understanding: It is not always easy to understand how a neural network came to a certain decision.

Despite these challenges, neural networks are a promising tool for environmental monitoring. They have the potential to improve our understanding of environmental problems, predict future changes, and develop more effective solutions for environmental protection [15, 32].

A web application for a neural network is software that allows users to interact with a neural network through a web browser [16-17]. Web applications can be used for various purposes, such as training, testing, and utilizing neural networks [19-37].

The aim of the study was to create a web application for image recognition using artificial neural networks to improve the efficiency of environmental monitoring.

3. Materials and Methods

Libraries and technologies used:
1) React.js is an open-source JavaScript library for creating user interfaces (UI). It is based on the concept of components, which are independent and interacting blocks that can be used to create complex UIs.

2) React-transition-group is a React.js library that allows you to create smooth transitions between components. It uses CSS transitions to create smooth effects such as smoothing, expanding, and contracting.

Main features of react-transition-group:
- Smooth transitions: react-transition-group uses CSS transitions to create smooth effects.
- Transition management: react-transition-group allows you to control transitions with JavaScript.
- Support for various components: react-transition-group supports various components such as text boxes, buttons, and images.

3) Material UI is an open-source React.js library that allows you to create user interfaces (UIs) based on Google's Material Design system. It contains sets of

components that can be used to create various UI elements such as buttons, input fields, menus, and navigation.

Main features of Material UI:

- Components: Material UI contains sets of components that you can use to create different UI elements.

- Style: Material UI supports Google's Material Design design system.

- Expansiveness: Material UI has a large and active community that develops many libraries and tools for Material UI.

4) TensorFlow.js: 1.0.1 is an open-source JavaScript library for machine learning that allows you to create and implement machine learning models in web browsers and Node.js. It is based on TensorFlow, a popular machine learning library for Python.

Main features of TensorFlow.js:

- Ability to create and implement machine learning models in web browsers and Node.js: TensorFlow.js allows you to create machine learning models that can be used in web browsers and Node.js.

- Supports various machine learning tasks: TensorFlow.js supports a wide range of machine learning tasks such as classification, regression, pattern recognition, and speech recognition.

- Ease of use: TensorFlow.js is relatively easy to use.

5) MobileNet: 1.0.0 is a neural network architecture for pattern recognition developed by Google. It was first introduced in 2017. It is designed for use in mobile devices. It is resource efficient, which allows it to run on devices with limited resources, such as smartphones.

MobileNet 1.0.0 consists of two main components:

- MobileNet base model: This is the base model that consists of 12 consecutive convolution layers.

- MobileNet extended model: This is an extended model that consists of 22 consecutive convolution layers.

MobileNet 1.0.0 was trained on the ImageNet dataset, which consists of over 1.2 million images and their classifications.

Main features of MobileNet 1.0.0:

- Resource-efficient: MobileNet 1.0.0 is resource efficient, enabling it to run on devices with limited resources.

- Ability to be used in mobile devices: MobileNet 1.0.0 has been designed to be used in mobile devices.

- Good results in pattern recognition: MobileNet 1.0.0 has shown good pattern recognition results on the ImageNet dataset.

4. Results and Discussion

The main components of a web application for a neural network are:
- Client interface: Users interact with the neural network through a client interface.
- Web server: The web server processes requests from the client interfaces and passes them on to the neural network.
- Neural network: neural network performs image recognition tasks.
    Important factors when developing a web application for a neural network:
- Reliability: the web application must be reliable and work without failures.
- Efficiency: the web application should be efficient and perform tasks quickly.

- Convenience: the web application should be easy to use and easily understandable for users.

The effectiveness of a web application for a neural network depends on several factors, including:

- The accuracy of the neural network: The more accurate a neural network is, the more efficient it will be.

- The speed of the neural network: The faster a neural network can perform tasks, the more efficient it will be.

- Ease of use of the web application: The easier it is to use a web application, the more effective it will be.

Benefits of using a web-based image recognition application for environmental monitoring (Fig. 1-5):

- Automation of tasks: web app can automate the task of recognizing objects in images. This can lead to significant time and cost savings.

- Improved accuracy: Web-based image recognition applications can use neural networks trained on large datasets. This can lead to improved object recognition accuracy.

- Speed: our web application can process large amounts of data quickly. This can be important for tasks that require a quick response.

Fig. 1. Image Classification Demo App

Fig. 2. Screenshot of the web application for image of bee recognition

Dowitcher

Confidence:68%
Genus of birds
Dowitcher The three dowitchers are medium-sized long-billed wading
birds in the genus Limnodromus. The English name &quot

Fig. 3. Screenshot of the web application for image of bird recognition

Daisy

Confidence:68%
Topics referred to by the same term
Daisy Look up Daisy or daisy in Wiktionary, the free dictionary. Daisy,
Daisies or DAISY may refer to: Bellis perennis, the common daisy, lawn
daisy or English

UPLOAD NEXT IMAGE

Fig. 4. Screenshot of the web application for image of flower recognition

Recent results:

Fig. 5. Screenshot of the web application for image recognition

We used Tensorflow.js together with React.js to build a one-page web application based on TensorFlow.js and the Mobilenet 1.0 artificial neural network model trained on the Imagenet2012 dataset to classify uploaded images and provide a short description about them from the MediaWiki API. The application stores the recent classification in the gallery. MobileNet is a class of convolutional neural network that was open-sourced by Google, and therefore, provides an excellent starting point for training classifiers that are insanely small and insanely fast.

React and artificial neural networks are two powerful tools that can be used to build web applications. React is a JavaScript framework for building user interfaces, and ANNs are a type of machine learning that can be used to train models that can predict or classify data.

Some of the main benefits of using React to build user interfaces include:
- Declarative Model: React uses a declarative model that makes the code more understandable and easier to maintain.
- Component-based architecture: React uses a component-based architecture that makes code more organized and scalable.
- Virtual DOM: React uses a virtual DOM that makes code more efficient and productive.
- Large community: React has a large and active community of developers who are constantly creating new tools and libraries.

One way to use React with ANNs is to create user interfaces that adapt to individual user needs. For example, an ANN can be used to train a model that can predict which UI features will be most useful to a particular user. This model can then be used to tailor the user interface to the user's individual needs.

Another way to use React with ANNs is to create user interfaces that can interact with the real world. For example, an ANN can be used to train a model that can recognize objects on a camera. This model can then be used to create a user interface that allows users to interact with objects on the camera.

TensorFlow.js is an open-source library developed by Google that allows for the training and deployment of machine learning models directly in the browser or on Node.js. It enables developers to build and run machine learning applications using JavaScript. MobileNet is a family of neural network architectures designed for efficient on-device computer vision, particularly suited for mobile and embedded applications.

Key Features:
- flexibility: TensorFlow.js supports both training and inference in the browser, which is useful for applications requiring real-time updates and interactivity;
- cross-platform: It works seamlessly on various platforms, including web browsers and Node.js, enabling a wide range of applications;
- TensorFlow.js can be integrated with other web technologies, allowing for the creation of interactive and dynamic web applications.

MobileNet is a family of neural network architectures designed for mobile and embedded vision applications. MobileNetV1, in particular, is known for its efficiency and ability to perform image classification with a relatively small computational footprint.

Key Features:
- MobileNetV1 uses depthwise separable convolutions, which reduce the number of parameters and computations compared to traditional convolutional layers.
- The architecture is designed to be lightweight and efficient, making it suitable for deployment on resource-constrained devices such as mobile phones and IoT devices.
- Pre-trained versions of MobileNetV1 are available, allowing developers to leverage transfer learning for tasks like image recognition.

TensorFlow.js provides pre-trained models, and MobileNetV1 is one of them. Developers can use MobileNetV1 in the browser for tasks such as image classification without the need for server-side computation. There is the web app code example using TensorFlow.js and React.js (fig. 6-7).

```
Code    Blame    136 lines (111 loc) · 5.16 KB                                      Raw

4       import ResultsGallery from './ResultsGallery';
5       import SingleImage from './SingleImage';
6       import { CSSTransition, TransitionGroup } from 'react-transition-group';
7
8       const MobileNet = require('@tensorflow-models/mobilenet');
9
10  ∨   const MainApp = () => {
11          const [results, setResults] = useState([]);
12          const [gigaState, setGigaState] = useState(false);
13          const fileInputRef = useRef(null);
14          const showWelcomeTitlesFlag = useRef(false);
15          const isImageBeingProcessed = useRef(false);
16          const [loadMobileNetModel, setMobileNetModel] = useState(null);
17          const [image, setImage] = useState({ src: null, title: null, excerpt: null, description: null, confidence: null });
18
19
20          useEffect(() => {
21              setMobileNetModel(async () => await MobileNet.load());
22          }, []);
23
24          useEffect(() => {
25
26              if (showWelcomeTitlesFlag.current) {
27                  showWelcomeTitlesFlag.current = false;
28                  isImageBeingProcessed.current = false;
```

Fig. 6. Screenshot of the project code

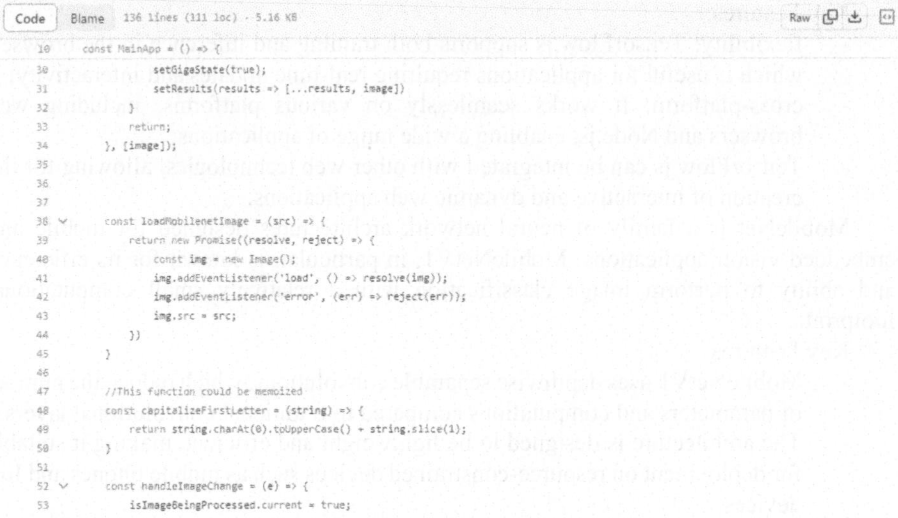

```
Code    Blame    136 lines (111 loc) · 5.16 KB                                    Raw

10    const MainApp = () => {
30              setGigaState(true);
31              setResults(results => [...results, image])
32          }
33          return;
34      }, [image]);
35
36
37
38  ∨   const loadMobilenetImage = (src) => {
39          return new Promise((resolve, reject) => {
40              const img = new Image();
41              img.addEventListener('load', () => resolve(img));
42              img.addEventListener('error', (err) => reject(err));
43              img.src = src;
44          })
45      }
46
47      //This function could be memoized
48      const capitalizeFirstLetter = (string) => {
49          return string.charAt(0).toUpperCase() + string.slice(1);
50      }
51
52  ∨   const handleImageChange = (e) => {
53          isImageBeingProcessed.current = true;
```

Fig. 7. The project code

Ensuring the reliability and accuracy of results in image recognition for environmental monitoring is crucial. Here are some critical steps to achieve this:

1) High-Quality Training Data. The start with a comprehensive and diverse dataset for training your neural network. The dataset should represent the types of images your application will encounter. Quality data is the foundation of accurate results.

2) Data Preprocessing. Preprocessing and cleaning the data to remove noise, artifacts, and inconsistencies. This step is essential to ensure the neural network learns from clean and relevant information.

3) Data Augmentation. Augmenting the dataset with variations of the original images, such as lighting, rotation, and scale changes. Data augmentation helps improve the model's generalization and robustness.

4) Cross-validation. Implementing cross-validation techniques to assess the model's performance. This involves splitting the dataset into multiple subsets for training and testing, providing a more comprehensive evaluation of the model's accuracy.

5) Hyperparameter Tuning. The experiment with various hyperparameters, such as learning rate, batch size, and network architecture. Fine-tuning these parameters can significantly impact the model's performance.

6) Regularization Techniques. Using regularization methods like dropout and L2 regularization to prevent overfitting. Overfit models may perform well on the training data but poorly on new, unseen data.

7) Ensemble Models. Considering using ensemble methods to combine predictions from multiple models. Ensemble methods often lead to more accurate results by reducing individual model biases.

8) Continuous Monitoring. Regularly monitoring the model's performance in a real-world environment. Retraining the model periodically to adapt to changing conditions and improve accuracy over time.

9) Confidence Scores. Implementing a confidence scoring system to gauge the model's certainty about its predictions. This allows us to filter out low-confidence results or seek human verification when necessary.

10) Human Oversight. Maintaining a human oversight component in the system. Experts review and validate a portion of the results to ensure accuracy, especially for critical applications.

11) Feedback Loops. Establishing feedback loops where user-provided feedback is used to improve the model. Correctly identifying inaccuracies or false positives can be fed back into the training process.

12) Error Analysis. Conducting thorough error analysis to identify common failure patterns. This can guide improvements in the model and data collection strategies.

13) Interpretability. Using interpretable models or techniques to make the model's decisions more understandable. Explainable AI can enhance trust in the model's results.

14) Documentation. Maintaining comprehensive documentation for the entire pipeline, including data sources, preprocessing steps, model architecture, and evaluation metrics. This ensures transparency and reproducibility.

15) Compliance and Regulations. Adhering to relevant regulations and standards for environmental monitoring, data privacy, and model deployment. Compliance contributes to the reliability of our results.

16) User Education. Educating users and stakeholders about the model's capabilities and limitations to manage expectations and enhance trust.

React and ANNs are rapidly evolving areas of technology. As these technologies improve, they have the potential to revolutionize web application development by making it more efficient, accessible, and informative.

5. Conclusions

The development of a web application for image recognition in environmental monitoring represents a significant advancement in the field. The application's capabilities offer several key advantages:

Task Automation: Automation is at the core of our web application, streamlining the identification and classification of objects in images. This not only results in substantial time and cost savings but also reduces the margin for human error.

Improved Accuracy: Our web-based image recognition application leverages neural networks trained on extensive datasets, which translates to a marked improvement in the precision of object recognition. This is particularly critical in environmental monitoring, where data accuracy is paramount.

Speed and Efficiency: Our application excels in processing vast volumes of data swiftly, a crucial aspect for tasks that demand immediate response, such as disaster management and early intervention in environmental challenges.

Image recognition technologies have rapidly become an integral part of contemporary environmental monitoring. These technologies are poised to significantly impact our understanding of environmental issues, forecast future changes, and craft more effective solutions for environmental protection.

However, it is vital to acknowledge and address the challenges inherent in the use of neural networks for environmental monitoring. Data requirements, overtraining, and the interpretability of neural network decisions are hurdles that must be overcome to harness the full potential of this technology. Moving forward, continued research is imperative to refine and enhance the accuracy and efficiency of neural network models. Furthermore, the establishment of standards for the training and evaluation of neural networks in the realm of environmental monitoring is essential to ensure the credibility and accuracy of these models.

In conclusion, the fusion of web development technologies and image recognition through artificial neural networks represents a substantial step forward in environmental monitoring. It provides a wealth of information crucial for solving environmental issues, promoting sustainability, and safeguarding ecosystems both locally and globally. As technology continues to evolve, the prospects for more accurate and efficient models in environmental monitoring remain promising.

Acknowledgment

This paper is supported by the National Research Foundation of Ukraine, project number 0123U103529 (2022.01/0009).

References

[1] Zhang et al. A review of deep learning for environmental monitoring. 2022, Sensors.

[2] Sun, L., Qin, H., Przystupa, K., Majka, M., & Kochan, O. Individualized Short-Term Electric Load Forecasting Using Data-Driven Meta-Heuristic Method Based on LSTM Network. Sensors, 22(20), 2022, 7900.

[3] Zhengbing, H., Jotsov, V., Jun, S., Kochan, O., Mykyichuk, M., Kochan, R., & Sasiuk, T. (2016, September). Data science applications to improve accuracy of thermocouples. In 2016 IEEE 8th International Conference on Intelligent Systems (IS), pp. 180-188.

[4] Kunrong Z., Tingting H., Shuang W., Songling W., Bilan D., Qifan Y. (2018). Application research of image recognition technology based on CNN in image location of environmental monitoring UAV. EURASIP Journal on Image and Video Processing. 50. pp. 1-11.

[5] Liu et al. Deep learning for environmental monitoring: A survey. 2022, IEEE Access.

[6] Zhengbing Hu, Yevgeniy V. Bodyanskiy, Nonna Ye. Kulishova, Oleksii K. Tyshchenko, "A Multidimensional Extended Neo-Fuzzy Neuron for Facial Expression Recognition", International Journal of Intelligent Systems and Applications (IJISA), Vol.9, No.9, 2017, pp.29-36.

[7] Wang et al. Application of deep learning in environmental monitoring. 2021, Earth Science Informatics.

[8] Zhang et al. Deep learning for environmental monitoring: A review of recent advances. 2020, IEEE Access

[9] Wang et al. Deep learning for environmental monitoring: A survey of methods and applications. 2019, IEEE Transactions on Geoscience and Remote Sensing.

[10] Zhang et al. Deep learning for remote sensing of the environment. 2023, Remote Sensing

[11] Wang et al. Deep learning for environmental data analysis. 2022, Environmental Science & Technology

[12] Zhang et al. Deep learning for environmental modeling. 2021, Environmental Modelling & Software

[13] Zhengbing Hu, Mykhailo Ivashchenko, Lesya Lyushenko, Dmytro Klyushnyk. Artificial Neural Network Training Criterion Formulation Using Error Continuous Domain", International Journal of Modern Education and Computer Science (IJMECS), Vol.13, No.3, 2021, pp. 13-22.

[14] Zhengbing Hu, Sergii V. Mashtalir, Oleksii K. Tyshchenko, Mykhailo I. Stolbovyi, "Video Shots' Matching via Various Length of Multidimensional Time Sequences", International Journal of Intelligent Systems and Applications (IJISA), Vol.9, No.11, pp.10-16, 2017.

[15] Karpinski M., V. Pohrebennyk V., Bernatska N., Ganczarchyk J., Shevchenko O. Simulation of Artificial Neural Networks for Assessing the Ecological State of Surface Water. 18th International Multidisciplinary Scientific GeoConference SGEM 2018. 2 July – 8 July 2018, Albena, Bulgaria. P. 693-700.

[16] Spencer MCDonald. Web-based decision support system tools: The Soil and Water Assessment Tool Online visualization and analyses (SWATOnline) and NASA earth observation data downloading and reformatting tool (NASAaccess). Environmental Modelling & Software. 2019. Volume 120. P. 1-12.

[17] Jun, S., & Kochan, O. (2015). Common mode noise rejection in measuring channels. Instruments and Experimental Techniques, 58, 86-89.

[18] Srivastava S., Vaddadi S., Sadistap S., Smartphone based System for water quality analysis. Applied Water Science, 2018., P. 129-130.

[19] Crimi A, Jones T. Sgalambro A. Designing a Web Spatial Decision Support System Based on Analytic Network Process to Locate a Freight Lorry Parking. Sustainability. 2019. 11. P. 1-14.

[20] Al-Rubaie F. Application of Artificial Neural Network and Geographical Information System Models to Predict and Evaluate the Quality of Diyala River Water, Iraq / F. Al-Rubaie, N. Al-Musawi // Association of Arab Universities Journal of Engineering Sciences, 2019, 26(1), pp. 160–169.

[21] Bernatska N., Dzhumelia E., Kochan O. Development of the web interface of the information-analytical system of environmental monitoring using the REACT library. Information technologies and society, 2023, No. 1 (7), pp. 6–12. (In Ukr.)

[22] Pohrebennyk, V., Dzhumelia, E. Environmental assessment of the impact of tars on the territory of the Rozdil state mining and chemical enterprise "Sirka" (Ukraine). Studies in Systems, Decision and Control, 2020, 198, pp. 201–214.

[23] Pohrebennyk, V., Korchenko O., Mitryasova O., Bernatska N., Kordos M. An Analytical Decision Support System in Prognostication of Surface Water Pollution Indicators. 19th International Multidisciplinary Scientific GeoConference SGEM 2019, 2019, 2.1, pp. 49-56.

[24] Pohrebennyk, V., Koszelnik, P., Mitryasova, O., Dzhumelia, E., & Zdeb, M. Environmental monitoring of soils of post-industrial mining areas. Journal of Ecological Engineering, 20(9), 2019, 53–61. https://doi.org/10.12911/22998993/112342.

[25] Al-Ashwal N.H., Al Soufy K.A.M., Hamza M.E., Swillam M.A. Deep Learning for Optical Sensor Applications: A Review. Sensors. 2023, 23(14):6486. https://doi.org/10.3390/s23146486.

[26] Chen, P. Visualization of real-time monitoring datagraphic of urban environmental quality (2019) Eurasip Journal on Image and Video Processing, (1), 2019, art. no. 42. doi: 10.1186/s13640-019-0443-6

[27] Chen, L., Zhang, L. Design of Ecological Environment Monitoring System Based on Internet of Things Technology. Wireless Communications and Mobile Computing, 2022, art. no. 2531425.

[28] Havrys, A., Yakovchuk, R., Pekarska, O., Tur, N. Visualization of Fire in Space and Time on the Basis of the Method of Spatial Location of Fire-Dangerous Areas. Ecological Engineering and Environmental Technology, 24 (2), 2023, pp. 28-37.

[29] Novak, R., Petridis, I., Kocman, D., Robinson, J.A., Kanduč, T., Chapizanis, D., Sarigiannis, D. Harmonization and visualization of data from a transnational multi-sensor personal exposure campaign. International Journal of Environmental Research and Public Health, 18 (21), 2021, art. no. 11614.

[30] Shpynkovska, M., Bakunova, A. Information system for visualization of the ecological state of the region (2015) Automation of Technological and Business Processes, 7, pp. 75-81.

[31] Sohor, A., Brydun, A., Yarema, N., Lozynskyi, V., Sohor, M. (2020) Interactive map of environmental pollution of the surface waters in Lviv Region, pp. 1-5.

[32] Fayyad, J., Jaradat, M.A., Gruyer, D., et al. Deep learning sensor fusion for autonomous vehicle perception and localization: A review. Sensors, 20(15), 2020, 4220 (3).

[33] Priya R. Maidamwar, Prasad P. Lokulwar, Kailash Kumar. Ensemble Learning Approach for Classification of Network Intrusion Detection in IoT Environment. International Journal of Computer Network and Information Security, Vol.15, No.3, pp.30-46, 2023.

[34] Mohammed Abduljabbar Zaid Al Bayati, Muhammet Çakmak. Real-Time Vehicle Detection for Surveillance of River Dredging Areas Using Convolutional Neural Networks. International Journal of Image, Graphics and Signal Processing, Vol.15, No.5, pp. 17-28, 2023.

[35] Dhekra El Hamdi, Ines Elouedi, Mai K Nguyen, Atef Hamouda. A Conic Radon-based Convolutional Neural Network for Image Recognition. International Journal of Intelligent Systems and Applications, Vol.15, No.1, pp.1-12, 2023.

[36] Banothu Balaji, T. Satyanarayana Murthy, Ramu Kuchipudi. A Comparative Study on Plant Disease Detection and Classification Using Deep Learning Approaches. International Journal of Image, Graphics and Signal Processing, Vol.15, No.3, pp. 48-59, 2023.

[37] Ihor Tereikovskyi, Zhengbing Hu, Denys Chernyshev, Liudmyla Tereikovska, Oleksandr Korystin, Oleh Tereikovskyi. The Method of Semantic Image Segmentation Using Neural Networks. International Journal of Image, Graphics and Signal Processing, Vol.14, No.6, pp. 1-14, 2022.

Artificial Intelligence, Medical Engineering and Education
Z.B. Hu et al. (Eds.)
doi:10.3233/ATDE231311

The Efficiency of University Resource Allocation Based on DEA Model

Fengcai QIN[a,1] , Chun JIANG[b]
[a] *Nanning University Division of Development Planning, Cooperation and Exchange, Nanning, China*
[b] *Nanning University School of Digital Economics, Nanning, China*

Abstract. The development of universities cannot be separated from the allocation of resources. Conduct empirical research on the efficiency of resource allocation in private universities to help them identify the current situation and problems of internal resource allocation, and promote high-quality development. This paper selects the undergraduate teaching status data of eight private undergraduate universities in Guangxi from 2018 to 2022, and uses DEA model to calculate the resource allocation efficiency of eight private undergraduate universities. The results show that the overall level of resource allocation efficiency of eight private undergraduate universities in Guangxi has maintained an upward trend, and the scale efficiency is significantly higher than the pure technical efficiency, which is the main factor affecting the overall efficiency improvement. Therefore, Guangxi private undergraduate universities should optimize the technical efficiency and management efficiency of resource allocation, strengthen professional construction and improve the quality of talent training.

Key words. Private universities; Resource allocation; Efficiency.

1. Introduction

Private universities refer to independent legal person educational institutions founded by funds and forces from all walks of life, approved and registered by the competent education department. Que Mingkun pointed out that since China's reform and opening up, higher education has undergone a historic leap forward development [1]. In 2019, the gross enrollment rate of higher education in China reached 51.6%, marking the beginning of the popularization stage of higher education in China. Wang Jun pointed out that china's vast population is a fundamental characteristic of the nation, and the unequal distribution of people across regions results in varying educational opportunities for students in different areas to access higher education[2].

Practice has proven that the development dependence of universities from the allocation of resources. Li Zhi defined resource allocation as the allocation of various resources such as human, financial, and material resources in different directions of use [3]. Koksal and Nalcaci believe that resource allocation is a complex and multi-level process that follows the principles of demand and allocates limited resources [4].

Based on the above research, internal resource allocation in universities refers to the process of reasonably allocating tangible resources, including human, financial, and

---

[1] Corresponding Author: Fengcai Qin, E-mail: 151273295@qq.com.

material resources, through certain measures, methods, and means, to enable educational resources to flow from low efficiency links and places to high efficiency links and places, in order to improve resource utilization. Empirical research on the efficiency of resource allocation in private universities not just helps to better understand the current situation and problems of private universities, and that helps to propose corresponding policy recommendations and promote the healthy development of universities.

Regarding the efficiency of internal resource allocation in universities, Wolszczak Derlacz and Parkeka conducted a bootstrapped truncated regression analysis on the educational efficiency of 259 universities in 7 European countries. The regression results showed that the number of female university employees and regional medical institutions can have a significant impact on university efficiency [5]. Wu Yingping used strategic positioning and university characteristics as independent variables, and university efficiency as dependent variable to explore the influencing factors of university efficiency using quantile regression [6].The algorithms and models developed by Azat Tashev, Zhanar Takenova, and Mukaddas Arshidinova can not only be used to solve the problem of load allocation between teachers, but also to solve resource allocation problems in other fields of institutions [7].

This paper is to explore the efficiency of resource in private universities, and evaluate the efficiency of private universities in Guangxi, China, through Data Envelopment Analysis (DEA).

2. Introduction of Data Envelopment Analysis

2.1 The Emergence and Development of Data Envelopment Analysis

In 1978, A.Charnes and W.W. Cooper of the United States proposed a quantitative analysis method called data envelopment analysis (DEA) [8].DEA method can be used to evaluate the relative effectiveness of the same type of units with multiple inputs and outputs, and is widely used in efficiency evaluation and effect analysis in various fields. DEA model has been widely used in the evaluation of resource allocation efficiency of private universities, and has achieved good results. Through DEA model, we can evaluate the resource utilization efficiency, management efficiency, technical efficiency and other aspects of private universities, and provide reference and guidance for private universities to improve the efficiency of resource allocation. Manjari Sahai, Prince Agarwal, Vaibhav Mishra, Monark Bag, Vrijendra Singh analyzed DEA by measuring the supplier performance of multinational telecommunications companies and manufacturing enterprises. The company uses this method to evaluate its suppliers based on their requirements and standards, and finds the best supplier among them [9].Its basic assumption is that all decision making units (DMUs) can reach the optimal efficiency level, but the input and output indicators of different DMUs may be different. The DEA model compares and measures the input and output indicators of different decision-making units to obtain the relative efficiency of each decision-making unit, and then provides reference and decision-making basis for decision makers.

CCR model and BCC model are the two most widely used models of DEA model.

CCR model (Charnes-Cooper-Rhodes model) is one of the earliest DEA models. It assumes that each decision making unit (DMU) has the same input and output weight [10].The basic idea of the model is to determine the relative efficiency of each DMU and calculate the relative efficiency score of all DMUs through linear programming. The CCR model can be used to evaluate the technical efficiency and scale efficiency of each DMU. The technical efficiency reflects whether a DMU has reached the maximum production capacity under the existing scale and resources, while the scale efficiency reflects the capacity of a DMU to expand its scale.

The BCC model (Banker-Charnes-Copper model) is an improved version based on the CCR model. The BCC model considers the differences between DMUs and allows each DMU to have different input and output weights. The basic idea of this model is to find a set of optimal input and output weights through linear programming, so that all DMUs can be evaluated to the maximum. The BCC model is more flexible when dealing with DMUs of different sizes, and can be used to evaluate the technical efficiency, scale efficiency and comprehensive efficiency of each DMU.

In general, CCR model and BCC model are two very useful DEA models. They can be used to evaluate the efficiency and difference of each DMU and provide valuable decision support information.

2.2 Application of Data Envelopment Analysis in The Research on The Efficiency of University Resource Allocation

In the research on the efficiency of university resource allocation, DEA method can help evaluate the relative efficiency of each university in resource utilization, find out the inefficient universities, and provide reference for the improvement of resource allocation.
(1) CCR model
CCR model is a model based on the assumption of fixed return to scale and multiple inputs and outputs, which can be used to evaluate the overall technical effectiveness of the entire decision-making unit.

Under the assumption of fixed return to scale, the university to be evaluated for efficiency is regarded as a decision-making unit (DMU). Suppose there are n DMUs, and each DMUj uses m input factors, the input vector is X= （X1，X2...XM）, and the output vector is Y= （Y1，Y2...YM）. Charnes, Cooper and Rhodes combined this multi-input and multi-output situation with the virtual circle Vi and Ui, and proposed the initial CCR model form, as follows:

$$
\begin{cases}
\max h_j = \dfrac{\sum u^T Y_0}{\sum v^T X_0} \\[2mm]
\dfrac{\sum_{r=1}^{s} U_\gamma Y_\eta}{\sum_{i=1}^{m} V_i X_\eta} \leq 1 \\[2mm]
U \geq 0, V \geq 0 \\[1mm]
j = 1,2,\dots n; i = 1,2,\dots m; r = 1,2,\dots s
\end{cases}
\tag{1}
$$

Where: X0 represents the input of the evaluated decision-making unit;
Y0 represents the output of the evaluated decision-making unit;
Xij represents the input of the jth DMUj to the ith input;
Yrj represents the output of the jth DMUj to the rth output;
Vi represents the weight of the ith input;
Ui represents the weight of the r-th input.
Charnes, Cooper and Rhodes defined V, U as the weight to evaluate the efficiency

value of the decision-making unit, and the selection method of this weight is more objective than the assignment method. However, because fractional programming is a nonlinear model, it will produce infinite solutions, so they converted the original CCR model into the form of linear programming of linear programming:

$$
\left\{
\begin{array}{l}
\max U^T Y_0 = \theta \\
V^T X_\eta - U^T Y_\eta \geq 0 \\
V^T X_0 = 1 \\
U \geq 0, V \geq 0 \\
j = 1,2, \dots n; i = 1,2, \dots m; r = 1,2, \dots s
\end{array}
\right.
\tag{2}
$$

And write its dual planning form according to the dual theory:

$$
\left\{
\begin{array}{l}
\min h_j = \theta \\
\sum_{j=i}^{n} X_\eta \lambda_j - s_j^- = \theta X_0 \\
\sum_{j=i}^{n} Y_\eta \lambda_j - s_r^- = Y_0 \\
\lambda j \geq 0 \\
j = 1,2 \dots n; i = 1,2, \dots m; r = 1,2, \dots s
\end{array}
\right.
\tag{3}
$$

Where: hj is the efficiency index of DMU, representing the technical efficiency value;

λj represents the weight multiplier of each decision-making unit;

S-, S+ are relaxation variables.

When $\theta 0 = 1$ and relative to S-0=0, S+0=0, Pareto optimization is achieved, then the DMU is said to be DEA total technology effective; When $\theta 0 < 1$ andS-0≠0, S+0≠0, it means that at least one input or output partial invalid rate is used, which is a non-DEA total count valid state.

According to Banker&Morey [11], In CCR model, $\sum \lambda$ The value of can be used to judge the scale return status of the evaluated unit as follows: when $\sum \lambda = 1$ means that the assessed unit is in the optimal production scale and belongs to fixed scale remuneration; $\sum \lambda < 1$ means that the appraisal unit is smaller than the optimal production scale, and belongs to the increase of scale returns; $\sum \lambda > 1$ means that the appraised unit is larger than the optimal production scale, and belongs to diminishing returns to scale. Pass $\sum \lambda$ To understand the scale return status of the assessed unit (DMU), which can be used to determine whether the allocation and utilization of resources are appropriate in management decision-making.

(2) BCC model

Because the CCR model is applicable to the evaluation of technical efficiency in the case of fixed returns to scale, some DMUs may not produce at the most suitable scale, but may produce under the increasing or decreasing variable returns to scale. Therefore, in 1984, Banker, Charnes and Cooper proposed the BCC model of variable returns to scale [12]. The relative efficiency measured by BCC model is pure technical efficiency. The model is as follows:

$$\begin{cases} \min h_j = \theta \\ \sum_{j=i}^{n} X_\eta \, \lambda_j + s_j^- = \theta X_0 \\ \sum_{j=i}^{n} Y_\eta \, \lambda_j - s_r^- = Y_0 \\ \sum_{j=i}^{n} \lambda_j = 1; \lambda j \geq 0 \\ j = 1,2 \dots n; i = 1,2, \dots m; r = 1,2, \dots s \end{cases} \tag{4}$$

Where: X0 represents the input of the evaluated decision-making unit;

Y0 represents the output of the evaluated decision-making unit;

Xij represents the input of the jth DMUj to the ith input;

Yrj represents the output of the jth DMUj to the rth output;

hj is the efficiency index of DMUj, representing the pure technical efficiency value (PTE);

λj represents the weight of the ith input;

S -, S+ are relaxation variables.

The BCC model has one more constraint than the CCR model, that is, the return to scale is variable，When θ0=1 and relative to S-0=0，S+0=0, the DMU is pure technical efficiency effective, otherwise it is pure technical efficiency ineffective.

3. Research Design

3.1 Selection of Input and Output Indicators

(1) Select and determine the decision unit (DMU)

When selecting DMUs, there must be homogeneity between DMUs. As for the selection of input and output items of each decision-making unit, Cooper and others have given the following requirements [13]:

1) For all DMUs, each input and output value can be achieved, and these values must be positive and positively correlated.

2) The selection of these project inputs, outputs and decision-making units should align with the concerns of analysts or managers regarding the assessment of decision-making units' relative effectiveness.

3) From the principle of efficiency ratio, the input value should be as small as possible, while the output value should be as large as possible.

4) Different input and output units are not required to be consistent. It can be the number of people, area, cost, etc.

Moreover, an abundance of input and output indicators can result in a higher effective number of decision-making units, thereby diminishing the efficiency of the DEA method in its evaluative function.[14]. Therefore, the evaluation indicators should be as simple as possible on the premise of meeting the purpose.

(2) Determination of input-output indicators

The objective of resource allocation optimization is to efficiently harness human, material, and financial resources to achieve the comprehensive goals of higher education, including nurturing talent, societal service, and scientific research, while minimizing resource consumption [15]. Based on the above considerations, the input indicators selected in this paper include: the number of full-time teachers in X1, the average school building area of students in X2, and the average teaching daily operating expenses of students in X3. The output indicators include: the number of full-time students in Y1, the sum of the number of papers published and the number of monographs published in Y2. The input indicators reflect the financial, material and human inputs of universities respectively, and the output indicators reflect the functions of universities in cultivating talents and scientific research. Considering that Guangxi is located in the western region of China, the overall education level ranks low, and the overall scientific research level of private universities is not high, there are basically not many measurable quantitative indicators in terms of social services, Therefore, social services are not included as output indicators for evaluation in this study [16].

3.2 Data Source Description

This paper takes the running data of eight private undergraduate universities in Guangxi from 2018 to 2022 as a sample, and carries out horizontal and vertical analysis to investigate the resource allocation efficiency of private universities. The indicator data used are from the annual undergraduate teaching status data of each university, various yearbooks and data collected from the business departments of private undergraduate universities.

4. Empirical Analysis and Results

Based on the input orientation, the CCR and BCC models are used to calculate and analyze the input and output data of the resource allocation of eight private undergraduate universities in Guangxi from 2018 to 2022. Since the global DEA analysis is used, the calculated efficiency values can be compared horizontally and vertically. At the same time, the comprehensive technical efficiency (TE), pure technical efficiency (PTE) and scale efficiency (SE) of university resource utilization can be obtained by using CRR model and BCC model. Table 1 shows the efficiency results.

Table 1. Resource allocation efficiency of eight private undergraduate universities in Guangxi (2018-2022)

Universities	Efficiency/Year	2018	2019	2020	2021	2022
BH	TE	0.689	0.709	0.782	0.644	0.622
	PTE	0.816	0.726	0.785	0.653	0.625
	SE	0.844	0.977	0.997	0.985	0.995
	Remuneration to scale	IRS	IRS	IRS	IRS	DRS
CM	TE	0.488	0.485	0.504	1.000	1.000
	PTE	0.562	0.559	0.686	1.000	1.000
	SE	0.869	0.868	0.735	1.000	1.000
	Remuneration to scale	IRS	IRS	IRS	-	-
GL	TE	0.973	0.850	0.914	0.852	0.892
	PTE	1.000	0.938	0.939	0.956	0.980
	SE	0.973	0.907	0.974	0.892	0.910

Table 1. Resource allocation efficiency of eight private undergraduate universities in Guangxi (2018-2022) (continued)

Universities	Efficiency/Year	2018	2019	2020	2021	2022
GL	Remuneration to scale	IRS	IRS	IRS	IRS	IRS
IT	TE	0.592	0.843	1.000	0.667	0.771
	PTE	0.757	0.878	1.000	0.670	0.773
	SE	0.782	0.960	1.000	0.995	0.998
	Remuneration to scale	IRS	IRS	-	DRS	IRS
LZ	TE	0.717	0.774	0.662	0.718	0.804
	PTE	0.793	0.815	0.674	0.739	0.820
	SE	0.904	0.950	0.982	0.972	0.981
	Remuneration to scale	IRS	IRS	IRS	IRS	IRS
NN	TE	1.000	1.000	0.961	1.000	1.000
	PTE	1.000	1.000	0.971	1.000	1.000
	SE	1.000	1.000	0.990	1.000	1.000
	Remuneration to scale	-	-	DRS	-	-
NT	TE	0.728	0.855	0.753	0.828	1.000
	PTE	0.793	0.861	0.762	0.833	1.000
	SE	0.917	0.993	0.987	0.993	1.000
	Remuneration to scale	IRS	IRS	IRS	DRS	-
XS	TE	1.000	0.998	1.000	0.762	1.000
	PTE	1.000	1.000	1.000	0.799	1.000
	SE	1.000	0.998	1.000	0.953	1.000
	Remuneration to scale	-	IRS	-	IRS	-

Note: "IRS, DRS, -" respectively mean increasing returns to scale, decreasing returns to scale and unchanged returns to scale.

4.1. Comprehensive Technical Efficiency Analysis

Figure. 1 shows the comprehensive technical efficiency of resource utilization in 8 universities from 2018 to 2022. It can be seen from the figure that the comprehensive technical efficiency of resource utilization of NN university and XS university is high. There are few universities that have achieved effective results in the early stage, but by 2022, the comprehensive efficiency of resource utilization of four of the eight universities has achieved effective results, indicating that the overall efficiency of resource utilization of these eight universities has improved. From the vertical perspective of universities, for example, the comprehensive efficiency of resource utilization of BH in universities has experienced "rise first and then fall", the comprehensive efficiency of resource utilization of LZ university has experienced fluctuations, while the comprehensive efficiency of resource utilization of CM in universities has increased year by year. From the perspective of horizontal analysis, by 2022, the comprehensive efficiency of resource utilization of BH and IT in universities will still be less than 0.8, which is not high. In view of this, we need to focus on the following analysis of pure technical efficiency and scale efficiency.

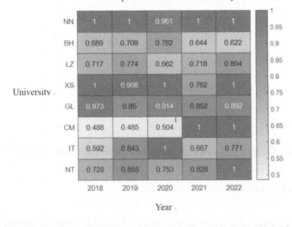

Figure 1. Comprehensive technical efficiency of resource allocation in 8 universities from 2018 to 2022

4.2. Pure Technical Efficiency Analysis

Figure. 2 shows the pure technical efficiency of resource allocation in 8 universities from 2018 to 2022. On the whole, the pure technical efficiency of NN university, XS university and GL university is relatively high. From the vertical perspective of universities, it is found that the pure technical efficiency of CM university has been greatly improved, while the pure technical efficiency of other universities fluctuates. From a horizontal perspective, it is found that by 2022, 4 of the 8 universities have achieved effective pure technical efficiency, which is more than that of other years. From the above analysis, it can be seen that in 2022, the comprehensive efficiency of resource utilization of BH university and IT university is less than 0.8, only 0.622 and 0.771 respectively. In 2022, the pure technical efficiency of BH university and IT university is only 0.625 and 0.773, respectively. It can be seen that the main reason for the low comprehensive efficiency of resource utilization in these two universities is the low level of pure technical efficiency. Therefore, in order to further improve the resource utilization efficiency of these two universities, it is necessary to focus on improving the management level of universities and allocating resources reasonably.

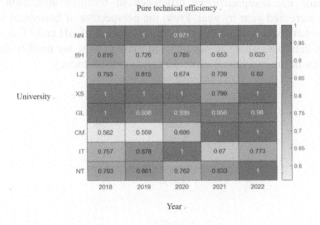

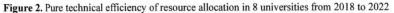

Figure 2. Pure technical efficiency of resource allocation in 8 universities from 2018 to 2022

4.3. Scale Efficiency Analysis

Figure. 3 shows the scale efficiency of resource allocation of eight universities in 2018-2022. On the whole, the scale efficiency of university resource allocation is relatively high, especially by 2022, the scale efficiency of four universities has reached effective, and the scale efficiency of the other four universities is also close to 1. From the perspective of time trend, in 2018, there were only 2 universities with effective scale efficiency, and the scale efficiency of other universities was also not high, which would be improved by 2022. This shows that, on the whole, the scale efficiency of university resources utilization is improved. By 2022, the space for improving the scale efficiency of university resource allocation has been limited. To further improve efficiency in the future, we need to start with improving pure technical efficiency.

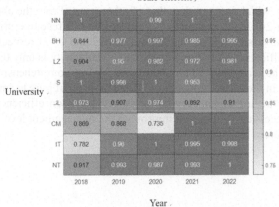

Figure 3. Resource allocation scale efficiency of 8 universities in 2018-2022

4.4. Overall Analysis

The comprehensive technical efficiency, pure technical efficiency and scale efficiency of resource allocation of 8 universities are averaged by year and visualized to obtain the overall resource allocation efficiency of these 8 universities from 2018 to 2022, as shown in Figure .4. It can be seen from the figure that, on the whole, the comprehensive technical efficiency has increased from 0.773 in 2018 to 0.886 in 2022, and there is still room for improvement. Through the decomposition analysis of the comprehensive technical efficiency, observations indicate that scale efficiency exhibits a notably higher level than pure technical efficiency, indicating that the pure technical efficiency is the main factor limiting the improvement of the efficiency of university resource allocation. Therefore, in order to further improve the efficiency of resource allocation in the future, it is necessary to improve the management level and reasonably allocate school resources.

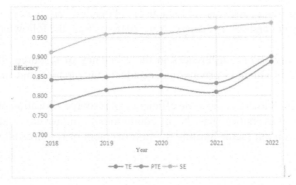

Figure 4. Overall situation of resource allocation efficiency of 8 universities in 2018-2022

In order to have an overall grasp of the resource allocation efficiency of each university, this paper calculates the annual average of the comprehensive technical efficiency of resource allocation of each university during the period 2018-2022, and visualizes it to obtain the average resource allocation efficiency of eight universities in 2018-2022, as shown in Figure. 5.

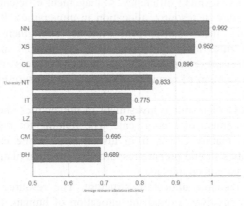

Figure 5. Average resource allocation efficiency of 8 universities in 2018-2022

According to Figure. 5, the top three universities in resource allocation efficiency are NN university, XS university and GL university. The comprehensive technical efficiency values of NN university and XS university both exceed 0.95, and the resource allocation efficiency is high. It can be seen that NN university and XS university are benchmarks that other universities need to learn in order to improve the efficiency of resource allocation. In addition, the comprehensive technical efficiency of CM　university and BH university is relatively low, both less than 0.7, and there is much room for improvement.

5. Conclusions And Recommendations

5.1. Conclusion

Based on the data analysis of resource allocation efficiency of eight private undergraduate universities in Guangxi from 2018 to 2022, the following conclusions can be drawn:

(1) There are certain differences in the efficiency of resource allocation between 2018 and 2022 in Guangxi private undergraduate universities, but the overall trend is upward;

(2) From 2018 to 2022, the scale efficiency of resource allocation of Guangxi private undergraduate universities has been continuously improved, and pure technical efficiency is the main factor limiting the improvement of resource allocation efficiency of universities.

5.2. Suggestions

In view of the above conclusions, the following suggestions are put forward:

(1) Optimize technical efficiency. Technical efficiency is an important part of the efficiency of university resource allocation. If it is optimized, it will help to improve the overall efficiency. It is suggested that universities should strengthen the construction of teaching staff, improve teaching facilities and technical equipment, introduce advanced information technology and management technology, and improve technical efficiency.

(2) Optimize management efficiency. Management efficiency is also a key factor affecting the efficiency of resource allocation in universities. It is recommended that universities improve their management systems, strengthen the formulation and implementation of rules and regulations such as financial management, personnel management, and asset management, strengthen process management, increase supervision and evaluation of resource allocation, and ensure effective monitoring of resource allocation.

(3) The intensity of resource investment in universities should keep up with the speed of the development of school scale. The funding for resource construction in private universities mainly comes from tuition fees. While expanding the scale of education, universities should prepare resource construction plans in advance to ensure that resources are guaranteed in place.

(4) Optimize resource allocation structure. The resource allocation of private universities mainly revolves around the allocation of human, financial, and material resources. Private universities should fully consider the characteristics of their education, prioritize the allocation of financial resources, link budget management with work

execution, achieve work monetization, and thereby improve the efficiency of education management.

In short, the efficiency of resource allocation in universities needs to be comprehensively optimized from various aspects such as technical efficiency, management efficiency, scale development, resource allocation speed, and resource allocation structure. If universities can strengthen these aspects of work, it will help improve the efficiency of resource allocation.

Acknowledgments

This project is supported by the 2022 private higher experts project of the 14th five-year plan of Guangxi educational science (2022ZJY3220) and the 2021 Professor Training project of Nanning University (2021JSGC15, 2021JSGC08)

Reference

[1]   Que Mingkun. Research on the generation mechanism of China's high-level private universities[D]. Xiamen University, 2020.

[2]   Wang Jun. The issue of equity in Chinese higher education and its countermeasures[J]. Education Development Research, (18):14-16.

[3]   Li Zhi, Li Kai, Li Yuhong. Research and practice of university material management[J]. Science and technology horizon, (23), 123-124.

[4]   Koksal and Nalcaci. Understanding and facilitating organizational change in the 21st century: Recent research and conceptualizations.ASHE-ERIC Higher Education Reports, 28(4), 1-187.

[5]   Wolszczak Derlacz and Parkeka. Discussion on the Rational Allocation of Physical Resources in universities. Education and Teaching Forum, (21), 71-72.

[6]   Wu Yingping. Research on the problems and countermeasures of university material resources allocation [J]. Science and Technology Wind, (11): 36-37.

[7]   Azat Tashev, Zhanar Takenova, Mukaddas Arshidinova, "Algorithms for Solving Problems of Resources Allocation in the Management of Business Processes in Educational Organizations", International Journal of Modern Education and Computer Science, Vol.15, No.5, pp. 14-27, 2023.

[8]   Charmes A, Cooper w.W, Rhodes E. Measuring the efficiency of decision making units[J]. European Journal of Operational Research, (2):429 444.

[9]   Manjari Sahai, Prince Agarwal, Vaibhav Mishra, Monark Bag, Vrijendra Singh, "Supplier Selection through Application of DEA", International Journal of Engineering and Manufacturing, vol.4, no.1, pp.1-9, 2014

[10] Banker, R. D., Charnes, A., & Cooper, W. W. (1984). Some models for estimating technical and scale inefficiencies in data envelopment analysis. Management science, 30(9), 1078-1092.

[11] Banker, R. D., & Morey, R. C. Efficiency analysis for exogenously fixed inputs and outputs.Operations Research, 34(4), 513-521.

[12] Wei Quanling. Evaluation of the relatively effective DEA method in the new field of operational research[M], China Renmin University Press, 1998:125-153.

[13] Cooper, W. W., Seiford, L. M., & Tone, K. Data envelopment analysis: a comprehensive text with models, applications, references and DEA-solver software. Springer Science & Business Media.

[14] Charmes A, Cooper w.W, Rhodes E. Measuring the efficiency of decision making units[J], European Journal of Operational Research, (2):429 444.

[15] M.Abbott, C.Doucoliagos. The efficiency of Australian university: a data envelopment analysis[J], Economics of Education Review, 1998, (22):89-97.

[16] Mintzberg, H. (1987). Crafting strategy. Harvard Business Review, 65(4), 66-75.

Artificial Intelligence, Medical Engineering and Education
Z.B. Hu et al. (Eds.)
© *2024 The Authors.*

doi:10.3233/ATDE231312

Aids to Navigation State Risk Assessment Model and Application Based on AHP and Entropy Weight Method

Liang HUANG[a,b], Xiaodie HUANG[c], Jingjing CAO[a,d], Dengfeng LI[e,1], Jinhui XU[f], Zhipeng WEN[d]

[a] *State Key Laboratory of Maritime Technology and Safety, Wuhan University of Technology, Wuhan, China*
[b] *National Eneineering Research Center for Water Transport Safety, Wuhan University of Technology, Wuhan, China*
[c] *Wuhan University of Technology, Intelligent Transportation Systems Research Center, Wuhan, China*
[d] *School of Transportation and Logistics Engineering, Wuhan University of Technology, Wuhan, China*
[e] *China Communications Information & Technology Group Co., Ltd., Beijing, China*
[f] *NavInfo Co., Ltd., Beijing, China*
ORCiD ID: Liang HUANG https://orcid.org/0000-0003-3233-4446

Abstract. The assessment and analysis of the operational status and safety risks associated with Aids to navigation hold paramount significance in ensuring the safety of maritime navigation. This paper constructs a risk assessment system for Aids to navigation based on the AHP (Analytic Hierarchy Process) and entropy weight method. The evaluation system employs the AHP to subjectively weight both discrete and continuous data, while the entropy weight method is applied to objectively weight data that can be continuously monitored. The subjective and objective weights are combined with nonlinear weights to construct a risk assessment model. The model has been applied to analyze and evaluate the Aids to navigation data of the waters of Guangzhou Maritime Safety Bureau in 2023. The evaluation results show that the power risk of the aids to navigation is the main risk of the existing aids to navigation.

Key words. Aids to navigation; Risk assessment; AHP; Entropy weight

1. Introduction

Aids to navigation are the navigational aid facilities for ship navigation, which have the role of calibrating obstructive objects. Aids to navigation are not only an indispensable component of the maritime and port safety systems, but also essential means of ensuring the safety of vessel navigation. The technical status of the Aids to navigation directly affects the safe navigation of the ship. However, the current remote control and telemetry technology for Aids to navigation fall short in providing comprehensive monitoring for them. Therefore, it is of paramount importance to comprehensively and effectively assess

---

[1] Corresponding Author: Dengfeng LI, E-mail: lidengfeng1@cccltd.cn

the status and risks associated with Aids to navigation.

The maintenance and management of early Aids to navigation were mainly based on manual patrol inspection, which was long, laborious and inefficient. With the development of Aids to navigation telemetry remote control technology, it has transcended the traditional forms of Aids to navigation maintenance and management, ushering in a higher quality of service [1]. Relevant research institutions at home and abroad carried multiple types of sensors on traditional Aids to navigation to dynamically manage and monitor Aids to navigation [2,3]. In the early stage, relevant R&D institutions have introduced information measurement and control technology into Aids to navigation management [4,5]. With the development of technology, Ma Jialin et al. applied NB-IoT technology to the telemetry remote control system of the Aids to navigation [6]. Yue Zhiyong et al. introduced Beidou satellite communication technology to the remote control telemetry system of the Aids to navigation, which improved the maintenance quality of the Aids to navigation [7]. However, in practical applications, various factors can lead to a significant number of false and missed alarms in Aids to navigation remote monitoring and control systems [8]. Therefore, it is essential to conduct a risk assessment of Aids to navigation. In the research of Aids to navigation evaluation and maintenance, Hye-Ri et al. developed objective indicators and evaluation models for Aids to navigation, using the AHP for the evaluation of these aids [9]. Nie Ziyi et al. combined Fuzzy and AHP to quantitatively evaluate the Aids to navigation [10], but the evaluation index system was incomplete. Deng Zhusen used the GM(1,1) model to forecast Aids to navigation workload in the northern waters of China [11]. They employed continuous grey differential equations to analyze system development, which has contributed to the management and maintenance of Aids to navigation.

Due to the presence of both continuous and discrete data in Aids to navigation risk assessment indicators, previous studies primarily addressed qualitative assessments of discrete indicators, lacking quantitative evaluations based on continuous data, and exhibiting an incomplete evaluation indicator system. Therefore, this paper establishes a risk evaluation index system for Aids to navigation in terms of lamps, power supply, appearance, and environment. Additionally, it endeavors to develop a Aids to navigation risk assessment model by amalgamating qualitative and quantitative methodologies.

2.   Evaluation System of Aids to Navigation System

According to the maintenance technical specifications of Aids to navigation in the Technical Specifications for Maintenance of Inland Waterways, this paper establishes a set of risk assessment indicators based on Aids to navigation, which are shown in Table 1.

The first level indicator of the evaluation system is the Aids to navigation. As for the second level, on one hand, the natural channel where the Aids to navigation are located has turbulent water flow and high air humidity, which is easy to cause the abnormality of the Aids to navigation and brings potential safety hazards to the passage of ships. Thus, it is necessary to evaluate the influence of hydrological and meteorological environment on the Aids to navigation. On the other hand, the appearance of the Aids to navigation is required to meet the relevant standards, with bright colors, long-lasting and bright lighting, and excellent lighting quality. Therefore, the second level consists of the main component structure of the Aids to navigation and the environment in which the Aids to navigation are located, including the Aids to navigation light, the appearance of the Aids to navigation, the power supply of the Aids to navigation, and the environment in which the beacon is located. All these indicators are recorded as the first-level indicators. The third level of the evaluation system is the specific evaluation index of the Aids to navigation, including voltage, power supply, light color, light range, light cycle, light rhythm, number of remaining bulbs, daylight threshold, voltage, internal resistance, battery temperature, appearance, color, location, structure, temperature, humidity, light intensity, water depth, flow rate, wind speed, which are recorded as the second-level indicators.

Table 1. Aids to navigation risk evaluation index system

The total indicator	The first-level indicators	The second-level indicators
		Light color (X_{11})
		Light range (X_{12})
	Aids to navigation light (X_1)	Light cycle (X_{13})
		Light rhythm (X_{14})
		Number of bulbs remaining (X_{15})
		Voltage (X_{21})
		Current (X_{22})
	Power supply (X_2)	Resistance (X_{23})
Aids to navigation		Temperature (X_{24})
		Appearance (X_{25})
		Color (X_{31})
	Appearance (X_3)	Location (X_{32})
		Structure (X_{33})
		Temperature (X_{41})
		Humidity (X_{42})
	Environment (X_4)	Light intensity (X_{43})
		The depth of the Water (X_{44})
		Water flow rate(X_{45})
		Wind velocity(X_{46})

3.   AHP-entropy Weight Method Aids to Navigation Risk Evaluation Model

The evaluation system of Aids to navigation includes discrete properties (such as appearance, etc.) and continuous properties (such as current, etc.). Among them, for discrete risk indicators, the common assessment method is to score experts; and for the evaluation index of continuous nature, the evaluation method of calculating the mathematical characteristic value is normally adopted. In this paper, for the risk evaluation of navigation standard equipment, the subjective weight of discrete and continuous index data are determined by analytic hierarchy method [13, 14], and the objective continuous index data is objectively weighted by the entropy method. Finally, the subjective and objective weights are combined nonlinear to determine the final weights. The calculation process is shown in Fig. 1.

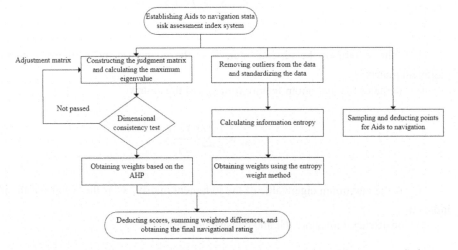

Figure 1. Calculation process of navigation mark risk system based on AHP-entropy method

3.1 Weight Calculation Based on the AHP Method

From the established risk evaluation index system of Aids to navigation, different risk factors of the same index layer are compared in pairs, so as to obtain a judgment matrix. The weight vector of the judgment matrix is calculated and the consistency test is performed as follows:

1) Build a judgment matrix

According to the established risk assessment system of Aids to navigation, the risk factors of the same index layer of Aids to navigation are compared. The comparative results were numerically quantified using relative measures, and the quantitative result values were given using T.L. Saaty's 1-9 scale method.

$$X = \left(x_{ij}\right)_{n \times n} = \begin{pmatrix} x_{11} & \cdots & x_{1n} \\ \vdots & \ddots & \vdots \\ x_{n1} & \cdots & x_{nn} \end{pmatrix} \tag{1}$$

X is the judgment matrix; x_{ij} is the ith row and jth column elements of matrix X; n is the order of the matrix.

2) Normalize X and Calculate the feature vector

$$\overline{w}_i = \left(\prod_{j=1}^{n} x_{ij} \right)^{\frac{1}{n}}, i, j = 1, 2, \ldots, n \tag{2}$$

x_{ij} is the element of the jth column of row i in the judgment matrix X; $\overline{w}_i$ is the geometric mean of row i in the judgment matrix X.

3) Calculate the weight vector

$$w_i' = \overline{w}_i / \sum_{i=1}^{n} \overline{w}_i, i = 1, 2, ..., n \tag{3}$$

w_i' is the weight of the ith indicator, $\overline{w}_i$ is the geometric mean of row i in the judgment matrix X

4) Calculates the maximum feature root $\lambda_{\max}$ of the matrix

$$\lambda_{\max} = \frac{1}{n} \sum_{i=1}^{n} \frac{(Xw')_i}{nw_i'} \tag{4}$$

$\lambda_{\max}$ is the maximum eigenvalue of the judgment matrix, w_i' is the weight of the ith indicator

5) Consistency indicators: CI and consistency ratio: CR

$$CR = \frac{CI}{RI} \tag{5}$$

$$CI = \frac{\lambda_{\max} - n}{n - 1} \tag{6}$$

n is the order of the judgment matrix X. The selection of RI is shown in Table 2. If CR< 0.10, the judgment matrix B of the risk assessment of the Aids to navigation is consistent.

6) Normalization determines indicator weights

If the judgment matrix is tested for consistency, the normalization of the feature vectors w_i' can obtain the weights of risk indicators at all levels in the risk evaluation of the Aids to navigation.

Table 2. RI comparison

n	1	2	3	4	5	6	7	8	9
RI	0	0	0.54	0.89	1.12	1.25	1.34	1.42	1.45

3.2 Weight Calculation Based on the Entropy Weight Method

The entropy weight method is objectively weighted, and the degree of influence of this index on the evaluation is determined by calculating the degree of discreteness of the index data [15, 16, 17], and this paper introduces the entropy weight method to calculate the weights for the third layer of continuous indicators $X-X_2-X_{21}$ and $X-X_2-X_{22}$.

3.2.1 Removing Extreme Values and Data Normalization

In order to reduce the influence of extreme values on entropy values, if the data values of a single sample exceed 20% of the total sum of the overall data, the data values are excluded after referring to relevant studies.

The entropy value is calculated logarithmically, and the data after extreme values are standardized by the critical value method with reference formula (7).

$$z_{i,t} = \frac{x_{i,t} - \min_t x_{i,t}}{\max_t x_{i,t} - \max_t x_{i,t}} \tag{7}$$

$x_{i,t}$ is the tth data in the monitoring data of the evaluation index i of the Aids to navigation.

$z_{i,t}$ is the tth data in the monitoring data of the Aids to navigation evaluation index i after removing the extreme value.

3.2.2 Entropy Calculation

The data set that excludes the extreme values is substituted into the formula (6)~(7), and the objective weights w_i'' are calculated.

$$H_i = -k \sum_{t=1}^{m} f_{it} \cdot \ln(f_{it}) \tag{8}$$

$$f_{it} = z_{it} / \sum_{t=1}^{m} z_{it} \tag{9}$$

$$k = \frac{1}{\ln m} \tag{10}$$

$$w_i'' = \frac{1 - H_i}{\sum_i (1 - H_i)} \tag{11}$$

w_i'' is the entropy weight of indicator i, m is the total number of samples after z_{jt} removed from extreme values. H_i is the entropy value corresponding to the Aids to navigation index i.

3.3 The Final Weight

The analytic hierarchy method subjectively determines the weights by experts, the entropy method determines the weights from objective information data, and the weights calculated by the analytic hierarchy method and the weights calculated by the entropy method are nonlinear weighted to obtain the final weight w_i.

$$w_i = \frac{w_i' w_i''}{\sum_i^t w_i' w_i''} \tag{12}$$

w_i' is the subjective weight determined by analytic hierarchy. w_i'' is the objective weight determined by entropy method.

3.4 The Total Score of the Risk Assessment of the Aids to Navigation

Points are deducted from the evaluation indicators, multiplied by the corresponding weights and then summed, and the calculation formula is shown in equation (9).

$$D = \sum_i w_i d_i \tag{13}$$

D—Weighted total demerit points for Aids to navigation
d_i—The demerit value of the evaluation indicator i of the Aids to navigation
Referring to the current assessment specifications, this paper divides the risk level of the beacon into three levels, as shown in Table 3, of which the level 1 risk is the smallest risk, the level 2 risk is the medium risk, and the level 3 risk is the larger risk.

Table 3. navigation risk classification

Risk level	Level I risk	Level II risk	Level III risk
Score interval	(0,25)	(25,40)	(40,100)

4.   Research on the Application of Risk Evaluation System for Aids to Navigation

4.1 Evaluation Process

This paper explores the historical data of navigation beacons in the waters of the Guangzhou Maritime Safety Bureau to take sensor data from 8 am to 12 am on March 21, 2023.

According to the chromatographic analysis method, the first-level factors set $U=\{X_1, X_2, X_3, X_4\}=\{$Aids to navigation lamp, power supply, appearance, environment$\}$ are established, and the judgment matrix of the Aids to navigation index is constructed. Through the investigation of the Aids to navigation, after the analysis of the Aids to navigation failure, relevant experts were invited to make judgment decisions on this matrix, and the judgment matrix of the criterion layer to the target layer was obtained, as shown in Table 4.

Table 4. Judgment matrix for the first-level indicators

	X_{11}	X_{12}	X_{13}	X_{14}
Aids to navigation light	1	1/3	5	3
Aids to navigation power supply	3	1	7	4
Aids to navigation appearance	1/5	1/7	1	1/2
Waterway environment	1/3	1/4	2	1

According to the judgment matrix in Table 3, the weight of the first-level indicators are calculated, and the calculation process is as follows:

1) The judgment matrix B of the criterion layer for the target layer.

$$X = \begin{bmatrix} 1 & \dfrac{1}{3} & 5 & 3 \\ 3 & 1 & 7 & 4 \\ \dfrac{1}{5} & \dfrac{1}{7} & 1 & \dfrac{1}{2} \\ \dfrac{1}{3} & \dfrac{1}{4} & 2 & 1 \end{bmatrix}$$

2) According to formulas (2)-(3), calculate the eigenvector w_i' of the criterion layer relative to the target layer.

$$w_i' = \begin{bmatrix} 0.272 \\ 0.549 \\ 0.063 \\ 0.116 \end{bmatrix}$$

3) According to formula (4), calculate and judge the maximum eigenvalue $\lambda_{max}=4.07$ of matrix X.

4) According to the formula (5) and (6), calculate and judge the matrix consistency index CI and the consistency ratio CR.

CI=0.023, CR=0.026, because CR=0.026<0.1, so the judgment matrix meets the requirements.

Similarly, the judgment matrix formula (2)-(6) of the construction scheme layer for the criterion layer calculates the subjective weight w' of each evaluation index of the third level as shown in Table 5-8 and the total ranking of the consistency test level, CR is less than 1, which meets the consistency requirements.

Table 5. X_{1j}'s judgment matrix and weight for X_1 （j=1,2,3,4,5）

X_1-X_{1j}	X_{11}	X_{12}	X_{13}	X_{14}	X_{15}	w_{1j}
X_{11}	1	1/3	1/3	2	1/3	0.1
X_{12}	3	1	2	3	1/2	0.26
X_{13}	3	1/2	1	2	1/3	0.17
X_{14}	1/2	1/3	1/2	1	1/5	0.07
X_{15}	3	2	3	5	1	0.41

Table 6. X_{2j}'s judgment matrix and weight for X_2 （j=1,2,3,4,5）

X_2-X_{2j}	X_{21}	X_{22}	X_{23}	X_{24}	X_{25}	w_{2j}
X_{21}	1	1	1/2	2	5	0.23
X_{22}	1	1	1/2	2	5	0.23
X_{23}	2	2	1	3	4	0.36
X_{24}	1/2	1/2	1/3	1	2	0.12
X_{25}	1/5	1/5	1/4	1/2	1	0.06

Table 7. X_{3j}'s judgment matrix and weight for X_3 （j=1,2,3）

X_3-X_{3j}	X_{31}	X_{32}	X_{33}	w_{3j}
X_{31}	1	1/3	3	0.26
X_{32}	3	1	5	0.64
X_{33}	1/3	1/5	1	0.1

Table 8. X_{4j}'s judgment matrix and weight for X_4 （j=1,2,3,4,5,6）

X_4-X_{4j}	X_{41}	X_{42}	X_{43}	X_{44}	X_{45}	X_{46}	w_{4j}
X_{41}	1	2	1/3	2	1/5	1/5	0.08
X_{42}	1/2	1	1/3	1	1/5	1/4	0.06
X_{43}	3	3	1	2	1/3	1/3	0.14
X_{44}	1/2	1	1/2	1	1/5	1/5	0.06
X_{45}	5	5	3	5	1	2	0.38
X_{46}	5	4	3	5	1/2	2	0.29

The weights w'' of the indicators X-X_2-X_{21} and X-X_2-X_{22} of continuity are calculated by formulas (8)-(12), and the final weight calculation results are shown in Table 9.

Table 9. The final calculated weight for the secondary metric

Evaluation indicators	w_i'	w_i''	w_i
X-X_1-X_{11}	0.1	-	0.1
X-X_1-X_{12}	0.26	-	0.26

Evaluation indicators	w_i'	w_i''	w_i
$X-X_1-X_{13}$	0.17	-	0.17
$X-X_1-X_{14}$	0.07	-	0.07
$X-X_1-X_{15}$	0.41	-	0.41
$X-X_2-X_{21}$	0.23	0.231	0.23
$X-X_2-X_{22}$	0.23	0.769	0.55
$X-X_2-X_{23}$	0.36	-	0.36
$X-X_2-X_{24}$	0.12	-	0.12
$X-X_2-X_{25}$	0.06	-	0.06
$X-X_3-X_{31}$	0.26	-	0.26
$X-X_3-X_{32}$	0.64	-	0.64
$X-X_3-X_{33}$	0.1	-	0.1
$X-X_4-X_{41}$	0.08	-	0.08
$X-X_4-X_{42}$	0.06	-	0.06
$X-X_4-X_{43}$	0.14	-	0.14
$X-X_4-X_{44}$	0.06	-	0.06
$X-X_4-X_{45}$	0.38	-	0.38
$X-X_4-X_{46}$	0.29	-	0.29

4.2. Analysis of Evaluation Results

The weight calculation based on the combination of AHP and the Entropy Weight Method addresses the limitations of subjective assessments and allows for the comprehensive consideration of both subjective and objective factors. This approach enhances the overall comprehensiveness, objectivity, and accuracy of the evaluation results. Based on Equation (13), the final calculated total score is 23 points, indicating a Level I risk. Because the total score of the Aids to navigation risk is close to the level II risk score, it has certain potential risks and needs to be strengthened maintenance and overhaul. The results of the existing risk analysis of the Aids to navigation show that the existing risk of the Aids to navigation mainly has four first-level factors: the Aids to navigation light, the power supply of the Aids to navigation, the appearance of the Aids to navigation, and the channel environment. The weights of its indicators are 0.27, 0.55, 0.06, 0.116, respectively. It can be seen that the risk of the power supply of the Aids to navigation is the main risk of the existing Aids to navigation, followed by the Aids to navigation light, and the environmental safety risk of the waterway is the smallest.

5.   Conclusion

In this paper, the risk evaluation system of the Aids to navigation is constructed, which is divided into four first-level indicators and nineteen second-level indicators, and the analytic hierarchy method-entropy method is used to evaluate the navigation target in a certain water area in Guangzhou.

1) In this paper, the analytic hierarchy method is used to determine the subjective weight, the entropy method is used to determine the objective weight, and the subjective evaluation and objective evaluation are combined to obtain the final weight.

2) Taking the Aids to navigation in a certain water area in Guangzhou as an example for risk evaluation, it is concluded that the total demerit points of this navigation beacon risk are in the first-level risk range, but close to the second-level risk range, and the buoy needs to be maintained and overhauled.

3) This paper calculates the weights of individual evaluation criteria for Aids to navigation and arranges them in order of importance. This information can offer valuable guidance and recommendations for prioritizing the treatment of high-risk indicators, as well as determining inspection and maintenance frequencies for Aids to navigation.

4) In this paper, a static risk assessment of Aids to navigation is conducted using the AHP-entropy method. However, as a future research direction, it is recommended to explore dynamic methods for assessing the dynamic risks associated with Aids to navigation.

Acknowledgment

This project is supported by the National Key Research and Development Program of China (No.2021YFB2600300)

References

[1]   Zhang Xiaocai, Zhao Lining, Wang Haibao, et al. Classification Method of Navigational Aids in Inland Waters Based on Big Data[C]. Ninth International Conference on Frontier of Computer Science and Technology. Dalian, China: IEEE, 2015: 203-208.

[2]   Peng Guojun, Zhang Xingguo, Ke Ranxuan, et al. Research on Navigation-Aids Information System[C]. International Conference on Cyberworlds. Hangzhou: IEEE, 2008: 601-604.

[3]   Chen Liping, Zhang Xinggu. The Application and Research of navigation-aids inspection and maintenance based on video surveillance[J]. Procedia Engineering, 2011, 15: 3088-3092.

[4]   Li Hui, Sang Lingzhi. On the Research and Realization of Standardized Telemetry and Telecontrol System for AtoN[J]. China Maritime Safety, 2019(6): 36-39+45 (in Chinese).

[5]   Wang Wei. Design and Application of the Buoy Telemetry and Telecontrol System of the South China Sea[D]. South China University of Technology, 2010 (in Chinese).

[6]   Ma Jialin. Research on beacon telemetry remote control system based on NB-IoT technology[J]. China Water Transport, 2018, 18(7): 51-52 (in Chinese).

[7]   Yue Zhiyong, Tian Yongzhong, Fan Shuqin, et al. Beidou satellite communication technology in the beacon telemetry remote control system Applied thinking. [J]. China Water Transport, 2021(5): 74-79 (in Chinese).

[8]   Li Xin, Wenquan, Li Yiting. Discussion on threshold of navigation service status index in navigation telemetry remote control system[J]. Journal of Waterway and Harbor, 2022, 43(4): 543-548 (in Chinese)

[9]   Hye-Ri, Park, Seung-Gi, et al. A Study to Develop an Efficiency Analysis Model to Aids to Navigation [J]. Journal of the Korean Society of Marine Environment and Safety, 2016, 22(6): 647-653.

[10]   Nie Ziyi, Jiang Zhonglian, Chu Xiumin, et al. Efficacy Evaluation of Maritime AtoN by Fuzzy AHP Approach[C]. 5th International Conference on Transportation Information and Safety. Liverpool, United Kingdom: IEEE, 2019: 247-251.

[11]   Deng Zhusen. Application of GM (1,1) Model in Sea Navigation Mark Operation Management[C]. 5th International Symposium on Computer, Communication, Control and Automation. Colombo, SRI LANKA, 2018. 3-7.

[12] Li Xueliang, Wu Kuihua, Wang Fei, et al. A Comprehensive Benefit Evaluation Model for Distributed Energy Systems Based on AHP-entropy Weight Method[C]. 5th Asia Conference on Power and Electrical Engineering. 2020. 928-933.

[13] Liu Yan, Eckert C M, Earl C. A review of fuzzy AHP methods for decision-making with subjective judgements[J]. Expert Systems with Applications, 2020, 161:113738.

[14] Yang Shuwen, He Jun, Fan Yaxiang. Analysis of Digital Economy Development Based on AHP-Entropy Weight Method[J]. Journal of Sensors, 2022, 2022: 1-8.

[15] Guzelci O Z, Sener S M. An Entropy-Based Design Evaluation Model for Architectural Competitions through Multiple Factors[J]. Entropy, 2019, 21(11): 1064.

[16] Apurwa Singh, Roshan Koju, "Healthcare Vulnerability Mapping Using K-means ++ Algorithm and Entropy Method: A Case Study of Ratnanagar Municipality", International Journal of Intelligent Systems and Applications, Vol.15, No.2, pp.43-54, 2023.

[17] Rama Mercy. S., G. Padmavathi, "Self-healing AIS with Entropy Based SVM and Bayesian Aggregate Model for the Prediction and Isolation of Malicious Nodes Triggering DoS Attacks in VANET", International Journal of Computer Network and Information Security, Vol.15, No.3, pp.90-105, 2023.

Artificial Intelligence, Medical Engineering and Education
Z.B. Hu et al. (Eds.)
© 2024 The Authors.

doi:10.3233/ATDE231313

Impact of the New Individual Income Tax Reform on Resident Consumption-Based on Empirical Data from Hubei Province

Yeye ZHOU[1], Kan WANG

School of Economics and Management, Wuchang Shouyi University, Wuhan, China
ORCiD ID: Yeye ZHOU https://orcid.org/0000-0002-0173-5530

Abstract: Tax reform, as an important measure of national macroeconomic regulation, is of great significance in stimulating resident consumption. The article selects data on individual income tax and resident consumption levels in Hubei Province from 2016 to 2021 as research samples, and uses SPSS software to empirically analyze the impact of the 2019 new individual income tax reform on resident consumption. The research results indicate that individual income tax reform can effectively promote resident consumption expenditure, and reducing residents' tax burden is beneficial for promoting resident consumption. Based on this, the article proposes suggestions from three aspects: the individual income tax collection system, the individual income tax rate structure, and the tax regulatory system, providing theoretical reference for deepening the individual income tax reform.

Key words: New individual income tax reform; Resident consumption; Tax regulatory system

1. Introduction

At present, various government agencies and departments have specifically pointed out that "vigorously developing domestic demand" is an important work content, to connect various aspects of production, circulation, and consumption, in order to improve resident consumption level. With the gradual development of the economy, the income distribution gap among residents in China is still large, and social development still faces the problem of insufficient consumption demand. In order to expand social consumption demand, the government has taken the tax system as the key point of reform, of which individual income tax is regarded as the main tax reform point because of its function of regulating residents' income, and it is also a key factor in promoting the optimization of consumption expenditure and consumption structure. Individual income tax is directly related to residents' disposable income, and deepening the regulation of income redistribution is an effective way to expand domestic demand and promote consumption. How to continuously deepen the reform of individual income tax and better play the role of individual income tax in economic development remains an important task for China in the future.

The individual income tax reform in 2019, China's first combination of classified

---

[1] Corresponding Author: Yeye ZHOU, E-mail: 610643847@qq.com.

collection and comprehensive collection of individual income tax, together with the further improvement of standard deductions and the increase of six special additional deductions, is a major step in the reform of individual income tax, which has significantly changed the disposable income and consumption expenditure of residents. Therefore, analyzing whether the reform of individual income tax can effectively stimulate resident consumption and to what extent it can promote consumption is increasingly attracting attention from all sectors of society.

Based on this, the paper mainly conducts empirical research around the impact of the new individual income tax reform on resident consumption, aiming to put forward policy recommendations for deepening the reform of the individual income tax collection system in the future, and strive to improve the consumption environment, improve the consumption level, and promote social fairness, to optimize China's future economic development model.

2. Research Basis and Research Design

2.1. Research Basis

At present, domestic and foreign scholars have conducted a profound analysis of the effects of individual tax policies mainly from two aspect, namely, the relationship between individual income tax and resident income and the impact of individual income tax on resident consumption, which provides a solid theoretical basis for the country to further optimize individual income tax policy and improve the level of residents' consumption.

2.1.1. The Relationship between Individual Income Tax and Resident Income

Domestic and foreign scholars agree that the individual income tax has an obvious regulatory effect on resident income. Hidayat Amir examines the impact of income tax reform in Indonesia on factors such as poverty and income distribution. Studies have shown that a reduction in individual income tax has led to a slight decline in the poverty rate; However, tax cuts are more beneficial to high-income households and therefore lead to increased income inequality [1]. Sérgio Wulff Gobetti & Rodrigo Octávio Orair analyzed the effect of income distribution before and after the individual income tax reform in Brazil, and believed that the tax exemption policy for dividends and dividends has a reverse adjustment effect on the income distribution effect [2]. Silvia Avram conducted a study on the redistribution effect of individual tax in several European countries through micro-simulation methods, and the results showed that the deduction of individual income tax is more obvious for middle- and upper-income groups [3]. Roberto Ramos, Nezih Guner and Javier López-Segovia found that the more progressive taxes, the lower the work income and quality of life of residents [4]. Li Jing and Niu Xuehong analyzed that the distribution effect of individual income tax income after the 2019 reform has weakened compared to before [5]. Liu Pengyan and Yang Xiaomei stated that the progressivity of individual income tax and its proportion of income affect the effectiveness of income redistribution regulation, and progressive taxation is conducive to narrowing the income gap [6].

2.1.2. The Effect of Individual Income Tax on Resident Consumption

Domestic and foreign scholars agree that the individual income tax reform has a significant impact on resident consumption. Hüseyin Şen and Ayşe Kay empirically analyzed the influence of resident consumption in Turkey by the tax policy of the country, and the results showed that among all international tax systems, the highest impact on residents' living consumption is value-added tax and individual income tax [7]. Jason DeBacker selected income tax data from the federal administration of Kansas from 2010 to 2014 as a research sample, and empirically showed that the reform of individual income tax increased economic activities such as consumption [8]. Mitja studied the effectiveness of the individual income tax reform during the financial crisis in Slovenia. The results showed that personal consumption further increased in the short term, but over time, the growth of personal consumption has been decreasing [9]. Maren Froemel and Charles Gottlieb found that the income tax credit system can increase household savings and improve the consumption situation of impoverished households [10]. Mao Jun pointed out that the redistribution effect of individual income tax can adjust income distribution, achieve social fairness, and improve the consumption capacity of the overall residents [11]. Li Zhaoqi pointed out that the newly added six special deductions have played a positive role in stimulating resident consumption potential and expanding their consumption demand [12].

2.1.3 Literature Review

Looking at existing literature, most scholars at home and abroad believe that reducing the individual income tax burden has a significant promoting effect on resident consumption. However, some scholars believe that the positive impact of individual income tax reform on resident income distribution is relatively unstable, and there are some problems in promoting consumption, and corresponding improvement suggestions have been proposed.

Although relevant research at home and abroad has deeply analyzed the significance of the impact of individual income tax on resident consumption, and generally concluded that the individual income tax reform has a significant impact on resident consumption; however, in terms of empirical analysis, many studies only focus on the current consumption situation after the individual income tax reform. Due to the influence of various factors, consumers often have lagging consumption tendencies, so they will affect the accuracy of the research results. Therefore, future research should further expand the selection range of research data [13,14].

2.2. Research Design

2.2.1. Research Hypothesis

Friedman proposed two concepts in the theory of persistent income: persistent income and temporary income. The viewpoint holds that persistent consumption is determined by persistent income, while temporary consumption is determined by temporary income. The consumption expenditure of residents will not increase in a short period of time due to temporary income increases, and consumption expenditure will only increase with the increase of residents' permanent income. It can be seen that the temporary tax reduction policy of the government will not have a positive impact on the consumption behavior of residents, but will increase the savings behavior of residents. Therefore, the government should take long-term tax reduction measures to increase residents' persistent income, thereby increasing residents' consumption expenditure, and the promotion effect on resident consumption will be more significant.

Based on this, the article proposes the corresponding hypothesis that the reform of individual income tax has a significant impact on the resident consumption level.

2.2.2. Sample Selection and Data Sources

The research compiles relevant data from the official website of the National Bureau of Statistics and the China Statistical Yearbook. In order to ensure that the research results are more targeted and enhance their indicative role in regional development, the research will select relevant data on individual income tax, resident income, and consumption in Hubei Province from 2016 to 2021, to research the impact of individual income tax on resident consumption levels.

2.2.3. Variable Setting

The dependent variable: per capita consumption expenditure of residents, mainly reflecting the degree of changes in the resident consumption level in Hubei Province before and after the individual income tax reform.

Explanatory variable: per capita individual income tax of residents, mainly reflecting the tax burden level of individual income tax in Hubei Province.

Control variables: select the added value of the financial industry and the expenditure value of the general public budgeting as the control variables, respectively reflecting the service provided by financial institutions in Hubei Province to convert savings into investment and the distribution and use of funds raised by the finance.

2.2.4. Model Building

Based on the above analysis, a linear regression equation is established as follows:

$$Y = \alpha X_1 + \gamma_1 X_2 + \gamma_2 X_3 + \beta \tag{1}$$

Where, Y represents the per capita consumption expenditure of residents, X_1 represents the per capita individual income Tax, X_2 represents the added value of the financial industry, and X_3 represents the expenditure value of the general public budgeting, α, γ_1 and γ_2 represents the coefficients of each variable, β is a constant term.

3. Empirical Analysis

3.1. Descriptive Statistical Analysis

The descriptive statistical analysis results of each variable are shown in Table 1.

According to Table 1, the consumption status of residents during the observation period was relatively ideal, and the average consumption expenditure per capita is 19504.00, indicating that the average consumption level of residents was relatively good and the overall consumption status was at a relatively high level. In addition, the minimum average consumption expenditure of residents is 15889.00, while the maximum value is 23846.00, with a difference of 7957. This indicates that there is a significant change in resident consumption expenditures in Hubei Province from 2016 to 2021, and there is likely to be some room for improvement in the level of residents' consumption.

The average individual income tax per capita of residents is 70040.27, while the maximum value is 86415.55, and the minimum value is 55859.19. The individual income tax per capita of residents changes greatly, reflecting the obvious tax reduction effect of individual income tax reform, which has a great relationship with the level of regional economic development. With the continuous development of the economy, the tax payable of residents has increased, and the per capita individual income tax of residents has also increased, which has also increased the per capita disposable income of residents.

The average added value of the financial industry is 2792.90, indicating that the relevant income brought by the financial industry to residents has always been considerable; the average value of general public budgeting expenditure is 7474.03, and the maximum value is 8443.00, indicating that the government has gradually increased its efforts in economic construction.

Table 1. Statistics of descriptive statistical analysis results for each variable

Variable	Minimum	Maximum	Mean	Std. Dev.
Y_1	15,889.00	23,846.00	19,504.00	2,926.75
X_1	55,859.19	86,415.55	70,040.27	11,328.82
X_2	2,318.87	3,432.74	2,792.90	392.26
X_3	6,423.00	8,443.00	7,474.03	734.75

3.2. Correlation Analysis

In order to test the relationship between the explained variable and various indicators in the data, the section uses SPSS software to conduct correlation analysis on various indicators based on Pearson correlation theory, and studies the significance of the relationship between various indicators. The correlation calculation results of various indicators are shown in Table 2.

Table 2. Statistics of the correlation analysis results of each variable

Variable	X_1	X_2	X_3
X_1	1	-0.043	0.753
X_2	—	1	-0.269
X_3	—	—	1

Note: ** and * represent significant at the 1% and 5% levels

According to the data of Table 2, there is no significance between the three variables of per capita individual income Tax, added value of the financial industry and general public budgeting expenditure, and the model that do not exist independent variable multiple linear problems.

3.3. Regressive Analysis

The results of linear regression analysis are shown in Table 3.

Table 3. Regression analysis results statistics

Variable	Non standardized coefficient		Standardized Coefficient	t	Sig.
	Coefficient	Std. Error	Coefficient		
(β)	8448.244	2509.896	—	3.366	0.078
X_1	0.426	0.061	1.647	6.974	0.020
X_2	-3.041	1.446	-0.408	-2.103	0.067
X_3	-1.372	0.546	-0.359	-2.515	0.128
R^2	0.989		Durbin-Watson stat	1.756	
Adjusted R^2	0.972		F-statistic	58.836	

The coefficient R^2 is an indicator for evaluating the rationality of regression equations. When R^2 is greater than 0.75, it indicates that the model has a good fit. From the regression result, the calculated R^2 is 0.989, and R^2 is greater than 0.75, indicating that the regression model has a good fit and a high degree of interpretability for the dependent variable. Based on the above analysis, the model is adjusted. After adjustment, the R^2 value changes slightly from the original 0.989 to 0.972, which shows that the fitting degree of the equation is good, indicating that the per capita individual income tax, the added value of the financial industry, and the general public budgeting expenditure value of local finance have 97.2% of the explanation degree of per capita consumption expenditure. The Durbin-Watson value is an effective method to test whether a model has autocorrelation, and when it is between 1.5 and 2.5, it indicates that the model does not have significant autocorrelation issues. The Durbin-Watson value of the model is 1.756, indicating that there is no significant sequence correlation and no abnormal issues in the model. The F-statistic of the model is 58.836, passing the F-test at the 1% significance level, indicating that the overall regression effect of the model is relatively ideal.

The regression equation obtained from the regression coefficient is:

$$Y = 0.426X_1 - 3.041X_2 - 1.372X_3 + 8448.244 \qquad (2)$$

3.4. Analysis of Results

The empirical analysis results show that the per capita individual income tax is positively correlated with the resident consumption expenditure, and the hypothesis is valid. This is because with the continuous development of the economy, the resident income will increase, and the individual income tax will also increase, which will ultimately affect the resident consumption expenditure. The significance of both is 0.020, indicating that the T-test has been passed at a significance level of 5%, indicating that promoting resident consumption requires implementing tax reduction and burden reduction policies in the context of continuous economic development to reduce resident tax burden.

There is a negative correlation between the added value of the financial industry and resident consumption expenditure, and it is significant at the 10% level. The higher the added value of the financial industry, the higher the resident savings rate; the more preventive savings behaviors occur, the more restrained consumer spending will be.

The value of general public budgeting expenditure of finance has a negative correlation with resident consumption expenditure, but it is not significant and has not passed the significance test. On the one hand, the expenditure value of the general public budgeting will reduce resident consumption, on the other hand, it will promote output, thus increasing resident consumption. The two are not significant. It may be that the distribution is unreasonable and the use efficiency is not high, which indicates that the general public budgeting expenditure in the future should be more reasonably distributed and the expenditure structure should be improved.

The results of the study further validate the previous views of domestic and foreign scholars, and the sample selection includes data from three years before and after the individual income tax reform, providing more sufficient evidence for the establishment of this viewpoint.

4. Suggestions on Deepening the Individual Income Tax Reform

According to the above analysis, to further promote resident consumption and deepen the reform of individual income tax, the ideas are: first, increase resident income level by relying on relevant tax reduction policies of the individual income tax collection system, so as to increase resident consumption expenditure; the second is to adjust the income distribution gap, make income distribution more fair, and reduce the preventive savings behavior of people with consumption potential. Therefore, the chapter puts forward suggestions on deepening the reform of individual income tax from the aspects of individual income tax collection system, individual income tax rate structure and tax regulatory system.

4.1. Improve the Individual Income Tax Collection System

Increasing resident disposable income can effectively promote resident consumption, and individual income tax is closely related to resident income, so the government can improve the special deduction items and expense deduction mechanism in the individual tax collection system, reduce residents' tax burden, and improve residents' wage income.

4.1.1. Improve Special Additional Deduction Items

With the gradual opening of China's fertility policy, households are paying more attention to their children's education and increasing their education expenses. However, raising children not only requires education expenses, but also bears expenses such as food, housing, medical care, and transportation, which account for a significant proportion of household expenses. Therefore, the deduction scope should be appropriately expanded to cover the majority of childcare expenses as much as possible.

In addition, the special additional deduction items in China only apply different deduction standards for housing rent based on the size of the city, while the deduction standards for other items are fixed and unchanged. With the increase of price levels, the quota deduction mechanism lacks rationality, and expenses for children's education, elderly care, and other projects are also related to regional economic development.

Therefore, the deduction of additional expenses should fully consider setting up a deduction mechanism that can reflect regional development differences, and achieve regional balance and fairness. If the deduction standard is linked to the price level, dynamic adjustments should be made in a timely manner to ensure that the special additional deduction policy can effectively reduce the tax burden on residents and increase their willingness to consume.

4.1.2. Adjusting the Basic Expense Deduction Mechanism

The establishment of a basic cost deduction mechanism is essentially to ensure the basic living expenses of residents. With the rise of domestic prices and the uneven regional development level in China, there is regional heterogeneity in resident consumption levels. If the expense deduction standard is not adjusted in time, the basic living income of some residents in underdevelopment will also be included in the collection scope of individual income tax. Therefore, the reform of individual income tax can consider linking the expense deduction standard with the consumer price index, creating a dynamic adjustment mechanism, combining the expense deduction mechanism with the changes in the consumer price index of residents, and also using resident income, consumption expenditure, etc. as reference basis to make more scientific adjustments. In this way, not only can residents' wage income be effectively increased, but also the impact of rising prices on resident consumption can be optimized.

4.2. Optimize the Structure of Individual Income Tax Rates

In the 2019 new individual income tax reform, the gap between the three low tax rates was expanded and the gap between the 25% tax rates was reduced, while the gap between the three high tax rates remained unchanged. The adjustment has increased the per capita disposable income of low-income residents, but the high-end tax rate has not changed, so the effect of policy adjustment on high-income groups is not significant. As for the middle-income group, the ideal disposable income and high-level consumption demand jointly promote the improvement of their consumption level. However, the consumption demand of the high-income group has gradually saturated, making it difficult to develop higher-level consumption demand. It can be seen that the main potential of social consumption is composed of middle-income groups with large base numbers and high consumption potential. Therefore, it is possible to consider reducing the tax rate hierarchy, adjusting the tax rate structure appropriately, reducing the tax burden, and promoting increased consumption.

Reducing the hierarchy of middle and low tax rates can effectively reduce the tax burden on low and middle-income groups, stabilize their income capacity, and stimulate resident consumption potential; reducing the hierarchy of high-level tax rates and adopting higher tax rates can stimulate the redistribution effect of taxation and improve the efficiency of the entire society. Targeted individual income tax reform not only promotes resident consumption and upgrades their consumption structure, but also deeply explores China's potential domestic demand.

4.3. Improve the Tax Regulatory System

With the rapid development of information technology, China's tax collection and payment methods have been constantly enriched. However, due to the asymmetry of information between the two parties, some residents have missed the tax preferential time or improper operation, and have not been able to enjoy the tax reduction brought about by the individual income tax reform; in addition, there are also some middle to high income individuals who use tax regulatory deficiencies to engage in illegal activities such as tax evasion. Therefore, we should further improve the tax regulatory system, coordinate the tax system, tax rate structure and regulatory system, and maximize the positive role of individual income tax on resident consumption.

Firstly, the government should improve tax regulatory policies. The improvement of tax laws should keep pace with the times, reduce tax planning space, and establish strict punishment systems to crack down on illegal activities that harm national interests, evade taxes, and increase the cost of illegal activities.

Secondly, the government should improve its tax supervision level, enhance citizens' tax awareness through publicity and education, promote a composite tax model that combines residents' active declaration and corporate withholding and payment, and open up online and offline multi-channel service channels to help taxpayers solve relevant tax issues and reduce tax compliance costs.

Finally, the government should improve the informatization of tax supervision, improve the individual income tax information management system, and use Internet technologies such as artificial intelligence and Big data to achieve intelligent supervision; at the same time, we should strengthen information sharing, create a comprehensive sexual network service platform, provide taxpayers with timely information about tax policies, solve the problem of information asymmetry, ensure that taxpayers can effectively enjoy relevant tax preferential policies, and reduce the tax burden of residents to promote consumption.

5. Conclusions

Through empirical research on the impact of the 2019 individual income tax reform on resident consumption in Hubei Province, it can be concluded that the individual income tax reform has a significant impact on resident consumption. The innovation of this paper is that the empirical research on the impact of individual income tax on resident consumption does not select the national sample data, but takes Hubei Province as a research case, which makes the research content more detailed, the research results more targeted, enhances the indicative role of the paper, more specifically reflects the impact of individual income tax reform, and plays a role in promoting the future deepening of individual income tax reform.

In recent years, China's industrial structure has undergone continuous optimization. Expanding internal demand and promoting resident consumption will be the main development direction for China in the future, in order to further promote economic growth. The article explores the impact of individual income tax on resident consumption expenditure, which is beneficial for the government to consider the actual situation when improving the tax system in the future, implement the current national policies to promote consumption, and strengthen the overall consumption strength of society. For residents, the article also provides new ideas from the perspective of individual income tax to stimulate consumption, enhance people's well-being, and improve residents' living standards.

References

[1] Hidayat Amir, John Asafu-Adjaye, Tien Ducpham. The impact of the Indonesian income tax reform: A CGE analysis[J]. Economic Modelling, 2013.

[2] Sérgio Wulff Gobetti & Rodrigo Octávio Orair. "Taxation and distribution of income in Brazil: new evidence from personal income tax data" [J]. Brazilian Journal of Political Economy, 2017: 267-286.

[3] Silvia Avram. Who benefits from the "hidden welfare state"? The distributional effects of personal income tax expenditure in six countries[J]. Journal of European Social Policy, 2018, 28(3): 271-293.

[4] Roberto Ramos, Nezih Guner, Javier López-Segovia. Reforming the individual income tax in Spain[J]. SERIEs, 2020, 11 : 369-406.

[5] Li Jing, Niu Xuehong. Research on the income distribution effect of individual income tax based on income structure[J]. Macroeconomic Research, 2022, (02): 16-26 (in Chinese).

[6] Liu Pengyan, Yang Xiaomei. The internal logic and optimization path of direct tax to promote common prosperity[J]. Tax Research, 2022, (10): 12-17 (in Chinese).

[7] Hüseyin Şen, Ayşe Kaya. Taxes and private consumption expenditures: a component-based analysis for Turkey[J]. Turkish Studies, 2016, 17(3).

[8] Jason DeBacker, Bradley T. Heim, Shanthi P. Ramnath, Justin M. Ross. The impact of state taxes on pass-through businesses: Evidence from the 2012 Kansas income tax reform[J]. Journal of Public Economics, 2019.

[9] Mitja Čok, Boris Majcen. Distribution of personal income tax changes in Slovenia[J]. Post-Communist Economies, 2020, (10): 123-135.

[10] Maren Froemel, Charles Gottlieb. The earned income tax credit: targeting the poor but crowding out wealth[J]. Canadian Journal of Economics, 2021, 54(1): 193-227.

[11] Mao Jun. Quantitative analysis of financial and tax policies and resident Consumption[M]. Beijing: Economic Science Press, 2020 (in Chinese).

[12] Li Zhaoqi. Implementation status and optimization analysis of the new individual income tax special additional deduction[J]. Bohai Rim Economic Outlook, 2021, (07): 119-122 (in Chinese).

[13] Paul E. Shao, Mussa Ally Dida, "Embedding Stock Tracking Module into Electronic Fiscal Device Machine and its Management System to Reduce Tax Evasion: A case of Tanzania", International Journal of Information Engineering and Electronic Business, Vol.11, No.5, pp. 24-32, 2019.

[14] Mihuandayani, Ema Utami, "Design Concept Integration Tax Payment System with Implementing Financial Technology", International Journal of Information Engineering and Electronic Business, Vol.10, No.5, pp. 15-22, 2018.

Artificial Intelligence, Medical Engineering and Education
Z.B. Hu et al. (Eds.)
© *2024 The Authors.*

doi:10.3233/ATDE231314

Analysis of Risk Prevention and Control Paths for Government Procurement in Universities in the Information Age

Wenzhe ZHAO, Qin SU[1], Qiang CHEN

Procurement and Tendering Office of Wuhan University of Technology, Wuhan, China

Abstract. Government procurement is an important link in promoting the operation and development of universities, which contains a series of risks. In the era of information technology, new types of risk vulnerabilities require advanced means and prevention. This article analyzes the risks of university government procurement from key aspects such as procurement document preparation, review process, and performance acceptance, forms a risk list, and establishes a process optimization matrix. It proposes response and prevention measures for university government procurement risks in the information age, in order to provide reference and reference for university government procurement work.

Keywords: Information age; Universities; Government procurement; Risk prevention and control

1. Introduction

Higher education institutions are places for cultivating high-level talents, which to some extent directly determine the development of a region or even a country [1-3]. The operation of higher education institutions requires the procurement of materials. In order to ensure the stable and orderly operation of school work, government procurement in universities provides strong material support for the development of universities, supporting various units of universities to assist in the smooth implementation of education, teaching, scientific research, management services, and other work, laying the foundation for achieving the connotation oriented development of universities [4, 5]. The scale of government procurement in universities is huge, involving complex and diverse funds and projects, and facing various risks. Conducting risk analysis and taking corresponding prevention and control measures is conducive to ensuring the fairness, impartiality, and transparency of government procurement in universities [6]. The above measures are of great significance for achieving the connotative development of universities and improving their educational level [7-9].

Domestic and foreign scholars have conducted relevant research on the risks in bidding procurement from different perspectives. Rusk S. believes that reducing risk is important for all projects. By means of adapting strategies to address economic, technical, environmental and social risks - and their increasing impact, if these risks are carried forward - risks can be reduced and project feasibility protected [10]. Hallikas analyzed the probability and possible outcomes of risk occurrence, and evaluated the risk [11].

---

[1] Corresponding Author: Qin SU, Email: 565791435@qq.com

Neu D. Everett J. proposed that Preventing corruption within government procurement: Constructing the specified and ethical subject is very important [12]. Liu Lihua and others analyzed the problems in actual bidding procurement in universities and proposed corresponding countermeasures and suggestions [13]. Zhou Xingyu and others analyzed the problems in internal control of university procurement business and proposed relatively comprehensive suggestions [14]. Li Huan, Wu Yang, and others have proposed in multiple papers the management mechanism and improvement measures of procurement organizations in the purchase of university equipment [15,16]. Strengthening security assessment and reducing procurement risks are also topics of common concern to the public [17,18].

The rapid development of technology in the information age has accelerated the pace of digital, networked, and intelligent transformation of traditional procurement [19, 20, 21]. It is of great significance to effectively avoid various potential risks and strive to achieve the goal of high-quality and cost-effective procurement [22-25].

2.   Risk Analysis of Government Procurement in Universities

2.1. Current Situation of Government Procurement Work in Universities

In recent years, with the reform of institutional mechanisms and the improvement of governance capabilities in universities, most universities have established specialized procurement and bidding management agencies to uniformly manage various procurement and bidding work in the school. The names of these agencies include the Procurement and Bidding Center, the Bidding and Equipment Procurement Center, and the Procurement and Bidding Management Office. Unlike ordinary enterprises, the tasks in university procurement appear in a bottom-up manner, driven by the scientific agenda of university researchers. However, the actual situation varies among universities, and there are still differences in the specific responsibilities of their procurement and bidding management agencies. Government procurement in universities requires the collaboration of many departments and personnel, which involves huge amounts of funds, complex procedures, diverse interests, and other characteristics during organization and implementation. Therefore, they face various risks, which may lead to problems such as waste of funds and unfair competition.

2.2. Government Procurement Risks in Universities

The government procurement of universities is a complex and complete organizational process, among which the most important key links are three: the preparation of procurement documents, the process of bid opening and evaluation, and the contract and performance (see Figure 1).

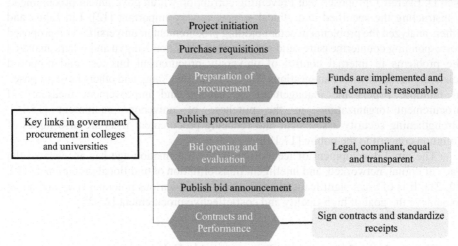

Figure 1. Key links of government procurement in universities

2.2.1. Risk of Procurement Document Preparation

The complete and accurate preparation of procurement documents is of great significance for achieving project objectives. When preparing procurement documents, the purchaser should implement the requirements of national government procurement regulations. At the same time, it is necessary to ensure the implementation of funds and reasonable demand.

The main contents of this type of risk include: technical parameter risk; Financial and competitive risks.

2.2.2 Review Process Risks

The most concise expression of the evaluation process is bid opening and evaluation. The evaluation of government procurement projects in universities should follow the principles of fairness, impartiality, and openness, ensuring that all potential suppliers can participate in competition on an equal footing. To comprehensively consider the capabilities, performance, and product performance of suppliers, select suitable suppliers to ensure the quality and effectiveness of the project.

It mainly includes three aspects, namely organizational risk, expert review risk, and corruption risk.

2.2.3 Contract and Performance Risks

The purchaser and supplier bind the rights and obligations of both parties by signing contracts, and performance acceptance is of great significance for quality control, risk management, project progress control, and cooperation relationship maintenance in contract performance. Performance acceptance is the last hurdle in the government procurement work of universities, and it is a key link to ensure that the government budget meets the originally set performance goals. Doing a good job in supervising performance acceptance can effectively reduce procurement risks.

The specific categories include contract risk, supplier risk, supervision risk, and policy risk.

3.   Risk Assessment and Process Optimization

3.1. Procurement Risk Assessment

Identify the degree of risk in the form of a list for the purpose of proposing prevention and control measures. The risk score and impact degree are divided into three levels, with values assigned as 3 points, 2 points, and 1 point. The higher the score, the higher the importance. Risk comprehensive score=risk score × The score of impact degree indicates that a result greater than or equal to 6 is an important risk, a result less than 3 is a minor risk, and the rest is a general risk.

The setting of risk score and impact degree score is directly related to the success or failure of risk identification. In an effort to accurately reflect the risk scores and impact levels of each risk point, this article uses the Delphi method to select 10 experts and scholars with years of experience in government bidding and procurement work in universities. They anonymously express their opinions and assign risk scores and impact levels to experts through three rounds of investigation. The arithmetic mean method is used as the result.

$$M_j = \frac{1}{n}\sum_{i=1}^n m_{ij} \tag{1}$$

Among them, M_j is the arithmetic mean of the indicator $j(j=1,2)$, $j=1,2$, representing the risk score and impact degree score, n is the number of experts, and m_{ij} is the score of the second expert on the indicator j. And the degree of coordination of expert opinions is reflected through the coefficient of variation:

$$CV_j = \frac{\sigma_j}{M_j}\sum_{i=1}^n m_{ij} \tag{2}$$

Among them, σ_j is the standard deviation of all experts' evaluation of indicators j.

$$\sigma_j = \sqrt{\frac{1}{n}\sum_{i=1}^n (m_{ij} - M_j)^2}\sum_{i=1}^n m_{ij} \tag{3}$$

The smaller the CV value, the higher the degree of coordination and convergence of expert opinions. After repeated consultation, induction, and modification, it was finally summarized into a consensus among experts, and the risk level was identified in the form of a list. The risk list of government procurement in universities is shown in Table 1.

In the table, the risk score and its coefficient of variation are denoted as $M1$ and $CV1$, respectively; The impact degree score and its coefficient of variation are represented by $M2$ and $CV2$; $M1 \times M2$ is the comprehensive score. The last column is the determined risk level, where * * represents important risks, and * represents general risks.

Table 1. List of risks in government procurement by universities

Risk Link	Type of risk	M1	CV1	M2	CV2	M1×M2	Grade
Documentation	Technic risk	3.00	0.00	3.00	0.00	9.00	**
	Financial risk	2.70	0.17	2.90	0.10	7.83	**
	competitive risk	2.00	0.00	2.10	0.14	4.20	*
Review process	Organizational risk	2.80	0.14	2.70	0.17	7.56	**
	Review expert risks	2.60	0.19	2.90	0.10	7.54	**
	Corruption risk	2.10	0.14	2.00	0.00	4.20	*
check and accept	Contract risk	2.00	0.00	1.90	0.15	3.80	*
	Supplier risk	2.70	0.17	2.80	0.14	7.56	**
	Supervision risk	1.90	0.15	2.00	0.00	3.80	*
	Policy risk	2.00	0.00	2.10	0.14	4.20	*

The results of the above risk analysis show that the coefficient of variation for each indicator score is less than 0.2, indicating a high degree of coordination and good convergence of expert opinions. According to the comprehensive score, there are 5 important risks and 5 general risks.

3.2. Key Process Optimization Matrix

Based on the key links identified in the procurement risk assessment, and in accordance with the principles of legal compliance, equal rights and responsibilities, hierarchical management, and classified exercise, a process optimization matrix for key links in government procurement is established (Table 2) to further strengthen the supervision of key links throughout the entire government procurement process (pre, during, and post), ensuring the smooth progress of government procurement work in universities.

Table 2. Optimization matrix for key processes in government procurement

Principle		Comply with the law, equal rights and responsibilities, hierarchical management, and classified exercise of power			
Beforehand	Key link	Separation of compilation and review of procurement documents			
	Process optimization	Centralized department	Technical experts	Agency Company	Countersign approval
During the process	Key link	Review process - compaction responsibility, fairness and impartiality			
	Process optimization	Party A's Representative	Collection of experts	expert training	Sound screen retention
Afterwards	Key link	Contract and performance - equal rights and responsibilities			
	Process optimization	Classification processing	Hierarchical implementation	Synchronous verification	Acceptance certificate

4.   Risk Prevention and Control of University Procurement in the Information Age

4.1. Basic Measures for Preventing Procurement Risks in Universities

Universities can take the following basic measures to prevent procurement risks.

(1) Improve institutional construction

Universities should establish a sound procurement management system, establish standardized procurement processes, clarify procurement procedures and the responsibilities of relevant personnel, focus on strengthening the construction of supervision mechanisms for important positions and key links, and ensure the compliance and transparency of procurement activities.

(2) Strengthen demand management

Universities should recognize the importance of procurement demand management, expand the breadth and depth of procurement demand management, and in the stage of procurement demand preparation, combine practical issues such as demand investigation, demand review, and procurement plan implementation to do a good job in procurement demand management.

(3) Improve personnel quality

Adopting various methods such as education and training, exchange and discussion, and case analysis to enhance the business capabilities of university procurement staff. At the same time, establish a reasonable incentive mechanism and performance evaluation system to promote the enthusiasm and initiative of procurement staff in universities.

(4) Strengthen performance acceptance

Universities should organize multiple departments, including finance, procurement, auditing, and purchasing units, to conduct joint acceptance based on the technical and commercial terms stipulated in the procurement contract. The departments participating in the acceptance work should jointly issue proof materials of acceptance after passing the acceptance.

4.2. Digital Procurement Platform Architecture in the Information Age

In the era of informatization, procurement business is gradually moving towards digitization and intelligence. There is an advanced concept that believes that digital procurement can turn the procurement department into a value creation center for enterprises, rather than just ensuring supply when "buying things".

Figure 2 shows the architecture design of a digital procurement platform. The three main components are the one-stop expenditure management platform, online matchmaking and collaboration platform, and the integration and centralization of procurement business.

The one-stop expenditure management platform can be seen as a "cloud + end" resource sharing and collaboration platform. It is a one-stop procurement mall with multiple terminals in parallel and full process cloud operation, connecting the reimbursement process and improving the overall financial efficiency of the enterprise. Transform the traditional two-party game, either overt or covert, into a transparent and controllable tripartite collaboration, reduce management difficulty, and effectively implement supplier performance evaluation.

The online matchmaking and collaboration platform includes full supplier management, sourcing management, contract management, physical inventory management, supplier collaboration portal, etc. Support all procurement needs of the enterprise through an integrated platform. The matchmaking platform is more valuable in the future and can effectively achieve credit warning work.

The integration and centralization of procurement business is also an important aspect. The middle platform refers to a comprehensive capability platform between the front and back ends, which can effectively connect the front and back ends, and has new rapid response capabilities. The deployment of a series of new technologies, such as in memory multidimensional databases, distributed computing, data visualization, intelligent data analysis, machine learning, etc., can be rapidly expanded and applied in procurement.

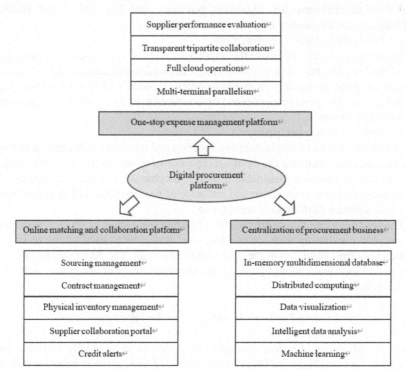

Figure 2. Architecture of a digital procurement platform

4.3. Procurement Risk Prevention Measures in the Information Age

The prevention of procurement risks in the information age requires building strong defenses from all aspects and leaving no loopholes. In addition to strengthening employee education and cultivating their sense of responsibility, it is also necessary to continuously enhance their ability to respond through technical means.

(1) Establish a digital procurement management platform

Procurement work should scientifically utilize information technology, establish a full process procurement management platform, and create a paperless, green, sustainable, and efficient procurement bidding model. By utilizing information technology, we ensure that the procurement process is traceable, data information can be queried, and improve procurement supervision capabilities and service levels.

(2) Building a standardized procurement document database

We should focus on procurement needs, establish a standardized procurement document database that includes various procurement categories and covers various procurement needs, provide demonstrations and templates for subsequent procurement projects, and accelerate the promotion of quality and efficiency improvement in university procurement work.

(3) Accelerate the digital development of procurement management

We should use information technology to comprehensively and systematically analyze data by capturing information such as demand, price, market, suppliers, and risks, in order to continuously optimize the government procurement workflow in universities and build an intelligent and flexible digital procurement system.

5. Conclusion

Government procurement in universities is an important task in their economic activities. It is directly related to the future development of the school. To conduct risk analysis of university procurement in the information age, it is necessary to conduct risk assessment and process optimization from a scientific perspective. Measures such as improving institutional construction and establishing a digital procurement management platform should also be taken to effectively reduce risks in the government procurement process of universities and promote high-quality development of government procurement work.

With the help of advanced technologies such as artificial intelligence and big data, the efficiency and reliability of procurement work will continue to improve, and the degree of intelligence will also become increasingly advanced. However, risk prevention is not a one-time solution, and the government procurement work in universities still needs to be continuously improved and improved. It is necessary to continuously improve personnel, systems, and technology, strengthen personnel training and technology promotion and implementation, in order to adapt to the development and changes of the new situation and achieve continuous improvement and innovation of government procurement work in universities.

References

[1]   Li Jing, He Shengsheng. Spatial econometric analysis of factors influencing the development of higher education in China[J]. 2021, (6): 6-11 (in Chinese).
[2]   Rae, John. Connecting for creativity in higher education[J]. Innovative Higher Education, 2022: 1-17.
[3]   Jiang Fan, Li Yuqian. How to promote innovation in higher education and the construction of world-class universities-- Summary of the Summit Forum on "Innovative Development of Higher Education and the Construction of World Class Universities"[J]. 2021, (4): 83-88 (in Chinese).
[4]   WU Guanyi. Whole Process Management of Government Procurement Suppliers in Colleges and Universities.[J]. Research & Exploration in Laboratory, 2019, .38(11): 282-300
[5]   Yue Tongwen, Hou Yi. A study of university procurement performance based on big data on government procurement[J]. Academic Journal of Business & Management, 2023, .5(4): 77-86
[6]   Zhu Bao. Analysis of strategies for improving the quality of university procurement work from the perspective of intensive development[J]. China Modern Equipment Education, 2022, (8): 41-42+46 (in Chinese)
[7]   Schmidt A. T. Construction supply chain welcomes new report on government infrastructure procurement[J]. Highway Engineering in Australia: Transport Infrastructure·Traffic Management·Intelligent Transport Systems, 2022, (3): 53.
[8]   Wirahadikusumah R, Abduh M, Messah Y. Framework for sustainable procurement - identifying elements for construction works[J]. Applied Mechanics and Materials, 2020, 897:245-249.

[9]   Anstis, Siena. Government procurement law and hacking technology: The role of public contracting in regulating an invisible market[J]. Computer Law & Security Review 41(2021):105536.

[10] Rusk S. Front-end strategies to reduce project risks[J]. CIM Magazine, 2019, (2):14.

[11] J.Hallikas, V.Virolainen, M. Tuominen. Risk Analysis environments: a dyadic case study[J]. Journal and Assessment in Network of Production Economics, 2002, (07): 45-55.

[12] Neu D. Everett J., Rahaman A. S. Preventing corruption within government procurement: Constructing the disciplined and ethical subject[J]. Critical Perspectives on Accounting, 2015, 28: 49-61.

[13] Liu Lihua. Discussion on the problems and solutions of university bidding procurement[J]. Journal of Liaoning University of Technology (Social Sciences Edition), 2018, 20, (01): 51-53 (in Chinese).

[14] Zhou Xingyu. Research on internal control of procurement business in public universities in China[D]. Nanjing: Nanjing Audit University, 2017 (in Chinese).

[15] Li Huan, Liu Juan, Cui Yunpeng, et al. Problems and improvement measures in the sharing management mechanism of large-scale instruments and equipment in agricultural research institutions: Taking the Chinese academy of agricultural sciences as an example[J]. Agricultural Science and Technology Management, 2021,40(2): 48-52 (in Chinese).

[16] Wu Yang, Zhang Mingqing, Chen Jianxin. Exploration of procurement organizational structure and informationization procurementJ]. Experimental Technology and Management, 2017, 34(6): 9-13 (in Chinese).

[17] Zhang Jianfang. Improving internal control mechanisms to make procurement risks controllable[N]. Government Procurement Information Report, 2021-09-13 (8) (in Chinese).

[18] Ou Yang Y P. Shieh H M,Tzeng G H. A VIKOR technique based on DEMATEL and ANP for information security risk control assessment[J]. Information Sciences, 2013.232(Complete):482-500.

[19] Hashimova Kamala, "Intelligent Management of a Network of Smart Billboards on the IoT Platform in Industry 4.0", International Journal of Information Technology and Computer Science, Vol.14, No.6, pp.39-46, 2022.

[20] Muhammad Aqeel, Hammad Shahab, Muhammad Naeem, Muhammad Sikander Shahbaz, Faizan Qaisar, Muhammad Ali Shahzad, "Intelligent Smart Energy Meter Reading System Using Global System for Mobile Communication", International Journal of Intelligent Systems and Applications, Vol.15, No.1, pp.35-47, 2023.

[21] Bisrat Betru, Fekade Getahun, "Ontology-driven Intelligent IT Incident Management Model", International Journal of Information Technology and Computer Science, Vol.15, No.1, pp.30-41, 2023.

[22] Mustapha A. Mohammed, Seth Alornyo, Michael Asante, Bernard O. Essah, "Intelligent Detection Technique for Malicious Websites Based on Deep Neural Network Classifier", International Journal of Education and Management Engineering, Vol.12, No.6, pp. 45-54, 2022.

[23] Aya S. Noah, Naglaa E. Ghannam, Gaber A. Elsharawy, Abeer S. Desuky, "An Intelligent System for Detecting Fake Materials on the Internet", International Journal of Modern Education and Computer Science, Vol.15, No.5, pp. 42-59, 2023.

[24] Wang P Y, Zhang B. Information service of a government procurement cloud platform based on the value chain model[J]. Journal of digital information management, 2021(3):19.

[25] Domashova J, Kripak E. Application of machine learning methods for risk analysis of unfavorable outcome of government procurement procedure in building and grounds maintenance domain[J]. Procedia Computer Science, 2021, 190:171-177.

Artificial Intelligence, Medical Engineering and Education
Z.B. Hu et al. (Eds.)
doi:10.3233/ATDE231315

Revisiting the Relation of Environmental Regulation and China's OFDI

Deyun XIAO, Luyao GAO[1], Jun TANG
School of Economics, Wuhan University of Technology, Wuhan, China
ORCiD ID: Luyao Gao https://orcid.org/0009-0002-2156-123X

Abstract. Since the reform and opening up, the rough-and-ready development model has brought about economic take-off, but it has also paid a huge price in terms of resources and environment. Under the double pressure of slowing economic growth and serious damage to the ecological environment, the intensity of China's environmental regulations has been increasing, and in 2013, eight provinces and municipalities began to implement a pilot policy of carbon emissions trading. At the same time, the scale of China's Outward Foreign Direct Investment (OFDI) has been increasing. Regarding the relationship between environmental regulation and OFDI, most scholars currently study it from the perspective of host-country environmental regulation, and fewer study home-country environmental regulation. Using provincial panel data for a total of 11 years from 2009 to 2019, this paper constructs a double-difference model based on the carbon emissions trading pilot policy in eight provinces and cities in China as a quasi-natural experiment and explores the relationship of home-country environmental regulation on China's OFDI.

Keywords. Environmental regulation; Outward Foreign Direct Investment (OFDI); Double differentiation; Carbon emissions trading.

1. Introduction

At present, China is facing increasingly serious environmental problems, and environmental pollution and destruction continue to emerge. These environmental problems not only affect people's health and waste resources, but also restrict the process of China's sustainable economic development. Du and Zhang [1] found that when the economic growth rate is too high, economic growth will inevitably cause environmental pollution. And a good ecological environment is both the cornerstone of people's pursuit of a happy life and the support of sustainable economic and social development [2]. The construction of China's ecological civilization has been advancing, and in this process, the intensity of China's environmental regulation has been gradually increasing. Against this backdrop, the state has proposed to co-ordinate the promotion of high-quality economic development and gradually transform China's economic system into a state of green, low-carbon and recycling development [3]. Starting from 2013, the pilot carbon emissions trading policy has been implemented in Beijing, Shanghai, Tianjin, Shenzhen, Guangdong, Hubei, Chongqing, and Fujian, to realize the development goals of carbon peaking and carbon neutrality as scheduled.

---

[1] Corresponding Author: Luyao GAO, Email: 2829349963@qq.com.

Based on existing research on environmental regulation and China's OFDI, this paper provides an in-depth investigation of how home country environmental regulation affects China's OFDI from the perspective of home country environmental regulation [4,5]. The innovative perspective of this study helps to understand the impact mechanism of environmental regulation on China's OFDI more comprehensively and puts forward relevant policy recommendations for achieving high-quality economic development and provides reference for national governments to formulate development strategies.

2.   Literature Review

Environmental regulation is a product of the combination of environmental and regulatory economics [6]. The environmental problems not only affect people's health and waste resources, but also restrict the process of China's sustainable economic development. In early studies, economists regarded the environment as a "public good", and Bovenberg and de Mooij [7] regarded environmental regulation as a manifestation of government intervention in economic development and environmental pollution, with the main purpose of preventing enterprises from focusing on their immediate interests without regard to the harm they do to resources and the environment, i.e., to reduce the negative impacts of corporate negative impacts caused by environmental pollution.

Many studies on the effects of environmental regulation mainly focus on macro and micro aspects. Tao [8] argues that environmental regulation can directly shift technological progress from pollution-intensive technology to green technology, thus directly contributing to the decrease of environmental pollution and improvement of the ecological environment. Li et al. [9] study Chinese firms and find that environmental regulation and the high-quality development of the economy called for by the Party Central Committee can complement each other. In a recent study, Xie et al. [10] found that the transfer of polluting industries due to environmental regulation has an N-shaped relationship between the economy and the environment.

Many scholars have studied the relationship between environmental regulation and OFDI. Liu [11] found that China's environmental regulation and foreign direct investment showed a significant inverted U-shaped relationship. Yin and Zhu [12] studied the relationship between China's two types of environmental regulations and China's OFDI and found that the impact of the two regulatory methods on outward foreign investment is diametrically opposite. The formal environmental regulations guaranteed by the government's coercive power will inhibit outward foreign direct investment, but the informal environment in which the public and social media participate can promote outward foreign investment.

In the past, more studies have explored environmental regulation and FDI, or environmental regulation and OFDI's reverse technology spillover effect, and most of them stand in the host country's environmental regulation perspective, while fewer studies have examined how the home country's environmental regulation influence China's OFDI, and even fewer studies have taken the carbon emissions trading pilot as a quasi-natural experiment [13,14]. When exploring the impact of environmental regulations on China's OFDI, there is no deeper exploration of their intrinsic mechanisms. The research mainly focuses on the moderating effects of environmental regulations on China's OFDI in terms of enterprises' intrinsic financing constraints.

3.   Theory and Assumptions

3.1. The Mechanisms of Environmental Regulation Affecting China's OFDI

OFDI can bring multiple advantages. First, by setting up production bases in countries with less stringent environmental regulations, enterprises can reduce the cost of pollution control [2]. Secondly, OFDI can bring more market opportunities and resources to further enhance the economic strength and competitiveness of enterprises. Finally, OFDI can also enhance the visibility and brand value of enterprises in the international market, establish the image of focusing on green environmental protection and strong sense of social responsibility, and lay the foundation for long-term development of enterprises [3]. The current Chinese environmental regulations on China's OFDI promotion effect, compared with the "Porter's hypothesis" put forward by the compensation effect of green technological innovation, more, dominated by the "pollution shelter" hypothesis led to the "high pollution and high energy consumption outward investment". In summary, there is a certain relationship between the strength of environmental regulation and China's OFDI, but the specific impact needs to be further explored. Accordingly, hypothesis 1 of this paper is proposed:

H1: Home country environmental regulation will promote China's OFDI.

3.2. The Mediating Effect of Production Cost Avoidance

The pollution haven hypothesis holds that under the trend of globalization and international integration, pollution-intensive industries will transfer from countries with strict environmental regulation to countries with loose environmental regulation. Carbon emissions trading, as a type of market-incentivized environmental regulation, will have a direct impact on the production costs of enterprises. Carbon emissions rights trading will have a direct impact on the cost of enterprises, so some enterprises may choose to make foreign direct investment in order to avoid the impact of rising costs brought about by carbon emissions rights trading. Accordingly, hypothesis 2 of this paper is proposed:

H2: Home country environmental regulation will increase enterprise costs by increasing the cost of enterprises, so that enterprises out of cost aversion considerations and outward direct investment.

4.   Empirical Analysis

4.1. Benchmark Regression Model Setting

In order to test the impact of environmental regulations on China's OFDI, a double difference model is constructed as follows:

$$OFDI_{it}=\alpha_1+\alpha_2 Carb_{it}\times Post_{it}+\alpha_3 Control_{it}+\lambda_t+\mu_i+\varepsilon_{it} \qquad (1)$$

Where the explanatory variable $OFDI_{it}$ is China's OFDI, indicating the OFDI flow of province i in year t. $Carb_{it}\times Post_{it}$ is the core explanatory variable in this paper, which is the cross-multiplier of the grouping dummy variable ($Carb_{it}$) and the time dummy variable ($Post_{it}$), $Carb_{it}$ is the dummy variable indicating that it is located in the pilot region of carbon emissions trading. $Carb_{it}$ is a dummy variable that indicates the location of the carbon emissions trading pilot region, $Carb_{it}$ is taken as 1 for the pilot region, and 0 for the non-pilot region. $Post_{it}$ is taken as 1 after the implementation of the policy (from 2013 to 2019), otherwise it is taken as 0. $Carb_{it}$ represents a series of control variables, and there is a total of 8 of them, including: the level of regional economic development, the degree of dependence on foreign investment, the regional industrial structure, the ownership structure of the industrial enterprises, the strength of the financial support, the governmental expenditure on energy conservation and environmental protection, infrastructure security and human capital. λ_t represents the year fixed effect, μ_i represents the province fixed effect, ε_{it} is the random error term, and I and t denote the province and year, respectively.

4.2. Mediation Effects Modelling

The previous study shows that the implementation of carbon emissions trading pilot policy may affect China's OFDI, in order to further study whether environmental regulation can affect China's OFDI through the mediating effect of $Cost_{it}$ the following mediating effect model is constructed with reference to the method of Wen et al (2005):

$$OFDI_{it} = \alpha_1 + \alpha_2 Carb_{it} \times Post_{it} + \alpha_3 Control_{it} + \lambda_t + \mu_i + \varepsilon_{it} \tag{2}$$

$$Cost_{it} = \beta_1 + \beta_2 Carb_{it} \times Post_{it} + \beta_3 Control_{it} + \lambda_t + \mu_i + \varepsilon_{it} \tag{3}$$

$$OFDI_{it} = c_1 + c_2 Carb_{it} \times Post_{it} + c_3 Cost_{it} + c_4 Control_{it} + \lambda_t + \mu_i + \varepsilon_{it} \tag{4}$$

4.3. Variable Selection and Data Sources

This paper uses China's provincial panel data for a total of 11 years from 2009 to 2019, excluding Xinjiang and Tibet, covering 29 provinces (autonomous regions and municipalities directly under the central government), with data from the State Intellectual Property Office, EPS database.

5. Empirical Testing and Analysis of Results

5.1. Descriptive Statistics

The descriptive statistics of all the variables are shown in Table 1, and the difference between the maximum and minimum values of the explanatory variable China's OFDI flow is very large, which indicates that there is a big gap between the OFDI capacity of China's provinces, providing room for interpretation of the possible influence mechanism in the middle. Among the control variables, there are also gaps in the level of economic development of provinces and cities, foreign investment dependence, government expenditure on energy conservation and environmental protection, human capital, financial support, regional industrial structure, and the development of industrial enterprises.

Table 1. Descriptive Statistics

Variable	Sample	Mean	STD	Min	Median	Max
OFDI	319	0.141	0.248	0.000	0.051	1.593
Cost	319	0.136	0.140	0.004	0.094	0.978
lnpgdp	319	10.715	0.499	9.241	10.697	12.009
depend	319	0.383	0.402	0.060	0.206	3.729
indus	319	0.454	0.098	0.286	0.440	0.835
soer	319	0.099	0.066	0.011	0.077	0.280
fina	319	3.017	1.063	1.506	2.862	7.575
lnenvir	319	-3.364	0.312	-4.251	-3.394	-2.552
infra	319	0.056	0.040	0.014	0.039	0.236
lnhc	319	-5.352	0.305	-6.383	-5.339	-4.717

5.2. Baseline Regression

(1) Regression Result

Table 2 presents the basic regression results and some robustness tests of the pilot emissions trading policy on China's OFDI using the double difference method. From the results in column (1) of Table 2, the regression coefficient of the policy interaction term $did = Carb_{it} \times Post_{it}$ is 0.265, which is significantly positive at 1% confidence level, indicating that the pilot policy of emissions trading in the market incentive environmental regulation promotes China's OFDI. The hypothesis H1 is proved.

Table 2. Double Difference Analysis of the Impact of Emissions Trading Pilot Policies on China's OFDI

	(1)	(2)
	OFDI	PSM-DID
did	0.265***	0.138**
	(4.09)	(2.00)
Control	YES	YES
N	319	209
R^2	0.724	0.749

(2) PSM-DID Test

The double-difference method may suffer from selectivity bias, i.e., it cannot ensure that pilot and non-pilot provinces and cities have exactly the same individual characteristics before and after policy implementation, i.e., there may be unobservable and time-varying differences, and the strength of response to the policy may be different across pilot provinces and cities, even if they are in the same experimental group. Considering that the pilot carbon emission rights policy provinces and cities are distributed in various regions of the country, and the economic development of these regions is not balanced, so in order to prevent policy estimation bias due to the emergence of these differences, this paper also adopts the double-difference propensity score matching method (PSM-DID) to conduct the test. Screening the provinces and cities similar to the experimental group in the control group as a new experimental group, the test results are shown in column (2) of Table 2, the regression coefficient of the policy interaction term $did = Carb_{it} \times Post_{it}$ is 0.138, and it is significant at 1% confidence level, which indicates that the results are very robust and the policy effect is credible.

5.3. Robustness Tests

An important assumption of the double-difference approach to assessing the impact of environmental regulation is that, assuming that all provinces and municipalities are free of environmental regulation as a policy shock, they should all have essentially the same trend. Instead, provinces and municipalities that adopt environmental regulation and those that do not will have differentiated trends after the implementation of the regulation. As can be seen from Figure 1, before 2013, the temporal development trend of OFDI in the experimental group and the control group is consistent, and after 2013 there is an obvious difference, and the gap is gradually getting bigger, therefore, the policy effect of market incentive environmental regulation measured by the carbon emissions trading pilot policy exists, which is consistent with the results of the previous analysis.

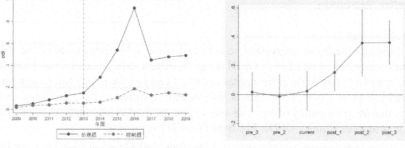

| **Figure 1.** Parallel Trend Test 1 | **Figure 2.** Parallel Trend Test 2 |

Similarly, as can be seen from Figure 2, the coefficients fluctuate around 0 and are insignificant before the current year, i.e., 2013, the year of policy occurrence, indicating that the development trend of China's OFDI in the control group and the experimental group is the same before the occurrence of the carbon emissions trading pilot policy; whereas, the coefficients are significantly positive and getting bigger after the current year, i.e., 2013, the year of policy occurrence, suggesting that the carbon emissions trading pilot has the policy effect of promoting China's OFDI.

5.4. The Mediating Effect of Production Cost Avoidance

(1) Regression Result
The results are shown in Table 3, the regression coefficient of the policy interaction term $did = Carb_{it} \times Post_{it}$ in column (1) is 0.265, which is significantly positive, the coefficient of the policy interaction term $did = Carb_{it} \times Post_{it}$ with the cost of production in column (2) is significantly positive, the coefficient of the policy interaction term $did = Carb_{it} \times Post_{it}$ with the cost of production in column (3) is also significantly $did = Carb_{it} \times Post_{it}$ and the coefficient 0.211 of production cost on China's OFDI is also significantly positive, which suggests that there is a partial mediating effect of production cost avoidance, i.e., environmental regulations do promote OFDI by making firms consider production cost avoidance. At this point, hypothesis H2 is proved.

(2) Robust Test

After replacing the measure of the explanatory variables and replacing OFDI flows with OFDI stock, the results are shown in Table 3, the regression coefficient of the policy interaction term $did = Carb_{it} \times Post_{it}$ in column (4) is 1.644 significantly positive, the coefficient of the policy interaction term $did = Carb_{it} \times Post_{it}$ with the production cost in column (5) is 0.0392 significantly positive, and the coefficient of the policy interaction term $did = Carb_{it} \times Post_{it}$ with production cost in column (6) is 0.0392 significantly positive for OFDI from China. 0.0392 is significantly positive, and the coefficient of the interaction term of policy $did = Carb_{it} \times Post_{it}$ and production cost on Chinese OFDI in column (6) is also significantly positive at 1.017, which also indicates that there is a part of the mediation effect, i.e., the results of the test of mediation effect of cost of production avoidance are robust.

Table 3. Mediating Effects of Production Cost Avoidance

	(1)	(2)	(3)	(4)	(5)	(6)
	OFDI	Cost	OFDI	OFDI	Cost	OFDI
did	0.265***	0.0392*	0.211***	1.644***	0.0392*	1.017***
	(4.09)	(1.75)	(3.85)	(3.25)	(1.75)	(3.52)
Control	YES	YES	YES	YES	YES	YES
N	319	319	319	319	319	319
R^2	0.724	0.912	0.776	0.707	0.912	0.851

6. Conclusions

The environmental problems not only affect people's health and waste resources, but also restrict the process of China's sustainable economic development. Through theoretical analysis and empirical test, this paper takes the pilot policy of carbon emission trading as a quasi-natural experiment, constructs a difference-in-difference model to test the applicability of the "pollution haven hypothesis" and the "Porter hypothesis" in China, and further examines the mediating effects of production cost avoidance. This paper mainly draws the following conclusions: The pilot policy of carbon emission trading as a market-incentive environmental regulation has a significant role in promoting China's OFDI, that is, the stronger the environmental regulation, the more China's OFDI. Environmental regulation can not only increase the production cost of enterprises, so that enterprises are forced to invest abroad to avoid higher costs, but also promote the compensation of green technology innovation, encourage enterprises to independently develop cleaner and more efficient production technology, enhance the competitiveness of enterprises, and enhance the initiative of OFDI. The level of marketisation development can play a positive moderating role in the process of environmental regulation to promote China's OFDI, the higher the level of marketisation, the stronger the promotion effect of environmental regulation on China's OFDI.

China is facing increasingly serious environmental problems, and environmental pollution and destruction continue to emerge. It is true that environmental regulation can promote Chinese OFDI, and it can be indirectly promoted through the intermediaries of production cost avoidance and green technological innovation, and the level of marketisation also plays a positive moderating role. However, it has to be said that the current Chinese environmental regulations on China's OFDI promotion effect, compared with the "Porter's hypothesis" put forward by the compensation effect of green technological innovation, more, dominated by the "pollution shelter" hypothesis led to the "high pollution and high energy consumption outward investment". High-pollution and high-energy-consumption outward investment, i.e., the motivation of enterprises for independent R&D and innovation is still insufficient, and high-quality OFDI resulting from technological innovation is still lacking.

References

[1]   Du, Zhang. Research on the role mechanism of economic growth and environmental pollution under the new normal[J]. Soft Science, 2017, 31(04): 1-4. (in Chinese)
[2]   Francis J, Zheng C, Mukherji A. An institutional perspective on foreign direct investment[J]. Management International Review, 2009, 49(5): 565-583.
[3]   García-Canal E, Guillén M F. Risk and the strategy of foreign location choice in regulated industries[J]. Strategic Management Journal, 2008, 29(10): 1097-1115.
[4]   He, Xu K. a study on the impact of the economic systems of the countries along the belt and road on China's OFDI[J]. International Trade Issues, 2018(01): 92-100. (in Chinese)
[5]   Taylor R. Globalization strategies of Chinese companies: current developments and future prospects[J]. Asian Bus Manage. 2002, 1, 209-225.
[6]   Kolstad I, Wiig A. What determines Chinese OFDI[J]. Journal of World Business, 2012, 47(1): 26-34.
[7]   Bovenberg A L, Ruud A M. Environmental levies and distortionary taxation: reply[J]. American Economic Association, 1997, 87(1), 252-253.
[8]   Tao, Ding Yu. Does dual environmental regulation promote or inhibit the skill premium [J]. Research and Development Management, 2019, 31(05): 114-12. (in Chinese)
[9]   Li S., Yu D. S., Yu J. Spatial spillover effects of heterogeneous environmental regulations on carbon productivity-based on spatial durbin model[J]. China Soft Science, 2020(04): 82-96.
[10] Xie. Green technology progress, positive externalities and environmental pollution governance in China[J]. Management Review, 2021, 33(06): 111-121. (in Chinese)
[11] Liu, Liu Y, Ma Q. Research on the two-way feedback effect of environmental regulation and high-quality economic development[J]. Economic and Management Review, 2021, 37(03): 111-122.
[12] Yin K D, Liu L, Huang C et al. Can the transfer of polluting industries achieve a win-win situation for both the economy and the environment? Research based on the Perspective of Environmental Regulation[J]. Environment, Development & Sustainability, 2022, 1-26.
[13] Bitat A. Environmental regulation and eco-innovation: the porter hypothesis refined[J]. Eurasian Business Review, 2018, 8(3): 299-321.
[14] Globerman S, Shapiro D. Global foreign direct investment flows: the role of governance infrastructure[J]. World Development, 2002, 30(11): 1899-1919.

Artificial Intelligence, Medical Engineering and Education
Z.B. Hu et al. (Eds.)
© 2024 The Authors.
This article is published online with Open Access by IOS Press and distributed under the terms
of the Creative Commons Attribution Non-Commercial License 4.0 (CC BY-NC 4.0).
doi:10.3233/ATDE231316

Construction of Talent Quality Evaluation Index System in Hydropower Industry Under the Background of Digital Transformation

Lihong HAO, Tao LIU, Jiwei TANG[1]

Dadu River-hydropower Development Co. Ltd, 610000, Chengdu, China

Abstract. Digital transformation and upgrading pose new requirements for talent quality. Taking human resources positions as an example, this article constructs a "3+X" talent quality evaluation index system that includes knowledge, ability, attitude, and professional skills. Based on the data characteristics of 55 employees in human resources positions, a combination weighting model, entropy method, and BP neural network model are used, and an evaluation index system and weight evaluation index system suitable for the quality characteristics of talents in China's hydropower industry have been constructed. The research results show that employee competence is an important indicator for driving digital transformation, with knowledge and professional skills playing a relatively central role, and attitudes being less differentiated. Finally, the research significance and shortcomings of the study are summarized, and the prospects for future development are provided.

Key words. Digital transformation; Talent quality characteristics; Evaluation index; BP neural network; Entropy method.

1. Introduction

In recent years, the digital economy has had a profound impact and transformation on resource allocation, economic form, and competition rules globally, playing a core role in promoting global development [1-3]. The Party and government repeatedly emphasize the need to "accelerate the development of the digital economy, promote the deep integration of the digital economy and the real economy, and create a digital industry cluster with international competitiveness." The rapid development of the digital economy has also brought new opportunities and challenges to traditional industries [4]. This is the case not only in China, but also around the world [5].

In the wave of digital economy transformation, talents with digital knowledge are indispensable [6, 7]. The construction of a talent evaluation system is undoubtedly a crucial issue [8-10]. At present, China's power enterprises are facing an important stage of institutional reform, especially with the arrival of the era of big data and artificial intelligence [11]. The traditional talent evaluation system in the hydropower industry is no longer sufficient to support enterprises in adapting to changes in the economic environment and cannot accurately describe their employment needs [12,13]. According

---

[1] Corresponding Author: Jiwei TANG, E-mail: 547272841@qq.com.

to the decision and deployment of the Party Central Committee and the State Council on the three-year action of state-owned enterprise reform and the work requirements of the Country owned Assets Supervision and Administration Commission, as well as the comprehensive implementation of the "Implementation Opinions on Deepening the Three System Reform of the National Energy Group" (National Energy Organization [2021] No. 176), in order to adapt to the requirements of the group company's reform and development and create world-class demonstration enterprises, and in combination with the characteristics of the new era represented by the digital economy, establish a scientific and focused hydropower industry A reasonable job talent evaluation system is a vital issue for Daduhe Company to maintain stability and long-term development.

In response to the above matters, this paper takes the human resources positions in Guoneng Daduhe Company as the research object, uses SPOT team guidance technology to jointly create an evaluation index system for the talent quality characteristics of human resources positions, and then uses entropy method and BP neural network to explore the index weights, constructing an evaluation index system suitable for the talent quality of the hydropower industry [14,15].

2. Research Methods and Evaluation Indicator System Construction

2.1. SPOT Team Guidance Technology

From the perspective of origin, SPOT team leadership technology is a team participatory decision-making method developed by Parab Naidu et al. (2014) [16]. It is guided by four elements: space, process, outcome, and time. Within a given time, team members engage in team interaction to achieve value co creation of a certain task.

In the actual operation process, the SPOT team guidance technology follows the 4D rule as the standard, communicates and interacts with team members through visual signage, and finally forms team members' identification with a certain goal through continuous correction and discussion.

2.2. Evaluation Index System for Talent Quality Characteristics in the Hydropower Industry

The construction of the evaluation system for the quality of talents in the hydropower industry should start from the evaluation dimension of quality characteristics, in order to find a way to construct the indicator system.

(1) The Evaluation Dimension and Construction of Talent Quality Characteristics Construction refers to the concepts formed through the understanding, expectation, evaluation, and thinking of people, things, and things in the environment. Based on SPOT team guidance technology, this article recruited more than 30 members specializing in human resource management from 25 subsidiaries of Guoneng Daduhe Group to participate in the seminar. According to Li Yang and Pan Haisheng, digital ability refers to the collective term for the knowledge, abilities, attitudes, and other skills that people must possess to integrate into the digital society [17].

In 2016, the European Union mentioned in the "Council Recommendation on Key Competences for Lifelong Learning" that digital capability is a survival capability formed by focusing on communication technology, utilizing internet communication and information governance [18]. In the EU Citizen Quality and Literacy Framework

(DigComp2.1), citizens' quality and literacy are divided into four levels [19]. Considering the social attributes of human resource management positions, in the team guidance process, the three elements of "knowledge, ability, and attitude" are considered as the "universal qualities" of talent quality characteristics and set as the criterion layer. At the same time, due to the professionalism of human resources positions, "professional skills" are regarded as the professional qualities of human resources positions and added to the criteria layer, forming a "3+X" talent quality characteristic evaluation dimension [20].

(2) Construction of Evaluation Index System for Talent Quality Characteristics in the Hydropower Industry

As an important functional position in enterprises, human resource management positions play a momentous role in human resource planning, personnel recruitment, personnel selection, motivation, and assessment. In order to improve the efficiency of personnel utilization in enterprises, human resource positions exhibit professional characteristics; On the other hand, in the context of digital empowerment of traditional enterprise transformation and upgrading, enterprise human resource management needs to use information systems and tools to improve work efficiency. Therefore, the job characteristics of human resources show a trend of digitization. Therefore, based on domestic and foreign literature research and SPOT team guidance, this article combines the actual situation of Daduhe Group to construct a total of 15 evaluation indicators related to the quality characteristics of talent in human resources positions, as shown in Figure 1.

3. Determination of the Weight of Evaluation Indicators for Talent Quality Characteristics

The applicability and accuracy of the evaluation model for the quality characteristics of job talents depend on the determination of weight indicators. 55 employees are selected in human resources positions within Guoneng Daduhe Group as the research object; In order to avoid data errors caused by subjective and objective scoring methods as much as possible, this article constructs a combination weighting model based on entropy method and principal component analysis method; Finally, by calculating the weights of each indicator, countermeasures and suggestions are provided for the digital transformation, upgrading, and management practices of enterprises.

3.1. Entropy Method

Entropy method is an approach of evaluating the orderliness of system elements, which can largely avoid the impact of subjective scoring methods such as Analytic Hierarchy Process (AHP) on system results. This research processes the data as follows:

Step 1: Define the dataset. Assumption: In the talent quality characteristic evaluation model, there are a total of $i(i = 1, ..., 38)$ scoring factors and $j(j = 1, ..., 55)$ employee data. So, dataset Y_{ij} can be expressed as:

$$Y_{ij} = \begin{bmatrix} y_{11} & \cdots & y_{1j} \\ \cdots & \cdots & \cdots \\ y_{i1} & \cdots & y_{ij} \end{bmatrix} \tag{1}$$

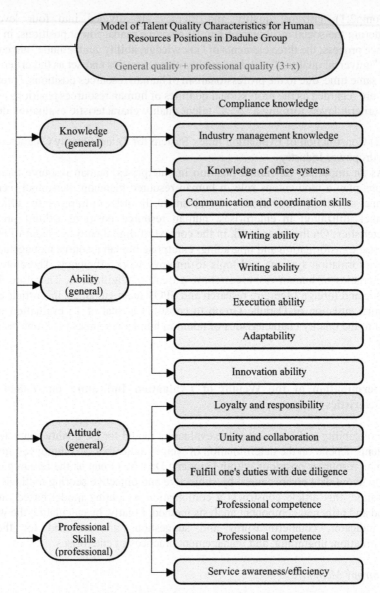

Figure 1. Evaluation Model for Talent Quality Characteristics of Human Resources Positions

Step 2: Data processing. Due to the different calculation units and statistical methods used in the original data. To eliminate the impact of different dimensions on the evaluation results, this article processes the original as follows:

$$y'_{ij,\text{Positive indicators}} = \frac{y_{ij}-\min\{y_{ij}\}}{\max\{y_{ij}\}-\min\{y_{ij}\}} \tag{2}$$

$$y'_{ij,\text{Negative indicator}} = \frac{\max\{y_{ij}\}-y_{ij}}{\max\{y_{ij}\}-\min\{y_{ij}\}} \tag{3}$$

Step 3: Calculate information weights. The paper assumes that the value range of information entropy e_j is [0,1]. Meanwhile, the information weight of the i-th scoring factor is expressed as w_j. So, the weight of factor i in the indicator system can be expressed as:

$$w_i = \frac{1-e_i}{\sum_{i=1}^{n}(1-e_i)} \qquad (4)$$

wherein, $e_i = -\ln m \times \sum \frac{y'_{ij}}{\sum_{i=1}^{n} y'_{ij}} \times \ln \frac{y'_{ij}}{\sum_{i=1}^{n} y'_{ij}}$.

Meanwhile, considering that the evaluation index results in formulas (2) and (3) may be taken as 0, and the true value range of the natural logarithm is (0, +∞). Then, it is stipulated that when $y'_{ij} = 0$, $n\frac{y'_{ij}}{\sum_{i=1}^{n} y'_{ij}} = 0$.

3.2. BP Neural Network

BP neural network is a model of neural network proposed by Rumelhart in 1986, which is a method of parameter prediction using the sigmoid function. The basic principle is shown in Figure 2. Through data analysis and processing in three stages: input layer, intermediate layer (also known as hidden layer), and output layer, nonlinear data can be effectively predicted and processed.

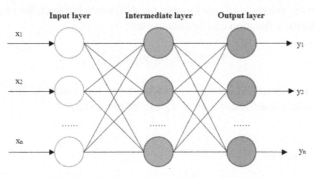

Figure 2. Structure diagram of BP neural network

In a neural network, if there are n nodes in the input layer and m nodes in the output layer, the number of intermediate layers h can be expressed as:

$$h = \sqrt{m+n} + a \qquad (5)$$

Among them, a is the adjustment constant, with values ranging from [1,10].

In this study, the first $I_{ij} = [I_{1j}, I_{2j}, I_{3j}, ..., I_{ij}]^T$ (i≤38) column in dataset Y_{ij} was set as the input matrix, and the remaining columns were set as the output matrix $L_i (i \leq 38)$. Based on the viewpoints of Sun Jinghao and He Haiyan et al. [15,21], the observation error $Error_{ij}$ between training result T_{ij} and actual result Y_{ij} can be expressed as:

$$Error_{ij} = \frac{1}{2}\Sigma(Y_{ij} - T_{ij})^2 \qquad (6)$$

Meanwhile, according to the viewpoint of reference [21], the correction formula for the intermediate layer can be expressed as:

$$\Delta w_{ij}(k) = -\eta \frac{\partial Error_{ij}}{\partial w_{ij}} \qquad (7)$$

If the error between the training results and the actual results meets the threshold, the expected weight can be output. Otherwise, the model training will be repeated until the requirements are met.

3.3. Objective Combination Weights

This article calculates the combination weight based on two objective weight calculation methods: entropy method and BP neural network, and the combination weight $W_q(q = 1,2)$ can be expressed as:

$$W_q = \Sigma \lambda_q w_q^T \qquad (8)$$

Among them, $w_q^T(q = 1,2)$ represents the weight coefficient matrix calculated based on entropy method and BP neural network.

Based on the principle of maximizing the difference between the evaluated objects, an objective function can be constructed:

$$W_q = \Sigma \lambda_q w_q^T y_{ij}' \quad \text{s.t.} \quad \Sigma \lambda_q = 1 \qquad (9)$$

So, by performing Lagrangian calculations on equation (9), the objective combination weight coefficient matrix λ_q' can be obtained.

4. Empirical Analysis

Based on the above analysis, an empirical analysis on the data of 55 employees in human resources positions at Guoneng Daduhe Group is conducted. The specific situation is as follows.

4.1. Weight Calculation Based on Entropy Method

Based on the actual data situation, two researchers screened the actual data of 55 employees, and then used Matlab R2016b to write a weight algorithm, ultimately obtaining the weight matrix W_1 (see Table 1).

Table 1. Indicator System and Weights of Talent Quality Characteristics Criteria for Human Resources Positions

Target layer	Criterion layer	weight		
		Entropy method	BP neural network	Combination weight
Ability (0.397)	communication skills	0.079	0.074	0.076
	Writing ability	0.079	0.082	0.081
	learning ability	0.079	0.073	0.075
	Adaptability	0.080	0.086	0.083
	Innovation ability	0.052	0.059	0.056
	Execution ability	0.026	0.024	0.025

4.2. Weight Calculation based on BP Neural Network

In the neural network model [22-24], the structure of initial data matrix Y_{ij} is 38×55. In the parameter setting, the raw data of 55 employees is used as input values. According to the algorithm of BP neural network, the gradient parameter is set to 0.01 in Matlab, and after 50 iterations, the predicted weight result is calculated (see Table 2 for details), with a correlation coefficient of $R^2 = 0.9135$.

4.3. Calculation of Objective Combination Weights

Table 2. Index System and Weights of Talent Quality Characteristics Factor Layer for Human Resources Positions

Target layer	Factor layer	weight		
		Entropy method		
Ability (0.397)	Communication and collaboration	0.026	0.025	0.026
	Language ability	0.026	0.021	0.023
	Number of organizational meetings	0.026	0.028	0.027
	Official document/system writing	0.026	0.028	0.027
	News promotion	0.027	0.033	0.030
	Paper/monograph	0.026	0.022	0.024
	continuing education	0.027	0.024	0.025
	Professional qualifications	0.026	0.023	0.024
	Internal trainer	0.026	0.025	0.026
	Multiple job experiences	0.027	0.035	0.031
	Physical condition	0.027	0.028	0.027
	Psychological resilience	0.026	0.024	0.025
	Innovation Awards	0.025	0.032	0.029
	intellectual property right	0.027	0.028	0.027
	performance appraisal	0.026	0.024	0.025

Based on the calculation results of entropy method and BP neural network, using Matlab to calculate equations (8) and (9), a normalized coefficient matrix $\lambda'_q =$ (0.4236,0.5764) can be obtained. The weight calculation results are shown in Table 2.

Both Tables 1 and 2 are studied using competency indicators as an example. From these two tables, it can be seen that the weight difference calculated using the three methods is relatively small, indicating that each indicator has a certain degree of stability in evaluating talents in human resource management positions.

5. Conclusion

Digital transformation has become an inevitable choice for the hydropower industry. It can not only improve the management level and production efficiency of the hydropower industry, but also promote the optimal allocation and utilization of hydropower resources, thereby providing strong support for the construction of ecological civilization, national energy security, and the realization of the "dual carbon" goals. This article takes the human resource management position as an example to construct an evaluation system for talent quality characteristics, achieving theoretical basis, traceable data, and executable operation, laying the foundation for further building a digital management evaluation system.

There are also shortcomings in this article. Firstly, this article only uses 55 employees as an example to calculate weights, which poses problems such as insufficient data and inaccurate calculations. Secondly, digital transformation is interconnected, and this article only completed the construction of talent evaluation index system for human resource management positions. Thirdly, in the digital era, rapid technological progress and ever-changing market demand have led to a shortened applicability of evaluation indicators. In subsequent practice, it is necessary to continuously maintain and update the talent evaluation index system to keep up with the times and ensure the effectiveness of the evaluation.

Acknowledgment

This project is supported by "Research on the Evaluation Model of Typical Job Indicators in the Hydropower Industry" (DSJ-KY-2022-018).

References

[1]   Zhao Tao, Zhang Zhi, Liang Shangkun. Digital economy, entrepreneurship activity, and high-quality development: empirical evidence from Chinese cities[J]. Management World, 2020, 36 (10): 65-76 (in Chinese).

[2]   Zhang Xun, Wan Guanghua, Zhang Jiajia, et al. Digital economy, inclusive finance, and inclusive growth[J]. Economic Research, 2019, 54 (08): 71-86 (in Chinese).

[3]   Бабкин, А. В;Алексеева, Н. С. A Methodology for assessing the intellectual capital of an innovative-active industrial cluster in the context of the digital economy. [J]. Ekonomika i Upravlenie / Economics & Management, 2020, 26(7): 739-749.

[4]   Zhang Yuzhe. Development ideas and main tasks for the digital economy driving industrial structure towards the mid to high end[J]. Economic Review, 2018, 394 (09): 85-91 (in Chinese).

[5]   Wei Qian, Huan Liu, Fanghui Pan. Digital economy, industry heterogeneity, and service industry resource allocation[J]. Sustainability, 2022, 14(13): 8020.

[6]   Zhang Hui, Shi Lin. Digital economy: new power in the new era[J]. Journal of Beijing Jiaotong University (Social Science Edition), 2019, 18 (02): 10-22 (in Chinese).

[7]   Lifang Chen, Yuan Liu, Fei Chen, Jie Zhang, Jing Lu. Research on the teaching system of creative and entrepreneurial software engineering (digital media technology) talents training[J]. Computer Education, 2018, (12): 75-81.

[8]   Prashant M. Dolia, "Evaluation: The New Philosophical Roles & Psychological Means", International Journal of Modern Education and Computer Science, vol.5, no.7, pp. 34-40, 2013.

[9]   Yong Gu, Di Liu and Zhiping Liu. Training and evaluation system of intelligent supply chain talent based on digital teaching and collaborative innovation[J]. Advances in Computer Science for Engineering and Education, 2022, 134.

[10]   Dong Wei, Ling Guo and WenRan Dong. Analysis on the classification and evaluation system of talents in colleges and universities from the perspective of AHP[J]. Mobile Information Systems, 2022.

[11]   Yue Shujing, Zhang Xinhe. Research on the impact of digital economy on energy intensity[J]. Journal of Nanchang University (Humanities and Social Sciences Edition), 2023, 54 (01): 77-90 (in Chinese).

[12]   rikshat, Verma;Patel, Parth. Digital talent management: Insights from the information technology and communication industry[J]. Thunderbird International Business Review, 2023, 65(2): 253-254.

[13]   Umasankar Murugesan, Padmavathy Subramanian, Shefali Srivastava, Ashish Dwivedi. A study of artificial intelligence impacts on human resource digitalization in industry 4.0[J]. Decision Analytics Journal, 2023, 7: 100249.

[14]   Xiong Ziyue, Zhang Yi, Wang Yanan. A study on the coupling and coordination of scientific research investment and achievement transformation in universities under the background of industry education integration[J]. Jiang Ke Academic Research, 2022, 17 (4): 1-8 (in Chinese).

[15]   Sun Jinghao, He Haiyan. Research on the influencing factors of scientific and technological innovation performance of State Key Laboratory in universities based on BP neural network[J]. Scientific Management Research, 2022,40 (04): 48-54 (in Chinese).

[16]   Palab Naidu, Lai Meiyun. SPOT team guided technology - ignite the wisdom of group management[M]. Nanjing: Jiangsu People's Publishing House, 2014 (in Chinese).

[17]   Li Yang, Pan Haisheng. The action logic and reform direction of integrating digital abilities into vocational education in the European Union[J]. Comparative Education Research, 2022, 44 (10): 76-85 (in Chinese).

[18]   Lan Guoshuai, Guo Qian, Zhang Yi, et al. The digital literacy framework for eu educators: key interpretation and enlightenment[J]. Modern Distance Education Research, 2020, 32 (06): 23-32 (in Chinese).

[19]   Liu Ping, Chen Weizheng. Analysis of the value and pricing of human capital[J]. Financial Science, 2007, No.230 (05): 81-88 (in Chinese).

[20]   Ge Minglei, Zhang Lihua, Jia Guangyu, et al. Contradictions and management of multiple institutional logic in human resources consulting projects[J]. Management Review, 2022, 34 (09): 254-270 (in Chinese).

[21]   Abdul Rahman Abuduaini. Evaluation of cross-border e-commerce logistics business based on game theory combination weighting model[J]. Statistics and Decision, 2022, 38 (19): 184-188 (in Chinese).

[22]   Indhumathi .J, Balasubramanian .M, Balasaigayathri .B, "Real-Time Video based Human Suspicious Activity Recognition with Transfer Learning for Deep Learning", International Journal of Image, Graphics and Signal Processing, Vol.15, No.1, pp. 47-62, 2023.

[23]   Dhekra El Hamdi, Ines Elouedi, Mai K Nguyen, Atef Hamouda, "A Conic Radon-based Convolutional Neural Network for Image Recognition", International Journal of Intelligent Systems and Applications, Vol.15, No.1, pp.1-12, 2023.

[24]   Duong Thang Long, Truong Tien Tung, Tran Tien Dung, "A Facial Expression Recognition Model using Lightweight Dense-Connectivity Neural Networks for Monitoring Online Learning Activities", International Journal of Modern Education and Computer Science, Vol.14, No.6, pp. 53-64, 2022.

Artificial Intelligence, Medical Engineering and Education
Z.B. Hu et al. (Eds.)
© 2024 The Authors.
This article is published online with Open Access by IOS Press and distributed under the terms
of the Creative Commons Attribution Non-Commercial License 4.0 (CC BY-NC 4.0).
doi:10.3233/ATDE231317

The Effect of AI Product Image Anthropomorphism on Consumer Purchase Intention

Li LI[a,b], Dhakir Abbas ALI[a,1], Lumian YIN[b]

[a] *Faculty of Business and Accountancy, Lincoln University College, Selangor, Malaysia*
[b] *School of Business, Nanning University, Nanning, China*
ORCiD ID: Dhakir Abbas ALI https://orcid.org/0009-0000-6842-0157

Abstract. The study focused on deconstructing the image of AI anthropomorphism in the casual food industry and investigating its impact on consumers' intention to purchase. This was done by examining impression-based cues and interaction-based cues, while also considering the role of psychological distance and information processing fluency. Additionally, the study explored the moderating role of consumers' self-constructed type. Previous research has shown that factors like AI anthropomorphic impression-based cues and interactive cues significantly influence consumers' purchase intention. Notably, the influence of interactive cues appears to be stronger. Furthermore, it has been found that both psychological distance and information processing fluency partially mediate the effect of AI anthropomorphism of product image on consumer purchase intention. Furthermore, the influence of anthropomorphic interactive cues on consumer purchase intention is contingent upon the type of consumer self-construction. Notably, individuals who possess interdependent self-construal are more inclined to purchase AI anthropomorphic product images that incorporate interactive cues, as opposed to those who possess independent self-construal. Conversely, there is no substantial disparity in the willingness to purchase AI anthropomorphic product images with impressionistic cues among consumers with different self-construal.

Keywords. Product Image AI Anthropomorphism; Purchase Intention; Psychological Distance; Information Processing Fluency

1. Introduction

With the advent of the market economy, enterprises are increasingly enhancing their core competitiveness through product upgrades and innovations. Furthermore, there is a growing emphasis on the establishment of product image within enterprises. Notably, the utilization of AI anthropomorphic product image has garnered significant attention due to its distinct advantages. Consequently, the application of product image AI anthropomorphic marketing strategy has emerged as a prominent research topic among scholars. Existing studies primarily concentrate on investigating the disparities in marketing effectiveness between AI anthropomorphism and non-AI anthropomorphism [1]. Additionally, scholars have explored a range of psychological processes, attitudes, evaluations, and purchasing behaviors that may arise when consumers are confronted

---

[1] Corresponding Author: Dhakir Abbas ALI, E-mail: drdhakir@lincoln.edu.my.

with product images or products bearing human-like characteristics [2]. Furthermore, a few researchers have delved into the impact of AI anthropomorphic communication on consumer attitudes and behaviors [3], as well as the effects of AI anthropomorphic images associated with various product attributes (such as competence or warmth) on consumer behaviors [4].Overall, existing studies have taken product image AI anthropomorphism as an independent unidimensional variable to conduct relevant empirical research, Wang Tao et al[5], proposed that product image AI anthropomorphism should be defined as a multidimensional concept, however, when it comes to assessing the marketing effectiveness of product image AI anthropomorphism, purchase intention is considered a more suitable measure, there is a lack of research exploring the specific mechanisms through which product image AI anthropomorphism influences purchase intention.

As marketing research evolves, Guo Guo Qing et al argue that certain fundamental concepts and theories from psychology and sociology can effectively elucidate the influence of product image marketing strategies on consumer behavior [6]. Product image AI anthropomorphism emphasizes the portrayal of human characteristics in product images to evoke consumer associations. This approach facilitates consumer comprehension of the conveyed information, reduces unfamiliarity with the product image, and establishes a closer connection between the consumer and the product image.

Consequently, these factors ultimately shape consumer attitudes and preferences towards the product. This paper examines the marketing impact of AI anthropomorphic product image shaping, specifically focusing on two dimensions: impression-based cues and interaction-based cues. It also investigates the influence of psychological distance and information processing fluency on consumers' purchase intention in relation to the AI anthropomorphism of product image. Additionally, the role of consumer self-construction as a moderating variable is explored to determine if there are discrepancies in the effect of AI anthropomorphism on purchase intention among consumers with different construct types.

2. Related Works

Product image AI anthropomorphism is mainly composed of three dimensions: external, internal and social, which can be used by enterprises to stimulate consumers' product image AI anthropomorphism perception. The external dimension of product image AI anthropomorphism can be easily perceived by consumers. Empirical studies have shown that consumers associate certain features of beverage bottles, such as a thin middle and wide ends resembling a human "waist", with the product image design. By incorporating elements like "mouth" and "ears" into the design, consumers perceive the product image as a person [7]. The intrinsic dimension of product image AI anthropomorphism reflects the unique personality of a product image and represents its culture and values. Each product image should possess its own personality, as this makes it easier for consumers to perceive it as having human-like qualities [8]. The personality of a product image can also help consumers find a product image that aligns with their own personality, which can impact their decision to consume. In the social dimension, AI anthropomorphism enables the product or product image to autonomously communicate and interact with consumers. Through language, such as greetings, the product or product image can initiate the consumer's perception of AI anthropomorphism, thereby enhancing the customer's emotional experience and gaining trust and favor [9]. To interact with consumers, AI anthropomorphic product image strategy will also shape different roles and images. Combined with the marketing practice of product image AI anthropomorphic role shaping, scholars have discovered that consumers tend to perceive AI anthropomorphic product image roles as either partners or servants. The study further reveals that consumers are more likely to engage in effective social interactions with AI anthropomorphic product images that align with social norms [10]; Additionally, the utilization of different types of AI anthropomorphic images enables more targeted and personalized communication and interaction with consumers, resulting in the perception of the product image as a real individual. This perception ultimately contributes to enhancing consumer sentiment towards the product image [11].

Psychological distance can systematically influence people's preference and choice decisions, and its important value and role in understanding consumer behavior has received increasing attention from scholars, and more and more scholars have introduced psychological distance into the study of consumer behavior. Existing research mainly focuses on the effects of psychological distance on the persuasive effect of information and on the evaluation of consumers' products or product image, purchase decision and purchase intention. Providing marketing persuasive messages with different levels of explanation matching the time distance for different purchase points of consumers can effectively improve the persuasive effect and influence of these messages, for example, when consumers are going to buy a certain product in the near future, messages with low levels of explanation (e.g., price discounts and purchasing convenience) have a greater influence on consumers' evaluation of the product[12]. When the advertising message matches the psychological explanation level of consumers, i.e., when the psychological distance is close, the advertising message has a stronger persuasive effect and can effectively promote consumers' purchase behavior. In a study conducted by Kim and John [13], the authors explored how two important dimensions of psychological distance, namely temporal distance and social distance, affect consumers' evaluations of products. The findings revealed that consumers tend to prioritize product attributes that can be easily explained when making future purchases at a greater temporal distance or for someone else at a greater social distance. Huang Jing et al found that when the product image offense event occurs, the degree of negative evaluation of the product image by consumers is affected by the psychological distance (spatial distance, social distance), compared to the psychological distance far, the degree of negative evaluation of consumers is higher when the psychological distance is close [14].

Scholars have conducted research on the influence of information processing fluency on consumer behavior. It has been discovered that information processing fluency has a favorable effect on consumer perceptions, evaluations of products or product images, and consumer decisions. Ferraro et al have determined that high information processing fluency can enhance an individual's familiarity with the information presented, resulting in increased knowledge of the processing object[15]. This, in turn, boosts the individual's confidence, which positively impacts their consumption choices, attitudes, and other specific behaviors[16]. Information processing fluency also has the potential to positively influence consumers' impulsive purchasing intentions. When individuals experience information processing fluency, they tend to have a positive and pleasurable experience, which increases the likelihood of impulsive purchasing behavior. Jin Fei and Zhu Huawei have also confirmed the impact of information processing fluency on consumers' impulse purchase intentions [17]. They found that high information processing fluency can stimulate positive information valence and promote consumers' intention to make a purchase.

The concept of self-construal plays a significant role in influencing various aspects of consumer behavior, such as self-motivation, value judgment, and attitude preference. Consumers with different types of self-constructs exhibit distinct perceptions, attitudes, and purchasing decisions towards products or product images. Lalwani and Shavit have argued that individuals with different self-constructing tendencies process information differently, thereby impacting their evaluation of products [18]. Those with interdependent constructs tend to integrate information and seek connections between various pieces of information, adopting a holistic thinking approach that often leads to more emotionally driven behavioral decisions. On the other hand, individuals with independent constructs prefer processing information autonomously, adopting an analytical thinking style that tends to result in more rational behavioral decisions. Thus, individuals possessing interdependent constructs exhibit a greater inclination to perceive connections among product components than individuals with independent constructs. Regarding impulsive buying behavior, individuals with interdependent self-construal display a heightened propensity for impulsive purchases compared to individuals with independent self-construal [19]. This is attributed to the former's reliance on emotions during decision-making, while the latter tend to adopt a more rational and evidence-based approach [20]. Furthermore, individuals with independent self-construal possess the ability to restrain their own consumption impulses. The field of consumer behavior has extensively explored the moderating impact of self-construal on attitudes and behaviors from diverse perspectives [21-23].

3. Research Hypothesis and Modeling

3.1. Research Hypothesis

The effect of product image AI anthropomorphism on consumer purchase intention. AI anthropomorphic features can stimulate consumers' cognitive patterns, enhance their perceptual fluency, and stimulate positive emotional responses, and these emotional positives will be transmitted to the product or brand image, which will improve consumers' attitudes and evaluations [2]. At the same time, AI anthropomorphic design helps to reduce the risk perceived by consumers [1], reduces hesitation in purchasing, and prompts consumers to be more inclined to purchase. In addition, the interaction between the AI anthropomorphic product image and consumers satisfies human social needs, through which consumers can satisfy basic social needs, establish social connections and emotional bonds, and ultimately form positive product image attitudes and purchase behavior [6]. For this reason, this paper proposes the following hypotheses.

- H1: Product image AI anthropomorphism has a positive effect on consumer purchase intention.
- H1a: Product image AI anthropomorphic impression-based cues have a positive effect on consumer purchase intention.
- H1b: Product image AI anthropomorphized interactive cues have a positive effect on consumer purchase intention.

The mediating role of psychological distance. Prior studies have demonstrated that imbuing product images with human characteristics, thoughts, and emotions can elicit a sense of friendliness, trust, and persuasion among consumers. Gupta et al discovered that interactive communication between AI anthropomorphized product images and consumers fosters a closer relationship between the two parties [24], with increased communication leading to greater trust and emotional connection. Furthermore, researchers examining psychological resistance theory found that when AI anthropomorphized communication incorporates unrelated information alongside product images, consumers perceive it as less persuasive compared to traditional promotional messaging. Consequently, this reduces psychological resistance towards the product image or the product itself and shortens the psychological distance between consumers and the product image. As a result, consumers' attitudes towards the product image are improved[5]. Notably, the reduction in psychological distance can directly or indirectly influence consumers' purchase intentions[25]. In addition, Zhou Fei and Sha Zhen Quan studied the effect of product image AI anthropomorphism on consumers' ability and warmth perception, and found that psychological distance plays a mediating role. To this end, the following hypotheses are formulated in this paper.

- H2a: Product image AI anthropomorphic impression-based cues can bring consumers closer to the psychological distance of the product image.
- H2b: Product image AI anthropomorphic interactive cues can bring consumers closer to the psychological distance of the product image.
- H3: The closer consumers are psychologically to the product image, the greater their willingness to buy the product image (product).
- H4: Psychological distance mediates the effect of AI anthropomorphism of product image on consumer purchase intention.
- H4a: Psychological distance mediates the effect of product image AI anthropomorphic impression-based cues on consumer purchase intention.
- H4b: Psychological distance mediates the effect of product image AI anthropomorphic interactive cues on consumer purchase intention.

The mediating role of information processing fluency. Oppenheimer highlighted the significance of enhancing information processing fluency in enhancing consumers' attitudes and purchase intentions towards products or product images. Information processing fluency can be categorized into two dimensions: perceptual fluency and conceptual fluency. Perceptual fluency pertains to the ease or difficulty in identifying a target stimulus based on its physical attributes, such as size, shape, color, and other observable characteristics. On the other hand, conceptual fluency refers to the ease or difficulty in identifying the target stimulus through the analysis of its semantic and other intricate information attributes. In light of this, this paper puts forward the following hypotheses.

- H5: Product image AI anthropomorphism has a positive effect on information processing fluency.
- H5a: Product image AI anthropomorphic impressionistic cues have a positive effect on information processing fluency.
- H5b: Product image AI anthropomorphic interactive cues have a positive effect on information processing fluency.
- H6: Information processing fluency has a positive effect on consumer purchase intention.
- H7: Information processing fluency mediates the effect of AI anthropomorphism of product image on consumer purchase intention.
- H7a: Information processing fluency mediates the effect of product image AI anthropomorphic impression-based cues on consumer purchase intention.

- H7b: Information processing fluency mediates the effect of product image AI anthropomorphic interactive cues on consumer purchase intention.

3.2. Model Construction

Based on the above literature compilation and analysis, the conceptual model of this study is proposed (see Figure 1).

Figure 1. Conceptual framework

4. Research Design and Computational Analysis

4.1. Design and Inspection

This scholarly paper has selected the product image within the leisure food industry as the subject of empirical investigation. The study was carried out over the period spanning from January 2020 to the end of January 2020. A total of 250 questionnaires were distributed, out of which 238 valid questionnaires were successfully collected, resulting in a commendable recovery rate of 95.2%. Through the analysis of descriptive statistical data derived from the valid questionnaires, it was observed that the samples exhibited a wide distribution and demonstrated a high level of representativeness. This approach aimed to minimize the impact of random factors on the research findings as much as possible.

Within this scholarly paper, an examination of descriptive statistical analysis and correlation testing was conducted using SPSS *22.0*. The resulting data presents the following: The average value for the impression-based cue dimension of AI anthropomorphism within the product image is 5.8655, whereas the average value for the interaction-based cue dimension is *4.9160*. Notably, both of these dimensions possess average values that surpass the median of *3.5*, indicating a relatively high level of anthropomorphism. Consequently, this signifies that consumers hold a favorable overall assessment regarding the extent of AI anthropomorphism within the sample product image, thus reinforcing the validity of our product image selection. The Cronbach's alpha coefficients for product image AI anthropomorphism, psychological distance, information processing fluency, purchase intention, and self-construal all exceed 0.8. The reliability of these variables was assessed by removing the question items, and no increase in reliability was found. This indicates that the formal research data is highly reliable. Furthermore, the KMO value and Bartlett's spherical test were conducted on the data for product image AI anthropomorphism, psychological distance, information processing fluency, purchase intention, and self-construction. The KMO value exceeded 0.7, and the p-value for Bartlett's spherical test was 0.000, which is much smaller than 0.01, demonstrating high significance. Finally, the Pearson correlation test revealed a significant correlation between the independent variables, mediator variables, and dependent variables.

4.2. Calculation and Analysis

This study will utilize SPSS 22.0 to perform a regression analysis on the variables, aiming to examine the hypotheses put forth. To evaluate causality in the regression analysis, a significance p-value below 0.05 and a t-value exceeding 1.96 are deemed as indicators. Table 1 presents the detailed outcomes of the hypothesis testing conducted in this research.

Table 1. Results of hypothesis testing

Suppose that	Hypothetical content	Test results
H1a	Product image anthropomorphizing impression-based cues have a positive effect on consumer purchase intention	be tenable
H1b	Product image anthropomorphic interactive cues have a positive effect on consumer purchase intention	be tenable
H2a	Product image anthropomorphic impression-based cues can bring consumers closer to the psychological distance of the product image	be tenable
H2b	Product image anthropomorphized interactive cues can bring consumers closer to the psychological distance of the product image	be tenable
H3	The closer the consumer is psychologically to the product image, the greater their willingness to buy the product image (product)	be tenable
H4a	Psychological distance plays a mediating part in the effect of anthropomorphic impressionistic cues of product image on consumers' purchase intention	be tenable
H4b	Psychological distance plays a mediating part in the effect of product image anthropomorphic interactive cues on consumer purchase intention	be tenable
H5a	Product image anthropomorphic impressionistic cues have a positive effect on information processing fluency	be tenable
H5b	Product image anthropomorphizing interaction-based cues have a positive effect on information processing fluency	be tenable
H6	Information processing fluency has a positive effect on consumer purchase intention	be tenable
H7a	Information processing fluency plays a mediating part in the effect of anthropomorphic impressionistic cues of product image on consumer purchase intention	be tenable
H7b	Information processing fluency plays a mediating part in the effect of anthropomorphic interactive cues of product image on consumer purchase intention	be tenable

5. Conclusion

5.1. The Role of Product Image AI Anthropomorphism on Consumer Purchase Intention

Product image AI anthropomorphism is an emerging marketing tool that has the potential to positively influence consumers' purchase intention, regardless of impression-based or interaction-based cues. Empirical analysis further supports this notion, indicating that the interactive cues of AI anthropomorphism in product images have a greater impact on consumers' purchase intention compared to the responses generated by impression-based cues. This can be attributed to the fact that when product images incorporate interactive AI anthropomorphic cues, such as expressing emotions and personalities, as well as interacting with consumers, it becomes easier for consumers to perceive them as real-life "human-like" individuals. This enhances the relationship between consumers and the product image, ultimately boosting consumers' purchase intention.

5.2. The Mediating Role of Psychological Distance

Both the impression-based cues and interaction-based cues of product image AI anthropomorphism could reduce the psychological distance between consumers and the product image. This closer psychological distance has a significant impact on consumers' love for the product image as well as their intention to purchase the product. The mediating role of psychological distance is evident in the influence of product image AI anthropomorphism on consumers' purchase intention. Interestingly, the study findings indicate that interactive cues of product image AI anthropomorphism are more effective in reducing the psychological distance between consumers and the product image compared to impression-based cues. In this context, psychological distance refers to the mental connection between consumers' perception and the product image. The interactive cues primarily focus on the communication and interaction between the product image and consumers. Through this communication and interaction, consumers develop a deeper perception of AI anthropomorphism, which ultimately increases their willingness to purchase the product and brings them closer to the psychological distance with the product image.

5.3. The Mediating Role of Information Processing Fluency

Both impression-based cues and interaction-based cues of product image AI anthropomorphism have the potential to enhance consumers' information processing fluency, thus positively impacting their purchase intention towards the product. The influence of product image AI anthropomorphism on purchase intention is partially mediated by information processing fluency. Moreover, the study results indicate that impression-based cues of product image AI anthropomorphism have a greater impact on consumers' perceived information processing fluency compared to interactive cues. These impression-based cues are more intuitive and simpler in presenting product image or information, thereby reducing the difficulty consumers face in understanding the product. Additionally, these cues do not emphasize interactivity, allowing consumers to process information more easily without needing to actively participate in interactions.

5.4. The Moderating Role of Self-Construal

The consumer's self-construction type partially moderates the influence of product image AI anthropomorphism on their purchase intention. However, self-construction does not moderate the influence of product image AI anthropomorphism impressionistic cues on purchase intention. Additionally, there is no significant difference in the purchase intention of consumers with different construct types when exposed to impressionistic AI anthropomorphic product images. On the other hand, self-construction does play a moderating role in the effect of product image AI anthropomorphic interaction type cues on purchase intention. Furthermore, interdependent self-constructed consumers exhibit stronger purchase intention for interaction type AI anthropomorphic product images compared to independent self-constructed consumers.

Acknowledgment

This project is supported by Nanning University ideological and political construction team "Market research ideological and political course team based on necklace model teaching" (2022SZJXTD09).

References

[1]   KIM S, MCGILLAL. Gaming with Mr. Slot or gaming the slot machine? Power, anthropomorphism, and risk perception [J]. Journal of consumer research,2011, 38(1): 94-107.
[2]   AGGARWAL P, MCGILL A L. When brands seem human, do humans act like brands? Automatic behavioral priming effects of brand anthropomorphism[J]. Journal of consumer research, 2012, 39(2): 307-323.
[3]   MA Yu Zhe, WANG Lin, ZHANG Yong Qiang, et al. A study on the impact effect of AI anthropomorphic communication on new product adoption[J]. Science and Science and Technology Management, 2017(8): 133-143
[4]   Zeng Xiang, Yang Guang Yu. Which brand AI anthropomorphic image is more favored - the moderating effect of attributional needs and boundaries[J]. Nankai Management Review, 2017(3): 135-143.
[5]   WANG Tao, XIE Zhipeng, ZHOU Ling, et al. A rooted study of brand AI Anthropomorphization[J]. Journal of Marketing Science,2014(1):1-20.
[6]   Guo Guo Qing, CHEN Feng Chao, LIAN Yi. Recent Research Progress and Implications of Brand AI Anthropomorphism Theory[J]. China Circulation Economy,2017(7):64-69.
[7]   LANDWEHR J R, MCGILL A L, HERRMANN A. It's got the look: the effect of friendly and aggressive "facial" expressions on product liking and sales[J]. Journal of marketing, 2011,75(3):132-146.
[8]   GUIDO G, PELUSO A M. Brand anthropomorphism: conceptualization, measurement, and impact on brand personality and loyalty[J]. Journal of brand management, 2015,22(1):1-19.
[9]   HASSANEINK, HEADM. The Impact of infusing social presence in the web interface: an investigation across product types[J]. International journal of electronic commerce,2005,10(2):31-55.
[10] Zhou Yi Jin, Mao Shiman, Chen Xiaoyan. Status compensation: The effect of "servant" branding on purchase intention[J]. Foreign Economics and Management, 2020(2):43-58.
[11] C. Nobata, J. Tetreault,   A. Thomas,   Y. Mehdad,   and Y. Chang, "Aabuseive Language Detection in Online User Content,   " in 25th International Conference on World Wide Web,   2016,   pp. 145–153
[12] CASTA R, SUJAN M, KACKER Mal. Managing consumer uncertainty in the adoption of new products: temporal distance and mental simulation[J]. Journal of marketing research,2008,45(3):320-336.
[13] KIM H, JOHN D R. Consumer response to brand extensions: construal level as a moderator of the importance of perceived fit[J]. Journal of consumer psychology,2008,18(2):116-126.
[14] HUANG Jing, WANG Xingang, TONG Zelin. The effects of space and social distance on the evaluation of erring brands[J]. China Soft Science,2011(7):123-130.
[15] FERRARO R, BETTMAN J R, CHARTRAND T L. The power of strangers: the effect of incidental consumer brand encounters on brand choice [J]. Journal of consumer research,2009,35(5):729-741.
[16] TSAI C I, THOMAS M. When does feeling of fluency matter? How abstract and concrete thinking influence fluency effects [J]. Psychological science,2011,22(3):348-354.
[17] Savchenko, V., Akhramovych, V., Dzyuba, T., Laptiev S., Lukova-Chuiko, N., Laptieva T. Methodology for calculating information protection from parameters of its distribution in social networks. 2021 IEEE 3rd International Conference on Advanced Trends in Information Theory, ATIT 2021 - Proceedings, 2021, Pp. 99–105.
[18] Y. Li, M. Potkonjak, and W. Wolf, "Real-time operating systems for embedded computing," Proc. - IEEE Int. Conf. Comput. Des. VLSI Comput. Process., no. December 1998, pp. 388–392, 1997, doi: 10.1145/288548.289349.
[19] ZHANGY, SHRUML. The influence of self-construal on impulsive consumption[J]. Journal of consumer research, 2009,35(5):838-850.
[20] HONG J, CHANG H H. "I" follow my heart and "we" rely on reasons: the impact of self-construal on reliance on feelings versus reasons in decision making[J]. Journal of consumer research,2015,41(6):1392-1411.

[21] Savchenko, V., Akhramovych, V., Dzyuba, T., Laptiev S., Lukova-Chuiko, N., Laptieva T. Methodology for calculating information protection from parameters of its distribution in social networks. 2021 IEEE 3rd International Conference on Advanced Trends in Information Theory, ATIT 2021 - Proceedings, 2021, Pp. 99–105.

[22] Zhang D., Pee L.G., Cui L. "Artificial intelligence in e-commerce fulfillment: A case study of resource orchestration at Alibaba's Smart Warehouse". International Journal of Information Management, 2021, volume 57, pp.102-304

[23] Win win Y.M. The role of information technology in e-commerce. International Journal of Scientific & Technology Research, 2019, volume 8, issue 1, pp.173-176.

[24] GUPTAS, MELEWARTC, BOURLAKISM.A relational insight of brand personification in business-to-business markets [J]. Journal of general management,2010,35(4):65-76.

Artificial Intelligence, Medical Engineering and Education
Z.B. Hu et al. (Eds.)
© 2024 The Authors.
This article is published online with Open Access by IOS Press and distributed under the terms
of the Creative Commons Attribution Non-Commercial License 4.0 (CC BY-NC 4.0).
doi:10.3233/ATDE231318

Decoupling Elasticity Analysis of Transportation Structure and Carbon Emission Efficiency of Transportation Industry in the Context of Intelligent Transportation

Shengrong LU, Yao LIU[1]
School of Business Administration, Wuhan Business University, Wuhan, China

Abstract. Transportation industry is a pillar industry for the development of the economy of a nation, and is indispensable in improving the operational efficiency of national economy and enhancing social and economic benefits. However, transportation industry has characteristics of high energy consumption, pollution and emissions, it requires an effective balance between development and carbon reduction in the context of the "Carbon neutrality and carbon reduction Goals". The problem of Poor transportation structure in China's transportation industry is relatively serious, so optimizing the transportation structure has been urgent to be solved. Based on the TAPIO decoupling elasticity analysis theory, this article takes the Yangtze River Economic Belt region for example to analyze the decoupling elasticity between transportation structure and carbon emission efficiency. The results indicate that the overall decoupling elasticity of carbon emissions, carbon emission efficiency, and transportation structure is respectively characterized by strong negative decoupling and weak negative decoupling. In other words, when the proportion of iron and water converted turnover decreases, the carbon emissions increase, and carbon emission efficiency decreases in company.

Keywords. Transportation Structure; Carbon Emission Efficiency; Decoupling Elasticity Analysis

1. Introduction

Transportation industry plays a fundamental, leading, and service-oriented role in national economy and social development, and is also a typical "high energy consumption, pollution and emissions" industry. With the formulation and implementation of strategic decisions for the development of the Yangtze River Economic Belt, fruitful achievements have been made in the transportation infrastructure construction, and the scale of transportation network is constantly expanding. According to the author's calculation, the major input-output indicators of the transportation industry, such as fixed assets investment, number of employees, and converted turnover, account for more than 40% of the nation, and they are expanding, which shows their position and role in the national transportation industry. Transportation energy consumption has increased from 6.5 million tons of standard

---

[1] Corresponding Author: Yao LIU, E-mail: 332556138@qq.com.

coal in 2009 to 14.5million in 2020 (average annual growth rate:6.92%). As one of the main pollutants in the transportation industry, carbon dioxide emissions increased from 139.933 million tons in 2009 to 307.9455 million tons in 2020, an increase of more than 1.2 times. Transportation industry development has paid a huge energy and environmental cost.

How to calculate and analyze the carbon emissions and carbon emission efficiency of transportation industry is a hot topic in current research. Salvatore Saija (2002) applied a "top-down" model to calculate the carbon emissions of Italian road transportation [1]. Wang (2011) and Wang (2012) applied the "top-down" model to calculate China's passenger and road freight carbon emissions respectively [2-3]. Lin (2010) compared transportation carbon emissions levels of five parks in Taiwan from 1999 to 2006 [4]. Xu (2016) used a panel data model to study the regional differences in carbon dioxide emissions between 2000 and 2012 [5]. Zhou (2010) compared the carbon emission efficiency levels of 18 countries with the highest total carbon emissions using the MCPI index [6]. Risto (2012) used the SFA method to measure emission efficiency based on inter provincial panel data [7]. Greening (1999) summarized and studied the temporal patterns of carbon emissions per unit of freight turnover in 10 OECD countries [8]. Ehrlich (1970) proposed that population, affluence, and technological level are the three major factors that affect environmental conditions [9]. Tae Hyeong Kwon (2005) used the IPAT model to study the main factors affecting carbon emissions from private car travel in the UK from 1970 to 2000 [10]. Xu (2015) studied the influencing factors in China's transportation industry using dynamic non parametric regression models from 2000 to 2012 [11].

China is the world's largest carbon dioxide emitter and faces enormous pressure from the international community to reduce emissions. In 2015, China proposed the goal of "reducing carbon dioxide emissions per unit of GDP by 60-65% in 2030 compared to 2005. In 2020, China proposed the goals of "carbon peaking" by 2030 and "carbon neutrality" by 2060. With the socioeconomic development of the Belt, the demand for infrastructure, transportation equipment, and transportation services in the transportation industry will continue to grow fast on the basis of its original scale in the future. The energy consumption and total transportation carbon emissions may show a sustained growth trend. Based on this trend, the contradiction between the development of transportation and resource and environmental constraints will become increasingly apparent, and carbon peaking and neutrality goals may be difficult to achieve. Therefore, improving emission efficiency and reducing carbon emissions through stronger management measures and more efficient technological means has become an inevitable choice to support and ensure the achievement of the national dual carbon goals. It is also an effective measure to implement the concepts of "green transportation", "green development", as well as the requirements of "efficiency transformation", "improving total factor productivity", and "high-quality development" proposed by the 19th National Congress.Among the above measures, the priority of optimizing transportation structure is extremely high.

2. Definition of Relevant Concepts

2.1. Transport Structure

Transportation structure means the proportion and composition of different aspects that are interconnected within and outside the transportation industry. The usual form of expression is to examine the composition of various transportation modes within the transportation industry, as well as the proportion relationships required to achieve reasonable division of labor and cooperation, such as the network size and regional distribution of various transportation modes, transportation capacity ratio, and so on.

This article uses proportion of railway and waterway transportation converted turnover in the total converted turnover to represent. Among them, converted turnover is an indicator that reflects the total turnover of passenger and freight department. We convert passenger turnover into ton kilometers using a fixed coefficient.

2.2. Carbon emission efficiency

Carbon Emission Efficiency(CEE) is a comprehensive consideration of input factors such as capital, manpower, energy, as well as output factors such as GDP and carbon emissions. Due to the unexpected output of carbon emissions, the smaller the value, the better. Therefore, CEE is defined as the maximum GDP and minimum carbon emissions that can be achieved by investing a fixed amount of capital, manpower, and energy elements at a certain level of technology.

This article constructs a directional SBM-GML index model based on the directional distance function to measure the CEE of the transportation industry in the Belt. The input variables include employees, capital stock, and energy input, while the output variables include converted turnover and carbon emissions.

Table 1. Description of input-output variables

Classification	Variables	Method of calculation
Input variables	Manpower	The average of employees in the previous year and the current year
	Capital stock	Perpetual inventory method
	Energy	Conversion of terminal energy consumption into standard coal
Output variables	Converted turnover	Passenger turnover is converted into freight turnover
	Carbon emissions	The top-down method

3. Model Construction of Decoupling Elastic Analysis

Decoupling refers to the breakdown of the coupling relationship between two variables, meaning that two variables are related to each other and become independent of each other. The OECD first applied this theory to study agricultural policies, and later scholars gradually expanded it to study the relationship of economy and environment. Currently, a large amount of literature applies this theory to study the relationship of economy and carbon emissions. The process of weakening and disappearing of the relationship is called carbon emission decoupling. At present, there are two main models for decoupling analysis: the OECD index and the Tapio elasticity model. This article adopts the second one [12].

Tapio (2005) introduced elasticity based on the OECD index [13], defining the decoupling elasticity as the ratio of pollutant growth rate to economic output growth rate. The decoupling states are generally divided into three categories: connected, unhooked, and negative unhooked. According to the index value, there are 8 types of the decoupling states: strong decoupling, weak decoupling, expansionary connection, expansionary negative decoupling, strong negative decoupling, decaying connection, weak negative decoupling, and decaying decoupling [14]. The specific division of the 8 states is shown in Figure 1.

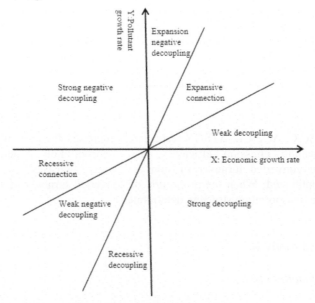

Figure 1. Division of the 8 decoupling states

The formula for Tapio decoupling elasticity index is:

$$e = P/G \qquad (1)$$

In Equation (1), e is the elasticity index; P is the growth rate of pollutants; G is the growth rate of economy. The comparison between elasticity index value and decoupling status is shown in Table 2.

Table 2. Description of decoupling status

P	G	e	decoupling status	
>0	>0	e>1.2	Expansion	
<0	<0	0≤e<0.8	Weak	negative decoupling
>0	<0	e<0	Strong	
<0	<0	e>1.2	Recessive	
>0	>0	0<e<0.8	Weak	decoupling
<0	>0	e<0	Strong	
>0	>0	0.8≤e≤1.2	Expansive connection	connected
<0	<0	0.8≤e≤1.2	Recessive connection	

Tapio decoupling elasticity model uses the growth rate of variables in previous year and the current year, effectively solving the problem of base period selection for the OECD model. The Tapio decoupling elasticity index calculation formula is as follows:

$$T_C = \left(\frac{\Delta C}{C}\right) \Big/ \left(\frac{\Delta TS}{TS}\right) \tag{2}$$

$$T_{CE} = \left(\frac{\Delta CE}{CE}\right) \Big/ \left(\frac{\Delta TS}{TS}\right) \tag{3}$$

Where $\Delta C/C$, $\Delta CE/CE$, $\Delta TS/TS$ respectively represent the growth rate of carbon emissions, carbon emission efficiency, and transportation structure. When the proportion of converted turnover of iron and water increases, the transportation structure is optimized; When the proportion of converted turnover of iron and water decreases, the transportation structure deteriorates.

4. Results and Analysis

4.1. Calculation Results

According to Equation (2) and (3), we calculate the decoupling elasticity of carbon emissions and transportation structure, carbon emission efficiency and transportation structure. The results are shown in Tables 3 and 4, respectively.

Table 3. The decoupling states of carbon emissions and transportation structures

year	$\Delta C/C$	$\Delta TS/TS$	T_C	Decoupling state
2010-2011	0.128	0.004	34.137	Expansion negative
2011-2012	0.080	-0.163	-0.492	Strong negative
2012-2013	0.042	-0.022	-1.940	Strong negative
2013-2014	0.094	0.072	1.297	Expansion negative
2014-2015	0.062	-0.058	-1.078	Strong negative
2015-2016	0.061	-0.031	-1.951	Strong negative
2016-2017	0.018	-0.058	-0.315	Strong negative
2017-2018	0.069	0.055	1.263	Expansion negative
2018-2019	0.054	-0.022	-2.446	Strong negative
2019-2020	0.096	-0.027	-3.527	Strong negative
2010-2020	0.967	-0.240	-4.035	Strong negative
average value	0.070	-0.025	-2.80	Strong negative

Table 4. The decoupling states of carbon emission efficiency and transportation structures

year	ΔCE/CE	ΔTS/TS	T_{CE}	Decoupling state
2010-2011	0.026	0.004	6.936	Expansion negative
2011-2012	-0.015	-0.163	0.092	Weak negative
2012-2013	0.015	-0.022	-0.704	Expansion negative
2013-2014	-0.057	0.072	-0.788	Strong
2014-2015	-0.017	-0.058	0.288	Weak negative
2015-2016	0.059	-0.031	-1.902	Expansion negative
2016-2017	0.049	-0.058	-0.842	Expansion negative
2017-2018	-0.029	0.055	-0.538	Strong
2018-2019	-0.016	-0.022	0.728	Weak negative
2019-2020	-0.018	-0.027	0.671	Weak negative
2010-2020	-0.009	-0.240	0.037	Weak negative
average value	-0.001	-0.025	0.040	Weak negative

4.2. Result Analysis

According to Table 3, during the research period, the decoupling elasticity index of carbon emissions and transportation structure fluctuated significantly, with an overall downward trend. The index value ranges from -3.527 to 34.137, and the decoupling relationship presents two states: expanding negative and strong negative. Among them, expanding negative occurs three times and strong negative occurs seven times. The decoupling elasticity index in the first and last years is -4.035, and the average value during the research period is -2.8, both showing a strong negative decoupling state, namely: the transportation structure continues to deteriorate and carbon emissions increase. Transportation carbon emissions are far from decoupling from the transportation structure, and there is a strong correlation.

According to Tables 4, the fluctuation of the decoupling elasticity index between the CEE and transportation structure during the study period is relatively small, with an overall trend of decreasing first and then increasing. Index value ranges from -1.902 to 6.936, and the decoupling relationship presents four states: expanding negative, weak negative, strong negative and strong decoupling, with occurrences of 1, 4, 3, and 2 respectively. The index between CEE and transportation structure in the first and last years is 0.037, and the average value during the study period is 0.04, showing a weakly negative decoupling state. The CEE of the transportation industry in the Belt has not been decoupled from the transportation structure, resulting in a deterioration of the transportation structure and a decrease in carbon emission efficiency.

The overall decoupling elasticity of carbon emissions, CEE and transportation structure is characterized by strong negative decoupling and weak negative decoupling.

5. Conclusion and Suggestions

According to the above analysis, the overall relationship between transportation structure and CEE is manifested as a decrease in the proportion of iron and water converted turnover, an increase in carbon emissions, and a decrease in CEE.

From 2009 to 2020, the proportion of converted turnover of railway and waterway transportation was generally on a downward trend, while the proportion of converted turnover of highway and air transportation rapidly increased. Compared with railway and waterway transportation, highway and air transportation is relatively high in terms of the per unit turnover energy consumption, and the dependence of highway and air transportation on high carbon emission factors such as diesel, gasoline, and aviation fuel is stronger.

Therefore, reducing the proportion of road and air transportation and increasing the proportion of the other transportation are important ways to improve the CEE and reduce carbon emissions. From the perspective of transportation industry governance, the priority of adjusting transportation structure is even higher.

The reform of the transportation supply side structure is a key task for the transportation industry during China's 13th Five Year Plan period, and the core of deepening the transportation supply side structure reform is to make up for the shortcomings of transportation infrastructure.

(1) The transportation industry should coordinate and optimize the comprehensive transportation network layout, significantly improve regional accessibility, improve transportation convenience and interchangeability of transportation methods, and better leverage the network and scale effects of transportation. For example, while paying attention to the connectivity between large cities and small and medium-sized cities, we will also focus on the inter-connectivity between them, forming a more fully functional railway transportation network, vigorously promoting the construction of high-level inland waterways, and constructing an inland shipping network centered on the Yangtze River, ultimately forming a green comprehensive transportation system with railways and waterways as the main body.

(2) It is necessary to optimize the ratio between various transportation modes to form differences and compartmentalizes in the functions of transportation modes. In terms of passenger transportation, we will accelerate the organic integration of various transportation modes, minimize transfer distances, build a large capacity fast passenger transportation system mainly composed of high-speed railways and intercity railways, reduce long-distance road passenger transportation routes, and thereby increase the proportion of railway passenger transportation and reduce the proportion of highway passenger transportation.

(3) In terms of freight transportation, fully leverage the comparative advantages of railways and waterways in bulk cargo and long-distance transportation, and reduce the proportion of various types of heavy-duty freight vehicles; Relying on the Yangtze River and its tributary ports to carry out multi-modal transportation business of iron and water, forming a major import and export freight channel for the Yangtze River's golden waterway; Encourage the development of railway express products and increase the proportion of container and bulk cargo rail water inter-modal transportation; Reduce the "return empty travel" in the highway transportation industry and promote "drop and drop transportation".

In summary, in the context of the "supply side reform of transportation", the competent department of transportation industry should seize the opportunity to coordinate and optimize the layout of the comprehensive transportation network, supplement the shortcomings of infrastructure, improve the interchangeability of transportation methods, guide the transfer of passenger and freight flows to railway and waterway transportation modes with lower energy intensity and carbon emissions per unit converted turnover, and thereby optimize the transportation structure; By promoting efficient transportation organization methods such as "Multi-modal transportation, drop and hang transportation", we aim to improve the level of transportation organization and reduce transportation intensity. At present, the potential for reducing emissions and improving efficiency in optimizing the transportation industry structure has not been effectively utilized. If the transportation structure can be effectively optimized in the future, the CEE of the transportation industry will be significantly improved.

Acknowledgment

This project is supported by Philosophy and Social Sciences Research Project of Hubei Provincial Department of Education(22G082).

References

[1] Salvatore Saija, Daniela Romano. A methodology for the estimation of road transport air emissions in urban areas of Italy [J]. Atmospheric Environment, 2002, 36(34):5377-5383.

[2] Wang Haikun, Fu Lixin, Bi Jun. CO2 and pollutant emissions from passenger cars in China [J]. Energy Policy, 2011, 39:3005-3011.

[3] Wang Tianyi, Li Hongqi, Zhang Jun, et al. Influencing Factors of Carbon Emission in China's Road Freight Transport [J]. Procedia-Social and Behavioral Sciences, 2012, 43:54-64.

[4] Lin Tzu-Ping. Carbon dioxide emissions from transport in Taiwan's national parks [J]. Tourism Management, 2010, 31(2):285-290.

[5] Xu Bin, Lin Boqiang. Differences in regional emissions in China's transport sector: Determinants and reduction strategies [J]. Energy, 2016, 95:459-470.

[6] Zhou P, Ang B W, Han J Y. Total factor carbon emission performance: A Malmquist index analysis [J]. Energy Economics, 2010, 32(1):194-201.

[7] Risto Herrala, Rajeev K. Goel. Global CO2 efficiency: Country-wise estimates using a stochastic cost frontier [J]. Energy Policy, 2012, 45(7):762-770.

[8] Greening L A, Ting M, Davis W B. Decomposition of aggregate carbon intensity for freight : Trends from 10 OECD countries for the period 1971-1993[J]. Energy Economics, 1999, 21(4):331-361.

[9] Ehrlich P R, Ehrlich A H. Population, resources, environment: issues in human ecology [M]. San Francisco: Freeman, 1970.

[10] Tae-Hyeong Kwon. Decomposition of factors determining the trend of CO2 emissions from car travel in Great Britain (1970-2000) [J]. Ecological Economics, 2005, 53:261-275.

[11] Xu Bin, Lin Boqiang. Factors affecting carbon dioxide (CO2) emissions in China's transport sector: a dynamic nonparametric additive regression model [J]. Journal of Cleaner Production, 2015, 101:311-322.

[12] OECD. Environmental indicators-development, measurement and use [R]. Paris: OECD, 2003:13.

[13] Vehmas J, Kaivo-oja J, Luukkanen J. Comparative De-link and Relink Analysis of Material Flows in EU-15 Member Countries [C]. Wuppertal: Con Account Conference, 2003.

[14] Tapio P. Towards a theory of decoupling: Degrees of decoupling in the EU and the ease of road traffic in Finland between 1970 and 2001[J]. Transport Policy, 2005, 12(2):137-151.

Artificial Intelligence, Medical Engineering and Education
Z.B. Hu et al. (Eds.)
© 2024 The Authors.
This article is published online with Open Access by IOS Press and distributed under the terms
of the Creative Commons Attribution Non-Commercial License 4.0 (CC BY-NC 4.0).
doi:10.3233/ATDE231319

Technical Scheme for Optimizing Urban and Rural Logistics Operations and Improving the Informatization of Rural Logistics

Zhong ZHENG[a,b], Wanxian HE[c,1], Ganglan WEI[d]

[a] *College of Business, Nanning University, Nanning, China*
[b] *King Mongkut's Institute of Technology Ladkrabang, Bangkok, 10520, Thailand*
[c] *Artificial intelligence Research Institute, Guangxi Academy of Sciences, Nanning, China*
[d] *Administration Section, Guangxi Mingyang Farms, Nanning, China*

Abstract. In order to optimize the core problems encountered in the operation of urban and rural logistics and improve the informatization degree of rural logistics, the authors of this paper conduct research on the application of big data, cloud computing, and other technologies in urban and rural logistics and informatization. Based on the current problems, the authors adopt the hierarchical design, C/S architecture, and cloud API technology to improve the low level of informatization in urban and rural logistics, as well as optimize the dispersion and repetitive construction of logistics resources for logistics enterprises in urban and rural areas. Overall, a feasible sharing technology solution for urban-rural logistics informatization has been provided, providing a certain reference for optimizing urban-rural logistics operations and improving rural informatization issues.

Keywords. Urban and rural Logistics; Big data; Cloud computing; Informatization

1. Introduction

With the continuous development of China's economy and society, the rapid advancement of urbanization and industrialization, and the comprehensive development of rural revitalization strategy, opening the two-way circulation channel of "industrial products going to the countryside and agricultural products entering the urban" has become a hot spot of attention of theoretical circles and practical managers. More and more experts, scholars, and industry enterprise managers have accumulated certain achievements in theoretical and practical research on the integration mode and technology of urban and rural logistics.

In terms of theoretical research, experts analyze the development model, necessity, and effectiveness of urban and rural logistics service systems from a macro perspective. And experts analyze the characteristics of urban-rural logistics in the context of the new era, explore the driving force of urban-rural logistics integration, study the construction

---

[1] Corresponding Author: Wanxian HE, E-mail: hewx2022@163.com.

of new models of urban-rural logistics [1-3]. And focus on the research of information technology on the innovation of urban and rural logistics modes in the context of the Internet age. and analyze the effect of integrated services of urban and rural logistics [1, 3, 4]. There are experts based on the consumption of residents and urban and rural logistics needs for analysis [5]. In terms of resource allocation, many experts have studied the problems in the allocation of urban and rural logistics resources and proposed solutions [6-7]. At the same time, many experts put forward suggestions on the application of information technology such as big data and blockchain to cope with the development of urban and rural logistics and achieved certain results [8-12].

In the process of industrial development and practical application, large enterprises such as ZTO Express, JD.com, and Cainiao (A logistics brand) have laid out the integrated operation of urban and rural logistics [13]. By empowering the supply chain logistics and e-commerce platform in both directions, ZTO Express innovates the "express + e-commerce" model deeply in the origin and provides services such as setting up express stations, centralized receipt and delivery, direct distribution special lines, and e-commerce sales in rural areas. JD Logistics continues to improve its infrastructure construction, promote the sinking of its logistics network, and have achieved the coverage of large and small item networks in all administrative regions and counties in mainland of China. Cainiao proposed the concept of "technology going to the countryside", hoping to use a series of "feasible and user-friendly" technologies to digitize rural outlets, fill the gaps in rural logistics, activate rural market consumption power, and boost the rural economy.

The main research of experts is focused on the macro level, and the research on specific technology applications is not in-depth enough, and the research on key technologies is still in the initial stage. In terms of industrial applications, major enterprises are also beginning to lay out the integration of urban and rural logistics, and the development of urban and rural logistics integration has urgent needs and broad market space.

Based on current theoretical research and industry operations analysis, the core issues encountered in urban and rural logistics operation include three aspects. First, the degree of information is low. At present, logistics in counties, townships, and villages mainly exist in the form of franchises, with a relatively small operating entity and a lack of motivation for logistics informatization. Moreover, there is a lack of investment in logistics technology research and development, resulting in a relatively low level of logistics informatization in urban and rural areas. The data structure of logistics systems adopted by different franchised logistics enterprises is different, the information level is different, and the knowledge representation is not uniform. The inability to use semantic information systematically is an urgent problem for the efficient development of urban and rural logistics. Secondly, it has high costs, low efficiency, and slow delivery time. The delivery time is generally 4-5 days, which is a significant difference compared to 2-3 days for urban delivery. It is difficult to return or exchange goods, and the challenges faced include low volume, low profits, high costs, and high seasonal fluctuations, which make it difficult for express delivery to enter the village. Thirdly, the integration of resources is weak, making it difficult to achieve economies of scale. However, currently in China, rural logistics resources and businesses are scattered, with duplicate construction and a self-contained system. The current model is difficult to sustain, mainly due to the inability to balance costs and benefits well, and enterprises cannot proceed without subsidies. Rural areas are vast and different from urban centralized residences, the logistics business in rural areas is relatively scattered, the frequency of orders is low, and the integration of resources is small and cannot play the scale economy, which are important reasons for the high cost of urban and rural logistics. Therefore, it is necessary to effectively integrate urban and rural logistics resources.

To solve the above problems, there is a need for a platform that can collect the overall resource information of urban and rural logistics enterprises, including the size of enterprises, regional distribution, and the amount of logistics assets invested [6,13]. At the same time, it is necessary to collect information on the logistics needs of each township, as well as information on the unique products and material needs of each township. By collecting and analyzing information to provide appropriate feedback to logistics enterprises and urban and rural residents.

In this way, on the one hand, it is possible to analyze the overall distribution of logistics and determine how to optimize and dispatch logistics resources overall. On the other hand, logistics companies can understand the logistics and material needs of various regions and consider whether they need to invest in adding post stations, logistics personnel, etc. based on their own enterprise situation. At the same time, urban and rural residents can also choose appropriate logistics methods based on their own needs by understanding the distribution of logistics resources, prices, timeliness, and other information. By showcasing the local specialties and material needs of townships, to some extent, it can also stimulate consumption and increase logistics demand. Guided by this idea, the authors of this paper study the application of big data [14-16], cloud computing [17-19], and other technologies in urban and rural logistics and informatization and propose a technical scheme to optimize urban and rural logistics operations and improve rural logistics informatization.

2. The Application of Big Data and Cloud Computing Technology in Urban and Rural Logistics and Rural Informatization

2.1. Big Data and Cloud Computing Technology

The most obvious feature of big data is "large". From a technical point of view, the problems that big data can solve are divided into three main aspects: effective management of data, data analysis, and data application. Data management involves operations such as data collection, cleaning, storage, and security. Data analysis mainly involves performing specific operations on data based on scenarios, which is also the process of achieving data value. The application of data depends on the export of big data applications, such as analyzing and screening out useful information for logistics enterprises and individuals from a big number of logistics information and providing external output.

Cloud computing is an emerging method of shared infrastructure that unifies the management of a mass of physical resources and virtualizes them, forming a huge pool of virtualized sources. Cloud computing is an emerging method of shared infrastructure that unifies the management of lots of physical resources and virtualizes them, forming a huge pool of virtualized sources. The cloud is a quasi-parallel and distributed system consisting of clusters of virtual computers that can be interconnected. These dynamically deployed virtual machines exist as unified computing resources and comply with service-level agreements.; Online games; Online medical care; Transportation logistics; Financial investment. Other aspects such as smart home, storage of video data, but also remote dialogue, monitoring, and so on.

2.2. The Application of Big Data and cloud Computing Technology in Urban and Rural Logistics and Rural Informatization

The application of big data and cloud computing technology in urban and rural logistics and rural logistics informatization is aimed at the low degree of urban and rural logistics informatization. The purpose is to design a cloud data center for information storage, analysis, and processing, as well as a rural APP for information collection and sharing for individual users. Through the rural APP, individual users can register and upload personal basic information, submit daily logistics demand information, retrieve personal scarce items information, etc. Cloud data centers can use big data technology to store, clean, analyze, mine, predict and other processing of these data. At the same time, the cloud data center uses cloud computing technology to provide cloud API interface services to various logistics enterprises. Logistics enterprises can access the cloud data center through the cloud API, upload the resource information of logistics enterprises, seek or provide logistics sharing information, and retrieve potential logistics business information, so as to optimize the logistics resources in urban and rural areas and improve the low degree of information technology in rural logistics.

From the concept design, system architecture design, and system module design of the system, the authors of this paper will elaborate on how to use big data and cloud computing technology to design a technical scheme to optimize the operation of urban and rural logistics and improve the informatization degree of rural logistics.

3. Urban and Rural Logistics Information Sharing Technology Scheme Based on Big Data and Cloud Computing Technology

3.1. Conceptual Design of the System

The Conceptual design of urban and rural logistics information system is shown in Figure 1.

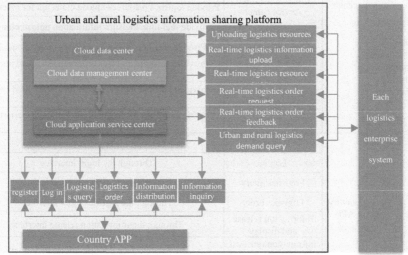

Figure 1. System deployment architecture diagram

3.1.1. Deployment Architecture Design

First, from the perspective of deployment architecture, the objects involved in this technical solution are: cloud data center, rural app, logistics enterprise system. A cloud data center includes a cloud data management center and a cloud application service center.

1) Cloud data center: using big data technology to store, clean, analyze, mine, forecast, and other processes of these data, and providing external cloud computing application services.

2) Rural APP: Completing registration and uploading personal basic information, submitting daily logistics demand information, searching for personal scarce item information, and other functions.

3) Enterprise logistics system: Accessing cloud data centers through cloud APIs, uploading resource information of logistics enterprises, and seeking or providing logistics sharing information, searching for potential logistics business information, etc.

3.1.2. Functional Design

Table 1. Function design of the system

System name	subsystem	Modular function	Functional Description
Urban and rural logistics information sharing platform	Cloud data center	Cloud data management center	Use big data technology to store, clean, analyze, mine and predict these data
		Cloud application service center	Provide registration interface for app
			Provide login interface for app
			Provide logistics query interface for app
			Provide logistics order interface for app
			Provide an information query and browsing interface
			Provide an information publishing interface for app
			Provide logistics resources upload cloud api for enterprises
			Provide real-time logistics information upload cloud api
			Provide real-time logistics resource query cloud API
			Provide real-time logistics order request cloud api for logistics enterprises
			Provide real-time logistics order feedback cloud api for logistics enterprises
			Provide cloud api for logistics enterprises to query urban and rural logistics demand
	Country APP	Register	Through the registration interface
		Log in	Through the login interface
		Logistics query	Through the logistics query interface
		Logistics order	Through the logistics order interface
		Information release and display	Through the information release interface
		Information retrieval browsing	Browse interface through information query
		Other functions	

The function of the system includes cloud data center and country APP, as Table 1 shown.

3.2. System Architecture Design

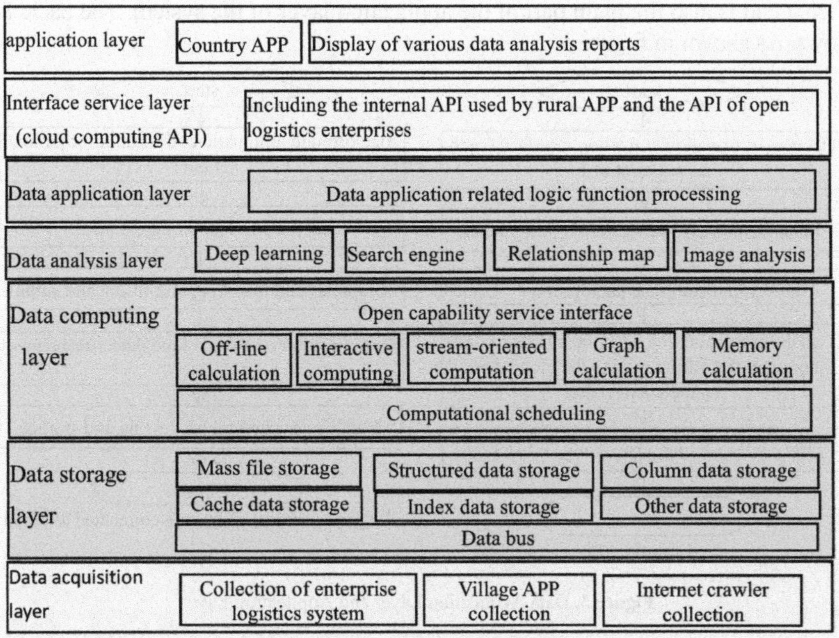

application layer	Country APP	Display of various data analysis reports			

Figure 2. System architecture diagram

As shown in the figure 2 above, the overall hierarchical design method is adopted, and the interaction between the server and the app client is built using the C/S architecture. Referring to the big data technology architecture design, it is divided into interface service layer, data application layer, data analysis layer, data calculation layer, data storage layer and data acquisition layer.

1) Data collection layer: Mainly collecting information on logistics enterprises, logistics and material demand information of urban and rural residents;

2) Data storage layer to data application layer: It is a general big data technology architecture reference structure level to complete big data-related technical functions;

3) Interface service layer: Completing the interface functions of logistics enterprises and rural apps.

4) Application layer: rural app client and various report displays.

3.3. System Module Design

Since the data storage layer to the data application layer is a general big data technology architecture reference structure level to complete big data-related technical functions, this chapter mainly introduces the data acquisition layer, interface service layer, and application layer.

3.3.1. Data Collection Layer and Application Layer

The data acquisition layer is mainly concentrated in the rural APP and the system of various logistics enterprises that access the cloud API, and the interface design involving the front end is also the main part of the application layer of the system. The basic logic follows. As shown in Figure 3.

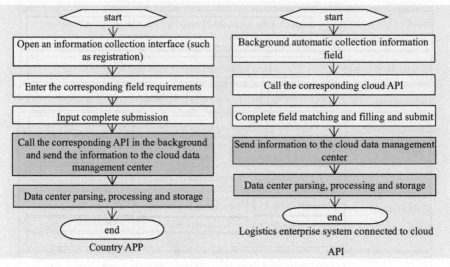

Figure 3. Data Acquisition Layer and Application Layer

3.3.2. Interface Service Layer

Logistics enterprise system parameter design is shown in Table 2- Table 13.
1) Logistics Resources Upload Cloud API, using http-post mode, input parameter:

Table 2. Logistics Input Parameter

Parameter meaning	Parameter name	Type	Is it required	Explain
Name of logistics enterprise	Logistics Name	String	Y	
Enterprise taxpayer identification number	Tax ID	String	Y	
Brief introduction of logistics enterprises	Logistics Info	String	N	
Ordinary express unit price	Regular Price	Float	Y	Yuan
Unit price of heavy-duty express delivery	Weight Price	Float	Y	Yuan/kg
Number of post stations	Delivery Station Num	Int	Y	
Number of vehicles transported by enterprises	Vehicles Num	Int	Y	
Post distribution information	Delivery Station Info			Json array

Return parameter:

Table 3. Logistics Return Parameter

Parameter meaning	Parameter name	Type	Is it required	Explain
Success or Fail	Success	Int	Y	0-Success，1-Failure
Cause of failure	Error Msg	String	N	Cause of failure

2）Real-time Logistics Information Upload Cloud API, using http-post mode, input parameter:

Table 4. Real-time Logistics Information Upload Cloud API Input Parameter

Parameter meaning	Parameter name	Type	Is it required	Explain
Name of logistics enterprise	Logistics Name	String	Y	
Enterprise taxpayer identification number	Tax ID	String	Y	
Station number	Delivery Station ID	String	Y	
Post address	Delivery Station Addr	String	Y	
Type and quantity of inventory information	Goods Type Num	Int	Y	
Inventory information	Goods Info			Json array

Return parameter:

Table 5. Real-time Logistics Information Upload Cloud API Return Parameter

Parameter meaning	Parameter name	Type	Is it required	Explain
Success or Fail	Success	Int	Y	0-Success，1-Failure
Cause of failure	Error Msg	String	N	Cause of failure

3）Cloud Resource Query Interface (API) initiated by Cloud Center, adopts http-get mode, input parameter:

Table 6. Cloud Resource Query Interface (API) Input Parameter

Parameter meaning	Parameter name	Type	Is it required	Explain
The sender's address	Sender Addr	String	Y	
Address of the recipient	Recipient Addr	String	Y	

Return parameter:

Table 7. Cloud Resource Query Interface (API) Return Parameter

Parameter meaning	Parameter name	Type	Is it required	Explain
Success or Fail	Success	Int	Y	0-Success，1-Failure
Cause of failure	Error Msg	String	N	Cause of failure
Specific logistics information	Logistics Info		N	

4）The Cloud Center initiates a single-interface Cloud API under the logistics, using the http-post mode, input parameter:

Table 8. Cloud Center initiates a single-interface Cloud API Input Parameter

Parameter meaning	Parameter name	Type	Is it required	Explain
Order request number	Order ID	String	Y	
The sender's address	Sender Addr	String	Y	
Address of the recipient	Recipient Addr	String	Y	

Table 8. Cloud Center initiates a single-interface Cloud API Input Parameter (continued)

Parameter meaning	Parameter name	Type	Is it required	Explain
Address of the recipient	Tax ID	String	Y	
Post address	Delivery Station Addr	String	Y	
Station number	Delivery Station ID	String	Y	
Selected courier type	Delivery Type	Int	Y	Value: 1 is ordinary express, 2 is heavy express

Return parameter:

Table 9. Cloud Center initiates a single-interface Cloud API Return Parameter

Parameter meaning	Parameter name	Type	Is it required	Explain
Success or Fail	Success	Int	Y	0-Success，1-Failure
Cause of failure	Error Msg	String	N	Cause of failure

5）Logistics enterprise orders Feedback Cloud API, using http-post mode, input parameter:

Table 10. Logistics enterprise orders Feedback Cloud API Input Parameter

Parameter meaning	Parameter name	Type	Is it required	Explain
Request number	Order ID	String	Y	
Whether to take orders or not	Is Agreed	int	Y	Value: 1 agree to take the order, 0 disagree to take the order

Return parameter:

Table 11. Logistics enterprise orders Feedback Cloud API Return Parameter

Parameter meaning	Parameter name	Type	Is it required	Explain
Success or Fail	Success	Int	Y	0-Success，1-Failure
Cause of failure	Error Msg	String	N	Cause of failure

6）Urban and rural logistics demand Query Cloud API, input parameter：

Table 12. Urban and rural logistics demand Query Cloud API Input Parameter

Parameter meaning	Parameter name	Type	Is it required	Explain
place name	Place Name	String	Y	It can be the name of a city, county, township, etc
Regional number	Place ID	String	Y	According to the national unified number

Return parameter

Table 13. Urban and rural logistics demand Query Cloud API Return Parameter

Parameter meaning	Parameter name	Type	Is it required	Explain
Success or Fail	Success	Int	Y	0-Success，1-Failure
Cause of failure	Error Msg	String	N	Cause of failure
Logistics demand	Logistics Needs	String	N	Average monthly logistics order volume and transaction amount, with the unit of RMB.
Local specialty products	SpecialProduct	String	N	List the top 5 items.

4. Conclusion

In order to optimize the core problems encountered in the operation of urban and rural logistics and improve the informatization degree of rural logistics, the authors of this paper carry out research on the application of big data, cloud computing, and other technologies in urban and rural logistics and informatization. In combination with the existing problems, hierarchical design, C/S architecture, and cloud API technology are adopted to improve the low degree of information technology in urban and rural logistics, and to optimize the dispersion and repeated construction of logistics resources in urban and rural areas. Overall, a feasible sharing technology scheme for logistics informatization in urban and rural areas is provided, and a certain reference for optimizing logistics operations in urban and rural areas and improving rural informatization is provided.

The shortcomings of this paper are that it is not designed in conjunction with a specific scenario, and there is a lack of specific data input. Therefore, the next step is to apply the system designed in this paper with actual cases and verify the effect through data input and calculation. And the design has not been implemented and ill-considered or the design is not ideal and needs to be more systematically studied and demonstrated.

Acknowledgment

This paper is supported by: Young and middle-aged teachers basic ability improvement project of Guangxi University "Research on Key Technologies of Urban and Rural Logistics Integration Operation Based on Big Data and Cloud Computing" (2023KY1862) and Guangxi Education Department teaching reform project(2022JGB440).

References

[1]   Zhao Dongqiang. Construction of an Integrated Urban-rural Logistics Model in the Context of the Internet[J]. Journal of Commercial Economics.2020, (17):93-96.
[2]   Wu Susu. Exploring and Promoting the Integrated Development of Urban and Rural Logistics Services[J]. Chinese Journal of Agricultural Resources and Regional Planning. 2022, 43(06):184+241.
[3]   Dai Xiaoting & Hu Yongshi. Research on Measuring the Development Level of Urban Rural Logistics Integration[J]. Journal of Technical Economics & Management. 2021, (04):72-77.
[4]   Ji Lianggang & Wang Jiahao. Research on the Integration Mode of Urban and Rural Commercial Circulation under the Background of "Internet ＋"[J]. Economy and Management. 2020,34(02):77-84.
[5]   Zhao Xingjun & Lou Feng. Coupling and Coordination Analysis of Urban-rural Circulation Integration and Resident Consumption[J].   Journal of Commercial Economics.2022, (17):46-50.
[6]   Zhang Mei. Research on Optimizing the Allocation of Urban and Rural Commercial Logistics Service Resources[J]. Journal of Commercial Economics.2020, (17):101-104.
[7]   Li Ziyuan & Ge Xiaowei. Research on Reconstruction of Urban and Rural Commercial Circulation Network in the Big Data Era[J]. Journal of Commercial Economics. 2017, (17):15-17.
[8]   Tao Juncheng, Pan Lin & Chu Yeping. Research on Reconstruction of Urban and Rural Logistics Network in the Era of Big data[J]. China Business and Market.2016,30(11):22-32. DOI: 10.14089/j.cnki.cn11-3664/f.2016.11.003.
[9]   Chen Kun. The Impact of Internet Technology on the Integrated Development of Urban Rural Bilateral Commercial Circulation from the Perspective of Overall Planning[J]. Journal of Commercial Economics. 2022, (21):14-17.
[10] Zhang Yanling. The Impact of Urban-rural Information Integration on the Development of Integrated Logistics in the Context of Digital Rural Areas[J]. Journal of Commercial Economics. 2022, (13):175-178.

[11] Chien C F, Dauzère-Pérès S, Huh W T, et al. Artificial intelligence in manufacturing and logistics systems: algorithms, applications, and case studies[J]. International Journal of Production Research, 2020, 58(9): 2730-2731.

[12] Woschank M, Rauch E, Zsifkovits H. A review of further directions for artificial intelligence, machine learning, and deep learning in smart logistics[J]. Sustainability, 2020, 12(9): 3760.

[13] Boute R N, Udenio M. AI in logistics and supply chain management[M]//Global Logistics and Supply Chain Strategies for the 2020s: Vital Skills for the Next Generation. Cham: Springer International Publishing, 2022: 49-65.

[14] Halil ARSLAN, Mustafa YALCIN and Yasin ŞAHAN, "SBIoT: Scalable Broker Design for Real Time Streaming Big Data in the Internet of Things Environment", International Journal of Information Technology and Computer Science, Vol.13, No.4, pp.47-52, 2021.

[15] Asma Omri, Mohamed Nazih Omri, "Towards an Efficient Big Data Indexing Approach under an Uncertain Environment", International Journal of Intelligent Systems and Applications, Vol.14, No.2, pp.1-13, 2022.

[16] Iram Mehmood, Sidra Anwar, AneezaDilawar, IsmaZulfiqar, Raja Manzar Abbas, "Managing Data Diversity on the Internet of Medical Things (IoMT)", International Journal of Information Technology and Computer Science, Vol.12, No.6, pp.49-56, 2020.

[17] Rasim M. Alguliyev, Rashid G. Alakbarov, "Integer Programming Models for Task Scheduling and Resource Allocation in Mobile Cloud Computing", International Journal of Computer Network and Information Security, Vol.15, No.5, pp.13-26, 2023.

[18] S. Sureshkumar, G. K. D. Prasanna Venkatesan, R. Santhosh, "Detection of DDOS Attacks on Cloud Computing Environment Using Altered Convolutional Deep Belief Networks", International Journal of Computer Network and Information Security, Vol.15, No.5, pp.63-72, 2023.

[19] Prabhakara B. K., Chandrakant Naikodi, Suresh L., "Ford Fulkerson and Newey West Regression Based Dynamic Load Balancing in Cloud Computing for Data Communication", International Journal of Computer Network and Information Security, Vol.15, No.5, pp.81-95, 2023.

Artificial Intelligence, Medical Engineering and Education
Z.B. Hu et al. (Eds.)
© *2024 The Authors.*
This article is published online with Open Access by IOS Press and distributed under the terms
of the Creative Commons Attribution Non-Commercial License 4.0 (CC BY-NC 4.0).
doi:10.3233/ATDE231320

Research on Scheduling of Terminal Frontier Resources Based on Multi-Objective Optimization

Min LIU[a], Hanbin XIAO[a], Yangyi LOU[a], Zengtao GENG[b] and Lingxin KONG[a,1]

[a] *School of transportation and Logistics Engineering, Wuhan University of Technology, Wuhan, 430063, China*

[b] *Shandong Port Technology Group Qingdao Co., Ltd, Qingdao 266000, China*

ORCiD ID: Min Liu https://orcid.org/0009-0008-5103-0740

Abstract. To achieve a balance between operational effectiveness and service efficiency in container terminals has become a critical issue with the rapid growth of container trade. In this paper, the scheduling problem of frontier operation resources of container terminals is proposed and studied. And a scheduling optimization method is proposed for the container terminal frontier operation resources. Considering the mutual influence between multiple resources, a joint scheduling optimization model of container terminal frontier operation resources is established. A multi-objective fusion algorithm is designed to carry out the solution.

Keywords. Container terminal; Joint scheduling; Multi-objective fusion algorithm

1. Introduction

As the increase of container trade volume, how to balance the operational effectiveness and service efficiency in the production operation process has become the focus of the optimization and upgrading in the container terminal. The service capacity of container terminals is closely related to the scheduling of frontier operation resources such as berths, quay cranes and container trucks. Therefore, various factors of the daily operation of terminals should be considered to obtain the optimal resource scheduling plan. The current studies have analyzed the development status of each port in depth from several perspectives, which can be the theoretical support for the rational scheduling optimization of port resources [1-4].

At present, the research on the optimization problem of resource scheduling for container terminal frontier operations aims to coordinate the relationship between different operational resources to ensure the efficient and smooth operation of terminal operations. And the research content extends from simple strategies to single resource scheduling and then to joint scheduling of multiple resources. Several scholars have introduced heuristic algorithms into the study of this problem, such as genetic algorithms, simulated annealing algorithms, and particle swarm algorithms [5-8]. Then the mathematical models have been continuously adapted according to the actual operational scenarios of the terminals. Agra et al proposed a solution to the berth assignment problem

---

[1] Corresponding Author: Lingxin KONG, E-mail: konglingxin@whut.edu.cn.

for heterogeneous cranes, which utilizes both rolling level and branch cutting methods based on the relative position formulation to find a RHH (Rolling Horizon Heuristic) solution [9]. Soroush et al analyzed various factors that can affect the vessel's access to the port to perform a numerical simulation of port operations with tidal impact, draft depth, and safe distance of the vessel as indicators [10]. Xie et al integrated to obtain an operational decision model for berth and quay crane scheduling and used a branching pricing algorithm to obtain the results of the main problem by solving a pricing subproblem for each vessel [11]. Zhong et al designed the fuzzy self-integrating algorithm GA-PSO to apply the optimal joint berth-quay crane and collector truck scheduling scheme, which has a faster solution speed and higher solution quality in the algorithm comparison experiment [12]. Liu et al improved the NSGA-II to make it more appropriate for working out the optimization problem of berth scheduling and channel cooperative scheduling [13].

In summary, the current studies mainly focus on the rational scheduling of existing resource conditions, and most of them consider one or two resources in terminal operations for scheduling optimization. At the same time, few of them systematically study the overall operating cost and operational effectiveness of container terminals by combining the changing rule of the number of arriving vessels. Considering the actual terminal operation, the frontier operation resources exist strongly correlated, and the comprehensive capacity of the terminal can be improved with a reasonable resource scheduling scheme. Therefore, distinguishing from the existing literature, a resource scheduling optimization method is proposed based on the main line of the container terminal operation process in this study. The multi-objective fusion algorithm is designed to solve the optimal operation plan by integrating the frontier operation resources of the terminal.

2. Problem Definition

As important terminal frontier resources of container terminals, the berths, quay cranes and trucks have strong interactions, the mutual influence and constraints among these three must be considered in formulating operation plans. An optimal berth-quay crane scheduling scheme is established in this paper by considering the influence of container trucks in terminal logistics transportation and operation plan based on the joint berth-quay crane scheduling problem. In the terminal operation process, continuous berths are more practical than discrete berths, and the scheduling are more applicable. In this paper, the joint continuous berth-quay crane scheduling problem is converted into a planar coordinate axis represented by a space-time diagram, as shown in Figure 1.

In Figure 1, i denotes the vessel number, V_i denotes the arriving vessel i; B_{Pi} denotes the optimal berthing position of vessel i; B_i denotes the actual berthing position of vessel i; T_{Ai} denotes the actual arrival time of vessel i; T_{Si} denotes the starting operation time of vessel i; T_{PLi} denotes the planned departure time of vessel i; T_{Li} denotes the actual departure time of vessel i.

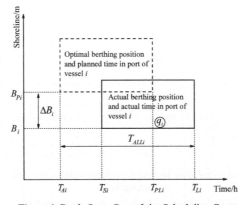

Figure 1. Berth-Quay Crane Joint Scheduling Gantt Chart

In Figure 1, the difference ΔB_i between the optimal berthing position and the actual berthing position of the vessel i can be described as Equation (1):

$$\Delta B_i = \left| B_{Pi} - B_i \right| \tag{1}$$

The delayed departure time T_{Wi} can be calculated in Equation (2):

$$T_{Wi} = T_{Li} - T_{PLi} \tag{2}$$

The total time in port T_{ALLi} can be calculated in Equation (3):

$$T_{ALLi} = T_{Li} - T_{Ai}, \forall i \tag{3}$$

To address the problem of joint scheduling of resources for container terminal frontier operations, the berthing offset factors and quay crane interference factors proposed by Meisel and Bienvirth are used in this study [14]. The impact produced by container trucks on the terminal operation plan is under consideration. The optimal berthing positions are usually prioritized when the berthing of incoming vessels is arranged. In the actual terminal operation, the berthing position of a vessel is influenced by various factors, such as the cost of container trucks. If a vessel deviates from the optimal berthing position, it will impact the efficiency of subsequent operations. For purpose of these effects, the cost of deviating from the optimal berthing position is considered as a penalty cost in this paper. The internal trucking route as a vessel deviates from the optimal berthing position is described in Figure 2.

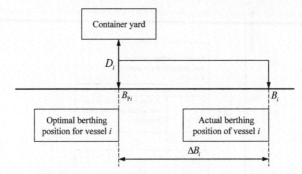

Figure 2. Schematic diagram of the internal container trucking route as the vessel deviates from the optimal berth

In Figure 2, the horizontal transportation distance of container at the terminal can be denoted as D_i when vessel i is at the optimal berthing position. And the distance becomes $D_i + \Delta B_i$ when the vessel i is at the actual berthing position. The berthing deviation coefficient α_i is specified as the ratio of the distance of horizontal transportation of container carried by vessel i through the internal truck and the distance difference between its optimal and actual berthing positions, as shown in Equation (4):

$$\alpha_i = \frac{D_i + \Delta B_i}{\Delta B_i} \tag{4}$$

However, when an incoming vessel is serviced by multiple quay cranes simultaneously, there will be interacted between quay cranes. So, the interference coefficient β is introduced to describe its impact on the operation plan. When the required operating time of quay crane is given as $m_i = W_i/v$, the distance of berth offset ΔB_i, the number of allocated quay cranes q_i and the operating time ϕ_i can be calculated as follow:

$$\phi_i = \left[\frac{(1 + \alpha_i \Delta B_i) m_i}{(q_i)^{\beta}} \right] \tag{5}$$

The maximum distance of berth offset $\Delta B_i^{\max}$ for the arbitrary vessel is shown in Equation (6):

$$\Delta B_i^{\max} = \max \left\{ L - B_i, B_i \right\} \tag{6}$$

Thus, the expression for the maximum and minimum working time of each vessel can be derived as shown in Equation (7) and Equation (8):

$$\phi_i^{\min} = \frac{m_i}{\left(q_i^{\max}\right)^\beta} \tag{7}$$

$$\phi_i^{\max} = \frac{\left(1 + \alpha_i \Delta B_i^{\max}\right) \cdot m_i}{\left(q_i^{\min}\right)^\beta} \tag{8}$$

3. Optimization Model

3.1 Model Assumption

The assumptions of the model are as follows:

1) Neglect the physical constraints such as shoreline water depth, the vessel can berth, loading and unloading at any position within the quay shoreline.

2) The number of the quay cranes is fixed during handling process.

3) Neglect the movement time of the quay cranes.

4) The arrival time of the vessel is fixed.

5) Each vessel can wait in the lying anchorage.

6) The berth position cannot be changed after berthing and each vessel can only berth once.

7) The distance between vessels must exceed the safe distance;

8) Each vessel has an optimal berth, and a certain cost will be incurred if the vessel deviates from the optimal berth;

9) The vessel length satisfies the shoreline space constraint.

3.2 Related Concepts and the Symbolic Representation

The vessels set: $V = \{1, 2, ..., N\}, i, j \in V, N$ is the total number of vessels. The quay cranes set: $Q = \{1, 2, ..., M\}, q \in Q, M$ is the total number of quay cranes. The time units set in the planning cycle: $T = \{1, 2, ..., H\}, t \in T, H$ is the total number of time units.

L is the length of the terminal, in 10m segments; Q is the total number of available quay cranes at the terminal; W_i is the container loading and unloading volume of the vessel i; l_i is the length of vessel i (neglect the safety distance of the vessel); $q_i^{\max}$ and $q_i^{\min}$ is the maximum and minimum number of quay cranes allowed to provide service at the same time when vessel i operated; v is the handling efficiency of the quay crane (TEU/h); C_1 is the operating cost per time unit for each quay crane; C_2 is the operating cost per truck; C_3 is the cost per time unit for delayed departure of vessel i; C_4 is the penalty coefficient of overdue time in port for vessel i; M is an infinity constant.

q_{it} is the number of quay cranes dispatched to vessel i at time t; B_i is the actual berthing position of vessel i; ϕ_i is the operating time of vessel i with the quay cranes interfering with each other; T_{Si} is the actual starting operating time of vessel i; T_{Ei} is the actual departure time of vessel i; x_{it} is a 0-1 variable, it shows 1 when vessel i is operated at berth at time t, and otherwise shows 0; y_{ij} is a 0-1 variable, it shows 1 when the berthing position of vessel i is to the left of the berthing position of vessel i, and otherwise shows 0; z_{ij} is a 0-1 variable, it shows 1 when the end operation time of vessel i is earlier than the start berthing time of vessel j, and otherwise shows 0; ω_{ijt} is a 0-1 variable, it shows 1 when vessel i and vessel j are operated at the same time t, and otherwise shows 0; θ_{it}^q is a 0-1 variable, it shows 1 when vessel i is served by quay crane q at moment t, and otherwise shows 0.

3.3 Modeling

To formulate a resource scheduling plan for vessels arriving in the planning period and optimize terminal operation cost and total time vessel in port, a container terminal frontier operations resource scheduling optimization model is established in this paper.
Two objective functions are introduced as follows:

$$\min f_1 = \sum_{i \in V} \left(C_1 \cdot q_{it} + C_2 \cdot W_i \cdot \alpha_i \cdot \Delta B_i + C_3 \cdot T_{Wi} \right) \tag{9}$$

$$\min f_2 = \sum_{i \in V} \left(T_{ALLi} + (C_4 - 1) \cdot (T_{Li} - T_{Pi}) \right) \tag{10}$$

Equation (9) is the objective function to minimize the terminal operation cost. Equation (10) is the objective function to minimize the total time for vessel in port.

The berths are allocated according to the frontier operation resource scheduling plan when the vessels arrive at the port. The berthing range of the vessels should satisfy Equation (11). And the difference between the actual berthing position and the optimal berthing position should satisfy Equation (12).

$$B_i + l_i \leqslant L, \forall i \in V \tag{11}$$

$$\Delta B_i \geq |B_i - B_{Pi}|, \forall i \in V \tag{12}$$

The vessel should wait at the distance of 60 nautical miles from the port until it receives the berthing signal from the terminal. And the vessel can start the operation only when it reaches the berthing position after receiving the berthing signal. As shown in Equation (13).

$$T_{Si} \geq T_{Ai}, \forall i \in V \tag{13}$$

The operating time of any incoming vessel at the terminal is expressed as follows.

$$\sum_t x_{it} = T_{Ei} - T_{Si}, \forall i \in V, \forall t \in T \tag{14}$$

$$\phi_i^{min} \leq \sum_t x_{it} \leq \phi_i^{max}, \forall i \in V, \forall t \in T \tag{15}$$

$$\sum_t (q_{it})^\beta \geq (1 + \alpha_i \Delta B_i) m_i, \forall i \in V, \forall t \in T \tag{16}$$

$$W_i = \sum_t x_{it} \cdot q_{it} \cdot v, \forall i \in V, \forall t \in T \tag{17}$$

Any two incoming vessels should ensure that they do not conflict in their actual berthing positions and actual berthing times, constrained as follows.

$$B_j + M(1 - y_{ij}) \geq B_i + l_i, \forall i, j \in V, i \neq j \tag{18}$$

$$T_{Sj} + M(1 - z_{ij}) \geq T_{Ei}, \forall i, j \in V, i \neq j \tag{19}$$

$$y_{ij} + y_{ji} + z_{ij} + z_{ji} \geq 1, \forall i, j \in V, i \neq j \tag{20}$$

A certain number of quay cranes will be allocated for loading and unloading after the vessel comes into port and berths according to the forward operation resource allocation plan. At time t, the arranged number of quay cranes cannot exceed the total number of quay cranes configured by the terminal. And the number of quay cranes serving the same vessel should meet the constraints of maximum and minimum number as follows:

$$\sum_{i=1}^m q_{it} \leq Q, \forall i \in V, \forall t \in T \tag{21}$$

$$q_i^{min} \leq q_{it} \leq q_i^{max}, \forall i \in V, \forall t \in T \tag{22}$$

The numbers of quay cranes serving for vessel i should be consecutive and constrained by the principle of non-crossover, shown as follows:

$$\theta_{it}^{q} + \theta_{it}^{q'} \leq 2 - y_{ij}, \forall q, q' \in Q, q < q', \forall i, j \in V, i \neq j, \forall t \in T \tag{23}$$

$$\theta_{it}^{q+1} \geq \theta_{it}^{q} + \theta_{it}^{q'} - 1, \forall q, q' \in Q, q+1 < q', \forall i \in V, \forall t \in T \tag{24}$$

One quay crane can serve only one vessel at the same time. The relationship between the total number of quay cranes in service at time t and the number of that assigned to each vessel in service are denoted as follows.

$$\sum_{i} \theta_{it}^{q} \leq 1, \forall q \in Q, \forall i \in V, \forall t \in T \tag{25}$$

$$q_{it} = \sum_{i} \theta_{it}^{q}, \forall q \in Q, \forall i \in V, \forall t \in T \tag{26}$$

ω_{ijt} is defined as follows.

$$M\omega_{ijt} \geq x_{it} x_{jt}, \forall i, j \in V, i \neq j, \forall t \in T \tag{27}$$

$$M(\omega_{ijt} - 1) < x_{it} x_{jt}, \forall i, j \in V, i \neq j, \forall t \in T \tag{28}$$

The serial number of quay crane assigned to the vessel with the berthing position on the left should be smaller than that on the right, it is restricted as follow.

$$\theta_{it}^{q} + \theta_{jt}^{q} \leq 1 + (M - M\omega_{ijt}) + (M - My_{ij}),$$
$$\forall q \in Q, \forall i, j \in V, i \neq j, \forall t \in T \tag{29}$$

The range of the decision variables in the model is defined as follows.

$$y_{ij}, z_{ij} \in \{0,1\}, \forall i, j \in V, i \neq j \tag{30}$$

$$x_{it}, \omega_{ijt}, \theta_{it}^{q} \in \{0,1\}, \forall q \in Q, \forall i, j \in V, i \neq j, \forall t \in T \tag{31}$$

4. Algorithm Design

The container terminal frontier resource scheduling optimization problem is an NP-hard problem [15-17]. Due to its complexity, a global search algorithm may lead to a very high computational complexity and may not be able to dig deeply into each searched local optimal solution. Therefore, a multi-objective fusion algorithm is designed by setting the NSGA-II algorithm and SA algorithm as the main fusion framework and the auxiliary algorithm respectively. The basic flow of the joint resource scheduling optimization algorithm for container terminal frontier operations is shown in Figure 3.

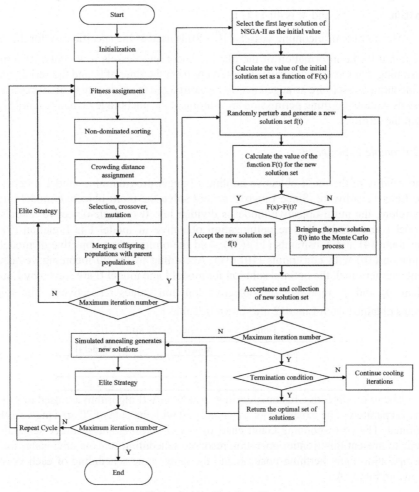

Figure 3. Algorithm flow diagram

5. Numerical Example

5.1. Example Parameters

The existing production and operation data of a container terminal are taken as an example to carry out the data simulation experiment. Taking 1 hour as one unit of time, and the safety distance is 10% of the vessel length. The parameters of this container terminal are set as follows: the length of the terminal shoreline is 1500 meters, the number of quay cranes is 15, C_1 is 180 RMB/h, C_2 is 50 RMB/(TEU·m^{-1}), C_3 is 20 RMB/h, C_4 is 1.5, and v is 40 TEU/h.

The number of incoming vessels ($|I|$=20) is used as the specific case for the testing according to the information of the planned incoming vessels in a container terminal. Assuming that the vessels arrive successively from the time of 0, and the serial numbers of incoming vessels are arranged in order according to the arrival time of 20 vessels. The vessels without berthing permission are waiting at the anchorage 60 nautical miles away from the terminal.

5.2 Example Experiment

The validity of the multi-objective nonlinear integer programming model is verified by the Lingo12 software. Since Lingo12 cannot solve the multi-objective model directly. Therefore, the multi-objective model is divided into two single-objective models, i.e., Model I and Model II. The optimization objective of model I is Equation (9) with constraint (4) and constraints (11)-(31). And the optimization objective of model II is Equation (10) with constraints (10)-(31). According to the 20 incoming vessels of a container terminal, the optimal solution for model I and model II are solved by Lingo12, where f_1 and f_2 represent the objective function values respectively. The solution results obtained from Lingo12 are shown in Table 1.

Table 1. Solution results of Lingo12

$|I|$	Model I f_1	Model II f_2
20	311236.62	71.27

The multi-objective fusion algorithm and NSGA-II algorithm are used to solve the cases separately. The experiments are conducted with the data of 20 arriving vessels at a terminal. The corresponding Gantt chart of vessel berthing and resource scheduling is made to present this frontier operation resource scheduling scheme obviously, showing the operation time, berthing position and the quay crane scheduling of each vessel, as shown in Figure 4.

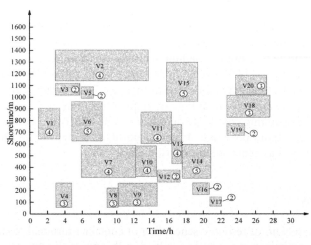

Figure 4. The Gantt chart corresponding to the optimal solution

The utilization of the quay crane in each period is shown in Figure 5. The maximum utilization rate of the quay crane is approaches 100%, the minimum utilization rate is 13.3%, and the average utilization rate is 60.95%.

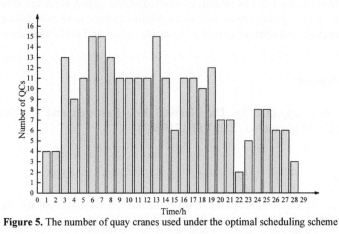

Figure 5. The number of quay cranes used under the optimal scheduling scheme

5.3 Analysis of Experimental Results

A solution result of single-objective optimization is chosen to compare with the set of Pareto optimal solutions of the multi-objective fusion algorithm, as shown in Table 2.

Table 2. Single-objective optimization versus multi-objective optimization

Optimization Strategies	Terminal operating costs/yuan	Total time vessel in port/h
Consider only optimal terminal operating costs	311236.62	79.43
Consider only the minimum total time vessel in port	326326.85	71.27
Combined consideration of two objectives optimal	315797.67	74.77

From the results in Table 2, the results show that the optimization of two conflicting objectives cannot be achieved at the same time. Therefore, in order to achieve the multi-objective optimization, it is necessary to weigh the relationship between different objectives and pursue the optimal solution of multiple objectives.

The optimal solution obtained by the optimization algorithm shows that the cost is ¥315,797.67 and the total time of the vessels in port is 74.77 hours. Adopting the multi-objective optimal scheme, the total time of ships in port can be increased as much as possible, and the operating cost of the terminal can be effectively controlled. It can be verified that the multi-objective fusion algorithm designed for multi-objective optimization model has better solution performance.

6. Conclusions

Aiming at the problem of resource scheduling of container terminal frontier operation, the scheduling optimization method is studied in this paper. Firstly, the joint resource scheduling optimization model is established and the optimization algorithm is designed to solve the model based on the terminal operational effectiveness and service efficiency. Then the actual operation data of a port is used for experiment, and the results reveal that the joint resource scheduling optimization model is effective.

In addition to the frontier resources studied in this paper, there are other resources, such as tugs, AGVs, gantry cranes and so on. Multi-resource joint scheduling is the future research direction and content to realize joint allocation and collaborative scheduling.

Acknowledgment

This work was supported by The National Key Research and Development 1102 Program of China (Grant No. 2020YFB1710803).

References

[1] Yang Xue, Ni Likun, Tong Fengming, et, al. Optimal management and allocation of superior resources in port industries[J]. Journal of Coastal Research, 2019, 94: 500-504.
[2] Lu Bo, Wang Qian. Port collaborative development based on rough set theory[J]. Soft Computer, 2020, 24(9): 6409-6419.
[3] Deng Zhao, Duan Wei, Zhou Yutao. Analysis of port transportation functions based on the structure of cargo types[J]. Applied Spatial Analysis and Policy, 2022, 8: 1-23.
[4] Wan Min, Kuang Haibo, Yu Yue, et, al. Evaluation of the competitiveness of the container multimodal port hub[J]. Scientific Report, 2022, 12(1): 19334.
[5] Jiao Xiaogang, Zheng Feifeng, Liu Ming, et, al. Integrated berth allocation and time-variant quay crane scheduling with tidal impact in approach channel[J]. Discrete Dynamics in Nature and Society, 2018: 1-19.
[6] Hsu H-P, Chiang T-L. An improved shuffled frog-leaping algorithm for solving the dynamic and continuous berth allocation problem (DCBAP)[J]. Applied Sciences-Basel, 2020, 2019(9): 4682.
[7] Ma Shoufeng, Li Hongming, Zhu Ning, et, al. Stochastic programming approach for unidirectional quay crane scheduling problem with uncertainty[J]. Journal of Scheduling, 2021, 24: 137-74.
[8] Malekahmadi A, Alinaghian M, Hejazi S. R, et, al. Integrated continuous berth allocation and quay crane assignment and scheduling problem with time-dependent physical constraints in container terminals[J]. Computers and Industrial Engineering, 2020, 147: 106672.

[9]   Agra A, Oliveira M. MIP approaches for the integrated berth allocation and quay crane assignment and scheduling problem[J]. European Journal of Operational Research, 2018, 264(1): 138-48.
[10] Fatemi-Anaraki S, Tavakkoli-Moghaddam R, Abdolhamidi D, Vahedi-Nouri B. Simultaneous waterway scheduling, berth allocation, and quay crane assignment: A novel matheuristic approach[J]. International Journal of Production Research, 2021, 59(24): 7576-93.
[11] Xie Fanrui, Wu Tao, Zhang Canrong. A Branch-and-price algorithm for the integrated berth allocation and quay crane assignment problem[J]. Transportation Science, 2019, 53(5): 1427-54.
[12] Zhong Meisu, Yang Yongsheng, Zhou Yamin, et, al. Adaptive autotuning mathematical approaches for integrated optimization of automated container terminal[J]. Mathematical Problems in Engineering, 2019, 2019(4): 1-14.
[13] Liu Guowei, Ren Hongxiang, Xu Fuquan, et, al. Application of improved NSGA-II algorithm in ship entry and exit dispatching[C]. 2021 IEEE 12th International Conference on Software Engineering and Service Science (ICSESS), Beijing: IEEE, 2021. 277-281.
[14] Bierwirth C, Meisel F. A follow-up survey of berth allocation and quay crane scheduling problems in container terminals[J]. European Journal of Operational Research, 2015, 244(3): 675-689.
[15] Zahid Ullah, Muhammad Fayaz, Su-Hyeon Lee, " An Efficient Technique for Optimality Measurement of Approximation Algorithms", International Journal of Modern Education and Computer Science, Vol.11, No.11, pp. 13-21, 2019.
[16] G.Narendrababu Reddy, S.Phani Kumar, "MACO-MOTS: Modified Ant Colony Optimization for Multi Objective Task Scheduling in Cloud Environment", International Journal of Intelligent Systems and Applications, Vol.11, No.1, pp.73-79, 2019.
[17] Sangeetha Muthuraman, V. Prasanna Venkatesan, "A Qualitative Study of Model based Approach with the Existing Approaches for Solving Combinatorial Optimization Problems Using Hybrid Strategies", International Journal of Modern Education and Computer Science, Vol.9, No.12, pp. 17-25, 2017.

Artificial Intelligence, Medical Engineering and Education
Z.B. Hu et al. (Eds.)
© *2024 The Authors.*
This article is published online with Open Access by IOS Press and distributed under the terms
of the Creative Commons Attribution Non-Commercial License 4.0 (CC BY-NC 4.0).
doi:10.3233/ATDE231321

Application and Development Research of Artificial Intelligence Technology in the Field of Transportation

Xiaoyi HU[1]

Wuhan Railway Vocational College of Technology, Wuhan, China

Abstract: Artificial intelligence technology is a new technological engine of a new round of science and technology and industrial revolution. After more than 60 years of development, it has gradually moved from technology to application, and will soon become a modern science that changes human economy and society. At present, the most popular branch technology of artificial intelligence is deep learning. Starting from the research content and application fields of artificial intelligence, this paper summarizes the basic model of artificial intelligence - neuron model, and then discusses the main application fields of artificial intelligence. In the field of transportation, the current research scope is wide, and the research depth is deep in the field of unmanned driving technology. Through sensing, decision-making, mapping and vehicle networking technologies, autonomous driving realizes fully autonomous driving of vehicles, providing significant technical support for improving the efficiency of transportation and ensuring safety.

Keywords. Artificial intelligence, transportation, deep learning, driverless

1. Introduction

1.1 Research Content of Artificial Intelligence Technology

Artificial intelligence technology since Dartmouth conference 1956 focused discussion led to this concept to 1977 the fifth International Conference on Artificial Intelligence knowledge engineering concept was formally proposed, a large number of expert systems appeared, but because of the limited learning ability of computer systems, unable to meet the requirements of science and technology and production, the important field of machine learning appeared. Later, the emergence of the concept of deep learning further promoted the development of artificial intelligence. The relationship between artificial intelligence, machine learning, and deep learning is shown in Figure 1.

At present, deep learning is widely used and widely sought after. The multi-layer neural network built by deep learning is evolved from the neuron model. In the first M-P neuron model, the neuron receives input signals from N other neurons, and then transmits them through weighted connections. After that, neuron output is generated by activation function. The M-P neuron model is shown in Figure 2.

Deep learning is a kind of machine learning, which is essentially to carry out data statistics, summarize models in big data, and then carry out a large number of operations.

---

[1] Corresponding Author: Xiaoyi HU, E-mail: lloveless@126.com

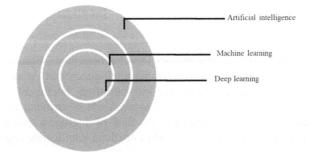

Figure 1. Relationship between artificial intelligence, machine learning and deep learning

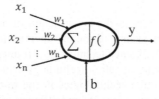

Figure 2. The M-P neuron model

1.2 Application Fields of Artificial Intelligence

From the perspective of the basic support layer, artificial intelligence is mainly composed of big data, computing power and algorithms, of which big data is composed of first-hand data from various industries or scenarios, as well as data obtained through various ways of data mining. Computing power requires hardware support such as GPU and FPGA, combined with neural network chips and cloud computing. A variety of algorithms, including supervised learning, unsupervised learning, reinforcement learning, and transfer learning underlie artificial intelligence in the context of neural networks and deep learning, as well as other machine learning [1].

From the view of technical point, artificial intelligence can achieve dynamic recognition, character recognition, image recognition and face recognition on the basis of computer vision. Through speech recognition and natural language understanding to achieve voice interaction, machine translation and other functions, so that machines can understand and understand the human world and human language, and even realize communication with humans, research human intelligence activities, learning human activities, etc., on this basis, artificial intelligence applications are very wide [2].

The application areas of artificial intelligence include static content recognition, dynamic content recognition, natural language processing, human-computer interaction and biotechnology, etc., and the next layer of applications can achieve search transformation, photo management, intelligent security, three-dimensional analysis, VR/AR and unmanned driving [3]. From the industry, the most concerned is medical finance and travel, for any industry, artificial intelligence is a cost reduction and efficiency can achieve industrial upgrading tools, in these three industry areas, artificial intelligence to achieve cost reduction and efficiency is the most likely.

2. Application Research Status of Artificial Intelligence Technology in Transportation Industry

In the "New Generation of artificial Intelligence Development Plan", China issued a plan to promote the innovation integration of artificial intelligence and various industries, among which intelligent logistics, intelligent transportation, intelligent delivery and other transportation fields are among the main applications of artificial intelligence in the field of transportation are concentrated in the field of intelligent transportation, of which unmanned driving is the current hot field of artificial intelligence application.

2.1 Application of Artificial Intelligence in the Field of Intelligent Transportation

Intelligent transportation refers to the construction of an efficient and safe integrated transportation management system through the Internet of Things, big data, cloud computing and artificial intelligence technologies. It integrates information technology, sensing technology and communication technology with today's cutting-edge artificial intelligence, big data and other technologies in the transportation industry to form a large-scale, all-round, real-time, accurate and efficient integrated traffic control system. In the future, intelligent transportation will be the first to realize intelligent perception coordination system to provide traffic data with timeliness, comprehensiveness and effectiveness. [4]The second most reliable communication system, through artificial intelligence technology, in the abnormal traffic environment, improve the reliability and effectiveness of communication system; The third comprehensive safety assessment system, through the comprehensive supervision and control of traffic behavior, to achieve real-time and effective tracking and handling of traffic risks; Fourth, intelligent travel decision-making, according to travel needs, the use of real-time comprehensive traffic and transportation data combined with the characteristics of transport vehicles to plan the best travel routes, to provide a variety of transportation services; Fifth, driverless, the use of deep learning, computer information and other artificial intelligence technology, combined with high-precision positioning system, to achieve vehicle driverless.

2.2 Application of Artificial Intelligence in the Field of Unmanned Driving

The most concerned application of artificial intelligence in the field of transportation is driverless technology. Driverless cars are outdoor wheeled mobile robots, which cooperate with artificial intelligence, sensors, positioning systems and navigation systems to achieve automatic and safe operation of motor vehicles without any human active operation [5].

Driverless is a process in which the driver surrenders control and improves safety, as shown in Figure3.

Automatic driving registration

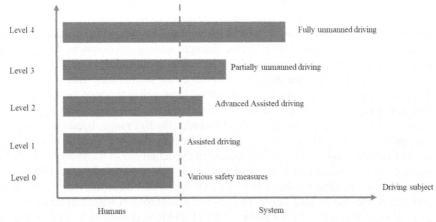

Figure 3. Driverless control right

3 . The AI Technologies Involved in Autonomous Driving

In general, the AI technologies involved in autonomous driving mainly include perception, decision making, mapping and car networking, It can be expressed as Driverless technology = environment awareness + positioning navigation + path planning + decision control [5]. The artificial intelligence technology in automatic driving specifically includes environment perception, path planning, control decision, communication interconnection, speech recognition, natural language interaction, gesture recognition and driver monitoring.

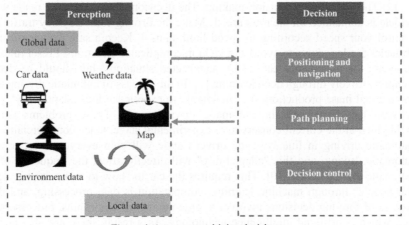

Figure 4. Autonomous driving decision

In the process of automatic driving, on the one hand, local data of the vehicle and its surrounding environment is obtained through sensor data; on the other hand, global data is constructed by combining weather and high-precision map data. Then, the data is integrated and coordinated with the decision-making level, the auxiliary system is used for positioning and navigation, the planned path is obtained by combining the algorithm model, and the vehicle steering and speed are controlled through vehicle technology. Thus, the automatic driving is realized. Figure 4 shows the process.

(1) The first is perception, which is the basic premise for a car to realize autonomous driving. The underlying logic is that perception is a process of data acquisition. Autonomous vehicles need to perceive the surrounding environment through sensors, and the perception function of vehicles is mainly acquired through sensors, just like human eyes, to perceive the dynamic changes of the surrounding area. And then there's the gyroscope. At present, the main perception approach is to shoot through the camera, and then image and video recognition to determine the surrounding environment of the vehicle. Important parameters of LiDAR include effective range, lateral and longitudinal recognition range, and angular resolution. Effective distance, generally speaking, the current vertical can be 200-300 meters, and in the actual use of the process, the decision-making process is generally not much to deal with obstacles beyond 100 meters.[7] Regarding the resolution, the current LiDAR horizontal direction reaches 0.1 degrees, and it may only be divided into 8-16 sector channels to deal with it in actual use. Local field of view (such as 110°) 8.16 or 32 line LiDAR is conducive to embedding in the vehicle body, facilitate complete vehicle design, and will be highly weighted in the front-loading market. At present, the main perception approach is to shoot through the camera, and then image and video recognition to determine the surrounding environment of the vehicle. The perception principle of camera includes three layers: image processing, pattern recognition and binocular positioning. Its advantages include lower cost, less data required, and more mature technology. However, the camera is greatly affected by the external environment, including light and weather.

At present, the cameras installed on the driverless car mainly include:

1) monocular camera;

2) Rear view camera;

3) Binocular camera;

4) 360-degree view camera [8].

(2) The next step is decision-making. The decisions that need to be made when the vehicle is unmanned on the road are: 1. Make the driving route 2. Obey traffic rules 3. Control your speed according to speed limit signs 4. Keep a safe distance from other obstacles 5. Slow down to avoid and yield in complicated situations. Preset rules cannot eliminate the uncertainty caused by unexpected situations, but should be dealt with comprehensively through deep learning [9]. In the process of automatic driving entering commercial mass production, it is inevitable to experience the "adaptability" problem between the driver and the automatic driving mode. These problems cannot be highlighted at the current conservative experimental stage. Once commercialized, only automatic driving in line with the driver's style will gain everyone's recognition of automatic driving, and this "adaptability" will directly affect the frequency of use of automatic driving mode [10]. This requires the car to "how to make driving decisions like people" through machine learning, computation is data processing, and then the process of forming decisions involves a large number of algorithms, processors, chips, etc., which is artificial intelligence technology. As a result, there are also many chip giants involved in unmanned driving.

3)Navigation technology helps driverless cars determine the speed, direction and path information, and integrates environmental information and body information into a systematic whole. High-precision maps are the basis for driverless path planning and provide assistance for autonomous driving. Path planning technology can provide the optimal driving path for unmanned driving [11]. In the process of driving the driverless car, starting from the travel demand, drawing a non-collision and passable path from the starting point to the target point based on the high-precision map and the road network and macro traffic information (including the calculation of road length, speed, section grade, traffic exit waiting time, etc.). Then the optimal route selection is made according to the local environmental data and its own state data collected by the vehicle in the process of driving.

4)Now the "Internet" is developing to the "Internet of Things", and the "Internet of vehicles" of automatic driving is an important application of the "Internet of everything", the Internet of vehicles technology to achieve intelligent control of people, cars, roads and traffic facilities, the ultimate realization of unmanned driving is bound to rely on the Internet of vehicles, in addition to the Internet of vehicles can provide more over-the-horizon information for unmanned driving to ensure driving safety. It can also optimize the driving route of the vehicle and improve the operating efficiency of the entire traffic system.

4. The Social and Economic Value of the Autonomous Driving

Autonomous driving has great social and economic value. BCG pointed out in the report "Back to the Future: The Road to Autonomous Driving": in the United States, for example, if autonomous vehicles are popularized, it can reduce the number of traffic accident deaths by more than 30,000 per year, save more than 40% of the cost of travel time, and reduce fuel consumption by 40%, and the value of these social benefits is as high as $1.3 trillion. Wang Jin, president of Baidu's autonomous driving division, said the spread of driverless technology could save 500 lives a day in car accidents in China

5. Conclusion

After 60 years of development, artificial intelligence, supported by deep learning, massive data and high-performance computing, has now entered the initial stage of industrial application. In 2016, deep learning-based intelligent voice, image recognition, intelligent driving and other technologies began to penetrate into various application fields, and the scale of the global artificial intelligence industry grew rapidly. In order to seize the high ground of artificial intelligence, Google, Microsoft, IBM, Facebook and other enterprises have further prominent strategic layout in the field of artificial intelligence, and innovation and entrepreneurship around artificial intelligence have further flourished. The United States, Japan and other countries have also introduced AI related policies and national plans to create a good ecological environment for industrial development.

Driven by deep learning technology and open-source platform, the threshold of artificial intelligence technology is gradually lowered, and forced by the urgent demand for global downstream applications, artificial intelligence has won a golden period of accelerated development, and applications and innovations around artificial intelligence continue to emerge. In 2015, the global AI industry reached 8.22 billion and is expected to exceed 10 billion in 2016. According to the BBC, the global artificial intelligence market is expected to reach 18.3 billion by 2020. In the next 10 years or even longer, artificial intelligence will be the breakthrough point for the development of many intelligent industry technologies and applications.

In addition to the rapid growth of the industrial scale, the number of startups around artificial intelligence has also increased significantly. According to Venture Scanner's statistics on artificial intelligence companies in 71 countries around the world, as of the third quarter of 2016, the number of artificial intelligence startups in the world has reached 1,287, of which 585 have received investment, with a total investment amount of 7.7 billion dollars. More than $3.1 billion was invested in the United States.

Since the end of 2015, starting with Baidu, several major manufacturers of intelligent driving vehicles in the world have released a timeline for the commercial and mass production of unmanned vehicles.

The United States IHS Automotive Information consulting company published a report in June 2016 that pointed out that by 2020, the United States will become the first country to allow driverless cars on the road, and there will be thousands of driverless cars on the road in the United States. Global sales of driverless cars will reach 600,000 by 2025. Over the next 10 years, sales will continue to grow at an annual rate of 43% as these vehicles are accepted in all key markets around the world [12].

Global sales of driverless cars will reach 21 million by 2035, significantly higher than the 11.8 million estimated two years ago. Sales in the United States will grow to 4.5 million, and China will be the largest market for autonomous vehicles with 5.7 million units sold. Sales in Europe will reach 4.2 million, while sales in Africa and the Middle East will reach 1 million. Meanwhile, 1.2 million driverless cars will be sold in Japan and South Korea.

In China, the current L1-L3 level technology has been partially commercialized and mass-produced, that is, high-end models equipped with adaptive cruise, highway automatic driving, automatic parking and other advanced driving assistance systems, and some laboratory stage unmanned vehicles have been able to achieve some road conditions and even full operating conditions of unmanned driving. KPMG predicts that L3 and L4 smart cars will be industrialized in 2018 and 2020, respectively. The promotion of intelligent driving services combined with mobile Internet, big data and cloud computing is expected to be gradually popularized in 10 years.

McKinsey predicts that driverless cars could generate $200 billion to $1.9 trillion by 2025. Hu Bo, chief marketing officer of Volkswagen Group (China) Greater China and ASEAN region, believes that "it is expected that by 2030, the proportion of driverless cars in all cars sold can be as high as 15%, and the proportion of semi-autonomous driving can reach about 50%", when the smart cars of traditional car companies and technology companies will account for half of the Chinese auto market.

In the future, urbanization and population growth will drive the average population density of cities to increase, and the resulting traffic congestion will greatly increase people's demand for efficient mobility. The three trends in the future of mobile travel are electrification, sharing and automation, among which electrification is a supplement to travel environment friendliness, sharing as a supplement to public transport system will inevitably be the backbone in the future, and automation is an important way to improve travel efficiency and improve traffic efficiency. As the most forward-looking technology in the artificial intelligence industry in the field of transportation, autonomous driving and even driverless driving are the focus of research in the world. In the future, autonomous driving can facilitate people with serious vision problems or physical defects to travel in the private driving scene, solve the problem of serious mismatch between the demand and supply of parking Spaces, and reduce the number of cars purchased. In the scenario where the road conditions are not complicated, the driverless driving lesson system assists the truck and truck drivers to complete the driving on the high-speed road with long distance and easy fatigue; During commuting time as a supplement to the first and last kilometer of public transport.

Reference

[1] Hyunjin Kim, Sang Hong, Jinsul Kim, Jaecheol Ryou. Intelligent Application Protection Mechanism for Transportation in V2C Environment[J]. IEEE Access,2020,8(8).

[2] Artificial Intelligence; Investigators from Swinburne University of Technology Target Artificial Intelligence (Applications of Artificial Intelligence In Transport: an Overview) [J]. Journal of Engineering,2019(in Chinese)

[3] Rusul Abduljabbar, Hussein Dia, Sohani Liyanage, Saeed Asadi Begole. Applications of Artificial Intelligence in Transport: An Overview[J]. Sustainability,2019,11(1).

[4] Chao DENG, Xue ZHANG, Yun bing YAN, et al. Construction of Traffic and Transportation Engineering Innovation Lab Based on Artificial Intelligence[C]. 2021 International Conference on Electronic Commerce, Engineering Management and Information Systems,2020.

[5] Martínez-Plumed Fernando, Gómez Emilia, Hernández-Orallo José. Futures of artificial intelligence through technology readiness levels[J]. Telematics and Informatics,2021,58(58).

[6] S. Rajesh, S. Geetha, Babu Sudarson S, Ramesh S, "Deep Learning based Real Time Radio Signal Modulation Classification and Visualization", International Journal of Engineering and Manufacturing, Vol.13, No.5, pp. 30-37, 2023.

[7] Koushal Kumar, Gour Sundar Mitra Thakur. Advanced Applications of Neural Networks and Artificial Intelligence: A Review[J]. International Journal of Information Technology and Computer Science, vol.4, no.6, pp.57-68, 2012.

[8] Adnan Qayyum, Junaid Qadir, Muhammad Bilal, Ala Al-Fuqaha. Secure and Robust Machine Learning for Healthcare: A Survey[J]. 2020 IEEE Reviews in Biomedical Engineering (Vol. 14).

[9] A comparison of methods to avoid overfitting in neural networks training in the case of catchment runoff modelling. Adam P. Piotrowski;;Jarosław J. Napiorkowski[J]. Journal of Hydrology, 2013.

[10] Density and viscosity of ternary Al-Cu-Si liquid alloys. Hidekazu Kobatake; Julianna Schmitz;Jürgen Brillo[J]. Journal of Materials Science,2014

[11] Phadke A. G. Synchronized phasor measurements in power systems[J]. IEEE Computer Applications in Power, 2013, 6(2): 10-15.

[12] Phadke A. G, Pickett B, Adamiak M, et al. Synchronized sampling and phasor measurements for relay and control[J]. IEEE Trans. on Power Delivery, 2014, 9(1): 442-452.

Artificial Intelligence, Medical Engineering and Education
Z.B. Hu et al. (Eds.)
© *2024 The Authors.*
This article is published online with Open Access by IOS Press and distributed under the terms
of the Creative Commons Attribution Non-Commercial License 4.0 (CC BY-NC 4.0).
doi:10.3233/ATDE231322

The Challenges and Countermeasures of ChatGPT-Type Generative Artificial Intelligence on Information Subjects' Right to Know

Yingying JIANG[1]

School of Law, University of Macau, Macau, China

Abstract. While ChatGPT's technological innovation has attracted worldwide attention, the risk of personal information leakage is particularly significant. Upon analysis, the primary cause for people's apprehension lies in the ambiguous origin of ChatGPT and the uncertain utilization of users' input information. These substantive issues can be distilled into challenges to the information subject's right to know. This paper takes ChatGPT, a representative generative artificial intelligence, as a case study to elucidate its effects on the information subject's right to know throughout various stages. To balance technological innovation and the rights of information subjects, priority is given to guarantee the rights through technical means. It is proposed to explore a path towards countermeasures through collaborative efforts of industry, administrative and judiciary authorities.

Keywords. Generative artificial intelligence; ChatGPT; The right to know; Personal information.

1. Introduction

Artificial intelligence has developed tremendous rapidly in recent years. The launch of new content-generating artificial intelligence tools represented by ChatGPT, has been greatly recognized by the market since its public test on November 30, 2022, and has sparked global attention. Chinese domestic technology companies have also joined the development of such generative AI tools. Moreover, the speed of iterative development of such AI tools is mind-boggling. Three months after the release of ChatGPT, OpenAI Inc. quickly launched GPT-4, a multimodal pre-trained big model that has further improved in image recognition capability, answer accuracy and number of input words.

Some experts believe that ChatGPT is another important breakthrough in artificial intelligence after AlphaGo, marking the establishment of an intelligent computing paradigm with a large model at its core and "opening the door to general artificial intelligence [1]". After the initial buzz, people begin to calm down and start to worry about the adverse effect brought about by this technological innovation. Concerns like generating inappropriate content for children [2]; generates glaring mistakes and

---

[1] Corresponding Author: Yingying JIANG, E-mail: yc27201@umac.mo.

disturbing responses [3]; cheating (as students use this AI chatbot to do schoolwork) [4]; bias, lack of transparency and accountability [5]; risk of privacy leakage triggered by hacking etc. [6]. Among all the concerns, the safety of personal privacy and information has been mentioned a lot [7-8]. It is well known that the three core elements of AI are: data, algorithm, and computing power. Among them, data is the nutrient and the basis for carrying out AI tasks. These data are often collected regularly for other purposes [9]. As a large language model, ChatGPT uses big data training and reinforcement learning with human feedback to generate human-like text. Its potential applications are vast, ranging from virtual assistants to automated content creation. However, as with any new technology, the risks associated with its development and use must be carefully considered. The risk of user information leakage is particularly significant among the many potential risks associated with this new technology. People are very concerned about the source and scope the training data of ChatGPT. Furthermore, after launching into the market, the extensive use by users further trains this language model. Concerns on information safety and privacy have been repeatedly mentioned since ChatGPT was launched and are worthy of in-depth discussion and research from legal aspect.

In previous literature, legal scholars have mostly explored AI in an abstract manner, attempting to describe the problem and give legal solutions in a general way. In the current context of widespread AI development, a bottom-up approach is necessary to conduct scientific and in-depth research on a new topic [10]. There is a large body of research on the legal risks of AI, and this paper focuses on the new issues raised by ChatGPT, a groundbreaking new technology. This paper attempt to analyze and clarify the impact of ChatGPT-type generative AI on information subjects' right to know from the contextual texts of the Personal Information Protection Law of the People's Republic of China and the EU General Data Protection Regulation and propose possible countermeasures. The research methodology is based on a literature review of relevant legal texts, industry reports, and academic research on this topic.

2. The Challenges of ChatGPT-type Generative Artificial Intelligence on Information Subjects' Right to Know

2.1. Brief Introduction of ChatGPT and Generative Artificial Intelligence

ChatGPT is a public tool based on the GPT language model technology [11], developed by OpenAI,a research laboratory founded in 2015 [12]. It is a large language model (LLM), a machine-learning system that autonomously learns from data and can produce sophisticated and seemingly intelligent writing after training on a massive data set of text [13], which is capable of fulfilling a wide range of text-based requests [14] by leveraging its extensive data stores and efficient design to understand and interpret user requests, and then generating appropriate responses in nearly natural human language [15]. ChatGPT and other Generative AI techniques belong to the category of Artificial Intelligence Generated Content (AIGC), which involves the creation of digital content, such as images, music, and natural language, through AI models [16].

2.2. Challenges on the Right to Know

The use of generative AI like ChatGPT poses several challenges for the security of personal information. One of the main concerns is the lack of clarity in the source of training data for these models. ChatGPT, for example, is trained on massive amounts of text scraped from the internet, without explicit consent from the original authors or sources. This raises questions about ownership of the data and the ethical implications of using it without permission. Additionally, there is a lack of clarity in how user input information is used. These concerns are not limited to ChatGPT alone but are applicable to similar generative AI models as well. As a matter of fact, the essence of all the concerns relies on the challenges of ChatGPT-type generative artificial intelligence on the right to know of personal information subjects or data subject. The terms "data subject" in GDPR and "information subject" in PIPL essentially refer to the same concept, which is an individual whose personal information is being processed. Both terms are used to describe the person whose personal data or information is being collected, stored, used, or transmitted.

The right to know is a fundamental right of information subject that underpins privacy and information protection laws in many countries [17]. It gives individuals the right to know of what personal data is being collected about them, how it is being used and etc. According to Article 44 of t*he Personal Information Protection Law of the People's Republic of China* (hereafter referred to as PIPL), individuals have the right to know about the processing of their personal information. This right includes being informed prior to the processing of their personal information, requesting that the personal information processor disclose their processing rules, and the right to access, copy and consult [18]. As in *General Data Protection Regulation* (hereafter referred to as GDPR) of the European Union, individuals have the right to know of what personal data is collected, used, or otherwise processed, as well as to be informed of the risks, safeguards, and their rights regarding the processing required by the transparency principles [19]. The right to know is enshrined in Article 13 and Article 14 of the GDPR. Article 13 pertains to instances in which personal data is gathered directly from the individual concerned, whereas Article 14 is relevant in cases where personal data is acquired from sources other than the data subject [20]. Both articles outline the information that must be provided to the data subject, and the conditions under which it must be provided.

The right to know is particularly important in the context of AI systems like ChatGPT, which rely on large amounts of personal data to operate effectively. A primary worry surrounding ChatGPT and the right to know centers on the potential lack of awareness among data subjects regarding the utilization of their data for training the system. ChatGPT is trained on a vast corpus of text data, which includes user-generated content from social media and other sources. This data is used to teach ChatGPT how to understand and respond to human language. However, users may not be aware that their data is being used in this way, or that their interactions with ChatGPT may be recorded and stored for future use. Another concern about ChatGPT and the right to know is that data subjects may not understand how their data is being used or how it is being processed. ChatGPT uses complex algorithms and natural language processing techniques to analyze and respond to users' input. These processes are not transparent to the average user, which makes it difficult for users to understand how their data is being used or how ChatGPT is making decisions about their interaction, as shown in Table 1.

Table 1. Right to Know in PIPL and GDPR

	PIPL
Article 44	individuals have the right to know about the processing of their personal information
Article 45	subordinate right: the right to access, copy and consult
	GDPR
Article 13	information to be provided where data are collected from the data subject
Article 14	information to be provided where data have not been obtained from the data subject

2.3. Challenge on the Right to Know What Personal Data is Being Collected

According to the information provided by OpenAI, the developer of ChatGPT, ChatGPT undergoes pre-training using existing text and data.The data source of ChatGPT comes from a diverse range of sources, including books, articles, websites, and other forms of text on the internet. The specific details of its training data are not publicly available, but it consists of vast amounts of text that have been fed into deep learning algorithms to train it to understand and generate human-like language.

It is observed that this model is trained on a large corpus of text data, such as web pages, books etc. Because of the non-transparency and algorithm black box, it is very difficult to verify all the sources of training data. In other words, it's impossible for data subject to identify whether their data has been collected. The risk of privacy and personal information leakage remains high. Alexander Hanff, who is a member of the European Data Protection Board's (EDPB) support pool of experts, has stated that "just because something is available online does not automatically make it legal to obtain". He also argues that gathering massive amounts of data from websites that have explicitly stated in their terms and conditions that the data cannot be obtained by third parties would be a violation of the contract. Additionally, it is important to consider individuals' rights to have their data protected under the EU's GDPR, ePrivacy directive, and Charter of Fundamental Rights [21]. What's worse, Some AIGC companies' databases hold substantial amounts of private data, including personal photos, without obtaining users' informed consent. This practice significantly jeopardizes users'personal privacy and information security [22].

As discussed above, according to PIPL, the personal information processor shall first assume the obligation to inform the personal information subject before processing [23]. Even if the training data is obtained from disclosed information source, individual still have the right to expressly refuse the processing [24].According to GDPR, when personal data is acquired from a source other than the individual, the same information must be provided to that individual as if the data had been obtained directly. In addition, the controller must inform the individual of the sources from which the personal data originated and whether it was publicly available. The information provided to the individual must be clear, concise, transparent, and easily accessible [25]. As for ChatGPT and the other similar generative artificial intelligence tool, the issue lies in the lack of transparency regarding what information has been input into the training process, making it seemingly impossible for individuals to identify. This raises significant concerns about the invasion of personal information security.

2.4. Challenge on the Right to Know How Personal Information is being used

When using generative AI applications like ChatGPT, the information input by users during the interaction phase becomes a vital source of data for further training the artificial intelligence,particularly since people are often more forthcoming about their personal details when conversing with machines This data can then be utilized for user profiling and model training. However, the collection, usage, and transmission of personal information are faced with security hurdles [26]. According to the operation principle of ChatGPT, after imputing a question by one user, the question will first be transmitted to OpenAI company in the U.S., ChatGPT will then respond the corresponding answer [27]. Whenever an attorney prompts the tool to review a legal document or a professor asks it to proofread an academic draft, those data would be involved into ChatGPT's database and could be used to further training this model [28]. People may not be aware of their imputing information are collected and are likely to unintentionally disclose sensitive information about personal, financial, and bio logical information when using this technology, resulting in sensitive personal information leakage. Open AI claims that their company employs methods such as differential privacy and data anonymization to prevent personal information from being disclosed or used inappropriately to protect users' privacy and comply with their privacy policy and applicable laws [29]. However, the mere statement in Open AI's privacy policy is clearly not enough. Due to the non-transparency and algorithm black box, as mentioned above, data subject still has no idea when and how their personal information will be used. That does not seem to comply with PIPL and GDPR. In PIPL, the information processor shall truthfully, accurately and completely inform the individuals before collecting and processing personal information. That requires the size, font, and color of the text are sufficient to attract the individual's attention. According to the explanation of right to know in GDPR, if personal data is collected directly from the individual, the individual must be informed of certain key pieces of information in a timely and transparent manner like the purpose and legal basis for processing the data. Only when users fully understand that the information they input will be used for further AI training can they truly exercise the right to choose and decide autonomously whether to input content involving personal information into ChatGPT. After the Italian Data Protection Authority issued a ban on ChatGPT and gave a 20-day deadline for remedies, OpenAI has made improvements in personal information security, which will be discussed in detail in the section on possible countermeasures.

3. Possible Countermeasures

Both in the field of privacy protection and in the field of intellectual property protection, there is a trend of using technological measures to defend people's rights [30]. Using technological measures may be a more efficient approach to addressing concerns about the use of personal data in AI. With the rapid pace of technological advancement, legislation struggles to keep up and fully comprehend the scope of the issue at hand. Achieving a balance between protecting citizens' fundamental rights and encouraging

AI technology development is a crucial issue that lawmakers at the national and international levels must confront.Faced with the challenges posed by generative artificial intelligence, represented by ChatGPT, the approach is twofold. Firstly, for those aspects that technology can address, it's advisable to prioritize technical solutions. For instance, techniques like synthetic data generation can be employed to remove personal information content. However, when technology cannot or is unwilling to solve the problem, legal intervention should promptly and appropriately step in. This can be achieved by establishing proactive security assessment standards and implementing post-facto accountability measures to ensure the healthy and orderly development of the artificial intelligence industry. In order to strike a balance between protecting citizen's fundamental rights and promoting the development of science and technology, it is essential to emphasize the collaborative efforts of research and development companies, the artificial intelligence industry, administrative bodies, judicial authorities, and the public. By harnessing the collective power of various stakeholders, a conducive ecosystem for the harmonious development of technological progress and rights protection could be established.

3.1. The Safeguarding Path on the Right to Know What Personal Data is Being Collected

As mentioned earlier, the primary challenge to the right to know is the lack of transparency in data sources, making it impossible to determine whether personal information is included in the data. If the issue of unidentified sources can be resolved or personal information can be removed from the data, ensuring that training data does not contain any personal information, this problem can be addressed.

● *Synthetic Data*

Further application of synthetic data could be a promising solution to tackle with the personal information concern caused by Generative AI. Synthetic data is created using a model trained to replicate the characteristics and structure of original data, resulting in artificial data that is similar to the original one. Consequently, both synthetic and original data should yield similar results when subjected to the same statistical analysis. The accuracy of synthetic data as a representation of the original data is a key indicator of the usefulness of the method and the model employed. This evaluation assesses the likelihood of identifying data subjects within the synthetic data and the amount of new information that would be revealed about them because of successful identification. There have been some assumptions among researchers that synthetic data, as it is not obtained from real-world personally identifiable information, is exempt from any privacy-related issues [31].

● *Public Data Pool*

Another possible solution is encouraging the industry to establish a public data pool and allowing reasonable use to train models of AI companies. Many scholars hold the idea that it would be both effective and safe to set up a public domain where data could be reasonable use to train AI model [32]. Professor Mark Lemely argue the use of data by artificial intelligence should be based on fair use, applying the principle of fair learning. In Lemley's view, it would be costly for AI to learn data if it had to obtain permission to do so. AI should be able to make fair use of data or even databases that are only used for learning [33]. Thus, setting up a public data pool for training AI models could be helpful, which can greatly reduce the cost for training AI. Besides, a public data pool can lead to improvements in the quality of AI models. By training models on a diverse range of data, bias can be reduced, and accuracy can be increased, resulting in better and more reliable results. Above all, a public data pool can address data privacy concerns by reducing the need for organizations to collect and store large amounts of sensitive data. By using public data pool to train AI models, the risk of data breaches or misuse can be minimized. Despite the numerous benefits, it is still quite costly and difficult to set up such a public data pool. To achieve that, it requires the joint efforts of the industry and the support of government.

3.2. The Safeguarding Path on the Right to Know How Personal Information is Being Used

The author has noticed an improvement in ChatGPT following the adjustments required by the Italian Data Protection Authority. Prior to user interactions, a hovering dialogue box now appears in the chat interface, advising users not to share sensitive information with it. This is a significant step forward. The author recommends having a prominently positioned notification box in the chat interface for an extended duration to remind users that the information they input will be incorporated into the database for further model training. Additionally, the notification text should be sufficiently large, in an attention-grabbing font and color. Besides, both ChatGPT and other similar generative AI systems in the domestic context should pay special attention to distinguishing the data subjects. Just as OpenAI has implemented security enhancements in compliance with GDPR requirements, including the 'requesting the specification of the birthdate on the service registration page to prevent access for users under the age of 13 and requiring users between the ages of 13 and 18 to confirm they have obtained parental or guardian consent.' In the Chinese context, for individuals under the age of fourteen, consent from their parents or other guardians is required. Artificial intelligence tools should establish differentiated notification procedures based on the specific requirements of the target user groups in their respective regions to ensure the right to know for different data subjects.

3.3. Legal Solution

Artificial intelligence requires a flexible and responsive governance framework to maximize its ability to respond to continuously changing risks and issues [34]. Addressing the issue of personal information protection from AIGC can be accomplished at the national level by reinforcing the regulatory process throughout the entire chain, which includes pre-input compliance assessment for AI systems like ChatGPT and implementing a hierarchical market access list system. Furthermore, improving the mechanism for addressing complaints including reporting regarding personal information protection and conducting interviews, ordering rectification, and imposing administrative penalties on AI R&D companies and responsible individuals who violate the privacy or information protection regulations [35].

Though ChatGPT is not currently open for use in mainland China, the research of it still has practical significance. Once it is available for mainland Chinese Internet users in the future, the rules in the Personal Protection Law can certainly apply based on the circumstances in which it provides services to natural persons in the country. Moreover, since the develop and use of generative AI is very promising in China, related research should also follow. It can be predicted that more Chinese hi-tech companies will be deeply involved in the field of artificial intelligence and more generative AI will be used in the market. Thus, it is both necessary and urgent to study the challenges and countermeasures to the protection of personal information caused by such type of AI models.

4. Conclusion

There are lots of concerns regarding of using new technical tool. People are worried about privacy and personal information leakage with the use of ChatGPT. With the non-transparent feature and algorithmic black box of this new technology, information subjects are not aware of what information of them will be collected and how the content imputed will be processed when using such AI tool.

This paper attempt to analyze and clarify the impact of ChatGPT-type generative AI on information subjects' right to know and propose possible countermeasures. Since too strict legal regulation may hinder the innovation of technology, it is recommended to apply technical tools prior to legal measure in tackling with the risks and challenges of ChatGPT and similar Generative Artificial Intelligence on the information subjects' right to know. Since Generative AI is still a novelty and related research is still in its preliminary stages, how to balance technological development and personal information rights protection remains an important issue for further study.

References

[1] ZHAO, G. Has ChatGPT opened the door to general artificial intelligence? [J]. China Science Daily.2023 (3):165-184.

[2] Tilley, A. Apple blocks update of ChatGPT-powered app, as concerns grow over AI's potential harm; iPhone maker asks email app with AI-language capabilities to set a 17-and-older age restriction[N]. Wall Street Journal, 2023-03-02.

[3] Bellman, E. Microsoft puts caps on new bing usage after AI chatbot offered unhinged responses; software giant seeks to address concerns about search engine powered by the technology behind ChatGPT[N]. Wall Street Journal, 2023-02-18.

[4] Lukpat, A. ChatGPT Banned in New York City Public Schools Over Concerns About Cheating, Learning Development; Education officials say students could use the artificial intelligence chatbot to do their schoolwork[N]. Wall Street Journal ,2023-01-06.

[5] Van Dis, E. A., Bollen, J., Zuidema, W., van Rooij, R., & Bockting, C. L. ChatGPT: five priorities for research[J]. Nature, 2023(614):224-226.

[6] Tlili, A., Shehata, B., Adarkwah, M.A. et al. What if the devil is my guardian angel: ChatGPT as a case study of using chatbots in education[J]. Smart Learning Environments,2023(10):15.

[7] Aljanabi, M. ChatGPT: Future Directions and Open possibilities[J]. Mesopotamian Journal of CyberSecurity, 2023:16-17.

[8] Helberger, N., & Diakopoulos, N. ChatGPT and the AI Act[J]. Internet Policy Review, 12.1 (2023). Web. 30 Mar. 2023.

[9] Wischmeyer, T. Reguli rung intelligenter systeme [J]. Archiv des öffentlichen Rechts, 2018(1):1-66.

[10] March, N. Fundamental Rights in the Era of Artificial Intelligence and Data Protection: Opening Doors for Innovation and Protection. In AI and Law Dialogue[D]. Shanghai: Shanghai People's Publishing House. (H. Li, Trans.), 2020:52.

[11] Kirmani, A.R. Artificial intelligence-enabled science poetry[J], ACS Energy Letters, Vol. 2022(8):574-576.

[12] Brockman, G., Cheung, V., Pettersson, L., Schneider, J., Schulman, J., Tang, J. and aremba, W. (2016), "OpenAI gym", arXiv.1606.01540.

[13] Van Dis, E. A., Bollen, J., Zuidema, W., van Rooij, R., & Bockting, C. L. ChatGPT: five priorities for research[J]. Nature, 2023 (614):224-226.

[14] LIU, X., ZHENG, Y., DU, Z., et al. "GPT understands, too", arXiv.2103.10385,2023.

[15] Lund, B.D. and Wang, T. (2023), "Chatting about ChatGPT: how may AI and GPT impact academia and libraries?", Library Hi Tech News, Vol. ahead-of-print No. ahead-of-print. https://doi.org/10.1108/LHTN-01-2023-0009.

[16] CAO, Y., LI, S., LIU, Y., et al. A Comprehensive Survey of AI-Generated Content (AIGC): A History of Generative AI from GAN to ChatGPT. arXiv preprint arXiv:2303.04226,2023 (in Chinese).

[17] ZHANG, X.B. On the Exercise of the Right to Be Informed in Personal Information Protection Requests[J]. Tribune of Political Science and Law, 2023(02): 26-37(in Chinese).

[18] SHEN, W.X. On the Construction and Systematization of the Right to Personal Information[J]. Journal of Comparative Law, 2021(5): 1-13(in Chinese).

[19] EU Agency for Fundamental Rights (FRA), Handbook on European Data Protection Law 207 (Publications Office of the European Union 2018).

[20] General Data Protection Regulation,ch. 3, art. 13,art. 14. See https://gdpr-info.eu/art-13-gdpr/; https://gdpr-info.eu/art-14-gdpr/.

[21] https://gdpr-info.eu/issues/right-to-be-informed/.

[22] https://www.infosecurity-magazine.com/news-features/chatgpts-datascraping-scrutiny/

[23] Jack Qiao, Legal Risks and Compliance Responses of AIGC from the Perspective of ChatGPT,Zhong Lun Law Firm, https://www.lexology.com/library/detail.aspx?g=ee42b3f1-3db5-4d9c-b9b3-d342a8834453, accessed March 7, 2023.

[24] Personal Information Protection Law, Ch. 2, art. 27. See https://personalinformationprotectionlaw.com/PIPL/article-27/.

[25] https://gdpr-info.eu/issues/right-to-be-informed/.

[26] ZHANG, L. H. Logical update and system iteration of deep synthesis governance: China's path for governing generative AI such as ChatGPT[J]. Science of Law (Journal of Northwest University of Political Science and Law), 2023(03):38-51.

[27] https://openai.com/policies/privacy-policy.

[28] https://theconversation.com/chatgpt-is-a-data-privacy-nightmare-if-youve-ever-posted-online-you-ought-to-be-concerned-199283.

[29] https://theconversation.com/chatgpt-is-a-data-privacy-nightmare-if-youve-ever-posted-online-you-ought-to-be-concerned-199283.

[30] YU, X.Z., ZHENG, G., DING, X. D. Generative Artificial Intelligence and Law: A Case Study of ChatGPT[J]. China Law Review, 2023(3):1-19(in Chinese).

[31] S. Koperniak, "Artificial data give the same results as real data—without compromising privacy," MIT News[N]. Available: http://news.mit.edu/2017/artificial-data-give-same-results-as-real-data-0303.2017-03.

[32] YU, X.Z., ZHENG, G., DING, X. D. Generative Artificial Intelligence and Law: A Case Study of ChatGPT[J]. China Law Review, 2023(3):1-19(in Chinese).

[33] Lemley, Mark A. and Casey, Bryan, Fair Learning. Available at SSRN: https://ssrn.com/abstract=3528447 or http://dx.doi.org/10.2139/ssrn.3528447,2023-01-30.

[34] WalterG.Johnson, DianaM.Bowman, A survey of Instruments and Institutions Available for the Global Governance of Artificial Intelligence[J], IEEE Technology and Society Magazine,2021(40):72.

[35] DENG.J. P, ZHU.Z.C.Legal Risks of ChatGPT Model and countermeasures[J],Journal of Xinjiang Normal University(Edition of Philosophy and Social Sciences),2023:1-11 (in Chinese).

Artificial Intelligence, Medical Engineering and Education
Z.B. Hu et al. (Eds.)
doi:10.3233/ATDE231323

Analysis of the Framework of Short Video News Reporting on Crisis Events - Take People's Daily's Tiktok Coverage of the COVID-19 Outbreak as an Example

Yan ZHU[1], Kuok Tiung LEE
University Malaysia Sabah, faculty of social sciences and humanitiess, 100004, Sabah, Malaysia

Abstract. With the continuous advancement of the information age, all kinds of short videos have exploded and gained an extremely large audience. Short video news has become an important way of news reporting because of its characteristics of easy production, fragmentation and fast transmission. As a representative of China's mainstream new media, Tiktok account of People Daily has the credibility of traditional media and the flexibility and diversity of new media. Among the short video reports on the COVID-19 outbreak in 2019, its attention and influence ranked first. Based on the theory of crisis communication and framework, this study uses content analysis method to analyze the "three-level" framework of People's Daily's Tik Tok news coverage of the COVID-19s outbreak, and analyzes the framework of People's Daily Tik Tok short video news coverage of the COVID-19s outbreak, providing useful references for other mainstream media when reporting similar crisis events.

Key words. Mainstream media; Short video news; People's Daily Douyin; COVID-19; Crisis event; Media frame

1. Introduction

The In recent years, crises have occurred frequently. Such as SARS in 2003, Middle East Respiratory Syndrome in 2012, Ebola virus in 2014, COVID-19 in 2019. The COVID-19 is the world's largest emergency public health event in the past decade and another representative global public health emergency after SARS [1]. As an early outbreak of the epidemic in China, mainstream media played an important role in news coverage. People pay a lot of attention to the reporting of such incidents, which brings great challenges to the reporting of news media. The public's perception and acceptance of crisis events is often based on the information they receive through the media, especially the news. An irresponsible media can easily create a moral panic through their coverage. Media coverage during the SARS outbreak has been extensively studied in the past. On the whole, during the critical period when the SARS crisis was transformed from latent to outbreak, the media in general lacked functions and were responsible for the spread of the epidemic [2]. With the development of communication technology, China's media

---

[1] Corresponding Author: Yan ZHU, Email: 2272151566@qq.com.

ecology has changed. As a new way of content production, short video is favored by users and concerned by mainstream media news producers. According to the Research Report on China's Online Audiovisual Development in 2023, the number of online audiovisual users in China has reached 1.04 billion, of which the number of short video users has reached 1.012 billion, of which 79% of Internet users obtain news information through short videos, indicating that short video news has become the main way to obtain news information. The spread of the COVID-19 on the Tiktok account of People's Daily, which this article will discuss, is a typical example of the public health crisis spread through short video news.

2. Reality Construction and Media Framework

This study uses the theory of reality construction and frame, and takes the short video of People's Daily's Tik Tok report on the COVID-19 epidemic as the research object to analyse its media frame.

2.1. Reality Construction

The media constructs reality by selecting and highlighting certain aspects [3]. As Lippmann said, news reporting is not a mirror reflection of reality, but a selection and processing based on news stance and value standards. News reporting reflects the aspirations of stakeholders, government policies, and the gatekeeping process by which reporters and editors inform, educate, persuade, and entertain the public, as well as construct reality. Especially in the face of sudden crisis events, people generally get information from the news. When the media provides people with the right public health information, people's perceptions can mitigate threats and risks. The failure of the media to disseminate this information creates uncertainty and panic for news consumers [4].

2.2. Media Framework

The term "frame" was first proposed by Bateson, who believed that frame refers to the mutually agreed rules of interpretation on how to understand each other's symbols [5]. Goffman believes that frames enable people to locate, perceive, understand, and summarize a wide range of specific information [6]. According to Kitling, framing is selection, emphasis and exclusion [7]. According to Entman, the framework contains two functions: selection and prominence [8]. Pan and Kosicki focus on conceptualizing news texts as experientially operable syntactic, scripted, thematic, and rhetorical dimensions [9]. In 1999, Taiwan scholar Zang Guo-ren proposed the famous "three-level framework structure", which divides news into three parts: social reality, symbolic reality and subjective reality, and defines each part as having three levels: high (theme), middle (structure of the entire news event) and low (language use). Based on Zang Guoren's three-level framework theory, this study explores what kind of news framework was constructed by People's Daily Tiktok News to make choices, emphasize or exclude the coverage of the COVID-19s outbreak. Thus, it can provide useful reference for other mainstream media's new media practice. Over the past few decades, many scholars from various countries have conducted extensive research on news discourse and media frameworks, and have achieved guiding results [10-12].

3. Methodology

In crisis events, how do mainstream media short video news reports "present" or "reproduce" this compelling public health issue of COVID-19? This paper takes the short video news about the COVID-19s pneumonia of People's Daily Tiktok as an example.

3.1. Research Questions

The following questions guide this study.

Q1: How did Tiktok account of People's Daily frame the issue of COVID-19?

Q2: How does Tiktok account of People's Daily construct a high-level framework for reporting on the COVID-19 epidemic?

Q3: How does Tiktok account of People's Daily construct a mid-level framework for reporting on the COVID-19 epidemic?

Q3: How does Tiktok account of People's Daily construct a low-level framework for reporting on the COVID-19 epidemic?

3.2. Research Method

Through the content analysis method [13-15], this study applied Zang Guiren's three-level framework theory to construct a high, medium and low-level framework for the epidemic news samples of People's Daily Tik Yin. By using quantitative content analysis method and qualitative method in category construction and research analysis, we can not only carry out objective coding analysis of short video news text data of the epidemic situation, but also carry out qualitative in-depth analysis of coding results, so as to objectively, systematically and qualitatively describe the framework of People's Daily Tik Yin's COVID-19 epidemic report.

3.3. Sampling

This study chooses People's Daily Tiktok number as the research object. Through horizontal and vertical data analysis of the four major mainstream media on the Tiktok platform, People's Daily, Xinhuanet, News broadcast and CCTV News, it is found that the Tiktok account of People Daily has the highest number of fans and likes and ranks first in the influence of short videos related to the epidemic. The time frame is limited to December 31, 2020 to April 28, 2020. On December 31, 2019, the People's Daily Tiktok published the first news about the COVID-19s. On April 28, 2020, Wuhan announced the lifting of the lockdown, and the national epidemic entered normal management. The sample covers the incubation period, outbreak period, spread period and resolution period of the epidemic. Finally, 450 short video news about the new pneumonia epidemic were captured as analysis samples.

3.4. Frame Category Construction

Based on Zangguoren's three-level framework theory, this study constructs three dimensions and nine categories of indicators.

1) High-level framework: includes three first-level indicators: release time, number of reports, and category of reports. Published from December 31, 2019 to April 8, 2020, the number of stories refers to the daily number of stories during this period, as well as the total number of stories. Report categories refer to attributes of information.

2) Middle-level framework: including three first-level indicators: report theme, report object and report tone.

3)Low-level framework: Including expression tone, presentation of three first-level indicators. The tone of the report is positive, neutral and negative. The expression tone includes statement, imperative and question. The presentation mode includes text, pictures, video, soundtrack and dubbing.

4.Results

4.1. Number and types of reports under the high-level framework

1) Large number and long duration of reports.

It can be found from Figure 1 that from December 31, 2019 to April 28, 2020, 450 messages were posted, an average of five messages per day. It peaked at 16 on January 30. It peaked at 26.03 million likes. In general, continuous follow-up, without interruption. However, since the first epidemic information was released on the Tiktok account of People's Daily on December 31, 2019, it was not followed up until January 20, during which no news about the epidemic was reported, and there were problems of lagging information release in the early stage and media aphasia.

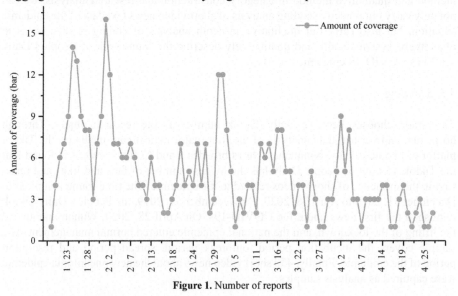

Figure 1. Number of reports

2) The categories of coverage are diverse.

Emotional interaction and epidemic news accounted for 37% and 25%, respectively, see Figure 2. This shows that in its coverage of the COVID-19, Tiktok account of People Daily continues the values of mainstream media and insists on positive guidance and public opinion guidance by publicizing touching stories. The international epidemic situation and national image accounted for 13% and 12% respectively, which was reflected in the middle and later stages of the epidemic. People Daily increased its attention to the international epidemic situation and the national image.

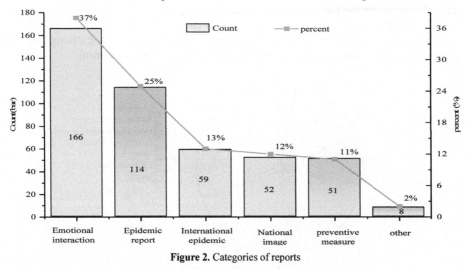

Figure 2. Categories of reports

4.2. Report Theme, Object and Tone Under the Framework of Middle Level

1) focus on touching stories, pay attention to emotional publicity
In this study, the topics of coverage are divided into 9 categoriesBut the bias in reporting is clear, shown in Figure 3. Touching stories topped the list, accounting for 28 %.

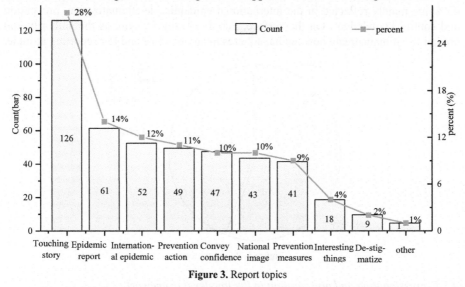

Figure 3. Report topics

This highlights the role of mainstream media in guiding public opinion and strengthening the emotional infection of the audience through touching stories.
2) Subject diversification and building interworking space

Among the 450 short video news, 139 mainly reported on the government, accounting for 30.89%. 98 cases were mainly reported on the anti-epidemic support, accounting for 21.78%. The Figure 4 shows that People's Daily, as a mainstream media, actively speaks for the Party and the government and pays attention to shaping the image of the government. At the same time, the overall target of the report is rich and diverse, indicating that People's Daily pays attention to building dialogue space among different groups and contributing media power to epidemic prevention and control.

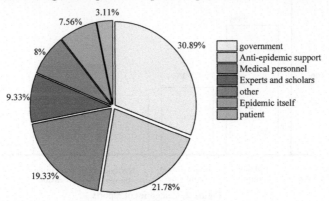

Figure 4. Report objects

3) Give priority to positive guidance and focus on social stability

In the 450 stories, 201 were positive, accounting for nearly 45 %. With touching stories, national image as the main features, it promoted the high attention of the government, the selfless dedication of supporters, positively affirming the actions of the government, presented in Figure 5. A total of 193 neutral reports, accounting for nearly 43%, are mainly reflected in the international epidemic, de-stigmatization, prevention and control knowledge . On the surface, People's Daily Douyin, as the authority and credibility of mainstream new media, adheres to an objective and fair reporting attitude.

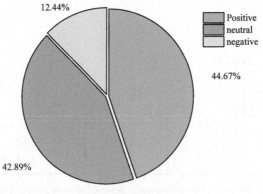

Figure 5. Reporting tone

4.3 Expression tone and presentation in the low-level framework

1) Use more imperative tone to strengthen emotional infection. In the study sample, there are 225 reports of imperative mood, accounting for 50%, which mostly contain positive words such as positive, praise, affirmation, imperative, exclamation and so on, which are

shown in Figure 6. For example: regardless of life and death! Seven doctors in Wuhan pressed the red handprint on the petition, let's pay tribute to the hero! Good news! The first case in Hubei! Wuhan University Central South Hospital successfully treated pneumonia patients with ECMO technology.

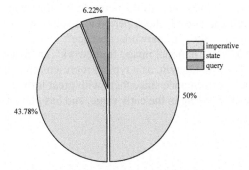

Figure 6. Expressing tone

2) Audio-visual dual effect to create a sense of scene. There are 291 subtitle + video + soundtrack articles, accounting for nearly 65%, which are mainly reflected in the reports of touching stories; It is clearly presented in Figure 7 that a total of 129 videos, pictures and music were included, accounting for 29%, mainly in epidemic notification. which reflects its active use of the characteristics of new media to strengthen the communication effect on the basis of retaining traditional communication methods. This kind of detailed display through text and pictures, combined with video and music, brings emotional rendering, making the report more shocking.

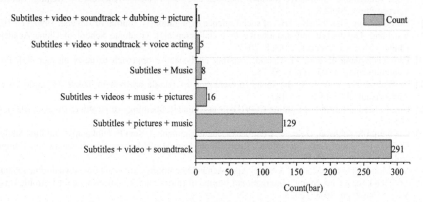

Figure 7. Reporting method

5. Conclusion

Through the analysis of the three-level framework of People's Daily's Tiktok epidemic report, it was found that it continued to pay attention to and report the COVID-19, and paid attention to public opinion guidance and agenda setting, reflecting the authority and influence of mainstream media. The categories of information reports are rich, the themes of reports are diverse, and most of them are emotional renderings of touching stories, highlighting the human touch framework. The diversification of the reporting objects, with the government and the anti-epidemic support as the main body, reflects the government leadership of the media. The tone of the report is positive, and the tone of the report is more imperative, focusing on the positive guidance of the audience. In addition, the combination of "subtitles + soundtrack + video" strengthened the audio-visual effect and enhanced the appeal of the news. In the four stages of the development incubation period, outbreak period, shock period and solution period of the epidemic, it successively experienced the "framework absence", "human interest framework", "emotional framework" and "national image framework". In general, in the reporting of the epidemic, People's Daily Douyin, as a typical representative of the mainstream new media, has outstanding performance since then, with great influence and appeal, despite the problem of delayed reporting in the early stage, and has played a good anti-epidemic effect.

References

[1] Shen J Y. Research on the framework of Chinese mainland media coverage of COVID-19[D]. Chengdu: Southwest Jiaotong University, 202: 11-12.

[2] Zhang Xiaoqun. SARS crisis highlights media credibility[J]. China Quality Miles, 2003, (07): 70-71.

[3] Ningrum, N. S. Framing Indonesian Women Leaders during the COVID-19 Pandemic in the mass media[J]. Community Empowerment and Engagement, 2021, 5: 80-85.

[4] Mutua, S. N. Online news media framing of COVID-19 pandemic[J]. European Journal of Interactive Multimedia and Education, (2020). 1(2): 13-20.

[5] Bateson, G. A theory of play and fantasy[J]. Psychiatric Research Reports, (1955). 2, 39–51.

[6] Goffman, E. Frame analysis: An essay on the organization of experience[J]. Harvard University Press. (1974).

[7] Chen Xiangming. Qualitative research methods and social science research[M]. Beijing: Educational Science Press, 2000: 8.

[8] Guo Guichun. The "Noah's Ark" of social science exploration[J]. Journal of Jinyang, 1990, (1): 10.

[9] Wu Fang. Qualitative and quantitative in social science[J]. Graduate School of China Academy of Chinese Medical Sciences, 2013, 8: 20-25.

[10] Pan, Zhongdang & Kosicki, Gerald. Framing analysis: An approach to news discourse[J]. Political Communication, 1993, 10(1) : 55-75.

[11] Bi Weina, Ma Yuefei. Media image presentation of female athletes in Tokyo Olympic Games[J]. Audiovisual, 2021, (12): 186-187.

[12] Gui, L. Media framing of fighting COVID-19 in China[J]. Sociology of Health & Illness, (2021), 43(4), 966-970.

[13] Oladipupo S. Johnson, Helen O. Edogbanya, Jacob Emmanuel, Seyi E. Olukanni, "Stability Analysis of COVID-19 Model with Quarantine", International Journal of Mathematical Sciences and Computing, Vol.9, No.3, pp. 26-45, 2023.

[14] Md. Motaleb Hossen Manik, "A Novel Approach in Determining Areas to Lockdown during a Pandemic: COVID-19 as a Case Study", International Journal of Information Engineering and Electronic Business, Vol.15, No.2, pp. 30-37, 2023.

[15] B. Premamayudu, Chavala Bhuvaneswari, " Covid-19 Automatic Detection from CT Images through Transfer Learning", International Journal of Image, Graphics and Signal Processing, Vol.14, No.5, pp. 84-95, 2022.

Artificial Intelligence, Medical Engineering and Education
Z.B. Hu et al. (Eds.)
143
doi:10.3233/ATDE231324

Little Red Book Brand Communication Strategy Analysis

Qinxian CHEN[a], Nian LONG[b], Saipeng XING[c1], Yang XING [d]

[a] *School of Economics and Management, Wuchang Shouyi University, Wuhan, China*
[b] *South Central University For Nationalities, Wuhan, China*
[c] *School of Management, Wuhan Technology and Business University, Wuhan, China*
[d] *School of Energy and Power Engineering, Lanzhou Technology University, Lanzhou, China*

Abstract. The rapid development of the Internet era has better linked the relationship between people and society, and also brought about the emergence and vigorous development of social media. The steady development of Little red book as an emerging social media platform is also worthy of in-depth study. Based on the development status of Little red book platform, this paper introduces the basic development status of Little red book platform and the characteristics of its own development, and further studies the brand communication strategy of Little red book platform in depth, focusing on visual communication, endorsement communication, accurate communication, etc. At the same time, the problems existing in the current development of Little red book and corresponding solutions are analyzed.

Keywords. Social media; Little red book; Brand communication.

1. Introduction

With the rapid development of the 5G era [1-4], whether major emerging brands can maintain their own advantages in the fierce competition for long-term development is the key to the problem. This paper is based on the research of the development status of the brand of Little red book, in-depth excavation of the main mechanism of Xiaohong book to attract users to deep retention, and analysis of the problems existing in the current development of Little red book and corresponding solutions. In this way, social media platforms including Little red book can be invincible in the era of rapid update and iteration, and the brand communication ability and user retention ability of Little red book platform can be Little red book improved.

1.1. Brand Communication

Brand communication is an information management process in which brand owners adhere to the core values of the brand and, within the overall framework of brand identification, achieve brand management tasks through communication methods such as advertising, public relations, and marketing promotion [5]. Brand communication is

---

[1] Corresponding Author: Saipeng XING, Email: xingsaipeng@163.com

the most important work in the construction of internet brands, and its essence is to complete the entire process of shaping corporate brands through the transmission of information from the dissemination subject to the dissemination object.

1.2. Brand Communication Strategy

In the context of social media, the communication strategy of a brand is nothing more than through social media advertising, interpersonal network, appeal to emotion and fan effect.

CIS theory is an abbreviation of corporate identity system, which consists of three parts: corporate concept identification, behavior identification and visual identification. The brand information of Little red book can include brand name, brand logo, brand logo, brand packaging and other visual identity brand communication elements. The brand visual system can often leave the first impression of the brand when the user contacts the brand and then form the first cause effect. Therefore, for the brand, the corporate visual image identification is extremely critical [6].

2. Little Red Book Platform Introduction

Little red book is a platform for users to create and share content launched by Xingyin Information Technology Co., Ltd. in 2013. At the beginning of its establishment, Little red book was only an APP for sharing overseas shopping guides [7]. However, through a series of explorings, Little red book successfully broke the circle by making efforts in the field of algorithm recommendation, conducting a large number of advertisements and inviting celebrities to settle in, and successfully built a national grass planting community. Users can record life and share lifestyle on Little red book platform through short videos, pictures and other forms, and have a series of interactions based on users' own interests in the form of consumption experience and lifestyle. Such sharing and interaction of lifestyle not only increases the popularity of Little red book platform, but also improves users' daily activity. The retention of interactive relationships can greatly enhance user stickiness and brand loyalty, and the current monthly active users of Little red book have exceeded 260 million, and the daily active users have exceeded 90 million.

3. Little Red Book Brand Communication Strategy and Effectsecond

The positioning of the Little red book platform is young female users in first and brand to accurately capture users' demands and carry out brand communication and related work.

3.1. Visual Communication under CIS Theory

The brand name is Little red book, and a catchy and easy to understand brand name is easier for users to memorize. "Book" represents knowledge, indicating that Little red book can help users understand various aspects of knowledge, expand their knowledge range, and also reflect the comprehensive knowledge in Little red book. The brand logo is the visual image that Little red book often displays in front of the audience. The brand logo of Little red book is a red background box with the white handwriting "Little red book" in the middle, which is also its most classic logo [8]. The brand logo is also the brand slogan, and the brand slogan of Little red book is "Mark my life".

3.2. Under the Celebrity Effect, Endorsement and Dissemination

Through in-depth observation of the celebrity endorsement selection on the Little red book platform, it can be found that Little red book has always been committed to seeking the spokesperson with the best internal fit with the brand and has also continuously gained popularity through the use of the spokesperson [9]. At the beginning of Little red book, the public's impression of Little red book remained on overseas shopping sharing community platforms, establishing differentiation between overseas and domestic e-commerce platforms. Therefore, Little red book chose Hu Ge, who became popular in popular dramas such as "The Disguiser" and "Langya Bang" at the time, as the brand spokesperson. Hu Ge not only focused on work, but also understood that the tone of enjoying life was consistent with Little red book's brand tone. The popularity of popular stars can greatly enhance the brand's visibility and exposure.

Under the continuous growth trend of the platform, Little red book continuously conveys a brand image that is more in line with the current stage to users. Little red book has chosen Liu Haoran and Gu Ailing as brand spokespersons [10]. On the one hand, social media weakens the restriction of accessibility, making it possible to see relatively low accessibility Spaces in small streets and alleys. On the other hand, it is possible for any store to take advantage of the huge traffic on social media platforms. The scale effect of agglomeration as shown in Figure 1.

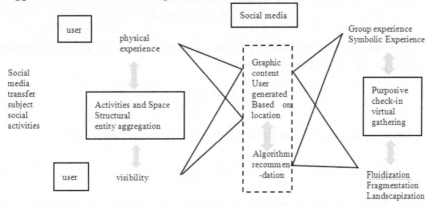

Figure 1. Leisure space under the influence of social media behavioral interaction mechanism

3.3. Cases Accurate Communication under Social Media

The Little red book platform, similar to other social media platforms, cannot do without algorithm recommendations and the support of big data. Based on obtaining user information and generating user profiles, precise marketing is carried out based on user interests and hobbies. Through in-depth observation of the Little red book platform, it has a highly insightful user experience. After analyzing the topic views, it was found that various imitations and makeup designs were the top among female topic views, while fashion and fashion were the top among male topic views. After that, the relevant topics were exposed on the platform to better create popularity and hot topics [11]. The users of the Little red book platform are mainly female users, accounting for over 80% of the total. Precise recommendations are made for the user group on the platform. Before new users use Little red book, they first fill in the user's gender and age information, and then launch 31 interest tags for users to choose based on their interests. After selecting, users open Little red book and see mostly high-quality content recommended based on their interests, perform precise push after accurately capturing user interests [12].

Comparison of the overall distribution pattern of The Little red book check-in areas: standard deviation ellipse, kernel density estimation, and head tail interruption method.

The results of kernel density estimation will be assigned to the interpolated data values of each analysis unit, and the result values will be grouped using the head tail interruption method as the basis for comparing the number of cores and distribution positions.

$$D(x,y) = \frac{1}{(r)^2} \sum_{i=1}^{n} \left[\frac{3}{\pi} p_i \left(1 - \left(\frac{d_i}{r}\right)^2\right) \right] \qquad (d_i < r) \qquad (1)$$

Concentration: Hotspot Analysis (Getis Ord G), Use the ratio of the number of leisure spaces in the hotspot cluster area to the total number of leisure spaces as the criterion for judging the degree of concentration (equation (2)). The higher the ratio, the higher the concentration of leisure spaces.

$$G_i^* = \frac{\sum_{j=1}^{n} W_{i,j} X_j - X \sum_{j=1}^{n} W_{i,j}}{S \sqrt{n \sum_{j=1}^{n} W_{i,j} - \left(\sum_{j=1}^{n} W_{i,j}\right)^2}} \qquad (2)$$

In the formula: xh is the number of leisure spaces located in the hotspot cluster area; Xtotal It is the total number of leisure spaces.

$$CCR = \frac{x_h}{x_{total}} \qquad (3)$$

Clustering Degree: Density Based Clustering Algorithm (DBSCAN)

$$CLR = \frac{x_c}{x_{total}} \qquad (4)$$

From the perspective of distribution, the regularity, and new characteristics of the leisure space of Xiaohongshu check-in under the influence of social media have been preliminarily revealed. However, the effectiveness of these regular features in different cities and regions still needs to be tested, especially with the rapid iteration of network trends, and research on cross-sections and single platforms may be limited by factors such as user characteristics, which cannot fully reveal the changing characteristics.

3.4. Appeal to Emotional Public Welfare Communication

Observation and analysis of Little red book's dissemination activities in recent years are not uncommon. Little red book has been committed to exploring the path of public welfare, combining public welfare activities with its own product characteristics around the keyword "community", and moving users with culture and warmth. As early as 2021, Little red book helped renovate the old community sports field in Shanghai, and later launched a street and alley store assistance program. It launched a renovation documentary on five small stores in Shanghai, selecting small stores that grew out of old streets and alleys and still maintained a lively atmosphere in urban self-renewal. It showcased stories of people and life that could connect small and large stores, allowing people to feel warmth in the details. In addition, on the eve of Women's Day, Little red book also prepared a "cardamom gift" for sixth grade girls in rural primary schools in Henan, donating 4 million yuan to support education in the Henan region. Little red book's commitment to public welfare has greatly enhanced users' reputation for the Little red book brand, and this emotional appeal to users often reflects the brand's values, Thus, it shifts from appealing to emotions to appealing to rational demands of values, thereby better enhancing users' liking for the brand and brand stickiness [13].

3.5. Little red book Brand Communication Effect

Little Red Book can be called a very magical platform. Since its inception, through a series of brand communication activities, it has been able to attract nearly 200 million users who pursue quality of life to stay active, thus becoming a real competitor feared by Tiktok, WeChat and other head social media platforms. In terms of the current APP downloads and 90 million daily activities on the Little red book platform, the brand communication of Little red book itself has received excellent results. It has successfully entered the social media platform market with young female users as a breakthrough point and achieved breakthroughs through a series of brand communication behaviors, from the original beauty and fashion field to various industries, Let Little red book truly become an experience sharing social platform that marks users' lives. From Table 1, Whether from the perspective of ordinary users or content creators on the Little red book platform, the Little red book app itself provides a very Smooth product experience and simple interaction process with products within the community.

Table 1. Types and quantities of two types of leisure space in Wuhan in 2022

Primary classification	Secondary classification	Number of leisure spaces/proportion (%)	Number of leisure check-in cards/proportion (%)
Catering services	Catering facilities; Tea House; Cake restaurant; cafe Western restaurant; Cold drink shops; Dessert shops; Leisure dining venues; Chinese Restaurant	24669/56	2369/63
Scenic Spots	Scenic spots: Scenic spots related; Park Plaza	561/1	347/9
Shopping services	Supermarkets; Cosmetics stores; Flower and bird beetle market; Home building materials market;	8931/26	650/17

Table 1. Types and quantities of two types of leisure space in Wuhan in 2022 (Continued)

Science, education, and cultural services	Museums; Exhibition Center; Science and Technology Museum; Scientific and educational cultural venues; Art Museum; Library; Cultural Palace;	1866/4	158/4
Sports and leisure services	Vacation and recuperation facilities; Sports and leisure service venues; Leisure venues; Cinema; Entertainment venues	4164/10	44/1
Accommodation services	Hotels and Resorts; Hotel guesthouses; Accommodation services related	3297/8	190/5

4. Brand Communication Issues of Little red book

4.1. Deterioration of Brand Ecology under Profit Pursuit

After the rise of the B2K2C model, brand recommendation advertisements under the trend of profit replaced the original pure sharing nature of recommendations, and eye-catching titles such as "use big from a young age" and "annual good items" replaced the original lifestyle scenes. Any blogger who shares interesting notes such as life experiences on the Little red book platform, once a certain number of fans accumulate their notes, cannot do without brand elements and soft advertising implantation, and currently, over 81% of users within the platform with an average monthly disposable income of over 4000 yuan may develop a desire to purchase due to note content. The grass planting economy, which was originally unique to the Little red book platform, has repeatedly experienced the phenomenon of being "planted" in the previous second and "pulled out" in the next second due to excessive commercialization. This excessive commercialization phenomenon seriously interferes with the original ecological environment of the Little red book platform, greatly reducing the user experience.

4.2. Brand Lacks Core Competitiveness under Social Media

Most social media platforms adopt algorithmic recommendation mechanisms, and users are trapped in the information cocoon formed by their own interests. Therefore, the social media platforms they use mostly recommend content based on their interests. It is difficult to highlight the brand's characteristics and truly embody the core values of the brand itself [13]. In the context of social media, if Little red book, as a social media platform, cannot create its own core competitiveness and produce truly high-quality content and features that attract users, it is extremely easy to be replaced by other social media platforms. Users can obtain content recommended based on their own interest algorithms in addition to other platform features on other social media platforms [14].

4.3. Brand Image Damage Driven by Traffic

In the current fast-paced development of society, many bloggers excessively focus on choosing note titles to gain attention or traffic, while neglecting content production itself. In the era of fragmentation, titles can even directly determine whether users choose to open notes for browsing [15]. Therefore, various exaggerated and superficial titles are ubiquitous on the Little red book platform, Titles such as "things that only 1% of people know" and "misconceptions that 90% of people find difficult to avoid" are common, but users who take notes out of interest in the title often feel disappointed, which greatly reduces the user's sense of experience and thus reduces their liking and reputation for the brand. Based on this sense of contrast, users will have a strong sense of deception, distrust of the Little red book platform, and even trigger a crisis of trust and language criticism in the entire society towards the platform.

4.4. Lack of Offline Promotion Through Social Media

Since its brand communication, Little Red Book Platform has focused on social media to carry out online brand communication activities, actively invited stars to speak on the microblog platform, released video promotions on the Tiktok platform, and so on. Offline activities are very limited, mainly for offline public welfare activities, such as the transformation of the old community sports ground in Shanghai, the support plan for the managers of coffee shops, small pubs, and so on, the communication activities have all received good communication results [16]. However, the brand communication of Little red book itself is far from enough. In addition to the public welfare activities of Little red book itself, offline sales and promotion activities can also be appropriately invested, so that users can truly feel the brand temperature and power of Little red book brand in the context of social media, and thus close the distance with users.

5. Suggestions for Brand Communication of Little Red Book

5.1. Regulations Introduced to Rebuild Brand Ecology

The Little red book platform cannot give up on social benefits while seizing economic benefits. When there is a conflict between the two, it is necessary to prioritize social benefits and meet user needs. Putting users at the center is the core and key to the long-term development of the brand. Over commercialization only brings short-term economic benefits and long-term user loss. Only by implementing regulations to strictly prevent excessive commercialization can we provide users with a truly harmonious and clear online atmosphere, allowing Little red book's original community experience and life sharing, a friendly brand ecological environment, to be seen by more users and achieve deep user retention.

5.2. Creating High-quality and Distinctive Content on the Platform

The lack of distinctive and homogeneous content essentially stems from the platform's recommendation mechanism, which can recommend content based on users' interests. However, a large amount of homogeneous content inevitably reduces users' perceived value. Therefore, the platform can fully utilize technical means for appropriate screening during review and will not approve a large amount of homogeneous content that appears over a period of time, At the same time, interview bloggers who have failed multiple note reviews and encourage them to produce high-quality content.

5.3. Integrated Communication of Brands on Social Media

Due to the false marketing driven by traffic, Little red book's brand image will be greatly threatened and damaged. It is necessary to comprehensively utilize various social media platforms to shape a good Little red book brand image for integrated marketing communication, to promote the development of Little red book's brand communication. For example, Little red book can invite stars to speak for it, choose stars who are consistent with Little red book's overall brand tone to speak for it, and make official announcements on social media platforms with high daily activity such as Weibo Tiktok. Using the fan effect of stars can greatly reverse the brand reputation, so as to create a good brand image.

5.4. Focusing on Offline Promotion of Brand Temperature

While Little red book's online brand communication activities are in full swing, they also need to be synchronized offline, fully combining online and offline to create a closed-loop brand communication. Little red book can carry out activities online and simultaneously offline. For example, Little red book can invite celebrities to endorse the brand online and promote it on social media platforms. Offline, celebrities can be invited to carry out offline promotional activities and posters.

6. Conclusion

The development of social media will change towards search engines in the future, which requires social media platforms to constantly improve their own supervision and incentive mechanisms for content production, encourage more producers of high-quality content to devote themselves to creation, and output more high-quality content for the platform, so that users can get content that fully meets their needs every time they search. In addition, the city is an interrelated and complex system. Although the behavior of punching cards is more bound to young people, social media users and leisure activities, the influence of the technology behind it on residents' behavior may penetrate into all aspects of life. Brands need to constantly retrieve the relevant information they need and want to know through social media platforms, and at the same time, make in-depth publicity through social media to create an image to promote more potential users to become real users, enhance user stickiness and promote users' deep retention in all aspects, so as to truly realize the healthy brand communication of Little Red Book platform under the social media background.

Acknowledgment

This project is supported by Key Projects of Education Scientific Planning in Hubei Province "Research on the management mode and operation mechanism of Teacher Development Center in Applied Undergraduate Colleges" (2019GA064), and this project is supported by Scientific research project of Hubei Provincial Department of Education "Research on the influence mechanism and management strategy of R & D team empowerment on team creativity of small and medium-sized scientific and technological enterprises in Hubei Province" (B2020294).

References

[1] Sourav Debnath, Samin Ahmed, S. M. Shamsul Alam, "Performance Comparison of OFDM, FBMC, and UFMC for Identifying the Optimal Solution for 5G Communications", International Journal of Wireless and Microwave Technologies, Vol.13, No.5, pp. 1-10, 2023.

[2] Mohammed Hussein Ali, Ghanim A. Al-Rubaye, "Performance Analysis of 5G New Radio LDPC over Different Multipath Fading Channel Models", International Journal of Computer Network and Information Security, Vol.15, No.4, pp.1-12, 2023.

[3] Mohammed H. Ali, Noora H. Sherif, "Design and Implementation of Adaptive Universal Filtered Multi Carrier for 5G and Beyond", International Journal of Computer Network and Information Security, Vol.14, No.6, pp.14-22, 2022.

[4] K. Pandey, R. Arya, "Robust Distributed Power Control with Resource Allocation in D2D Communication Network for 5G-IoT Communication System", International Journal of Computer Network and Information Security, Vol.14, No.5, pp.73-81, 2022.

[5] Xie Lulu, Analysis of communication strategies for female bloggers on Little red book platform[D]. Guangzhou: Guangzhou Institute of Sports, 2022 (in Chinese).

[6] Yin G, Zhen F, Tang F H, et al. Leisure behavior under the influence of information technology: A conceptual analysis framework[J]. Geography and Geo-Information Science, 2018, 34(1): 53-58 (in Chinese).

[7] Fan Qunlin. Research on marketing strategy innovation of Little red book social E-commerce platform [J]. Journal of Tianjin Business Vocational College, 2021, 6: 66-68 (in Chinese).

[8] Zhang Jingjing Research on internet celebrity brand communication based on the Little red book platform[D]. Dalian: Northeast University of Finance and Economics, 2022 (in Chinese).

[9] Zhou J, Lin G. The impact of the internet on physical stores: A case study of internet-sensation cafes in Guangzhou[J]. Modern Urban Research, 2021, (2): 114-120, 125 (in Chinese).

[10] Zhang A X, Ma B B, Lu J. W., et al. Spatial pattern and driving mechanism of leisure tourism in Lanzhou[J]. Journal of Arid Land Resources and Environment, 2022, 36(11): 200-208 (in Chinese).

[11] Todoric J, Yamashkin A, Vuksanovic Macura Z. Spatial patterns of entertainment mobility in cities[J]. Journal of the Geographical Institute Jovan Cvijic, SASA, 2022, 72(2): 207-220.

[12] Zhang Ting. Transformation and strategy optimization of brand communication in the new media environment[J]. Journal of Harbin University, 2022, 43 (12): 36-38 (in Chinese).

[13] Wang Yidan. Research on the brand bommunication strategy of Gansu's "Yang Straw" agricultural products[J]. Modern Agriculture Research, 2022, 28 (12): 32-35 (in Chinese).

[14] David Priestland. The big reach of the Little Red Book[J]. New Statesman, 2019, 148(5479): 48-49.

[15] Moisescu OvidiuIoan, Gică OanaAdriana, Herle FlaviaAndreea. Boosting eWOM through social media brand page engagement: the mediating role of self-brand connection[J]. Behavioral Sciences, 2022, 12(11): 411-411.

[16] Marmat Geeta. Online brand communication and building brand trust: social information processing theory perspective[J]. Global Knowledge, Memory, and Communication, 2022, 71: 6-7.

Artificial Intelligence, Medical Engineering and Education
Z.B. Hu et al. (Eds.)
© *2024 The Authors.*
This article is published online with Open Access by IOS Press and distributed under the terms
of the Creative Commons Attribution Non-Commercial License 4.0 (CC BY-NC 4.0).
doi:10.3233/ATDE231325

Risk Analysis and Evaluation of Cross-Border Supply Chain of Overseas Engineering Projects Based on PEST-RS-SVM Driven by "Belt and Road" Trade

Lei ZHANG[1]
School of Management, Guangzhou City University of Technology, Guangzhou,
China

Abstract. Driven by the "One Belt and One Road" trade, overseas engineering projects have become the embodiment of cooperation with countries along the "One Belt and One Road", thus bringing frequent material exchange of cross-border supply chains among countries. In order to achieve smooth and rapid development of cross-border supply chain, reduce risks and strengthen control, it is necessary to screen the risk factors of cross-border supply chain, establish a system and make correct and reasonable evaluation. In this paper, PEST method is adopted to analyze the risk factors of external cross-border supply chain of energy enterprises under the background of "One Belt and One Road", and corresponding evaluation index system is established. The risk evaluation model of external cross-border supply chain was established by combining the rough set theory and support vector mechanism, and the risk evaluation model of phoenix risk was used to comprehensively evaluate the risk of cross-border supply chain along the "Belt and Road", and corresponding countermeasures were put forward.

Keywords. One Belt and One Road; Cross-border supply chain; PEST-RS-SVM

1. Introduction

The Belt and Road Initiative refers to the joint efforts of many countries to build the Silk Road Economic Belt and the 21st Century Maritime Silk Road.

"One Belt and One Road" Initiative is a major innovation since the reform and opening up and even the founding of the People's Republic of China. Since the initiative was put forward, China's foreign trade has been greatly improved in both quantity and quality. The growth of foreign trade will inevitably bring about an increase in the demand for foreign trade services [1].

"Belt and Road" involves 66 countries in the world. These countries have huge differences in policies and laws, economy and culture, natural environment and geography, logistics and communication technology [2]. With the rapid development of trade, these countries have huge differences in policies and laws, economy and culture, natural environment, geography, culture and technology. The imperfect laws and regulations, imperfect management system, inadequate infrastructure, low clearance

---

[1] Corresponding Author: Lei ZHANG, Email: 495997665@qq.com

efficiency, high cost, poor timeliness, insufficient reliability, imperfect cross-border reverse logistics system, and shortage of management professionals in cross-border supply chain all bring hidden dangers to the security and stable development of cross-border supply chain. How to coordinate the relationship between the two is an important topic that needs in-depth study [3].

The development of cross-border supply chain is the driving force of "Belt and Road" countries to seek the maximization of interests in the pursuit of common development, and it has become the connection and link of the economic development of many countries [4]. "Extensive consultation" emphasizes equality, mutual respect, seeking common ground while shelving differences, consultation and cooperation, and accommodates the interests of all parties [5]. "Joint contribution" is an open and inclusive system of cooperation on a voluntary basis. "Sharing" is to achieve mutual benefit and win-win results, take fair, balanced and sustainable development as the purpose and goal, and build a community of common prosperity and security [6]. Therefore, with the common development of economic security and stability of China and the rest of the world, the cross-border supply chain needs to be completed and shared through extensive consultation [7]. In addition, it needs to form and clarify the rights, responsibilities and obligations of each country in the mechanism of security and development, and gradually enjoy the benefits brought by the security and development. Therefore, the cooperation of cross-border supply chain security and development is of great significance to the economic growth of China and countries along the "Belt and Road" [8].

2. Brief Introduction to the Construction Principle of Risk Analysis Evaluation Model

2.1. Principle of PEST

PEST analysis model is an analysis tool for enterprise macro environment, where P for politics, E for economics, S for society, T for technology. PEST analysis can be used to analyze the macro strength of an enterprise and its related factors, as shown in Figure 1.

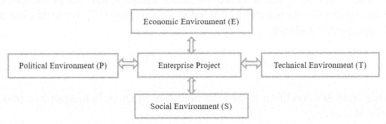

Figure. 1. PEST analysis model

In Figure 1, political environment (P) refers to the social system and institutional nature of the country where the enterprise is located. Economic environment (E) mainly consists of macro environment and micro environment. The macro environment reflects the state and level of national economic development, while the micro environment reflects the economic environment of the enterprise, such as the consumption and savings of local residents and the employment degree of the local population; Technological environment (T) mainly refers to the status and level of technological development in the place where the enterprise is located; Social environment (S) includes a country's residents' education level, customs, values, cultural level, etc., all of which directly or indirectly affect residents' recognition of enterprises [9].

2.2. Rough Set Theory

In 1982, Polish scientists first proposed Rough Set theory (RS), which is a new mathematical tool to deal with fuzzy and uncertain knowledge. Rough set theory can effectively analyze all kinds of incomplete information such as inaccuracy, inconsistency and incompleteness. It can also analyze and reason data to discover hidden knowledge and reveal potential laws and reasoning. The core of rough set theory is attribute reduction, that is, by calculating the dependence degree of decision attribute value on feature attribute, the index with zero importance degree is deleted, and the expressive ability of knowledge representation system is not affected. Rough set theory can effectively solve the problems of ambiguity and uncertainty in the evaluation, calculate the relative importance of indicators, and make the evaluation and strategy selection more reasonable [10]. Rough set theory can be understood by the following definitions:

If the prediction object is W and an equivalence relation on W is R, then k =(W,R) is called an approximate space.

If x,y ∈ W and x,y ∈ R, then x and y are uncontestable on k, and R is an indistinguishable relation.

If property set P ⊆ R and P indicates phi, so IP is P a indiscernibility relation, ind (P); If the attribute r ∈ P and ind(P)=ind(P-(r)), then r is omitted on P.

Then, the attribute r has little effect on the description of features and is a redundant attribute. The omitted attribute will not affect the description of attribute features [11].

2.3. Support Vector Machine Theory

Support vector Machine (SVM) theory is a new general learning method based on statistical learning theory. It can effectively realize the accurate fitting of high-dimensional nonlinear systems based on small samples, and adopt the principle of minimum structural risk, which has a good generalization [12]. Its regression function can be expressed as follows:

$$y_i[(w \bullet x_i) + b] - 1 \geq 0 \quad i = 1,..., \quad n \tag{1}$$

When Mercer's condition is met, the objective function is transformed into a high-dimensional space:

$$Q(\alpha) = \sum_{i=1}^{n} \alpha_i - \frac{1}{2} \sum_{i,j=1}^{n} \alpha_i \alpha_j y_i y_j K(x_i, x_j) \tag{2}$$

the corresponding classification function becomes:

$$f(x) = \text{sgn}\{(w^* \bullet x) + b^*\} = \text{sgn}\left\{\sum_{i=1}^{n} \alpha_i^* y_i K(x_i, x_j) + b^*\right\} \tag{3}$$

Gaussian radial basis kernel function is the most widely used in support vector machine, has a wide convergence area and only contains one parameter, so this paper uses radial basis kernel function for calculation. By constructing Lagrange function, the dual of the original function is obtained. The above problem eventually becomes a convex quadratic programming problem [13]. These ideas and ways to solve the problem is also very useful in many different fields, such as the fault diagnosis of mechanical equipment, the information recognition in video, and the development of commercial market sales plans [14-17].

3. PEST Based Cross-Border Supply Chain Risk Analysis of Overseas Engineering Projects

An overseas engineering project of an energy engineering enterprise is selected as the research object, and the status quo of this enterprise project and the risk factors it may face in the external cross-border supply chain are studied by PEST analysis model. Combined with literature reading method and practical analysis method, the risk factors of overseas engineering project enterprises mainly include financial risk, market risk and financial risk under economic environment.

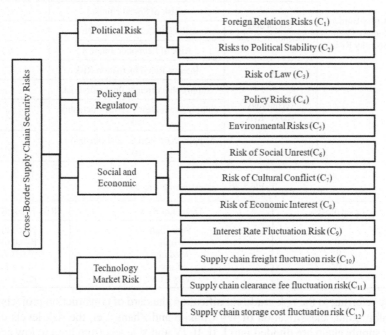

Figure. 2. PEST analysis model

Diplomatic relations in the political environment and political stability in the host country; Laws, policies and environmental protection in policies and regulations; Social unrest, cultural conflicts, and economic interests in the social economy; Interest rate fluctuation, supply chain freight fluctuation, supply chain clearance cost fluctuation, supply chain storage cost fluctuation under the technology market.

The evaluation index system of external cross-border supply chain should follow the three principles of systematic principle, scientific principle and comparability principle to ensure the construction of a scientific, reasonable, feasible and reliable risk evaluation system.

The evaluation index system of external cross-border supply chain designed this time is shown in Figure 2.

In the PEST analysis model in Fig.2, there are 4-criteria layer indexes and 12 indicator layer indexes, according to which the initial indicator set of evaluation can be established, as shown in Table 1.

Table 1. Initial index set of cross-border supply chain risk assessment

Target Layer	Layer of Criterion	Indicator Layer	Serial Number
Cross-Border Supply Chain Security Risks	Political Risk	Foreign Relations Risks	C_1
		Risks to Political Stability	C_2
	Policy and Regulatory Risks	Risk of Law	C_3
		Policy Risks	C_4
		Environmental Risks	C_5
	Social and Economic Risks	Risk of Social Unrest	C_6
		Risk of Cultural Conflict	C_7
		Risk of Economic Interest	C_8
	Technology Market Risk	Interest Rate Fluctuation Risk	C_9
		Supply chain freight fluctuation risk	C_{10}
		Supply chain clearance fee fluctuation risk	C_{11}
		Supply chain storage cost fluctuation risk	C_{12}

Table 2. Risk assessment grade standards

Level of Risk	Degree of Risk	Risk Grade Range
I	Very High	[1.0,0.8)
II	High	[0.8,0.6)
III	Medium	[0.6,0.4)
IV	Low	[0.4,0.2)
V	Very Low	[0.2,0.0)

By referring to the risk grade classification standard of construction projects and the risk safety grade classification of Wu Chukuo and Zhang Lei, the risk levels of cross-border supply chain are divided into I, II, II, IV and V levels from high to low according to the possibility of occurrence of risk events, risk loss and social impact.

This paper divides the risk criteria into five levels, as shown in Table 2.

4.   Risk Assessment Model of Overseas Project Cross-Border Supply Chain Based on Rough Set and Support Vector Machine

4.1. Risk Assessment Model

(1) Evaluation data preparation

The above evaluation index set is taken as the conditional attribute in the decision table. $\{C_1, C_2 \dots C_{12}\}$ indicates that the sample data is taken for attribute reduction processing, and then the sample classification is carried out.

(2) Rough set data reduction

The simple steps for the evaluation index intensification with the rough set calculation and analysis tool are as follows:

1) Establish a decision table for the research data according to the rough set theory.

The decision attributes of the decision table include: risk assessment level *{extremely high, high, medium, low, very low}* is a single decision attribute represented by {d}.

Set up the information system

$$S= \{U, R, V, f\}, U= \{X1, X2,\dots Xn\},$$

$$R=C \cup D, C = \{C1, C2\dots C12\}$$

and D {d} are conditional and decision attributes respectively.

2) Data preprocessing, including decision table data completion, decision table discretization.

3) Select the Algorithm for reduction and use Johnson's algorithm method.

(3) SVM for sample classification

After the rough set is used to reduce the attributes of the sample data of cross-border supply chain risk evaluation index, the core attributes of risk evaluation are retained, the calculation amount is reduced, and the calculation process is simplified. Then the evaluation index is classified according to the reduced core attributes.

1) Select kernel function and parameters. At present, there are three types of inner product kernel functions which are widely used. Generally, radial basis function is considered first when selecting kernel function, mainly because of its relatively few parameters and small numerical difference.

2) Sample training. The sample data were classified by SVM multi-classification method, and a 2-level support vector machine classifier was established to distinguish two evaluation levels ({extremely high, high, medium, low, very low}).

3) Sample test. After the sample training is completed, the test sample data is input into the trained 2-level support vector machine classifier. According to the output results, different sample evaluation levels can be distinguished.

4.2. Empirical Analysis

The evaluation index set is taken as the conditional attribute in the decision table.

{C_1, C_2 \dots C_{12}} indicates that the sample data is taken for attribute reduction processing, and then the sample classification is carried out.

The research period of this paper is 2018-2021, and the data are collected from China Statistical Yearbook.

(1) Sample data selection.

Data are used as learning samples, as shown in Table 4. C_1-C_{12} in the table are 12 evaluation indexes of cross-border supply chain risk respectively.

(2) *RS* reduction.

Johnson's Algorithm was used to reduce the attributes of the preprocessed decision table, and the reduction result was obtained by taking the intersection of the two.

(3) SVM classification.

Rosetta, a rough set calculation and analysis tool, was used to reduce the attributes of the sample data of evaluation indicators, and four core attributes were retained, so as to carry out multi-level classification of cross-border supply chain risks.

The risk coefficient sample set was divided into the training sample set and the test sample set, and the 9 groups of samples in Table 3 were randomly selected as the training sample set to construct the multi-layer SVM model. The remaining 3 groups of samples are used as test specimen sets to test the generalization ability of the model, as shown in Table 3, where the meanings of letters A-D are shown in Table 4.

Table 3. Sample data table of risk coefficient evaluation model

No.	A	B	C	D	E	F	G	H	I	J	K	L
1	0.13	0.11	0.12	0.23	0.23	0.12	0.12	0.25	0.23	0.23	0.22	0.22
2	0.24	0.14	0.21	0.22	0.17	0.21	0.21	0.21	0.22	0.17	0.19	0.19
3	0.23	0.17	0.15	0.19	0.25	0.15	0.15	0.19	0.19	0.25	0.23	0.24
4	0.12	0.21	0.22	0.15	0.23	0.22	0.22	0.22	0.24	0.21	0.12	0.23
5	0.21	0.15	0.16	0.22	0.32	0.16	0.32	0.25	0.23	0.23	0.21	0.12
6	0.15	0.22	0.24	0.19	0.21	0.23	0.19	0.23	0.12	0.22	0.15	0.21
7	0.22	0.19	0.12	0.23	0.15	0.12	0.23	0.12	0.21	0.19	0.22	0.15
8	0.16	0.23	0.21	0.17	0.22	0.21	0.17	0.21	0.15	0.23	0.16	0.22
9	0.24	0.17	0.22	0.25	0.36	0.25	0.27	0.15	0.32	0.17	0.24	0.16
10	0.18	0.25	0.19	0.21	0.24	0.22	0.21	0.33	0.16	0.25	0.12	0.24
11	0.21	0.14	0.23	0.12	0.22	0.16	0.15	0.26	0.23	0.21	0.31	0.23
12	0.18	0.16	0.23	0.12	0.22	0.15	0.22	0.23	0.22	0.25	0.15	0.22

The specific operation process is to write a program on the MATLABr2016a platform, use the LIBSVM toolbox, radial basis function as the kernel function, and use the RS object reduction of 9 groups of training sample data (Table 3) for sample training of the SVM model. After the training, the regression estimation method was used to carry out back judgment on the 9 groups of samples in Table 3, and the misjudgment rate of the back judgment was 0, indicating that the training results of the prediction model were highly correct and could be applied to actual engineering practice.

Table 4. The meanings of 12 letters A-L

A	Risk of diplomatic relations	G	Risk of cultural conflict
B	Political stability risk	H	Economic interest risk
C	Legal risk	I	Interest rate fluctuation risk
D	Policy risk	J	Freight fluctuation risk
E	Environmental risk	K	Risk of fluctuation of customs clearance fee
F	Social unrest risk	L	Risk of warehouse expense fluctuation

It can be seen that the combined prediction model based on RS-SVM established in this paper has high prediction accuracy and clear significance for cross-border supply chain risk prediction. As can be seen from the results, the risk situation of cross-border supply chain is relatively severe, still in grade II, in a high-risk state, the future cross-border supply chain risk is still facing many challenges.

The above results show that cross-border supply chain has been in a high-risk situation, it is necessary to take measures to prevent and deal with the occurrence of risks.

5.   Conclusion

In this paper, PEST, rough set and support vector machine are combined, and mathematical tools Matlab and Rosetta are used for practical calculation and analysis of the model. The model has a high accuracy and can be well applied to cross-border supply chain risk assessment to obtain a more accurate prediction rate, which can play a role in security early warning. The risk evaluation index system can also be used as a reference to evaluate the quantitative basis of cross-border supply chain risk.

According to the evaluation results, in the evaluation period, the risk of cross-border supply chain is generally in the high-risk range. In addition, international political, social and economic risks continue to rise, which seriously restricts cross-border supply chains.

The development of "The Belt and Road" is closely related to the expansion of overseas projects. With the expansion of the scope of project development activities, the cross-border supply chain will extend to a wider range, and its security risks will also be affected by more comprehensive factors. In order to reduce risks and promote the stable development of "One Belt and One Road" initiative, this study analyzes the risk factors under the background of "One Belt and One Road" through PEST analysis method, establishes the corresponding risk evaluation index system, proposes the feasibility of the risk evaluation system and evaluation model, and carries out the evaluation. However, the applicability and validation of the risk rating model are insufficient, the selection of indicators is limited, and the relevant data is not universal and historical. Therefore, it is necessary to broaden the research horizon and depth in the future, and continue to deepen the relevant research in this field.

In the development of cross-border supply chain driven by the "Belt and Road" trade, there are many high-risk factors, and various measures should be taken to avoid and reduce the occurrence of risks:

First, from the government level, build a logistics information platform, improve the cross-border supply chain infrastructure, improve the efficiency of the supply chain from the hard link, and reduce the risks in the flow of materials;

Second, standardize the management of cross-border supply chain enterprises, improve the level and efficiency of customs clearance and clearance, accelerate the steady development of supply chain, and reduce the risk of differentiation between regulations and laws between countries;

Third, from the enterprise level, improve the level of professional technology, establish a standardized system, promote modern technology in all links of the supply chain, improve the efficiency of the supply chain with scientific and technological means, complete the work in the fastest time and speed, reduce risks;

Fourth, cross-border supply chain enterprises should actively connect with cross-border trade e-commerce service platform, accelerate the informatization of cross-border supply chain, and jointly build logistics informatization platform;

Fifth, strengthen the cooperation between cross-border e-commerce platform and more cross-border supply chain enterprises, extend the breadth and depth of supply chain, achieve scale efficiency, and resist the occurrence of high risks.

Acknowledgment

The research is funded by Key Research Base of Humanities and Social Sciences in Universities of Guangdong Province: Research Base for Digital Transformation of Manufacturing Enterprises (2023WZJD012) and supported by Research Center for Hubei Business Service and Development, Key Research Base of Humanities and Social Science of Hubei Province.Hubei Business Service Development Research Center Fund Project: Hubei Intelligent Logistics Development Support System Research (2020Z01).

References

[1]   Wang Yuling. Research on the Collaborative development of cross-border e-commerce and cross-border logistics in China[J]. Reform and Strategy, 2017, 33(9): 16-19(in Chinese).

[2]   Tian Qing, Li Gui E. Discussion on optimization path of cross-border e-commerce logistics alliance mode operation[J]. Price Monthly, 2021(6): 14-17.

[3]   Li Hezhou, Liu Cunjing. The Influence of the eurasian geostrategy of the United States, Russia, India and Europe on the construction of "The Belt and Road"[J]. Russian, Eastern European and Central Asian Studies, 2020(1): 32-51, 156.

[4]   Liu Xiaojun, Zhang Bin. Cross-border logistics cooperation between China and countries along the "Belt and Road"[J]. China Circulation Economy, 2016, 30(12): 15-18(in Chinese).

[5]   He Jiang, Qian Huimin. Empirical study on the synergistic relationship between cross-border E-commerce and cross-border logistics[J]. Journal of Dalian University of Technology (Social Sciences Edition), 2019(9): 26-28(in Chinese).

[6]   Fang Ji, Zhang Xiaheng. Cross-border e-commerce logistics model innovation and development trend[J]. China Circulation Economy, 2015(6): 23-26(in Chinese).

[7]   Dong Qianli. Industrial linkage development based on the "Belt and Road" cross-border logistics network construction[J]. China Circulation Economy, 2015, 29(10): 34-41(in Chinese).

[8]   Wu Shouxue. Lack of cross-border e-commerce logistics coordination and its realization path[J]. Logistics Management, 2018(9): 12-17(in Chinese).

[9]   Huang Xuemei, Wang Wei, Huang Yongqin. Research on the construction of military archive knowledge service system based on PEST Model[J]. Archives of Shanxi Province, 2020, (3): 98-102+97(in Chinese).

[10]   Yang Fan, Tan Fei, Cui Xiang. Research on credit risk assessment of construction enterprises based on RS and SVM[J]. Journal of Wuhan University of Technology: Information and Management Engineering, 2016(1): 33-36(in Chinese).

[11]   Zhang Lei. Evaluation of China's petroleum security system: based on rough set and support vector machine[J]. China Soft Science, 2022(11): 13-19(in Chinese).

[12] Vapnik V. The nature of statistical learning theory[M]. Zhang Xuegong, trans. Beijing: Tsinghua University Press, 2000: 56-112.

[13] Zhang Lei, Zheng Pi'e, Wang Zhongquan, et al. Analysis of petroleum security in China based on Support vector machine[J]. Industrial Engineering, 2010, 13(4): 40-47, 52(in Chinese).

[14] Lianying Zhou, Daniel M. Amoh, Louis K. Boateng, Andrews A. Okine. Combined appetency and upselling prediction scheme in telecommunication sector using support vector machines[J]. International Journal of Modern Education and Computer Science, 2019, 11(6): 1-7.

[15] Om Prakash Yadav, G L Pahuja. Bearing fault detection using logarithmic wavelet packet transform and support vector machine[J]. International Journal of Image, Graphics and Signal Processing, 2019, 11(5): 21-33.

[16] Sivaiah Bellamkonda, N.P. Gopalan. A facial expression recognition model using support vector machines[J]. International Journal of Mathematical Sciences and Computing, 2018, 4(4): 56-65.

[17] Thuy Nguyen Thi Thu, Vuong Dang Xuan. Supervised support vector machine in predicting foreign exchange trading[J]. International Journal of Intelligent Systems and Applications, 2018, 10(9): 48-56.

Artificial Intelligence, Medical Engineering and Education
Z.B. Hu et al. (Eds.)
© 2024 The Authors.
This article is published online with Open Access by IOS Press and distributed under the terms
of the Creative Commons Attribution Non-Commercial License 4.0 (CC BY-NC 4.0).
doi:10.3233/ATDE231326

Intelligent Measurement of Total Factor Carbon Emission Efficiency of Logistics Industry in Hubei Province Under Low Carbon Constraints

Yao LIU[a], Zhaojun WU[b,1]

a School of Business Administration, Wuhan Business University, Wuhan, China
a School of General Education, Wuhan Business University, Wuhan, China

Abstract. Under the background of "dual carbon", Hubei Province has always attached great importance to the low-carbon-logistics transformation and has made green and efficient the focus of logistics industry development. The article takes energy and unexpected output into account and takes unit carbon emission added value and unit carbon emission conversion turnover as output factors. It constructs an SBM-DEA model to measure the carbon emission efficiency of the logistics industry in Hubei China. Finally, based on the research results, a carbon emission reduction path for the logistics industry in Hubei Province is proposed, including strengthen policy guidance and reasonably set freight rates; transfer of high carbon emission transportation methods; extend the logistics value chain and carry out logistics technology innovation.The research conclusion can provide theoretical support for the government.

Keywords. Low Carbon Constraints; Logistics; All Elements; Carbon Emission Efficiency.

1. Introduction

With the arrival of the new "retail revolution" era, Logistics industry becomes a significant guarantee for driving consumption and promoting economic development. Hubei Province, as the intersection of China's economic sectors, has favorable congenital conditions for developing the logistics industry. However, Logistics industry is also one of the most significant sources of carbon emissions, accounting for 18.9% of the total amount. It is the only sector among the five major industries of agriculture, industry, construction, and commerce where the proportion of carbon emissions continues to rise. Therefore, the government has paid much attention to the low-carbon transformation of logistics and has made the low-carbon development model a key focus of the logistics development.

At present, there is relatively little research on the carbon emission efficiency (CEE) of the logistics industry both domestically and internationally. More scholars are studying the CEE of the transportation industry, mainly focusing on traditional single factor CEE [1-5]. There is even less research on the comprehensive CEE of the logistics

---

[1] Corresponding Author: Zhaojun WU, E-mail: 3230810@qq.com.

industry based on production function theory and considering energy input and carbon emission output [6-7]. In addition, DEA and its improved models are the main methods for measuring CEE, but there is almost no research on measuring the efficiency of all factor CEE using the SBM model based on relaxed variables and the improved DEA model based on the common frontier Meta Frontier production function [8-11]. The research of this project has high reference value for how to achieve higher logistics output and minimize environmental pollution with fewer resources, labor, and energy inputs. It has important theoretical significance for filling the research gaps and gaps in the field of CEE measurement.

2. Definition of Core Concepts

2.1. Single Factor/Total Factor CEE

The current definition of CEE in research is based on two perspectives: single factor and total factor.

Single factor CEE: refers to the ratio of carbon emissions to individual input variables, such as carbon emissions per unit energy consumption (i.e., carbon index). There are currently some studies that consider carbon emissions per GDP (i.e., carbon intensity) as CEE, but generally speaking, low carbon intensity does not necessarily indicate high CEE.

Total factor CEE: refers to the CEE that comprehensively considers input factors such as capital, manpower, energy, as well as output factors such as GDP and carbon emissions. Due to the unexpected output of carbon emissions, the smaller the value, the better. Therefore, the total factor CEE is defined as the maximum GDP and minimum carbon emissions that can be achieved by investing a fixed amount of capital, manpower, and energy elements at a certain technological level.

2.2. Total Factor CEE of Logistics Industry

The input factors of Logistics industry are similar to other industries, including capital, labor, energy, etc. Unlike other industries, the essence of logistics services is "providing displacement of people and things". Therefore, this article believes that the output indicators of Logistics industry should choose the physical form indicator - transportation turnover. In addition, since energy consumption data related to Logistics industry cannot be directly obtained, and Transportation, Warehousing, and Postal industries can approximately represent Logistics industry, and the data can be directly used from statistical yearbooks. This article uses data from Transportation, Warehousing, and Postal industries in Hubei Province to represent the logistics industry.

The total factor CEE of Logistics industry means: the maximum conversion turnover and minimum carbon emissions that can be achieved by investing a fixed amount of capital, manpower, and energy elements at a certain level of technology. The total factor CEE of Logistics industry is a relative efficiency, which ranges from 0 to 1.

3. Calculation of Logistics Carbon Emission in Hubei Province

There are significant distinctions when calculating carbon emissions and carbon dioxide emissions. This study focuses on the carbon dioxide emissions, and the descriptions of carbon emissions in the study all represent carbon dioxide emissions. According to the IPCC (2006), greenhouse gases mainly composed of carbon dioxide, in addition to those generated by nature itself, mainly come from fossil fuels combustion. The calculation methods are divided into two types: the "top-down" and the "bottom-up" method. This article uses the "top-down" method. The calculation formula is as follows:

$$C = \sum_i C_i = \sum_i E_i F_i \tag{1}$$

In Formula (1), i represents form of energy; C represents carbon emissions; Ci is emission of the i-th energy form; Ei is consumption amount of the i-th energy form; Fi is carbon emission factor. The carbon emission factors of different fossil fuels are shown in Table 1.

Table 1 Carbon Emission Factors for Each Energy Type   Unit: kgCO2/kg or m3

Energy type	Raw Coal	Crude Oil	Gasoline	Kerosene	Diesel Oil	Fuel Oil	Natural Gas
Emission factors	1.9003	3.0202	2.9251	3.0179	3.0959	3.1705	2.1622

According to Formula (1) and Table 1, the carbon emissions of Hubei's logistics industry from 2012 to 2022 can be calculated as shown in Figure 1.

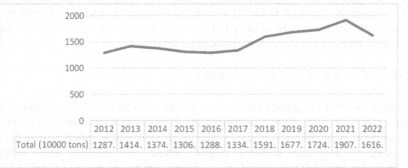

	2012	2013	2014	2015	2016	2017	2018	2019	2020	2021	2022
Total (10000 tons)	1287.	1414.	1374.	1306.	1288.	1334.	1591.	1677.	1724.	1907.	1616.

Figure 1 Logistics industry carbon emissions in Hubei Province

4. Measurement of Total Factor CEE of Logistics Industry in Hubei Province

4.1. Production Technology Collection

Assuming that Logistics industry is a DMU (denoted as O), each DMU has M input elements, and the element set is denoted as $x = (x_1, x_2, x_3, \dots x_{a,}) \in R_+^M$; N expected output elements, with the element set denoted as $y = (y_1, y_2, y_3, \dots y_{b,}) \in R_+^N$; Type I non expected output elements, with the element set denoted as $z = (z_1, z_2, z_3, \dots z_{c,}) \in R_+^I$; The production technology set for the t-th :

$$P^t(x^t) = \begin{cases} (y^t, b^t) \mid \sum_{q=1}^{O} \lambda_q^t y_{qn}^t, n = 1, \dots, N \\[2mm] \sum_{q=1}^{O} \lambda_q^t x_{qm}^t \le x_m^t, m = 1, \dots, M \\[2mm] \sum_{q=1}^{O} \lambda_q^t b_{qi}^t = b_i^t, i = 1, \dots, I \\[2mm] \sum_{q=1}^{O} \lambda_q^t = 1, \lambda_q^t \ge 0, q = 1, \dots, Q \end{cases} \tag{2}$$

In equation (2), λ_q^t represents the weight of the input and output values of the qth DMU in the t-th period. When the Constant Returns to Scale (CRS) of production technology remains unchanged, $\lambda_q^t \ge 0$; When the variable returns to scale (VRS) of production technology is variable, $\sum_q^O \lambda_q^t = 1, \lambda_q^t \ge 0$.

The above production technology concentration data is the observed values under the production technology level of the t period, without considering the non-synchronicity of the reference technology, and there is a certain deviation in the measured efficiency results. To ensure the synchronization of reference technologies, some scholars have proposed a global production technology set:

$$P^G(x) = \begin{cases} (y^t, b^t) \mid \sum_{t=1}^{T} \sum_{q=1}^{O} \lambda_q^t y_{qn}^t \ge y_n^t, n = 1, \dots, N \\[2mm] \sum_{t=1}^{T} \sum_{q=1}^{O} \lambda_q^t x_{qm}^t \le x_m^t, m = 1, \dots, M \\[2mm] \sum_{t=1}^{T} \sum_{q=1}^{O} \lambda_q^t b_{qi}^t = b_i^t, i = 1, \dots, I \\[2mm] \sum_{q=1}^{O} \lambda_q^t = 1, \lambda_q^t \ge 0, q = 1, \dots, Q \end{cases} \tag{3}$$

In equation (3), $P^G(x) = P^1(x^1) \cup \dots \cup P^t(x^t)$, the global production technology set is the union of the production technology sets for each period, that is, the sample data for periods 1 to t use the same production frontier, making the measured efficiency comparable.

4.2. Construction of Directional SBM-GML Index Measurement Model

In traditional radial DEA models, one of the basic requirements is to minimize input while maximizing corresponding output. In this regard, some scholars have expanded and generalized the non-radial and non-angular directional distance function based on the previous work [12-14]. This article draws inspiration from this processing method and obtains the global directional SBM model as follows:

$$S_v^G(x_o^t, y_o^t, b_o^t; g^x, g^y, g^b) = \max_{s^x, s^y, s^b} \frac{\frac{1}{M}\sum_{m=1}^{M}\frac{S_m^x}{g_m^x} + \frac{1}{N+I}(\sum_{n=1}^{N}\frac{S_n^y}{g_n^x} + \sum_{i=1}^{I}\frac{S_i^b}{g_i^b})}{2}$$

$$s.t. \begin{cases} \sum_{t=1}^{T}\sum_{q=1}^{O}\lambda_q^t x_{qm}^t + S_m^x = x_{mO}^t, m=1,...,M \\ \sum_{t=1}^{T}\sum_{q=1}^{O}\lambda_q^t y_{qn}^t - S_n^y = y_{nO}^t, n=1,...,N \\ \sum_{t=1}^{T}\sum_{q=1}^{O}\lambda_q^t b_{qi}^t + S_i^b = b_{iO}^t, i=1,...,I \\ \sum_{q=1}^{O}\lambda_q^t = 1, \lambda_q^t \geq 0, q=1,...,O \\ S_m^x \geq 0, S_n^y \geq 0, S_i^b \geq 0 \end{cases}$$

(4)

In the formula, x_O^t are the vectors of the input elements, y_O^t are the expected output elements, and b_O^t are the unexpected output elements ; g^x、g^y、g^b are the corresponding direction vector; S_m^x、S_n^y、S_i^b are the corresponding relaxation vector.

4.3. GML index model

The M index is an indicator that measures the fluctuate of CEE. To study the changing efficiency including unexpected outputs, this article draws on the research methods of other scholars and further decomposes the GML index into pure efficiency change (GPEC), technological progress rate (GPTC), and scale efficiency change (GSEC) based on the global directional SBM. The relevant calculation formulas are as follows:

$$GML_t^{t+1} = \frac{1 + \vec{S}_v^G(x^t, y^t, b^t; g^t)}{1 + \vec{S}_v^G(x^{t+1}, y^{t+1}, b^{t+1}; g^{t+1})} = GPEC_t^{t+1} \times GPTC_t^{t+1} \times GSEC_t^{t+1}$$

$$GPEC_t^{t+1} = \frac{1 + \vec{S}_v^t(x^t, y^t, b^t; g^t)}{1 + \vec{S}_v^{t+1}(x^{t+1}, y^{t+1}, b^{t+1}; g^{t+1})}$$

$$GPTC_t^{t+1} = \frac{\left[1 + \vec{S}_c^G(x^t, y^t, b^t; g^t)\right] / \left[1 + \vec{S}_c^t(x^t, y^t, b^t; g^t)\right]}{\left[1 + \vec{S}_v^G(x^{t+1}, y^{t+1}, b^{t+1}; g^{t+1})\right] / \left[1 + \vec{S}_v^{t+1}(x^{t+1}, y^{t+1}, b^{t+1}; g^{t+1})\right]}$$

$$GSEC_t^{t+1} = \frac{\left[1 + \vec{S}_v^G(x^t, y^t, b^t; g^t)\right] / \left[1 + \vec{S}_c^G(x^t, y^t, b^t; g^t)\right]}{\left[1 + \vec{S}_v^G(x^{t+1}, y^{t+1}, b^{t+1}; g^{t+1})\right] / \left[1 + \vec{S}_c^G(x^{t+1}, y^{t+1}, b^{t+1}; g^{t+1})\right]}$$

(5)

In the formula, GML_{t+1}、$GPEC_{t+1}$、$GPTC_{t+1}$、$GSEC_{t+1}$ are greater than 1 (less than 1), respectively, indicating an increase (decrease) in total factor carbon emission efficiency, an increase (decrease) in pure technical efficiency, a reversal of technological progress, and an increase (decrease) in scale efficiency; $GML_{t+1} = 1$, it means that the total factor CEE level remains unchanged.

4.4. Input output variable selection

The basic principle of DEA is to establish a production frontier by the input and output variable data of each DMU and calculate the relative efficiency value by measuring the degree of deviation between each DMU and the production frontier. Therefore, the selection of variables directly determines the size of efficiency.

Based on the above considerations and the availability of variable data, combined with the concept of the total factor CEE of the logistics industry, this paper selects three resources, namely labor, capital, and energy, as input factors. When these three elements are input into the transportation production process, in addition to obtaining expected output (converted turnover), they will also bring unexpected output (carbon emissions).

Table 2 Explanation of input-output variables

Classification	Variables	Method of calculation
Input variables	Manpower	The average of employees in the previous and the current year
	Capital stock	Perpetual inventory method
	Energy	Conversion of terminal energy consumption into standard coal
Output variables	Converted turnover	Passenger turnover is converted into freight turnover
	Carbon emissions	The top-down method

4.5. Measurement of Total Factor CEE

Before applying DEA model, it is necessary to test whether each input and output variable has "Isotonicity", that is, whether the input and output variables are correlated. This article uses Pearson correlation analysis for validation, and the results are shown in Table 6. The correlation coefficients of each input and output variable are greater than 0.5 at the 5% significance level. Therefore, the selection of variables is relatively reasonable and suitable for DEA analysis.

Table 3 Correlation Test of Input and Output Variables

	Conversion turnover	Carbon emissions
Practitioners	0.589**(0.000)	0.744**(0.000)
Capital stock	0.846**(0.000)	0.730**(0.000)
Energy input	0.832**(0.000)	0.999**(0.000)

Based on the variable data of the logistics industry in Hubei Province from 2012 to 2022 and the directional SBM-GML index model, this section uses MaxDEA6.8pro software to calculate the total factor CEE of the logistics industry. The results are presented in Figure 2.

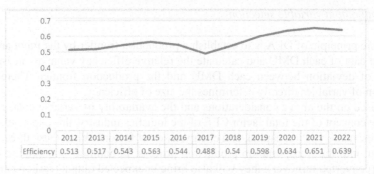

	2012	2013	2014	2015	2016	2017	2018	2019	2020	2021	2022
Efficiency	0.513	0.517	0.543	0.563	0.544	0.488	0.54	0.598	0.634	0.651	0.639

Figure 2 Carbon Emission Efficiency of Logistics Industry in Hubei Province from 2012 to 2022

From the results, we can notice that the overall CEE of the logistics industry in Hubei Province from 2012 to 2017 was relatively low, due to the rapid development of society and economy in Hubei, with a large amount of capital investment and relatively complete transportation infrastructure. However, the large, expected output generated by these investments is not enough to cover up the lack of producing massive, unexpected outputs, resulting in a low level of overall factor CEE. From 2018 to 2022, CEE steadily increased. The increase from 0.54 to 0.64 reflects that after transportation infrastructure construction, the CEE of logistics has also improved. However, the average CEE over the years is only 0.56, which is at a moderate level. This indicates that there is ample room for Logistics industry carbon emission reduction in Hubei Province.

5. Research on path of logistics industry carbon emission reduction in Hubei Province

Against the backdrop of the country's vigorous promotion of carbon emission reduction, Hubei Province can scientifically and effectively guide prices in combination with carbon tax policies; Focusing on railway and waterway transportation with lower carbon emissions, enhancing the optimization level of transportation routes and improving the efficiency of multi-modal transportation networks; Seize the important opportunity of industrial digitization, develop smart logistics, and extend the logistics value chain; Strengthen the information construction, improve technological content, and accelerate high-quality development.

Acknowledgment

This project is supported by Research topic of China Society of Logistics (2023CSLKT3-146)

References

[1]   Salvatore Saija, Daniela Romano. A methodology for the estimation of road transport air emissions in urban areas of Italy [J]. Atmospheric Environment, 2002, 36(34):5377-5383.
[2]   Schipper L, Marie-Lilliu C, Gorham R. Flexing the Link between Urban Transport and CO2 Emissions: A Path for the World Bank[C]. International Energy Agency, 2000.

[3] Mensink C, IDE Vlieger, J Nys. An urban transport emission model for the Antwerp area [J]. Atmospheric Environment, 2000, 34:4595-4602.

[4] He Kebin, Huo Hong, Zhang Qiang, et al. Walsh. Oil consumption and CO2 emissions in China's road transport: current status, future trends, and policy implications [J]. Energy Policy, 2005, 33:1499-1507.

[5] Lin Tzu-Ping. Carbon dioxide emissions from transport in Taiwan's national parks [J]. Tourism Management, 2010, 31(2):285-290.

[6] T.V. Ramachandra, Shwetmala. Emissions from India's transport sector: Statewise synthesis [J]. Energy Policy, 2009, 37:3259-3267.

[7] Risto Herrala, Rajeev K. Goel. Global CO2 efficiency: Country-wise estimates using a stochastic cost frontier [J]. Energy Policy, 2012, 45(7):762-770.

[8] Rungrapee P, Roengchai T. Dynamic impacts of energy efficiency, economic growth, and renewable energy consumption on carbon emissions: Evidence from Markov Switching model[J]. Energy Reports,2023,9(S12):332-336.

[9] Kgaugelo R M, Khumbulani M, Tijani O A. Energy and Carbon Emission Efficiency Prediction: Applications in Future Transport Manufacturing[J]. Energies,2021,14(24):8466-8466.

[10] Greening L A, Ting M, Davis W B. Decomposition of aggregate carbon intensity for freight: Trends from 10 OECD countries for the period 1971-1993[J]. Energy Economics, 1999, 21(4):331-361.

[11] Färe.R, Grosskopf.S. Directional distance functions and slacks-based measures of efficiency [J]. European Journal of Operational Research, 2010:1(1):320-322.

[12] FUKUYAMA H, WEBER W L. A directional slacks -based measure of technical inefficiency [J]. Socio-Economic Planning Sciences, 2009, 43(4):274-287.

[13] Tone.K. A Slacks based Measure of Efficiency in Data Envelopment Analysis [J]. European Journal of Operational Research, 2001(130):498-509.

[14] M' baye A. Carbon Emission Efficiency Best Practices: A Case Study in an Industrial Site[J]. Journal of Energy Research and Reviews,2022:10-23。

Artificial Intelligence, Medical Engineering and Education
Z.B. Hu et al. (Eds.)
© *2024 The Authors.*

doi:10.3233/ATDE231327

Modernization of E-Commerce and Logistics Platforms of Enterprises Based on Artificial Intelligence Technology

Alovsat G. Aliyev[1], Roza O.Shahverdiyeva, Ulker H.Hagverdiyeva
Institute of Information Technology, Baku, Azerbaijan
E-mail: alovsat_qaraca@mail.ru[1]; shahverdiyevar@gmail.com; ulker_haqverdiyeva@mail.ru
ORCID ID: *orcid.org/0000-0002-1174-8036 (Alovsat Aliyev)*
ORCID ID: *orcid.org/0000-0003-0842-7300 (Roza Shahverdiyeva)*

Abstract. E-commerce systems have become one of the global trends in the current era when large-scale technological innovations are rapidly applied to all fields of activity. In particular, in recent times, the digital transformation of the economy and society has created conditions for the massive replacement of traditional trade with electronic trade. The rapid development of e-commerce has led to the emergence of many modern trends in the activity sectors, the formation of new requirements for e-commerce systems, and the beginning of a new era in logistics and supply chain management. An overview analysis of relevant scientific research works was conducted and the state of problem solving was studied. Providing a personalized approach to customers, optimizing supply chain operations, and responding to customer inquiries in a timely and accurate manner are the problems that await their solution. For this reason, in the presented article, directions for improving the performance of e-commerce systems and optimizing supply chain management processes by applying innovative technologies such as artificial intelligence, the Internet of Things, and big data have been studied. A conceptual model of intelligent e-commerce systems has been proposed based on the application of these technologies. Appropriate recommendations were given for modernizing e-commerce and logistics platforms applied at the national, regional, and enterprise levels based on new digital transformation technologies.

Keywords: *digital transformation, e-commerce and logistics platforms, single window, artificial intelligence technologies*

1. Introduction

E-commerce systems involve the display of products and services to consumers through the Internet and the implementation of the online purchase and sale process. For this purpose, e-commerce systems and platforms based on various models are used. E-commerce systems operate as complex system that includes ICT technologies such as appropriate technical means, software products, Internet protocols, and human resources that enable the automation of numerous operations [1]. These systems, on the one hand, allow buyers to review a wide range of product catalogs offered by various companies and purchase the desired product through online payment at any time, from any location,

---

[1] Corresponding Author: Alovsat Aliyev. E-mail: alovsat_qaraca@mail.ru.

simply by accessing the Internet. On the other hand, it allows enterprises to show their products to more customers at a lower cost, engage in trade on a global scale, and respond more quickly to the modern demands of the market [2]. For this reason, at present, almost many enterprises use e-commerce systems to display their products on the Internet. Thus, the sharp increase in the participants in the e-commerce market has led to the strengthening of competition in this sector, the emergence of new global trends, as well as deficiencies in the existing infrastructure of e-commerce systems [3]. Despite all the mentioned superior features, in the modern era, there is a need for the application of modern technologies such as artificial intelligence, the Internet of Things, and big data analytics in e-commerce to strengthen the position of e-commerce systems and technologies in the international economic arena, as well as to optimize the process of organizing e-commerce activities at the national, regional and enterprise levels. These problems are quite important, their solution is in the center of attention of the society as an urgent issue.

The purpose of the study. The main goal of conducting scientific research is to create a conceptual model for the modernization of information systems and other platforms of innovative production and sales enterprises on e-commerce and logistics based on the application of artificial intelligence methods and technologies, as well as to develop the basis of a scientific-theoretical and methodological approach to the study of prospective development problems. was. Here, on the basis of the wide application of the digital technologies of the Industry 4.0 platform, attention was paid to the development of recommendations on the overall improvement of the e-commerce platforms of enterprises and the modernization of its components. Digital technologies of Industry 4.0, including the application of artificial intelligence methods in various fields, have been studied. Based on the application of digital innovative technologies, the initial version of the conceptual model of the intellectualization of E-commerce systems has been developed.

The importance of conducting research is to transfer them to modern and effective e-commerce systems by improving e-commerce and logistics platforms based on the digital technologies of the Industry 4.0 platform, based on international trends and requirements. Effective management of the sales, logistics, and equipment chain in modern e-commerce systems and logistics platforms of enterprises, optimization of supply chain operations, prompt and accurate response to customer inquiries, and automation of technological processes performed at delivery points by means of IoT technology. Artificial intelligence methods are used to analyze sales records, current trends in the market, current trends in social media, etc. allows to perform intellectual analysis of such data. In this process, the improvement of e-commerce systems based on the principle of a single window with the application of artificial intelligence, a unified customer experience, intelligent search capabilities, customer support, managing customer inquiries of artificial intelligence chatbots, providing real-time support and assisting in the execution of tasks with various customer services, the formation of appropriate solution mechanisms in the processes of demand forecasting, fraud detection, and security assurance can be considered as important issues.

Research methods used. Systematic analysis, data analysis, correlation analysis, econometric modeling methods, multi-criteria expert evaluation method, information theory, algorithmization, CRM systems, artificial intelligence technology, and ICT in the modernization of e-commerce and logistics platforms of innovative production and sales enterprises, in the development of its prospective development directions and so on. such research methods were used.

Research methodology. In the article, the e-commerce and logistics platforms of innovative production and sales-type enterprises and the prospective development directions of their modernization are taken as the object of research.

The issue of effective application of artificial intelligence to e-commerce and logistics platforms is included in the research subject.

A systematic approach was implemented to determine the prospective development directions of the modernization of e-commerce and logistics platforms of enterprises on the basis of artificial intelligence technology. The methodological requirements of the application of the main technologies of e-commerce systems to the development of the digital economy on the Industry 4.0 platform have been taken into account. The scientific-theoretical and methodological foundations of the formation of intellectual systems were used in the development of the conceptual structure model of the intellectual e-commerce system. Methodical proposals and recommendations for increasing the level of stability of e-commerce systems have been developed. Global economic development trends, requirements of high ICT technologies, and methodological requirements of the main trends of the 4.0 Industry platform were also taken into account in ensuring the sustainability of electronic commerce systems.

2. An Overview Analysis of Relevant Related Scientific Research Works and the State of the Problem

E-commerce and logistics platforms of innovative production and sales enterprises increase their operational efficiency. The development of mechanisms for solving the problems of their modernization on the basis of artificial intelligence methods and technologies is distinguished by its importance, modernity, and relevance. Nevertheless, that field has not yet been properly formed. In the scientific literature, there is still no systematic development and multifaceted analysis of its conceptual foundations. Therefore, the existing theoretical and practical aspects of the problems of modernization of e-commerce and logistics platforms of enterprises on the basis of artificial intelligence technology should be further analyzed and researched. It is necessary to study the processing aspects and semantic content of the existing concepts in that field, as well as to study the perspectives and limitations of the transition of production and consumption to a new management system. It should be noted that the authors of the articles, like other researchers, have many publications in this field in different years, in different databases, including in different scientific journals indexed in the MECS database [1-6, 8-16].

In this regard, it should be noted that [4] in the post-coronavirus period, regulation of e-commerce systems and prospective development problems were studied. The advantages that lead to the strengthening of the position of e-commerce in the international economic space have been revealed. The functions of electronic business models corresponding to the commercial stages of the enterprise's activity have been explained. In the article, the issues of the application of modern technologies such as 3D modeling, the Internet of Things, artificial intelligence, and big data in electronic commerce systems were considered. The application characteristics and regulation mechanisms of E-commerce systems, which have a direct stimulating effect on economic growth, in real economic sectors have been investigated.

[5] is devoted to the development of ecobot intelligent conversational agent for e-commerce applications using the Deep learning method. The importance of this research is to reduce the system's human dependency and improve customer support by providing

human-like natural responses using a deep learning method on specially designed data. Here, based on the creation of a common data set that is used for all types of products, the user's intentions during queries are precisely determined by the bot through deep learning.

[6] have conducted studies on QR code behavior on commercial-based platforms using Machine learning. A "quick response" code, or QR code, is designed to quickly decode large amounts of information. Any controlled device, such as a smartphone, can hold it and it is easy to access by simply scanning the 2D matrix code. The dataset is analyzed using machine learning techniques, such as matrix calculus, which is used for the Bayesian algorithm. QR code generation is extended to cover all products. Customers are provided with advantages such as fast, error-free access and the ability to store large amounts of data. Generally, many people use online payment for any transaction and it can be done anytime anywhere. Cash is not a good option for large payments. Therefore, many retailers are joining e-wallet systems and making payments with flexible and faster transactions.

In [12], the trends of expanding the application of IoT technology in the development stages of e-commerce were analyzed. Along with the advantages of applying IoT technology in logistics processes in the e-commerce sphere, the challenges ahead from a technical point of view were also deeply investigated in the research work. An intelligent logistics system architecture based on the application of IoT technology is proposed for the optimization of logistics operations in e-commerce systems.

In [13], it is shown that the application of big data analytics, cloud computing, the Internet of Things, mobile Internet, social media, and other innovative technologies in e-commerce are quite relevant. With the application of these technologies, a unified architecture of intelligent e-commerce systems with higher operational efficiency and greater business opportunities has been proposed. The author has explored the main problems related to intelligent e-commerce systems and made recommendations on possible research directions.

In [14], the current situation of the logistics network in cross-border e-commerce was analyzed in-depth, and detailed information was given about the existing problems. In the research work, the issue of the application of the wide possibilities of artificial intelligence in logistics processes was considered, the effectiveness of the application of artificial intelligence in such directions as optimization of the delivery process, realization of unmanned delivery, intelligent management of the warehouse, intelligent management of transport in both domestic and cross-border e-commerce was carried out.

In [15], a comparative analysis of various logistics models applied in the e-commerce process in North America, Europe, Asia, and other regions and the technical equipment used in the implementation of these models was conducted.

3. Application of the Latest ICT and Artificial İntelligence Technologies in E-Commerce and Supply Chain Operations Optimization

It is known that the massiveness of E-commerce systems requires the collection of large amounts of data. Therefore, the demand for large-scale data processing in the management work of that field has increased [8].

The high demand for protection and management of all this data created by consumers and businesses is also driving the creation and development of data centers built on cloud providers [11].

In addition, one of the most important factors affecting customer satisfaction in the e-commerce sector in modern times is logistics performance. Thus, delays in the delivery of orders and other emerging problems cause great dissatisfaction among consumers. This ultimately leads to the loss of regular customers and a decrease in income. In this regard, one of the most important factors in organizing the efficient operation of e-commerce systems, in general, is the optimal management of the supply chain [14]. Supply chain management refers to the management of all processes from raw materials to product production and delivery of the manufactured product to the end user. These processes include 1) Execution of orders; 2) Inventory management; 3) Transportation; 4) Reception, storage, transportation, and packaging of goods; 5) Establishing a unified logistics network. In order to ensure the implementation of all these processes, Supply Chain Management (SCM) systems integrated into e-commerce systems are used. SCM systems coordinate the activities of suppliers, manufacturers, logistics partners, wholesale distributors, retailers, and end consumers, in short, all participants of the supply chain and control this wide network.

In contrast to traditional logistics, the concept of modern logistics, formed under the influence of the e-commerce environment, has a number of new features. So, if traditional logistics included the organization of inventory, storage, transportation, and distribution, modern logistics takes into account many factors such as operational flexibility, optimal management, technical and technological equipment, and economic efficiency. In this regard, the management of logistics processes to ensure the timely and accurate delivery of orders given by consumers is a very complex issue that requires the implementation of intellectual activity with the application of modern technologies [15].

Today, the Internet of Things technology, which is widely used in "smart" homes, transportation, health care, agriculture, military, commerce, and other fields, is a dynamic distributed environment and includes intelligent devices that can understand the processes happening around. The application of IoT technology in e-commerce, which enables the creation of a single infrastructure that connects all objects within the organization, plays an important role in improving logistics services, which are an integral part of the e-commerce process in particular [12]. Thus, thanks to IoT technology, interconnected physical devices record data related to physical processes occurring in the environment through special sensors and transmit those data to cloud resources for processing via wireless communication. Here, the process of obtaining information from raw data is carried out using big data analytical processing methods. Based on the resulting useful information, those physical devices can make automatic decisions, as well as interact with each other and people in real-time. The real-time analysis of the data obtained about the condition of the product at various stages of the supply chain allows the enterprise to ensure the transparency of the logistics process and minimize possible threats and cases of fraud. Also, by equipping products with special IoT tags, consumers have the opportunity to dynamically track the movement of their parcels [12]. At the same time, IoT technology enables the automation of processes performed at delivery points and thus allows to minimize of a number of problems such as incorrect placement of products in the warehouse, slow and incorrect delivery of the order, and incorrect packaging.

4. Prospects of Application of Artificial İntelligence Technology in E-Commerce and Logistics Systems

In modern times, artificial intelligence is one of the most widely used technologies in creating innovative mechanisms aimed at optimizing and improving operations performed not only in logistics but also in e-commerce as a whole. Thus, with the application of IoT technology, a very large amount of raw data is collected from various sensors, as well as from various other sources, and the only way to benefit from these data is their intelligent analysis. This can only be done with the application of artificial intelligence technology methods such as machine learning and deep learning methods. The application of this technology in logistics platforms, which involves the creation of intelligent computer systems that can think like humans, and perform human-like behavior such as problem-solving, decision-making, and reasoning, allows for improvements in the following areas:

- *Demand forecasting and inventory management.* Artificial intelligence allows for intellectual analysis of data such as sales records, current trends in the market, current trends in social media, etc. This, in turn, allows SCM systems to more accurately predict market demand and determine the amount of inventory corresponding to that demand. Such optimal inventory management allows for ensuring the constant availability of goods in high demand, as well as avoidance of unnecessary loading in the warehouse [16].
- *Real-time route optimization.* Through the application of machine learning and deep learning methods, determining the optimal route for delivery is ensured by taking into account a large number of different factors such as road conditions, weather conditions, priority destinations, vehicle capacity, etc. This allows to increase efficiency in logistics operations. Due to the continuous processing and analysis of data collected from various sources (sensors, systems) in real-time, the system dynamically generates the optimal route. This allows to reduce transportation costs and increase customer satisfaction. Thus, the system allows dispatchers to adapt to changing conditions and make informed decisions, significantly increasing the efficiency of distribution and also reducing traffic congestion [14].
- *Supplier Management.* Based on various indicators, intelligent assessment of the service quality of suppliers, and analysis of positive and negative trends in their activity, it is possible to identify reliable suppliers and predict potential disruptions in activity or quality-related problems in advance. This enables proactive management of suppliers in general by preventing potential risks, improvement of cooperative relationships established with suppliers, and selecting reliable suppliers.
- *Equipment optimization and maintenance forecasting.* Artificial intelligence can be used to monitor the performance of vehicles, machinery, and other logistics equipment, as well as technical failures. Intelligent analysis of data generated by machines, collected from various sensors and technical records with the application of machine learning algorithms will enable the prediction of potential technical failures that may occur in equipment operating in the warehouse, logistics, and production processes, as well as maintenance needs, and optimization of maintenance schedules. Thus, it is possible to minimize unexpected downtime due to technical failure in the work process, increase equipment reliability and optimize maintenance costs [17, 18].

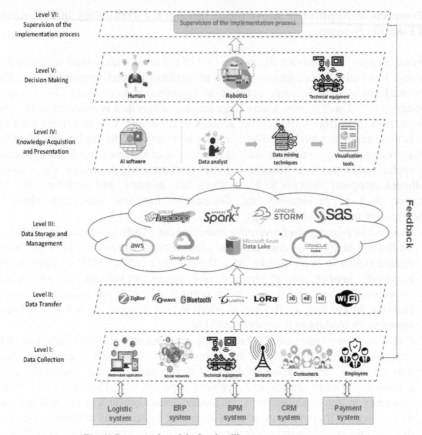

Fig. 1. Conceptual model of an intelligent e-commerce system

5. Conceptual Model Of Intellectualization of E-Commerce Systems

The rapid development of modern technologies and their application in e-commerce and logistics systems allow the intellectualization of traditional e-commerce systems. Due to the joint application of big data, the cloud, the Internet of Things, artificial intelligence, and other innovative technologies, a modern and intelligent e-commerce model with features such as high operational efficiency, intelligent information processing, and decision-making is being formed [13]. Taking into account the mentioned possibilities and perspectives, the conceptual model of the modern intellectual e-commerce system was developed as shown in Figure 1.

In the presented conceptual scheme, the architecture of intelligent e-commerce systems (IES) is described from the point of view of data flow. Here, the processes of converting data collected from various sources into information, information into knowledge, and making and applying decisions based on knowledge are reflected. In this regard, the conceptual scheme of IES has been built on a 6-level architecture:

Level I: Data Collection. This is the lowest level. According to the scheme, the data collected during the activity of the e-commerce ecosystem are mainly generated in the various subsystems that make up it. Thus, data comes from various subsystems, as well as web/mobile applications, social media, hardware, sensors, mobile devices, consumers, employees, and other sources [9]. Thus, due to the application of physical and virtual sensors, data on the status of both consumers and individual structures (enterprises) that make up the e-commerce ecosystem are recorded in IES.

Level II: Data Transfer. Different methods of data transfer and different standards are used at this level, as the data is obtained from very different sources and there are inconsistencies between them. Examples of these are ZigBee, Zwave, Bluetooth, 4G/5G, WiFi, etc. can be noted. As you can see, both human-to-machine and machine-to-machine connections are supported here. As a result, a large number of communication modes are applied at the data transmission level.

Level III: Data storage and management. At this level, the storage and management capabilities of traditional e-commerce systems cannot handle the large volume of data generated. Therefore, at this level, cloud technology and other IT solutions are applied to store, manage, analyze, and visualize the results of large volumes of data. Currently, many large IT companies provide users with cloud services that include these capabilities [10]. Examples of these are Oracle Cloud, AWS (Amazon Web Services) Cloud, Google Cloud, Microsoft Azure Data Lake, etc. can be noted. In addition, Apache Hadoop, Apache Spark, Apache Storm, SAS, etc., provide big data processing and analysis in a distributed computing environment. various software tools, as well as unstructured data storage and management NoSQL type database management systems, are applied [7]. Thus, structured, semi-structured, and unstructured data collected from various sources are transferred to the cloud using various network standards and stored there, and processing of this raw data is ensured by the application of big data processing tools. Thus, the necessary information is obtained from the data.

Level IV: Knowledge acquisition and presentation. At this level, knowledge acquisition from the information obtained is done. Here, the acquisition of knowledge is performed by both human experts and various hardware and software based on artificial intelligence. Useful information, that is, knowledge, is obtained by applying various methods and algorithms of knowledge acquisition. Then, by using various visualization tools, the acquired knowledge is put into an understandable format for the decision-maker, visualized and presented in various reports, charts, personalized recommendations, etc. submission is executed.

Level V: Decision Making. This level is characterized by making decisions in real-time based on the acquired knowledge. It should be noted that, unlike traditional e-commerce systems, both human specialists (managers) and robots, and various technical equipment equipped with sensors act as decision-makers in IES. Decisions made at this level help employees at all other levels take action with more confidence.

Level VI: Supervision of the implementation process. Actions performed on the basis of previously made decisions at this level create feedback with the first layer, and as a result, new data are obtained. In other words, all these steps or processes are repeated throughout the activity of the e-commerce ecosystem.

Thus, the intellectual e-commerce model, built on a unified network that integrates traditional e-commerce systems with technologies such as cloud computing, the Internet of Things, big data, etc., supports various types of interactions, including human-to-human, human-to-machine, and machine-to-machine. By enabling real-time analysis of collected data, it facilitates the decision-making process based on knowledge.

In addition, we would like to make some predictions about the application of the latest achievements and trends in the ICT sphere. Thus, in modern e-commerce and logistics systems, within the framework of artificial intelligence technology, ChatGPT, a new language model, can be effectively applied to improve customer support and experience, provide personalized recommendations, and help in product search and selection. Some of its main applications include the following:

1. Improving customer service. ChatGPT can handle customer inquiries and participate in real-time responses to inquiries. He can answer frequently asked questions, solve common problems, and guide customers through the purchasing process. This helps reduce the workload of human operators performing the same task and minimize response time.

2. Product recommendations. ChatGPT can analyze customers' preferences, purchase histories, and behavioral patterns to create personalized product recommendations. Thus, it can identify products that match the interests of consumers and increase the likelihood of sales by offering them to consumers.

3. Product search and selection. ChatGPT can help buyers find the right products by understanding customer requirements and making relevant offers. Thus, customers can describe their needs in plain language without dealing with different interfaces of different e-commerce platforms. A chatbot can help narrow down choices, suggest alternatives, or provide detailed information about specific products based on this description.

4. Involvement of consumers. Thanks to the aforementioned capabilities, ChatGPT provides customers with a more interactive and personalized experience, driving increased customer satisfaction and loyalty.

It is important to note that while ChatGPT can significantly improve an e-commerce system, it needs human supervision to ensure accuracy, manage complex situations, and protect data privacy and security.

6. Improvement of E-Commerce Systems Based on the Single-Window Principle with the Application of Artificial Intelligence

The single-window e-commerce model involves the creation of a single platform for customers that integrates various e-commerce services. Artificial intelligence can be applied in several directions in the improvement of e-commerce systems based on a single window:

1.A seamless customer experience. With the application of artificial intelligence, the analysis of existing trends in the market, as well as by use of customer data, personalized recommendations, discounts, as well as the automatic presentation of private content to each customer or customer group can be achieved.

2. Intelligent search capabilities. AI-powered search algorithms can improve the product search process within a one-stop e-commerce model. Advanced methods such as natural language processing and machine learning can improve search accuracy, offer relevant product suggestions, and help customers find the right products quickly and efficiently.

3.Customer support. AI-powered chatbots can handle customer inquiries, provide real-time support, and assist with various customer service tasks. Chatbots can be integrated into a one-stop e-commerce platform to answer customer queries, provide product information and resolve common issues. This reduces the burden on human agents and provides round-the-clock assistance for customers.

4.Demand forecasting. Artificial intelligence algorithms can analyze sales history, customer behaviors, and market trends to provide demand forecasting. By understanding customer preferences and predicting future demand, a one-stop shop can optimize inventory management on an e-commerce platform, ensure product availability, and prevent stock-outs or excess inventory.

5.Fraud detection and security. Artificial intelligence can enhance the security of a one-stop e-commerce platform by detecting and preventing fraudulent activities. Artificial intelligence algorithms can analyze transaction data, user behavior patterns, and other relevant information to identify potential fraudulent activities such as unauthorized access or suspicious transactions and take appropriate measures to mitigate risks and protect sensitive customer information.

Integrating artificial intelligence technologies into a one-stop e-commerce model can improve customer experience, simplify operations, increase efficiency, and drive growth. It provides valuable information for decision-making to business enterprises while providing a more personalized, intelligent, and accurate e-commerce experience for customers.

7. Conclusion

In modern times, the acceleration of the digital transformation process creates conditions for the formation and development of a global digital environment and virtual relationships in many fields of activity. As this process affects most sectors of activity, it also affects the e-commerce sphere and causes the emergence of a number of global trends and the formation of the modern concept of commerce and logistics. There is a need to modernize e-commerce and logistics systems with the application of innovative technologies to ensure adaptation to these trends and meet the modern demands of the market. In e-commerce, the integrated application of artificial intelligence with modern technologies such as big data, the cloud, Internet of Things ensures the creation of a comprehensive service platform with automatic perception, identification, and visualization capabilities, and the seamless integration of transitions between separate transactions that make up the e-commerce process. It creates conditions for the effective distribution of resources at the national and regional level, optimization of inventory management, optimization of logistics processes in general, significant reduction of costs, and improvement of service quality.

Results and discussion. Wide application of artificial intelligence technologies is necessary to promote the sustainable development of e-commerce/commercial and logistics platforms in order to ensure the innovative development of the regional and national economy on an inclusive basis. Despite the acceptance of the worldwide consequences of such a global development trend, there is still a need to discuss this problem at the local, regional, and national level, and to be used by large groups of people and enterprises.

Modernization of e-commerce and logistics platforms on the basis of artificial intelligence technology, e-commerce systems on the Internet and their types, increasing the effectiveness of e-commerce systems on the Industry 4.0 platform, developing recommendations for strengthening the prospective development directions of e-commerce, should form the basis of future discussions and research.

Further modernization of e-commerce and logistics platforms on the basis of artificial intelligence technology should be among the main directions. In the development of e-commerce and logistics processes, the wide application of modern ICT corresponding to the Industry 4.0 platform should be stimulated. Payment and delivery on e-commerce platforms, the Internet of Things, artificial intelligence and machine learning, big data analytics digital technologies should be the subject of a wide discussion in order to justify the improvement of the operational efficiency of e-commerce systems.

Contributions. Modernization of enterprises' e-commerce, including logistics platforms based on artificial intelligence methods and technologies can give a serious boost to the development and sustainability of the digital economy. In this work, a conceptual structural model of the intellectualization of the e-commerce system was proposed. In the presented conceptual model, the architecture of intelligent e-commerce systems is described from the point of view of data flow and analytical processing. Here is the conceptual structural model of intelligent e-commerce systems Level I-Data collection, Level II-Data transmission, Level III-Data storage and management, Level IV-Knowledge acquisition and presentation, Level V-Decision making, Level VI-Execution process built on a 6-level architecture model as a control. The main digital technology trend of the modern era, the solutions to the problems of the application of artificial intelligence methods and technologies can be considered as a tool or mechanism in the development of e-commerce and logistics platforms of enterprises in solving its existing problems.

References

[1]   Aliyev A.G., Shahverdiyeva R.O., Hagverdiyeva U.H. Activity characteristics and perspective development directions of electronic trade platforms in Azerbaijan. Problems of Information Society, 2023, vol.14, no.1, pp.32-42.
[2]   Golubeva A.S. i dr. Rynok elektronnoy kommertsii: Mirovyye tendentsii i Rossiyskiye realii. Ekonomika: vchera, segodnya, zavtra, 2020 t.10, №6-1, c.157-168.
[3]   Kayli Yan. Sovremennyye tendentsii v elektronnom biznese i elektronnoy kommertsii // V sbornike: Materialy mezhdunarodnoy nauchno-prakticheskoy konferentsii «Innovatsii v upravlenii sotsial'no-ekonomicheskimi sistemami» (ICIMSS). Tema plenarnogo zasedaniya: Digital technologies in the management of the crisis and recession, 2020, s.260-264.
[4]   Alovsat Garaja Aliyev, "Problems of Regulation and Prospective Development of E-commerce Systems in the Post-coronavirus Era", International Journal of Information Engineering and Electronic Business, Vol.14, No.6, pp. 14-26, 2022.
[5]   Maria Zafar, "Developing Smart Conversation Agent ECOM-BOT for Ecommerce Applications using Deep Learning and Pattern Matching", International Journal of Information Engineering and Electronic Business, Vol.15, No.2, pp. 1-10, 2023.
[6]   Archana Uriti, Surya Prakash Yalla, "Exploration on Quick Response (QR) Code Behaviour in Commerce based Platforms Using Machine Learning", International Journal of Information Engineering and Electronic Business, Vol.15, No.5, pp. 1-12, 2023.
[7]   Aliguliyev R.M., Hajirahimova M.Sh. Big Data phenomenon: problems and opportunities. Information Technology Problems, 2014, No.2, pp.3-16.
[8]   Feng L., Yuxin Yu. Innovation of e-commerce service mode in the era of Big Data // 7th International Conference on Social Network, Communication and Education (SNCE 2017). Advances in Computer Science Research, 2017, volume 82. pp.874-877.
[9]   Ilieva G. et al. Big Data based system model of electronic commerce. Trakia Journal of Sciences, 2015, vol.13, suppl. 1, pp.407-413.
[10]   David R. et al. Data Age 2025 – The Digitization of the World from Edge to Core. International Data Corporation (IDC), November 2018. https://www.seagate.com/files/www-content/our-story/trends/files/Seagate-WP-DataAge2025-March-2017.pdf
[11]   Mariam Al-Jaberi et al. E-commerce cloud: Opportunities and challenges. proceedings of the 2015 International Conference on Industrial Engineering and Operations Management Dubai, United Arab Emirates (UAE), March 3 – 5, 2015. 978-1-4799-6065-1/15. IEEE.
[12]   Sharma V. et al. Internet of Things (IoT) on e-commerce logistics: A review. Journal of Physics: Conference Series. ICACSE 2020, Ser. 1964 062113, pp.1-9.
[13]   Zhiting S. et al. Smart e-commerce systems: Current status and research challenges. Electron Markets, 2019, 29, pp.221–238. https://doi.org/10.1007/s12525-017-0272-3.

[14] Jihua Shi. Research on optimization of cross-border e-commerce logistics distribution network in the context of Artificial Intelligence. Hindawi Mobile Information Systems, volume 2022, Article ID 3022280, 11 pages. https://doi.org/10.1155/2022/3022280.

[15] Ying Yu et al. E-commerce logistics in supply chain management: Practice perspective. Elsevier Procedia CIRP 52 (2016), pp.179–185.

[16] Hicham K. et al. The rising trends of smart e-commerce logistics. IEEE Open Access Journal, 2023, volume 11, pp.33839-33857.

[17] Morozova O.YU. Internet veshchey v logistike. Ekonomika: vchera, segodnya, zavtra, 2021, T.11, №6-1, s.296-302.

[18] Ikramov M.M., Dzhumaniyazova M.YU. Rol' iskusstvennogo intellekta v razvitiye elektronnoy kommertsii // Ekonomika i biznes: teoriya i praktika, 2021, №5-2(75), s. 21-24.

Artificial Intelligence, Medical Engineering and Education
Z.B. Hu et al. (Eds.)
© 2024 The Authors.
This article is published online with Open Access by IOS Press and distributed under the terms
of the Creative Commons Attribution Non-Commercial License 4.0 (CC BY-NC 4.0).
doi:10.3233/ATDE231328

Engineering Solutions Synthesis Based on Morphological Knowledge-Based Engineering

Dmitry RAKOV[1]

Mechanical Engineering Research Institute of the Russian Academy of Sciences (IMASH RAN), Moscow 101000, Russia

ORCiD ID: Dmitry Rakov https://orcid.org/0000-0002-0585-0827

Abstract. Engineering knowledge is an important step for creating innovative products. This paper discusses the morphological knowledge-based engineering (KBE). The development of science and technology is characterized by the increasing complexity of created technical means, a sharp increase in the cost of their development, production, operation, as well as rapid obsolescence. In this connection, the solution of the problem of creating machinery with a high technical level acquires special importance. A huge number of factors of structural, technological, operational, and economic nature, affecting the process of creating new equipment, predetermined the need to use system analysis and synthesis of knowledge in the synthesis of engineering systems. All this increases the number of possible implementations of both individual units and devices, and engineering systems. The need to improve the overall design methodology (and technological processes) is constantly increasing, which is a consequence of high rates of scientific and technological progress. Requirements for the maximum reduction of time spent on the entire cycle of creating a system or technological process have increased sharply. Morphological approaches correspond to these objective processes. They are considered in this paper and an example of the creation of an innovative aerostats system is given. The purpose of the article is to analyze the application of advanced morphological approaches. The approach is based on the application of set theory and agglomerative clustering of solutions. The paper describes the approach and results of using the proposed approach. As a result, the analysis and synthesis of innovative engineering solutions were carried out and recommendations for further development of the methodology were given. The use of the approach is considered as a continuous process of improving the technical level of engineering systems.

Keywords. Knowledge engineering, knowledge management, KBE, morphological matrix, discursive methods, innovative aerostats system.

1. Introduction

The development of science and technology nowadays represents a continuous flow of implementation of innovative solutions. This development allows simultaneously improving the technical level and efficiency of synthesized systems, which leads to an increase in the quality of life and products created. Consequently, it is necessary to create methods and tools to enhance the creative potential of designers. Methods and tools

---

[1] Corresponding Author: Dmitry Rakov, e-mail: rdl@mail.ru.

should ensure the synthesis of new ideas for solutions, the dissemination of knowledge, and the creation of innovations.

Project development includes several stages. At the beginning of the project, the market is analysed, the needs of the target audience and competitors are studied. Then the main goals and objectives of the project are defined, which should be specific, measurable, and achievable.

The analysis of design stages shows that there are no clear delimitations between them. The works started in the previous stages are continued and developed in the subsequent stages. For example, the analysis and selection of principal engineering solutions begins at the conceptual design stage and ends at the preliminary design stage. If some set of fundamentally different solutions is possible, then often the conceptual design stage is preceded by the pre-design research stage, which selects options for further consideration.

At the beginning of the design, the purpose and objectives of the project are determined. The project goal is the result that is intended to be achieved. Project objectives are the steps that need to be taken to achieve the project goal. The project goal should be specific, measurable, achievable, relevant, and time bound. A specific objective makes it clear what is to be achieved. A measurable goal allows the criteria for achieving it to be defined. An achievable goal must be realistic, considering available resources and capabilities. A relevant goal should be related to the overall goals of the realization or project. A temporally constrained goal must be achieved within a specific time frame.

The importance of the different stages of engineering systems development is summarized in Figure 1. The most important stage is the conceptual design stage. At this stage, the idea of a new device takes the shape of a commercially successful product. Competitors are evaluated and a comparative table with competing solutions is drawn up. Developers choose the optimal combination of functional and technical characteristics of the product and determine the business model of the entire project. Conceptual design is the basis for all work on its development and realization. The success of the project depends on the correctness and quality of the design.

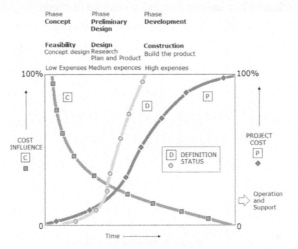

Figure 1. Importance of the different stages of engineering systems development.

2. Statement of the Problem

Scientific and technological progress and the explosive use of information technology are expanding the possibilities of implementing knowledge engineering. For the developers of innovative products, the constant expansion and importance of knowledge is of increasing importance. And the main factor is not only the quantity but also the quality of knowledge. Developers act as both a consumer and a synthesizer and analyzer of knowledge. Knowledge engineering is considered as a set of synthesis of ideas, modeling, and design of technical systems together with technological processes [1-3]. This process is based on extensive use of information technology. The process is based on the creation and use of scientific knowledge and considers the laws of retrospective and development of engineering systems. Knowledge engineering be considered in close connection with value engineering [4,5].

Knowledge engineering must be used in conjunction with management engineering. It is this connection that ensures the successful organization and implementation of innovative tasks. Existing technologies are mainly focused on communication and information management tasks, not on knowledge engineering. Modern information systems should be based on and focused on knowledge itself, i.e., on the processes of decomposition, synthesis, and analysis, as well as their dissemination and use. One of the main directions of development of knowledge engineering is data mining. Morphological approaches can be successfully used to solve this problem.

A morphological approach can be applied to evaluate engineering solutions (ES) [6,7]. It consists in constructing a morphological matrix (MM), filling it with possible attributes and alternatives, and selecting the best solutions from the whole set of combinations (Fig. 2). The approaches are widely used in various applied technical fields [8,9]. These methods are used to build artificial intelligence and student learning systems [10-12].

The life cycle of a system begins with an idea, the synthesis of a series of engineering solutions, and the creation of a prototype, and the development of a production system, as well as the production, distribution, and use of the product. Morphological approaches occupy a significant place among discursive creative methods (Fig. 3) [13].

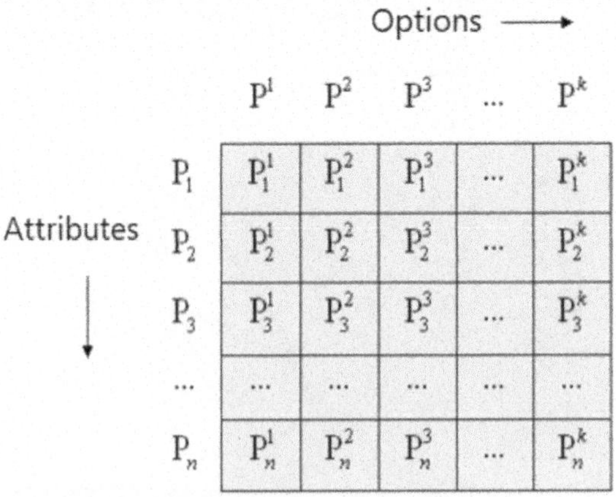

Figure 2. Morphological matrix.

	intuitive	discursive	heuristic
Generation of alternatives	Brainstorming Brainwriting 6-3-5 Method Mindmapping	Morphological box	SCAMPER Inventor heuristics
Challenging assumptions	Reversal method/ Anti-solution Forced connection	Theory of inventive problem solving (TIPS/TRIZ)	Heuristic principles of TIPS/TRIZ Inventor heuristics

Figure 3. Creativity techniques and heuristics [12].

3. Methodology and Advanced Morphological Approach in KBE

Among the problems of application of classical morphological methods are most often mentioned: poor access to support software which can address the combinatorial explosion generated by multi-parameter problem spaces inherent in the use of morphological analysis; insufficiently flexible processes that address users' operational constraints; seen to be overly generic, disguising identification of specific application areas of interest [14]. To address these shortcomings, a method was developed that later became known as the Advanced Morphological Approach (AMA). The AMA is based on the use of cluster analysis [15], set theory, set of rules allows to identify the clusters of innovative systems combining high performance potential with robustness regarding requirement changes and design uncertainties [16]. The proposed approach consists of the following main elements [17]:

- MM Synthesis
- Synthesis and evaluation of criteria
- Analysis and entry of reference variants
- Generation and pre-selection of variants
- Agglomerative clustering of options
- Analysis of solutions and clusters
- Selection of rational options.
- Conclusions

Let the initial X^*_0 and the desired engineering solution (ES) X^* belong to the set of engineering solutions X (Fig. 4).

$$X^*_0 \in X \qquad (1)$$
$$X^* \in X \qquad (2)$$

As a rule, the process of finding ES X* is iterative and consists in a sequential enumeration of ESs:

$$X^{*0} \to X^{*1} \to X^{*2} \to ... \to X^* \qquad (3)$$

In the object under study there is a set of basic features X_p. Depending on the task, from this set of features significant X_n are selected, i.e. capable of greatly affecting the solution of the problem.

$$X_n \leq X_p \qquad (4)$$

$$X_n = (x_1, x_2, x_3, ..., x_n) \qquad (5)$$

where n is the number of ES attributes and belongs to the morphological set of X_M from MM (Fig. 5), where the set of attributes X_n corresponds to n, where X_M is a subset of the set of ES X (Fig. 6).

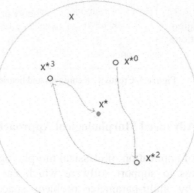

Figure 4. Iterative process of solutions search.

	Options						
	x^1	x^2	x^3	...	x^i	...	x^k
	x_1	x_1^1	x_1^2	x_1^3	...	x_1^i	...	x_1^{k1}
	x_2	x_2^1	x_2^2	x_2^3	...	x_2^i	...	x_2^{k2}
	x_3	x_3^1	x_3^2	x_3^3	...	x_3^i	...	x_3^{k3}
Attributes	...	...	...	...	...	...	...	...
	x_j	x_j^1	x_j^2	x_j^3	...	x_j^i	...	x_j^{km}
	...	...	...	...	...	...	...	...
	x_n	x_n^1	x_n^2	x_n^3	...	x_n^i	...	x_n^{kl}

Figure 5. Complete MM.

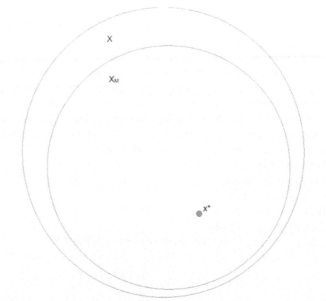

Figure 6. The morphological set of solutions X_M and the required variant X^*

For example, the set of attributes X_n can be identified from the claims. For each feature, the elements, i.e. possible variants of its performance or implementation are selected

$$X_M \subset X \tag{6}$$

The sought TP X^* consists of a set of elements

$$X^* = \{ x_1^*, \ x_2^*, x_3^*, \ ..., \ x_n^* \} \tag{7}$$

and the set of elements X^k

$$X^k = (x^1, x^2, x^3, ..., x^k) \tag{8}$$

where k is a row of MM elements.

The power of the morphological decision set (MMR) Xm is

$$| X_M | = \prod_{j=1}^{n} X_j \tag{9}$$

The morphological set of solutions:

$$X_M = \{X_{mi}, i = 1, p\}, \tag{10}$$

where X_{mi} is the i-th option of ES and

$$p = |X_M| \tag{11}$$

where n is the number of ES variants (the power of the morphological set), i.e., $|X_M| =$ n; x_{Mi} – is the i-th ES variant.

4. Morphological Approach in Shaping the Shape of Innovative Aerostatic Systems

Further development of aerostats and airships is currently associated not so much with the development of designs involving the improvement of existing systems, but with the introduction of new solutions capable of providing reliable and safe mode of flight and performance of assigned tasks. The variety of design solutions provided to the designer in choosing the appearance of new aerostatic platforms that meet the same requirements can vary significantly.

One of the main problems in the design of aerostats is the choice of how to regulate the lifting force. Balloons are lifted due to excess aerostatic force. A change in flight altitude during lift is achieved by increasing the lifting force by dropping some ballast or by increasing the temperature of the lift gas, and during descent by decreasing the lifting force by releasing some gas through a special valve or by cooling the lift gas.

For the analysis and subsequent synthesis, the MM "Principles of lifting force control" is constructed. As the main features Pi were chosen:

• Pressure change.
• Temperature change.
• Change of volume.
• Ballasting system.
• Aerodynamic control.

A matrix and reference alternatives were constructed (Fig.7,8).

	P^1	P^2	P^3	P^4
P_1	P_1^1	P_1^2	P_1^3	
P_2	P_2^1	P_2^2	P_2^3	P_2^4
P_3	P_3^1	P_3^2	P_3^3	
P_4	P_4^1	P_4^2	P_4^3	
P_5	P_5^1	P_5^2	P_5^3	

Figure 7. The morphological matrix "Principles of lifting force control"

	P^1	P^2	P^3	P^4
P_1	P_1^1	P_1^2	P_1^3	
P_2	P_2^1	P_2^2	P_2^3	P_2^4
P_3	P_3^1	P_3^2	P_3^3	
P_4	P_4^1	P_4^2	P_4^3	
P_5	P_5^1	P_5^2	P_5^3	

a

	P^1	P^2	P^3	P^4
P_1	P_1^1	P_1^2	P_1^3	
P_2	P_2^1	P_2^2	P_2^3	P_2^4
P_3	P_3^1	P_3^2	P_3^3	
P_4	P_4^1	P_4^2	P_4^3	
P_5	P_5^1	P_5^2	P_5^3	

b

	P^1	P^2	P^3	P^4
P_1	P_1^1	P_1^2	P_1^3	
P_2	P_2^1	P_2^2	P_2^3	P_2^4
P_3	P_3^1	P_3^2	P_3^3	
P_4	P_4^1	P_4^2	P_4^3	
P_5	P_5^1	P_5^2	P_5^3	

c

	P^1	P^2	P^3	P^4
P_1	P_1^1	P_1^2	P_1^3	
P_2	P_2^1	P_2^2	P_2^3	P_2^4
P_3	P_3^1	P_3^2	P_3^3	
P_4	P_4^1	P_4^2	P_4^3	
P_5	P_5^1	P_5^2	P_5^3	

d

	P^1	P^2	P^3	P^4
P_1	P_1^1	P_1^2	P_1^3	
P_2	P_2^1	P_2^2	P_2^3	P_2^4
P_3	P_3^1	P_3^2	P_3^3	
P_4	P_4^1	P_4^2	P_4^3	
P_5	P_5^1	P_5^2	P_5^3	

e

	P^1	P^2	P^3	P^4
P_1	P_1^1	P_1^2	P_1^3	
P_2	P_2^1	P_2^2	P_2^3	P_2^4
P_3	P_3^1	P_3^2	P_3^3	
P_4	P_4^1	P_4^2	P_4^3	
P_5	P_5^1	P_5^2	P_5^3	

f

Figure 8. Reference variants in the MM (a) air balloon, b) hot air balloon, c) helicopter, d) thermal airship "Thermoplane", e) balloon with air ballast, f) airship with air ballast)

To study the principles of lifting force control, a structural synthesis of engineering solutions was made, generation of variants was carried out and a morphological space was built. Based on the results of the synthesis, schemes for controlling the aerostatic lifting force by compressing part of the carrier gas have been proposed (Fig.9).

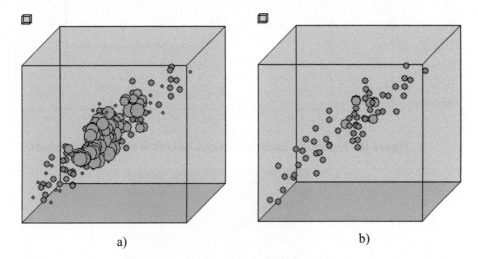

a)   b)

Figure 9. ES variants in the morphological space a) maximum number of ESs, b) selected set of ESs (screen forms)

5. Results

Based on the results of the analysis, a number of alternatives were selected from the matrix and modelling was carried out. The proposed concepts are characterized by the following advantages over existing ones:
- Interaction with simultaneous volume and pressure variation in lifting force control.
- Possibility to control the lifting force in two directions.
- Universal applicability for various balloon and hybrid concepts.

- Short reaction times.
- Increased reliability.
- High manufacturability.
- Low mass of the entire system.

Based on the results of analysis and synthesis, aerodynamic calculations were carried out and the demonstrator model was built. The model confirmed the theoretical studies (Fig.10,11).

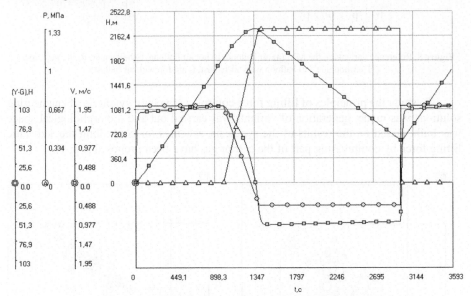

Figure 10. Trajectory characteristics of a ballastless balloon (screenshot).

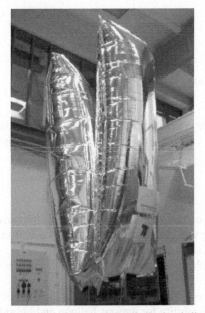

Figure 11. Demonstrator of the principle of ballastless balloon operation

Compared to the technology that uses air injection into cylinders, the proposed one allows to adjust the lifting force by creating a slight pressure increase in the shell, and using hydrogen or helium, pump the carrier gas out of the main shell of the balloon, which results in a reduction of the mass and reaction speed of the system.

Future research is envisioned in refining expert judgment, selecting criterions, and expanding clustering options.

6. Conclusion

KBE is an important step for creating innovative products. The development of science and technology is characterized by the increasing complexity of created technical means, a sharp increase in the cost of their development, production, operation, as well as rapid obsolescence. In this connection, the solution of the problem of creating machinery with a high technical level acquires special importance.

Morphological approaches correspond to these objective processes. They are considered in this paper and an example of the creation of an ecological aerostat system is given.

The purpose of the article is to analyze the application of morphological approaches. The paper describes the approach and results of using the proposed approach. The proposed approach is based on the application of set theory and agglomerative clustering of solutions. As a result, the analysis and synthesis of innovative engineering solutions were carried out and recommendations for further development of the methodology were given. The use of the approach is considered as a continuous process of improving the technical level of engineering systems.

References

[1] Rocca G. Knowledge based engineering: Between AI and CAD. Review of a language-based technology to support engineering design. Advanced Engineering Informatics. 2012. 26. Pp. 159–179. doi: 10.1016/j.aei.2012.02.002.

[2] Kügler P, Dworschak F, Schleich B, Wartzack S, The evolution of knowledge-based engineering from a design research perspective: Literature review 2012–2021, Advanced Engineering Informatics, 55, 2023, 101892, doi: 10.1016/j.aei.2023.101892.

[3] Zamboni J, Zamfir A, Moerland E. Semantic knowledge-based-engineering: The codex framework. In Proceedings of the 12th International Joint Conference on Knowledge Discovery, Knowledge Engineering and Knowledge Management, 2020, Pp. 242–249.

[4] Setti P, Canciglieri O, Estorilio C. Integrated product development method based on Value Engineering and design for assembly concepts, Journal of Industrial Information Integration, 21,2021,100199. doi: 10.1016/j.jii.2020.100199

[5] Putnik GD, Putnik Z, Pinheiro P, Alves C. Engineering is Design and only Design – Part I: The value of making a distinctive sign. Procedia CIRP 2022. doi: 10.1016/j.procir.2022.05.313

[6] Zwicky F. Morphology of aerial propulsion Helvetica Physica Acta. 1948. V. 21(5). Pp. 299–340.

[7] Zwicky F. Discovery, Invention, Research – Through the Morphological Approach. Toronto: The Macmillan Company, 1969.

[8] Aziz DH, Razak NH, Zulkafli NI, Jaromír Klemeš JJ. Systematic framework to select the sustainable best design for an automated fertiliser blending system, Journal of Cleaner Production, 2023,139107, doi: 10.1016/j.jclepro.2023.139107.

[9] Ngatiman NA, Mohd Shariff AQ, Sutikno T, Wardiyono S, Manap M, Jopri MH. Personal air-conditioning system using evapolar as heat waste management. Bulletin of Electrical Engineering and Informatics [Internet]. 2021 Dec 1;10(6):2953–63. doi: 10.11591/eei.v10i6.3283

[10] Alvarez-Dionisi L, Mittra M, Balza R. Teaching Artificial Intelligence and Robotics to Undergraduate Systems Engineering Students. International Journal of Modern Education and Computer Science, 2019, 11(7): 54-63.

[11] Njenga S, Oboko R, Omwenga E, Maina E. Use of Intelligent Agents in Collaborative M-Learning: Case of Facilitating Group Learner Interactions. International Journal of Modern Education and Computer Science, 2017, 10:18–28.

[12] Sumaiya S, Sumaiya E, Nayeem M, Akinul I, Dip N. A Comparison of Opinion Mining Algorithms by Using Product Review Data[J]. International Journal of Information Engineering and Electronic Business, 2022, 14(4), 28-38.

[13] Deckert C, Mohya A. Innovation without Creativity? – Teaching Creative Problem Solving to Prospective Engineers. In SEFI (eds.). Proceedings of the 48th SEFI Annual Conference "Engaging Engineering Education" (758-767), 2020 Brüssel: SEFI.

[14] Garvey B. Combining quantitative and qualitative aspects of problem structuring in computational morphological analysis, PhD thesis, Imperial College London. 2016.

[15] Rakov D. Morphological synthesis method of search for promising technical system. IEEE Aerospace and Electronic Systems Magazine 1996, 11, Pp. 3–8. doi:10.1109/62.544791.

[16] Bardenhagen A, Rakov D, Advanced Morphological Approach in Aerospace Design During Conceptual Stage. Facta Universitatis, Series: Mechanical Engineering 2019, 17, 321–332. doi:10.22190/FUME180110005B.

[17] Todorov VT, Rakov D, Bardenhagen A. Enhancement Opportunities for Conceptual Design in Aerospace Based on the Advanced Morphological Approach. Aerospace, 2022, 9, 78. doi: 10.3390/aerospace9020078.

Artificial Intelligence, Medical Engineering and Education
Z.B. Hu et al. (Eds.)
© 2024 The Authors.
This article is published online with Open Access by IOS Press and distributed under the terms
of the Creative Commons Attribution Non-Commercial License 4.0 (CC BY-NC 4.0).
doi:10.3233/ATDE231329

Management Problems of Information Support of Technical and Economic Systems Based on Artificial Intelligence Technologies

Alovsat G. Aliyev[a,1], Roza O.Shahverdiyeva[a], Sunyakhanim A.Salimkhanova[b]

[a]Institute of Information Technology, Baku, Azerbaijan
[b]Azerbaijan University of Architecture and Construction
E-mail: alovsat_qaraca@mail.ru[a]; shahverdiyevar@gmail.com[a]; sunye.selimxanova@gmail.com[b]
ORCID ID: *orcid.org/0000-0002-1174-8036 (Alovsat Aliyev)*
ORCID ID: *orcid.org/0000-0003-0842-7300 (Roza Shahverdiyeva)*

Abstract: In the article, the problems of management of the information support of regional technical and economic systems based on the digital technologies of the Industry 4.0 platform are defined and their relevance is justified. With the application of artificial intelligence technologies, some problems related to the effective management of information support in technical and economic systems, including innovative enterprises, were explained. Some aspects of the essence and activity of technical-economic systems and their information support were analyzed. An overview analysis of relevant scientific research works was conducted and the state of problem solving was studied. Digital technologies of Industry 4.0, as well as the main functions of artificial intelligence technologies, and some global development trends related to their application in various fields, were studied. An architectural-technological structure model was proposed based on the application of artificial intelligence technologies of technical-economic systems, as well as information support of innovative-industrial enterprises. In the conditions of the transfer of digital innovations, directions for increasing the sustainable activity of technical-economic systems and innovative enterprises have been determined. The level of importance of industrial-digital technologies applied in the activity of technical-economic systems and innovative enterprises is indicated. Based on artificial intelligence technologies, relevant recommendations were given on the mechanisms for solving the problems of management of the information support of technical and economic systems.

Keywords: digital transformation; technical and economic systems; innovative enterprises; information support; artificial intelligence technologies; Industry 4.0 platform

1. Introduction

In the era of modern digital transformation, the construction of technical and economic systems, including the information support of innovative industrial production enterprises based on artificial intelligence technologies, and their effective management based on modern digital technologies are considered urgent issues. (https://president.az/articles/51299). Artificial Intelligence (AI) technologies are increasingly

---

[1] Corresponding Author: Alovsat Aliyev. E-mail: alovsat_qaraca@mail.ru.

applied in various aspects of the active operation of technical and economic systems and create new opportunities for increasing its effective operation. Effective management of information support of technical and economic systems based on artificial intelligence technologies is of particular importance for decision-making, resource allocation, and general activity [1]. With the application of artificial intelligence technologies, new opportunities and challenges arise to use the potential of information management. For this reason, the presented article is dedicated to the investigation of some problems related to the effective management of information support in technical-economic systems and innovative enterprises using artificial intelligence technologies.

There are various reports and many scientific publications dedicated to the problems of effective management of the information support of technical and economic systems based on artificial intelligence technologies [2-7]. Although most of them are of a general nature, some of them also address specific problems. In order to solve the problems related to the general research work, appropriate mechanisms should be developed taking into account the recommendations of international organizations, as well as the new management models of the Industry 4.0 platform, and the perspectives of the application of new technological components. Although there are enough difficulties in solving the existing problems in this field, there are also opportunities and potential. It is very important to identify these problems and their solutions and include them in the functional cycle. In general, although certain scientific research works are carried out on the regional, international, and global scale in the analysis of the problems of effective management of the information support of technical and economic systems based on artificial intelligence technologies, this field has been poorly researched. There is a great demand for comprehensive deep scientific-technical and practical research in a similar sphere.

The purpose of the research. The main purpose of the scientific research conducted in the article is to analyze the issues of effective management of the information support of innovative enterprises acting as a synthesis of technical and economic systems based on artificial intelligence technologies, to develop its conceptual model, as well as the basics of the scientific-methodological approach to the study of prospective development problems. has been processed. In the article, based on the digital technologies of the Industry 4.0 platform, some considerations were given and recommendations were made for increasing the efficiency of the effective management of the information support of innovative enterprises. The study of the functional aspects of the information support of enterprises is included in the list of research objectives. The global development trends related to the application of digital technologies of Industry 4.0, as well as artificial intelligence technologies applied in the activities of innovative enterprises in various fields, were studied. An architectural-technological structural model of information support of innovative industrial enterprises was developed based on the application of artificial intelligence technologies. Features characterizing the level of importance of industrial-digital technologies applied in their activity have been determined. Certain recommendations have been made on the mechanisms for solving the problems of effective management of information support based on artificial intelligence technologies of innovative enterprises.

Research methods used. On the basis of artificial intelligence technologies, the following research methods were used in solving the problems of effective management of the information support of enterprises, in studying prospective development directions, in working out their scientific-methodological and theoretical bases: information theory, systematic analysis, correlation analysis, econometric modeling methods, expert evaluation method, artificial intelligence technologies and methods, algorithmization, ICT tools, and technologies, etc.

Research methodology. The appropriate methodological apparatus and approach were used for the synthesis of technical and economic systems based on artificial intelligence technologies, as well as for the determination of the problems of effective management of the information support of enterprises, and prospective development directions. A systematic review of the digital technologies of the Industry 4.0 platform, as well as the technical and technological features of artificial intelligence technologies applied in enterprises, was conducted. Relevant methodological principles have been taken into account in the applications of digital technologies of the Industry 4.0 platform in enterprises.

The requirements of the application of artificial intelligence technologies in the formation of the information support system of enterprises were proposed, and the development of the architectural-technological structural model was taken into account. International economic development trends, requirements of high and modern digital technologies, and the main trends of the Industry 4.0 platform are the basis of the relevant methodological approach in ensuring the sustainability of enterprises.

2. An Overview Analysis of Relevant Related Scientific Research Works and the State of Problem

Despite the importance and relevance of the development of effective management problems of the information support of enterprises as a result of the synthesis of technical and economic systems based on artificial intelligence technologies and the mechanisms for its solution, that field has not yet been properly formed. A systematic multidisciplinary analysis of its conceptual foundations is still lacking in the scientific literature. Therefore, the existing theoretical and practical aspects of the problems of effective management of technical and economic systems of various purposes, including the information support of innovative enterprises based on Artificial Intelligence technologies, should be studied more. It is necessary to study the processing aspects and semantic content of existing concepts in that field, as well as to examine the perspectives and limitations of the transition of production and consumption to a new management scheme. It should be noted that the authors of the articles, like other researchers, have many publications in this field in different years, in different databases, including in different scientific journals indexed in the MECS database [2-12].

In this regard, it should be noted that [2] on the application of artificial intelligence in enterprises and organizations until 2021 in 31 journals of information systems, business, and management, and a systematic analysis of published articles on operations management was carried out. In this work, a conceptual structural model for the application of artificial intelligence in enterprises and organizations is proposed.

[8] is dedicated to the development and implementation of the conceptual model of efficient management of innovative enterprises based on digital twin technologies. A perspective conceptual development model of industrial-economic systems based on innovative digitization processes has been proposed. A SWOT analysis of the process of using digital twins in the management of innovative industrial-economic systems was carried out. The creation of digital twins for the organization and management of the activities of this type of enterprise and the expanded architectural structure of its concept were proposed.

[9] addressed multi-factor authentication issues to improve the security of enterprise resource planning systems. Multi-factor authentication has been developed as a state-of-the-art technology to strengthen the authentication security of user-owned information systems that combine several authentication factors. Here, stratified, random, and purposive sampling methods were used to identify the target group. The dependent variable for the study was limited to privacy, completeness, accessibility, and security rating regarding implementation of use. Independent variables are limited to security, authentication mechanisms, infrastructure, information security policies, vulnerabilities, and user adequacy. Through correlation and regression analysis, vulnerabilities, information security policies, and user training were identified to have a higher impact on system security.

[10] analyzed the methods of identifying cyber threats based on machine learning technology for the information system in real-time. It has been shown that by means of the proposed method, it is possible to independently detect cyber threats to information systems and perform countermeasures to eliminate them, and increase the functional stability of the system operating in real-time.

[11], the features of the application of Big Data technologies in cyber-physical systems and digital manufacturing on the Industry 4.0 platform were investigated. It was noted that digital manufacturing is a new technology based on the use of computers and interconnected modern technologies to manage the entire production process. The application of key technologies such as the Internet of Things, Cloud computing, Machine-to-Machine (M2M) communications, 3D printing, and Big Data in Industry 4.0 is shown in the work.

3. Functional Aspects of Information Support of Technical and Economic Systems

The information support of technical and economic systems plays a decisive role in supporting the efficient operation and development of the digital technological economy [12]. It includes various components, technologies, and processes that facilitate the collection, storage, processing, and dissemination of information in systems. These can be attributed to some functional aspects of information support in technical and economic systems. *1. Data collection and management.* The infrastructure includes mechanisms for collecting and managing relevant data within the region. This involves the creation of data collection systems, data warehouses, and databases that include various economic indicators, market trends, demographic data, and other relevant data sources. *2. Information exchange and cooperation.* Regional technical and economic systems and innovative industrial enterprises require effective information exchange and collaboration platforms. This includes the development of digital platforms, networks, and communication channels that facilitate the exchange of information and knowledge between different stakeholders such as businesses, government agencies, research institutes, and community organizations. *3. ICT Infrastructure.* ICT infrastructure is the basis of information support infrastructure. It includes hardware, software, networks, and communications that enable efficient data transfer and processing. This infrastructure includes Internet connection, servers, data centers, communication networks, and other ICT resources necessary for data exchange and processing. *4. Electronic Government services.* Information provision supports the delivery of e-government services in regional economies. It includes online portals, digital platforms, and electronic systems that enable citizens and businesses to use government services, submit credentials, make payments, and communicate with government agencies seamlessly and efficiently. *5. Business intelligence and analytics.* The infrastructure consists of the relevant mechanisms, tools, and technologies for business intelligence and analytics. It includes data analysis software, visualization tools, and statistical models that enable businesses to extract valuable insights from data, make informed decisions, and identify opportunities for growth and development within a regional economy. *6.Cyber security and data privacy.* Information support should prioritize cybersecurity and data privacy measures. This includes robust security protocols, encryption mechanisms, access controls, and data protection procedures to protect sensitive information and prevent unauthorized access or data breaches. *7. Increasing skills.* The effective operation of the information support is based on qualified professionals who can manage and use the available resources. This requires ongoing training and capacity-building programs to improve the digital literacy and technical skills of those involved in data collection, analysis, and data management. *8.Cooperation of interested parties.* Information support should foster collaboration between various stakeholders, including government agencies, businesses, research institutes, and community organizations. This includes creating partnerships, information-sharing agreements, and collaborative platforms to leverage collective knowledge and expertise within the regional economy. Effective management and development of technical and economic systems information support help in better decision-making, policy formulation, and resource allocation in the region [1, 13]. It facilitates the creation of an environment that supports innovation, entrepreneurship, and sustainable economic growth.

4. Architectural-technological Structural Model of Technical-Economic Systems and Innovative Enterprises İnformation Support Based on Artificial Intelligence Technologies

Artificial intelligence expert systems, machine learning, robotics, natural language processing, machine vision, speech recognition, etc. have some basic functions [6].

Industry 4.0 offers new perspectives on how manufacturing can use new technologies to create value with maximum output and minimum resource use. The digital technologies of the Industry 4.0 platform applied in technical and economic systems can be given as in Figure 1.

Each of the indicated technologies has characteristic features of the application in the operation of technical-economic systems, including industrial-innovative enterprises [12, 14]. Their application at different levels leads to obtaining different results. In this sense, their choice should be justified.

The application of artificial intelligence technologies, which is one of the main digital technologies of the Industry 4.0 platform, in the information support of technical-economic systems and innovative enterprises, and the development of a conceptual model of modern information support based on it are particularly important issues. Regarding the situation related to the application of artificial intelligence technologies in the world, it can be noted that some notable functional development trends related to the application of artificial intelligence technologies on a global scale include: *1)Research and development.* Many countries are investing heavily in AI-related research and development to foster innovation. Countries such as the United States, China, Canada, and the European Union have launched relevant funding programs to support AI research, encourage collaboration between academia and industry, and attract AI best practices.

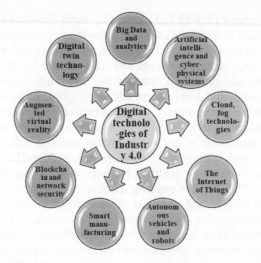

Fig.1. Digital technologies of Industry 4.0 applied in technical-economic systems and innovation enterprises *(Compiled by the authors based on the analysis of scientific literature)*

2)Diagnostics and medical processes. Artificial intelligence is revolutionizing healthcare by enabling advanced diagnostics, personalized medicine, and effective therapeutic care. AI-powered systems can analyze medical images, detect diseases, assist in surgical procedures, and improve drug discovery processes. Artificial intelligence is also being used to improve telemedicine services and remote patient monitoring. *3)Finance and banking.* The financial industry uses artificial intelligence for tasks such as anomaly detection, risk assessment, trading, and customer service. AI-powered chatbots and virtual assistants are being used to provide personalized financial advice. Natural language processing algorithms are used for sentiment analysis and market forecasting. *4)Logistics management and routing.* Artificial intelligence technologies are transforming the transportation sector with advances in autonomous vehicles, route optimization, and traffic management. Self-driving cars and trucks are being tested and implemented in the logistics management of different countries. Artificial intelligence algorithms are used to optimize transport networks, reduce congestion and improve safety. *5)Production systems and robotics.* Artificial intelligence is driving automation and optimization in the manufacturing industry. Robots and cobots equipped with artificial intelligence capabilities are used for tasks such as assembly, quality control, and predictive maintenance. AI-powered algorithms analyze production data to optimize processes, minimize downtime and increase productivity. *6)Customer services.* AI-based chatbots and virtual assistants are increasingly dominating customer service. These AI systems can provide fast and personalized responses, manage customer inquiries and assist with transactions. Natural language processing and machine learning algorithms allow chatbots to continuously improve their interactions with customers. *7)Smart cities.* Artificial intelligence technologies are being used to build smart cities to improve infrastructure, energy management, and public services. AI-powered systems can optimize energy use, monitor and manage traffic flow, improve waste management, and enhance public safety through video analytics and predictive policing. *8)Social impact.* Artificial intelligence is also used for social services and humanitarian purposes. It is applied in disaster response and management, access to health care in remote areas, and environmental protection. AI-powered solutions help in wildlife conservation, climate change research, and disaster risk assessment.

In addition to presenting numerous opportunities, the introduction of artificial intelligence technologies also raises regulatory considerations. Ensuring data privacy, addressing issues of bias and fairness, and creating transparent and accountable AI systems are critical to its responsible implementation.

In general, the widespread adoption of artificial intelligence technologies in various sectors around the world is increasing the scope, driving transformative changes, and creating new opportunities for innovation, efficiency, and social development. The architectural-technological structure model of technical-economic systems and information support of the enterprise is composed of structures and components that make up the system that is important for the collection, storage, processing, and distribution of information within the organization. This model describes the main elements and their relationships in the information support system.

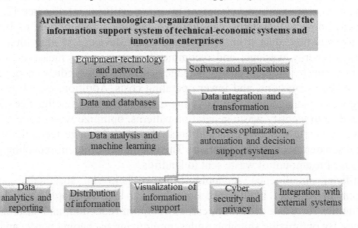

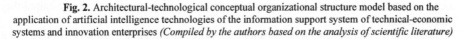

Fig. 2. Architectural-technological conceptual organizational structure model based on the application of artificial intelligence technologies of the information support system of technical-economic systems and innovation enterprises *(Compiled by the authors based on the analysis of scientific literature)*

Based on the application of technical-economic systems and artificial intelligence technologies in the information support of the enterprise, the architectural-technological conceptual structure model can change depending on the specific goals of the organization. The proposed architectural-technological structure model and its constituent elements can be given as in Figure 2.

Based on the application of artificial intelligence technologies in technical-economic systems and enterprises' information support systems, the following can be attributed to the essence and content of the architectural-technological structural model: 1) Equipment-technology infrastructure. 2) Software and applications. 3) Data and databases. 4) Network infrastructure. 5) Data integration and transformation. 6) Data collection, integration, storage, and management. 7) Data analytics and reporting. 8) Data analysis and machine learning. 9) Visualization of information support. 10) Decision support systems. 11) Optimization and automation of processes. 12) Continuous learning and improvement. 13) Cyber security and privacy. Integration with external systems.

The architectural-technological structural model of the information support system can change depending on the specific requirements of the innovative enterprise. It is important to implement the system in a way that aligns with organizational goals and supports effective information management and decision-making processes [7]. It is important to note that the specific application of artificial intelligence technologies in technical and economic systems and innovative enterprises will depend on factors such as industry, organizational structure, available resources, and strategic goals [2-4]. Each organizational structure must adapt the model to its specific needs and take into account the expected consequences of using artificial intelligence technology.

5. Directions for Improving the Sustainable Activity of Technical and Economic Systems and Enterprises in the Conditions of the Transfer of Digital Innovations

Artificial intelligence technologies play an important role in promoting the sustainable operation of technical and economic systems and innovation enterprises. Enterprises can improve their economic-environmental performance, and resource efficiency and contribute to sustainable development by using artificial intelligence [2, 3]. Artificial intelligence-powered systems can optimize energy consumption in businesses. By analyzing real-time data from sensors and smart devices, AI algorithms can identify patterns of energy wastage, and recommend energy-saving measures and automated control systems for efficient energy management. This helps reduce energy consumption, reduce carbon emissions, and lower operating costs. Additionally, AI technologies are helping waste management and recycling efforts. Artificial intelligence algorithms can analyze data to identify waste generation patterns, optimize waste collection routes and improve recycling processes. In addition, AI-powered image recognition systems can sort and separate recyclable materials. This facilitates efficient recycling practices and can reduce the amount of waste sent to landfills.

Artificial intelligence technologies also help in sustainable supply chain management. Artificial intelligence algorithms can analyze supply chain data to identify opportunities for waste reduction, carbon footprint reduction, and sustainable sourcing practices. By optimizing shipping routes, minimizing packaging waste, and ensuring the use of essential resources, businesses can improve their supply chain sustainability performance.

Artificial intelligence technologies support sustainable product design and development. Machine learning algorithms can analyze data about customer preferences, market trends, and environmental impact to inform product design decisions. AI-powered simulations and optimization models can help identify environmentally friendly materials, reduce product lifecycle impacts, and improve the overall sustainability performance of products.

Artificial intelligence technologies enable businesses to monitor and manage their environmental impact. Sensors and monitoring systems powered by artificial intelligence can analyze data on air quality, water quality, and other environmental parameters in real time, detect anomalies, and provide early warning systems to reduce potential socio-economic-technical-environmental risks. Artificial intelligence algorithms can evaluate different scenarios, assess environmental impacts and make recommendations for sustainable decision-making. This helps innovative businesses align their strategic and operational decisions with sustainability goals [4, 5].

In general, artificial intelligence technologies are applied in many technical and economic sectors to optimize the use of resources and minimize environmental impacts [1, 7]. Artificial intelligence algorithms can analyze data from sensors, satellite images, and weather patterns to provide a real-time factor in certain processes. This includes optimization of production/service processes. This leads to an increase in production productivity, a decrease in resource consumption, and minimization of environmental pollution. Artificial intelligence technologies facilitate the transition to a circular economy by ensuring efficient use of resources and waste management. Artificial intelligence algorithms can identify product reuse, remanufacturing, and recycling opportunities. By optimizing logistics processes, predicting demand for recycled materials, and supporting circular business models, businesses can contribute to a more sustainable and resource-efficient economy.

Many industrial-digital technologies play an important role in increasing efficiency, productivity, and competitiveness in the operation of technical-economic systems and innovation enterprises [3, 4, 12]. The main industrial digital technologies widely used by innovative enterprises are 1)Internet of Things (IoT). 2)Artificial intelligence and machine learning technologies. 3)Big Data Analytics. 4)Robotics and automation. 5) Augmented Reality and Virtual Reality, 6)Cloud computing. 7)Digital Twin.

The aforementioned Industrial-digital technologies improve the performance of enterprises in various sectors. By using these technologies, businesses can improve efficiency, productivity, and innovation, gain better operational results, and a competitive advantage in the marketplace. The application of digital technologies that are able to correctly assess the specific needs of enterprises and align with the relevant business objectives is very important in the current era (Table 1).

Table 1. The level of importance of industrial digital technologies applied in the operation of technical-economic systems and innovative enterprises *(Source: 2021. Top-15 digital technologies in the industry. https://issek.hse.ru/ news/494926896.html)*

Rating	Digital technologies	Significance index
1.	Industrial robots	1
2.	Artificial intelligence	0,86
3.	Machine learning	0,68
4.	Digital prototyping	0,56
5.	Sensors	0,42
6.	Wireless technologies	0,3
7.	Blockchain technologies	0,21
8.	Big Data	0,2
9.	Virtual and augmented reality	0,12
10.	Automation of product/service production processes	0,09
11.	Computer (machine) vision	0,03
12.	Smart contracts	0,03
13.	Industrial Internet of Things	0,03
14.	Digital twins	0,02
15.	Smart factories and plants	0,01

As it can be seen from the table, the main digital innovative technologies are Industrial robots, Artificial intelligence, and Machine learning.

6. Conclusion

Currently, the artificial intelligence technologies of the Industry 4.0 platform are of particular importance in the effective management of technical-economic systems and information support of innovative enterprises. Real-time data monitoring and analysis, predictive maintenance, intelligent automation, supply chain optimization, improved product quality and customization, intelligent resource management, application of digital twin technology, information-based decision-making, innovative enterprises have higher productivity, minimal costs, improved products, etc. such issues should be resolved. Modern technologies of Industry 4.0 open up new opportunities for the future of production in technical and economic systems, including innovative enterprises. These provide businesses with new opportunities to remain competitive in the digital environment. Effective management of information support in technical and economic systems based on artificial intelligence technologies creates both new opportunities and new problems. Addressing issues related to data quality, privacy, scalability, trust, and collaboration are critical to harnessing the full potential of AI in information management. By overcoming these difficulties, regional-economic-technical systems can improve decision-making and optimize resource allocation. As a result, the application of artificial intelligence technologies in the activities of technical and economic systems and innovative enterprises changes the way enterprises operate and provides efficiency, innovation, and competitive advantage. By leveraging AI-powered analytics, automation, and decision-making systems, enterprises can optimize manufacturing/service operations, improve customer experiences, reduce risk, and drive sustainable growth in a dynamic business landscape. The application of artificial intelligence technologies in the operation of technical-economic systems and innovative enterprises can increase sustainability by improving energy management, waste reduction, supply chain sustainability, sustainable product design, environmental monitoring, and decision-making. By integrating artificial intelligence into their operations, businesses can achieve greater resource efficiency, reduce negative environmental impacts and further contribute to a more sustainable future.

Results and discussion. Effective management of technical and economic systems, including the information support of enterprises, requires the wide application of artificial intelligence and other digital technologies. Despite the acceptance of the results of such a development trend on a global scale, there is still a need to discuss this problem at the regional and national level and to accept and use it by large population groups. Digital twin, artificial intelligence, Internet of Things, etc. on the basis of digital transformation technologies such as increasing the efficiency of the management of the information support of enterprises, developing recommendations on strengthening the prospective development directions of the enterprise, should form the basis of future discussions and research. Development of enterprises based on digital technologies, effective management, development, and further improvement of the conceptual structure model of effective management of its information support should be included among the main directions of future research. The improvement of the effective management of the information support of enterprises should be stimulated by modern ICT solutions corresponding to the Industry 4.0 platform. The justification of raising the level of effective management of its information support by means of digital technologies such as artificial intelligence and machine learning, big data analytics in enterprises should also be the subject of research discussion in the form of the benefits that these technologies can bring.

Contributions. Effective management of the information support of innovative enterprises based on artificial intelligence technologies can give a serious impetus to sustainable development and increase of the stability of the digital economy. Accordingly, relevant recommendations and proposals were developed based on the study of the characteristics of the formation of the information support of innovative enterprises based on artificial intelligence technologies.

An architectural-technological structure model was proposed based on the application of artificial intelligence technologies for information support of innovative industrial enterprises. 1)Hardware, technology, and network infrastructure, 2)Software and applications, 3)Data and databases, 4)Data integration and transformation, 5)Data analysis and machine learning, 6)Process optimization, automation, and decision support systems, 7)Data analytics and reporting, 8)Visualization of information support, 9)Cyber security and privacy, 10)Integration with external systems, etc. such structural elements have been determined.

The level of importance of industrial-digital technologies applied in the activity of innovative enterprises has been determined. The solutions to the problems of the application of artificial intelligence technologies, which are the digital technology trends of the modern era, can be considered as a tool or mechanism for investigating the solutions to existing problems in the development of enterprises. By using artificial intelligence technology, it is possible to increase the efficiency of innovative enterprises, their effective management, and sustainable development. The proposals presented in this direction can lead to effective results for more stable and sustainable innovative enterprises based on artificial intelligence technologies.

The interaction of the proposed main components of the digital platform environment can be considered an improved conceptual structural model of the information support of enterprises. This can have a positive effect on increasing the operational efficiency of the enterprise and decision-making issues for its effective management.

The usefulness of the obtained result and application in practice. The problems of effective management of information support of technical and economic systems based on artificial intelligence technologies and prospective development directions can be applied in the development of other regional enterprises and in the development of solution mechanisms and options.

The analysis of the results of the application of artificial intelligence technologies in the efficient management of the information support of enterprises can serve as a platform for a comprehensive assessment of the activities of other enterprises in general. The application of artificial intelligence technologies in the improvement and effective management of enterprises' information support provides a basis for making appropriate management decisions. The proposed methodological and conceptual approach to efficient management of enterprises based on artificial intelligence technologies can be applied in other regional and sectoral enterprises.

References

[1] Alovsat G. Aliyev, "Development of Models of Manufacturing Processes of Innovative Products at Different Levels of Management", International Journal of Information Technology and Computer Science, Vol.11, No.5, pp.23-29, 2019.

[2] Maggie C.M. et al. The implementation of artificial intelligence in organizations: A systematic literature review. Information & Management, 2023, volume 60, Issue 5, 103816. https://doi.org/10.1016/j.im.2023.103816.

[3] Mansoori S.Al. et al. The impact of artificial intelligence and information technologies on the efficiency of knowledge management at modern organizations: A systematic review. In book: Recent Advances in Intelligent Systems and Smart Applications, 2021, pp.163-182.

[4] Haefner N. et al. Artificial intelligence and innovation management: A review, framework, and research agenda. Technological Forecasting & Social Change, 2021,162, pp.120392.

[5] Jun Liu et al. Influence of artificial intelligence on technological innovation: Evidence from the panel data of China's manufacturing sectors. Technological Forecasting and Social Change, 2020, 158(2), 120142.

[6] Collins C. et al. Artificial intelligence in information systems research: A systematic literature review and research agenda. International Journal of Information Management, 2021, 60, 102383.

[7] Zhidko Ye.A., Ukhov S.V., Rudenko A.I. Intellektualizatsiya informatsionnykh i organizatsionnykh protsessov v upravlenii sotsial'no-ekonomicheskimi sistemami. Informatsionnyye tekhnologii v stroitel'nykh, sotsial'nykh i ekonomicheskikh sistemakh, 2022, №4(30), s.60-64.

[8] Alovsat G. Aliyev, Roza O. Shahverdiyeva, "Development of a Conceptual Model of Effective Management of Innovative Enterprises based on Digital Twin Technologies", International Journal of Information Engineering and Electronic Business, Vol.15, No.4, pp. 34-47, 2023.

[9] Carolyne Kimani, James I. Obuhuma, Emily Roche, "Multi-Factor Authentication for Improved Enterprise Resource Planning Systems Security", International Journal of Information Technology and Computer Science, Vol.15, No.3, pp.42-54, 2023.

[10] Volodymyr Tolubko, Viktor Vyshnivskyi, Vadym Mukhin, Halyna Haidur, Nadiia Dovzhenko, Oleh Ilin, Volodymyr Vasylenko, "Method for Determination of Cyber Threats Based on Machine Learning for Real-Time Information System", International Journal of Intelligent Systems and Applications, Vol.10, No.8, pp.11-18, 2018.

[11] Lidong Wang, Guanghui Wang, "Big Data in Cyber-Physical Systems, Digital Manufacturing and Industry 4.0", International Journal of Engineering and Manufacturing, Vol.6, No.4, pp.1-8, 2016.

[12] Aliyev A.G., Shahverdiyeva R.O. A conceptual approach to the formation of a digital innovation economy based on artificial intelligence technologies. Artificial Societies, 2022, v.17, issue 4, pp.1-16.

[13] Somov A.G. Razrabotka metodov i instrumentov podderzhki prinyatiya upravlencheskikh resheniy na osnove iskusstvennogo intellekta. Innovatsii i investitsii, 2023, №4, s.305-308.

[14] Han Y., Shevchenko T., Yannou B., Ranjbari M. Et al. Exploring how digital technologies enable a circular economy of products. Sustainability 2023, 15, 2067. https://doi.org/ 10.3390/su15032067.

Artificial Intelligence, Medical Engineering and Education
Z.B. Hu et al. (Eds.)
doi:10.3233/ATDE231330

Mental Health State Prediction Method of College Students Based on Integrated Algorithm

Na GUO[1]

College of Resources and Environment, Wuhan University of Technology, Wuhan,
Hubei 430070, China
ORCiD ID: Na Guo https://orcid.org/0000-0002-7677-6820

Abstract. Psychological health is an important issue faced by college students, therefore conducting relevant research is meaningful. The use of Adaboost algorithm for ensemble learning, combined with the application of decision tree algorithm, can fully utilize the information in mental health test data and improve the prediction accuracy of the classifier. The C4.5 decision tree algorithm is a commonly used classification algorithm that can classify and distinguish samples based on feature attributes, so it has been selected as the basic algorithm for this study. In order to verify the effectiveness of this method, we selected the mental health test data of 2780 students from a certain university in 2020 for the experiment. Through analyzing experimental results, we found that the method can accurately identify sensitive psychological problems among students. In practical applications, this method can serve as an auxiliary tool to help schools accurately understand the distribution of students' mental health problems, and thus develop corresponding educational measures and intervention plans. In summary, the mental health prediction method based on Adaboost algorithm proposed in the article, combined with the application of decision tree algorithm, can effectively identify psychological problems among college students. In the experiment, this method demonstrated high accuracy and robustness.

Keywords. Adaboost algorithm; University students; Mental health; Prediction methods; Decision trees

1. Introduction

With rapid socio-economic development and increasingly fierce competition in employment, contemporary university students are facing unprecedented pressure from academic, employment and interpersonal relationships, which has led to the emergence of psychological disorders and the occurrence of malicious incidents. Students are more prone to mental health problems such as confusion, anxiety, anxiety, low self-esteem, rebellion and even hate psychology due to their studies and employment. Therefore, the use of technology to identify the mental health problems timely and to take measures to educate, guide and treat them has become an important topic of research in mental health education in higher education. Data mining is a knowledge discovery process that uses algorithms to search for hidden information from a large amount of

---

[1] Corresponding Author: Na GUO, E-mail: 234074489@qq.com.

data, allowing intelligent and efficient analysis and processing of big data. The application of data mining methods to the analysis of university students' psychological problems and crisis warning has attracted widespread attention from researchers in China.

2. Related Technical Studies

The level of individual mental health has always been a major variable in shaping and promoting their growth and development [1]. China has clearly stated the importance of psychological counseling and improving mental health education. In recent years, relevant policies on improving public mental health have been continuously improved and strengthened to enhance public awareness of mental health. However, the problem of public mental health has not been fully resolved [2]. With the further attention of the state and people on this issue, more and more experts in the field of psychology have invested in the research of mental health problems [3]. They gain a deeper understanding in the field of the treatment and prevention of mental health problems, and in the continuous research, the methods and models of mental health prediction have been also continuously developed. However, the research on mental health still cannot keep up with the pace of social development, and there is a problem of asynchronous development [4]. So far, domestic experts' research on mental health mainly in facing psychological problems, coping strategies, challenges, reasons and how to predict and deal with them in time. Some scholars mainly analyze the root causes, solutions, and challenges faced by current college students' mental health problems [5]. For the prediction of psychological problems, two main methods are used, one is based on research on network user data.

They analyze user behavior to predict user psychological states by obtaining network behavior data of APP users, such as Weibo and Twitter [6]. For example, through analyzing students' network behavior data and using support vector machine algorithm, random forest algorithm, etc., they can predict students' psychological health. Using Weibo active user data, based on the Big Five personality assessment scale, the personality variables can be classified and predicted through robust multi-task learning model. Through data analysis from Weibo data, they can predict risks using MLP model. However, there is a problem in these studies, that is, only through users' network behavior for prediction, so these prediction results may not be accurate [7].

Another method is to directly obtain first-hand psychological data through designing and distributing mental health questionnaires, and then analyze these data to predict mental health. Questionnaire surveys are more direct and accurate than the first method, without further analysis of the underlying psychological state of the user. For example, using multiple regression analysis to analyze the impact of positive psychological traits on mental health in college students; conducting questionnaire surveys among freshmen, and using a BP neural network model to predict students' mental health [8].

The core idea is to adjust the distribution probability of each sample in a set of psychological data to form different training sets, and integrate these basic classifiers using different weights to generate a powerful classifier. As the number of iterations increases, the upper limit of the training error rate decreases, while effectively avoiding the overfitting problems common in other algorithms, thus improving the classification accuracy of the classifier [9].

3. Mental Health Prediction Model

The decision tree algorithm is a tree-structured classification and regression method that combines classification and regression. As a classification method, it is based on the classification of feature attributes and builds a model based on the principle of minimizing the loss function. until it reaches the leaf node, and the category in the corresponding leaf node is the decision result of the model. In a decision tree, only the leaf nodes can represent the final classification, with different leaf nodes representing different classifications and other non-leaf nodes representing features or attributes [10]. The ultimate goal is to be able to correctly classify the dataset. As the model structure is a tree structure, the classification decision is made through layers of conditions, which is intuitive and easy to understand, and has the advantages of high accuracy and simple model. The decision tree algorithms used commonly include ID3 and C4.5, etc. In this paper we will use the C4.5 algorithms. The classification weights are used as parameters to adjust the sample weight distribution D. After several iterations of training, the classification of each basic classifier and its weights are obtained. The model is shown in Figure 1. The mental health prediction model is shown in Figure 1.

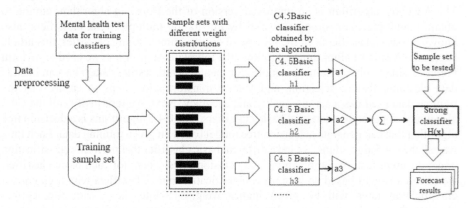

Figure 1. Mental health prediction model

4. Key Technologies

4.1. Basic Classifier Generation Algorithm

In this article, we used the C4.5 decision tree algorithm, which is a basic classifier generation algorithm. The decision tree model is a rule-based reasoning model that can learn from training samples, establish classification rules, and then classify new samples. The information gain rate is used in the C4.5 decision tree algorithm as the criterion for selecting branch attributes, which solves the problem of simply using information gain that tends to prefer attributes with more values. In addition, C4.5 also has the ability to handle incomplete and non-discrete data. Incomplete data refers to the presence of missing values in the training set, while non-discrete data refers to attributes that are not only discrete values, but also include continuous values or other forms of data. In summary, the C4.5 algorithms, which is regarded as an improved decision tree algorithm, uses information entropy and information gain rate for classification, and has high efficiency and flexibility in processing non-numeric data, selecting branch attributes, and handling incomplete and non-discrete data. By the decision tree model generated in the C4.5 algorithms, we can better classify new samples.

The following is a new description of the specific steps of the C4.5 decision tree algorithm:

(1) Initialize the starting node of the decision tree, also known as the root;

(2) If all samples S belong to a certain category C, return Root as the leaf node and label it with category C;

(3) For each element $A \in$ in the tribute Set, calculate its information gain ratio (A);

(4) Select the attribute Set with the largest Gain ratio(A) value as the test attribute for Root, that is, the optimal segmentation attribute Attest;

(5) This new leaf node will be marked as the category with the largest number of samples included in the node.

4.2. Adaboost Process for Constructing Strong Classifiers

The Adaboost algorithm is an improved version of the Boosting algorithm, aiming to obtain a high-precision strong classifier by integrating multiple weak classifiers (also known as basic classifiers). In the process of constructing a strong classifier, this article adopts the Adaboost algorithm and follows the following steps. First, we need to perform preprocessing to obtain training samples for mental health testing data. This can include data cleaning, feature selection, and feature transformation steps to ensure that the training data used has a certain quality and accuracy. Next, we repeatedly call the C4.5 algorithms to generate a series of basic classifiers. The C4.5 algorithms is a decision tree algorithm that can generate a decision tree model based on given training data. Each time we call the C4.5 algorithms, we get a different basic classifier that performs classification under different feature combinations and decision rules. Then, for each basic classifier, we assign a weight based on its correct classification rate. Classifiers with high correct classification rates will be given higher weights, while those with low correct classification rates will be given lower weights. The purpose of this is to make those classifiers that perform well in the training data play a greater role in the final strong classifier. Finally, we combine all the basic classifiers to obtain the final strong classifier. When some new samples are detected, we provide these samples in parallel to all the basic classifiers, and add the weights of those classifiers that have the same classification result. Finally, the highest weight of the classification result will be chosen as the output of the strong classifier. This method of using Adaboost to build a strong classifier can improve the accuracy and stability of classification. By integrating the prediction results of multiple basic classifiers, we can leverage their respective strengths to obtain a more reliable and accurate classification result.

The logistic regression model is solved using a gradient ascent/descent algorithm for optimization. If you want to minimize the loss function you use gradient descent, if you want to maximize the likelihood function you use gradient ascent, they are essentially the same thing. Firstly, a sample set containing N training samples of mental health data is inputted.

$$D = \{(x_1, y_1), \cdots, (x_i, y_i), \cdots, (x_N, y_N)\} \; x_i \in X, y_i \in Y \tag{1}$$

X is the sample set, Y is the sample class, $Y = \{-1, +1\}$ and each sample x_i contains the K-dimensional feature .

In the second step, the weight distribution of the sample set is initialized.

$$D_1 = \{w_1(x_i)\}, w_1(x_i) = \frac{1}{N}, i = 1, 2, \cdots, N$$

(2)

In the third step, perform a loop on any $t \in \{1, 2, \cdots, T\}$ (where T is the number of basic classifiers).

Using samples with a weight distribution of D_t for learning, a basic classifier h_j is trained for each $v_j(x)$.

$$h_j = \begin{cases} 1, p_j v_j(x) < p_j \theta_j \\ -1, p_j v_j(x)..p_j \theta_j \end{cases}$$

(3)

θ_j is the threshold value, p_j is the bias value and $p_j \in \{-1, 1\}$.
The weighted error rate is calculated.

$$\varepsilon_j = \sum_{i=1}^{n} w_t(x_i) |h_j(x_i) \neq y_i|$$

(4)

The error rate ε_j minimum value h_j corresponding to ε_t is used as the basic classifier for this loop h_t

(2) Calculation of the weighting parameter α_t for h_t .

$$\alpha_t = \frac{1}{2} \ln\left(\frac{1-\varepsilon_t}{\varepsilon_t}\right)$$

(5)

(3) Update the weighting distribution using the weighting parameter α_t .

$$D_{t+1} = \{w_{t+1}(x_i)\}, w_{t+1}(x_i) = \frac{w_t(x_i)e^{(-\alpha_t y_i h_t(x_i))}}{Z_t} \quad i = 1, 2, \cdots, N$$

(6)

Z_t For the normalization factor, $Z_t = \sum w_t(x_i)e^{(-\alpha_t y_i h_t(x_i))}$.

In the fourth step, the final strong classifier is constructed through the T optimal basic classifiers obtained from the T rounds of training $H(x)$.

$$H(x) = \text{sign}\left(\sum_{t=1}^{T} \alpha_t h_t(x)\right)$$

(7)

5. Experiments and Analysis of Results

This study collected data from students in the class of 2015 in a university to test their mental health and personality traits. The mental health test used the SCL-90 scale, including 90 items divided into 10 factors. Each factor has 5 items, and participants are required to choose 1 (none), 2 (very slight), 3 (moderate), 4 (serious), or 5 (extremely serious) to indicate the degree of psychological symptoms of the corresponding item based on their own situation. In addition, the personality test used the Eysenck Personality Questionnaire (EPQ). The questionnaire consists of four scales. Through the collection and analysis of these tests, we will be able to gain a deeper understanding of the mental health status and personality traits of the college student population. This will help provide them with better mental health support and intervention strategies to promote their all-round development. The first three scales represent three separate dimensions of personality structure, while L is the validity scale, which represents fictive personality traits and the level of social simplicity and infantilism. The version of the scale used in this paper is the Eysenck Personality Questionnaire Short Form Chinese version (EPQ- RSC).

Model evaluation plays an important role in the entire data mining process [11-13]. Before each prediction model is implemented, it is difficult to know the specific strengths and weaknesses of the prediction model in the research direction. Therefore, multiple prediction model experiments are required, and model evaluation metrics are used to evaluate each model based on the prediction results, in order to select the optimal prediction model for the research direction. As the possible response options for a scale entry are discrete values, missing values are filled in by counting the most frequent values for that entry. To facilitate data processing by the algorithm, the values taken for all questionnaire items are abstracted into codes.

The experiments were carried out on a Dell Inspiron 3650-D1838 machine and the algorithms were programmed in Python. The test samples were divided into a training set and a test set. Of these, 1,800 were training samples and 980 were test samples. The Adaboost integrated learning classifier was trained using the training samples, and the positive and negative samples were classified based on the expert assessment of the samples by the school's mental health counselling center. The final test set was tested and compared with the Mental Health Assessment Centre's assessment data. To observe the final performance of the classifier, the following two indicators were considered.

$$\text{Recall} = \frac{PP}{PP + NP}$$

(8)

The final classifier was tested on 980 test samples and the results were compared with the results of the basic classifier based on the decision tree algorithm C4.5 on the same dataset and the statistics are shown in Table 1.

Table 1. Classifier classification results

Classified ware	Number of positive samples	Negative sample size	PP	PN	NP	NN	Recall	Accuracy
Adaboost + C4.5	28	952	26	12	2	940	0.9286	0.9857
C4.5	28	952	25	27	3	925	0.8928	0.9694

The results in Table 1 indicate that the performance of the classifier based on the integrated learning Adaboost algorithm has improved significantly in terms of accuracy and recall [14].

6. Conclusion

This article proposes a method that combines the C4.5 decision tree algorithm and Adaboost ensemble learning algorithm to construct a classifier for predicting the mental health problems that college students may face. The experimental results show that the ensemble learning classifier using this algorithm has significant improvements in both accuracy and recall. This algorithm can provide support to mental health counselors, student administrators, and counselors understand students' psychological development, main symptoms of mental health problems, and personality traits, enabling them to focus on students who may have mental health problems, provide deeper care, guidance, and psychological therapy, and prevent them from encountering mental health problems in the future.

The research of the college students' mental health is an important and promising field. With the increasing complexity of the social environment, college students are facing increasing psychological stress [15]. With the ubiquity of mental health issues, many researches are paying more and more attention to the development of mental health education curriculum, and exploring how to integrate it into the university curriculum. The rapid development of digitization and information technology has made online psychological counseling possible, and this form has been applied in many places. This article hopes to provide services to more college students who need help through online platforms. Depending on different sources of stress, college students' coping strategies will differ; this article hopes to find the most effective coping strategies to help college students deal with various pressures. For those special groups that are easily affected by psychological stress, this article hopes to gain a deep understanding of their mental health status in order to provide effective intervention and help. In general, research in the field of college students' mental health is constantly expanding to meet society's needs. In the future, we may see more innovative research methods and strategies being used to improve the mental health of college students.

Reference

[1] Prodipto Bishnu Angon, Sujit Mondal, Chandona Rani Das, Mintu Kumar Bishnu. Behavioral Changes of Children Intelligence for the Extreme Affection of Parents [J]. International Journal of Education and Management Engineering (IJEME), 2021, 11(6): 20-28.

[2] Yu Jiayuan. Application of fuzzy comprehensive evaluation based on genetic algorithm in psychometric measurement [J]. Journal of Psychology, 2009(10): 1015-1023 (in Chinese).

[3] Ahuja, R., & Banga, A. Mental stress detection in university students using machine learning algorithms [J]. Procedia Computer Science, 2019, 152: 349–353.

[4] Kim, J. Y., Liu, N., Tan, H. X., & Chu, C. H. Unobtrusive Monitoring to Detect Depression for Elderly with Chronic Illnesses [J]. IEEE Sensors Journal, 2017, 17(17): 5694–5704.

[5] Andrews, G., Bell, C., Boyce, P., Gale, C., Lampe, L., Marwat, O., Wilkins, G. Royal Australian and New Zealand College of Psychiatrists clinical practice guidelines for the treatment of panic disorder, social anxiety disorder and generalised anxiety disorder [J]. Australian and New Zealand Journal of Psychiatry, 2018, 52(12): 1109–1172.

[6] He Guangdong. Research on the application of data mining technology in the analysis of college students' psychological problems [D]. Baoding: Hebei University, 2013 (in Chinese).

[7]   Muruka C. and Muruka, A. Guidelines for Environmental Health Management in Children's Homes in Sub-Sahara Africa [J]. International Journal of Environmental Research and Public Health. 2007, 4(4): 319-331.

[8]   Alan Abelsohn, John Frank and John Eyles. Environmental Public Health Tracking/Surveillance in Canada: A Commentary [J]. Healthcare Policy, 2009, 4(3): 37-52.

[9]   Adebayo P. Idowu, Emmanuel R. Adagunodo, Olapeju A. Esimai. Development of a Web Based Environmental Health Tracking System for Nigeria [J]. International Journal of Information Technology and Computer Science, 2012, 4(7): 61-71.

[10] Nor Safika Mohd Shafiee, Sofianita Mutalib. Prediction of Mental Health Problems among Higher Education Student Using Machine Learning [J]. International Journal of Education and Management Engineering, 2020, 10(6): 1-9.

[11] Snigdho Dip Howlader, Tushar Biswas, Aishwarjyo Roy, Golam Mortuja, Dip Nandi, "A Comparative Analysis of Algorithms for Heart Disease Prediction Using Data Mining", International Journal of Information Technology and Computer Science, Vol.15, No.5, pp.45-54, 2023.

[12] Md. Al Muzahid Nayim, Fahmidul Alam, Md. Rasel, Ragib Shahriar, Dip Nandi, "Comparative Analysis of Data Mining Techniques to Predict Cardiovascular Disease", International Journal of Information Technology and Computer Science, Vol.14, No.6, pp.23-32, 2022.

[13] P. Amaranatha Reddy, MHM Krishna Prasad, " Sliding Window Based High Utility Item-Sets Mining over Data Stream Using Extended Global Utility Item-Sets Tree", International Journal of Image, Graphics and Signal Processing, Vol.14, No.5, pp. 72-83, 2022.

[14] Sabourin, A. A., Prater, J. C., & Mason, N. A. Assessment of mental health in Doctor of Pharmacy Students [J]. Currents in Pharmacy Teaching and Learning, 2019, 11(3): 243–250.

[15] McLafferty, M., Lapsley, C. R., Ennis, E., Armour, C., Murphy, S., Bunting, B. P., O'Neill, S. M. Mental health, behavioural problems and treatment seeking among students commencing university in Northern Ireland [J]. PLoS ONE, 2017, 12(12): 1–14.

Artificial Intelligence, Medical Engineering and Education
Z.B. Hu et al. (Eds.)

213

doi:10.3233/ATDE231331

Financial Original Voucher Classification and Verification System Based on Deep Learning

Wenhao YAO[a,1], Wen HUA[b,2], Huiying WANG[b]

[a]*International business school, Xi'an jiaotong-Liverpool University*
[b]*Finance Office, Wuhan University of Technology, Wuhan, China*
ORCiD ID: Wenhao.YAO https://orcid.org/0009-0009-9437-7856

Abstract. Aiming at the problems of voucher preparation errors, numerous verification rules, lengthy audit cycle and low efficiency in the process of voucher preparation and audit of financial reimbursement in Colleges and universities, based on the implementation process of financial reimbursement process, this paper designs a framework of financial original voucher classification and verification system based on deep learning, and proposes a deep learning algorithm to identify the key contents of financial original vouchers, so as to support the voucher preparation process of financial reimbursement personnel Review and verification process of financial personnel. By testing the existing financial reimbursement process, the original voucher can be accurately classified according to the requirements of the national tax system for the classification of goods, for the identification of the type of daily reimbursement; based on the preprocessing of bills, FRCNN algorithms in deep learning can be applied to identify the key contents of bills.

Keywords. Deep learning, Classification and verification, Financial original voucher

1. Introduction

In recent years, with the rapid development of artificial intelligence, big data, and information technology, the applications of deep learning have become increasingly broad, especially in the fields of finance and taxation [1-4]. In the daily operation of enterprises and institutions, the financial management system plays an essential role. These systems including financial accounting, financial analysis, financial sharing and industry finance integration, to help enterprises and institutions achieve efficient financial management. Financial accounting is the basis for data storage and financial analysis of the entire system. Financial accounting consists of original voucher review, bookkeeping voucher preparation, banking system settlement and additional links. For financial accounting, it is necessary to verify the authenticity of the original vouchers. On this basis, the financial staff will review the reimbursement form and corresponding original vouchers filled in by the reimbursement applicant, and prepare accounting

---

[1] Corresponding Author: Wenhao YAO, Email: Wenhao.Yao21@student.xjtlu.edu.cn.
[2] Corresponding Author: Wen HUA, Email: 598526841@qq.com.

vouchers. Finally, the cashier will complete the bank settlement. However, in the financial reimbursement system of colleges and universities, the reimbursement applicant needs to select the corresponding reimbursement entry according to the content of the original voucher when filling in the reimbursement form. Due to limited financial knowledge errors are inevitable when choosing a particular type of reimbursement. After being reviewed by the financial staff, the reimbursement form is returned to its original state and the reimbursement applicant has to repeat the above voucher preparation process, which is a huge waste of time. Therefore, the original reimbursement voucher must be initially verified and classified to reduce the unnecessary turnover process in the reimbursement process and improve the efficiency of financial reimbursement.

In order to make accounting more accurate, efficient and automatic, optical recognition technology (OCR) has been gradually applied to the recognition of financial bills. The invoice text contains highly significant information [5-6]. Making full use of this information can considerably improve the recognition effect of invoices. However, because the collection of financial bills is formed by scanning or photographing, the layout of financial bills is diverse, including a variety of different fonts, sizes, colors and backgrounds, as well as mixed Chinese and English characters, resulting in the complexity of financial bills, which makes OCR technology face great challenges in identifying and extracting bill information. Image recognition technology, especially the application of image recognition technology based on deep learning, provides necessary support for accurate recognition and efficient processing of financial original vouchers. At present, among the deep learning algorithms, the text recognition algorithms include fast RCNN, mask RCNN [7], YOLOs [8], Textboxes [9], Graph Convolutional Network [10], and the character recognition algorithms include CRNN [11-12], RARE [13], and FOTS [14]. These algorithms are implemented by training on a large amount of sample data, and deep learning models are able to learn the features and patterns of different types of vouchers to accurately match vouchers in a graph with known vouchers. This accuracy is not only reflected in the identification of the voucher itself, but can also be extended to the identification of the words, numbers, and other key information in the voucher. At the same time, the image recognition technology based on deep learning can complete the processing of a large number of vouchers in a relatively short time.

Therefore, this paper designs a system framework of financial original voucher classification and verification based on deep learning, and proposes a deep learning algorithm to realize the identification of the key content of the original bill, and support the preparation process of the financial reimbursement person, the review and verification process of the financial person.

2. Process and Framework of Classification and Verification System

2.1 Voucher Processing Process

With the digital transformation of financial governance, the delivery reimbursement is the current mode of use in colleges and universities. It places an online voucher delivery machine in the school, and the reimbursement applicant can put the reimbursement form into the delivery machine in time according to his own situation without waiting at the financial site. In this mode, the reimbursement applicant will put the reimbursement form approved by the project leader into the delivery machine, and the delivery machine will allocate the reimbursement form to the financial accounting personnel, who will receive the reimbursement form for financial processing by themselves. At the same time, combined with the online feedback function of the financial system, the reimbursement results will be pushed to the reimbursement applicant by SMS. When the reimbursement document is approved, the system will automatically send a message of successful reimbursement to the operator after the accounting staff generates an accounting voucher for review. When there is a problem with the reimbursement form, the accounting personnel can also send a text message to inform the reason through the financial system, and the handler will go to the financial operator to continue processing after receiving the text message.

The processing flow of financial reimbursement vouchers is shown in Figure 1.

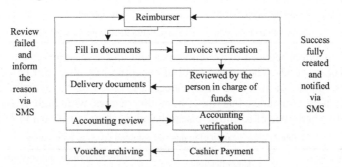

Figure 1. Delivery reimbursement flow chart

In the current financial system, the reimbursement applicant needs to select the reimbursement category according to the original voucher when filling in the reimbursement form, such as daily reimbursement and asset reimbursement. Due to the limited financial expertise of the reimbursement applicant, it is usually unable to accurately determine the corresponding category, resulting in the filling error of the reimbursement form, which needs to be modified and re delivered after being returned by the financial staff. At present, the use of technical means to scan and identify the authenticity of invoices has been widely used in financial reimbursement practice, but the scanning and verification technology only records the contents of the original voucher invoice and associates it with the bookkeeping voucher, and cannot judge the contents of the original voucher and drive the reimbursement applicant to the correct reimbursement category entry. This paper takes the selection of daily reimbursement form and asset reimbursement form as an example, by identifying the two key information of "goods or taxable services, service name" and "unit price" on the original voucher invoice, the system independently judges and selects the correct reimbursement category to ensure the accuracy of voucher preparation.

2.2 Identification Characteristics of Financial Vouchers

In the selection of financial reimbursement category, the "name of goods or taxable services and services" on the original voucher invoice is related to the classification code of goods and services tax implemented by the State Administration of Taxation on May 1st, 2016. Tax classification codes, which are the identity codes of goods, taxable services or services, are composed of 19 digits and are classified according to different levels to strengthen collection management. The first level is divided into six categories:

goods, labor services, services, intangible assets, real estate, and non-taxable items without sales actions, as shown in Table 1.

Table 1. Tax Code Level 1 Classification

Tax classification code	First level classification
1000000000000000000	Goods
2000000000000000000	Labor services
3000000000000000000	services
4000000000000000000	intangible assets
5000000000000000000	real estate
6000000000000000000	Non taxable items without sales behavior

The distinction between daily reimbursement and asset reimbursement in finance mainly involves goods. The second level of encoding is further split based on the first level, where goods are involved in 10 categories. Based on the actual situation of W University, it is concluded that the commodity names with high frequency in the administrative activities of scientific research and teaching are shown in Table 2.

Table 2. Classification of goods and common goods in universities

Second layer coding of goods	Classification	Goods categories commonly involved in universities
105	Wood products and furniture products	Office desks, chairs, laboratory supplies storage cabinets, etc
106	Paper, printed goods, software, cultural and educational, handicraft products	Printing paper, notebooks, neutral pens, books, etc
107	Petroleum, chemical, pharmaceutical products	Chemical materials such as ethylene ether, asphalt, gasoline diesel lubricating oil, etc
108	Metal and non-metallic products	Pliers, steel plates, deck structures, anti-static and impact resistant flooring, etc
109	Machinery and equipment products	Electronic components, sensors, computers and their accessories, etc

2.3 Financial Voucher Classification and Verification System Process and Framework

According to the financial reimbursement process, in the classification and verification process of financial original vouchers, whether the goods need to be reimbursed for asset acceptance depends on its category and unit price amount. Taking this as one of the judgment criteria, the process and implementation framework of the financial voucher classification and verification system are designed in combination with invoice recognition technology, as shown in Figure 2.

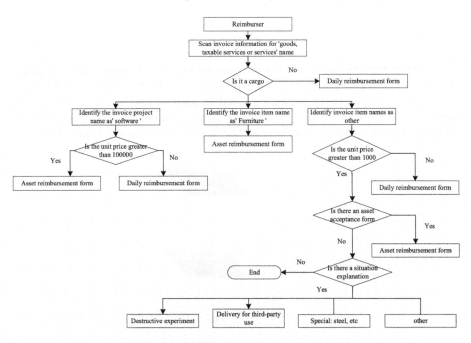

Figure 2. Process and implementation framework of financial voucher classification and verification system

3. Invoice Image Recognition Algorithm based on Deep Learning

The fast RCNN algorithm is mainly used in invoice recognition processing. It is mainly divided into four steps: Invoice region segmentation, invoice text correction, text region detection, and text recognition, as shown in Figure 3.

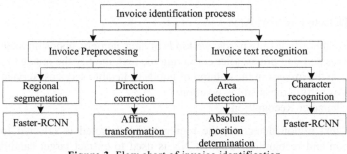

Figure 3. Flow chart of invoice identification

3.1 Invoice Preprocessing

Invoice image preprocessing refers to invoice area recognition and direction correction, so that the image entering the subsequent text recognition can maintain a single invoice area, remove the non-invoice background, and make the text direction more consistent with the recognition direction.

- Invoice area segmentation

There are numerous sources of invoice images and various shooting methods. Some images contain only a single bill, leaving a large background area. These unimportant factors can have an impact on invoice recognition, and invoice region segmentation is essentially to take the invoice region as the target object and detect it in the image. In area segmentation processing, this paper selects the rapid RCNN algorithm to realize the invoice area segmentation function. Fast RCNN combines RPN and fast RCNN. The former is responsible for extracting high-quality suggestion area boxes, while the latter classifies them by learning their features. The flow chart is shown in Figure 4.

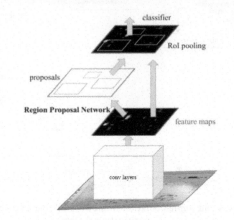

Figure 4. Flow chart of faster RCNN

● Invoice direction correction

The text recognition algorithm used is based on a horizontal image of a single row text field. The actual angle of the invoice image is random, so it is necessary to correct the horizontal direction of the invoice area obtained by the fast RCNN.

3.2 Invoice Text Recognition

● Detection of Text Area

Because this article only needs two kinds of data, namely, goods or taxable services, service names and unit prices, after correcting the text, modify the image to a fixed size, and then crop the images in the column of goods or taxable services, service names and unit prices by setting the absolute position.

● Character Recognition

After text region detection, the region to be detected is selected for character segmentation and recognition. Fast RCNN is used to extract target candidate regions from the feature maps given by the backbone network, and then ROI region features of the same size are obtained by ROI merging, which are sent to multiple classifiers for target classification and location regression. Fast RCNN is a single and unified object detection network with high detection accuracy and speed, As shown in Figure 5.

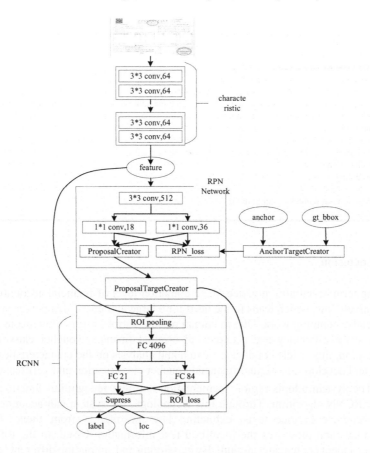

Figure 5. Fast RCNN processing

4. System Example Result Analysis

To test the feasibility of this method, the system inputs different types of invoices for testing. For more complex invoices, such as name classes with multiple lines for different items and multiple lines for the same item, the results of the operation are shown in Figure 6 and the procedure of the operation algorithm is shown in Table 3.

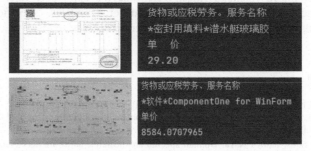

Figure 6. Example demonstration of invoice recognition algorithm

Table 3 Invoice recognition algorithm

(1) Read all images in the folder to the image set images
(2) Loop 1: traverse all images
(3) Using fast RCNN to remove background
(4) Correcting text by affine transformation
(5) Determination of detection position by relative position
(6) Using fast RCNN to recognize characters to get name data set, number of name lines and number set
(7) Index1, unit price data set price, unit price line number set index2
(8) End cycle 1
(9) Loop 2: traversing data1
(10) Judgment 1: if there is no * sign at the beginning of the line
(11) Delete turn mark
(12) End judgment 1
(13) End cycle 2
(14) New dataset name for output data1
(15) Output price

5. Conclusion

In long-term accounting practice, the automation level of financial accounting systems is relatively low, which leads to the need for a large amount of manpower investment in financial accounting work. Due to human reason, various errors often occur. In order to improve the efficiency and accuracy of original financial voucher classification and verification, this article conducts research and analysis on the characteristics of invoice texts, and develops an original financial voucher classification and verification system.

The system adopts region segmentation and text recognition functions based on Faster RCNN algorithm. Through this technology, the system can accurately segment and recognize invoice texts, extracting key information from them. This article categorizes and processes the identified text information based on the differences in reimbursement content and amount. By classifying and annotating different types of text, the system can display the details of each transaction more clearly, avoiding repetitive operations in the reimbursement and verification process caused by human error, greatly reducing the time and cost of manual operation, and improving overall work efficiency and quality.

For the designed system, in practical applications, the following work should also be done well:

1) Data collection and preparation: Ensure that sufficient invoice text samples are collected as training datasets, and clean and preprocess the data.

2) Customized financial rules: Determine the applicable rules based on actual financial needs, such as customized voucher templates, specific project policy requirements, and standardized reimbursement processes.

References

[1] Eugene Charniak. Introduction to deep learning[M]. The MIT Press, 2019.

[2] Feng Xin, Jiang Youni, Yang Xuejiao, et al. Computer vision algorithms and hardware implementations: A survey[J]. Integration, 2019 (69): 309–320.

[3] Angel I. Solis, Patrica Nava. Domain specific architectures, hardware acceleration for machine/deep learning[C]. Proc. SPIE 11013, Disruptive Technologies in Information Sciences II, 1101307. Baltimore : International Society for Optics and Photonics, 2019. 1101307.

[4]   Mukesh Jha, Madhur Kabra, Sahil Jobanputra, et al. Automation of cheque transaction using deep learning and optical character recognition[C]. 2019 International Conference on Smart Systems and Inventive Technology (ICSSIT), Tirunelveli : IEEE, 2019. 309–312.

[5]   Zhang H, Zheng Q, Dong B, et al. A financial ticket image intelligent recognition system based on deep learning[J]. Knowledge-Based Systems, 2021, 222: 106955.

[6]   Zhang H, Dong B, Zheng Q, et al. All-content text recognition method for financial ticket images[J]. Multimedia Tools and Applications: An International Journal. 2022,81(20):28327-28346.

[7]   A. K. M. Fahim Rahman, Mostofa Rakib Raihan, S.M. Mohidul Islam. Pedestrian Detection in Thermal Images Using Deep Saliency Map and Instance Segmentation[J]. International Journal of Image, Graphics and Signal Processing, 2021. 13(1):40-49.

[8]   Ashutosh Kumar Tiwari, Sandeep Varma Nadimpalli. Learning Semantic Image Attributes Using Image Recognition and Knowledge Graph Embeddings[J], International Journal of Image, Graphics and Signal Processing. 2020, 12(5):44-52.

[9]   Liao Minghui, Shi Baoguang, Bai Xiang, et al. Textboxes: A fast text detector with a single deep neural network[EB/OL]. 2016, arXiv preprint arXiv:1611.06779.

[10]   Thomas N. Kipf, Max Welling. Semi-supervised classification with graph convolutional networks[EB/OL]. 2016, arXiv preprint arXiv:1609.02907.

[11]   Lokeshwar S, Vadiraja Rao M. K, Sujay Kumar P. S, et al. Analog Document Search Using CRNN and Keyphrase Extraction[J]. International Journal of Image, Graphics and Signal Processing. 2021, 13(2):16-24.

[12]   Shi Baoguang, Bai Xiang, Yao Cong. An end-to-end trainable neural network for image-based sequence recognition and its application to scene text recognition[J]. IEEE Trans. Pattern Anal. Mach. Intell. 2016,39 (11): 2298–2304.

[13]   Shi Baoguang, Wang Xinggang, Lyu Pengyuan, et al. Robust scene text recognition with automatic rectification[C]. Proceedings of the IEEE Conference on Computer Vision and Pattern Recognition. Las Vegas: IEEE, 2016. 4168–4176.

[14]   Liu Xuebo, Ding Liang, Shi Yan, et al. Fots: Fast oriented text spotting with a unified network[C]. Proceedings of the IEEE Conference on Computer Vision and Pattern Recognition. Salt Lake City :IEEE, 2018. 5676–5685.

Artificial Intelligence, Medical Engineering and Education
Z.B. Hu et al. (Eds.)

doi:10.3233/ATDE231332

Analysis of Psychological Health Data for College Students Based on Data Mining

Qin JIN[1]

College of Resources and Environment, Wuhan University of Technology, Wuhan,
Hubei 430070, China
ORCiD ID: Qin Jin https: //orcid.org/0009-0004-9330-1482

Abstract. The backlog of pressure from multiple parties has led to a variety of psychological problems and has also led to many irreparable tragedies. It is very important for college student management to pay attention to the mental health problems of college students, and to discover and guide the mental health development of college students in time. This paper uses data mining technology to set up a questionnaire with 90 questions reflecting mental health as a sample. Using the "SCL-90 Symptom Self-Rating Scale" as the evaluation standard, data were collected, a data set was established, and data analysis was carried out, so as to detect and adjust psychological problems in time and avoid the aggravation of problems and lead to suicide and other irreversible problems.

Keywords. Mental health of college students; SCL-90 symptom self-rating scale; Data mining; Prediction model

1. Introduction

For a long time, people did everything they could for their physical health, but the low level of economy and consumption made people unconcerned about mental health. At the same time, due to limited awareness, people did not realise the importance of mental health, and physical health was basically all people knew about health. This view has long been embedded in people's minds, and even now many people still disdain mental health and consider psychological problems to be insignificant. While physical health is essential, psychological health is also vital [1]. Physical health and psychological health are indispensable, and neither can be called healthy without the other.

There are a variety of definitions of mental health, and specific measures vary. The American scholar Cambs analyzed and researched from the perspective of personality traits and believed that mental health should include traits such as positive perceptions, identification with others, open acceptance and confrontation with reality, clear understanding of oneself and one's surroundings and environment, rich experience and the ability to call on experience to solve problems when encountering them. Orbolt, on the other hand, has studied from the perspective of mature human nature and believes that a healthy personality should have the ability to extend itself, good interpersonal relationships, emotional security and identity, perceptual objectivity, and a unified and correct outlook on life [2].

---

[1] Corresponding Author: Qin JIN, E-mail: txcf2000@163.com.

In general, psychological health is defined as a positive state of all aspects and processes of human psychological activity, the ability to harmonise relationships, and the ability to adapt to the environment [3]. In the context of positive psychology, the main criteria for the mental health of university students include the following: self-acceptance, open-mindedness, the ability to accept both strengths and weaknesses and face them objectively, constantly developing self-awareness and facing people and events in life positively, positive and optimistic, maintaining enthusiasm for life, not being negative in the face of setbacks, being able to summarize the reasons for failure in time and solve problems calmly, good empathy, being able to feel hope for a better future and find a sense of meaning, always feeling a sense of happiness in life, forming a perfect personality, good empathy, being able to feel a sense of happiness in life, being able to feel a sense of meaning in life [4]. They are hopeful, full of hope for a better future and able to find a sense of meaning, always feeling a sense of happiness in life and forming a perfect personality, good empathy, able to feel the emotions of others and care about their feelings, with the ability to think differently, able to agree with the views and attitudes of others and accept their advice, good interpersonal relationships the student should be able to live in harmony with others, not to malign and hate others, and to live in harmony with others [5]. University students should be aware of their own state of being, in their daily lives.

Studies on prevalence reveal that a considerable proportion of college students experience psychological distress, with common disorders being anxiety, depression, and substance abuse. The research on causes reproduces a wide range of contributing factors from academic performance pressures, social isolation, to financial difficulties.

While notable work has been done to map the extent and underpinnings of psychological health issues in college students, there remain gaps in understanding how to effectively interpret the data obtained and adapt it into effective strategies for prevention and intervention. Studies on management and intervention have largely focused on individual counseling, group therapies, and helpline services, but there is a dearth of research analyzing the efficacy of these strategies based on collected psychological health data.

In light of the existing research, several important questions emerge: How can psychological health data for college students be effectively utilized to improve prevention and intervention strategies? What are the key indicators in the data that could help facilitate early detection of these disorders? How can digital technology improve psychological health data collection and analysis efficiency?

These questions underscore the need for more empirical research focused on the meaningful interpretation of psychological health data, which can provide insights on tailoring more effective mental health programs for college students. This review suggests that further research is necessary to address these pressing concerns and bridge the gap in our understanding of college students' psychological health.

2. Factors Influencing the Mental Health of University Students

At present, the mental health problems of university students are emerging and showing an increasing trend of seriousness, and their influencing factors are various, the main factors include the following aspects.

(1)Physiological factors. Mental health problems can have not only psychological but also physiological causes. Research has shown that abnormalities in the functioning of the neuro-endocrine-immune network system can lead to abnormal moods in the body, with pentazocine and norepinephrine being the most representative substances in this system.

(2)Self-factor. Many students may have the wrong perception of appearance, taking appearance as an important criterion for judging a person, and there is no lack of people who combine beauty and wisdom among university students, which may devalue themselves in comparison [6]. Secondly, university students begin to face emotional problems, they are all new to relationships and may have misconceptions in their cognition in the face of complex emotional problems, and their immature view of love may lead to falling out of love and emotional problems [7].

(3)Family factors. Many students' families have more or less problems. Some parents may be divorced, or their parents may be away for a long time, making the child a left-behind child, and the lack of affection may make the child have low self-esteem, be more sensitive and withdrawn, and may have some problems in interacting with others. In addition, for some parents, they devote all their efforts to their children, hoping that they will become the best of the best, and that they will become outstanding in the future, so there may be excessive emphasis on academic achievement, making their children attend a variety of tutorial classes at the expense of their inner needs, and completely arranging their children's lives, making them unable to take charge of their own lives, which in the long run will lead to a lack of self-confidence, lack of initiative and timidity. In the long run, the child will become unconfident, lacking in initiative, timid, etc.

(4)The school factor. The university life tests students' ability in all aspects and is no longer limited to academics. This requires students to be self-monitoring, which can lead to academic anxiety for those who have poor self-control, over-indulgence or neglect of their studies, as they may experience poor academic performance and may have a significant psychological gap. Secondly, university is no longer judged on academic criteria alone, but also on social skills, practical skills, and the ability to work in the classroom.

This can be a big shock to students who are known for their grades in secondary school, and other deficiencies such as personal strengths can gradually become apparent, leading to an inferiority complex. The changes in all areas may not be a quick adjustment for university students who have just left high school life.

(5)Social factors. For students nearing graduation, the influence of social factors may be more pronounced [8]. The increasing competitiveness of employment has placed higher demands on the qualifications and knowledge level of university students, especially It is the uninterrupted emergence of the new crown pneumonia epidemic in recent years that has put many small and medium-sized companies at risk of bankruptcy, greatly reducing employment opportunities and leading to a more difficult employment situation, with many university students unable to find suitable jobs and facing the risk of unemployment upon graduation.

(6)The internet factor. The rapid development of the Internet has brought about a variety of problems. Social software has become more mature, and basically all university students are used to surfing online, so it is highly likely that they will face the problem of online violence, and the collision of ideas may lead to strong online arguments or even online attacks, which will seriously damage the psychological health of university students. Also, although college students are already adults, many of them are not yet mentally mature and cannot perfectly handle the problem between online games and studies, and may waste their studies to the extent that they face failure and difficulties in graduation [9].

3. Psychological Data Collection and Processing

The dataset for this paper is derived from online mental health questionnaires for undergraduate students at a number of universities in 2018-2020, all using the SCL-90 symptom self-assessment scale, and integrating data from each university to obtain a total of 11, 897 mental health data.

3.1. Questionnaire Design Principles

Questionnaires are about providing valuable data to the investigator by understanding targeted, purposeful questions, analysing and researching the data to derive the basis for what is needed. Therefore, the design of the questionnaire is particularly important. A good questionnaire can both communicate the questions clearly and understandably to the respondents, and at the same time make the respondents enjoy themselves and gain their support. Therefore, the questionnaire set up both to follow certain principles, but also need to be skillful. The principles of questionnaire design are as follows [10] .

(1) Clarity of purpose. The main purpose of the questionnaire is to obtain the data needed by the investigator, and the questions set must be indispensable, with no irrelevant questions. The subject is clear, the objective is clear and focused.

(2) Be logical. Questions should not be arranged randomly, but in a logical order, easy first, then difficult, set in a regular sequence, with difficult questions placed later.

(3) Easy to understand. The questionnaire is aimed at the general population, the questions should be set clearly and unambiguously, do not beat around the bush and do not use professional vocabulary, if the questions are too advanced and difficult to understand, it will reduce the interest of the respondents, the respondents can easily refuse or give up, so use a simple and easy to understand presentation.

(4) Reasonable length. The questionnaire should not be too long, too much length will cause respondents to lose patience and may give up answering, or they may answer indiscriminately to save time, resulting in less credible results.

3.2. Data Optimization

Once the data has been obtained, it needs to be optimized. A total of 11897 data were obtained in this paper, and the data were processed using Python, using data.isnull().any() to see if there were missing values in the mental health data obtained in this paper for university students, and using data.duplicated().sum() to see if there were duplicate values in the mental health data obtained in this paper for university students, and the results of the run showed that The obtained data is perfect and there are no missing values or duplicate values, this is because the score of the survey questions in this paper is limited and within a manageable range, therefore the possibility of outliers is very small. After data processing, it was found that the data set in this paper was of high quality and the sample size of the data after processing was still 11897 data items. Some of the data obtained are shown in Table 1 below.

Table 1. Selected sample data sheets

F1	F2	F3	F4	F5	F6	F7	F8	F9	Other
1.33	1.9	1	1.08	1	1.33	1.14	1	1.2	1.57
1.42	2	1.67	1.85	1.8	1.33	1.14	1.5	1.4	1.14
1	1	1	1	1	1.17	1	1	1	1
1	1.1	1	1.08	1	1	1	1	1	1
1	1.2	1.44	1.08	1.3	1	1.29	1.33	1.2	1
1.5	1.9	1.78	1.38	1.3	1.33	1.29	1.17	1.3	1.86
1.25	1.5	1.33	1.15	1.3	1	1	1.17	1.1	1.14
1.17	2	1.89	1.69	1.6	1.33	1.43	1.67	1.5	1.43
1.08	1.6	1.11	1.15	1.2	1.17	1	1.17	1	1.14
1.25	1.6	1.44	1.23	1.7	1.17	1	1.5	1.7	1.86
1.92	2.9	2.56	2.23	2.2	1.83	3.14	2	1.4	1.29
1.17	1.2	1.56	1.31	1.3	1	1.43	1.33	1.3	1.57
1	1.2	1.89	1	1.2	1.17	1.29	1.67	1.1	1
1.08	1.3	1.56	1.38	1.5	1.17	1.43	1	1.4	1.14
1	2.1	1.89	1	1.2	1.17	1.29	1.33	1.1	1
1.5	2	1.56	1.46	1.6	1.17	1.29	1.67	1.3	1.86
1.08	1.5	1.67	1.15	1.2	1.17	1.29	1.5	1	1
1.08	1.3	1.33	1.23	1.1	1.33	1	1.33	1.6	1.57

Relational sensitivity with 9 items, F4 for depression with 13 items, F5 for anxiety with 10 items, F6 for hostility with 6 items, F7 for terror with 7 items, F8 for paranoia with 6 items, F9 for psychoticism with 10 items, and other with 7 items.

4. Correlation Analysis of Variables

In this paper, there are 14 variables affecting the mental health of college students, namely total score, total mean score, mean score of positive items, number of positive items, depression, anxiety, interpersonal sensitivity, psychoticism, obsessive-compulsive disorder, paranoia, hostility, somatization, phobia, and others. In order to analyze the degree of correlation between the variables, this paper obtains a heat map based on person's correlation coefficient, as shown in Table 2. From the table we can see that the correlation coefficients for all variables were above 0.4, with strong correlations for total score, total mean score, and suppressed the correlation coefficients for depression, anxiety, number of positive items, interpersonal sensitivity, and psychoticism reached 0.8 or more, with stronger correlations relative to the other variables.

Table 2. Table of predictive model variables

Variable name	Meaning of variables	Variable type	Variable length
TOTAL_SCORE	Total score for psychological survey questions	Int	64
DEPRESSION	Depression	Float	64
ANXIETY	Anxiety	Float	64
NUMBER_OF_POSITIVE ITEMS	Number of positive items	Int	64
INTERPERSONAL_SENSITIVITY	Interpersonal sensitivity	Float	64
PSYCHOTIC	Psychogenic	Float	64
OBSESSIVE-COMPULSIVE_DISORDER	Obsessive Compulsive Disorder (OCD)	Float	64
PARANOID	Paranoia	Float	64
OTHER	Other	Float	64
HOSTILITY	Hostile	Float	64
SOMATIZATION	Somatization	Float	64
FEAR	Horror	Float	64

5. Statistical Analysis of Psychological Data

In terms of the psychological status of university students, of the 11897 data obtained from the sample of university students' mental health in this paper.The sample data for those without psychological problems was 8537, representing a proportion of the total student mental health sample of the number of data samples with psychological problems was 3360, accounting for 28.24% of the total number of students' mental health samples, but this aspect alone cannot clearly and concretely show the distribution of psychological problems. In this section, we will classify and count the mental health data obtained from university students, obtain the overall variables such as total score, total mean score, number of positive items and mean score of positive items, analyse the data from different perspectives such as local and overall, and draw the data distribution of each influence factor, total score, total mean score, number of positive items and mean score of positive items to show the distribution of mental health level and problems of university students from multiple perspectives. The data distribution of each impact factor, score, total mean score, number of positive items and mean score of positive items are plotted to show the distribution of mental health and problems among university students from multiple perspectives [11].

5.1. Analysis of the Distribution of Factors Influencing Psychological Problems

The data mining methods used in this article include:
(1) Pearson Correlation Coefficients: Measures the degree of linear correlation between two variables.

$$r = \frac{\sum (x_i - \bar{x}) * (y_i - \bar{y})}{\sqrt{\sum (x_i - \bar{x})^2 * (y_i - \bar{y})^2}} \tag{1}$$

(2) Decision Tree: An algorithm used for classification or regression problems.

$$F(x) = \text{argmax}_c \sum_{y[i]=c} [h(x,c) - y[i]] + \alpha \cdot \text{Count}(C) \tag{2}$$

(3) K-Nearest Neighbor (KNN): An algorithm used for classification or regression problems.

$$P(x) = \text{argmax}_c \sum [kNN(x, \text{train}[c]) < d(\text{train}[c], x)] \cdot (y[\text{train}[c] == c) \tag{3}$$

(4) Neural Network: An algorithm used for classification or regression problems.

$$y = \text{Sigmoid}(\omega x + b) \tag{4}$$

These formulas are only a small part involved in data mining, and when used, appropriate algorithms and formulas need to be selected based on specific problems and datasets.

5.2. Analysis of Total Score Distribution

The higher the total score is, the worse the mental health level is, and the more teachers and counsellors need to pay attention to it. When the total score does not exceed 160, it means that the student is less likely to have mental health problems, when the total score exceeds 160 but is not higher than 200, it means that the student may have mild psychological problems, but not serious, when the total score exceeds 200 but is not higher than 300 When the total score is above 160 but not above 200, the student is likely to have a moderate psychological problem, and when the total score is above 300, the student is highly likely to have a serious psychological disorder.

Among the 11897 students in the mental health sample, 10243 had a total score of 160 or less, accounting for 86.10% of the total sample. The number of students with a total score of more than 160 but not more than 200 is 1114, accounting for 9.36% of the total sample. These students have mild psychological problems, so counsellors need to communicate with these students from time to time to understand their inner thoughts, find out where the problems lie, and regularly understand their status. Compared to students with mild psychological problems, these students need the help of teachers and counsellors to help them solve their psychological problems and regulate their psychological state, and to inform their parents about their psychological condition, so that parents and schools can work together to help students and relieve their psychological pressure. There are 30 people with a total score of over 300, accounting for 0.25% of the total sample. These people are suffering from very serious psychological problems and are in an unstable and extreme state of psychological emotions, and may have thoughts of light-heartedness, and need psychological assistance from a professional counselling teacher or more systematic and professional treatment at a psychological clinic. For students who may be mentally ill, counsellors should contact parents in a timely manner and send students home for medical treatment to avoid accidents.

5.3. Analysis of the Total Mean Score Distribution

The total mean score is an extension of the total score and is an objective description of the average level of psychological problems of students. In 3.5.2, the total score is divided into four levels, no, mild, moderate and severe, so the corresponding total mean score will also be divided into four levels, no, mild, moderate and severe, which are no more than 1.78, no more than 1.78 but no more than 2.22, no more than 2.22 but no more than 3.22, no more than 1.78 but no more than 2.22 and no more than 3.22. over 1.78 but no higher than 2.22, over 2.22 but no higher than 3.33, over 3.33, and Although the total score and the mean score represent different meanings, they are consistent in terms of the level of mental health of the students and the number of students in each level remains the same, so this section does not analyse the data on the total mean score in detail.

5.4. Analysis of the Distribution of the Number of Positive Items

Although the data on the mental health of university students have been analysed from the perspective of total and mean scores, the analysis from the overall perspective is still rather thin as there is a certain degree of consistency between the total and mean scores, and they overlap to a considerable extent. The number of positive items refers to the total number of items with a score of more than 2. The questionnaire in this paper contains 90 items, and according to the results of the SCL-90 Symptom Self-Rating Inventory, we can see that when the number of positive items exceeds 43, the student has a high probability of having mental health problems. Therefore, in this paper, the number of positive items obtained from the psychological survey in the mental health data set was categorised using 43 items as the classification boundary.The majority of these students (more than 47 items) scored below 2, indicating that in the majority of the 90 survey items in this paper did not show any psychological problems, so on the whole, these people are less likely to have mental health problems, but it should not be ignored that there are still some university students whose number of positive items is at the border of 43, which is within the normal range but still has a certain risk. Therefore, we should not ignore this group of university students and should conduct psychological surveys from time to time to pay attention to their psychological health and prevent them from developing psychological problems due to the occurrence of other problems [14].

The number of positive items exceeded 43, accounting for 19.79% of the total sample. The number of positive items indicates that most of them have mental health problems and need the help of teachers and counsellors. For those students who are positive for most of the items, they need not only psychological counselling, but also professional psychological staff to diagnose and analyse their problems and seek medical treatment in time.

5.5. Analysis of the Mean Score Distribution of Positive Items

The mean score of positive items is the average score of all items with a positive test result, i.e. those with a score of 2 or more. The value is the ratio of the total score of positive items to the number of positive items, which is an objective description of the average level of positive items, as it is only for items that present a positive result. As there are no positive items for those with a mean positive score of no more than 2, and all items are in a normal state, this paper does not examine them, but only those with a mean positive score of more than 2. This paper examines the mean positive item scores in the mental health dataset.The classification is based on a scale of 3 and 4, and is divided into those with a score of more than 2 but not more than 3, those with a score of more than 3, and those with a score of more than the three levels of scoring, not higher than 4 and more than 4, are categorised and counted. The number of people who scored more than 2 but not more than 3 was 8180, which is the percentage of the total sample 68.76%, those scoring more than 3 but not more than 4 were 353, or 2.97% of the total sample.The number of people with a score of more than 4 was 35, representing 0.29% of the total sample. From the above data we can see that the majority of people with a positive score are in the mild stage and not yet severe enough to warrant intervention. This is because the mean score of positive items is a measure of the severity of positive items, not a measure of the overall distribution of psychological problems among university students. The mean score of positive items is higher than 2, so that those who do not score above 2 are those who do not have any of the 90 items.For those with a positive score of more than 2, we can only judge the presence of positive items but not the number of positive items, and therefore we cannot judge whether the university student has a mental health problem. If this item is used as an indicator to evaluate whether a university student has a psychological problem, there is a high risk of misjudgment for those students who have 43 positive items or less, so it can be used to determine whether the average level of positive items is mild, moderate or severe, but it cannot be used as a criterion to evaluate whether a university student has a psychological problem.

Therefore, in order to prevent overfitting, we can select one of the predictor variables and discard one, in this paper, we choose to discard the total mean score. In addition, the mean score of positive items is the average score of all positive items. When the number of positive items does not exceed 43 and the mean score of each factor does not exceed 2, there may be cases where the mean score of positive items is high. Therefore, this indicator is not used as a predictor variable in this paper. As each of the other factors exceeds the corresponding value, it is possible that there is a mental health problem, and the purpose of psychological prediction is to identify and improve the psychological condition of students with mental health problems as much as possible, so each variable has an important value.

6. Conclusion

In recent years, the proportion of college students suffering from depression has increased. Especially since the COVID-19 in 2020, many smaller enterprises are facing the crisis of development difficulties or even bankruptcy, which has led to a sharp reduction in the number of social recruitments, increasing employment pressure on college students, which has greatly increased the living and psychological pressure on college students. Students with insufficient psychological endurance are prone to depression, Therefore, it is very important for universities to promptly identify students with psychological problems and provide professional psychological guidance. This article obtained psychological health data of some college students through a questionnaire survey, and fully utilized data mining technology to analyze the sample data. Multiple prediction models were used to predict the psychological health of college students.

Reference

[1]   Chawla N V, Bowyer K W, Hall L O, et al. SMOTE: synthetic minority over-sampling technique[J]. Journal of Artificial Intelligence Research, 2002, 16(1): 321-357.

[2]   Brathwaite R, Rocha B M, Kieling C, et al. Predicting the risk of future depression among school-attending adolescents in Nigeria using a model developed in Brazil[J]. Psychiatry Research, 2020, 294: 113511.

[3]   Cho S E, Geem Z W, Na K S. Predicting depression in community dwellers using a machine learning algorithm[J]. Diagnostics, 2021, 11(8): 1429.

[4]   Y Bengü, üzer Ahmet. The relationship between internet addiction, social anxiety, impulsivity, self-esteem, and depression in a sample of turkish undergraduate medical students[J]. Psychiatry Research, 2018, 267: 313.

[5]   A, Herran-Boix, I, et al. The role of personality in the prediction of hospitalization duration in mental health[J]. Personality and Individual Differences, 2014, 60(Suppl): S75.

[6]   Mohammed J. Zaki, Wagner Meira, Jr. Data mining and analysis: fundamental concepts and algorithms[M]. Cambridge University Press, 2014.

[7]   Burnap P, Colombo G, Amery R, et al. Multiclass machine classification of suicide-related communication on Twitter[J]. Online Social Networks and Media, 2017, 2: 32-44.

[8]   Gaur M, Kursuncu U, Alambo A, et al. Let me tell you about your mental health! Contextualized classification of Reddit post to DSM-5 for web-based intervention[C]//Proceedings of the 27th ACM International Conference on Information and Knowledge Management, Torino, Italy: ACM, 2018: 753-762.

[9]   Wei Xinjuan. A Review of the Relationship between Psychological Capital and Mental Health of College Students[J]. Research on Communication Power, 2019, 3(29): 260 (in Chinese).

[10]   Lu Liming. Psychological health education for college students under the guidance of the "Healthy Personality Theory". Journal of Higher Education, 2015, (09): 230-231 (in Chinese).

[11]   Tianye. Psychological health standards and educational strategies for college students based on positive psychology[J]. International Education, 2020, 10 (11): 89-90 (in Chinese).

[12]   Akhrorov Voris Yunusovich, Farruh Ahmedov, Komiljon Norboyev, Farrukh Zakirov. Analysis of experimental research results focused on improving student psychological Health[J]. International Journal of Modern Education and Computer Science, 2022, 14(2): 14-30.

[13]   Han Xiyang. A visual analysis of the research on the use of mobile phones by college students based on VOSviewer[J]. International Journal of Education and Management Engineering, 2020, 10(6): 10-16.

[14]   Chuanmei Wang. An Investigation and Structure Model Study on College Students' Studying-interest[J]. International Journal of Modern Education and Computer Science, 2011, 3(3): 33-39.

232

Artificial Intelligence, Medical Engineering and Education
Z.B. Hu et al. (Eds.)
© *2024 The Authors.*
This article is published online with Open Access by IOS Press and distributed under the terms
of the Creative Commons Attribution Non-Commercial License 4.0 (CC BY-NC 4.0).
doi:10.3233/ATDE231333

Empirical Study on the Influencing Factors of Satisfaction of Logistics Service Quality of Cross-Border Import E-Commerce Based on KANO Model

Li LI[a,1], Zhixiang CHEN[b]

[a]*School of Logistics, Wuhan Technology and Business University, Wuhan, China*
[b]*School of Management, Sun Yat-sen University, Guangzhou, China*

Abstract. The development of cross-border e-commerce cannot be separated from the coordination of cross-border logistics. Structural equation model is used to explore the influencing factors of logistics service satisfaction of cross-border import e-commerce. The results show that the service quality of cross-border logistics and its three dimensions namely basic service quality, value-added service quality and supply chain service quality have significant positive influence on customer satisfaction, and the supply chain service quality has the greatest influence on satisfaction, followed by basic service quality and value-added service quality; the logistics service quality and satisfaction of different cross-border e-commerce companies and different import logistics modes differ. The research has certain guidance and reference significance for cross-border import e-commerce to improve the satisfaction of logistics service.

Keywords. Cross-border e-commerce; Logistics service quality; Customer satisfaction; Structural equation model; KANO Model

1. Introduction

After the outbreak of COVID-19, consumers have shifted to online consumption on a large scale, stimulating the rapid development of the global e-commerce retail industry [1-5]. China's cross-border e-commerce has become a new growth point of foreign trade. Cross-border logistics plays an important role in connecting domestic and foreign trade, but the development of cross-border logistics lags behind, which limits the further development of cross-border e-commerce; the evaluation index system of cross-border logistics service plays an important role in standardizing the operation of cross-border logistics and improving the business level of cross-border logistics enterprises [6].

SERVQUAL model evaluates the service quality from five dimensions: tangible, assurance, empathy, reliability and responsiveness [7]. The LSQ model evaluates the logistics service quality from nine dimensions: personnel communication quality, order release quantity, information quality, ordering process, goods accuracy, goods integrity, goods quality, error processing and timeliness [8]. Some scholars have studied the

---

[1] Corresponding Author: Li LI, E-mail: 36845399@qq.com.

influencing factors of cross-border logistics service satisfaction based on SERVQUAL and LSQ models. For example, the cross-border e-commerce logistics service quality was divided into economy, responsiveness, flexibility, reliability and empathy five dimensions, their influence on customer satisfaction was explored through the structure equation model, and the results showed that empathy was the biggest influence on satisfaction, followed by flexibility and economy, finally the reliability and responsiveness [9]. Using a similar scale, Liu Xingwang et al. found that the impact of economy on satisfaction was not significant, and the significant influence of the other four dimensions changed from large to small for personnel service quality, flexibility, reliability and timeliness [10]. Song Shuaiyu established the import bonded mode logistics service evaluation index system through project analysis and factor analysis and other statistical methods, with the availability, responsiveness, empathy, economy and security five dimensions, and found their importance in the customer from large to small was availability, responsiveness, empathy, security and economic [11]. As can be seen from the above literature, there are many factors affecting the satisfaction of cross-border logistics service. It is not easy to classify them based on SERVQUAL or LSQ models. Different scholars summarize different dimensions and indicators, and the importance of dimensions and indicators obtained through empirical studies is also different.

In the KANO model, the factors that affect satisfaction can be divided into five types, including basic demand, expected demand, excited demand, indifference demand and reverse demand [12]. Wang Yan and Kou Changhua discussed the needs of consumers for different levels of terminal cold chain distribution based on KANO model, and suggested the construction of a composite terminal cold chain mode to meet the basic demand, a whole supply chain cold chain mode to meet the desired demand and an innovative terminal cold chain mode to meet the exciting demand [13]. Based on Maslow's hierarchy of needs theory and the definition of international standards for service quality, Chen Yangyang divided the cross-border logistics service quality into basic service quality and value-added service quality [14]. Through online comment clustering analysis, Wei Rui found that in the cross-border e-commerce environment, customers attached great importance to the supply chain service capability of e-commerce to supply global new products [15]. Based on the reality of cross-border e-commerce logistics and KANO model, this paper evaluates cross-border logistics service from three dimensions: basic service quality, value-added service quality and supply chain service quality. Basic service includes the accuracy and integrity of goods in the LSQ model, value-added service includes error processing and timing in the LSQ model, and supply chain service include the modes of imported goods, supply channels and etc.

In addition, there are many qualitative studies on cross-border logistics models. Lin Qiaoli analyzed the development status and main problems of China's cross-border e-commerce overseas warehouse [16]. Zhang Xiaheng and Li Doudou summarized the types and existing problems of overseas warehouses and put forward suggestions such as the preferential use of public overseas warehouse mode, and the construction of intelligent operation system of overseas warehouses, and making full use of the resources of the destination country [17]. Zeng Rong analyzed the problems and difficulties existing in the current bonded logistics logistics mode and put forward a strategy to improve the problems of the bonded logistics mode in cross-border e-commerce [18]. Shen Tong analyzed several logistics modes of cross-border retail e-commerce in China, analyzed the existing problems of cross-border import e-commerce logistics and gave corresponding suggestions [19]. The above literature does not take into account customers' understanding or acceptance of these cross-border logistics modes. Therefore, this paper also quantitatively studies the influence of different import logistics modes on customer satisfaction.

2. Research Hypothesis and Model Construction

In the cross-border e-commerce environment, customers place orders to buy imported goods on the e-commerce company, and the e-commerce company delivers the goods to customers through cross-border logistics. Compared with traditional e-commerce logistics, cross-border e-commerce logistics involves international transportation, customs declaration and inspection, domestic transportation, bonded warehousing, and other affairs, so it faces various uncertainties and risks. The quality of cross-border e-commerce logistics service has a significant impact on consumers' shopping experience and satisfaction [9, 20]. Therefore, propose the hypothesis:

H1: The quality of cross-border e-commerce logistics service has a significant positive impact on customer satisfaction.

Cross-border logistics will lead to weather, force majeure and human factors. The delivery of cross-border logistics service to the designated place is the most basic requirement for cross-border logistics service. Through empirical research, scholars found that the reliability, availability or security in cross-border logistics service had a significant impact on customer satisfaction [9-11, 15]. Therefore, propose the hypothesis:

H2: Basic service quality has a significant positive impact on customer satisfaction.

Due to the many links and long distance of cross-border logistics, customers need to wait for a long time to receive the goods after placing an order, and the return of money is also very complicated. Customers want cross-border e-commerce to promise when the goods will deliver and arrive, and can track the logistics information of the goods at any time; if quality problems occur, customers want e-commerce to process returns quickly. When Hsiao et al. studied cross-border logistics service, they found that 'logistics abnormal warning', 'delivery commitment' and 'APP service' as value-added service items would affect customers' willingness to use them [21]. Expected arrival time and allowing returns shall affect consumers' shopping motivation [22]. Based on this value-added service, customers will compare the logistics service quality of different cross-border e-commerce companies, so as to affect customer satisfaction and loyalty to e-commerce companies. Therefore, propose the hypothesis:

H3: The quality of value-added service has a significant positive impact on customer satisfaction.

Due to differences in policy, culture, economic development level and product production standards in different countries, coupled with logistics cost and space distance, some commodities cannot meet customer demand in time or even through cross-border transactions. The product supply capacity of cross-border e-commerce to consumer demand significantly affected the logistics service satisfaction [15]. Although customers buy imported goods through cross-border e-commerce companies, they often do not know what good goods are available overseas. If cross-border e-commerce can provide customers with a wide range of products from all over the world and launch new products soon, then customers will be very surprised and their satisfaction will increase. Therefore, propose the hypothesis:

H4: Supply chain service quality has a significant positive impact on customer satisfaction.

Based on the above assumptions, a theoretical model of cross-border e-commerce logistics service satisfaction is constructed, as shown in Figure 1.

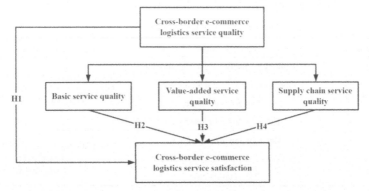

Figure 1. Theoretical model of satisfaction of cross-border e-commerce logistics service

3. Questionnaire Design and Survey

3.1. Questionnaire Design

This paper uses a structural equation model to study the relationship between basic service, value-added service, supply chain service, and customer satisfaction. After a small-scale pre-investigation and listening to expert suggestions, a formal questionnaire is formed. The main body of the questionnaire is made of the four dimensions of the theoretical model and 5-level Likert scales of 13 question items (1 dissatisfied, 2 unsatisfactory, 3 general, 4 satisfied, and 5 very satisfied), as shown in Table 1.

3.2. Questionnaire Survey

The formal survey was distributed and collected through the Questionnaire Star Mini-program. A total of 233 questionnaires were collected. After excluding invalid questionnaires such as no cross-border online shopping experience and misfilling, the remaining 204 valid questionnaires were found, with an effective recovery rate of 87.6%. The sample background information questions of the questionnaire included gender, age, occupation and annual family income, as well as the preferred cross-border e-commerce companies and import logistics model. Descriptive statistical analysis of the above sample background information is shown in Table 2; each item is reasonable and representative.

4. Empirical Results

4.1. Reliability and Validity Test

The Cronbach α coefficients are all greater than 0.9, indicating the high reliability quality of the data. In addition, the 'α coefficient of the deleted item' indicates that the reliability coefficient will not increase significantly after any item is deleted, so it indicates that the item should not be deleted. Validity is verified using KMO and Bartlett tests, and the

KMO value is 0.945 and p value is 0.000, indicating that the data are suitable for extracting factor information with good validity.

Table 1. Design of the questionnaire variables

Dimension	Question item	Scale source
Basic service	The goods themselves are intact and tidy	The LSQ model; the KANO model; Quan Chunni and Fan Yueqiao (2018); Dai Ying, etc. (2021)
	Goods are consistent with the order	
	Delivery is accurate	
	Delivery does not lose parts	
Value added service	Delivery and arrival on time	The LSQ model; the KANO model; Hsiao(2016); Zhang(2018)
	Logistics information update timely	
	The return is fast	
Supply chain service	There are many merchandises to choose from	KANO model; Wei Rui (2021)
	The new product is available quickly	
	Strong global supply capacity	
Customers satisfaction	Overall evaluation of logistics service	Dai Ying, etc. (2021); Chen Yangyang (2021)
	Evaluation compared with other cross-border e-commerce logistics	
	Buy again	

4.2. Confirmatory Factor Analysis

The confirmatory factor analysis (CFA) analysis is performed for the above 4 factors and 13 analysis items. The effective sample size is 204, 10 times beyond the number of analyzed items, with a moderate sample size. The absolute value of the standardized load system is greater than 0.6 and significant, indicating a good measurement relationship between the latent and dominant variables. The AVE values corresponding to all the 4 factors are greater than 0.5, and all the CR values are higher than 0.7, which means that the data has good aggregation (convergence) validity. The AVE square root values of the four factors are greater than the absolute inter-factor correlation coefficient values, implying good discriminatory validity.

4.3. Hypothesis Test

The first-order model composed of H2, H3 and H4 is fitted. The common indicators are within the judgment criteria, indicating that the overall fit degree of the first-order model is within the acceptable range (χ^2/df=1.511<3, GFI=0.942>0.9, RMSEA=0.050<0.10, RMR=0.011<0.05, CFI=0.991>0.9, NFI=0.973>0.9, AGFI=0.911>0.9). As can be seen from Table 3, the three dimensions of logistics service quality of cross-border e-commerce all have a significant positive impact on satisfaction, that is, H2, H3 and H4 are all established. According to the degree of influence, supply chain service, basic service and value-added service are in descending order, with the path coefficients of 0.390, 0.370 and 0.228, respectively.

The second-order model composed of H1, H2, H3 and H4 is fitted The common indicators are within the judgment criteria, indicating that the overall fit degree of the second-order model is within the acceptable range ($\chi^2/df=1.554<3$, GFI=0.938>0.9, RMSEA=0.052<0.10,   RMR=0.013<0.05,   CFI=0.990>0.9,   NFI=0.972>0.9, AGFI=0.908>0.9). The second order path coefficient is shown in Table 4, which can be seen that logistics service quality has a significant positive impact on satisfaction, and the path coefficient is 0.951, that is, H1 is established.

Table 2. Descriptive statistical analysis

Name	Option	Frequency □	Percentage (%)□
Sex	Man	77	37.75
	Woman	127	62.25
Age	Under 30	63	30.89
	30-39 Years old	67	32.84
	Age 40 and over	74	36.27
Occupation	Student	33	16.18
	Civil servants and employees of public institutions	59	28.92
	Enterprise worker	72	35.29
	Freelancer or otherwise	40	19.61
Family annual income	Less than 30,000	21	10.29
	30,000-80,000	46	22.55
	80,000-300,000	67	32.84
	More than 300,000	70	34.31
More preferred cross-border e-commerce companies	Tmall International	104	50.98
	JD International	77	37.75
	Other	23	11.27
More preferred import logistics mode	Overseas direct shipping	41	20.10
	Overseas warehouse delivery	13	6.37
	Bonded warehouse delivery	81	39.71
	Domestic delivery	26	12.75
	Don't care where the goods are shipped from	43	21.08
Amount to		204	100.0

4.4. Variance Test

In order to further verify the practicability of the model, the questionnaires of Tmall International and JD International are selected from the valid questionnaires, and the logistics service satisfaction of the two cross-border e-commerce companies is compared by variance analysis. Although the average value of basic service quality, value-added service quality, supply chain service quality and customer satisfaction of JD International are all higher than that of Tmall International, they are not significant, so there is no significant difference between the logistics service satisfaction of the two cross-border e-commerce companies.

Under the two e-commerce companies, customers prefer to deliver goods from bonded warehouses or domestic warehouses, and the average value of logistics service satisfaction is also higher. In Tmall International, the value-added service quality of different import logistics modes shows significant differences; in JD International, the basic service quality of different import logistics modes shows significant differences. For the two cross-border e-commerce companies, there is no significant difference in the supply chain service under different import logistics modes.

Table 3. First-order path coefficients

Path relationship		Non-standardized regression coefficients	SE	z	p	Standardized regression coefficient
H2: Basic service	→ Customers satisfaction	0.352	0.073	4.804	0.000	0.370
H3: Value-added service	→ Customers satisfaction	0.206	0.065	3.184	0.001	0.228
H4: Supply chain service	→ Customers satisfaction	0.360	0.060	5.956	0.000	0.390

Table 4. Second-order path coefficients

Path relationship		Non-standardized regression coefficients	SE	z	p	Standardized regression coefficient
Logistics service quality	→ Basic service	1.000	-	-	-	0.914
Logistics service quality	→ Value added service	1.013	0.072	14.058	0.000	0.876
Logistics service quality	→ Supply chain service	0.987	0.071	13.913	0.000	0.873
H1: Logistics service quality	→ Customers satisfaction	0.993	0.059	16.792	0.000	0.951

5. Conclusions and Revelation

Existing literature were mostly based on SERVQUAL and LSQ model to study the influencing factors of cross-border logistics service quality. This paper has innovatively used three dimensions of the basic service, value-added service and supply chain service based on KANO and LSQ model to establish the cross-border logistics service quality satisfaction equation model and studied the influence of different logistics import modes on satisfaction. The following conclusions are drawn from the empirical study:

1) The three dimensions of logistics service quality of cross-border e-commerce all have a significant positive impact on satisfaction, among which supply chain service has the greatest impact, followed by basic service and value-added service. Cross-border e-

commerce companies should constantly optimize their cross-border supply chain, improve the global supply capacity, increase the variety of goods, and quickly get new, and truly realize global sales. In addition to supply chain service, customers are very concerned about the basic service of complete and correct delivery of goods, followed by value-added service with faster logistics information update, faster delivery, and faster return goods. Cross-border e-commerce should first complete cross-border logistics with both quality and quantity guaranteed, and then complete it faster.

2) In general, customers are satisfied with various import logistics modes, and the satisfaction evaluation is above 3.5 points. Since the bonded warehouse mode has been implemented for many years, customers more accept and love it, and the satisfaction of logistics service under this mode is also higher. In recent years, the enterprise has just adopted the overseas warehouse mode. In contrast, customers have less understanding of the overseas warehouse mode, and their satisfaction is also low. For Tmall International, there are significant differences in value-added service under different import logistics modes, so the responsiveness of cross-border logistics service should be strengthened. For JD International, there are significant differences in basic service under different import logistics modes, so the reliability of cross-border logistics service should be strengthened. It is worth noting that there is no significant difference in the supply chain service under different import logistics modes. The quality of supply chain service delivered from overseas or overseas warehouses should be better because they can provide personalized purchasing and delivery service to customers; the non-significant difference result may be due to the limitation of sample data and the randomness of sample survey.

In future studies, questionnaires should combine online and offline to increase face-to-face communication with customers and improve the scientificity of the scale; and expand the scope of sample collection to make more samples for each option to obtain more representative data. In addition, the credibility of e-commerce companies and the government can be taken as the intermediary in the model.

Acknowledgment

This project is supported by China Society of Logistics and China Federation of Logistics and Purchasing Research Project Plan (2022CSLKT3-172).

References

[1] Mirza Waseem Hussain, Tabasum Mirza, Malik Mubasher Hassan. " Impact of COVID-19 Pandemic on the Human Behavior ", International Journal of Education and Management Engineering, Vol.10, No.5, pp.35-61, 2020.

[2] Debadrita Panda, Sabyasachi Mukhopadhyay, Amit Kumar Bachhar, Moumita Roy, "Multi Criteria Decision Making based Approach to Assist Marketers for Targeting BoPs Regarding Packaging Influenced Purchase during Covid-19", International Journal of Intelligent Systems and Applications, Vol.14, No.3, pp.1-17, 2022.

[3] Debadrita Panda, Sabyasachi Mukhopadhyay, Rajarshi Saha, Prasanta K. Panigrahi, "BoPCOVIPIP: Capturing the Dynamics of Marketing Mix Among Bottom of Pyramid Consumers during COVID-19", International Journal of Intelligent Systems and Applications, Vol.14, No.4, pp.37-51, 2022.

[4] Taufik Hidayat, Rahutomo Mahardiko, Ali Miftakhu Rosyad, "A Model Statistical during Covid-19 Future E-Commerce Revenue for Indonesia Aviation", International Journal of Information Engineering and Electronic Business, Vol.15, No.1, pp. 51-57, 2023.

[5]   Md. Motaleb Hossen Manik, "A Novel Approach in Determining Areas to Lockdown during a Pandemic: COVID-19 as a Case Study", International Journal of Information Engineering and Electronic Business, Vol.15, No.2, pp. 30-37, 2023.

[6]   Du Zhiping, Qu Yuxian. Research status, hotspot and trend analysis of cross-border logistics based on CiteSpace[J]. Price Monthly, 2021, (04): 77-86.

[7]   Parasuraman A., Zeithaml V.and Berry L. SERVQUAL: A multiple-item scale for measuring consumer perceptions of service quality[J]. Journal of Retailing, 1998, 64: 12-40.

[8]   Mentzer John T., Flint Daniel J., Kent John L. Developing a logistics service quality scale[J]. Journal of Business Logistics, 1999, 20(1): 9-32.

[9]   Dai Ying, Li Yu, Yu Xiaodong, and Song Han. An Empirical study on the influencing factors of logistics service satisfaction in cross-border e-commerce[J]. Journal of Chongqing University of Technology (Social Sciences), 2021, 35 (01): 60-69 (in Chinese).

[10] Liu Xingwang, Che Xiaoying, Chi Weiming. Influencing factors and empirical study on the satisfaction of cross-border e-commerce logistics service in Qinzhou[J]. Commercial economy, 2022, (01): 56-60 (in Chinese).

[11] Song Shuaiyu. Research on logistics Service Quality Evaluation of cross-border e-commerce —— Take Tmall International and JD Global as an example[D]. Beijing: Beijing University of Posts and Telecommunications, 2019 (in Chinese).

[12] Kano Noriaki. A Perspective on Quality Activities in American Firms[J]. California Management Review, 1993, 35(3): 12-31.

[13] Wang Yan, Kou Changhua. Research on fresh e-commerce and terminal cold chain distribution based on KANO model[J]. Business Economics Research, 2019, (12): 97-99 (in Chinese).

[14] ChenYang-yang. Study on customer satisfaction of B2C cross-border e-commerce logistics service based on SEM[D]. Shaanxi Province: Xidian University, 2021 (in Chinese).

[15] Wei Rui. Study on customer satisfaction of imported cross-border e-commerce logistics service based on online reviews[D]. Shaanxi Province: Xidian University, 2021 (in Chinese).

[16] Lin Qiaoli. Research on the development of overseas warehouses of Cross-border E-commerce in China in the Era of Big Data[J]. Logistics Technology, 2021, 44 (07): 68-71 (in Chinese).

[17] Zhang Xiaheng, Li Doudou. Types and development measures of cross-border e-commerce overseas warehouse[J]. ICBC Financial Technology, 2021, (01): 72-80 (in Chinese).

[18] Zeng Rong. Dilemmas and improvement approaches facing the development of bonded stock logistics mode of cross-border e-commerce[J]. Economist, 2021, (06): 40-41 + 44 (in Chinese).

[19] Shen Tong. Analysis of logistics mode of Cross-border retail e-commerce in China: Based on the perspective of import[J]. Business Economics Research, 2020, (18): 109-112 (in Chinese).

[20] Quan Chunni, Fan Yuejiao. Empirical study on the impact of logistics service quality on customer satisfaction in the context of cross-border online shopping-takes perceived value as the intermediary[J]. Journal of Harbin University of Commerce (Social Science Edition), 2018, (05): 98-107 + 116 (in Chinese).

[21] Hsiao Y.H., Chen M.C., and Liao W.C. Logistics service design for cross-border E-commerce using Kansei engineering with text-mining-based online content analysis[J]. Telematics & Informatics, 2017, 34(4): 284-302.

[22] Ma S., Chai Y., and Zhang H. Rise of cross-border e-commerce exports in China[J]. China and the World Economy (English version), 2018, 26 (3): 25.

Artificial Intelligence, Medical Engineering and Education
Z.B. Hu et al. (Eds.)
© 2024 The Authors.
This article is published online with Open Access by IOS Press and distributed under the terms
of the Creative Commons Attribution Non-Commercial License 4.0 (CC BY-NC 4.0).
doi:10.3233/ATDE231334

A Study on Leaving of Tibetan Cadres Under the Perspective of Psychological Contracts-Take Teachers and Civil Servants as an Example

Ya'nan WANG[1]

School of Economics and Management, Tibet University, Lhasa, 850000, China
ORCiD ID: Ya'nan Wang https://orcid.org/0000-0002-7849-1335

Abstract. The high turnover rate of Tibetan cadres has seriously affected the development of Tibet. Existing studies have mainly explored the turnover of rural teachers, and primary and secondary school teachers, and have paid less attention to the extra-occupational factors. In this paper, we take teachers and civil servants working on the Tibetan Plateau as examples to explore the turnover problems, and analyze their mediating and moderating mechanisms. The study finds that psychological contract breakdown significantly and positively affects the turnover intention of Tibetan cadres, while job satisfaction, job embeddedness, and perceived opportunities play a mediating role, and kinship responsibility moderates the relationship between job satisfaction, job embeddedness, and turnover intention. The results of this study expand the antecedents of job embeddedness theory and turnover modeling studies, enrich the mediation and boundary mechanisms of turnover research, explain the reason and internal mechanism of Tibetan cadres leaving and retention, and provide ideas for Tibetan cadres' retention.

Keywords. psychological contract, turnover intention, job embeddedness, job satisfaction, perceived opportunity, kinship responsibility

1. Introduction

Talent is the source of the organization's continuous development and progress, with the increasing importance of human capital, the research heat about the employee leaving continues to climb and has become one of the focuses of attention in the management and psychology circles. Frequent employee job-hopping will inevitably bring explicit and implicit losses to the organization, such as the loss of human capital investment, and resources reconfiguration costs, then, affecting the psychology and behavior of retained employees, and undermining the cohesion of the organization. For organizations, analyzing the reasons for employees to leave, understanding the behavior of employees to leave, and targeted retention is the key to grasping the first opportunity in the fierce talent war.

After combing the relevant literature at home and abroad, It can be found that the exit research model is broadly divided into two categories, one is the traditional model,

---

[1] Corresponding Author: Ya'nan WANG, E-mail: 513867761@qq.com.

which mainly uses job satisfaction or organizational commitment as the mediating variables to analyze "why employees leave". The other is the diversified, multi-path model [1], which analyzes "what motivates employees to stay " from the perspective of job embeddedness.

At present, there is still a controversy about which of the two theories is better or worse, although some scholars have shown that job satisfaction can better explain employee' leaving behavior relative to job embeddedness [2], Griffeth & Hom (2000) pointed out that the traditional model is not strong enough to explain the leaving behavior, and that the strength of satisfaction in explaining the actual leaving behavior is only 3.6% [3]. Wang and Deng (2017) found that the effects of traditional variables such as job satisfaction, organizational commitment, and job opportunities cannot be ignored when analyzing leaving, and they should be considered in an integrated manner to make the understanding of the leaving problem more comprehensive and closer to reality [4].

Based on this, this paper intends to construct a conceptual model including the above two modeling ideas to explore the reasons for employee retention and leaving. At the same time, to make up for the lack of research on job-embedded antecedent variables and specific groups in the Chinese context, this paper takes Tibetan cadres as an example to explore the impact of psychological contract breakdown on the turnover intention of teachers and civil servants, and the specific conceptual model is as follows:

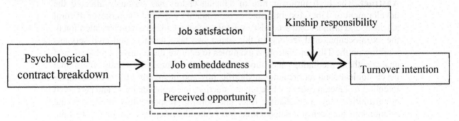

Figure 1. Conceptual model

2. Theoretical Foundations and Research Hypotheses

2.1. Psychological Contract Breakdown and Turnover Intention

A psychological contract is an implicit, informal, and unstated mutual expectation that exists between an organization and an employee [5]. As a foundational indication in the study of the employment relationship, the psychological contract plays an increasingly important role in defining and explaining the characteristics of contemporary employment relationships [6]. Psychological contract breakdown affects employees' work attitudes and behaviors, such as job satisfaction [7], organizational citizenship intentions [8], organizational citizenship behaviors [9], and retention intentions [6], etc. Reviewing the literature, it can be found that the current conclusions about the relationship between psychological contract breakdown and turnover are more consistent, and scholars generally agree that there is a positive relationship between psychological contract breakdown and employee turnover, thus proposing that Hypothesis 1:

H1: There is a positive relationship between psychological contract breakdown and turnover.

2.2. The Mediating Effect of the Psychological Contract Breakdown and Turnover Intention

The establishment, breakdown, and violation of the psychological contract are jointly influenced by individual, organizational, and environmental factors. Not all employees take specific actions after the psychological contract breakdown, it is only a necessary but not sufficient condition for the turnover intention, and there are also a large number of moderating and mediating variables between the psychological contract breakdown and employees attitudes and behaviors [10].

- The mediating effect of job satisfaction

Job satisfaction is an employee's subjective feeling about the work itself and its related environment [11], in traditional leaving research, scholars have studied the relationship between job-related variables and leaving, and take "job satisfaction" as a mediator variable to explain the reasons why employees leaving. The study found that job satisfaction is a prerequisite for employee turnover, and there is a significant negative correlation between job satisfaction and employee turnover [12], and the higher the employee's job satisfaction, the lower the tendency to leave.

Psychological contract fit can increase employees' satisfaction, which in turn reduces their willingness to leave. Although few scholars have studied the mediating mechanism of job satisfaction between psychological contract breakdown and leaving, some useful explorations have been conducted by scholars, Gu et al., (2014) confirmed that job satisfaction plays a mediating role between psychological contract fit and employee leaving behavior and job performance [13]. Based on this, this paper proposes the following hypotheses:

H2a: Psychological contract breakdown is negatively related to job satisfaction

H2b: Job satisfaction mediates the relationship between psychological contract breakdown and turnover intention

- The mediating effect of job embeddedness

Job embeddedness represents the degree of association between employees and non-work factors. Mitchell & Holtom (2001) divided job embeddedness into three dimensions: job connection, job matching, and job sacrifice, and pointed out that with the deepening of employees' connection to their jobs, the match between the employees and the organization and environment improves, and the material and spiritual costs of leaving the job continue to increase [1]. A large number of empirical studies have also shown that there is indeed a negative correlation between job embeddedness and turnover intention [14].

Existing studies have explored the effects of demographic variables, organizational performance, organizational ethical climate, error aversion culture, and organizational justice on job embeddedness, but have not analyzed the effects of psychological contract breakdown on job embeddedness. Based on the social exchange theory, it can be found that after the psychological contract breakdown, employees will consciously reduce their positive work attitudes and behaviors to achieve the rebalancing of the exchange relationship, so there may be a negative correlation between psychological contract breakdown and job embeddedness. Ballou's (2013) study also proved that psychological contract fit is positively correlated with job embeddedness and negatively correlated with turnover intention [15]. Based on this, the following hypotheses is proposed:

H3a: Psychological contract breakdown is negatively related to job embeddedness

H3b: Job embeddedness mediates the relationship between psychological contract breakdown and turnover intention.

- The mediating effect of perceived opportunity

Employees' reasons for leaving can be categorized into two aspects: job attitude and ease of leaving, considering that the pull effect of job attitude has already been discussed, this section focuses on the push effect of ease of leaving. Ease of leaving refers to the perceived opportunities and the actual unemployment ratio [2], Lambent (2001) argued that optional job opportunities can significantly predict employees' willingness to leave [14], and Griffeth et al.'s (2000) study also showed that there is a correlation between job opportunities and employees' leaving behavior [3].

Some scholars have found that the material incentives, environmental support, and development opportunities in the psychological contract are positively correlated with job satisfaction and negatively correlated with turnover intention [16]. After the psychological contract breakdown, employees' organizational identity declines, organizational commitment decreases, and they are very likely to tend to leave their jobs once a new job opportunity arises or they perceive the ease of job mobility, based on which, the following hypotheses is proposed:

H4a: Psychological contract breakdown is positively related to perceived opportunity.

H4b: Perceived opportunity plays a mediating role between psychological contract breakdown and turnover intention.

2.3. The Moderating Effect of Kinship Responsibilities

Work and life are two inseparable components of human beings in the real world [3], with the continuous development of flexible employment, the boundaries between work and family are blurring, and people begin to switch roles arbitrarily in two distinct areas, and the influence of family on work has been magnified. Lee et al. (1999) argued that individuals in the Chinese context pay more attention to family life, and family factors such as spouses and children are more predictive of turnover behavior than organizational commitment [2]. Yang (2019) also pointed out that various factors such as geographic, social, and family factors affect employees' occupational embeddedness, which in turn affects the choice of job [17].

Based on the limiting effect of kinship responsibility on employee mobility, some scholars have begun to analyze the moderating effect of kinship responsibility. Van & Kirk (2003) also conducted a related study but found that the moderating relationship did not exist [18]. This study concluded that kinship responsibilities moderated the relationship between job satisfaction (H5a), job embeddedness (H5b), perceived opportunity (H5c), and turnover intention.

3. Methods

3.1. Subjects

Tibetan cadres refer to national or local civil servants and institution workers who have been working in Tibet for a long time. This paper takes the Tibetan cadres as a research object mainly based on the following considerations: (1) the Tibetan cadres are crucial to the regional stability and the national border construction, and the study of their leaving has certain practical meaning. (2) Previous research mostly focused on enterprise employees or teachers but did not analyze the leaving problems of several groups at the same time. (3) Due to the influence of the plateau climate, Tibetan cadres may face more serious problems of kinship responsibilities (such as long-distance marriages, left-behind children, etc.), which can be used as a good example to analyze the border effect of family responsibilities.

3.2. Samples

This research distributed 450 questionnaires, and recovered 421, after removing 130 invalid or non-Tibetan cadres questionnaires, finally got 291 valid questionnaires, with a validity rate of 69.12%, and the specific statistical information can be seen in Table 1.

Table 1. Demographic information

Item		Proportions	Item		Proportions
Genders	male	52.92%	Education	high school and below	0.34%
	female	47.08%		polytechnic	3.34%
Marital status	unmarried	28.18%		undergraduate	44.33%
	married	71.82%		master's degree or above	51.89%
Age	under 30	32.65%	Seniority	under 5	30.24%
	30-35	32.65%		5-10	33.33%
	35-40	15.81%		10-15	14.78%
	40-45	9.97%		15-20	8.93%
	above 45	8.93%		above 20	12.71%

3.3. Measurement

Well-established domestic and international scales were selected for conceptualization measurement. All scales were scored using the Likert-7 except for the control variables, where 1 indicates complete disagreement and 7 indicates complete agreement.

Psychological contract breakdown was measured using the scale developed by Morrison (2000) [19], with 7 items, an example of which is "So far, none of the promises made by the organization at the time of recruitment have been fulfilled". Job satisfaction was adopted from the scale developed by Johlke & Duhan (2000) [20], with 5 items, and the sample item was "I feel that my job is satisfactory". Job embeddedness was adopted from Wen et al. (2018) developed in the Chinese context [21], with a total of 10 items, and the sample question was "I adapt to the unit's cultural atmosphere". The scale developed by Zhao et al. (2018) was used for the perceived opportunity and kinship responsibility [22], in which perceived opportunity contains 3 items, with an example "I feel that I can find a better job than the current one in other companies more easily", and kinship responsibility contains 4 items, with an example "My income is the main source of my family". The scale developed by Lee et al. (2017) was used for the turnover intention [23], with a total of 4 items, and the sample question was "I have always wanted to quit my current job".

Gender, age, seniority, marital status, and education were selected as control variables, while all control variables were transformed into dummy variables for statistical convenience.

4. Statistics and Results

4.1. Common Method Bias Test

In this study, Harman's one-way test was used to check the common method bias, and the results of the principal component analysis showed that the unrotated first factor explained 31.682% of the original variance, which is smaller than the discriminant criterion proposed by Podsakoff et al., (2003) [24], therefore, this research's common method bias is not a significant problem.

4.2. Reliability Measures

The consistency test was first performed by calculating Cronbach's alpha coefficient, considering that some of the constructs had too many items, the constructs with more than 3 items were packed, and the final composition of the constructs and Cronbach's alpha coefficient can be seen in Table 2.

Table 2. Cronbach's alpha coefficient of constructs

Variables	Code	Number of items	Cronbach's alpha
Psychological Contract Breakdown	PCB	3	0.887
Job Embeddedness	JE	3	0.907
Job Satisfaction	JS	3	0.703
Perceived Opportunity	PO	3	0.671
Kinship Responsibility	KR	4	0.691
Turnover Intention	TI	4	0.875

Observing the Cronbach's alpha coefficient of the constructs, it was found that the coefficients were located between 0.671-0.907, where Cronbach's alpha coefficient of PO and KR were close to the judgmental criterion of 0.7, and therefore could be considered to pass the reliability measures.

4.3. Validity Measures

- Convergent validity

Confirmatory Factor Analysis was conducted by AMOS and found that the factor loadings were located between 0.709-0.918, greater than the discriminant criterion of 0.7; the AVE values were located between 0.5236-0.8446, greater than the discriminant criterion of 0.5, and the CR values were located between 0.8145-0.9422, greater than the discriminant criterion of 0.8, which shows that the questionnaire has high convergent validity.

- Discriminant validity

Comparing $\sqrt{AVE}$ and correlation coefficient of variables, the results showed that the minimum value of $\sqrt{AVE}$ is 0.7805, which is greater than the maximum correlation coefficient(0.7805>0.682, see Table 3 for details), indicating that the questionnaire has good discriminant validity.

- Discriminant validity

To test the overall model fitness, AMOS software was used to construct 6 models respectively. After comparing the model fitness indexes it can be found that the 6-factor model had the highest fitness (χ^2/df =2.558, CFI=0.938, NFI=0.903, GFI=0.906, TLI=0.926, IFI=0.939, RMSEA=0.063), and all of them met the model fit criteria (1< χ^2/df <3, CFI, NFI, GFI, TLI, IFI are all greater than 0.9, and RMSEA<0.08), which indicates that the 6-factor model has a good fit.

4.4. Correlation Analysis

Correlation analysis [25, 26] was conducted with the help of SPSS 25.0, and the results showed that psychological contract breakdown was positively correlated with turnover intention (r=0.420**) and perceived opportunity (r=0.373**), negatively correlated with job satisfaction (r=-0.260**), and job embeddedness (r=-0.473**), which preliminarily verified that H1, H2a, H3a, and H4a.

Table 3. Correlation analysis

Concepts	Mean	SD	PCB	JE	TI	JS	PO	KR
PCB	3.54	1.50	0.9027					
JE	4.05	1.18	-.473**	0.9190				
TI	3.68	1.46	.420**	-.521**	0.8531			
JS	4.36	1.32	-.260**	.682**	-.461**	0.8012		
PO	3.59	1.21	.373**	-.209**	.425**	-.093	0.7805	
KR	5.01	1.15	.061	.090	.038	.209**	.050	0.7326

Note: ** indicates significant correlation at the 0.01 level (two-tailed).

4.5. Hypothesis Tests

- Direct effect test

In this study, AMOS software and SPSS software were used for hypothesis testing, after analyzed the path coefficients of SEM, it showed that PCB was significantly and positively related to TI (β=0.405, P<0.001), and PO (β=0.364, P<0.001), so H1, H4a were verified. Meanwhile, PCB was significantly negatively related to JS (β=-0.313, P<0.001) and JE (β=-0.239, P<0.001), thus H2a and H3a were tested.

- Mediation effect test

This study used the PROCESS program to test for mediation effects. The results showed that the mediating effect of JS between PCB and TI was 0.0833, with a 95% confidence interval of [0.0346,0.1448], and the confidence interval did not contain 0, which indicated that the mediating effect of JS was established (H2b was proved). Besides, the mediating effect of JE was 0.1724 with a 95% confidence interval of [0.1082,0.2455], indicating that the mediating effect of JE was established (H3b was proved). In the meantime, the mediating effect of PO to be 0.1149, with a 95% confidence interval of [0.0645,0.1760], indicating that the mediating effect of PO holds (H4b was proved).

To further test the mediation effect and verify the moderation effect at the same time, multilevel regression analysis was conducted, firstly, the control variables were included in the model to generate M_1, and then the control variables were included in the model together with the independent variables to generate M_2, immediately after that, the control variables, independent variables, and mediation variables were included in M_3, and finally, the control variables, independent variables, mediation variables, moderation variable, and interaction terms were included to generate M_4. It is worth noting that to reduce the multicollinearity problem in the multilevel regression process, the interaction variables was centred in advance, and the specific analysis results can be seen in Table 4.

Table 4. Results of multilevel regression analysis

Variables		M_1	M_2	M_3	M_4
	Gender	0.149***	0.108*	0.111*	0.087*
	Age	-0.058	-0.085	-0.096	-0.111
Control variables	Marital status	0.06	0.019	-0.018	-0.027
	Education	0.043	0	-0.002	-0.008
	Seniority	-0.027	-0.075	-0.078	-0.097
Independent variables	PCB		0.404***	0.138**	0.124*
	JS			-0.192**	-0.18**
Mediation variables	JE			-0.246***	-0.278***
	PO			0.291***	0.297***
Moderation variable	KR				0.122**
	KR*JS				-0.155*
Interaction terms	KR*JE				0.16*
	KR*OP				0.008
R^2		0.136	0.297	0.498	0.519
$\triangle R^2$		0.111	0.272	0.474	0.489
F		5.526***	11.843***	21.123***	17.343***

Observing M_3 in Table 4, it can be found that, consistent with the results of the PROCESS program analysis, JS, JE, and PO all play mediation roles between PCB and TI. Since the main effect of PCB on TI remains significant after the introduction of the mediating variables, it can be determined that JS, JE, and PO are all partial mediators. Further comparing the effect values, the result showed that PO had the largest mediating effect, JE was the second largest, and JS was the lowest.

- Moderation effect test

The results of M_4 showed that KR*JS was significantly negatively related to TI (β=-0.155, P<0.05), indicating that KR exacerbated the negative relationship between JS and TI (i.e., the greater the KR, the greater the negative impact of JS on TI), thus H5a was verified. KR*JE was significantly positively related to TI (β=0.16, p<0.05), indicating that KR weakens the negative relationship between JE and TI (i.e., the greater the KR, the lower the negative effect of JE on TI, and H5b was tested. At the same time, there was no significant correlation between KR*PO and TI, H5c was not tested.

5. Discussion

5.1. Conclusions and Implications

This study analyzed the leaving problem from the psychological contract perspective, verified the mediation role of job satisfaction (JS), job embeddedness (JE), and perceived opportunity (PO) between psychological contract breakdown (PCB) and turnover intention (TI), as well as the moderating role of kinship responsibility (KR), and provided new ideas for further understanding and explaining employees' retention and leaving behaviors. The study found that, firstly, the PCB of Tibetan cadres is significantly and positively related to TI. Second, PCB of Tibetan cadres was significantly negatively correlated with JS and JE and significantly positively correlated with PO. Third, JS, JE, and PO played a mediating role between PCB and TI, with PO playing the largest mediating role, JE the next largest, and JS the lowest. Fourth, KR moderated the relationship between JS, JE, and TI.

The theoretical significance of this study is mainly manifested in four aspects. First, this study expands the antecedent studies of job satisfaction and job embeddedness and provides empirical support for enriching job embeddedness theory and turnover modeling studies. Second, this study validates the multi-path turnover model and enriches the mediation and boundary mechanisms of turnover research. Third, this study considered the mediating variables of both the traditional turnover model and the new turnover model, compared the magnitude of the mediating effect, and practiced the research outlook proposed by Wang and Deng (2017) [4]. Fourth, this study takes Tibetan cadres as an example and also considers multiple samples such as teachers and civil servants, expanding the sample study in the Chinese context.

Meanwhile, this study also has certain practical meaning. First, this study focuses on the plateau workers and analyzes the problem of leaving, which can draw the attention of society to the Tibetan cadres. Second, this study explored the effects of psychological contract breakdown on turnover intention and analyzed the mediating effects of job satisfaction, job embeddedness, and kinship responsibility, which can help us better understand the causes of talent loss in the plateau. Again, the establishment of the moderating effect of kinship responsibility can provide ideas for solving the problem of leaving, such as paying more attention to the life of the workers, and solving the problems of long-distance marriages and left-behind children.

5.2. Shortcomings and Prospects

All data in this study were obtained through a one-time questionnaire, and although we controlled the common methodological bias by anonymously filling, balancing the order of the questions, and adjusting the prompt presentation, it was still unable to derive the causal relationship between the variables. Future research can try the multi-temporal data collection method to explore the intrinsic factors affecting employees' leaving behavior through regular follow-up surveys. In addition, due to the sample size limitation, this paper did not compare the differences between different groups, and future research can further analyze the turnover behavior of the same region and different types of employees while expanding the sample size.

Acknowledgment

This project is supported by Research on the Turnover Behavior of Tibet's Employees under the Perspective of a Plateau Environment (zdbs202320)

References

[1]   Mitchell,T.R., Holtom,B.C., Lee,T.W., Erez,M. Why people stay: using job embeddedness to predict voluntary turnover. [J]. Academy of Management Journal, 2001, 44(6): 1102-1121.

[2]   Lee,T.W., Maurer, S. The effects of family structure on organizational commitment, intention to leave and voluntary turnover. [J]. Journal of Managerial Issues, 1999, (11): 493-513.

[3]   Griffeth, R.W., Hom, P. W., Gaertner, S. A meta-analysis of antecedents and correlates of employee turnover: Update, moderator tests, and research implications for the millenniums. [J]. Journal of Management, 2000, 26(3): 463-488.

[4]   Wang,L.,& Deng,S. Study on mechanism for turnover intention of new generation of migrant workers: the perspective of job embeddedness.[J]. Rural Economy, 2017, (01): 118-123. (in Chinese).

[5]   Rousseau,D.M. Psychological Contract in Organizations: understanding written and unwritten agreements. [M]. Sage Publications, London, 1995.

[6]   Shao,G.L.,Li,J.Z.,Fan, X.C. Psychological contract, employee satisfaction and turnover intention: the moderating effect of self-efficacy.[J]. Journal of Business Economics, 2009, (06): 29-35. (in Chinese).

[7]   Turnley,W.H., Feldman,D.C. Re-examining the effects of psychological contract violations. [J]. Journal of organizational behavior, 2000, 21: 25-42.

[8]   Shore,L.M., Wayne,S.J. Commitment and employee behavior: comparison of affective commitment and continuance commitment with perceived organizational support.[J]. Journal of Applied Psychology, 1993, 78(5): 774-780.

[9]   Zhao, H., Wayen, S. J., Glibkowski, B. C., et al. The impact of psychological contract breach on work related outcomes: a meta-analysis.Personnel psychology,2007, 60: 647-680.(in Chinese).

[10] Peng,C.Y. An Empirical Study on the relationship between psychological contract and organizational citizenship behavior and turnover intention of R&D employees in High-Tech enterprises. [J]. Science and Technology Management Research, 2009, 29(05): 380-383. (in Chinese).

[11] Hoppock, R. Job satisfaction of psychologists. [J]. Journal of Applied Psychology, 1937, 21(3): 300-303.

[12] Porter, L.M., Steers, R.M. Organizational work and personal factors in employee turnover and absenteeism. [J]. Psychological Bulletin, 1973, 80(2): 151-176.

[13] Gu, Y. K., He, X., Chen, L. Y. Research on influence mechanism of psychological contract fit on employee's behavioral intentions. [J]. Commercial Research, 2014, (12): 93-100. (in Chinese).

[14] Lambent, E. G. The impact of Job Satisfaction on Turnover Intent: a Test of a Structural Measurement Model Using a National Sample of Workers. [J]. Social Science Journal, 2001, 38(2): 233-251.

[15] Ballou, N. S. The effects of psychological contract breach on job outcomes. [D]. San Jose State University ,2013.

[16] Zhou, L. A Study on the Effect of Psychological Contract on Employees' Turnover Intention. [J]. Academic Forum, 2014, 37(06): 140-144. (in Chinese).

[17] Yang, C.J., Liu,D., Mao,C.C. Job embeddedness in China: an analysis of concept, structure and scale.[J]. Journal of Industrial Engineering Management, 2019, (01): 122-133. (in Chinese).

[18] Van, Dijk. P., Kirk-brown. The relationship between job embeddedness and Intention to Leave an organization. [J]. Australian Journal of Psychology,2003, (Supplement): 232.

[19] Morrison,R.E.W. The development of psychological contract breach and violation: a longitudinal study. [J]. Journal of Organizational Behavior, 2000, 21(5): 525-546.

[20] Johlke, M. C., Duhan, D. F. Supervisor Communication Practices and Service Employee Job Outcomes. [J]. Journal of Service Research, 2000, 3(2): 154-165.

[21] Wen, K., Yu, G.F., Lu,J.L., Su,H.Y.Job embeddedness, research institutional environment and turnover intention: analysis on the influencing factors of brain drain of CAS.[J]. Science of Science and Management of S.& T. 2018, 39(11): 132-143. (in Chinese).

[22] Zhao,J.X., Wang,M.Q.,& Zhao, D. L. Research on the factors influencing employees turnover in internet companies based on Price-Mueller Model. Journal of Hebei University of Economics and Business, 2018(5): 93-101. (in Chinese).

[23] Lee, Xianyin, YANG, et al. The influence factors of job satisfaction and its relationship with turnover intention: taking early-career employees as an example. [J]. Anales De Psicología, 2017, 33: 697-707.

[24] Podsakoff P M, MacKenzie S B, Lee J Y, et al. Common method biases in behavioral research: A critical review of the literature and recommended remedies[J]. Journal of Applied Psychology, 2003, 88: 879-903.

[25] Mengjin Yu, Huiyun Bai, "Study on Influencing Factors of Regional Economy Based on Multilevel Model", International Journal of Mathematical Sciences and Computing, Vol.9, No.4, pp. 29-43, 2023.

[26] Kasliono, Suprapto, Faizal Makhrus, "Point Based Forecasting Model of Vehicle Queue with Extreme Learning Machine Method and Correlation Analysis", International Journal of Intelligent Systems and Applications, Vol.13, No.3, pp.11-22, 2021.

Artificial Intelligence, Medical Engineering and Education
Z.B. Hu et al. (Eds.)
© 2024 The Authors.
This article is published online with Open Access by IOS Press and distributed under the terms
of the Creative Commons Attribution Non-Commercial License 4.0 (CC BY-NC 4.0).
doi:10.3233/ATDE231335

High-Quality Development of Wuhan Deeply Integrated into the "Belt and Road"

Wenjie XIONG[1], Yanni ZHANG, Lei YE
Wuhan Business School, School of Business Administration, Wuhan, China

Abstract. Focusing on the high-quality development of the Belt and Road in Wuhan in the future, this paper makes an in-depth analysis of the current situation and conditions and uses the experience of the development of brother cities for reference to determine the measurement indicators of the efficiency and effectiveness of the high-quality development of the Belt and Road in Wuhan. In the study, the evaluation system of the efficiency and effectiveness of high-quality development of Wuhan integrated into the "the Belt and Road" was constructed, and the evaluation model of high-quality development of Wuhan was designed. At the same time, the weight of evaluation indicators was determined using Analytic Hierarchy Process, and the fuzzy comprehensive evaluation method was used to evaluate the high-quality development level of Wuhan. Targeted countermeasures and suggestions were proposed to provide suggestions for the development of Wuhan.

Keywords. Yangtze River Economic Belt; The high-quality development of Wuhan City; The Belt and Road initiative; Analytic Hierarchy Process

1. Introduction

Deeply integrating into "the Belt and Road" initiative has become a powerful engine to promote the sustainable economic development of China and countries along the Belt and Road [1-3]. In this new context, which is the gradual formation of a new development pattern with domestic circulation as the main body and domestic and international dual circulation promoting each other, strengthening the development of the Yangtze River Economic Belt has become an important part of the national strategic policy [4].

Actively responding to the new situation, Wuhan should seize the location advantage of the middle reaches of the Yangtze River and bravely undertake its historical mission as the intersection point of the "east-west two-way" opening-up strategy and an important connection point for the construction of the "Yangtze River Economic Belt" and "Silk Road Economic Belt" [5-8]. We will promote the linkage of land, domestic and overseas, and the two-way opening of east and west, focus on building an important node for the integrated development of the Yangtze River Economic Belt and the "one Belt and one Road", and achieve high-quality economic integration of Wuhan and cities along "the Belt and Road" to play the role of an engine of economic and industrial development [9,10]. It is very important to seize the strategic opportunity period, policy opportunity period, innovation opportunity period, and prospect opportunity period of Wuhan's development, and through means such as advantage diffusion, resource complementarity, industrial clusters, intellectual innovation, and institutional innovation,

---

[1] Corresponding Author: Wenjie XIONG, Email: 719695038@qq.com

to carry out cross-border and intensive allocation of capital, human resources, and natural resources, and achieve "internationalization, modernization, and ecology" in Wuhan. Only in this way can we play the leading role of the "National Strategic Center City", promote high-quality economic development in Wuhan, and accelerate its entry into the fast lane of high-quality development [11]. This is the original intention and purpose of this study.

Building a scientific evaluation system to evaluate the current situation and requirements of high-quality development in Wuhan is a correct approach [12-14]. There are many similar studies both domestically and internationally on the analysis and evaluation of urban development that can be used for reference [15-17]. The research perspectives vary, from discussing urban logistics and green spaces to fresh product distribution, with a focus on the economic development of cities [18-21]. These studies can help us identify shortcomings in the development process, adopt scientific thinking to clarify the direction of future efforts, and provide useful suggestions for government decision-making [22-24].

2. The Evaluation System for Wuhan's Integration into the High-Quality Development of "the Belt and Road"

Driven by the "Belt and Road" engine, the high-quality development of Wuhan can be studied from many aspects through the analytic hierarchy process.

2.1. Construction of Hierarchical Structure Model

The evaluation system for high-quality development in Wuhan is shown in Figure 1, and the discussion is conducted from five aspects, which are the development of innovation, coordination, environmental protection, openness, and sharing. They are set as primary indicators. On this basis, the paper selected 15 secondary indicators, such as "acquisition and transformation of achievements ", "high-level talent cultivation and introduction", "high-tech investment", coordinated urban-rural development", "harmonized development of industries ","integrated progress of culture and economy", "urban greening and environmental protection", "treatment of sewage and waste", "assurance and improvement of air quality", "foreign capital introduction", "export of domestic labor force to the outside world", "exchange between different cultures". The structural model of Analytic Hierarchy Process is composed of "mass cultural services", "medical and healthcare services", "public services of public libraries", etc., to form the structural model of the Analytic Hierarchy Process.

2.2. Construction and Consistency Testing of Comparative Discriminant Matrices

Matrix of comparative discrimination is used to determine the importance of two factors within one hierarchy. The comparative discriminant matrix of this article adopts the *1-9* scale method and based on the hierarchical structure pattern in Figure 1, a relevant questionnaire is designed to survey relevant experts in the field.

In the comparison discrimination matrix of S, λ *Max=5.287, CI=0.072, CR=0.064<0.1*, passed the consistency test. The validation results of the five comparative discriminant matrices *A, B, C, D*, and *E* in the criterion layer are shown in Table 1, all of which have passed the consistency test.

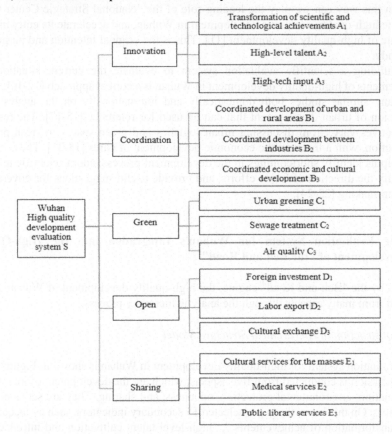

Figure 1. Hierarchy model of Wuhan high quality development evaluation system

Table 1. Consistency test of criterion layer discriminant matrix

Criteria layer content	λ_{max}	CI	CR	Consistency inspection results
A-Innovation	3.054	0.027	0.046<0.1	
B-Coordination	3.018	0.009	0.016<0.1	
C-Greenness	3.054	0.027	0.046<0.1	All passed consistency check
D-Openness	3.023	0.011	0.019 <0.1	
E-Shareability	3.025	0.012	0.021<0.1	

3. Empirical Analysis of the Evaluation System for High-Quality Development in Wuhan based on FCE

3.1. Method and Steps of Fuzzy Comprehensive Evaluation

FCE is typically a method that uses fuzzy mathematics theory to quantitatively analyze various factors with unclear boundaries and to get clear judgments.

The fuzzy comprehensive evaluation method can be divided into the following stages.

Step 1, determine the indicator set $U=\{U1, U2, U3, U4..., Un\}$, Ui $(i=1, 2, 3,... n)$ to represent the i-th indicator of the evaluated object. This step is to establish an evaluation index system and clarify the relationship between evaluation indicators at all levels.

Step 2, determine the weight of evaluation indicators $Wi=\{Wi1, Wi2, Wi3, Wi4...,$ $Win\}$, where Wi represents the weight of the i-level indicator. The weight of the evaluation indicator indicates its importance in the set.

Step 3, establish a comment set $V=\{V1, V2, V3, V4..., Vn\}$, typically using 4 or 5 evaluation levels.

$$\begin{pmatrix} r_{i11} & r_{i12} & \cdots & r_{i1n} \\ r_{i21} & r_{i22} & \cdots & r_{i2n} \\ \vdots & \vdots & \ddots & \vdots \\ r_{in1} & r_{in2} & \cdots & r_{inn} \end{pmatrix} \tag{1}$$

Step 4, establish an evaluation membership matrix R, where Ri represents the membership matrix of the i-level evaluation index.

Step 5, comprehensive evaluation. $Ti=Wi \times Ri$ and Ti represent the i-th level fuzzy comprehensive evaluation.

3.2. Establishment of Evaluation Indicators and Weights

Based on the hierarchical structure model in Figure 1, this article establishes a fuzzy comprehensive evaluation index system for "high-quality development in Wuhan". Calculate the weights of each factor in the matrix, which is the evaluation index weight of "high-quality development in Wuhan".

3.3. Questionnaire Design and Data Analysis

During the questionnaire design process, the project team determined that $V5=\{Excellent, Good, Medium, Passable, Poor\}$.

The questionnaires were collected through online distribution and on-site distribution and received 137 valid questionnaires. This article uses SPSS software to test the data, and *Cronbach's* α values of five indicators A, B, C, D, and E are obtained as *0.867, 0.908, 0.851, 0.873* and *0.832* respectively.

It is clearly shown that the values of *Cronbach's* α for each indicator are greater than 0.8, which indicate that the questionnaire data is of high reliability.

The fuzzy evaluation set of each element presented in Table 2 was obtained by processing the questionnaire data.

Table 2. A collection of vague evaluations of Wuhan's high-quality development

Target layer	Criteria layer		Object layer		Evaluation set				
	First-level	Weight	Second-level	Weight	Excellent	good	Medium	Fair	poor
Wuhan high- quality development evaluation system	Innovative development	0.110	Transformation of scientific and technological achievements A_1	0.140	0.117	0.241	0.540	0.066	0.037
			High-level talent A_2	0.333	0.139	0.394	0.380	0.051	0.037
			High-tech input A_3	0.528	0.095	0.336	0.438	0.066	0.066
	Coordinated development	0.202	Coordinated development of urban and rural areas B_1	0.320	0.095	0.292	0.489	0.095	0.029
			Coordinated development between industries B_2	0.558	0.058	0.270	0.547	0.073	0.051
			Coordinated economic and cultural development B_3	0.122	0.080	0.292	0.504	0.088	0.037
	Green development	0.266	Urban greening C_1	0.249	0.175	0.416	0.285	0.102	0.022
			Sewage treatment C_2	0.594	0.080	0.226	0.402	0.234	0.058
			Air quality C_3	0.157	0.088	0.161	0.438	0.226	0.088
	Open development	0.071	Foreign investment D_1	0.228	0.102	0.219	0.533	0.117	0.029
			Labor export D_2	0.092	0.095	0.234	0.584	0.073	0.015
			Cultural exchange D_3	0.680	0.102	0.314	0.496	0.073	0.015
	Shared development	0.351	Cultural services for the masses E_1	0.200	0.131	0.248	0.518	0.073	0.029
			Medical services E_2	0.683	0.110	0.270	0.467	0.110	0.044
			Public library services E_3	0.117	0.139	0.336	0.445	0.080	0.000

Calculate the comprehensive evaluation value of high-quality development in Wuhan based on the data in Table 2. Taking the first of the five secondary indicators in the criteria layer as an example, the calculation process is as follows.

$$T21 = W21 \times R21 =$$

$$(0.140 \quad 0.333 \quad 0.528) \begin{pmatrix} 0.117 & 0.241 & 0.540 & 0.066 & 0.037 \\ 0.139 & 0.394 & 0.380 & 0.051 & 0.037 \\ 0.095 & 0.336 & 0.438 & 0.066 & 0.066 \end{pmatrix}$$

$$= (0.113 \quad 0.342 \quad 0.433 \quad 0.061 \quad 0.052)$$

The calculation method for the other four secondary indicators is in the same manners. Count the summary of the first level indicators as below.

$T1 = W1 \times R1 =$

$$(0.110 \quad 0.202 \quad 0.266 \quad 0.071 \quad 0.351) \begin{pmatrix} 0.113 & 0.342 & 0.433 & 0.061 & 0.052 \\ 0.073 & 0.280 & 0.523 & 0.082 & 0.042 \\ 0.105 & 0.263 & 0.379 & 0.200 & 0.054 \\ 0.101 & 0.285 & 0.513 & 0.083 & 0.018 \\ 0.118 & 0.273 & 0.475 & 0.099 & 0.036 \end{pmatrix}$$

$$= (0.104 \quad 0.280 \quad 0.457 \quad 0.117 \quad 0.042)$$

Based on the above analysis, it is distinctly displayed that the probability of identifying the evaluation result as "excellent" is 10.4%, with 28% of the evaluation results being "good", 45.7% believing that the level is "moderate", 11.7% believing that it is "passable", and the probability of persisting in believing that it is "poor" is 4.2%.

Using the principle of maximum number of members to queue values,

$$0.457 > 0.280 > 0.117 > 0.104 > 0.042.$$

Analysis shows that the evaluation result of high-quality development in Wuhan city is "medium". This result of evaluation still falls short of the expectations of the municipal government and all citizens of Wuhan. It still requires the continuous efforts of the entire city.

4. Suggestions for High-Quality Development in Wuhan City

On the base of the above comprehensive evaluation, the following countermeasures and suggestions are proposed for the high-quality development of Wuhan deeply integrated into the "the Belt and Road" initiative.

(1) Clear positioning and active integration into the top-level design of "the Belt and Road"

With the development concept of innovation, coordination, green, openness and sharing, Wuhan should strengthen top-level design and layout in accordance with the principle of "moderately advanced, planning led, and systematic layout", so as to orderly promote the integration of high-quality construction into "the Belt and Road".

(2) Breaking the administrative system and establishing a coordinated organizational structure for domestic development strategies

It is necessary to balance the interests of "the Belt and Road" administrative regions, coordinate industrial division, promote industrial integration and complementary advantages, and strive to build a new open economic system compatible with "the Belt and Road" construction through deepening reform.

(3) Optimize space and layout the development system

Firstly, promote regional linkage development; Secondly, leverage regional comparative advantages; Thirdly, create new economic growth points; The fourth is to create a node city and a peaceful Taiwan style city; Thus, a comprehensive development system is laid out.

(4) Strengthen industrial development and build an industrial system

To build a world-class advanced manufacturing cluster and cultivate strategic emerging industries. Prioritize the growth of various strategic emerging industries based on local technological advantages; It is also necessary to support the construction of advantageous industrial clusters along the Yangtze River and the construction of a modern industrial system.

(5) Improving the environment and promoting high-quality urban development

Creating a good environment, aligning with national strategies, formulating industrial policy plans, and building the Wuhan Free Trade Zone not only brings into play the free trade effect within the zone, but also needs to do a good job in the linkage between inside and outside the zone, and leverage the radiation effect of the free trade zone.

(6) Gathering excellent talents and showcasing intellectual advantages

Fully leverage Wuhan's advantages in science, education, and talent; Support the introduction and cultivation of discipline leaders, science and technology leading talents and high-level entrepreneurial talents in relevant fields, especially in high-tech fields, promote the reform of talent training pattern in universities and colleges, promote talent training cooperation in different countries and separate regions along "the Belt and Road", and ensure that Wuhan is at the height of intelligence.

5. Conclusion

Located in the geographical center of China, the huge Wuhan bears the mission of connecting the east, west, north, south, and promoting the construction of a strong country. It plays an important role in the construction of "the Belt and Road". To promote the high-quality development of Wuhan city, it is necessary to have a global perspective from both China and the world, comprehensively analyzing the advantages and weakness of innovation, harmony, greenization, openness, and sharing. Using the Analytic Hierarchy Process, design primary and secondary indicators, establish a synthetical evaluation system for analysis, and determine the focus of urban construction and development work.

Through the distribution of questionnaires and the analysis of the data in the collected results, it can be concluded that the evaluation level of Wuhan's development level is "medium", indicating that there is significant development space. In view of the practical shortcomings existing in the urban development, the research of this project has put forward corresponding constructive opinions and suggestions from various aspects, such as top-level design, organization construction, development space construction, industrial system design, environmental improvement, talent intelligence advantages, etc., expecting to make certain contributions to the deep integration of Wuhan into the "Belt and Road" construction and future high-quality development.

Acknowledgment

This paper is the research result of the key bidding project of Wuhan Federation of Social Sciences (WSKLW [2019] No. 4-3).

References

[1] Reeves J. China's Silk Road Economic belt initiative: network and influence formation in Central Asia[J]. Journal of Contemporary China, 2018, 27(112): 502-518.

[2] Bogojevi S., Zou M. Making Infrastructure 'visible' in environmental law: the belt and road initiative and climate change friction[J]. Transnational Environmental Law, 2021, 10(1): 35-56.

[3] Mitrovic D. The belt and road: China's ambitious initiative[J]. China International Study, 2016, 59: 76.

[4] Krupp F. How to keep belt and road green[J]. World Environment, 2015, 000(004): 29-31.

[5] Huiqing K. Research on the risk of foreign investment of Chinese energy enterprises under the "One Belt and One Road" initiative[D]. Beijing: University of International Business and Economics 2018.

[6] A, Erik Lichtenberg, C. D. B. Local officials as land developers: Urban spatial expansion in China[J]. Journal of Urban Economics, 2009, 66(1):57-64.

[7] Moser S , Mayrhofer J , Schmidt R R ,et al. Socioeconomic cost-benefit-analysis of seasonal heat storages in district heating systems with industrial waste heat integration[J]. Energy, 2018, 160(10): 868-874.

[8] Kantor P, Savitch H. V. How to study comparative urban development politics: a research note[J]. International Journal of Urban & Regional Research, 2010, 29(1): 69-72.

[9] Li Jinchang, Shi Longmei, Xu Aiting. Discussion on the evaluation index system for high quality development[J]. Statistical Research, 2019, 36 (01): 4-14 (in Chinese).

[10] Boonstra B. Self-organization in urban development: towards a new perspective on spatial planning: Urban Research & Practice[J]. 2011, 4(2): 124-129.

[11] Li Chang'an, Zhang Yufen. The formation and development of Wuhan City and the evolution of Human land relations[J]. Journal of Geology, 2021, 95 (03): 940-942 (in Chinese).

[12] Alipouri E., Sarvar R., Panahi MVS. Analysis, measurement, and evaluation of sustainable development in Aleshtar City using AHP-Fuzzy and TOPSIS Models[J]. Semnan University, 2020, 11: 497-510.

[13] Wolnowska AE., Konicki W. Multi-criterial analysis of oversize cargo transport through the city, using the AHP method[J]. Transportation Research Procedia, 2019, 39: 614-623.

[14] Salemi A. Prioritizing the effective criteria in locating green spaces using AHP Approach (Case Study: Mahmoudabad Nemuneh City) [J]. Indian Journal of Innovations and Developments, 2019, 8(8): 2277-5390.

[15] Du Yupei, Zhang Di, Zou Yue. Sustainable supplier evaluation and selection of fresh agricultural products based on IFAHP-TODIM model[J]. Mathematical Problems in Engineering, 2020: 1-15.

[16] Deng Yuling, Selection of cold chain logistics suppliers for fresh agricultural products based on AHP[J]. Logistics Technology, 2017, 04: 91-93, (in Chinese).

[17] Xinling, An Xiaoning. Construction and measurement analysis of the evaluation system for high quality agricultural development in China[J]. Economic Perspective, 2019 (05): 109-118 (in Chinese).

[18] Felix Escolano, et al. Strategies on Reuse of Clayey Expansive Soils as Embankment Material in Urban Development Areas: A Case Study in New Urbanized Zones[J]. Applied Sciences, 2018, 8(5):764-771.

[19] Han Junhui, Shakhzod Shokirov, Liu Yang. Research on comprehensive evaluation of high quality development based on entropy method[J]. Technology and Industry, 2019, 19 (06): 79-83 (in Chinese).

[20] Xu Yongbing, Luo Peng, Zhang Yue. Construction and measurement of high quality development indicator system - taking Hebei Province as an example[J]. Journal of Hebei University (Philosophy and Social Sciences Edition), 2019, 44 (03): 86-97 (in Chinese).

[21] Liu Lixia, Sun Chunhua. Comprehensive evaluation and analysis of high quality economic development in western provinces[J]. Journal of Inner Mongolia University of Finance and Economics, 2019, 17 (03): 13-15 (in Chinese).

[22] Liu Shuliang. Research on strategies for transforming Wuhan's science and education resource advantages into development advantages[J]. Operations Research and Fuzziness, 2023, 13 (4): 10 (in Chinese).

[23] Narayan G R, Natalia Herran, Reymond C. E, et al. Local persistence of Large Benthic Foraminifera (LBF) under increasing urban development: A case study from Zanzibar (Unguja), East Africa[J]. Journal of Earth Sciences: English Edition, 2022, 33(6):17.

[24] Shouming Chen, Jiasi Fan. Measuring corporate social responsibility based on a fuzzy analytical hierarchy process[J]. International Journal of Computer Network and Information Security, 2011, (03): 13-22.

Artificial Intelligence, Medical Engineering and Education
Z.B. Hu et al. (Eds.)
© 2024 The Authors.
This article is published online with Open Access by IOS Press and distributed under the terms
of the Creative Commons Attribution Non-Commercial License 4.0 (CC BY-NC 4.0).
doi:10.3233/ATDE231336

Research on Influence Factors of Resilience Capability in Fresh Cold Chain Logistics Based on DEMATEL-ISM Method

Yang HU[a,1], Aiman Magde Abdallah Ahmed[b]

a School of Econnomics and Management, Wuchang Shouyi University, Wuhan, China
b Faisal AI Islam Bank, Khartoum, Sudan
ORCiD ID: Yang HU https://orcid.org/ 0009-0003-0851-0240

Abstract. The capacity for resilience is becoming more and more crucial to the sustainable development of cold chain logistics in China, particularly in the event of an unexpected public security incident. This is because agricultural cold chain logistics is particularly susceptible to shocks due to its wide spatial and temporal distribution and large number of participating subjects. On residents' daily lives, even small disruptions in cold chain logistics can have a big effect. Thus, strengthening the cold chain logistics for agriculture's resilience is essential for sustainable development. From a resilience standpoint, this paper examines the cold chain logistics for agriculture's emergency management path. Five resilience factor dimensions are used to contextualize the resilience capability and investigate the relationship between these indicators and the resilience of fresh cold chain logistics, based on the DEMATEl-ISM model. Lastly, a multilevel structural model for the variables influencing the fresh cold chain logistics' resilience is constructed by the paper. The findings indicate that the primary factors influencing the resilience of fresh cold chain logistics are the deterioration and loss of fresh agricultural products during transit, the low delivery punctuality, and the high operating costs. The study's findings may serve as a guide for new cold chain logistics companies looking to raise service standards, boost productivity, lower costs, and minimize risk.

Keywords. Fresh cold chain logistics resilience, Resilience capability, DEMATEL-ISM method

1. Introduction

Nowadays unexpected public safety incidents, such as the COVID-19 pandemic, have happened more often. While cold chain logistics capacity is restricted by COVID-19 lockout, people' demand for fresh agricultural products has been steadily increasing. This leads to a high frequency of interruption and delay situations. The complexity and multiplicity of the linkages and subjects involved in cold chain logistics make it susceptible to breakage, hence limiting the extent to which agricultural cold chain operations can be expanded. To reduce the risk of disruption, agricultural cold chain logistics must be made more resilient to unforeseen public security events [3]. Cold chain

---

[1] Corresponding Author: Yang HU, E-mail: huyang730@163.com.

logistics must also improve operators' marketability through sustainable development, expand the cold chain industry's standardization system, and consistently raise the bar on standardized services [4]. Furthermore, in order to achieve long-term growth in cold chain logistics for fresh agricultural products, it is critical to understand the causes of cold chain logistics breakdowns and to propose appropriate solutions and recommendations to strengthen the cold chain's resilience [7].

One of the most important characteristics of supply chain systems in dealing with the uncertainty caused by the most recent environmental, economic, and social crisis is resilience. Building a more resilient and adaptable agri-food supply chain system, particularly in the agri-food supply chain, is critical. More research on agricultural cold chain logistics resilience could be conducted. Some researchers have only looked at the essential components of a strong agri-food supply chain [10]. Given the flaws in agricultural product logistics research theory, some academics employ rooted theory to construct a theoretical system based on factual data and phenomena that provides concepts for the study of agricultural product resilience. Many of the components of evolutionary resilience can be used to boost resilience.

They must, however, be carefully chosen and implemented in accordance with the relevant stages of disruption, and their overall impact on the supply chain must be evaluated. The primary research focus must be on the overall impact on the supply chain [15]. Because of the numerous participants and intricate systems found in agricultural products' cold chain logistics systems, some researchers apply reliability analysis concepts found in reliability engineering theory to the problem of cold chain logistics system failure. They make the abstract issue concrete by taking into account the system's operational characteristics, the causal relationship between events, and the resulting fault tree. The evolution of resilience is viewed as an uncertain event, with Bayesian networks used for inference. To assess the overall risk, key influencing factors are identified and subjected to sensitivity analysis using Bayesian network modeling and simulation [17]. Using fuzzy set theory, essential risk factors are identified by predicting and computing the probability of each root node. Methods to reduce the likelihood of broken chains have been investigated [18]. Most current research focuses on efficiency and risk, and most academics look at agricultural cold chain logistics resilience from a static perspective. There is a severe lack of dynamic research on resilience development. The majority of prior research has used system dynamics and Bayesian networks to examine the effectiveness and risk of cold chain logistics [7]. Although these studies are not as comprehensive as the current one, they do provide a theoretical framework for investigating uncertainty and contextual evolution, which is the focus of this paper's investigation.

The Decision-Making Trial and Evaluation Laboratory (DEMATEL), which is based on the 4M1E method, is used to analyze the significance of various influencing factors on the resilience of logistics services in the cold chain for fresh agri-food. In order to study the resilience influencing factors of logistics service in fresh agricultural cold chain, a multi-layer hierarchical structure model was built using Interpretative Structural Modeling (ISM), with the categories and roles of each factor identified. To reduce the risk of disruption and increase the efficiency of fresh cold chain logistics operations, the hierarchical relationship between different influencing factors was examined. The study illustrates the importance of resilience and offers guidelines for businesses and the government to improve fresh cold chain logistics' resilience and withstand the effects of unforeseen public events.

2. Identification of Factors Influencing the Resilience of Fresh Cold Chain Logistics

A unique supply chain system known as "fresh cold chain logistics" handles all phases of agricultural product lifecycle management, including harvesting, processing, warehousing, transportation, distribution, and retail, while maintaining a constant low temperature control environment, which emphasizes the selection and distribution of fresh agricultural products, describes how fresh e-commerce businesses send goods into front-end warehouses for refrigeration through the cold chain, load them, and deliver them to customers' homes after receiving orders. The 'last mile' of fresh cold chain logistics consists of packaging and delivery services. Serving as a middleman between buyers and sellers, the warehouse plans delivery routes, assigns delivery staff and refrigerated trucks, sorts items based on the specific items and time constraints in user orders. The logistics process of the fresh cold chain is shown in Figure 1:

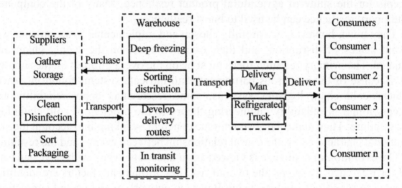

Figure 1. Flow chart of fresh cold chain logistics

This paper summarizes and extracts the resilience influencing factors of fresh cold chain logistics mentioned in previous literature based on relevant consumer evaluation and statistics on the logistics service problems of fresh cold chain, combined with research on the logistics process of fresh cold chain. The factors affecting the resilience of logistics services in the fresh cold chain were identified from five dimensions: man, machine, material, method, and environment, with reference to the established 4M1E risk management method. "Machine" refers to the facilities and equipment used in the logistics service process; "Material" refers to the fresh agricultural products in the logistics process; and "Man" refers to all personnel involved in the fresh cold chain logistics service process; The term "environment" refers to the internal and external environments that have an impact on the fresh cold chain's logistical operation. "Method" refers to the management system, operational regulations, etc. in the logistics process. Table 1 displays the causal diagram used to determine the resilience factors influencing the caliber of logistics services in the fresh cold chain.

Table 1. Factors affecting resilience of fresh cold chain logistics

Dimensions	Factors	References
Man	Manager's emergency awareness A1	Yu Z et al. 2021[1]
	Employee knowledge and skill level A2	Xie Ruhe et al. 2022[2]
	Employee work collaboration A3	Luo Qianfeng et al. 2021[3]
Machine	Real time monitoring system for product quality A4	Xiao Hu Xing et al. 2020[4]
	Cold chain low temperature control and support capability A5	Nodali et al. （2019）[5]
	Fresh agricultural product traceability system A6	Shankar et al. （2018）[6]
Material	Fresh agricultural product qualityA7	Zhang Xicai et al.(2021)[7]
	Cost of damage to fresh agricultural products in transit A8	Tromp et al. （2016）[8]
	Differences in temperature requirements for fresh agricultural products A9	J.Vieira et al. （2017）[9]
	Government emergency supply A10	Kontopanou et al.(2022)[10]
Method	Delivery punctuality A11	Maliheh et al. （2016）[11]
	Design of delivery path for fresh agricultural products A12	Huang et al. （2018）[12]
	Fresh product logistics operation cost A13	Yang et al. （2016）[13]
	National reserve system A14	Martin et al. （2016）[14]
Environment	Industry safety pressure A15	Stone et al.(2018)[15]
	Market price fluctuation of fresh agricultural products A16	Macheka et al. （2017）[16]
	Consumer risk culture A17	Zheng Chaoyu et al. (2020)[17]
	Corporate innovation development A18	Chen H et al.(2021)[18]

3. Correlation Analysis of Factors Influencing Resilience in Fresh Cold Chain Logistics Based on DEMATEL-ISM Method

The United States National Laboratory developed the DEMATEL method in 1971 as an analytical technique for resolving challenging display issues. It does this by combining matrix methods and graph theory. This method determines the hierarchical structure and significance of each factor in complex systems by analyzing the relationships between the factors in the system, creating an impact matrix, and obtaining the analysis results of the degree of influence, degree of influence, centrality, and degree of cause of each influencing factor. The main way that this method is currently applied is in an efficient combination with other methods to solve the problem of jointly identifying key factors in a variety of fields.

The primary functions of an Interpretative Structural Model (ISM) are to sort out many complex system elements and create a clear, hierarchical system structure. ISMs also analyze the relationships of mutual influence between system elements. The four main analysis steps of Interpreting the Structural Model (ISM) are: (1) identifying the influencing factors; (2) sorting out the relationships between the influencing factors to establish adjacency and reachability matrices; (3) obtaining the reachability matrix and dividing it into regions and levels; and (4) building a hierarchical system matrix diagram based on the hierarchical division's outcomes.

The comprehensive impact matrix is obtained by applying the DEMATEL method to the direct impact matrix, which is determined by the strength relationship of the influencing factors in the integrated DEMATEL-ISM method. Following transformation, the complete impact matrix is produced, from which the degree of each influencing factor's influence, centrality, origin, and degree of influence can be determined. Perform corresponding transformations based on the previously constructed direct influence matrix to obtain the adjacency matrix of the ISM method. Process the adjacency matrix in accordance with the ISM method to obtain a multi-level hierarchical structure model with strong explanatory power.

3.1. DEMATEL Modeling of the Factors Influencing Resilience in Cold Chain Logistics

1) Building a direct impact matrix for indicators

There are four dimensions and eighteen indicators in the resilience index system. The mutual influence relationship between indicators is represented by the notation A_{ij}, which indicates the extent to which indicator A_i influences indicator A_j. The indicator set is designated as $A=\{A01, A02,..., A18\}$. When i=j, $A_{ij}=0$, the indicators are said to have no influence on themselves because the relationship between their mutual influence is unequal. According to the mutual influence relationship between the indicators, relevant experts are asked to assign A_{ij} values using the Delphi method. The direct impact matrix of resilience indicators, $B=(A_{ij})$ 18 × 18, is obtained by assigning values of 3, 2, 1, and 0 to the strong, medium, weak, and no levels, respectively (See Figure 2). By normalizing the direct impact matrix of the indicators, the normalized direct impact matrix C of the indicators is obtained.

A_{ij}	A01	A02	A03	A04	A05	A06	A07	A08	A9	A10	A11	A12	A13	A14	A15	A16	A17	A18
A01	0	2	3	0	1	2	1	0	0	0	0	0	0	0	0	0	0	3
A02	0	0	1	0	0	0	0	1	0	0	0	0	0	0	0	0	0	0
A03	0	0	0	1	2	0	0	2	0	0	0	2	1	0	0	0	0	1
A04	0	0	0	0	2	0	0	0	0	3	0	0	0	0	0	0	0	0
A05	0	0	0	0	0	3	0	0	0	0	0	0	0	0	0	0	0	0
A06	0	0	0	0	1	0	0	0	0	0	0	0	0	0	0	0	0	0
A07	0	0	0	0	0	0	0	0	1	0	0	0	0	0	0	0	0	0
A08	0	0	0	0	0	0	0	0	0	0	0	0	0	0	0	0	0	0
A9	0	0	0	0	0	0	0	0	0	0	0	1	3	0	1	0	0	0
A10	0	0	0	0	0	0	0	0	0	0	3	0	0	0	0	0	3	0
A11	0	0	0	0	0	1	2	0	0	0	0	0	0	3	2	0	0	0
A12	0	0	0	0	0	0	0	0	0	0	0	0	0	0	0	0	0	0
A13	0	0	0	0	0	0	0	0	2	0	0	1	0	0	0	0	0	0
A14	0	0	0	1	0	0	0	2	0	0	2	0	2	0	3	0	0	0
A15	0	0	0	0	0	0	0	0	0	0	0	0	0	0	0	0	0	0
A16	0	0	0	0	0	0	0	0	0	0	0	1	0	0	0	0	0	0
A17	0	0	0	0	0	0	0	1	2	0	0	1	0	0	0	0	0	0
A18	0	0	0	0	0	0	0	0	0	0	0	0	0	0	0	1	0	0

Figure.2 Direct Impact Matrix Diagram of Resilience Indicators

Divide each influence relationship A_{ij} obtained in the direct impact matrix B by the maximum value of the sum of influencing factors in each row to obtain a new normalized direct impact matrix. Formula 1 is calculated as follows.

$$C = (c_{ij})_{18 \times 18} = \frac{1}{MAX \sum_{1}^{n} A_{ij}} B \tag{1}$$

2) Calculate the comprehensive impact matrix T, centrality M_i, and causal degree N_i of the indicators

Calculate the comprehensive impact matrix of indicators $T[T=(t_{ij})18 \times 18]$ to determine the comprehensive impact of various indicators relative to the highest level indicators in the Resilience Index System, formula 2 is used as the unit matrix in formula 1.

$$T = C(I-C)^{-1} \tag{2}$$

For the rows and columns in the comprehensive impact matrix T of the indicator, use the formula 2 above, where I is the identity matrix. Calculate the centrality M_i and causal degree N_i of each indicator using the formula:

$$f_i = \sum_{i=1}^{18} t_{ij} (i = 1,2,\ldots,18) \tag{3}$$

$$e_i = \sum_{j=1}^{18} t_{ij} (i = 1,2,\ldots,18) \tag{4}$$

$$M_i = f_i + e_i (i = 1,2,\ldots,18) \tag{5}$$

$$N_i = f_i - e_i (i = 1,2,\ldots,18) \tag{6}$$

The formula, which is used to indicate the significance of the indicator in the evaluation indicator system, uses the variables f_i, e_i, and M_i to represent the degree of influence, centrality, and importance of the indicator, respectively, of the indicator A_i. The more central the indicator, the more significant it is. The indicator A_i's causal degree, or N_i, is a measure of how big of a part it plays in the evaluation indicator system. An indicator is considered causal if it has a larger causal degree, which also indicates that the indicator has a greater role in the evaluation indicator system. In the evaluation indicator system, the indicator is more strongly indicative of a result indicator the smaller the causal degree. Table 2 displays the results of the calculations for the centrality and causal degree of the different indicators.

Table 2. Calculation results of centrality and causality of various indicators resilience system of Fresh Cold Chain Logistics

Identifier	Influence degree	Affected degree	Centrality	Causality
A01	1.33577697	0	1.33577697	1.33577697
A02	0.240634963	0.166666667	0.40730163	0.073968297
A03	0.88761956	0.347222222	1.234841782	0.540397338
A04	0.674632122	0.228067523	0.902699646	0.446564599
A05	0.276595745	0.655073093	0.931668838	-0.378477348
A06	0.106382979	0.710297626	0.816680604	-0.603914647
A07	0.125	0.343058705	0.468058705	-0.218058705
A08	0	0.663920121	0.663920121	-0.663920121
A09	0.5	0.624721757	1.124721757	-0.124721757
A10	0.84746466	0.307016881	1.15448154	0.540447779
A11	0.973191972	0.55835223	1.531544202	0.414839742
A12	0	0.709124147	0.709124147	-0.709124147
A13	0.333333333	0.750046967	1.083380301	-0.416713634
A14	1.107306894	0.389588057	1.496894952	0.717718837
A15	0	0.742515866	0.742515866	-0.742515866
A16	0.083333333	0.113522377	0.19685571	-0.030189043
A17	0.416666667	0.32675422	0.743420887	0.089912446
A18	0.090277778	0.362268519	0.452546296	-0.271990741

3.2. Result Analysis of the Factors Influencing Resilience in Fresh Cold Chain Logistics

1)Analysis of the importance of indicators
According to the index centrality calculated by the DEMATEL-ISM model, the importance curve of business environment evaluation can be drawn, as shown in Figure 2. The centrality of the indicator is positively correlated with its importance in the evaluation indicator system. The indicators that have a significant impact on the resilience are the delivery punctuality (A11), national reserve system (A14), manager's emergency awareness (A1), and employee work collaboration (A3); Secondly, the government emergency supply (A10), differences in temperature requirements for fresh agricultural products (A9), fresh product logistics operation cost (A13), cold chain low temperature control and support capability (A5), real time monitoring system for product quality (A4), fresh agricultural product traceability system (A6), design of delivery path for fresh agricultural products (A12), consumer risk culture (A17), industry safety pressure (A15), and cost of damage to fresh agricultural products in transit (A8); The less important ones are fresh agricultural product quality (A7), corporate innovation development (A18), employee knowledge and skill level (A2), and market price fluctuation of fresh agricultural products (A16).

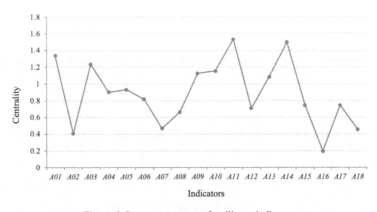

Figure 3. Importance curve of resilience indicators

2)Category analysis of indicators

According to the causal degree of the indicators calculated by the above model, a causal diagram of the business environment evaluation indicators can be drawn, as shown in Figure 2. Manager's emergency awareness (*A1*), employee knowledge and skill level (*A2*), employee work collaboration (*A3*), real time monitoring system for product quality (*A4*), the government emergency supply (*A10*), delivery punctuality (*A11*), real time monitoring system for product quality (*A14*), and consumer risk culture (*A17*) are the reason indicators in the resilience factors system; The outcome indicators in the resilience factors system include cold chain low temperature control and support capability (*A5*), fresh agricultural product traceability system (*A6*), fresh agricultural product quality (*A7*), cost of damage to fresh agricultural products in transit (A8), design of delivery path for fresh agricultural products (*A12*), differences in temperature requirements for fresh agricultural products (*A9*), fresh product logistics operation cost (*A13*), industry safety pressure (*A15*), and corporate innovation development (*A18*); The other indicators are located in the middle and serve as transitional indicators from cause indicators to outcome indicators.

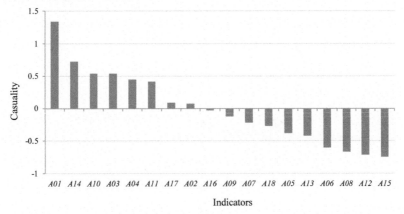

Figure 4. Causality diagram of resilience indicators

3.3 Analysis of the Structure of Factors Influencing Resilience in Cold Chain Logistics Based on ISM

1)Calculate the overall impact matrix H and reachability matrix K of indicators
Overall Impact Matrix of Indicators $H[H=(h_{ij})_{18\times18}]$The calculation formula for is

$$H=I+T \tag{7}$$

Given a threshold based on the overall impact matrix H of the indicator $\lambda=1$, Calculate the reachability matrix of indicators through K $K[K=H=I+T(k_{ij})_{18\times18}]$:

$$k_{ij}=1 \ \unicode{x5F53}\ h_{ij}\geqslant\lambda(i,j=1,\ 2...18) \tag{8}$$

$$k_{ij}=0,\unicode{x5F53}\ h_{ij}<\lambda(i,j=1,\ 2...18) \tag{9}$$

Define the cutoff λ. Simplifying the system structure and getting rid of influence relationships between indicators that have less influence are the goals. The division of the system structure and the make-up of the reachability matrix are directly impacted by its size. Stronger independence between indicators and a simpler system structure are associated with larger threshold values; however, expressing the impact relationship between indicators clearly is more challenging when the threshold value is smaller. Conversely, more complex impact relationships and intricate system structures are associated with smaller threshold values, but more challenging to express the system's overall nature. To get the best system structure model, multiple value analysis and threshold verification are therefore required.

2)Analysis of the multi-level hierarchical structure model of the system
The reachability matrix is broken down into levels and divided into regions based on the reachability matrix that was previously obtained.

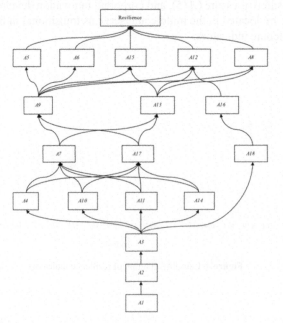

Figure 5. Multilevel hierarchical structural model for factors affecting resilience

Figure 5 illustrates the construction of a hierarchical structural model based on the outcomes of the hierarchical division.

According to the ISM model, the influencing factor system of resilience in fresh cold chain logistics is a multi-level hierarchical structure with 7 levels, which determines the hierarchical and hierarchical relationships between various influencing factors. Among them, the influencing factors include direct layer factors, intermediate layer factors, and root layer factors.

The direct factors affecting the resilience in fresh cold chain logistics are cold chain low temperature control and support capability ($A5$), fresh agricultural product traceability system ($A6$), industry safety pressure ($A15$), cost of damage to fresh agricultural products in transit ($A8$) and design of delivery path for fresh agricultural products ($A12$). That is to say, the most direct way to optimize the resilience in fresh cold chain logistics is to start from these aspects. In addition, as shown in Figure 5, the five factors not only have a direct impact on the resilience in fresh cold chain logistics, but also are influenced by the next level of factors. Therefore, when improving these aspects, it is necessary to consider the next level of factors comprehensively.

Differences in temperature requirements for fresh agricultural products ($A9$), fresh product logistics operation cost ($A13$), Market price fluctuation of fresh agricultural products ($A16$), price supervision and fresh agricultural product quality ($A7$), consumer risk culture ($A17$) and corporate innovation development ($A18$) in the ISM model are intermediate factors. Because they interact with the second and lower level factors, they are at the center of the relationship in the model. The relationship between these factors is extremely close, and it is difficult to solve a single problem effectively. It is necessary to intervene in multiple problems simultaneously to produce results.

The root cause factors that affect the resilience are those that affect or indirectly affect other factors, but are not affected by any factors. Real time monitoring system for product quality (A4) at the bottom of the model, the government emergency supply ($A10$), delivery punctuality ($A11$), real time monitoring system for product quality ($A14$), manager's emergency awareness ($A1$), employee knowledge and skill level ($A2$), employee work collaboration ($A3$) are all root causes. Managing these root causes is the easiest to operate and most effective.

4. Conclusion

The following findings from the study are derived from the literature review and Delphi method used to extract 18 influencing factors involving the resilience of fresh cold chain front-end warehouses; the correlation between various influencing factors was studied using the DEMATEL integrated decision-making laboratory analysis method and the Interpretative Structural Model (ISM); the influencing factors were categorized based on cause and centrality; and a resilience system model was established for the fresh cold chain logistics.

1)Real time monitoring system for product quality, government emergency supply, delivery punctuality, manager's emergency awareness, employee knowledge and skill level, employee work collaboration and national reserve system are the basic indicators that affect the resilience of fresh cold chain logistics.

2)In order to improve the resilience of fresh agricultural products, the government needs to introduce a series of policy measures to guide the logistics of fresh cold chain towards standardization, security and sustainability, and provide policy support for the development of fresh e-commerce enterprises.

3)Consumers also need to continuously strengthen their awareness of food safety, encourage fresh e-commerce enterprises to pay more attention to product quality, invest more costs in quality control of cold chain logistics, and achieve the sustainable development of the fresh cold chain industry.

The theoretical foundation for increasing the effectiveness of logistics operations and lowering risks for new e-commerce businesses is presented in this paper. To achieve a more in-depth evolutionary study of the resilience in fresh cold chain logistics, more verification and improvement of the chosen research method is necessary, even though it has a certain degree of objectivity and scientificity. Nevertheless, the number of factors that affect the resilience of fresh cold chain logistics that are identified in this paper is limited.

Acknowledgment

This project is supported by Institute of Distribution Research, IDR (IDR2021YB004).

References

[1]   Yu Z, Liu Y, Wang Q, et al. Research on food safety and security of cold chain logistics[J]. IOP Conference Series: Earth and Environmental Science, 2021, 647(1):012176 (6pp).
[2]   Xie Ruhe, Hong Huang, Yuan Zhang and Peiyun Yu. Coupling relationship between cold chain logistics and economic development: A investigation from China[J]. PLoS One, 2022, 17 (2): e0264561.
[3]   Luo Qianfeng, and Zhang Liyang. Theoretical interpretation and realization path of the high-quality development of agricultural cold chain logistics[J]. China Business and Market, 2021, 35(11): 3-11 (in Chinese).
[4]   Xiao Hu Xing, Zhi Hua Hu, Wen Ping Luo. Using evolutionary game theory to study governments and logistics companies' strategies for avoiding broken cold chains[J]. Annals of Operations Research, 2020(2).
[5]   Ndraha N, Sung W. C, Hsiao H. I. Evaluation of the cold chain management options to preserve the shelf life of frozen shrimps: A case study in the home delivery services in Taiwan[J]. Journal of food engineering, 2019, 242(2): 21-30.
[6]   Shankar R , Gupta R , Pathak D K .Modeling critical success factors of traceability for food logistics system[J]. Transportation Research Part E Logistics & Transportation Review, 2018, 119(11): 205-222.
[7]   Zhang Xicai, Huo Di. Analysis and countermeasures of weak links in cold chain logistics of fresh agricultural products in China[J]. Agricultural Economics and Management, 2021, 67(03): 93-102.
[8]   Tromp S O , René Haijema, Rijgersberg H, et al. A systematic approach to preventing chilled-food waste at the retail outlet[J]. International Journal of Production Economics, 2016, 182: 508-518.
[9]   José Geraldo Vidal Vieira, Toso MR, Ribeiro PCC. An AHP- based framework for logistics operations in distribution centres[J]. International Journal of Production Economics, 2017, 187: 246-259.
[10]   Kontopanou M, Tsoulfas G T, Rachaniotis N P, The compatibility of the triple-a agri-food supply chain with the United Nations Sustainable Development Goals[J]. IOP Conference Series: Earth and Environmental Science, 2021, 899(1): 012002.
[11]   Ghajargar M, Zenezini G, Montanaro T. Home delivery services: innovations and emerging needs[J]. IFAC PapersOnLine, 2016, 49(12): 1371-1376.
[12]   Huang Y, Savelsbergh M, Zhao L. Designing logistics systems for home delivery in densely populated urban areas[J]. Transportation Research Part B: Methodological, 2018, 115(9): 95-125.
[13]   Yang X, Strauss A, Currie C S M, et al. Choice-based demand management and vehicle routing in e-fulfillment[J]. Transportation Science, 2016, 50(2): 473-488.
[14]   Ron Martin, Peter Sunley, Ben Gardiner, Peter Tyler. How regions react to recessions: resilience and the role of economic structure[J]. Regional Studies. 2016, 50(4): 561-585.

[15] Stone, Jamie and Shahin Rahimifard. Resilience in agri-food supply chains: a critical analysis of the literature and synthesis of a novel framework[J]. Supply Chain Management, 2018,23(3): 207-238.

[16] Macheka L, Spelt E, et al. Exploration of logistics and quality control activities in view of context characteristics and postharvest losses in fresh produce chains: A case study for tomatoes[J]. Food Control, 2017(77): 221-234.

[17] Zheng Chaoyu, et al. Operational risk modeling for cold chain logistics system: a Bayesian network approach[J]. Kybernetes: The International Journal of Systems & Cybernetics, 2020, 50(2): 550-567.

[18] Chen H, Zhang Q, Luo J, et al. Interruption risk assessment and transmission of fresh cold chain network based on a fuzzy bayesian network[J]. Discrete Dynamics in Nature and Society, 2021(2021): 1-11.

Artificial Intelligence, Medical Engineering and Education
Z.B. Hu et al. (Eds.)
© 2024 The Authors.
doi:10.3233/ATDE231337

Machine Learning Driven Strategies for Safeguarding India's Digital Environment Against Cyberstalking

Chintan Singh[a], Himanshu Khajuria[a,1], Biswa Prakash Nayak[a]
[a]*Amity Institute of Forensic Sciences, Amity University, Noida, Sector 125, U.P., India*

Abstract. The ubiquity of the internet and mobile phones has drastically shifted the physical world into a virtual realm, encompassing individuals of all age groups, from schoolchildren to seniors. People now utilize social media and various internet-based platforms to connect and invest their time. However, within this virtual environment, the ability to conceal or impersonate one's identity presents an opportunity for criminal activity to go unnoticed. Despite India's progression towards becoming a digital nation, there exists a shortage of regulations and technological resources to address the challenges stemming from this digital paradigm shift. Cybercrime refers to any illicit behavior involving the use of a computer as a tool, target, or weapon. One subset of cybercrime is cyberstalking, which encompasses actions where a perpetrator employs a computer or associated technologies to induce fear in their victim. This chapter aims to delve into the definition, typology, detection, prevention, and the imperative need for cybercrime education. Its primary objective is to investigate the surge in internet stalking cases in India, exploring the definition, categories, and underlying causes of cyberstalking. Additionally, this article scrutinizes the Indian legal framework and judicial precedents related to these issues.

Keywords. Cyberstalking, cybercrime, spyware, Information technology act, machine learning framework

1. Introduction

The Internet has grown exponentially in the last millennium, advancing almost every aspect of modern life and becoming widely available and accessible throughout the vast majority of the globe [1]. The Internet is primarily responsible for taking global business to previously unimaginable heights, promoting tremendous improvements in education and healthcare, and permitting previously limited and costly global communication [2]. The Internet has, nevertheless, a dark side because it has exposed previously unimagined criminal prospects that not only present a challenge but also surpass all physical boundaries, frontiers, and confines for the detection, prosecution, and mitigation of what appears to be a growing global social issue. Social media has become an integral element of human life, allowing users to share personal experiences with the rest of the world. Social networks are solidifying, and social media is influencing people in a variety of good ways. However, a large amount of data is generated and disseminated during this process. In many cases, the public fails to recognise that a user's social media activity

---

[1] Corresponding Author: Himanshu Khajuria, hkhajuria@amity.edu.

serves as a starting point for determining that person's preferences, personal and professional details, and can lead to additional attacks on that person. According to studies, there is a lack of understanding among young people about topics such as social media privacy, which could be one of the reasons why young people are targeted for cyberstalking and cyberbullying [3].

An entirely novel and distinct species of criminal known as the cyber stalker has practically emerged on the Internet. The term "cyber stalker" refers to someone who uses the Internet as a weapon or tool to prey on, harass, threaten, and induce fear and trepidation in the minds of their captives utilising modern stalking approaches that are sometimes misunderstood and, in some circumstances, legal. Since these attacks are carried out remotely without the attacker departing their dwelling, cyberstalking and bullying are far more widespread online than conventional stalking and bullying. Attackers also profit from the fact that, for a variety of reasons, including fear of defamation, few individuals publicly discuss their issues on social media [4].

The societal problem of cyberstalking is one that is becoming more and more prominent and well-known worldwide. According to a survey, about 20% of respondents have experienced cyberstalking when using internet applications [5,6]. According to available evidence, cyberstalking instances will continue to rise in an unforeseen manner. Machine learning, with its capacity to process vast amounts of data and identify patterns, offers promising solutions for cyberstalking detection and prevention. This research seeks to explore the potential of machine learning techniques in addressing cyberstalking in the Indian context and assess their effectiveness. It also aims to provide a comprehensive overview of the current state of cyberstalking in India. It will include an analysis of the prevalence, patterns, and trends of cyberstalking incidents, taking into account the diverse cultural, social, and demographic factors that influence this phenomenon.

1.1. Nature of stalking

Cyberstalking is a form of stalking whereby the victim is harassed or threatened through technological devices. The right to life, liberty, and security are only a few of the fundamental human rights that are violated by cyberstalking, which can also seriously interfere with the victim's confidentiality, connections, or communication. According to the conclusions of the survey, cyberstalkers have virtually no restrictions in terms of age, gender, marital status, sexual orientation, ethnic, cultural, economic, or intellectual background, and it appears that cyberstalking will grow more frequent [7]. It's critical that instructional programmes cover these online dangers, as well as the numerous strategies used by criminals, so that potential victims can minimise the chances available to cyberstalkers.

Victims, offenders, and authorities (law enforcement officers, police officers, school teachers, and others) are unaware of the crime's malicious and hazardous nature until the victim is physically abused or his or her personal property is damaged [8]. It is notable that more than 38% of cyberstalking victims were unaware of their harassers' identities yet nonetheless experienced considerable psychological distress. This is crucial for two reasons: first, a large proportion of cyberstalking events include stalkers who are strangers to the victimisation, and second, victims can feel painful psychological symptoms in the absence of physical contact with their stalker. Surveys have shown that most stalkers have a history with their victims, shedding doubt on the claims of those who favour treating stalking both online and offline concurrently. Individuals who support the simultaneous management of both online and offline intimidation disagree with this vantage point.

1.2. Psychological reason behind stalking

Cyberstalkers frequently believe they can stay hidden and maintain inconspicuous. In other words, the biggest strength of a cyber stalker is that they depend on the anonymity that the internet provides them, enabling them to keep checks on their victim's actions without revealing their identity. Severe narcissism, anger, rage, retribution, envy, obsession, psychiatric disorder, power and control, sadomasochistic fantasies, sexual deviance, internet addiction, or religious fanaticism are among psychological causes for stalking [9]. Fig. 1. demonstrate some of the main factors that enhance cyberstalking

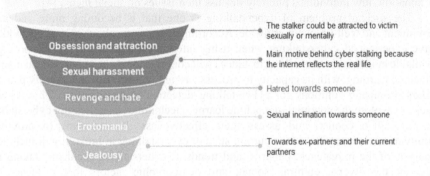

Figure 1. Psychological factors that influence cyberstalking

2. Cyberstalking trend in India

2.1. By gender and age

Table 1 shows the number of survey respondents who reported being 'cyberstalked,' given as a percentage of the total number of respondents. Two-thirds of the survey respondents were female, indicating a higher rate of male victimisation (about one-third), which is higher than the 17 percent reported in some studies of offline stalking [12]. The most common age group in the current 'cyberstalked' group was 20-39 years old, while ages ranged from 14 to 74 years old.

Table 1. Cyberstalking victimization percentage by gender and age

Age Category	Total (N=353)	Male	Female
14-19	7.7	5.6	7.9
20-29	25.7	22.4	27.2
30-39	32.9	29.0	35.1
40-49	22.9	32.7	18.4
50-59	8.9	7.5	9.6
60-69	1.7	1.9	1.7
70-74	0.3	0.9	0.0

2.2. Victim and Harasser relationship

Data about the harasser's relationship with the responders was also obtained, and this information is shown in Table 2. Table 3 shows the main categories found in the stalking literature; however, a considerable proportion of respondents (35%) classified the stalker as belonging to a different category. These people were then asked to explain their relationship with the stalker, which resulted in the creation of six new groups. Table 3 shows all of the categories that were identified by respondents.

Table 2. Percentage relationship reported in stalking relationship

Harasser	Male %	Female %	Total %
Acquaintance	10.5	17.8	16.0
Stranger	18.9	13.8	15.4
Friend	1.1	3.6	2.8
Work Colleague	7.4	4.0	4.9
Casual Date	11.6	20.9	17.9
Lived with someone	3.2	1.9	1.7
Spouse	0.0	0.4	0.3
Other	46.3	30.7	35.2

Table 3. Percentages categories of harasser identified by respondents

Harasser	Male %	Female %	Total %
Acquaintance	14.1	22.5	20.4
Stranger	23.9	20.7	21.7
Pupil	1.1	0.0	0.3
Casually dated person	12.0	21.2	18.2
Close Friend	1.1	5.0	3.8
Business	1.1	0.0	0.3
Married Person	8.7	10.4	9.7
Unknown Person	25.0	13.1	16.4
Colleague	10.9	4.5	6.3
Relative	1.1	0.9	0.9
Ex-Partner	1.1	1.4	1.3
Spouse	0.0	0.5	0.3

3. Machine Learning based Framework for Cyberstalking Detection and Documentation

A hybrid machine learning framework is required for cyberstalking identification and documentation. As shown in Fig. 2., the proposed machine learning system will function on textual non-spam email data. It includes multiphase approach in the form of seven main modules which are –

A. Email Pre-Processing - Email data will be acquired from a worldwide dataset in this step, and then filtered and standardised to a specified format using the keywords collected.

B. Feature Extraction - Using the extraction of spam and non-spam text, a feature dictionary and feature vectors will be created in this phase. Machine learning approaches will also employ the feature dictionary and feature vectors as input for training and testing the data classifier.

C. Spam Classification using Machine Learning Techniques - Machine learning classifier techniques will be applied to email documents in this phase.

D. Spam Email Detection - Spam email detection module will filter, detect, and classify emails into spam or non-spam email categories based on feature extraction and machine learning classifier.

E. Cyberstalking Pre-Detection - After email filtering and spam classification, the next goal will be to detect cyberstalking in non-spam email. The Cyberstalking Pre-Detection module was utilised for this. The proposed Cyberstalking Pre-Detection will detect cyberstalking data before transferring the email to the next phase of the cyberstalking detection module, thanks to the help of a worldwide data dictionary and database.

F. Data Classification using Machine Learning Techniques - Machine learning classifier techniques such as Naive Bayes, Logistic Regression, Random Forest, K-Nearest Neighbour, and Support Vector Machines will be utilised in this lesson to detect cyberstalking on non-spam email. The analysis of non-spam email content, header, sender, and hyperlinks text is performed using the machine learning classifier and data dictionary, and then non-spam email is classed as genuine email or cyberstalking email.

G. Stalking Message & Evidence Collection - This module will assist other users in predicting and preventing cyberstalking when using email. For cyberstalker documentation, the IP address of the cyberstalking email and the domain name information will be transmitted to WHOIS and other IP geo-location services.

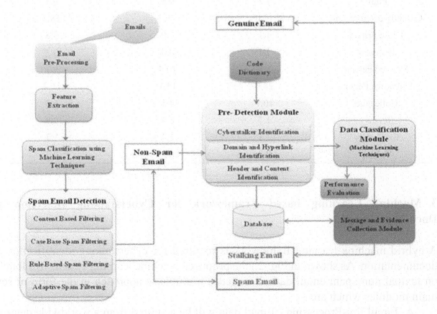

Figure 2. The recommended Machine Learning Framework for Cyberstalking Detection and Documentation on non-spam e – mail

4. Prevention Strategies

Education is frequently the first step in prevention. According to Marcum et al. (2019) [13], increasing public knowledge of cyber-stalking is necessary. Agencies at the municipal and federal levels may become more focused on preventative measures as a result of raising public knowledge of the problem, which could lead to multi-agency awareness campaigns [14]. Experts agree that the best approach to avoid becoming a victim of cyberstalking is to educate yourself about the crimes and to seek professional help from law enforcement and other organisations if you feel a cybercrime has occurred [13].

Cyberstalking can be prevented or reduced with the help of victim advocates, support organizations, and prosecutors' offices. According to Hensen et al. (2011, p. 3446), victims with protection orders reported a 35.3 percent reduction in stalking activity and 15.4 percent said it had completely stopped [14].

Nonetheless, the responsibility for prevention should not be primarily attributed to law enforcement, and there are distinct actions that the general public can adopt to reduce their vulnerability to victimization. For instance, young individuals who refrain from engaging with unknown individuals on the internet are less likely to become victims. When it comes to online conversation with strangers, especially if they are eager to share personal information, teenagers should exercise caution. Prior to starting internet use, it is highly suggested that youths be educated about the dangers of online communication, and that adults (most likely parents and instructors) set clear norms for adolescents online etiquette. Social networking sites can also serve as platforms for enabling cyberstalking. It is advisable for individuals to acquaint themselves with online security practices and employ these tactics to regulate the accessibility of their personal data on platforms such as Facebook and Myspace in order to mitigate the risk of cyberstalking incidents.

Facebook: Because most people use their real names on Facebook, tracking them is simple. The site, on the other hand, makes it rather simple to keep others from seeing what you're up to, which seems like a reasonable trade-off. And you have a lot of possibilities here. To begin, make sure your posts aren't visible to the public. Simply select "privacy shortcuts" from the question mark symbol in the upper right corner, then change "who may see my posts" to "friends." This means that only the individuals you've added as friends can see what you're up to. This is all you need to do if you haven't friended someone yet.

Snapchat: Blocking someone from seeing your Snapchat Story is the simplest way to get rid of them on Snapchat. Open the programme, drag downwards, then hit the "settings" icon in the upper right corner, then go to the "who can" area. Click the term "custom" to the right of the "view my story" heading, and then just click on the name of the person you wish to keep from seeing your Story. If you like, you may add them back in later. You can also entirely ban someone, so they don't appear on your friend's list. They will not be able to add you as a friend again. Return to the settings page, select "my friends," and then simply press the name you want to block. Choose "block," confirm your decision, and then done.

Instagram: Blocking someone on Instagram is a two-step process, but it's rather straightforward. The first step is to block the individual. To block someone, go to their profile page and click the three small dots in the upper right corner, then "block" and confirm. After that, you'll need to make your account private so that anyone attempting to add you will need to prove their identity (to stop the person just following you again). Toggle on "private account" from your profile page by clicking the three small dots in the top right corner. Your followers will be able to see your content, but everyone else will have to first ask your permission.

Twitter: This will be a two-step procedure. To begin, you'll need to block the individual. Simply browse to the profile of the person you want to block and select "block@username" from the little gear icon next to the Follow button. Done. You have the option to quit immediately, but there is nothing to prevent the person from following you again. As a result, you may want to make your Tweets private once more. Go to your profile page, click the tiny circle with your profile picture in the upper right corner, and then select "settings and privacy." Select "privacy and safety" from the left-hand menu, then tick the box next to "guard my Tweets." Only your followers may see your content now, and new followers will need your permission to see tweets.

5. Conclusion

Cyberstalking is a new and challenging type of cybercrime that is causing users of online applications to be afraid. The conflict between cyberstalkers and researchers in the future will be fascinating, as will pandemic difficulties for secure internet application usage. As a result, there is currently little methodological precedent for a researcher wishing to investigate online abuse and harassment qualitatively. The use of machine learning-driven strategies offers a promising approach to detect and prevent cyberstalking incidents in India. This research has shed light on the potential of machine learning in this context, revealing its effectiveness in identifying patterns and anomalies that may signal cyberstalking behavior. The victim's life and calm are disrupted by cyber stalking, which is frightening and potentially hazardous. Cyberstalking is becoming a more serious issue in schools and in society. Society should be more aware of the existence of such significant issues and take steps to avoid becoming a victim of cyber stalkers.

References

[1]. L. McFarlane, P.B.-F. Update, and U. 2003, Cyberstalking: defining the invasion of cyberspace, Research.Aston.Ac.Uk. (2003).
[2]. Bodunde Akinyemi, Oluwakemi Adewusi, Adedoyin Oyebade, "An Improved Classification Model for Fake News Detection in Social Media", International Journal of Information Technology and Computer Science, Vol.12, No.1, pp.34-43, 2020.
[3]. P. Potgieter, The Awareness Behaviour of Students on Cyber Security Awareness by Using Social Media Platforms: A Case Study at Central University of Technology, 2019: pp. 272–262. doi:10.29007/gprf.
[4]. N. Parsons-Pollard, and L.J. Moriarty, Cyberstalking: Utilizing what we do know, Victims and Offenders. 4 (2009) 435–441. doi:10.1080/15564880903227644.
[5]. K. K. Sindhu, B. B. Meshram, "Digital Forensic Investigation Tools and Procedures", International Journal of Computer Network and Information Security, vol.4, no.4, pp.39-48, 2012.
[6]. Singh C, Khajuria H, Nayak BP. A Study of Implementing a Blockchain-Based Forensic Model Integration (BBFMI) for IoT Devices in Digital Forensics. In International Conference on Computer Science, Engineering and Education Applications 2023 Mar 17 (pp. 318-327). doi: 10.1007/978-3-031-36118-0_28.
[7]. I. Vasiu, and L. Vasiu, Cyberstalking Nature and Response Recommendations, Academic Journal of Interdisciplinary Studies. (2013). doi:10.5901/ajis.2013.v2n9p229.

[8]. S. Sarkar, and B. Rajan, Materiality and Discursivity of Cyber Violence Against Women in India, 1Journal of Creative Communications. 18 (2023) 109–123. doi:10.1177/0973258621992273

[9]. K. K. Sindhu, B. B. Meshram, "Digital Forensic Investigation Tools and Procedures", International Journal of Computer Network and Information Security, vol.4, no.4, pp.39-48, 2012.

[10]. L. McFarlane, and P. Bocij, An exploration of predatory behaviour in cyberspace: Towards a typology of cyberstalkers, First Monday. 8 (2003). doi:10.5210/fm.v8i9.1076.

[11]. C. Lalji, D. Pakrashi, S. Saha, S.S.- Perspectives, and U. 2021, Countering violence against women with awareness creation and self-defence training, Ideasforindia. In. (2021).

[12]. Liubov Pomytkina, Yuliia Podkopaieva, Kateryna Hordiienko, " Peculiarities of Manifestation of Student Youth' Roles and Positions in the Cyberbullying Process", International Journal of Modern Education and Computer Science, Vol.13, No.6, pp. 1-10, 2021.

[13]. L. Cox, and B. Speziale, Survivors of stalking: Their voices and lived experiences, Affilia - Journal of Women and Social Work. 24 (2009) 5–18. doi:10.1177/0886109908326815.

[14]. B. Henson, B.W. Reyns, and B.S. Fisher, Security in the 21st century: Examining the link between online social network activity, privacy, and interpersonal victimization, Criminal Justice Review. 36 (2011) 253–268. doi:10.1177/0734016811399421.

Artificial Intelligence, Medical Engineering and Education
Z.B. Hu et al. (Eds.)
© 2024 The Authors.

doi:10.3233/ATDE231338

Cold Chain Logistics Demand Forecasting Based on Improved BP Neural Network Model

Xudong DENG, Boheng ZHANG[1], Yong WANG

School of Management, Wuhan University of Science and Technology, Wuhan, China

Abstract. According to the characteristics of continuous value prediction and the imitation of the sample data size of cold chain logistics demand, an improved BP neural network model based on gating mechanism and GELU is proposed. Through gating mechanism, neural network pays more attention to important features in input, and GELU is used as the activation function of neural network, which can provide better nonlinear ability. In the empirical process, the model is used to forecast the demand of cold chain logistics of agricultural products in Hubei Province. The improved BP neural network achieves 96.07% similarity on the test dataset, which represents the state of the art in cold chain logistics demand forecast.

Keywords. Cold chain logistics demand forecast; BP neural network; Gating mechanism; GELU; Adam optimizer; Sub-models.

1. Introduction

Forecasting and analyzing the cold chain logistics demand of fresh agricultural products is an important basis for measuring the current level of cold chain logistics, which can promote the process of restoring economic development to ensure that cold chain logistics services achieve a relative balance between supply and demand, and then improve the operational efficiency of cold chain logistics.

With the development of emerging technologies such as the Internet of Things, big data, and blockchain, machine learning methods are also more used in the field of prediction. For example, in the industrial sector, Awad et al. constructed artificial neural networks using different types of optimization algorithms, successfully predicting the water demand in the Jenin city of Palestine [1]. In the aviation field, Mamdouh et al. utilized machine learning to build a model for predicting ground service resource demand by constructing future flight schedule resource demand curves, which has been proven to have good accuracy [2]. In the medical field, Howlader et al. compared naive Bayes, decision trees, random forests, and logistic regression using data mining techniques and accurately predicted heart diseases [3].

This paper introduces state-of-the-art deep learning techniques into cold chain logistics demand forecasting. The bp neural network is improved through GELU and the gating mechanism, the Adam optimizer is used in the training process, and the sub-model prediction input is used when performing the forecast, which not only improves the

---

[1] Corresponding Author: ZHANG Boheng, E-mail: boxdada@qq.com.

accuracy of the prediction results, but also improves the stability of the model. This study can not only provide reference and suggestions for cold chain logistics demand forecasting, but also provide new perspectives and ideas for research related to continuous value forecasting. Effective demand management based on the prediction and analysis results, guiding funds from all aspects of society to reasonably enter the field of agricultural product cold chain logistics services, is conducive to scientific and effective logistics system planning development of cold chain logistics, and effectively avoiding resource waste and overcapacity.

2. Literature Review

2.1. Research Status

Currently, traditional logistics demand forecasting methods include time series analysis, causal analysis, and random analysis [4]. Due to the advantages of machine learning and various algorithm optimizations, neural networks often have higher accuracy compared to traditional forecasting methods [5]. In recent years, many scholars have used neural networks to predict logistics demand. For example, Eksoz C used a neural network model and grey model to comprehensively analyze factors affecting demand forecasting and scientifically predict short-term cold chain logistics demand [6]. Huang L et al. used the GM (1,1) model and BP neural network model to simulate and forecast logistics demand. The results showed that the BP neural network model had smaller prediction errors and more stable results [7]. Munkhdalai L et al. compared and analyzed multiple linear regression models, MLP models, LSTM models, UBER-LSTM models, and MLP-SUL models, and concluded that the MLP-SUL model was the most effective for predicting logistics demand in Korea [8]. Ma H et al. combined the logistic regression algorithm to construct a neural network algorithm model and predicted logistics demand through examples [9]. Yu N et al. combined ant colony algorithm with support vector machine (SVM) to predict urban logistics demand. The experimental results showed that the improved SVM had higher prediction accuracy, stronger stability, lower error rate, and more realistic prediction results [10]. Zhang G et al. proposed a combination forecasting model that combines the ARIMA time series forecasting model with BP neural network. Through simulation experiments, it was found that the combination forecasting model could more comprehensively reflect the changing patterns of logistics demand [11].

When selecting logistics demand influencing factors, scholars have established diverse logistics demand forecasting indicator systems based on different situations. For example, Nguyen TY proposed from the perspective of Southeast Asian logistics development that GDP, regional logistics volume growth rate, logistics regional attractiveness, regional logistics distribution, and regional distance had an inseparable impact on logistics demand [12]. Du B et al. proposed that national freight volume represented logistics demand and selected four indicators as factors affecting logistics demand [13].

Many scholars have established diverse logistics demand forecasting indicator systems based on different situations. Feng Y selected social logistics volume as a substitute variable to predict fresh agricultural products cold chain logistics demand. He predicted social logistics volume by constructing a prediction model that combined BP neural network and principal component regression analysis [14]. At the level of fresh agricultural product consumption, Wang S selected 14 indicators affecting fresh agricultural product consumption from five aspects: regional development level, market supply and demand factors, industry structure level, location advantage factors, and logistics industry factors, and then constructed a combined prediction model based on SVR [15]. Wang X predicted fresh agricultural product consumption from five aspects: agricultural product supply, cold chain level, socio-economic indicators, logistics demand scale, and human development angle, and optimized neural network using genetic algorithm [16].

2.2. Innovation

Different from the above research, this paper is more focusing on introducing the state of the art deep learning techniques into cold chain logistics demand forecast. The major contributions are: 1. Utilizing GELU and gating mechanism in the neural network. 2. Leveraging Adam optimizer during training. 3. Using sub-models to predict input when doing forecasting.

Current research only utilizes machine learning at a primary level, and majorly focuses on feature engineering. However, with more advance techniques, the most learn the relationship between the input and the label. For example, most of the research mentioned above use RELU as activation function, but GELU as an update on RELU has been proved to be much more effective in a wide range of applications. Although RELU function has the advantages of simple calculation, fast speed and outstanding performance in solving parallel data, RELU function has only two output situations, and completely ignores the negative part of input, which may lead to the activation function not making full use of input information, thus affecting the forecasting effect. Therefore, this paper uses GELU to retain more useful information in the data, so that it can bring better nonlinear ability in the process of forecasting agricultural logistics demand.

At the same time, in the process of model training, facing the pain points such as limited data volume of cold chain logistics prediction, most of the existing researches use Attention mechanism to train the prediction model. Although Attention mechanism is widely used in AI and other scenarios as the mainstream, it usually needs a large amount of data to learn reasonable weight parameters, and cannot learn the sequence relationship in the sequence [17]. Therefore, the Attention mechanism may not be effective in predicting continuous values with limited data.

The reason why this paper did not choose the SGD optimizer used by most scholars is that SGD is unstable and prone to local optimality. Therefore, this paper chooses to use the more advanced Adam optimizer. Adam adds second-order momentum based on SGD. Adam adds second-order momentum based on momentum SGD and controls the step size through adaptive learning. When the gradient is small, the overall learning rate will increase, otherwise it will shrink. Therefore, in general, Adam has a faster and more stable convergence speed than SGD. Finally, the existing literature on cold chain logistics demand forecasting describes the input very simply when forecasting. This method can easily lead to the accumulation of errors. Therefore, we use sub-models to eliminate errors and improve the final forecasting results. accuracy.

3. Research Method

3.1. Model Introduction

In essence, the prediction of the total output value of agricultural products belongs to the continuous value prediction problem.

Suppose we have k eigenvalues in a single sample represented by x, then the j-th eigenvalue for each sample is denoted as , x_j, $0 <= j <= k$. Suppose we have n data, then x^i $o_{i=1..n}$ ur data set is denoted , $D = \{x^i\}_{i=1..n}$. Our objective function is:

$$\max_w \quad \sum_{i=1}^n I(y^i, t^i) \tag{1}$$

$y = f(x)$ is the predicted value of the model, t is the true value, and the function return $I(\ )s$ 1 if equals, y^i otherwise t^i it is 0.

We use neural network to learn the mapping relationship between input space and output space, and introduce gating mechanism to help control the inflow of information.

3.2. Neural Network Model Structure

Because the forecast data of agricultural products can only come from annual statistics, the amount of data is greatly limited, and various data augmentation technologies are difficult to use. Therefore, the model structure should be flatter and avoid over-fitting, so we only use one hidden layer.

GELU function and its Derivative showed in Fig. 1. For the activation function of hidden layer, GELU is a better function to introduce nonlinear relationship. Compared with the traditional RELU, GELU will change it to 0 according to Bernoulli distribution based on its numerical value. If a value is smaller, it has a greater chance of being converted to 0, and vice versa. Therefore, GELU can retain more useful information than RELU.

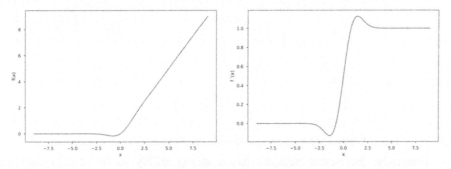

Figure 1. GELU function and it's derivative

3.3. Gating Mechanism

For the input of forecasting the total output value of agricultural products, some features have some similar characteristics. For example, per capita GDP and added value of primary industry can be regarded as data to measure the level of economic development. When we divide the input features into multiple feature groups according to their physical meanings, the importance of the features in each group relative to the information that the feature group wants to represent will be different from each other. The gating mechanism can adaptively control the information amount of each feature group involved in neural network calculation.

There are two main uses of gating mechanism, one is to act on the feature embedding layer, and the other is to act on the hidden layer. Because there is only one hidden layer in the model and the amount of training data is limited, if the gate control is applied to the hidden layer, it will be counterproductive, which will be mentioned in the introduction of the experiment. Therefore, the gating mechanism is applied to every feature group in the input layer, and the bit-wise mode is adopted. Compared with vector-wise, bit-wise can control the amount of information on each input value, which means that the processing accuracy of information will be higher than vector-wise. The excellent performance of bit-wise is also verified in the follow-up experiments.

For each input sample x, suppose there are m feature groups, where $m < = k$. Then the input after gate control is:

$$g_i = \sigma(W_i \cdot x_i) \quad for\ i\ in\ [0, m] \tag{2}$$

$$x_{gated} = concat(g_i \odot x_i) \quad for\ i\ in\ [0, m] \tag{3}$$

Where $\sigma()$ is signmoid function to control the inflow size of information, and W_i is used as a learnable parameter. The model structure is showed as Fig. 2.

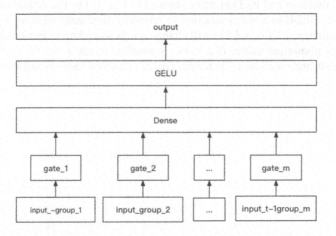

Figure 2. Improved BP neural network model structure based on gating mechanism

Generally, the neural network has a strong ability to fit various mapping relationships. The gating mechanism makes the neural network pay more attention to the important features in the input, while GELU can bring better nonlinear ability to the neural network and improve the model capacity.

4. Establish a Prediction Model

4.1. Data Sources

Based on the existing research results in the field of cold chain logistics demand and consumption of fresh agricultural products, and following the principles of availability, practicality and comprehensiveness, this paper selects five first-level indicators: economic development level, supply and demand level, transportation development level, cold chain logistics support level and cold chain logistics sustainable development level, and systematically summarizes and screens out 21 second-level indicators, as shown in Table 1.

Relevant data come from the statistical data of China Statistical Yearbook, China Cold Chain Logistics Development Report, China Logistics Yearbook and related websites from 2001 to 2022, which are directly quoted or indirectly calculated and collated.

Table 1. Index system of influencing factors of logistics demand

First-class index	Secondary index	Variable
Level of economic development	Per capita GDP	X1
	Added value of tertiary industry	X2
	Total retail sales of social consumer goods	X3
	Added value of primary industry	X4
	Residents' consumption expenditure	X5
Supply and demand level	Resident population	X6
	Fruit yield	X7
	Meat production	X8
	Output of aquatic products	X9
	Commercial price quantity of agricultural products	X10
	Freight volume	X11
Development level of transportation	Goods turnover	X12
	Added value of transportation, warehousing and postal services	X13
	Railway operating mileage	X14
	Total mileage of highway	X15
Support level	Number of outlets	X16
	Road mileage	X17
	Quantity of express delivery	X18
	Warehouse holdings	X19
Sustainable Development Level of Cold Chain Logistics	Number of college graduates	X20
	Fixed investment in scientific and technological research	X21

Therefore, we selected 22 pieces of data from 2001 to 2022 from the data source. The input of each data consists of 5 characteristic groups and 21 characteristics, including economic development level (5 characteristics), supply and demand level (6 characteristics), transportation development level (4 characteristics), cold chain logistics support level (4 characteristics) and cold chain logistics sustainable development level (2 characteristics). The label is the total output value of agricultural products, which is a continuous value.

Among the 22 pieces of data, we selected 18 pieces of data from 2001 to 2018 as training sets and 4 pieces of data from 2019 to 2022 as test sets.

4.2. Evaluation Criteria

We use the average error method to evaluate the performance of the model. The formula is as follows:

$$similarity = \frac{1}{n}\sum_{i=1}^{n} 1 - \frac{|y^i - t^i|}{t^i} \tag{4}$$

where similarity has a value range of $(-\infty, 1]$. When the similarity is higher, we think the model performance is better, and vice versa, the worse the model performance.

4.3. Trainer

4.3.1 Loss Function

Because this task is to predict continuous values, we choose MSE as the loss function. The advantage of MSE is that it can fully learn the mapping relationship from feature space to output space when the amount of training set data is small and the noise is small. The formula is as follows:

$$Loss = \frac{1}{n}\sum_{i=1}^{n}(y^i - t^i)^2 \tag{5}$$

4.3.2 Optimizer

We chose Adam as the optimizer. Adam absorbs the advantages of both Momentum and RMSProp, and is more stable in the weight update direction and update step size, thus finding the global optimum. The formula is as follows:

$$m_t = \beta_1 m_{t-1} + (1 - \beta_1)g_t \tag{6}$$

$$v_t = \beta_2 v_{t-1} + (1 - \beta_2)g_t^2 \tag{7}$$

$$\hat{m}_t = \frac{m_t}{1 - \beta_1^t} \tag{8}$$

$$\hat{v}_t = \frac{v_t}{1 - \beta_2^t} \tag{9}$$

$$\theta_{t+1} = \theta_t - \frac{\eta}{\sqrt{\hat{v}_t} + \epsilon} \hat{m}_t \tag{10}$$

where g_t is the gradient of the parameter, β_1 and β_2 are the attenuation coefficients of the two exponentially weighted averages, $\hat{m}_t$ and $\hat{v}t$ are the moving averages of the gradient after deviation correction, $\theta t + 1$ is the updated parameter, η is the learning rate, and ϵ is a small constant to avoid dividing by 0.

Among them, $[\beta_1, \beta_2]$ we choose $[0.98, 0.98]$ and the initial learning rate is set to 5e-6. From Table 2, we tested the epoch number of 50, 100, 200, 500, 1000, and found that when the epoch is 100, the model performs best in the test set. The training convergence state curve are showed as Fig. 3.

Table 2. similarity of different epoch

epoch	Similarity
50	92.77%
75	95.03%
100	96.07%
125	95.12%
150	94.36%

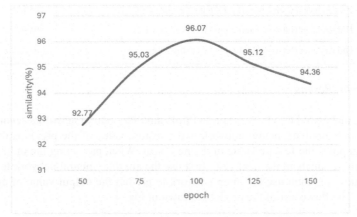

Figure 3. Training convergence state curve for BP neural networks

4.4. Comparison of Model Structures

We mainly compare three ways: no gating mechanism, gating mechanism in hidden layer and gating mechanism in input layer. Among them, the method of using gating mechanism in hidden layer is as follows:

$$g = \sigma(W_{gate} \cdot h) \tag{11}$$

$$h_{gated} = g \odot h \tag{12}$$

Where h represents the output of GELU, $\sigma()$ is the signmoid function to control the inflow of information, and W_{gate} is a learnable parameter. Intuitively speaking, we use gating mechanism on GELU output to control how much information will be used to predict the total output value of agricultural products.

In the gating mechanism, for the learnable parameter W_i or W_{gate}, it can either map x_i or h to 1 dimension, which we call vector-wise, or it can map to the same dimension as x_i or h, which we call bit-wise.

Therefore, we can get the similarity using different model structures, showed as Table. 3:

Table3. similarity using different model structures

Model structure	similarity
No Gating mechanism is used	94.96%
Gating mechanism (vector-wise) in the hidden layer	95.04%
Gating mechanism (bit-wise) in the hidden layer	94.63%
Gating mechanism in the input level (vector-wise)	95.24%
Gating mechanism in the input level (bit-wise)	96.07%
Hidden layer (vector-wise) and input layer (vector-wise)	95.21%
Hidden layer (vector-wise) and input layer (bit-wise)	95.83%
Hidden layer (bit-wise) and input layer (vector-wise)	94.42%
Hidden layer (bit-wise) and input layer (bit-wise)	95.22%

4.5. Forecast Results

When we make predictions, we train multiple auxiliary neural networks separately. The input of each auxiliary neural network is the feature value of the previous three years, and the output is the feature value of the next year. When predicting the output value of agricultural products in the next year, first use the auxiliary neural network to obtain all input values, and then use the main network to predict the output value of agricultural products. The flowchart of the model is shown in Fig. 4.

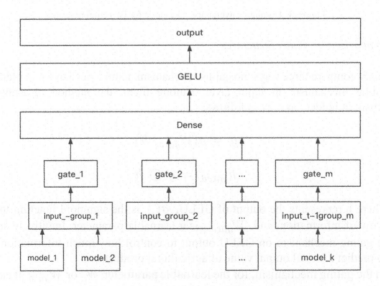

Figure 4. Improved BP neural network flowchart

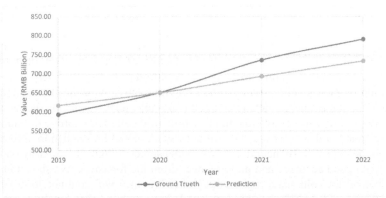

Figure 5. The contrast of ground truth and predicted value.

Our final prediction model of output value of agricultural products is a neural network model with bit-wise control mechanism in feature layer, a hidden layer with 42 neurons, activation function GELU, loss function MSE, optimizer Adam and 100 epoch training. The contrast of ground truth and predicted value is shown in Fig. 5.

Our auxiliary model consists of six neurons in multiple hidden layers, GELU in activation function, MSE in loss function and Adam in optimizer. Each model trains 25 epoch neural networks. Therefore, our forecast of the output value of agricultural products from 2023 to 2026 is shown in Table.4.

Table 4. Forecast of cold chain logistics demand in Hubei Province in the next 4 years

Year	Predicted value (RMB Billion)
2023	861.27
2024	920.91
2025	980.16
2026	1035.84

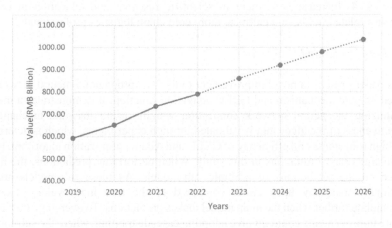

Figure 6. Hubei Province agricultural products cold chain logistics demand forecast curve.

5. Conclusion

Based on the above analysis, aiming at the characteristics and limited data volume of continuous value prediction in the relevant factors of agricultural product logistics demand forecasting, a gating mechanism is introduced to adaptively extract the information of each feature group. At the same time, in view of the slow convergence speed of common BP neural networks and the unstable defects in the prediction results, GELU is introduced to improve the training time of the model, improve the stability of the model, and build an improved BP neural network model for prediction. Experiments show that the improved BP neural network model achieves 96.07% similarity on the test dataset, with good accuracy and performance. From the forecast curve shown in Figure 6, the demand for cold chain logistics in Hubei Province will continue to grow in the future, and the cold chain logistics industry will continue to develop, but the development speed will slow down slightly.

5.1. Suggestion

The research results have certain reference value and can provide a certain reference basis for relevant departments in Hubei Province to formulate policies. In order to further promote the development of regional cold chain logistics industry in Hubei Province, in view of the influencing factors of cold chain logistics demand, combined with the development of agriculture and logistics industry in Hubei Province, the following suggestions are put forward: 1. Strengthen the cold chain logistics service system and build a cold chain logistics system that meets the characteristics of the local industrial structure and meets the needs of economic and social development. 2. Improve the low-temperature processing capacity of agricultural product production areas, expand the supply of high-quality fresh agricultural products, and support the development of cold chain logistics industry. 3. Improve the research and development of key technologies and advanced equipment in cold chain logistics, promote the establishment of a statistical evaluation system for cold chain logistics, and improve the standard system of cold chain logistics. 4. Increase investment in scientific research and education in cold chain logistics related fields, and cultivate more cold chain logistics professionals.

5.2. Deficiencies and Prospects

This paper presents a novel improvement to the backpropagation neural network model based on gate mechanism and GELU activation function. It demonstrates a method for optimizing the neural network connection weights using the gate mechanism. The effectiveness of the algorithm is validated through experiments, which is determined by the high robustness and efficiency of GELU and Adam optimization algorithm. However, there are certain limitations in this study. When performing predictions, the inputs are based on the predictions of multiple sub-models. As these sub-models are trained separately and may have errors compared to the true input values, these errors accumulate further when the main model makes predictions. To overcome this limitation, future improvements could involve adopting cascade training, where the sub-models and the main model are trained together to reduce the accumulation of errors.

Acknowledgment

This project is supported by Major Project of Philosophy and Social Science Research in Hubei Province Higher Education Institutions (22ZD046); The Ph.D. Scientific Research and Innovation Foundation of Sanya Yazhou Bay Science and Technology City (HSPHDSRF-2022-03-032); The WUST & Int-plog Research Project (2022H20537); The CSL & CFLP research project plan (2023CSLKT3-306); The Department of Education of Hubei Province Young and Middle-Aged Talents Project (20211102).

References

[1]   Awad M, Zaid-Alkelani M. Prediction of water demand using artificial neural networks models and statistical model[J]. International Journal of Intelligent Systems and Applications, 2019, 11(9): 40.

[2]   Mamdouh M, Ezzat M, Hefny H. Optimized Planning of Resources Demand Curve in Ground Handling based on Machine Learning Prediction[J]. International Journal of Intelligent Systems and Applications, 2021, 13(1).

[3]   Howlader S, Biswas T, Roy A, Mortuja G, Nandi D. A Comparative Analysis of Algorithms for Heart Disease Prediction Using Data Mining[J]. International Journal of Intelligent Systems and Applications, 2023, 15(5).

[4]   Heikkurinen P, Forsman - Hugg S. Strategic corporate responsibility in the food chain[J]. Corporate Social Responsibility and Environmental Management, 2011, 18(5): 306-316.

[5]   Benkachcha S, Benhra J, El Hassani H. Demand forecasting in supply chain: Comparing multiple linear regression and artificial neural networks approaches[J]. International Review on Modelling and Simulations, 2014, 7(2): 279-286.

[6]   Eksoz C, Mansouri S A, Bourlakis M, et al. Judgmental adjustments through supply integration for strategic partnerships in food chains[J]. Omega, 2019, 87: 20-33.

[7]   Huang L, Xie G, Zhao W, et al. Regional logistics demand forecasting: a BP neural network approach[J]. Complex & Intelligent Systems, 2021: 1-16.

[8]   Munkhdalai L, Park K H, Batbaatar E, et al. Deep learning-based demand forecasting for Korean postal delivery service[J]. IEEE Access, 2020, 8: 188135-188145.

[9]   Ma H, Luo X. Logistics demand forecasting model based on improved neural network algorithm[J]. Journal of Intelligent & Fuzzy Systems, 2021, 40(4): 6385-6395.

[10] Yu N, Xu W, Yu K L. Research on regional logistics demand forecast based on improved support vector machine: A case study of Qingdao city under the New Free Trade Zone Strategy[J]. IEEE Access, 2020, 8: 9551-9564.

[11] Zhang G, Xu X. A logistics demand forecasting model based on ARIMA-BPNN [J]. Control Engineering, 2017, 24(05): 958-962(in Chinese).

[12] Nguyen T Y. Research on logistics demand forecast in southeast Asia[J]. World Journal of Engineering and Technology, 2020, 8(03): 249.

[13] Du B, Chen A. Research on logistics demand forecast based on the combination of grey GM (1, 1) and BP neural network[C]//Journal of Physics: Conference Series. IOP Publishing, 2019, 1288(1): 012055.

[14] Feng Y. Research on demand forecast of agricultural products cold chain logistics in Beijing [D]. Beijing. North China Electric Power University (Beijing), 2016(in Chinese).

[15] Wang S. Research on cold chain logistics demand forecast of fresh agricultural products [D]. Xi'an: Xi'an Engineering University, 2017(in Chinese).

[16] Wang X, Yan F. Demand forecast of cold chain logistics of urban agricultural products in Beijing based on GA-BP model [J]. Practice and Understanding of Mathematics, 2019, 49 (21): 17-27(in Chinese).

[17] Wu P, Lei Z, Zhou Q, et al. Multiple premises entailment recognition based on attention and gate mechanism[J]. Expert Systems with Applications, 2020, 147: 113214.

Artificial Intelligence, Medical Engineering and Education
Z.B. Hu et al. (Eds.)
© 2024 The Authors.

doi:10.3233/ATDE231339

Logistics Delivery Path of *S* Electronics Company Based on Ant Colony Algorithm

Lijun JIANG, Zhong ZHENG[1], Hanzhi HE, Jing LI, Ling ZHU
Business School of Nanning University, Nanning, China

Abstract. Optimizing logistics delivery paths using artificial intelligence technology is an important way for enterprises to achieve cost reduction and efficiency increase. Based on the analysis and research of several main distribution path optimization methods, and based on the characteristics of each method, the article chooses to use ant colony algorithm to carry out the research of this paper. This paper expounds the principle and algorithm process of the ant colony algorithm and based on the actual problems and data of S Electronics' logistics distribution, conducts modeling research on its logistics distribution path, and then compares and analyzes the results of its empirical research with those under the traditional algorithm. The conclusion is that although the total distance of the ant colony algorithm is slightly increased compared to traditional algorithms, it can save one transportation vehicle and its labor costs for enterprises, and help enterprises greatly save delivery costs. Compared to traditional algorithms, the ant colony algorithm has better performance.

Keywords. Logistics distribution; Vehicle path; Ant colony Logistics costs.

1. Introduction

In logistics and its basic functional links, distribution is a very important content [1,2]. Choosing a reasonable delivery route is of great significance for both enterprises and society [3,4]. By optimizing delivery routes, delivery time and mileage can be reduced, delivery efficiency can be improved, vehicle utilization can be increased, and delivery costs can be reduced [5,6]. At the same time, it can also accelerate logistics speed, deliver goods to customers on time and quickly, and improve customer satisfaction [7,8]. Realizing the rationalization of the distribution operation process can improve the efficiency of enterprise operations, which is beneficial for enterprises to improve competitiveness and efficiency.

Driven by modern information technology, although modern logistics technology has made significant progress, due to multiple factors such as increased fuel and labor costs, logistics distribution costs still account for a large proportion of the overall operating costs of enterprises [10-12]. Most enterprises, especially small and medium-sized enterprises, have not yet been able to use artificial intelligence technology to scientifically plan distribution routes due to the lack of information technology talents, resulting in resource waste and failure to achieve the goal of reducing costs and increasing efficiency. Currently, enterprises are facing greater competitive pressure for survival, and they are placing greater emphasis on optimizing distribution issues,

---

[1] Corresponding Author: Zhong ZHENG, Email: 932370009@qq.com

reducing costs, and enhancing competitiveness [13,14]. The progress of science and technology can effectively solve this problem [15-18]. Adopting advanced technological means and methods, such as the ant colony algorithm discussed in this article, as well as other technologies such as particle swarm optimization and genetic algorithm, can achieve the goal of optimizing distribution paths and fundamentally improve the efficiency of logistics systems [19, 20].

2. Research Methods for Optimizing Delivery Routes

2.1. Method Selection

The existing methods for solving vehicle routing problems can be divided into precise algorithms and heuristic algorithms. Accurate algorithms include branch and bound method, branch and cut method, set coverage method, etc; Heuristic algorithms include savings method, simulated annealing method, deterministic annealing method, tabu search method, genetic algorithm, neural network, ant colony algorithm, and so on [21].

Accurate algorithms refer to methods for finding the best target. It is mainly suitable for solving small-scale vehicle path optimization problems with simple transportation networks and a small number of customers. As the number of customers increases, precise algorithms become complex and computationally intensive.

Unlike precise algorithms, heuristic algorithms that search for the optimal target through general search can partially compensate for the shortcomings of local optima and produce better solutions. In practice, heuristic algorithms are more suitable for the impact of factors such as complexity and limited computing resources. Heuristic algorithms can improve computational efficiency and accuracy without requiring too much human intervention. Therefore, current research on solving algorithms is usually developed on the base of existing heuristic algorithms.

In heuristic algorithms, although tabu search has advantages such as ease of understanding, it can only find the optimal solution locally and is not suitable for global development; The particle swarm optimization algorithm is also limited by local optima; Although the simulated annealing method has strong stability and is suitable for parallel processing, it cannot guarantee that the final solution obtained is indeed the optimal solution in the previous process; Both genetic algorithm and ant colony algorithm can be combined and improved with other algorithms to obtain the optimal solution of the solution. Ant colony algorithm has high robustness. This study is based on ant colony algorithm to achieve the optimization of logistics distribution paths.

2.2. Ant Colony Algorithm

Ant colony algorithm is an optimization algorithm that simulates ant behavior, solving complex problems by simulating the information exchange and collaboration of ants in finding food, establishing routes, and other behaviors [22-24].

2.2.1. Principle

The first study on the foraging behavior of ants in forests was conducted in 1991. An ant that discovers food will quickly emit a pheromone to its companions, and the aggregated ant colony will continue to release more pheromones, forming a positive feedback. By utilizing the "bait" effect of ants, the optimal path is found to obtain the shortest distance. The ant colony algorithm developed based on the principle of pheromone publishing and search has the following characteristics:

(1) In the optimal problem, each ant path is the entry point for the optimal problem, and they form the entry point for the optimal problem;

(2) As time goes on, the pheromone secreted by ants along the short-circuit path increases, the concentration of pheromones accumulated on the short-circuit path increases, and the number of ants choosing this path also increases. Finally, all ants will focus on the optimal path that matches the optimal solution to the optimization problem;

(3) Ant colony algorithm adopts a positive feedback mechanism to continuously converge the search process and ultimately approach the optimal solution.

2.2.2. Algorithm Process

The process of the algorithm includes the following steps.

(1) Initialize relevant parameters

Ant quantity m, pheromone importance factor α、   Heuristic Function Importance Factor β、   Pheromone volatilization factor ρ、   The pheromone constant Q and the maximum number of iterations n. Among them, α The higher the value, the greater the likelihood that the ant will choose the path it has previously traveled, and the weaker the randomness of the search path, α The smaller the value, the smaller the search range of the ant colony, and it is easy to fall into local optima. β The larger the value of, the greater the role of the heuristic function in the transition, that is, the higher the probability of transferring to nodes with shorter distances, the easier it is for the population to choose shorter paths locally, and the faster the convergence speed of the algorithm. However, it has low randomness and is prone to falling into local relative optima.

(2) Constructing Solution Space

Randomly place a single ant at different starting points and determine its current set of candidate paths for each ant colony. Each ant selects the node to pass through for the next action based on its pheromone concentration until completing the entire path.

The probability formula for ants to select the next node is:

$$P_{ij}(t) = \begin{cases} \dfrac{[\tau_{ij}(t)]^{\alpha}[\eta_{ij}]^{\beta}}{\sum_{s\in I_{\kappa}}[\tau_{ij}(t)]^{\alpha}[\eta_{ij}]^{\beta}}, s \in I_{\kappa} \\ 0, s\notin I_{\kappa} \end{cases} \quad (1)$$

In the formula, $\tau_{ij}(t)$ is the pheromone concentration between point i and point j during the t-th iteration, $I_{\kappa} = 1,2,3,\ldots,n$ represents the set of ants' next available delivery points.

$\eta_{ij}(t)$ is a heuristic function, and its formula is:

$$\eta_{ij}(t) = \frac{1}{\sqrt{(x_i-x_j)^2+(y_1-y_2)^2}} \quad (2)$$

As the value of the heuristic function increases, more ants will choose this route before all ants have completed transportation and returned to the transportation center.

(3) Update pheromones

Calculate the length $L_\kappa(\kappa = 1,2, \dots, m)$ of the path traveled by the κth ant, record the best solution (*i.e.* the shortest path) within the current iteration. At the same time, the concentration of pheromones is continuously updated on the connection path of each node.

The update rules for pheromones are as follows:

$$\tau_{ij}(t + 1) = (1 - \rho)\tau_{ij}(t) + \Delta\tau_{ij}(t) \qquad (3)$$

Among them, the volatility factor ρ represents the degree to which pheromones are lost over time. $\rho \in (0,1)$.

$$\Delta\tau_{ij} = \sum_{\kappa=1}^{m} \Delta\tau_{ij}^\kappa \qquad (4)$$

Among them, $\Delta\tau_{ij}^\kappa$ represents the pheromone content emitted by the k-th ant during the current cycle when passing through node i and node j.

$$\Delta\tau_{ij} = \begin{cases} Q/L_\kappa, The \ ant \ k \ accesses \ node \ J \ from \ node \ i \\ 0 \end{cases} \qquad (5)$$

Among them, Q is the pheromone constant, representing the total amount of pheromones released by ants in one cycle.

(4) Determine whether to terminate

When the number of iterations reaches its maximum, clear the record table of ant paths and return to step (2); On the contrary, the operation ends and the best result is obtained.

3. Logistics and Distribution Status of S Electronics Company

S Electronics Company was established in 2000 and is a high-tech enterprise specializing in the research and development, production, and sales of various chip components. Due to the rapid development of S Electronics in recent years, its own vehicles have increased every year. At present, S Electronics Company uses the same type of truck, with a load of 2 tons and a total of 10 vehicles, which can basically meet the delivery service from Shenzhen to the customer's destination. S Electronics Company has a distribution center in the Dafuyuan Industrial Park, providing customers with designated supply centers. The main problems the company faces in terms of distribution are as follows.

(1) Delayed delivery

Due to the lack of a scientific and efficient delivery plan by S Electronics Company, the time spent during the delivery process will exceed expectations, resulting in delayed delivery.

(2) Unreasonable distribution route allocation

Truck drivers only allocate vehicle routes based on experience, lacking support from information system data and decision-making foundations, and unable to determine the rationalization of the allocation route, often resulting in the truck not being able to operate fully. With the increase in vehicle loading, the company's truck resources cannot be used reasonably, and the transportation costs of transportation vehicles will significantly increase, and the costs paid by the company will also be very high.

4. Case Discussion and Analysis of Logistics Delivery Paths Based on *S* Electronics Company

4.1. Problem Description

For VRPTW, the vehicle path planning problem with time windows. Starting from the distribution center, the truck provides services at the designated time according to customer requirements, and returns to the distribution center after completing all tasks. Develop the optimal vehicle delivery plan under all constraints to minimize total costs and maximize benefits. Delivery time is an important limiting constraint in this problem.

4.2. Model Assumptions

Before establishing a mathematical model, make the following assumptions about the problem.

(1) Neglecting the characteristics, weight, etc. of each electronic component product;

(2) Without considering unexpected situations such as road conditions and climate, the shortest delivery distance is between any two points.

(3) The network between each node is fully open, and there is no impassable situation between nodes.

(4) The vehicle type is a single vehicle type, and the attributes of the vehicle (such as payload, volume, etc.) are known;

(5) The vehicle departs from the distribution center and must return to the distribution center after completing the delivery;

(6) All types of electronic components have no shortage issues, can be mixed and cannot be mutually exclusive;

(7) Knowing the expected service time and acceptable service time of each customer, without any temporary changes;

(8) The number of vehicles loaded cannot exceed the specified number of orders, and there is no limit on the distance traveled.

4.3. Mathematical Model

The relevant parameters of this model are as follows:

M: A collection of customer demand points;

P_0 and $P_i(i = 1,2, ... , M)$: coordinates of the distribution center and i customer demand points;

K: Number of delivery trucks;

k: The number of trucks delivered this time;

q_k: The loading capacity of each truck (in discs, where $k=1,2,..., K$), and the actual number of discs loaded with electronic components on the truck must be less than the maximum loading capacity specified by the vehicle;

d_{oi}: the distance between customer demand point i and the distribution center;

d_{ij}: The distance between customer demand point j and customer demand point i;

r_i: Number of electronic components required by each customer (unit: disk);

a: Unit distance delivery fee;

ET_i: Customer demand point i allows for the earliest arrival time of trucks;

LT_i: Customer demand point i allows for the latest arrival time of trucks;

WT_i: The departure time of the truck from customer demand point i;

RT_i: The time when the truck arrives at customer demand point i;

α: Hard time window penalty cost coefficient (resulting from non-compliance with customer delivery time regulations);

β: Soft time window penalty cost coefficient (resulting from non-compliance with customer delivery time regulations);

UT: The time for serving customer demand point i;

θ: Cost coefficient per kilometer of transportation;

v: Speed of delivery trucks;

T_{ij}: The travel time from customer demand point i to customer demand point j;

$$x_{ijk} \begin{cases} 1, \text{vehicle K is driving from point i to point j} \\ 0, \text{otherwise} \end{cases};$$

In order to meet the delivery time window set for customer demand point i, when delivering to customer demand point i, the truck arrival time RT_i must satisfy the following equation:

$$ET_i \leq RT_i \leq LT_i \qquad (6)$$

The travel time of the truck from customer demand point i to customer demand point j is:

$$T_{ij} = \frac{d_{ij}}{v} \qquad (7)$$

The time when the truck arrives at the next customer demand point j is:

$$RT_j = WT_i + UT_i + T_{ij} \qquad (8)$$

The coefficients of the time window penalty function are represented by the set W:

$$W = [\alpha, \beta] \qquad (9)$$

(1) Objective function (transportation cost + penalty cost)

$$\min z = \theta \sum_i \sum_j \sum_k d_{ij} x_{ijk} + \sum_W \sum_i \sum_j \sum_k \max [(ET_i - RT_i), 0] + \sum_W \sum_i \sum_j \sum_k \max[(RT_i - LT_i), 0] \qquad (10)$$

(2) Constraints:

Ensure that the number of delivery trucks k does not exceed the total number of company trucks k:

$$\sum k \in, \forall K \qquad (11)$$

Each customer demand point can only be delivered by one truck:

$$\sum_k y_{ki} = 1, \ i \in M, k \in 1,2,...,10 \qquad (12)$$

(3) Integer constraint

$$y_{ki} = \{0,1\}, \ i \in M; \forall k \qquad (13)$$

$$x_{ki} = \{0,1\}, \ i \in M; \forall k \qquad (14)$$

The delivery route is not closed, depart from the distribution center, and finally return to the distribution center:

$$\sum_i x_{ijk} = y_i k, \ i \in M; \forall k, i \in 1,2,...,20 \qquad (15)$$

$$\sum_j x_{ijk} = y_{ik}, \ i \in M; \forall k, j \in 1,2,...,20 \qquad (16)$$

Arrive within the appropriate time window:

$$RT_i \in [ET_i, LT_i], \ i \in M \qquad (17)$$

4.4. Parameter Selection

The important parameters that affect the performance of ant colony algorithm include: pheromone importance factor *alpha*, heuristic function importance factor *beta*, waiting time importance factor *game*, time window span importance factor *delta*, constant *Q* for updating pheromone concentration, pheromone volatilization factor *rho*, etc. It is necessary to try to achieve the optimal state of each parameter as a fixed parameter. In this study, the parameter assumptions of the ant colony algorithm are as follows: *alpha=1, beta=3, game=2, delta=3, Q=5, rho=0.85*, maximum number of iterations $N_c = 100$, number of ants *m=50*, etc.

4.5. Instance Verification

This study takes the order volume of S Electronics Company on a certain day (20 customers) as an example, and uses traditional algorithms and ant colony algorithm to obtain delivery plans, and analyzes and compares them.
    (1) Traditional algorithms
    The distribution center is represented by 0, and customer demand points are represented by 1-20. The distribution plan obtained by S Electronics Company using traditional algorithms is shown in Table 1.

Table 1. Distribution Vehicle Allocation of S Electronics Company Based on Traditional Algorithms

Vehicle No.	Delivery route	Total delivery distance
1	0->1->8->7->10->0	*24663.2337 Km*
2	0->17->0	
3	0->9->16->12->15->6->0	
4	0->11->19->14->0	
5	0->18->13->0	
6	0->4->0	
7	0->3->0	
8	0->2->20->5->0	

Data source: Compiled based on the optimization path results obtained from traditional algorithms.

S Electronics Company used traditional algorithms to develop a delivery plan, using a total of 8 vehicles with a total delivery distance of 24663.2337Km.

(2) Ant Colony Algorithm

The distribution route obtained by S Electronics Company using ant colony algorithm is shown in Figure 1.

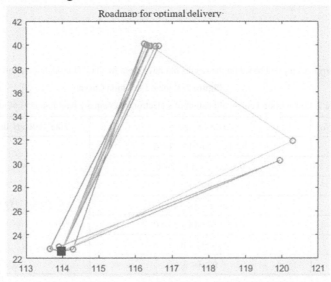

Data source: Compiled based on the results obtained from MATLAB model operation.

Figure 1. Ant colony algorithm optimal route distribution plan route map

The number of iterations and the objective function value are shown in Figure 2. As the number of iterations increases, the objective function value shows a continuous decreasing trend. When the number of iterations is greater than 30, the cost no longer changes, indicating that the optimal cost for the optimal delivery plan has been found.

Using ant colony algorithm to solve the optimization model in MATLAB software, the results obtained are the routes shown in Table 2. This plan uses 7 vehicles, with a total delivery distance of *25001.2253 km* for these 7 delivery routes.

(3) Comparative analysis

Use ant colony algorithm to solve the optimization model, form an optimization plan, and compare the optimization plan with the original distribution plan obtained using traditional algorithms. Compare the number of vehicles delivered and the total distance, as shown in Table 3.

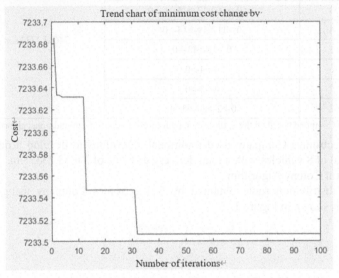

Data source: Compiled based on the results obtained from MATLAB model operation.

Figure 2. Fitness Evolution Curve

Table 2. Distribution vehicle allocation of s electronics company based on ant colony algorithm

Vehicle No.	Delivery route	Total delivery distance
1	0->16->10->19->1->0	
2	0->12->2->13->7->0	
3	0->9->11->0	
4	0->6->8->18->4->0	*25001.2253 km*
5	0->20->5->14->15->0	
6	0->17->0	
7	0->3->0	

Data source: Compiled based on the results obtained from MATLAB model operation.

Table 3. Comparison of Two Delivery Schemes

	Number of vehicles	Total distance
Traditional algorithm	8	24663.2337
Ant colony	7	25001.2253

Data source: Based on the analysis of the distribution plan results obtained by traditional algorithms and ant colony algorithm.

In terms of the number of delivery vehicles, S Electronics Company used traditional algorithms to obtain a delivery plan that used a total of 8 vehicles. After optimizing using ant colony algorithm, the number of vehicles used was 7, saving 1 vehicle compared to the original plan.

In terms of total delivery distance, S Electronics Company used traditional algorithms to obtain a delivery plan with a total delivery distance of 24663.2337Km, while the optimized total delivery distance was 25001.2253Km, a slight increase of 337.9916Km.

According to the above analysis, although the ant colony algorithm has increased the total distance by 337.9916Km compared to traditional algorithms, it can save enterprises one transportation vehicle and its labor costs. Overall, ant colony algorithm can significantly save transportation costs for enterprises. It can be seen that compared to traditional algorithms, ant colony algorithm performs better.

5. Conclusion

With the development of computer information technology and the improvement of transportation tools, people's demand for modern logistics distribution is also increasing. As a key link in logistics systems, vehicle routing distribution can provide customers with high-quality, efficient, and low-cost services. This study establishes an optimization model based on the vehicle routing problem based on the actual situation, and optimizes the vehicle routing problem based on this model. The main conclusions of this study are as follows.

(1) In terms of model construction: Empirical research was conducted using field research methods, and S Electronics Company's logistics has the main problem of "delayed delivery". A vehicle routing problem model was established for S Electronics Company under the optimal distribution route distance conditions.

(2) In terms of algorithm design: Based on research on ant colony algorithm and relevant literature, it was found that it still exhibits good global optimization performance in optimization problems. This study normalizes the pheromone function of the ant colony algorithm. The ant colony algorithm has strong robustness and can be used to solve vehicle path models and achieve optimal logistics distribution routes.

(3) In terms of example proof: Based on the customer demand situation of S Electronics Company on a certain day, the optimal delivery route plan obtained using MATLAB software and ant colony algorithm is to drive 7 vehicles, with a total distance of 25001.2253Km. Compared with traditional algorithms, it indicates that ant colony algorithm has better performance in solving vehicle routing problems, indicating that the vehicle routing problem model established in this paper has certain practicality.

Acknowledgment

This project is supported by the Guangxi Education Science Planning Project (2022ZJY2449) and the Nanning University Teaching Team Construction Project (2021XJJXTD05).

References

[1]   Coyle J. Mastering delivery logistics[J]. Butane-Propane News, 2021, (5): 53.

[2]   A. O. S., Karel Jeábek, Mária Stopková. Using the operations research methods to address distribution tasks at a city logistics Scale[J]. Transportation Research Procedia, 2020, 44: 348-355.

[3]   Friedrich C, Elbert R. Adaptive large neighborhood search for vehicle routing problems with transshipment facilities arising in city logistics[J]. Computers & Operations Research, 2022, (1): 137.

[4]   Kim T. H., Yoon S. J., Song S. H. Designing urban logistics network for last-mile delivery services: a case study in Seoul[J]. Journal of the Korean Society of Supply Chain Management, 2020, 20(1): 110-120.

[5]   Wang S., Yang L., Yao Y., et al. Equity-oriented vehicle routing optimization for catering distribution services with timeliness requirements[J]. IET Intelligent Transport Systems, 2022, (2): 16.

[6]   Liu, Guike , et al. Vehicle routing problem in cold Chain logistics: A joint distribution model with carbon trading mechanisms[J]. Resources Conservation and Recycling, 2020, (156): 104715.

[7]   Wang Y., Peng S., Guan X., et al. Collaborative logistics pickup and delivery problem with eco-packages based on time-space network[J]. Expert Systems with Applications, 2021, 170(3): 114561.

[8]   Gao Y., Wang X. Research on optimization model of dynamic distribution path based on intelligent logistics[J]. Journal of Physics Conference Series, 2020, 1650: 032169.

[9]   Bin Hou, Zhang Luxing, Wang Sujie, Wang Huanfang Optimization of rural low-carbon logistics distribution path based on improved multi-objective genetic algorithm [J] Journal of China Agricultural University 2023,28 (07): 224-237 (in Chinese).

[10] Ganji M., Kazemipoor H., Molana S. A green multi-objective integrated scheduling of production and distribution with heterogeneous fleet vehicle routing and time windows[J].   Journal of Cleaner Production, 2020, 259: 120824.

[11] Envelope K. H., Envelope V. K. G. Solving large scale vehicle routing problems with hard time windows under travel time uncertainty[J]. IFAC-Papers OnLine, 2022, 55(10): 233-238.

[12] Zhu W., Zhuoran A. O., Baldacci R., et al. Enhanced solution representations for vehicle routing problems with split deliveries[J]. Frontiers of Engineering Managemen, 2023, 10(3): 483-498.

[13] Lord Guona, Tang Xiaoping. Research on rural emergency logistics delivery path based on simulated annealing and floyd optimization algorithm[J]. Software Engineering 2022, 25(12): 9-12+8 (in Chinese).

[14] Zhao B., Gui H., Li H., et al. Cold chain logistics path optimization via improved multi-objectiveant colony algorithm[J]. Ieee Access, 2020, 8(1): 142977-142995.

[15] Chen Zhixin, Yan Haowei, Zhang Xinyu, Zhang Zhihao. Vehicle path optimization in B2B urban distribution mode based on improved ant colony algorithm[J]. Highway Transportation, 2023, 40(07): 231-238 (in Chinese).

[16] Xiong H. Research on cold chain logistics distribution route based on ant colony optimization algorithm[J]. Discrete Dynamics in Nature and Society, 2021, 2021(1): 134-139 (in Chinese).

[17] Guo Sen, Qin Guihe, Zhang Jindong. Research on particle swarm optimization algorithm for multi objective vehicle routing problem[J] Journal of Xi'an Jiaotong University, 2016, 50(9): 97-104 (in Chinese).

[18] Dewangan B., Jain A., Shukla R., et al. An ensemble of Bacterial Foraging, Genetic, Ant Colony and Particle Swarm Approach EB-GAP: a load balancing approach in cloud computing[J]. Recent Advances in Computer Science and Communications, 2022, (5): 15.

[19] Cui Y., Ren J., Zhang Y. Path planning algorithm for unmanned surface vehicle based on optimized ant colony algorithm[J]. IEEE Transactions on Electrical and Electronic Engineering, 2022, (7): 17.

[20] Kanso B., Kansou A., Yassine A. Open capacitated ARC routing problem by Hybridized Ant Colony Algorithm[J]. RAIRO - Operations Research, 2021, 55(2): 639-652.

[21] Wang Xuefeng, Chen Hao. Overview of vehicle path optimization problems based on logistics delivery[J]. Journal of Liaoning University of Technology (Natural Science Edition), 2022, 42(06): 386-392 (in Chinese).

[22] Nazia Tazeen, K. Sandhya Rani, "A Novel Ant Colony Based DBN Framework to Analyze the Drug Reviews", International Journal of Intelligent Systems and Applications, Vol.13, No.6, pp.25-39, 2021.

[23] Sepide Fotoohi, Shahram Saeidi, "Discovering the Maximum Clique in Social Networks Using Artificial Bee Colony Optimization Method", International Journal of Information Technology and Computer Science, Vol.11, No.10, pp.1-11, 2019.

[24] G.Narendrababu Reddy, S.Phani Kumar, "MACO-MOTS: Modified Ant Colony Optimization for Multi Objective Task Scheduling in Cloud Environment", International Journal of Intelligent Systems and Applications, Vol.11, No.1, pp.73-79, 2019.

Artificial Intelligence, Medical Engineering and Education
Z.B. Hu et al. (Eds.)
© 2024 The Authors.
This article is published online with Open Access by IOS Press and distributed under the terms
of the Creative Commons Attribution Non-Commercial License 4.0 (CC BY-NC 4.0).
doi:10.3233/ATDE231340

Big Data Analysis of TikTok in the Education of Traditional Chinese Opera

Yuejia YANG[1], Kuok Tiung LEE

Universiti Malaysia Sabah, faculty of social sciences and humanities, 100004, Sabah, Malaysia

Abstract. Opera is the essence of traditional art accumulated in Chinese history and civilization. In China, the inheritance of opera culture has been developed as an educational cause. However, in the era of the Internet, the once glorious and popular opera is also facing an existential crisis of losing a large number of audiences. How to reconstruct the communication ecology of opera with the help of new media has become an urgent problem for opera and media circles. In this paper, through big data of Douyin (Tiktok), to analyze the education of traditional Chinese opera, the ultimate hope as an innovative communication form combining traditional opera and mobile new media, short video of opera can expand the acceptance and influence of opera and promote the popularization and development of opera.

Keywords. Chinese opera; TikTok; Big data.

1. Introduction

The appearance of short videos has changed the audience's preferences. The audience watching Chinese opera, from the theater stage to the cinema to the TV program, until now everyone began to look at the mobile phone smart phone [1]. Driven by the power of science and technology, the Internet is rapidly updated, and the many advantages of network media provide soil for the innovative dissemination and modernization of Chinese opera. People who love Chinese opera may watch it on their mobile phones instead of going to the China Opera Academy [2]. As a result, lightweight, fragmented, and interactive transmission carriers like Tiktok, as popular phenomena on the Internet, have grown rapidly and attracted public attention. It caters to the audience's personalized media habits generated in a fast-paced lifestyle. Using mobile short videos to spread opera is a choice that fits the media environment. The emergence of short video shows that opera art is presenting itself to the audience with a new look full of the sense of The Times [3].

The modern communication theory is used to analyze this process using the method of satisfaction [4]. With the Internet era, the change of communication environment, communication concept and the diversification of entertainment modes have further squeezed the living space of opera. However, at present, the number of short video playback of traditional opera is still relatively high. The reasons for this are analyzed with the modern communication theory of use and satisfaction [5]. Taking the study of opera inheritance as an example, from the audience's perspective, this paper analyzes the key technologies of mainstream informatization such as satisfaction [6], digitalization

---

[1]Corresponding Author: Yuejia YANG, yangyj3@foxmail.com.

[7], big data [8], new media, Internet [9], and Chinese opera culture, and demonstrates and designs the main contents and basic methods of short video communication of Chinese opera culture. Finally, through the data analysis of the content and phenomenon of short drama video communication, it is found that the logic behind the research is conducive to the healthy development of drama art and short video media [10].

2. Research Scope

By combing the media communication process of short drama video, this paper explains the value and characteristics of this communication mode, and then introduces the short drama video method that inherits the communication content of short drama video and combines the communication of mobile application and shows the development status of its platform content and interactive function, script selection and market share. The paper mainly analyzes the communication mechanism and value of short drama video. It analyzes its communication ecological structure from the aspects of resource content, platform channel, user interaction, publicity and so on, and then explains the interwoven and expanded communication mechanism inside and outside the system and points out that the short drama video achieves stickiness through the use and satisfaction theory [11].

3. Research Process

This paper basically follows the idea of raising questions -- analyzing problems -- solving problems. Centering on the opera audio APP object, under the main framework of the use and satisfaction theory and Lasswell's 5W model, the paper focuses on the analysis of the role and function of each media and channel in the platform to the whole communication process, and expounds its communication mechanism about inheritance. And spread the social value of traditional opera art. Namely: APP developers -- content and elements -- platform design and communication strategies -- users and audiences -- communication effects [12]. The following research methods are used in this research process.

   The innovative communication of traditional opera in the era of mobile Internet new media is viewed from the short video of Tiktok, and the application platform of mobile phone new media is analyzed by means of communication theory. By analyzing what forms of content resources the platform has, what interfaces and functions it has designed, and what promotional behaviors it has done, the role and value of mobile short video in the dissemination of opera music and opera culture are explained.

3.1. Research Design

In order to verify the theoretical model of factors influencing the use behavior of fans of Tiktok and related operas, it is assumed that this paper mainly obtains research data through questionnaire survey. Therefore, this chapter first describes the design of the questionnaire in detail, and formulates the question scale for the established model variables, and determines the sample object. After the pre-test, the scale was adjusted and corrected, and finally the formal questionnaire was issued and the data samples were collected.

3.2. Measurement item design of key variables

The following is the measurement design of each variable in the model framework, including the independent variable in the model studied in this paper: Performance expectation, effort expectation, social influence, contributing factor, perceived entertainment, identity; Intermediate variable: intention to use; Dependent variable: use behavior.

3.3 Users use behavioral descriptive analysis

According to the survey, 113 people used Tiktok to watch more than 1 hour to 3 hours of Chinese opera related content in a week, and 157 people used Tiktok to watch more than 3 hours to 5 hours of Chinese opera related content in a week, accounting for 45.51% of the total respondents; In addition, 75 people will spend more than five hours a week watching Chinese opera content on Tiktok.

In terms of viewing time, 60 people watch Chinese opera related content for less than half an hour on Tiktok each time, 121 people spend half an hour to 1 hour on Chinese opera each time, 116 people watch Chinese opera content for more than 1 hour to 1.5 hours each time, 48 people spend the most time. They will watch more than 1.5 hours of Chinese opera content on Tiktok each time.

Table 1. Using behavioral descriptive analysis

Category Items		Number of people	Percentage
Time to watch Chinese opera using Tiktok during the week	More than 1 hour to 3 hours	113	32.75%
	More than 3 hours to 5 hours	157	45.51%
	5 + hours	75	21.74%
Classified item		Number of people	Percentage
Time to watch Chinese opera each time you use Tiktok	Within half an hour	60	17.39%
	Half an hour to 1 hour	121	35.07%
	More than 1 hour to 1.5 hours	116	33.62%
	1.5 + hours	48	13.91%

In terms of usage preference, the "like" function is the most frequently used Tiktok software function by respondents, which is simple to operate and convenient to use. Among the respondents, 128 people frequently like videos, and 165 people frequently use "like" function, accounting for 84.93%. The second is the search function, the content in Tiktok is massive, users often need to actively search to find the content they are interested in more accurately, 51 people always actively search for the videos or creators they want to watch, 197 people will often use this function, accounting for 71.88%; The frequency of use of the comment function is also higher, 109 people will often comment, 132 people will occasionally comment, both accounted for 69.85%; While sharing and active shooting behaviors are less, 109 people will occasionally share videos, 118 people rarely share videos, which is mainly related to the sharing function often requires cross-platform operation and more steps. However, due to the overall age of the respondents, the demand for self-display is not high, so the respondents often or more to take the initiative to shoot video only accounted for 36.23%.

Finally, the respondents have the least reward behavior, only 23 people often reward videos or creators, accounting for 6.67%, 148 people rarely reward, 65 people never reward, both accounting for 61.74%.

In addition, it was found that the interviewees were willing to learn the video content and would follow the video for opera singing or skill learning. Among them, 153 frequently learned the video content and 147 frequently learned the video content, accounting for 86.96% of the total sample.

Table 2. Analysis of respondents' use preference

	Always		Often		Occasionally		Rarely		Never	
	Number of people	Percentage	Number of people	Percentage	Number of people	Percentage	Number of people	percent	Number of people	Percentage
Make a comment	31	8.99%	109	31.59%	132	38.26%	60	17.39%	13	3.77%
Liking a video	128	37.10%	165	47.83%	46	13.33%	6	1.74%	0	0%
Share Videos	62	17.97%	49	14.20%	110	31.88%	118	4.20%	6	1.74%
Tipping Creators	0	0%	23	6.67%	109	31.59%	148	42.90%	65	8.84%
Search for videos of interest with creators	51	14.78%	197	57.10%	84	24.35%	13	3.77%	0	0%
Active video shooting	58	16.81%	67	19.42%	86	24.93%	106	0.72%	28	8.12%
Post Moments	0	0%	7	2.03%	53	5.36%	152	44.06%	133	38.55%
Learn video content	153	44.35%	147	42.61%	42	12.17%	2	0.58%	1	0.29%

In summary, among Chinese opera fans who use Tiktok for more than two hours in a week, there are more male users than female users, and the overall male sex ratio is about 6:4, which is more balanced. In terms of age, the majority of Chinese opera fans who use Tiktok are middle-aged, with high school education and college education, and mostly live in northwestern provinces and cities, with an equal proportion of rural users and urban users. Based on the above information, it can be concluded that the Chinese opera fans who use Tiktok are in line with the basic characteristics of Chinese opera lovers. They are older in age, live mostly in northwest China, and the proportion of users in rural towns is large. To some extent, this reflects that with the increasingly low cost of Internet access and the continuous improvement of infrastructure today, middle-aged and even elderly people have gradually become residents of the Internet. In addition, it is worth noting that Chinese opera fans' preference for Chinese opera content is not just a kind of entertainment consumption, more than 80% of the respondents have learning behaviors, which can reflect the quality and quantity of Chinese opera content in Tiktok is relatively considerable. However, users' content consumption habits are not fully formed -- only 6% of respondents often tip video creators, and most users' usage habits only stay at the level of content interaction [13].

4. Research model and hypothesis testing

Structural Equation Model is one of the important tools for multivariate data analysis [14, 15]. Compared with regression analysis, path analysis and other analysis methods, structural equation model can process multiple dependent variables at the same time and adjust the model according to the theoretical model and its fitting degree with the data, so as to measure the fitting degree of the whole model.

Commonly used structural equation model analysis software includes LISREL, Amos, EQS, etc. Due to the powerful function and simple operation of AMOS software, this paper contains eight latent variables "Chinese opera fans in Tiktok use behavior and its motivation and influencing factors" model is also more suitable for using SEM for research model and hypothesis testing. Therefore, the author chose to use AMOS24.0 software for model drawing and imported the sample data that had been tested for reliability and validity into the software to build the path relationship diagram between the variables, analyze the model fitting index, and then verify the research model and hypothesis in this paper.

The fitting index of the model is compared with the fitting standard range parameters as shown in the following table:

Table 3. Comparison of estimated parameters of the model

Fitting index	Fit standard range	Model index values
X^2/df	< 3	2.829
GFI	> 0.8	0.847
AGFI	> 0.8	0.814
RMSEA	< 0.08	0.073
CFI	> 0.8	0.901
PGFI	> 0.5	0.699
NFI	> 0.8	0.855
IFI	> 0.8	0.888

By comparing the fitting index of the model in this paper with the standard value, it can be seen that the theoretical model of "Influencing Factors of the use behavior of Chinese opera fans in Tiktok" in this study has a good fit with the sample data, and the path analysis can be continued.

Table 4 shows the path test analysis results of the model.

As can be seen from the above table, there are other relationships except that effort expectation and social influence have no significant influence on use intention.

All of them were significant (P<0.05). The coefficients of variables in the model are shown in Figure 1.

Table 4. model path check analysis results

The path relationship among latent variables	Eestimate	S.E.	C.R.	P	Salience
Willingness to use <-- Performance expectation	0.257	0.065	3.939	* * *	Significant
Willingness to use <-- Strive to expect	0.047	0.035	1.343	0.179	Non-significant
Performance expectations <-- effort expectations	0.388	0.047	8.194	* * *	Significant
Intention to use <-- social impact	0.031	0.055	0.565	0.572	Non-significant
Use behavior <-- contributing factors	0.328	0.062	5.288	* * *	Significant
Willingness to use <-- perceived entertainment	0.369	0.087	4.221	* * *	Significant
Use willingness <-- identity	0.122	0.058	2.107	0.035 *	Significant
Use behavior <-- willingness to use	0.363	0.363.065	5.629	* * *	Significant

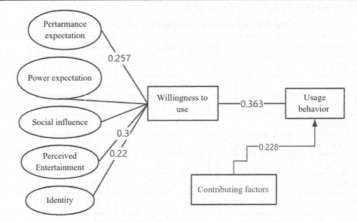

Figure 1. Model diagram of variable coefficients

Based on the path coefficient graph, this study calculated the mediating effects of 6 independent variables or intermediate variables on dependent variables.
The results are shown in the table 5.

It can be seen that performance expectation, perceived entertainment and identity have significant direct effects on use intention and significant indirect effects on use behavior respectively, while effort expectation and social influence have no significant direct and indirect effects on use intention and use behavior respectively.

In addition, since the direct effect of use intention on use behavior is significant, use intention plays an intermediary role in the influence of performance expectation, perceived entertainment and identity on use behavior.

Table 5. Effects of independent variables or intermediate variables on dependent variables

	Total effect		Direct effects		Indirect effects	
	Willingness to use	Use behavior	Willingness to use	Use behavior	Willingness to use	Use behavior
Performance expectations	0.361	0.336	0.361	0	0	0.336
Strive to expect	0.065	0.061	0.065	0	0	0.061
Social impact	0.033	0.03	0.033	0	0	0.03
Contributing Factors	0	0.369	0	0.369	0	0
Perceived Entertainment	0.392	0.364	0.392	0	0	0.364
Identity	0.112	0.104	0.112	0	0	0.104
Intention to use	0	0.929	0	0.929	0	0

5. Conclusion

Firstly, SPSS25.0 and AMOS24.0 software were used to conduct reliability and validity test, factor analysis and structural equation model test on 345 valid questionnaires collected. Then, in order to deepen the research results, in-depth interviews were conducted on some research subjects through random sampling. This chapter will summarize this research, summarize the conclusions obtained through empirical research and in-depth interview, and on the basis of the summary results, conduct a more in-depth discussion on the motivation of Chinese opera fans in Tiktok.

By verifying the research hypothesis proposed in this paper, we can draw the following conclusions:

1) Perceived entertainment and performance expectation can indirectly affect the use behavior of Chinese opera fans by influencing their use intention

The interpretation degree of perceived entertainment and performance expectation on usage intention is 36.9% and 25.7% respectively, indicating that perceived entertainment has the most significant positive impact on usage intention, followed by performance expectation. In this study, the two words most frequently used by users when referring to Tiktok are "useful" and "fun". Useful because Tiktok provides rich opera content, which is constantly confirmed in the following interview process, while fun is more reflected by user frequency and positive emotions -- many users are easily fascinated when using Tiktok. And the use of Tiktok can make them feel relaxed and happy.

2) Identity indirectly affects the use behavior of Chinese opera fans by influencing their willingness to use Tiktok

The explanation degree of identity to use intention is 12.2%, which indicates that the stronger the identity of Chinese opera fans as "fans" in Tiktok, the more inclined they are to use Tiktok. Through follow-up interviews, the author found that many users are satisfied with the community atmosphere in Tiktok, and the group chat function in Tiktok has been praised by users alike. This function greatly expands the social scene of users and enhances the opportunities for mutual exposure and interaction among users. Such strong sociability makes it easy to maintain user activity and high content popularity. Thus, the offline community of Chinese opera can be transferred to Tiktok more completely and conveniently, and the cultural atmosphere and fan stickability of Chinese opera fans are well maintained.

3)Usage intention and contributing factors will positively affect the usage behavior of Chinese opera fans in Tiktok.

The results show that the interpretation degree of usage intention is 36.3%, and the explanation degree of contributing factors is 32.8%, both of which have significant positive effects on usage behavior. There is no need to explain the influence of the intention to use on the use behavior, and the relationship between the two is also consistent with the common sense of life and the conclusion of psychological research. The contributing factors are the necessary objective conditions for the occurrence of use behavior. Only when users feel that their own material conditions and the external attraction of Tiktok are sufficient and perfect, will they be prompted to have actual use behavior.

References

[1]   Georgios Rigopoulos. Assessment and Feedback as Predictors for Student Satisfaction in UK Higher Education[J]. International Journal of Modern Education and Computer Science, 2022, 14(5): 1-9.

[2]   Yana Serkina, Alena Vobolevich, Irina Petunina, Aleksandra Zakharova. Analysis of the Information and Communication Technology in Blended Learning for Economics Students in the Context of Digitalization[J]. International Journal of Modern Education and Computer Science, 2023, 15(3): 33-43.

[3]   Asma Omri, Mohamed Nazih Omri. Towards an Efficient Big Data Indexing Approach under an Uncertain Environment[J]. International Journal of Intelligent Systems and Applications, 2022, 14(2): 1-13.

[4]   Qingqing Zhou, Minkang Yang, Hongyi Zhang, Rong Qian. Comprehensive introduction to Chinese traditional music[M]. Hollitzer Verlag, 2023, 12: 23-25 (in Chinese).

[5]   Liu Kaixuan, Lin Kai, Zhu Chun. Research on Chinese traditional opera costume recognition based on improved YOLOv5[J]. Heritage Science, 2023, 11(1):41-44 (in Chinese).

[6]   Si Zhengyu. An introduction to the use of Chinese Opera expressions in experimental drama[J]. SHS Web of Conferences, 2023, 158(1): 51-60.

[7]   Information Systems Mobile. Retracted: design of Chinese Opera Cultural Platform based on digital twins and research on international cultural communication strategies[J]. Mobile Information Systems, 2022, 2(2): 51-55.

[8]   Zhifei Chen. Kunqu Opera Film the Zidu: A case study of cross-media communication research of kunqu[J]. Art and Performance Letters, 2022, 3(4): 33-36 (in Chinese).

[9]   Chi Xia Bing, Belliveau George. Between tradition and modernity: developments in Xiqu (Chinese opera) actor training[J]. Theatre, Dance and Performance Training, 2022, 13(4):14-18 (in Chinese).

[10] Yang Zhiyong. Scientific and technological creative stage design using artificial intelligence[J]. Computers and Electrical Engineering, 2022, 103(1): 16-17 (in Chinese).

[11] Shanshan An. Research on the aesthetic connotation of Beijing opera mask culture and innovation of modern design[J]. Art and Design, 2022, 5(5): 126-128 (in Chinese).

[12] Xu Lisha, Johnston David. Between safeguarding and translating: Chinese classical opera and Spanish Golden Age theatre[J]. Translation Studies, 2022, 15(3): 99-107.

[13] Ma Li. Design of Chinese Opera Cultural Platform Based on digital twins and research on international cultural communication strategies[J]. Mobile Information Systems, 2022, 22(1): 56-57.

[14] Liang Hui, Dong Xiaohang, Liu Xiaoxiao, Pan Junjun, Zhang Jingyue, Wang Ruicong.A semantic‐driven generation of 3D Chinese opera performance scenes[J]. Computer Animation and Virtual Worlds, 2022, 33(3-4): 1-17 (in Chinese).

[15] Ma Haili. The missing intangible cultural heritage in Shanghai cultural and creative industries[J]. International Journal of Heritage Studies, 2022, 28(5): 19-27.

Artificial Intelligence, Medical Engineering and Education
Z.B. Hu et al. (Eds.)
© 2024 The Authors.
This article is published online with Open Access by IOS Press and distributed under the terms
of the Creative Commons Attribution Non-Commercial License 4.0 (CC BY-NC 4.0).
doi:10.3233/ATDE231341

A Bibliometric Analysis of Industry-Education Integration Research Based on Web of Science

Jing ZUO[a], Fang HUANG[c], Yanxin YE[b1]

a Nanning University, Nanning, China
b Guangxi Modern Polytechnic College, Hechi, China
c Xiangsihu College of Guangxi Minzu University, Nanning, China

ORCiD ID: Jing ZUO https://orcid.org/0000-0002-9118-1040

Abstract. This study aims to gain a deeper understanding of the research dynamics and trends in industry-education integration through a quantitative analysis of the literature in this field. Eight hundred ninety-five relevant articles were retrieved from the Web of Science Core Collection database, and the research focused on the annual publication trends, prominent authors, institutions and countries, highly cited articles, keywords, and collaborative networks. The study found that the field of industry-education integration has undergone three stages. Secondly, researchers from China and the United States ranked first and second in the number of publications in this field. Thirdly, highly cited articles have a particular influence on industry-education integration, but the overall citation count is relatively limited. Fourthly, keywords such as "cooperative education," "students," and "performance" are hot topics in this field. Finally, the analysis of collaborative networks revealed the existence of multiple communities, but the overall scale of collaboration is relatively small, and the influence is limited. This study provides profound insights into the academic research in industry-education integration. It helps scholars, policymakers, and practitioners better understand this field's development trends.

Keywords. Industry-education integration; Bibliometrics; Research trends

1. Introduction

Industry-education integration refers to the cooperation and integration between the industry and education sectors, aiming to improve the quality of education, promote industrial development, and cultivate talents that meet market demands [1]. Industry-education integration is essential for vocational education and a crucial approach to achieving high-quality products [2]. China has attached great importance to developing industry-education integration in recent years and has implemented policy measures to provide more robust support [3-5]. In this context, conducting scientific research and evaluating industry-education integration is essential. Bibliometrics analysis is a method for studying literature's characteristics and development trends. It can consider and analyze literature from multiple dimensions, such as quantity, quality, citations, authors, and institutions, to understand the development status and trends in the field of literature

---

[1] Corresponding Author: Yanxin YE, E-mail: dariayyx@126.com.

and provide support for academic research and discipline construction.

This article uses bibliometrics analysis to systematically analyze the literature on industry-education integration research in the Web of Science database. It seeks to uncover its development process, main characteristics, core themes, knowledge structure, influencing factors, and comparative analysis with relevant domestic literature to provide reference and inspiration for industry-education integration research in China.

The expected contributions of this article are as follows:

(1) This article is the first comprehensive and systematic bibliometric analysis of international industry-education integration research using the Web of Science database. It fills the domestic and international research gap and provides a global perspective and reference for industry-education integration research in China.

(2) This article adopts various bibliometric analysis techniques, such as literature statistics, co-word analysis, clustering analysis, and social network analysis. It explores industry-education integration research from different angles and levels, providing a multidimensional and multi-level analysis framework and methods for industry-education integration research in China.

(3) Based on the results of bibliometric analysis, this article provides insightful discussions on the development trends, disciplinary frontiers, hot issues, knowledge structure, and influencing factors of industry-education integration research. It offers new ideas and directions for industry-education integration research in China.

2. Literature Review

2.1. The Main Theories and Definition of Industry-Education Integration

Industry-education integration has multidimensional connotations and is defined differently in government policy documents. The General Office of the State Council defines it as a process promoting comprehensive integration of talent cultivation and industry demands [5]. The National Medium- and Long-Term Education Reform and Development Plan defines it as a process centered around market demands, industrial development, talent cultivation, innovation, and entrepreneurship, and win-win cooperation [4]. The National Vocational Education Reform Implementation Plan emphasizes the principles of school-enterprise cooperation and joint construction and sharing [2]. From an academic research perspective, industry-education integration can be categorized into cooperative development, integrated development, and regional economic service-oriented approaches [6-9].

The main theories of industry-education integration include the pluralistic shared governance perspective, which emphasizes the participation of multiple actors to maximize public interests; the transaction cost theory, which highlights the reduction of transaction costs to promote cooperation; the triple helix theory, which emphasizes the interaction and collaboration among government, industry, and education; the community theory, which highlights the establishment of a shared vision and a community to achieve a common goal; and the value orientation, which emphasizes the long-term development and quality [1, 6].

2.2. History and Development Trend of Industry-Education Integration

The integration of industry and education originated in China during the reform and opening-up period of the 1980s. With the changes in market demand and industrial structure, the education sector began collaborating with the industry, gradually forming an important educational model [1]. Over the past forty years, the integration of industry and education has gone through three stages: initial exploration, diverse innovation, and continuous deepening [6]. The active promotion by the government, as well as the attention and support from various levels of government and universities, have enabled the rapid development of the integration of industry and education [6].

The future development trends of the integration of industry and education can be divided into four main directions. Firstly, integrating industry and education will further innovate its forms and contents. It will include traditional internships and practical training and involve industrial research, technology transfer, and talent development in various fields. Emphasis will be placed on improving talent development's quality and innovative capabilities [7]. Secondly, integrating industry and education will expand its scope and domains, including international cooperation and cross-border integration. This will broaden the perspectives and resources for talent development, enhancing competitiveness [7]. The participation of social organizations and individuals will promote the diversity and influence of the integration of industry and education [9]. Thirdly, government support and guidance will continue optimizing the environment and conditions for integrating the sector and education. Formulating policies and measures will encourage and support the integration of industry and education [8]. Meanwhile, using the Internet and digital technologies will improve educational efficiency and quality [1]. Lastly, integrating industry and education will continuously enhance its effectiveness and value. Technological innovation and technology transfer will drive the development of the integration of industry and education [10]. The principles of sustainable development will guide the development of the integration of industry and education, aiming to achieve coordinated economic, social, and ecological development [10].

2.3. Major Practices and Experiences in the Integration of Industry and Education

Since its development, the integration of industry and education has accumulated a wealth of experience. In summary, in terms of the forms and contents of the integration of industry and education, it can be divided into the integration of industry, education, and research [10], joint development of industry and education [11], guidance of industry and education projects [7], and talent development and exchange [1]. There are three categories in terms of mechanisms and models of integrating industry and education. The first category is the school-enterprise cooperation mechanism [8, 1], the second category is modern management models [6], and the third category is diverse models [10]. Regarding influencing factors, the integration of industry and education can be divided into internal, external, and coupling factors [11]. These factors directly impact the depth and breadth of the integration of industry and education and need to be strengthened and optimized.

3. Methodology

3.1. Data Sources and Data Analysis

The Web of Science core ensemble database is selected, and relevant search keywords are extended based on industry-education integration. The search formula is written as: ("Industry-education integration") OR ("Production-education integration") OR (" School-industry collaboration") OR ("Cooperative education") OR ("School-industry partnership") OR ("Dual education system") OR ("Industry- linked capstone projects") OR ("academic-industry partnership"). The timeframe for the search was from the build to August 22, 2023. Eight hundred ninety-five relevant documents with the above search terms in the title and keywords were retrieved. The retrieved literature was analyzed econometrically using R 4.3.1 and Bibliometric.

4. Results and Discussion

4.1. Annual Trends in Literature Publication

The publication of literature on industry-education integration reflects the trends in research in this field. Figure 1 shows that this analysis can be divided into three phases. The first phase, from 1946 to 1960, had limited research activities. The second phase, from the 1960s to 2007, saw an increase in research on topics such as cooperative education models, academic and vocational benefits, international cooperation, and institutionalized cooperative education. The third phase, starting in 2008, has shown significant growth in research interest. Research on industry-education integration has remained consistently active, reflecting the growing recognition of its importance in higher education.

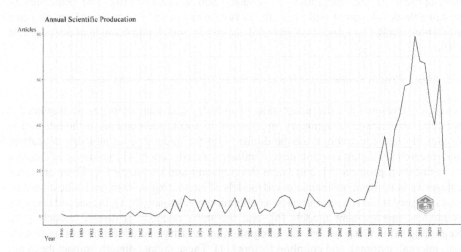

Figure 1. Annual literature publication trends in the field of industry-education integration research

4.2. Lead Authors, Institutions and Countries

Canadian authors T. Judene Prett and David Drewery have the highest number of publications in the field, with 10 and 9, respectively, with research focusing on cooperative education, work-integrated learning, and related topics aimed at understanding the impact of various factors in these areas on students and the workplace.

China has the highest number of publications at 27.2%, followed by the United States at 18.8%. This is likely due to their large education systems and strong collaborations between higher education and industry. However, research from other countries is also valuable for understanding industry-education integration in different regions.

Asia-Pacific Journal of Cooperative Education has the most publications, with 2.8%. Waterloo University in Canada is the most developed institution in the field, with 5.7%.

4.3. Highly Cited Literature

Highly cited literature refers to papers ranked in the top 1% regarding citation frequency, which are widely influential and well-known in the academic world and are often regarded as essential references in specific fields [12]. The top 10 highly cited literature in the field of integration of industry and education in this study are shown in Table 1. This highly cited literature dramatically influences the academic world and provides an essential theoretical and practical foundation for research on integrating industry and education.

At the top of the list is Developing Graduate Employability Skills and Attributes: Curriculum Enhancement through Work-integrated Learning. This article explores how work-integrated learning, WIL) is a crucial strategy for enhancing graduate employability skills. In industry-education integration, WIL provides students with opportunities to interact with natural work environments, facilitating the development of the skills and qualities they need in their careers [13]. This topic is crucial for the current needs of the job market, which is why this article is more influential. However, it is also important to note that although the highly cited literature at the top of the list has attracted a certain amount of attention from academics within the field of industry-education integration, the number of citations for these ten articles is not large, which reflects that the influence of these articles is limited to a certain extent, which may be affected by the narrowness of the field, the timeliness, the source of the data, and the timeframe for retrieval, among other factors. Despite the limited number of citations, we still need to consider the quality and depth of this highly cited literature. They may provide deep theoretical insights, practical methodologies, or unique insights into specific issues. As the field of industry-education integration may still be a relatively new area of research, more studies may generate more citations over time, thus increasing the impact of the literature.

Table 1. Top 10 highly cited literature

No.	Title of Literature	Periodical	TC	TC / year
1	Developing graduate employability skills and attributes: Curriculum enhancement through work-integrated learning	Asia-Pacific Journal of Cooperative Education	96	13.71
2	Are the benefits of tourism and cooperative education in UK undergraduate courses realized?	Tourism Management	57	2.38

Continued Table 1

No.	Title of Literature	Periodical	TC	TC / year
3	Cooperative education work assignments: The role of organizational and individual factors in enhancing ABET competencies and co-op workplace well-being	Journal of Engineering Education	54	2.84
4	The Impact of Cooperative Education on Academic Performance and Compensation of Engineering Majors	Journal of Engineering Education	53	2.65
5	Experiential education in the undergraduate curriculum	Communication Education	52	2.08
6	From sponsorship to partnership in academy-industry relations	R&D Management	46	1.92
7	Bridging science and technology through academic-industry partnerships	Research Policy	41	5.13
8	(How) Do work placements work? Scrutinizing the quantitative evidence for a theory-driven future research agenda	Journal of Vocational Behavior	40	8.00
9	Tourism and hospitality internship experiences overseas: A British perspective	Journal of Hospitality, Leisure, Sport & Tourism Education	37	4.11
10	Linking internships and classroom learning: A case study examination of hospitality and tourism management students	Journal of Hospitality, Leisure, Sport & Tourism Education	36	4.50

Note: TC= Total Citation.

4.4. Trend Topics

Keywords are a natural language that reflects the core content of the literature, and high-frequency keywords reflect the hot topics that are concentrated in this research field [14]. According to the frequency analysis, the top 10 keywords are cooperative education, students, performance, impact, model, university, work, experience, education, and higher education.

Keyword co-occurrence analysis is a data visualization method usually used to analyze and show co-occurrence relationships between multiple things or concepts [15]. The parameters are set as follows: Clustering Algorithm is Walktrap, Normalization is an association, the Number of Nodes selected is 50, the Repulsion Force is 0.1, the Minimum number of edges is 2, and isolated Nodes. To get the keyword co-occurrence network graph (see Fig. 2), the nodes' size and the edges' thickness can reflect the importance or strength of association between these keys.

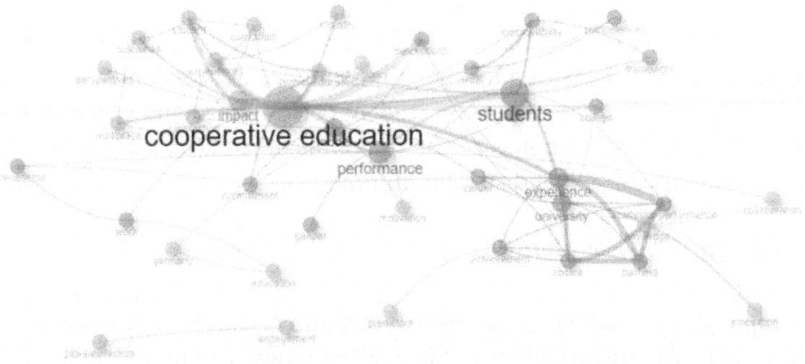

Figure 2. Keyword co-occurrence analysis network diagram

Table 2. Trend topics in industry-education integration research areas

Item	Freq	Year_q1	Year_med	Year_q3
work	12	2013	2014	2019
choice	6	2012	2014	2014
academic-performance	5	2013	2014	2014
antecedents	6	2015	2016	2017
career	6	2013	2016	2020
outcomes	6	2016	2016	2020
commitment	6	2016	2017	2018
engagement	5	2017	2017	2021
support	5	2017	2017	2020
experience	11	2014	2018	2019

Trend Topics indicate the hottest topics in a research field during a specific period. By analyzing these topics(see Table 2), we can identify key trends. "Work" is the most discussed topic, followed by "Career." Other popular topics include "Outcomes," "Commitment," and "Engagement." These trends reflect researchers' growing interest in products, dedication, and employment.

Trend Topics are usually used to indicate the hottest topics or keywords in a field or topic during a specific period, which can help researchers understand the current hot trends and focuses in the research field [14]. We can observe key trends based on the Trend Topics in this research area (see Table 2). First, the most frequently occurring topic in the research literature is "Work," which has received much attention in the past few years, especially reaching a peak in 2019. This demonstrates the continued influence of work-related research in academia. In addition, research on 'Career' also shows a long history of research, covering the period from 2013 to 2020. This reflects the exploration of career aspects. In addition, topics such as 'Outcomes,' 'Commitment,' and 'Engagement' have also received much attention recently, suggesting that researchers are interested in outcomes, commitment, and engagement. This indicates that research interest in products, dedication, and employment is rising.

In terms of high-frequency keywords and trends, we observed significant patterns. "Cooperative education" and "students" indicate a focus on integrating education and industry, highlighting the roles of educational institutions and students. "Performance" and "impact" show concern for the effects on student performance and social impact. "Higher education" and "university" emphasize the importance of these institutions in facilitating industry-education integration and student training.

4.5. Collaborative Network Analysis

Co-authorship network analysis provides insights into research collaboration relationships in the field [16]. We identified multiple communities within the network, reflecting collaborative dynamics. Three types of communities were observed: small neighborhoods of 2-3 researchers/entities, a significant linear community indicating a highly centralized collaborative relationship, and a large community with cross-connections indicating close relationships between sub-teams or research directions. Nodes represented by authors Wang Y, Drewery, and Pretti had higher centrality and influence within the co-authorship network.

Figure 3. Cooperative network diagram

Further analysis of the members, collaboration frequency, and joint research areas within these communities will help us better understand the characteristics and trends of research collaboration, providing valuable insights and guidance for future research and collaboration.

Through the observation of collaboration communities in the co-authorship network, it is worth noting that there are currently not many collaboration communities in the field of industry-education integration. Furthermore, most of the communities are relatively small in size, indicating limited influence. This suggests that industry-education integration has yet to establish more extensive and effective research groups. However, measures can be taken to enhance the power of the field. These measures may include promoting collaboration, increasing visibility, encouraging the participation of young researchers, and fostering interdisciplinary cooperation. By implementing these strategies, the field can strengthen its impact and establish more impactful research groups in industry-education integration.

5. Conclusion

The main objective of this study is to explore the research dynamics and trends in the field of industry-education integration, as well as to identify highly cited literature, keywords, and collaborative networks. Through the econometric analysis of 895 relevant literature in the Web of Science core ensemble database, we draw the following conclusions:

First, research activities in the field of industry-education integration have gone through different phases, including a starting phase, a phase of gradual growth, and a phase of rapid growth. This indicates that the field has attracted increasing academic attention and continues to grow.

Second, Canadian authors T. Judene Prett and David Drewery have the highest number of publications in the field, with China and the United States ranking first and second, respectively. This reflects that these two countries dominate the research activities in industry-industry integration.

Third, highly cited literature has a particular influence within the field of industry-teaching integration, but the overall number of citations is relatively limited. The narrowness of the area, timeliness, and data sources may influence this.

Fourth, the keyword analysis revealed that keywords such as "collaborative education," "students," and "performance" are hot topics in the field, reflecting the focus of the research.

Fifth, the collaborative network analysis revealed the existence of multiple communities, but the overall collaboration was relatively small and had limited impact.

This study provides a comprehensive perspective, revealing the research trends and critical participants in the field of industry-education integration. It helps scholars better understand the development dynamics of industry-education integration, guiding future research directions and providing some reference value for policymakers and practitioners. Although this study offers an in-depth understanding of the field of industry-education integration, there are still many future research directions worth exploring. These include further investigating the content and impact of highly cited literature, exploring industry-education integration models in different countries and regions, analyzing the evolution of collaborative networks, and analyzing key terms and trends over various periods to track the development direction of the field.

Acknowledgment

This project is supported by Project of Guangxi Higher Education Undergraduate Teaching Reform (2022JGA394), and Project for the Research Foundation Abilities Enhancement of Young and Middle-aged Teachers of Guangxi Universities(2023KY1455).

References

[1]   Liao Hongbing. Internal logic and implementation ways of industry-education integration[J]. Converter, 2021: 658-666.

[2]   Ministry of Education of the People's Republic of China. Circular of the state council on issuing the implementation program of national vocational education reform [EB/OL]// Government Portal of the

Ministry of Education of the People's Republic of China. [2023-09-08]. http://www.moe.gov.cn/jyb_xxgk/moe_1777/moe_1778/201904/t20190404_376701.html (in Chinese).

[3]   Xinhua. Xi Jinping proposes to raise the level of safeguarding and improving people's livelihoods and strengthen and innovate social governance [EB/OL]//China.gov.cn. (2017-10-18) [2023-09-08]. https://www.gov.cn/zhuanti/2017-10/18/content_5232656.htm (in Chinese).

[4]   Ministry of Education of the People's Republic of China. Outline of the national medium- and long-term education reform and development plan (2010-2020) [EB/OL]// Government Portal of the Ministry of Education of the People's Republic of China. (2010-07-29)[2023-09-08]. http://www.moe.gov.cn/srcsite/A01/s7048/201007/t20100729_171904.html (in Chinese).

[5]   Ministry of Education of the People's Republic of China. Several opinions of the general office of the state council on deepening the integration of industry and education [EB/OL]// Government Portal of the Ministry of Education of the People's Republic of China. (2017)[2023-09-08]. http://www.moe.gov.cn/jyb_xxgk/moe_1777/moe_1778/201712/t20171219_321953.html (in Chinese).

[6]   Qi Zhanyong, Wang Yufei. Changes and prospects of China's vocational education industry-education integration policies over the 40 years of reform and opening up[J]. China Higher Education Research, 2018(5): 40-45+67 (in Chinese).

[7]   Li Y, Zhou X, Pan Y, et, al. How engagement in the industry-education integration promotes one's attitudes toward energy efficiency: evidence from Chinese evidence from Chinese university students[J]. Sustainability, 2022, 14(23): 15890.

[8]   Peng Mengjiao. Research on Industry-Education Integration in Applied Undergraduate Colleges and Universities--Taking Chongqing Institute of Science and Technology as an Example [D]. Chongqing Normal University, 2016 (in Chinese).

[9]   Chen Nianyou, Zhou Changqing, Wu Zhuping. Connotation and realization way of industry-education integration[J]. China University Science and Technology, 2014(8): 40-42 (in Chinese).

[10]   Chen Xing. Research on the dynamics of industry-education integration in applied colleges and universities[D]. Chongqing: Southwest University, 2017 (in Chinese).

[11]   Yourong Liu, Gui'e Xiang, Jiancheng Wang. Research on industry-teaching integration mode and its influencing factors in applied undergraduate colleges[J]. China Higher Education Research, 2015(5): 64-68 (in Chinese).

[12]   Bornmann L. How are excellent (highly cited) papers defined in bibliometrics? A quantitative analysis of the literature[J]. Research Evaluation, 2014, 23(2): 166-173.

[13]   Rowe A D, Zegwaard K E. Developing graduate employability skills and attributes: Curriculum enhancement through work-integrated learning[M]//Asia-Pacific Journal of Cooperative Education: Volume 18. C/O Cooperative Education Unit, Fac Science, Univ Waikato, Private Bag 3105, Hamilton, 3240, New Zealand: Asia-Pacific Journal Cooperative Education, 2017: 87-99.

[14]   Chen G, Xiao L. Selecting publication keywords for domain analysis in bibliometrics: A comparison of three methods[J]. Journal of Informetrics, 2016, 10(1): 212-223.

[15]   Radhakrishnan S, Erbis S, Isaacs J A, et, al. Novel keyword co-occurrence network-based methods to foster systematic reviews of scientific literature[J]. PloS One, 2017, 12(3): e0172778.

[16]   Chen H, Song X, Jin Q, et, al. Network dynamics in university-industry collaboration: A collaboration-knowledge dual-layer network perspective[J]. Scientometrics, 2022, 127(11): 6637-6660.

Artificial Intelligence, Medical Engineering and Education
Z.B. Hu et al. (Eds.)
© 2024 The Authors.
This article is published online with Open Access by IOS Press and distributed under the terms
of the Creative Commons Attribution Non-Commercial License 4.0 (CC BY-NC 4.0).
doi:10.3233/ATDE231342

The Impact of Data-Based Boosting on User Click-Through Intention Under AI Personalized Recommendations

Li LI[a, b], Dhakir Abbas ALI[a, 1], Yuanting GUO[b]

[a] *Faculty of Business and Accountancy, Lincoln University College, Selangor, Malaysia*
[b] *School of Business, Nanning University, Nanning, China*
ORCiD ID: Dhakir Abbas ALI https://orcid.org/0009-0000-6842-0157

Abstract. As the main means of product information recommendation, data boost will have an important impact on consumers' purchasing behavior. Although there are a lot of research on data boost at present, they mainly focus on system design and algorithm research, and pay less attention to data aid under AI personalized recommendation. In view of this, this paper studies how the data boost pair under AI personalized recommendation has an impact on consumers' willingness to click. Through scenario simulation method, three experiments were carried out with college students as experimental objects to carry out empirical research. The results show that the data boost of AI personalized recommendation positively affects click intention; Under AI personalized recommendation, perceived benefits play an important intermediary role in consumer behavior; Privacy concerns play a moderating role in the influence mechanism of AI personalized recommendation on consumers' click intention.

Keywords. AI Personalized Recommendations; Data-based Boost; Perceived Benefit; Privacy Concern; Click-through Intention

1. Introduction

With the development of science and technology, precision marketing has gradually developed to the intelligent marketing stage of "thousands of people, thousands of faces", and the combination of personalized marketing and artificial intelligence (artificial intelligence, AI) has brought more convenience and benefits to consumers. However, it is worth thinking about whether intelligent marketing is more likely to be liked and accepted by consumers in any case, and whether the data-enabled promotion of AI technology will bring new influences on consumer behavior. Compared with traditional data-based boosting, under AI-based data-based boosting, intelligent algorithms can process all kinds of data more quickly and comprehensively, with the ability of independent learning and self-correction [1]. On the one hand, when consumers see the recommended choices that meet their needs and preferences under these data-based boosts, they may feel convenient because of the reduced search effort and time cost; on

---

[1] Corresponding Author: Dhakir Abbas ALI, E-mail: drdhakir@lincoln.edu.my.

the other hand, when their minds are speculated to be seen through, consumers are more likely to be averse to the AI algorithm-based data-based boosts if it involves their personal privacy [2].

As a result, the impact of data-based boosting of AI personalized recommendation on consumer behavior and the path of influence is quite uncertain, and the current Chinese research on the degree of AI personalization focuses on the personalized recommendation system and algorithmic model [3-5], and more often explores the effect of personalized recommendation, or reviews the existing research from the perspective of the review. Some scholars conduct a research review for deep learning-based recommender systems, explore the difference between them and traditional recommender systems, and sort out the problems and solutions in deep learning research related to information recommender systems in China [6,7]. Liu Huafeng et al. conducted a research review on the model of social recommendation based on model construction [8], and Zhang Yan bing et al. conducted a full-scale combing of theories on the influence mechanism between AI marketing and people [9].

Fewer studies have explored the influence mechanism of data-based boosting on consumers' clicking intention under AI personalized recommendation from the perspective of consumer behavior, and even fewer studies have been conducted on the boundary conditions of the influence of data-based boosting on consumer behavior. In addition, under the scenario of AI personalized recommendation, different consumption scenarios involving online disclosure of consumer information and personal privacy protection are also one of the important factors affecting consumer decision-making behavior. Therefore, this study explores the mechanism of the influence of the degree of data-fueled personalization on consumers' clicking intention in the context of AI by combining different consumption scenarios through an experimental approach to broaden the existing research in this field in terms of both breadth and depth, which is an important reference value for the development of intelligent marketing in the future.

2. Theoretical Analysis and Research Hypothesis

From a theoretical point of view, actual personalization occurs when a message sender (website or merchant, etc.) sends a modified and personalized recommendation message to a receiver via a digital boost based on previously collected data about the message recipient and modifies the generic recommendation based on this information and data [7]. It has been shown that digital boosting often recommended content selected by the user can help the user to reduce the difficulty of decision making, reduce the time and effort spent in the decision-making process, and select a more appropriate product. Thus, digital boosting may enhance users' willingness to click. Therefore, this study adopts the concept of whether data boosting enhances consumers' click willingness, and measures consumers' attitudes toward AI-based data-based boosting at this categorical level to explore the mechanism of the degree of personalization of data-based boosting on consumers' click willingness under data-based boosting from the perspective of the recipients of the pushed content.

2.1. Data-driven Promotion and Consumers' Willingness to Click

LI C. in the study of the path of the influence of data-based boosting on consumers suggested that the data-based boosting approach, by attracting the attention of consumers, triggers them to think more positively rather than negatively about the information processing, which creates a positive attitude towards the information as a whole, and ultimately improves the willingness of consumers to adopt the recommendation [10]. Li in the process of his research through 3 experiments found that perceived personalization, rather than actual personalization, is the psychological mechanism behind determining the impactful outcome of a message [11]. When the message receiver perceives the recommended content as personalized, whether it is personalized or not, data driven boosting leads to positive impact and outcomes [12]. In reality, when consumers are browsing the web, their behavior is often monitored in real time, and enterprise marketers can recommend the most appropriate products to customers at any time, which means that user profiling and segmentation of end consumers can be done more accurately and quickly, and big data processing based on the AI background is a favorable means to help data-based marketing [13]. And AI-based data-based boosting is more likely to attract consumers and meet their needs than traditional data-based boosting, and consumers are more willing to click. Therefore, this study proposes the hypothesis that.

H1: The higher the data-based boost under AI personalized recommendation, the higher the consumers' willingness to click on AI-based data-based boost.

2.2. Mediating Effects of Perceived Benefits

In the research on the influence mechanism of data-enabled boosting on consumers, many scholars have incorporated variables at the level of consumer perception. It has been argued that perceived usefulness plays a key role in the influence mechanism, and perceived usefulness also increases users' intention to adopt the information of data-based boosts for digital libraries as well as their willingness to purchase data-based boosts for mobile e-commerce [14,15]. Goldfarb A et al. showed that there is a positive influence relationship between perceived benefits and consumers' willingness to accept data-enabled boosts [16]; Snehlata Barde et al. incorporated perceived value as a mediating variable, and the study showed that good information presentation positively affects consumers' perceived value, which in turn positively affects their willingness to accept data-enabled boosts [17]. Kramer T. found that the negative impact of data driven push systems on consumers is less than the positive impact, and the positive impact is mainly due to the benefits and advantages that personalized services bring to consumers [18]. Compared with the traditional data-driven push system, the AI-based data-driven push system brings more convenience and benefits to consumers, which can be presumed to trigger consumers' perceived benefits, stimulate them to click on recommendations, and even ultimately generate purchasing behaviors. Therefore, this study proposes the hypothesis that.

H2: Perceived benefits play a mediating role in the influence of data-based boosting on consumers' clicking intention, i.e., under AI personalized recommendation, when data-based boosting is high, it can stimulate consumers' perceived benefits and thus increase their clicking intention on recommended content.

2.3. Moderating Effects of Privacy Concerns

Scholars construct theoretical models of privacy concerns from many different dimensions, Maslowska E et al. showed that consumers' personal traits significantly affect their privacy concerns [19]; according to Vieira A et al. AI learns people's preferences through algorithms and predicts that people's most favorite products or services are likely to be perceived in most cases as practical and convenient [20]. However, such AI services will be disliked by consumers when they themselves have a strong desire to explore and are willing to spend time and enjoy the process of finding the desired goods and services on their own [21]. De Keyzer F 's study shows that privacy concerns are an individual's personal endogenous character and attitude, and a level of consumer concern about speculations' behavior, and that consumers with different character have different attitudes and levels of trust about who has access to their information and how it is used when they are in an internet environment where information is disclosed [22]. Consumers' privacy concerns negatively affect users' willingness to purchase and adopt data-enabled boosts, and AI-based data-enabled boosts threaten consumers' privacy to a large extent, and the higher the degree of personalization perceived by consumers, the more likely it is to create a creepy feeling for people, as the recommended content and products show an overly close, overly familiar connection with the consumer, which in turn reduces the consumer's willingness to purchase the data-enabled boosts, willingness to purchase for data-enabled boosts [23,24]. Therefore, this study argues that in addition to the influence of the external environment (situational privacy concerns), consumer heterogeneity (privacy concerns) is also one of the important factors that need to be included in order to explore whether different types of consumers differ in their willingness to buy for data driven boosts. Therefore, this study proposes the hypotheses:

H3: Privacy concern plays a moderating role in the effect of datatization boosting on consumers' purchase intention.

H3a: When privacy concerns are low, consumers are more willing to purchase recommended content with high datatization boosts compared to recommended content with low datatization boosts.

H3b: When privacy concerns are high, the positive effect of data driven boosting on consumers' purchase intention is weakened compared to low data driven boosted recommended content.

This study explores the mechanism of the influence of data driven boosting on consumers' purchase intention under AI personalized recommendation, and how the mechanism of the influence of data driven boosting on consumers changes when the scenarios are different between high and low privacy concern, and between high and low privacy concern, and the conceptual model is shown in Figure 1.

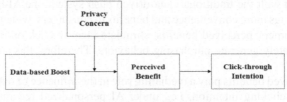

Figure 1. Conceptual framework

3. Experimental

To test the hypotheses, this study conducts 3 experiments. Experiment 1 selects an e-commerce takeout platform to explore the effect of data-based boosting on consumers' purchase intention, to verify H1; Experiment 2 selects a book website to explore whether perceived benefits play a mediating role in the effect of data-based boosting on consumers' purchase intention, to verify H2; and Experiment 3 selects different website service scenarios respectively to explore the moderating role of privacy concerns, to verify H3.

3.1. Experiment 1

3.1.1. Experimental Design

The questionnaires were distributed in two batches from March 6 to 30, 2023 through channels such as WeChat and Questionnaire Star, with the first batch of questionnaires distributed and collected from March 6 to 17, followed by the second batch of questionnaires, and a total of 268 valid questionnaires were collected in the two batches. Of the 68 samples, 160 or 76.92% were male; 108 or 51.92% were female. Finally, subjects were asked to fill out questionnaires measuring personalized data boosting, willingness to click, and personal information. Referring to the study by Van Doorn J, the questions measuring personalized recommendations were "This recommendation seems to be designed specifically for me" "This recommendation targets me as a unique user" [25]; referring to Mittal A et al. study, the question item measuring willingness to click was "I am willing to click on this recommendation for more detailed information" [26, 27]. All scales were measured using a Likert 7-point scale, with 1 being strongly disagree and 7 being strongly agree.

3.1.2. Experimental Results and Discussion

(1) Reliability analysis

From the results of the reliability analysis, it can be seen that the Cronbach's alpha value of the databased boosting scale is 0.852, indicating that the factors of the databased boosting scale are reliable, and the scores of each question item in the questionnaire are summed up and then averaged as the final value of the databased boosting, and then subjected to the main effect test.

(2) Correlation analysis

Before verifying the hypothesis, a preliminary correlation analysis of the relationship between the variables was carried out, and the results showed that the datatization boost was significantly positively correlated with the willingness to click, $r = 0.523$, $p < 0.010$, and further analysis of the variables could be done.

(3) Main effect test

Since the experimental process divides the data-based boosting of AI personalized recommendation into two groups, respectively pushing different contents, the manipulation test is carried out to verify whether the manipulation of data-based boosting is effective for the experimental group and the control group. Table 1 gives the results of the manipulation test of data-based boosting, through the independent samples t-test results show that the mean value of the low data-based boosting degree group is 4.306, with a standard deviation of 1.264; the mean value of the high data-based boosting group is 5.663, with a standard deviation of 1.053. $p < 0.001$, the results are significant, indicating that there is a significant difference in data-based boosting of the subjects in the two groups. the experimental process in the AI personalized recommendation system has been carried out in the experimental group and control group. recommender system is successful in manipulating the degree of data-based boosting.

Table 1. Data-based boosted independent sample T test results

Clusters	Sample size	Average value	Standard deviation	Standard Error Mean
Low-data-enabled	134	4.307	1.264	0.124
Supports low data volumes	134	5.708	1.053	0.103

To verify the influence of data-based promotion on consumers' clicking intention, independent sample t-test is conducted on the data of the two groups of subjects, and Figure 2 gives the consumers' clicking intention under different degrees of data-based promotion. The results show that the mean value of the high datatization boosting group is 5.663, and the standard deviation is 1.234; the mean value of the low datatization boosting group is 4.306, and the standard deviation is 1.528; and the impact of the high datatization boosting group on clicking willingness is significantly higher than that of the low datatization boosting group, with p<0.001, Cohen's d=0.888, and t(155)=6.798. H1 is verified.

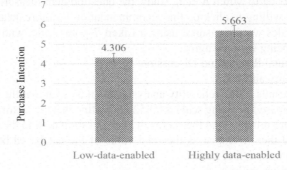

Figure 2(Experiment one). Click-through intention under different degrees of data-based boost

3.2. Experiment 2

3.2.1. Experimental Design
In Experiment 2, from April 1 to 16, 2023, the questionnaires were distributed in two batches through WeChat and Question star and other channels, the first batch of questionnaires were distributed and collected from April 1 to 8, after which the second batch of questionnaires were distributed and collected, a total of 300 questionnaires were distributed in the two batches, and 270 valid questionnaires were collected in the end. Among them, 145 (53.7%) were males and 125 (46.3%) were females. According to the questionnaire distribution batch, the subjects were divided into two groups of 135 each, high and low datatization boosting groups, and the difference between the experimental group and the control group was the same as in Experiment 1.

The subjects were informed that this was an experiment on memory, and the stronger the immersion when reading, the stronger the effect of memorization, to avoid the subjects guessing the intention of the experiment. The very first reading of the material was also about the characteristics of AI and the AI-based data-based boosting, to strengthen the consumers' knowledge about the characteristics of the AI-based data-based boosting.

3.2.2. Experimental Results and Discussion
    (1) Reliability analysis
    From the results of reliability analysis, it can be seen that the Cronbach's alpha value
of datatization boosting scale is 0.795, and the Cronbach's alpha value of perceived
benefit scale is 0.843, which indicates that these factors are reliable, and each item score
in the questionnaire is summed up and averaged as the final value of datatization boosting
and perceived benefit, and then the main effect and the main effect and the main effect
and the main effect are taken. Item scores in the questionnaire were summed and then
averaged as the final values of datatization boost and perceived benefit, and then the
main effect and mediation effect tests were conducted.
    (2) Correlation analysis
    The results of correlation analysis show that data-based boosting is significantly
positively correlated with clicking willingness, $r=0.609$, $p<0.010$; perceived benefit is
significantly positively correlated with clicking willingness, $r=0.420$, $p<0.010$; data-
based boosting is significantly positively correlated with perceived benefit, $r=0.239$,
$p<0.010$.
    (3) Main effects test
    Similar to Experiment 1, Table 2 gives the results of the manipulation test of
Experiment 2 on datatization boosting, from the independent samples t-test results, the
mean value of the low datatization boosting group is 3.569, and the standard deviation is
1.015; and the mean value of the high datatization boosting group is 5.525, and the
standard deviation is 0.754. $p < 0.001$, the results are significant, indicating that there is
a significant difference in the datatization boosting of the subjects in the two groups, and
the experimental manipulation is successful. Success.H1 was verified again.

Table 2(Experiment TWO). Data-based boosted independent sample T test results

Clusters	Sample size	Average value	Standard deviation	Standard Error Mean
Low-data enabled	135	4.307	1.264	0.124
Supports low data volumes	135	5.708	1.053	0.103

    (4) Mediating effect test
    To verify the mediating effect of perceived benefits, the Bootstrap method proposed
by PREACHE Retal was used to conduct the mediation test according to the mediation
effect test procedure summarized by ZHAO et al. The Process plug-in was installed in
spss and model 4 was selected with a confidence level of 95%. Input the datatization
boost as the independent variable, perceived benefit as the mediator variable, and click
willingness as the dependent variable into the model to verify whether the perceived
benefit plays a mediating role between datatization boost and purchase willingness. I test
whether the mediating effect is significant, i.e., the indirect effect of datatization boost
on purchase intention, the confidence interval is [0.036, 0.199], which does not contain
0, and passes the Sobel test, with $p < 0.050$, indicating that the mediating effect is
significant, and the value of the mediating effect is 0.100. ⅱ After controlling the
mediator variable of perceived benefit, test the direct effect of datatization boost on
purchase intention, which is given in Table 3. Table 3 gives the results of the mediation
effect test of perceived benefits. As shown in Table 3, after controlling the perceived
benefit, the direct effect of datatization boosting on purchase intention is still significant,
$\beta = 0.779$, $p < 0.001$, with a confidence interval of [0.605, 0.953], which does not contain

0. Therefore, the perceived benefit does not play a fully mediating role in the effect of datatization boosting on clicking intention and is not the only mediating variable. Therefore, H2 is validated.

Table 3. Mediating effect test results for perceived benefits

Variant	Perceived benefits			Willingness to buy		
	β	Standard error	t	β	Standard error	t
Intercept term perception	3.138***	0.357	8.783	1.172*	0.494	-2.373
Data-enabled boost	0.234**	0. 076	3. 095	0.779***	0.088	8. 847
Perceived benefits				0.430***	0.090	4.768
R^2	0.057			0.450		
F	9.578**			64.259***		

*** $p<0.001$, ** $p<0.010$, * $p<0.050$, two-sided test, same below.

3.3. Experiment 3

3.3.1. Experimental Design

Similar to Experiment 1 and Experiment 2, from April 20 to 31, 2023, the questionnaires were distributed in two batches through WeChat and Questionnaire Star and other channels, the 1st batch of questionnaires were distributed and collected from April 20 to 25, and then the 2nd batch of questionnaires were distributed and collected after that, and a total of 250 questionnaires were distributed in the two batches, and 228 valid questionnaires were collected in the end. Among them, there were 147 males, accounting for 64.601%; and 81 females, accounting for 35.398%.

Finally, subjects were asked to fill out questionnaires measuring datatization boosting, purchase intention, privacy concerns and personal information, while in the high and low datatization boosting groups under low privacy concerns, subjects also answered a few more questions about privacy concerns. The reason for choosing to measure the subjects' privacy concerns in the web service platform was to avoid that the high privacy concern scenario would exacerbate or more or less influence the consumers' responses.

3.3.2. Experimental Results and Discussion

(1) Reliability test

The reliability test of datatization boosting scale and privacy concern scale, the Cronbach's alpha value of datatization boosting scale is 0.875, the Cronbach's alpha value of perceived benefit scale is 0.842, and the Cronbach's alpha value of privacy concern scale is 0.869, and the scales of the three variables have a high degree of internal consistency. It indicates that these factors are reliable, and the scores of each question item can be summed up and averaged as the final values of datamining boost, perceived benefit and privacy concern.

(2) Correlation analysis

The results of correlation analysis show that datatization boost is significantly positively correlated with purchase intention, r = 0.461, p < 0.010; perceived benefit is significantly positively correlated with clicking intention, r = 0.320, p < 0.010; datatization boost is significantly positively correlated with perceived benefit, r = 0.312, p < 0.010; and privacy concern is significantly negatively correlated with datatization boost, clicking intention and perceived benefit, with correlation coefficients of -0.4% and -0.4%, respectively. The correlation coefficients are -0.415, -0.701, -0.363, p<0.010. Based on the above results, the variables can be further analyzed.

(3) Main effect test

From the results of independent sample t-test, it can be seen that the mean value of the low datatization boost group is 3.865, and the standard deviation is 0.735; the mean value of the high datatization boost group is 5.870, and the standard deviation is 0.642. p < 0.001, the results are significant, indicating that there is a significant difference in datatization boost of the two groups of subjects, and the experimental manipulation is successful. In order to verify the effect of databased boosting on consumers' click willingness, an independent sample t-test was conducted on the data of the two groups of subjects. The results show that the mean value of the high datatization boosting group is 5.872, and the standard deviation is 1.094; the mean value of the low datatization boosting group is 4.495, and the standard deviation is 1.566; the purchase intention of the high datatization boosting group on AI datatization boosting is significantly higher than that of the low datatization boosting group, with p < 0.001, Cohen's d = 0.879, and t(154)=7.141. H1 is verified.

(4) Moderating effect test of privacy concern

In order to study whether consumers' own privacy concern, that is, the concern for privacy, will affect the influence of data-based boosting on purchase intention, privacy concern is input into the model as a moderating variable, purchase intention as a dependent variable, and data-based boosting as an independent variable, and the moderating effect test is carried out. Table 5 gives the results of the moderating effect test of privacy concern, the interaction term of datatization boost and privacy concern has a significant effect on click willingness, $\beta = -0.154$, p < 0.010, R2 = 0.638; the results of the hierarchical regression show that putting the moderating variable into the regression equation brings about significant changes, $\Delta R2 = 0.025$, p < 0.010. Therefore, privacy concerns regulate the relationship between datamining boosts and purchase intentions.

Table 4. Independent -samples T test results for data-based boost

Clusters	Sample size	Average value	Standard deviation	Standard Error Mean
Low-data enabled	114	4.307	1.264	0.124
Supports low data volumes	114	5.708	1.053	0.103

Table 5 gives the direction of influence of the moderating effect of privacy concern, and it can be judged how the influence of databased boosting on consumer's click willingness is different when privacy concern is different, and Fig. 3 is plotted according to the results of Table 5.From Table 5 and Fig. 3, it can be seen that the privacy concern does not change the direction of the influence of high and low databased boosting on consumer's click willingness, i.e., the positive relationship between the two. The positive influence of data driven boosting on consumers' clicking intention is stronger for AI-based personalized recommendation.H3 is verified.

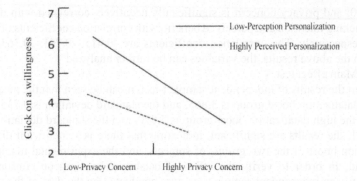

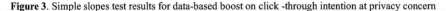

Figure 3. Simple slopes test results for data-based boost on click -through intention at privacy concern

4. Conclusion

This study investigates the influence mechanism of high or low data-enabled boosting of recommended content on consumers' click intention in the context of AI personalized recommendation, incorporating perceived benefit as a mediating variable. The results of this study show that: (i)AI personalized recommendation system positively affects clicking intention, and recommendation content with high data boost brings higher clicking intention, which is in line with the expectation of the study. (ii) Under AI personalized recommendation, perceived benefits play an important mediating role in consumer behavior, that is, consumers value the benefits brought to them by the data-enabled boost of AI recommendations. (iii) Privacy concerns play a moderating role in the mechanism of the influence of AI personalized recommendations on consumers' clicking intentions.

Acknowledgment

This project is supported by Nanning University ideological and political construction team "Market research ideological and political course team based on necklace model teaching" (2022SZJXTD09).

References

[1] Kietzmann J., Paschen J., Treen E. Artificial intelligence in advertising: How marketers can leverage artificial intelligence along the consumer journey[J]. Journal of Advertising Research, 2018, 58(3): 263-267.

[2] André Q, Carmon Z, Wertenbroch K et al. Consumer choice and autonomy in the age of artificial intelligence and big data[J]. Customer Needs and Solutions, 2018, 5: 28-37.

[3] Li Shiyu. Design and implementation of personalized recommendation system based on collaborative filtering algorithm[J]. Chinese Computer & Communication, 2018, (11): 53-54 (in Chinese).

[4] Cai Yong Jia, Li Guanyu, Guan Haoyuan. Personalized recommendation algorithm based on graph entropy in trust social network[J]. Journal of Computer Applications, 2019, 39(1): 176-180.

[5] Deng Lei, Yuan Chang Wei, Tian Gaohua. Application analysis and research of personalized recommendation system[J]. Digital Space, 2019, (3): 91.

[6] Huang Liwei, JIANG Bitao, LYU Shou ye, etal. Survey on deep learning based recommender systems. Chinese Journal of Computers[J], 2018, 41(7): 1619-1647 (in Chinese).

[7] Kai, Zhang Limin, Zhou Li jun. Survey of deep learning applied in information recommendation system[J]. Journal of Chinese Computer Systems, 2019, 40(4): 738-743 (in Chinese).

[8] Liu Huafeng, JING Liping, YU Jian. Survey of Matrix Factorization based recommendation methods by integrating social in-formation[J]. Journal of Software, 2018, 29(2): 340-362

[9] Zhang Yanbing，Lu Wei, Zhang Jia yu. Marketing re-search of Al: prospect and challenges[J]. Journal of Management Science, 2019, 32(5): 75-86.

[10] LI C. When does web-based personalization really work? The distinction between actual personalization and perceived personalization[J]. Computers in Human Behavior, 2016, 54: 25-33.

[11] Li C, Liu J. A name alone is not enough: A reexamination of web-based personalization effect[J]. Computers in Human Behavior, 2017, 72: 132-139.

[12] Gomez-Uribe C A, Hunt N. The netflix recommender system: Algorithms, business value, and innovation[J]. ACM Transactions on Management Information Systems (TMIS), 2015, 6(4): 1-19.

[13] West A, Clifford J, Atkinson D. "Alexa, build me a brand" An Investigation into the impact of Artificial Intelligence on Branding[J]. The Business & Management Review, 2018, 9(3): 321-330.

[14] Faggella D. Artificial intelligence in marketing and advertising-5 examples of real traction. Emerj[J]. 2019.

[15] Brinson N H, Eastin M S, Cicchirillo V J. Reactance to personalization: Understanding the drivers behind the growth of ad blocking[J]. Journal of Interactive Advertising, 2018, 18(2): 136-147.

[16] Goldfarb A, Tucker C E. Privacy regulation and online advertising[J]. Management science, 2011, 57(1): 57-71.

[17] Snehlata Barde et al. Scientific Approach of Prediction for Professions Using Machine Learning Classification Techniques. International Journal of Modern Education and Computer Science (IJMECS), 2023, 15(4): 30-42.

[18] Kramer T. The effect of measurement task transparency on preference construction and evaluations of personalized recommendations[J]. Journal of Marketing Research, 2007, 44(2): 224-233.

[19] Maslowska E, Smit E G, Van den Putte B. It is all in the name: A study of consumers' responses to personalized communication[J]. Journal of Interactive Advertising, 2016, 16(1): 74-85.

[20] Vieira A, Segal A. How banks can better serve their customers through artificial technology [M]// Unleashing the digital marketplace. Berlin, Heidelberg: Springer Berlin Heidelberg, 2017: 311-326.

[21] Verma S, Sharma R, Deb S, et al. Artificial intelligence in marketing: Systematic review and future research direction[J]. International Journal of Information Management Data Insights, 2021, 1(1): 100002.

[22] De Keyzer F, Dens N, De Pelsmacker P. Is this for me? How consumers respond to personalized advertising on social network sites[J]. Journal of Interactive Advertising, 2015, 15(2): 124-134.

[23] DAI Debao, LIU Xi yang, FAN Ti jun. Research on the adoption intention of online personalized recommender in the inter-net plus era[J]. China Soft Science, 2015(8): 163-172 (in Chinese).

[24] Singla M, Ghosh D, Shukla K K. A survey of robust optimization based machine learning with special reference to support vector machines[J]. International Journal of Machine Learning and Cybernetics, 2020, 11(7): 1359-1385.

[25] Van Doorn J, Hoekstra J C. Customization of online advertising: The role of intrusiveness[J]. Marketing Letters, 2013, 24: 339-351.

[26] Mittal A, Soundararajan R, Bovik A C. Making a "completely blind" image quality analyzer[J]. IEEE Signal processing letters, 2012, 20(3): 209-212.

[27] Qian Y. Image denoising algorithm based on improved wavelet threshold function and median filter[C]//2018 IEEE 18th International Conference on Communication Technology (ICCT). IEEE, 2018: 1197-1202.

Artificial Intelligence, Medical Engineering and Education
Z.B. Hu et al. (Eds.)
© *2024 The Authors.*
This article is published online with Open Access by IOS Press and distributed under the terms
of the Creative Commons Attribution Non-Commercial License 4.0 (CC BY-NC 4.0).
doi:10.3233/ATDE231343

Performance Evaluation System of University Government Procurement Under the Background of Integrated Central Budget Management

Wenzhe ZHAO, Qin SU[1], Qiang CHEN
Procurement and Tendering Office of Wuhan University of Technology, Wuhan, China

Abstract. With the promotion of the integration of central budget management, the importance of performance evaluation for university government procurement management is increasingly prominent. The establishment and improvement of the university government procurement performance evaluation system has become an urgent issue to be solved. This article analyzes relevant literature and combines the requirements of central budget management integration for university procurement work, designs performance evaluation indicators and constructs corresponding performance evaluation systems, in order to provide scientific decision-making basis for improving the quality and efficiency of university government procurement work.

Keywords. Integration of central budget management; Government procurement in universities; Performance evaluation system

1. Introduction

The management and transparency of fiscal budgets directly affect financial sustainability and even economic development [1, 2]. The integration of central budget management is one of the important contents of national financial management reform, aimed at improving the efficiency and transparency of financial resource utilization [3, 4]. The Notice of the Ministry of Finance on Promoting the Integration of Central Budget Management pointed out that each unit should recognize the important significance of budget management integration in improving the performance of financial fund utilization. As a public institution, universities' government procurement activities are also influenced by the integration of central budget management [5, 6]. To ensure the standardization, transparency, and effectiveness of university government procurement, establishing an efficient, orderly, and practical performance evaluation system for university government procurement is conducive to improving the efficiency of fund utilization and promoting the rational allocation of resources [7]. The research on the performance evaluation system of university government procurement at home and abroad provides a reference for this article [8]. Bolton Phoebe believes that the

---

[1] Corresponding Author: Qin SU, Email: 565791435@qq.com

performance evaluation of government procurement should focus on the economy and efficiency of financial funds.

Yue and Hou analyzed the procurement performance of universities using big data methods [9]. WU Guanyi explored the entire process management of university government procurement suppliers [10]. John Griffiths divided the indicators of the government procurement evaluation system into three aspects: cost, performance, and internal management [11]. Zhong Ming mentioned in the "Complete Book of Practical Operations for Chinese Government Procurement" that the fundamental goal of government procurement should be to maximize profits. During procurement, expenditure amounts should be strictly controlled and regulated, in order to reduce procurement costs [12]. Zhu Bao explored strategies to improve the quality of university procurement work from the perspective of connotation-based development [13]. Several other authors have conducted research on the sustainable development of government procurement and supply chain management from different perspectives [14-16]. Wang Xiaohong and others combined the principles of "3E" (economy, efficiency, and effectiveness) and added the principle of fairness, proposing the "4E" principle [17]. Xiao Ailin analyzed and optimized the performance evaluation index system of university government procurement from aspects such as value orientation, positioning mode, main structure, personnel arrangement, and content agreement, taking the relevant data of government procurement performance indicators of a certain university in Beijing as an example [18]. Analyzing the risk environment and proposing strategies and measures to reduce project risks are also important issues studied by scholars [19-21].

At present, most of the research focuses on the establishment and improvement of the government procurement performance evaluation system. Obviously, in the context of integrated central budget management, the research on the performance evaluation system of university government procurement has significant significance and challenges.

2. The Impact of the Integration of Central Budget Management on the Performance Evaluation of Government Procurement in Universities

Promoting the integrated reform of central budget management is to enhance the effectiveness of financial governance through integrated management methods and means. For universities, this is also a very important task.

(1) The government procurement work in universities has evolved from a relatively independent business to an important component of the central budget management integration system, which is more closely linked to budget management, fund payment, asset management, etc. Therefore, the performance evaluation of government procurement in universities needs to fully consider further expanding influencing factors and evaluation indicators.

(2) The integration of central budget management requires universities to carry out relevant management work based on procurement projects, implementing full lifecycle management for procurement project review, budget preparation, procurement, performance acceptance, fund payment, and asset warehousing, etc. This puts forward higher requirements for the accuracy of government procurement performance evaluation in universities.

3. Analysis of the Current Situation of Government Procurement Performance Evaluation in Universities

3.1. Current Situation of Performance Evaluation of Government Procurement in Universities

The problems in government procurement in universities are mainly reflected in the following three aspects.

(1) The system is not perfect. National laws, regulations, and policy requirements are the foundation for universities to carry out government procurement work. Currently, China has not yet introduced relevant regulations for government procurement performance evaluation work, and there is no relevant content in the government procurement rules and regulations of universities, which increases the difficulty of government procurement performance evaluation work in universities.

(2) Lack of management experience. The government procurement work in universities is characterized by strong professionalism, diversity, and complex funding sources. Currently, there are many problems in the performance management of government procurement in universities in China, such as lack of experience, incomplete performance management system, and superficial performance evaluation. In practice, the subjective judgment of workers is mainly relied on to solve problems.

(3) Deviation in regulatory direction. The supervision of government procurement work by universities mainly focuses on the compliance and legality of procurement procedures, with a focus on monitoring the work process of procurement departments. The supervision of performance management after the procurement process is relatively weak, and performance evaluation work needs to be strengthened.

3.2. Problems in the Performance Evaluation System of Government Procurement in Universities

There are still some shortcomings or weaknesses in the existing government procurement evaluation system in universities. It can be summarized as follows.

(1) The evaluation system is not perfect enough. The existing evaluation system mainly focuses on compliance and cost savings in the procurement process, but lacks consideration for the benefits, effectiveness, and efficiency of procurement. The evaluation results are not comprehensive and objective enough to truly reflect the actual benefits of procurement.

(2) The evaluation indicators are not scientific enough. At present, the various indicators within the evaluation system are independent of each other and mainly rely on quantitative indicators and financial data, with insufficient consideration given to non-quantitative indicators and qualitative factors. Resulting in a lack of persuasiveness in the evaluation results, making it difficult to reflect the actual situation.

(3) The evaluation method is not reasonable enough. In practical operation, a large number of evaluation indicators involving various aspects of government procurement are often selected, and the indicators generally have complex interrelationships. The existing evaluation methods mainly rely on experience and personal judgment, lacking scientificity and impartiality. This leads to a certain degree of subjectivity and one-sidedness in the evaluation results, making it difficult to convince the public.

4. Construction of a Performance Evaluation System for University Government Procurement

This article establishes the basic idea of constructing a performance evaluation system for university government procurement, as shown in Figure 1. That is, based on the relevant documents and systems of government procurement and performance management, following the principles of data standardization, full process, mobility, and intelligence, supported by the university management system, internal control system, and information system, to achieve the goal of optimizing the performance of university government procurement. The construction of an evaluation system mainly includes three aspects: performance evaluation indicator system, evaluation methods, and evaluation process.

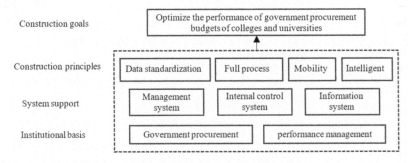

Figure 1. Construction ideas for the performance evaluation system of government procurement in universities

4.1. Design of Performance Evaluation Index System for University Government Procurement

4.1.1. Design Method of Evaluation Index System

The foundation of constructing the indicator system is the evaluation content. This article uses the Analytic Hierarchy Process to analyze the evaluation indicators based on the attributes of the evaluation content, and conducts top-down stratification. The Analytic Hierarchy Process (AHP) is based on in-depth analysis of the essence, influencing factors, and internal relationships of complex decision-making problems. It utilizes quantitative information to mathematize the thinking process of decision-making, thereby providing a simple decision-making method for complex decision-making problems with multi-objective, multi-criteria, or unstructured characteristics.

4.1.2. Design of Evaluation Index System

Government procurement in universities has the characteristics of large demand, complex projects, high timeliness requirements, and strong technical capabilities. The basic value orientation of its performance evaluation is oriented towards efficiency, order, fairness, and democracy. The construction of a performance evaluation system for university government procurement is limited to the self-evaluation within the university procurement department and user units, neglecting the interaction between the procurement department, user units, and suppliers. This evaluation system lacks external supervision and is not conducive to improving the performance management of university government procurement. Through literature review and the use of Analytic Hierarchy Process, combined with the actual government procurement work in universities, following the principles of fairness, impartiality, comprehensiveness, relativity, and operability, six primary indicators were designed, namely economy, efficiency, effectiveness, legality and openness, sociality, and innovation. Design 32 secondary indicators based on 6 primary indicators and construct a performance evaluation indicator system as shown in Figure 2.

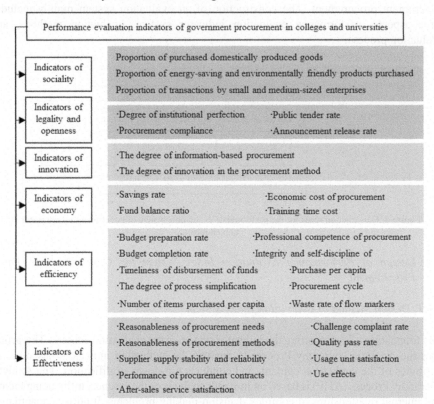

Figure 2. Framework of performance evaluation index system for university government procurement

Economy is the most fundamental factor in the procurement performance evaluation system. No matter which analysis method is used, economic factors cannot be ignored. Building a procurement performance evaluation system does not consider economic benefits, just like evaluating the performance of a car does not consider engine performance. Efficiency is a key factor in performance evaluation and one of the factors that can intuitively reflect government procurement work through data. Effectiveness is a comprehensive factor in performance evaluation and a collection of feedback from all stakeholders. Government procurement work in universities serves the entire governance of universities, and the effectiveness of procurement work plays an important role in the development of universities. Legitimacy and openness are the red lines of government procurement work and important factors in procurement performance evaluation.

Sociology refers to the degree to which government procurement work implements relevant national policies at the current stage. Universities should closely follow the government's footsteps and make contributions to social development. Innovation is the development trend and inevitable requirement of government procurement work in the information age. The performance evaluation system of university government procurement should have certain foresight for the future, which is in line with the development direction of government procurement work.

4.2. Performance Evaluation Methods for Government Procurement in Universities

The evaluation method includes a combination of qualitative and quantitative evaluation. Firstly, the properties of the 32 secondary indicators in the indicator system are defined, and then the weights of the 32 secondary indicators are determined through three rounds of Delphi method. Take the arithmetic mean method as the final result:

$$W_j = \frac{1}{n}\sum_{i=1}^{n} w_{ij}$$

(1)

Among them, W_j is the arithmetic mean of the j-th indicator, n is the number of experts, and W_{ij} is the scoring value of the i-th expert $i(i = 1, 2, \cdots, n)$ on the indicator j. And the degree of coordination of expert opinions is reflected through the coefficient of variation.

$$CV_j = \frac{\sigma_j}{W_j}$$

(2)

Among them, σ_j is the standard deviation of all experts' evaluation of indicator j:

$$\sigma_j = \sqrt{\frac{1}{n}\sum_{i=1}^{n} (w_{ij} - W_j)^2}$$

(3)

The smaller the value CV, the higher the degree of coordination and convergence of expert opinions. After repeated consultation, induction, and modification, the opinions of the experts were basically consistent. After summarizing and organizing, the weight results of each indicator are shown in Table 1. The last column in the table refers to the nature of the evaluation indicators, which can be divided into qualitative and quantitative categories, represented by Q_1 and Q_2 respectively.

Table 1. Analysis of the Performance Evaluation Index System for Government Procurement in Universities

Primary indicators		Secondary indicators		
Type	Weight	concrete content	Weight	Nature
Economy	0.17	Fund savings rate	0.1	Q_2
		Fund balance rate	0.01	Q_2
		Economic cost of procurement	0.04	Q_2
		Training time cost	0.02	Q_2
Efficiency	0.34	Budgeting rate	0.08	Q_2
		Budget completion rate	0.08	Q_2
		Timeliness of fund payment	0.03	Q_1
		Degree of process simplification	0.02	Q_1
		Per capita procurement amount	0.01	Q_2
		Number of procurement projects per capita	0.01	Q_2
		Procurement cycle	0.04	Q_2
		Professional competence of procurement personnel	0.01	Q_1
		Honesty and self-discipline ability of procurement personnel	0.01	Q_1
		Rejection rate of flow standard	0.05	Q_2
Effectiveness	0.17	Rationality of procurement requirements	0.02	Q_1
		Rationality of procurement method	0.01	Q_1
		Challenge and complaint rate	0.03	Q_2
		Supplier supply stability and reliability	0.02	Q_1
		Performance of procurement contracts	0.02	Q_2
		Quality qualification rate	0.01	Q_2
		User satisfaction	0.03	Q_1
		Usage effect	0.02	Q_1
		Satisfaction with after-sales service	0.01	Q_1
Legitimacy and Publicity	0.18	Degree of institutional improvement	0.05	Q_1
		Procurement compliance	0.03	Q_1
		Public bidding rate	0.03	Q_2
		Announcement release rate	0.07	Q_2
Sociology	0.12	Proportion of domestic goods purchased	0.04	Q_2
		Proportion of purchasing energy-saving and environmental protection products	0.04	Q_2
		Transaction proportion of small and medium-sized enterprises	0.04	Q_2
Innovation	0.02	Degree of information procurement	0.01	Q_1
		Innovation level of procurement methods	0.01	Q_1

4.3. Performance Evaluation Process for University Government Procurement

Based on factors such as school policies and government regulations, develop a performance evaluation process for university government procurement, including data collection, data processing, and feedback on evaluation results. The data collection stage mainly collects various data and information related to the procurement project, including the entire procurement process, procurement content, price, delivery cycle, supplier service quality, etc. In addition, it is also necessary to collect data on the capabilities, user satisfaction, and usage of procurement personnel. After collecting sufficient data, it is necessary to process and analyze it, and use information technology to clean, organize, classify, summarize, compare, and calculate the data, in order to obtain indicators that can reflect procurement performance. Based on the results of data processing, form a conclusion for performance evaluation, and then feedback this conclusion to relevant departments and personnel, which helps to propose more effective optimization strategies and implementation plans.

5. Conclusion

The new era background and special requirements faced by government procurement in universities. In today's integrated development of central budget management, it is an urgent task to comprehensively analyze the problems existing in the system and explore their root causes, in order to identify methods and approaches to solve the problems.

This article analyzes the problems in the practical process of the performance evaluation system for university government procurement, combines the principles and methods of constructing the performance evaluation system, designs evaluation indicators, and constructs a performance evaluation system, which plays a positive role in improving the management level of university government procurement. It is recommended that universities evaluate and improve their government procurement activities based on the performance evaluation system, with the aim of promoting the standardized and scientific development of government procurement work in universities.

References

[1]   Cuadradoballesteros B, Bisogno M, Grossi D. G. Budget transparency and financial sustainability[J]. Journal of Public Budgeting, Accounting & Financial Management, 2022, 34(6): 210-234.
[2]   Gill J, Sharma U. Public sector financial management in New Zealand central government: the role of?public sector accountants[J].Journal of Public Budgeting, Accounting & Financial Management, 2023, 35(1): 65-72.
[3]   Wang Xiaolong. Steadily promoting the integration of central budget management[J]. China Finance, 2022, (15): 3 (in Chinese).
[4]   Li Yanpei. Practice of integrated budget management reform in central budget units[J]. China Agricultural Accounting, 2023, 33 (15): 60-62 (in Chinese).
[5]   Huang Yixin. Exploration of comprehensive budget management in central budget units in the new era[J]. Finance News, 2019, (31): 1 (in Chinese).
[6]   Cao Guoqiang, Ding Jiangbin. Reflections and suggestions on performance management of government procurement in central budget units[J]. Chinese Government Procurement, 2018, (11): 34-38 (in Chinese).
[7]   Zhang Xiaoli, Sun Xuetong. Construction of a performance evaluation index system for government procurement in universities[J]. Knowledge Economy, 2018, (16): 89-91 (in Chinese).

[8]   Phoebe B. Government procurement as a policy tool in South Africa[J]. Journal of Public Procurement, 2007, 4: 43-51.

[9]   Yue Tongwen, Hou Yi. A study of university procurement performance based on big data on government procurement[J]. Academic Journal of Business & Management, 2023, .5(4): 77-86

[10]   WU Guanyi. Whole Process Management of Government Procurement Suppliers in Colleges and Universities[J]. Research & Exploration in Laboratory, 2019, .38(11): 282-300.

[11]   Griffiths J. Benchmarking using principal component analysis and the method of combining screening government procurement performance evaluation[J]. Governmental Purchasing, 2013, 5: 65-68.

[12]   Zhong Ming. Complete book of practical operations in Chinese Government Procurement[M]. Beijing: China Times Economic Publishing House, 2001 (in Chinese).

[13]   Zhu Bao. Analysis of strategies for improving the quality of university procurement work from the perspective of intensive development[J]. China Modern Equipment Education, 2022, (8): 41-42+46 (in Chinese)

[14]   Schmidt A. T. Construction supply chain welcomes new report on government infrastructure procurement[J]. Highway Engineering in Australia: Transport Infrastructure Traffic Management Intelligent Transport Systems, 2022, (3): 53.

[15]   Wirahadikusumah R, Abduh M, Messah Y. Framework for sustainable procurement - identifying elements for construction works[J]. Applied Mechanics and Materials, 2020, 897: 245-249.

[16]   Anstis, Siena. Government procurement law and hacking technology: The role of public contracting in regulating an invisible market[J]. Computer Law & Security Review, 2021, (41): 105536.

[17]   Wang Xiaohong, Zhang Baosheng, Pan Zhigang. Construction of performance evaluation index system for government procurement in China[J]. China Government Procurement, 2010, (3): 75-77 (in Chinese).

[18]   Xiao Ailin. Optimization of the indicator system for evaluating the performance of government procurement in universities: taking the practice of a university in Beijing as an example[J]. Dongyue Analects 2013, 34(11): 162-165 (in Chinese).

[19]   Rusk S. Front-end strategies to reduce project risks[J]. CIM Magazine, 2019, (2): 14.

[20]   J. Hallikas, V.Virolainen, M. Tuominen. Risk analysis environments: a dyadic case study[J]. Journal and Assessment in Network of Production Economics, 2002, (07): 45-55.

[21]   Neu D. Everett J., Rahaman A. S. Preventing corruption within government procurement: Constructing the disciplined and ethical subject[J]. Critical Perspectives on Accounting, 2015, 28: 49-61.

Artificial Intelligence, Medical Engineering and Education
Z.B. Hu et al. (Eds.)
© 2024 The Authors.
This article is published online with Open Access by IOS Press and distributed under the terms
of the Creative Commons Attribution Non-Commercial License 4.0 (CC BY-NC 4.0).
doi:10.3233/ATDE231344

Intelligent Identification and Analysis of Stakeholders in Waterway Engineering Projects

Yongchao ZOU[a], Peilin ZHANG[a], Shengrong LU[b,1]

ª School of Transportation and Logistics, Wuhan University of Technology, Wuhan, China

ᵇ School of Business Administration, Wuhan Business University, Wuhan, China

Abstract. The waterway engineering project belongs to a government public investment project, with the goal of emphasizing the harmony and unity of the economic benefits, environment, and social aspects of the waterway, and the needs of stakeholders represent the performance of different aspects of the waterway engineering project goals. Focusing solely on the needs of a certain type of stakeholders not only fails to ensure the sustainability of waterway engineering projects, but may also affect the smooth implementation of waterway engineering construction. This article starts from the factors that affect the interests of waterway engineering projects, preliminarily identifies stakeholders, and then identifies and classifies stakeholders in the decision-making stage of the project from the perspectives of initiative, influence, and interest. Core stakeholders, general stakeholders, and marginal stakeholders are identified, providing decision-making reference for waterway construction and governance.

Keywords. Waterway Engineering Project; Stakeholders; Recognition

1. Introduction

The concept of stakeholders originated from the Stanford University Research Institute and is defined as "stakeholders are all individuals and groups who can influence or be influenced by the process of achieving an organization's goals." The results of cooperation, influence, and constraints among stakeholders determine the degree to which an organization's ultimate goals are achieved, which is crucial for project success or improving project performance.

Stakeholders were first proposed by Freeman [1] and divided into one-dimensional categories. Subsequently, Clarkson [2], Wheelers [3], and Mitchell [4] conducted two-dimensional and combinatorial segmentation of stakeholders. In terms of identification, scholars such as Nguyen [5] adopt direct identification of stakeholders, and after providing a definition of stakeholders, they directly obtain the identification object. Scholars such as Newcombe [6], Famiyeh [7], Eskerod [8], and Lv Ping [9] use literature analysis and expert interviews to identify project stakeholders. In terms of analysis methods, scholars have proposed methods such as multidimensional subdivision, social network analysis, and role linkage matrix [10-13]. At present, when scholars use

---

¹ Corresponding Author: Shengrong LU, E-mail: 370013501@qq.com.

multidimensional analysis, there is no clear and unified analytical framework for dimension selection and quantity, and there is relatively little research on stakeholders in waterway engineering projects. Based on this, this article attempts to study the categories of stakeholders in waterway projects from the perspective of stakeholders and the actual situation, clarifying the differences in interest demands of different stakeholders, In order to fully consider the demands of stakeholders at all levels and make targeted decisions in future waterway project planning.

1.1. Concept of Stakeholders in Waterway Engineering

Referring to the concept of stakeholders mentioned earlier, stakeholders in waterway engineering projects refer to individuals or groups who can influence the goals of the waterway engineering project or are affected by the process of achieving the goals of the waterway engineering project.

1.2. Interest demands of stakeholders in waterway engineering projects

Carrying out waterway engineering construction in rivers involves numerous influencing factors. From the perspective of interest impact, the main concerns of stakeholders regarding waterway engineering include:

(1) The improvement effect of waterway engineering construction on waterway conditions, thereby promoting the development benefits of shipping and port industry.

(2) The impact of improving waterway conditions on resource development, industrial development, employment opportunities, and economic income.

(3) The impact of the implementation of waterway engineering on the production activities of residents and fishermen along the river.

(4) The water administration department is concerned about whether the waterway project will affect the connectivity of the river, and whether the construction of the project will have an impact on the flood control of the river.

(5) The environmental protection department is concerned about the impact of waterway engineering on river ecology and aquatic organisms.

(6) As participants in the construction of waterway engineering projects, the design party and construction party are concerned about the commercial benefits and social reputation brought by the engineering construction.

(7) The waterway operation and maintenance department is concerned about maintenance costs and subsequent safety hazards.

2. Stakeholder Analysis Based on System Dynamics

Based on the main concerns of stakeholders regarding waterway engineering, this study mainly adopts the following three steps for stakeholder identification: ① literature analysis: analyze and organize the literature on existing waterway engineering project stakeholders, and preliminarily define the stakeholders of waterway engineering projects; ② Expert judgment: Invite experts in the field of waterway construction to conduct interviews, allowing them to make comprehensive judgments from multiple fields and perspectives, and determine the final stakeholders; ③ System dynamics analysis: From the perspective of waterway engineering project construction, study various stakeholders as system variables and analyze the main causal relationships between variables; ④ Dimensional analysis, collecting and organizing data, and distinguishing the importance of stakeholders; ⑤ Construction cycle analysis: Conduct separate analysis of stakeholders in different project cycles to clarify their changing trends.

| Document Analysis | Expert Judgment | System Dynamics Analysis | Dimensional Analysis | Construction Cycle Analysis |

| Preliminary definition | Identify determine | Related relationships | Classification | Trend |

Figure 1. Stakeholder Identification and Analysis Steps

2.1. Identification of Stakeholders in Waterway Engineering Projects

Waterways belong to a type of public goods. The management and construction of waterways are the responsibility of the government.

1. Initial stakeholder list

Based on the analysis of existing literature, stakeholders of waterway engineering project have been preliminarily defined,including: Government (investors), Project Agent Units, Shipping Enterprise, Port Enterprises, Operation and Maintenance Units, The Public, Water Administration Departments, Environmental Protection Departments, Design Parties, Construction Parties, Material and Equipment Suppliers, Supervision Party, Audit Units, Scientific Research Institutions, Insurance Company, Medium.

2. Finalized stakeholders

In this expert interview, a total of 10 senior experts in the shipping industry were selected, and the interviews were mainly conducted face-to-face and telephone. Through organizing and summarizing the opinions of 10 experts, the following suggestions are obtained: ① The construction of waterway engineering is conducive to the development of ports along the line, and ports and shipping enterprises should be regarded as stakeholders, and shipping enterprises and ports can be merged as end users; ② Both the supervising party and the auditing unit are responsible for controlling and supervising the engineering project, and can be merged as the supervising and auditing party; ③ Insurance companies generally do not participate in waterway engineering construction and do not consider them as stakeholders; ④ Media participation is low and not a stakeholder.

Convene a special group discussion to discuss the list of stakeholders determined after expert interviews. Participants are requested to screen the confirmed stakeholders. Based on the above discussion, a total of 12 types of stakeholders for waterway engineering projects are defined based on the selection percentage exceeding 60%, including Government, Project Agent Units(Agent), End Users(Users), Operation and Maintenance Units(Operation), Social Public(Public), Water Administration Departments(Water), Environmental Protection Departments(Environment), Design Parties(Design), Construction Parties(Construction), Material and Equipment Suppliers(Material), Supervision and Audit Units(Supervision) and Scientific Research Institutions(Research).

2.2. Analysis of Stakeholder Relationships Based on System Dynamics

1. Objectives of the waterway engineering project system

The goal of the system can be expressed as: to coordinate and promote the construction of waterway engineering projects with social, economic development, and environmental protection.

2. Model Assumptions

In order to ensure the integrity of the model and accurately describe the actual causal process, factors with weaker correlation such as population level and consumption level are removed. From the perspective of waterway engineering project construction, the final user, operation and maintenance, social public, environmental protection and water conservancy are studied as variables in the waterway engineering project system.

3. Main causal relationships of waterway engineering project system

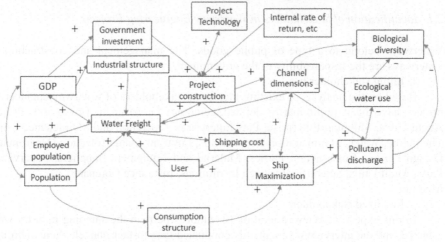

Figure 2. Correlation diagram of waterway engineering project system

The construction of waterway engineering projects has driven the growth of shipping demand in economic and social aspects, such as GDP, population, and water freight volume, which puts forward higher requirements for the construction level and navigation efficiency of the waterway. In terms of environmental protection and water conservancy, increasing the depth of the waterway will to some extent reduce the biodiversity of the aquatic ecosystem. Expanding the width of the waterway and increasing the number of renovation projects will damage the vegetation cover on both sides of the slope protection and the development of natural reserves. Therefore, increasing the scale of the waterway may have negative benefits for the sustainable development of the ecological environment in the watershed. In summary, there are complex relationships among stakeholders in waterway engineering projects. There is both positive and negative feedback, and it is necessary to take the system as a whole and coordinate its development.

3. Empirical Analysis

In recent years, with the construction of the 12.5 meter deep water channel below Nanjing on the Yangtze River trunk line and the formation of the upstream Three Gorges Reservoir area, the conditions of the upstream and downstream channels on the Yangtze River trunk line have been greatly improved. However, the section of the Yangtze River from Wuhan to Anqing is mostly curved or slightly curved, and the waterway conditions are complex, requiring waterway regulation.

For government investment projects, according to the general project lifecycle classification standards, the entire process of waterway engineering projects can be divided into four stages: project decision-making stage, design stage, project implementation stage, and completion acceptance stage. This article takes the classification of stakeholders in the project decision-making stage as an example, combining three dimensions of initiative, influence, and profitability to classify stakeholders. Finally, a dynamic dimension analysis of the lifecycle is carried out.

3.1. Dimensional analysis of stakeholders

By analyzing the literature and taking into account the characteristics of waterway engineering projects themselves, we can simplify the complexity and grasp the main contradictions, and summarize the analysis perspectives of stakeholders into three main dimensions: initiative, influence, and profitability.

1. Data collection

Considering the characteristics of waterway engineering projects, a survey questionnaire is designed. Based on the 5-level Likert scale, the initiative, influence, and interests of 13 stakeholders in waterway engineering projects are judged, with "1" representing very unimportant, "2" representing relatively unimportant, "3" representing average, "4" representing relatively important, and "5" representing non very important.

The survey questionnaire adopts two forms: paper questionnaire and online questionnaire. A total of 200 questionnaires were distributed, and 174 questionnaires were actually collected, with a recovery rate of 87%. Among them, 101 valid questionnaires were collected, with a response rate of 58.05%. In order to ensure the reliability of the questionnaire data, the Cronbach's Ahpha coefficients were calculated for the 101 questionnaires. The results showed that the coefficients for initiative, influence, and benefit were 0.784, 0.709, and 0.843, respectively, with coefficients greater than 0.7, indicating that the questionnaire data had high reliability.

2. Data analysis method - Mann Whitney U-test

The Mann Whitney U-test can be used to determine whether two populations are the same at the center, that is, to examine whether the median Mx of population X and the median My of population Y are equal. Therefore, the following hypothesis can be proposed:

$$H_0 : M_x = M_y$$
$$H_1 : M_x \neq M_y \tag{1}$$

If H0 is true, mix the data of M x and N y and arrange them together. If most of x is greater than y, or most of y is greater than x, it cannot be proven that n+m=N data come from the same population, and H0 is rejected. The statistical value of the Mann Whitney U-test is U. If the U-value is higher than a certain level of significance (usually set at 0.05), it indicates that there is no difference, and the H0 hypothesis is accepted. Otherwise, it indicates that there is a significant difference, and H0 should be rejected and H1 should be accepted.

3.Data Analysis

The statistical analysis conducted using the Mann Whitney U-test mainly includes:
1) whether there are differences in initiative among stakeholders in waterway

engineering projects; 2) Whether there are differences in influence; 3) Are there any differences in terms of interests.

Firstly, calculate the average initiative of each stakeholder in the construction of waterway engineering projects, and use the Mann Whitney U-test to determine whether there are differences in their contributions. The data analysis results are shown in the table below.

Table 1. Description of the mean of initiative among various stakeholders

Stakeholders	Mean value	Variance	Ranking	Significant differences
Government	4.787	0.685	1	8
Agent	4.632	0.651	2	8
Construction	3.578	1.236	11	3
Design	3.722	1.054	10	3
Material	3.402	1.366	12	2
Public	3.881	1.136	8	6
Supervision	4.472	1.042	5	7
Operation	4.49	1.038	4	6
Research	3.974	1.069	7	7
Environment	3.725	1.163	9	5
Water	4.382	0.946	6	5
Users	4.625	0.681	3	9

From the above table, it can be seen that the stakeholder with the most differences from other stakeholders is the Users, with a total of 9 stakeholders showing significant differences in initiative; The top 3 stakeholders in the average score of initiative, namely Government, Agent, and Users, are more consistent with those who show significant differences. Therefore, it is possible to consider the mean value of each stakeholder and the number of significant differences with other stakeholders.Identify stakeholders as shown in the table above.

By using similar methods for identifying stakeholders in terms of initiative as mentioned above, the stakeholders in terms of influence and profitability can be identified, resulting in the following results.

Table 2 Three dimensional classification results of project stakeholders in the decision-making stage

Dimension	Initiative	Impact	Benefit oriented
Core stakeholders	Government/Agent/ Users	Government/Agent/ Water/Environment	Government/Agent/ Users
General stakeholders	Water/Environment/ Operation/Supervisi on/Research	Supervision/Operation /Users/Design/ Construction/Material	Design/Construction/ Material/Operation/ Research/Supervision
Marginal stakeholders	Designer/Constructi on/Material/Public	Research/Public	Environment/Water/ Public

Based on the classification of stakeholders from three dimensions, the 12 categories of project stakeholders in the decision-making stage of waterway engineering projects can be classified as follows:

(1) Core stakeholders. At least two dimensions are core stakeholders who are indispensable and closely related to the project process. In the decision-making stage of waterway engineering projects, the core stakeholders are the Government and Agent. The Government is the ultimate decision-maker of the project, providing necessary resources and funds to ensure that the project results meet the needs. Their attitude and behavior are crucial for the impact of the project. Agent also plays an important role in the decision-making stage of waterway engineering projects. In addition, local governments promote the development of water transportation through waterway engineering renovation, thereby promoting the development of local economy.

(2) General stakeholders. At least two dimensions are general stakeholders. They often form a close relationship with the project, and their impact cannot be ignored. In the decision-making stage of waterway engineering projects, there are Operation, Users, Water, Environmental, Design, Construction, Material, Research, Supervision. The water administration department and environmental protection department have administrative approval power and play an important role in project decision-making. As beneficiaries of project results, end users have significant influence on the project and actively participate in the project.

(3) Marginal stakeholders. It scores at least two dimensions among marginal stakeholders, such as Public.

3.2. Stakeholder Changes at Different Stages of the Project Cycle

There are significant differences in the importance of the same stakeholders at different stages of the project construction lifecycle, exhibiting dynamic changes. By using the same method as in the decision-making stage, the classification of stakeholders in the design, implementation, and completion stages can be obtained, as shown in Figure 3.

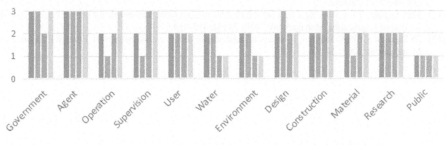

■ Decision ■ Design ■ Implementation ■ Project Acceptance

Note: The vertical axis 1 represents marginal stakeholders, 2 represents general stakeholders, and 3 represents core stakeholders.

Figure 3 Stakeholders at Each Stage of the Project Lifecycle

Stakeholder participation demonstrates the fairness and justice of public products in waterway engineering. Therefore, it is necessary to enhance the ability to scientifically identify stakeholders, strengthen the coordination and management of conflicts among stakeholders, improve the institutional mechanisms for stakeholder participation in decision-making of waterway engineering projects, and enhance the effectiveness of public participation, promoting transparency, legality, and scientificity in decision-making of waterway engineering projects Improvement of effectiveness.

Acknowledgment

This project is supported by Research Projects of China Society of Logistics(2023CSLKT3-310).

References

[1] Freeman, R, E, Strategic management: A stakeholder approach[M]. Boston, MA: Pitman, 1984
[2] Clarkson Me. A stakeholder framework for analyzing and evaluating corporate social performance[J]. Academy of Management Review, 1995,20 (1): 92-117.
[3] Wheeler D, Sillanpa M. Including the stakeholders: the business case[J]. Long Range Planning, 1998, 31 (2): 201-210.
[4] Mitchell A and Wood. Toward a theory of stakeholder identification and salience defining the principle of who and what really counts[J]. The Academy of Management Review. 1997.22 (4) 853-886.
[5] Nhat Hong Nguyen, Martin Skitmore, Johnny Kwok Wai Wong. Stakeholder impact analysis of infrastructure project management in developing countries: a study of perception of project managers in state-owned engineering firms in Vietnam[J]. Construction Management & Economics, 2009, 27 (11): 1129-1140.
[6] Robert Newcombe From client to project stakeholders: a stakeholder mapping approach[J]. Construction Management & Economics, 2003, 21 (8): 841-848
[7] Famiyeh, Samuel. Socially responsible mining using project stakeholder identification and management[J]. Journal of Global Responsibility, 2017, 8(2):151-168.
[8] Eskerod P, Huemann M, Savage G. Project stakeholder management-past and present[J]. Project Management Journal, 2015, 46(6): 6–14.
[9] Wang Jin, Xu Yujie. Classification of stakeholders in large engineering projects[J]. Journal of Railway Science and Engineering, 2009, 6 (5): 77-83.
[10] Lv Ping, Hu Huanhuan, Guo Shuping. Empirical study on stakeholder classification of government investment projects[J]. Journal of Engineering Management, 2013 (1): 39-43.
[11] Mao Xiaoping, Lu Huimin, Li Qiming. Stakeholder study on sustainable construction of engineering projects in China[J]. Journal of Southeast University (Philosophy and Social Sciences Edition), 2012, 14 (2): 46-50 (in Chinese).
[12] Shen Qiping, Yang Jing. Research on stakeholder management framework for construction projects[J]. Journal of Engineering Management, 2010, 24 (4): 412-419.
[13] Jia Shenghua, Chen Honghui. A review of methods for defining stakeholders[J]. Foreign Economics and Management, 2002, 24 (5): 13-18.

Part 2

Systems Engineering and Analysis:
Concepts, Methods, and Applications

Artificial Intelligence, Medical Engineering and Education
Z.B. Hu et al. (Eds.)

351

doi:10.3233/ATDE231346

New Approach to Assessing Structural Complexity

Nataliia VOZNA[1]

Department of Specialized Computer Systems, West Ukrainian National University,
Ternopil, Ukraine
The University College of Applied Science in Chelm, Chelm, Poland

ORCID ID: Nataliia Vozna https://orcid.org/0000-0002-8856-1720

Abstract. The work is devoted to solving a scientific problem of the development of methodology for improvement of multifunctional computing devices structures, which are the components of complex computer systems. Multifunctional data that are generated, transformed, transmitted, stored, processed and used in modern distributed IoT systems is defined. The use of this data simplifies the operations to be performed. New theoretical and applied bases of evaluation and calculation criteria of structural complexity of the created and applied components of complex distributed computer and cyber physical systems are determined and the existing ones are developed that allowed improving system characteristics of computerized systems components and using them efficiently in cyber physical systems due to the reduction of structural, hardware and time complexity.

Keywords. Structuring, structured multifunctional data, structural complexity criteria, distributed computer systems, functional, structural, entropy complexity.

1. Introduction

Information telecommunications systems and IT technologies for data generation, transmission, processing, storage and use are considered to be an important functional environment of modern society.

The concept of multifunctional data (MFD) refers to a wide range of information message types in physical, logical and virtual data environments, for example, analog and digital output sensor data and analog-to-digital converter output data, digital output compression encoder data, data on encryption and protection against errors, output data of special-purpose processors and controllers of digital information processing, modulated and manipulated signals of data transmission systems, physical and logical data in databases and knowledge bases, alphanumeric data, graphic information.

Advanced computer equipment can be developed due to the extension of its multifunctional characteristics by integrating algorithms, calculations and component structures of the computer system processors.

This research work focuses on the development of the method for assessing the structural complexity and a set of performance criteria, which is a completely new issue topic in scientific literature. This approach makes it possible to solve the applied

---

[1] Corresponding Author: Nataliia VOZNA, nvozna@ukr.net.

problems of comparing the structural complexity (SC) of different classes of data in order to improve their system characteristics, in particular, the time and hardware complexity of digital data generator structures, computing tools, algorithms, methods for multifunctional data encoding and converting.

Well-known scientists such as J.Martin, Thomas J. Harrison, A.S.Wilsky [1-3] pioneered certain issues of the theory of structural complexity development of various data classes.

Among modern scientists, investigating the above issues, Saeed V. Vaseghi, Dean Walter, Jukka Suomela, R. Miller, and others should be mentioned [4-11].

These ideas can also be found in monitoring and control systems and in the field of data protection, when transmitting signals in measuring channels [12-16].

However, the conducted review of literature has shown that the system of structural complexity criteria and a generalized approach to the problem of developing theoretical foundations, methodology, and methods of analysis and improving the structural data organization in computer systems were almost not considered in research works. Therefore, it became the subject of our research.

The purpose of the research is to develop a method for assessing the structural complexity of multifunctional data. This makes it possible to optimize the system characteristics of data and structural solutions of hardware and software in complex computer systems.

2. Concept of Data Structuring

The concept of structuring is associated with the processes of development and improvement of information systems: "Development aims not only at something complex but also at real World, i.e., structured under its realities." "Because everything that exists in the world is structured under its realities." [17].

The fundamental example of information conglomerates structuring is the structure and DNA information organization that demonstrates the role of selection and system survival of structurally more stable and informationally improved forms of living matter. This fundamental theoretical and logistical basis is the entropy principle of optimality. Therefore, understanding the concept of processes structuring, information data and generalization of fundamental theoretical bases is an urgent problem.

The rapid development of modern information technology, computer networks and computer systems set a research of structuring in given branch as the most promising task since almost all trends of modern civilization are closely related to the informatization of society and the proper structuring of information flows.

It is necessary to know the system structuring to better understand the role of information and use it effectively when operating. The highest level of information structuring is its singling out as a system for a particular item and associated subsystems. However, any system can be broken down to identify its indivisible units.

2.1. Classification of Attributes and Formalization of Data Structuring Processes

Statement of the concept of solution to the problem of information processes structuring allows us to generalize the fundamental theory of structuring and systematize the scientific disciplines which are the attributes and components of the theory and methodology of structuring. Figure 1 shows an example of such a systematization.

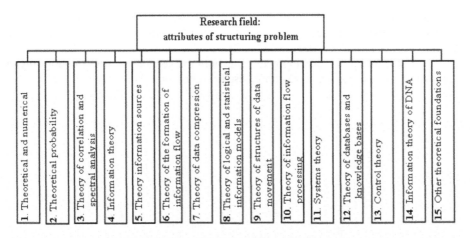

Figure 1. Structuring theory attributes classification.

Figure 2 shows generalized processes of information source flow structuring, where IS – information sources, S - sensory system, # - sampling processes in the Hamming space, FS - functional structuring, F(U, ∩) - operations of structural unification and separation.

Figure 2. The process of structuring.

2.2. Generalization of Theoretical Bases and Functions of the Data Structuring Concept

A successful solution to the problem of structured data (SD) formulation and processing in the distributed computer systems is conceptually related to the appropriate use of a wide class of fundamental theoretical principles of computer science, cybernetics and systems engineering. It is necessary to formulate the basic attributes and information provision procedures of the generalized theory of data structuring [18].

Theoretical and applied bases of such a synthesis can significantly promote math development, improve transmission and processing of digital data and increase the efficiency of components and algorithm functions, and efectiveness of using processed data in distributed computer systems [2, 3, 5].

Different data type structuring and complex computer system modeling is an urgent task that aims at improving the theory, methodology, design practice and diagnosis of functioning in real time. In terms of methodology, solving this problem requires consideration of the problem orientation, integrity and complexity, uncertainty, adaptability and versatility of computer system. The level of purposefulness and the aim of the system functioning, the possibility of the system description using only one model, evaluation of entropy that reflects the required amount of control information, the possibility of the system adaptation to external factors, and the system description using mathematical models that have the same structure regardless of the volume of objects - sources are defined alongside.

Analysis of data structuring methods, substantiation of the theoretical perspectives, methodology and techniques of structuring in modern computer systems is an urgent task today.

Data structuring for executing the functions of generation, transmission, digital processing, storage and structured frame use to control objects is shown in Fig. 3.

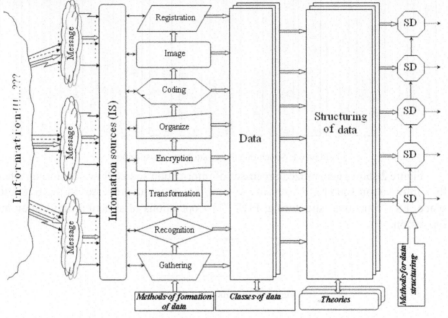

Figure 3. Generalized functions scheme of data structuring concept

Data structuring productive interaction functions scheme shows the way of data generation and algorithmic-mathematical data processing according to the task set, for example, pattern recognition, data compression, protection against unauthorized access, the results of the problem solved and others.

3. Investigating and Developing Criteria for Structural Complexity of Multifunctional Data

Synthesis and analysis of the DCS structures and components requires a clear definition of the system of criteria, on the basis of which, the comparison and optimization of the system characteristics of the developed software and hardware is carried out. The most common in modern practice of analyzing the system characteristics of computers, which are the components of DCS, are estimates of hardware and time complexity. In addition to the above, one more important criteria for assessing the perfection of the architecture of components, devices and MFD is the criterion of structural complexity.

Theoretical bases for estimating structural complexity were first proposed in the theory of graphs of Petri nets, which became the basis for calculating the structures of Petri nets [19]. Thus, effective application of theoretical bases of the estimate formalization of the structural complexity of the graphs representing Petri nets made it possible to systematize the ways of their structural representation, and also to formalize their functional transformations when pasting, differentiating, and presenting them in the form of trees, etc.

The result of the development of this direction of data structuring was the development of the theory and practical applications of the so-called "color" Petri nets, which are characterized by an extended functional description of the attributes of the network active nodes and edges. This made it possible to differentiate the attributes of the Petri net nodes such as information source, data processing and receiving points, data approval and use, which is shown in the research works of the author.

The functional transformations in the structure of Petri nets are performed according to adjacency (C_{ij}) and incidence (A_{ij}) matrices, which can be considered as initial estimates of structural complexity in DCSs that are represented by graphs of Petri nets:

$$C_{ij} = \begin{cases} V_j \to V_{j+1} = -1; \\ V_j \leftarrow V_{j+1} = +1, \end{cases} \qquad A_{ij} = V_i \& V_j \in \overline{0 \vee 1}.$$

The overall estimate of the structural complexity of Petri nets is determined by the ratio of the number of vertices (V_k) to the total number of one-directional (b_n) and bidirectional (b_m) edges:

$$k_c = \frac{V_k}{b_n + b_m},$$

where k, n, m - a number of vertices, a number of one-directional and bidirectional edges correspondingly.

The development of criteria for estimating the structural complexity of topologies and microelectronic components of computer operating devices is of great importance today. The first example of such an estimate is the Quine method [20] based on the estimate of the total number of inputs and outputs of the microelectronic structure, which is calculated according to the expression:

$$S_K = \sum_{i=1}^{n} X_i + \sum_{j=1}^{m} Y_j,$$

where X_i - inputs, $i \in 1, n$; Y_j - outputs, $j \in 1, m$;

n, m - the number of the structure inputs and outputs correspondingly.

The optimization criterion for the structure level according to Quine is determined by three criteria: the minimum number of logic gates in the structure, the minimum number of inputs and outputs in the structure, the minimum signal delay time. The last two criteria correspond to the estimates of hardware and time complexity of computing device structures.

The component of the criterion for estimating complexity according to Quine is the assessment of structural complexity by determining the hardware complexity of the device. This estimate is calculated determining the number of logic elements and gates in the structure of the devices with different numbers of hierarchies and types of components: single-level devices or components of different types - $A_\Pi = \sum_{i=1}^{n} A_i$

$$A_\Pi = \sum_{j=1}^{m}\sum_{i=1}^{n} A_{ij} \text{ , three-level devices } A_\Pi = \sum_{j=1}^{m}\sum_{i=1}^{n}\sum_{k=1}^{l} A_{ijk} \text{ , where}$$

A_Π - the overall assessment of hardware complexity, i, j, k - types of components or levels of the structure of the device, m, n, l - the corresponding number of types of different components or levels of the device structure.

The functional limitations of this criterion lie in the fact that it does not take into account the topology of types, a number of relations and their intersections, crystal dimensions, a number of inputs and outputs, etc., which are important characteristics in microelectronic design of PLDs, FPGAs and nanotechnology tools.

M. V. Cherkaskyi proposed a criterion that to some extent solves this problem [21] based on the SH-model of the algorithm, which takes into account hardware in the explicit form:

$$B = < D, Q, g_0, g_f, G, P, M >,$$

where D – a finite set of characters of the external alphabet; Q – a finite set of states of SH-model; q_0 and q_f – initial and finite states: $q_0, q_f \in Q$; G – hardware configuration of the model: $G = (X, U)$; X – a set of elementary converters: $\{x_1, x_2, ..., x_n\}$; U – a set of connections: $\{u_1, u_2, ..., u_m\}$; P – program; M – memory.

The concept of "elementary converter" x_i, used in this model, is a unit of hardware complexity which converts a certain set of initial input data d_i into a set of output data d_i': $x_i : \{d_i\} \rightarrow \{d_i'\}$.

When using the SH-model, such characteristics of complexity as hardware, time, capacity, software and structure are proposed to be used, where hardware complexity is the number of elementary converters and elements of RAM; time complexity is determined by the number of elementary converters in the maximum signal propagation path $L = |\max X_i|$; software complexity is determined by formula:

$$P = -F \log_2 \frac{F}{n \cdot m},$$

where $F = \sum_{L} f_l$; n – the number of control inputs; m – the number of time samples of the time chart; f_l – the number of control signals of the l-th fragment of the time chart; L – is the number of the time chart fragments, configurations of which are not repeated.

The structural complexity of the algorithmic device is determined by the following formula:

$$S = -E \log_2 \frac{E}{n(n-1)},$$

where E – the number of elements of the triangular adjacency matrix of the system; n – the number of vertices of the graph.

This criterion is used when estimating the structural complexity of operating devices and functional units of personal computers.

The functional limitation of such estimation lies in the fact that when calculating the structural complexity of homogeneous and regular environments $\log_2 = 1$ and differentiation of structural complexity becomes impossible.

The calculation of the structure time complexity is performed by determining the total number of micro-cycles of signal delay in the longest chain of series-connected logical or functional elements between the corresponding inputs and outputs of the device:

$$\tau = \sum_{j=1}^{m} \tau_j ,$$

where m - the number of series-connected elements; τ_j - signal delay in each j-th element.

In modern theory of binary and color digital image processing a wide range of mathematical expressions is used that makes it possible to classify, distinguish, recognize images by analyzing the structural complexity of components according to the appropriate algorithms and functionals.

The calculation of the structural complexity of the nodes of data movement matrix models based on the characteristics of emergence, proposed by J.Martin [1], corresponds to the ratio of the number of relations to the number of system components according to the estimate of the unit of data movement, and is as follows:

$$K_d = \frac{N_i}{N_0},$$

where N_i - the number of relations, N_0 - the number of components.

In [22], the symbolic attributes of Petri nets were expanded on the basis of data movement models (DMM), and the data movement coefficients, were taken into account:

$$K_{ed} = \frac{S_i \cdot G_0}{S_0 \cdot G_i},$$

where S_i, S_0, G_i, G_0 - the actual number of queries, the maximum possible number of queries, the actual number of records or updates, the maximum possible number of records or updates in the node of the matrix model respectively.

The structural complexity of microelectronic device topology, proposed by V.S.Glukhov [23], is estimated according to the total length of horizontal g_i and vertical v_i connections on the conventional FPGA:

$$L = \sum_{i=0}^{m-1} (g_i + v_i) \approx (1/2...3/4)m^2 , \text{ де } g_i = x_i + 1, \ v_j = m + d_i + 1$$

However, classification of the structure components with informative parameters and weight estimates of structural unit components were not included into the considered criteria.

We propose to estimate the structural complexity of circuit structures, graphic images and multifunctional data as follows [24,]:

$$k_c = \sum_{i=1}^{n} \alpha_i P_i, \qquad (1)$$

where $P_i \in (l, P, x, d, r, h, z, b, c, i, n, a, f)$ - informative parameters of structure attributes, α_i - weighting coefficients of expert estimates of structural complexity of structured data elements and components.

The proposed criterion, obtained on the basis of expert estimates, is one of the elements of building ontological models in the systems of intelligent data processing in organizational and technical complexes.

Table 1 shows symbol attributes of MFD structural components and expert estimates of the complexity coefficient α_i and the classified informative parameters $l, P, x, d, r, h, z, b, c, i, n, a$.

Table 1. Expert estimates of the structural complexity of MFD elements

№	Element designation identifier	The content of the element	Symbols	α_i	Symbols	α_i
1	l	Line		1		1,2
				1,5		1,2
				1,1		1,7
2	P	Turn		2		2,2
				2,2		
3	x	Intersection		3		3,1
4	d	Touch		2		2,2
5	r	Branching	,	4		6,2
6	h	Filling	,	2	,	2
7	z	Direction of a relationship		2		2,5
				3		3,4
				2,4		3,5
8	b	Letter	Аа...Яя, Аа...Яя, ...,	8-10	Аа...Zz, ..., Аа...Zz Аа...Zz	8-10
	c	Digit	1, 2,...0....	4	*1, 2,...0*	4
	i	Index	1, 2,...0, a, A	4	1, 2,...0, a, A	4
	s	Symbol	©, ®, π, ψ, ω, &, %,	4	☺, ☼ ♫, μ, $, *, €, ,	4
	n	Sign	+, -, <, >, =, ±, ≡, ≈..	2	≠, ≤, ≥, ¢, ", {, !, ?...	2

The proposed criterion for estimating structural complexity does not include the informative characteristics of the structure components, so MFD structure effectiveness criterion is proposed to determine the ratio between information and structural complexities according to the expression [24, 28, 29, 30]:

$$k_e = K \cdot \frac{F_C}{k_c} = K \cdot \frac{\sum\limits_{j=1}^{m} f_j}{\sum\limits_{i=1}^{n} \alpha_i P_i} \Rightarrow \max, \tag{2}$$

where K – MFD level identifier ($K = n$,... – for *n*-level structures correspondingly); F_C - information complexity of the device; f_j - functional information characteristics of the device structure.

Thus, the maximum increase in k_e value is a comparative characteristic of different implementations of the device structures and MFD. For example, at a given structural complexity k_c, the functionality of the structures is expanded, or at a given functionality, structural complexity is reduced. This can lead to changes in target characteristics by reducing hardware, time or computational complexities.

Functional and informative characteristics of the device structure can be represented by the following estimates:

1. Functional completeness of the device inputs-outputs, which is determined by the total estimate $f_j = \sum\limits_{i=1}^{n} \beta_i \cdot f_{input} + \sum\limits_{i=1}^{m} \lambda_i \cdot f_{output}$, where f_j - functional information characteristics of the device structure, β, λ - coefficients of input-output functions informativity, m, n - the number of inputs-outputs, f_{input}, f_{output} - input-output functions (e.g., input / output channel, input / output x / y n / m -bit buses, synchronization input, crystal selection c / s, power supply $+ / -$);

2. The degree of availability of certain functions in the formalized structures of data movement derivative models. An example of the calculation is carried out according to the expression:

$$f_j = \sum\limits_{j=1}^{m} f_i .$$

3. Evaluation of structural complexity based on entropy characteristics of input calculation and output information flows.

The entropy estimates are calculated according to coding (R. Hartley), probabilistic (K. Shannon) and correlation (Y. Nykolaychuk) information entropy measures [25-27]:

- R. Hartley: $H = n \cdot \hat{E}[\log_2 S] = n \cdot]\log_2 S[$;

- K. Shannon: $H = -k \sum\limits_{j=0}^{S} p_j \log p_j$;

- Y. Nykolaychuk: $I_x = n \cdot \hat{E}\left[\frac{1}{2}\log_2 \frac{1}{m} \times \sum\limits_{j=1}^{m} \left(D_x^2 - R_{xx}^2(j)\right)\right]$, where H – the amount of information; S – the number of independent equally probable states of the information source (IS); n – the number of samples; $\hat{E}[\bullet]$ – an integer-valued function with rounding to a larger whole; k – a positive coefficient that takes into account the base of the logarithm; p_j – the probability of the S_j-th state of the discrete IS; S – the number of independent IS states; $\overset{\circ}{x_i} = x_i - M_x$ – centered values of the data array; $D_x = \dfrac{1}{n}\sum_{i=1}^{n}(x_i - M_x)^2$ – dispersion x_i; $M_x = \dfrac{1}{n}\sum_{i=1}^{n}x_i$ – mathematical expectation; $R_{xx}(j) = \dfrac{1}{n}\sum_{i=1}^{n}\overset{\circ}{x_i}\cdot\overset{\circ}{x_{i+j}}$ – autocorrelation function (ACF); m – the number of points of the function $R_{xx}(j)$ on the correlation interval; $j = 0,1,....m$.

Thus, the estimation of the entropy functional complexity looks as follows:

$$f_j = I_{input} + I_X + I_{output},$$

where $I_{input}, I_X, I_{output}$ - quantification of entropy at the input, during the transformation and at the output of the structure, respectively.

Based on the proposed criterion (1), a method for estimating the structural complexity of the attributes of multi-level DCS data movement models, as well as alphanumeric and functional symbols, which are displayed on monitors and hard copies of physical data, is developed [24].

4. Examples of Estimating the Structural Complexity of Elementary Units of Computer Technology

The above systematization of structural elements formed the basis of the methodology for estimating the structural complexity of logical elements and structures of microelectronic devices in computer technology.

The logical element is the most elementary component in computer technology. Therefore, the estimation of the structural complexity of any component of DCSs (ADC, adders, multipliers, entropy measurement devices, processors, special-purpose processors, memory, etc.) is based on determining the structural complexity of the logical elements, taking into account the relationships between them.

Based on the criterion (1) and the data in Table 1, the structural complexity of the microelectronic components of the processors is estimated (Table 2).

The following tables show examples of estimating the structural complexity and informativity of various graphic images in electrical automatics, and crystals of logical and microelectronic components.

Table 2. Informative characteristics of the logical element structural complexity of computer technology.

№	Function, type of a component	Symbolic graphic notation	Criterion parameters for structural complexity $l, P, x, d, r, h, z, b, c, i, n$	Total estimate of structural complexity
1	Denial		2,3,-,3,-,-,-,-,-,-	14,8
2	Disjunction		1,2,-,3,-,-,-,-,-,-,-	11,6
3	Denial of disjunction		2,2,-,4,-,-,-,-,-,-	14,8
4	Conjunction		1,2,-,3,-,-,-,-,-,-	11,2
5	Denial of conjunction		2,2,-,4,-,-,-,-,-,-	14,4
6	Equivalency		2,2,-,3,-,-,-,-,-,-	12,8
7	Denial of equivalency		3,2,-,4,-,-,-,-,-,-	16
8	Implication		3,2,-,6,-,-,-,-,-	20
9	Prohibition		3,2,-,6,-,-,-,-,-	19,6

Table 3. Symbolic notation of graphic images in electrical automatics

№	Function, type of a component	Symbolic graphic notation	Total estimate of structural complexity
1	Disjunction		130
2	Conjunction		111
3	Denial		70

Table 4. Nonlinear diode transistor elements

№	Function, type of a component	Symbolic graphic notation	Total estimate of structural complexity
1	Element NO		180
2	Element OR		251
3	Element AND		315
4	Element OR-NO		368
5	Element AND-NO		393

Table 5. Symbolic notation of logical element crystals

№	Function, type of a component	Symbolic graphic notation	Total estimate of structural complexity
1	Examples of coefficient N_1 values	$N_1=3$ $N_1=8$ $N_1=2AND\text{-}2AND\text{-}3AND\text{-}3OR\text{-}NO$ $N_1=1$ a) b) c) d)	a) – 28 b) – 23 c) – 42 d) – 74
2	Majority elements	$N_p=3$ $N_p=4$ a) b)	a) – 177 b) – 232

An example of a multi-bit arithmetic processor component is a modified pseudo-random code sequence delimited feedback register (Fig. 4).

Вихідний біт

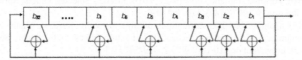

Figure 4. Modified feedback register

$$k_e = \frac{k_i}{n} + k_{e2} + k_{e3} = \frac{96}{n} + 3 + 17,$$

n - the number of regular elements, when $n = 1024$ $k_e \approx 21$

Possibility of structuring information and transition from one structure to another provides a basis for efficient analysis and evaluation, processing and regrouping.

5. Conclusions

Based on the analysis of modern theories and tools of formation, conversion, transmission and digital processing of information flows in complex CSs, the concept of structuring multifunctional analog and digital data processing is proposed, which makes it possible to improve the processes of synthesized generation and movement of structured data and implement computing tools with advanced functionality and reduced structural, hardware and time complexities.

The proposed criteria of structural complexity as a weighted sum of structural characteristics and the informative characteristics of multifunctional data structures, allow us to compare and improve the system characteristics (structural, hardware and time complexities) of the software and hardware being created, which form multifunctional data.

Since the method for assessing the structural data complexity is proposed for the first time, it is considered as a new one and needs further development and improvement.

Today, it is still hard to say exactly how perfect it is, and it is also difficult to compare it with any other method. Therefore, the development of the theory of structuring multifunctional data needs further elaboration, which will be discussed in our future research papers.

References

[1] James Martin (1990) Design and strategy for distributed data processing / J. Martin – NJ: Prentice Hall PTR Upper Saddle River. – 672p.

[2] Thomas J. Harrison (1978) Minicomputers in industrial control: An introduction Hardcover, Instrument Society of America.

[3] Wilsky A.S. (1979) Digital Signal Processing, Control and Estimation Theory: Points of Tangency, Areas of Intersection and Parallel Directions. MIT Press, Cambridge, MA.

[4] Zhengbing Hu, Igor A. Tereykovskiy, Lyudmila O. Tereykovska, Volodymyr V. Pogorelov, "Determination of Structural Parameters of Multilayer Perceptron Designed to Estimate Parameters of Technical Systems", International Journal of Intelligent Systems and Applications, Vol.9, No.10, pp.57-62, 2017.

[5] Vaseghi, Saeed V. Advanced digital signal processing and noise reduction / Saeed V. Vaseghi. — 3rd ed., 2006. - 451 p.

[6] Dean, Walter (2019). Computational Complexity Theory and the Philosophy of Mathematics. Philosophia Mathematica 27 (3):381-439.

[7] Jukka Suomela Structural Information and Communication Complexity. 23rd International Colloquium, SIROCCO 2016, Helsinki, Finland, July 19-21, 2016, Revised Selected Papers, Springer, Cham, 2016, 408 p. https://doi.org/10.1007/978-3-319-48314-6.

[8] Miller, R. (2017). Computable Transformations of Structures. In: Kari, J., Manea, F., Petre, I. (eds) Unveiling Dynamics and Complexity. CiE 2017. Lecture Notes in Computer Science, vol 10307. Springer, Cham. https://doi.org/10.1007/978-3-319-58741-7_9

[9] Okhotin, A., Salomaa, K.: State complexity of operations on input-driven pushdown automata. J. Comput. Syst. Sci. 86, 207–228 (2017)

[10] Jun, S., & Kochan, O. (2015). Common mode noise rejection in measuring channels. Instruments and Experimental Techniques, 58, 86-89.

[11] Zhengbing Hu, Ihor Tereikovskyi, Denys Chernyshev, Liudmyla Tereikovska, Oleh Tereikovskyi, Dong Wang, "Procedure for Processing Biometric Parameters Based on Wavelet Transformations", International Journal of Modern Education and Computer Science, Vol.13, No.2, pp. 11-22, 2021.

[12] Jun, S., Kochan, O. V., & Jotsov, V. S. (2015). Methods of reducing the effect of the acquired thermoelectric inhomogeneity of thermocouples on temperature measurement error. Measurement Techniques, 58(3), 327-331.

[13] Shu, C., & Kochan, O. (2013). Method of thermocouples self-verification on operation place. Sensors & Transducers, 160(12), 55-61.

[14] Sun, L., Qin, H., Przystupa, K., Majka, M., & Kochan, O. (2022). Individualized Short-Term Electric Load Forecasting Using Data-Driven Meta-Heuristic Method Based on LSTM Network. Sensors, 22(20), 7900.

[15] Zhengbing Hu, Ivan Dychka, Yevgeniya Sulema, Yevhen Radchenko,"Graphical Data Steganographic Protection Method Based on Bits Correspondence Scheme", International Journal of Intelligent Systems and Applications, Vol.9, No.8, pp.34-40, 2017.

[16] Vasylkiv, N., Kochan, O., Kochan, R., & Chyrka, M. (2009, September). The control system of the profile of temperature field. In 2009 IEEE International Workshop on Intelligent Data Acquisition and Advanced Computing Systems: Technology and Applications (pp. 201-206). IEEE.

[17] Workplace safety diagnostic information and control systems / edited by A. Drozd and V. Marchenko - National Aerospace University. M.Ye. Zhukovskoho "HAI", 2012. – 614 p.

[18] Vozna N.Y. Fundamentals of the theory of structuring multifunctional elements of complex systems // Bulletin of Khmelnytsky National University. – Khmelnytsky, 2015. – №2 (223). P. 204–208.

[19] Carl Adam Petri. Nets, time and space. Theoretical computer science, 153(12):3-48, 1996.

[20] Boychenko O.V. High-speed multiple combinaton type adders / O.V. Boychenko, Y.I. Toroshanko // Interuniversity Collection "Computer-integrated technologies: education, science, production", 2011 №3. – P.20–24.

[21] Cherkaskyi M.V. Analysis of the complexity of multiplication devices / M.V. Cherkaskyi, Murad Hussein Khalil // Bulletin of NULP "Computer systems design. Theory and practice". – Lviv: National University "Lviv Polytechnic", 2005. №548. – P.15-21.

[22] Nykolaichuk Ya.M. Structuring the movement of data in computer systems / Ya.M. Nykolaichuk, N.Ya. Vozna, I.R. Pitukh. - Ternopil: Terno-graf, 2013. - 284 p.

[23] Hlukhov V., Hlukhova A. Galois field elements multipliers structural complexity evaluation. Proceedings of the 6-th International Conference ACSN-2013. Sept. 16–18. – Lviv, 2013. – P. 18–19.

[24] Vozna N.Y. Structuring multifunctional data: theory, methods and tools / N.Y. Vozna // Monograph. – Ternopil: TNEU, 2018. – 378 p.

[25] Shannon C. E. (1948) A mathematical theory of communication. Bell Syst. Tech. J. 27: 379–423, 623–656.

[26] John Hartley, John R.Hartley (1983) Robots at Work, IFS (Publications) Limited, 191 p.

[27] Nykolaichuk Y.M. Theory of information sources / Y. M. Nykolaychuk – Ternopil: Ltd.: Terno-graf, 2010. –536 p.

[28] Aayush Juyal, Nandini Sharma, Pisati Rithya, Sandeep Kumar, "An Enhanced Approach to Recommend Data Structures and Algorithms Problems Using Content-based Filtering", International Journal of Intelligent Systems and Applications, Vol.15, No.5, pp.28-40, 2023.

[29] Ujwal U.J, Saleem Malik, "A Hybrid Weight based Feature Selection Algorithm for Predicting Students' Academic Advancement by Employing Data Science Approaches", International Journal of Education and Management Engineering, Vol.13, No.5, pp. 1-22, 2023.

[30] Snigdho Dip Howlader, Tushar Biswas, Aishwarjyo Roy, Golam Mortuja, Dip Nandi, "A Comparative Analysis of Algorithms for Heart Disease Prediction Using Data Mining", International Journal of Information Technology and Computer Science, Vol.15, No.5, pp.45-54, 2023.

Artificial Intelligence, Medical Engineering and Education
Z.B. Hu et al. (Eds.)
© 2024 The Authors.
This article is published online with Open Access by IOS Press and distributed under the terms
of the Creative Commons Attribution Non-Commercial License 4.0 (CC BY-NC 4.0).
doi:10.3233/ATDE231347

Design of an Improved Autonomous Tracked Vehicle Based on SLAM Algorithm

Xiaozhe YANG, Pizheng CHEN, Huiting LU
The Faculty of Intelligent Manufacturing, Nanning University, Nanning, 530299, China

Abstract. In the design of autonomous vehicles, relying solely on the SLAM algorithm for obstacle avoidance poses a certain response delay issue, which may affect the real-time safe driving of unmanned vehicles. To address this issue, a solution that identifies simulated obstacles by running YOLOv5 on the Jetson module is proposed to achieve optimized obstacle avoidance processing. At the same time, a tracked vehicle was designed using the ROS robot development system to achieve the specific effects of this solution. In the experiment, when the tracked vehicle encounters simulated obstacles during driving, it can automatically turn and deviate from the original driving trajectory, proving that this visual obstacle avoidance scheme is effective.

Keywords. Yolov5; Ros robot development; SLAM; Visual obstacle avoidance

1. Introduction

With the development of technology, autonomous driving technology has become a special concern in current society. It also represents an important direction in today's technological development to a certain extent [1,2]. To achieve autonomous driving technology, advanced sensors and increasingly optimized autonomous navigation technology are indispensable.

Autonomous navigation involves a series of core technologies such as environmental perception, map creation, autonomous positioning, and motion planning. The implementation of autonomous navigation technology for robots relies on research in many technical fields, such as the combination of perception technology, automation control technology, dynamic decision-making, path planning technology, etc., in order to build a complete robot system [5-7]. The combination of various advanced technologies enriches the functions of robots and provides them with more flexible obstacle avoidance methods, no longer limited to lidar or ultrasonic detectors [8,9]. Adding a camera to the robot not only allows for real-time acquisition of images in front for mapping, but also allows for visual recognition to check for obstacles ahead [10,11].

More and more mobile robots are extracting deep semantic features to perceive the surrounding environment through deep learning methods [12,13]. Continuous improvement and optimization are very important [14]. The method of environmental perception and autonomous navigation based on multi-sensor fusion has become a hot topic in current research [15]. It faces many challenges, and using improved algorithms can effectively solve various practical problems encountered.

2. Overall Design and Selection of Hardware and Software

Based on SLAM algorithm improvement and optimization for local obstacle avoidance, the main research method is to achieve the positioning, mapping, and path planning functions of tracked robots in the ROS system platform [16].

Use path planning algorithm to achieve global planning in the experimental site with simulated obstacles and use YOLOv5 visual recognition model to perform local obstacle avoidance to achieve dynamic obstacle avoidance of tracked robots during driving.

2.1 Overall Design Plan

The tracked vehicle is mainly composed of tracks, encoding motors, frame, battery, ROS robot STM32 drive board, Raspberry Pi 4B development board, and LiDAR. By installing cameras on the tracked robot and running YOLOv5 visual recognition on the Jetson module, the problem of the tracked robot being unable to quickly and effectively avoid obstacles in local avoidance is improved[17].

2.2 Hardware Selection of Tracked Vehicles

The RPLIDAR A1 LiDAR model can perform 360^0 laser ranging scans in all directions, up to 12 meters, and generate a two-dimensional raster map.

The ROS robot STM32 driver board consists of an STM32 chip, a USB driver chip, an attitude sensor module, a power processing chip module, a motor driver chip module, and a power circuit.

Raspberry Pi 4B is a Linux based microcomputer that can be used to run on the ROS development platform and achieve distributed multi machine communication through WiFi.

Jetson nano is a platform that supports the development of applications such as deep learning, machine learning, and computer vision, and can load YOLOv5 visual recognition onto robots on mobile platforms.

The GY-85 nine axis sensor is used to measure the speed, direction, and gravity of the equipment, and convert the data into PPM signals for feedback to the STM32 driver board.

A DC motor with an encoder can convert angular displacement or angular velocity into digital pulse signals, which are fed back to the Raspberry Pi through the STM32 driver board [18].

2.3 Software Platform - ROS Robot Development Platform

ROS is the abbreviation for robot operating system, which was proposed by Stanford University in the STAIR project in 2007, which is mainly driven by Willow Garage and developed in collaboration with other institutions. It is now widely used in robot development and provides a complete set of tools and frameworks for building, deploying, and maintaining robot systems. In the ROS system, massive, developed resource packages are collected to directly implement software functions, which increases the heavy usage rate of the software and makes the development of robots more convenient.

3. Map Construction and Path Planning

3.1 SLAM Mapping

SLAM is an abbreviation for Synchronous Localization and Mapping, first proposed by Hugh Durrant Whyte and John J. Leonard, mainly used to solve the problem of real-time localization and map building for robots running in unknown environments. Using SLAM can effectively solve the three major problems of where the robot is located, where the robot should go, and how the robot should go.

3.2 Gmapping Algorithm Mapping

Gmapping is an open-source SLAM algorithm based on 2D LiDAR that uses RBPF particle filter algorithm to separate the positioning and mapping processes, first performing localization and then mapping. The advantage of Gmapping is that it requires less computation and higher accuracy when building maps for small scenes. It is suitable for indoor robot mapping experiments in small scenes due to its low frequency requirements for LiDAR. Obtain the Gmapping function package on the ROS development platform, subscribe to the robot's depth information, IMU information, and odometer information, and complete the configuration of some necessary parameters to create a probability based 2D grid map.

3.3 Path Planning

After obtaining a map of the surrounding environment through the SLAM algorithm, the path planning algorithm enables the robot to find a collision free and safe path from the starting point to the endpoint within the specified range area.

The path planning algorithm can use the A * algorithm, which was originally published in 1968 by Peter Hart, Nils Nilsson, and Bertram Raphael of Stanford Research Institute. The A * algorithm is an extension of the Dijkstra algorithm, which improves the Dijkstra algorithm by proposing a heuristic function method that adds an estimated cost from the endpoint to the original one.

$$f(n) = g(n) + h(n) \tag{1}$$

In the function of the A * algorithm, $f(n)$ represents the comprehensive priority of the node, which is also the node closest to the starting point and the estimated distance to the endpoint. $g(n)$ represents the distance between the node and the starting point, while $h(n)$ represents the estimated distance between the node and the endpoint. There are three main methods for estimating the distance, namely Manhattan distance, Euclidean distance, and Chebyshev distance.

In the Manhattan distance calculation function, it represents the sum of the horizontal and vertical distances between node a and target node b.

$$h(n) = |x_a - x_b| + |y_a - y_b| \qquad (2)$$

The Euclidean distance calculation function represents the linear distance between node a and target node b.

$$h(n) = \sqrt{(x_a - x_b)^2 + (y_a - y_b)^2} \qquad (3)$$

The Chebyshev distance calculation function represents the maximum difference in coordinates between node a and target node b.

$$h(n) = max(|x_a - x_b|, |y_a - y_b|) \qquad (4)$$

3.4. Improvement Based on SLAM Algorithm

In the path planning of mobile robots, a global map is usually established using LiDAR, and then mobile navigation obstacle avoidance is achieved by combining global and local path planning. However, the Dynamic Window Algorithm (DWA) requires robot position, velocity, angular velocity, and surrounding obstacle information when processing dynamic obstacle avoidance, and is susceptible to sensor noise. Inaccurate sensors or sensor information not updated in a timely manner can affect the effectiveness of the DWA algorithm, and the obstacle avoidance effect for non-convex obstacles is also poor. Additionally, it may not be possible to avoid sudden obstacles when the robot is moving at high speeds. Therefore, this article proposes to add a camera to the robot and use the YOLOv5 algorithm for dynamic obstacle recognition to assist in dynamic obstacle avoidance during the movement process.

4. Experimental Verification

4.1. Train YOLOv5 Model

Collect relevant simulated obstacle images. This article collected 106 similar images of the wheels of the robot car and used the open-source image annotation tool (labelimg) to annotate the images. After labeling the images, use YOLOv5 code to train the model to obtain a visual recognition model for such items.

4.2. YOLOv5 Code Modification

Visual obstacle avoidance requires real-time detection in YOLOv5 to determine the position of the detected obstacle by recording the real-time position coordinates of the marked block diagram. Under YOLOv5 code, by obtaining the coordinated position of the marked block diagram through the *box_label* module recorded by the p1 and p2 arrays, the specific position coordinates of obstacles on the image can be obtained.

The coordinates of the center point of the obstacle in the marked block diagram can be calculated from the coordinates of the upper left and lower right corners. Set a standard safe distance pixel so that the tracked robot can offset in a certain direction to avoid the position of the obstacle when detecting it. Use a camera to capture the center point position coordinates (320320) of frame 640 * 640 and compare them with the x-axis values of the obstacle center point position coordinates and ensure that the pixel distance between these two points is maintained outside the safe pixel distance. Otherwise, make the tracked robot turn and offset, increasing the position between two points and maintaining it beyond a safe pixel distance. The modified code can output the center position coordinates of the marked block diagram in real-time in the image, and the coordinates will also be sent to the Raspberry Pi end for processing.

4.3. System Integration

Deploying a deep learning environment with a USB camera and running YOLOv5 code in the Jetson nano to detect obstacles in front of the car and connecting the Jetson nano to the Raspberry Pi 4B using a USB data cable. When the USB camera detects obstacles in front, the YOLOv5 code is used to select the frame and send binary messages through serial communication in a timely manner to transmit the position coordinates of the frame selection center to the control system of the car, Raspberry Pi 4B, for data processing. Figure 1 shows this process. Run the ROS system in Raspberry Pi 4B to receive center point coordinate messages sent by Jetson Nano, and process binary messages to convert them into coordinate position messages. Then, create a new message node to subscribe to the processed coordinate position information, and use the if function to determine whether the center point position coordinates meet the safety pixel distance. If not, publish the speed message cmd to the ROS system_ Vel, changes the rotational speed of the tracked robot to move away from obstacles.

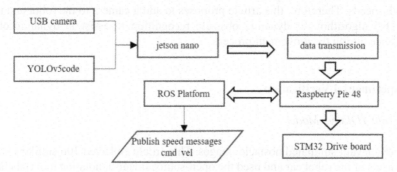

Figure 1. Visual Local Obstacle Avoidance System Diagram

4.4. Testing and Experimentation

Download the ROS robot platform from the Ubuntu system or the Ubuntu system running virtual machines on a PC. Start the power supply of the tracked vehicle, connect it to the tracked vehicle through the Ubuntu system ssh command on the PC, start the STM32 base plate, and run the LiDAR. The process of drawing is shown in Figure 2. Start the keyboard control node in the ROS terminal of the virtual machine, control the tracked robot to move, complete the mapping of the surrounding environment, and save the map.

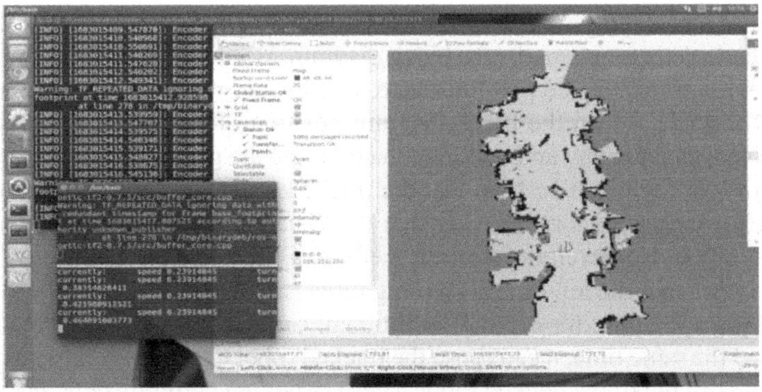

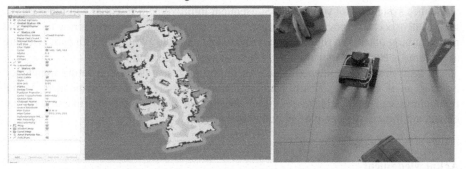

Figure 2. SLAM Mapping Process

The construction of the map is completed by connecting the virtual machine to the terminal of the tracked robot using SSH. The code in the navigate.launch file is activated to read the established map and automatically expand the contours of obstacles in the grid environment map.

Run the autonomous navigation algorithm shown in Figure 3 in the ROS terminal, use the robot simulation platform to view the working status of various sensors of the tracked robot, and calibrate the position of the tracked robot using the 2D Pose Estimate tool. Start the Jetson nano module to run YOLOv5 code to detect obstacles ahead. The actual environment is shown in Figure 4.

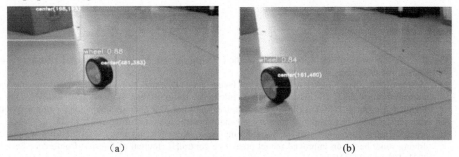

Figure 3. Autonomous Navigation Environment Map   **Figure 4.** Actual Environment Map

When dynamic obstacles appear during driving, the camera on the tracked robot takes real-time pictures of the front and uploads them to the Jetson nano module for image processing.

（a）   (b)

Figure 5. Effect diagram of obstacle avoidance process

As shown in the figure 5, when a wheel appears in front of the tracked robot, the YOLOv5 code detects and marks the block diagram. Because the block diagram position of the wheel is within a safe pixel distance, the tracked robot begins to turn and offset the wheel obstacle. When the block diagram position of the wheel is outside the safe pixel distance, stop turning and continue to complete the global path planning route.

From Figure 5, it can be seen that the tracked robot has turned and deviated from its original driving trajectory, proving that the visual obstacle avoidance module is an effective solution. However, the steering method of the tracked robot is too rigid, which only determines that the left or right turning movement cannot be well coordinated with the global path planning for driving. Additionally, when there are moving obstacles on both sides at the same time, it can cause the tracked robot to shake, leading to the problem of unsmooth driving of the tracked robot. These issues are currently deficiencies in visual obstacle avoidance, and we hope to strengthen code development in the future to better improve the occurrence of such problems.

5. Conclusion and Outlook

For improving the performance of autonomous vehicles, YOLOv5 can be run on the Jetson module to identify simulated obstacles and improve the automatic steering and obstacle avoidance functions of tracked vehicles. The research results of this article can achieve left and right turn obstacle avoidance for simple obstacles, but the visual obstacle avoidance system is not yet perfect. Subsequent improvement research will focus on the following aspects: achieving visual obstacle avoidance while also considering the global path planning of tracked robots. Integrating visual obstacle avoidance with path planning algorithms is expected to yield better obstacle avoidance solutions.

Visual obstacle avoidance is also an important research field in future unmanned driving, as it can more flexibly and effectively handle obstacle avoidance. Visual recognition can also achieve real-time analysis of road conditions, thereby further enhancing the safety guarantee of unmanned driving.

Acknowledgment

This project is supported by the project of 2022 Nanning University Educational reform （2022XJJG22）

References

[1]   Bai, Y. Accurate obstacle prediction method in unmanned vehicle driving. [J]. Advances in Transportation Studies, 2022, 1: 3-14.
[2]   Mushuang Liu, Ilya Kolmanovsky, H. Eric Tseng, et al. Potential game-based decision-making for autonomous driving[J]. IEEE Transactions on Intelligent Transportation Systems, 2023, 24(8): 1-14.
[3]   Vikram Raja, Dhruv Talwar, Akilesh Manchikanti & Sunil Jha. Autonomous navigation for mobile robots with sensor fusion technology[J]. Industry 4.0 and Advanced Manufacturing, 2022, 13-23.
[4]   Wang, Zengxi, Zhang, Qingyu, Jia, Tong; Zhang, Sulin. Research on control algorithm of a automatic driving robot based on improved model predictive control[J]. Journal of Physics: Conference Series, 2021, 1920(1): 012116.
[5]   Jinbiao Zhu, Dongshu Wang, Jikai Si. Flexible behavioral decision making of mobile robot in dynamic

environment[J]. IEEE Transactions on Cognitive and Developmental Systems, 2023, 15(1): 134-149.

[6] Xin Xiong, Runan Huang, Cuixian He. Research on intelligent path planning technology of logistics robots based on Giraph architecture[J]. International Journal of Computing Science and Mathematics, 2022, 16(3): 252-264.

[7] Zhang Lei, Li, Dezhong. Research on mobile robot target recognition and obstacle avoidance based on vision (Article)[J]. Journal of Internet Technology, 2018, 19(6): 1879-1892.

[8] Hekm, Zhang X. Y., Ren S Q, et al. Spatial pyramid pooling in deep convolutional networks for visual recognition[J]. IEEE Transactions on Pattern Analysis and Machine Intelligence, 2015, .37(9): 1904-1916.

[9] Giorgio Grisetti, Cyrill Stachniss, Wolfram Burgard. Improved techniques for grid mapping with rao-blackwellized particle filters. [J]. IEEE Trans. Robotics, 2007, .23(1): 34-46.

[10] Qilie Cai; Qiang Wang; Yulong Zhang, Zhibo He, Yuhong Zhang. LWDNet-A lightweight water-obstacles detection network for unmanned surface vehicles[J]. Robotics and Autonomous Systems, 2023, 166: 104453.

[11] Liu Yuzhe. Research and implementation of mobile robot obstacle avoidance algorithm based on machine vision[D]. Chongqing University of Posts and Telecommunications, 2021 (in Chinese).

[12] Qingyong, Liu. Research on visual recognition method of unmanned driving based on deep learning[J]. Journal of Physics: Conference Series, 2021, 2010(1): 012001.

[13] ZHU Chunhao. Design and implementation of SLAM System for mobile robot based on ROS[D]. Beijing: Beijing Jiaotong University, 2020 (in Chinese).

[14] Yan Han, Wang Wei, Cui Jinhua, Dai Didi, Wang Rujia. Research on SLAM_gmapping optimization based on AF and AS algorithm[J]. Journal of Jiangsu Institute of Technology,2022, 28(2): 93-101.

[15] Wang Linlin, Chen Yunfang. Diversity based on entropy: a novel evaluation criterion in multi-objective optimization algorithm[J]. International Journal of Intelligent Systems and Applications, 2017, 10: 113-124.

[16] Mohammad Zohaib, Muhammad Ahsan, Mudassir Khan, Jamshed Iqbal. A featureless approach for object detection and tracking in dynamic environments[J]. PloS one, 2023, 18(1): e0280476.

[17] Sithmini Gunasekara, Dilshan Gunarathna, Maheshi B. Dissanayake, Supavadee Aramith, Wazir Muhammad, "Deep Learning Based Autonomous Real-Time Traffic Sign Recognition System for Advanced Driver Assistance", International Journal of Image, Graphics and Signal Processing, 2022, 14(6): 70-83.

[18] B.V. Arun Kumar, G V Marutheswar, "Multi Quadrant Operation of Brushless Direct Current Motor Drive with PI and Fuzzy Logic Controllers", International Journal of Information Engineering and Electronic Business, 2019, 11(3): 25-32.

374

Artificial Intelligence, Medical Engineering and Education
Z.B. Hu et al. (Eds.)
© 2024 The Authors.

doi:10.3233/ATDE231348

System Dynamics Modeling for Contactless Delivery Strategy of Medical Supplies

Liwei LI, Zhong ZHENG[1], Quanli MO, Xiaofei MA
School of Traffic and Transportation, Nanning University, Nanning, China
ORCiD ID: Liwei Li https://orcid.org/0009-0007-3409-3259

Abstract. The contactless delivery of drugs under the novel coronavirus pneumonia epidemic has become one of the main research trends. In this paper, an optimization model of contactless distribution of drugs under the epidemic is constructed based on the system dynamics simulation, considering the medical prescriptions of spare drugs in the cabin and the workflow of contactless drug distribution by unmanned vehicles. Finally, the model and algorithm are validated by taking the drug delivery of Wuhan city mobile cabin hospital under the new coronavirus pneumonia epidemic as an example. By adjusting the parameters and continuously simulating and optimizing, we study the use of contactless technology in drug distribution in mobile cabin hospital, clarify the practical value of the technology, and analyze the distribution efficiency, distribution cost and inventory changes before and after its use. The results show that the model constructed in this paper takes into account the time delay caused by quarantine and disinfection in distribution, which can more realistically reflect the distribution scenarios and influencing factors in the hospital environment, reasonably plan the unmanned vehicle scheduling work, and maximize the benefits of the contactless drug distribution system.

Keywords. System Dynamics; Contactless Delivery; Medical Supplies; Drug Distribution.

1. Introduction

Since the new WHO International Health Regulations added "public health emergencies of international concern", the supply of medical protective materials and medicines has gradually come under the spotlight. It is reported that in the early stage of covid-19 epidemic in China, 1716 cases of medical staff were reported, accounting for 3.8% of the country; Hubei Province reported 1502 confirmed cases of medical staff, accounting for 87.5% of the confirmed cases of medical staff in China [1]. Therefore, under the COVID-19 epidemic, it has become an urgent problem to optimize the drug dispensing mode and minimize the infection rate of medical personnel by ensuring timely supply of drugs.

Although COVID-19 epidemic has promoted the continuous development of contactless distribution technology, but contactless distribution has been associated with higher technical costs, and there is a lack of a relatively quantitative evaluation scheme

---

[1] Corresponding Author: Zhong ZHENG, E-mail: 523201940@qq.com.

to determine the distribution costs and distribution efficiency of contactless technology. There are many factors affecting the contactless distribution of medical supplies. On the one hand, the characteristics of the unmanned vehicles themselves, such as different delivery modes of unmanned vehicles and different loads and power of different types of unmanned vehicles. On the other hand, logistics factors, such as drug demand, delay time, distribution cycle and inventory status. In short, the simulation of contactless distribution of medical supplies includes nonlinear dynamic feedback of multiple business processes in multiple situations [2]. The system dynamics simulation method is suitable for dealing with this kind of periodic high-order nonlinear dynamic complex systems. The problem of insufficient data in modeling can be solved by calculating and analyzing the causal relationship in the model.

Therefore, based on the system dynamics approach, this thesis investigates the unmanned distribution demand, distribution cost and efficiency of drugs in the mobile cabin hospitals designated for treatment during an epidemic outbreak, and continuously optimizes the simulation to seek the optimal dispatching scheme for the contactless technology. As far as possible, we provide theoretical and data support for the process of unmanned vehicle distribution of drugs in mobile cabin hospitals, and provide a suitable cost budget for the contactless distribution of drugs. It provides meaningful references for improving the safety of material distribution, reducing interpersonal contact, improving distribution capacity, promoting contactless distribution mode, and strengthening epidemic prevention and control.

1. Literature Review

1.1. Distribution of medical supplies under epidemic situation

From the perspective of medical supplies distribution outside the hospital, the rapid spread of the epidemic, the lack of raw materials and manpower reserves, the limited capacity of supplies, and the inefficiency of emergency supplies dispatch, it is not easy to consider the degree of priority of medical supplies and the uncertain dispatch of multi-point distribution under the conditions of insufficient supplies during the epidemic outbreak [1-3]. More importantly, medical supplies distribution during the epidemic increased the risk of infection among medical staff and reduced the labor force [4]. In general, the current medical supply distribution challenges under the epidemic mainly rely on contactless distribution technology to accomplish.

1.2. Contactless delivery of medical supplies

With the outbreak of covid-19 epidemic, the demand for contactless distribution of medical supplies in hospitals is increasing rapidly. Among them, uttam U. Deshpande et al. have developed an unmanned guided car for drug distribution, which has low cost and no track [5]. Chen, Shunda et al. to explore new drug dispensing pattern in mobile cabin hospitals under coronavirus disease 2019 (COVID-19) circumstances, the contactless drug delivery was carried out by using 5G cloud technology and unmanned vehicle [1]. Huilin Li et. al. designed an intelligent express box for contactless distribution of medical supplies, and optimized the distribution path based on the implementation points of sharing economy and open-loop distribution to achieve the goal of low-cost and low-carbon economy [6]. Debapriya Banik et al. proposed a contactless distribution scheme of UAV medical supplies applied to urban areas and remote rural areas [7].

In summary, scholars' research focuses on how to more effectively use unmanned vehicles, the Internet of Things, and artificial intelligence technologies, and focuses on contactless delivery of medical supplies from the perspectives of innovation of contactless technology, algorithm optimization of delivery paths, and location of delivery points [8,9].

1.3. Distribution and System Dynamics

In the face of complex dynamic systems, system dynamics is used to study the flow and stock, causality in the model through quantitative and qualitative methods, so that it can accurately simulate the model in reality and provide researchers with data for support and decision making [10-12]. System dynamics is widely used in the field of logistics, such as warehousing, distribution simulation and path optimization [13-14]. Distribution, as an important part of the supply chain, is usually integrated into the analysis of the supply chain during modeling and simulation.Many literature focuses on distribution route selection, distribution node design, and distribution costs in supply chains using system dynamics, and the objects are mainly urban logistics, commodity supply chains, or disaster relief and emergency logistics [15-17].

Although they have analyzed the optimization of distribution routes and the location layout of distribution points in the supply chain using system dynamics methods, it is worth mentioning that there are still few studies on the cost, cycle time, and benefits of contactless distribution of medical supplies within hospital premises [18-20]. To sum up, the design of a model for contactless distribution of medical supplies under an epidemic is an important research problem.

2. Methodology

System dynamics can observe the behavior trend and change trend of the system at different times by dynamically setting the control factors [21-22]. Therefore, this paper uses the system dynamics method to analyze the application of contactless distribution technology in fixed-point treatment hospitals, and further discusses the demand for contactless distribution of medical materials during the epidemic.

2.1. Background Analysis

The real distribution process and data of mobile cabin hospital in Wuhan Guanggu Science and Technology Exhibition Center are selected as the empirical background. The mobile cabin hospital of Guanggu Science and Technology Exhibition Center is an intelligent mobile cabin hospital with 5G cloud technology. It has a total area of about 10,000 square meters and can accommodate 850 beds. There are three wards of A1, A2 and A3, including four supporting service areas: entrance and exit, buffer zone, washing area and treatment room. It is mainly used for the treatment of mild patients with new coronavirus pneumonia infection. The hospital adopts the BXN-01 unmanned vehicle (Beijing White Rhino Cattle Zhida Technology Co., Ltd., size: 2.5m * 1.0m * 1.8m, loading capacity $2.15m^3$, endurance 100km, maximum speed 45km / h) to carry out drug dispensing and drug contactless distribution [1].

Since it is a designated hospital specializing in the treatment of New Coronary Pneumonia, which involves sterilization and quarantine, its drug dispensing and distribution model has special characteristics in order to reduce cross-infection. Before using the unmanned delivery technology, the process is as follows: First of all, the cabin doctor prescribes the medication medical advice before the end of the shift, and the pharmacist reviews the medical advice and then allocates the medication, next, the special person delivers it to the cleaning room of the mobile cabin hospital, and then, the receiving medical staff enters the cabin and brings it to the treatment room, and then distributes the medication. The process of using unmanned vehicles for in cabin drug distribution is as follows: First, the drugs enter the hospital from outside the hospital and are stored in the staging area, the physician reviews the medical prescription through the system, prints the medical prescription dispensing order, and dispenses the prescription, and after dispensing, the drugs are taken and packed according to the cabin partition, loaded into the unmanned vehicle, and sent to the backstage technician. The backstage operates the unmanned car through 5G technology to enter the cabin from the patient channel and arrive at the treatment room. The nurse inside the cabin scans the code and opens the box, distributes the medicine according to the medical prescription, and sends out the cabin command after completion. The backstage receives the instruction and turns on the car's built-in UV disinfection lamp to disinfect. The unmanned vehicle arrives at the buffer zone after leaving the cabin, disinfects for 1 hour, and is ready for use after disinfection [1].The highly automated drug distribution system can reduce human labor, reduce the demand for protective materials and improve the distribution efficiency. In particular, the risk of doctor-patient cross infection is greatly reduced.

2.2. System Boundary

This paper will establish a model around the drug distribution system within the hospital. Therefore, the definition of the model should be set around the loading link, the entry link, the killing link and the exit link of the drugs in the cabin. The boundary diagram of model is shown in Figure 1. The solid line frame represents the boundary of the system, in which the hospital drug delivery process covers the drug packaging vehicle area, treatment room and buffer zone of the hospital.

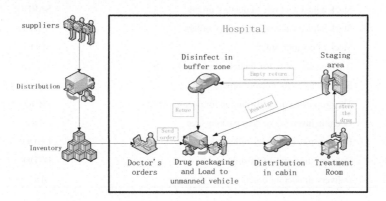

Figure 1. Boundary of delivery system diagram

2.3. Assumptions of the Simulation Model

The following assumptions are put forward when establishing the model:
   • There are three modes of medical prescription within the hospital: long-term medical prescription, temporary medical prescription and in-cabin standby. The medication

demand and drug distribution process of different medical prescription modes vary greatly, and the model only considers the distribution demand of in-cabin standby which is small in size, large in quantity and relatively single and repetitive in distribution.

• Extreme conditions in the distribution system are not considered during the study time period, i.e., unmanned vehicle equipment, medical personnel, etc., all proceed normally as planned.

• Patient demand during the study period was within a certain range and did not show extremes.

• The supply of drugs is sufficient and there is no shortage of stock.

• Assuming a treatment room safety stock of 100.

• Unmanned vehicles deliver drugs with a single fixed point of delivery, and there is no coordinated delivery.

2.4. Causal Loop Diagram

The causal loop diagram shows the causal behavior from the perspective of the system, which is helpful to intuitively understand the relationship between different variables in the system. According to the previous introduction of the in-hospital distribution system and the actual situation of the distribution process, as well as the parameters involved in the model, the Vensim Ple software was used to construct the causal loop diagram of the in-hospital distribution system of the mobile cabin hospital (The main variables in the model and their acronyms are shown in Table 1). These variables are connected by a causal chain representing positive feedback (plus sign) and negative feedback (minus sign) [23].

Table 1. Variables in the model

Number	Variable	Acronym
1	Doctors' orders	DO
2	The productivity of doctors' orders	PDO
3	Stock adjustment rate of doctors' orders	SARDO
4	Stock adjustment time of doctors' orders	SATDO
5	Stock of doctors' orders	SDO
6	A Time delay of redistribution for doctors' orders	TDRDO
7	Redistribution for doctors' orders	RDO
8	The proportion of redistribution for doctors' orders	PRDO
9	Opening inventory of drug packing area	PIDPA
10	Delivery rate of doctors' orders	DRDO
11	Delivery time of doctors' orders	DTDO
12	Delivery of doctors' orders	DDO

Table 1. *(continued)*

Number	Variable	Acronym
13	Inventory of drug packing area	IDPA
14	Stock adjustment rate of drug packing area	SARDPA
15	Stock adjustment time of drug packing area	SATDPA
16	Safety stock of drug packing area	SSDPA
17	Delivery time of drug packing area	DTDPA
18	Delivery rate of drug packing area	DRDPA
19	Opening inventory of drug in treatment room	OIDPA
20	Inventory of drug in treatment room	IDTR
21	Stock adjustment time of drug in treatment room	SATDTR
22	Stock adjustment rate of drug in treatment room	SARDTR
23	Safety stock of drug in treatment room	SSDTR
24	Delivery time of treatment room	DTTR
25	Delivery rate of treatment room	DRTR
26	Inventory of temporary storage area	ITSA
27	Opening inventory of temporary storage area	OITSA
28	Order rate of drug in temporary storage area	ORDTSA
29	Stock adjustment time of drug in temporary storage area	SATDTSA
30	Stock adjustment rate of drug in temporary storage area	SARDTSA
31	Safety stock of drug in temporary storage area	SSDTSA
32	Delivery time of drug in temporary storage area	DTDTSA
33	Opening inventory of external using	OIEU
34	External utilization rate	EUR
35	Potential needs of patients	PNP
36	Number of unmanned vehicles	NUV
37	Single cost of unmanned vehicle	SCUV
38	The change rate of distribution cost	CRDC
39	Distribution cost	DC
40	Inventory of utilization drug in temporary storage area	TUDTSA
41	Ratio of utilization drug in temporary storage area	RUDTSA
42	Utilization of utilization drug in temporary storage area	UUDTSA
43	Time delay of utilization drug in temporary storage area	TDUDTSA
44	The proportion of drug in temporary storage area	PDTSA
45	Time delay of drug in temporary storage area	TDDTSA
46	Stock adjustment time of drug in temporary storage area	SATDTSA
47	Order rate of drug in treatment room	ORDTR
48	Repackaging rate	RR

2.5. Simulation Model Formulation

2.5.1. Flow Stock Diagram

The flow stock diagram is a graphical representation that further distinguishes the nature of variables on the basis of the causal loop diagram, describes the logical relationships between system elements with more intuitive symbols, and clarifies the feedback forms and control laws of the system [24]. Through the analysis of each influencing factor of the drug distribution system within the mobile cabin hospital, the flow stock diagram of the contactless drug distribution system was drawn, as shown in Figure 2.

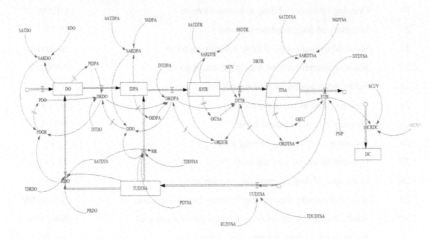

Figure 2. Flow stock diagram based on contactless drug distribution system

2.5.2. Mathematical Formulation

In this paper, combined with the actual data of the corresponding case, the mathematical equations of the variables are established. Among them, since the level variables and the rate variables are the key types of variables studied in the logistics distribution model, they are presented separately in a list, as shown in Table 2.

Table 2. The stock of equation

Number	The Stock of Equation	Unit
1	DO=INTEG((DELAY1I(PDO, 1 , 0) - DRDO + RDO,0)	Piece
2	IDPA=INTEG((DELAY1I(DRDO,1 ,0) - DRDPA + RR),0)	Piece
3	ITSA=INTEG(DELAY1I(DRDPA,1 , 0) - DTTR,0)	Piece
4	ITSA=INTEG(DELAY1I(DTTR, 1 , 0) - EUR,0)	Piece
5	TUDTSA=INTEG(UUDTSA - RR - RDO,100)	Piece
6	DC=INTEG(CRDC,0)	RMB

Meanwhile, the main rate variable equations in this paper are as follows:

$$DRDO=MIN(PIDPA/DTDO+PDO, DELAY1I(DDO, 5, 0)) \tag{1}$$

$$DRDPA=MIN(OIDPA/DTDPA+DRDO, DELAY1I(DTTR, 5, 0)) \tag{2}$$

$$EUR=MIN(OIEU/DTDTSA+DTTR, SMOOTH(PNP, 2)) \tag{3}$$

$$RDO=DELAY1(TUDTSA*PRDO/SATDTSA, TDRDO) \tag{4}$$

There are also some auxiliary variables as well as constants in the model, whose equations and coefficients are shown in Table 3.

Table 3. Auxiliary variables and parametric equations

Number	Auxiliary Variables and Parametric Equations	Type of variable
1	PIDPA=DELAY1I(DO, 1 , 0)	Auxiliary variable
2	SARDPA=(SSDPA - IDPA)/SATDPA	Auxiliary variable
3	ORDTR=DELAY1I(DTTR, 1 ,0) + SARDTR	Auxiliary variable
4	SADTO=3	constant
5	SSDPA=120	constant
6	PNP=1200*RANDOM NORMAL(1, 2 , 1.5 , 2 , 99)	constant
7	DTDO=2	constant
8	TDDTSA=1	constant
9	DTDTSA=2	constant
10	TDUDTSA=2	constant
11	RUDTSA=0.3	constant
12	DTDPA=2	constant
13	SATDTSA=2	constant
14	TDRDO=1	constant

2.6. Model Validation

System dynamics is the science of studying the behavior of systems and their structures. The rationality of system dynamics modeling requires testing of the model. only the following test items are usually completed: system boundary test; step size test; model structure and its behavior test; parameter estimation test; integration error test; consistency of magnitudes test; extreme scenario test; and sensitivity test [25].

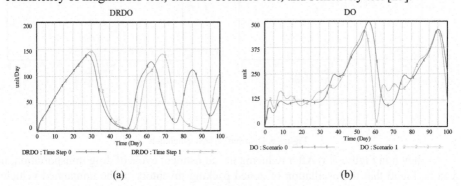

(a)   (b)

Figure 3. Test chart

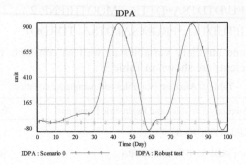

Figure 4. Test chart

In this paper, according to the actual situation, the above system boundary test, step size test, sensitivity test, extreme scenario test, and consistency test are selected to test and analyze the model, and finally pass the test to prove that the model can be used for subsequent simulation. All tests passed, the test results are shown in the Figure 3 and Figure 4.

3. Analysis of Experimental Results

3.1. Analysis of Key Influencing Factors of Distribution System

Tn order to study how to study the distribution efficiency and distribution cost influencing factors of the drug distribution system before and after the contactless distribution technology in a more cost-efficient way, the bullwhip effect of contactless distribution and the distribution cost are related to the analysis and focus on finding the key influencing factors.

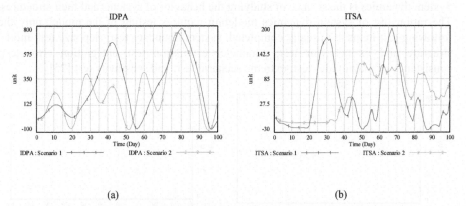

(a)   (b)

Figure 5. Distribution cost simulation

As shown in Figure 5(a) After reducing the adjustment cycle of drug transportation, it can be found that the oscillation of zoned packing inventory in the unmanned vehicle compartment is significantly reduced, which in turn significantly reduces the inventory cost in the distribution process, and thus improves the distribution and transportation efficiency. Therefore, reducing the adjustment cycle of drug transportation and improving the response speed in the distribution process can appropriately reduce the cost of distribution and improve the efficiency of distribution.

As shown inFigure 5(b) After reducing the adjustment period of drug transportation, it can be found that the stock shock of drugs in the staging area is significantly reduced. As the end node of distribution and handover in the shelter hospital, the temporary storage area can reduce the inventory shock, effectively reduce the distribution pressure, improve the distribution and transportation efficiency, reduce the backlog of drugs in stock in the distribution process, and improve the turnover and delivery rate of drugs.

After the adjustment cycle for drug transportation was reduced, the number of deliveries that needed to be made for later transportation was significantly reduced due to the significant reduction in the wave of materials that needed to be stored in the inventory of each segment, which in turn improved the efficiency of distribution and reduced the cost of later distribution. The model simulation data reveals that the distribution cost is reduced by about 28.6% after the adjustment cycle reduction is performed. As shown in Figure 6 .

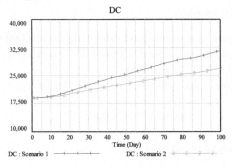

Figure 6. Distribution cost simulation

3.2. Requirement Analysis of Unmanned Vehicle Configuration

In order to objectively evaluate the demand for the number of unmanned vehicles in the mobile cabin hospital of the model from more angles, and quantify the research indicators, the number of unmanned vehicles simulation is carried out for the model. Considering the small area of the mobile cabin hospital, the demand for unmanned vehicles is only limited to the distribution of the medical prescriptions of spare drugs in the cabin, so six simulation scenarios are set, increasing from one vehicle to the next, including one vehicle, two vehicles, four vehicles, six vehicles, eight vehicles and ten vehicles. The simulation results are shown in Figure 7. The simulation results show that with the increase of the number of unmanned vehicles, the doctors'orders and inventory of temporary storage area show similar fluctuations. When the number of vehicles increases to 8, the fluctuation range becomes smaller, and the simulation fluctuations of 8 vehicles and 10 vehicles tend to be the same. This shows that when more than 8 vehicles are configured, the demand fluctuation of standby drug dispensing and the inventory fluctuation in the distribution system are the smallest, the distribution demand tends to be stable, the in transit inventory is reduced, the stable supply of drugs is ensured, and the backlog of drugs in stock is reduced. Therefore, it is the most economical for the mobile cabin hospital in Wuhan Guangdong science and Technology Exhibition Center in this model to be equipped with 8 unmanned vehicles. Of course, the model is also applicable to the number of unmanned vehicles in other hospitals.

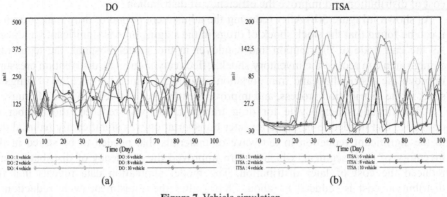

Figure 7. Vehicle simulation

3.3. Distribution Cost Analysis

In terms of cost, the cost of an unmanned vehicle needs 100,000 yuan, safe and reliable, low post-care costs, according to the design life of 5 years to record. Then the fixed cost of a single unmanned vehicle is as follows.

The residual value of the unmanned vehicle at the fifth year is:

$$100000\times5\%=5000 \; RMB \tag{5}$$

The annual depreciation charges are:

$$(100000-100000\times5\%)/5=19000 \; RMB \tag{6}$$

The annual depreciation expense is regarded as the fixed cost of the unmanned vehicle, while the equipment maintenance expense, management expense and other daily operating costs of the unmanned vehicle are included in the variable cost of the unmanned vehicle. According to the statistics of the unmanned Distribution Department of meituan company, the average distribution cost of unmanned aerial vehicles when delivering takeout is 7-8 RMB per order. Therefore, it is considered to set the daily operation cost of short-distance unmanned vehicles in the hospital as 1 yuan per order. By simulating the distribution cost of a single unmanned vehicle in the benchmark scenario and the optimization scenario, the simulation data of the distribution cost is obtained.

It can be seen from Table 4 that during 90 days of simulation, the cumulative cost of a single unmanned vehicle under the benchmark scenario is 30191 yuan, and the simulation result of the optimized model is 25961 yuan. The model simulation data show that the cumulative use cost of a single unmanned vehicle during the three months under the epidemic is about 25961-30191 yuan. The treatment cost of covid-19 mild patients is 17000 yuan, and the treatment cost of severe patients is higher, even up to 200000 yuan. According to the website of the State Commission for Discipline Inspection of the Central Commission for Discipline Inspection of China. According to the official wechat of the people's Bank of China, from January 22 to February 23, 2020, the national treasury at all levels allocated 61372 funds for epidemic prevention and control, with an amount of 8.93 billion yuan. This data does not include a large number of private material donations. In such a large economic consumption, the unmanned vehicle distribution mode can not only reduce the infection risk of medical personnel, but also save the consumption of human resources and protective materials.

Table 4. Distribution cost of single unmanned vehicle

Time (Day)	30	60	90
Scenario 1: Distribution cost	22487RMB	26747RMB	30191RMB
Scenario 2: Distribution cost	21066RMB	23669RMB	25961RMB

4. Conclusion

The sudden increase in demand for in-hospital drug delivery in sentinel hospitals during the epidemic, coupled with the risk of cross-infection between doctors and patients, has increased the complexity of the drug delivery process within mobile cabin hospitals, and thus highlighted the advantages of contactless delivery technology applied to hospital drug delivery. Therefore, hospitals should explore the benefits of deploying unmanned vehicles and quantify the value of contactless drug delivery. This study explores the delivery costs and configuration requirements of unmanned vehicle technology within a mobile cabin hospital in the context of a real-world case, taking into account not only the characteristics of the hospital's medical orders, but also the delays generated by the need for epidemic prevention in the delivery chain, and the contactless distribution behavior of drugs in the mobile cabin hospital is analyzed by constructing the system dynamics model. In order to achieve this goal, the actual situation of the mobile cabin hospital was first studied and the modules and logic of the system were specified. Then, the necessary data were collected and analyzed for the developed model, which was used to specify the mathematical functions of the variables in the model. Through continuous simulation and optimization, key influencing factors such as the adjustment period of drug transportation and the bullwhip effect of the distribution system were identified, and the configuration requirements of unmanned vehicles and the cost of single vehicle distribution of unmanned vehicles in the mobile cabin hospital under the background of the case are analyzed.

Acknowledgment

This project is supported by Guangxi young and middle-aged teacher's basic ability enhancement project (2021KY1807) and Guangxi young and middle-aged teacher's basic ability enhancement project (2018KY0744).

References

[1] Chen, Shun-Da, Tang, J., Ye, Q., Liu, D. Practice of contactless drug dispensing model in Fangzhai Hospital[J]. Pharmaceutical Herald,2020,39(07):940-942(in Chinese).

[2] Xu Y, Dong J, Ren R, et al. The impact of metro-based underground logistics system on city logistics performance under COVID-19 epidemic: A case study of Wuhan, China[J]. Transport policy, 2022, 116: 81-95.

[3]   Hu Hu, Tang Ziqi, Liu Fuxin, Wang Yuqin, He Xiongfei, Zhao Jiao. Optimization of "contactless" distribution of medical protective materials under epidemic[J]. China Management Science:1-11.

[4]   Lemke, M.K., Apostolopoulos, Y., Sonmez, S., 2020. Syndemic frameworks to understand the effects of COVID-19 on commercial driver stress, health, and safety. j. Transp. Health 18, 100877.

[5]   Deshpande U U, Malemath A B V S. Unmanned Drug Delivery Vehicle for COVID-19 Wards in Hospitals[J]. Journal of Computer Science Research, 2021, 3(3).

[6]   Li H, Xiong K, Xie X. Multiobjective Contactless Delivery on Medical Supplies under Open-Loop Distribution[J]. Mathematical Problems in Engineering, 2021, 2021.

[7]   Banik D, Hossain N U I, Govindan K, et al. A decision support model for selecting unmanned aerial vehicle for medical supplies: context of COVID-19 pandemic[J]. The International Journal of Logistics Management, 2022.

[8]   Luo J Y, Wang J Y, Yu H. A dynamic vehicle routing problem for medical supplies in large-scale emergencies[C]//2011 6th IEEE Joint International Information Technology and Artificial Intelligence Conference. IEEE, 2011, 1: 271-275.

[9]   Golroudbary S R, Zahraee S M. System dynamics model for optimizing the recycling and collection of waste material in a closed-loop supply chain[J]. Simulation modelling practice and theory, 2015, 53: 88-102.

[10]   Xia De 1, Fangru Wu. Towards More Sustainability: A Dynamic Recycling Framework of Discarded Products Based on SD Theory[J]. International Journal of Intelligent Systems and Applications, 2011, 3(1):43-50.

[11]   Yu Jianping. Design and dynamics simulation optimization of the Internet of Things system for pharmaceutical manufacturing enterprises[D]. Guangdong University of Technology, 2020(in Chinese).

[12]   Li Haoqi. Research on the optimization of cold chain distribution system for aquatic products based on system dynamics [D]. Qingdao University of Technology,2019(in Chinese).

[13]   Lewe, J.H., Hivin, L.F., Mavris, D.N., 2014. a multi-paradigm approach to system dynamics modeling of intercity transportation. transport. res. E Logist. transport. rev. 71, 188-202.

[14]   Angerhofer B J, Angelides M C. System dynamics modelling in supply chain management: research review[C]//2000 Winter Simulation Conference Proceedings (Cat. No. 00CH37165). IEEE, 2000, 1: 342-351.

[15]   Zhou Yunfeng. Research on the distribution of flood control materials based on system dynamics with multiple supply points and multiple demand points[J]. Modern Trade Industry,2019,40(14):42-46(in Chinese).

[16]   Lai C L, Lee W B, Ip W H. A study of system dynamics in just-in-time logistics[J]. Journal of materials processing technology, 2003, 138(1-3): 265-269.

[17]   Gui S, Zhu Q, Lu L. Area logistics system based on system dynamics model[J]. Tsinghua science and technology, 2005, 10(2): 265-269.

[18]   Zhang Zhiyong, Yang Liu, Shi Yongqiang, Lin Dansheng. Optimization of low-carbon urban distribution based on system dynamics[J]. Logistics Technology,2017,36(03):78-83(in Chinese).

[19]   Cruz-Cantillo Y. A system dynamics approach to humanitarian logistics and the transportation of relief supplies[J]. International Journal of System Dynamics Applications (IJSDA), 2014, 3(3): 96-126

[20]   D. Vlachos, P. Georgiadis, E. Iakovou, A system dynamics model for dynamic capacity planning of remanufacturing in closed-loop supply chains, Comput. Oper. Res. 34 (2) (2007) 367-394.

[21]   Guo Xin. Research on urban emergency logistics distribution based on system dynamics[D]. Shenyang University,2016(in Chinese).

[22]   Sterman, J., 2000. Business Dynamics: Systems Thinking and Modeling for a Complex World. irwin/McGraw-Hill, Boston.

[23]   Emberger, G., Pfaffenbichler, P., 2020. A quantitative analysis of potential impacts of automated vehicles in Austria using a dynamic integrated land Transport Pol. 98, 57-67.

[24]   Fontoura, W.B., Chaves, G.D.L.D., Ribeiro, G.M., 2019. The Brazilian urban mobility policy: the impact in Sao Paulo transport system using system dynamics. transport Pol. 73, 51-61.

[25]   Vijay Nehra 1. MATLAB/Simulink Based Study of Different Approaches Using Mathematical Model of Differential Equations[J]. International Journal of Intelligent Systems and Applications, 2014, 6(5):1-24.

Artificial Intelligence, Medical Engineering and Education
Z.B. Hu et al. (Eds.)

387

doi:10.3233/ATDE231349

Research on Digitization of Plate Cutting Based on DELMIA

Yan HONG, Qin HE[1], Haixia ZENG, Yi HUANG, Xiaoying XU
Mechanical and Electrical Engineering Department, Wenhua College, Wuhan, China
ORCiD ID: Yan HONG https://orcid.org/0009-0004-9891-8713

Abstract. With the development of the economy and the innovation of technology, enterprises are eager to have higher, efficient, energy-saving and environmental protection technology applied in the cutting process. There are a lot of problems in the cutting process right now, For example, there will be uneven cutting section, Cutting dust debris splashing around causes environmental pollution and other problems. So, it is still necessary to constantly improve the cutting equipment. This paper studies the simulation of plasma cutting machine based on DELMIA. The cutting path in AUTOCAD is imported into DELMIA, and the cutting nozzle is simulated according to this path. At the same time, the second development of DELMIA is conducted based on VB language. The information of different steel plates can be automatically matched with the cutting nozzle type, cutting speed, etc., and is associated with the motion speed in DELMIA software. Seek the shortest cutting path, reduce the empty path, increase the effective cutting working time, so as to improve the cutting efficiency; And take into account environmental protection to reduce pollution and reduce noise.

Keyword. Plate cutting; DELMIA; Secondary development; Digitization research.

1. DELMIA Introduction

DELMIA is a "digital manufacturing" simulation platform for design, manufacturing, maintenance and man-machine processes, covering the digital manufacturing of almost all mechanical products such as aviation, aerospace, automobiles and ships, involving spot welding, arc welding, cutting, assembly, painting, final assembly, gluing, handling, automation and many other professions [1-4].

The secondary development can make the software better serve the user, which has an important role in improving the work efficiency and work quality. For this reason, DELMIA provides users with secondary development interfaces and open internal command sets, which brings convenience to users' secondary development [5-7].

DELMIA mainly provides two secondary development interfaces, including the open component-based Application Programming Interface (CAA) and Automated Object Programming (V5 Automation) [8-9]. Based on the characteristics of the two development methods, this paper chooses to use Automation method to carry out secondary development of DELMIA, and the development environment chooses Visual Basic 6.0.

---

[1] Corresponding Author: Qin HE, E-mail: 267083084@qq.com.

2. The Simulation of Plate Cutting Path based on DELMIA

DELMIA's 3D simulation has been widely used in aircraft assembly, automobile body assembly, ship virtual assembly and other aspects [10-11]. Errors in product design, tooling design and process design should be found early before the product is put into actual production to reduce the rework and scrap of the product [12-16].

The amount of steel used in China's machinery industry has reached more than 300 million tons, and the amount of steel cutting is very large. However, in the actual machining process, often due to insufficient preparation work, or blindly shortening the construction period, resulting in the phenomenon of design, production, and modification, thus increasing cost and extending the construction period.

2.1. Establish Cutting Machine Simulation Model

The plasma cutting machine is composed of rails, beams and cutting guns and other components. In actual production, the cutting machine needs to be driven horizontally and vertically. In order to achieve the cutting effect in actual production, constraints are also added to the model in DELMIA, laying the foundation for the simulation of the cutting machine below.

2.1.1. Creating Mechanical Devices

In the "Device Building" module, select the first command "New Mechanism"; Then fix the base; Select the "Fixed part" command and select the guide rail as the base to fix it. Finally, add constraints between components.For example, the cutting machine body moves along the guide rail, you need to add a moving pair, select a line and surface that the fuselage fits with the guide rail, and check the length drive, you can make the fuselage move on the guide rail.

2.1.2. Setting the Device as a Robot

For convenience, the device can be set up as a software-recognizable robot, with all the characteristics and uses of the robot, and can drag the various parts of the cutting machine through the compass. First, "Frames of Interest" is established, click the Frames of Interes command, select the device to be created, that is, the cutting machine, click Fram Type, and select Tools as the type. Then grab the compass to the bottom of the cutting torch of the cutting machine, select the point where the cutting torch cuts the steel plate and the steel plate contact.

2.2. Cutting Process Simulation

In this paper, the nesting diagram of former one-stroke cutting is selected in the simulation, and DELMIA's DPM module is used to carry out the cutting machine Real-time simulation. The main Robot Arc Welding module provides different tools to create an efficient and intuitive simulation environment, often combined with two modules: Device Task Definition and Workcell Sequencing. Form a complete system to meet the needs of welding simulation.

2.2.1. Creating Tag Points

In Robot Arc Welding module ----Tag----Tag on Intersectin Parts, wait until the command icon turns yellow, select the steel plate plane first and then select the track. Flip Curve is to adjust the direction of the track line. If the arrow direction is wrong, click to reverse adjustment. To evenly create Tag points over a path, select Equal Spacing and enter the number of Tag points.

2.2.2. Create RobotTasks and Simulations

Tasks should be assigned to Process before simulation. To do this, select the new command from the file menu. Select Process Library from the dialog box, then enter the interface, select Create New Activity Type - Create New Activity Subtype - save and close.

Enter Workcell Sequencing module, the Activity Management toolbar and select Insert Activity Library - Activity Library file - Insert Activity - resource allocation, The created tasks can be assigned to the process for simulation. The simulation effect diagram is shown in Figure 1.

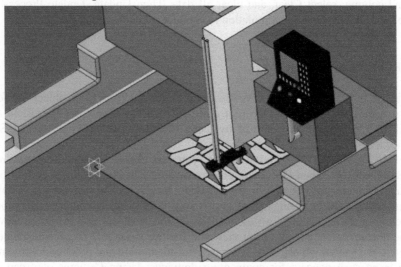

Figure 1. Simulation effect of cutting machine

In order to set the cutting nozzle speed, many parameters need to be modified to make it move at a uniform speed. The precision file in Controller - Flyby is selected ON, the intensive reading type is selected Speed, and the value is 100; Motion Profile is to enter the robot speed, generally choose absolute, enter the speed value can be. Multiple speeds can be defined and set to the current value.

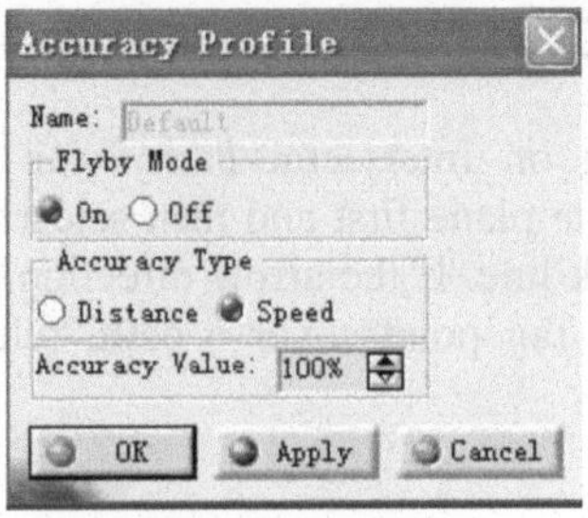

Figure 2. Motion Profile 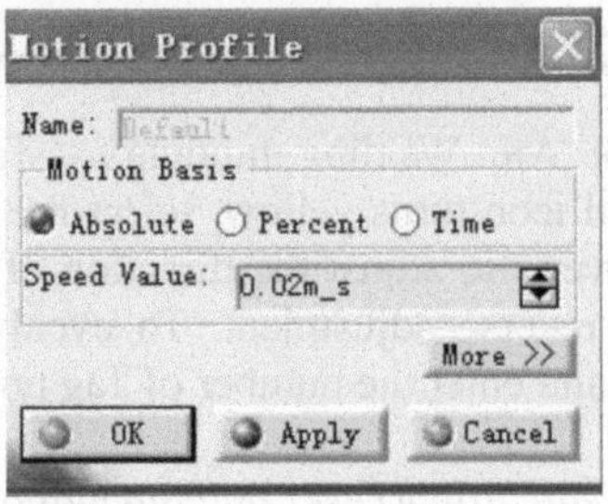   **Figure 3.** Accuracy Profile

2.3. Check the Cutting Speed

In order to ensure that the cutting process of the cutting machine maintains uniform motion, verification is required. Click the Data Readout command in the Simulation Analysis Tools toolbar to bring up the Option toolbar. Click the second command to bring up the dialog box.

Change Tcpspeed to Yes in the Selection list, then click Spread Sheed in the second column, select Clear, and clear all data. Then Update, Update Process Cycle Time, and click Robot Task Simulation to conduct simulation after the update.

3. DELMIA Object Structure

All data is blocked in DELMIA Automation, It takes the form of an object and forms a tree structure. Application is the root object, which is the entrance to DELMIA. All DELMIA objects can be obtained by using the Documents, Windows and System Service attributes of the root object.

First obtain the Application object, you can obtain Documents and Windows collection objects; Then Document objects such as Part and Product can be obtained through Documents object. For the created Document object, you can obtain the Document by saving, closing and other methods. For the object that needs 3D modeling, modeling operations can be carried out. The document object also stores the viewpoint of the document, such as the front view and the left view, etc. These view objects are stored in the camera object. This is for part documentation and product documentation, there is no such concept for engineering drawings; Using Cameras, you can obtain Camera objects Camera2D and Camera3D.

A Windows object is a collection of all open Windows, and a Window object is a specific window. The relationship between the two is similar to the relationship between Documents and Document objects. Viewer object is a property of Window object, generally using Window, ActiveViewer can get it, and then use many methods of Viewer object, such as Reframe, ZoomeIn, ZoomOut, you can zoom in and reorganize the view.

4.   Secondary Development of Plate Cutting based on DELMIA

In the plate cutting virtual simulation process, because the cutting parameters must be set each time, and for the steel plate with different plate thickness, the cutting nozzle model and cutting speed of the cutting machine have corresponding data, in order to avoid the trouble of adding parameters each time in the simulation and in order to better display all the parameter values in the cutting process, In this paper, the speed, cutting time, energy consumption and exhaust emission of cutting machine are controlled by DELMIA software secondary development method.

It is mainly to realize the selection of various commands and parameters on the cutting interface.

4.1. Insert Steel Plate Cutting Information

The program interface is set up plasma cutting machine, CNC cutting machine and laser cutting machine three types, and is equipped with semi-automatic and automatic options, you can make the whole cutting data at a glance.

Double-click the form, write its event code, and enter the following:
Add cutting machine type
CboCuttingMachine. AddItem "plasma cutting"
Add cutting speed
cboCuttingSpeed.AddItem "0.027"

4.2. Setting the Cutting Speed

There are a variety of options for steel cutting information in the interface. In order to reduce the workload, the software is edited to automatically select the corresponding cutting nozzle type and cutting speed when selecting the thickness.

Double-click the plate thickness form and write the event code as follows:
Private Sub cboThick_Click()
Select Case cboThick.Text
Case "5-15"
cboCuttingType = 1
cboCuttingSpeed = 0.08
End Select

4.3. Associated Cutting Speed

The previous section only set the cutting speed of the cutting nozzle on the program interface, but it is not related to the speed of the cutting machine, and it cannot play a role. In order to realize the control of the speed of the cutting machine on the window interface, I wrote a method program to obtain the speed of the robot.

Get the PPR object
Set currDoc = DELMIA.ActiveDocument. PPRDocument
Gets the resource object Set Res = currDoc.Resources
Get the robot object Set Rob = Res.Item(i)
Get controller object
Set RobCon = Rob.GetTechnologicalObject ("RobGenericController")
Get the MotionProfile
RobCon.GetMotionProfiles MPro
Gets the name of the MotionProfile and assigns a cut speed value
MPro.GetName Pname
MPro.SetSpeedValue cboCuttingSpeed

As shown in Figure 4, this program is to obtain the speed of the robot and make the cutting speed reflected in the cutting machine when the program is running.

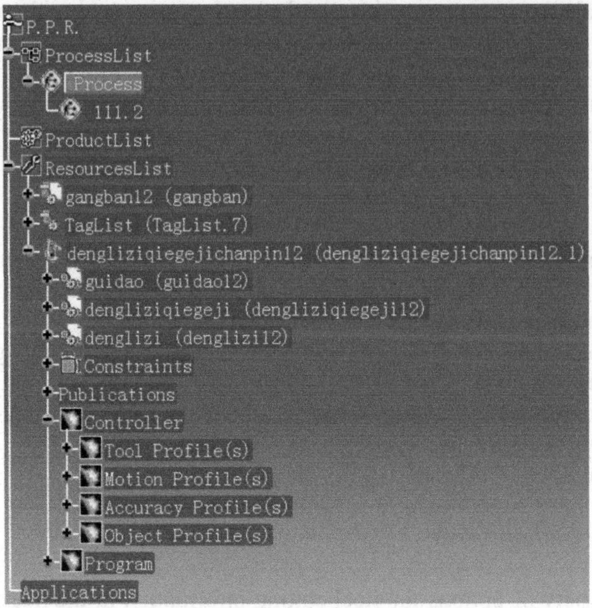

Figure 4. PPR structure

As mentioned earlier, the secondary development of DELMIA is accessed on a per-object basis in the PPR tree. First, access the PPR object, set the object to the current document, and then get the PPR resource object, there are multiple resources under the resource, The robot object is obtained through the Item method of the resource object, and then the GetTechnologicalObject method of the robot is used to access the Controller object. This sequence is broken through step by step. Multiple objects under the controller can be obtained by the Get method.

4.4. Simulation Results, Program Implementation

In DELMIA, there is a Gantt chart that records the time of each stage of the robot movement. After establishing the task, click on the Gantt chart command, and then it will prompt you to Select an Activity. Click the little man below Process to enter the Gantt chart page. This section is to implement this process in the program to obtain the movement time.

```
Set Doc = DELMIA.ActiveDocument
Set RootP = Doc.GetItem("Process")
Set Act = RootP.ChildrenActivities.Item(i)
oOCT = Act.CalculatedCycleTime
txtTime = Round (oOCT / 3600, 3)
```

5.   Conclusion

In this paper, the nesting diagram is successfully imported into DELMIA, and the cutting task of the cutting machine is created for real-time simulation, and then the cutting process is verified, a more accurate cutting process is obtained, and the digitalization of the cutting process of the cutting machine is realized. Then using V5 Automation interface, using VB language to DELMIA secondary development. The information of different steel plates can be automatically matched with the cutting nozzle type, cutting speed, etc., and associated with the motion speed in DELMIA software, and finally the cutting time can be obtained to calculate the energy consumption and gas emission during the cutting process. The program can be used to guide the actual production and facilitate the production management of the cutting process and even the entire processing process.

Acknowledgment

This study is supported by the first-class undergraduate specialty construction project in Hubei Province (J09007802) and the teaching quality and teaching reform project of Wenhua University (J09007014).

References

[1]   Zha Hongwen, Wang Hongtao. Robot 3D measurement simulation based on DELMIA[J]. Applied Science and Technology, 2013, 40(1): 19-21.
[2]   Dai H, Lv G, Huang W, et al. Research on the simulation process for the CFETR Divertor assembly in delmia[C]. Advanced Science and Industry Research Center. Proceedings of 2020 4th International Conference on Electrical, Automation and Mechanical Engineering, 2020: 6.
[3]   Yao Y, Tian Z, Cao W. A Simulation study on the assembly of an integrated transmission device of an armored vehicle based On DELMIA[C]. Institute of Management Science and Industrial Engineering.Proceedings of 2018 8th International Conference on Education, Management, Computer and Society. Francis Academic Press, 2018: 3.
[4]   H. D. Li, X.Y. Sheng, W. D. Zhang. Ergonomics analysis of hoisting large equipment based on DELMIA[C]. Information Engineering Research Institute, USA. Proceedings of 4th International Conference on Materials Engineering for Advanced Technologies. DEStech Publications, 2015: 5.
[5]   WU C. Research and application of DELMIA secondary development[J]. International Journal of Intelligent Information and Management Science, Hong Kong New Century Cultural Publishing House, 2014: 4.
[6]   Hu Ting, Wu Lijun. Technical basis of CATIA secondary development[M]. Beijing: Publishing House of Electronics Industry, 2006: 1-150.
[7]   Li Zisheng, Zhu Ying, Xiang Zhongfan. Secondary development technology based on CATIA software[J]. Journal of Sichuan Institute of Technology, 2003, 22 (1): 16-18.
[8]   Long Feng, Fan Liuqun. Discussion on secondary development Technology of CATIA V5[J]. Journal of Huaiyin Institute of Technology, 2005, 14 (5): 21-23.
[9]   Peng Huan. Research on secondary development technology of CATIA based on V5Automation[J]. Journal of Electronic and Mechanical Engineering, 2012, 28(2): 61-64.
[10] Wang Zhanhai, Zhai Qinggang. Preliminary study on secondary development Technology of DELMIA[J]. Journal of Xi 'an Aeronautical Technical College, 2010(1): 1-3.
[11] Wang Lidong , Wang Guanghui. Big Data in Cyber-physical systems, digital manufacturing and Industry 4.0[C]. International Journal of Engineering and Manufacturing, 2016, 6(4): 1-8.
[12] Farhan M. Nashwan, Khaled A. M. Al Soufy. An Intelligent system for detecting fake materials on the internet[C]. International Journal of Intelligent Systems and Applications, 2023, 4(15): 37-52.
[13] Hashimova Kamala. Intelligent management of a network of smart billboards on the IoT platform in Industry 4.0. International Journal of Information Technology and Computer Science, 2023, 6(14): 39-46.

[14] Guan Z, Cao L, Wang C, et al. Simulation of logistics system with aspect of pallet requirements optimization based on digital factory[C]. Proceedings of the 2011 International Conference on Automation and Robotics (ICAR 2011 V1), Springer, 2011: 10.

[15] Okumoto Y. Optimization of torch movements of welding of welding and cutting using ant colony method [J]. Journal of Ship Production, 2009, 25(3): 136-141.

[16] Davila-Rios, Torres-Trevino. On the implementation of a robotic welding process using 3D simulation environmen[J]. Electronics, Robotics and Automotive Mechanics Conference, 2008: 283-287.

Artificial Intelligence, Medical Engineering and Education
Z.B. Hu et al. (Eds.)
doi:10.3233/ATDE231350

Traffic Flow Characteristics of Road Sections Containing Double Speed Limit Zones

Lanxiang WEI[a], Wugang LI[a,1], Rongjian HUANG[b]

ᵃ School of Intelligent Manufacturing, Nanning University, Nanning, China
ᵇ School of Physics and Mechanical & Electrical Engineering, Hechi University, Hechi, China

Abstract. The establishment of speed limit zones on roads plays a role in ensuring driving safety, but speed limit zones are also a kind of traffic bottleneck, can also cause traffic congestion. In order to study the traffic flow characteristics of the speed limit area, based on the NaSch traffic flow model of the cellular automata, a traffic flow model suitable for the road section with double speed limit zone was established, and the influence of the maximum allowable speed and the length of the speed limit zone on the traffic flow was simulated and analyzed. It is concluded that the smaller the maximum speed allowed in the speed limit zone and the longer the speed limit zone, the smaller the traffic flow on the road and the smaller the average speed of vehicles, indicating that these two are important factors affecting road capacity.

Keywords. Cellular automaton; Speed limit zone; Traffic flow; Numerical simulation.

1. Introduction

Vehicle s driving on city roads, if the speed is too fast, it is easy to cause traffic accidents. For this reason, traffic management departments usually impose maximum speed limits on these sections of the road to ensure safe driving [1]. However, speed limit zones can cause traffic congestion on the road. Therefore, it is of practical significance to study the traffic problems in the speed limit area.

Cellular automata is composed of a number of evolutionary rules, one vehicle occupies one cell, all vehicles follow the same evolutionary rules, and the system forms a dynamic evolution through interaction between cells [2]. Among the various traffic flow models, the cellular automata model is easier to realize the numerical simulation of the real traffic situation on the computer than other models [3-6].

Scholars have conducted extensive research on traffic problems [7-15]. However, there are few theoretical studies on the traffic flow characteristics of speed limit sections in the existing literature. In this paper, a one-way single-lane cellular automaton model with double speed limit zones is established by using the NaSch traffic flow model of cellular automata, and the numerical simulation of the influence of the maximum

---

[1] Corresponding Author: Wugang LI, E-mail: wlx071102@163.com.

allowable speed of the speed limit zone and the length of the speed limit zone on the traffic flow is carried out on the computer, and the simulation results are analyzed and discussed.

2. Traffic Flow Model

The road system in this article is divided into four areas. The number of normal driving areas and speed limit areas is equal. The schematic diagram of the road section model is shown in Figure 1. Suppose the carriageway is composed of 1,000 cells, and the actual road length of each cell is 7.5m. Each car occupies one cell, the black cell means there is a car, and the blank cell means that there is no car there. The total length of the road is $L=L_{b1}+L_{a1}+L_{b2}+L_{a2}=7.5$km. Have the vehicle drive from left to right on a ring road, and when exiting the right boundary, start again from the left boundary [4]. The units of length in this paper are all in the unit of cells, and they are dimensionless.

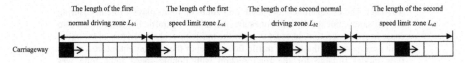

Figure 1. Schematic diagram of road section model with double speed limit zones

2.1. Provisions for Vehicle Speed and Probability of Vehicle Delay

Assume that there are N vehicles randomly distributed on the road. Each vehicle only occupies one cell. The state of each vehicle is represented by speed v. The value of v is an integer in $[0, v_{max}]$, that is, the speed of all vehicles. Distributed between 0 and the maximum speed. The maximum speed that vehicles are allowed to pass through in the first speed limit zone and the random delay probability of vehicles are represented by v_{max11} and P_{01} respectively; the maximum speed that vehicles are allowed to pass through and the random delay probability of vehicles in the second speed limit zone are represented by v_{max12} and P_{02} respectively; when the vehicle passes through the normal driving area, its maximum speed takes the larger value, represented by v_{max2}, $v_{max2}=5$ (moving 5 cells per second, the corresponding actual speed is 135km/h). At this time, the random delay probability takes the larger value. The small value is represented by P, $P=0.25$.

2.2. Vehicle Operation Rules Based on NaSch Model

There are four rules for vehicle operation:

1) Deterministic acceleration process: $v_n(t) \to \min(v_n(t)+1, v_{max})$;

2) Deterministic deceleration process: $v_n(t) \to \min(v_n(t), gap_n(t))$;

3) Random deceleration process: $v_n(t) \to \max(v_n(t)-1, 0)$ with probability P;

4) Location update process: $x_n(t) \to x_n(t)+v_n(t)$.

Among them, $v_n(t)$ and $x_n(t)$ are the speed and position of the nth vehicle at time t

respectively, $x_{n+1}(t)$ is the position of the $n+1$th vehicle at time t, $gapn(t)=x_{n+1}(t)-x_n(t)-1$ is the number of cells between the nth car and the immediately preceding car at time t. In each time step $t \rightarrow t+1$ (one time step is 1 second), all vehicles update their speed and position according to the above evolution rules.

3. Simulation and Results on the Computer

The calculation formula is as follows:

Vehicle density: $\rho = \dfrac{N}{L}$

Average traffic volume: $J = \rho \bar{v}$

Average speed of vehicle: $V = \dfrac{1}{S}\dfrac{1}{T}\dfrac{1}{N}\sum_{i=1}^{S}\sum_{t=t_0}^{t_0+T-1}\sum_{n=1}^{N}v_n(t)$

Let N cars be randomly distributed on 1000 cells, and the density of the vehicles is ρ, which is used as the starting point of timing. Each run of 40,000 time steps, due to the transient effect, the velocity $v_n(t)$ is not counted in the first 20,000 time steps, and only accumulates in the last 20,000 time steps. The average speed of each run is the average of the speed of 20,000 time steps. A total of 10 runs are run, namely $S=10$.

The values of the model parameters in this article are as follows: the random delay probabilities P_{01} and P_{02} of the vehicle in the speed limit area take a value of 0.4, 0.5, 0.6, and 0.7 respectively. When the vehicle passes through the normal driving zone, the maximum speed value is $v_{max2}=5$ (that is, 135km/h). When the vehicle passes through the speed limit zone, v_{max11} and v_{max12} take one of the values 1, 2, 3, and 4 respectively, corresponding to the actual speeds are 27km/h, 54km/h, 81km/h, and 108km/h respectively. The lengths L_{a1} and L_{a2} of the two speed limit zones take one of 100, 200, 300, and 400 respectively, and the corresponding actual lengths are 750m, 1500m, 2250m, and 3000m respectively.

3.1. The Impact V_{max11} and V_{max12} on Traffic Flow

Let $L_{a1}=L_{a2}=200$, $P_{01}=P_{02}=0.6$, v_{max11} and v_{max12} are taken as 1, 2, 3, and 4 respectively (the values of v_{max11} and v_{max12} are equal), and the basic diagram obtained is shown in Figure 2.

Observing Figure 2 (a), it can be seen that when the vehicle density is small, the distance between vehicles is larger, the vehicle driving is freer, and the average speed of the vehicle is large, the traffic flow is correspondingly large, and there is no traffic congestion. As the density increases, the flow-density curve shows a platform area, in which the traffic flow changes with the density is not obvious, and the flow is basically unchanged on the basic map, and the traffic congestion phenomenon can be eliminated or formed. When the vehicle density is high, the vehicle interval is relatively small, the vehicles affect each other, and the phenomenon of walking and stopping occurs when the average speed decreases rapidly, and the flow rate decreases quickly. When the vehicle density is about more than 0.8, the four curves in the figure coincide, that is, the road section is blocked at this time, and the maximum speed of the speed limit zone to restrict the traffic of vehicles no longer has an impact on the traffic capacity of the road. It can also be seen from Figure 2 (a) that the smaller the values of v_{max11} and v_{max12}, the smaller the J. When the density of vehicles in the road system is constant, the smaller the values of v_{max11} and v_{max12}, the smaller the traffic flow.

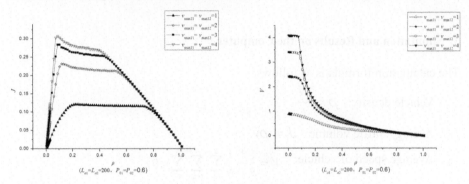

Figure 2. Basic diagram under different v_{max11} and v_{max12}

In Figure 2 (b), because there are speed limit zones on the road, both v_{max11} and v_{max12} are less than v_{max2}, vehicle speed reduction, and the rear vehicle should keep a safe distance and also slow down, the greater the vehicle density, the smaller the overall speed of the vehicle, so there is a trend that the average speed decreases with the increase of density. When the average speed of vehicles drops to zero, there is a traffic jam on the road. It can also be seen from Figure 2 (b) that the smaller the values of v_{max11} and v_{max12} at the same density, the smaller the average velocity.

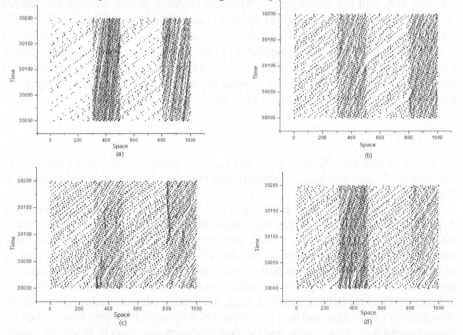

Figure 3. Spatiotemporal evolution patterns under different v_{max11} and v_{max12} (ρ=0.1,P_{01}=P_{02}=0.6, L_{a1}= L_{a2}=200, (a) v_{max11}=v_{max12}=1; (b) v_{max11}=v_{max12}=2; (c) v_{max11}=v_{max12}=3; (d) v_{max11}=2,v_{max12}=3)

Figure 3 is the time-space patch map of the road section with double speed limit area (parameter $\rho=0.1$, $P_{01}=P_{02}=0.6$, $L_{a1}=L_{a2}=200$). Among them, the vertical axis is 30000~30200 steps, the horizontal axis is 1000 cells, and the two speed limiting zones are located between 300~500 cells and 800~1000 cells. The black dot in the diagram indicates that there is a car in the cell, and the white dot indicates that there is no car in the cell. The maximum allowable speed in Figure 3 (a), (b) and (c) is the same, wherein (a) $v_{max11}=v_{max12}=1$, (b) $v_{max11}=v_{max12}=2$, (c) $v_{max11}=v_{max12}=3$, while Figure 3 (d) the maximum allowable speed of the two speed limiting zones is different, $v_{max11}=2$ and $v_{max12}=3$, respectively. The obvious black areas in Figure 3 (a), (b), (c), and (d) indicate the area of vehicle congestion, that is, the phenomenon of traffic congestion. According to the spatiotemporal evolution patch, the smaller v_{max11} and v_{max12}, the more serious the vehicle congestion. A comparison of (a), (b), (c), and (d) in Figure 3 also shows the changes in the basic diagram. Therefore, it can be concluded that v_{max11} or v_{max12} is one of the important factors affecting road traffic.

3.2. The Impact of Speed Limit Zone Lengths L_{a1} and L_{a2} on Traffic Flow

In the numerical simulation, $v_{max11}=v_{max12}=2$, $P_{01}=P_{02}=0.6$, L_{a1} and L_{a2} are 100, 200, 300 and 400 respectively (the values of L_{a1} and L_{a2} are equal), and the basic diagram obtained is shown in Figure 4.

The picture shows the basic flow-density diagram of the model in this article when $P_{01}=P_{02}=0.6$, $v_{max11}=v_{max12}=2$, and L_{a1} and L_{a2} are set to 100, 200, 300, and 400 respectively. By analyzing Figure 4 (a), when the vehicle density is small, the distance between vehicles is larger, the vehicle driving is freer, and V is large, J is correspondingly large, and there is no traffic congestion. When the vehicle density is in the medium range, the flow-density curve has a platform area, in which the traffic flow does not change significantly with the density, and the flow is basically unchanged on the basic diagram, and the traffic congestion can be eliminated or formed. In areas with high vehicle density, the distance between vehicles is relatively small, and the movement of vehicles is affected by other vehicles. They stop and go, the average speed decreases rapidly, and the traffic volume drops quickly.

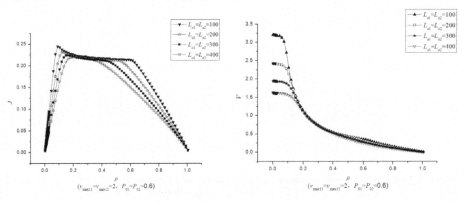

Figure 4. Basic diagram under different L_{a1} and L_{a2}

Figure 4 (b) shows the speed-density basic diagram obtained by the model in this article when $P_{01}=P_{02}=0.6$, $v_{max11}=v_{max12}=2$, and L_{a1} and L_{a2} are set to 100, 200, 300, and 400 respectively. In Figure 4 (b), because there are speed limit areas on the road, both

v_{max11} and v_{max12} are less than v_{max2}, the vehicle will decelerate, and the rear car should keep a safe distance and also slow down, the greater the vehicle density, the smaller the overall speed of the vehicle, so there is a trend that the average speed decreases with the increase of density. When the average speed of vehicles drops to zero, there is a traffic jam on the road.

Figure 5 is the spatio-temporal evolution pattern of a road section containing double speed limit zones (with certain parameters $\rho=0.1$, $P_{01}=P_{02}=0.6$, $v_{max11}=v_{max12}=2$). The lengths of the two speed limit zones in (a), (b) and (c) of Figure 5 are the same, where (a) Figure $L_{a1}=L_{a2}=200$, (b) Figure $L_{a1}=L_{a2}=300$, (c) Figure $L_{a1}=L_{a2}=400$; and Figure (d), the lengths of the two speed limit zones have different values, which are $L_{a1}=200$ and $L_{a2}=300$ respectively. The time-space patch map shows that the black spots are densely distributed in the speed restriction area. In the normal driving area, the black dots are sparsely distributed. This is because speed zones are slower than normal driving zones, and traffic congestion is more likely to occur in speed zones. When the length of the speed limit zone increases, the scope of traffic congestion becomes larger. The comparison of (a), (b), (c) and (d) in Figure 5 can also reflect the change of the Figure 4, which shows that L_{a1} or L_{a2} has a certain impact on the traffic flow and is one of the important factors causing traffic congestion.

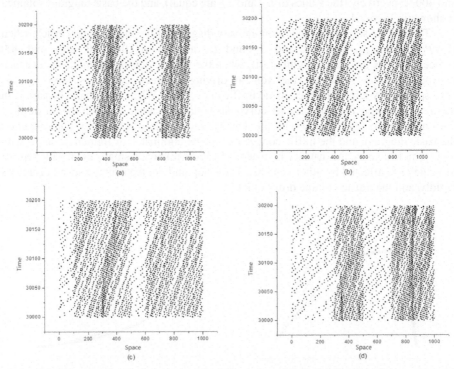

Figure 5. Spatiotemporal evolution patterns under different L_{a1} and L_{a2} ($\rho=0.1,P_{01}=P_{02}=0.6,v_{max11}=v_{max12}=2$, (a) $L_{a1}=L_{a2}=200$; (b) $L_{a1}=L_{a2}=300$; (c) $L_{a1}=L_{a2}=400$;(d) $L_{a1}=200,L_{a2}=300$)

4. Conclusion

In this paper, based on the NaSch traffic flow model of cellular automata, a traffic flow model suitable for road sections with double speed limit zones is established, and the traffic conditions of the road are numerically simulated by changing $v_{\mathrm{max}11}$ and $v_{\mathrm{max}12}$, L_{a1} and L_{a2} on a circular road. Based on the analysis of the basic map and the spatio-temporal evolution patch map obtained by simulation, it is concluded that the smaller the $v_{\mathrm{max}11}$ and $v_{\mathrm{max}12}$, and the longer L_{a1} and L_{a2}, the smaller the J and the smaller the V, indicating that these two are important factors affecting the road capacity. The above conclusions have certain reference value for the rational setting of speed limit zones and the study of solving the traffic congestion problem in speed limit zones.

Acknowledgment

This project is supported by Nanning University Professor Cultivation Engineering Project (Project No.: 2020JSGC01).

References

[1] Yang Xianqing, Zhang Wei, Qiu Kang, et al. Impact of speed limits on traffic flow [J]. Computational Physics, 2007, 24(4): 499-504 (in Chinese).

[2] Guo Siling. Research on phase change characteristics of cellular automaton traffic flow model and analysis of traffic measurements [D]. Nanning: Guangxi University, 2006: 15-22 (in Chinese).

[3] Xue Yu, Dong Liyun, Dai Shiqiang. An improved one-dimensional cellular automaton traffic flow model and the influence of deceleration probability [J]. Acta Physica Sinica, 2001, 50(3): 445-449.

[4] Liu Xiaoming, Wang Li. Cellular automata traffic flow model considering on-street parking [J]. Journal of Jilin University (Engineering Edition), 2012, 42(2): 327-333 (in Chinese).

[5] Chowdhury D, Santen L, and Schreckenberg A. Statistical physics of vehicular traffic and some related systems [J]. Phys. Rept., 2000, 329: 199-329.

[6] Fan Yanhong. Traffic flow modeling and research on traffic energy consumption and traffic accidents on some complex road sections [D]. Guilin: Guangxi Normal University, 2013: 13-22 (in Chinese).

[7] Wei Lanxiang, Liang Yujuan. Impact of delay probability and on-street parking strip length on road traffic[J]. Journal of Southwest Normal University (Natural Science Edition), 2016, 41(5):115-121 (in Chinese).

[8] Wei Lanxiang. A cellular automaton traffic flow energy consumption model considering on-street parking[J]. Science and Technology Bulletin, 2017, 33(1): 216-220 (in Chinese).

[9] Sun Dihua, Peng Guanghan, Fu Liping, et al. A continuum traffic flow model with the consideration of coupling effect for two-lane freeways[J]. Acta Physica Sinica, 2011, 27(2) :228-236.

[10] Nur Kumala Dewi. Review of vehicle surveillance using iot in the smart transportation concept[J]. International Journal of Engineering and Manufacturing.2021, 11(1): 29-36.

[11] Vo Hoai Viet, Huynh Nhat Duy. Object tracking: an experimental and comprehensive study on vehicle object in video[J]. International Journal of Image, Graphics and Signal Processing, 2022, 14(1): 64-81.

[12] Abdorreza Joe Afshany, Ali Tourani, Asadollah Shahbahrami, et al. Parallel implementation of a video-based vehicle speed measurement system for municipal roadways[J]. International Journal of Intelligent Systems and Applications, 2019, 11(11): 25-37.

[13] Yuanli GU, Lei Yu. Study on optimization of phase offset at adjacent intersections[J]. International Journal of Intelligent Systems and Applications, 2010, 2(1): 30-36.

[14] Ali Tourani, Asadollah Shahbahrami, Alireza Akoushideh, et al. Motion-based vehicle speed measurement for intelligent transportation systems[J]. International Journal of Image, Graphics and Signal Processing, 2019, 11(4): 42-54.

[15] Razib Hayat Khan. Quantitative analysis of RFID based vehicle toll collection system using UML and SPN[J]. International Journal of Information Technology and Computer Science, 2022, 14(4): 25-33.

Artificial Intelligence, Medical Engineering and Education
Z.B. Hu et al. (Eds.)
© 2024 The Authors.

doi:10.3233/ATDE231351

DHL Logistics Distribution Path Optimization Analysis

Weihui DU[a], Xiaoyu ZHANG[b,1], Yixuan WU[a]

ᵃ *School of Logistics, Wuhan Technology and Business University, Wuhan, China*
ᵇ *College of Humanities, Jianghan University, Hubei, China*

Abstract. With the continuous development of the market economy, logistics as the "third source of profit" continues to promote economic development, but how to maximize profits has become the top priority of enterprises. Logistics distribution is one of the most important links in logistics, so it is very important to optimize the logistics distribution path. This paper first analyzes the current situation of DHL logistics distribution, Through the current situation of its management system and vehicle scheduling, we find that there are too many DHL logistics distribution path loops, low full load rate and unreasonable path selection. Taking the distribution problem of DHL Wuchang service center as an example, the VRP mathematical model is established, and the optimal distribution route is obtained by using the mileage saving method, it is confirmed that the optimized route is better.

Keywords. DHL logistics; VRP; Distribution path.

1. Introduction

With the continuous development of science and technology of the times, China's economic strength has been greatly improved, and its various industries have also been affected and developed rapidly. Among them, the logistics and distribution industry is particularly prominent. However, while complying with the development, it is often the most serious problem. At present, the domestic logistics distribution industry is in chaos, the distribution environment is characterized by many, scattered, disorderly, weak and other large but incomplete phenomena. The service level of logistics distribution industry is uneven, internal management is low and chaotic, and there is no stable and balanced price system, and so on, which gives the impression that the industry is a kind of overall chaos. In addition, in the post epidemic era, in order to prevent the epidemic from spreading again, the logistics and distribution industry is facing a rapid expansion of problems, More advocate non-contact distribution, which will increase the logistics distribution of higher challenges [1-2].

The cost of logistics distribution accounts for nearly half of the cost of logistics enterprises. Therefore, reasonable and effective control of logistics distribution costs is the most important thing for logistics enterprises to survive. How to optimize the distribution path and grasp the efficiency of distribution is one of the core businesses. It can also greatly reduce the total transportation cost, complete the logistics service with the least money and the fastest speed, and improve the economic benefits, Provide better service for customers. The identification of key proteins has become an important

---
[1] Corresponding Author: Xiaoyu ZHANG, E-mail: zzxy_0317@163.com.

research task. In particular, the discovery of key proteins based on fuzzy ant colony clustering is a reference in exploring disease mechanisms and drug development [3-5].

2. Current Situation and Problem Analysis of DHL Logistics Distribution

2.1. DHL Company Profile

Up to now, DHL has more than one hundred and twenty-five employees of DHL, which is one of the world's largest logistics companies in the world, Customers in more than 1000 destinations provide fast and reliable service.

2.2. Current Situation of DHL Logistics Distribution Path

2.2.1. Composition of DHL Logistics Distribution Business

According to the different customs policies at the place of origin / destination, DHL's distribution business is mainly divided into document logistics distribution and non-document logistics distribution.

At the same time, document and non-document distribution can be divided into three categories according to the different transit time: products of the same day (SDI), products with limited time (TDI) and products with limited daily production (DDI). Among them, time limited products (TDI) are the core of DHL [6-8].

2.2.2. DHL Logistics Distribution Mode

The common logistics distribution mode in domestic logistics is three-level distribution mode, which goes from region to branch and then to subordinate stores. DHL mainly focuses on international logistics, which is not developed in China and has few logistics centers, and some regional systems will not be involved. In a simple point, take a county or city in Hubei Province as an example, foreign parts are loaded to Wuhan logistics service center after arriving at the domestic transfer center, When Wuhan logistics service center goes to the county and city, it needs the cooperation of other domestic logistics, such as SF, EMS, etc. to place an order to deliver the goods to customers. But it is also a ladder from the whole to the local.

As far as central China is concerned, the ports of Beijing, Shanghai and Guangzhou are the regional logistics centers, which can share the logistics inventory of the whole central China area. The export near the ports is convenient, which can reduce the logistics cost; As a branch logistics center, seven provinces in Central China (Hubei, Hunan, Hubei, Henan, Shanxi, Anhui and Jiangxi) have the same functions as regional logistics centers in controlling the logistics inventory of the province, These seven provinces have the main functions of logistics warehousing and distribution. For Hubei Province, Hankou, Hanyang and Wuchang three logistics service centers are the distribution points of branch logistics centers. Other logistics companies are required to assist in the distribution in areas not covered by the distribution scope [9-10].

This paper mainly discusses the problem of route optimization for the distribution and transportation of customers in the provincial branch logistics center. There are few logistics centers in the province, the route is complex and unstable, and the cost saving after optimization is relatively obvious. Figure 1 is flow chart of DHL logistics distribution mode.

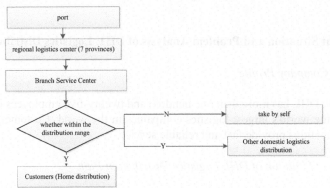

Figure1. Flow chart of DHL logistics distribution mode

2.2.3. DHL Logistics Distribution Grid Layout

DHL express delivery logistics network is mainly composed of regional logistics center, branch logistics center and distribution point. The regional logistics center is located in Beijing、 Shanghai and Guangzhou port, the branch logistics center is located in all provinces of the country, and the distribution point is located in the cities under each province. Taking central China as an example, the branch logistics centers are located in Hubei, Hunan, Hubei, Henan, Shanxi, Anhui and Jiangxi provinces, The distribution points of branch logistics centers in Hubei Province are located in Hankou, Hanyang and Wuchang.

2.3. Problems in DHL Logistics Distribution Path

2.3.1. There are Too Many Circuits

DHL express delivery is different from domestic logistics distribution in terms of the number of packages, which is less than that of domestic logistics. In terms of service scope, it adopts door-to-door service, but does not cooperate with other logistics in the service scope. In the area of door-to-door service, each DHL customer has multiple addresses, and there are uncertain factors for customers, this delivery complexity to several customers will result in different needs. The point-to-point distribution mode will result in a long distribution route. At the same time, DHL will rearrange the responsible Road area for a period of time according to the quantity of pieces and divide the road area continuously. The distribution personnel need time to adapt to the new road area, which deepens the multi loop route.

2.3.2. The Load Factor is Unstable

After arriving at the port, the express will be transported in different regions and arrive at the Branch Logistics Center at a fixed time every day. According to the normal operation, sometimes a foreign piece will arrive at the port in three or four days, but sometimes, due to the export policy of the sender's country and the lack of customs declaration materials, the service personnel at the delivery point start to work at a fixed time every day, it is possible that the full load rate of distribution vehicles on the same day is not high, and sometimes there is empty car distribution in the morning. The main reason is that the point-to-point distribution mode reduces the overall full load rate, thus reducing the enthusiasm and sense of responsibility of the distribution personnel. Therefore, it is necessary to stabilize the vehicle load rate and optimize the distribution path.

2.3.3. The Choice of Distribution Route is Lack of Planning

The branch logistics center mainly manages the vehicles, personnel and goods warehouse. There is no perfect distribution management system, no one-to-one planning for the distribution route. It only has the allocation of the road area. Then the distribution personnel can only arrange the distribution path according to their own driving experience, which is not reasonable in many aspects, as a result, it is difficult to guarantee the stability of distribution service if the self-selected distribution path is not scientifically planned and perfected. In this way, convection and circuitous transportation are often easy to occur, which greatly increases the distribution cost, and it is difficult to reduce the delivery time, so that the customer satisfaction is not easy to improve, and then the company's operating costs will be increased.

3. Establish DHL Logistics Distribution Path Model

3.1. VRP Mathematical Model

At the algorithm level, vehicle routing problem (VRP) can be abstractly solved in digraph, undirected graph, connected graph and network graph. The cities and warehouses arriving in the logistics distribution route are represented by points, and the connection between the points represents the water, land and air routes between the two cities, which can clearly reflect the connection between each point and point. The research models of vehicle routing problem (VRP) mainly include mathematical model and network graph model. The mathematical model has the advantages of large capacity, high flexibility and strong versatility than network graph model, so the mathematical model is often used.

The mathematical model of VRP is to start from a distribution center, distribute goods to multiple demand points, and then vehicles return to the distribution center on the same day, and require to arrange a suitable driving route to meet the demand points. For the known conditions of VRP Problem, including the number of vehicles, the weight of each vehicle, the demand point, the quantity of goods required per demand point, etc, Suppose that the number of vehicles owned by the distribution center is m, the number of each vehicle is k, and the carrying capacity of each vehicle is Wk $(k=1,2,...,m)$. The number of distribution demand points p is n, distribution demand point Pi, and the quantity of goods required is, Ri $(i=1,2,...,n)$. Then the cost from the distribution center to each demand point and the cost between each demand point is C_{ij}, $(i=1,2,...,n-1;$ $j=1,2,...,n;i<j,i-0)$. The constraints include that the total weight of the goods carried by each vehicle should not exceed the maximum carrying capacity of the vehicle itself, that each demand point can only be delivered by one vehicle, and that the starting and ending points of each route must be the distribution center [11-13].

$$min_z = \sum_{i=0}^{n} \sum_{j=1}^{n} \sum_{k=1}^{n} c_{ij} x_{ijk} \tag{1}$$

$$s.t. \sum_{i=1}^{n} R_i Y_{ki} \leq W_K, K = 1,2,\ldots,m \qquad (2)$$

$$\sum_{k=1}^{k} Y_{ki} = 1, \quad i = 1,2,\ldots,n \qquad (3)$$

$$\sum_{i=0}^{n} X_{ijk} = Y_{kj}, \quad j=0,1,2,\ldots,n; k=1,2,\ldots,m \qquad (4)$$

$$\sum_{j=0}^{n} X_{ijk} = Y_{ki}, \quad i = 1,2,\ldots,n; k = 1,2,\ldots,m \qquad (5)$$

$$Y_{ki} = 1 or 0, \quad i = 1,2,\ldots,n ; k = 1,2,\ldots,m \qquad (6)$$

$$X_{ijk} = 1 or 0, \quad i \neq j ; i, \quad i = 1,2,\ldots,n; k = 1,2,\ldots,m \qquad (7)$$

In the above model:

(1) Expression is expressed as objective function

(2) The formula indicates that the quantity of goods transported by each vehicle does not exceed its carrying capacity

(3) Each demand point is delivered by and only one vehicle

(4) From K to the distribution point

(5) The formula shows that vehicle K delivers goods to demand point I, and vehicle K will arrive at another point J after delivering the goods at that point

(6) The formula indicates that the distribution task of demand point I is completed by vehicle K. when the distribution task occurs, it is taken as 1; if it does not occur, it is taken as 0

(7) The formula indicates that vehicle K is from demand point I to demand point J. when time occurs, it is taken as 1; if it does not occur, it is taken as 0.

3.2. VRP Problem Description

Vehicle routing problem (VRP) refers to the fact that a certain number of customers have different requirements for receiving and delivering goods. Under certain constraints, the distribution center distributes goods to customers, and organizes appropriate driving routes to make vehicles pass through these customers orderly, so as to achieve the goals of shortest distance, less time and minimum cost, The constraints include the demand and delivery of goods, delivery time, time limit, vehicle capacity limit, etc. The VRP Problem is extended to consider that the demand point has some requirements on the vehicle arrival time, so the time window problem is added to the vehicle path (the waiting time caused by early arrival of a customer and the service time required by the customer), it extends to the vehicle routing problem with time windows (VRPTW). Most DHL delivery customers are for companies, and there will be no time window problem. If it is a single person, the customer will not deliver next time or Honeycomb will temporarily release. Therefore, this paper chooses VRP.

The components of VRP model mainly include road, demand point, distribution center and vehicle. Road is one of the core elements of vehicle routing problem, which connects distribution center with demand point and forms a network route map of distribution center demand point distribution center; Obviously speaking, demand is the object that needs to be served, which promotes vehicle transportation, At the same time, because of the different demand, the transportation time is also different; The distribution center plays the role of goods storage and the starting or ending point of each vehicle route; The vehicle is a tool to transport goods between points. The most important thing to consider when using a vehicle is the load capacity and volume, as well as the unit distance, cost and time of the vehicle [14-15].

3.3. Establishment of VRP Model for DHL Logistics Distribution Path

Multi loop transportation problem is a very common vehicle allocation problem in real transportation [16-17]. Especially for entities with a big number of service objects, VRP model can successfully solve most of the multi loop problems. Therefore, VRP model is established for DHL logistics distribution.

Known conditions: DHL Wuchang service center will fix a batch of wooden box goods every week, and now they need to be delivered to the regional customers involved, including Wuchang District, Hongshan District, Jiangxia District and Qingshan District. This paper assumes that there are 2 demand points in Wuchang District, 3 in Hongshan District, 2 in Jiangxia District and 1 in Qingshan District. The number of vehicles used in the distribution center is 8 golden cups, The rear of the vehicle is 3 meters*1.3 meters*1.6 meters, which can hold 6 cubic meters of goods. The average fuel consumption per 100 kilometers is 12 ltr, and 92 gasoline is 8.06 yuan per liter. In addition to the basic salary, the salary of distribution personnel also includes mileage salary, which is 1.5 yuan per kilometer within 50 kilometers, and 1.8 yuan per kilometer for parts exceeding 50 kilometers.

The goal of the model is to determine the number of vehicles to be arranged N and the distribution path of each vehicle, and arrange these vehicles to a loop (routing and scheduling of the loop), so as to maximize the benefit of the total transportation cost.

Restrictions:

Jinbei can hold 12 wooden cases of goods, not exceeding the vehicle volume limit.

Each vehicle will be returned to the Service Center w after delivery.

4. Logistics Route Optimization Based on DHL

4.1. DHL Logistics Distribution Optimization Data Source

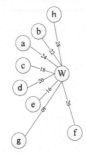

Figure 2. Original distribution route of DHL Wuchang Service Center

At present, the distribution route of DHL Wuchang service center is shown in Figure 2 (W is Wuchang Service Center).

The distribution volume of wooden box goods in a certain week at each demand point is shown in table 1.

Table 1. Distribution of goods at demand point

Demand point	Wuchang a	Wuchang b	Hongshan c	Hongshan d	Hongshan e	JiangXia f	JiangXia g	Qinshan h
Distribution volume	4	3	2	4	3	2	4	3

4.2. DHL Logistics Distribution Path Optimization Calculation

This paper uses the parallel method of saving mileage to optimize the distribution route.

Table 2. Transport distance of each demand point (unit: km)

Demand point	Center w	Wuchang a	Wuchang b	Hongshan c	Hongshan d	Hongshan e	Jiangxia f	Jiangxia g	Qinshan h
Center w	0	24	22	18	20	16	26	40	28
Wuchang a		0	6	8	10	9	18	36	13
Wuchang b			0	7	9	8	20	34	11
Hongshan c				0	5	4	9	14	21
Hongshan d					0	7	10	11	31
Hongshan e						0	8	7	29
Jiangxia f							0	17	27
Jiangxia g								0	7
Qinshan h									0

The best distribution route is calculated to make the running distance of the vehicle the shortest. According to the restriction conditions, the vehicle can carry 5 wooden boxes of goods, which cannot exceed the carrying capacity of the vehicle in the process of optimization.

According to the distance between Wuchang service centre to each demand point and each demand point to the point in table 2, the shortest distance between each other is calculated and the shortest distribution route matrix is obtained as shown in table 3.

From the shortest distribution route matrix, calculate the saving mileage of distribution route between each demand point, as shown in the table 4.

Table 3. Shortest distribution route matrix

	W								
a	24	a							
b	22	6	b						
c	18	8	7	c					
d	20	10	9	5	d				
e	16	9	8	4	7	e			
f	26	18	20	9	10	8	f		
g	40	36	34	14	11	7	17	g	
h	28	13	11	21	31	29	27	48	h

According to the distribution route saving odometer, the mileage saving is sorted from large to small. The sorting table of distribution route mileage is shown in table 5.

According to the table 5 distribution route mileage sorting table, the distribution route map is formed.

Case 1: Initial solution.

As shown in Figure 3, there are 8 distribution lines from Wuchang Service Center w to demand point, and the total vehicle running distance is 388 km.

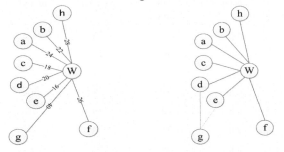

Figure 3. Initial solution   **Figure 4.** Quadratic solution

Table 4. Saving mileage of distribution route

	a	b	c	d	e	f	g	h
b	40	b						
c	34	33	c					
d	34	33	33	d				
e	31	30	30	29	e			
f	32	28	35	36	34	f		
g	28	28	44	49	49	49	g	
h	39	393	25	17	15	15	20	h

Case 2: Quadratic solution.

According to the order of saving mileage, d-g is connected and combined into distribution line 1. As shown in Figure 4, there are 7 distribution lines with a total running distance of 339 km. Because the total number of wooden boxes required by demand points d and g is 8, which is less than the carrying capacity of one golden cup, it can require 7 vehicles. After connecting e-g into distribution route 1, the total demand of demand points d, e and g is 11 boxes, the carrying capacity of a golden cup is less than 12 boxes, so it can be incorporated into distribution line 1. The optimized operation distance of distribution line 1 is 54 km, which is 98 km less than that of 152 km before optimization, and two distribution personnel are reduced.

Case 3: Cubic solution.

Then, according to the order of saving mileage, d-f, a-d, e-f, etc. may be incorporated into the distribution route 1 of the secondary solution. As a golden cup can only carry 12 cases of wooden box goods, and other demand points need more than one wooden box goods, so the distribution line 1 can't add more demand points, so connect a-b to form distribution line 2, as shown in Figure 5, the total demand of wooden boxes at demand points a and b is 7. Then connect a-h. the total demand of wooden boxes at demand points a, b and h is 10 cases, which is less than 12 boxes of a golden cup. Therefore, b-h is incorporated into distribution line 2, and then connected to b-c. the total demand of wooden boxes at demand points a, b, c and h is 12 cases, which is equal to the carrying capacity of a gold cup. Therefore, b-c is incorporated into distribution line 2, and distribution line 2 can't increase the demand point. There are 3 distribution lines with a total running distance of 178 km, and the operation distance of distribution line 2 is 72 km, which saves 112 km compared with 290 km of secondary solution.

Table 5. Sorting table of saving mileage of distribution route

Number	Connection	Saving algorithm	Number	Connection	Saving algorithm
1	d-g	49	15	c-d	33
2	e-g	49	16	a-f	32
3	f-g	49	17	a-e	31
4	c-g	44	18	b-e	30
5	a-b	40	19	c-e	30
6	a-h	39	20	d-e	29
7	b-h	39	21	a-g	28
8	d-f	36	22	b-f	28
9	c-f	35	23	b-g	28
10	a-c	34	24	f-h	27
11	a-d	34	25	c-h	25
12	e-f	34	26	g-h	20
13	b-c	33	27	d-h	17
14	b-d	33	28	e-h	15

Case 4: Final solution.

Through the above three-step solution, we can optimize the distribution route, leaving the demand point jiangxia f not incorporated into the optimized distribution route. Because the distribution route one and distribution route two in front can't be merged, we choose separate distribution for the demand point.

4.3. Analysis of DHL Distribution Route Optimization Results

4.3.1. Optimization Results

To sum up, the vehicle distribution route planning and design of Wuchang service center has been completed, as shown in Figure 6. There are three distribution routes, and three Jinbei minibuses are required, and the total running distance is 178 km. Among them, the operation distance of distribution line 1 is 54 km, that of distribution line 2 is 72 km, and that of distribution line 3 is 52 km. Compared with the optimized route of 38km, the total distance of the optimized distribution is 8 km, which is 8 km for the first and 8 km for the former.

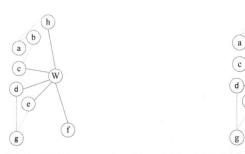

Figure 5. Cubic solution   **Figure 6.** Logistics distribution of DHL Wuchang
                                                              service center after optimization

To sum up, the vehicle distribution route planning and design of Wuchang service center has been completed, as shown in Figure 6. There are three distribution routes, and three Jinbei minibuses are required, and the total running distance is 178 km. Among them, the operation distance of distribution line 1 is 54 km, that of distribution line 2 is 72 km, and that of distribution line 3 is 52 km. Compared with the optimized route of 38km, the total distance of the optimized distribution is 8 km, which is 8 km for the first and 8 km for the former.

4.3.2. Comparative Analysis of Distribution Route Optimization Results

This paper uses the mileage saving method to optimize the distribution route, and obtains the final optimization scheme. Now, through a series of indicators such as the number of vehicles required, the total mileage of vehicle operation, the total fuel consumption, human resources and total cost, the optimized distribution route is evaluated and analyzed, as shown in table 6.

According to the comparison of the optimization results in table 6, from the perspective of vehicle demand, the optimized vehicle scheduling saves 37.5 percent vehicle demand and reduces the use of vehicles in Wuchang service center, which makes DHL Wuchang service center more flexible in vehicle scheduling arrangement; In terms of the total operating mileage of the vehicle, the total mileage after optimization is 178 km, Compared with the total mileage of 388 km before optimization, the mileage of 210 km is greatly reduced, which greatly reduces the loss of vehicle use and improves the utilization rate of resources; In terms of gasoline consumption, the gasoline consumption before optimization can reach 46.56 ltr, and the fuel consumption after optimization is reduced by 25.2 ltr compared with that before optimization, nearly half of the gasoline cost is reduced, and the utilization of social resources is protected; From the point of view of distribution personnel consumption, before the optimization, the distribution personnel need 8 people, but after optimization, only 3 people are needed, which reduces the cost and increases the flexibility of distribution personnel arrangement; Finally, it is obvious from the total additional cost that the optimized cost greatly saves more than half of the expenditure. To sum up, five vehicle routing optimization results are compared.

Table 6. Comparison of optimization results

Index	Before saving algorithm	After saving algorithm
The number of Jinbei cars	8	3
The number of cars reduction	5	
Car movement (Km)	388	178
The number of miles reduction (Km)	210	
Oil consumption (L)	46.56	21.36
Oil saving（L）	25.2	
The number of delivery persons	8	8
The number of saving manpower	5	
Total additional charges (CNY)	1058.67	477.58
Charge saving（CNT）	581.11	

4.3.3. Result Analysis

The results of Wuchang Service Center's distribution route optimization to customers at demand points are shown in Figure 7.

Figure 7. Route optimization

Wuchang Service Center w - Hongshan District d - Jiangxia District g - Hongshan e - Wuchang Service Center w is the first distribution route;

Wuchang Service Center w - Hongshan c - Wuchang b - Wuchang a - Qingshan District h - Wuchang Service Center w is the second distribution line;

If Jiangxia District f is incorporated into the above two distribution routes, its distribution cost will be increased. Therefore, Wuchang Service Center w-jiangxia District f will be taken as the third distribution route.

As an international logistics, it is difficult for DHL to achieve all aspects of domestic logistics after arriving at the distribution area. In this paper, according to the nine demand points of Wuchang service center, the route planning is carried out, and the calculation and analysis are carried out by using the mileage saving method. Through the benefit analysis of each index, it is proved that the optimized distribution mileage is shortened by 210 km, and the gasoline is saved by 25.2 ltr, so as to reduce the logistics distribution cost, Improve its enterprise efficiency.

5. Conclusion

In recent years, with the development of e-commerce, the business volume of the logistics industry has gradually increased. With the increase of business volume, the logistics cost will be higher and higher. The transportation cost accounts for half of the logistics cost, and the distribution cost is the primary expenditure item in the transportation cost. In the era of rapid development of Internet big data, enterprises need to keep up with the times, which is also necessary to improve the quality of development and strive to make the enterprise have a more refined operation, which can provide better services and meet the needs of the market. Based on the mileage saving method, this paper takes the DHL terminal distribution path as the goal optimization, combined with the case analysis, constructs the optimal distribution route from the service center to the customers at the demand point, and evaluates the optimized distribution route by comparing various indicators, Carry out the optimization work effectively and scientifically.

References

[1]   Liu Yajie et al. eds. Logistics distribution path optimization and distribution area division[M]. Beijing: National Defense Industry Press. 2015 (in Chinese).
[2]   Zhao Yanwei, Zhang Jingling. Vehicle path optimization method for logistics distribution[M]. Beijing: Science Press, 2014 (in Chinese).
[3]   Archett C, Feillet D, Speranza M. Complexity of routing problems with releasedates[J]. European Journal of Operational Research, 2015, 247(3): 797-803.
[4]   Archetti C, Speranza M, Boccia M, et al. A branch-and-cut algorithm for the inventory routing problem with pickups and deliveries [J]. European Journal of Operational Research, 2020, 282(3): 886-895.
[5]   Reyes D, Savelsbergh M, Toriello A. Vehicle Routing with Roaming Delivery Locations[J]. Transportation Research Part C: Emerging Technologies, 2017, 80: 71 -91.
[6]   Yuen Kum Fai, Wang Xueqin, Li Ting Wendy Ng, etc. An investigation of customers' intention to use self-collection services for last-mile delivery. Transport Policy, 2018, 66: 1-8.
[7]   Ozbaygin, Gizem; Karasan, Oya Ekin; Savelsbergh, Martin. A branch-and-price algorithm for the vehicle routing problem with roaming delivery locations[J]. Transportation Research Part B, 2017, 100: 115-137.
[8]   Li Jiahui. Research on urban logistics distribution vehicle path optimization method[D]. Changchun: Changchun University of Science and Technology, 2021 (in Chinese).
[9]   Deutsch Yael, Golany Boaz. A parcel locker network as a solution to the logistics last mile problem[J]. International Journal of Production Research, 2018, 56(1-2): 251-261.
[10] Shelbourne B, Battarra M, Potts C. The Vehicle Routing Problem with Release and Due Dates[J]. INFORMS Journal on Computing, 2017, 29(4): 705-723.
[11] Hu Xianman. Analysis of cold chain logistics distribution path optimization based on green supply chain[J]. China Logistics and Purchasing, 2021, (09): 71-72 (in Chinese).
[12] Song Saifeng, Zhang Meijie et al. Logistics distribution path optimization based on mileage saving method[J]. China Market, 2021, (05): 177-178 (in Chinese).
[13] Wu Jingpeng. Modern logistics distribution centre classification and planning analysis[J]. Logistics Technology and Application, 2020, 25(07): 159-163 (in Chinese).
[14] Pereira A, Urrutia S. Formulations and algorithms for the Pickup and Delivery Traveling Salesman Problem with Multiple Stacks [J]. Computers & Operations Research, 2018, 93: 1-14.
[15] Chitsaz M, Cordeau J, Jans R. A branch-and-cut algorithm for an assembly routingproblem [J]. European Journal of Operational Research, 2020, 282(3): 896-910.
[16] Nur Kumala Dewi, " Review of Vehicle Surveillance Using Iot in the Smart Transportation Concept ", International Journal of Engineering and Manufacturing, Vol.11, No.1, pp. 29-36, 2021.
[17] Abdorreza Joe Afshany, Ali Tourani, Asadollah Shahbahrami, Saeed Khazaee, Alireza Akoushideh, "Parallel Implementation of a Video-based Vehicle Speed Measurement System for Municipal Roadways", International Journal of Intelligent Systems and Applications, Vol.11, No.11, pp.25-37, 2019.

Artificial Intelligence, Medical Engineering and Education
Z.B. Hu et al. (Eds.)
© *2024 The Authors.*
This article is published online with Open Access by IOS Press and distributed under the terms
of the Creative Commons Attribution Non-Commercial License 4.0 (CC BY-NC 4.0).
doi:10.3233/ATDE231352

Investigation into the Long-Term Dynamics of Microbiomes in Hong Kong Outdoor Bioaerosols

Lingxiao XU[a,1], Xinzhao TONG[b]

[a] *Faculty of Natural Sciences, Imperial College London, London, UK*
[b] *Department of Biological Sciences, Xi'an Jiaotong-Liverpool University, Suzhou, China*

Abstract. The composition of outdoor microorganisms is dynamic in nature, often affected by factors such as geography, seasonality, environmental conditions. In this study, bioinformatic platform QIIME2 (v2022.8) was used to process the 93 outdoor air samples after 16S rRNA gene sequencing, aiming to understand the dynamics of the outdoor bioaerosol microbial communities in Hong Kong and identify the significant factor underlying such variations. The results suggested the diversity and composition of outdoor microorganisms in Hong Kong significantly varied by seasonal changes, with the outdoor air bacterial community being highest in summer and autumn and lowest in winter. The study also identified indicator species for the three seasons, spring, autumn and winter, to investigate the changes in bacterial habits, living conditions and environment during the different seasons. The results indicate that bacteria in the aquatic environment are more abundant during these seasons, and that spring has seen the emergence of bacteria often associated with human epidemics. However, within one season, geographic area had minimal influence on the bacterial community diversity and composition, suggesting outdoor airborne bacterial communities tended to be homogeneous across different locations on a city-wide scale within a season.

Keywords. Metagenomics; Microbial ecology; Environmental microbiology.

1. Introduction

In several cases in recent years, the experience of major infectious disease events has reinforced the conviction of researchers that exploring the substance of airborne microorganisms has a significant impact on the prevention and interdiction of pathogenic infectious agents. The major chemical constituents of outdoor air include particulate matter 2.5 (PM2.5) and the organisms, such as bacteria, fungi, and viruses [1]. Airborne pathogenic microorganisms may cause human respiratory infection after inhalation, especially during the cold and wet seasons. Hence, understanding the dynamic pattern of the outdoor bioaerosol microbiota lays a foundation for the prevention of the spread of outdoor infections and prediction of large-scale transmission of diseases in outdoor urban places [2].

Seasonality and geography are the two major factors significantly affecting the diversity and composition of outdoor airborne microbial communities. In most regions

---

[1] Corresponding Author: Lingxiao XU, E-mail: lx323@ic.ac.uk

of the world, the high humidity and temperature in summer favor the growth and reproduction of microorganisms. As a result, summer usually harbors the highest airborne microbial diversity [3]. The influence of geography on the diversity and composition of the atmospheric microbiome varies across different geographical scales, with significant differences detected between continents to even small local scales. However, due to the less vegetation in the city compared to the suburbs and rural areas, urbanization can result in the homogenization of the outdoor airborne microbial communities in urban areas [2].

In this study, the QIIME2(v2022.8) bioinformatics platform [1]was applied to study the diversity and composition of the outdoor airborne bacterial community in Hong Kong across four seasons and using the internal R language packages to calculate and visualize the resulting data, aiming to identify the factors significantly structuring the dynamics pattern of the outdoor airborne microbiome [4].

2. Sample Collection and Sequence Data Analysis

Previous researchers collected air samples for microbiome analysis from Hong Kong outdoor aerosol environment of commercial buildings, including five office buildings and three shopping malls, during the weekends to reflect the normal use of the outdoor environment of high-volume buildings with 3 days in each season and negative control samples. For each sample, three PCR reactions were performed in triplicate. The amplicons were pooled and filtered prior to institution construction, and then sequenced the platform. The 16S rRNA gene fragment sequences required for the experiments were finally obtained that could verify the bacterial species.

The raw sequences were downloaded from NCBI under the accession number PRJNA55682. The samples were grouped according to the seasons and sampling areas when and where they were collected. However, one air sample was removed from the study due to the incompleteness of data upon examination, resulting in a dataset consisting of 22 winter, 23 spring, 24 summer, and 24 autumn samples, plus a negative control sample.

In this study, QIIME2 (v2022.8) was used for bioinformatics analyses [1]. The import command was used to demultiplex and import raw paired-end fastq files into QIIME2. Using the DADA2 denoise-paired plug-in utility, the DADA2 algorithm was executed to generate amplicon sequence variants (ASVs) [2]. with a minimum read length of 250 bp and a maximum of two expected errors per read, the imported paired-end sequences were filtered, truncated, de-noised, and de-replicated. Additionally, chimeric and singleton sequences were eliminated [5].

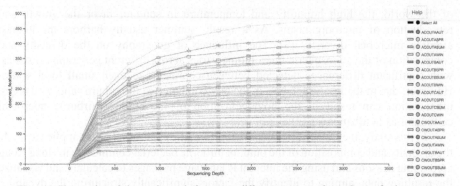

Figure 1. The number of observed sample features at different sequence shows the rarefaction curves.

Using a feature classifier trained with the SILVA database and truncated to the V4 hypervariable region of the 16S rRNA gene, taxonomy was ascribed to all ASVs. Representative sequences were aligned with MAFFT and deployed in QIIME2's FastTree for phylogenetic reconstruction. Mitochondrial, chloroplast, and contaminant sequences removed from all the samples. Based on the blank sample, lineages of taxa with a relative abundance exceeding 5% were deemed contaminants. After contamination filtering, 11,018 unique ASVs were retained for subsequent analysis [2]. After removing the six contaminant samples from the control group, the samples were re-tested for feature analysis again, with the result that when the sequence depth was taken to 2956, the number of discoverable features for essentially all samples would level off and no longer increase, then a very minimal sample size could be kept missing to obtain the lowest level of error value (Figure 1).

At the beginning of the analysis of the data, to obtain the approximate composition of the microbial communities in the four seasons in the most visual and extensive way, R (v3.4.4) packages 'ggplot2' (v3.4.2) and 'dplyr' (v0.7.8) were used to plot histograms with the three taxonomic levels 'phylum', 'class' and 'genus' for the taxonomic classification of the samples in each of the four seasons, providing a visual understanding of the changes in the relative abundance.

The alpha and beta diversity metrics were computed using the core-metrics-phylogenetic command in QIIME2. At a normalized depth of 4476 reads per sample, three alpha diversity metrics, including the observed features (ASVs), faith's phylogenetic diversity, and shannon diversity index, were calculated for each sample. QIIME2's "alpha rarefaction" command was used to generate rarefaction curves of alpha diversity at different read depths. The "alpha-group-significance" command was utilized to execute the Kruskal-Wallis (KW) test to identify statistically significant differences between the four seasonal groups and the eight geographic groups [2]. Based on the weighted (structure) and unweighted (membership) UniFrac distances, beta diversity was determined. Using the Vegan utility, PCoA graphs based on the weighted and unweighted UniFrac distances were generated. To evaluate the significance of influential factors, the permutation multivariate analyses of variance (PERMANOVA) pseudo-F statistic test based on 999 permutations was implemented [2]. The Benjamin-Hochberg method was used to ascertain significance (adjusted-$p < 0.05$) in alpha and beta diversity assessments when multiple comparisons were performed. Using the arithmetic "stat ellipse" in the R package ggplot2 and the multivariate normal distribution with a 95% confidence interval, seasonal samples were grouped using ellipses. The "dplyr" and "Indicspecies" (v1.7.12) in R was used to identify indicator taxa at the specificity and sensitivity values of 0.70 for each season and location in respective outdoor communities using triplicate samples [2].

3. Taxonomic Composition of Bacteria in Seasonal Aerosol Samples

3.1. Taxonomic Overview of the Outdoor Air Microbiome at the Phylum, Class, and Genus Levels.

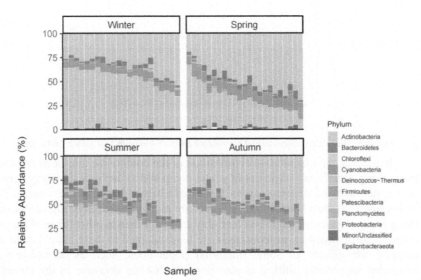

Figure 2. The relative abundance of the outdoor air microbiome in four seasons at the phylum level

In all four seasons, actinobacteria (about 47%) and proteobacteria (about 41%) were the predominant phyla, followed by firmicutes nearly 10% (Figure 2). The relative abundance of proteobacteria was higher than that of actinobacteria in winter, while the opposite pattern was observed in the other three seasons. Other bacterial phylum, such as chloroflexi, cyanobacteria, and epsilonbacteraeota, remained at low levels lower than 5% in all four seasons, suggesting their rarity in outdoor environments. (Figure 1) Overall, the microbial composition of outdoor air was highly similar across four seasons at the phylum level.

At the genus level, cutibacterium dominate all the samples. Cutibacterium is derived from the actinobacteria class, primarily from human skin and sweat, consistent with the dominance of actinomycetota in all the samples (Figure 3). As Hong Kong is one of the most densely populated cities in the world, residents' flaking epidermis may discharge cutibacterium [2]. Halomonas and shewanella dominated the winter samples, reaching nearly 25% and 11% while presented in low abundances or even absent in the other seasons. The remaining microbial populations, such as enhyfrobacter, bacillus and staphylococcus, remained low, with a relative abundance of < 5% in all seasons (Figure 3).

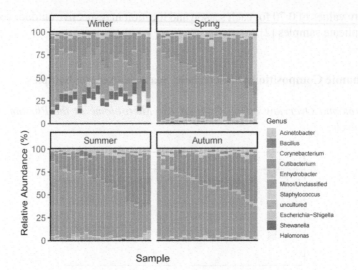

Figure 3. The relative abundance of the outdoor air microbiome in four seasons at the genus level

In general, the quantitative composition of the outdoor air microbial community in Hong Kong was slightly different in winter compared to the high similarity between the spring, summer, and autumn seasons. It showed a higher degree of unevenness. This may be because the natural conditions in winter are more variable in a tropical location like Hong Kong, e.g., temperature and humidity are lower than in other times of the year, and microorganisms such as proteobacteria are more adapted to these natural conditions. In contrast, the growth of some microbial populations, such as actinobacteria, was somewhat suppressed. Still, it is also possible that the decrease in the abundance of bacterial members belonging to actinobacteria, such as cutibacteria, which are adapted to grow on the surface of the skin, is because people go out less in winter due to the low temperature and the reduction in skin exposure.

3.2. Investigating Indicator Species in Outdoor Aerosol Microorganisms during Different Seasons.

Table 1 indicates the species and their corresponding coding (ASV), domain, genus, fidelity, relative abundance, and standard deviation, which occur in autumn, winter, and spring. Indicator analysis identified bacteria that strongly indicate a specific season. EHydrobacter and burkholderiaceae are indicator bacteria for the outdoor air microbiome in autumn, with relative abundance of 0.557%, 0.692%, 0.747%, and 0.452%, respectively.

In autumn, both enhydrobacter and burkholderiaceae occur frequently in aquatic environments, probably associated with Hong Kong being a coastal city. Possible causes of this phenomenon [6], apart from the humidity temperature in autumn, may be since autumn is the change of season in Hong Kong, when the wind direction may change and may blow more air from around the waters towards the urban areas [7]. This may then allow aquatic bacteria to enter the air in the urban area with the air currents. Another reason is that Hong Kong is sometimes affected by typhoons and monsoons in autumn, resulting in increased rainfall. The rain may wash bacteria from the surface and water bodies into the air, thus leading to increased levels of aquatic bacteria in the air.

Table 1. Species and their corresponding codes (ASV), domain, genus, fidelity, relative abundance, standard deviation

Season	ASV	Genus	Fidelity	Average Relative Abundance	Standard Deviation
Autumn	2916	*Enhydrobacter*	1	0.557	0.330
	3f77	*Enhydrobacter*	1	0.692	0.363
	8c68	*Enhydrobacter*	1	0.747	0.356
	c5ec	*Burkholderiaceae*	1	0.452	0.329
Winter	c946	*Shewanella*	1	3.887	1.380
	34f3	*Shewanella*	1	3.886	1.127
	07f8	*Halomonas*	1	4.450	1.419
	8836	*Halomonas*	1	4.387	1.445
	8ab9	*Halomonas*	1	4.386	1.626
	b868	*Halomonas*	1	3.698	1.179
	d38d	*Halomonas*	1	4.526	1.567
Spring	d908	*Corynebacterium*	0.783	1.099	1.567

Shewanella and halomonas strongly indicated winter outdoor microbiome, accounting for 3.887%, 3.886%, 4.450%, 4.387%, 4.386%, 3.698% and 4.526% in the relative abundance. Fidelity levels for the indicator species were 1 in both seasons, with standard deviations of less than 0.400 for the autumn indicator species and less than 1.700 for the winter indicator species, yielding data of high reference value in both seasons (Table 1).

In winter, shewanella is a rod-shaped bacterium that lives mainly in the marine environment [8]. Halomonas belongs to the γ-Amastigotes class of marine halophilic bacteria [9]. A possible reason for them being winter indicator species is that shewanella and halomonas (Table 1), as marine bacteria, may enter the outdoor air with changes in tides, wind direction and marine aerosols. Winter weather conditions and wind direction may contribute to the dispersal of these bacteria in the air. In addition, there may be specific climatic phenomena in winter, such as temperature reversals and air stability, which may affect the distribution and dispersal of airborne bacteria.

Corynebacterium was the only bacterium strongly indicative of spring outdoor microbiome, accounting for 1.099% in the relative abundance. However, the fidelity of the spring indicator species was 0.783 and the standard deviation was also relatively large at 2.390 due to the low availability of reference data (Table 1). Corynebacterium are bacteria that are widely distributed in the natural environment, including soil, water, and air. Some of them are pathogenic to humans, such as corynebacterium diphtheriae and corynebacterium judicium, and may cause diseases of the human immune system [10]. One of the reasons for their appearance in spring may be human activity, as spring temperatures are moderate, outdoor activities increase and people have increased exposure to bacteria in the outdoor air. In addition, spring is the time when plants are flowering and pollen and spore numbers are high, and corynebacterium may attach to these particles and with them enter the outdoor air [11].

3.3. Investigating Influences of Season and Geography on the Outdoor Microbiomes by Alpha-diversity.

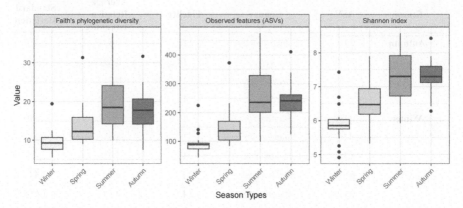

Figure 4. The four seasonal factors that influence the microorganisms in outdoor aerosols were evaluated via three methods: observed features (ASVs), faith's phylogenetic diversity, and shannon diversity index

Before diversity analysis, rarefaction was performed to eliminate the difference caused by the unequal sample reads. Rarefaction analysis revealed that the implemented rarefaction depth could encompass the diversity of the microbial communities (Figure 4). The results showed significant seasonal differences in alpha diversity of outdoor air microbiota were observed between the four seasons regardless of the metrics used (Table 2). The observed difference is the difference observed from two or more data; the critical difference is used to determine whether the observed differences are large enough so that they can be considered statistically significant; and the p-value is used to determine whether the observed differences are statistically significant.

Table 2. Kruskal-Wallis (alpha < 0.05) was used to verify the significance of microbial diversity between seasons

	Observed Difference	Critical Difference	Adjusted-p KW	Statistical Significance
Winter-Spring	21.706	21.346	0.021	TRUE
Winter-Summer	50.686	21.018	0.007	TRUE
Winter-Autumn	49.519	21.018	0.012	TRUE
Spring-Summer	28.980	20.778	0.001	TRUE
Spring-Autumn	27.813	20.778	0.008	TRUE
Summer-Autumn	1.167	20.556	0.312	FALSE

Interestingly, a gradual increase in diversity was observed with time, with the lowest microbial diversity found in winter and the highest diversity in the summer and autumn (adjusted p = 0.312 > 0.050, KW), highlighting the critical role of seasonality in governing the dynamics of outdoor air microbial diversity.

4. Investigating Influences of Season and Geography on the Outdoor Microbiomes by Beta-diversity.

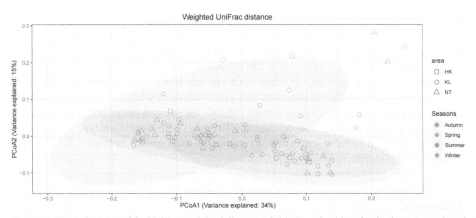

Figure 5. PCoA diagrams of the UniFrac weighted distance of airborne microbiota for the three categories of areas.

The difference in microbial communities between samples was studied using Weighted and Unweighted UniFrac distance metrics and visualized using PCOA. The significance of seasonality and geography on the composition of outdoor airborne microbial communities were investigated using the PERMANOVA test [12]. The heterogeneous dispersion effect had little impact on the PERMANOVA results because the dataset was largely balanced within each group (i.e., each group had nearly the same sample size) when each of the aforementioned factors was considered [2].

As Figure 5 shows, the statistics were calculated using 999 permutations and the PERMANOVA test. The colored ellipses are based on the 95% confidence intervals of the multivariate normal distribution. When the weighted UniFrac distance was considered, the two dimensions explained a total of 49% variance. As can be seen from the graph, the samples in autumn were distinct from that in other seasons for Kruskal-Wallis alpha $p = 0.001 < 0.05$, suggesting that autumn outdoor air microbiomes were different from other seasons in composition. However, the samples in the other three seasons were highly overlapped, suggesting a high similarity in their microbial community composition. Graphical location showed no significant influence on the areas and composition of the outdoor air microbiome (permanova $p = 0.119 > 0.05$, $R^2 = 0.511$, and pseudo-F $= 34.428$). Taken together, our findings suggested that seasonal change was the primary cause of dynamics in outdoor microbial composition and structure in Hong Kong, with the geographical location only showing a minor effect.

5. Conclusion

Our study highlights the important role of seasonality in shaping the diversity and composition of the Hong Kong outdoor airborne microbiomes. The dominant genera remained stable at each location across the four seasons in outdoor environments, this is likely because Hong Kong's climatic conditions vary within a relatively narrow range despite having four seasons [2]. Nevertheless, indicator bacteria were detected for the three seasons. These findings suggest that environmental conditions are likely to have a more significant effect on the less abundant members of microbial communities or that some microbial members may be boomed in a specific season. Consistent with this, the beta-diversity analysis demonstrated that the season was a weak but significant driver of the membership and structure of outdoor airborne microbiome.

The community status of outdoor microbial samples fluctuated the most under the influence of seasonal changes, the aerosol microbial diversity peaks in summer and autumn and is lowest in winter, while the influence of regional location was slight than the season factor, suggesting outdoor airborne bacterial communities tended to be homogeneous across different locations on a city-wide scale within a season. By studying the bacterial composition of Hong Kong's outdoor air, we can better understand the role of microorganisms in the urban ecosystem. This will help develop urban planning and environmental protection measures to maintain ecological balance and promote sustainable development.

References

[1]   Bolyen, E., Rideout, J. R., Dillon, M. R., & al., e. (2019). Reproducible, interactive, scalable and extensible microbiome data science using QIIME 2. Nature biotechnology, 37(8), 852-857.
[2]   Zhou, Y., Lai, Y., Tong, X., & al., e. (2020). Airborne bacteria in outdoor air and air of mechanically ventilated buildings at city scale in Hong Kong across seasons. Environmental Science & Technology, 54(19), 11732-11743.
[3]   Prussin, A. J., 2nd, Garcia, E. B., & Marr, L. C. (2015). Total Virus and Bacteria Concentrations in Indoor and Outdoor Air. Environ Sci Technol Lett, 2(4), 84-88. doi: 10.1021/acs.estlett.5b00050
[4]   Chen, X., Ran, P., Ho, K., & al., e. (2012). Concentrations and Size Distributions of Airborne Microorganisms in Guangzhou during Summer. Aerosol and Air Quality Research, 12(6), 1336-1344. doi:10.4209/aaqr.2012.03.0066
[5]   Zhou, Y., Leung, M. H. Y., Tong, X., & al., e. (2021). City-Scale Meta-Analysis of Indoor Airborne Microbiota Reveals that Taxonomic and Functional Compositions Vary with Building Types. Environmental Science & Technology, 55(22), 15051-15062. doi: 10.1021/acs.est.1c03941
[6]   Carrión, V. J., Cordovez, V., Tyc, O., & al., e. (2018). Involvement of Burkholderiaceae and sulfurous volatiles in disease-suppressive soils. The ISME journal, 12(9), 2307-2321.
[7]   Staley, J. T., Irgens, R. L., & Brenner, D. J. (1987). Enhydrobacter aerosaccus gen. nov., sp. nov., a gas-vacuolated, facultatively anaerobic, heterotrophic rod. International journal of systematic bacteriology, 37(3), 289-291.
[8]   Holt, H., Gahrn-Hansen, B., & Bruun, B. (2005). Shewanella algae and Shewanella putrefaciens: clinical and microbiological characteristics. Clinical microbiology and infection, 11(5), 347-352.
[9]   Mata, J. A., Martínez-Cánovas, J., Quesada, E., & al., e. (2002). A detailed phenotypic characterisation of the type strains of Halomonas species. Systematic and applied microbiology, 25(3), 360-375.
[10]   Eggeling, L., & Bott, M. (2005). Handbook of Corynebacterium glutamicum: CRC press.
[11]   Lee, J.-Y., Na, Y.-A., Kim, E., & al., e. (2016). The actinobacterium Corynebacterium glutamicum, an industrial workhorse.
[12]   Jiang, S., Sun, B., Zhu, R., & al., e. (2022). Airborne microbial community structure and potential pathogen identification across the PM size fractions and seasons in the urban atmosphere. Science of The Total Environment, 831, 154665. doi: https://doi.org/10.1016/j.scitotenv.2022.154665

Artificial Intelligence, Medical Engineering and Education
Z.B. Hu et al. (Eds.)

doi:10.3233/ATDE231353

Planning and Design of Intelligent Scheduling System for Subway Staff

Haitao DENG [a,1], Mengmeng DONG[b], Zhenqing ZHANG[b]

a School of Transportation, Nanning University, Guangxi, China
b Rail Transit Group Co, LTD, Guangxi, China

Abstract. With the rapid development of urban rail transit, the number of workers on the front line of urban rail transit is increasing. With the increase in rail transit network density in most cities, the total number of staff in a single station and the number of staff in the same shift is increasing, which adds difficulty to the overall scheduling of subway staff. At present, most urban subway station staff are arranged manually, in order to reduce manual participation in the process of scheduling, save labor costs, and enhance the rationality of working time arrangement. According to the actual demand, the intelligent scheduling system of subway staff is planned and designed.

Keywords. Urban rail transit; Subway stations; Intelligent scheduling system.

1. Introduction

With the rapid development of urban rail transit, by the end of 2022, Chinese mainland of 55 cities on the mainland have opened and operated more than 10,000 kilometers of urban rail transit lines, with the operating mileage reaching 10,291.95 kilometers [1]. The number of urban rail transit stations has reached 6,861, and the total number of station operation and management personnel is more than 200,000 [2,3]. In the daily work of the station, the staff scheduling is a common and complicated problem, in fact, the essence of the staff scheduling is a combination optimization problem, when the scale of the problem is large, it will become very complicated [4,5].

Through the field visit and investigation, it is found that most stations currently complete the next month's work plan of all personnel through manual scheduling, and the scheduling work of most stations is carried out by the stationmaster, who mainly uses Excel tables or statistical reports to make scheduling plans [6,7]. Manual scheduling has some disadvantages, such as being time-consuming and laborious, easy to make mistakes, and too random, so it is difficult to ensure the rationality of the scheduling plan [8].

2. Intelligent Scheduling System Design Requirements

In order to reduce the degree of manual participation in the process of scheduling work, enhance the rationality of the working time arrangement of staff in various positions, improve work efficiency, reduce the scheduling burden of each work scene group, and

---

[1] Corresponding Author: Haitao DENG, E-mail: 549465788@qq.com.

solve the difficulties of scheduling time and error, intelligent scheduling system needs to be designed from the top level [9,10]. The main requirements are as follows:

(1). The system needs to establish a big data center based on the position details of railway companies and station personnel, use long-term precipitation data, summarize the rules of personnel transfer and promotion, and use data to analyze the dynamic situation of personnel at each station of the line network, to achieve intelligent management of personnel information [11].

(2). The system needs to realize online and real-time on-the-job dynamic monitoring of personnel and support the interconnection with mobile devices.

(3). The system should realize the automatic generation function of the station staff scheduling plan, be able to identify the rest days independently set by staff, and automatically complete the adjustment work of idle positions in relevant periods based on the analysis of total working hours difference data [12].

3. The Overall Function of an Intelligent Scheduling System

Based on the demand analysis of the intelligent scheduling system, the relevant departments of the railway Company for operation and management personnel are decomposed, and the research and development of the intelligent scheduling and attendance system is carried out according to the comprehensive analysis of the company's personnel attendance system, scheduling principles, and the scheduling needs of different first-line departments such as stations. The overall functions and implementation methods of the intelligent scheduling system are as follows:

(1) Employee information management function. It is mainly manifested in: the management of employees' personal information including the updating of academic information and technical title information; Employee account management; and Staff position information. Through the personnel department, the company will carry out the entry procedures for new employees, input their personal information, and assign post departments. Personal information is entered into the system, and search queries can be conducted within the system by number and name.

(2) Intelligent scheduling function. The main performance is automatic scheduling of the station, automatic scheduling of the dispatching center, automatic scheduling of crew, and automatic scheduling of vehicle plants. After the staff log in to the scheduling system and pass the information verification, they can enter the scheduling link through the submenu. After entering the system, they can view the personal scheduling situation, select the scheduling position, set the transfer date, etc., for automatic scheduling Settings, and finally confirm the submission, they can export and print the scheduling table. These functions are realized in the scheduling management module.

(3) Post-dynamic management function. The main performance is the automatic deployment of support personnel, the traceable query of historical duty personnel information, the query of leave personnel on any date, the query of duty personnel information on the same day, the query of job vacancy details. Based on big data technology, the scheduling system can always analyze and evaluate the overall staff on the job that day, and when an emergency occurs in a station or other work scene and additional manpower is temporarily needed, the system can judge and release support information to the terminal equipment of the corresponding personnel.

(4) Attendance management function. The main performance is the attendance statistics and analysis of the personnel in the passenger transport branch center, the

attendance statistics and analysis of the station personnel, and the attendance statistics and analysis of the individual. The system can conduct comprehensive attendance statistics and analysis by week, month, and year according to the data information of the staff's duty arrangement, leave transfer, leave, and so on.

4. Systematic Planning and Design Ideas

4.1. The Overall Structure of the Intelligent Scheduling System

The intelligent scheduling system is a deeply integrated technology based on big data and personnel information comprehensive management platform, which can realize real-time monitoring, dynamic deployment, and automatic generation of scheduling plans for on-duty personnel, achieve a reasonable and efficient dynamic personnel management mechanism, and achieve the goal of saving labor costs for enterprises and improving the overall work efficiency. The overall framework scheme is shown in Figure 1.

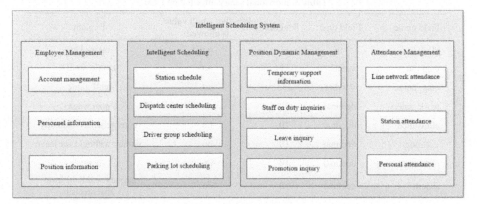

Figure 1. Overall architecture scheme of intelligent scheduling system

4.2. Datasheet Design

The intelligent scheduling system can use MYSQL as the background database, and the specific data structure type of the data table is designed as follows:

(1). Employee attendance information table, as shown in Table 1.

Table 1. Employee attendance information table

Field name	Field type	Length	Whether a null value is allowed	Explain
attend_id	int	11	no	major key
emp_no	varchar	11	no	employee ID
emp_name	varchar	255	no	staff name
attend_begin_time	timestamp	0	no	time to punch in
attend_end_time	timestamp	0	no	time to clock out

(2). Leave record information table, as shown in Table 2.

Table 2. Leave record information table

Field name	Field type	Fength	Whether a null value is allowed	Explain
vacation_id	int	11	no	major key
emp_no	varchar	11	no	employee ID
emp_name	varchar	128	no	staff name
begin_time	date	0	no	start time
end_time	date	0	no	end time
reason	varchar	128	no	reason for leave
approve_name	varchar	128	no	name of the handler
approve_no	varchar	11	no	agent job number
remark	varchar	128	no	remarks

(3). Personal salary information table, as shown in Table 3.

Table 3. Individual salary information table

Field name	Field type	Fength	Whether a null value is allowed	Explain
id	int	11	no	major key
emp_no	varchar	11	no	employee ID
emp_name	varchar	255	no	staff name
work_salery	decimal	10	no	post wage
allowance	decimal	10	no	comprehensive subsidy
vacation	decimal	10	no	money withheld for leave
reward	decimal	10	no	bonus
absent	decimal	10	no	money withheld from absenteeism
total	decimal	10	no	total wage bill
createtime	date	0	no	issue date

(4). User login information table, as shown in Table 4.

Table 4. User information table

Field name	Field type	Fength	Whether a null value is allowed	Explain
userID	varchar	11	no	major key
admin_name	varchar	5	no	login ID
admin_password	varchar	11	no	password
role_name	varchar	255	no	character name
role_description	varchar	255	no	role description

4.3. Part of the module function implementation of the operation flow design

Operation flow is an important part of system design. Whether the operation process is convenient is a key factor in reflecting whether a system is mature and intelligent. The operation process often needs constant adjustment and optimization during the application of the system.

(1). Employee management module, the administrator enters the main page of the system, searches the employee information, clicks Add employee, fills in the employee information, and submits it when completed, otherwise it can be canceled and the execution is over. The specific execution process is shown in Figure 2.

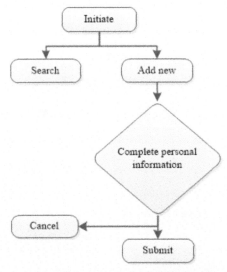

Figure 2. Add an employee information flow chart

(2). Scheduling management module, the administrator logs in to the system, clicks scheduling, enters the time and class system, clicks scheduling, and finally exports the scheduling table. The specific execution process is shown in Figure 3.

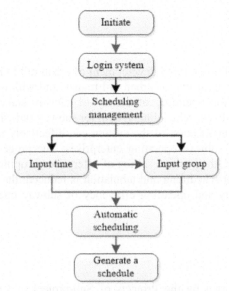

Figure 3. System scheduling flow chart

(3). In the leave management module, the administrator logs in to the system, clicks on leave management, applies for leave, fills in the basic information, and finally the administrator approves and sells leave. The specific execution process is shown in Figure 4.

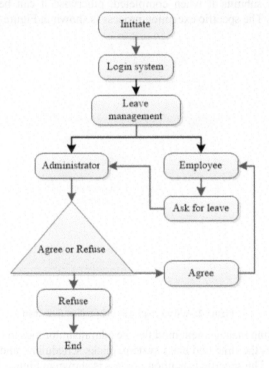

Figure 4. Leave management flow chart

5. Conclusion

Under the background of the rapid development of urban rail transit and the increasing number of staff at the front line of urban rail transit, and with the future development focus on improving the operating efficiency of subway stations, the research and application of the intelligent scheduling system for subway staff should be paid attention to. The research and application of the system can effectively improve the personnel management level of subway operating enterprises. The process of shift scheduling operation is simplified, the position setting of enterprises is optimized, the workload of repetitive manual shift scheduling and tabulation is reduced, the labor cost is reduced, and the service quality and operating efficiency of subway operating enterprises are improved.

Acknowledgment

This project is supported by the Projects of Sub-project of Construction of China-ASEAN International Joint Laboratory for Comprehensive Transportation (Phase I),No,GuiKeAA21077011-6, the Projects of Research and Design of Subway Station

Scheduling Management System Based on Web in Nanning University(2019XJ10).

References

[1] Overview of urban rail transit lines in Chinese mainland 2022[J]. Urban Rail Transit,2023,83(01):10-11 (in Chinese).

[2] Azhdar R, Nazemi A. Modeling of incentive-based policies for demand management for the Tehran subway[J]. Travel Behaviour and Society, 2020, 20: 174-180.

[3] Zhao P, Li S. Bicycle-metro integration in a growing city: The determinants of cycling as a transfer mode in metro station areas in Beijing[J]. Transportation research part A: policy and practice, 2017, 99: 46-60.

[4] Roukouni A, Basbas S, Kokkalis A. Impacts of a metro station to the land use and transport system: the Thessaloniki Metro case[J]. Procedia-Social and Behavioral Sciences, 2012, 48: 1155-1163.

[5] Luo Z, Zhang Y, Li L, et al. A hybrid method for predicting traffic congestion during peak hours in the subway system of Shenzhen[J]. Sensors, 2019, 20(1): 150.

[6] El Hamshary O, Abouhamad M, Marzouk M. Integrated maintenance planning approach to optimize budget allocation for subway operating systems[J]. Tunnelling and Underground Space Technology, 2022, 121: 104322.

[7] Sun J, Yao J, Wang M. Subway passenger flow analysis and management optimization model based on AFC data[J]. Journal of Intelligent & Fuzzy Systems, 2021, 41(4): 4773-4783.

[8] Yan X, **e Z, Wang A. Real-Time Monitoring System for Passenger Flow Information of Metro Stations Based on Intelligent Video Surveillance[C]//Proceedings of the 4th International Conference on Electrical and Information Technologies for Rail Transportation (EITRT) 2019: Rail Transportation Information Processing and Operational Management Technologies. Springer Singapore, 2020: 329-335.

[9] Rasim M. Alguliyev, Rashid G. Alakbarov, "Integer Programming Models for Task Scheduling and Resource Allocation in Mobile Cloud Computing", International Journal of Computer Network and Information Security, Vol.15, No.5, pp.13-26, 2023.

[10] Mijanur Rahaman, Md. Masudul Islam, "Optimal and Appropriate Job Allocation Algorithm for Skilled Agents under a Server Constraint", International Journal of Education and Management Engineering, Vol.13, No.1, pp. 10-17, 2023.

[11] Nasim Soltani Soulegan, Behrang Barekatain, Behzad Soleimani Neysiani, "MTC: Minimizing Time and Cost of Cloud Task Scheduling based on Customers and Providers Needs using Genetic Algorithm", International Journal of Intelligent Systems and Applications, Vol.13, No.2, pp.38-51, 2021.

[12] Ankita, Sudip Kumar Sahana, "An Automated Parameter Tuning Method for Ant Colony Optimization for Scheduling Jobs in Grid Environment", International Journal of Intelligent Systems and Applications, Vol.11, No.3, pp.11-21, 2019.

Artificial Intelligence, Medical Engineering and Education
Z.B. Hu et al. (Eds.)
© 2024 The Authors.
This article is published online with Open Access by IOS Press and distributed under the terms
of the Creative Commons Attribution Non-Commercial License 4.0 (CC BY-NC 4.0).
doi:10.3233/ATDE231354

Disposal for the Pinching People and Objects Accidents in Fully Automated Operation Urban Rail Transit Lines Based on Fault Tree Analysis

Jianrong FENG[a], Jie SHANG[b,c,d,1], Ahmad Nazrul Hakimi Ibrahim[d]

[a] *Nanning Rail Transit Co., Ltd. Co., Guangxi 530000, China*
[b] *Department of Traffic and Transportation, College of transportation, Nanning University, Nanning, 530000, China*
[c] *Guangxi Key Laboratory for International Join for China-ASEAN Comprehensive Transportation, Nanning, 530000, China*
[d] *Department of Civil Engineering, Faculty of Engineering and Built Environment, Universiti Kebangsaan Malaysia, Bangi, 43600, Malaysia*

Abstract. The Fault Tree Analysis (FTA) method was used to analyze the accidents of high-speed trains with people and objects caught in fully automatic operation lines of urban rail transit. A fault tree was established to describe the top event, intermediate event, and basic event in the accident tree of high-speed trains with people and objects caught in train doors and platform doors. The minimum path set, and structural importance parameters of the accident were analyzed and calculated, and the equivalent tree of the accident tree was drawn. The four shortest path sets with shorter chains were selected for analysis, and effective measures were proposed to prevent the occurrence of high-speed train accidents involving people and objects.

Keywords. Urban rail transit; Fully automatic line; Fault tree analysis; Clamping people and objects

1. Introduction

Transportation largely determines the development of a country and region. Traffic safety has always been and will always be a crucial topic [1, 2]. According to data released by the Ministry of Transport, as of August 2023, a total of 297 urban rail transit lines have been opened and operated in 54 cities in China, with an operating mileage of 9771.8 kilometers [3]. As of the end of 2022, a total of 15 cities in mainland China, including Beijing, Shanghai, Tianjin, Chongqing, Guangzhou, Shenzhen, Wuhan, Nanjing, Chengdu, Suzhou, Ningbo, Nanning, Jinan, and Taiyuan Wuhu, have opened fully automated operation system lines (FAO), with a total of 30 lines, forming a scale of 716.83 kilometers of fully automated operation lines [4]. Fully automatic operation lines, due to their significant reliability and economy, are the trend of future urban rail transit development, and also bring new challenges to line operation work [5, 6].

---

[1] Corresponding Author: Jie SHANG, E-mail: 2158655849@qq.com.

FAO adopts Grade of Automation 4 (GOA4) level unmanned driving technology, which does not require a driver to drive throughout the entire operation. Therefore, compared to traditional routes, it is not possible to judge the closing status of train doors and platform doors through manual observation during departure. Instead, the safety detection function of train doors and platform doors replaces this process [7,8]. Once the system experiences inaccurate judgment or improper fault handling, it may lead to a high-speed train accident involving people, objects, and passengers' lives and property may be damaged [9,10]. Therefore, the risk point that urban rail transit fully automatic operation line operators need to pay close attention to is the high-speed train with people and objects caught, and corresponding measures must be taken to prevent the occurrence of high-speed train accidents with people and objects caught in train doors and platform doors [11-13]. At the same time, it is even more necessary to do a good job in prediction and prevention through deep learning and other technical means, to effectively ensure the safety and reliability allowed by rail transit [14,15].

2. Literature Review of Fault Tree Analysis

Fault tree analysis (FTA) originated from fault tree analysis and is one of the important analysis methods in safety systems engineering. It was first applied in the military field [16-18]. It sets the specific accident to be analyzed as the top event and analyzes the reasons that induce it until the basic cause of the accident is identified. These most fundamental reasons are also known as fundamental events. The fault tree analysis method can identify and evaluate the hazards of various systems, not only analyzing the direct causes of accidents, but also deeply revealing the potential causes of accidents. Therefore, this method is widely used in the field of safety analysis [19].

Gui Siping and Sun Hongyin analyzed and explored the anti-pinch measures based on the reasons for the occurrence of people and objects being caught between the subway platform doors and the train gaps [20]. Han Lingshan, Li Xiaopu, and others have designed an infrared detection safety protection system based on a 51 microcontroller. This system can be used not only for detecting people and objects in straight platforms, but also for detecting people and objects in curved platforms [21]. Li Yanfeng reviewed typical cases, analyzed the reasons, and proposed prevention and control measures from the aspects of employee behavior, equipment and facility improvement, operation management optimization, and safety riding promotion to reduce safety risks [22].

Lei Huanyu and Liu Weiming proposed a K-means based method for detecting foreign object surfaces in subway platforms to address potential safety hazards such as personnel and objects being trapped in the gap between subway screen doors and train doors. Through experiments on real video data, the results show that the proposed algorithm has good robustness to changes in lighting, can accurately detect various foreign objects, and can assist drivers in making pre driving decisions [23]. Wang Xinyan used Fault Tree Analysis (FTA) based on the fault data of Zhengzhou Metro Line 1 Phase I, combined with the structural characteristics of the gantry crane system, to establish a fault tree for the gantry crane system. Through qualitative and quantitative analysis, the probability of top event faults was obtained. Based on the importance calculation results, typical fault causes, and weak links of the gantry crane system were identified, and an optimization plan for platform gantry crane system faults was proposed [24]. Pang Yanzhi et al. used the fault tree method to analyze the feasibility of the train delay accident caused by the air brake relief relay failure on Nanning Metro Line 1 and provided relevant suggestions for driving safety [25]. Faults and their prevention have received attention from countries around the world [26, 27].

Most of the above studies have used FTA methods to study accidents under the Automatic Train Operation mode, proposing optimization measures for operation or improving the detection performance of shielded doors, in order to reduce the occurrence of accidents involving people and objects. However, it is rare to conduct targeted in-depth research on people and objects caught accidents based on the characteristics of FAO operating lines.

3. Establishment and Analysis of Accident Trees

3.1. Establishment of Accident Tree

Set the train door and platform door collision accident as a top event, based on operation and maintenance management experience, sort out the various links that led to the occurrence of the top event, analyze the internal mechanism between the basic events and the cause events, and draw a fault tree for the train door and platform door collision accident on fully automatic operation lines, as shown in Figure 1.

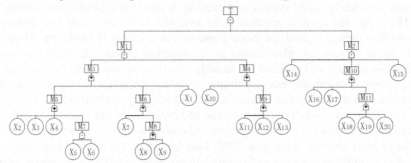

Figure 1. Accident tree of high-speed trains with people and objects caught in fully automatic operation of urban rail transit lines

3.2. Fault Tree Description

The meanings of various elements contained in the accident tree of train doors and platform doors clamping people and objects on fully automatic operation lines, as well as the corresponding events represented (top event, intermediate event, basic event), are detailed in Table 1, where the "intermediate event" are abbreviated as "Interm-event".

Table 1. Fault Tree symbols and event description for high-speed rail vehicles with people, objects, and objects in fully automatic operation of urban rail transit lines

Symbol	Event	Description
T	Top events	People and object gripping accidents in fully automatic operation lines of high-speed trains
M_1	Interm-event	The passenger's body and belongings are trapped or located between the train doors and platform doors
M_2	Interm-event	Train departure
M_3	Interm-event	The passenger's body and belongings are located on the platform and in the carriage
M_4	Interm-event	The anti pinch function of train doors and platform doors is not activated
M_5	Interm-event	Passengers are unable to board the train in a timely manner
M_6	Interm-event	Passengers are pushed onto the vehicle
M_7	Interm-event	Passenger flushing door
M_8	Interm-event	Crowded platform
M_9	Interm-event	No abnormality detected in the anti pinch function
M_{10}	Interm-event	The safety detection system for train doors and platform doors did not detect any abnormalities
M_{11}	Interm-event	Platform door gap detector does not alarm
X_1	Basic event	Passengers hesitate to enter or exit the carriage
X_2	Basic event	Crowded carriages
X_3	Basic event	Passengers carrying large luggage and items
X_4	Basic event	Short stop time
X_5	Basic event	The departure interval is large, and passengers are unwilling to wait for the next train
X_6	Basic event	No one to dissuade, insufficient publicity
X_7	Basic event	Too many passengers getting off the train, unable to get on the train in a timely manner
X_8	Basic event	Insufficient platform design capacity
X_9	Basic event	Train delay
X_{10}	Basic event	No anti pinch function designed
X_{11}	Basic event	Anti pinch function failure
X_{12}	Basic event	Low sensitivity
X_{13}	Basic event	Small size of the clamped part or item
X_{14}	Basic event	Interlocking receives and detects no abnormal departure signal

Table 1. Fault Tree symbols and event description for high-speed rail vehicles with people, objects, and objects in fully automatic operation of urban rail transit lines (continued)

Symbol	Event	Description
X_{15}	Basic event	Foreign objects still invade the vehicle door and platform door after the fault is removed
X_{16}	Basic event	Undesigned detection function
X_{17}	Basic event	Train door and platform door system malfunction
X_{18}	Basic event	Gap detector failure
X_{19}	Basic event	The gap detector was manually cut off
X_{20}	Basic event	Gap detector has detection blind spots

3.3. Calculation of the Minimum Path Set of the Accident Tree

The path set refers to the set of basic events in the accident tree. The minimum path set of the accident tree refers to the minimum set of basic events that cannot cause the occurrence of the top event. As long as all basic events within one of the minimum path sets do not occur, the top event will not occur. According to the definition of the minimum path set, accidents can be avoided by controlling each minimum path set. Based on this, it can be concluded that the accident tree for the fully automatic operation of high-speed trains with people and objects in the line contains a total of 8 minimum path sets, and the equivalent tree drawn is shown in Figure 2.

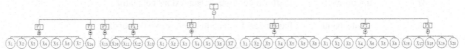

Figure 2. Equivalent tree of high-speed train accidents caused by people and objects clamping on fully automatic operation lines

3.4. Structural Importance Analysis

Structural importance analysis is an important means of analyzing the impact of basic events on top events in the fault tree, and providing information for improving system safety. The main methods used in this paper are approximate judgment and precise calculation. The approximate judgment calculation method is used to calculate the structural importance using the minimum diameter set. The calculation formula is:

$$I(i) = \frac{1}{k} \sum_{j=1}^{n} \frac{1}{n_j} (j \in k_j) \tag{1}$$

In the equation:

k : Total number of minimum path sets;

k_j : The *j-th* minimum path set;

n_j : Number of basic events contained in the *j-th* minimum path set.

According to formula (1), the structural importance of the minimum path set is calculated, and the structural importance is sorted and layered from highest to lowest. The basic events can be divided into 7 layers, as shown in Table 2.

Table 2. Analysis of the importance of basic event structure

Hierarchy	Basic events	Event Description	Structural Importance
1	X_{14}	Interlocking receives and detects no abnormal departure signal	1.0000
	X_{15}	Foreign objects still invade the vehicle door and platform door after the fault is removed	
2	X_{10}	No anti pinch function designed	0.1250
	X_{11}	Anti pinch function failure	
	X_{12}	Low sensitivity	
	X_{13}	Small size of the clamped part or item	
3	X_1	Passengers hesitate to enter or exit the carriage	0.0906
	X_2	Crowded carriages	
	X_3	Passengers carrying large luggage and items	
	X_4	Short stop time	
4	X_{16}	Undesigned detection function	0.0625
	X_{17}	Train door and platform door system malfunction	
	X_{18}	Gap detector failure	
	X_{19}	The gap detector was manually cut off	
	X_{20}	Gap detector has detection blind spots	
5	X_7	Too many passengers getting off the train, unable to get on the train in a timely manner	0.0615
6	X_5	The departure interval is large, and passengers are unwilling to wait for the next train	0.0464
	X_6	No one to dissuade, insufficient publicity	
7	X_8	Insufficient platform design capacity	0.0310
	X_9	Train delay	

Table 2 presented that basic events can be classified into safety condition categories (Level *1*), design function categories (Levels *2, 4,* and *7*), passenger subjective factors categories (Level *3*), and operation department passenger flow organization categories (Levels *5* and *6*). From a macro perspective, the events with the greatest impact are the safe operation of the system and manual intervention to confirm on-site safety in case of faults, while the events with the least impact are insufficient platform design capacity and train delays. From a micro perspective, in the design functional category, the event with anti-pinch function type has the greatest impact (structural importance=*0.1250*), while the event with insufficient platform design capacity has the smallest impact (structural importance=*0.0310*).

In addition, subjective factors of passengers have a certain impact on accidents. Due to individual behavior being difficult to control, direct measures cannot be taken for control. However, management can be carried out through publicity and education, on-site guidance, and other forms to reduce the probability of such basic events occurring. At the same time, subjective factors are also related to the organizational mode of urban rail transit transportation, the supply and demand relationship between transportation capacity and travel demand. Therefore, for the purpose of improving transportation capacity, measures such as passenger flow relief, passenger flow control, and passenger guidance should also be taken to intervene, avoiding the accumulation of time and space during peak hours for passengers, and thus preventing the occurrence of people and objects accidents.

4. Analysis of the Results of a High-Speed Train Accident Involving People and Objects Being Caught

To avoid accidents involving people and objects in high-speed trains, an equivalent tree is drawn based on the minimum path set. As long as one of the minimum path sets is controlled, the top event can be avoided. The composition of the *P2* and *P3* path sets is the simplest, only containing one basic event. It is an ideal control plan for preventing accidents involving people and objects in high-speed trains. The *P4* path set includes 4 basic events, while the *P8* path set includes 5 basic events, making it a relatively simple control scheme. The composition of the *P1, P5, P6,* and *P7* path sets is relatively complex, making it more difficult to control compared to the aforementioned schemes. Based on this, this paper selects four relatively simple path set analysis methods to develop control measures, as shown detailed in Table 3.

Table 3. Optimal control measures for preventing accidents involving people and objects in high-speed trains

Scenario	Minimum path set	Control measures
1	$P_2 = \{X_{14}\}$	If there is an abnormality and the interlocking cannot receive the departure signal, there will be no accident of people or objects being caught in the train.
2	$P_3 = \{X_{15}\}$	If the fault of the train door and platform door is manually removed and there is no invasion of the safety limit on site, there will be no accident of people or objects being caught in the high-speed train
3	$P_4 = \{X_{10}, X_{11}, X_{12}, X_{13}\}$	The train doors and platform doors are designed with anti-pinch function, which is normal and has high sensitivity. If the size of the clamped parts or items is normal, there will be no accident of people or objects being caught in the high-speed train.
4	$P_8 = \{X_{16}, X_{17}, X_{18}, X_{19}, X_{20}\}$	The design of train doors and platform doors has detection functions. If the system of train doors and platform doors is normal, the gap detector is normal, and the gap detector has not been manually cut off, and there is no detection blind area for the gap detector, then there will be no accident of people or objects being caught in the train.

Among the four control measures mentioned above, Scheme 1 is a requirement for the safe operation of the signal system. It can be used as a control measure by improving equipment reliability and redundancy, strengthening equipment inspection and regular maintenance, and has strong feasibility. Option 2 is to organize the train to depart after manually confirming the on-site safety in case of fault handling. Measures such as strengthening staff training, developing standardized operation procedures, and pressing the emergency stop button on the platform for protection during fault handling can be taken as control measures, which have strong feasibility. Both Scheme 3 and Scheme 4 are system functional requirements, and their control measures can be fully demonstrated and incorporated into the overall requirements during the construction phase, or technical upgrades and renovations can be carried out on existing line equipment, both of which can achieve the goal of preventing accidents. However, they have many influencing factors and can be used as technical auxiliary means to reduce the probability of accidents.

5. Conclusion

Safety is the lifeline. The fundamental way to prevent accidents involving people, objects, and high-speed trains in fully automatic operation is, on the one hand, to ensure that the system equipment is sufficiently reliable, and relevant requirements are fully considered in the design stage. After being put into operation, complete maintenance procedures are formulated to ensure the safe operation of the system. On the other hand, there is a higher requirement for the emergency response level of staff, and a comprehensive plan and regular training mechanism should be developed. In addition, it is necessary to strengthen passenger flow guidance. While doing a good job in relieving peak passenger flow, it is also necessary to do a good job in promoting and educating safe riding and improve awareness of safe riding.

The use of fault tree methods to identify and evaluate the hazards of various systems, establish the calculation of the minimum path set and analyze the structural importance, identify the direct causes of accidents, and deeply reveal the potential causes of accidents. From a systematic perspective, it has been proven to be scientific and effective to eliminate hidden dangers of accidents.

Acknowledgment

The funding support for this paper includes: (1) Guangxi Science and Technology Base and Talent Project (Guike AD23026029); (2) Nanning City Science Research and Technology Development Plan Project (20223230); and (3) Transportation Operation Subsidy Project of Guangxi Key Laboratory for International Join for China-ASEAN Comprehensive Transportation in 2021 (21-220-21).

References

[1] Xie Guo, Shangguan Anqi, Fei Rong, Hei Xinhong, Ji Wenjiang, Qian Fucai. Unmanned system safety decision-making support: analysis and assessment of road traffic accidents[J]. IEEE-ASME Transactions on Mechatronics, 2021, 26(2): 633-644.

[2] Lin Zuo. Public safety risk prediction of urban rail transit based on mathematical model and algorithm simulation [EB/OL]: Springer Science and Business Media Llc, 2023. http://dx.doi.org/10.1007/s00500-023-08919-x. 10.1007/s00500-023-08919-x.

[3] Ministry of Transport of the People's Republic of China quick report on urban rail transit operation data for August 2023 [DB/OL] https://www.mot.gov.cn/fenxigongbao/yunlifenxi/202309/t20230905_3908942.html.

[4] China urban rail transit association statistical and analysis report on urban rail transit in 2022 [DB/OL] https://www.camet.org.cn/tjxx/11944.

[5] Xinyu Jiao, Junjie Chen, Kun Jiang, Zhong Cao, Diange Yang. Autonomous driving risk assessment with boundary-based environment model[J]. IEEE Transactions on Intelligent Vehicles, 2023, :1-15.

[6]   Yunfang Ma, Jose M Sallan, Oriol Lordan. Motif analysis of urban rail transit network[J]. Physica A: Statistical Mechanics and its Applications, 2023, .625: 129016.

[7]   V. Ganesh Kumar. Driverless train technology[J]. International Journal of Technology and Engineering Science, 2013, .1(6).

[8]   Fei Yan, Junqiao Ma, Mo Li, et al. An automated accident causal scenario identification method for fully automatic operation system based on STPA[J]. IEEE Access, 2021, 9: 11051-11064.

[9]   Yuan Cao, Xiang Liu, Guo Xie, Clive Roberts. AAP - Technology in rail safety - applications of advanced technologies in rail safety[J]. Accident; analysis and prevention, 2023, :107152.

[10]   Yuan Cao, Xiang Liu, Guo Xie, Clive Roberts. AAP - Technology in rail safety - Applications of advanced technologies in rail safety[J]. Accident; analysis and prevention, 2023, 5:107152.

[11]   Sobolevska, Maryna (Sobmb@I.Ua), Telychko, Igor. Passive safety of high-speed passenger trains at accident collisions on 1520 mm gauge railways[J]. Transport Problems, 2017, .12(1):51-62.

[12]   Feifan Liu, Fulin Zhou, Lei Ma. An automatic detection framework for electrical anomalies in electrified rail transit system[J]. IEEE Transactions on Instrumentation and Measurement, 2023, 72: 1-13.

[13]   Noble, Fergus. Driving safety for consumers[J]. GPS World, 2022, .33(9): 28.

[14]   Deyun Wang. Intelligent detection of vehicle driving safety based on deep learning[J]. Wireless Communications and Mobile Computing, 2022, .2022.

[15]   AlKheder S, Al-Rashidi M. Bayesian hierarchical statistics for traffic safety modelling and forecasting[J]. International journal of injury control and safety promotion, 2020, .27(2): 99-111.

[16]   Silvia Tolo, John Andrews. Fault tree analysis including component dependencies[J]. IEEE Transactions on Reliability, 2023, 6:1-9.

[17]   Signoret, Jean Pierre, Leroy, Alain. Fault tree analysis (FTA)[J]. Springer Series in Reliability Engineering, 2021, 6: 209-225.

[18]   Yazdi, Mohammad, Mohammadpour, Javad, Li He, et al. Fault tree analysis improvements: A bibliometric analysis and literature review[J]. Quality & Reliability Engineering International, 2023, .39(5):1.

[19]   Xiao Guiping, Zhu Xiaoning. Traffic safety engineering (second edition) [M] Beijing: China Railway Publishing House, 2016: 152 (in Chinese).

[20]   Gui Siping, Sun Hongyin. Exploration of anti-pinch measures for subway platform doors[J]. China Equipment Engineering, 2019, (23): 107-108 (Chinese).

[21]   Han Lingshan, Li Xiaopu, Sun Kangmeng, et al. Design of infrared detection safety protection system for the gap between subway trains and platform doors[J]. Electromechanical Technology, 2019, (05): 36-38 + 60 (Chinese).

[22]   Li Yanfeng. Risk prevention and control analysis of personnel and objects caught in platform doors and train doors of subway stations[J]. Journal of Nanyang Normal University, 2018, 17(06): 59-61 (Chinese).

[23]   Lei Huanyu, Liu Weiming. Foreign object detection in subway platforms based on K-means algorithm[J]. Computer and Modernization, 2018, (06): 42-46 (Chinese).

[24]   Wang Xinyan. Reliability analysis of platform door operator system based on FTA[J]. Journal of Zhengzhou Railway Vocational and Technical College, 2020, 32(01): 28-31 (Chinese).

[25]   Pang Yanzhi, Chen Jianqiu, Chen Jiali. Research on abnormal train operation of urban rail transit based on FTA[J]. Railway Communication Signal, 2020, 56 (02): 71-74 (Chinese).

[26]   Hongfei Meng, Xuejian Kang, Yabin Yan, et al. Reliability analysis of the third rail system based on fault tree[C]//2020 5th International Conference on Electromechanical Control Technology and Transportation (ICECTT 2020): IEEE, 2020: 599-602.

[27]   Thi Hoai An Nguyen, Jochen Trinckauf, Tuan Anh Luong, et al. Risk analysis for train collisions using fault tree analysis: case study of the Hanoi Urban Mass Rapid Transit[J]. Urban Rail Transit, 2023, 8(2): 193.

Artificial Intelligence, Medical Engineering and Education
Z.B. Hu et al. (Eds.)
© *2024 The Authors.*
This article is published online with Open Access by IOS Press and distributed under the terms
of the Creative Commons Attribution Non-Commercial License 4.0 (CC BY-NC 4.0).
doi:10.3233/ATDE231355

439

Influencing Factors of Community Logistics Service Satisfaction at Cainiao Station

Xiaofen ZHOU[1], Genping XIE
Wuhan Technology and Business University, Wuhan 430065, Hubei, China

Abstract. The rise of e-commerce has led to the rapid development of community logistics in the last mile of end-to-end distribution. However, the rapidly developing community logistics also faces various management issues, especially the satisfaction of consumers with community logistics services. This article examines the factors influencing residents' satisfaction with community logistics from the perspective of consumers. Using questionnaire surveys, it collects data on residents' satisfaction with various services in the community logistics Cainiao station. Using multiple linear regression, it analyzes the impact of the five aspects of service (tangibility, reliability, responsiveness, assurance, and empathy) on customer satisfaction in the community Cainiao station. The study shows that reliability, responsiveness, and assurance are the three most significant indicators affecting community logistics satisfaction. This conclusion provides a reference for enterprises related to community logistics distribution to improve their logistics service quality and enhance customer satisfaction.

Keywords. Community logistics; Satisfaction; Cainiao Station; SERVQUAL model.

1. Introduction

The e-commerce market in China is consistently expanding, with online shopping having become the primary method of daily consumption for individuals. The logistics industry has rapidly developed in tandem with the increasing demand of e-commerce consumption mode [1]. The quality of logistics service directly impacts the consumer's choice of e-commerce consumption platform. The logistics services of e-commerce are increasingly becoming the main competitive field among various e-commerce platforms, especially in the community logistics at the end of logistics services. The quality of community service logistics directly influences the consumer experience and has a profound effect on their satisfaction with online shopping [2-4].

Community logistics refer to the logistical activities organized by groups of residents within a community to fulfill their daily needs. Its primary service targets are residents within the community, encompassing individuals or families, as well as different units (enterprises) [5]. Viewing community logistics from the standpoint of logistics, it is a rapidly emerging and developing type of logistics within the context of e-commerce. And from the perspective of service model, community logistics is enabled

---

[1] Corresponding Author: Xiaofen ZHOU, E-mail: 103343280@qq.com.

by modern information technology, establishing an "information highway" between consumers and suppliers.

The quality of community logistics services refers to the direct feelings customers have during the process of enjoying logistics services, and is a major factor affecting customer satisfaction [6]. It includes factors such as express delivery, packaging, personnel, and processes. Unlike general logistics services, the purpose of community logistics services is to meet the personalized and diverse shopping needs of community residents.

The research on logistics service quality evaluation methods and evaluation index systems has received a certain degree of attention in the academic community at home and abroad, and has formed a set of highly recognized measurement methods for logistics service quality, as well as diversified evaluation and analysis methods for logistics service quality. The construction and measurement of evaluation indicators are generally based on the SERVQUAL model proposed by PZB [7].

2. Construction of Indicator System for Influencing Factors

Based on previous research, combined with the logistics services provided by Cainiao Express, such as package collection, improved timeliness, and enhanced user experience, and drawing on the SERVQUAL model proposed by PZB (1988) [8], five representative primary indicators were constructed, including tangibility, reliability, responsiveness, assurance, and empathy. The relationship diagram is shown in Figure 1. Combining the content and characteristics of the logistics services provided by the community "Cainiao Station" and the specific content of the first-level indicators, the corresponding second-level indicators were reasonably adjusted, and an index system for evaluating the satisfaction of community logistics services provided by Cainiao Station was constructed, as shown in Table 1.

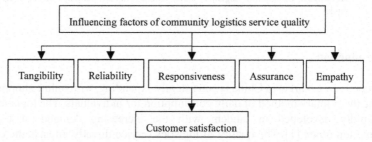

Figure 1. Relationship diagram of primary indicators of influencing factors.

The satisfaction index of community logistics services mainly consists of five aspects: tangibility, reliability, responsiveness, assurance, and empathy [9]. Among them, tangibility refers to the impact of the external image of community logistics on residents, mainly measured from five aspects: logistics service facilities of the community station, the appearance of service personnel, the attractiveness of facilities, the matching degree of facilities and services, and the cleanliness of the community station environment. Reliability refers to the ability of community logistics services to fulfill their service commitments with accuracy and reliability, mainly measured from five aspects: the efficiency of pickup notifications, the accuracy of item distribution, the rationality of the distribution and layout of relay stations, the flexibility of service time, and the timeliness of service process information updates [10]. Responsiveness refers to the ability of community logistics services to meet residents' requests for mailing and picking up items in a relatively short period of time, mainly measured from four aspects: the active service awareness of the station, the waiting time for mailing and picking up items, the efficiency of handling claims issues, and the timeliness of advisory services [11]. Guarantee refers to that the community logistics service meets the requirements of residents in terms of express privacy protection, which is mainly measured from four aspects: integrity of express goods, transparency and rationality of charges, progressiveness of logistics system and security of personal information [12].

Table 1. The index system of influencing factors of community logistics service satisfaction of Cainiao stations

constituent elements	Influencing factors	Indicator Code
Tangibility	logistics service facilities of the station	A1
	the appearance of service personnel	A2
	the attractiveness of facilities	A3
	the matching degree of facilities and services	A4
	the cleanliness of the station environment	A5
Reliability	the efficiency of pickup notifications	B1
	the accuracy of item distribution	B2
	the rationality of the distribution and layout of relay stations	B3
	the flexibility of service time	B4
	the timeliness of service process information updates	B5
Responsiveness	the active service awareness of the station	C1
	the waiting time for mailing and picking up items	C2
	the efficiency of handling claims issues	C3
	the timeliness of advisory services	C4
Assurance	integrity of express goods	D1
	transparency and rationality of charges	D2
	progressiveness of logistics system	D3
	security of personal information	D4
Empathy	the diversity of courier services	E1
	the effectiveness of communication with customers	E2
	the level of respect for customers	E3
	customer satisfaction with complaint handling	E4
Customer satisfaction	I will consider using the community post service again	Y
	I will recommend my relatives and friends to use the community post service	
	I am satisfied with the community post service	

Empathy refers to the ability of community logistics to provide personalized services that meet customer needs, measured mainly in terms of the diversity of courier services, the effectiveness of communication with customers, the level of respect for customers, and customer satisfaction with complaint handling. The secondary indicator scale evaluation is shown in Table 1.

3. Research Methods and Empirical Analysis

The SERVQUAL model is a quantitative method proposed based on the gap model of service quality, considering five indicators of service quality, and is an effective method to test the relationship between service quality and customer satisfaction. The paper proposes an indicator system of factors affecting community logistics service satisfaction based on the SERVQUAL evaluation model, and adopts the "Likert five-level scale method" to transform the indicator system into a questionnaire, and conducts a survey. The questionnaire is mainly divided into two parts: the first part is the personal information of the survey object, including five items. The second part is mainly composed of 22 logistics service quality indicator items, as shown in Table 1.It was launched through a network platform, and a total of 130 valid questionnaires were received.

3.1. Reliability and Validity Analysis

To ensure the credibility of the questionnaire survey data, the reliability analysis and testing of the questionnaire were conducted using the Cronbach's alpha method of SPSS software [13]. The test results are shown in Table 2. The closer the Cronbach's alpha value is to 1, the higher the credibility and internal consistency of the questionnaire data. It can be seen from Table 2 that the overall Cronbach's alpha coefficient is 0.951, and the Cronbach's alpha coefficients for each indicator are *0.709, 0.785, 0.745, 0.764, 0.773,* and *0.701*, indicating that the credibility of this questionnaire is high and the survey results are true and reliable.

Table 2. Reliability analysis

Indicators	Cronbach's α coefficient	Overall Cronbach's α coefficient
Tangibility	*0.709*	
Reliability	*0.785*	
Responsiveness	*0.745*	*0.951*
Assurance	*0.764*	
Empathy	*0.773*	
Customer satisfaction	*0.701*	

Validity refers to the consistency between the survey objectives and survey results. The higher the validity, the higher the consistency [14]. To ensure the consistency between the survey objectives and survey results, it is necessary to conduct a validity analysis on the survey data. This article uses KMO and Bartett's sphericity test to measure the effectiveness of the overall scale validity. The validity analysis of the questionnaire was conducted using SPSS software, and the analysis results are shown in Table 3. The KMO value is 0.912, which is above *0.7,* indicating that the survey has high validity. The Bartett's sphericity test result is *0.000*, and its significance is lower than *0.001*, indicating that there is a certain correlation between different scale variables.

Table 3. KMO test and Bartlett's test

KMO value		0.912
Bartlett's Test of Sphericity	Approximate Chi-squared value	1920.186
	df	300
	P	0.000***

Note: ***、 **、 * represent significance levels of 1%, 5%, and 10%, respectively

3.2. Correlation Analysis

To explore the main factors affecting the satisfaction of community logistics Cainiao stations, Pearson coefficient was used to test the correlation and dependence between two distance-based variables. The correlation analysis was conducted on the customer satisfaction index system and the five influencing factors. The test results are shown in Table 4.

Table 4. Pearson correlation analysis

	Customer satisfaction	Responsiveness	Tangibility	Empathy	Reliability	Assurance
Customer satisfaction	1 (0.000***)	0.793 (0.000***)	0.76 (0.000***)	0.737 (0.000***)	0.787 (0.000***)	0.768 (0.000***)
Responsiveness	0.793 (0.000***)	1 (0.000***)	0.856 (0.000***)	0.853 (0.000***)	0.754 (0.000***)	0.819 (0.000***)
Tangibility	0.76 (0.000***)	0.856(0.000***)	1(0.000***)	0.855 (0.000***)	0.734 (0.000***)	0.881 (0.000***)
Empathy	0.737 (0.000***)	0.853 (0.000***)	0.855 (0.000***)	1(0.000***)	0.749 (0.000***)	0.823 (0.000***)
Reliability	0.787 (0.000***)	0.754 (0.000***)	0.734 (0.000***)	0.749 (0.000***)	1 (0.000***)	0.739 (0.000***)
Assurance	0.768 (0.000***)	0.819 (0.000***)	0.881 (0.000***)	0.823 (0.000***)	0.739 (0.000***)	1 (0.000***)

Note: ***、 **、 * represent significance levels of 1%, 5%, and 10%, respectively

When the Pearson coefficient is above 0 and the confidence level is below 0.01, it indicates that there is a significant relationship between them [15]. All variables in the following table are below the 0.01 confidence level, indicating that the five indicators of community logistics service quality are positively correlated with customer satisfaction. This reflects the close relationship between community logistics service quality and customer satisfaction.

3.3. Multivariate Linear Regression Analysis

The above analysis verifies the reliability and validity of the questionnaire, and concludes the correlation between the five indicators and customer satisfaction. Therefore, the paper further analyzes the relationship between customer satisfaction and the five indicators using multiple linear regression analysis in SPSS software. Multiple regression analysis describes the influence of multiple independent variables on the dependent variable [16]. This article sets tangibility, reliability, responsiveness, assurance, and empathy as independent variables in the factors affecting customer satisfaction in community logistics, and sets customer satisfaction as the dependent variable for regression analysis. The final regression constant of the equation is 0.296, the regression coefficient of responsiveness is 0.323, the regression coefficient of tangibility is 0.058, the regression coefficient of empathy is -0.044, the regression coefficient of reliability is 0.375, and the regression coefficient of assurance is 0.213. The multiple regression model of the factors affecting customer satisfaction in Cainiao logistics service is as follows:

$$Y=0.296+0.323X_1+0.058X_2-0.044X_3+0.375X_4+0.213X_5.$$

Among them, Y in the regression equation represents the dependent variable, community logistics overall satisfaction, X_1 represents the independent variable, responsiveness, X_2 represents the independent variable, tangibility, X_3 represents the independent variable, empathy, X_4 represents the independent variable, reliability, X_5 represents the independent variable, assurance, and 0.296 is the constant term of the model. The specific parameters are shown in Table 5.

As shown in Table 5, the adjusted R^2 of the five indicators on customer satisfaction is 0.717, the adjusted R^2 of the five indicators on customer satisfaction is 0.717, indicating that the factors that affect community logistics service satisfaction included in the regression equation can explain 71.7% of the model, reflecting the high level of explanation of the model. This indicates that the independent variables can better explain the dependent variables. In the analysis of variance, the F value of the model is 66.276, and the significance level is 0.000, which is less than 0.05, indicating that there is a strong linear correlation between the five indicators and customer satisfaction, indicating that the model passes the significance test and is suitable for using linear regression model to analyze the correlation between the five indicators of community logistics Cainiao Station service and customer satisfaction.

Table 5. Multiple linear regression analysis results

	Unstandardized Coefficients		Standardized Coefficient	t	P	VIF	R^2	R^2 Adjust	F
	B	Standard Error	Beta						
constant	0.296	0.2	-	1.479	0.142	-	0.728	0.717	$F=66.276$ $P=0.000$***
Responsiveness	0.323	0.104	0.329	3.118	0.002***	5.061			
Tangibility	0.058	0.116	0.06	0.506	0.614	6.468			
Empathy	-0.044	0.097	-0.048	-0.455	0.650	5.025			
Reliability	0.375	0.076	0.379	4.928	0.000***	2.697			
Assurance	0.213	0.11	0.205	1.932	0.050*	5.142			
dependent variable: Customer satisfaction									

Note: ***、 **、 * represent significance levels of 1%, 5%, and 10%, respectively

To further ensure the accuracy and reliability of the regression model, the multicollinearity of the model was tested. The VIF value represents the severity of multicollinearity and is used to test whether the model exhibits multicollinearity, that is, there is a highly correlated relationship between explanatory variables (VIF should be less than 10 or 5, strictly 5). If VIF appears inf, it indicates that the VIF value is infinite, and it is recommended to check for multicollinearity [17].

As can be seen from Table 5, the VIF values of the five independent variables are all around or below the critical value of *5*, indicating that there is no multicollinearity between the dependent variable and the independent variables, and the model is well constructed. Therefore, the multiple regression model constructed in this paper is reasonable.

In the multiple linear regression analysis, when *P<0.05*, it indicates that the hypothesis is established and has good significance. In the analysis results shown in Table 5, the significance P values of the regression coefficients of tangibility and empathy are *0.614* and *0.650*, respectively. Both of which are greater than *0.05*, indicating that the relationship between customer satisfaction and tangibility and empathy is not significant. The significance P values of the regression coefficients of customer satisfaction and reliability, responsiveness, and assurance are all below *0.05*, indicating that there is a significant positive relationship between customer satisfaction and reliability, responsiveness, and assurance.

4. Conclusion

In the above analysis, a model of factors affecting the satisfaction of community logistics Cainiao stations was constructed through the evaluation indicators proposed by PZB, exploring the relationship between each indicator and customer satisfaction. Multivariate linear regression analysis was used to verify the influence of tangibility, reliability, responsiveness, assurance, and empathy in community logistics services, providing a certain basis for improving community logistics satisfaction. According to the research data, reliability, responsiveness, and assurance are the three most significant indicators affecting community logistics satisfaction. Among the regression coefficients of all variables, the reliability coefficient is the largest, followed by responsiveness, and finally assurance. This indicates that residents have significant demands for reliability, responsiveness, and assurance in community logistics, and it is necessary to focus on improving these three aspects. Among them, residents' experience of convenience and reliability of express delivery is the most important, that is, whether the notification of pickup is timely, whether the distribution of stations is reasonable, whether the signs in the store are accurate, whether the time of pickup and delivery is flexible, and whether the goods are in good condition, which have the greatest impact on customer satisfaction.

Through the above quantitative analysis, it was found that tangibility and empathy cannot effectively affect customer satisfaction, but there are certain differences from the actual situation. The possible reasons can be attributed to the following three points: First, the insufficient sample size obtained from the recycling may make the research results less representative; second, due to the low quality of the data collected in the questionnaire, some deviations in the two dimensions of tangibility and empathy appear in the survey results; third, in reality, although the community logistics has a relatively complete system, in terms of providing services to customers, both software and hardware are not perfect, and customer complaints and other aspects of service fail to meet customer expectations. The above problems can be the direction for continuous research and improvement in the future.

Acknowledgment

This project is supported by Distinguished Young and Middle-aged Team Program for Scientific and Technological Innovation in Higher Education of Hubei, T201938, "Smart Logistics Park Service Innovation and Support Technologies Driven by Big-data"

References

[1]   Gang Li, Xin Shi. An Empirical Study on Consumers' Continuance Intention Model of Online Group-buying [J], International Journal of Engineering and Manufacturing, 2012, 2(05):83-95.
[2]   Raj Raval, Tarun Sankhla, Rushabh Shah, Swati Nadkarni, "Developing Markerless Augmented Reality for Furniture Mobile Application", International Journal of Education and Management Engineering, Vol.11, No.1, pp. 11-18, 2021.
[3]   Ashish K. Sharma, Sunanda Khandait, "A Novel Software Tool to Generate Customer Needs for Effective Design of Online Shopping Websites", International Journal of Information Technology and Computer Science, Vol.8, No.3, pp.85-92, 2016.
[4]   Ian-rong Li,"The Online Shopping System of the Web Service Technology with B2B Framework", International Journal of Education and Management Engineering, vol.2, no.12, pp.21-27, 2012.
[5]   Wang chenglin, Xiao Shan, Liang Jiayu. Research on the development of community logistics service[J]. Supply management, 2021, 2(01): 119-128 (in Chinese).
[6]   Oliver R L. A cognitive model of the antecedents and consequences of satisfaction decisions[J]. Journal of Marketing Research, 1980, 17(4): 460-469.
[7]   Parasuraman, A., Zeithaml, V. A., & Berry, L. L. A conceptual model of service quality and its implications for future research [J]. Journal of Marketing, 1985, 49(4): 41-50.
[8]   Markus Blut, Nivriti Chowdhry, et al. E-Service quality: a meta analytic review [J]. Journal of Retailing, 2015, 91(4): 679-700.
[9]   Laisak A H, Rosli A, Sa'Adi N. The effect of service quality on customers' satisfaction of inter-district public bus companies in the central region of Sarawak, Malaysia [J]. International Journal of Marketing Studies, 2021(2).
[10] Xie Guangying. Review of the measurement of logistics service quality in B2C and C2C online shopping: a conceptual model and theoretical framework[J]. Management Review, 2016, 28(4): 15 (in Chinese).
[11] Peng Runhua, Lin Xiaoxiao, Yang Zhenqing. Construction and testing of an evaluation index system for terminal logistics service quality[J]. Business Economics Research, 2018, 759(20): 83-86 (in Chinese).
[12] Wang Hong. Research on the problems and countermeasures of new rural community logistics services under the background of rural revitalization[J]. Logistics Technology, 2022, 45(14): 65-67 (in Chinese).
[13] Zhou Zhengsong, Shi Guohong. Research on service quality evaluation of logistics enterprises based on SERVQUAL and LSQ Models[J]. Science and Technology Management Research, 2012, 32(06): 27-29+34.
[14] Han Panpan, Tang Minting. Research on the optimization strategy of community logistics in the last kilometer of e-commerce mode - taking the Emerald Oasis Community in Guangzhou as an example[J]. Foreign Trade and Economic Cooperation, 2022(02): 108-111(in Chinese).
[15] Rong Taisheng. SPSS and research methods: statistical products and services solution[M]. Dongbei University of Finance & Economics Press, 2012 (in Chinese).
[16] Nahla M. Aljojo, Abeer Alkhouli. An Empirical Investigation of the Relationships between Learning Styles based on an Arabic version of the Felder-Silverman Model [J], International Journal of Modern Education and Computer Science, 2015,7(04):42-52.
[17] Anitha P, Malini M. Patil. A Review on Data Analytics for Supply Chain Management: A Case study [J]. International Journal of Information Engineering and Electronic Business, 2018,10(05): 30-39.

Artificial Intelligence, Medical Engineering and Education
Z.B. Hu et al. (Eds.)
doi:10.3233/ATDE231356

Exploration and Application of Marine Magnetic Field Information Based on Ocean Measurement Technology

Muxuan LI[1]

School of Marine Science and Technology, Northwestern Polytechnical University, China

ORCiD ID: Muxuan LI https://orcid.org/0009-0000-8222-0207

Abstract. Marine surveying technology, as an important component of marine science and technology, plays a very important role in safeguarding marine rights, developing marine resources, warning marine disasters, protecting the marine environment, strengthening national defense construction, and seeking new development space. It is also an important symbol of a country's comprehensive national strength. In recent years, China's ocean measurement technology has made great development. On the basis of a brief introduction of the basic characteristics of Marine magnetic field, the application status of Marine magnetic field measurement technology in ocean engineering and military struggle is summarized, and combined with the current situation of technology development and the development trend of Marine magnetic field measurement is discussed. Keywords. Ocean magnetic field; Ocean magnetic field measurement; Ocean engineering; Military application. Research has shown that marine magnetic measurement technology belongs to weak magnetic field detection technology. The task of marine magnetic measurement is to obtain the distribution and variation characteristics of the geomagnetic field in the ocean region through various means, providing basic data support for further research, interpretation, and application of marine magnetic information.

Keywords. Marine magnetic field; Marine magnetic field measurement; Ocean engineering; Military applications

1. Introduction

Ocean is the widest area on Earth, accounting for 71% of the Earth's surface area. Currently, there is still 95% of the unknown world on the seabed [1]. The 21st century is the ocean century, and the military struggle around marine resources and maritime territory is becoming increasingly fierce [2,3]. Whether it is a superpower, a traditional maritime power, or a coastal developing country, they all consider developing and managing the ocean as an important national policy, and strive to build a navy and develop maritime power to obtain the maximum ocean benefits. After efforts in recent years, China's marine magnetic field measurement technology has made significant progress in multiple research and application fields, with its applications specifically reflected in both marine engineering and military fields [4].

---

[1] Corresponding Author: Muxuan LI, E-mail: 1191127227@qq.com.

The ocean magnetic field changes with space and time, and the geomagnetic field detected by geomagnetic sensors is actually a composite field composed of many overlapping and influencing magnetic field sources. According to its origin, it can be divided into four parts:

$$B(r,t) = B_m(r,t) + B_c(r) + B_d(r,t) + B_s(r,t) \tag{1}$$

In the formula, $B_m(r,t)$ is the magnetic field caused by the current generated by the outer core of the Earth's liquid metal as it rotates with the Earth, accounting for over 99% of the ocean magnetic field; $B_c(r)$ is a magnetic anomaly generated by crustal rocks; $B_d(r,t)$ is the magnetic field caused by weak currents in the ionosphere and magnetosphere around the Earth, while $B_s(r,t)$ is the magnetic field caused by seawater movement, which is the calculation objective of this article. Since $B_m(r,t)$ is the main component of the Earth's magnetic field, the calculation of $B_s(r,t)$ can be obtained by the induced magnetic field generated by seawater movement under the action of $B_m(r,t)$, the main component of the Earth's magnetic field.

In the ocean, seawater moving at speed $\vec{V}$ in the geomagnetic field $\vec{B}$ generates a conductive current $\vec{J}$, which is expressed as:

$$\vec{J} = (\sigma\vec{E} + \mu_0\vec{V} \times \vec{B}) \tag{2}$$

In the formula, $\vec{E}$ represents all electric fields, including induced electric fields; $\vec{B}$ is the induction intensity of the Earth's magnetic field; σ is the conductivity of seawater, and its value is generally 3-5 S/m. At the typical frequency of seawater fluctuations, displacement current is relatively small compared to conduction current. Due to the thermal effect of the current generated by the electric field, its energy is quickly absorbed by seawater, so $\vec{E}$ quickly disappears, so formula (2) can be simplified as:

$$\vec{J} = \sigma\vec{V} \times \vec{B} \tag{3}$$

According to Ampere's law, the induced electromagnetic field satisfies the following equation:

$$\Delta \times \vec{H} = \mu_0\vec{J} \tag{4}$$

Bringing equation (3) into the above equation leads to the following equation:

$$\Delta \times \vec{H} = \sigma\mu_0\vec{V} \times \vec{B} \tag{5}$$

The calculation of $\vec{H}$ in equation (5) can be simplified as the simulation and calculation of the distribution of seawater velocity $\vec{V}$, corresponding to different ocean phenomena, such as waves, currents, and internal waves. The motion mode of $\vec{V}$ is different, and its induced magnetic field is also different, so it needs to be discussed separately.

2. Basic Characteristics of the Ocean's Magnetic Field

The geomagnetic field is a fundamental physical field in the Earth system, which directly affects the motion characteristics of all moving charged or magnetic objects in the system [5-7]. The geomagnetic field is an inherent physical property of the Earth, providing a natural coordinate reference frame for aviation, aerospace, and navigation. It is widely used for positioning, orientation, and attitude control of spacecraft and naval vessels [8]. The geomagnetic field mainly consists of three parts: basic magnetic field, abnormal magnetic field, and external magnetic field [9]. The basic magnetic field originates from the Earth's core, accounting for about 95% of the Earth's magnetic field; The anomalous magnetic field originates from crustal magnetic activity, accounting for about 4% of the Earth's magnetic field; The external magnetic field is related to the current system in near-Earth space, with a very small magnitude, accounting for only about 1% of the Earth's magnetic field [10].

The average intensity of the basic magnetic field on the Earth's surface is about 50000 nanoteslas (nT), about 35000nT in the equatorial region, and about 70000 nT near the poles. The geomagnetic field intensity in the waters of China is approximately between 40000 and 60000nT. The anomalous magnetic field intensity in most areas of the Earth's surface is generally small, but in igneous rock areas, magnetic anomalies can reach hundreds of nT, and in magnetite distribution areas, magnetic anomalies can reach several thousand nT. On magnetic calm days, the variation of external magnetic fields generally does not exceed 100nT, but on magnetic storm days, the variation of magnetic fields can reach up to thousands of nT.

Magnetic measurement can be divided into land magnetic measurement, ocean magnetic measurement, aerial magnetic measurement, and satellite magnetic measurement according to different measurement areas [11,12]. Currently, marine magnetic measurement in China mainly focuses on ship magnetic measurement and aerial magnetic measurement [13].

Ocean currents are independent circulation systems or eddies that flow from one sea area to another under the influence of sea surface wind and salinity, and ultimately back to the original sea area. Due to the fact that in magnetotelluric research and the measurement of velocity using electromagnetic current meters, the horizontal component of the field is measured, we only need to study the magnetic field excited by the ocean current under the action of the vertical component of the magnetic field.

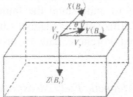

Figure 1. Current induced magnetic field reference coordinate system.

The seawater layer with a thickness of M flows horizontally, and the flow velocity is uniform between layers, which is a constant. Taking the center of the surface of the unit current as the origin and taking the coordinate system shown in Figure 1, the geomagnetic field is divided into three-dimensional components, and only the vertical component (Z-axis direction) is considered to affect the motion of seawater.

3. The Application of Marine Magnetic Field Measurement in Ocean Engineering

In recent years, with the continuous development of marine magnetic measurement related technologies, the technology has become more and more mature, and the application range of marine magnetic measurement technology in the civilian field is becoming wider and wider. For example, ocean magnetic surveys have discovered seafloor banded magnetic anomalies, providing an important basis for plate tectonics theory. Marine magnetic measurement technology has broad potential in the development of marine engineering.

3.1. Application of Marine Magnetic Field Measurement in Submarine Optical Cable Laying

Marine magnetic detection technology is used to detect and locate submarine cables by detecting changes in the Earth's magnetic field caused by submarine cables. The distribution of the geomagnetic field is relatively complex. In areas susceptible to interference from the magnetic field in the sea (such as the presence of magnetic substances such as sea sand mines on the seabed), shallow (less than 1m) submarine cables can be detected, and their relative variation in the geomagnetic field (25000~65000nT) is about 50nT. Based on this, submarine power cables, submarine communication cables, and submarine optical cables can be detected. Other methods such as saturation magnetometer detection, proton magnetometer detection, and optical pump magnetometer detection can all achieve good detection accuracy, and can detect and locate submarine cable fault points and laying routes.

3.2. Application of Marine Magnetic Field Measurement in Site Selection of Large Ocean Engineering

Large marine engineering must ensure the stability and reliability of its foundation, which is similar to ground airport runways. Marine related engineering also requires measurements of the geomagnetic environment to ensure regional stability. The application of marine magnetic measurement technology can not only identify harmful obstacles such as shipwrecks on the seabed, but also effectively avoid the construction of heavy engineering on seabed minerals, which will affect future development and use. The most important thing is to understand the faults and other geological structures within the engineering area. Utilize marine magnetic measurement technology combined with seismic exploration and borehole data to provide geological interpretation of geological anomalies.

3.3. Application of Marine Magnetic Field Measurement in Environmental Monitoring

The accumulation of pollutants on the seabed and sea surface can have a serious impact on marine life and human daily marine activities. Therefore, countries are actively carrying out marine environmental governance. Compared to traditional dense sampling, the use of marine magnetic measurement can comprehensively monitor and control the pollution situation of the marine environment on a large scale, wide sea area, and multiple levels.

4. The Application of Marine Magnetic Field Measurement in Military Affairs

Marine magnetic field information is an essential element in the construction of the naval battlefield environment. The application of key technologies such as marine magnetic target detection and recognition technology, ocean geomagnetic matching navigation, etc. all require the support of marine magnetic field measurement technology and marine magnetic measurement data.

4.1. Application of Marine Magnetic Field Measurement in Submarine Exploration

Marine magnetic field measurement can effectively obtain underwater and surface magnetic field and change information, and its prominent role in military affairs is first reflected in the detection of magnetic objects in the ocean (submarines, mines, sunken ships, etc.). If the Earth's magnetic field (i.e., background field) has already been measured in advance, the magnetic field generated by magnetic ships and other objects will be superimposed on the Earth's magnetic field, causing distortion of the Earth's magnetic field, resulting in local magnetic anomalies. Once a magnetometer detects this local magnetic anomaly, it can provide a very practical means for detecting and identifying magnetic objects. It can also be combined with airborne magnetic field measurement to detect submarine targets under complex background field conditions. The world's advanced airborne magnetic detection system can accurately locate submarines at a distance of 300-800 meters above them.

4.2. Application in Submarine Demagnetization Stealth

Submarine exploration and anti-submarine exploration are two opposing aspects of marine magnetic field information in military applications on the sea battlefield. In order to address the threat of magnetic anomaly detection, military powers around the world have invested a large number of financial resources in researching submarine magnetic stealth technology to enhance its survival ability.

Due to the current practice of comparing local magnetic fields with geomagnetic fields and detecting local magnetic anomalies to identify the position of submarines, geomagnetic background field information is an extremely important fundamental data for achieving magnetic protection of submarines. In the past, demagnetization stations or demagnetization fields were used for demagnetization, but due to the large magnetic field of submarines themselves, it is difficult to obtain information close to the Earth's background field. In addition, the magnetic changes in different sea areas are unknown, so it is difficult to ensure the demagnetization effect by eliminating fixed magnetic fields. Modern demagnetization technology often uses magnetic cancellation technology, which obtains real-time magnetic field information in the current sea area through marine magnetic measurement technology. After geomagnetic calculation, demagnetization equipment is used to cancel the magnetism of the submarine itself, making magnetic weapons and magnetic detection lose (or difficult to capture) signal sources, thereby achieving the goal of improving the submarine's magnetic protection ability.

For traditional demagnetization methods, the demagnetization field must be selected in the sea area where the Earth's background magnetic field changes gently and the absolute value of the Earth's total magnetic field strength is relatively small, otherwise it will be difficult to ensure the demagnetization effect and cannot play a stealth role. For the solution-based demagnetization method, it is more necessary to support global background magnetic field data, especially the magnetic field information of submarine activity areas. The combat vessels of various navies, including submarines, undergo degaussing at least once a year, and must undergo degaussing before each major training mission. The efficiency of demagnetization depends on the specific demagnetization method used, but more importantly, it depends on whether to master high-precision ocean magnetic field information.

4.3. The Application of Marine Magnetic Field Measurement in Ship Navigation and Weapon Guidance

Geomagnetic navigation is one of the fields of marine military applications. The development of marine magnetic measurement technology has achieved the combination of geomagnetic navigation with GNSS, inertial systems, etc., providing more advanced and scientific choices for navigation and guidance. It has the advantages of passive, non-radiative, all day, all weather, all earth, small size, and low energy consumption.

Heading is an important parameter for navigation, and geomagnetic orientation is an accurate, reliable, and efficient orientation technology with important application value. Magnetic heading measurement instruments, also known as magnetic compasses, are devices that use the Earth's magnetic field to measure direction. Electronic magnetic compass is a compass composed of magnetic sensors, electronic circuits, and microprocessors that can output electrical signals. It has been widely used in the automation systems of aircraft, tanks, ships, or other means of transportation. However, it should be noted that due to the fact that the Earth's rotation axis does not coincide with the geomagnetic axis, there is an angle called geomagnetic declination between the geomagnetic heading and geographic direction. Therefore, the magnetic heading or azimuth measured by geomagnetic sensors must be corrected for magnetic declination before obtaining the geographic heading or azimuth of the navigation carrier. The geomagnetic declination is an important parameter of the Earth's magnetic field and a traditional spatial geographic element loaded on military maps and nautical charts. Accurate calculation of geomagnetic declination must be based on high-precision geomagnetic field observation data. Submarines need to continuously control and correct their heading during prolonged underwater navigation. Geomagnetic declination navigation technology has many advantages such as simplicity, reliability, anti-interference, and affordability, making it an essential auxiliary means for submarine navigation. As an important basis for submarine underwater navigation, the accuracy of ocean geomagnetic declination maps directly affects the survival ability of submarines. Traveling mine navigation systems also typically use magnetic declination navigation technology, which is also inseparable from the support of magnetic declination data in mined areas.

In recent years, with the rapid development of missiles, satellites, aerospace, and aviation technologies, the requirements for navigation systems have become increasingly high. At present, geomagnetic navigation systems have been successfully applied in many fields such as near-Earth satellite attitude control, motion carrier heading and position calculation, and have shown a development trend of optimizing integrated navigation together with GPS satellite navigation and gyro inertial navigation, becoming an important technological force driving modern new military transformation.

5. Prospects for the Development of Marine Magnetic Field Measurement

With the continuous development and maturity of magnetic field measurement sensor technology, marine magnetic field measurement is moving towards high-precision, high-efficiency, miniaturization, and interdisciplinary applications. At the same time, in order to cope with the new round of world military transformation, our military's modernization construction and development are facing unprecedented severe challenges and rare development opportunities. We must re understand the surveying and mapping support role of battlefield environment construction with a new perspective, carefully plan the surveying and mapping support overall situation of marine battlefield environment construction with a new thinking, and seriously explore the military application value of marine magnetic field information with higher standards.

5.1. Measurement Sensors Tend to be High-precision and Miniaturized

Marine magnetic measurement has evolved from early products such as magnetic saturation fluxgate magnetometers and nuclear precession proton magnetometers to more miniaturized, high-precision, and widely used products such as optical pump magnetometers, superconducting quantum interference magnetometers, and atomic magnetometers. With the advancement of computer technology, data processing methods have also undergone a transformation from analog signals to digital signals. Miniaturization, portability, digitization, and high accuracy are the future development directions of ocean magnetometers. Therefore, in order to meet the application needs of various aspects, strong support should be given to the research and development of high-precision miniaturized magnetometers.

5.2. Marine Magnetic Field Information Measurement Carriers are Becoming More Diverse

With the development of unmanned aerial vehicle technology, unmanned underwater vehicle technology, and satellite technology, marine magnetic measurement carriers have shown diverse characteristics, including shipborne, manned, unmanned aerial vehicles, satellites, and underwater vehicles. We need to coordinate various means of obtaining marine magnetic field information such as ocean surveys and monitoring, establish a comprehensive data collection system consisting of space-based, space-based, shore-based, sea-based, submarine based, and seabed-based data collection methods, and form a marine magnetic field information acquisition system with reasonable distribution density and complete monitoring elements.

5.3. Exploring the Military Application Value of Marine Magnetic Gravity Information with High Standards

At present, China's military application research in the field of marine magnetic and gravity field information is still in its infancy, and there is still a significant gap from the advanced level of countries such as the United States, Japan, and Russia. It is recommended to focus on the following areas of work in the near future.

- Precise detection of heavy and magnetic fields in important sea areas
- Technical transformation of marine shipborne magnetic measurement mode

- Research on magnetic potential exploration technology
- Research on ocean magnetic and gravity field assisted navigation technology
- Research on compensation technology for marine magnetic and gravity fields

References

[1]	Wang D, Cheng C. The analysis of marine magnetic field detection influenced by the platform migration[J]. Applied Mechanics and Materials, 2013, (2560): 347-350.
[2]	Huang Motao, Zhai Guojun, Ouyang Yongzhong, et al. Current status and prospects of military application research on marine magnetic and gravity field information[J]. Ocean Surveying and Mapping, 2011, 31(01): 71-76 (in Chinese).
[3]	Li Hongping, Zhang Haibin. Simulation and calculation of marine background magnetic field and surface magnetic field distribution in the East China Sea[J]. Ocean Technology, 2008, (03): 70-74 (in Chinese).
[4]	Aaron Hornschild, Julien Baerenzung, Jan Saynisch-Wagner, et al. On the detectability of the magnetic fields induced by ocean circulation in geomagnetic satellite observations[J]. Earth, Planets and Space, 2022, 74(1): 1-19.
[5]	Su, Wei. Magnetic anomaly data detection of local marine geomagnetic field model considering robust trend surface scientific calculation algorithm. [J]. Scientific Programming, 2022, 2022: 1-10.
[6]	Valet Jean-Pierre Bassinot, Franck Simon, Quentin Savranskaia, et al. Constraining the age of the last geomagnetic reversal from geochemical and magnetic analyses of Atlantic, Indian, and Pacific Ocean sediments. [J]. Earth & Planetary Science Letters, 2019, 506: 323-331.
[7]	J.S. Gee, D.V. Kent. 5.12 – Source of oceanic magnetic anomalies and the geomagnetic polarity timescale[J]. Treatise on Geophysics (Second Edition), 2007, .5: 419-460.
[8]	Wang D, Chi C. The analysis of marine magnetic field detection influenced by the platform migration[P]. isccca-13, 2013.
[9]	Modern Day. Marine military exposition 2009 modern day marine exposition to spotlight marine aviation[J]. Defense & Aerospace Business, 2008, 2008(1): 6.
[10]	Y. Niiro, H. Yamamoto. The international long-haul optical-fiber submarine cable system in Japan[J]. Communications Magazine, IEEE, 1986, 24(5): 24-32.
[11]	Ankita Modi, Faruk Kazi. Magnetic-Signature Prediction for Efficient Degaussing of Naval Vessels[J]. IEEE Transactions on Magnetics, 2020, 6(9): 1-6.
[12]	Sun Hao, Li Zhiwei, Xiong Xiong. Application and development status of marine magnetic measurement technology [J]. Ocean Painting, 2019, 39 (06): 5-8+20 (in Chinese).
[13]	Kwangkook Lee, Mijin Jeong, Dong Hun Kim. Software-in-the-loop based modeling and simulation of unmanned semi-submersible vehicle for performance verification of autonomous navigation[J]. IOP Conference Series: Materials Science and Engineering, 2017, 280(1): 012-042.

Artificial Intelligence, Medical Engineering and Education 455
Z.B. Hu et al. (Eds.)
© 2024 The Authors.
doi:10.3233/ATDE231357

Multiprocessing as a Way to Optimize Queries

Nataliia KHRYSTYNETS [1], Kateryna MELNYK, Svitlana LAVRENCHUK,
Oksana MISKEVYCH, Serhii KOSTIUCHKO
Lutsk National Technical University, Lutsk 43017, Ukraine
ORCiD ID: Nataliia KHRYSTYNETS https://orcid.org/0000-0002-4836-7632
Kateryna MELNYK https://orcid.org/0000-0002-9991-582X
Svitlana LAVRENCHUK https://orcid.org/0000-0002-5453-3924
Oksana MISKEVYCH https://orcid.org/0000-0002-5009-2391
Serhii KOSTIUCHKO https://orcid.org/0000-0002-1262-6268

Abstract. Developing an effective web application involves the use of various methods and techniques to ensure fast and efficient processing of requests. Sometimes it is not possible to solve the problem of multiprocessing with a single tool, such as a programming language or framework. This work investigates the use of asynchronous methods of processing requests using queues. Job operation in background and non-background modes relative to the main web process is studied. Analytics are provided to analyze a web application with 13,000 requests to process daily. It is proposed to optimize the processing by using the Laravel framework and the Python server dual-tasking using the Supervisor tool on Linux, as well as using a task scheduler for each task. The paper presents positive findings about this algorithm, which contributes to the efficiency of web development and provides a great user experience on the website. Fast processing of web application requests can be a valuable competitive advantage for a business or organization. Research in this field helps to maintain their high competitiveness. In addition, the study of query processing speed is important in scientific research, as it contributes to the development of new algorithms, optimization methods and technologies.

Keywords. Multiprocessing; web-application; query; requests; data processing; server; Laravel

1. Introduction

Web development projects typically involve integration with a large number of external services, platforms, and systems in today's digital world. The operation of web applications in practice is often accompanied by data parsing to obtain, analyze, and process information [1-3]. Commercial websites, news portals, social media platforms, blogs, forums, transportation websites, and more – are just a few examples of areas where the processing of a large number of requests needs to be taken into account.

There are general approaches to implement this task, such as web scraping and using HTTP clients [4]. However, these mechanisms are often not universal. The most famous method, in our opinion, is the ARI public method for executing queries, but excessive requests can lead to IP address blocking or other limitations. Development of

---

[1] Corresponding Author: Nataliia KHRYSTYNETS, E-mail: hrystynets.at.ua@gmail.com.

web applications [5-8], such as online stores, may require handling a large number of server requests.

This can pose challenges to the performance and scalability of the developed application [9-11]. It is important to utilize effective techniques and tools to optimize server interactions and ensure speed and productivity during development in such situations.

One of the main goals of the research is to improve the quality of user service. A quick response to requests will increase the satisfaction of customers and users of the web resource. Reducing the processing time of requests and the response of the server can help improve the productivity of the workflow and the business in general.

2. Literature Review

rom a review of literary sources, many ways of improving the operation of web systems are known. In work [12], the authors investigated that "to increase the efficiency of a web server by using a load balancing system to manage a large number of requests," six servers and three load balancing algorithms were proposed. The authors achieved a high response speed and stability of the response time, but the implementation of this method requires expensive equipment - additional servers. In [13], a study was proposed to automate the customer support for inquiries of a business company that currently handles customer support requests manually. Research was conducted using traditional machine learning approaches. These studies are important, they use parameters for each learning algorithm and data set in terms of the query sampling distribution. However, in our opinion, only framework tools can be used for effective traffic of small companies. Asynchronous query optimization methods are explored in [14], but it is not clear whether people can "use asynchrony when updating data, because the user interface is dynamically updated and changes can be difficult to interpret."

From the review of the literature, it can be concluded that the proposed research of the authors is valid, especially in terms of the use of asynchronous methods. In our opinion, it is possible to achieve a reduction in request processing time using multiprocessing tools of the Laravel framework. It fully meets the intended purpose.

3. Research Methodology

Parsing research methods can be divided into three categories [15]. In the first, programming languages are used to facilitate the construction of data analysis systems. The second group uses artificial intelligence methods. It should be noted here that machine learning methods are quite time-consuming. The methods of the third category consist in the application of automated systems to detect patterns of query behavior, which include data segmentation and field extraction.

The methods of the first group were used in the research work.

Often, when creating high-capacity web applications, you need to make a large number of requests to a third-party website for monitoring. To do this, you can use different methods of integration with the website, depending on the available tools. For parsing a large number of products, it is recommended to use asynchronous processing of background tasks in Laravel. This will allow efficient processing of a large amount of data without blocking the main flow of web requests.

Technologies and tools for creating web applications were used to achieve the goal. Initially, Laravel tools were used to support multiprocessing and configuration file settings, and PHP language was used to design database library elements. Further editing of the web application scripts was performed using the Python language. The selected tools are free software, so they are universal and accessible to developers from all over the world. The Supervisor toolkit on Linux was used to process and monitor background processes. Classical framework methods and Google Analytics were used for data collection and analysis.

According to this methodology, it is possible to carry out a complex implementation of parsing of web resources and thus get rid of the problem of lengthy processing of requests. First paragraph.

4. Multiprocessing and methods of implementation in web development

Asynchronicity is one way to optimize the handling of multiple database queries in web development. The use of the Queues in the Laravel framework allows efficient management of executing heavy or long operations in the background. This improves the performance of the web application and enhances the user experience. Queues in Laravel operate based on the «producer-consumer» concept. This allows adding job to the queue and then asynchronously executing them using workers. Workers check the queue for pending tasks and perform them in the background. The tasks are implemented following the scheme (Fig. 1).

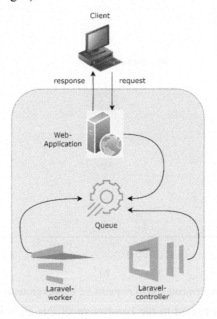

Figure 1. Using the Queues in the Laravel framework

This scheme will be used to solve the problem of multi-threaded processing of requests. For this, the Laravel framework supports asynchronous multiprocessing through the use of functional built-in mechanisms. However, the PHP development language itself is not multi-threaded. Therefore, to manage the queue of tasks in the database, we will use the Jobs table, which stores information about tasks awaiting execution [16]. For the efficiency of their use and communication, we will use the mechanisms connects. It should be noted here that the Jobs implementation mechanism is possible in the Background Jobs and Non-Background/Synchronous Jobs mode [17]. The difference between them is schematically presented in Fig. 2. In the background mode (Fig. 2a) tasks are performed asynchronously and run separately from the main web process, with the support of various drivers. In non-background mode (Fig. 2b), tasks are performed synchronously, which means that they are performed directly in the context of a web request.

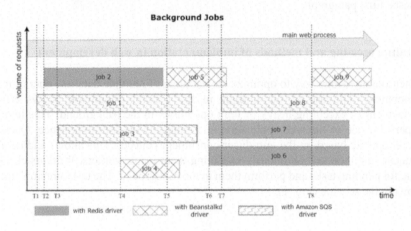

a)

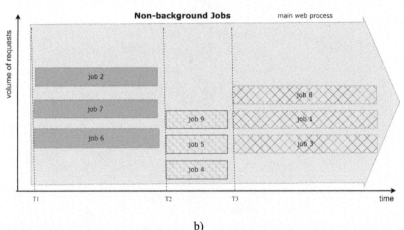

b)

Figure 2. Temporary implementation of requests in: a) background and b) synchronous mode

All data that was passed to the constructor of this class is in JSON format [18]. Fields that allow you to store and track information about tasks waiting to be executed in the database queue are important for performing further tasks of multiprocessor processing. Among them are the «payload» table field, which contains serialized data, and the «queue» field – a queue field that distinguishes each job. The default value of the «queue» field for a task in the queue is specified in the application settings in Laravel.

When «queue» is set to «sync», tasks in the queue are executed synchronously. If the process is asynchronous, we can configure these queues.

Parsing of a well-known online store with tens of thousands of products was provided, and these products were periodically updated and changed. Background tasks were running to update the goods, the update process was started every night at 02:00. Initially, the application processed only one job for each time period, and in this mode, updating 13,000 products (since such many of requests were planned for daily processing) took too long. Analytical data of request processing was analyzed, average indicators were calculated according to tabular data and, as a result of calculations, the graphic representation of traffic has the following form:

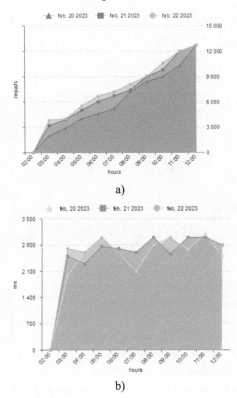

a)

b)

Figure 3. Analysis of request processing in the period from February 20 to February 23, 2023:
a) processing time; b) average request time

As can be seen from Fig. 3 a), about 13,000 requests were processed in three days, and the time of complete processing was about 10 hours. The duration of the request (Fig. 3b) is from 2 to 3 seconds. Such a process is quite slow and needs improvement for the efficiency of the developed application.

The problem of such lengthy processing was identified. Note that the problem of such a plan often occurs when organizing multiprocessing. A site with a large number of products is a powerful application. It was possible to use traffic sniffers to monitor network traffic that passes through the web application interface. Then it would be possible to access the data packets sent over the network and analyze their content and make decisions about optimizing their work [19]. Different frameworks allow you to solve this problem with your own methods. Solving the issue is possible through the use of a Python library as an implementation of the Laravel framework for developing web applications that interact with scripts written in the Python programming language. Python is not the fastest programming language, and PHP, as a language specialized in web development, has some advantages in the speed of executing web queries and interacting with databases. Therefore, for an ideal solution, it was worth rewriting the site library with a huge number of products in PHP. Or, in the case of not fully using the functionality, such as only updating prices, availability of goods and some categories, solve the issue by contacting the IP of your own development using the Job class (Fig. 4)

```
namespace App\Jobs;

use App\Models\Product;
use Illuminate\Bus\Queueable;
use Illuminate\Contracts\Queue\ShouldQueue;
use Illuminate\Foundation\Bus\Dispatchable;
use Illuminate\Queue\InteractsWithQueue;
use Illuminate\Queue\SerializesModels;

class UpdateProductAvailabilityJob implements ShouldQueue
{
    use Dispatchable, InteractsWithQueue, Queueable, SerializesModels;

    public $tries = 1;
    public $timeout = 3600;

    private const LIMIT = 1000;


    public function handle()
    {
        $offset = 0;

        $productIds = $this->getProductIds($offset);

        while(count($productIds)) {
            foreach ($productIds as $productId) {
                ProductAvailabilityJob::dispatch($productId)->onQueue('update-one-product');
            }

            $offset += self::LIMIT;

            $productIds = $this->getProductIds($offset);
        }
    }

    private function getProductIds($offset): array
    {
        return Product::where('sync_at', '<', date('Y-m-d'))
            ->whereNotNull('sync_at')
            ->offset($offset)
            ->limit(self::LIMIT)
            ->pluck('id')
            ->toArray();
    }
}
```

Figure 4. A code snippet of a program to make a request to your own IP address using the Job class

Let's move on to solving the issue of multiprocessing and optimization of the web application developed on Laravel [20, 21]. With the help of this framework, it is possible to make settings so that in the Config directory, where the configuration file is located, a separate configuration file database_connect.php was specified, where the settings for a new connection will be specified in this file, so that the job is executed on a specific connection.

The work uses the popular Supervisor tool for managing background processes on a server running the Linux OS. It allows us to monitor the state of processes, monitor their execution, automatically restart them in case of a crash. The Supervisor is a powerful tool for ensuring the stability and continuity of background processes on the server, in particular for managing the background tasks of web applications that use Laravel or other frameworks.

The Supervisor's role in resolving the issue is as follows: When the Supervisor starts a queue process, it caches the code and settings used to process the queue. When we change the code or setting for a particular queue, we must restart the corresponding queue process in Supervisor for the changes to take effect. This is because the Supervisor is responsible for managing background processes, including queue handling. If we do not restart the queues, then processing will be performed with old data, and this will be incorrect relative to the expected results. Note that restart is a supervisor setting.

Going back to multiprocessing, the following was done to speed up query processing. When processing the queue, the simultaneous execution of five jobs is planned. This means that in the Non-Background mode (which is schematically presented earlier in Fig. 2b), the parallel execution of several jobs works simultaneously, which helps to reduce the execution time of the entire queue.

As a result of such planning, the update time was reduced from 10 to 4 hours, which is a significant positive indicator. Now, when the process was started at 2 in the morning, it was completed by 6 in the morning (Fig. 5a).

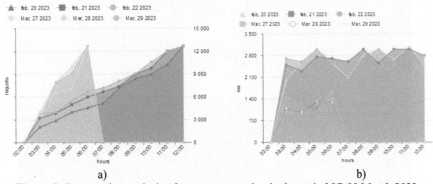

a)   b)

Figure 5. Comparative analysis of request processing in the period 27-29 March 2023:
a) processing time; b) average request time

Reducing the update time has its advantages, especially for an online store where the timeliness of information is important. At the same time, the average request time was significantly reduced (Fig. 5b): from 1900-3000 ms to 800-1450 ms. To execute the update command in the online store, the following software structure was used in the Laravel console (Fig. 6):

```php
class ProductAvailabilityJob implements ShouldQueue  1 usage
{
    use Dispatchable, InteractsWithQueue, Queueable, SerializesModels;

    public $tries = 1;  no usages
    public $timeout = 60 * 15;
    public int $productId;
    public Product $product;

    public function __construct(int $productId)  no usages
    {
        $this->productId = $productId;
    }

    public function handle()
    {
        $this->product = Product::find($this->productId);

        $code = trim($this->product->code);

        if (Str::is('*-*', $this->product->code)) {
            $code = substr($code, offset: 0, strpos($code, needle: "-"));
        }

        if (strlen($code) < 5) {
            return;
        }

        $availability = app(ProductAvailability::class)->getAvailability($code);

        if (is_null($availability)) {
            $this->product->update([
                'quantity' => 0,
                'sync_at' => date( format: 'Y-m-d H:i:s')
            ]);
            return;
        }

        $this->product->update([
            'price' => $availability['price'],
            'quantity' => $availability['quantity'],
            'sync_at' => date( format: 'Y-m-d H:i:s')
        ]);
    }
}
```

Figure 6. Job code that is dispatched to the queue

Laravel can execute its commands in the console using a built-in engine (Artisan). This command is implemented programmatically as follows. Laravel's built-in task scheduler mechanism in the developed project automatically starts it for execution every day at a fixed time, at 02:00. The planned and implemented mechanism is flexible, and the logic of the command can be adjusted according to the requirements and the type of job to be called. Therefore, planning organized in this way allows you to optimize the operation of the application according to your own needs.

5. Conclusion

This article solves the problem of long data processing in the process of parsing a web application. The initial data of processing 40 thousand requests with a request duration of 2 to 3 seconds showed an unsatisfactory result of contacting the server - the request processing time lasted for 10 hours. This indicated a rather slow process that needed improvement. As a result of the study, multiprocessing was applied to the original data set using the proposed methodology using the specified tools.

Six experiments were conducted during February-March 2023. They were defined as follows: the original data set in the form of requests to the server was launched at a fixed time of 02:00. For these experiments, the data was pre-processed by the Supervisor using the data caching method. As a result of the programmed elements of the system, five jobs simultaneously participated in the processing of requests. This significantly reduced the processing time of requests from 10 to 4 hours.

The reliability and accuracy of the results are ensured by the analytical data of the framework and the Google Analytics audit. That is, the proposed method is actually confirmed by a series of six experiments, which allows you to see the stability and effectiveness of multiprocessing as a result of web application server parsing.

The results of the study are a significant acceleration of the processing of requests. Improvements in long-running query processing can have practical applications in real-world scenarios, such as computing systems, databases, Internet searches, and medical research. The practical significance of the conducted experiments, the popularization of research and the publication of its results will contribute to the improvement of the field and increase the level of knowledge, encouraging other scientists to further research and development.

References

[1] Ashish K. Sharma, Sunanda Khandait, "A Novel Software Tool to Generate Customer Needs for Effective Design of Online Shopping Websites", International Journal of Information Technology and Computer Science, Vol.8, No.3, pp.85-92, 2016.

[2] Atia Bano Memon, Kyrill Meyer, "Why We Need Dedicated Web-based Collaboration Platforms for Inter-organizational Connectivity? A Research Synthesis", International Journal of Information Technology and Computer Science, Vol.9, No.11, pp.1-11, 2017.

[3] Amini, Mahyar, et al. Mahamgostar.com as a case study for adoption of laravel framework as the best programming tools for php based web development for small and medium enterprises. Journal of Innovation & Knowledge, ISSN (2021): 100-110.

[4] Laaziri, M., Benmoussa, K., Khoulji, S., & Kerkeb, ML (2019). A comparative study of PHP frameworks performance. Procedia Manufacturing, 32, 864-871.

[5] Sunardi, Andri, et al. MVC architecture: a comparative study between Laravel framework and Slim framework in freelancer project monitoring system web based. Procedia Computer Science, 2019, 157: 134-141.

[6] Yamao, Yasuo, et al. Protocol to acquire time series data on adverse reactions following vaccination using a smartphone or web-based platform. STAR protocols, 2023, 4.2: 102284.

[7] Mourato, Sandra, et al. An interactive Web-GIS fluvial flood forecast and alert system in operation in Portugal. International Journal of Disaster Risk Reduction, 2021, 58: 102201.

[8] Permana, Putu Adi Guna; Triandini, Evi. Performance with Eloquent and Query Builder in Crowdfunding System with Laravel Framework. 2021.

[9] Rojas, Hesmeralda; ARIAS, Kevin A.; Renteria, Ronald. Service-oriented architecture design for small and medium enterprises with infrastructure and cost optimization. Procedia Computer Science, 2021, 179: 488-497.

[10] Bottani, Eleonora, et al. Wearable and interactive mixed reality solutions for fault diagnosis and assistance in manufacturing systems: Implementation and testing in an aseptic bottling line. Computers in Industry, 2021, 128: 103429.

[11] Pulmano, Christian E., et al. MIND Plug-in: Development of an Electronic Medical Record based data collection tool for research in autism and neurodevelopmental disorders. Procedia Computer Science, 2019, 164: 646-653.

[12] Antunes, Mário; Maximiano, Marisa; GOMEZ, Ricardo. A Customizable Web Platform to Manage Standards Compliance of Information Security and Cybersecurity Auditing. Procedia Computer Science, 2022, 196: 36-43.

[13] Fawzy, Ahmed Hany; Wassif, Khaled; MOUSSA, Hanan. Framework for automatic detection of anomalies in DevOps. Journal of King Saud University-Computer and Information Sciences, 2023, 35.3: 8-19.

[14] Chyrvon, Andrii & Lisovskyi, Kostiantyn & Kyryndas, Nikita. (2023). The Main Methods of load Balancing on the Nginx Web Server. 10.36074/logos-26.05.2023.040.

[15] Arias-Barahona, María & Arteaga Arteaga, Harold & Orozco Arias, Simon & Flórez-Ruíz, Juan & Valencia-Díaz, Mario & Tabares Soto, Reinel. (2023). Requests classification in the customer service area for software companies using machine learning and natural language processing. PeerJ Computer Science. 9. e1016. 10.7717/peerj-cs.1016.

[16] Divya Rishi Sahu, Deepak Singh Tomar, "DNS Pharming through PHP Injection: Attack Scenario and Investigation", International Journal of Computer Network and Information Security, vol.7, no.4, pp.21-28, 2015.

[17] Anosh Fatima, Nosheen Nazir, Muhammad Gufran Khan, "Data Cleaning In Data Warehouse: A Survey of Data Pre-processing Techniques and Tools", International Journal of Information Technology and Computer Science, Vol.9, No.3, pp.50-61, 2017.

[18] Parreira, Vinícius da Silva Coutinho, et al. ExVe: the knowledge base of orthologous proteins identified in fungal extracellular vesicles. Computational and Structural Biotechnology Journal, 2021, 19: 2286-2296.

[19] Sonmez, Rifat; Ahmadisheykhsarmast, Salar; Güngör, Aslı Akçamete. BIM integrated smart contract for construction project progress payment administration. Automation in Construction, 2022, 139: 104294.

[20] Fotakis, Emmanouil A., et al. VectorMap -GR: A local scale operational management tool for entomological monitoring, to support vector control activities in Greece and the Mediterranean Basin. Current Research in Parasitology & Vector-Borne Diseases, 2021, 1: 100053.

[21] LARBI Abdelmadjid, MALKI Mimoun, BOUKHALFA Kamel, "Fuzzy Ontology-based Approach for the Requirements Query Imprecision Assessment in Data Warehouse Design Process near Negative Fuzzy Operator", International Journal of Information Technology and Computer Science, Vol.10, No.2, pp.18-32, 2018.

Artificial Intelligence, Medical Engineering and Education 465
Z.B. Hu et al. (Eds.)
© *2024 The Authors.*
This article is published online with Open Access by IOS Press and distributed under the terms
of the Creative Commons Attribution Non-Commercial License 4.0 (CC BY-NC 4.0).
doi:10.3233/ATDE231358

Research of Digital Characteristics of the Step Cycle in Forensic Medicine

Elena FOMINA[a][1], Dmitry ZYBIN[b]

[a]*Tver State Technical University, Tver 170026, Russian Federation*
[b]*Federal State Institution Research Institute of Information Technologies of the*
Federal Penitentiary Service of Russia, Tver, 170100, Russian Federation
ORCID ID: Elena Fomina http://orcid.org/0000-0002-1028-0750
ORCIR ID: Dmitry Zybin https://orcid.org/0009-0007-8749-4101

Abstract: This article presents the results of a study devoted to the analysis of the characteristics of the human step cycle as an indicator that allows you to identify a person on video by the signs of gait. Video recordings of volunteers walking on an electric treadmill were used as the research material. A software package has been developed that allows calculating the parameters of the step cycle used for processing the material. The average values of such characteristics of the step cycle were obtained and analyzed, such as the duration of the transition period and double support as a percentage of the step cycle and seconds, the length of the step cycle in seconds, walking frequency, walking pace separately for men, women and for the entire sample as a whole. The change of the listed indicators depending on the walking speed is investigated, the change in the frequency of steps with increasing speed is analyzed. A method of identifying a person in a video based on the characteristics of a step cycle is proposed, which allows comparing the digital characteristics of steps and making a reasonable conclusion about their similarity or difference. A software package has been developed to determine the anthropometric parameters of an individual in a video based on the characteristics of the step cycle. The obtained results can be used in forensic medicine for conducting expertise on identification of a person by signs of gait.

Keywords: Characteristics of the step cycle, gait signs, identity identification, analysis of video materials.

1. Introduction

The modern level of development of information technologies and technical means contributes to improving the effectiveness of measures to investigate and solve crimes [1-3].

Video surveillance systems are one of the tools that help law enforcement agencies in investigating crimes [4-5]. They allow to record information that is later used in investigative measures [6-8].

In the case then a person's face is clearly fixed on the video, or any special signs are visible, the task of portrait identification of a person does not cause difficulties. Nevertheless, expertise in which a person's face is not visible on the video (since it is hidden by a mask, or the shooting was made at an unsuccessful angle) are relevant [9-10].

---

[1] Corresponding Author: Elena Fomina, f-elena2008@yandex.ru.

When working with such video material, the only sign that characterizes the individual in the video is the gait. Gait has a large complex of dynamic characteristics. However, there is a problem in choosing such a set of significant signs that are clearly recorded regardless of the shooting angle.

Recently, interest in the problem of identifying a person in a video by signs of gait has especially grown. The proposed methods are based on the analysis of human movement characteristics but use different tools.

The first group of techniques is based on the use of neural networks. Their essence lies in recording the primary signs of gait and transmitting them to the input of a neural network, which, by processing the data, generates a signal about the identity or difference of individuals. The difference lies in the set of input information and network architecture. For example, in articles [11, 12], the input information was blocks of optical flow maps. In article [13], the neural network was trained based on data from binary silhouette masks. In research [14], the source of primary information is a three-channel image, including black and white frames and components of optical flow maps.

The second group of methods uses the analysis of basic gait signs, for example, such as gait energy [15-17], the position of joints and main parts of the body [18, 19], and the trajectory of movement of figure points during walking [20].

Each method has its own implementation signs. Methods based on the use of neural networks are characterized by high computational costs, and for methods based on the analysis of basic signs, difficulties are associated with the analysis of video material from an unsuccessful angle.

Thus, due to the large number of conditions affecting the manner of human movement and its presentation in video, the problem of identification by gait still does not have a sufficiently accurate solution.

In forensic medicine, the urgent task is to study the signs of gait and developing methods that allow for a comparative analysis of the gait signs of several individuals presented in different videos and to draw a conclusion about their similarities or differences, as well as to form informed expert opinions that can be presented as an evidence base.

In this work, we study such a dynamic gait sign as the step cycle.

The purpose of this research is to study the digital characteristics of the step cycle as one of the parameters that allow identification of a person by the signs of gait.

2.　Collection and Processing of Materials for the Organization of Research

2.1.　Research Materials

The step cycle is the time from the beginning of contact with the support of a fixed leg to the next contact with the support of the same leg. The step cycle includes two periods that are repeated twice - the period of double support, when both legs are in contact with the support, and the transfer period (or the period of single support) [21] (Figure 1).

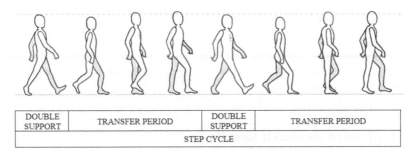

DOUBLE SUPPORT	TRANSFER PERIOD	DOUBLE SUPPORT	TRANSFER PERIOD
STEP CYCLE			

Figure 1. Step cycle.

To analyze the characteristics of the step cycle, video recordings of walking were analyzed. On the video recordings the volunteers walked on an electric treadmill with a speed of 3 to 7 km/h.

The shooting time was 20-30 seconds for each speed mode. During this period, the volunteer took 7-10 steps of natural walking without bending his torso and touching his hands with the handrails or the scoreboard of the track, stabilizing his movement. A prerequisite for fixation was a complete hit in the shot of the track platform and the legs of the subject, as well as a clear visualization of the contact with the platform of both feet.

Each video was supplemented with accompanying information, including the gender, age, height and body weight of the individual. The frame rate was recorded for each recording. The resulting videos corresponding to different speed modes were decomposed into a video sequence. A cyclogram corresponding to four consecutive steps was extracted from each video sequence to identify the characteristics of an individual's walking with support on the left and right legs. Cyclograms were loaded into the «Software package for calculating the characteristics of the step cycle» [22], designed to calculate the parameters of the step cycle.

2.2. Research Method

A software package was developed to calculate the characteristics of the step cycle. The software package includes the following modules:

1. Module for entering source information into a database (examination number, date, gender, height, body weight, age, number of frames per second, distinctive signs).

2. Module for calculating the characteristics of the step cycle. When working with the module, the expert loads frames on which the full cycle of the step is recorded. Next, the frame numbers corresponding to the beginning and end of each period are recorded. Fixation begins either with a period of double support, or with a period of transfer. When fixing, a record is made of which leg (left or right) the cycle in question begins. In automatic mode, the calculation of such indicators of the step cycle as:

- the length of the first and second periods of the double support in seconds and percentages of the step cycle;
- the length of the first and second transfer periods in seconds and percentages of the step cycle;
- step cycle length in seconds;
- walking frequency;
- walking pace.

As a result of the processing of video recordings, a «Database of human step cycle characteristics» was formed [23], containing information about the digital characteristics of the steps 129 individuals aged 16 to 60 years.

The processing of four steps was carried out in order to identify the individual characteristics of the subject's walking with support on the left and right legs, as well as in order to obtain stable results.

3.   Analysis of Research Results

3.1.   *Checking the Reproducibility of the Results*

At the first stage of the analysis of the results, their reproducibility was checked. The same videos were processed by different experts, then measurements were compared. The discrepancy in the data obtained by different experts was no more than 1%, which indicates good reproducibility and the possibility of using the digitization algorithm and the software package both to study the numerical characteristics of the step cycle and to solve the identification problem.

For further data analysis, the step cycle indicators for four steps were averaged at each speed mode for each individual.

The study of the results was carried out in the following areas:

- study of the digital characteristics of the step cycle as a parameter that allows for identification of an individual.

- analysis of the general regularities of the characteristics of the step cycle.

3.2.   *Descriptive statistics*

The second stage of the study is the calculation of descriptive statistics for each speed mode. This article presents the results for a speed limit of 5 km/h, which corresponds to the natural pace of walking. The length of each double support period averages about 14.3% of the step cycle, and the length of each transfer period averages 35.5%. The total time of double support per step cycle is on average 29%, and the transfer time is 71% of the step cycle, which corresponds to 0.29 seconds and 0.73 seconds, respectively.

According to the data obtained, the average duration of the step cycle when walking at a speed of 5 km / h is 1.03 seconds, the average walking frequency is 116.4 steps per minute.

The above indicators were separately analyzed for men and women. The result is presented in Table 1.

Table 1. Characteristics of the step cycle at a walking speed of 5 km/h for men and women

Characteristic	Men	Women
Average duration of the double support period:		
in % of the step cycle	15,00	14,00
in seconds	0,16	0,14
Average duration of the transfer period:		
in % of the step cycle	34,80	35,9
in seconds	0,37	0,38
Average duration of the step cycle, in seconds	1,06	1,04
Average walking frequency, steps per minute	111,08	118,36

Men are characterized by longer periods of double support and shorter periods of transfer than women. Also, the average duration of the step cycle in men is longer than in women, and women are characterized by a high frequency of walking.

For a more detailed analysis, the Student's t-test was calculated in the difference between the average values for men and women and it was found that the differences in the average values are statistically significant for all indicators of the step cycle at each speed mode. Table 2 shows the indicators for the speed of 5 km/h.

Table 2. P-values for the Student's t-test

Indicator	t-value	p-value
The first period of double support (sec)	-4,48	0,000016
First transfer period (sec)	-2,37	0,021419
Second period of double support (sec)	-5,05	0,000001
Second transfer period (sec)	-2,17	0,031419
First period of double support (%)	-2,75	0,006819
First transfer period (%)	4,19	0,000051
Second period of double support (%)	-3,67	0,000348
Second transfer period (%)	2,40	0,017588
Average duration of the step cycle, in seconds	-4,47	0,000017
Average walking frequency, steps per minute	4,32	0,000031

Using data from the numerical characteristics of the step cycle and the anthropometric parameters of individuals, a software package was developed to determine the height, weight and gender of a person captured on video footage [24].

The software package is based on the Random Foresrt algorithm, which is a machine learning method that involves using an ensemble of trees to solve regression, classification and clustering problems. The Random Forest algorithm allows us to mitigate the problem of overfitting, generate a fairly stable solution, and increase classification accuracy. Another important advantage of the algorithm is the ability to evaluate the measure of information content of each variable.

The algorithm made it possible to determine the most informative signs, i.e. signs that are most important for prediction: values of the periods of transfer and support as a percentage of the step cycle.

Below is an example of how classification algorithms work for a specific expert case. As a result of the analysis of the characteristics of the step cycle, the expert recorded the following average values of indicators (Table 3).

Table 3. Input data

№	Sign	Value in % of the step cycle	Value in seconds
1.	Duration of the first period of double support	16,89	0,22
2.	Duration of the second period of double support	17,63	0,23
3.	Duration of the first transfer period	32,64	0,43
4.	Duration of the second transfer period	32,83	0,43
5.	The duration of the step cycle in seconds	1,3	
6.	Number of steps per minute	90,10	

The presented information was uploaded as input data to the software package [24]. As a result of data processing, the following results were obtained (Table 4).

Table 4. Input data

Parameter	Height	Weight	Gender
Predicted value (Random Forest)	164,7	62	2
Real value	162	58	2

The developed software package can be used to determine the anthropometric parameters of a person on a video recording during a forensic medical examination if there are no objects on the video whose dimensions are known.

3.3.   The study of Indicators in Dynamics

The study of the indicators of the step cycle in dynamics showed that with an increase in walking speed, there is a decrease in the duration of the periods of support and transfer in seconds. For the same indicators, as a percentage, there is a decrease in the period of double support as a percentage of the step cycle and an increase in the duration of the transfer period as a percentage of the step cycle.

The length of the step cycle also decreases with increasing speed, and the step frequency increases (Table 5, Figure 2-5).

Table 5. Average indicators of the step cycle in dynamics

Speed	Double support period		Transfer period		Step cycle	Step frequency
	sec	%	sec	%		
3 km/h	0,25	18,71	0,41	31,29	1,32	91,70
4 km/h	0,20	16,88	0,39	33,12	1,18	102,46
5 km/h	0,15	14,35	0,37	35,64	1,04	116,49
6 km/h	0,13	12,98	0,36	37,02	0,97	124,00
7 km/h	0,13	12,87	0,35	37,13	0,95	128,49

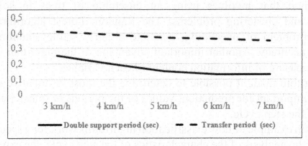

Figure 2. The lengths of periods in %.

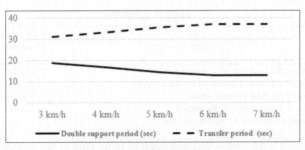

Figure 3. The lengths of periods in sec.

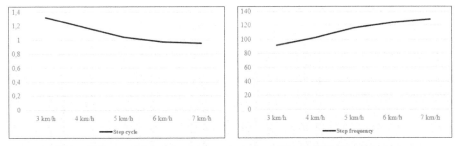

Figure 4. Step cycle length. **Figure 5.** Walking frequency.

Having data on the relationship between the characteristics of the step cycle and the walking speed, it is possible to compare, comparative research and further examination of the identification of individuals when they move at different speeds on video footage.

3.4. Study the Characteristics of Walking

Studying the signs of the step cycle allows us to conclude that individuals can be divided into groups:

- depending on the characteristics of the single support period:

1) individuals whose period of single support on the left leg is longer than the period of single support on the right leg;

2) individuals whose period of single support on the right leg is longer than the period of single support on the left leg;

3) individuals whose periods of single support on the left and right leg are the same (about 5% of cases in the sample);

- depending on the characteristics of the double support period:

1) individuals who have a longer period of double support before the transfer of the left leg;

2) individuals who have a longer period of double support before transferring the right leg;

3) individuals whose periods of double support are the same (about 9% of cases in the sample).

It is established that the "symmetry" of the periods is preserved with a change in velocity. This feature makes it possible to compare the durations of periods when moving at different speeds.

The obtained results allow us to propose an identification algorithm based on the characteristics of the step cycle, which may consist of the following stages:

identification of rare walking signs that are not characteristic of the bulk of individuals (lameness, special foot position when supporting, etc.);

decomposition of a video recording into a video sequence and selection of four consecutive steps from a cyclogram;

digitization of the step cycle;

comparative analysis of the periods of the step cycle, assessment of the «symmetry» of periods, classification of individuals depending on belonging to a particular group;

calculation of anthropometric parameters.

As a result, an expert opinion on the comparative analysis can be formed.

An example of an expert opinion comparing the digital characteristics of the steps of three individuals is presented in Table 6.

Table 6. Expert opinion

Video	First transfer period / Support on the left leg, transfer of the right leg	The first period of double support / The period of support before the transfer of the left leg	Second transfer period / Support on the right leg, transfer of the left leg	Second period of double support / The period of support before the transfer of the right leg	Average duration of the step cycle (sec)	Average walking frequency (steps per minute)
1	0,36 sec	0,14 sec	0,35 sec	0,12 sec	0,97	123
	37,01 %	14,37 %	36,01 %	12,60 %		
	0,36 sec> 0,35 sec		37,01 % > 36,01 %			
	0,14 sec> 0,12 sec		14,37 %> 12,60 %			
2	0,36 sec	0,16 sec	0,38 sec	0,15 sec	1,05	114
	34,50 %	15,25 %	36,40 %	13,87 %		
	0,36 sec < 0,38 sec		34,50 %< 36,40 %			
	0,16 sec > 0,15 sec		15,25 %> 13,87 %			

Prediction of height, weight, and gender based on the characteristics of the step cycle: video №1 - height 170 cm, weight 84 kg, and female gender; video №2 - height 165 cm, weight 80 kg, and female gender.

Conclusion: the individual shown in video No. 1 is characterized by a longer period of single support on the left leg unlike the individual in video No. 2; the individual in video No. 2 has a longer average duration of the step cycle and a lower average walking frequency. It can be concluded that the digital characteristics of the steps of individuals in video No. 1 and No. 2 are different.

4.   Conclusions

The article describes the results of a study devoted to the analysis of the characteristics of the step cycle, as one of the gait parameters, allowing comparison of individuals in video footage.

A collection of materials was made, representing video recordings of the volunteers walking on an electric treadmill. A «Software package for calculating the characteristics of the step cycle» has been developed, which made it possible to digitize information. As a result of the processing of video materials, a «Database of human step cycle characteristics» was formed, which is a material for statistical analysis.

The analysis of the periods of the step cycle is carried out and an algorithm for identifying an individual by his characteristics is proposed.

The analysis of the indicators of descriptive statistics of the characteristics of the step cycle was carried out, a statistically significant difference was found in the average values of the periods of support and transfer (in seconds and percentages of the step cycle) for men and women: men are characterized by longer periods of double support and shorter periods of transfer than for women, a longer average duration of the step cycle and a lower frequency walking.

The analysis of indicators in dynamics (i.e., with a change in walking speed) is carried out: with an increase in walking speed, the lengths of the first and second periods of double support in seconds, as well as the first and second periods of transfer in seconds, the length of the step cycle decrease, which simultaneously leads to an increase in the frequency of the step.

An algorithm has been proposed and a software package has been developed to determine the anthropometric parameters of a person in a video.

The developed software systems can be used for diagnostics during forensic and forensic examinations, as well as in investigative activities.

References

[1]   Smakhtin EV., Shcherbich SV. The use of video recording systems in the disclosure and investigation of crimes. Altai Legal Bulletin, 2017, 1(17): 137-141.

[2]   Zvyagin VN., Rakitin VA., Fomina EE. The application of the «Biometriclal dactylography 17.0» program complex for the digital interpretation of the finger dermatoglyphic signs. Sudebno-Meditsinskaya Ekspertiza, 2018, 61(2): 31-35, doi: 10.17116/sudmed201861231-35.

[3]   Nur Kumala Dewi, Arman Syah Putra. Application of Greedy Algorithm on Traffic Violation Enforcement. International Journal of Education and Management Engineering, 2021, 11(1): 1-10.

[4]   Kustov AM., Kokorev RA. Problems of using video recordings in the investigation of crimes against the person. Proceedings of the Academy of Management of the Ministry of Internal Affairs of Russia, 2018, 1 (45): 73-77.

[5]   Anupam Dey, Fahad Mohammad, Saleque Ahmed, Raiyan Sharif, A.F.M. Saifuddin Saif. Anomaly Detection in Crowded Scene by Pedestrians Behaviour Extraction using Long Short Term Method: A Comprehensive Study. International Journal of Education and Management Engineering, 2019, 9(1): 51-63.

[6]   Nabiev RF., Belov EA. Socio-psychological aspect of personality identification. Habitology in the system of public administration. Bulletin of the Kazan Law Institute of the Ministry of Internal Affairs of Russia, 2020, T. 11, 4 (42): 519-526, doi: 10.37973/KUI.2020.34.12.023.

[7]   Skvortsov DV. Clinical analysis of movements. Gait analysis. Ivanovo: Publishing house of SPC «Stimul», 1996: 344.

[8]   Wei Liu, Ran Wang, Jun Su. An Image Impulsive Noise Denoising Method Based on Salp Swarm Algorithm. International Journal of Education and Management Engineering, 2019, 10(1): 43-51.

[9]   Dipti Pawade, Avani Sakhapara, Raj shah, Siby Thampi, Vignesh Vaid. Blockchain Based Secure Traffic Police Assistant System. International Journal of Education and Management Engineering, 2020, 10(6): 34-41.

[10]   Moroz VM., Yoltukhovsky MV., Vlasenko OV., Moskovko GS., Bogomaz OV., Rokunets IL., Tishchenko IV., Kostyuk LV., Suprunov KV. Sexual characteristics of walking while performing cognitive tasks. Bulletin of Morphology, 2019, 25(2): 5-15.

[11]   Castro FM., Marín-Jiménez MJ., Guil N., de la Blanca N.P. Automatic learning of gait signatures for people identification. LNCS. Proc. IWANN, 2017, 10306: 257-270. doi: 10.1007/978-3-319-59147-6_23.

[12]   Sokolova A., Konushin A. Gait recognition based on convolutional neural networks. Int. Arch. Photogramm. Re-mote Sens. Spatial Inf. Sci., 2017, XLII-2/W4: 207-212. doi: 10.5194/isprs-archives-XLII-2-W4-207-2017.

[13]   Zhang X., Sun S., Li C., Zhao X., Hu Y. DeepGait: A learning deep convolutional representation for gait recogni-tion. LNCS. Proc. Biometric Recognition, 2017, 10568: 447-456. doi: 10.1007/978-3-319-69923-3_48.

[14]   Wolf T., Babaee M., Rigoll G. Multi-view gait recognition using 3D convolutional neural networks. Proc. IEEE ICIP, 2016, 4165-4169. doi: 10.1109/ICIP.2016.7533144.

[15]   Sokolova A., Konushin A. Methods of identifying a person by gait in a video. Tr. ISP RAS. 2019, 31(1): 69-82. doi: 10.15514/ISPRAS-2019-31(1)-5.

[16]   Chhatrala R., Jadhav D. Gait recognition based on curvelet transform and PCANet. Pattern Recognition and Image Analysis, 2017, 27(3), 525-531. doi: 10.1134/s1054661817030075.

[17] Chen C., Liang J., Zhao H., Hu H., Tian J. Frame difference energy image for gait recognition with incomplete silhouettes. Pattern Recognition Letters, 2009, 30(11): 977-984. doi: 10.1016/j.patrec.2009.04.012.

[18] Arseev SP., Konushin AS., Lyutov VS. Recognition of a person by gait and appearance. Programming. 2018. T. 44. 4. C. 258-265. doi: 10.31857/S000523100000515-0.

[19] Whytock T., Belyaev A., Robertson N.M. Dynamic distance-based shape signs for gait recognition. J. Math. Imaging Vis., 2014, 50(3): 314-326. doi: 10.1007/s10851-014-0501-8.

[20] Castro F.M., Marín-Jiménez M.J., Carnicer R.M. Pyramidal Fisher motion for multiview gait recognition. Proc. XXII Int. Conf. on Pattern Recognition, 2014, 1692-1697. doi: 10.1109/ICPR.2014.298.

[21] Moroz VM., Yoltukhovsky MV., Vlasenko OV., Moskovko GS., Bogomaz OV., Rokunets IL., Tishchenko IV., Kostyuk LV., Suprunov KV. Age-related signs of walking while performing cognitive tasks. Biomedical and Biosocial Anthropology, 2019, 1(34): 68-76.

[22] Fomina EE., Leonov SV., Kosukhina OI. Software package for calculating the characteristics of the step cycle. Certificate of state registration of the computer program No. 2022682014 dated 17.11.2022.

[23] Kosukhina OI., Fomina EE., Leonov SV. Database of characteristics of the step cycle. Certificate of state registration of the database No. 2022623085 dated 11.24.2022.

[24] Fomina EE., Zybin DG. A program for determining human anthropometric parameters based on the characteristics of the step cycle using the random forest algorithm. Certificate of state registration of the computer program No. 2023661287 dated 30.05.2023.

Artificial Intelligence, Medical Engineering and Education
Z.B. Hu et al. (Eds.)

475

doi:10.3233/ATDE231359

The Efficient and Secure Digital Management System for Radiologists

Maksim IAVICH [a,1] , Lasha SHARVADZE [b]

a Caucasus University, 1 Paata Saakadze St, Tbilisi 0102, Georgia
b Georgian Technical University, 68, Merab Kostava St, Tbilisi, 0108, Georgia
ORCiD ID: Maksim IAVICH https://orcid.org/0000-0002-3109-7971

Abstract: This article describes the authors' research on a unified digital management system for the clinic. The system is focused on the use of radiologists and medical imaging. The goal of the research is to develop a unified, secure, and efficient management system for the clinic. The system uses a single-window principle, fully integrates all clinic management systems into one environment, and fully digitizes them. Due to the scattered processes across different areas, the current clinical management systems do not have all the necessary structures, processes, data, and systems integrated into a single electronic environment. This article describes one of the medical visualization modules of the new research-based medical facility management software, which will be integrated into a unified hospital management system. The system has a Web-based interface and is compatible with a variety of mobile devices. The system provides security features such as password policies and user role management. The system works in a secure network environment. Experiments conducted in a test environment have revealed that the new system improves the efficiency of delivering medical services and reduces the time needed to deliver a medical service. The significance lies in the potential to transform clinic management, optimize clinical processes, and ultimately enhance the quality of patient care. The findings have relevance not only for the medical community but also for technology developers and policymakers aiming to advance healthcare systems.

Keywords. PACS, security, radiologists, digital.

1. Introduction

PACS (Picture Archiving and Communication Systems) is a system used to connect servers, computers, and medical devices for storing, retrieving, using, and managing medical radiology images. PACS systems handle images in a variety of formats. The most common format for digital images and communication in PACS systems is (DICOM) [1-4].

PACS (Picture Archiving and Communication Systems) is a medical imaging technology used mainly in healthcare organizations for the secure storage and use of electronic images and clinically important information by the medical personnel [5-7]. Using PACS eliminates the need to manually store, retrieve and send sensitive medical information, images and records. Instead, medical records and images can be securely stored on the clinic's servers and accessed/used through encrypted channels from

---

[1] Corresponding Author: Maksim IAVICH, E-mail: miavich@cu.edu.ge.

anywhere in the world using various communication devices (computer, tablet, cell phone, etc.). Medical image storage technologies such as PACS are becoming increasingly important and necessary as the volume of digital medical images increases in the healthcare industry and the analysis of these image data becomes more and more common. The use of such systems by radiologists has shown us its advantage, need and necessity, and under this system, various areas of medicine using visualized data such as computed tomography, magnetic resonance tomography, X-ray, ultrasound, nuclear medicine, cardiology, pathology, radiation, oncology, dermatology, endoscopy, bronchoscopy, gynecology, plastic surgery - have all been integrated into this system.

Medical images are captured and used for clinical analysis, diagnosis and treatment as part of the patient's care plan [8, 9]. The information collected can be used to identify any anatomical and physiological pathology, evaluate treatment progress, and maintain a database of patient images.

PACS systems consist of four main components:

1.   Image processing devices;
2.   A secure network environment to share patient images and data;
3.   A workstation, computer or mobile device for viewing, processing and interpreting images;
4.   Electronic archive for storage and future use of images and related documentation.

PACS imaging information systems have replaced the need to store and manage printed materials and media in desks and rooms. Instead, medical images, medical records, and other clinical data can be securely stored digitally on-site or on the cloud server.

Vendors often use a hybrid cloud system in which master images are stored locally and backups are stored in the cloud. Additional types of storage architecture and security, such as direct-attached storage (DAS), network attached storage (NAS) or storage area network (SAN), can be configured and connected to a PACS server, each providing updates and connectivity, enhancements and additional security. Imagine you have been injured and need to go to hospital. When you arrive at the hospital, you will be checked in based on your personal information survey, and this information will be entered into the hospital information system. After a short wait, you are seen by a doctor for a consultation. The doctor will examine you and prescribe a series of tests to assess your health, including X-rays and blood tests. This information is also included in the HIS (Hospital Information System). This information is now needed by other medical personnel in their computer system to continue the process of diagnosing and treating your illness. The communication language for clinical, laboratory, and radiology devices in clinical management systems is the HL7 (Health Level 7) protocol [10,11].

HL7 is a set of standards for sharing clinical and administrative data between hospital information systems. It is like a language that describes you and your medical information across all the hospital information systems, and what is most important is that all systems speak the same language. Thus, as an HL7 message is received by another computer system, it can be processed and used by the medical staff.

The HL7 message has the following structure:

```
MSH|^~\&|HL7Soup|HIS|HL7Soup|HIS|201407271408||ADT^A04|1817457|D|2.5.1|E
VN|A04|AL
PID||0493575^^^2^ID1|454721||DOE^JOHN^^^^|DOE^JOHN^^^^|19480203|M||B|25
4E238ST^^Howick^OH^3252^USA||
(216)631-4359|||M|AGN|400003403~1129086|999-|
```

NK1||CONROY^MARI^^^^|SPO||(216)731-4359||EC|||||||||||||||||||||||
PV1||O|O/R||||277^ALLEN^BONNIE^J^^^||||||||
||2688684|||||||||||||||||||||||201407271408||||||002376853

The workflow in PACS systems is as follows:

A patient registers in the system with his/her personal information, for an examination by a certain physician. The physician/assistant then begins examining the patient. During the examination, he/she monitors the patient and the imaging process in the program and, if necessary, adds additional programs to the examination (examinations consist of programs) or relaunches certain programs. After the examination, the doctor performs a detailed examination of each medical image, determines the size and structure of organs and abnormalities, marks/measures problem areas and clinical significance, marks/measures problem areas and their clinical significance, and determines the anatomy of the organs to examine. He/she then writes the conclusion in the program and completes the examination. If the system is connected to a CD recorder and medical tape printer, the system automatically sends the examination to an external storage device (CD-ROM) for recording and printing on a tape.

This research endeavors to achieve several critical objectives:

- Unified PACS System: Develop a unified Picture Archiving and Communication System (PACS) to efficiently manage medical radiology images, with a focus on the DICOM format.
- Medical Imaging Management: Provide healthcare organizations with a secure, comprehensive system for electronic image and data storage and access.
- Global Accessibility: Enable secure global access to medical records and images from various devices.
- Integration Across Specialties: Create a unified platform for diverse medical fields, including radiology, cardiology, and pathology.
- Workflow Optimization: Streamline healthcare processes by centralizing records and images, enhancing patient care efficiency.

Existing solutions are often fragmented and manual, but the proposed system aims to bridge these gaps, although specific limitations are not detailed in the introduction. The author's aspiration is to offer a practical, efficient solution that streamlines healthcare management, benefiting medical professionals and patients alike.

2.   Literature Review

The literature surrounding medical image management, radiology, and the integration of technology in healthcare presents a diverse landscape of research and innovations. J. Randolph et al. introduce a Blockchain-based Medical Image Sharing framework that automates critical-results notification through blockchain technology, promising advancements in secure data sharing and patient care. B. P. Tinashe, C. Wu, and R. Zhou discuss the transformative potential of AI in radiology, particularly in image diagnosis within healthcare, highlighting the AI Transformation in Radiology [11-13].

A. Haddad et al. conduct a systematic review on AI and blockchain-based e-healthcare records management systems, providing insights into the development of secure and efficient healthcare data systems [14]. I. E. Ivanov and B. Ivanov propose a

Unified National Digital Framework for Medical Image Information, offering a blueprint for improving the accessibility and standardization of medical images [15].

K. Loizidou, G. Skouroumouni, C. Nikolaou, and C. Pitris explore automated breast mass segmentation and classification, advancing image processing techniques for breast cancer diagnosis [16]. E. O. Zulu and L. Phiri delve into the challenges and opportunities associated with Enterprise Medical Imaging in the Global South, shedding light on healthcare scenarios and technology integration challenges in these regions [17]. Collectively, these sources provide a comprehensive view of ongoing developments in medical image management, AI and blockchain integration, and the challenges and opportunities in healthcare imaging, both in developed and developing regions.

3.   Current Issues

PACS systems are presented as standalone software rather than part of an overall clinic management system. This makes it difficult to access some of the most essential patient information, because physicians have to work in multiple programs and it is difficult to see the picture in a single view[18-20]. Transferring this information to other related systems and reporting are also complicated.

To solve this problem, PACS system manufacturers offer integration with existing clinic management systems, but all common integrations are incomplete and once integrated, the patient's DICOM data can be viewed only if the software transfers them into the PACS system (the data link is integrated, not the data itself) and the medical recording option is also very limited. It also fails to provide complete reporting and history. Mostly the personal data of the patient and the study being performed are integrated, but not the link to the location of the imaging itself.

Medical imaging is one of the most essential and often the only source of information for patient diagnosis and treatment planning/course. This information is used by virtually all physicians, surgeons, and other medical personnel [21-22].

4.   Market Study

We have reviewed and studied the PACS systems of the key vendors. All systems are tailored to the workflow of radiologists and diagnosticians, are difficult for other clinicians to access, and even after integration with a unified clinic management system, cannot provide a complete unified picture in one window.

We studied the current situation of clinics in the area of medical image scanning systems and the results, unfortunately, are very poor. We surveyed 50 large clinics and found that only 7 of them have comprehensive medical image and data storage systems (PACS). In other cases, the data are recorded on electronic media (CD, USB, cassette) and given to the patient. If the electronic medium is damaged or lost, the results of the study are also lost. These data are also difficult to use as a single presentation of the patient's medical history for use by physicians or other medical personnel. This type of information also does not make its way into electronic clinic management system reports and distorts statistical data. See table 1.

Table 1. Clinics' data

Number of clinics	Equipped with PACS system	Not equipped with PACS system
50	7	43

PACS systems are quite expensive to maintain. After all, the size of medical images in many cases is quite large and can be several gigabytes. It needs powerful processors, a lot of RAM, even more hard drives, and a well-protected and fast network environment for stable operation. Server and network infrastructure is necessary for the proper and fast operation of these systems. Often, all medical devices and PACS servers are on a confined network to prevent overloading the network with additional traffic, data loss or system slowdowns.

Our research has shown that only few clinics in countries other than Georgia have introduced PACS systems because they are quite expensive to maintain. These systems are most developed and implemented in many clinics in America, Germany, and Turkey, where PACS systems are being actively developed and optimized. One of the biggest challenges in this area is the size of the medical examinations. Although the DICOM format allows for compression and reduction of image file size without compromising quality, the study size remains quite large. Because of the large size, it is difficult and expensive to maintain them.

Studies have been conducted with radiologists, clinicians, surgeons and other medical personnel who need access to patient data in PACS to treat patients or diagnose diseases. The study considered the need for the PACS system in their workflow and the ease of interacting with the program. All interviewees reported a need for such a system in their workflow. Most medical staff (radiology physicians and junior radiology personnel) working directly in the medical imaging, noted that the software is quite user-friendly and easy to use. And the remaining majority stated that it is not so easy to work with this software.

5. Suggested Methodology

Based on these studies, we determined that there is a need for a PACS system that connects easily to the clinic management system and completely shares data, with medical images flowing into the patient history for complete and convenient management. The HL7 protocols and DICOM reader need to be integrated into a single clinical management system so that the system can process these types of messages independently and have its own complete database of these data. With this method, all medical personnel will have access to medical images in their unified system as part of the patient's medical history, and they will be easy to view and use chronologically.

Our goal is to create a medical imaging module that will capture all the necessary information from the image, such as: the examined organ, the area, the deviation, the dimensions, etc. This information in the image format will be automatically inserted by the system into the relevant place in the patient's medical history.

Our goal is to create a PACS system according to the specified model, which will be as affordable and accessible as possible for the health sector. We have started to work on its implementation and real-world implementation and expect the first results in the near future.

Proper integration of the PACS system into a unified clinical management system will also create more opportunities for the use of artificial intelligence in medicine. The future of radiology will make extensive use of artificial intelligence, which will help the radiologist to analyze each pixel in detail and identify abnormalities. It should be noted that creating a suitable database for AI is possible with the cooperation of clinicians and other allied health professionals, who must be involved in the machine learning process.

The AI tool must be well-trained. There must be a back-up monitoring and testing mechanism to ensure strict quality control. AI tools are difficult to control, so they need to be implemented through process authorization. Implementing strict quality control will increase the reliability of the clinical and analytical data being processed and give us the opportunity to develop it. Artificial intelligence will assist medical personnel in making medical decisions. Finding the best and latest treatments for a patient's specific case and providing the right care requires a lot of resources from physicians. Using artificial intelligence-based technologies, medical professionals can simplify the process of retrieving relevant information from the latest biomedical data and electronic medical records. Some tools have natural language processing capabilities, allowing physicians to ask questions just like their medical colleagues and receive quick and reliable answers.

In diagnostics, the use of artificial intelligence to analyze medical images is also important. A typical clinical trial can accumulate thousands of images of data that need to be analyzed one by one. Artificial intelligence facilitates their decoding and the detection of certain patterns. In addition, such technologies are also used in everyday processes in the medical field, when analyzing the results of CT or MRI scans and making a diagnosis. With the help of artificial chatbots, users can get relevant answers to various health-related topics, such as payment processes, diseases, and symptoms. Virtual health assistants are responsible for such things as managing patient medical information, hiding sensitive data, scheduling appointments with doctors, sending reminders, etc.

The mathematical model for the system can be introduced as following:

Patient data structure: P = {Demographics, MedicalHistory, MedicalImages}   (1)

Demographics = {Age, Gender, etc.}   (2)

MedicalHistory = {Diagnosis, Treatments, Medications, etc.}   (3)

MedicalImages = {Image1, Image2, ..., ImageN}   (4)

PACS System Model:

A mathematical representation of PACS might include: (5)

Image storage: PACS_storage(image) = StorageLocation   (6)

Data retrieval: PACS_retrieve(PatientID, ImageID) = MedicalImage   (7)

Data extraction: ImageProcessing(MedicalImage) = ExtractedData   (8)

Clinical Management System Model:

Patient record storage and retrieval: CMS(PatientID) = PatientRecord   (9)

Integration of PACS data into the patient record:

CMS(PatientID).MedicalImages = MedicalImages   (10)

AI Model: A representation of AI model is offered as:

AI_model(MedicalImage) = Diagnosis   (11)

AI_train(Data, Labels) = ModelParameters   (12)

Integration Model: Data flow between systems:

CMS(PatientID).MedicalImages = PACS_retrieve(PatientID, ImageID)   (13)

AI_model(MedicalImage) = Diagnosis   (14)

CMS(PatientID).Diagnosis = Diagnosis   (15)

Cost and Resource Model:

Cost = HardwareCost + SoftwareCost + PersonnelCost   (16)

HardwareCost is calculated based on the number of servers, storage capacity, etc. SoftwareCost could involve licensing fees and software development costs.

PersonnelCost considers salaries and maintenance costs.

Quality Control Model:

Quality metric: QC(Diagnosis, GroundTruth) = QualityScore (17)

Threshold for acceptable QualityScore: ThresholdQualityScore (18)

Natural language interaction is user model:

NLP(UserQuery) = AI_response (19)

AI_response involves a response to a medical query. In this model, we consider two key aspects of scalability: data scalability and user scalability.

Data Scalability: Data scalability refers to the system's ability to handle increasing volumes of medical data, including images and patient records.

Let D represent the current data capacity of the system (e.g., storage capacity in terabytes). Let D_max represent the maximum data capacity the system can handle without a significant drop in performance. A formula for data scalability can be written as follow:

Data_Scalability = D_max / D (20)

This formula provides a ratio that indicates how close the system is to reaching its maximum data capacity. A higher value indicates better data scalability.

User Scalability: User scalability focuses on how the system can accommodate more users, such as medical professionals accessing patient records and AI algorithms. Let U represent the current number of concurrent users. Let U_max represent the maximum number of concurrent users the system can support without degradation in response times.

A formula for user scalability can be written as follows:

User_Scalability = U_max / U (21)

This formula provides a ratio indicating how many more concurrent users the system can handle before performance starts to decline.Optimization Objectives:

Objective function to maximize: Maximize(DesiredObjective)

The proposed methodology aligns with the research objectives by integrating HL7 protocols and DICOM readers into a unified clinical management system. This integration automates data entry, improving accuracy and accessibility. The research aims to create a cost-effective PACS system, promoting affordability and accessibility for healthcare facilities. The methodology also integrates artificial intelligence, enhancing image analysis and diagnosis. Quality control mechanisms ensure data reliability. This approach is grounded in data integration, automation, cost-effectiveness, AI utilization, and quality control, all contributing to improved healthcare services and patient outcomes.

6. Results and Discussion

The implementation of the PACS system integrated with HL7 protocols and DICOM readers has shown significant promise. Medical images now seamlessly merge into unified patient records, improving accessibility for medical personnel, reducing manual errors, and saving time. This approach aligns with our research goal of creating a cost-effective and accessible system for healthcare facilities. Initial real-world trials have yielded positive results, with ongoing implementation expected to reinforce its efficacy. Additionally, the introduction of artificial intelligence into medical image analysis demonstrates great potential for enhancing diagnostic accuracy and efficiency. AI models, when trained on comprehensive medical image datasets, exhibit promise in identifying abnormalities and assisting healthcare professionals in making diagnoses. Our stringent quality control measures contribute to the reliability of clinical and analytical data, ultimately elevating healthcare service quality.

In summary, our proposed methodology, emphasizing data integration, automation, cost-efficiency, AI utilization, and quality control, presents a substantial opportunity for improving healthcare services and patient outcomes. The initial results are encouraging, and ongoing endeavors are likely to validate the methodology's effectiveness.

7. Experiments

The experiments were conducted in a test environment. First, we calculated the time in an existing decentralized environment for a physician who needs to see the results of an imaging study to find a medical image of a patient, and then manually transfer this data to the patient history in another system and analyze the patient history as a single picture. It was found that this process takes 30-45 minutes, and then, according to our methodology, we automatically transferred the data of the simulated test image into a single patient history.

The experiment revealed that this time was reduced by a factor of 6 at best. This was because the processes were scattered across different programs and it was necessary to find and analyze the patient data in all systems separately.

8. Conclusion

The needs throughout the study are that all digital clinic management systems should be integrated into one large complete clinic management system, and it should integrate the major areas of medicine and data in an appropriate chronology and sequence. In this process, it is very important that the information the system collects around patient care be sorted chronologically, adapted to the various management or peripheral devices. The system should provide accurate, consistent, and convenient reporting in all areas.

Creating such a system and adapting it to such simple portable equipment as a tablet and a cell phone greatly simplifies and speeds up the process of monitoring and treating patients. Storing patient medical images, creating a history, and accessing them from the brain allows for faster and better disease diagnosis, shorter treatment times, minimization of errors, and avoidance of unnecessary examinations. Digital systems also increase the security of a patient's personal data and reduce the time it takes to receive medical services. The need for improving the patient's medical history data gives us an opportunity to create a platform for the widespread use of artificial intelligence in medicine. The combination of properly structured electronic data and electronic production of calculations has improved the quality of care, the reliability of information, and dramatically accelerated the time for diagnosis and establishment of a treatment regimen. Physicians were able to easily monitor the patient's condition in one window and learn about all the necessary data and patient results. The system has been updated, refined, and improved several times, and research and innovation are still underway.

The system is constantly evolving and expanding. The research, development and optimization of this project is done intensely with the medical staff. At this stage, the aforementioned system has been updated/optimized several times, and we are still researching, implementing new systems and expanding the system in the direction of digitalization of processes and data. In conclusion, our research significantly advances healthcare informatics by introducing a unified digital clinic management system. This addresses the need for integrated patient data across medical domains, improving efficiency, security, and access to information. The system's potential extends to various healthcare applications and paves the way for AI integration in healthcare decision-making. It provides a foundation for future healthcare informatics developments. This innovative approach enhances healthcare systems, benefiting medical professionals and patients. Ongoing research and system expansion will further improve healthcare delivery and patient outcomes.

References

[1] Phadke A. G. Synchronized phasor measurements in power systems[J]. IEEE Computer Applications in Power, 2013, 6(2): 10-15. Iavich, M., Sharvadze, L. (2023). The Model of the Novel One Windows Secure Clinic Management Systems. In: Hu, Z., Wang, Y., He, M. (eds) Advances in Intelligent Systems, Computer Science and Digital Economics IV. CSDEIS 2022. Lecture Notes on Data Engineering and Communications Technologies, vol 158. Springer, Cham. https://doi.org/10.1007/978-3-031-24475-9_29.

[2] Smith, G. (2006). Introduction to RIS and PACS. In: Dreyer, K.J., Thrall, J.H., Hirschorn, D.S., Mehta, A. (eds) PACS. Springer, New York, NY. https://doi.org/10.1007/0-387-31070-3_2

[3] Bick, U., Lenzen, H. PACS: the silent revolution. Eur Radiol 9, 1152–1160 (1999). https://doi.org/10.1007/s003300050811

[4] Siegel, E.L., Reiner, B. Work Flow Redesign: The Key to Success When Using PACS. J Digit Imaging 16, 164–168 (2003). https://doi.org/10.1007/s10278-002-6006-9

[5] G. Pearce, J. Wong, L. Mirtskhulava, S. Al-Majeed, K. Bakuria and N. Gulua, "Artificial Neural Network and Mobile Applications in Medical Diagnosis," 2015 17th UKSim-AMSS International Conference on Modelling and Simulation (UKSim), Cambridge, UK, 2015, pp. 61-64, doi: 10.1109/UKSim.2015.34.

[6] Mirtskhulava, M. Iavich, M. Razmadze and N. Gulua, "Securing Medical Data in 5G and 6G via Multichain Blockchain Technology using Post-Quantum Signatures," 2021 IEEE International Conference on Information and Telecommunication Technologies and Radio Electronics (UkrMiCo), Odesa, Ukraine, 2021, pp. 72-75, doi: 10.1109/UkrMiCo52950.2021.9716595.

[7] P. Chinnasamy and P. Deepalakshmi, "Design of Secure Storage for Health-care Cloud using Hybrid Cryptography," 2018 Second International Conference on Inventive Communication and Computational Technologies (ICICCT), Coimbatore, India, 2018, pp. 1717-1720, doi: 10.1109/ICICCT.2018.8473107.

[8] M. J. McAuliffe, F. M. Lalonde, D. McGarry, W. Gandler, K. Csaky and B. L. Trus, "Medical Image Processing, Analysis and Visualization in clinical research," Proceedings 14th IEEE Symposium on Computer-Based Medical Systems. CBMS 2001, Bethesda, MD, USA, 2001, pp. 381-386, doi: 10.1109/CBMS.2001.941749.

[9] E. Nasr-Esfahani et al., "Melanoma detection by analysis of clinical images using convolutional neural network," 2016 38th Annual International Conference of the IEEE Engineering in Medicine and Biology Society (EMBC), Orlando, FL, USA, 2016, pp. 1373-1376, doi: 10.1109/EMBC.2016.7590963.

[10] Lee, H.W., Ramayah, T. & Zakaria, N. External Factors in Hospital Information System (HIS) Adoption Model: A Case on Malaysia. J Med Syst 36, 2129–2140 (2012). https://doi.org/10.1007/s10916-011-9675-4

[11] Ahmadian, L., Khajouei, R., Nejad, S.S. et al. Prioritizing Barriers to Successful Implementation of Hospital Information Systems. J Med Syst 38, 151 (2014). https://doi.org/10.1007/s10916-014-0151-9

[12] J. Randolph et al., "Blockchain-based Medical Image Sharing and Automated Critical-results Notification: A Novel Framework," 2022 IEEE 46th Annual Computers, Software, and Applications

Conference (COMPSAC), Los Alamitos, CA, USA, 2022, pp. 1756-1761, doi: 10.1109/COMPSAC54236.2022.00279.

[13] B. P. Tinashe, C. Wu and R. Zhou, "AI (Artificial Intelligence) Transformation in Radiology: Image Diagnosis in Healthcare," 2022 Euro-Asia Conference on Frontiers of Computer Science and Information Technology (FCSIT), Beijing, China, 2022, pp. 170-172, doi: 10.1109/FCSIT57414.2022.00042.

[14] A. Haddad, M. H. Habaebi, M. R. Islam, N. F. Hasbullah and S. A. Zabidi, "Systematic Review on AI-Blockchain Based E-Healthcare Records Management Systems," in IEEE Access, vol. 10, pp. 94583-94615, 2022, doi: 10.1109/ACCESS.2022.3201878.

[15] I. E. Ivanov and B. Ivanov, "Unified National Digital Framework for Exchange and Storage of Medical Image Information," 2022 10th International Scientific Conference on Computer Science (COMSCI), Sofia, Bulgaria, 2022, pp. 1-7, doi: 10.1109/COMSCI55378.2022.9912601.

[16] K. Loizidou, G. Skouroumouni, C. Nikolaou and C. Pitris, "Automatic Breast Mass Segmentation and Classification Using Subtraction of Temporally Sequential Digital Mammograms," in IEEE Journal of Translational Engineering in Health and Medicine, vol. 10, pp. 1-11, 2022, Art no. 1801111, doi: 10.1109/JTEHM.2022.3219891.E. O. Zulu and L. Phiri, "Enterprise Medical Imaging in the Global South: Challenges and Opportunities," 2022 IST-Africa Conference (IST-Africa), Ireland, 2022, pp. 1-9, doi: 10.23919/IST-Africa56635.2022.9845508.

[17] E. O. Zulu and L. Phiri, "Enterprise Medical Imaging in the Global South: Challenges and Opportunities," 2022 IST-Africa Conference (IST-Africa), Ireland, 2022, pp. 1-9, doi: 10.23919/IST-Africa56635.2022.9845508.

[18] Ruth G. Luciano, Rhoel Anthony G. Torres, Edward B. Gomez, Hardly Joy D. Nacino, Rodmark D. Ramirez, "Medicine Management System: Its Design and Development", International Journal of Education and Management Engineering, Vol.13, No.3, pp. 11-18, 2023.

[19] Vusumuzi Maphosa, "E-health Implementation by Private Dental Service Providers in Bulawayo, Zimbabwe", International Journal of Information Engineering and Electronic Business, Vol.15, No.1, pp. 20-28, 2023. DOI:10.5815/ijieeb.2023.01.02.

[20] ZENG Jian-hong,"Products Selection Modeling of Medicine Manufacturing Industry Development in Beibuwan Economical Zone", International Journal of Wireless and Microwave Technologies, vol.2, no.4, pp.52-58, 2012.

[21] Beladgham Mohammed, Habchi Yassine, Moulay Lakhdar Abdelmouneim, Bassou Abdesselam, Taleb-Ahmed Abdelmalik, "New Contribution on Compression Color Images: Analysis and Synthesis for Telemedicine Applications", International Journal of Information Engineering and Electronic Business, vol.6, no.2, pp.28-34, 2014.

[22] Shakil Mahmud Boby, Shaela Sharmin, " Medical Image Denoising Techniques against Hazardous Noises: An IQA Metrics Based Comparative Analysis", International Journal of Image, Graphics and Signal Processing, Vol.13, No.2, pp. 25-43, 2021.

Artificial Intelligence, Medical Engineering and Education
Z.B. Hu et al. (Eds.)
doi:10.3233/ATDE231360

Research on Arena Simulation Application for Parcel Pickup Queuing System

Xudong DENG[a], Yajun WU[a], Yong WANG[a,b,c,1] and Qian LU[b,c]

[a] *School of Management, Wuhan University of Science and Technology, Wuhan, China*
[b] *Sanya Science and Education Innovation Park of Wuhan University of Technology, Sanya, China*
[c] *Department of Production Engineering, KTH Royal Institute of Technology, Stockholm, Sweden*
ORCiD ID: Yajun WU https://orcid.org/0009-0002-3466-5812

Abstract. With the continuous improvement of people's living standards, especially under the influence of shopping festivals such as "618", "Double 11," and "Double 12", the competition in the express delivery industry is becoming increasingly fierce. Since there is no express cabinet in many areas, it is necessary to go to the express station to pick up the parcel in person. Therefore, pick-up efficiency affects the customer's satisfaction with the express station. To improve customer satisfaction, we must first improve the efficiency of pick-up. Many express companies now adopt a combination of self-service and manual methods to solve the problem of too long waiting times in picking up parcels. However, it is still inevitable that there will be too long waiting times in shopping festivals due to the explosion of express delivery. In order to improve the pick-up efficiency, this paper uses Arena to establish a simulation model to simulate the pick-up waiting situation and allocate the number of self-service pick-up machines and manual services to solve the problem of excessively long waiting times during pick-up.

Keywords. Arena software, Simulation, Pick up the parcel

1. Introduction

With the rapid development of the economy, the rise of e-commerce, and the continuous improvement of people's living standards, the express delivery industry has become an indispensable part of our lives. Especially in the "618", "Double Eleven," "Double Twelve," and other shopping carnival activities, the express delivery business has shown explosive growth, and the competition in the express delivery industry has become increasingly fierce. However, many regions do not have universal delivery cabinets. Customers need to pick-up parcels in person at the Courier point, and pick-up efficiency significantly impacts customer satisfaction. Therefore, how to improve delivery efficiency to enhance customer satisfaction has become an urgent problem to be solved in the express delivery industry.

Many scholars have carried out relevant research on the problem of picking up items. Wen H et al. proposed a DeepRoute model to predict the future pick-up route of couriers based on the decision-making experience of couriers' historical spatiotemporal behavior. This model can help the scheduling system more intelligently assign packages to couriers,

---

[1] Corresponding Author: Yong WANG, E-mail: Swedenwang-yong@wust.edu.cn

thus improving pick-up efficiency [1]. Wang Y et al. established a collaborative alliance and allocated truck transportation resources based on time-space (TS) network attributes to minimize the total operating cost. They designed an optimal collaboration strategy to solve the collaborative logistics pick-up problem of CLPDPE [2]. Hong F et al. proposed a new package receiving and receiving mode and system in which multiple drones and automatic devices work together. In this mode, automatic devices are set up in the free area on the top of residential buildings as delivery and pick-up points for packages, and drones are used to transport packages between buildings and warehouses [3]. In order to optimize parcel collection and delivery in rural areas, Yang C et al. established a vehicle routing model integrating parcel collection and delivery in rural areas. To solve the model, they designed a two-stage algorithm based on an improved K-means clustering algorithm and a genetic algorithm [4]. Scholars have much research on the pick-up problem, but there is a lack of discussion on the problem of too long queuing time during the pick-up process.

At present, many express delivery companies adopt a combination of self-help and manual methods to solve the long waiting time problem in picking up items. A self-service pick-up machine enables customers to complete the pick-up at the express point, significantly reducing the waiting time in line. However, how to allocate the number of self-service pick-up machines and manual services to ensure the efficiency of pick-up while not causing a waste of resources is a problem that needs in-depth research. Especially during the shopping carnival, due to the explosion of express delivery volume, the problem of long queuing time is more prominent. This problem affects the customer's pick-up experience and challenges the service quality of express delivery companies. Therefore, how to rationally allocate the number of self-service pick-up machines and manual services scientifically to improve pick-up efficiency is an urgent problem for the express delivery industry.

This paper aims to use Arena to build a simulation model to simulate the pick-up queuing situation and optimize the number of self-service pick-up machines and manual services to solve the problem of too long queuing time during pick-up. Through this research, we hope to provide a scientific and effective method for the express delivery industry to improve pick-up efficiency and enhance customer satisfaction to promote the sustainable development of the express delivery industry.

2. Literature Review

With the continuous development and upgrading of Arena software, its functions and applications have been further expanded. Guseva E et al. used Arena to establish a simulation model of patient service management to evaluate the workload of clinicians to determine the number of doctors such as general practitioners, surgeons, and other specialists required for patient services [5]. In order to shorten the waiting time of patients and optimize the staffing, Sasanfar et al. used Arena simulation technology to simulate the new layout of the emergency department of a hospital and gave layout design suggestions based on the research results, which significantly improved the work efficiency of the emergency department [6]. Aziati A. N et al. used Arena simulation software to simulate patients' waiting time and service time at the outpatient counter and proposed corresponding strategies to improve patients' waiting time and service rate by observing problems in the simulation process [7]. Tavakoli M et al. simulated the patient flow process through Arena software to predict the situation of future patients entering the hospital. Simulations showed that the system crashed after 14 days. Researchers improve the system by analyzing the problems in the simulation [8]. Kalwar MA et al. used Arena software to model and simulate the queuing system of the outpatient department of gastroenterology in the hospital, analyze the waiting time of patients in four scenarios, and adjust the number of doctors and work schedule according to the simulation results to solve the problem of excessively long waiting time of patients [9]. Derni O et al. aims to minimize the total waiting time to increase patient flow and improve the quality of patient monitoring. They used Arena software to build models and conduct simulation experiments to assess the impact of the proposed solution [10].

In order to study the production process of aluminum brake brackets in the factory, find out the bottleneck in the production, and calculate the production efficiency and workforce demand of the unit, Neeraj R et al. used Arena software to conduct a discrete event simulation of a manufacturing unit, and combined the process analyzer (PAN) with Opt Quest to propose a better model [11]. In order to expand the application research of computer simulation technology in the production line balance of the garment industry, Sime H et al. adopted Arena software for modeling and simulation [12]. In order to analyze the current situation of A manufacturing industry and design a future state diagram to optimize the process flow, Mishra A K et al. used Arena software to simulate the method. The research results show that this method can reduce the cost and the impact on the environment [13]. To mitigate the consequences of the channel closure so that a new bridge could be built over the channel, Rahimikelarijani B et al. used the discrete event model in Arena to conduct a simulation analysis of ship traffic and operations in the Houston Channel. By simulating different shutdown scenarios, the shutdown scheme with the least waiting time is selected [14]. In order to solve the problems in the sewing stage and improve garment productivity, Yemane A et al. used Arena software to simulate and measure the existing and proposed pants sewing thread models and conducted statistical analysis on the collected data to determine the statistical significance and determine the expression for simulation modeling, to develop a new sewing assembly line model [15]. Bajjou MS et al. developed a lean simulation model using Arena software to study the impact of lean building principles on the performance of these processes. Studies have found that lean principles effectively improve the performance of selected construction processes [16]. In summary, Arena simulation software has been widely used in many fields and will continue to be used in other aspects.

3. Model Building

Arena simulation software is used to collect the user's arrival time and pick-up parcel service time during the user's pick-up process, and the pick-up time is used to represent the user's waiting time. The simulation results are analyzed, and the scientific number of self-service pick-up machines and pick-up service personnel are allocated to the express station.

The pick-up simulation system has two pick-up modes: self-service and manual. After receiving the parcel, the user determines whether it is small. If it is a small parcel and meets the conditions of self-service pick-up, the user directly goes to the self-service pick-up machine to pick up the parcel and leave. If the conditions for self-service pick-up are not met, go to the manual service desk for manual processing. If it is not a small parcel, enter the manual acceptance area; if it meets the manual acceptance conditions, directly pick up the parcel and leave. The manual service desk is used for manual processing if the manual acceptance conditions are unmet. The parcel pick-up flow chart is shown in Fig. 1. Arena software was used to establish a simulation model for the above pick-up process, as shown in Fig. 2.

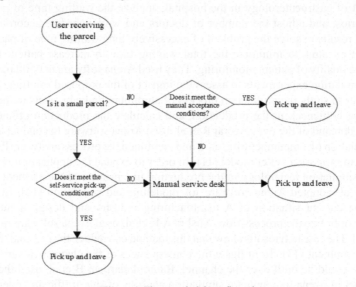

Figure 1. The parcel pick-up flow chart

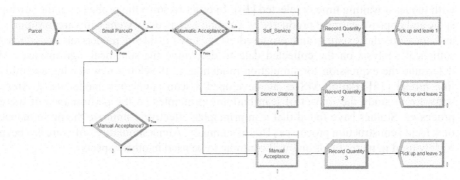

Figure 2. Pick up parcel simulation model diagram

Module and parameter setting:

(1) First, create a create module to simulate the user receiving the parcel. The module, named "Parcel," follows an exponential distribution with an average of 2 minutes, the number of arrivals is 1, the maximum number of arrivals is infinite, and the initial value is 0.

(2) Create three decide modules of type 2-way by chance. The first one is called "Small Parcel?" to determine whether it is a small parcel, and the pass rate is 70%. The second one is called "Automatic Acceptance?" to check whether the conditions for self-service pickup are met. The pass rate is 95%. Moreover, the third one is called "Manual Acceptance?" to determine whether the manual acceptance conditions are met, and the pass rate is 80%.

(3) Create three process modules. The first is named "Self_Service," indicating the self-service pick-up machine. Action selects Seize Delay Release; delay type is

Triangular with the minimum value of 1, the maximum value of 5, and the value of 2; the unit is minutes, and the number of automatic pick-up machines is 1. The second is named "Service Station" for a human service desk. Action selects Seize Delay Release; delay type is Triangular with a minimum value of 5, a maximum value of 8, and a value of 6; the unit is minutes, and the number of manual service stations is 1. The third is called "Manual Acceptance," which means manual acceptance. Action selects Seize Delay Release; delay type is Triangular with a minimum value of 3, a maximum value of 6, and a value of 5; the unit is minutes, and the number of manual acceptance workers is 1.

(4) Create three record modules to record the fetching information, named "Record Quantity 1", "Record Quantity 2", and "Record Quantity 3", respectively.

(5) Create three dispose modules to indicate that users pick up and leave, respectively named "Pick up and leave 1", "Pick up and leave 2", and "Pick up and leave 3".

(6) Set operating conditions. The daily working time is 8 hours or 480 minutes, and the operating cycle is ten days.

4. Output Report Analysis

A partial report of the output of this pick-up simulation model is shown in Fig. 3. Table 1 shows the data from ten simulations. After analysis, the following conclusions can be obtained:

(1) The average number of people waiting for self-service pick-up is 2.96, and the average waiting time is 8.74 minutes. The waiting time is long, so the number of self-service pick-up machines can be appropriately increased to reduce the waiting time;

(2) The average number of people waiting for manual acceptance is 1.14, and the average waiting time is 8.72 minutes. Although the waiting time is long, the number of people waiting is small, which is more feasible;

(3) The average number of people waiting at the manual service desk is 0.42, and the average waiting time is 8.74 minutes. The number of people waiting is less than one, which is also feasible.

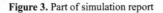

Unnamed Project					Replications: 10
Replication 1	Start Time:	0.00	Stop Time:	480.00	Time Units: **Minutes**

Queue Detail Summary

Time

	Waiting Time
Manual Pickup.Queue	5.77
Self_Service.Queue	4.83
Service Station.Queue	5.32

Other

	Number Waiting
Manual Pickup.Queue	0.53
Self_Service.Queue	1.52
Service Station.Queue	0.21

Figure 3. Part of simulation report

Table 1. Waiting Time

	Waiting Time			Number Waiting		
	Self-Service	Manual Acceptance	Service Station	Self-Service	Manual Acceptance	Service Station
1	4.83	5.77	5.32	0.53	1.52	0.21
2	9.23	6.18	8.97	3.19	0.83	0.42
3	7.35	8.46	7.16	2.71	1.26	0.30
4	5.99	9.37	8.52	1.97	0.90	0.41
5	6.01	4.04	4.72	1.99	0.42	0.13
6	10.99	4.72	4.61	3.99	0.55	0.21
7	3.64	15.32	15.35	1.12	2.07	0.70
8	4.65	11.01	14.52	1.43	1.26	0.80
9	27.85	7.25	6.54	10.17	1.01	0.22
10	6.90	15.07	11.70	2.49	1.59	0.81
average	8.74	8.72	8.74	2.96	1.14	0.42

5. Conclusion

In order to solve the problem of too long queuing time of pick-up the parcel, this paper uses Arena to establish a simulation model to simulate the queuing situation and optimize the number of self-service pick-up machines and manual services. Through the application of a simulation model, this paper simulates and analyzes different pick-up strategies to find the best pick-up strategy. The simulation results show that the waiting time can be reduced effectively, and customer satisfaction can be improved under the appropriate strategy. The research results of this paper provide helpful references and enlightenment for express companies in the face of the shopping carnival and other rush hours.

First, according to the simulation results, we can find that the reasonable allocation of self-service pick-up machines and manual services is crucial to improving pick-up efficiency. During the shopping carnival, express delivery companies can ease the queuing pressure by increasing the number of self-service pick-up machines and, simultaneously, ensure a certain number of manual services to cope with emergencies and meet special needs.

Secondly, express companies must adjust the pick-up strategy according to the situation. For example, during peak periods such as shopping carnivals, measures such as temporarily increasing the number of self-service pick-up machines and manual services and extending business hours can be taken to cope with many pick-up demands in a short period. Regularly, resources can be reasonably allocated according to customer needs and business volumes to improve operational efficiency.

Finally, express companies can use extensive data analysis and other technical means to understand customers' pick-up habits and need to develop a more accurate pick-up strategy. In addition, express delivery companies can strengthen cooperation with partners such as e-commerce platforms, promote the coordinated development of the express delivery industry and e-commerce industry, and improve pick-up efficiency and customer satisfaction.

In short, by using Arena to establish a simulation model, this paper optimizes the number of self-service pick-up machines and manual services. It provides an effective strategy to solve the problem of waiting in the pick-up queue. These strategies are of great significance to improve customer satisfaction, reduce operating costs, and provide certain competitive advantages for express delivery companies in an environment facing fierce competition.

Acknowledgment

The research was funded by The Major Project of Philosophy and Social Science Research in Hubei Province Higher Education Institutions (22ZD046); The Ph.D. Scientific Research and Innovation Foundation of Sanya Yazhou Bay Science and Technology City (HSPHDSRF-2022-03-032); The WUST & Int-plog Research Project (2022H20537); The CSL & CFLP research project plan (2023CSLKT3-306); The Department of Education of Hubei Province Young and Middle-Aged Talents Project (20211102).

References

[1]   Wen H, Lin Y, Wu F, et al. Package pick-up route prediction via modeling couriers' spatial-temporal behaviors[C]//2021 IEEE 37th International Conference on Data Engineering (ICDE). IEEE, 2021: 2141-2146.

[2]   Wang Y, Peng S, Guan X, et al. Collaborative logistics pickup and delivery problem with eco-packages based on time–space network[J]. Expert Systems with Applications, 2021, 170: 114561.

[3]   Hong F, Wu G, Luo Q, et al. Logistics in the sky: A two-phase optimization approach for the drone package pickup and delivery system[J]. IEEE Transactions on Intelligent Transportation Systems, 2023, 24(9): 9175-9190.

[4]   Yang C, Shu T, Liang S, et al. Vehicle routing optimization for rural package collection and delivery integrated with regard to the customer self-pickup radius[J]. Applied Economics, 2023, 55(41): 4841-4852.

[5]   Guseva E, Varfolomeyeva T, Efimova I, et al. Discrete event simulation modelling of patient service management with Arena[C]//Journal of Physics: Conference Series. IOP Publishing, 2018, 1015: 032095.

[6]   Sasanfar S, Bagherpour M, Moatari-Kazerouni A. Improving emergency departments: Simulation-based optimization of patients waiting time and staff allocation in an Iranian hospital[J]. International Journal of Healthcare Management, 2021, 14(4): 1449-1456.

[7]   Aziati A H N, Hamdan N S B. Application of queuing theory model and simulation to patient flow at the outpatient department[C]//Proceedings of the International Conference on Industrial Engineering and Operations Management Bandung, Indonesia. 2018: 3016-3028.

[8]   Tavakoli M, Tavakkoli-Moghaddam R, Mesbahi R, et al. Simulation of the COVID-19 patient flow and investigation of the future patient arrival using a time-series prediction model: a real-case study[J]. Medical & Biological Engineering & Computing, 2022, 60(4): 969-990.

[9]   Kalwar M A, Mari S I, Memon M S, et al. Simulation based approach for improving outpatient clinic operations[J]. Mehran University Research Journal of Engineering & Technology, 2020, 39(1): 153-170.

[10]   Derni O, Boufera F, Khelfi M F. Modeling and optimizing patients' flows inside emergency department based on the simulation model: A case study in an algerian hospital[J]. International Journal of Information Engineering and Electronic Business, 2019, 11(4): 24-32.

[11]   Neeraj R R, Nithin R P, Niranjhan P, et al. Modelling and simulation of discrete manufacturing industry[J]. Materials Today: Proceedings, 2018, 5(11): 24971-24983.

[12]   Sime H, Jana P, Panghal D. Feasibility of using simulation technique for line balancing in apparel industry[J]. Procedia Manufacturing, 2019, 30: 300-307.

[13]   Mishra A K, Sharma A, Sachdeo M, et al. Development of sustainable value stream mapping (SVSM) for unit part manufacturing: A simulation approach[J]. International Journal of Lean Six Sigma, 2020, 11(3): 493-514.

[14]   Rahimikelarijani B, Abedi A, Hamidi M, et al. Simulation modeling of Houston Ship Channel vessel

traffic for optimal closure scheduling[J]. Simulation Modelling Practice and Theory, 2018, 80: 89-103.

[15]	Yemane A, Gebremicheal G, Meraha T, et al. Productivity improvement through line balancing by using simulation modeling[J]. Journal of Optimization in Industrial Engineering, 2020, 13(1): 153-165.

[16]	Bajjou M S, Chafi A. Lean construction and simulation for performance improvement: a case study of reinforcement process[J]. International Journal of Productivity and Performance Management, 2021, 70(2): 459-487.

Artificial Intelligence, Medical Engineering and Education
Z.B. Hu et al. (Eds.)
doi:10.3233/ATDE231361

Application of Autonomous Driving Algorithm Based on HSV and Yolov5 in Micro Intelligent Vehicles

Xiaozhe YANG[1], Huiting LU, Junjie MO, Guobiao HUANG, Yongzhu LONG

The Faculty of Intelligent Manufacturing, Nanning University, Nanning, 530299, China

Abstract. Artificial intelligence driving technology has become the main direction of technological progress in intelligent vehicles. To address the issue of road recognition and traffic sign recognition response in the field of intelligent vehicle autonomous driving, a vehicle autonomous driving algorithm based on HSV road detection and yolov5 traffic sign recognition is proposed and applied to micro intelligent vehicles. The hardware of the mini smart car is controlled by NVIDIA Jetson AGX Orin, and the software method is embedded in the Ubuntu system. The yolov5 neural network is used to solve the classification and location problems of traffic signs. The results of experimental testing prove that micro intelligent vehicles can drive according to regulations on simulated roads and accurately recognize road signs, and can make corresponding actions accurately. The research results provide certain reference value for the application and development of vehicle autonomous driving.

Keywords. Intelligent vehicles; Autonomous driving; Target identification; Embedded systems

1. Introduction

The concept of autonomous driving has been in people's sight for nearly a century. Computer vision and artificial intelligence have continuously promoted and developed it [1,2]. Unmanned driving technology is a synthesis of multiple cutting-edge disciplines such as sensors, computers, artificial intelligence, communication, navigation and positioning, pattern recognition, machine vision, intelligent control, etc. [3-5]. It brings disruptive changes to the business model of automobiles and has good development prospects [6,7].

The implementation of autonomous driving benefits from the rapid development of recognition technology and deep learning algorithm technology [8]. The development of these disciplines has made the concept of autonomous driving a reality. At present, road detection and recognition technology mainly rely on sensor technology to obtain environmental information and uses computer vision and deep learning for data analysis and processing [10-12]. Computer vision algorithms and models enable object detection and tracking, while deep learning technology enables pattern recognition and decision reasoning, thereby achieving autonomous navigation and driving decision-making

---

[1] Corresponding Author: Xiaozhe YANG, E-mail: 970423706@qq.com

[13,14]. The design of software and hardware, as well as system communication, are important design contents [15-18].

The core technology system of autonomous driving can be mainly divided into three levels: perception, decision-making, and execution [19-21]. Currently, intelligent assisted driving has become the mainstream in the transformation and development of the automotive industry. In the future, unmanned driving technology will drive the research and application of information technologies such as artificial intelligence, the Internet of Things, big data, and cloud computing, and promote the process of China's economic transformation and upgrading [22].

To improve the safety and reliability of micro intelligent vehicles, it is necessary to strengthen research in various aspects such as hardware and software. The study of algorithms is one of the important contents.

2. Overall Design and Differential Steering Analysis of Micro Intelligent Vehicles

The object of this design is a micro intelligent vehicle on urban roads. The overall design concept, vehicle analysis, and vehicle design content are as follows.

2.1. Overall Design

The urban road recognition intelligent vehicle system designed in this article uses NVIDIA Jetson AGX Orin as the core control unit, detects track information through PCBA-imx1080P camera, collects grayscale images of the track using CMOS camera, generates a binary image array through dynamic threshold algorithm, extracts white guide lines, and uses them for track recognition; By detecting the real-time speed of urban road recognition intelligent vehicles through motor encoders and adjusting the speed of the driving left and right motors using PID control algorithms, closed-loop control of vehicle movement speed and direction is achieved. In order to improve the speed and stability of intelligent vehicles, extensive hardware and software testing has been conducted on the system. The experimental results indicate that the system design scheme is feasible.

2.2. Vehicle Analysis

The micro intelligent car is composed of a frame body and four coded deceleration motors, with each wheel having an independent power system to achieve four-wheel drive. The vehicle uses a self-developed circuit board based on the STM32 microcontroller as the control center. The camera pillar is located at the front of the vehicle and is equipped with a high-definition industrial camera on the top, which can collect map data in a wide range and with high accuracy. The main control unit adopts NVIDIA Jetson AGX Orin, which is small in size and fast in computation, and can quickly analyze map data and send commands. The battery is placed under the vehicle to lower the center of gravity and improve stability. Use wireless HDMI to connect NVIDIA Jetson AGX Orin and computer screen for vehicle debugging. The vehicle is equipped with a 15V lithium battery, which is stabilized to 12V using a DC-DC voltage reduction module to drive the vehicle.

Figure 1. Intelligent vehicle physical object

2.3. Vehicle Design

As shown in Figure 1, the intelligent vehicle chassis uses 3D MAX for autonomous 3D modeling design, and undergoes CNC (Computer numerical control) precision machining. The smart car uses lightweight, high-strength, corrosion-resistant, and long-life aluminum alloy materials. The surface of the car body has reserved holes for fixing structures such as motor brackets and camera bases.

The installation of cameras is one of the main objectives of this project. Therefore, in the design of the mechanism, it is necessary to comprehensively consider the perspective and balance of the camera. The design aims to increase the free adjustment range of the camera and reduce its weight. By using UG (NX12.0) for design and printing with ABS material, a set of connecting mechanisms has been created, allowing for flexible adjustment of camera angles within a certain space.

2.4. Differential Steering Analysis of Micro Intelligent Vehicles

Differential steering generates steering torque by controlling the speed difference between the left and right wheels of the vehicle, thereby causing the vehicle to turn. Differential steering can provide the required steering force by increasing the speed of the inner wheel or decreasing the speed of the outer wheel.

Differential is a mechanical device used in a vehicle's transmission system, whose main function is to make the wheels move at different speeds, so that the vehicle can travel better. The basic principle of differential is achieved through the combination of gear transmission and differential gears.

The entire differential steering control logic is shown in Figure 2.

The specific differential steering control logic may vary depending on the vehicle type, differential transmission system, and electric suspension system design. In addition, the control of differential steering also needs to consider safety and stability to ensure that the vehicle remains stable and controllable during differential steering. Therefore, in practical applications, the differential steering control logic requires professional modeling, validation, and adjustment to achieve the best results.

3. Driver Circuit Design

3.1. Circuit Principle and Component Selection

The main control board of the circuit board uses STM32 as the intelligent control center, mainly including the main control circuit module, motor drive module, sensor module, and UART module. The STM32 chip controls the TB6612 chip to drive a DC motor to achieve vehicle movement.

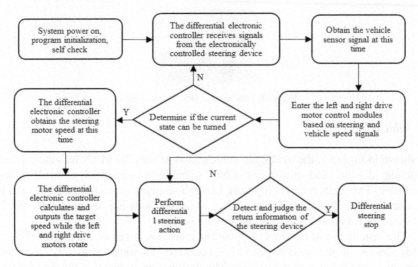

Figure 2. Control logic for differential steering

The GY-85 sensor module is used to measure the attitude and direction of intelligent vehicles, achieving navigation and positioning. The circuit board provides various regulated power supplies and LDO regulated power supplies to ensure stable power supply of the system. The smart car can communicate with other devices through the UART module and the CH340 serial port. The circuit board is equipped with Type-C and USB interfaces for convenient data transmission and charging.

3.2. Circuit Module Implementation

Considering the stability, reliability, efficiency, practicality, and simplicity of the system, Altium Designer was used in the design process of this article for schematic and PCB design, fully considering the electrical characteristics of each functional module and their coupling.

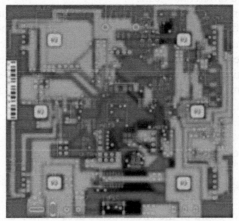

Figure 3. PCB diagram of the circuit board

The modules that are susceptible to interference have added electromagnetic shielding measures to prevent external interference. Figure 3 shows the PCB layout.

3.3. Sensor Module

The sensor module mainly consists of a GY-85 gyroscope and related circuits. The GY-85 gyroscope integrates sensor modules of a three-axis accelerometer, a three-axis gyroscope, and a three-axis magnetometer.

3.4. UART Module

The main function of the UART part is to communicate with computers or other external devices. It is a serial communication module that can convert data into serial signals for transmission, thereby achieving data exchange with other devices.

4. Deep Learning Intelligent Vehicle Software Design

4.1. Track Data Extraction and Optimization Processing

By using the Canny edge detection algorithm, the actual edges in the image can be identified as much as possible in road recognition, while minimizing the probability of missed detection of real edges and false detection of not-an-edge. This algorithm can determine whether the position of the edge point is closest to the actual edge point, or the minimum deviation between the edge point and the actual edge point caused by noise. The edge points detected by the operator should have a one-to-one correspondence with the actual edge points.

4.2. Identification of Road Signs

Using Pytorch to train the model can accurately identify landmarks. We need to prepare training datasets and testing datasets. In Python, reading datasets requires two classes: Dataset and DataLoader. Dataset is responsible for reading data, and the read content includes each data and its corresponding label; The image is labeled. The DataLoader is responsible for packaging the data read by the Dataset and then feeding it into the neural network in batches. Record the changes in the training and testing processes through Tensorboard, define the number of training sessions, testing sessions, training rounds, start time, and end time. After each round of training, save the trained model.

Table 1. Results of Target Recognition

Label	Predicted as 1 (predicted object)	Predicted as 0 (no object predicted)
1 (presence of objects)	True (TP)	False Negative (FN)
0 (no object present)	False positive (FP)	True Negative (TN)

After loading GPU on PyTorch for training, you can view the trained model curves. By observing the model curves, it may be found that some models perform poorly during the marking stage, resulting in significant fluctuations in the model curves. To evaluate the effectiveness of target detection, a table can be used to display the evaluation results as shown in table 1.

$$Accuracy=(TP+TN)/(TP+FN+TN+F\_P) \tag{1}$$

$$Accuracy=TP/(TP+FP) \tag{2}$$

$$Recall\ rate=TP/(TP+FN) \tag{3}$$

Result analysis: As shown in table 1, this design conducted on-site research on the model and loaded it into the intelligent vehicle designed in this design.

4.3. Programming

Install the official system image on the Jetson AGX Orin platform, configure the environment, and install opencv, sys, torch, etc. Opening Python on the terminal and programming is extremely inconvenient. To achieve this, it is necessary to install the Pychar IDE, which facilitates program modification and debugging. Use Python to lead the entry and import other written programs.

Define global speed and global variables. Choosing the range of HSV is crucial for road recognition, and it is particularly important to follow the path. By using a camera to identify the road, in addition to relying on the difference in speed between the left and right wheels, the image identification value can also be adjusted. The resolution of the image captured by the camera is 640x640, with offset representing the identification value, and x being the x-axis of the maximum resolution value. Offset=x-320 is the most central marking position. A value greater than 320 indicates that the smart car needs to lean to the left, while a value less than 320 indicates the opposite. In addition, each section of the road is assigned a speed, identification value, and two wheel speed separately. The following is the assignment of two-wheel speeds:

The following is the assignment of two-wheel speeds:

$$Rightspeed=(speed)*(1-speed\_e)-100+245+right\_speed\_limit$$

$$Leftspeed=(-(speed)*(1+speed\_e)-135-100+limit\_left\_speed)$$

In summary, the program flowchart is shown in Figure 4.

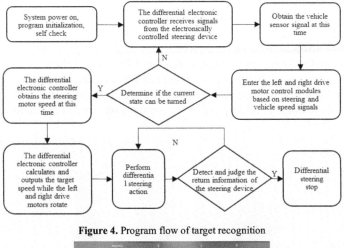

Figure 4. Program flow of target recognition

Figure 5. Identifying pedestrian crossings and stopping

4.4. Practical Testing of Micro Intelligent Vehicles

The micro intelligent vehicle was tested under the selected urban road conditions. The smart car detects pedestrian crossings and uphill signs after passing a left turn from the starting point. The road signs start to stop for one second after the pixel value in the image is greater than or equal to the set value. This process is shown in Figure 5.

After the turn, followed by a deceleration sign, the processing speed of Jetson AGX Orin can handle this situation. Upon recognizing the deceleration sign, perform the third action of deceleration - deceleration driving. During deceleration driving, a T-shaped intersection will appear, so it is necessary to increase the left wheel speed during deceleration driving. Slow down and continue driving until the speed limit sign is lifted, and perform the fourth action - restore driving speed. The deceleration section is shown in Figure 6.

Immediately after, the S-bend arrived. The purpose of setting up this S-turn is to test the flexibility and stability of the smart car. The center of gravity of the smart car designed in this design is low, and the wheelbase is reasonable, making the smart car more sensitive and able to run the S-turn perfectly. After turning S and reaching the intersection, the Canny detection will detect all road surfaces, which may lead to the possibility of the smart car driving in both directions. So, this design added the fifth action at the intersection - straight ahead at the intersection. When the smart car reaches an intersection and recognizes the intersection, the speed limit on the left and right wheels is set by the actual direction of the smart car's deflection. After passing the intersection, enter a major right turn and turn left at the traffic lights. The S-turn test tests the flexibility and stability of smart cars. The center of gravity of the smart car designed in this design is low, and the wheelbase is reasonable, making the smart car more sensitive and able to run the S-turn perfectly. After turning S and reaching the intersection, the Canny detection will detect all road surfaces, which may lead to the possibility of the smart car driving in both directions. This design added the fifth action at the intersection - straight ahead at the intersection. When the smart car reaches an intersection and recognizes the intersection, the speed limit on the left and right wheels is set by the actual direction of the smart car's deflection. After passing the intersection, enter a big right turn and turn left at the traffic lights.

Figure 6. Deceleration section   **Figure 7.** Recognition of red light stop and prepare to turn left

Due to the presence of numerous road signs during the movement of stopping at traffic lights and turning left, errors are prone to occur. So in this design, a program that only recognizes traffic lights when recognizing left turn signs is added to the program. When the red light is recognized and reaches the set pixel value, the sixth action is executed - parking. It is important to note whether the parking position is within the line, as shown in Figure 7.

Until the green light comes on, recognize the green light and perform the seventh action - drive forward and start ranging. Turn left, recognize the left turn sign and start measuring the distance from the traffic lights. After reaching the set distance value, perform the eighth action - turn left.

When the smart car completes a left turn, it begins to recognize the finish line and executes the ninth action - delay the set time and stop, causing the smart car to run past the finish line and stop.

5. Conclusion

The artificial intelligence driving technology based on YOLOv5 is a visual perception technology based on urban road recognition, which can achieve autonomous navigation and obstacle avoidance for intelligent vehicle autonomous driving. Yolov5 is an efficient object detection algorithm that can achieve real-time detection while maintaining high accuracy. In the field of intelligent vehicle autonomous driving, YOLOv5 can be used to detect objects such as roads, vehicles, pedestrians, and traffic signs, thereby helping intelligent vehicles achieve autonomous navigation and obstacle avoidance. Based on Yolov5's artificial intelligence driving technology combined with Canny detection, a complete artificial intelligence driving system is implemented. At the same time, for the purpose of ensuring the safety of artificial intelligence driving, it is also necessary to process and analyze data in real-time, as well as conduct real-time risk assessment and decision-making.

Artificial intelligence driving technology based on YOLOv5 is an efficient, accurate, and real-time visual perception technology that can provide autonomous navigation and obstacle avoidance capabilities for unmanned vehicles. It is one of the important directions for the development of future artificial intelligence driving technology. The disruptive transformation effect of the development of autonomous driving technology on the automotive manufacturing industry and the boosting effect on modern industrial upgrading will gradually become apparent. It has great advantages in solving road congestion, air pollution, and traffic accidents, and can bring huge benefits to society. Further research is highly necessary.

Acknowledgment

This project is supported by the project of scientific research and basic ability improvement for young and middle-aged teachers of Guangxi universities（2022KY1781）

References

[1]   Giannoulas J. V., Mosxopoulou H., Drosos C. V. The contribution of unmanned systems to updating forest maps. International Conference on Remote Sensing and Geoinformation of Environment, 2018, 10773: 107731I.

[2]   Thompson W., Fleming R., Creem-Regehr S., et al. Visual perception from a computer graphics perspective[M]. Taylor and Francis; CRC Press: 2013-12-12.

[3]   Ling L., Tao J., Wu G. Pedestrian detection and feedback application based on YOLOv5s and deep SORT[C]. Proceedings of the 34th China Conference on Control and Decision Making, 2022: 456-461 (in Chinese).

[4]   Oscar R, C. J R,Oleg S, et al. Fast template match algorithm for spatial object detection using a stereo vision system for autonomous navigation[J]. Measurement, 2023, 220: 113299.

[5]   Vikram Raja, Dhruv Talwar, Akilesh Manchikanti & Sunil Jha. Autonomous navigation for mobile robots with sensor fusion technology[J]. Industry 4.0 and Advanced Manufacturing, 2022, 2: 13-23.

[6]   Xin Xiong, Runan Huang, Cuixian He. Research on intelligent path planning technology of logistics robots based on Giraph architecture[J]. International Journal of Computing Science and Mathematics, 2022, 16(3): 252-264.

[7]   Wang, Zengxi, Zhang, Qingyu, Jia, Tong;Zhang, Sulin. Research on control algorithm of a automatic driving robot based on improved model predictive control[J]. Journal of Physics: Conference Series, 2021, 1920(1): 012116.

[8]   Qingyong, Liu. Research on visual recognition method of unmanned driving based on deep learning[J]. Journal of Physics: Conference Series, 2021, 2010(1): 012001.

[9]   Futao N., Jian Z., Ertugrul T. Development of a moving vehicle identification framework using structural vibration response and deep learning algorithms[J]. Mechanical Systems and Signal Processing, 2023, 201: 110667.

[10] Ruiyuan Liu, Jian Mao. Research on improved canny edge detection algorithm[J]. MATEC Web of Conferences, 2018, .232: 3053 (in Chinese).

[11] Faheem Zaid Bin, Ishaq Abid, Rustam Furqan, et al. Image watermarking using least significant bit and canny edge detection[J]. Sensors, 2023, 23(3): 1210.

[12] Bai, Y. Accurate obstacle prediction method in unmanned vehicle driving [J]. Advances in Transportation Studies, 2022, 4: 3-14.

[13] Zheng C. Bayesian network based computer vision algorithm for vehicle classification from incomplete data[C]. Proceedings of 2017 2nd International Conference on Computational Modeling, Simulation and Applied Mathematics (CMSAM 2017). DEStech Publications, 2017: 453-458.

[14] Jinbiao Zhu, Dongshu Wang, Jikai Si. Flexible behavioral decision making of mobile robot in dynamic environment[J]. IEEE Transactions on Cognitive and Developmental Systems, 2023, 15(1): 134-149.

[15] Liu Haowen,Li Ripeng. Design of stepper motor driver based on STM32[J]. Journal of Physics: Conference Series, 2021, 2082(1): 012009.

[16] Jian Huang. Development of DC motor drive based on TB6612[C]. Proceedings of the 5th International Conference on Frontiers of Manufacturing Science and Measuring Technology (FMSMT 2017), 2017, 737-740.

[17] Fengyun L., Shaohua L., Shaobo H., et al. Dynamical analysis and accelerated adaptive backstepping control of MEMS triaxial gyroscope with output constraints[J]. Nonlinear Dynamics, 2023, 111(18): 17123-17140.

[18] Wanzhen L., Di L., Lingzhi Z., et al. Design of a sensor terminal serial communication module for power transmission and distribution equipment based on data protocol of sensors in Internet of Things[P]. State Grid Information and Telecommunication Group Co., Ltd. (China), 2022 (in Chinese).

[19] Zhang Lei, Li, Dezhong. Research on mobile robot target recognition and obstacle avoidance based on vision[J]. Journal of Internet Technology, 2018, 19(6): 1879-1892.

[20] Qingyong, Liu. Research on visual recognition method of unmanned driving based on deep learning[J]. Journal of Physics: Conference Series, 2021, 2010(1): 012001.

[21] Qilie Cai;Qiang Wang;Yulong Zhang, Zhibo He, Yuhong Zhang. LWDNet-A lightweight water-obstacles detection network for unmanned surface vehicles[J]. Robotics and Autonomous Systems, 2023, 166: 104453.

[22] Mohammad Zohaib, Muhammad Ahsan, Mudassir Khan, Jamshed Iqbal. A featureless approach for object detection and tracking in dynamic environments[J]. PloS one, 2023, 18(1): e0280476.

[23] Monga V., Li Y. Eldar Y C. Algorithm unrolling: interpretable, Efficient Deep Learning for Signal and Image Processing[J]. IEEE Signal Processing Magazine, 2021, 38(2):18-44.

Artificial Intelligence, Medical Engineering and Education
Z.B. Hu et al. (Eds.)
doi:10.3233/ATDE231362

Inverse Method to Study the Effects of Factors of the Curve on Traffic Flow

Lanxiang WEI[a], Yujuan LIANG[b,1]

[a] *School of Intelligent Manufacturing, Nanning University, Nanning, China*
[b] *School of Mathematics and Physics, Hechi University, Hechi, China*

Abstract. The curve is a very typical traffic bottleneck. When turning, the vehicle must slow down, otherwise they will likely fly to the outside of the corner due to inertia. The objective practice shows that the bigger the bend curvature is, the slower the speed permitted is when vehicle turning. Therefore, based on the classical NaSch traffic flow model, setting up a cellular automaton model including a corner on the condition of open boundary, and if the bend curvature and the maximum speed of vehicle permitted on the curve is inversely proportional, we can separately study the effects of the curvature and the arc length of the curve on traffic flow. The results of research show that the influence of the bend curvature on traffic flow is greater than that of the arc length, which is quite similar to the results obtained by other research methods. Thus, we can think that in a certain range of error, this method is desirable.

Keywords. curve; curvature; arc length; NaSch model; bottleneck effect.

1. Introduction

Curves are a key part of the road, and due to their low curvature, vehicles are less stable at curves, which can easily lead to traffic congestion and traffic accidents [1]. Therefore, curves are regarded as a typical traffic bottleneck. In order to improve the capacity of curves, various traffic flow models have been used to study the traffic characteristics of curves. The cellular automata model is a rule-based model whose rules can be flexibly adjusted according to the needs, and it can effectively simulate various real traffic situations on the computer. Therefore, it has been widely used and developed in the study of traffic flow [2-8]. References [3] assumed that the inclination angle of a curve superelevation is directly proportional to the permissible critical speed of the curve based on the cellular automata model and investigated the effect of superelevation on traffic flow. The results of this study are similar to those obtained by other methods and can truly reflect the actual situation. References [4], also based on the cellular automata model, assumed that the inclination of a ramp is inversely related to the maximum speed of a vehicle on the ramp, and investigated the effects of the inclination and length of a motorway ramp on traffic flow. The results are also consistent with the actual traffic situation.

In this paper, a single-lane cellular automaton model including curves is developed under open boundary conditions using the NaSch traffic flow model for cellular automata. At the same time, it is assumed that the curvature of the curve is inversely proportional

---

[1] Corresponding Author: Yujuan LIANG, E-mail: wlx071102@163.com.

to the maximum permissible vehicle speed of the vehicle on the curve. On this basis, the effects of curvature and arc length of the curve on traffic flow are investigated separately, which provides a new research method to explore the traffic flow characteristics of the curve. In addition, this method can also be applied in quantitative analysis of vehicle tolls [9], vehicle monitoring [10], vehicle speed measurements [11-12], and intersection measurements [13].

2. Theoretical Foundation

According to Newton's second law of motion, when a particle moving on the curved section, it must be impacted by a centripetal force F:

$$F = ma = m\frac{v^2}{r} \tag{1}$$

Here m, a, v respectively stands for the particle mass, centripetal acceleration and linear speed along the curve tangent direction, and r is the radius of the curve. F and a are in the same direction, which point to the center of curvature.

The vehicle is not always doing linear motion, sometimes uphill and downhill, sometimes turning and changing to do curvilinear motion [2-6]. In order to simplify the problem, taking the vehicle as particle, when the vehicle is cornering, formula (1) still applies. Assuming μ is the static friction coefficient between the wheels and the road, and g is the acceleration of gravity. For planar curve, when vehicle cornering, the centripetal force F is given by normal static friction μmg, then [2]:

$$m\frac{v^2}{r} = \mu mg \tag{2}$$

$$v = \sqrt{r\mu g} \tag{3}$$

（3）type is the limited speed of vehicle safety turning, known as the critical speed, which depends on the parameters of r, μ, g, and usually g is a constant. Only when the speed is below the critical speed can vehicle turn safely. But for the super corner, namely, the outside is higher than the inside corners, supposing the dip of ultra-high as θ (θ is smaller), the critical speed of turning safely is given in reference [2]:

$$v = \sqrt{rg(\theta + \mu)} \tag{4}$$

Compared (4) and (3), obviously, the critical speed of the ultra-high bend is larger, and the passing speed allowed becomes larger with the ultra-high value increases.

The formula (3), (4) shows that the vehicle must slow down in order to safely pass the curve. In addiction, the smaller the bend radius is, the bigger curvature is, hence, bottleneck limiting effect is more obvious. Vehicles on the straight part is equivalent to the fast car and on the bend part is equivalent to the slow car. Therefore, here, we similarly assume the bend curvature and the maximum speed of the vehicle on the curved section is directly proportional, using cellular automata model to study the effect of the curvature and arc length of the curve on traffic flow, and compare the results of the research with that of other methods.

3. Model and Rules

In order to simplify the problem, assuming that the road system researched containing only one corner, and only one type of cars, and path length is by 1D discrete lattice 1000 cellular structure chain. Each lattice point in every moment is either empty or occupied by a car. The states of the vehicle is standed by v, $v \in (0, v_{max})$, and v_{max} is the maximum speed of the vehicle. The maximum speed is divided into two types: on the straight section, the maximum value is v_{max1}, while v_{max2} is on the curve section, and $v_{max1} > v_{max2}$. Delay probability of vehicles on the road differs because of different road conditions and various vehicle dynamic performance. Because here we respectively take different maximum speed on straight section and curve section , and here is only one type of cars, therefore, we take the same delay probability for all vehicles. The actual road is an open system; therefore, we adopt the open boundary condition. The rules of the classic NaSch [7] traffic flow model of the cellular automata is amended as follows:

1) Define the maximum speed: If vehicle is on the curve section, take $v_{max} = v_{max2}$, else, take $v_{max} = v_{max1}$;

2) Acceleration: $v_n(t) \rightarrow \min (v_n(t)+1, v_{max})$;

3) Deceleration: $v_n(t) \rightarrow \min (v_n(t), gap_n(t))$;

4) Random deceleration with probability p: $v_n(t) \rightarrow \max (v_n(t)-1, 0)$;

5) Vehicle motion renew: $x_n(t) \rightarrow x_n(t)+v_n(t)$.

Here, $v_n(t)$ and $x_n(t)$ are respectively the speed and the position of vehicle n at the moment of t, and $x_{n+1}(t)$ is the position of vehicle $n+1$ at the moment of t. $Gap_n(t) = x_{n+1}(t) - x_n(t)-1$ denotes the number of empty cells between vehicle n and its near prior vehicle $n+1$ at the moment of t. The rule of this model is added first step compared with classic NaSch model. All vehicles on the road in each time step synchronously update their speed and position in accordance with the above rules.

4. Numerical Results and Analysis

The parameters of the model are set as follows: a time step is for 1s; each lattice point length is 7.5m; the total length L of the road is 7.5km; the stochastic delay probability of vehicle p=0.25; to simplify the problem, the lattice is a unit of length and dimensionless processing, take v_{max1}=5, corresponding to that, the actual speed is 135km/h; take v_{max2}=4,3,2,1, and its corresponding actual speed is 108km/h, 81km/h,54km/h, 27km/h, respectively. Because the critical speed of vehicle safely turning decreases with the increase of the bend curvature and thus, assuming that the curvature S of the curve is inversely proportional to the maximum speed v_{max2} of vehicle allowed in curved section [2-3], that is $S=k/v_{max2}$. Here k is the proportional coefficient. Take k=1, and then S =1/v_{max2}. When v_{max2}=4, 3, 2, 1, S=1/4, 1/3, 1/2, 1. S=1/4 stands that the bend radius is very large while the curvature is very small; S=1 stands that the bend radius is minimum, while the curvature is maximum. Let the initial density of vehicles is 0.5, and vehicles are randomly distributed on the lattice with the speed of v. For the road, the disappearing probability of vehicles on the right boundary is 1 and the entering probability on the left boundary increases gradually from 0.05 to 1. If N is the total number of vehicles on the road at time t, the density of vehicles, average speed and average flow are defined as follows:

The density of vehicles: $\rho = N/L$

Average speed: $v_t = \dfrac{1}{N}\sum_{n=1}^{N} v_n(t)$, $\bar{v} = \dfrac{1}{T}\sum_{t=t_0}^{t=t_0+T-1} v_t$

Average flow: $J = \rho \bar{v}$

Simulated evolution total time step is 10×10^5. The first $t_0 = 5 \times 10^5$ time steps are discarded in order to remove the transient effects and then the data are recorded in successive $T = 5 \times 10^5$ time steps. The obtained average speed v_t for each time step is the average value of $v_n(t)$, and average speed $\bar{v}$ for each run is the average value of v_t at the last $T = 5 \times 10^5$ time steps, then the average flow of $J = \rho \bar{v}$. In order to eliminate the influence of randomness of the results, retake an average of 5 samples, and the simulation results is shown in Figure 1~Figure. 4. Each point on the graph is an average of 5 runs.

4.1. Effect of Curvature on Traffic Flow

Figure 1 and Figure 2 are the relationships of the average flow, average speed of the road system changing with the entering probability under different bend curvature. We can know from Figure 1:

（1）The flow increases in linearity with the increasing of entering probability of vehicle, and until it reaches a saturation flow platform, capacity reaches a maximum value;

（2）The flow platform increases with the decrease of curvature, and the corresponding saturation flow values of $S=1$, 1/2, 1/3, 1/4 are 0.259, 0.399, 0.476, 0.508;

（3）The critical entering probability of the saturation flow decreases while the length of the platform of the flow increases with the increase of the curvature, and the corresponding critical entering probability of $S=1$, 1/2, 1/3, 1/4 are 0.3, 0.48, 0.62, 0.72, namely the greater the curvature, the earlier the system entries crowded traffic state. Thus, bend bottleneck effect significantly enhanced with the increase of the bend curvature.

It is clearly shown by Figure 2 that:

（1）There is a greater speed platform in the low entering probability range. In the case of the low entering probability, vehicles on the road are less, and their interactions are weak, and the movement of the vehicles is in larger freedom so they can travel to the desired speed, thus the flow chart reflects that on smaller entering probability range, the flow increases linearly with the increase of entering probability;

（2） hen the entering probability is greater than the critical entering probability, the speed decreases rapidly, and then keep a certain value unchangs, and then the second speed platform appears with smaller value, thus the system comes into a forced flow state in low speed, and vehicles queue with slow.The corresponding compulsory flow speed of $S=1$, 1/2, 1/3, 1/4 are 0.749 (20.22km/h), 1.714 (46.28km/h), 2.866 (77.38km/h), 3.681 (99.39km/h) which are corresponding to the saturated flow values in Figure 1, the forced flow state disturbance often make the system have a traffic jam;

（3）The critical entering probability decreases with the increase of the curvature, therefore, the greater the curvature,the earlier the system comes into the crowded traffic flow state, and the corresponding critical entering probability is the same with Figure 1;

(4) The smaller the curvature is, the greater the value of speed platform is, the smaller bend bottleneck effect is. It is obvious that speed and entering probability diagram can also show that the effects of the bend curvature on traffic flow is great.

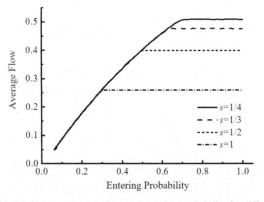

Figure 1. Relationship between average flow and entering probability for different values of *S*

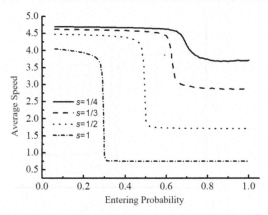

Figure 2. Relationship between mean speed and entering probability for different values of *S*

4.2. Effect of Arc Length on Traffic Flow

In order to highlight the effect of the arc length of the curve on traffic flow, take constant curvature and change of arc length to do numerical simulation. The parameters of the model are: curvature $S=1/3$, arc length $C=10$cells, 30cells, 50cells, 70cells. The simulation results are shown as Figure 3~ Figure 4. it is obvious that the two diagrams are respectively similar to Figure 1 and Figure 2. ①The effects curve of different arc length are relatively close; ②With the increase of the arc length, the saturated flow value, average speed and the critical entering probability are reduced in small amplitude. Obviously, the arc length of the curve has greater impact on traffic flow, but which is smaller than that of curvature.

Comparing the results of the method and that of literature [1], although the method can not study the effects of friction coefficient in the curve section on traffic flow, its researching results and that of method in literature [1] are similar when studying the effects of radius (or curvature) and arc length of the curve on traffic flow, and they are consistent with the actual situation which can explain that the influencing factors of the bend bottleneck limits on traffic flow. Therefore, this assumed researching method is desirable.

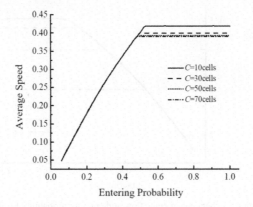

Figure 3. Relationship between mean flow and entering probability for different values C

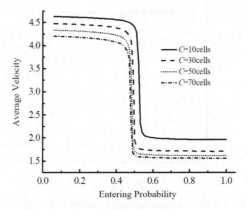

Figure 4. Relationship between mean velocity and entering probability for different values C

5. Conclusion

In this paper, the single-lane cellular automata model including curves is constructed under open boundary conditions based on the classical NaSch traffic flow model. It is assumed that the curvature of a curve is inversely proportional to the maximum permissible speed of a vehicle on the curve, and the study focuses on the effects of curve curvature and arc length on traffic flow. The results show that the effect of curve curvature on traffic flow is more significant than the effect of arc length on traffic flow, which is similar to the results obtained using other methods. Therefore, it can be concluded that this method is feasible within a certain margin of error and can truly reflect the complexity of traffic flow on curves. The conclusions drawn from the above study are of great practical value for optimising the traffic congestion problem in the bottleneck area of curves and improving the stability of traffic flow operation.

Acknowledgment

This project is supported by Nanning University Professor Cultivation Engineering Project (Project No.: 2020JSGC01).

References

[1] Shi Yingjie. Vehicle movement modeland stability analysis of urban expressway curve[D]. Qingdao: Qingdao University of Technology, 2018: 1- 6 (in Chinese).
[2] Liang Yujuan. A study on properties of traffic flow based on road turning impact[J]. Gong Lu, 2011, 3: 115-118 (in Chinese).
[3] Liang Yujuan. Dynamic analysis and numerical simulation on the road turning with Ultra-High[J]. Internation Conference on Computing, Information and   Con trol, 2011, Part VI, 236 : 173-178.
[4] Li Shengchun, Kong Lingjiang, Liu Muren. The effect of uphill gradient bottleneck on freeway traffic [J]. Guangxi Sciences, 2008, 15(1): 47-51 (in Chinese).
[5] Rui Jiang, Wu Qingsong, and Wang Binghong. Cellular automata model simulating traffic interactions between on-ramp and main road [J]. Physical review E, 2002, 66:036104-1~036104-6.
[6] Pan Jiaxiu, Xueyu, Liang Yujuan, et al. Effect of road structure on the capacity of a signalized road intersection[J]. Chinese Physics B, 2009, 18(10): 4169-4176.
[7] Dai Shiqiang, Lei Li, Dong Liyun. Analysis of traffic flow at intersections near ramps of overhanging freeways[J]. Acta Mechanica Sinica, 2003, 35(5):513-518 (in Chinese).
[8] Nagel K, Schreckenberg M. A cellular automaton model for freeway traffic[J]. Phys. I France, 1992, 2:2221-2229.
[9] Razib Hayat Khan. Quantitative analysis of RFID based vehicle toll collection system using UML and SPN[J]. International Journal of Information Technology and Computer Science, 2022, 14(4): 25-33.
[10] Nur Kumala Dewi. Review of vehicle surveillance using iot in the smart transportation concept[J]. International Journal of Engineering and Manufacturing, 2021, 11(1): 29-36.
[11] Ali Tourani, Asadollah Shahbahrami, Alireza Akoushideh, et al. Motion-based vehicle speed measurement for intelligent transportation systems[J]. International Journal of Image, Graphics and Signal Processing, 2019, 11(4): 42-54.
[12] Abdorreza Joe Afshany, Ali Tourani, Asadollah Shahbahrami, et al. Parallel implementation of a video-based vehicle speed measurement system for municipal roadways[J]. International Journal of Intelligent Systems and Applications, 2019, 11(11): 25-37.
[13] Yuanli GU, Lei Yu. Study on optimization of phase offset at adjacent intersections[J]. International Journal of Intelligent Systems and Applications, 2010, 2(1): 30-36.

510

Artificial Intelligence, Medical Engineering and Education
Z.B. Hu et al. (Eds.)
© 2024 The Authors.
This article is published online with Open Access by IOS Press and distributed under the terms
of the Creative Commons Attribution Non-Commercial License 4.0 (CC BY-NC 4.0).
doi:10.3233/ATDE231363

Designing an Improved VMD-CNNs-DS Algorithm for the Port Crane Bearing Fault Diagnosis

Shu WU[a,b,1], Xinxin LEI[a], Jinghua ZHANG[c], Xing CHEN[a]

a School of Transportation and Logistics Engineering, Wuhan University of Technology, Wuhan, China
b Engineering Research Center of Port Logistics Technology and Equipment, Ministry of Education, China
c CCCC Second Harbor Consultants Co., Ltd., Wuhan, China
ORCiD ID: https://orcid.org/0000-0002-9175-892X

Abstract. Accurate diagnosis of bearing faults is crucial for detecting faults in rotating machinery. However, the variability and complexity of recorded vibration signals present a significant challenge in distinguishing unique characteristic fault features. To address this issue, we proposed VMD-CNNs-DS, a novel bearing fault diagnosis algorithm based on data-level and decision-level bipolar fusion network. The adaptive variational mode decomposition (VMD) method based on parameter optimization is employed to transform multiple sensor raw vibration signals into time-frequency analysis. The convolutional neural network (CNN) takes as input a graph of the features of the vibration signals from the two sensors. Improve DS theory for decision blending. An extensive evaluation of the fault diagnosis performance of VMD-CNNs-DS on various data sets shows that VMD-CNNs-DS achieves better results than a single CNN network model by fusing complementary or conflicting evidences from different models and sensors and adapting to different load conditions.

Keywords. Bearing fault; Image classification; DS evidence theory; Information Fusion; Deep learning

1. Introduction

Rolling bearings, as crucial components of cranes and other rotating machinery, are prone to failure, making them one of the primary causes of machine malfuctions. Therefore, detecting and diagnosing bearing issues is ensuring proper functioning of rotating machinery. Liu et al. assert that bearing failure signals can manifest through various means, such as vibration, temperature, acoustic emission, current, and speed signals [1]. At the same time, as identified by Zhang et al. vibration signals contain abundant information about machine health [2]. Diagnosis and monitoring progressive bearing failures in rotating machinery through vibration signal measurements have been employed for some time now and have become more cost-effective and reliable in recent years [3-4]. Therefore, serve as the foundation for effective fault detection and diagnosis.

Over the past two decades, extensive research has been conducted on conventional

---

[1] Corresponding Author: Shu WU, E-mail: wushu@whut.edu.cn.

fault diagnosis methods based on feature extraction from vibration signals [5-6]. Liu et al. and Cheng et al. utilized the EMD method for signal decomposition [7-8]. However, EMD is a recursive mode decomposition technique that accumulates errors gradually during the decomposition process. To overcome these limitations, Dragomiretskiy et al. introduced a variable-scale processing method called VMD in 2014 [9]. Subsequently, Liu et al. proposed a feature extraction method based on parameter-optimized VMD and sample entropy, which significantly improved the accuracy of rolling bearing fault diagnosis [10]. However, due to limited prior knowledge available for selecting features, choosing appropriate features becomes increasingly challenging over time. Consequently, intelligent deep learning techniques have been employed to address these challenges in bearing fault diagnosis research.

However, in challenging operational environments, the reliability of fault diagnosis solely based on single-sensor data may be compromised. Therefore, the incorporation of an ensemble of classifiers can significantly enhance the accuracy and robustness of the system [11]. Due to their strong information fusion capability, CNN also exhibit great potential for "multi-information fusion" in recognition tasks [12,13]. In the field of rotating machinery fault signal recognition, Li et al. proposed IDSCNN, a novel bearing fault diagnosis algorithm based on ensemble deep convolutional neural networks and an improved Dempster-Shafer based evidence fusion approach [14]. Hoang et al. employed deep belief networks to train and classify signals from different sensors and implemented fusion decisions using DS theory [15].

While contemporary research based on CNN and DS theory fusion has achieved some success in rolling bearing fault diagnosis, there are still some shortcomings. Building upon the aforementioned research, this paper presents a novel framework for bearing fault diagnosis by integrating multiple Convolutional Neural Networks (CNNs) and enhancing DS evidence theory for dual fusion at both the data and decision levels.

The main contributions of this study are as follows:

- The optimized VMD method is employed to decompose the sensor vibration signal, enabling extraction of non-sensitive fault information embedded within the signal. Moreover, a novel approach is proposed for generating signal feature maps that effectively preserve the time-frequency domain characteristics of the signal.
- The effectiveness of AlexNet, VggNet, and ResNet in the diagnosis of rolling bearing faults is evaluated. The proposed fusion model addresses two inherent limitations in the traditional DS evidence theory: considering the significance of evidence subjects and resolving conflicts arising from diverse sources.
- A novel algorithm is proposed that integrates CNNs and multi-sensor information based on the DS evidence theory for crane gearbox bearing fault diagnosis. This algorithm achieves two levels of information fusion, operating at both the data layer and decision layer, enabling the combination of multiple uncertain pieces of evidence to generate fused decision results by incorporating consistent information while excluding conflicting information.

2. Materials and Methods

2.1. Pre-Processing Methods

The raw gas pedal signals captured by two sensors during bearing failure experiments were processed using a sliding window approach, employing a specific window size and shift step. This method ensures overlap of data points between consecutive samples, satisfying the training requirements of convolutional neural networks and preventing loss of signal edge features that may occur with conventional interception methods. After conducting experiments, it has been determined that the highest accuracy of 99.6% can be achieved by using a sample length of approximately 600 for the test set. Therefore, in this experiment, utilized a sliding window with a size of 600 and a shift step of 400 to scan the signal and generate original data samples.

2.2. Variational Mode Decomposition (VMD)

The selection of the VMD parameter combination [k, α] can significantly impact the effectiveness of decomposition, and improper parameter choices may result in false component results such as under-decomposition or overdecomposition. To address this, current research focuses on adaptively optimizing the parameter combinations in VMD. In this paper, we employ a trial-and-error parameter selection method combined with the general rule of VMD model parameter selection to determine the appropriate model parameters. Through multiple training and testing experiments, we identify the parameters that yield optimal test results. After conducting extensive experiments, we observe that when using a parameter combination of [3, 5100], the model performs optimally in terms of frequency domain segmentation and effective separation of the components.

2.3. Convolutional Neural Network (CNN)

CNN are a type of deep learning algorithm specifically designed for analyzing two-dimensional data. In fact, researchers have found that CNN consistently outperform artificial neural networks in mechanical fault classification studies involving both large and small datasets [16]. Since the CNN was first used for the fault diagnosis of gearbox bearings and gears in 2016, and the fault diagnosis rate has increased by 6%, various popular CNN models such as LeNet5, AlexNet, GoogLeNet, ResNet, VggNet have been gradually used for the identification and classification of bearing fault signals. The experimental results are shown in Table 1.

Table 1. Comparison between the Results of CNN Model Work

Work	Based on	Dataset	Domain	Goal	Accuracy
Shi et al. [17]	AlexNet	CWRU	Time and frequency	Failure detection	97.92%
	GoogLeNet				89.88%
Kaya et al. [18]	GoogleNet	Own	Time and frequency	Failure detection	96.67%-99.11%
	AlexNet				98.21%-100%
	ResNet				98.25%-100%
	Vgg16				99.12%-100%
Pinedo-Sanchez [19]	AlexNet	IMS/ CWRU	Time and frequency	Failure detection	98.64%-99%
Qian et al. [20]	ResNet	Own	Tim e and frequency	Failure detection	100%
Tang et al. [21]	AlexNet	CWRU	Time and frequency	Failure detection	98.43%
Hemmer et al. [22]	AlexNet	Own	Frequency	Failure detection	91.96%

The ResNet, AlexNet, and VggNet architectures highlighted have demonstrated their effectiveness in identifying and classifying bearing fault signals across various datasets. These networks have shown promising results on diverse datasets. Considering the experimental results of previous studies and considering factors such as model size and network depth, this paper selects a CNN model based on the AlexNet, ResNet18, and Vgg16 network architectures as the fault signal classifier.

2.4. Improved D-S Evidence Theory

This study adopts Wei's proposed method that integrates the degree of difference and exclusion between evidence into the decision-making process, aiming to overcome the constraints of DS evidence theory [23]. Firstly, we calculate the degree of discrepancy and exclusion between each piece of evidence to determine their importance. Secondly, based on their respective importance levels, quantitative determination is conducted along with assigning different weights accordingly. Subsequently, a new body of evidence is obtained through weighted averaging. Finally, we apply the DS combination rule to achieve fusion results.

(1) Calculate the degree of difference between each two pieces of evidence.

Assuming that the corresponding BPAs of the two evidences on the discriminative framework are m_1 and m_2, the corresponding subsets are A_i and A_j, the degree of difference between evidence m_1 and evidence m_2 is defined as

$$\text{dif}(m_1,m_2) = \sum_{A_i \cap A_j = \varnothing} m_1(A_i) \cdot m_2(A_j) \tag{1}$$

Assume that there are n pieces of evidence in the same discriminative frame and if they are identical, their difference degree is defined as 0. The difference degree between evidence m_i and evidence m_j can be calculated using Eq. (3) and is expressed as the difference degree matrix Dif.

$$Dif = \begin{bmatrix} 0 & dif_{12} & \cdots & dif_{1j} & \cdots & dif_{1n} \\ \vdots & \vdots & \ddots & \vdots & \ddots & \vdots \\ dif_{i1} & dif_{i2} & \cdots & dif_{ij} & \cdots & dif_{in} \\ \vdots & \vdots & \ddots & \vdots & \ddots & \vdots \\ dif_{n1} & dif_{n2} & \cdots & dif_{nj} & \cdots & 0 \end{bmatrix} \tag{2}$$

(2) The degree of exclusion of each piece of evidence is determined. The degree of exclusion $\text{Exc}(m_i)$ for evidence m_i is

$$\text{Exc}(m_i) = \sum_{i=1,i\neq j}^{n} dif_{ij}, (i, j = 1, 2, \ldots, n) \tag{3}$$

(3) Weights are assigned to each piece of evidence. The weight w_i of each evidence mi is given by the following equation:

$$w_i = \frac{\left[Exc(mi)\right]^{-1}}{\sum\limits_{i=1}^{n}\left[Exc(mi)\right]^{-1}} \tag{4}$$

(4) New evidence is determined. Based on the weights assigned in Eq. (6), new evidence is obtained by weighted averaging, as shown in Eq. (7):

$$\bar{m} = \sum\limits_{i=1}^{n} w_i m_i, (i = 1, 2, \ldots, n) \tag{5}$$

(5) The fusion results are solved. Based on the new evidence obtained from Eq. (7), the final fusion result can be solved by using DS evidence theory fusion.

3. Experimentation and Data Collection

3.1. Experimental Feature Extraction and Feature Map Generation

The experimental feature maps obtained from various sensors underwent experimental analysis, and sample sets representing different fault types (NOR, IRF1, ORF1, and BEF1) were selected as inputs for training the CNN. Each classification category comprised approximately 778 sample sets. For the training process, 80% of the samples were randomly selected as the training set, while the remaining 20% were used as the test set.

3.2. Evaluation index

In this study, we evaluated the performance metrics of the CNN architecture using several key performance metrics, including accuracy, recall, precision, and F1-score. These metrics are calculated as follows:

$$Accuracy = \frac{TP + TN}{TP + TN + FP + FN} \tag{6}$$

$$\mathrm{Re}\,call = \frac{TP}{TP + FN} \times 100\% \tag{7}$$

$$\mathrm{Pr}\,ecision = \frac{TP}{TP + FP} \times 100\% \tag{8}$$

$$F1 - Score = \frac{2 \times \mathrm{Pr}\,ecision \times Sensitivity}{\mathrm{Pr}\,ecision + Sensitivity} \times 100\% \tag{9}$$

where, TP: true positive, FP: false positive, TN: true negative, and FN: false negative are expressed.

4. Experimental Results

The primary aim of this study is to enhance the CNN architecture and develop a VMD-CNNs-DS network for bearing fault signal feature classification. To achieve this, distinct fault signal image datasets were generated using VMD on original data samples obtained from various sensors. These datasets were then utilized to train improved AlexNet, ResNet, and Vgg16 networks that extracted features from the NOR, IRF1, ORF1, and BEF1 training sets for each sensor. Based on performance analysis, the two best CNN networks were selected, and their SoftMax layer outputs served as input for the DS method which led to determining the VMD-CNNs-DS network architecture. Table 2 presents classification results of different CNNs on the test set.

Table 2. CNN fault feature classification results

Classifier	Signal Source	Test Data	Accuracy
VMD-Vgg16	Sensor1	155	90.1%
	Sensor2	155	89.8%
VMD-ResNet	Sensor1	155	94.7%
	Sensor2	155	94.4%
VMD-AlexNet	Sensor1	155	94.5%
	Sensor2	155	95.0%

According to the results presented in Table 2, it is determined that the VMD-CNNs-DS network proposed in this paper, utilizes the ResNet architecture for fault signal classification from Sensor1, and employs the AlexNet architecture for fault signal classification from Sensor2.The adaptive feature extraction capability of the convolutional network is demonstrated in Fig. 1, showcasing the improved AlexNet and ResNet networks' superior performance in extracting features from the bearing fault signal dataset compared to the original data features.

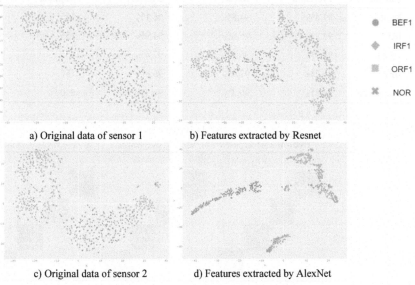

a) Original data of sensor 1   b) Features extracted by Resnet

c) Original data of sensor 2   d) Features extracted by AlexNet

Figure 1. Adaptive extraction of features for visualization

Furthermore, the Table3a-3c presents comprehensive results of various performance metrics for the convolutional networks. Upon careful examination of all the metrics in the table, it is evident that both AlexNet and ResNet convolutional neural networks consistently achieve macro avg values of approximately 95% across all recognition performance metrics. Consequently, we select the outputs from these improved models as inputs to our proposed VMD-CNNs-DS network. Finally, we compare and analyze the classification outcomes of the VMD-CNNs-DS network with those obtained from VMD-ResNet and VMD-AlexNet. Fig. 2 shows confusion matrices for the three identification models.

Table 3. Performance Test Results

(a) VMD-ResNet Performance Test Results

Classes	Precision	Recall	F1-score	Support	Accuracy
NOR	96.6%	92.3%	94.4%	155	92.3%
IRF1	94.8%	94.8%	94.8%	155	94.8%
ORF1	96.1%	94.8%	95.5%	155	94.8%
BEF1	91.5%	96.8%	94.0%	155	96.8%
Macro avg	94.8%	94.7%	94.7%	620	94.7%

(b) VMD-AlexNet Performance Test Results

Classes	Precision	Recall	F1-score	Support	Accuracy
NOR	98.0%	95.5%	96.7%	155	95.5%
IRF1	89.8%	96.8%	93.2%	155	96.8%
ORF1	96.6%	91.6%	94.0%	155	91.6%
BEF1	96.1%	96.1%	96.1%	155	96.1%
Macro avg	95.1%	95.0%	95.0%	620	95.0%

(c) VMD-CNNs-DS Performance Test Results

Classes	Precision	Recall	F1-score	Support	Accuracy
NOR	97.4%	94.8%	96.1%	155	96.1%
IRF1	93.2%	96.8%	94.9%	155	96.8%
ORF1	98.7%	96.1%	97.4%	155	94.8%
BEF1	96.2%	97.4%	96.8%	155	97.4%
Macro avg	96.3%	96.3%	96.3%	620	96.3%

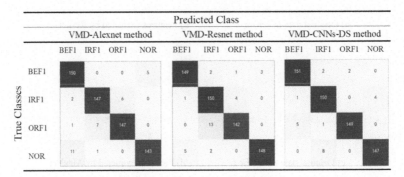

Figure 2. Fault classification situation

It can be observed that CNNs-DS outperforms only one CNN network in terms of accuracy, and Fig. 2 shows the confusion matrix for the bearing fault NOR, IRF1, ORF1, and BEF1 bearing state classification cases. It can be observed that the VMD-CNNs-DS model proposed in this paper outperforms the identification of the bearing states for different wear states in all cases than the CNN network alone. The results indicate a significant improvement in classification accuracy for the proposed VMD-CNNs-DS model compared to the individual VMD-CNN models. This indicates the effectiveness of the fusion of multiple CNN models with the DS evidence theory in improving the fault classification performance for different types of bearing faults.

5. Conclusions

The proposed paper presents an improved model, VMD-CNNs-DS, for bearing fault diagnosis using an integrated approach of DS evidence theory and CNN. Firstly, the VMD decomposition process is optimized by searching for suitable parameter combinations. Secondly, the traditional DS evidence theory is enhanced by incorporating evidence credibility, which helps to resolve paradoxical evidence problems. Furthermore, the mainstream CNN architectures were improved and applied to the bearing dataset for network training and model selection. Experimental results demonstrate that the VMD-CNNs-DS model, with its two-layer fusion of data and decision layers, outperforms single CNN models in handling various common fault bearing classifications. Overall, the proposed approach provides a feasible and robust approach for non-contact, multi-sensor vibration signal fusion combined with CNN recognition, facilitating accurate identification and quantification of bearing faults.

Acknowledgment

This research was funded by the National Key R&D Program of China (No.2022YFB2602300)

References

[1]　Liu Haobin, Yang Fengyu, Yang Zhiyong, et al. Detection method of bearing end surface defects based on yolov5[J]. Failure Analysis and Prevention, 2021, 16(6): 392-397 (in Chinese).

[2]　Zhang Xinpeng, Hu Niaoqing, Hu Lei, et al. A bearing fault diagnosis method based on the low-dimensional compressed vibration signal[J]. Advances in Mechanical Engineering, 2015, 7(7): 1687814015593442.

[3]　Lei Yaguo, Li Naipeng, Guo Liang, et al. Machinery health prognostics: A systematic review from data acquisition to rul prediction[J]. Mechanical systems and signal processing, 2018, 104: 799-834.

[4]　Ahmed H, Nandi A. K. Condition monitoring with vibration signals: Compressive sampling and learning algorithms for rotating machines[M]. John Wiley & Sons, 2020.

[5]　Song Xiangjin, Zhao Wenxiang. A review of rolling bearing fault diagnosis approaches using ac motor signature analysis[J]. Proceedings of the CSEE, 2022, 42(04): 1582-1596 (in Chinese).

[6]　Md. Rayhan Ahmed, Towhidul Islam Robin, Ashfaq Ali Shafin, " Automatic Environmental Sound Recognition (AESR) Using Convolutional Neural Network", International Journal of Modern Education and Computer Science, Vol.12, No.5, pp. 41-54, 2020.

[7]　Liu Bao, Riemenschneider S, Xu Y. Gearbox fault diagnosis using empirical mode decomposition and hilbert spectrum[J]. Mechanical Systems and Signal Processing, 2006, 20(3): 718-734.

[8]　Cheng Junsheng, Yu Dejie, Yang Yu. Fault diagnosis approach based on intrinsic mode singular value decomposition and support vector machines[J]. Acta Automatica Sinica, 2006, 32(3): 475-480 (in Chinese).

[9]   Dragomiretskiy K, Zosso D. Variational mode decomposition[J]. IEEE transactions on signal processing, 2013, 62(3): 531-544.

[10] Liu Jianchang, Quan He, Yu Xia, et al. Rolling bearing fault diagnosis based on parameter optimization VMD and sample entropy[J]. Acta Automatica Sinica, 2022, 48(3): 808-819 (in Chinese).

[11] Ahmed Iqbal, Shabib Aftab, " A Classification Framework for Software Defect Prediction Using Multi-filter Feature Selection Technique and MLP ", International Journal of Modern Education and Computer Science, Vol.12, No.1, pp. 18-25, 2020.

[12] Zhang Lizhi, Jing Luyang, Xu Weixiao, et al. A composite fault diagnosis method of gearbox combining with convolution neural network and DS evidence theory[J]. Mechanical Science and Technology for Aerospace Engineering, 2019, 38: 1582-1588. (in Chinese).

[13] Jaykumar M. Vala, Udesang K. Jaliya, "Deep Learning Network and Renyi-entropy Based Fusion Model for Emotion Recognition Using Multimodal Signals", International Journal of Modern Education and Computer Science, Vol.14, No.4, pp. 67-84, 2022.

[14] Li Shaobo, Liu Guokai, Tang Xianghong, et al. An ensemble deep convolutional neural network model with improved DS evidence fusion for bearing fault diagnosis[J]. Sensors, 2017, 17(8): 1729.

[15] Hoang D. T, Tran X. T, Van M, et al. A deep neural network-based feature fusion for bearing fault diagnosis[J]. Sensors, 2021, 21(1): 244.

[16] Iqbal M, Madan A. K. CNC machine-bearing fault detection based on convolutional neural network using vibration and acoustic signal[J]. Journal of Vibration Engineering & Technologies, 2022, 10(5): 1613-1621.

[17] Shi Xiaoyu, Qiu Gen, Yin Chun, et al. An improved bearing fault diagnosis scheme based on hierarchical fuzzy entropy and alexnet network[J]. IEEE Access, 2021, 9: 61710-61720.

[18] Kaya Y, Kuncan F, ERTUNÇ H. M. A new automatic bearing fault size diagnosis using time-frequency images of cwt and deep transfer learning methods[J]. Turkish Journal of Electrical Engineering and Computer Sciences, 2022, 30(5): 1851-1867.

[19] Pinedo-Sanchez L. A, Mercado-Ravell D. A, Carballo-Monsivais C. A. Vibration analysis in bearings for failure prevention using CNN[J]. Journal of the Brazilian Society of Mechanical Sciences and Engineering, 2020, 42(12): 628.

[20] Qian Lu, Pan Qing, Lv Yaqiong, et al. Fault detection of bearing by resnet classifier with model-based data augmentation[J]. Machines, 2022, 10(7): 521.

[21] Tang Guiji, Tian Yinchu, Tian Tian. Multi-working condition rolling bearing fault identification method based on the alexnet-adaboost algorithm[J]. Journal of Vibration and Shock, 2022, 41(02): 20-25 (in Chinese).

[22] Hemmer M, Van Khang H, Robbersmyr K. G. Fault classification of axial and radial roller bearings using transfer learning through a pretrained convolutional neural network[J]. Designs, 2018, 2(4): 56.

[23] Wei Jianfeng, Zhang Faping, Lu Jiping, et al. Fault diagnosis method for machinery based on multi-source conflict information fusion[J]. Measurement Science and Technology, 2022, 33(11): 115007.

Artificial Intelligence, Medical Engineering and Education
Z.B. Hu et al. (Eds.)

519

doi:10.3233/ATDE231364

Application of EIQ-ABC Analysis in the Layout Planning of P E-Commerce Preposition Warehouse

Meng FU[a,1], Xin GAO[b]

[a] *School of Logistics, Wuhan Technology and Business University, Wuhan, China*
[b] *Wuhan Suning Yigou Sales Co., Ltd*
ORCiD ID: Meng FU https://orcid.org/0009-0002-9987-7517

Abstract: New retail fresh instant delivery has changed the traditional sales model of fresh products, and its emergence and development can to a certain extent solve the problems of traditional fresh food retailing industry such as inflexibility, high storage costs, and excessive loss, which has brought a new profit model to the fresh food retail industry. However, the new retail consumption model has generated new problems such as unreasonable layout of preposition warehouse, low distribution efficiency, and consumers' inability to intuitively feel the quality of products, etc., and its development path is still difficult. Based on the above background, this paper takes the operation of P e-commerce preposition warehouse as an example, through the use of EIQ analysis and ABC classification method to statistically analyze the customer order data of the warehouse, summarize the characteristics and laws of customer orders, and classify the customer orders and the products of the distribution center, then use this as the basis for optimizing the layout and storage arrangement of the preposition warehouse, improving the operational efficiency of the warehouse, and ultimately satisfying the customer's order requirements.

Keywords. EIQ analysis method; ABC classification method; Preposition warehouse

1. Introduction

The development of social economy and the development of emerging technologies represented by big data has continuously guided the domestic consumption upgrading, and at the same time accelerated the updating and development of the traditional retail industry. Under the background of the development of internet information technology in the new era and the policy support of the national "digital economy", the business model of new retail fresh food supermarkets has emerged with the help of e-commerce and mobile payment technologies [1]. In this context, the customer's orders show the characteristics of multiple batches, varieties, small batches, short cycle and high frequency demand, which puts forward higher requirements for the distribution center's distribution service level [2]. At the same time, to reduce costs and improve efficiency, distribution centers need to continuously optimize the storage of goods and picking operations to improve the efficiency of warehouse management. Warehousing

---

[1] Corresponding Author: Meng FU, E-mail: 735068543@qq.com.

operations as the key to improve the overall distribution service level has become the focus of scholars' research.

Manoche proposed a corresponding optimization scheme for the layout of workshop functional areas through SLP method when studying the workshop layout problem [3].Berg.JP and others compared the three storage methods such as random memory, locational memory and hierarchical memory, summarized their advantages and disadvantages, and explored how to distribute the optimal storage space in the optimal selecting the optimal scheme [4].Riccardo constructed a corresponding mathematical model based on the turnover rate of goods to determine the storage location according to the turnover rate of goods, which achieved the purpose of improving the efficiency of work [5].Yu L established a warehouse space optimization model based on the mixed-order sequencing by simulating the warehouse of an actual enterprise to reduce the racking centering and reduce its handling time [6].Najlae A used electronic technology to determine the optimal storage location of goods in warehouse space by analyzing the distribution of warehouse space [7]. Qian Feng used the method of cargo space distribution to optimize the arrangement of the storage area, established a cargo distribution model based on the aggregation of materials, and solved the model using the ILOGCPLEX software, and adjusted the arrangement of the warehouse based on the results of the calculation [8]. Quan Liu established a multi-objective model by using Fishbone's warehouse layout planning method and obtained the optimal shelf arrangement scheme in Fishbone's warehouse by solving it [9]. Lili Bi obtained the optimization scheme of warehouse cargo space by classifying the original warehouse goods [10]. Zhilan Song and others took the steel logistics park of Company M as the research object and used EIQ-ABC analysis to optimize the unreasonable cargo space allocated in the steel logistics park of Company M [11].

This paper combines P e-commerce's own situation, draws on the theories and methods in the above research content, and adopts the EIQ and ABC classification method to optimize the layout of P e-commerce's preposition warehouse.

2. EIQ-ABC Theory

2.1 EIQ Theory

The EIQ analysis method was first proposed by a Japanese logistics expert, Suzuki Chen. This method is a kind of analysis method focusing on enterprise orders by organizing and analyzing the items, quantities and order times of customer orders, summarizing the distribution characteristics and shipping characteristics of logistics distribution centers, and providing a basis for the reasonable layout and picking methods of distribution centers .The contents of EIQ analysis are mainly EQ (order quantity), EN (number of order items), IQ (number of items), IK (ordering times).The specific analysis steps of EIQ analysis method are: collection and sampling of customer order information, decomposition and organization of order information, making and interpreting analysis charts, planning improvement and application.

2.2 ABC Theory

ABC Classification (Activity Based Classification) is also known as Plato's analysis. Enterprises classify goods into three categories, A, B and C, according to the relevant characteristics of the goods, and adopt different management methods for different categories of goods. Among them, goods of category A are best-selling products with high frequency of storage and shipment; goods of category B are better-selling, with high frequency of storage and middle shipment; goods of category C are slow-moving products with low frequency of storage and small shipment. Differentiated management of different kinds of products can compress the total amount of inventory, reduce financial pressure, optimize the inventory structure and improve management efficiency [12].

2.3 EIQ-ABC Analysis

An EIQ analysis table is established for the goods in each warehouse. By randomly selecting 10 sales orders, the data is analyzed by EIQ, and the EIQ statistical table is established. According to the statistical data, the EQ (order quantity), EN (number of order items), IQ (number of items), IK (ordering times) are analyzed, so as to derive the ABC classification level of the goods, which is used to make suggestions for the warehouse location planning.

3. P E-Commerce Preposition Warehouse Layout and Problem Analysis

3.1 P E-Commerce Preposition Warehouse Layout Status Quo

Take the preposition warehouse of a store of P e-commerce as an example. At present, the layout of the P e-commerce front warehouse needs to be optimized, the distribution of goods in the storage area is chaotic, and the goods are shelved randomly. Goods with large picking volume and high picking frequency are shelved at the far end of the warehouse, resulting in long picking distances and congested aisles during peak periods, affecting operational efficiency. The existing warehouse layout is not planned according to the ABC classification of goods, resulting in storage space is not fully utilized.

By collecting order picking anomaly data from a front warehouse of a store of P e-commerce in July 2023, it can be seen that the existing warehousing layout has a great impact on the picking efficiency. (Table 1)

The total number of orders picking anomalies in this warehouse in July was 886, of which the percentage of order picking overtime reached 82.51%, which is due to the unreasonable warehouse layout, resulting in order peaks that are prone to picking routes congested, picking distances far away and other problems. Ultimately, the phenomenon of overtime picking occurs, thus affecting the distribution time of fresh goods.

Table 1. Statistics of Order Picking Anomalies in a Store of P Ecommerce, July 2023

anomaly	pick more	pick less(in stock)	pick less (out of stock)	faulty pick	damaged	order picking timeout	lack of supplies	total
quantity	6	36	2	6	63	731	42	886
percentage	0.68%	4.06%	0.23%	0.68%	7.11%	82.51%	4.74%	100%

Meanwhile, by collecting and organizing all customer complaint cases within July

2023, it can be seen that delivery overtime and substandard delivery services account for a large proportion of customer complaint issues, as shown in Table 2. It can be seen that order delivery overtime seriously affects the consumer's consumption experience, and may also cause the quality of fresh products to decline.

Table 2. Statistics of Customer Complaints in a Store of P Ecommerce, July 2023

grounds for complaint	quality	delivery timeout	lack of supplies	pick less	delivery service	irregular packaging	total
quantity	22	37	5	3	12	4	83
percentage	26.51%	44.58%	6.02%	3.61%	14.46%	4.82%	100%

3.2 Problems in the Layout of P E-Commerce Preposition Warehouse

1) Arbitrary placement of goods

P e-commerce preposition warehouse currently follow the logic of traditional retail supermarkets for merchandise layout, i.e., shelf distribution based on product category names, and are not categorized according to the ABC classification. This practice leads to farther picking paths for pop-up goods, which can easily cause problems such as longer picking times and congestion in the aisles during peak hours.

(2) Commodity warehouse space is not updated in time

Due to the complexity of consumer demand for fresh products, the number of daily arrivals of fresh commodities varies greatly. Therefore, it will cause the problem that the commodity storage space is sometimes not enough, and sometimes too empty. If the commodity replacement of warehouse space is not timely in the warehouse management system to update the warehouse code, it is easy to cause the picking staff cannot find the goods, wrong picking, leakage picking and so on.

(3) Commodity inventory is not timely

P e-commerce preposition warehouse conduct a comprehensive inventory once a month for general merchandise and frozen storage areas, and once a day for fruit and vegetable and fishpond storage areas. The long inventory frequency and the large number of inventoried goods can result in low stock and out-of-stock cold goods, affecting consumers' consumption experience.

4. EIQ-ABC Analysis and Application of P E-Commerce Preposition Warehouse Layout

4.1 The Process of EIQ-ABC Analysis

The main business of P Ecommerce is fresh products, daily department stores and alcoholic beverages and snacks. Since fresh goods require different environments and temperatures, the preposition warehouse are divided into ambient, low-temperature and frozen storage areas.

Next, an EIQ analysis table is created for the items in each area, and EIQ statistics are created by randomly selecting 10 sales orders and analyzing the data for EIQ. Based on the statistical data, the EQ (order quantity), EN (number of order items), IQ (number of items), IK (ordering times) are analyzed. Thus, the ABC classification level of the goods is derived, which is used to make suggestions for the warehouse planning of the P e-commerce preposition warehouse.

1) ABC classification of goods in ambient storage areas

Ambient storage goods are mainly categorized into: I1-Bulk beverages, I2-Convenience foods, I3-Snacks, I4-Dried fruits, I5-Breads, I6-Pasta sauces, I7-Daily necessities, I8-Toiletries, I9-Baby products, I10-Paper products.

Table 3. EIQ Statistics for Ambient Cargo Orders

Customer Orders	Outgoing items										EQ	EN
	I1	I2	I3	I4	I5	I6	I7	I8	I9	I10		
E1	1						1	2			4	3
E2	6	1								1	8	3
E3	7		4		1	1					13	4
E4	2	1								1	4	3
E5	1				4						5	2
E6	3						4	1		1	9	4
E7	4		2	1	1	1					9	5
E8	1	1		4							6	3
E9	1	2	1	1	4						9	5
E10					1	3				1	5	3
IQ	26	4	8	6	10	3	8	3	0	4	72	
IK	9	3	4	3	4	3	3	2	0	4		35

By randomly selecting 10 orders of ambient goods, the data were analyzed by EIQ and an EIQ statistical table was established, as shown in Table 3. Based on the statistical data, the EQ (order quantity), EN (number of order items), IQ (number of items), IK (ordering times) are analyzed.

IQ represents the number of goods out of stock, and all the IQs are arranged from largest to smallest, and the cumulative percentage is obtained by accumulating them sequentially, and the IQ-ABC analysis chart is drawn, as shown in Figure 1. Among them, the products corresponding to IQ1, IQ5, IQ3, and IQ7 account for 72.2% of the total number of products, which have a large number of goods out of the warehouse and need to deploy more inventory and require more shelf space. Products corresponding to IQ4, IQ2, and IQ10 accounted for 19.4% of the total, and the outgoing quantity of these products is average, which can be appropriately controlled by inventory and requires less shelf space. The products corresponding to IQ6, IQ8 and IQ9 only account for 8.3% of the total, and this kind of product has less outgoing volume, so the storage control can be more relaxed.

IK represents the number of times the goods have been ordered. Similarly, all the IKs are arranged in order from largest to smallest to get the cumulative percentage, and the IK-ABC analysis chart is drawn, as in Figure 2. The products corresponding to IK1, IK5, IK3, and IK10 account for 60% of the total number of picks, which are picked more often and therefore need to be placed closer to the shipping gate to shorten the picking distance and facilitate shipping. 28.5% of the total number of picks are corresponded to IK2, IK4, and IK6, which are picked moderately and can be placed in a location a little farther from the shipping gate. Products corresponding to IK7, IK8, and IK9 accounted for only 14.2% of the total number of picks, and their low picking frequency allowed them to be placed at the far end of the shipping gate.

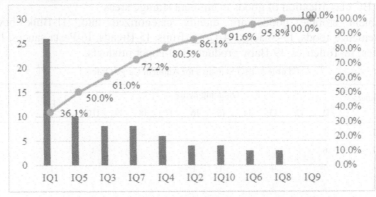

Figure 1. Pareto Analysis of IQ-ABC in Ambient Storage Area

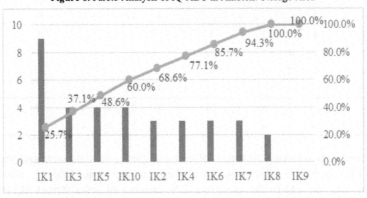

Figure 2. Pareto Analysis of IK-ABC in Ambient Storage Area

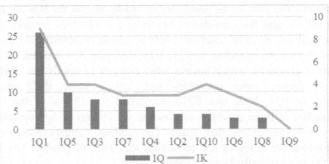

Figure 3. IQ-IK Cross-analysis Plot in Ambient Storage Area

Finally, the IQ-IK cross-tabulation analysis was performed, as shown in Figure 3. The categories of bulk beverages, bread, snacks, and daily necessities accounted for 72.2% of the total number of products, and the number of picking times accounted for 57.1% of the total number of picking times, which were classified as Category A products according to the ABC classification. Convenience foods, dried fruits, and paper products accounted for 19.4% of the total number of products, and the number of picks accounted for 28.5% of the total number of picks and were classified as Category B products. Noodle sauces, toiletries and baby products accounted for 8.3% of the total number of products and 14.2% of the total number of picks and were classified as Category C products.

2) ABC classification of goods in low-temperature storage areas

Low-temperature storage goods are mainly categorized into: I1-fresh meat, I2-leafy vegetables, I3-tomato melons and fruits, I4-root and stem vegetables, I5-fruits, I6-pure vegetables, I7-beans, I8-legumes, I9-yoghurt, I10-mushrooms.

Table 4. EIQ Statistics for Low-temperature Cargo Orders

Customer Orders	Outgoing items										EQ	EN
	I1	I2	I3	I4	I5	I6	I7	I8	I9	I10		
IQ	8	13	4	2	9	1	2	4	3	4	50	
IK	5	7	4	2	5	1	2	4	2	3		35

Similarly, 10 orders of products in the low-temperature storage area were randomly selected, and the data were analyzed by EIQ to establish an EIQ statistical table, as shown in Table 4. IQ-ABC analysis and IK-ABC analysis are performed based on the data in the EIQ statistical table, as shown in Figures 4.

Combined with the above figure and table analysis to conclude the classification of goods in the low-temperature warehouse area. Leafy vegetables, fruits, fresh meat, tomatoes and fruits accounted for 68% of the total number of products, the number of picking times accounted for 60% of the total number of pickings, according to the ABC classification method is classified as Class A products. Soybean products, mushrooms and yogurt accounted for 22% of the total number of products, and the number of picking times accounted for 25.7% of the total number of picking times, which were classified as B products. Root vegetables, beans, and net vegetables accounted for 10% of the total number of products, and the number of picking times accounted for 14.3% of the total number of pickings times, and were classified as C products.

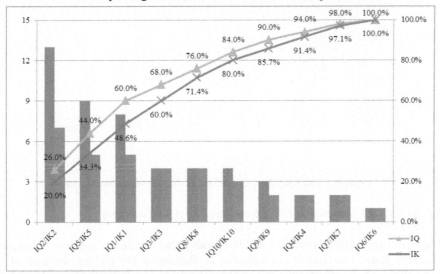

Figure 4. Pareto Analysis of IQ-ABC and IK-ABC in Low-temperature Storage Area

3) ABC classification of goods in frozen storage areas

The goods stored in the frozen area are mainly categorized into: I1-ice-cream, I2-hotpot meatballs, I3-frozen dumplings, I4-frozen aquatic products, I5-frozen meats, and I6-frozen cakes. As above, 10 orders of products in the frozen storage area were randomly selected, and the data were analyzed by EIQ to establish an EIQ statistical table, as shown in Table 5. IQ-ABC analysis and IK-ABC analysis are performed based on the data in the EIQ statistical table, as shown in Figures 5.

Table 5. EIQ Statistics for Frozen Cargo Orders

Customer Orders	Outgoing items						EQ	EN
	I1	I2	I3	I4	I5	I6		
IQ	2	2	13	1	8	1	27	
IK	1	2	7	1	6	1		18

Combined with the above figure and table analysis to conclude the classification of goods in the frozen warehouse area. Frozen dumplings and frozen meat accounted for 72.2% of the total number of products, and the number of picking times accounted for 72.2% of the total number of pickings times and were classified as Category A products according to the ABC classification. Hot pot meatballs and ice cream accounted for 19.4% of the total number of products, and the number of picking times accounted for 16.7% of the total number of picking times, which were classified as category B products. Frozen aquatic products and frozen cakes accounted for 8.3% of the total number of products and 11.1% of the total number of picks and were categorized as Category C products.

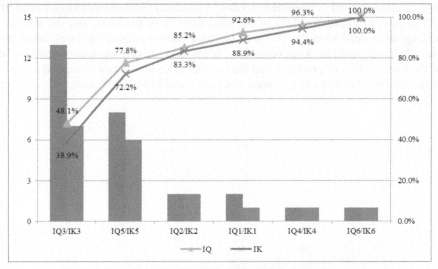

Figure 5. Pareto Analysis of IQ-ABC and IK-ABC in Frozen Storage Area

4.2 Analysis of Optimization Effect Based on EIQ-ABC Taxonomy

The layout after ABC classification of the goods in the warehouse is shown in Figure 6. The new warehouse layout is conducive to shortening the picking distance of the best-selling goods, shortening the distance between the hot-selling goods and the packing table, and shortening the distance between the related goods, which facilitates the store picking staff to improve the efficiency of picking, thus shortening the picking time and improving the service quality.

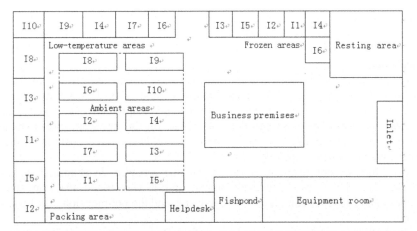

Figure 6. Optimized Layout of P E-commerce Preposition Warehouse

Table 6. Statistics of Order Picking Anomalies in a Store of P Ecommerce, August 2023

anomaly	pick more	pick less(in stock)	pick less (out of stock)	faulty pick	damaged	order picking timeout	lack of supplies	total
quantity	3	6	0	6	45	114	31	205
percentage	1.46%	2.93%	0.00%	2.93%	21.95%	55.61%	15.12%	

After the optimization of the layout of the preposition warehouse, the picking order anomalies of the store were counted again. As can be seen from Table 6, the order picking timeout in August was greatly reduced compared to July, and the cases of faulty picking were also reduced.

Thanks to the shortening of the picking time and the rationalization of the goods layout, the customer complaints about the delivery time and out-of-stock leakage problems in this store during August were also greatly reduced, as shown in Table 7, which further improved the service quality of the P-commerce company and brought a better shopping experience to the consumers.

Table 7. Statistics of Customer Complaints in a Store of P Ecommerce, August 2023

grounds for complaint	quality	delivery timeout	lack of supplies	pick less	delivery service	irregular packaging	total
quantity	31	12	2	0	23	0	68
percentage	45.59%	17.65%	2.94%	0.00%	33.82%	0.00%	100%

5. Conclusion

This paper analyzes the storage layout within the preposition warehouse of a store of P e-commerce and combines the operational data and abnormalities of P e-commerce to analyze the problems existing in its preposition warehouse layout. In response to these problems, EIQ-ABC analysis is carried out on the goods in different temperature zones within the store of P e-commerce, so as to obtain the optimized layout within the store, and the effectiveness of the optimization is analyzed.

The main research conclusions are as follows:

(1) Through the research on abnormal orders and customer complaints, the current

situation of P E-commerce's preposition warehouse has been deeply analyzed, and its current problems such as the arbitrary placement of goods, commodity warehouse space is not updated in time, and the commodity inventory is not timely have been understood.

(2) Based on the analysis of the current situation, for the problems existing in the warehouse layout, the EIQ-ABC classification method is used to optimize the cargo space, placing the category of goods with a larger shipment volume and a greater frequency of shipments closest to the exit, and so on for emissions, positioning each type of goods for storage, and each type of goods has a fixed position in order to improve the efficiency of picking.

(3) After the optimization of the layout, the research on abnormal orders and customer complaints was conducted again, and it was found that the abnormal situations and customer complaints were reduced, and the optimization effect was more obvious.

Through the optimization of the layout of the P e-commerce preposition warehouse, the operational efficiency of the store is further improved, and the purpose of improving the service quality of the store is finally achieved.

References

[1]   Mbida Mohamed. Smart Warehouse Management using Hybrid Architecture of Neural Network with Barcode Reader 1D / 2D Vision Technology. International Journal of Intelligent Systems and Applications, 2019,11:16-24.

[2]   Anitha P, Malini M. Patil. A Review on Data Analytics for Supply Chain Management: A Case study. International Journal of Information Engineering and Electronic Business, 2018, 10(5): 30-39.

[3]   Djassemi M. Improving factory layout under a mixed floor and overhead material handling condition. Journal of Manufacturing Technology Management, 2017, 18(3): 281-291.

[4]   J. P. Berg, A. Gademann, H. D. Hoff. An Order Batching Algorithm for Wave Picking in a Parallel-aisle Warehouse. IIE Transactions, 2016, 33(5): 385-398.

[5]   Manzini R, Accorsi R, Gamberi M, et al. Modeling class-based storage assignment over life cycle picking patterns. International Journal of Production Economics, 2015, 170: 790-800.

[6]   Yue L, Guan Z, He C, et al. Slotting optimization of automated storage and retrieval system (AS/RS) for efficient delivery of parts in an assembly shop using genetic algorithm: a case Study. IOP conference series: materials science and engineering. IOP Publishing, 2017, 215(1): 012002.

[7]   Najlae A, Abdelouahid L, Abdelfettah S. Product driven system for the optimal assignment of warehouse locations. International Journal of Logistics Systems and Management, 2019, 33(3): 322-352.

[8]   Qian Feng, Meilong Le, Yi Zhao. Optimization of warehouse space assignment under material clustering analysis. Journal of Liaoning University of Engineering and Technology (Natural Science Edition), 2015, 34(10): 1207-1212.

[9]   Quan Liu. Warehouse layout optimization model based on genetic algorithm and determination of optimal angle. Journal of Hebei North College (Natural Science Edition), 2016, 32(03): 21-27.

[10] LiLi Bi. Optimization of warehouse layout of logistics company based on EIQ-ABC method. Logistics Technology, 2015, 34(20): 145-148.

[11] Zhilan Song. Optimization of storage space in steel logistics park of company M based on EIQ-ABC method. Logistics Technology, 2019, 38(07): 135-139.

[12] P. Sreeramana Aithal, Suresh Kumar P.M. "ABC Model of Research Productivity and Higher Educational Institutional Ranking". International Journal of Education and Management Engineering, 2016,6(6):74-84.

Artificial Intelligence, Medical Engineering and Education
Z.B. Hu et al. (Eds.)
doi:10.3233/ATDE231365

Exploration and Practice of Volunteer Service Model Based on Alleviating Emotional Disorders in Children with Leukemia

Haojie LIU[a], Jiangbiao WANG[a], Ruofan HU[a], Xiaohuan LI[a], Luqing LIU[a], Yuyang HAN[a], Xiangxing YAN[b,1]

[a] *School of Information Engineering, Wuhan University of Technology, Wuhan, China*
[b] *Personnel Department, Wuhan University of Technology, Wuhan, China*

Abstract. In recent years, the long-term quality of life of children with leukemia has received widespread attention as the prevalence of the disease has increased and the cure rate has improved. To alleviate the negative emotions of children with leukemia and their families and ensure the socialization process of children, this paper actively explores the volunteer service model based on caring for children with leukemia with emotional disorders and establishes the "REAL" service model, aiming to form a four-way volunteer system of self-reduction, environmental simulation, affectionate companionship, and social support. The aim is to form a four-way volunteer system of self-reduction, environmental simulation, affectionate companionship, and social support to provide professional volunteer services for children with leukemia and their families to alleviate the emotional disorders of children with leukemia and improve their quality of life. Meanwhile, this paper verified the alleviating effect of the service model on the emotional state of children through Pearson correlation analysis, and designed a recommendation system of "REAL" service model for different types of children based on SCARED and DSRCS scores to propose treatment plans for different children.

Keywords. Leukemia children; Emotional disorder; Voluntary service; Service model; Recommendation system.

1. Introduction

At present, there are 4-6 leukemia patients in every 100,000 people in China, 40% of whom are children, and they are mostly 2-7 years old. For leukemia children, long-term hospitalization will isolate them from the colorful world. The children face medical staff in a white coat every day and lead monotony life [1]. Children can not release the pursuit of happiness nature, easily producing anxiety. The kind of emotional disorders affected the socialization of leukemia children and even caused some psychological and behavioral problems [2]. Taking into account the current situation and the needs of the socialization process of leukemia children, we have formed a volunteer team and created a place with recreational, rest and learning functions for hospitalized children. Meanwhile, we explored the voluntary service model to improve the problem of emotional disorders in leukemia children, so as to achieve the effect of complementary

---

[1] Corresponding Author: Xiangxing YAN, E-mail: yanxx@whut.edu.cn

treatment [3].

2. Causes of Emotional Disorders in Leukemia Children

The emotion changes of children are closely related to social factors such as family, school, peer group and mass media. Most leukemia children are hospitalized for long periods of time [4]. With the change of family environment and learning environment, isolation from peer group, excessive contact with the mass media during treatment, the children gradually appear various emotional disorders [5].

2.1. The Negative Effects Of Native Family

The families of leukemia children are prone to generate negative emotions due to heavy psychological burden and economic pressure, which can lead to family conflicts and have a negative impact on the emotion of children. On account of the child's illness, family conflicts occur frequently. The tension in the family leads to pessimism, contradiction, anxiety, neuroticism and other problems in children. In addition, the potential reasons why the child have impetuous, pessimistic attitude, other personality defects and love to lose temper also include the lack of interaction with parents, the over-indulgent from family, or the existence of parents' quarrel. The unhealthy living atmosphere of the family can make children feel more restless and irritable [6]. And to some extent, they feel guilty about their illness and think that they are the root cause of family conflict. The feeling of self-blame and inferiority decreases the motivation of children's social interaction [7].

2.2. Lack of Communication with Peer Group

Leukemia children have been separated from the original peer group due to repeated and long-term chemotherapy, isolation treatment [8]. For the leukemia children, lacking mutual imitation and learning with their peers are prone to a strong sense of inferiority, which affects their confidence in the future and their return to normal life. Some parents even think that their children will be discriminated against when they return to school after their illness, so choose to hide the fact from their children. This not only cuts off all connection between the children and peer group, schools, but also leads to a deepening sense of exclusion in children to some extent [9].

2.3. Too Far Away from Campus Life

Most leukemia children are suspended from school to receive treatment. Changes in the environment and interruption of learning have caused a huge psychological gap for the children, making them anxious and ambiguous. At the same time, the children's social communication skills and learning abilities decline [10]. Especially for school-age children, the strong desire to learn at this stage will also produce a strong sense of loss and inferiority. At the same time, because they are far from normal school life, children cannot clearly understand their future positioning, and their self-identity is reduced. They are more likely to choose ways to escape when faced with difficulties, and their ability to solve problems cannot be improved [11].

2.4. Excessive Exposure To Mass Media

It is undeniable that mass media brought entertainment and convenience to leukemia children during their hospitalization [12]. However, children with leukemia who have been treated for a long time, lack of contact with the outside world, are easily addicted to electronic devices and resist daily social behavior. Moreover, the mass media's voices that discriminate against leukemia are more quickly transmitted to the children, which also indirectly leads to psychological problems such as social anxiety, self-doubt, and self-evasion in leukemia children [13].

3. Exploring the Volunteer Service Model of Alleviating Emotional Disorders of Leukemia Children

3.1. Explore and Establish "REAL" Service Model

According to a series of practical activity forms effective in improving the emotional disorders of leukemia children, we explore and establish the "REAL" service model (REAL is the abbreviation of Reduce, Environment, Accompany and Love), forming a voluntary service system promoted by self-decompression, environmental simulation, family companionship and social support. Through developing all-round and continuous voluntary service activities, we devote to walking into the hearts of leukemia children, bringing the most practical care to the children, helping them to relieve various emotional disorders and increase courage to fight against the disease, and improving the living quality of the children, finally making them " a really cured child". The four main themes of the volunteer service system are as follows [14].

Self-decompression. Self-decompression is to relieve the inner stress and anxiety of leukemia children. We carry out painting and handmade activities to understand the true inner world of leukemia children and encourage children to express themselves bravely, which can also promote the development of more targeted follow-up activities. We carry out Fun reading clubs, watching cartoons and other activities to give leukemia children more interaction and companionship, distract the children 's attention, and alleviate their inner anxiety about the illness. Besides, we carry out the propaganda and publicity about the knowledge of nursing and diet of leukemia children, helping the children and their families cooperate more scientifically with treatment and reduce their inner fear [15].

Campus simulation. Building a "Love Cabin", a place integrating entertainment, rest, and learning functions, is to create a natural external environment, reducing the pressure and tension caused by the special environment of the hospital to patients. We carry out theme lessons, teaching basic subject knowledge, learning news, etc. to narrow the distance with the children and make up for their regrets about the lack of classrooms. We carry out Anniversary, Festival-themed activities, Social identity games, etc. to further promote the growth of children, so that they can better understand the social living environment. At the same time this form can promote the communication between children and peer groups and enhance their basic social skills[16].

Family companionship. Family companionship is an indispensable part of the treatment of leukemia children. We carry out the "Family Portrait" and "Our Group" theme painting activities to promote the interaction between children and their parents and we also carry out activities such as Lectures to the family members of the children, Parent-child exchanges, and Cards convey love, so that the children and their parents can open their hearts to express their love and the mutual communication between the two parties can be strengthened, which has a positive effect on reducing the psychological burden on patients and their families and increasing confidence in treatment[17].

Love relays. Social attention and support are the important guarantee for the treatment of leukemia children. Our volunteer team provides direct help for the treatment of leukemia children through activities such as Charity sales, Social donations, and Love boxes in the ward, helping reduce the financial pressure and psychological burden of the children and their families. Our Dream claiming activity allows leukemia children 's dreams to fly out of the ward and attracts loving people to help realize their dreams. These encouragements from society can strengthen the confidence of leukemia children in treatment and help them establish a positive treatment attitude. In addition, we make the volunteer service team cooperate with other caring organizations, build a public welfare platform and carry out promotional activities, appealing to the society to care for leukemia children, and using the power of social media to make leukemia children and families feel the warmth of society [18].

3.2. Customized System Design of "REAL" Service Model Based on Recommendation Algorithm

The "REAL" service model is a larger service model system, mainly divided into four aspects: self-reduction, environmental simulation, affectionate companionship, and social support. In the outcome test, we found that the psychotherapeutic effects of the REAL service model differed when the same child faced different aspects of the REAL service model, and the psychotherapeutic effects of the REAL service model differed when different children faced the same process. The psychological treatment effects of the same REAL service model vary from child to child. Therefore, we consider using a recommendation algorithm to quantify which REAL service method is best for the same type of child [19].

The system begins with a classification of the child based on the factors that influence the psychological outcome. The common method of classification is the cosine similarity calculation, and a threshold is set so that when two children are within a certain range of similarity, they are considered to be in the same category. The cosine similarity is measured by calculating the cosine of the angle between vectors to measure the similarity of users. The calculation formula is shown in Equation (1).

$$Sim\ (u_1, u_2) = cos\ (V_{u1}, V_{u2}) = \frac{|V_{u1} \cap V_{u2}|}{\sqrt{|V_{u1}|V_{u2}|}} \tag{1}$$

The formula shows that the smaller the angle between the vectors, the greater the similarity. If the angle is 0, the vectors are considered identical, i.e., the similarity is 1.

After the classification is completed, different aspects of the "REAL" service for the child need to be performed, and each service needs to be evaluated by SAS and SDS scores, and the best service method for the child is determined by quantitative comparison. When the amount of data is large enough, the system can predict the therapeutic effect of a certain aspect of "REAL" service for the child, and the difference between the predicted value and the real value can be evaluated by the root mean square error, so as to improve the reliability of the prediction and provide data support for the doctor's psychological treatment plan for the child [20].

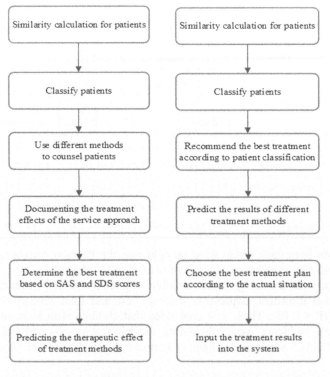

Figure 1. System Design Process   **Figure 2.** System Operation Process

The design flow of "REAL" service model customization system based on the recommendation algorithm is shown in Figure 1. The operation flow of the "REAL" service model customization system is shown in Figure 2.

3.3. Actual Case Tests

Objective: To investigate the psychological changes of children with leukemia after "REAL" service and explore the effective "REAL" service model. Methods: 60 children with leukemia were randomly divided into two groups, 30 cases in each group.

Table 1. Low year group before and after treatment test results

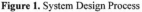

Factor	The test group		The control group	
	Before treatment	After treatment	Before treatment	After treatment
Terrified	5.97 ± 4.19	2.82 ± 1.88	4.23 ± 4.09	4.01 ±3.13
Separation anxiety	6.46 ± 3.74	2.72 ± 1.89	5.83 ± 4.01	5.01 ± 2.89
Extensive anxiety	5.73 ± 3.63	3.27 ± 2.24	5.69 ± 2.61	5.47 ± 3.16
Fear of school	2.23 ± 2.11	1.22 ± 1.05	2.12 ± 1.40	2.05 ± 1.35
Social phobia	5.29 ± 2.58	3.37 ± 2.13	5.33 ± 2.86	5.14 ± 4.01

The trial group was given REAL service on the basis of routine chemotherapy, while the control group was given routine chemotherapy. The children were assessed with (SCARED) and self-rating depression scales (DSRSC).

Table 2. High year group before and after treatment test results

Factor	The test group		The control group	
	Before treatment	After treatment	Before treatment	After treatment
Terrified	6.19 ± 4.21	2.32 ± 1.28	5.53 ± 3.99	4.61 ±3.23
Separation anxiety	6.76 ± 3.74	2.62 ± 1.49	5.93 ± 4.21	5.31 ± 2.69
Extensive anxiety	5.73 ± 3.73	2.77 ± 2.34	5.89 ± 2.71	5.67 ± 3.16
Fear of school	2.43 ± 2.11	1.02 ± 1.15	2.82 ± 1.55	2.55 ± 1.45
Social phobia	5.39 ± 2.68	1.99 ± 2.13	5.63 ± 2.56	5.23 ± 3.71

The data from each group were brought into the Pearson correlation coefficient formula, and the correlation coefficient was 0.651, while there was a significant difference between the two groups of children with leukemia after treatment in terms of anxiety mood disorders, depression disorder test and total scores of anxiety and depression ($P < 0.05$). Thus, it is concluded that children with leukemia have more psychological problems, especially during the initial diagnosis and treatment phase. Effective "REAL" services can help to improve the quality of life of children with leukemia.

4. Effectiveness of Volunteer Service Model for Alleviating Emotional Disorders of Leukemia Children

4.1. Relieve Emotional Disorders Of Leukemia Children

After exploration and practice, this article summarizes an effective form of volunteering for the emotional disorder of leukemia children. Through a series of self-decompression activities, volunteers understand the true inner world of the children during the interactive communication, encourage children to express themselves bravely, and relieve the stress and anxiety in children; the series of activities on the simulated campus create a comfortable and relaxing external environment for the children, relieve the sense of helplessness and loss of children away from school. In addition, carrying out theme lessons and social role-playing activities can let children understand more about the outside world, enhance the communication between children and peer groups, enhance their basic social skills, and ensure the socialization process; the series of activities about family companionship can promote the communication and interaction between children and the parents, help to close the parent-child relationship, thereby improving the family conflicts caused by the disease, and alleviate the psychological pressure of the parents and the children; through the love relays, we extensively seek social support and attention, so that the public's goodwill will continue to flow into the ward, helping the families to reduce financial pressure and psychological burden.

4.2. Promote Volunteers' Self-Improvement

For all volunteers participating in voluntary service activities, long-term adherence and practice on the path of caring for the leukemia children not only improves the volunteer's own comprehensive ability, but also makes them deeply understand the volunteer spirit, "dedication, friendship, mutual assistance, progress "and enhances the sense of social responsibility. In addition, our volunteer team has been repeatedly rated as "Excellent Volunteer Service Team of Concord Hospital Caring School", which affirmed the social value of volunteers. The sense of accomplishment gained by volunteers make them more willing to improve the quality of volunteer services and serve the society, which becomes a continuous source of social volunteer service.

4.3. Strengthen the Positive Attention and Support of the Society

The problem of leukemia children is not only a problem that the patients have to bear, a problem that their families have to face, but also a problem that our society needs to pay attention to and find a solution. The medical environment, living environment, learning environment, and social environment of leukemia children will be continuously improved to fundamentally solve the problem only if the support of social forces can be increased. Our volunteer team cooperated with other loving organizations to build a public welfare platform and conduct extensive social publicity. We have published news on Jingchu.com, Yangtze.com and other websites to appeal attention and support. We also published news on Chutian Metropolis Daily, Wuhan Evening News and other off-campus media to call on more people to join the volunteer service activities for caring leukemia children, which has improved the social benefits of volunteer service activities.

The exploration of volunteer service model for alleviating emotional disorders of leukemia children, although it is currently in the initial stage, there are many imperfections, but we will continue to actively explore and improve in practice to provide a realistic path. The path is to alleviate emotional disorders and the environment of leukemia children.

5. Conclusion

This article explores and practices the voluntary service model for the emotional disorder of leukemia children during treatment. We analyzed the causes of emotional problems of children with leukemia from the aspects of family, school, mass media, etc. , explored the volunteer service model for the reasons, formulated a voluntary service plan and established a "REAL" service model, forming a voluntary service system promoted by self-decompression, environmental simulation, family companionship, and social support. Our activities have effectively alleviated the emotional disorder of children with leukemia, and have received positive attention and support in the society. However, caring for the emotional disorder of leukemia children and ensuring the socialization of children are a social issue. The corresponding support mechanism needs to be improved, and there is still a long way to go in the future.

Acknowledgment

This project is supported by Humanities and Social Sciences Research Project of Independent Innovation Research Fund of Wuhan University of Technology (2020-XX-C1-30)

References

[1] Du Guangli. Effect of anticipatory nursing interventions on psychological mood and complications in patients with acute leukemia[J]. Tibetan Medicine, 2022, 43(01): 119-121 (In Chinese)

[2] Li Qiuyue, Ke Meitao. The role of group cognitive behavioral care in improving psychological status and sleep quality of pediatric leukemia chemotherapy patients[J]. World Journal of Sleep Medicine, 2021, 8(12): 2198-2200.

[3] Li Lulu. Effect of anticipatory care combined with psychological intervention on complications and psychological status of patients with acute leukemia[J]. China Pharmaceutical Science, 2021, 11(15): 131-134 (in Chinese).

[4] Hou XR, Tao YJ. Effects of cognitive psychotherapy on negative emotions and cancer-caused fatigue in leukemia chemotherapy patients[J]. Chinese Journal of Health Psychology, 2021, 29(10): 1496-1501 (In Chinese).

[5] Liu Xiaoxiao, Li Shuangyan. Effects of positive relaxation training on psychological state and sleep quality of chemotherapy patients with leukemia[J]. International Journal of Nursing, 2021, 40(05): 854-857.

[6] Sun Peijuan, Xing Wei, Ren Mengmeng. Effect of psychological care in leukemia chemotherapy patients[J]. Chinese National Health Medicine, 2021, 33(01): 191-192 (In Chinese).

[7] Md. Rayhan Ahmed. Leveraging convolutional neural network and transfer learning for cotton plant and leaf disease recognition[J]. International Journal of Image, Graphics and Signal Processing, 2021, 13(4): 47-62.

[8] Nasim Soltani Soulegan, Behrang Barekatain, Behzad Soleimani Neysiani. MTC: Minimizing time and cost of cloud task scheduling based on customers and providers needs using genetic algorithm[J]. International Journal of Intelligent Systems and Applications, 2021, 13(2): 38-51.

[9] Roman peleshchak, Vasyl lytvyn, Oksana bihun, Ivan peleshchak. Structural Transformations of Incoming Signal by a Single Nonlinear Oscillatory Neuron or by an Artificial Nonlinear Neural Network [J]. International Journal of Intelligent Systems and Applications, 2019, 11(8): 1-10.

[10] Atish Kumar Dipongkor, Rayhanul Islam, Nadia Nahar, et al. Reduction of Multiple Move Method Suggestions Using Total Call-Frequencies of Distinct Entities[J]. International Journal of Information Engineering and Electronic Business, 2020, 12(4): 21-29.

[11] Alexandros Deligiannis, Charalampos Argyriou. Designing a Real-Time Data-Driven Customer Churn Risk Indicator for Subscription Commerce[J]. International Journal of Information Engineering and Electronic Business, 2020, 12(4): 1-14.

[12] Alovsat Garaja Aliyev, Roza Ordukhan Shahverdiyeva. Scientific and Methodological bases of Complex Assessment of Threats and Damage to Information Systems of the Digital Economy[J]. International Journal of Information Engineering and Electronic Business, 2022, 14(2): 23-38.

[13] Md. Tofail Ahmed, Md. Humaun Kabir and Sujit Roy. Web Based Student Registration and Exam Form Fill-up Management System for Educational Institute[J]. International Journal of Information Engineering and Electronic Business, 2022, 14(2): 47-62.

[14] Day Bert R. Mariñas, Roberto R. Coloma, Lin V. Tadeja, et al. Development of an Intelligent Tutoring System for English Reading Comprehension: Design Based on Philippine Public School Flexible Learning Experience[J]. International Journal of Information Engineering and Electronic Business, 2021, 13(5): 9-23.

[15] Joseph O. ADIGUN, Eric A. IRUNOKHAI, Oluwafemi A. ADENIJI, et al. Role of Coronavirus Outbreak on Adoption of Electronic Education in New Bussa, Niger State, Nigeria[J]. International Journal of Education and Management Engineering, 2021, 11(5): 13-22.

[16] Mohamed Zaim Shahrel, Sofianita Mutalib, Shuzlina Abdul-Rahman. PriceCop – Price Monitor and Prediction Using Linear Regression and LSVM-ABC Methods for E-commerce Platform[J]. International Journal of Information Engineering and Electronic Business, 2021, 13(1): 1-14.

[17] Adewale Olumide S., Boyinbode Olutayo K., Salako E. Adekunle. An Innovative Approach in Electronic Voting System Based on Fingerprint and Visual Semagram[J]. International Journal of Information Engineering and Electronic Business, 2021, 13(5):24-37.

[18] Muhammad Hassaan. A Comparative Study between Cloud Energy Consumption Measuring Simulators [J]. International Journal of Education and Management Engineering, 2020, 10(2): 20-27.

[19] Ismail Aliyu, A. F. D. Kana, Salisu Aliyu. Development of Knowledge Graph for University Courses Management[J]. International Journal of Education and Management Engineering, 2020, 10(2): 1-10.

[20] Sudhir Anakal, P Sandhya. Decision Support System for Drug-Drug Interaction Pertaining to COPD and its Comorbidities[J]. International Journal of Education and Management Engineering, 2022, 12(2): 1-6.

Part 3

Education Reform and Innovation

Artificial Intelligence, Medical Engineering and Education
Z.B. Hu et al. (Eds.)
© 2024 The Authors.
This article is published online with Open Access by IOS Press and distributed under the terms
of the Creative Commons Attribution Non-Commercial License 4.0 (CC BY-NC 4.0).
doi:10.3233/ATDE231367

Research on the Correlation Between College Students' Financial Status and Feedback Awareness

Zhifang HUANG[1]
Finance Department, Wuhan City Polytechnic, Wuhan, China
ORCiD ID: Zhifang HUANG https://orcid.org/0009-0005-2619-1911

Abstract: Student funding is an important project that ensures people's livelihoods and warms the hearts of the people, which is related to poverty alleviation and social equity. In the continuous progress of society, China's student aid policy is also gradually improving, and its focus has shifted from basic guarantee based aid to development based aid. But it is worth studying how college students' feedback awareness after financial status. This article takes 51 subsidized college students from vocational colleges in Wuhan as the research sample, and uses Eviews13 software to empirically study the correlation between college students' financial status and feedback awareness. The research conclusion shows that there is a significant correlation between financial status and feedback awareness, indicating that funded college students are grateful and know how to give back to society. Receiving drips of water when in need, and returning the kindness with a spring.

Keywords: College students; Financial status; Regurgitation feeding.

1. Introduction

With the continuous development of society, the policy and implementation of student aid in Chinese universities are becoming more and more perfect, and the student aid policy is also gradually improving with the progress of society. The focus of its work has shifted from satisfying basic security assistance to development assistance, and the goal of cultivating funded college students has expanded from economic security to valuing them as useful talents in the motherland. So how do college students feel after receiving funding, and are they willing to give back to the society and help others? There is currently little literature on the situation of college students after they are funded. Therefore, the article takes 51 funded college students from vocational colleges in Wuhan as the research sample, collect the specific information of their amount of feedback amount of funded, monthly household income and monthly living expenses, and use empirical analysis method to analyze the correlation between college students' financial status and feedback awareness.

---

[1] Corresponding Author: Zhifang HUANG, E-mail: 12528286@qq.com.

2. Theoretical Analysis and Research Hypotheses

Domestic and foreign scholars have mainly conducted research in four aspects: The first is the research on the development history, system, mode, method, path of funding by college students. Scholars Cui Yuan and Xue Yuan analyzed students with financial difficulties, and proposes that colleges and universities should change their funding concepts and establish a unified standard funding recognition system [1]. Doyle, W. R. compared student funding activities between different states in the United States in terms of policy objectives, recipients, selection criteria, and the amount of funding [2]. Lee, Jungmin analyzed the changes in tuition and accommodation fees of college students in the United States from 1987 to 2009, and proposed that higher education funding can promote sponsored students to better complete higher education [3]. The second is a comparative study of funding systems between China and foreign countries. Scholar Mark Stater conducted a survey of first-year students at three public universities in the United States and proposed that college students' financial aid is decisive for their choice of major [4]. Scholar Li Zhijie conducted in-depth research on the situation of foreign college student funding policies and put forward suggestions on China's college student funding policies [5]. Scholar Ronald J. Peters, JR. analyzed the difficulty of financial aid for 180 African-American college students enrolled in the fall of 2010 found that the difficulty of financial aid was related to the mental health and behavior of college students [6]. The third is research on performance evaluation and monitoring research of grant management. Scholar Qu Shaowei analyzed the performance of college student funding in 120 colleges and universities in 2013, and proposed that the performance evaluation of college student funding should start from four aspects [7]. Scholar Jacob P. Gross surveyed Americans and found that 75% think college tuition is too expensive, and due to the impact of the recession, the state government is giving less and less funding to students, leading to major changes in the federal government in higher education funding [8]. Scholar Cerin, Lindgren savage introduced the current status of for-profit higher education in the United States in recent years, the process of evaluation and review, and the process of supervision and management by the Federal Department of Education. Suggestions were made for the effectiveness of the review and evaluation of the behavior of the education supervision and management department [9]. Scholars Loris Vergolini and Nadir Zanini investigate the educational program launched in the Italian province of Trento, which aims to reduce inequalities in access to higher education and foster low incomes College enrollment for home-based students. However, the survey found that the program had no significant impact on enrolment [10]. The fourth is research on the functional development and evaluation of ideological and political education channels funded by college students. Scholar Zhao Guichen proposed that the student funding system has functions such as institutional guidance, institutional norms, rule of law education, gratitude education, and caring for others education [11]. Bekishev K. conducted an in-depth analysis of the advantages and shortcomings of Kazakhstan's higher education enrollment system, and suggested that students' innovative thinking, scientific research ability, cultural quality, practical skills and other abilities should be used as the selection criteria for higher education entrance examination and national scholarships [12-15].

In summary, it is not difficult to find that research on the relevant issues of college student funding, whether foreign scholars or domestic scholars, has achieved fruitful results. However, the research on whether the funded college students are willing to feed back the society after receiving the funding is not deep enough. Therefore, it is of practical significance to study the correlation of college students' funding situation and feedback awareness. Generally speaking, people have a sense of gratitude. As the saying goes: "The kindness of dripping water should be reported by a gushing spring". Based on this, this article proposes the following hypothesis:

Hypothesis H: There is a positive correlation between the level of financial status and the feedback awareness.

3. Research Design

3.1. Sample Selection

The collection scope selected by this research institute is data from 51 funded college students in vocational colleges in Wuhan, and the specific information collected is related to the feedback of funded college students within this scope. After completing the collection, further data analysis was carried out. The platform Jinshan document used during the collection process.

3.2. Indicator Selection

3.2.1. Dependent Variable

The standard measure of subsidized college students feeding back to the society is not relatively unified. However, after comprehensive consideration, this article uses the amount of feedback as a measure, which refers to the fact that funded college students have a sense of feedback after receiving funding and are willing to use monetization to give back to society in the future. By analyzing the amount of feedback, we can better grasp the willingness and practical actions of current funded college students to feedback society.

3.2.2. Independent Variable

The college students' financial status, represented by the amount of funding received, refers to the amount of funding received by the state, society, schools, and other entities.

3.2.3. Control Variables

Choosing reasonable controllable variables can effectively improve the accuracy of empirical results. At present, through research on funded college students, it has been found that there are various factors that affect their feedback, such as household income, living expenses, and the number of times they receive funding. Strengthening research on relevant factors can better determine the true willingness of funded college students' giving back to the society. In the study, the following indicators will be selected as controllable variables.

1) Monthly household income

Monthly household income refers to the monthly income of the entire household of funded college students.

2) Monthly living expenses

Monthly living expenses refer to the monthly living expenses of funded college students during their school years.

3.3 Research Model

Based on the selected relevant variables and data characteristics mentioned above, this article will conduct research and analysis using Eviews13 software. In the study, the data of 2022 is formed into a time series, and the data of 51 funded college students are cross-sectional data. Based on the Panel data model, the author has established the following regression equation:

$$Y = C + A_1 X_1 + A_2 X_2 + A_3 X_3 \qquad (1)$$

In the above equation, Y refers to the amount of feedback, X1 refers to the amount of funded, X2 refers to the monthly household income, X3 refers to the monthly living expenses, C refers to the coefficient, and A1 -A3 are the regression coefficients of each variable.

4. Empirical Analysis

4.1 Descriptive Analysis

According to the statistical results described in Table1, the average amount of funded is 5828.431, the maximum value is 18000, the minimum value is 200, the standard deviation is 4207.853, and the difference between the maximum and minimum values is 17800. It can be seen that there is a significant difference in the supported amount received by the funded college students. The average monthly household income is 4492.157, with a maximum value is 10000 and a minimum value is 1000. The standard deviation is 2203.347, and the maximum value is 10 times the minimum value. This indicates that there is a significant difference in monthly household income of funded college students. The average monthly living expenses is 1176.471, the maximum value is 2000, the minimum value is 600, and the standard deviation is 281.1322. It can be seen that the monthly living expenses of funded college students are relatively low, and their household income is not high. The state, society, schools, and other entities should help students with poor living conditions more. The average amount of feedback is 18856.86, with a maximum value is 40000 and a minimum value is 200. The standard deviation is 9610.791, indicating a significant difference in the amount of feedback for funded college students.

Table 1. Statistical Table of Variable Description

Variable	Mean	Maximum	Minimum	Std. Dev.
Y	18856.86	40000	200	9610.791
X_1	5828.431	18000	200	4207.853
X_2	4492.157	10000	1000	2203.347
X_3	1176.471	2000	600	281.1322

4.2　Autocorrelation analysis

It can be seen from Table 2 that there is no Multicollinearity between the three variables, namely, there is no substitutability.

Table 2. Independent variable correlation test table

Variable	X_1	X_2	X_3
X1	1	-	-
X2	0.058452 （0.6837）	1	-
X3	0.260179 （0.0652）	0.223772 （0.1144）	1

4.3　Regression Analysis

The regression results between various factors and the amount of feedback are shown in Table 3.

Table 3. Regression Results Table

Variable	Coefficient	Std. Error	t-Statistic	Prob.
X_1	1.8300	0.2087	8.7706	0.0000
X_2	0.5999	0.3948	1.5198	0.1353
X_3	-3.6191	3.1989	-1.1314	0.2636
C	9753.54	3778.493	2.5813	0.013
R-squared	0.6343	F-statistic		27.1751
Adjusted R-squared	0.6110	Prob(F-statistic)		0.0000

From the regression results, it is clear that the fitting degree of the model is 0.6343, and the adjusted fitting degree is 0.6110. This indicates that the amount of subsidies, monthly household income, and monthly living expenses have a 61.1% explanatory degree for the amount of feedback. The F-test statistic of the model is 27.1751, passing the F-test at the 1% significance level, indicating that the overall regression effect of the model is relatively ideal.

The regression equation of the model can be obtained from the regression coefficients:

$$Y = 9753.54 + 1.8300X_1 + 0.5999X_2 - 3.6191X_3 \tag{2}$$

4.4　Empirical Results

The experimental results show a positive correlation between the amount of funded and the amount of feedback, and the two have passed the T-test at the 1% level, indicating a significant positive correlation between the two. The reason is that the larger the amount of financial aid that college students receive, the greater the amount of social feedback. Therefore, the hypothesis H of this article holds.

There is a positive correlation between monthly household income and the amount of feedback, indicating that the higher the monthly household income of the funded college students, the more willing they are to feedback society, and the amount of feedback will be more, but the significance between the two is not high. There is a negative correlation between monthly living expenses and the amount of feedback, indicating that the lower the monthly living expenses, the stronger the consciousness of feedback society, and the more the amount of feedback. However, the significance between the two is not high.

The above research was carried out on the theoretical basis of the predecessors, and the results were obtained by the empirical analysis method, which makes the theory more convincing and provides a basis for the subsequent research.

5. Ways to Enhance the Feedback Will among Funded College Students

5.1 Strengthen the Diversified Construction of Campus Culture

Campus culture is the general term of Material culture construction, spiritual culture construction and institutional culture construction, which takes students as the main body and campus as the main space, and covers all teachers and staff of the school. It is the epitome of school culture, an important channel for students to absorb various cultures, and also a concentration place for the school to cultivate high-quality talents for the country. Schools are not only places for learning cultural knowledge, but also important places for educating people. Campus culture as an environmental education force, is a place where the country needs talents, an important place for spreading socialist spiritual civilization and socialist culture, and a second external environment for college students to survive. It has an indelible, subtle and lasting impact on the healthy growth of college students. College students who receive education in schools have strong plasticity and imitation ability. Without a good environment, students are more likely to go astray. Therefore, schools should fully mobilize the subjective initiative of college students according to national policies, educational objectives, and cultivation goals, organically combine morality, intelligence, physical fitness, and aesthetics, and dissolve them in cultural activities. They should also rely on the long-term and delicate influence of their surroundings, Creating an excellent educational environment that is suitable for the comprehensive development of college students' mental health cannot simply cultivate students' thoughts and qualities through the teaching of cultural knowledge. Only in this way can college students adapt to the development of the times, resist the erosion of negative factors, and meet the requirements of the motherland. Therefore, the construction of campus culture in universities should be at the forefront of the times, giving full play to its exemplary and radiating role, and building an excellent campus culture. It is necessary to create an atmosphere for college students to cultivate their sentiments, build a sound and healthy personality, and improve their comprehensive quality. This will generate positive and upward spiritual power for college students, and encourage them to constantly strive forward.

5.2 Establishing the Role of Teachers' Words and Deeds

Teachers are those who preach, impart knowledge, and dispel doubts. They are not just simple teachers, but role models for students to learn from. The words and actions of teachers affect the formation of students' personality traits and the healthy growth of students, which puts forward high requirements for teachers. In teaching, teachers should not only reserve a certain amount of knowledge, but also adopt appropriate teaching methods to impart knowledge that students can accept, understand, absorb, and apply. They should not only teach courses well, but also do a good job in teaching and research. They should not only engage in social practice, but also solve students' active doubts. They should also possess noble moral character and great personality charm, Give college students a subtle influence, integrate ideological and political education and the fine traditional education of the motherland into their daily teaching activities, reform the routine professional cultural courses, and integrate them into the study of ideological and political courses, so that college students can strengthen their own ideological and political cultivation in learning professional cultural courses, and fully mobilize their enthusiasm and initiative, Integrating students' active learning with teacher teaching, guiding college students in self-management, self-service, and self-education, continuously improving their political consciousness, and gradually forming themselves as the pillars of the motherland. The prosperity of the motherland has my obligation, and I must take on the responsibility of building a beautiful motherland, and encourage more people to provide help to those in need, contributing to what needs to be done.

5.3   Creating a Good and Comfortable Social Environment

College students are the future of our country. They live in society and are constantly influenced by the social environment, which influences their healthy growth from various aspects and prepares them for a strong spiritual food. News, newspapers, magazines and periodicals, and various publicity venues should actively carry forward the traditional Chinese virtues, national spirit and the Zeitgeist; Actively developing network resources, continuously improving and innovating, forming diversified online education activities, seizing the initiative of network resources, firmly grasping the correct direction, purifying the network environment, effectively enhancing the positive impact of the network, and creating a healthy, comfortable, quiet and peaceful environment; Regularly or irregularly organize advanced representatives from various industries to give lectures to college students, continuously influence their correct ideological guidance with vivid and advanced models, and vigorously exert the power of role models, so that college students can grow up healthy and happy under the care and care of society, become useful talents in society, and realize personal self-worth.

6. Conclusion

College students are the wealth of the country, the future of the country, and the hope of schools and families. It is the duty of the country to cultivate college students. Cultivating college students in line with the needs of the motherland cannot be separated from the influence of the society, education from schools, and guidance from teachers. I hope that while cultivating the future pillars of our country, while ensuring the basic needs of college students, the country can continuously optimize the social environment and create a good campus environment. Through the guidance of exemplary models in various industries and using different channels of information exchange, we can help them establish correct views on life and form a sound personality. It is expected that under the cultivation of the motherland, more and more college students can gradually improve their own goals, with the motto " soldiers who do not want to be generals are not good soldiers ", constantly inspiring and demanding themselves with strict and noble standards, doing everything around them with a serious and meticulous heart, infecting and influencing people around them with love, and driving more like-minded individuals to fully utilize their strengths with practical actions, to better give back to our motherland, inherit and carry forward the fine traditional virtues of China, and make our country increasingly strong.

References

[1]   Cui Yuan, Xue Yuan. Research on the construction of a precise subsidy system for students from economically difficult families in colleges and universities[J]. Reform & Openning, 2017, (18): 101 - 102 (in Chinese).

[2]   Doyle, W. R. Adoption of Merit-Based Student Grant Programs: An Event History Analysis[J]. Educational Evaluation and Policy Analysis, 2006, (28): 259 - 285.

[3]   Lee, Jungmin. Does merit - based aid improve college affordability? Testing the bennett hypothesis in the ear of merit - based aid[J]. Journal of Student Financial Aid, 2016, (46).

[4]   Mark Stater. Financial Aid, Student Background, and the Choice of First-year College Major[J]. Eastern Economic Journal, 2011, (37).

[5]   Li Zhijie. Analysis of federal college student assistance policies in the United States[D]. Shanghai: East China Normal University, 2012 (in Chinese).

[6]   Ronald J. Peters, JR. The relationship between psychpological distress, behavioral indicators and african American student financial aid attainment difficulty[J]. American Journal of Health Studies, 2011, (3).

[7]   Qu Shaowei. Research on the performance evaluation of the funding management for college students - Based on the empirical analysis of 120 universities directly under the Central government[J]. Educational Research, 2015, (08) (in Chinese).

[8]   Jacob P. Gross. Introduction: reauthorization: an opportunity for substantive change in how students pay for college[J]. Journal of Student Financial Aid, 2015, (45).

[9]   Cerin Lindgren savage. Regulatory oversight of student financial aid through accreditation of institutions of higher education[J]. Journal of Law and Education, Summer, 2016, (45).

[10]   Loris Vergolini, Nadir Zanini. Away, but not too far from home. The effects of financial aid on university enrolment decisions[J]. Economics of Education Review, 2015, (49).

[11]   Zhao Guicheng. A study on the characteristics of the moral education function of the university student assistance system[J]. Modern Education Science, 2010, (06) (in Chinese).

[12]   Bekishev K. Trends in Development of the Educational System in the Republic of Kazakhstan[J]. Russian Journal of General Chemistry, 2013, (83) 3:594-603.

[13]   Souvik Sengupta, "Towards Finding a Minimal Set of Features for Predicting Students' Performance Using Educational Data Mining", International Journal of Modern Education and Computer Science, Vol.15, No.3, pp. 44-54, 2023.

[14]   Yana Serkina, Alena Vobolevich, Irina Petunina, Aleksandra Zakharova, "Analysis of the Information and Communication Technology in Blended Learning for Economics Students in the Context of Digitalization", International Journal of Modern Education and Computer Science, Vol.15, No.3, pp. 33-43, 2023.

[15]   Juma'zoda Malika, Farruh Ahmedov, "Effective Pedagogical Aspects of the Development of Creative Qualities in Students", International Journal of Education and Management Engineering, Vol.13, No.1, pp. 35-40, 2023.

Artificial Intelligence, Medical Engineering and Education
Z.B. Hu et al. (Eds.)
© *2024 The Authors.*
This article is published online with Open Access by IOS Press and distributed under the terms
of the Creative Commons Attribution Non-Commercial License 4.0 (CC BY-NC 4.0).
doi:10.3233/ATDE231368

A Discussion of the Pedagogical Benefits of Nodal Knowledge in University Physics

Fengmei CHEN, Fanbin TANG, Lanxiang WEI, Yao SU, Yanghao YAN, Wugang LI[1]

School of Intelligent Manufacturing, Nanning University, Nanning, China

ORCiD ID: Wugang LI https://orcid.org/0009-0000-8177-9228

Abstract. Focusing on nodal knowledge in university physics, this paper describes the definition and categorisation of nodal knowledge, revealing its characteristics and its connection to core knowledge. Through in-depth analyses, it is found that nodal knowledge is an important link in the physics subject that promotes and extends core knowledge, embodying the characteristics of fundamentality, selectivity, transition and diversity. In addition, this paper also highlights the superiority of using nodal knowledge for teaching, which not only helps students reduce the burden of memorisation, but also promotes the construction of a clear structure in the knowledge network and the understanding of the ins and outs of knowledge. Crucially, nodal knowledge makes it easier for students to understand and derive subject knowledge, thus helping them to master it more effectively.

Keywords. University physics, Nodal knowledge, Teaching superiority.

1. Introduction

The teaching of core knowledge, which is the mainstay of the knowledge structure, has always received a lot of attention in both Chinese and foreign educational circles. Educators and researchers generally agree that mastery of important core knowledge is crucial for students' future cognition as well as thought formation [1-2]. In China, for example, in education from primary school to university, teachers repeatedly emphasise the importance of core knowledge and require students to understand and memorise core knowledge until they master it [3-4]. For the West, in fact, as early as the 1990s, the United States as a representative of the science curriculum reform, which is highlighted by the following feature: "Emphasis is placed on core knowledge as the centre and main line of organizing the content of the science curriculum [5-7]. In the UK, core knowledge was incorporated into the national curriculum program to emphasize the teaching of core knowledge [8]. In addition, many international educational organizations are also advocating the importance of teaching core knowledge, for example, the PISA test of the organization for Economic Co-operation and Development (OECD) also focuses on examining students' core knowledge and competence [9]. In short, whether in China or in the West, the teaching of core knowledge has been receiving much attention and emphasis.

However, this paper argues that a more important aspect of teaching and learning than core knowledge, and one that has gone unnoticed, is what is referred to in this paper as "Nodal knowledge". If educators pay attention to the use of nodal knowledge in

---

[1] Corresponding Author: Wugang LI, E-mail: 13407720832@163.com.

teaching and learning, it will be more effective than using core knowledge alone. Therefore, this paper discusses the concept, characteristics, classification, and pedagogical advantages of nodal knowledge using a university physics course as an example.

2. Definition and Classification of Nodal Knowledge

2.1. Definition of Nodal Knowledge

In the process of scientific research, the acquisition of knowledge can be an instantaneous outburst; while in the process of teaching, the acquisition of knowledge requires a process [10-11]. For example, from the perspective of knowledge system, what is in the first position should be the most basic concepts, principles and laws, such as "source knowledge", and on the basis of these source knowledge, the next derivation or calculation will reach "nodal knowledge", and then, through further reasoning, it will eventually develop into "core knowledge". Nodal knowledge is a very important link between source and core knowledge. These nodal knowledge can be developed independently as a core knowledge point, or sometimes they can be differentiated into multiple core knowledge points. Additionally, they also can be the core concepts, core principles or key skills of the subject, which are essential for understanding and mastering the subject knowledge.

If the structure of a fruit tree is compared to the structure of a knowledge system, then the roots of the tree can be regarded as the source knowledge, and the trunk and branches can be regarded as the derivation process. Through derivation, the source knowledge firstly derives the nodal knowledge, and then the nodal knowledge derives the nodal knowledge or core knowledge, so the nodal knowledge can be regarded as the fork joints of the trunk and branches. Or, the nodal knowledge is then deduced or acted out to finally get the core knowledge, which are just like the fruit of the tree's blossom. As shown in Figure 1, the basic knowledge structure of source, nodal and core knowledge and their interrelationships can be visualized in a single diagram. It is clearly reflected in this figure that the status of nodal knowledge is very important.

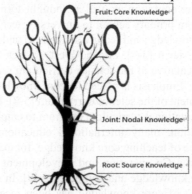

Figure 1. Diagram of the relationship between source, nodal and core knowledge

In order to more clearly elaborate the concept, classification, characteristics of nodal knowledge and its advantages in university physics teaching, this paper takes the university physics course as the research object and proposes that the nodal knowledge of the university physics discipline refers to those that are in line with the requirements of the educational objectives, can be adapted to the development of the cognitive structure of the students, and are between the source knowledge and the core knowledge, which mainly includes the physical concepts, the physical principles, and the regularity of the physical content.

2.2. Classification of Nodal Knowledge

There are various types of nodal knowledge identified in university physics textbooks, which can be broadly categorised into the following five types:

1) Single Line Type

"Single Line" means that in a knowledge structure, the knowledge of the previous node is obtained through a series of logical deduction to the knowledge of the subsequent node, both of which are key node knowledge. The latter node knowledge is deepened and developed downwards to form the core knowledge point, and there is no more branching. Taking the form of vector components as an example, it is used as the knowledge of the previous nodal which is gradually deduced to form the knowledge of the latter nodal, the vector components of light, which further leads to the core knowledge point of Marius' law $I = I_0 \cos^2 \alpha$. The simple structure diagram of this type is shown in Figure 2. (Note: Solid indicates nodal knowledge and hollow indicates core knowledge. The same applies to all the following.)

Figure 2. Single line type

2) Bifurcated Type

"Bifurcated Type" means that in a knowledge structure, a nodal knowledge point can be derived from multiple core knowledge points after derivation. For example, in the interwoven knowledge system of mathematics and physics, taking the section of dot product $\vec{A} \cdot \vec{B} = |A||B|\cos(A,B)$ and fork product of vectors $\vec{A} \times \vec{B} = |A||B|\sin(A,B)$ as an example, if this knowledge point is first understood and grasped, the related core knowledge points of the formula for work done by a variable force $W = \int_a^b \vec{F} \cdot dt$, the formula for work done by a torque $W = \int_a^b \overline{M}d\theta$, momentum torque $\vec{L} = \vec{r} \times \vec{p}$, torques $\overline{M} = \vec{r} \times \vec{F}$, etc. can be understood and grasped more easily. This suggests that one should have the courage to break the boundaries of knowledge and transcend boundaries in the study of subjects such as mathematics and physics. An example can also be given of Newton's second law $\overline{F} = \dfrac{d\vec{p}}{dt}$ as a nodal knowledge point on which to base the derivation of the momentum theorem, the angular momentum theorem, and the kinetic energy theorem for a mass. A diagram of this simple structure can be seen in Figure 3.

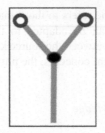

Figure 3. Bifurcated type

3) Single Line - Bifurcated Type

"Single Line - Bifurcated Type" means that in a knowledge structure, there are two progressive main nodal of knowledge, in which the knowledge of the former nodal is obtained through a series of derivations to obtain the knowledge of the latter nodal, and the latter nodal is further derived from the derivation algorithms to derive a number of core knowledge points. Taking the dot product of vectors as an example of section knowledge, the formula for work done by a variable force is obtained through derivation, and based on this, the loop theorem of electrostatic field $\oint_L \vec{E} \cdot d\vec{l} = 0$ and the amperometric loop theorem $\oint_L \vec{B} \cdot d\vec{l} = \mu_0 \Sigma_{(\text{inside } L)} I$ can be derived respectively. In addition, the phase difference between two partial vibrations $\Delta\varphi$ can be used as an example to obtain the wave-travel difference between two columns of waves δ_{wave} or two beams of light δ_{light} by expanding the wave-travel difference, and on the basis of this, the enhancement and attenuation conditions for wave interference and the interference conditions for two beams of light can be obtained, respectively. A diagram of this simple structure can be seen in Figure 4.

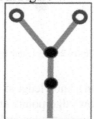

Figure 4. Single line - bifurcated type

4) Multi Type

The term "Multi Type" refers to a body of knowledge in which multiple nodes of knowledge are derived from a certain predecessor knowledge through a series of derivations. These nodal knowledge are further derived from multiple core knowledge points based on the pre-nodal knowledge after another derivation. For example, in the field of electromagnetism, the electrical flux formulas $\phi_e = \oint_s \vec{E} \cdot d\vec{S}$ and magnetic flux formulas $\phi_B = \oint_s \vec{B} \cdot d\vec{S}$ are derived using the dot-multiplication operation of vectors as the pre-nodal knowledge. These two formulas are used as nodal knowledge to derive two core knowledge points, Gauss's Theorem $\oint_s \vec{E} \cdot d\vec{S} = \frac{1}{\varepsilon_0} \Sigma_{(\text{inside } S)} q_i$ and Gauss's Theorem in Magnetic Fields $\oint_s \vec{B} \cdot d\vec{S} = 0$, respectively. A diagram of this type of simple structure is shown in detail in Figure 5.

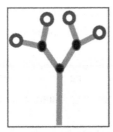

Figure 5. Multi type

5) Composite Type

"Composite Type" means that in a knowledge system, a knowledge point can be both a nodal knowledge point and a core knowledge point, and a new core knowledge point can be derived through derivation. For example, the kinematic formula of the compound pendulum $\dfrac{d^2\theta}{dt^2}+\dfrac{3g}{2l}\theta=0$ is both a core knowledge point and a nodal knowledge point,

and the kinematic formula of the single pendulum $\dfrac{d^2\theta}{dt^2}+\dfrac{g}{l}\theta=0$ can be obtained

directly through derivation, thus deriving a new core knowledge point. In addition, the point of Newton's second law is both a core knowledge point and a nodal knowledge point, and in its formula, if the acceleration is made equal to zero, the point of Newton's first law can be deduced. A diagram of this simple structure can be seen in Figure 6.

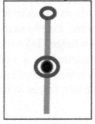

Figure 6. Composite type

3. Characteristics of Nodal Knowledge and Comparison with Core Knowledge

3.1. Characteristics of Nodal Knowledge

The four characteristics of node knowledge are shown below.

1) Fundamental

The nodal knowledge of physics contains basic physical concepts, principles and formulas, etc. Core knowledge is often built on the basis of nodal knowledge, so nodal knowledge plays a pivotal role in laying the foundation in the development of physics. In the teaching of physics, due to the key position of nodal knowledge, students can construct core knowledge logically and progressively through learning and applying nodal knowledge under the guidance of teachers.

2) Transitional

Nodal knowledge is crucial in the knowledge system, which is between the source knowledge and core knowledge, and has a clear hierarchical structure and logical relationship between the knowledge points. As a specific knowledge point with the role of starting and ending, nodal knowledge plays a decisive role in building a complete knowledge system and promoting the interconnection between knowledge points.

3) Selectivity

The selection of nodal knowledge of physics may take into account a degree of personal subjectivity in addition to the principle of objectivity. For example, both "Derivation of displacement vectors $\dfrac{d\vec{r}}{dt}$ " and "Displacement versus time $\vec{r}(t)$ " can be used as nodal knowledge, but choosing " $\dfrac{d\vec{r}}{dt}$ " as nodal knowledge may be more appropriate than " $\vec{r}(t)$ ". However, "Derivation of displacement vectors" as a node knowledge may be more suitable for teaching than "Relationship between displacement and time". In physics, one derivation of the displacement vector yields the instantaneous velocity, another derivation yields the instantaneous acceleration, and the integration of the velocity yields the equation of motion. Therefore, the " $\dfrac{d\vec{r}}{dt}$ " is in the key position of describing the physical quantities of the object's motion, and teaching it as a nodal knowledge can connect these physical quantities more quickly, which is convenient for students to learn and master.

4) Diversity

Nodal knowledge of physics does not exist in isolation, but has several different nodal knowledge, which are often followed by higher nodes. These nodes get more knowledge of other nodes through various derivations and derivatives, forming an intricate but ordered network of knowledge. At the same time, the physical knowledge points themselves can be both node knowledge and core knowledge. Take the formula of work done by variable force as an example, it can be regarded as a nodal knowledge point, but from the perspective of teaching objectives, it is also a core knowledge point. Based on this, we can derive formulas for work done by various forces to further enrich our knowledge system.

3.2. Comparison of Nodal and Core Knowledge

The following compares nodal and core knowledge in terms of quantity, status and role:

1) In Terms of Quantity

Quantitatively, node knowledge can be derived to infer multiple core knowledge, which makes node knowledge often less quantitative than core knowledge. Take the dynamics part of university physics as an example, the core knowledge stipulated in the teaching objectives are: Newton's three laws, the momentum theorem, the impulse theorem, the law of conservation of momentum, the equation of work done by force, the theorem of kinetic energy, and the law of conservation of mechanical energy, etc. *23*, but the ones that can be categorised as nodal knowledge are Newton's second law, the expression of work done, the theorem of momentum, and the theorem of angular momentum are just *4*, which is fewer than the number of core knowledge.

Core knowledge is the expansion and refinement of nodal knowledge, which is an important part of the subject system. The mastery of nodal knowledge can not only help learners better understand core knowledge, but also enable them to have a more comprehensive understanding of the entire subject system. Therefore, in the process of education, teachers should pay attention to the teaching of nodal knowledge in order to help students better master the core knowledge and improve the learning effect.

2) In Terms of Status

In terms of status, nodal knowledge can be regarded as the knowledge point of the process, which is located in a key link or pivotal position in the discipline system. Core knowledge, on the other hand, is in the terminal position and is the final goal and outcome in the discipline system [12]. Nodal knowledge is the connection and transition point between different knowledge points in the discipline system, which connects different knowledge points and makes the discipline system more systematic and structured. Core knowledge, on the other hand, is the final outcome in the disciplinary system, which represents the most basic, important, and central concepts, principles, or methods in the subject area. Therefore, both nodal knowledge and core knowledge should be valued and paid attention to in the process of education and learning. Nodal knowledge is the foundation and key to understanding and mastering core knowledge, while core knowledge is the expansion and deepening of nodal knowledge. But mastering nodal knowledge is more conducive to mastering core knowledge, so that we can better understand and master the subject system and improve the learning effect and knowledge application ability.

3) In Terms of Role

Nodal knowledge is a key point in the derivation process, which is often an important concept, principle or method in the subject system, the core of derivation and arithmetic, and an important step or turning point in the derivation of a series of core knowledge. Nodal knowledge plays a role in the derivation process, which can connect different knowledge points to form a complete knowledge system. In some cases, node knowledge itself may also become core knowledge, because node knowledge is one of the most important knowledge points in the subject system, which represents important concepts, principles or methods in the subject area. The mastery of nodal knowledge plays a crucial role in the smoothness of the deduction process and the understanding and mastery of core knowledge. Without the mastery of nodal knowledge, the deduction process will not be able to proceed or will be hindered, and at the same time, it will also affect the understanding and memorisation of the core knowledge. Therefore, the teaching and mastery of nodal knowledge should be emphasised in the education and learning process in order to better deduce and deepen the core knowledge. Only by mastering these key nodal knowledge can students be helped to understand and remember the core knowledge points and better understand and master the subject system.

4. Teaching Advantages of Nodal Knowledge

4.1. Reducing the Burden of Memory

The amount of nodal knowledge is less than the core knowledge, but nodal knowledge plays a crucial role in physics. University physics courses involve many complex concepts and theories, in order to help students reduce their learning burden and improve their learning efficiency, teachers can summarise the nodal knowledge of the course content and focus on these nodal knowledge. By mastering these nodal knowledge, students can understand and master the relevant physics concepts and theories more easily. In addition, students can use this nodal knowledge to deduce and explain other related physical phenomena and formulas. This not only reduces students' burden of memorisation, but also improves their comprehension and application skills. Although core knowledge also has its importance in physics, they are more often regarded as more complicated and complex physical concepts, principles and formulas compared to nodal knowledge [13]. Therefore, by summarising and explaining nodal knowledge, students can understand and master the fundamental concepts and theories of physics more effectively. After mastering the nodal knowledge, it is logical for the core knowledge to be mastered. Thus learning nodal knowledge allows students to memorise fewer unnecessary formulas, theorems and laws and reduces the memory burden.

4.2. Clearer Lines of Knowledge

Physical node knowledge plays a key role in the structure of the knowledge system and serves as a bridge between different knowledge links and systems. It connects different knowledge points to form a systematic knowledge network. When students are able to remember these key nodal knowledge in the knowledge system and learn to remember and understand through association, they are able to grasp the ins and outs of physics knowledge more clearly. Therefore, understanding and remembering the core knowledge associated with these nodal knowledge can significantly improve learning efficiency and is an important part of our ability to better understand a small system of knowledge or even the entire subject system. For learners, nodal knowledge is an important breakthrough in learning the subject of physics; for educators, it is the key to designing efficient teaching programmes. Therefore, nodal knowledge is an indispensable part of learning physics, and it is essential to pay attention to it.

4.3. Easier to Understand and Derive

In the past, teachers may have tended to overlook the importance of nodal knowledge as it is often easier to understand and derive than core knowledge. However, once students are proficient in node knowledge, teachers only need a little guidance and they are able to understand the subsequent core knowledge points naturally. Therefore, mastery of nodal knowledge is helpful for students to better understand and apply the core knowledge points. In addition, if students show forgetfulness of a particular knowledge point, they can also derive the core knowledge point through nodal knowledge. This means that even if students forget some specific knowledge points, they can still derive them through nodal knowledge to better apply what they have learnt. Therefore, nodal knowledge is an important tool to consolidate learning and help students apply their physics knowledge more flexibly to solve real-world problems. This means that nodal knowledge not only plays a key role in understanding the subject system, but also supports students' long-term memory and knowledge application. Overall, nodal knowledge is an important part of the learning process in the subject of physics. It is essential for teachers to pay attention to and develop students' nodal knowledge, which can help students understand the knowledge system of the Physics subject in a deeper way and improve their learning outcomes and knowledge application.

4.4. Facilitates Retention of Core Knowledge

Usually, when a teacher explains a core knowledge point, students often find it difficult to understand and remember this knowledge point because the speed of explanation is too fast, and they can easily forget it. Although this way of teaching seems natural and covers all the knowledge points to be mastered [14], students do not remember the follow-up deeply enough because they are not made to pay special attention to this key point. If students can be made to deeply understand and remember this node of knowledge, then they will be more likely to master this core knowledge point [15, 16]. Taking the teaching of Marius' law as an example, if the teacher just lists out the formula and lets students briefly recognise this knowledge, it will be easy to forget it afterwards. However, if the operations of vectors and the vectorial nature of light are emphasized, even if students forget the specific content of Marius' law, they will be able to deduce it quickly through vector operations. Therefore, mastering the knowledge of knots is crucial for learning the subject of physics.

5. Conclusion

In this paper, a new concept of "nodal knowledge" is innovatively proposed, and the characteristics, types and pedagogical benefits of nodal knowledge are discussed in depth from the perspective of the university physics discipline. Through detailed elaboration and analysis, the characteristics of basic, selective, transitional and diversified nodal knowledge as well as the five different types of nodal knowledge are comprehensively understood. Meanwhile, the key role of nodal knowledge in the process of understanding and deriving core knowledge points is highlighted through comparison with core knowledge. In addition, this paper also focuses on the pedagogical benefits of nodal knowledge, especially in helping students to form a more scientific physical mindset, which is more conducive to effectively linking physical knowledge together, restructuring the architecture of physical knowledge, and forming a three-dimensional physical mindset. It provides new ideas and methods for optimising university physics teaching. Although the research in this paper has achieved some results, there are still many issues that deserve further exploration and research. For example, the use of nodal knowledge and core knowledge for comparative teaching, through the pre-test and post-test to compare their teaching effect and the formation of physical mindset and so on. In the future, we will continue to pay attention to the research progress of nodal knowledge and keep exploring new teaching methods and strategies to better optimise university physics teaching and help students form scientific thinking as well as a structured knowledge system.

Acknowledgment

This project is supported by Guangxi Education Science "14th Five-Year Plan" 2022 Private Higher Education Special Topic. (Project No.: 2022ZJY3241)

References

[1]   Wei Guangming. Elongating the process of construction: The contingent choice of core knowledge teaching[J]. Jiangsu Education Research, 2017(11): 8-13+2. (in Chinese)
[2]   Core Knowledge Foundation. Core implementation practices: a guide to effective implementation of core knowledge[R]. Core Knowledge Foundation, 2019: 11-12.
[3]   Liu Xiaoping. Research on the teaching of core knowledge of primary school mathematics based on the development of key competences in the discipline[J]. JiangSu Education, 2019(01): 37-41. (in Chinese)
[4]   Zhai Shuang. Research on teaching core knowledge of high school physics[D]. Northeast Normal University, ChangChun, 2015. (in Chinese)
[5]   HIRSCH Jr. E D. The making of americans: democracy and out schools[M]. New Haven: Yale University Press, 2009: 8.

[6]   Core Knowledge Foundation. Core knowledge sequence: content and skill guidelines for preschool[S]. Charlottesville: Core Knowledge Foundation, 2022: 1.

[7]   Core   Knowledge   Foundation.   Knowledge-   Based   Schooling   [EB/OL].   2023-05-20. https://www.coreknowledge.org/our-approach/knowledge-based-schools/.

[8]   E. D. Hirsch Jr. American Ethnicity: a Sense of Commonality[M]. Charlottesville: Core Knowledge Foundation, 2022: 149.

[9]   Dehart Hurd. New Directions in Teaching Secondary School. Chicago[J]. Rand McNally & Company. 1971, 247.

[10]   Wu, Yuanyue. Research on Knowledge Acquisition and Its Criteria [D]. Huazhong Normal University, WuHan, 2016. (in Chinese)

[11]   Swanand K. Navandar, Arvind W. Kiwelekar, Manjushree D. Laddha, "A Performance Analysis of the Impact of Prior-Knowledge on Computational Thinking", International Journal of Modern Education and Computer Science, Vol. 15, No. 2, pp. 54-61, 2023.

[12]   Long Baoxin. Towards core knowledge teaching: The contemporary implications of efficient classroom teaching[J]. Global Education Prospects, 2012, 41(3): 19-24. (in Chinese)

[13]   Zhang Lichang. Creating an efficient classroom based on core knowledge mapping[J]. Curriculum. Teaching Materials. Teaching Methods, 2014, 34(08): 26-31. (in Chinese)

[14]   Walid Mestadi, Khalid Nafil, Raja Touahni, Rochdi Messoussi, "Knowledge Representation by Analogy for the Design of Learning and Assessment Strategies", International Journal of Modern Education and Computer Science, Vol. 9, No. 6, pp. 9-16, 2017.

[15]   Swanand K. Navandar, Arvind W. Kiwelekar, Manjushree D. Laddha, "A Performance Analysis of the Impact of Prior-Knowledge on Computational Thinking", International Journal of Modern Education and Computer Science, Vol.15, No.2, pp. 54-61, 2023.

[16]   Ismail Aliyu, A. F. D. Kana, Salisu Aliyu. " Development of Knowledge Graph for University Courses Management ", International Journal of Education and Management Engineering, Vol.10, No.2, pp.1-10, 2020.

Artificial Intelligence, Medical Engineering and Education
Z.B. Hu et al. (Eds.)
© 2024 The Authors.
doi:10.3233/ATDE231369

Optimization Path of College Network Classroom in Teaching Practice in Post-Epidemic Era

Lifang SU, Xixi GU[1]

Wuhan Railway Vocational College of Technology, Wuhan, China

Abstract. The rapid development of Internet technology provides technical support for online classroom. Since the COVID-19, online classroom has been widely promoted and integrated with traditional classroom. However, the practice of online classroom in China is short and the experience is not yet rich. Through the survey of online classroom use and satisfaction of college students, it is found that the evaluation of online classroom is mixed. It is mainly attributed to students' learning attitude, outdated teaching methods of teachers, imperfect teaching management and other problems. To solve these three problems, we should increase the publicity of online classroom to correct students' learning attitude. Teachers should use network technology resources to realize the diversification of teaching methods, and schools should use multiple evaluation to improve teaching supervision, so as to promote the high-quality development of online classroom.

Key Words. Post-pandemic era; Online classroom; Practice of teaching

1. Introduction

After the outbreak of COVID-19, universities and colleges have started the online teaching mode of "continuous suspension of classes". Online classroom is an online learning mode advocated and encouraged by the Chinese government and the Ministry of Education in order to actively prevent and control the epidemic, ensure health and safety, and not delay the study of college students. Although online classes played an important role in the critical period when the epidemic was raging, there was a mismatch between teaching and learning in online classes under the condition of the normalization of the epidemic, which led to the inefficient learning state of college students [1]. How to correctly open the online classroom "without suspension", after nearly three years of online classroom teaching practice, explore the optimization path of online classroom in college teaching, to provide a reference for the promotion of online classroom to daily teaching.

2. The Relationship Between Network Classroom and Traditional Classroom

Network classroom is a long-distance online interactive classroom based on the Internet network. Generally, network transmission technologies such as audio and video

---

[1] Corresponding Author: Xixi GU, Email: 526350860@qq.com.

transmission and data collaboration are adopted to simulate the real classroom environment and provide students with an effective teaching and learning environment through the network [2,3]. The network classroom is not only an empty place of pure materialization, but also a unity of materiality, spirituality and sociality, that is, the classroom should be a place for teachers and students to carry out spiritual, cultural and emotional communication and dialogue. Compared with the traditional classroom, the teaching subject, teaching content, teaching organization, teacher-student relationship and evaluation methods of the network classroom are rooted in the traditional classroom, but on the basis of the traditional classroom, great changes have taken place.

2.1 The Innovation of Network Classroom to Traditional Classroom

With the extensive promotion of Internet technology in the field of teaching, based on the expansion of the Internet field, new online classes such as MOOC, micro-courses, intelligent education cloud and YY Open Class have emerged [4-6]. These online classes initially move the traditional classroom teaching methods to the network platform with the help of the network terminal, breaking through the time and space restrictions of the traditional classroom administrative class, so that the classroom teaching can be carried out anytime and anywhere. Online classroom enables students to have a brand new learning experience inside and outside the classroom. Massive online information not only broadens college students, but also creates fair and high-quality education resources. But looking at the world, college teaching still follows the traditional class teaching system, the network classroom is just a teaching auxiliary way, the traditional classroom is the basis of teaching, the network classroom is the expansion of the traditional classroom.

2.2 The Online Classroom Is the Product of the Information Technology of Traditional Classroom Teaching

The traditional classroom is mainly taught by teachers, focusing on basic knowledge and theoretical knowledge. The traditional classroom is subject to time, teaching facilities and equipment and other factors, teaching means and paradigm are relatively simple, even with the use of multimedia, teaching whiteboard and other auxiliary equipment, the traditional classroom teaching mode has not changed, students still take listening to the lecture as the main task in class. With the popularization of 5G technology, online classroom can collect and filter complicated network information, present cutting-edge and valuable knowledge to students, and share teaching resources through online classroom. Through information-based teaching, the teaching content is presented in a richer way.

2.3 The Network Classroom Will Transform the Traditional Classroom into A Diversified Teaching Model

Traditional classroom only involves two teaching subjects, teachers and students, and they use textbooks as media to build the interactive relationship between teachers and students. Confined to the traditional classroom for the majority of classroom teaching, teacher-centered, so the classroom is unified. The online classroom breaks the unitary teaching mode of the traditional classroom. With the help of network information technology and media, the online classroom can establish a diversified, virtual and interactive classroom [7,8]. Teachers can pay attention to students' independent learning ability through online classroom, expand knowledge learning related to their major, and provide all-weather services [9]. Students can take extended learning and online tests through the online classroom to achieve two-way interaction between teachers and students [10-13]. In addition, the online classroom can also introduce experts, scholars, famous people to participate in the classroom teaching[14-18].

3.   Survey on The Use and Satisfaction of Online Classroom in The Post-Epidemic Era

China's online classroom started in 1994, but it was relatively late and developed slowly compared with foreign countries. Until the popularization of 5G technology, college students have become the most active group in online activities, which provides the possibility for the promotion of online classroom. In addition, after the outbreak of COVID-19, the Ministry of Education's requirement of continuous suspension of classes has made online classroom have a large number of teaching practices. Although the network classroom and the traditional classroom is two integral ones, has its irreplaceable role. However, there are some problems that need to be solved in the practice of online classroom in recent years. In order to accurately understand the use of online classes in colleges and universities, we conducted a survey through the questionnaire star. 300 college students were selected to issue questionnaires, and 286 valid questionnaires were collected to make a statistical analysis on the use status and satisfaction of online classes.

3.1 Basic Information about the Research Object

Among the valid questionnaires collected, 190 undergraduates accounted for 66.5%, and 96 junior college students accounted for 33.5%. From the retrieved questionnaires, the teaching equipment (FIG. 1), learning style (FIG. 2) and average daily online time (FIG. 3) used by them in the online class were counted respectively.

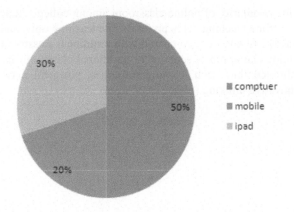

Figure 1. The teaching equipment used in the network class

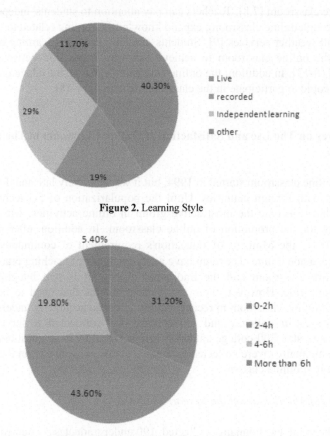

Figure 2. Learning Style

Figure 3. Average online study time per day

3.2   *Application of Network Classroom in Colleges and Universities*

According to the popularity of online classroom among college students, 73% of them prefer online + offline teaching, 21% prefer offline teaching only, and 6% prefer online teaching (Figure 4). In addition, compared with traditional classroom, college students believe that online classroom is superior to traditional classroom in terms of learning selectivity, unlimited time, rich learning resources, powerful network platform and stimulating innovative thinking (FIG. 5).

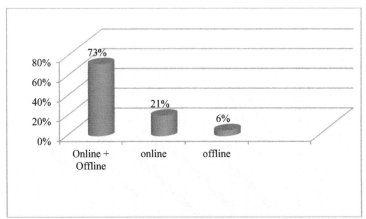

Figure 4. College students identify with online classroom

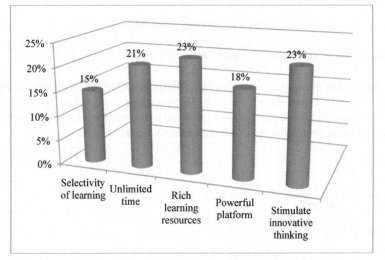

Figure 5. Network classroom advantage identification

3.3 The Use of Online Classroom Platform for College Students

The development of the Internet has led to the rise of a large number of online classroom platforms. Many college majors use different online classroom platforms in combination with their own school and specialty characteristics. Through the survey data, it is found that the mainstream online classroom platforms are MOOC, iCVE, and other online classroom teaching resources are relatively small (Figure 6).

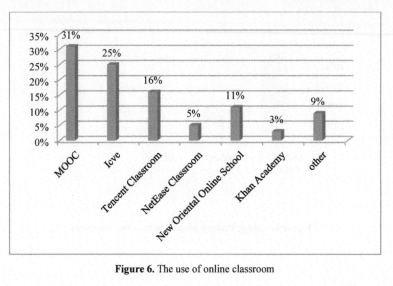

Figure 6. The use of online classroom

3.4 College Students' Satisfaction with Online Classroom Experience

When it comes to the satisfaction of online classroom experience, college students show obvious opposite views. From the collected questionnaires, it can be found that the number of students who support the continuation of online classes after the epidemic and the number of students who oppose it are basically equal. (Figure 7)

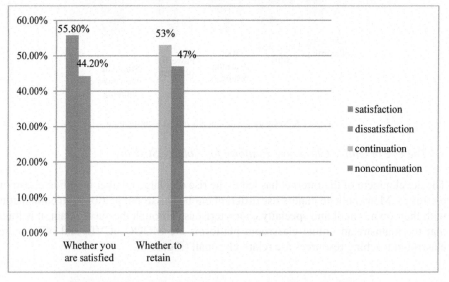

Figure 7. College students' satisfaction with online classroom experience

3.5 The Difficulties Encountered by College Students in Online Classroom Learning

In order to better analyze the factors influencing the effect of online classroom, the questionnaire sets open questions: "What are the difficulties encountered in online classroom learning?" After statistical analysis of the collected questionnaires, it is found that college students have various difficulties in online classroom learning, which are mainly manifested as lack of a good learning environment, weak self-control, low efficiency of classroom interaction and discussion, inability to use campus network resources, and difficulty in completing practical course content, (see Figure 8).

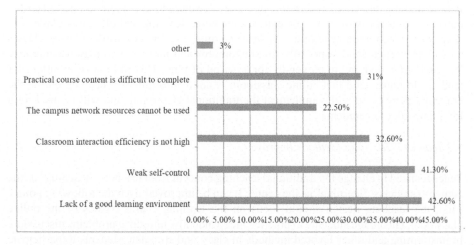

Figure 8. The difficulties encountered by college students in online classroom learning

4.   An Analysis of Factors Affecting the Satisfaction of Online Classroom

From the results of the questionnaire survey, it can be found that the implementation effect of online classroom teaching is mainly affected by three factors. One is the students' own learning attitude. Some students have relatively weak self-control, and after signing up, they don't pay attention to the classroom learning and start to do their own things. Some students' self-learning ability is poor, unable to keep up with the teaching progress of the network class, the completion of homework is not ideal. Second, teachers' teaching methods need to be improved. Many teachers still use traditional classroom teaching for online teaching, and the teaching resources are not fully prepared and the interaction with students is not enough to stimulate students' interest in online learning. At the same time, it also neglects the feedback of students' learning situation, fails to find the problems of online class in time, and adjusts the teaching methods of online class. Third, the network classroom supervision is weak. Due to the wide space of the online classroom, the school cannot carry out remote supervision of the classroom teaching effect, let alone realize the full coverage of the inspection, resulting in the loose discipline of the online classroom, teaching evaluation effect is not satisfactory. In view of the above three factors, it is necessary to improve from three aspects: students' learning attitude, teachers' teaching methods and school teaching management.

5. Countermeasures to Strengthen the Construction of Online Classroom in the Post-Epidemic Era

5.1 Students' Learning Attitude Should be Correct

It is necessary for school counselors and class teachers to cooperate to strengthen the education of students who are not enthusiastic about learning and often mix classes, so as to correct their learning attitude. At the same time, the publicity work of online classes should be strengthened, especially for sophomores and juniors, who may become lazy and tired after studying in university for a period of time. Therefore, it is important for students to understand that online classroom is not a substitute for teaching during the epidemic period, but will complement the traditional classroom, and will be used for a long time after the epidemic.

5.2 Teachers' Teaching Methods Improved

Teachers need to change the traditional teaching concept from teachers' "teaching" as the center to students' "learning" as the center. It can be improved from the following points. First, the teaching design should focus on the learning characteristics of the online classroom, encourage students to practice independently, introduce problems discussion, brainstorming and other favored methods in class, and stimulate students to participate in the classroom learning. Second, make arrangements before, during and after class. Assign preview tasks before class and let students bring questions into class. Increase classroom activities in class, pay attention to the data feedback of students' classroom activities, timely report the quality of classroom interaction, and increase the proportion of process assessment of online classroom activities. After class, homework is assigned on the network platform, and the results of students' homework can be clearly reported on the platform data. Teachers solve students' confusion in learning by means of QQ group and platform Q&A. Third, increase the construction of network teaching resources. The short videos and micro lessons that students like are introduced into the teaching resources. Students can learn and supplement their own knowledge anytime and anywhere through these short videos.

5.3 The Improvement of School Network Classroom Management

Good teaching management is indispensable to high-quality online classroom. On the one hand, schools need to strengthen the construction of curriculum resources, encourage teachers to actively build online resource courses, strengthen the guidance of teaching teams, organize teachers with good online classroom teaching effect to promote and exchange experience, and help and guide the construction of curriculum resources. On the other hand, it is also necessary to increase the teaching inspection of online class, from teaching plans, teaching plans, online class construction materials, organization of online lectures and other management methods, and feedback to the teacher, to ensure the completion of teaching objectives. In addition, it is also necessary to pay attention to the time arrangement of the network class. The class hours and time of the network class should be reasonably arranged. It should not be too long, otherwise it is not conducive to the physical and mental health of the students.

6. Conclusion

During the epidemic period, the online classroom played its advantages of time and field, and realized the suspension of classes without suspension. Teaching in the digital age should keep up with The Times. While giving full play to the advantages of the network classroom, the drawbacks of the traditional classroom single teaching are corrected, so that students' learning from "I learn" to "I learn". The formation of multiple evaluation of school teaching management will play a positive role in promoting educational equity in the future.

References

[1]   Jiao Wei, Xu Jicun. Classroom Space: Essence and Reconstruction[J]. Curriculum and Teaching, 2012, (19): 16-19.
[2]   Guo Bingjie., Give full play to the advantages of "Internet + Classroom" to Comprehensively improve the quality of education and teaching [J]. Educational Practice and Research. 2018, (3): 57-59.
[3]   Cao Zhongqiu, Zhang Chenyang, Kang Yadan. Investigation and countermeasure analysis of the current situation of college students' online classroom learning[J]. Education and Teaching Forum. 2020, (14): 317−319.
[4]   Du Yuhua, Ding Jin. Study on the existing problems and countermeasures of college students' online course learning[J]. Rural economy and Science and technology. 2020, 31(10): 344−354.
[5]   Xiao Junquan. Online courses accelerate the reform of "teaching and learning"[N]. China Teachers' News. 2020-04-22 (004).
[6]   Wang Zhijun, Chen Li. Connectionism: ontology of "internet + education"[J]. Distance Education in China. 2019, (8): 1-9.
[7]   Badugu S, Rachakatla B. Student's performance prediction using machine learning approach[C]. In Data Engineering and Communication Technology. Singapore: Springer; 2020. 3: 333–340.
[8]   Hooshyar D, Pedaste M, Yang Y. Mining educational data to predict students' performance through procrastination behavior[J]. Entropy, 2020; 22(1): 12.
[9]   Aqr M, Fors U, Tedre M. How the study of online collaborative learning can guide teachers and predict students' performance in a medical course[J]. BMC Med Educ. 2018, 18(1): 1–14.
[10]   T. Zhang, X. Shi, D. Zhang, and J. Xiao. Socio-economic development and electricity access in developing economies: A long-run model averaging approach[J]. Energy Policy, 2019. 132: 223–231.
[11]   L. D. Prasojo, A. Mukminin, A. Habibi, R. Hendra, and D. Iqroni, Building quality education through integrating ICT in schools: Teachers' attitudes, perception, and barriers[J]. QualityAccess to Success, 2019, 20(172): 45–50.
[12]   J. Wang, D. E. H. Tigelaar, and W. Admiral. Connecting rural schools to quality education: Rural teachers' use of digital educational resources[J]. Comput Human Behav, 2019, 101: 68–76.
[13]   Issah Baako, Prosper Gidisu, Sayibu Umar. Access to electricity in ghanaian basic schools and ICT in education policy rhetoric: empirical quantitative analysis and access theory approach[J]. International Journal of Education and Management Engineering, 2023, 13(5): 23-33.
[14]   Nyme Ahmed, Dip Nandi, A. G. M. Zaman, "Analyzing Student Evaluations of Teaching in a Completely Online Environment", International Journal of Modern Education and Computer Science, Vol.14, No.6, pp. 13-24, 2022.
[15]   K. Kashinath, R. L. N. Raju, "An Empirical Research on the Effectiveness online and Offline Classes of English Language Learning based on Student's Perception in Telangana Schools", International Journal of Modern Education and Computer Science, Vol.15, No.2, pp. 40-53, 2023.
[16]   Yana Serkina, Alena Vobolevich, Irina Petunina, Aleksandra Zakharova, "Analysis of the Information and Communication Technology in Blended Learning for Economics Students in the Context of Digitalization", International Journal of Modern Education and Computer Science, Vol.15, No.3, pp. 33-43, 2023.
[17]   Salah Al Khafaji, Sriram. B, "A Concept Review on MOOCs Research Findings – A Qualitative Approach", International Journal of Education and Management Engineering, Vol.13, No.4, pp. 19-25, 2023.
[18]   Soumi Majumder, Soumalya Chowdhury, Sayan Chakraborty, "Interactive Web-interface for Competency-based Classroom Assessment", International Journal of Education and Management Engineering, Vol.13, No.1, pp. 18-28, 2023.

568

Artificial Intelligence, Medical Engineering and Education
Z.B. Hu et al. (Eds.)
© *2024 The Authors.*
This article is published online with Open Access by IOS Press and distributed under the terms
of the Creative Commons Attribution Non-Commercial License 4.0 (CC BY-NC 4.0).
doi:10.3233/ATDE231370

Logical Path and Implementation Effect of Ideological and Ethical Curriculum with Different Courses with the Same Value Mode

Kaibo LV[1], Wei YUE, Wenting YANG, Zhuo CHEN

School of Environmental and Biological Engineering, Wuhan Technology and Business University, Wuhan 430065, China

Abstract. There are both differences and commonalities between the construction logic of ideological and ethical courses in colleges and universities and the mode of "different courses with the same education" in implementing the reform. "Different courses, Same education" is a lesson preparation activity for the same course and subject through the "four in one" links of expert guidance, teaching demonstration, free seminar and expert Q&A. The four Characteristics of Marxist Community Thought, the implementation of the fundamental task of moral education and the superiority of other models of lesson preparation are the theoretical logic, practical logic and comparative logic of this model. Respect each other's similarities and differences, seek common ground while reserving differences, pay attention to the unification of value orientation, the unification of methodology education, the unification of independence and openness between courses, and effectively form a collaborative education mechanism.

Key words. Ideological and ethical course in colleges and universities; "Different courses with same values"; Pattern building; effect

1. Introduction

Entering the new era, the future of national rejuvenation is arduous. At the 19th National Conference on Propaganda and Ideological Work and the National Symposium on Ideological and ethical Education Teachers, the General Secretary delivered an important speech, repeatedly emphasizing that education should aim at establishing morality and cultivating talents and cultivating new people of the era who shoulder the important mission of national rejuvenation [1]. As we all know, the curriculum system plays a vital role in cultivating talents [2].

The ideological and ethical theory course is called "thinking course", which is the key course to implement the fundamental task of educating people in the curriculum. Therefore, the ethical feature of the curriculum, the unity of teaching activities, the diversity of teachers are the basic requirements to improve the teaching quality of the curriculum [3,4]. However, there still exists some problems, such as narrow participation, non-standard course preparation process, and weak sense of gain. The

---

[1] Corresponding Author: Kaibo LV, E-mail: 32969265@qq.com.

courses research team has explored the different courses with the same values model since 2020, which was greatly supported by the teachers who teach ideological and ethical theory [5-7]. At present, the differences of "curriculum thinking mode" and "curriculum thinking mode" reform and the formation of a joint education mechanism require a further study and a summary combined with the goal of establishing morality and cultivating talents. This paper systematically represents its logical mechanism, practice route and value.

2. The Logical Mechanism of Different Courses with Same Values in Ideological and Ethical Courses in Colleges

"Different courses with same values " refers to different teaching design for the same teaching content, thus forming different teaching structures [8,9]. With its distinct "comparative" feature, "different courses with same values have become an important means to implement educational competition and evaluation activities in primary education, but there are few research and practices in the higher education.

2.1. The Theoretical Logic: The Inevitable Requirement of Marxist Community Thought

The thought of Community is an important part of Marxist theory, which embodies Marx and Engels' ideal for the future society. Marxist Community thought pays attention to the development of people, advocates the realization of people's free individual in the community, promotes all-round development of human being and achieves the harmonious unity of community and individual freedom. It provides a solid theoretical support for our current university ideological and ethical courses to Education Community". The Community affirmed by Marx, different from the illusory community is a real community. In class society, only the dominant minority can obtain freedom, as Marx pointed out, "individual freedom exists only for individuals who develop in ruling class" [10]. From Marx we find the weakness of illusory community, but also noticed the importance of community for human freedom. Therefore, in order to allow teachers who teach ideological and ethical theory gain freedom in teaching, it is necessary to build a integrated and united Teaching and Research Community.

2.2 Realistic Logic: the Requirement of the Times to Implement the Fundamental Task of Establishing Morality and Cultivating Talents.

Ideological and ethical course is an important to implement the fundamental task of establishing morality and cultivating talents. The key to having a good ideological and ethical course lies in teachers and the key to learning the ideological and ethical course well lies in students. In 2019, the General Office of the Communist Party of China Central Committee and The General Office of the State Council printed and issued "Several Opinions on Deepening the Reform and Innovation of Ideological and ethical Theory Courses in Schools in the New Era" (hereinafter referred to as the "Opinions"). It is required to generally implement the system of ideological and ethical teachers and establish a lesson preparation mechanism for ideological and ethical teachers hand in hand. To carry out different courses with same values in ideological and ethical courses in colleges is not only to put the requirements of the "Opinions" into effect, but also to comply with the requirements of the times of implementing the fundamental task of establishing morality and cultivating talents, which is shown in Figure 1.

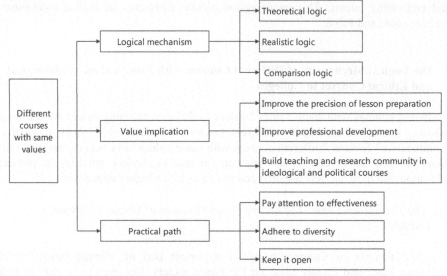

Figure 1. Model building process of "Different courses with same values"

The different courses with same values in ideological and ethical courses of colleges and universities aims to improve teachers' teaching level, but it is not the fundamental purpose. The fundamental purpose is to make students fall in love with ideological and ethical courses and enhance students' sense of gain. The reason why the lesson preparation activity can enhance students' sense of gains is that the lesson preparation is centered on students which takes students' professional differences and cognitive differences into consideration. Each teacher's teaching demonstrations should be based on the students' actual situation. In the process of demonstrations, the analysis of learning situation should be displayed so that the lesson preparation directly serves the students.

2.3. Comparison Logic: Four Typical Features that are Superior to Other Lesson Preparation Modes

Compared with other lesson preparation modes, different courses with same values in ideological and ethical courses of colleges and universities boosts four typical features - participants all over the country, standardized process, expert guidance for direction control, experts to answer questions and solve doubts by free discussion and brainstorming. Therefore, "different courses with same values" activity has strong advantages of precision, joint research and popularization.

First, adhere to expert guidance and direction control. In the class preparation meeting, experts generally focus on the teaching objectives, put forward guiding suggestions on how to carry out teaching design, how to talk about important and difficult points, how to effectively carry out teaching, etc., and offer suggestions for the same courses, control the theoretical direction and practical direction, which has a strong "precision" advantage.

Second, adhere to the model of demonstrating lesson examples. The difference of subjectivity and connotation derived from difference courses whose key is to respect the difference of subjectivity and show their strengths. The participants of the conference are ideological and ethical teachers of different levels, types and regions. They will provide reference with alternative samples, excellent quality, wide participation strong demonstration and distinctive characteristics for their peers. It not only reflects the differences of teachers' subjectivity, but also the differences of teaching design. At the same time, on the base of "difference courses", the meeting closely stick to the teaching theme and achieve the common teaching objectives to realize the organic unity of university and individuality.

Third, adhere to free discussion and concentrated wisdom. "Different courses with same values" focuses on building a platform for ideological and ethical teachers to cooperate and gather wisdom. "Joint research" has obvious advantages. It requires a free state of research, so the free speech is essential. In the free speech, teachers can share their experience about the experts' answer and teaching demonstration. They can share their own teaching experience and put forward puzzles.

Fourth, adhere to experts' answer to eliminate confusion. In the process of teaching and preparing lessons, there are often various puzzles. To solve these puzzles, we must be engaged in ideological and ethical teaching research for a long time, invite the experts with many years of front-line teaching experience to answer. In the "different courses with same values", there are both problems collected in advance and problems raised on the day of preparation. Experts and teachers of ideological and ethical courses have online exchanges and dispel doubts about common problems in teaching.

3. The Value Implication of "Different Teaching Design and the Same Content" in Ideological and Ethical Courses in Colleges and Universities

For the teaching of ideological and ethical courses in colleges and universities, the promotion of "different courses with same values " can not only optimize the teaching concept of ideological and ethical courses teachers and improve the teaching ability of ideological and ethical courses in colleges and universities, but also improve the accuracy of the preparation of ideological and ethical courses in colleges and universities and the effectiveness of joint research, expand the sharing of resources and help create a new model of high-quality ideological and ethical courses in colleges and universities.

3.1. Improve the Precision of Lesson Preparation and Enhance the Effectiveness of Ideological and Ethical Teaching

Accurate preparation is the most important value pursued by "different courses with same values". The key to accurate lesson preparation is to grasp the "pain points", carry out targeted lesson preparation discussions for specific topics and problems so that the pain points can be eliminated and then improve the teaching quality of ideological and ethical courses. "Different courses with same values" is oriented by problem awareness.

By collecting teachers' feedback and concerns before the meeting, the question-answering session is set up in the meeting to effectively solve the problems encountered by teachers, so as to ensure the accuracy of the content. "Different courses with same values" set up expert counseling and answer, and the purpose is to control the ethical, theoretical and practical direction. Direction and correctness are closely related, and incorrect guidance is not helpful for people to find the right direction, nor does expert guidance. different courses with same values" is different from the preparation meeting organized by the teaching and research office. If the preparation meeting is carried out several times in the teaching and research office and there is no high-level expert to participate, the preparation of lessons will fall into a low level cycle. In addition to the existing or potential competition mechanism and culture in some institutions, the evaluation of professional titles and annual assessment require the evaluation of teaching as the quantitative standard. Therefore, it is easy to cause conflicts of interest among teachers. The psychology of ride-sharing and competition is common among members and some teachers are afraid to share their teaching experience and results with colleagues in order to win the competition, thus affecting the quality of the meeting among teachers.

3.2. Improve Professional Development and the Overall Strength of Ideological and Ethical Teachers

In a narrow sense, the professional development of teachers refers to the dynamic process in which teachers, as individuals, gradually realize the transformation from childish to mature and grow from new teachers to expert teachers through the practical improvement of personal professional knowledge and skills. Teacher professional development is concerned with the quality of the individual's education, the cooperation way in career, how the educator integrates the knowledge and skills with job responsibilities, the relationships with colleagues, and the contractual and ethical relationships with those he or she serves." The professional development of ideological and ethical teachers includes educational cognition and design ability, implementation and management ability, evaluation and reflection ability, research, and innovation ability, etc."   It is based on the attribute dimension of ideological and ethical courses, firm ethical stance and communist belief, full theoretical literacy and education also includes affinity, stable understanding and transformation ability of Marxist theory, and keen time Ideological qualities such as sense of smell and ethical feeling." In the process of teachers' professional growth, especially the young teachers', the imparting and sharing of teaching experience is very important. The main responsibility of the ideological and ethical course teacher is to teach the ideological and ethical course well, but the ideological and ethical course has many disciplines, the teaching content changes quickly. Therefore, there is a high requirement for teachers. "Students put forward sensitive and sensitive issues about deep theory and practical problems." In terms of the title, it is not easy to explain these things clearly." "It is not easy to teach the ideological and ethical course well because this course is very demanding" [11].

3.3. Mutual Learning and Joint Research to Build Teaching and Research Community in Ideological and Ethical Courses

Ferdinand Tienis Tonnes, a famous German sociologist, 1855-1936, first proposed the sociological concept that "community is a lasting and true common life" and "it is the complete unity of human will in the original or natural state" [12]. Once the concept of community is incorporated into different contexts, it will rebuild the ethical community, economic community, learning community, etc. The nature of teachers' work determines that it is difficult to build a teaching and research community among teachers. The work of education is essentially a personal work, which depends on the individualized independent work of teachers to complete." The complexity and uncertainty of the educational also act as a resistance to teacher's cooperation. Different teachers have different understandings and preferences of educational goals, and the standards for education evaluation are also different. [13] Teachers who are confident in their own education do not easily absorb the educational advice of others. A teacher who is not confident in his own education is reluctant to show it to others. Therefore, trust is the basic premise of building the teaching and research community, and cooperation and sharing is the basic requirement of maintaining the teaching and research community. The "different courses with same values" teaching and research community is committed to building an expert-led, cooperative and shared teaching and research community, and strives to solve the three problems of "teaching", "learning" and "research" of ideological and ethical courses: The first is to focus on the key and difficult problems of education and the exploration of teaching methods and teaching modes and look forward to achieving more effective teaching; The second is to use the new platform to share teaching resources to ensure that teachers continue to learn; The third is to carry out horizontal and vertical integration research among teachers of ideological and ethical courses in colleges and universities and among teachers of ideological and ethical courses in large and middle schools to promote teachers' in-depth research[14, 15]. Some scholars have conducted research on the ideological and ethical course meeting of different courses with same values and pointed out that different courses with same values have strong characteristics of educational community from the perspective of model design, implementation and effect and is the physical manifestation of the concept of education community [16-18].

4. The practical path of "Different courses with same values" in ideological and ethical courses in Colleges and Universities

It is not only the process of the exchange of teaching ideas and the sharing of teaching experience, but also the same process of the teaching community. It needs careful organization and planning, especially in the aspects of effectiveness, diversity, and openness.

4.1. Pay Attention to Effectiveness: Keep Pace with the Daily Teaching Progress and Go Hand in Hand with Teaching Experts and Famous Teachers

For activities based on voluntary participation, "effectiveness" is the most important principle that education in different classes should follow. Without "effectiveness", the lesson preparation meeting will not have lasting cohesion and vitality. To improve the actual effect and enhance teachers' sense of achievement, "education in different classes" should pay attention to the following two points.

The school organized the first network meeting of "co-education in different courses and collaborative research" in time. There are three online teaching methods:

the combination of "synchronous" and "asynchronous", the combination of "1-to-1 centralized tutoring" and "1-to-1 separate teaching", and the combination of "individual questions" and "common questions". Reached a consensus on the teaching of online education that "the classroom is carefully managed, the content is carefully designed, and the process is fully interactive".

Second, go with education experts and celebrities. To achieve effectiveness, high-level expert guidance is very important. Therefore, when inviting the keynote expert, we should grasp the following two principles. First, the main lecturer must be an ideological and ethical teacher who teaches in the front line and has rich teaching experience. with professional title and honor, they do research on teaching materials as well. Second, with profound theoretical background, experts must conduct in-depth research on the specific topics of the courses and chapters they have prepared. The charm of ideological and ethical course lies in "responding to students with thorough theoretical analysis, persuading students with thorough ideological theory, and guiding students with the power of truth".

4.2. Adhere to Diversity: Highlight "Different Types", "Different Ideas" and "Different Methods"

"Different courses with same values " is to strengthen the "different structure" on the basis of "the same education", showing the different characteristics of different schools, different ideas with different examples, different methods with different students. Further "seek common ground", return to the same teaching materials, the same teaching requirements, the same teaching objectives, so that teachers can choose the most appropriate methods and examples according to teaching objects and teaching contents, and form a teaching consensus.

First of all, emphasize the "different types" of educational display. The purpose of "heterogeneous mixing" is to facilitate mutual learning and reference, realize the collision of wisdom, and broaden the way of thinking. When holding the exhibition, efforts should be made to select the keynote teachers, optimize the composition of teachers, and select college ideological and ethical teachers from different levels, different types, different industries and different regions to share teaching. The invited ideological and ethical teachers have made a wonderful teaching display based on the characteristics of their respective colleges and universities and students, which provides a good opportunity for ideological and ethical teachers of different levels and types of colleges and universities to identify and learn from each other in "heterogeneity" and set up a platform for mutual communication.

Secondly, it shows the "difference of thinking mode" in the process of education. Different teachers will have different understandings of the same content, so they will naturally have different teaching ideas and teaching designs. Professor L puts forward strategic requirement of "training new people of the times who undertake the great task of national rejuvenation" based on the 19th CPC National Congress, and focuses on the questions such as why college students have ideals, what kind of ideals they should have, why they have abilities, what kind of abilities they should have, why they have responsibilities, and what kind of responsibilities they should have, which strengthen the freshmen' s sense of responsibility.

4.3. Keep It Open: Teachers' Participation, Solicitation and Resource Sharing

Different courses with same values should always adhere to openness, specifically to the following points: first, adhere to teachers' participation in opening up. "the same education in different classes" adheres to the concept of "opening the door to prepare lessons". For ideological and ethical teachers in colleges and universities across the country, teachers participating in training must submit necessary lesson preparation materials. At the same time, standardize the operation mechanism, deeply integrate with the current digital media technology and network technology, realize online and offline synchronization, and teachers can participate online at any time during the meeting in different regions and different occasions which have effectively broken the space restrictions on the exchange of ideological and ethical teachers in schools, and effectively reduced the cost of teachers' participation.

Secondly, adhere to the opening of enrollment issues. Before the preparation meeting, we should collect the difficult problems in teaching and learning from the teachers and students of ideological and ethical course all over the country. This kind of open enrollment can widely understand the actual situation of teachers and students, make lesson preparation targeted and better solve practical problems.

Finally, adhere to the openness of resource sharing. Sharing is a basic condition for establishing a loose partnership. Different from the traditional forms of teachers' organization, such as teaching and research departments and teaching and research groups, "co-education in different classes" is a loose cooperative organization in which teachers participate spontaneously, and the participating teachers hope to achieve their own educational growth through lesson preparation. Otherwise, they will withdraw from the preparatory meeting one after another. At the same time, we should find new problems in teaching, transform teaching problems into teaching topics for research, promote teaching, study teaching, and strive to improve the pertinence and effectiveness of ideological and ethical teaching.

5. The Implementation Effect of the "Different Courses with Same Values" Mode of Ideological and Ethical Courses in Colleges and Universities

The implementation effect of the "Different courses with the same values" mode of ideological and ethical courses after two years of practice and exploration in WGS University, 26 undergraduate ideological and ethical courses have been approved as demonstration courses and implemented with the model. With 25 teachers and nearly 3438 students as the analysis objects, the implementation effect evaluation was carried out from four dimensions, teachers' evaluation of the implementation effect of the mode, teachers' evaluation of students' education effect, students' support degree before the implementation of the mode, and students' satisfaction degree after the implementation of the mode. The results are shown in the Figures 2-5.

The results showed that there was a certain correlation between the teachers' self-evaluation of the implementation effect of the mode and the teachers' evaluation of the students' education effect ($R^2=0.74$). There was also a positive correlation between teachers' self-evaluation of the implementation effect and students' support before the implementation ($R^2=0.74$).

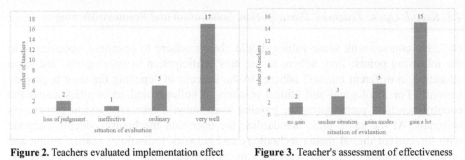

Figure 2. Teachers evaluated implementation effect   **Figure 3.** Teacher's assessment of effectiveness

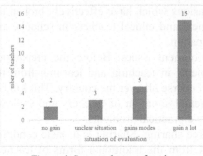

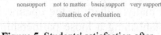

Figure 4. Support degree of students   **Figure 5.** Students' satisfaction after
before Implementation   implementation

The results show that the effect of different classes and teachers' preparation and recognition have a great influence on the results. Students' support and understanding of curriculum reform have great influence on curriculum implementation.

6. Conclusion

After several years of practice and development, colleges and universities have added the content of ideological and ethical education to the overall teaching design.

On the base of previous practice, "Different courses with same values " is constantly exploring "new methods", intercollegiate cooperation "hand in hand" and answering questions "face to face". Online efforts to carry out offline "deep integration", focus on the theme "target", large, small and medium-sized ideological and ethical courses "integration" and other preparatory activities, to explore the establishment of multi-agent problem collection mechanism. The vertical connection of ideological and ethical courses in colleges and universities, the horizontal connection of ideological and ethical courses, the depth and refinement mode of multi-subject, multi-level, omni-directional collaborative research and collaborative improvement, and constantly sum up experience, solidify achievements and expand influence effectively enhance the overall strength of ideological and ethical teachers, so that the team of ideological and ethical teachers is more balanced and develop.

Acknowledgment

The project was funded by the key project of Hubei Education Science Planning in 2022, "Research on the Mode of Different Courses with Same Value with the help of "double cycle" and "double Integration"(2022GA105); School-level Ideological and Ethical Demonstration Course-Microbiology and Immunology.

Reference

[1] Coulter Robert W. S., Onufer Lindsay. Using Student-Led Discussions and Snapshot Lectures to Stimulate Active Learning and Accountability: a mixed methods study on teaching an implementation science course[J]. Pedagogy in Health Promotion, 2022, 8(1): 30-40.

[2] China Encyclopedia Publishing House editorial department. Encyclopedia of China (Education) [M]. Beijing: Encyclopedia of China Publishing House, 1985: 20 (in Chinese).

[3] Yuan qun. Application of PDCA model in teaching management of logistics management major[J]. Education and Teaching BBS, 2016, (12):7-8.

[4] Mengya Zhang, Zhiping Liu, Kun Chen, Qingying Zhang, Jinshan Dai. Quality evaluation of mechanical experiment teaching under the background of emerging engineering education[J]. Advances in Artificial Systems for Medicine and Education III, 2020, (1126): 345-353.

[5] Chen Honghua, Shi Xiaoyun, Yu Aihua. Reflections on the construction of college teaching quality management system under the concept of OBE[J]. Heilongjiang Education (Higher Education Research and Evaluation), 2021, (2): 3-5.

[6] Ma Linyuan, Guo Chunyan, Yang Zongzhi. Research on the construction of experimental teaching system for economics and management majors[J]. Experimental Science and Technology, 2020, 18(1): 120-124.

[7] Zhang Hai, Fu Wei. Construction of experimental teaching system for mechanical engineering specialty for engineering education certification[J]. Experimental Technology and Management, 2017, 34(10): 166-169, 186.

[8] Yuan qun. Application of PDCA model in teaching management of logistics management major[J]. Education and Teaching BBS, 2016, (12):7-8.

[9] Shuang Liu, Peng Chen. Research on Fuzzy comprehensive evaluation in practice teaching assessment of computer majors[J]. International Journal of Modern Education and Computer Science, 2015, 7(11): 12-19.

[10] Karl Marx, Friedrich Engels. Selected Works by Marx and Engels (Volume 1) [M]. Beijing: People's Publishing House, 2012: 199+10 (in Chinese).

[11] Xi Jinping. Ideological and ethical course is the key course to implement the fundamental task of moral education[J]. Seeking Truth, 2020 (17): 1-18. (in Chinese)

[12] Ferdinand Tennes. Community and Society[M]. Lin Rongyuan, trans. Beijing: Peking University Press, 2010: 2 (in Chinese).

[13] Feng Shengyao, Li Zijian. The expression, cause and significance of teacher culture[J]. Education Guide, 2002, (7): 32-34 (in Chinese).

[14] Enitan Olabisi Adebayo, Ibiyinka Temilola Ayorinde, "Efficacy of Assistive Technology for Improved Teaching and Learning in Computer Science ", International Journal of Education and Management Engineering, Vol.12, No.5, pp. 9-17, 2022.

[15] Prathamesh Churi, N. T. Rao, "Teaching Cyber Security Course in the Classrooms of NMIMS University ", International Journal of Modern Education and Computer Science, Vol.13, No.4, pp. 1-15, 2021.

[16] Liu Feping. The idea and practice of building a teaching community of ideological and ethical courses in colleges and universities in the new Era[J]. Hubei Social Sciences, 2020 (11): 162-168 (in Chinese).

[17] Yuhuang Zheng. Research on innovation and entrepreneurship teaching system of engineering graphics course group[C]. Proceedings of 4th International Conference on Social Science and Higher Education (ICSSHE 2018) (Advances in Social Science, Education and Humanities Research), 2018, (181): 492-494.

[18] Zuo J, Wu X, Zhang G, et al. Statistical analysis based on students' evaluation of teaching data in an Application-Oriented University[C]//2022 International Conference on Educational Innovation and Multimedia Technology (EIMT 2022). Atlantis Press, 2022: 490-498.

Artificial Intelligence, Medical Engineering and Education
Z.B. Hu et al. (Eds.)
© *2024 The Authors.*
doi:10.3233/ATDE231371

Blended Teaching Research Under 1 + X Certificate System - Take Big Data Financial Analysis as an Example

Yiming WANG[a,1], Luxia YI[b]

aGuangzhou City University of Technology, Guangzhou, China
bGuangzhou Industry and Commerce College, Guangzhou, China
ORCiD ID: Yiming Wang https://orcid.org/0009-0000-0931-8128

Abstract. A new round of scientific and technological revolution is booming, and new technologies such as big data, artificial intelligence, and block-chain promote comprehensive innovation in the economy and society. The digitization process in various industries and fields is accelerating, and the accounting industry is also deeply affected. The cultivation of intelligent compound accounting talents is imminent, and universities play a vital role in talent training. Based on the application-oriented undergraduate colleges and universities, based on the era of digital economy, the 1+X certificate system and the background of school-enterprise cooperation, this study takes the mixed teaching of big data financial analysis based on the DEEP platform as an example to explore the transformation from traditional accounting talents to intelligent compound accounting talents. The new path of training promotes the integration of production and education, and provides reference for the training program, curriculum, and teaching of accounting talents in colleges and universities.

Keywords. Big data financial analysis; 1+X certificate system; School-enterprise cooperation; Blended Teaching

1. Introduction

In the current era, data has become an important factor of production and a driving force for promoting the quality and efficiency of economic and social development. Under the impetus of information technology, accounting personnel should not only have professional skills but also have information technology literacy, and colleges and universities that cultivate accounting talents have a long way to go. How to cultivate intelligent compound accounting talents has become a problem that education and teaching must pay attention to and think about. In vocational colleges and application-oriented universities, the pilot work of academic certificate + several vocational skill level certificates system (hereinafter referred to as 1+X certificate system) is launched to improve the vocational education and training system, deepen the integration of production and education, school-enterprise cooperation, and cultivate compound technical talents for enterprises.

This study adopts the blended teaching mode to carry out curriculum reform in order

---

[1] Corresponding Author: Yiming WANG, E-mail: 849162395@qq.com, wangym@gcu.edu.cn.

to cultivate intelligent compound accounting talents. From the domestic literature, He Kekang pointed out that the advantages of traditional teaching and the advantages of Blending Learning should be combined to promote each other [1]. Huang Hongmei and others used the hybrid teaching method combining the chemical simulation experiment platform with the mobile phone We-Chat platform to better solve the problem of teaching status such as untimely communication between teachers and students [2]. Li Xuan and others designed five steps based on the online+offline blended teaching model: pre-class preparation, classroom teaching, experimental training, after-school summary evaluation, knowledge expansion, which effectively improved students' interest in learning and reduced the demand for class hours compared with traditional teaching [3]. From the relevant foreign literature, the blended teaching model is also a concept identified by the American Simon League, which integrates traditional teaching and online teaching to create a new teaching method [4]. EralpAltun, Barıs Demirdag et al.created a virtual laboratory (SANLAB) in 2019, which promoted learning activities based on active learning methods, and students can conduct interactive experiments in a computer environment [5]. Peng X s article puts forward how to use the online+offline blended teaching mode in colleges and universities, and puts forward the use of flipping classrooms, micro-classes, MOOCs online and offline teachers teaching, which can not only effectively improve students self-learning ability but also improve the teaching effect [6]. Jin X demonstrates the advantages of the online+offline blended teaching model compared with traditional teaching and online teaching, but it points out that choosing the appropriate online teaching platform is the top priority for the quality of this teaching model [7].

To sum up, the mixed teaching mode has become the main trend of curriculum teaching reform. In foreign countries, there are many virtual laboratories and MOOCs as online teaching tools. The main scope of implementation is the same as that in China, and it is mostly used in higher education [8-10]. Research shows that the online+offline blended teaching mode can improve the teaching effect, reduce the pressure of teachers, and promote students self-learning ability [11-13].

2. Application-oriented Undergraduate Colleges and Universities Mathematical Intelligence Compound Accounting Personnel Training Needs and Difficulties

2.1. The Demand for Accounting Talents in the Era of Big Data Intelligence

According to the Top Ten Information Technology Selection Reports Affecting Chinese Accountants issued by Shanghai National Accounting Institute in 2021, financial cloud, electronic invoice, accounting big data analysis and processing technology, electronic accounting archives, robot process automation, new generation ERP, mobile payment, data platform, data mining and intelligent process automation are the top ten information technologies affecting accountants. Technological innovations such as artificial intelligence, big data, and block-chain have spawned new industries, new formats, and new models. This urgently requires accelerating the training of a group of high-quality accounting talents who are proficient in both professional and information technology and have strategic thinking and innovation capabilities. Since the release of the Accounting Industry Medium and Long-term Talent Development Plan (2010-2020), although the construction of accounting talent team has been significantly improved, from the actual development of accounting talents, structural imbalances still exist. There are more people engaged in basic accounting, and the supply of high-end accounting talents with new era development concepts, global strategic vision, and management innovation capabilities is insufficient.

2.2. Dilemma of Accounting Talent Training in Application-Oriented Universities

For colleges and universities, due to the special attributes of financial work, it is difficult for accounting majors to find enough positions to organize students practical training, resulting in low practical ability of students. For enterprises, the number of accounting students is huge, but there are not many people who can get started quickly, and there are few people who can have data thinking and use big data tools to deal with financial problems. The key to solving these problems lies in the training of accounting professionals in colleges and universities. How to set up a technical curriculum system, build big data professional courses, build training conditions, organize internships, and how to integrate production, education, and research has become a problem faced by various colleges and universities. At the same time, because the colleges and universities did not have strong big data technology teachers, courses, and training conditions before, the training of new accounting talents under the economic situation of data intelligence is facing difficulties [14-16].

2.3. School-Enterprise Cooperation to Promote 1+X Vocational Skill Level Certificate System

The 1+X certificate system aims to jointly develop talent training programs between schools and enterprises, break through the barriers between academic education and vocational training, closely combine professional knowledge with job demand skills training, strengthen students entrepreneurial and employment ability, and accelerate the cultivation of compound technical talents. The institutional foundation for alleviating structural employment conflicts. This project is a course offered by Shouguan Technology Co., Ltd.in cooperation with Yuelan (Shanghai) Data Service Co., Ltd.on the DEEP cloud platform. Not only to carry out teacher training, but also to encourage and organize students to obtain 1+X big data financial analysis professional qualification certificate after the completion of the course teaching, so as to realize the deep integration of industry, university and research.

3. The Course of Big Data Financial Analysis Opens a New Path for the Cultivation of Accounting Talents

3.1. Research on Students Intention to Lay the Foundation of Curriculum Demand

The course of Big Data Financial Analysis adopts a mixed teaching mode based on the DEEP platform. Guided by the 1 + X professional qualification certificate of big data financial analysis, it uses a variety of teaching methods to organically integrate big data data technology with enterprise financial analysis theory, and introduces teaching in the form of typical work tasks to cultivate compound accounting talents qualified for big data financial analysis positions. Before the start of the course, a questionnaire was issued to collect students learning intentions. According to the questionnaire, students pay more attention to employment and the difficulty and practicability of professional courses.

Table 1. Students' confusion in the learning process of professional courses

Option	Proportion
It is difficult to learn professional courses.	53.67%
No interest	16.06%
Will not learn to be useful	45.87%
There is no direction of employment	62.39%
Disagree with the assessment method	18.81%
The classroom form is not novel enough	31.19%
Others	12.84%

From Table 1, senior students generally have a sense of employment anxiety. They pay attention to the difficulty and practicability of their professional courses, pay attention to the combination of theory and practice, and are eager to master more frontier information of the times, develop their horizons, broaden their knowledge of modern information technology and big data analysis and application, and expand their employment direction. This requires teachers to pay attention to the acceptance and practicability of the teaching content when teaching, as well as to provide students with relevant suggestions on employment. The course of Big Data Financial Analysis opens up new employment channels for students' employment.

Table 2. The professional skills that students think accounting major must have

Option	Proportion
Accounting processing capacity	93.58%
Management ability	61.47%
Language competence	49.54%
Financial software application ability	84.86%
Tax business processing capacity	77.06%
Financial management ability	72.94%
Organization and coordination ability	48.17%
Financial big data application analysis ability	76.15%
Practical ability	66.97%

At the same time, the survey shows that students believe that in addition to accounting ability, the accounting profession should also have the ability to apply and analyze financial big data, software application ability and practical ability, reflecting students' needs and expectations for big data financial analysis. It also shows that big data financial analysis is a practical course.

3.2. School-Enterprise Co-construction Provides Platform Technical Support

Strengthen the integration of school-enterprise cooperation, build a big data financial analysis course group, and provide students with comprehensive financial data analysis and learning resources. This paper selects the 1 + X certificate system series of teaching materials for big data financial analysis, takes the   professional skill level standard of big data financial analysis   as the benchmark, relies on the DEEP big data financial analysis platform, and integrates the latest technologies such as data collection, processing, analysis and mining, data visualization and the latest applications of the industry into the teaching materials and training according to the big data processing process, so as to provide strong support for the latest skills requirements of big data financial analysis positions. The learning resources support online open courses, operation videos, PPT teaching courseware, internship and training operations and other resources. Some of the selected resources in the teaching materials are embedded in the two-dimensional code link. Readers can learn by scanning the code on the mobile terminal anytime and anywhere to meet the needs of blended teaching. Strengthen the cooperation between schools and enterprises to build curriculum resources, and continue to expand and improve education and teaching resources on the basis of the original curriculum materials, videos, and micro-classes, including curriculum syllabus, lesson plans, learning cases, papers, question banks, network resources, etc. Enrich the mixed teaching process and achieve sustainable improvement.

3.3. Open up a New Direction for the Training of Mathematical Intelligence Compound Accounting Talents

The big data financial analysis provides a breakthrough for the cultivation of new accounting talents. It not only combines the background of the digital intelligence economic era, but also combines with the vocational skill qualification examination to cultivate students' ability to process the whole link of big data and form the thinking of using data to solve practical work problems. Combined with accounting expertise, big data technology is used for data collation, processing, analysis, and data visualization, so as to deal with financial statement analysis, audit analysis, cost analysis, budget analysis and other issues.

4. The Design and Research of Blended Teaching Mode Based on DEEP Platform

4.1. DEEP Platform and Experimental Project Content

Big Data Financial Analysis relies on the DEEP training platform and is supported by the Windows operating system. The DEEP big data analysis system adopts the C/S system architecture, and the experimental training environment can be constructed in the way of cloud server or LAN server. The course includes two major sections and eleven experimental projects, which constitute the workflow of big data full-link processing. As shown in Figure 1.

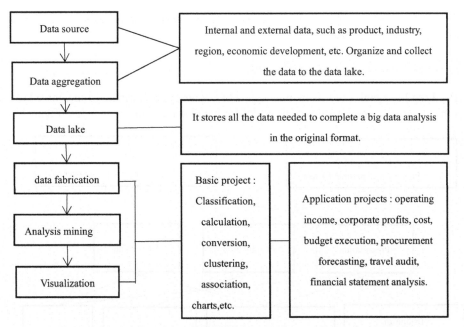

Figure 1. Big data financial analysis Full link processing workflow and project content

4.2. Introducing the IMPACT Cycle Model to Help Students Establish Data Analysis Thinking

University of Arkansas Sam. Vernon.J.Richardson, a professor of accounting at Walton Business School, believes that accountants do not need to become data scientists, but in the big data environment, accounting talents need to master seven kinds of data analysis thinking, namely, data analysis thinking mode, data cleaning and data preparation, data quality, descriptive data analysis, manipulation of data to perform data analysis, problem solving through statistical data analysis, data visualization and data reporting [17]. The big data financial analysis course is not only to train students to operate software, but also to cultivate students' big data analysis thinking in each project training. Therefore, the IMPACT cycle model is used to describe the data analysis process to students. In the continuous intensive training, students' big data thinking is trained to use linked data to solve business problems. As shown in Figure 2.

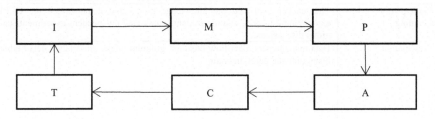

Figure 2. IMPACT cycle model

The steps of IMPACT cycle model are Identify the question, Master the data, Perform the test plan, Address, and refine the results, communicate insights, Track the outcomes. Then, according to the results, further research questions are put forward.

Through the training of each experimental project, accounting students are trained to gradually establish data analysis thinking.

4.3. Using Diversified Teaching Methods

Big Data Financial Analysis mainly adopts two stages of online and offline, three links in the classroom, and six steps of BOPPPS for blended teaching, as shown in Figure3.

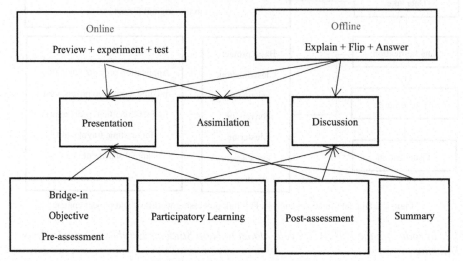

Figure 3. Multi-teaching method design

The classroom examples of multi-teaching mode are as follows:

Table 3. Multi-teaching model example classroom

procedure	Examples of first-class teaching activities
Self-study before class (Online)	Introduction and development trend of big data financial analysis, big data thinking and full chain processing workflow.
Bridge-in (Offline)	The installation of DEEP training platform introduces the development prospect of big data financial analysis and mobilizes students' enthusiasm for learning.
Objective (Offline)	Master the visual data processing skills in DEEP, cultivate students' aesthetic ability, drawing ability, data graphic typesetting ability.
Pre-assessment (Offline)	Ask EXCEL drawing types and steps, understand the current knowledge level of students, and answer the difference between EXCEL and DEEP in visualization.
Participatory Learning (Offline)	The teacher explained the knowledge points and demonstrated the DEEP experimental project, and the students conducted independent experiments and group discussions.
Presentation	Data management, data flow creation, grouping table, cross table, detail table, histogram and point diagram.

Table 3. Multi-teaching model example classroom (Continued)

procedure	Examples of first-class teaching activities
Assimilation	Students complete all the experimental projects in the DEEP system and think about the logical relationship of the data. To be able to demonstrate the experimental project on stage.
Discussion	Group discussion was conducted on the doubtful points of this course, and the problems that could not be solved were submitted to teachers for answers.
Post-assessment (Online +Offline)	Students carry out group experiments and teachers and students evaluate together. The teacher arranges the homework after class, the students complete it independently, and the problem discussion summary is retained in the next class in the classroom discussion [18].
Summary (Offline)	Teachers summarize the knowledge points of this course and comment on the students learning process. Pre-announce the content of the next class, arrange online preview work: thermal point map, line chart, area map, rectangular block map, pie chart, text map.
Afterclass feedback (Online +Offline)	Teachers reflect on the teaching of this course, receive feedback on students learning effects through learning, and optimize and adjust teaching methods and teaching progress.

5. Conclusion

The accounting major in application-oriented universities should keep up with the pace of the times, and the professional construction should move towards big data intelligence, and strive to cultivate application-oriented compound accounting talents with solid professional foundation, reasonable knowledge structure, strong innovation and practice ability and high information literacy. Colleges and universities should attach importance to and strengthen the construction of theoretical courses, practical courses and training bases related to accounting informatization and big data, cooperate with software companies to carry out some related teaching, and combine teaching work, scientific research work with new technologies, new methods, and new tools in the field of practice to achieve coordinated development [19]. Starting from the course of big data financial analysis as the starting point of the cultivation of intelligent compound accounting talents, in the process of exploring the mixed teaching research, in response to the 1 + X certificate system, deepen the cooperation between schools and enterprises, and point to area, the following conclusions are summarized, which can provide reference for the application-oriented undergraduate colleges and universities to improve the training program and curriculum setting and teaching of accounting talents.

1) Blended teaching is student-centered, starting before class, through class and after class. The pre-class activity is an online activity. Students need to complete the teacher s preview task and give the problem to the group supervisor to feedback to the teacher. The classroom activity is the key and difficult point of the teacher s intensive teaching, and the students are divided into groups to carry out the operation steps of the flipped classroom demonstration experiment. After-class activities Students need to complete their homework and conduct mutual evaluation [20].

2) When launching online activities, the teacher publishes courseware, videos and DEEP experimental projects related to pre-class preview, and then the students complete the experimental operation. The teacher divides the students into several groups through the teaching platform, and each group assigns student representatives to be responsible for the organization of online learning activities and the guidance and supervision of offline learning. When launching offline activities, the teacher will elaborate on the key

points and difficulties and demonstrate the DEEP platform to visualize the relevant experimental projects. The team members can submit the problems encountered in their preview to the group discussion group [21].

3) Teachers evaluation of students learning effect: pre-class evaluation, through the way of questions (teachers ask students to answer or students ask each other to answer) to evaluate students' knowledge of last class and the preview of this class; in-class evaluation, explain the new content in the process of constantly throwing problems in order to evaluate the degree of understanding of students and the difficulty of teaching content; after-school evaluation, arrange after-school assignments to evaluate students learning of this class.

Students' evaluation of teachers teaching methods and contents: students can regularly feedback and evaluate the learning effect and teachers teaching methods and progress, including oral feedback, written feedback, platform feedback, group feedback and other forms, improve students' participation in the classroom, help teachers optimize teaching methods and adjust teaching progress in time.

Acknowledgment

This project is supported by the following topics: Key Research Base of Humanities and Social Sciences in Universities of Guangdong Province: Research Base for Digital Transformation of Manufacturing Enterprises (2023WZJD012); Guangdong Province first-class professional accounting construction point (JY214501); Guangdong Province Special Talent Training Plan ' New Liberal Arts Big Data Accounting Experimental Class Talent Training Plan of Guangzhou City University of Technology ' (JY220202); Guangdong Service Trade " Double Circulation " Research Center, a key research base for humanities and social sciences in Guangdong universities (2021WZJD002).

References

[1]   He Kekang. A new development of educational technology theory from blending learning[J]. Information Technology Education in Primary and Secondary Schools, 2004 (04): 21-31(in Chinese).

[2]   Huang Hongmei, Yan Hailin, Wu Tunyan, Ran Ming. Reform and practice of experimental teaching of chemistry teaching theory in normal universities based on information technology[J]. Chemistry Education (Chinese and English), 2020,41 (20): 59-63(in Chinese).

[3]   Li Xuan, Wang Yan. The application of online and offline hybrid teaching mode in the course of Organic Chemistry Experiment -Taking the preparation of benzoic acid as an example[J]. Chemical Design Communication, 2022,48 (08): 112-115(in Chinese).

[4]   Allen I E, Seaman J. Sizing the Opportunity: The quality and extent of online education in the United States,2002 and 2003[J]. Sloan Consortium,2003,23: 65-67.

[5]   Altun E, Demirdağ B, Feyzioğlu B, et al. Developing an interactive virtual chemistry laboratory enriched with constructivist learning activities for secondary schools[J]. Procedia-Social and Behavioral Sciences,2009,1(1): 1895-1898.

[6]   Peng X, Wei L. Exploration of online and offline hybrid teaching of pathophysiology[J]. Open Journal of Social Sciences,2021,9(9): 433-438.

[7]   Jin X, Zhang C, Su J. Exploring strategies for quality assurance in online-offline hybrid teaching under the background of smart cities[J]. Security and Communication Networks,2022: 1-5.

[8]   Salah Al Khafaji, Sriram. B, "A Concept Review on MOOCs Research Findings – A Qualitative Approach", International Journal of Education and Management Engineering, Vol.13, No.4, pp. 19-25, 2023.

[9]   Li Nan, Zhang Yong, "Improvement and Practice of Secondary School Geography Teachers' Informatization Teaching Ability Based on the Perspective of MOOCs", International Journal of Education and Management Engineering, Vol.12, No.1, pp. 11-18, 2022.

[10] Abderrahim El Mhouti, Azeddine Nasseh, Mohamed Erradi, "Stimulate Engagement and Motivation in MOOCs Using an Ontologies Based Multi-Agents System", International Journal of Intelligent Systems and Applications, Vol.8, No.4, pp.33-42, 2016.

[11] Serge Dolgikh, "Categorization in Unsupervised Generative Self-learning Systems", International Journal of Modern Education and Computer Science, Vol.13, No.3, pp. 68-78, 2021.

[12] Ahmed AbdulQader Al-Bakeri, Abdullah Ahmad Basuhail, "ASR for Tajweed Rules: Integrated with Self-Learning Environments", International Journal of Information Engineering and Electronic Business, Vol.9, No.6, pp.1-9, 2017.

[13] Yevgeniy V. Bodyanskiy, Oleksii K. Tyshchenko, Anastasiia O. Deineko, "An Evolving Neuro-Fuzzy System with Online Learning/Self-learning", International Journal of Modern Education and Computer Science, vol.7, no.2, pp.1-7, 2015.

[14] Asma Omri, Mohamed Nazih Omri, "Towards an Efficient Big Data Indexing Approach under an Uncertain Environment", International Journal of Intelligent Systems and Applications, Vol.14, No.2, pp.1-13, 2022.

[15] Essaid EL HAJI, Abdellah Azmani, " Proposal of a Digital Ecosystem Based on Big Data and Artificial Intelligence to Support Educational and Vocational Guidance", International Journal of Modern Education and Computer Science, Vol.12, No.4, pp. 1-11, 2020.

[16] Jesslyn Noverlita, Herison Surbakti, "Streamlining Stock Price Analysis: Hadoop Ecosystem for Machine Learning Models and Big Data Analytics", International Journal of Information Technology and Computer Science, Vol.15, No.5, pp.25-34, 2023.

[17] Vernon J. Richardson, Shan Yuxin, Ryan A. Tite, Katie L. Teller. Accounting data analysis[M]. Beijing: Machinery Industry Press, 2021: 3-5.

[18] Lai M, Lam K, Lim C.P. Design principles for the blend in blended learning: a collective case study[J]. Teaching in Higher Education, 2016, 05, 13: 716-729.

[19] Porter W W, Graham C R, Spring K A, et al. Blended learning in higher education: institutional adoption and implementation[J]. Computers&Education,2014,75(3): 185-195.

[20] Hrastinski S. What do we mean by blended learning? [J]. Tech Trends, 2019,63(5): 564-569

[21] Barnum C, Paarmann W. Bringing introduction to the teacher: a blended learning model[J]. T H E Journal, 2002, 30 (2): 56-64.

588

Artificial Intelligence, Medical Engineering and Education
Z.B. Hu et al. (Eds.)
© 2024 The Authors.
This article is published online with Open Access by IOS Press and distributed under the terms
of the Creative Commons Attribution Non-Commercial License 4.0 (CC BY-NC 4.0).
doi:10.3233/ATDE231372

Multi-Interactive College English Teaching Under the Network-Based Multimedia Environment

Zhilan ZENG[a,1]
a School of Humanities, Hunan City University, Yiyang, China
ORCiD ID: Zhilan ZENG https://orcid.org/0000-0003-0586-2825

Abstract. As a new teaching method, multi-interactive teaching has been more and more recognized by educators in this fast-growing information age due to its advantage of facilitating communication. However, more empirical studies still need to be done to investigate its effect. This study aims to investigate the impact of multi-interactive teaching method on college students' English proficiency and their learning motivation through a quasi-experimental design. The Experimental Group (44 students) was taught using multi-interactive teaching approach while the Control Group (44 students) learned English in a conventional way over a span of 14 weeks. T-test was adopted to examine whether there was significant difference in English proficiency (listening, reading, writing, and translation) and their learning motivation between the two groups. The findings revealed that except writing, the Experimental Group obtained significantly higher scores than the Control Group. Hence, it is recommended that multi-interactive teaching be used as an effective method to promote students' English proficiency and learning motivation in College English classes.

Keywords. Multi-interactive teaching; College English; English Proficiency; Motivation.

1. Introduction

The fast-evolving Internet technology in the past decades has significantly boosted the efficiency and initiative of work and study. The reorganization of the education system and the redistribution of resources accelerates the integration and sharing of education resources, so that education is moving toward a more diversified and scientific direction. Internet provides a platform for information resource sharing and cooperative learning. In the virtual reality established by Internet, learners can imitate and explain the simulated world, and they can experience the whole process of knowledge acquisition instead of just getting facts or conclusions from teachers. Liberating students from traditional teacher-centered mode, Internet-aided teaching allows learners immersed in a more social environment where their interest and motivation in learning can be promoted [1-2].

College English is a compulsory course for non-English majors in universities in China. Influenced by the nationwide reform of College English course, EFL (English as

---

[1] Corresponding Author: Zhilan ZENG, E-mail: 35159476@qq.com.

a foreign language) teachers are encountered with great challenges because of shortened teaching time yet increased requirements. Nowadays, EFL college students are not only required to have a good command of the basic language knowledge of English, but also learn how to use English in their life and future work. Solely relying on classroom teaching and learning is far from achieving the desired learning effect. The blossoming of network information technology can bring its superiority into full play and be helpful in promoting English teaching effect. Multi-interaction refers to the mutual communication and understanding between two or more interactive elements. Multi-interactive teaching not only involves the interaction between teachers and students, but also the interaction between learners and learners, and between learners and information technology. The use of network multimedia allows students to study actively and participate in classroom activities instead of passively accepting the knowledge imparted by teachers [3-5]. Multi-interactive teaching approach advocates effective interaction between different elements. Changing their mindset, teachers reset their role in classroom, and guide students to actively acquire knowledge, so that students reconstruct knowledge based on previously acquired knowledge to form deep understanding. Under the background of network multimedia, this research designs a mode of multi-interactive College English teaching under the network-based multimedia environment, and verifies its teaching effect in practice, in order to provide reference for English teaching and learning at universities.

The research questions are as follows.

Question 1: Can multi-interactive teaching method improve students' English proficiency (in writing, listening, reading and translation)?

Question 2: Can multi-interactive teaching method promote students' learning motivation?

2. Literature Review

Multi-interactive teaching method originated from interaction theory, the core of which is interaction hypothesis which means that when difficulty occurs in communication, both sides of the communication must conduct meaning negotiation, so that the input can be understandable and language acquisition is achieved [6-7]. Interaction theory has been continuously updated and developed in the long-term research, laying a solid foundation for multi-dimensional interactions. Multi-interactive teaching refers to a series of teaching activities where various elements interact with each other to encourage students to actively participate in learning and achieve high-quality learning results. In multi-interactive teaching model, a comprehensive and multi-level harmonious interaction is formed through optimizing the way of teaching interaction, making full use of various elements related to learning, mobilizing and promoting students' initiative and enthusiasm to learning [8-10].

Multi-interactive teaching advocates the interaction between students and students, teachers and students, students and technology, students and learning materials. Its theoretical basis mainly includes constructivist learning theory, situated cognition theory, metacognitive learning strategy theory. Constructivist learning theory emphasizes the cognitive subject of learning and the collaboration between students and teachers. Multi-interactive teaching allows language learners to subtly comprehend the required knowledge. The tacit knowledge hidden in people's behavior and event comes into play while learners interact with peers, teachers, learning materials or situations. According to situated cognition theory, real, meaningful and purposeful learning activity is an important way for learners to acquire knowledge. For students, learning is not just about acquiring a mass of factual knowledge, but also about how to construct meaning and form solutions to problems through learning and collaboration. Multi-interactive teaching helps students build cooperative communities where they participate in community activities, interact with others, and work together on the social construction of the knowledge they have learned. Meta-cognition refers to human's thinking about their own behavior in the process of acquiring knowledge, which can be interpreted as thinking about the way of thinking. Learners not only need to know what method is most beneficial to their learning, but also understand the learning process and choose effective learning strategies. In multi-interactive teaching, teachers skillfully combine meta-cognitive strategy with foreign language teaching through providing autonomous learning guidance, and conducting various classroom activities to help students grasp some learning skills and develop good learning habit [11-15].

Compared with the traditional teaching method, the multi-interactive teaching method has the following characteristics: 1) The integration of teaching elements. It blends teaching methods, teaching content, and teaching structure together, turning relatively abstract educational ideas into concrete strategies, and encouraging students to feel, judge, practice, and adjust their learning behavior in an all-round way; 2) The openness of teaching environment. The interactive teaching actually gives students greater learning initiative and autonomy, so that students' learning space is expanded. The information technology environment facilitates the collaboration between students and teachers; 3) Diversity of teaching forms. The multi-interactive teaching promotes the active interaction of various teaching elements. It focuses on students' proactive and cooperative acquisition of knowledge, attaches importance to learning ability, and promotes students' all-round development; 4) Multiple levels of interaction. Interactive teaching does not insist on the uniformity in the learning methods, learning process, and use of media. Instead, it is a kind of approach with student-centered, task-based, interest-focused characteristics; 5) Equality of teacher-student relationship. In the interactive teaching model, teachers respect students' personality and experience, encourage students' exploration, collaboration and innovation, and try to construct relaxed and harmonious atmosphere where students can learn language in accordance with their own needs; 6) Diversity of assessment system. Teaching evaluation in the network technology environment includes summative and formative assessment, the latter of which is done by evaluating students' in-class and extra-curricular performance, students' autonomous learning on different learning platforms and so on, to promote students' maximal engagement [16-18].

In recent decade, with the diversification of society and the in-depth study of multi-interactive theory, researchers have carried out extensive research from different perspectives. Fruitful developments in the construction of interactive teaching and learning, specific implementation of interactive approach in class, and its effects are witnessed [19-21]. In spite of fruitful study in interaction theory in education, there is still in need of empirical study into the application of multi-interactive teaching method in foreign language class. And how to bring network technology into full play in education should be on the list of things worth studying. Interaction between human and network information technology, between human and teaching resources, distance teaching technology, distance teaching concepts carried by modern technology in EFL teaching and learning should be taken into full consideration [22-24].

3. Methodology

This research is carried out in a public university in Hunan, China, which has hardware equipment such as digital language laboratory, network multimedia classroom, independent learning center based on information technology such as computer network, which provides necessary guarantee for the implementation of the interactive teaching mode in College English class. A quasi-experimental study was employed in this study. Eighty-eight second-year students aged from 18 to 20 in two classes are the research objects. Class A is the Control Group, with 44 students majoring in Civil Engineering, and Class B is the Experimental Group with 44 students majoring in Management. There is no significant difference in students' English proficiency between the two groups before the experiment.

The experiment lasted 14 weeks, about 3 months. The Control Group followed the conventional teachers-centered way, in which teachers explained linguistic knowledge, especially vocabulary and grammar. In textual analysis, the teacher in control group usually selected key sentences and explain them sentence by sentence through structure analysis and translation. The Experimental Group adopted a multi-interactive teaching mode, aiming at cultivating students' language skills, encouraging their participation and promoting their learning motivation. In this teaching model, students were divided into small groups, and they completed curricular and extracurricular assignments in groups. The teachers adopted information network technology such as Rain Classroom, Unipus, WeChat, QQ to develop students' skills in listening, reading, writing, and translation. The interaction between teachers and students, between students and students, between students and machines ran through the whole teaching process.

Figure 1 is the operation chart of the multi-interactive teaching model. To begin with, teachers design the multi-interactive teaching model and work as facilitators to guide students to construct knowledge based on specific teaching objectives, students' proficiency and teaching resources. On the other hand, students construct knowledge through participating in learning activities and cooperating with teachers. Secondly, students interact with teachers, other students, and machines (computers, mobile phones, network facilities, and so on) in three-dimensional environments such as classrooms, extracurricular activity places, and online virtual spaces. Teachers make necessary adjustments in the organization and regulation of the teaching design. Thirdly, guided by the teaching design and the course requirements, students complete the meaning construction through individual efforts and group cooperation, and externalize the acquired language knowledge into specific learning outcomes. Finally, teachers and students conduct timely evaluations of the learning outcomes for the improvement of future teaching and learning, and prepare for a new round of process.

Pre-test and post-test covering listening, reading, writing and translation were conducted, and the data were collected and analyzed through statistical tool. Additionally, the questionnaire surveys were carried out before and after the experiment to investigate the participants' motivation of learning English. The questionnaire consisted of 15 items, adapted from Kellers' (2010) Motivational Design for Learning and Performance [25]. Through the comparative analysis between the experimental group and the control group, the influence of student-centered multi-interactive teaching method on university students' English proficiency and motivation has been studied and relevant conclusions have been drawn.

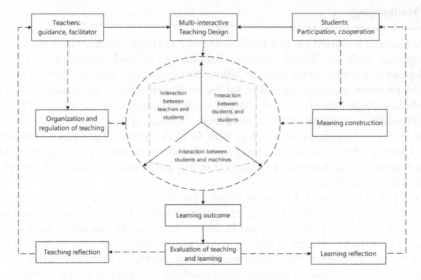

Figure 1. The multi-dimensional interactive teaching model

4. Results and Discussions

The aim of T-Test was adopted to see whether there is significant difference between the Experiment Group and the Control Group in the English proficiency test covering writing, listening, reading and translation, and students' motivation to learn English. Following are the results of the T-Test.

Ho1: There is no significant difference in the mean scores for the English proficiency test between the Experimental Group (interactive teaching method) and the Control Group (conventional method).

Table 1. Comparison of mean scores on English proficiency test in the pre-test

Group	N	Mean	SD	MD	t-value	df	p-value
Experimental	44	58.36	5.969	.205	.147	86	.883
Control	44	58.16	7.008				

Level of significance is at p<0.05

Before the experiment, Independent T-Test was employed to compare the mean scores for English Test between the Experimental and Control group. As can be seen from Table 1 that the mean score was *58.36* for the Experimental Group and *58.16* for the Control Group. The results show that there is no significant difference in students' performance in English Test between the experimental Group and the Control Group in the pretest (*Mean difference=.205, t=.147, df=86, p=.883*).

Table 2. Comparison of the mean scores for English proficiency test in the post-test

Group	N	Mean	SD	MD	t-value	df	p-value
Experimental	44	61.60	5.743	3.182	2.455	86	.016
Control	44	58.41	6.395				

Level of significance is at p<0.05

Table 2 demonstrates the students' performance in English proficiency test after the experiment. In the post-test, the students in the Experimental Group obtained higher scores (*Mean=61.60, SD=5.743*) than those in the Control Group (*Mean=58.41, SD=6.395*). The results from the Independent T-test displayed that there was significant difference in English proficiency test between the two groups after the experiment (*Mean difference=3.182, t=2.455, df=86, p=.016*).

Ho1a: There is no significant difference in the mean scores for listening in English proficiency test between the Experimental Group and the Control Group.

Table 3. Comparison of mean scores for listening in the pre-test

Group	N	Mean	SD	MD	t-value	df	p-value
Experimental	44	13.52	1.705	-.091	.264	86	.816
Control	44	13.61	1.944				

Level of significance is at p<0.05

Table 3 showed that before the experiment, the mean score for listening in English proficiency test was *13.52* for the Experimental Group and *13.61* for the Control Group. The results reveal that there is no significant difference in students' performance in listening between the experimental Group and the Control Group in the pre-test (*Mean difference=-.091, t=-.264, df=86, p=.816*).

Table 4. Comparison of mean scores for listening in the post-test

Group	N	Mean	SD	MD	t-value	df	p-value
Experimental	44	14.43	1.885	.864	2.215	86	.029
Control	44	13.57	1.771				

Level of significance is at p<0.05

The students' performance in listening in English proficiency test after the experiment can be shown in Table 4. In the post-test, the students in the Experimental Group (*Mean=14.43, SD=1.885*) scored higher than those from the Control Group (*Mean=13.57, SD=1.771*). The results from the Independent T-test displayed that there was significant difference in listening between the two groups after the experiment (*Mean difference=.864, t=2.215, df=86, p=.029*).

Table 5. Comparison of mean scores for reading in the pre-test

Group	N	Mean	SD	MD	t-value	df	p-value
Experimental	44	14.50	1.94	.159	.369	86	.713
Control	44	14.34	2.10				

Level of significance is at p<0.05

Ho1b: There is no significant difference in the mean scores for reading in English proficiency test between the Experimental Group and the Control Group.

Similarly, Independent T-Test was employed to compare the mean scores for reading between the Experimental and Control group before the experiment. Table 5 showed that the mean score was *14.50* for the Experimental Group and *14.34* for the Control Group. The results reveal that there is no significant difference in students' performance in reading between the experimental Group and the Control Group in the pretest (*Mean difference=.159, t=.369, df=86, p=.713*).

Table 6. Comparison of mean scores for reading in the post-test

Group	N	Mean	SD	MD	t-value	df	p-value
Experimental	44	15.39	2.104	.886	2.05	86	.043
Control	44	14.50	1.947				

Level of significance is at p<0.05

Table 6 displays the students' performance in reading in English proficiency test after the experiment. In the post-test, the students in the Experimental Group (*Mean=15.39, SD=2.104*) outperformed those from the Control Group (*Mean=14.50, SD=1.947*). The results from the Independent T-test displayed that there was significant difference in reading between the two groups after the experiment (*Mean difference=.886, t=2.05, df=86, p=.043*).

Ho1c: There is no significant difference in the mean scores for writing in English proficiency test between the Experimental Group and the Control Group.

Table 7. Comparison of mean scores for writing in the pre-test

Group	N	Mean	SD	MD	t-value	df	p-value
Experimental	44	15.75	1.894	.114	.262	86	.794
Control	44	15.64	2.168				

Level of significance is at p<0.05

It can be seen from Table 7 that in pre-test, the mean score for writing in English proficiency test was 15.75 for the Experimental Group and 15.64 for the Control Group. The results show that there is no significant difference in students' performance in writing between the experimental Group and the Control Group in the pretest (*Mean difference=.114, t=.262, df=86, p=.794*).

Table 8. Comparison of mean scores for writing in the post-test

Group	N	Mean	SD	MD	t-value	df	p-value
Experimental	44	16.36	1.464	.500	1.325	86	.189
Control	44	15.86	2.030				

Level of significance is at p<0.05

As is shown in Table 8, in the post-test, even though the students in the Experimental Group (*Mean=16.36, SD=1.464*) scored higher than those from the Control Group (*Mean=15.86, SD=2.03*) in the part of writing, the difference between the two groups was not significant (*Mean difference=.500, t=1.325, df=86, p=.189*).

Ho1d: There is no significant difference in the mean scores for translation in English proficiency test between the Experimental Group and the Control Group.

Table 9. Comparison of mean scores for translation in the pre-test

Group	N	Mean	SD	MD	t-value	df	p-value
Experimental	44	14.59	1.530	.023	.064	86	.949
Control	44	14.57	1.810				

Level of significance is at p<0.05

Table 9 demonstrated that in pre-test, the mean score for translation in English proficiency test was *14.59* for the Experimental Group, very close to the Control Group,

14.57. The results display that there is no significant difference in students' performance in translation between the two groups in the pre-test *(Mean difference=.023, t=.064, df=86, p=.949)*.

Table 10. Comparison of mean scores for translation in the post-test

Group	N	Mean	SD	MD	t-value	df	p-value
Experimental	44	15.41	1.945	.932	2.289	86	.025
Control	44	14.48	1.874				

Level of significance is at p<0.05

The students' performance in translation in English proficiency test after the experiment can be shown in Table 10. In the post-test, the students in the Experimental Group *(Mean=15.41, SD=1.945)* obtained higher scores than those from the Control Group *(Mean=14.48, SD=1.874)*. The results from the Independent T-test showed that there was significant difference in translation between the two groups after the experiment *(Mean difference=.932, t=2.289, df=86, p=.025)*.

Ho2: There is no significant difference in students' motivation between the Experimental Group and the Control Group.

Table 11. Comparison of students' motivation between two groups in pre-test

Group	N	Mean	SD	MD	t-value	df	p-value
Experimental	44	37.61	5.899	-.182	-.146	86	.884
Control	44	37.80	5.793				

Level of significance is at p<0.05

Table 11 showed that in pre-test, the mean score for the Experimental Group's motivation in questionnaire survey was *37.61*, coming close to the Control Group, *37.80*. The results display that there is no significant difference in students' motivation between the two groups in the pre-test *(Mean difference=-.182, t=-.146, df=86, p=.884)*.

Table 12. Comparison of students' motivation between two groups in post-test

Group	N	Mean	SD	MD	t-value	df	p-value
Experimental	44	42.18	4.731	3.909	3.782	86	.000
Control	44	38.27	4.962				

Level of significance is at p<0.05

Students' responses in questionnaire survey in Table 12 showed that in the post-test, the students in the Experimental Group *(Mean=42.18, SD=4.731)* scored higher in motivation than the Control Group *(Mean=38.27, SD=4.962)*. The results revealed that the difference in students' motivation between the two groups after the experiment was significant *(Mean difference=3.909, t=3.782, df=86, p=.000)*.

Table 13. Comparison of students' motivation between pre-test and post-test

		Mean	SD	t-value	df	p-value
Control	Pretest-Posttest	-.477	1.677	-1.887	43	.066
Experimental	Pretest-Posttest	-4.568	2.386	-12.70	43	.000

Level of significance is at p<0.05

Paired-Samples T-test results in Table 13 also demonstrated that in the questionnaire survey, there was no significant difference in the Control Group's motivation between the pre-test and post-post (*Mean=-.477, df=43, p=.066*). However, there was significant difference in the Experimental Group's motivation between the pre-test and the post-test (*Mean=-4.568, df=43, p=.000*). The students from the Experimental Group were more motivated in learning English in multi-interactive teaching mode than those from the Control Group studying English in conventional teaching environment.

The above findings show that the multi-interactive teaching model has a positive impact on students' English proficiency in listening, reading and translation, which are in consistent with some researchers' study that multi-interactive teaching method allowed each student to experience the interactive process of information search, interpretation, evaluation, which was a kind of learning in itself. Compared with traditional teaching environment, foreign language learning under the network-based multimedia context makes the input more optional, "i+1" input more feasible and operable, which is conducive to reducing students' learning anxiety. More importantly, the diversity of online resources exposes students to versatile English used by native English speakers, promoting students' language awareness, and the ability of discerning, correlating and using information. It can also be seen from the above results that even the Experimental Group makes no significant progress in writing. It was understandable there was no significant difference in students' writing ability after 14-week's interactive teaching, because it was challenging for students to make rapid progress in writing without a great deal of time and energy.

The questionnaire survey showed that in multi-interactive learning environment, students' learning motivation had been significantly improved. Inside and outside the classroom, the interaction between students and students, students and teachers, students and machines (modern technology) went through the whole teaching process, which made students study in a state of being emotionally and mentally at peace. Teaching tasks combining individuality and integrity make teaching process more dynamic, evaluation more accurate and objective, learning more autonomous, thereby mobilizing students' enthusiasm. The sense of accomplishment after completing tasks and receiving teachers' appropriate feedback triggered their learning motivation.

5. Conclusion

This study was carried out in a university in China, lasting about three months. Taking the advantage of information network technology, it designed a multi-interactive teaching mode and applied it into College English class, in hope of improving students' English language proficiency. The results of the research showed that this teaching model has a positive impact on students' motivation as well as English ability in listening, reading and translation. Through creating a multi-level curriculum system, multi-dimensional teaching and learning environment, multiple evaluation methods and multi-interactive practice, this teaching mode fully utilizes network teaching platform and information technology, aiming to meet the reform requirements of College English today, the needs of contemporary college students.

Aside from analyzing the results of the experiment, the study has also carried out some reflections. Firstly, in multi-interactive teaching model, teachers can help students develop their online autonomous learning ability. Internet is an open learning environment filled with infinite information, which is challenging for students to distinguish. To resist various temptation on Internet, students need to foster their autonomous learning ability. Teachers could play their role in strengthening the management of online learning and offer support whenever students are in need. Specifically, teachers can make full use of online learning platform to aid teaching, such as recommending learning materials, assigning and marking homework, giving feedback, to ensure that students learn English in a good environment. Secondly, the evaluation system could be optimized. One way is to conduct longitudinal evaluation instead of vertical one, to put more emphasis on students' development. The other way is to highlight the weight of formative evaluation, during which students benefit through reflection. Thirdly, teachers' digital literacy needs to be promoted. University teachers should embrace the trend in this information technology era, improving their ability in identifying information, designing teaching activities, and carrying out teaching in virtual environment according to teaching content, students' proficiency and characters, and equipment conditions.

While adopting the multi-interactive approach under the network-based multimedia environment, EFL teachers need to establish teaching objectives and specific requirements according to specific situations. To be specific, it is suggested that teachers consider the following principles: 1) Group collaboration needs to be fully valued. Computer-assisted group collaboration requires each group member to clarify individual and group responsibilities, and work together to complete learning tasks. Additionally, group collaboration requires members' mutual trust, complement and encouragement. Centered on topics, discussions can be conducted, so that students can exchange opinions and get inspirations from others; 2) Evaluation needs to be fully valued. A comprehensive evaluation involving students' knowledge, skills, learning strategies, attitudes, and value is preferable to a single evaluation in which knowledge and skill is regarded as the sole criterion. Meanwhile, self-evaluation is also encouraged. Students can promote their motivation, understanding of learning through reflecting on and making critical analysis of their own efforts.

The research is not without its shortcomings. First, the research object of this study only involves 88 students from two faculties. To make the study more generalized, future study should involve more students from more faculties such as medical, arts, English. Second, the experiment only lasted one semester, about three months. For a comprehensive course covering listening, speaking, reading, writing and translation, it is recommended that the future experimental research period be appropriately extended so as to reveal more about the changes in students' learning attitudes, concepts, and language skills. Third, due to the small proportion of speaking in actual College English class in China, students' speaking ability has not been investigated in the research. As an important element of learners' communicative competence, it is suggested that the development of students' speaking ability be studied by researchers in future.

References

[1] Li Y, Zhao S, Ma Q, Qian C, Lin, Q. A feature analysis of regional classroom teaching in the trend of interactive instruction[J]. Interactive learning Environments, 2019, 27(2): 137-162.
[2] Shcherbakova I, Ilina M. Foreign language communicative competence formation of university students by using interactive teaching methods[J]. The New Educational Review, 2019, 57(3): 173-183.
[3] Suanyot S, Dibyamandala J, Mangkhang C, & Wannapaisan C. Enhancing communicative competence in English as a foreign language through hybrid learning[J]. Journal of Positive School Psychology, 2022, 6(3): 9617-9822.
[4] Ristic J, Capozzi F. Interactive cognition: An introduction[J]. Visual Cognition, 2022, 30(1): 1-5.
[5] Yang L. An "Interactive Learning Model" to enhance EFL students' lexical knowledge and reading comprehension[J]. Sustainability, 2023, 15(8): 6471.

[6] Gao Y. Problems and countermeasures of multi-dimensional interactive classroom teaching mode in College English[J]. Contemporary Foreign Language Studies, 2014, (05): 36-39 (in Chinese).

[7] Majumder S, Chowdhury S, Chakraborty S. Interactive Web-interface for Competency-based Classroom Assessment[J]. International Journal of Education and Management Engineering, 2023, 13, (1): 18-28.

[8] Taslibeyaz E. The effect of scenario-based interactive videos on English learning[J]. Interactive Learning Environment, 2020, 28(7): 808-820.

[9] Wu J. Impact of foreign language proficiency and English uses on intercultural sensitivity[J]. International Journal of Modern Education and Computer Science, 2016, 8(8): 28-35.

[10] Zeng G, Gao Y. Learner engagement in mixed-proficiency triadic interactions in the online muti-interaction environment: A case study of a collaborative writing task[J]. Foreign Languages and their Teaching, 2022, (05): 53-64, 146 (in Chinese).

[11] Agarwal Y, Vamsi P. R, Jain S, Goel J. CodeUP: A web application for collaborative question-answering system[J]. International Journal of Information Technology and Computer Science, 2023, 15(4): 33-49.

[12] He X, Zhou D. The predictive effects of extrinsic motivation on learner engagement in online College English instruction[J]. Foreign Languages and their Teaching, 2022, (05): 95-106, 148 (in Chinese).

[13] Huo W, Rui Y. The mediating effect of L2 motivation between self-efficacy and English proficiency[J]. Journal of Xi'an International Studies University, 2020, (2): 54-58 (in Chinese).

[14] Lile R, Kelemen G. Results of researchers on strategies of teaching/learning/assessment based on interactive learning methods[J]. Procedia-Social and Behavioral Sciences, 2014, 163: 120-124.

[15] Zhang S. Reflections on the diversified and interactive College English teaching model[J]. Computer-Assisted Foreign language Education in China, 2011, (07):76-80 (in Chinese).

[16] Kashinath K, Raju R. L. N. An empirical research on the effectiveness online and offline classes of English language learning based on student's perception in Telangana schools[J]. International Journal of Modern Education and Computer Science, 2023, 15(2): 40-53.

[17] Nafosat Z, Nasiba A, Ozoda N, Baktior D. Interactive Strategies and Methods of Education[J]. The International Journal of Recent Technology and Engineering, 2019, (8): 7667–7670.

[18] Nikolaeva N A, Zonova M V, Sosnina N G. Project work in English language as a method for developing the managerial skills of the future managers of service industry[J]. Modern Education, 2017, 73(3): 73-82.

[19] Fu Z. A study of College English learning motivation in the New Century: Achievements, problems and paths[J]. Journal of Southwest University (Social Sciences Edition), 2022, 48(03): 224-234 (in Chinese).

[20] Yang L. An "Interactive Learning Model" to enhance EFL students' lexical knowledge and reading comprehension[J]. Sustainability, 2023, 15(8): 6471.

[21] Zhang Z, Hyland, K. Fostering students engagement with feedback: An integrated approach[J]. Assessing Writing, 2022, (51): 100586 (in Chinese).

[22] Shyam R. Sihare, "Colleges Require ICT Facilities to Enhance Educational and Employment Prospects", International Journal of Modern Education and Computer Science, Vol.15, No.3, pp. 16-32, 2023.

[23] Fumiko Harada, Rin Nagai, Hiromitsu Shimakawa, "Predicting Online Student Effort with Accelerometer, Heart Rate Sensors, and Camera Using Random Forest Regression Model", International Journal of Modern Education and Computer Science, Vol.14, No.5, pp. 10-23, 2022.

[24] Abdessamad Binaoui, Mohammed Moubtassime, Latifa Belfakir, "The Effectiveness and Impact of Teaching Coding through Scratch on Moroccan Pupils' Competencies", International Journal of Modern Education and Computer Science, Vol.14, No.5, pp. 44-55, 2022.

[25] Keller J. M. Motivational Design for Learning and Performance: The ARCS Model Approach[M]. New York, NY: Springer. 2010.

Artificial Intelligence, Medical Engineering and Education
Z.B. Hu et al. (Eds.)
doi:10.3233/ATDE231373

599

Challenges and Innovations in Teaching Business Administration Majors in the Digital Economy Era

Wenjie XIONG[1]

Wuhan Business University, School of Business Administration, Wuhan, China

Abstract. On the basis of exploring the teaching requirements and changes of business management majors in application-oriented undergraduate colleges under the new situation, this paper analyzes many problems and their causes in professional teaching and talent cultivation, explores the new challenges posed by the digital economy era to the teaching of business management majors in application-oriented undergraduate colleges, and proposes innovative teaching methods and approaches for business management majors in application-oriented undergraduate colleges in the digital economy era.

Keywords. digital economy; Applied undergraduate program; Major in Business Administration; Teaching Innovation

1. Introduction

The basic function of education is to cultivate people, who are useful to society and capable of continuous development and progress [1,2]. Business management majors have been established for over a century. In the process of continuously adapting to talent needs and serving economic and social development, we have never stopped self innovation and evolution [3,4]. Compared to regular undergraduate programs, applied undergraduate programs have distinct technical application characteristics. It cultivates higher technology applied talents who meet the needs of production, construction, management, and service frontlines [5-7]. In terms of training mode, it takes adapting to social needs as the goal, cultivating technology application ability as the main line, designing students' knowledge, ability, quality structure and training plan, constructing curriculum and teaching content system with "application" as the main theme and characteristics, and emphasizing the cultivation of students' technology application ability [8-11].

In the era of the digital economy, the education industry, like other industries, faces enormous challenges [12,13]. The business management majors in applied universities, including business management, marketing, accounting, financial management, international business, logistics and supply chain management, human resource management, auditing, asset evaluation, franchise management, cultural industry management, etc., have completely different requirements and characteristics from before. Therefore, high requirements have been put forward for the teaching and reform of applied business management majors [14,15].

---

[1] Corresponding Author: Wenjie XIONG, Email: 719695038@qq.com

In recent years, scholars have conducted several explorations in the field of business administration education regarding the teaching characteristics, models, methods, and other aspects of applied undergraduate colleges, which have always shown a clear sense of modernity and foresight [16,17]. In terms of theoretical research, more and more scholars are focusing on studying how to promote the teaching effectiveness of business majors, integrating theory into practical operations, and seeking methods and approaches to cultivate more efficient and adaptable applied talents to market changes [18,19]. At the same time, business management majors have also made significant progress in practice. Many domestic universities have effectively integrated internal and external resources based on student characteristics and their own advantages, and have taken strong actions in exploring practical teaching models. On the one hand, some universities have enriched the content of practical teaching activities through experimental training platforms; On the other hand, the construction of a "industry university research" oriented school enterprise cooperation in universities has expanded the practical teaching form of business management majors. The challenges and innovations in teaching business management majors are of great significance [20,21].

2. Shortcomings in the Teaching of Business Management Majors in Application-Oriented Undergraduate Colleges

Due to the development of the times, especially the advent of digital generations, there are many shortcomings in the teaching of business management majors in applied undergraduate colleges. Analysis can be conducted from multiple perspectives.

2.1. Employment Status of Business Administration Students in Applied Universities

Compared to ordinary universities and even key universities, the salary level of graduates majoring in applied undergraduate business management is generally lower, as shown in Figure 1.

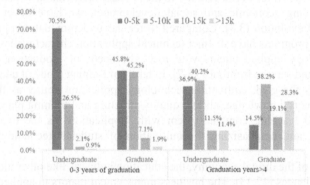

Figure 1. Salary levels of graduates majoring in business administration in applied universities

It is obvious that the proportion of newly graduated undergraduate students with a monthly salary of 0-5k exceeds 70%. Even for graduate students who have graduated for more than 4 years, only 28.3% can earn a salary of over 15k. This is very different from the situation of graduates from key universities, and there is also a significant gap compared to graduates from ordinary universities.

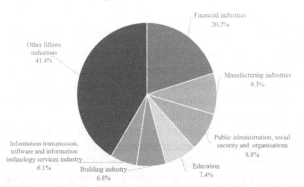

Figure 2. Industry Destinations of Applied Undergraduate Business Administration Graduates

From Figure 2, it is exhibited that the industry destinations of undergraduate graduates majoring in business administration in applied universities are very scattered, and do not reflect the professional advantages of working in business administration. The relatively concentrated financial industry practitioners only account for one fifth, while the rest have no obvious employment trends or advantages.

2.2. Shortcomings in the Teaching of Business Administration In Applied Universities

Although China has made certain achievements in the teaching and research of business management majors in applied undergraduate colleges, compared to Western countries with relatively complete and mature teaching systems, there are still many shortcomings and areas for improvement in theory and practice, mainly manifested in the traditional teaching style, which cannot keep up with the development of the times and economy

The traditional teaching model of "knowledge transfer + case teaching" is no longer suitable for cultivating talents in the digital economy era. However, the teaching style of many application-oriented undergraduate colleges remains unchanged, with textbook content as the focus and knowledge is mainly taught through PPT, blackboard writing, and other methods. The phenomenon of teachers and students completing all teaching content (teacher speaking, student listening) in the classroom still exists. The main shortcomings in professional teaching are as follows.

(1) Weak faculty and lagging teaching transformation behind the development of the digital economy

The teaching philosophy of teachers is relatively outdated, and the teaching content is outdated. They use indoctrination teaching, preaching from the book, and the theory is disconnected from reality, which is not conducive to the development of students' personalities and the exploration of their personal potential.

(2) The single assessment mode is not conducive to the growth of comprehensive outstanding talents

At present, application-oriented undergraduate colleges mainly use a single exam paper assessment model for students, rarely adopting flexible and diverse assessment methods, which cannot accurately assess students' ability to apply knowledge, imprisons students' thinking ability, and is not conducive to cultivating comprehensive outstanding talents.

(3) Backward textbook construction, unable to meet the requirements of digital economy development

The selection of textbooks mostly follows the classic textbooks and Western textbooks used by key universities, with high theoretical difficulty. Not in line with the positioning and cultivation of applied management talents. Formalization is inevitable in teaching and it is difficult to achieve the expected teaching effect.

(4) Theory and practical teaching are disconnected, and students' practical abilities cannot keep up with the pace of the times

The practical teaching of business management majors has long been attached to theoretical teaching, neglecting practical teaching. The conditions for practical teaching on campus are insufficient, and the construction of training rooms and off campus internship bases is not given enough attention, resulting in low practical abilities of students.

(5) Students have a weak sense of subjectivity and cannot fully play their role as the main body

Applied undergraduate colleges do not place enough emphasis on students' subjectivity, and their enthusiasm for self-directed learning is not high. The authoritative role of teachers leads to a lack of passion and impulse for self-exploration and learning among students, as well as a lack of innovative spirit.

3. The Digital Economy Era Poses New Challenges to the Teaching of Business Management Majors in Applied Undergraduate Colleges and Universities

The digital economy refers to the economic form of identifying, selecting, filtering, storing, and using big data (digitized knowledge and information) to guide and achieve rapid optimization and regeneration of resources, and to achieve high-quality economic development. The new round of technological revolution and industrial transformation is deepening, and digital transformation has become the trend. Influenced by multiple internal and external factors, the situation faced by China's digital economy development is undergoing profound changes, and the cultivation of business management talents is facing unprecedented opportunities and challenges.

(1) Integrating Digital Technology into Teaching Practice, the Paradigm of Digital Education Training Needs to be Reconstructed

With the rapid development and large-scale application of technologies such as the Internet, big data, and the Internet of Things in teaching, students' cognitive patterns and learning behaviors are undergoing changes, and the training paradigm of higher education is also undergoing reconstruction. There are higher requirements for improving practical teaching, learning methods, thinking patterns, and cognitive abilities.

(2) Accurately connecting with the transformation needs of the digital industry, the talent cultivation system needs to be improved

The arrival of the digital economy era is closely related to the development of applied education and applied talent cultivation in universities. Digital capabilities and technology are reshaping digital productivity while also driving industrial transformation. With the deep integration of digital technology and the real economy, the innovation of productivity and production relations, and the rapid rise of emerging formats such as intelligent management and platform-based enterprises, higher requirements have been put forward for the construction of talent cultivation systems in universities. It is urgent to reconstruct the digital entrepreneurial talent cultivation system.

(3) Driven by the development of business formats and technology, the concept of talent cultivation needs to be updated

The exponential growth of multidimensional information driven by data directly impacts the cultivation of traditional business talents, and there may be gaps and gaps between knowledge supply and demand. The construction and transmission of knowledge system content require new connotation driving forces. The increasing sophistication of the data economy era has led to revolutionary changes and challenges in talent cultivation concepts, value judgments, and cognitive thinking in applied university business management majors.

(4) The widespread penetration of the digital economy and the need to expand the space for talent development

In the new era, information can be fully shared and updated beyond the boundaries of time and space, and the intersection, infiltration, integration, and symbiosis between different disciplines are conducive to deepening the connotation of knowledge theory and the extension of practice. The cultivation of business management talents is more concerned than any other era. Guiding business management talents to have a more proactive and in-depth understanding of the objective world can better meet the development requirements of "individualized teaching" in talent cultivation in the new era [22-23].

4. Innovative Teaching Paths for Business Administration Majors in Applied Undergraduate Colleges in the Digital Economy Era

To address the aforementioned challenges, in the digital economy era, in order for applied undergraduate colleges and universities to achieve leapfrog progress in business management majors, it is necessary to innovate teaching ideas and methods. Figure 3 shows the seven effective paths for teaching innovation.

4.1. Improve the Goal System of Business Management and Integrate Interdisciplinary Teaching Resources

Promoting the improvement of the teaching objective system for business management has become a fundamental requirement in the digital economy era. We should focus on internationalization, target the training standards for high-quality applied talents, and form cross professional integration.

4.2. Reforming the Teaching Mode of Business Management Majors, Focusing on Students as the Main Body

By fully utilizing technologies such as artificial intelligence, big data, and blockchain, we aim to "student-centered" and enhance the digital abilities of teachers and students, promoting the transformation of traditional teaching models to smart teaching, and creating a digital education ecosystem.

4.3. Strengthen the Combination of Teaching and Learning, and Create a Teaching Team with "Thick Theory and Strong Practical Experience"

The two core resources in the digital economy era are talent and digital. Schools should formulate policies to encourage teachers to continuously learn. Teachers should use modern educational methods to make teaching more dynamic and vibrant.

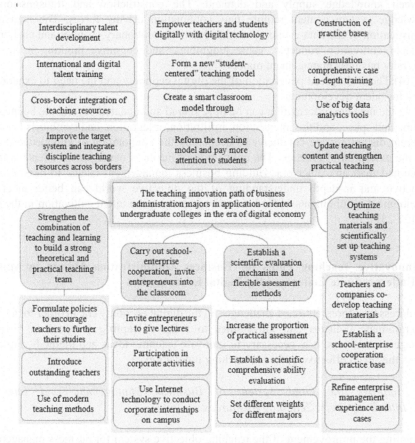

Figure 3. Innovative Teaching Paths for Business Administration Majors in Applied Undergraduate Colleges

4.4. Update Professional Teaching Content and Strengthen Practical Teaching

Abundant simulation comprehensive cases are cited in teaching, which can enable students to conduct in-depth training and cultivate their big data analysis skills and thinking patterns. The management of practical teaching should be strengthened, and the construction of internal and external internship bases should be built to cultivate more outstanding talents.

4.5. Flexible Professional Assessment Methods and Establishment of Scientific Assessment Mechanisms

Establish a diversified and comprehensive three-dimensional assessment model, change the previous practice of setting scores based on one test paper, and cultivate talents with comprehensive development.

4.6. Optimize Textbook Construction and Build a Scientific Teaching System

Guided by ability development, collaborate with enterprises to jointly develop or compile textbooks with professional characteristics. Improve the construction of the curriculum system, broaden students' knowledge base and employment channels.

4.7. Explore the Path of School Enterprise Cooperation and Invite Entrepreneurs into the Classroom

Actively promote school enterprise cooperation and carry out two-way exchanges. Establish "online teaching practice bases" in different industries, move the workplace to the classroom, and enable students to understand society in advance and familiarize themselves with the future work environment.

5. Conclusion

In the era of digital economy, talent cultivation in application-oriented universities not only requires comprehensive knowledge and strong practical skills, but also continuous improvement of digital and intelligent abilities, and comprehensive improvement of overall quality. Faced with the coexistence of opportunities and challenges in the era and new requirements, application-oriented undergraduate colleges should deeply reflect, identify the problems and shortcomings in teaching business management majors, and comprehensively promote teaching reform.

We should take student growth as the basic guidance, based on the needs of enterprises, cultivate students' abilities in self-directed inquiry learning, digital analysis and application, develop new talent training plans, improve curriculum systems and designs, strengthen the three-dimensional construction of textbooks, enhance teacher qualifications, and adhere to the close combination of theory and practice. Continuously improve practical teaching methods and methods. Through comprehensive reform and innovation, we aim to deliver professional talents that meet the needs of the big data era to society and provide better services for the digital economy era.

Acknowledgment

This project is supported by the 2018 project "Investigation and Research on the Current Situation and Improvement Strategies of Undergraduate Teaching in Business Administration Majors in Municipal Universities" (No. 2018A041) approved by the 13th Five Year Plan of Wuhan Education and Science.

References

[1]   Liu Zhiqin, Fei Jianguo, Wang Fang, Deng Xin. Study on higher education service quality based on student perception[J]. International Journal of Education and Management Engineering, 2012, 2(4): 22-27.

[2]   Hansen Rune. The use of learning goals in mathematics education[J]. Scandinavian Journal of Educational Research, 2021, 65(3): 510-522.

[3]   Gong Yuting. Exploration of applied talent training models in business administration education[J]. Industry and Technology Forum, 2019, (7): 2 (in Chinese).

[4]   Ke Xue. New exploration of the training model for undergraduate business administration talents in local universities[J]. Qilu Weekly, 2021, 000(004): 64-66 (in Chinese).

[5]   Ma Botao, Sha Haiqin. Analysis of the training path for applied talents in business administration[J]. Journal of Changji University, 2021, (2): 4 (in Chinese).

[6]   Tao Aixiang, Liu Chu, Chen Lu, et al. Research on talent cultivation strategies for business administration in applied universities based on new development concepts[J]. Industry and Technology Forum, 2022, 21(8): 2 (in Chinese).

[7]   Huimin M A, Shao X .Research on the training mode of "three-quality talents" in application-oriented universities based on OBE[J]. Asian Agricultural Research, 2022, 14(12): 51-53.

[8]   Wu Yuping. Research on the construction of a curriculum group for business administration based on ability cultivation[J]. Business Intelligence, 2022, (1): 0110-0112 (in Chinese).

[9]   Gao Yanli. Research on the reform of college business english course system from the perspective of professional ability training[J]. Overseas English, 2021, (10): 2.

[10] Xiao Xiaohong, Liu Siqian, Chen Jiangtao. Innovation in practical teaching of business administration majors based on real case construction[J]. Education Observation, 2020, 9 (29): 4 (in Chinese).

[11] Chen Jiangkun. Building a business administration talent training model with outstanding employment ability[J]. Business Culture, 2021, 000 (025): 126-127 (in Chinese).

[12] Kang Wei, Jiang Bao. Analysis of the connotation, challenges, and countermeasures of the digital economy[J]. Journal of University of Electronic Science and Technology: Social Science Edition, 2018, 20(5): 7 (in Chinese).

[13] Li Sanxi, Wu Yufan, Li Jiaqi. Digital economy and chinese path to modernization: significance of the times, opportunities, challenges and path exploration[J]. Economic Review, 2023, (2): 12 (in Chinese).

[14] Xu Wei. Research on the training path of entrepreneurship talents in universities in the digital economy era[J]. Information Systems Engineering, 2021, 000 (001): 157-160 (in Chinese).

[15] Bian Yuetang. Innovative research on talent cultivation in business administration in the digital economy era[J]. Frontiers of Social Science, 2021, 10(12): 6 (in Chinese).

[16] Huimin M A., Shao X. Research on the training mode of "three-quality talents" in application-oriented universities based on OBE[J]. Asian Agricultural Research, 2022, 14(12):51-53.

[17] Deák Csaba, Kumar Baibhaw, Szabó István, et al. Evolution of new approaches in pedagogy and STEM with inquiry-based learning and post-pandemic scenarios[J]. Education Sciences, 2021, 11(7): 319.

[18] Syamsidah, Ratnawati, Amir Muhiddin, Mithen Lullulangi. Effectiveness of learning devices with inquiry learning models to increase skills creative thinking students[J]. Education, Language and Sociology Research, 2020, 1(1): 128-136.

[19] Fan Xumei. Teachers' perspectives on the evaluation of teacher effectiveness: A focus on student learning objectives[J]. Teaching and Teacher Education, 2022, 110: 1-12.

[20] Bureau Julien S., Howard Joshua L., Chong Jane X. Y., et al. Pathways to student motivation: a meta-analysis of antecedents of autonomous and controlled motivations[J]. Review of Educational Research, 2022, 92(1): 46-72.

[21] Hui Chen, Zhanming Li, Wei Li, Haijie Mao. Discussion on teaching pattern of cultivating engineering application talent of automation specialty[J]. International Journal of Education and Management Engineering, 2012, 2(11): 30-34.

[22] Ibrahim Ouahbi, Hassane Darhmaoui, Fatiha Kaddari, "Visual Block-based Programming for ICT Training of Prospective Teachers in Morocco", International Journal of Modern Education and Computer Science, Vol.14, No.1, pp. 56-64, 2022.

[23] Nyme Ahmed, Dip Nandi, A. G. M. Zaman, "Analyzing Student Evaluations of Teaching in a Completely Online Environment", International Journal of Modern Education and Computer Science, Vol.14, No.6, pp. 13-24, 2022.

Artificial Intelligence, Medical Engineering and Education
Z.B. Hu et al. (Eds.)
© 2024 The Authors.
This article is published online with Open Access by IOS Press and distributed under the terms
of the Creative Commons Attribution Non-Commercial License 4.0 (CC BY-NC 4.0).
doi:10.3233/ATDE231374

The Preliminary Construction of an Evaluation Index System for Digital Competence of University Leaders in the Context of Digital Transformation

Yingbin SONG[1]

School of Art and Desings, Wuhan Technology and Business University, Wuhan, China

Abstract. Digital transformation puts forward new requirements for colleges and universities. This paper takes university leaders as an example and combines the competence model of "knowledge-ability-attitude" to construct the evaluation index system of digital competence of university leaders under the background of digital transformation. Through the expert scoring method, this paper has measured the weights of the evaluation index system with G1 method, principal component analysis and combined weighting model. The results of the study show that in the weighting system, the digital competence characteristics of leaders show a trend of "ability (0.4218) > knowledge (0.2586) > attitude (0.1965)". Finally, based on the results of the weight calculation, the conclusions and shortcomings of this paper are summarized, and insights for future studies are presented.

Keywords. Digital transformation ; University leaders ; Digital competence ; Evaluation index system ; Portfolio Empowerment Model.

1. Introduction

The term "digital competence" can be traced back to the 2007 EU publication 《Key Competences for Lifelong Learning : A European Reference Framework"》 [1]，which aims to promote the upgrade of economic and society by raising the level of informatization of the whole population to cope with the impact of information and communication technologies (ICT) [2]. The Education Informatization 2.0 Action Plan issued by the Ministry of Education proposes to use education informatization as an endogenous variable for educational transformation in order to support and lead the development of China's education modernization [3]. On the one hand, under the impact of 5G technology and the COVID-19 epidemic, the informatization of higher education in China has mainly taken the role of emergency respondent [4], but in turn has to some extent contributed to the digital transformation of higher education. On the other hand, the report of the 20th National Congress of the Communist Party of China in 2022 once

---

[1] Corresponding Author: Yingbin Song, E-mail: 1692231619@qq.com

again mentions the need to build a strong country with digitization and network. It can be seen that promoting the digitalization and information reform of higher education has become the only way to drive the high-quality development in the field of education in China.

The digital literacy of university leaders, who are the leaders and decision makers in the digitalization of universities, has a direct impact on the digital transformation of higher education institutions [3,5]. Different from the Digitization and Digitalization, the digital transformation of colleges and universities includes three levels: cultural transformation, labor force transformation and technological transformation [6]. Among them, cultural transformation is efficiency-driven and emphasizes changes in the way universities manage to increase flexibility and agility; in the workforce transformation, there is a need to focus on developing the capacity of the workforce to acquire new technologies and skills; in the technology transformation, leaders are focusing on adopting new technologies and implementing new processes to drive innovative development of workflows and teaching methods in universities [7]. Therefore, the digital transformation of universities has put forward new requirements on the competence of university leaders, not only requiring them to be able to effectively identify the impact of data and new technologies on traditional education and teaching processes [6,7] , but also requiring them to be able to coordinate the relationship between the development strategy of universities and the construction of information technology to promote the stable digital transformation of universities. However, at present, most of the academic research on the digital transformation in universities focuses on how emerging technologies affect the digital transformation [8] and the realization path [9]. Few studies have analyzed how the leadership characteristics can enable the digital transformation of universities from the perspective of digital competence.

Based on the above, this study starts from the digital competence of university leaders, derives the evaluation index system of digital competence of university leaders under the background of digital transformation through literature research method, and then calculates the evaluation index weight of university leaders based on the combined empowerment model. At last, this paper provides countermeasures and suggestions for promoting the digital transformation and upgrading of colleges and universities from the perspective of university leaders.

2. Literature Review

Digital Competence was originally conceived as a theoretical basis for the development of policies in the EU countries in response to the changing environment of the digital age in society, with the aim of developing and nurturing the digital skills of the population so as to cultivate the digital ability that workers need in the employment, development and social survival [7]. With the popularization and application of Information and communications technology (ICT)， in 2007, the EU regarded the three elements of "knowledge, ability and attitude" as a fusion of "competence", interpreted as "the ability of individuals to achieve and meet personal development and achievement needs, to use ICT technology in work, leisure time and communication"[2]. Along with the impact of digital technology on the education sector, the EU issued the EU Framework for Digital Competence for Educators (DigCompEdu) in 2017, which distinguishes the competences of educators into three categories: professional competence, learning competence and teaching competence, and proposes six competence domains and 22 specific digital competences [10]. Domestic scholars' research on digital competence mainly focuses on the construction of knowledge service system in university libraries and how user information competence affects knowledge acquisition. For example, Fu studied how to build university libraries' knowledge service system to meet the needs of readers [11]. Ying analyzed how digital competence reshaped the development pattern of higher education in the era of digital economy from the perspective of organizational change [12]. Zhu provided countermeasures and suggestions for the construction of university library in China by comparing the digital competence education in foreign university libraries [13].

To sum up, most scholars have chosen university libraries as their research object, and used case analysis, linear regression analysis and other measures to explore how digital competence affects the construction and development of colleges and universities and have achieved certain results. However, few studies have explored the role of digital competence of university leaders, as the decision-makers and helmsmen of digital reform in universities, in the digital construction of universities.

3. Construction of the Factor Sets of the Evaluation Index System

In the context of digital transformation and upgrading of universities, the digital competence of university leaders plays an important role. From the perspective of leadership, Avolio first put forward the concept of "E-leadership", and systematically discussed its connotation and extension [14]. Li also explored the leadership of digital enterprises and put forward 8 important dimensions [15]. Therefore, based on the results of previous studies and combined with the digital leadership theory, 24 influence factors were preliminarily extracted, as shown in Table 1.

4. Research Methods and Empirical Analysis

This paper adopts the principal component analysis method and the G1 method to measure the weight of the evaluation index system respectively. Subsequently, a subjective assignment model is introduced in this paper to determine the final weights.

4.1 Principal Component Analysis

Principal component analysis is an indicator dimensionality reduction method that can be used to determine the relative size of data when multiple factors are presented, and each factor is strongly correlated with the other.

First, assume that there is a total of $n(n = 1, ..., n)$ samples in the evaluation index system, as well as $j(j = 1, ..., 24)$ evaluation factors employee data. Then, the normalised data set Y_{ij} can be expressed as:

$$Y_{nj} = [y_1, ..., y_j] = \begin{bmatrix} y_{11} & \cdots & y_{1j} \\ \cdots & \cdots & \cdots \\ y_{n1} & \cdots & y_{nj} \end{bmatrix} \tag{1}$$

Then, the covariance matrix R for calculating the normalized samples can be expressed as:

$$R = \begin{bmatrix} r_{11} & \cdots & r_{1j} \\ \cdots & \cdots & \cdots \\ r_{i1} & \cdots & r_{ij} \end{bmatrix} \tag{2}$$

Among them,

$$r_{ij} = \frac{\sum_{i=1}^{n}(x_{ij}-\overline{x_j})(x_{in}-\overline{x_n})^2}{\sqrt{\sum_{i=1}^{n}(x_{ij}-\overline{x_j})^2 \sum_{i=1}^{n}(x_{in}-\overline{x_n})^2}}, \quad \overline{x_j} \text{ and } \overline{x_n} \text{ denotes the sample mean.}$$

Secondly, the eigenvalue of formula (2) is calculated using the function eig (R) in matlab, $\lambda = [\lambda_1, \dots, \lambda_j]^T$.

Table 1. Impact factor sets for leaders' digital competence

Tier 1 index	Tier 2 index	Tier 3 index	Tier 1 index	Tier 2 index	Tier 3 index
Knowledge	Use of ICT technology	Knowledge of the ICT technology S_1 Use of social software S_2 Online office abilities S_3 Text writing S_4	Ability	Ability to change	Introduction of a new information system S_{13} Construction of digital culture S_{14} Workflow innovation S_{15}
	Administration management	Digital team management S_5 Virtual team building S_6 Digital communication skills S_7		Ability of innovation	Organization structure adjustment S_{16} Digital talent recruitment S_{17}
	Communication ability	Virtual identity management S_8 Public relationship coordination S_9		Talent development	Digital talent management S_{18} Digital team building S_{19}
Ability		Interdepartmental coordination S_{10}		Digital strategic thinking	Perception of technology policies S_{20} Mastery of the technical development situation S_{21}
	Coordination ability	Digital trust ability S_{11}	Attitude		Digital vision building S_{22} Mastery of the strategy and direction S_{23}
		Digital social etiquette S_{12}		Performance duties and responsibilities	Completion of the work within the role S_{24}

Thirdly, according to the size of the eigenvalue matrix λ, the sample weight is calculated by formula (3):

$$\theta = \frac{\lambda_j}{\sum_{j=1}^{n} \lambda_j} \tag{3}$$

Finally, the weight size of $\theta = [\theta_1, \dots, \theta_j]^T$ can be obtained.

4.2 G1 Method

G1 method, also known as the order relationship analysis method, is a weight calculation method that reflects the influence size of each index according to the order of indicators. Specifically:

First, recruit l experts to determine the importance of the index y_{j-1} and y_j by the following formula:

$$r_i = \frac{w_{i-1}}{w_i} \qquad (4)$$

Specifically, r_i is the relative important degree, and w_i is the weight of the ith indicator in the G1 method.

Second, calculate the weight of the nth index in w_i according to r_i, with the following formula:

$$w_i = (1 + \sum_{i=2}^{n} \prod_{k=1}^{n} r_k)^{-1} \qquad (5)$$

Third, if among l experts, the ratio of the same order and the same importance degree are $l_1 \text{、} l_2 \text{、} \ldots \text{、} l_s$, then there is:

$$w_j^s = \frac{1}{l} \sum_{k=1}^{l_s} w_{kj}^s \qquad (6)$$

where w_j^s represents the weight size of the sth expert in w_j.

Fourth, the sample weight is calculated by using Equation (7):

$$\vartheta_{ij}^s = \frac{l_1}{l} \vartheta_{ij}^1 + \frac{l_2}{l} \vartheta_{ij}^2 + \cdots + \frac{l_h}{l} \vartheta_{ij}^h \qquad (7)$$

Finally, the weight size of the index system $\vartheta = [\vartheta_1, \ldots, \vartheta_j]^T$ can be obtained.

4.3 Portfolio Empowerment Model

This paper uses a subjective assignment model to determine the size of the weights of the evaluation indicator system, and the portfolio weights $\alpha_q(q = 1,2)$ can be expressed as:

$$W_q = \alpha_1 \theta + \alpha_2 \vartheta \qquad (8)$$

Where α_1 and α_2 represent the weight coefficient matrix calculated based on the main component analysis method and the G1 method.

Then, the objective function can be constructed according to the principle of difference maximization of evaluation objects:

$$W_q = \sum \alpha_q w_q^T Y_{nj} \ s.t. \sum \alpha_q = 1 \qquad (9)$$

Finally, a Lagrangian calculation was performed on equation (9), and by solving for the extremes, a matrix of subjective portfolio weighting coefficients α_q can be obtained.

4.4 Empirical Analysis

Based on the G1 method and the principal component analysis method, this paper took the middle-level leaders of a university in Wuhan as the survey sample for empirical analysis, a total of 14 valid questionnaires were collected, and the portfolio empowerment model was used to determine the weight of the digital competence evaluation index system (as shown in Table 2), where the size of the calculated combined weight matrix is $\alpha_q = (0.3245, 0.6755)$

Table 2. The evaluation index weight of leaders' digital competence

Tier 1 index weight	Tier 2 index weight				Factors	Tier 3 index weight		
	Factors	G1	Principal componen t analysis	Portfolio weight		G1	Principal componen t analysis	Portfolio weight
	Use of ICT		0.1254	0.1246	S1	0.0407	0.0418	0.0415

	technology	0.1228			S2	0.0471	0.0416	0.0434
Knowledge 0.2586					S3	0.0350	0.0419	0.0397
					S4	0.0590	0.0416	0.0472
	Administration management	0.1543	0.1243	0.1340	S5	0.0615	0.0407	0.0475
					S6	0.0338	0.0420	0.0393
					S7	0.0465	0.0418	0.0433
	Communication ability	0.1455	0.1258	0.1322	S8	0.0444	0.0422	0.0429
					S9	0.0545	0.0418	0.0459
					S10	0.0409	0.0418	0.0415
	Coordination ability	0.1470	0.1245	0.1318	S11	0.0425	0.0410	0.0414
					S12	0.0636	0.0418	0.0489
Ability 0.4128	Ability to change	0.0780	0.0827	0.0812	S13	0.0273	0.0413	0.0367
					S14	0.0507	0.0415	0.0445
	Ability of innovation	0.0838	0.0838	0.0838	S15	0.0409	0.0417	0.0415
					S16	0.0428	0.0420	0.0423
					S17	0.0223	0.0415	0.0353
	Talent development	0.0980	0.1246	0.1160	S18	0.0034	0.0424	0.0298
					S19	0.0723	0.0407	0.0509
					S20	0.0429	0.0420	0.0423
	Digital strategic thinking	0.1211	0.1686	0.1532	S21	0.0337	0.0423	0.0395
Attitude 0.1965					S22	0.0077	0.0424	0.0312
					S23	0.0368	0.0418	0.0402
	Performance of duties and responsibilities	0.0496	0.0403	0.0433	S24	0.0496	0.0403	0.0433

5. Conclusion

This study is proposed a digital competence evaluation index system for higher education leaders and conducted weighting calculations. The following findings were obtained:

Firstly, this paper constructs an evaluation index model for digital competence of leaders in the context of digital transformation. Through literature research, a total of 24 factors are selected as evaluation elements, and an evaluation index system is constructed by combining the "knowledge-ability-attitude" framework. The weights of the indicators are measured by expert evaluation, which provides a basis for promoting the quality transformation of universities.

Secondly, the weight of Ability dimension in the evaluation index system is much higher than that of knowledge and attitude, showing a trend of "ability (0.4218) > knowledge (0.2586) > attitude (0.1965)". This indicates that, as the helmsman of the digital transformation of universities, the leader's competence plays an important role compared to knowledge and attitude. In terms of the internal structure of competencies, communication skills (0.1455) and coordination skills (0.1470) are the most critical indicators.

Finally, the study also found that administration (0.1543) and digital strategic thinking (0.1211) are more important within the two dimensions of knowledge and attitude. This shows that leaders also need to have strategic thinking to actively perceive the changes of relevant national science and technology policies, and at the same time to create the vision and goal of digital transformation within the organization, so as to promote the digital transformation of colleges and universities.

References

[1] European Commission. Key competences for lifelong learning: European reference framework [EB/OL]. [2023-03-01]. https://op.europa.eu/en/publication-detail/-/publication/5719a044-b659-46de-b58b-606bc5b084c1/language-en/format-PDF/source-262349883.

[2] Graham M, Hjorth I, Lehdonvirta V. Digital Labour and Development: Impacts of Global Digital Labour Platforms and the Gig Economy on Worker Livelihoods, 2017, 23(2): 135-162.

[3] Dong Tong-qiang. Research on Informationization Leadership Model of Principals of Higher Vocational Colleges [J]. Modern Education Technology, 2020, 30(11): :77-83 (in Chinese).

[4] Zhang Yi, Wang Yanan, Zhao Yunjing. The Historical Context Hotspots and Frontier Analysis of Education Informatization of China[J]. Academic Research of JXUT, 2022, 17(1): 9-16 (in Chinese).

[5] Telukdarie A, Munsamy M. Digitization of higher education institutions[C]//2019 IEEE International Conference on Industrial Engineering and Engineering Management (IEEM). IEEE, 2019: 716-721.

[6] Christopher D B, McCormack M. Driving digital transformation in higher education . ［EB /OL］. [2023-04-01] . https://library. educause. edu /resources /2020 /6 /driving-digital-transformation-in-higher-education.

[7] Gençer M S, Samur Y. Leadership styles and technology: Leadership competency level of educational leaders[J]. Procedia-Social and Behavioral Sciences, 2016, 229: 226-233.

[8] Jones K, Rubel A , Leclere E . A Matter of Trust: Higher Education Institutions as Information Fiduciaries in an Age of Educational Data Mining and Learning Analytics[J]. Journal of the Association for Information Science and Technology, 2019. (71): 1227-1241.

[9] Fernández A, Gómez B, Binjaku K, et al. Digital transformation initiatives in higher education institutions: A multivocal literature review[J]. Education and Information Technologies, 2023: 1-32.

[10] Ferrari, A. DIGCOMP: A Framework for Developing and Understanding Digital Competence in Europe [EB/OL]. [2023-04-01]. https://publications.jrc.ec.europa.eu/repository/bitstream/JRC83167/lb-na-26035-enn.pdf.

[11] Fu Luyao, Liu Wenyun, Shen Yajie, et al. Research on Knowledge Service System and Strategy of University Library from the Perspective of Digital Literacy[J]. Library, 2023, (01):58-64 (in Chinese).

[12] Qin Ying, Gou Shouliang, Zhou Mingshan. Connotations and Direction of the Organizational Reform in Colleges and Universities in the Digital Economy Era[J]. Education Research Monthly, 2022, (05):64-71 (in Chinese).

[13] Zhu Menggang. Practice and Enlightenment of Digital Literacy Education in Foreign University Library[J]. Library Work and Study, 2021, (08):54-61 (in Chinese).

[14] Avolio B J, Kahai S, Dodge G E. E-leadership: Implications for Theory, Research, and Practice[J]. The Leadership Quarterly, 2000,11(4): 615-668.

[15] Li Yanping, Miao Li. The Structural Dimensions of Enterprise Digital Leadership and Its Impact[J]. Wuhan University Journal (Philosophy & social science), 2020, 73(6):125-136 (in Chinese).

614

Artificial Intelligence, Medical Engineering and Education
Z.B. Hu et al. (Eds.)
© 2024 The Authors.
This article is published online with Open Access by IOS Press and distributed under the terms
of the Creative Commons Attribution Non-Commercial License 4.0 (CC BY-NC 4.0).
doi:10.3233/ATDE231375

Study on Cultivation Mechanism for Intelligent Navigation Talents Based on "Discipline Crossing, Interdisciplinary Integration"

Yuan LI[a], Hongxu GUAN[b], Kang LIU[b,1]
ª Institute of Higher Education Policy, Wuhan University of Technology, Wuhan, China
ᵇ School of Navigation, Wuhan University of Technology, Wuhan, China

Abstract: The advancement of intelligent navigation will lead the shipping industry and a profound change in our country's navigation higher education. Based on the analysis of the current problems faced by China's navigation education and the demand for intelligent navigation, this paper puts forward the general ideas and strategies for the reform of the training mechanism of compound intelligent navigation talents based on the integration of navigation technology, Marine engineering and multi-disciplines, and explores the training path of compound intelligent navigation talents, which can be used for reference for the training of "Emerging Engineering Education" talents in navigation in China's higher education.

Key words: discipline crossing, interdisciplinary integration, compound talents, intelligent navigation, Emerging Engineering Education

1. The Historical Background of Intelligent Sailing Talent Cultivation

Sea freight is national transportation. "An economic power must be a maritime power and a sea transportation power", and "to develop the economy and strengthen the country, transportation, especially shipping, must be stronger first," specified by General Secretary Xi Jinping has profoundly clarified the relationship between sea transportation and the [1]economy,as well as between sea transportation and national strategy, and clearly demonstrating the direction for the future development of China's sea transportation industry [1].

In recent years, the undergraduate nautical colleges taken as the main fronts for training nautical talents, have extended to the current 16 institutions from the traditional 4, namely, Dalian Maritime University, Wuhan University of Technology, Shanghai Maritime University, and Jimei University, reaching a total amount of nautical talent training which has already met the needs of traditional nautical talents in China. In the strategic context of a great transportation power and maritime power, waterway transportation is being profoundly integrated with new energy technology, modern information technology, and artificial intelligence technology while the shipping

---

[1] Corresponding Author: Kang LIU, E-mail: liukang_88@whut.edu.cn.

industry is presenting a green, intelligent, and flexible technological development trend as a whole with a new generation of shipping systems characterized by "shore-based remote driving control dominance, and few people on board terminal assistance" developing into a new direction for industry development. The American Society for Engineering Education (ASEE) believes that innovation in engineering education requires constant interaction between educational research and practice [2]. This critical period of restructuring the important waterway transportation technology system has made it extensively necessary and urgent to cultivate a high-quality and highly qualified crew that can adapt to the needs of future waterway transportation development, and to train complex intelligent nautical talents who can adapt and take the lead in developing the industry.

2. Analysis of the Cultivation Needs of Complex Intelligent Nautical Talents

As a national control major, the nautical major will carry out performance competent education under the requirements of the STCW Convention, with generally the same curriculum systems for undergraduate and senior high school nautical colleges, consistent talent training positioning from an appropriate perspective, and a focus on competent education and sailing skills education. Its standard is mainly on training qualified seafarers, and the cultivation is directing at mastering the operation, maintenance and repair of ships, their equipment and systems, and ship operation management and personnel management. Relatively, the professional curriculum system is single, and the knowledge level is narrow. Meanwhile, the system knowledge reserves for related fields such as intelligent control, data science, and information technology are scarce while the problem of lacking capable persons to drive and manage new intelligent ships has shown up with the advent and promotion of intelligent ships [3].

Regarding the above issues, it is imperative to probe into the hierarchical and classified cultivation of nautical talents and develop new nautical engineering science. On the basis of policy literature analysis, relevant research on the issues such as the relations of higher engineering education: teaching, research and social services, professional education and humanity education, ability education and knowledge education, theoretical teaching and practical teaching, development of education and development of national and regional economy has been conducted in this study in which the research samples including academicians [4], experts from the State Maritime Administration's crew department, university professors, and business representatives are selected for semi-structured interviews (refer to Table 1 for sample distribution) according to the principles of representation, independence, and comprehensiveness of the research samples.

Table 1. Distribution of interview samples

	University experts	Marine Bureau experts	Enterprise representatives	Alumni	Outstanding graduates
Interviewees	25	16	16	20	20
Interview period	3 hours	2.5 hours	2.5 hours	2.5 hours	2 hours

After arranging the interviewed contents, the main indicators for cultivating complex intelligent nautical talents are summarized as follows:

1) Considering the academic positioning and cultivation models, it is a must for

higher nautical education to orient towards intelligent shipping, to clarify the cultivation goals of intelligent nautical talents, take serving the "transportation power", "maritime power" and "shipping power" strategies as the overall goal, center on intelligent shipping, rely on scientific and technological innovations such as 5G+, AI+, BDS+, and big data+ to drive industry development in intelligent ships, intelligent ports, intelligent shipping services, intelligent shipping services, intelligent shipping protection, intelligent shipping supervision, etc., and develop a talent training knowledge system to carry out key tasks such as scientific and technological theory innovation, bottleneck technology breakthroughs, and equipment application system promotion. It is also necessary to aim at the cutting edge of intelligent shipping development, regard industry demands as the guidance, deem balance between rivers and seas as the cultivation positioning, perform comprehensive system reform, and focus on breaking through the complex nautical talent training mechanism for intelligent shipping, following the development trend of intelligent shipping, and exploring a model for cultivating complex intelligent sailing talents.

2) In allusion to the subject and professional structure, while meeting the appropriate requirements of modern ships, the complex intelligent navigation professional curriculum system should also pay attention to industry development, deeply integrate key disciplines such as transportation engineering, marine engineering, environmental science and engineering, emergency safety and engineering, and establish a curriculum system meeting the needs of the future development of the shipping industry. To establish the core professional curriculum, the IMO model curriculum system can be referred to with the emphasis laid on the consistency between the demonstration course and the STCW Convention. Besides, the general knowledge and elective curriculum should focus on intelligent ship technology, assisted driving technology, while strengthening the tracking of the development frontier of the discipline of great navigation, exploring and developing comprehensive courses, multi-perspective problem-solving courses, interdisciplinary discussion courses, etc. in addition to promoting the updating of teaching content with cutting-edge disciplines, industry and technology developments related to intelligent ships, unmanned ships, etc., and establishing a curriculum system that meets the needs of future shipping industry development [5].

3) Considering talent training and output, complex intelligent nautical talents should both meet the job suitability requirements of the current industry and be equipped with a deep mathematical and scientific foundation as well as backed by a strong interdisciplinary background. In terms of competency composition, in addition to strong practicality, more emphasis is placed on cultivating the ability to solve complex engineering problems, innovation and entrepreneurship, etc in order that a large number of high-quality reserve talents can be accumulated for the future development of the industry. The output of intelligent nautical talents can greatly ease the demand for new jobs. Shore-based support and assisted driving will make navigation a "more decent job". Meanwhile, it is also an important part of the cultivation of new maritime engineering talents to promote the cultivation of innovative spirit through technological change, to realize the inheritance of maritime culture through cultural confidence, and to carry out the ideological and political development of the course through the education of national conditions and values.

3. Suggestions on the Cultivation Needs of Complex Intelligent Nautical Talents

In the context of the strategies for becoming a transportation and maritime powerhouse, there is a deep integration of waterway transportation with new energy technologies, modern information technology, and artificial intelligence. The shipping industry is generally showing a trend towards green, intelligent, and flexible technologies. A new generation of shipping systems characterized by "remote onshore control as the mainstay and minimal manning onboard as assistance" is emerging as the new direction for the industry's development. At this critical period of reconstructing the key waterway transportation technology system, it is necessary and urgent to cultivate a high-quality and high-caliber crew that can adapt to the future development needs of waterway transportation, as well as to foster compound intelligent navigation talents who can adapt to and lead the industry's development [6]. At the same time, the cultivation of maritime professionals is a systematic project that requires collaborative efforts from maritime authorities, institutions of higher education, industries, and society to jointly create an environment conducive to the cultivation of high-quality maritime professionals.

3.1. Scientific Positioning, Hierarchical Classification, and Achieving Differentiated Training of Higher Nautical Talents

Accurately identify changes, scientifically respond to changes, and proactively seek changes from the aspects of the expansion of the connotation, technical extension, and regional extension of nautical majors. Further clarify the orientation of talent training in higher nautical education and achieve differentiated nautical talent training for undergraduates, higher vocational education, and specialized secondary education. National first-class undergraduate majors should not only be positioned to meet the needs of large ships, special ships, new ships, intelligent ships, etc. For qualified personnel, but also be positioned to cultivate nautical system and engineering personnel under the background of intelligent navigation, focusing on cultivating high-end nautical technology personnel for intelligent shipping.

3.2. Serve the National Strategy, Lead Industry Development, and Focus on Cultivating Intelligent Nautical Talents

In terms of positioning the goal of intelligent nautical talent cultivation, we take serving the strategies of becoming a "powerful transportation country," a "powerful maritime country," and a "powerful shipping country" as the overall objective. We focus on intelligent shipping, relying on technological innovations such as 5G+, AI+, BDS+, big data+ to drive industry development. We construct a knowledge system for talent cultivation in the directions of intelligent ships, intelligent ports, intelligent shipping services, intelligent navigation protection, and intelligent shipping supervision. We carry out key tasks such as scientific and technological theoretical innovation, breakthroughs in bottleneck technologies, equipment system research and development, and technology application promotion. We aim at the forefront of intelligent shipping development, take industrial needs as the guidance, take river and sea integration as the training orientation, reform comprehensively and systematically, make key breakthroughs in facing intelligent shipping with a focus on cultivating compound-type nautical talents. We follow the development trend of intelligent shipping and explore ways to cultivate compound-type intelligent nautical talents.

3.3. Overall Planning of Resources, Perfection of Mechanisms, and Creation of a Coordinated Support System for the Cultivation of Intelligent Nautical Talents

The guarantee system for the cultivation of intelligent nautical talents requires internal and external coordination, improvement of institutional mechanisms, and linkage of resources from all parties. In terms of external guarantees, it is necessary for the state and industry to improve relevant systems and mechanisms, further enhance the social status, income, and occupational security of nautical personnel, thereby enhancing their professional attraction and sense of honor, improving the attractiveness of nautical majors, and laying a solid foundation for high-quality professional students in intelligent nautical fields. In terms of internal guarantees, universities need to accelerate the construction of an intelligent nautical talent training mechanism based on the traditional nautical talent training system, the "double-qualified" teacher team building mechanism, and the practical experimental condition guarantee mechanism [7]. They also need to accelerate the exploration of comprehensive collaborative training in intelligent navigation, adopt collaborative methods, achieve multi-level, multi-directional, and multi-channel collaborative education, build school-enterprise collaboration, interdisciplinary collaboration, industry-education collaboration, and international cooperation multi-collaborative training modes, and ensure the quality of intelligent nautical talent training.

4. Exploration of the Training Path for Compound Intelligent Navigation Talents

Under the guidance of "serving the national strategy and docking the needs of industry", WHUT has carried out profound exploration and practice in the fields of training positioning, training program, curriculum system, curriculum ideology & politics, condition construction, training mode and implement approach for intelligent navigation talents, accelerating transformation and upgrading of the "Emerging Engineering Education" majors. WHUT comprehensively promoted training reform for the compound intelligent navigation talents.

4.1. Intelligence-oriented and Interdisciplinary, Scientific Positioning of Compound Intelligent Navigation Talents

In order to comply with a future imperative field and meet the training needs of "Emerging Engineering" for intelligent navigation talents [8-10], relying on two of national first-class professional construction points, namely navigation technology and marine engineering, and on the basis of intelligence navigation class in the direction of ship navigation and control in 2017, WHUT has added a navigation technology & marine engineering integration class in 2021, massive effort has been conducted to cultivate high-end leading talents for intelligent navigation. The training objective of this class is to service national strategy: transportation power, maritime power, shipping power, to comprehensively master the professional theory and practical skills of two majors, to hold a multidisciplinary background of transportation engineering, navigation & information engineering, data science & engineering, safety &emergency engineering, to adapt the development of domestic and foreign shipping industry, to cultivate highly qualified and compound intelligence talents with comprehensive dynamic adaptability, innovation and entrepreneurship ability. Henceforth, the overall structure of three classified training system for navigation talents has been basically completed: competent talents based on "Two orientations, three stages and school-enterprise cooperation", intelligence talents based on "Interdisciplinary and international collaboration", innovative and entrepreneurial talent based on "Two Collaborations". The homogenization of navigation education, and the structural imbalance between talent training and industry demand has been eased, value-added classified education has been promoted.

4.2. Goal-oriented and Student-centered, Constructing Cross-dimensional Curriculum Matrix

WHUT has comprehensive constructed interdisciplinary, integrated, multi-dimensional curriculum matrix system for intelligent navigation which support the requirements of talent training objectives. Curriculum system for both major courses and professional courses were centered on multi-disciplinary cross-training system which includes transportation engineering, navigation & information engineering, data science & Engineering, and safety & emergency engineering, etc. A further "Navigation + X" interdisciplinary and professional courses integrated system were proposed, WHUT has emphasized curriculum system of two directions (ship communication navigation and ship remote control) within three modules (competency, communication, control), and opened professional cutting-edge courses for smart ships and unmanned cargo ships. Intelligent navigation talents training curriculum system were formed and showed in Fig 1. In accordance with the construction standards of "advanced, innovative and challenging", and focusing on the core courses of intelligent navigation and marine engineering, the curriculum system and teaching content were designed from a holistic, systematic and cutting-edge perspective. On this basis, the curriculum standards for the training of new navigation engineering talents were formulated. In view of the new characteristics of students' learning in the information age, additional extracurricular content and credit hours were added, the depth, breadth and communication of specialized courses were reasonably expanded by blended teaching.

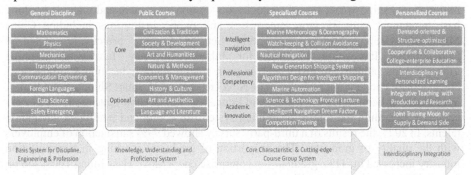

Fig 1. Interdisciplinary and dimensional curriculum system for intelligent navigation

4.3. Competency-priority and Innovation-highlighted, Establishing Practical Training Teaching System Based on Profession-innovation Integration

In 2017, MIT proposed the "New Engineering Education Transformation" (NEET) program. This program clearly states that "the center of engineering education should emphasize the development of students' thinking [11]. "WHUT laid out and established a series of intelligent shipping practical innovation platforms, promoted interdisciplinary talent training, industry-university-research collaboration and guidance on innovation and entrepreneurship, put forward measures maritime competency training, and innovative & entrepreneurship training as important foothold for training of intelligent navigation talents. On the basis of competency experimental training platforms, such as two 45,000-ton training ships, six DOFs ship maneuvering simulation platform, Huangpi Water Training Base, WHUT highlighted training of innovative practical ability and teaching system, intensified "industry competency ", "intelligent technology", "innovation & entrepreneurship" three types of practical capabilities, created competency-oriented virtual simulation + "marine campus" internship ship platform, intelligent-oriented marine emerging engineering integrated practical platform, scientific innovation-oriented Smart Shipping Creator Zoom, and established comprehensive Intelligent Navigation Integrated Practical Platform. A six-grades platform "Experimental Platform -Practical Platform - Practical Base - Competition Platform - Research platform - Innovation platform" was built, a five-levels process "Cognitive Practice - Individual training - Confrontation Drill - Comprehensive Assessment - Innovation & entrepreneurship" was implemented. The arrangement for progressive and successional practical training system would last for full period of student's cultivation. Students' thinking habits and learning patterns were rebuilt and intelligent navigation education supply system were improved [12]. The graduates have acquired practical & innovative ability for further employment and development (refer to Table 2 for sample distribution).

4.4. Expanding Actively and Multi-party Cooperation, Constructing New Model of Collaborative Training of Intelligent Navigation Talents

WHUT has actively explored multivariate cooperation of training modes under the background of new era and emerging navigation, coordinated various resources such as enterprises, research bases, intramural practice platforms, international colleges and multinational shipowners, signed strategic cooperation agreement and practice teaching base agreement with 35 large enterprises and public institutions including China Merchants Group, Eastern Navigation Service Center, principally organized Collaborative Innovation Platform for Inland Waterway Intelligent Shipping Transportation Industry, Ministry of Transport, and "Science, education & production" Development cooperation body for "The Next Generation of Smart Shipping and Ports", Yangtze River Economic Belt, Ministry of Education. Remarkable education results were achieved, regarding the reform of training system for compound intelligent navigation talents. In 2021, the results of a third-party survey showed 99% satisfaction of employers with the quality of graduates. The proportion of graduates working in transportation industry increased by 11%, graduates in enterprise cooperative class found 100% job on board, 43% of students in intelligent navigation class were examined or through exam - free recommendation for master degree in interdiscipline. The proportion of employment in the world's top 500 and strategic emerging industries were 52.2%, and the proportion of graduates with overseas exchange study experience increased by 10%. Students have achieved superb results in innovation fields, more than 80 achievements at or above the ministerial level have been obtained in the past three years, e.g "Internet Plus" college Student Innovation and Entrepreneurship Competition silver award, First prize of National Traffic Science and Technology Competition, national invention patent.

Table 2. Progressive and successional practical training system for navigational experiments

Time		Training Process	Organizational Forms	Experimental Platform	Supported Platform
1st Year	Cognitive Practice Single Training	The courses focus on ship cognition experiment, physics experiment and computer basic software experiment to cultivate general knowledge foundation	General experiment Professional experiment	Experimental Platform	Ship Cognition Experiment Platform, Intelligent Navigation Experiment Teaching Platform
2nd Year	Competency Training Engineering Practice	The courses focus on basic skills training for seafarers., rely on the innovation and entrepreneurship training to carry out project research, cultivate professional ability and scientific research awareness	Independent experiment Individual practical training Innovation & entrepreneurship training	Practical Platform Practice Base Research Platform	Six DOFs Ship Maneuvering Simulation Platform Huangpi Water Training Base Intelligent Navigation Integrated Practical Platform
3rd Year	Science & Technology Competition Innovation & Entrepreneurship	Carry out practical courses via virtual simulation and practice ship, set up interactive and cooperative navigation operation, confrontation exercises; Carry out the competition practice On the basis of innovation and entrepreneurship projects	Comprehensive ability training Cutting-edge practice of science and technology Innovation & entrepreneurship training	Practice Base Research Platform Research Platform Innovative Platform	Changhang Training Ship, Ship Traffic Big Data Platform, Water Traffic Accident Inversion Platform National University Student Social Practice and Science Contest on Energy Saving and Emission Reduction, National Ocean Vehicle design and production competition, National Competition of Transportation Science and Technology for students Intelligent Navigation Integrated Practical Platform Smart Shipping Creator Zoom
4th Year	Comprehensive Evaluation Innovation & Entrepreneurship Guided	The courses focus on the training for second/third officer competency certificate; Carry out graduation practice on employmentative training ship and intelligent ship research base; Dissertation writing, focus on transformation and promotion of achievements, economic benefits and social value.	School-enterprise collaborative practice Dissertation (Design) Research popularization	Practice Base Practical Platform Innovative Platform	Changhang Training Ship, Intelligent Ship Research Base Intelligent Navigation Integrated Practical Platform Smart Shipping Creator Zoom

5. Conclusion

Starting for the strategy of serving the national "transportation power" and "maritime power", and keeping a close watch at the evolution of the content of nautical specialties, carrying out "driving integration" research and practice on training new engineering talents in navigation with the goal of meeting the needs of intelligent shipping talents is a new and far-reaching exploration after the adjustment of the "integrated driving communication" specialty. On the basis of "driving-machine integration", its deep integration with communication engineering, navigation and information engineering, data science engineering, safety emergency engineering and other disciplines to create a multi-disciplinary new maritime engineering talent training mode, and focus on the training of high-end maritime talents are conducive to achieving the transformation and upgrading of higher nautical education in China, leading domestic higher nautical education from competent education to strong foundation and wide-caliber talent training, accelerating the classification and classification of sailing education in China's nautical colleges and universities, and comprehensively enhancing the service competitiveness and service capabilities of the maritime industry.

Acknowledgments

This project is supported by the Teaching Reform & Research Project of the Higher Education Institutions of Hubei Province (No. 2021107), the Research Project of Education & Teaching Reform, The Advisory Sub-committee on Teaching Nautical Science Major, The National Advisory Committee on Teaching Transportation to Majors in Higher Education under the Ministry of Education (No. 2022jzw007), the Research Project of Educational Science, China Institute of Communications Education (No. JT2022YB035 & No. JT2022YB134).

References

[1]   Lirong Xu. Economic power must be a maritime power and shipping power[J]. Pearl River Water Transport, 2019,20:76-83. (in Chinese)
[2]   Jamieson, L., & Lohmann, J. Creating a culture for scholarly and systematic innovation in engineering.education. [J]. Washington, DC: American Society for Engineering Education.2009.
[3]   Sean Trafford. Maritime safety[M]. Brighton: Book Guild Publishing, 2009.
[4]   Guangshe Jia,Chengbin Xiao.Research on five stakeholders & five relationships of higher engineering education in China[J]. International Journal of Modern Education and Computer Science, 2009, 1:30-38.
[5]   Ke Zhou. Exploration of the engineering ability training mode of "interdisciplinary learning and integration of industry and education"[J]. Research in Higher Education of Engineering, 2019(3): 33-39 (in Chinese)
[6]   Helen Sampson. International seafarers and transnationalism in the twenty-firstcentury[M]. Manchester: Manchester University Press, 2013.
[7]   UNESCO. The International Center for Engineering Education. Engineering education and engineering capacity building for the future [M]. Higher Education Press, 2018.7: 35.
[8]   Fudan consensus of "Emerging engineering education" construction[J]. Research in Higher Education of Engineering, 2017, (1): 10-11 (in Chinese)
[9]   "Emerging engineering education" construction action route ("Tianjin University Action")[J]. Research in Higher Education of Engineering, 2017, (2):24-25. (in Chinese)
[10] "Emerging engineering education" construction cuide ("Beijing Guide")[J]. Research in Higher Education of Engineering, 2017, (4): 20-21 (in Chinese)

[11] Graham R. The global state of the art in engineering education[J]. Massachusetts Institute of Technology (MIT), Massachusetts, USA, 2018.

[12] XinLiang Ou, John Wang, Huafu Liu, Dan Wen, Wende He, Yi Pan. Research on the reform of practical teaching driven by practical training under constructivism[J]. International Journal of Modern Education and Computer Science, 2011, 1: 77-83.

624
Artificial Intelligence, Medical Engineering and Education
Z.B. Hu et al. (Eds.)
© 2024 The Authors.
doi:10.3233/ATDE231376

Reform and Practice of the Teaching System of Combining Virtual and Real Teaching in the Experimental Course of "Asphalt and Asphalt Mixture"

Wen XU[1], Ruiqi CHEN, Linbo ZHANG, Jian TONG, Tingting HUANG
[a] School of Transportation and Logistics Engineering, Wuhan University of Technology
Wuhan, China
ORCiD ID: Wen Xu https://orcid.org/0000-0003-0136-4204

Abstract. Experimental teaching is an important carrier for cultivating innovative spirit and practical ability. By using the combination of virtual and real methods, the breadth and depth of experimental teaching content are expanded, the time and space of experimental teaching are extended, and the quality and level of experimental teaching are improved. This article introduces the overall framework of the virtual reality combination teaching system for the "Asphalt and Asphalt Mixture" experimental course. Through teaching reform, the effectiveness of experimental teaching has been effectively improved, students' basic experimental skills and techniques have been better trained, and students' further understanding and consolidation of basic theoretical knowledge have been deepened. Finally, taking the "Three Major Indicators of Asphalt" experiment as an example, the architecture and teaching methods of the virtual reality combination experimental teaching system were elaborated in detail, as well as the role of cultivating students' experimental skills and independent innovation ability.

Keywords. Asphalt experiment; Combination of virtual and reality; Teaching reform and practice.

1. Introduction

With the implementation of major strategies such as "Made in China 2025", "the Belt and Road" and "Internet plus", the new economy represented by new technologies, new formats, new models and new industries is booming, which puts forward higher requirements for engineering science and technology talents and urgently needs reform and innovation in higher engineering education [1, 2]. The "Emerging Engineering Education" is a reform aimed at higher engineering education. Practical teaching of engineering majors is a crucial teaching link in cultivating applied talents in higher engineering education, and the Road and Bridge and River Crossing Engineering majors are engineering majors with strong practicality. In the context of the construction of Emerging Engineering Education disciplines, only through practical teaching and strengthening the cultivation of students' engineering abilities can we achieve the

---

[1] Corresponding Author: Wen XU, E-mail: wenxu@whut.edu.cn.

cultivation of high-quality composite engineering and technical talents who can solve practical engineering problems [3]. Therefore, it is particularly necessary to promote the reform of practical teaching by combining the theoretical and practical teaching of road and bridge and river crossing engineering majors.

At present, in the reform of practical teaching in undergraduate colleges, reforms have been mainly carried out in the construction of engineering training bases, strengthening cooperation with enterprises, academia, and research, as well as improving the team of practical teachers, and good reform results have been achieved [4][5]. However, for asphalt and asphalt mixture courses, due to their long teaching cycle and lack of practical links, it is difficult for students to deeply learn relevant theoretical knowledge, and they lack the practical operation ability of experiments, making it difficult to connect with engineering practice [6]. Through classroom teaching alone, students have difficulty understanding the design and performance of asphalt and asphalt mixtures, and do not have the ability to solve practical engineering problems. The "Asphalt and Asphalt Mixture" experiment is an important foundational course in the field of road and bridge engineering. This course plays an important role in students' systematic understanding and mastery of theoretical knowledge [7].

Experimental teaching is an important carrier for cultivating innovative spirit and practical ability. By using the combination of virtual and real methods, the breadth and depth of experimental teaching content are expanded, the time and space of experimental teaching are extended, and the quality and level of experimental teaching are improved [8]. The experiment of "asphalt and asphalt mixture" is a traditional experimental teaching project in the course of road construction materials. However, due to the long time and strong comprehensiveness, it is usually demonstrated by teachers during undergraduate teaching, and students watch or watch video animations to complete it. Students have fewer opportunities to hands-on operation [9]. This passive learning method is difficult to stimulate students' interest. In this context, conducting research and practice on the virtual reality combined teaching system for asphalt and asphalt mixture experiments not only improves experimental efficiency and saves teaching costs, but also deeply changes teaching concepts and methods, which is of great significance for cultivating students' professional practical and innovative abilities.

2. Introduction to the Experimental Course of "Asphalt and Asphalt Mixtures"

The "Asphalt and Asphalt Mixture" experiment is a fundamental course in studying the performance technology of asphalt pavement materials [10]. Through courses and experimental teaching, students can understand the technical performance and testing methods of asphalt pavement materials, explore the relationship between the internal composition and technical performance of materials, and master the technical performance and improvement methods of materials.

Basic requirements for experimental teaching of "asphalt and asphalt mixture":

1) Understand the structure, function, operating procedures, and metrological calibration methods of the main experimental instruments;

2) Understand the testing methods for the technical performance of commonly used asphalt pavement materials and master the testing methods;

3) Master the design methods of asphalt mixtures;

4) Master the processing methods of experimental data.

3. The Experimental Teaching Model of Combining Virtual and Real

3.1 Objectives

The objectives to be achieved in this study are as follows. Firstly, in conjunction with the transformation and upgrading of majors in the context of Emerging Engineering Education, we aim to enhance professional vitality and cultivate high-quality road engineering talents. Secondly, Enrich teaching resources: Through the combination of virtual and real, stimulate students' interest in learning and improve their understanding of professional knowledge.

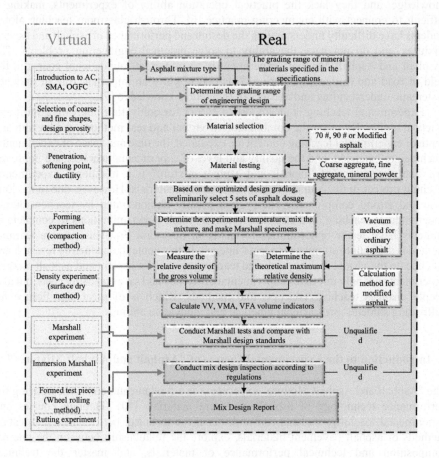

Figure 1. Research content on the combination of virtual and real

3.2 Research Contents

This study adheres to the principle of "combining virtual and real, and complementing each other", and takes the design of dense asphalt concrete mix proportion as the main line [11], as shown in Figure 1. Starting from several major modules such as virtual simulation overall design, material selection and testing, specimen forming and testing, interaction and assessment design.

4. Experimental Cases of "Three Major Indicators of Asphalt"

4.1. Penetration Experiment

4.1.1 Purpose and Scope of Application

Suitable for measuring the penetration of road petroleum asphalt, polymer modified asphalt, and liquid petroleum asphalt distillation or emulsified asphalt evaporation residue, measured in 0.1mm. The standard experimental conditions are temperature 25 ℃, load 100g, and penetration time 5s.

The penetration index PI is used to describe the temperature sensitivity of asphalt. It is recommended to measure the penetration at three or more temperature conditions such as 15℃, 25℃, and 30℃, and calculate it according to the specified method. If the penetration at 30℃ is too large, 5℃ can be used instead. The equivalent softening point T_{800} is equivalent to the temperature at which the penetration of asphalt is 800℃, used to evaluate the high-temperature stability of asphalt. The equivalent brittleness point $T_{1.2}$ is the temperature equivalent to a penetration of 1.2 for asphalt, used to evaluate the low-temperature cracking resistance of asphalt.

4.1.2 Experimental Methods

1) Preparation
- Prepare the sample, adjust the constant temperature water tank to the required experimental temperature
- Inject the sample into the test mold, with a height exceeding 10mm of the needle penetration value, and cover the test mold
- Cool in air for 1.5 to 3 hours, then keep it warm for 1.5 to 3 hours in a water tank at a test temperature of ±0.1℃, adjust the penetrometer to be level

2) Procedure
- Place the test mold on the instrument tripod, with a water depth of no less than 10mm above the surface of the sample
- Slowly lower the connecting rod, coarse bar → fine adjustment, just make contact and return to zero
- Press the release button, the timing and standard needle drop start simultaneously, and automatically stop at 5 seconds. The schematic diagram of the penetration experiment is shown in Figure 2.
- Read the displacement value of the display window, accurate to 0.1mm
- At least three parallel tests shall be conducted on the same sample, and the distance between each measuring point and the edge of the container shall not be less than 10mm. The temperature should be accurately controlled during each test, and the standard needle should be replaced or wiped clean during each test
- For samples with a needle penetration greater than 200, use at least three standard needles. After each test, leave the needles in the sample until the test is completed and removed

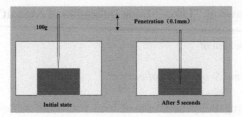

Figure 2. Schematic diagram of penetration experiment

4.2. Softening Point Experiment

4.2.1 Purpose and Scope of Application

Suitable for measuring the softening point of road petroleum asphalt and polymer modified asphalt, as well as the softening point of liquid petroleum asphalt, coal tar asphalt distillation residue, or emulsified asphalt evaporation residue.

The softening point is an indicator reflecting the thermal stability of asphalt materials and a measure of asphalt viscosity.

4.2.2 Experimental Methods

1) Preparation
● Place the sample ring on the base plate coated with isolation agent, inject asphalt into the sample ring, and fill it slightly higher than the inside of the ring surface; Slightly raised for easy scraping of the mold
● Cool at room temperature for 30 minutes and scrape flat with a hot scraper, as shown in Figure 3

2) Procedure
● Place the sample together with the base plate in a water tank at 5±0.5℃ for 15 minutes, while placing the bracket, steel ball, and positioning ring in the same water tank
● Inject distilled water that has been boiled and cooled to 5℃ into the beaker, with the water surface slightly lower than the depth mark on the vertical pole
● Place the sample ring in the circular hole in the middle of the bracket and cover it with a positioning ring; Put the whole support into the beaker, adjust the water level to the mark, and keep the water temperature at 5±0.5℃
● Insert the thermometer through the center hole of the upper plate, so that the temperature measuring head is flush with the bottom of the sample ring
● Place the steel ball in the middle of the positioning ring, activate the electromagnetic stirrer, and start heating
● The sample gradually drops when heated, and the instrument automatically obtains the temperature value when in contact with the floor. The schematic diagram of the softening point experiment is shown in Figure 4

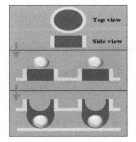

Figure 3. Scrape the softening point sample

Figure 4. Schematic diagram of softening point experiment

4.3. Ductility Experiment

4.3.1 Purpose and Scope of Application

Suitable for measuring the ductility of materials such as road petroleum asphalt, polymer modified asphalt, liquid petroleum asphalt distillation residue, and emulsified asphalt evaporation residue.

The test temperature and tensile rate for asphalt ductility can be used according to requirements. The commonly used test temperature is 25℃, 15℃, 10℃ or 5℃, and the tensile rate is 5±0.25cm/min. When using 1±0.5cm/min for low temperature, it should be noted in the report.

4.3.2 Experimental Methods

1) Preparation
- Mix glycerol and talcum powder in a ratio of 2:1 by mass and apply a evenly mixed isolation agent to the inner surface of the base plate and copper mold, and then assemble it
- The asphalt sample is injected back and forth from one end of the mold to the other end, slightly higher than the mold
- After cooling the specimen at room temperature for 1.5 hours, use a hot scraper to scrape it flat and place it in a constant temperature water bath at the specified temperature for 1.5 hours, as shown in Figure 5

2) Procedure
- After curing, remove the test piece from the bottom plate, place its two ends on the metal columns at the sliding plate and groove ends, and remove the side mold. The water surface should be no less than 25mm from the surface of the test piece
- Start the ductility tester and observe the extension of the sample carefully
- When the specimen is pulled apart, read the reading on the display screen in cm, as shown in Figure 6

 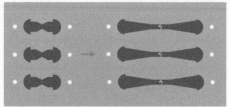

Figure 5. Scrape the ductility sample   **Figure 6.** Schematic diagram of ductility experiment

4.4 Case Analysis

According to the basic architecture of the experimental teaching system that combines virtual and real elements, different methods of combining virtual and real elements are designed for each experimental project according to the experimental teaching content, teaching methods, and equipment. Take the experimental project of "Three Major Indicators of Asphalt" as an example to elaborate in detail.

The "Three Major Indicators of Asphalt" experiment is a key experimental project for evaluating asphalt materials, involving the grading, high and low temperature performance of asphalt materials [12][13]. In the experiment, students can learn to use instruments and equipment correctly, master various testing methods, understand relevant engineering concepts, and obtain experimental skill training based on the experimental principles.

The first level requirement of the experiment is to measure the basic properties of asphalt materials provided by the laboratory. The second level requirement is to improve the experimental plan or method in order to minimize the error of the experimental data as much as possible. The third level requirement: if encountering abnormal test data, it is necessary to analyze whether the data is incorrect or within a reasonable range through the material synthesis mechanism, and study how to obtain the required performance of the material by adjusting the formula reasonably.

The teaching implementation process mainly includes three parts: first, pre-experiment preview, through the provided materials and virtual simulation experiments. The second is to conduct on-site experimental testing, where students select appropriate instrument settings in the laboratory based on pre class preparation to correctly complete material performance testing. Finally, it is necessary to complete the experimental summary and write an experimental report, which also includes discussions on the thinking questions proposed by the professor to further stimulate students' thinking.

5. Improvement of Teaching Methods

1) Reasonably arrange teaching content

Regarding the existing teaching materials on asphalt and asphalt mixtures, reduce the amount of theory appropriately and focus on practice. Update and supplement some content during teaching. For example, in response to the rapid changes in norms and standards, when understanding new norms and provisions, consult information to update knowledge. On this basis, the content of each chapter in the original textbook is screened, and the new norms and standards are integrated into the teaching, explaining the purpose and implementation methods of the modifications to students [14].

2) Adopting multimedia teaching

In the case of limited teaching hours, teaching more content within the specified time will inevitably result in teachers being overwhelmed, students not having time to think, and difficult to accept. The use of multimedia and a combination of virtual and real teaching methods can solve this problem. For example, collecting a large amount of materials such as photos, videos, and design drawings. [15].

3) Combining engineering case teaching to guide students to actively learn

In the teaching process, change the teacher centered cramming teaching method and replace it with a heuristic, and self-learning discussion based active teaching method model of "student-centered, with ability development as the goal", thus turning students into active and active knowledge explorers. For example, in the news, it was reported that a large area of asphalt pavement had been damaged several months after being paved. During the teaching process, relevant news reports and on-site pictures were first displayed to students, and then combined with the teaching content, students were guided to discuss the cause of the accident. Finally, the teacher came to the conclusion. [15].

4) Excellent students participating in scientific research projects

Not only graduate students, but also outstanding undergraduate students can enhance their understanding of asphalt and asphalt mixture majors by participating in scientific research. Integrating research projects into undergraduate teaching and involving some interested outstanding students is of great benefit in enhancing the understanding of asphalt and asphalt mixture professional knowledge and understanding the forefront of the discipline.

5) Change the course assessment method

Traditionally, asphalt and asphalt mixture courses are mostly assessed through closed book exams. The drawbacks of this assessment method are obvious. Students will adopt a rote memorization approach and ask the teacher about the scope of the exam. By using course papers or experimental reports for assessment, students will have enough time to think and search for information, allowing them to fully understand the knowledge points.

6. Conclusion

1) The paper aims to reform teaching methods and models, and embrace the multiple strategic opportunities and challenges of professional development with a holistic approach of "Emerging Engineering Education", providing strong talent protection and intellectual support for the upgrading of the transportation industry and social development.

2) The combination of virtual and real can effectively solve the problems of high cost and energy consumption, long time consumption, and difficulty in conducting traditional experiments. In the process of combining virtual and real, the guidance of educational theory was taken into account.

3) This study is a practical application of the "Emerging Engineering Education" reform in the field of road engineering, which can enhance professional competitiveness and enhance students' employment practical abilities. At the same time, it has certain reference significance for the talent cultivation mode and practical teaching reform of other engineering majors.

Acknowledgment

This project is supported by Teaching Research Reform Project from Wuhan University of Technology (W2020064), and The National Innovation and Entrepreneurship Training Program for College Students (S202310497183).

References

[1]   Zhou Guping, Kan Yue. The talents supporting and educational solutions to the "Belt and Road Initiative" [J]. Educational Research, 2015, 36(10): 4-9+22 (in Chinese).

[2]   [1] Memon S, Bhatti S, Thebo L A et al. A Video based Vehicle Detection, Counting and Classification System[J]. International Journal of Image, Graphics and Signal Processing, 2018(9).

[3]   Wang X. Discussion Reform of Forestry Panorama Course Teaching[J]. International Journal of Education and Management Engineering, 2012, 2(12):41-45.

[4]   Zhang S, Wei G, Zhang S, et al. The Thought and Practice in Teaching Reform of "Soil Mechanics"[J]. International Journal of Education and Management Engineering, 2013, 3(1):55-59.

[5]   Zhao J, Ying F. Research on the Teaching Reform Strategy of Professional Engineering Survey Course for Architecture Specialty based on the Internet under the Background of MOOC[J]. Journal of Physics Conference Series, 2021, 1744(3):032114.

[6]   Zhang L, Zhang M, Shao L et al. Analysis of effective innovation strategies on electronic information engineering specialized practical teaching[J]. Metallurgical and Mining Industry, 2015, 7(6):233-237.

[7]   Xu W., Luo R. Evaluation of interaction between emulsified asphalt and mineral powder using rheology[J]. Construction and Building Materials, 2022, 318:125990.

[8]   Chen Weiping et al. Exploration and practical research on teaching reforms of engineering practice center based on 3I‐CDIO‐OBE talent‐training mode[J]. Computer applications in engineering education, 2021(1).

[9]   Ma G., Jiang J., Shang S. Visualization of Component Status Information of Prefabricated Concrete Building Based on Building Information Modeling and Radio Frequency Identification: A Case Study in China[J]. Advances in Civil Engineering, 2019, 2019:1-13.

[10] Ministry of Transport of the People's Republic of China. Technical specification for construction of highway asphalt pavement JTG F40-2004[S], China Communication Press, Beijing, 2004 (in Chinese).

[11] Xu W., Guan Y., Shah Y I., et al. Study on curing characteristics of cold-mixed and cold-laid asphalt mixture based on electrical properties[J]. Construction and Building Materials, 2022, 330:127223.

[12] Xu, W., Luo, R., Zhang, K., Feng, G., & Zhang, D. Experimental investigation on preparation and performance of clear asphalt[J]. International Journal of Pavement Engineering, 2018, 19(5), 416–421.

[13] Xu, W., Shah, Y. I., Luan, D., & Tian, S. Evaluation of moisture damage of cold patch asphalt using the surface free energy method[J]. Arabian Journal for Science and Engineering, 2021, 46(11): 11277–11277.

[14] Heck T., Peters I., Mazarakis A., et al. Open science practices in higher education: Discussion of survey results from research and teaching staff in Germany[J]. Education for Information, 2020, 36(2):1-23.

[15] Chen Yongzhen. Exploring the Teaching Reform of "Asphalt and Asphalt Mixture" with Emphasis on the Combination of Theory and Practice[J]. Technology Perspective, 2020, (14): 33-35 (in Chinese).

Artificial Intelligence, Medical Engineering and Education
Z.B. Hu et al. (Eds.)
© 2024 The Authors.
This article is published online with Open Access by IOS Press and distributed under the terms
of the Creative Commons Attribution Non-Commercial License 4.0 (CC BY-NC 4.0).
doi:10.3233/ATDE231377

Survey and Reflection on the Current Situation of Chinese Farmers' Education and Training in the Context of Rural Revitalization

Lingyun ZHANG, Hongmei GAO[1]
School of Economics and Management, Tianjin Agricultural University, China

Abstract. Farmers are the foundation for the modernization and development of agriculture and the countryside, and they are the backbone of the implementation of the rural revitalization strategy. Seriously doing a good job of training farmers and building a high-quality rural human resources team can lay a solid foundation for the implementation of the rural revitalization strategy and ensure that poverty eradication and the rural revitalization strategy are effectively linked. Therefore, in the new period, we should focus on the goal of rural human resources development, accelerate the adjustment and optimization of human resources structure, effectively improve the overall quality of agricultural and rural professionals, and ensure that the trained talents can master the work methods and management methods, so as to promote the implementation of the rural revitalization strategy more effectively, and to improve the economic income of farmers. Through the examination of the actual situation of rural education and training, this paper has a broader and deeper understanding of the problem of farmers' education and training in China and puts forward relevant measures and solutions.

Keywords. Rural rejuvenation; Chinese farmers; Education and training

1. Introduction

At present, the overall level of education of China's agricultural labor force is generally low, and the aging of the rural labor force is becoming increasingly evident leading to serious constraints on the development of modern agriculture. The key to the strategy of rural revitalization lies in the revitalization of human resources, and the most direct and effective way to improve the scientific and cultural quality of the rural labor force and to build a strong human resource base for the country is to provide farmers with high-quality education and training [1]. Since 2005, the State Council has proposed 'actively cultivating practical and technical talents in the countryside' and for the first time made clear the requirement to train professional farmers [2]. In February 2021, the General Office of the CPC Central Committee and the General Office of the State Council issued the "Opinions on Accelerating the revitalization of Rural Talents". The document points out that it is necessary to focus on the need to comprehensively promote the revitalization of the countryside, comprehensively cultivate all kinds of talent, increase the total number of talents, improve the quality of talent, and optimize the structure of talent.

---

[1] Corresponding Author: Hongmei Gao, Email: gaohongmei@126.com

Farmer training is the key to accelerating the formation of a high-quality agricultural team [3]. An efficient education and training model for a new generation of high-quality farmers should be formed, with vocational needs as the guide and the cultivation of practical skills as the goal.

2. Survey on the Status of Education and Training of Chinese Farmers

2.1 Survey of Farmers' Own Conditions

From Table 1, we can observe that 66 percent of China's farmers have received junior high school education or below, and only 8 percent have received university education or above, thus reflecting the low level of knowledge of China's farmers themselves, most of whom have never systematically learn modern technology and scientific theories, resulting in low comprehensive quality, narrow vision and low awareness of self-improvement. In addition, the aging phenomenon of our farmers is serious, with relatively few young adults, which is unfavorable to the long-term and stable development of modern agriculture in China.

Table 1. Gender composition, education level and age composition of farmers in China

Categories	Content	Percentage%
Gender Composition	Male	58.4
	Female	41.6
Educational Attainment	Primary School	30
	Junior High School	36
	High School	18
	College	8
	University and above	8
Age Composition	30 years old and below	18.6
	31~40 years old	22.4
	41~50 years old	31.6
	51 years old and above	27.4

2.2. Survey on the Reasons, Objectives and Types of Farmers' Participation in Training

From Table 2, most farmers are neither willing nor interested in participating in training, but some participate in training to improve their skills and learn. Only a small number of farmers participate in training for the sole purpose of furthering their education, seeking profit or recruiting labor, which also indicates that farmers do not have strong business management skills. At present, the training that farmers participate in is mainly comprehensive quality training and agricultural technology training, with less training for new vocational farmers, and the teaching and training methods are generally single and not innovative enough, and the match between the farmers' own situation and the society's demand for training and development is not high. All these data tell us that we need to improve the current education and training, and that we have a serious shortage of professionals in this field, which is crucial for the future development of high-quality agriculture.

Table 2. Survey on the reasons, objectives and types of farmers' participation in training

Categories	Content	Percentage%
Reasons for Farmers to Participate in Training	Participation is required by the village	43
	Encouraged and supported by the government	16
	Interested in training	12
	Helpful to myself	17
	Watching others participate, I also participate	12
Purpose of Farmers' Participation in Education	Finding a job	5
	Getting subsidized	3
	Increase production	5
	Improve skills	36
	Others	2
	Learning the relevant knowledge	49
Main Types of Farmers' Participation in Education and Training	Scientific farming training	15
	Comprehensive quality education	42
	New vocational farmers	2
	Planting and breeding skills	41

2.3. Construction of the Education and Training System for Chinese Farmers

Talent is the basis for strengthening and developing agriculture, and since 'the Thirteenth Five-Year Plan', the education and training of farmers have taken a new step forward. At present, there are a total of 540,000 available talent in rural areas across the country, including more than 17 million high-quality farmers. The central financial authorities have invested 300 million yuan to support the training of new types of farmers around the country, achieving full coverage of agricultural areas and focusing on training poverty-alleviation leaders, entrepreneurial and innovative talents who have returned to their hometowns, and those who specialize in the farming industry [4]. China has expanded its resources for farmer development, and a new model of farmer training has emerged that combines short-term education, secondary and tertiary education, and vocational training. These changes are inextricably linked to more focused goals, more diverse training channels and more standardized training methods in China's farmer education and training. Together with the reform of higher agricultural education, this has led to the high-quality development of farmer education and training in China. However, there are still some areas that need to be further improved, on top of which agricultural education and training can be brought to a higher level.

2.3.1. The Education and Training System Needs Further Organizational and Managerial Strengthening

At present, China's education and training organizations are still led by government departments, but there is insufficient integration of existing education and training resources, a lack of a unified coordination mechanism, and many of the institutions involved in training do not really play their proper roles [5]. Individual education and training programme are still superficial and not in-depth enough, and no commissioners have been sent to review the results of farmers' education and training, resulting in the implementation of the relevant responsibilities not being in place, and the results of the training not meeting expectations, nor being able to guarantee its effectiveness [6].

2.3.2. The Education and Training System is Relatively Unstructured

To improve the effectiveness of farmers' education and training, joint efforts by many parties are needed. In China's current structural system, there are few opportunities for voluntary participation in training by leading enterprises, cooperatives, relevant research institutions, and existing training resources are not fully utilized. Functional transformation of major government departments is not in place, and social participation is not high. The integration and coordination capacity of the relevant institutions needs to be improved, and the lack of continuity in farmers' education and training is due to the fact that training programme are not formulated in advance.

3. Status of Education and Training of Farmers Abroad

According to each country's agricultural resource endowment, population size, geographic situation and level of economic development has led to the formation of farmers' education and training methods with their own characteristics in practice, in general, foreign farmers' training can be roughly divided into three modes, namely, the East Asian model, the North American model and the Western European model.

3.1. The East Asian Model Represented by Japan

The East Asian model applies to the characteristics of agricultural production where the per capital area of arable land is lower than the global average and where it is difficult to establish large-scale farms, with the government taking the lead in providing multi-level and multi-faceted training to farmers through different levels and types of training organizations.

3.1.1. Strong Government Support

Because of the relative scarcity of natural resources in Japan, the government attaches great importance to agricultural education and technical training, and since the 1990s Japan has introduced a series of relevant policies and measures, and set agricultural education as a general education that must be mastered by all citizens. Coupled with some legislative systems and financial support to ensure the implementation of agriculture, the development of modern agriculture in Japan has created favorable conditions.

3.1.2. Diversified Education and Training System for Farmers

In Japan, the demand for agricultural personnel for research and teaching has been met through the provision of education for a wide range of groups, from the highest to the lowest level, in accordance with the needs of agricultural production. In the course of the programme, the wishes of the farmers themselves are taken into account, and the contents of the training programme are designed to meet the needs of the farmers to the fullest extent possible.

3.2. Western European Model Represented by Germany

The German Government and civil agricultural organizations attach great importance to the education and training of farmers and have enacted special vocational education and training laws to promote this [7]. For example, 'The Vocational Education Act' it affirms vocational and technical education as a basic education system in Germany, laying a good foundation for the vocational education and training of German farmers. Vocational education in Germany is known for its 'dual system model'. This model consists of a combination of schooling and enterprise training, with students receiving one day of theoretical instruction per week followed by three to four days of enterprise training, enabling them to acquire both knowledge and practical skills [8].

3.3. North American Model Represented by the United States

The main features of the North American model are that agricultural production is basically mechanized and operated on a large scale, and that the agricultural science and technology system is relatively complete, with the organic integration of agricultural technology training, agricultural technology promotion, agricultural education, science and technology research and development. The United States mainly adopts the 'three-in-one' farmer training system, namely, education, research, extension of the three aspects of the integration of the education system, the system pays great attention to the actual problems faced by farmers in agricultural production, through technical education and training not only to give farmers theoretical guidance on technology, but also in the face of the problem of the first time to the feedback to the scientific research institutions, thus facilitating the scientific research institutions to carry out targeted research. This is conducive to the conduct of targeted research by scientific research institution, and promotes the transformation of theory into productivity.

4. Problems Faced by Chinese Farmers' Education and Training in the Context of Rural Revitalization

4.1. Farmers' Own Conditions Need to be Improved

The overall level of China's farmers is low, their living environment, cultural level, the level of awareness of social development and the cognitive ability of lifelong learning are lacking, the government departments as the leading to pay attention to, strengthening the weak links, to guide the farmers to better invest in learning the relevant knowledge and technology, so that they understand the importance of it [9].

4.2. Low Willingness of Farmers to Participate Actively in Education and Training

The above data show that most farmers do not go voluntarily, but rather cope in order to fulfill their tasks. Government departments and grass-roots cadres lack the capacity to widely publicize and organize this type of education and training, failing to give farmers a clear understanding of the purpose and significance of the training, and failing to organize it in a systematic and standardized way.

4.3. Most of the Farmers Trained Reported little Gain from Education and Training

Not according to the different regions to tailor the training, not in line with local product characteristics, not to understand clearly what local farmers really need, targeted, timeliness is weak, are rigid knowledge, optical will be the knowledge of the books but will not be used in life, our ultimate task is to learn on the basis of going into practice, in practice to find problems to solve the problem, so that it is an effective training.

4.4. Mismatch between the Actual Needs of Farmers and the Effective Supply of Education

4.4.1. The Lack of Coordination in the Organization of Training has Led to Uneven Levels of Education among Farmers

Agricultural education and training are carried out by various types of organizations, especially in the implementation of poverty eradication and rural revitalization strategies, and training is organized by agricultural education-related departments at all levels in all provinces, and departments at all levels are actively carrying out relevant training. However, each department works in its own way without a unified system, training materials are not updated in a timely manner, training plans and objectives are duplicated, and some places where information is relatively closed miss out on training because they cannot access information in a timely manner, resulting in a waste of resources that are not put to better use. These farmers regard training as a burden and thus reject it, depriving those who would like to participate in training of valuable opportunities and information [10].

4.4.2. The Lack of Individualized Teaching Leads to Low Efficiency of Farmer Training

A large part of the training unit is to complete the task, relatively passive, they do not have a prior understanding of the training object, their needs as well the current development of the current situation and trends in this industry without in-depth research and analysis, and not in accordance with the development of modern agriculture changes in a timely and effective adjustment [11].

4.5. Lack of Emphasis on the Construction of Farmers' Training Teachers

4.5.1. Unreasonable Structure of the Teaching Staff

A large proportion of the teachers joining the training programs are recruited through formal channels, but some of them are temporarily borrowed or are substituting for classes on a temporary basis, and they do not have a thorough understanding of the relevant knowledge, nor do they meet the requirements for attending classes at all.

4.5.2. Farmer-trained Teachers have a low sense of Identity

Currently, our farmer training teachers generally have low course fees because they are not well known, and therefore do not have a high degree of social dissemination. However, teachers need to spend a great deal of time and energy preparing their lessons, so many of them teach farmers purely out of love for the work of 'Agriculture, rural areas and farmers' and a sense of responsibility to serve them.

4.5.3. Farmer-trained Teachers have few Opportunities for Self-improvement

Teachers need to explore, understand and analyze farmers' psychology and behavior in a comprehensive manner, improve their teaching methods and techniques according to their cognitive and learning characteristics, and continuously acquire the latest information technology and update their professional knowledge. However, at present, there is little training for teachers in agricultural education institutions, and the number of participants is relatively small. Seminars, academic exchange activities, knowledge competitions, etc., on this subject are even more virtually non-existent.

5. Countermeasures and Suggestions for Chinese Farmers' Education and Training in the Context of Rural Revitalization

5.1. Strengthening Publicity and Encouragement to Increase Farmers' Motivation for Education and Training

Nowadays, there are still many farmers who do not understand what farmer education and training is and do not know how to take part in it, thus leading to a very small number of people taking the course, and those who take it well are even fewer in number. Therefore, the relevant departments should step up publicity in this regard, so that everyone understands the importance of this course, in the hope that everyone can participate in the in-depth learning and exploration of agriculture-related professional knowledge and technology. The Government should also play a leading role in stepping up its efforts to educate and publicize farmers.

5.2. Stimulate Farmers' Intrinsic Motivation to Participate in Training and Enhance its Effectiveness

Effectively stimulate the farmers themselves to participate in the training of intrinsic motivation is a long-term solution, so as to improve the effectiveness of training, to let the farmers spontaneous, targeted and motivated to learn in order to really learn, which is the most effective. In addition, we also need to strengthen the farmers' demand for research, know what they really need, carefully design the training content, stimulate their interest, improve the farmers' consciousness, and further improve the training effect. Theory is linked to practice in order to really solve the actual problems of farmers.

5.3. Encourage Young and Middle-Aged Farmers to Participate in Education and Training according to Local Conditions

As China's current labor force is mostly composed of older people, with fewer and fewer young adults, we need to take effective measures to encourage young farmers, workers and outstanding migrant workers to return to their hometowns to start their own businesses. In response to this phenomenon, the State has introduced favorable policies to support the entrepreneurship of young farmers. The situation varies from region to region, but assistance can take the form of capital, technology, education and taxes.

5.4. Improving the Assessment and Evaluation System and the Supervision and Management Mechanism

From the experience of farmers' education and training in various countries, the formulation and implementation of relevant laws have provided a good foundation and guarantee for farmers' training in many countries. Farmer education and training departments should improve and update the evaluation system and assessment methods in a timely manner, aiming at the target requirements of rural revitalization for agricultural modernization, and should strictly supervise the process and finally accept it through assessment.Uniform assessment standards should be formulated and the assessment process should be standardized. To pay attention to the effect of training, a commissioner can be arranged to visit the training site, and better and more comprehensive supervision and inspection mechanisms and safeguards should be established according to the actual situation. A correct attitude should be adopted to closely integrate the training policy with the national guidelines, clarify the objectives, take effective measures according to the actual situation, and strengthen the field inspection, not be an armchair strategist.

5.5. Strict Control of the Quality of Teachers and Establishment of an Overall Education and Training Mechanism

A strict entry system has been set for teacher training for farmers abroad, and developed countries have relatively high requirements for teachers engaged in agricultural education, with particular emphasis on the practical skills of teachers. In the United States, it is necessary not only to obtain a bachelor's degree in agricultural education, but also to complete programme in education and agriculture and other related disciplines. We can target new farmers, strengthen the construction of teaching staff in the country, train a group of farmers' expert teachers with rich practical experience in different industries and specialties, build a teaching master teacher bank and subject groups, jointly develop some high-quality courses combining theory and practice with the help of some key universities and scientific research institutes, and set up some practical training bases, so that the combination of theory and practice can better expand the coverage of education and training of farmers in our country. This combination of theory and practice can better expand the coverage of education and training for farmers in China.

5.6. Training Content should be up-to-date, with Equal Emphasis on Theory and Practice

One of the distinctive features of farmer training in developed countries is that it focuses on combining theory and practice and on the practicality of the training. They constantly optimize their courses according to the needs of society and the changing development of the market. Training institutions in the United States and the United Kingdom usually conduct rigorous market research and analysis before the start of the course, the teachers are to be trained in counterpart training, and the curriculum is not only basic technical training, gradually integrated into the management and operation of the content, to cultivate better composite talents, which is exactly what our country needs to learn and continue to improve the place.

6. Conclusion

High-quality farmers are the foundation for the implementation of the rural revitalization strategy and the modernization of China's agriculture and rural areas. By analyzing the educational policies, methods and characteristics of advanced capitalist countries abroad [12-14], it will be of great benefit to construct a system of education and training for farmers that is in line with China's actual situation and has Chinese characteristics. Constructing a standardized and scientific education and training system to train an excellent team of farmers in the shortest possible time is a new prerequisite for actively adapting to the new situation of progress in agricultural science and technology, changes in the organization of agricultural production, the accelerated formation of new industries and new forms of business, and the coordinated development of urban and rural areas [15].We should fully understand the strategic significance of farmers' education and training in rural revitalization, take 'patriotism and industriousness' as the basic requirement for training, and take 'love of agriculture, knowledge of technology, good management and good management' as the main connotation of a good farmer, and keep focusing on successful experiences. We are constantly focusing on successful experiences and drawing on useful nutrients. Through ongoing education and training of high-quality farmers, we can more effectively promote the development of rural industries, generate good social and economic benefits, and promote the prosperity of 'Agriculture, rural areas and farmers' [16].

References

[1] Yu Z. A Study on the Realistic Path of Tourism Industry Helping Rural Rejuvenation −Taking Shaanxi Rural Tourism Demonstration Village as an example[J]. E3S Web of Conferences, 2021, 235.

[2] Yufang HUANG, Li MING, Fang LIU. Current status and future development trend of research on education and training of high-quality farmers in Guizhou Province under the background of rural revitalization[J]. Agricultural Machinery Use and Maintenance, 2022(02): 123-125. (in Chinese)

[3] Chunjuan GAO, Baochen XU, Jiazhai CHEN. Research on the supply and demand of farmers' education and training under the perspective of rural talent revitalization and strategies for improving quality and efficiency--Taking Zhejiang Province as an example[J]. Modern Agricultural Science and Technology, 2021(22): 172-176+180. (in Chinese)

[4] Mao Y. Technological Thoughts on Scientific and Technological Innovation Promoting Rural Rejuvenation[J]. E3S Web of Conferences, 2021, 235.

[5] Wei Z, Wang X. Research on the Difficulties in Rural Renovation Through Art Intervention Under the Background of Rural Rejuvenation and Countermeasures[P]. 2021 International Conference on Culture, Design and Social Development (CDSD 2021), 2022.

[6] Wang M, Burgess J, Xiao Y. Literature analysis of the evaluation of public training programmes in the USA, Europe and China: Implications for the evaluation of farmer training programmes in China[J]. Pacific Economic Review, 2019, 24(1).

[7] Shuai LIU, Ping WANG. Implications of foreign farmers' vocational education for innovation and entrepreneurship training of migrant workers in China[J]. Journal of Chuzhou College, 2019, 21(06): 28-32. (in Chinese)

[8]   Xiaoru GUO, Wenxing XU. Experience and inspiration of new vocational farmer training in foreign countries[J]. Journal of Jilin College of Engineering and Technology, 2015, 31(05): 46-48. (in Chinese)

[9]   Wang X. The Role of Traditional Culture in Rural Rejuvenation[J]. Organic Chemistry: An Indian Journal, 2017, 14(3).

[10] Wan A, Zhang A Z. The New Type of Agricultural Management Main Body and Its Education and Training Mode in the Rural Rejuvenation Period[J]. E3S Web of Conferences, 2020, 189.

[11] Li L. Research on Improving the Willingness of Chinese Farmers to Participate in Vocational Skills Training[J]. Journal of Social Science and Humanities, 2022, 4(4).

[12] Salah Al Khafaji, Sriram. B, "A Concept Review on MOOCs Research Findings – A Qualitative Approach", International Journal of Education and Management Engineering, Vol.13, No.4, pp. 19-25, 2023.

[13] Aurelia De Lorenzo, Alessandro Nasso, Viviana Bono, Emanuela Rabaglietti, "Introducing TCD-D for Creativity Assessment: A Mobile App for Educational Contexts", International Journal of Modern Education and Computer Science, Vol.15, No.1, pp. 13-27, 2023.

[14] Musaddiq Al Karim, Md. Mahadi Masnad, Mst. Yeasmin Ara, Mostafa Rasel, Dip Nandi, "A Comprehensive Study to Investigate Student Performance in Online Education during Covid-19", International Journal of Modern Education and Computer Science, Vol.14, No.3, pp. 1-25, 2022.

[15] Luo C, Wei Q,Zheng Y, et al. Research on the Demand of New Farmers Training in Beijing[P]. Proceedings of 3rd International Symposium on Social Science (ISSS 2017), 2017.

[16] Li G. Research of the Role that Local University Libraries Played in the Service for the" Three Rural Issues"[P]. Proceedings of the 2016 2nd International Conference on Economy, Management, Law, and Education (EMLE 2016), 2016.

Artificial Intelligence, Medical Engineering and Education
Z.B. Hu et al. (Eds.)
© 2024 The Authors.
This article is published online with Open Access by IOS Press and distributed under the terms
of the Creative Commons Attribution Non-Commercial License 4.0 (CC BY-NC 4.0).
doi:10.3233/ATDE231378

A Discussion of the Causes and Effects of Wrong Pen Grip Posture Based on Mechanical Analysis

Wugang LI [a], Yushu HUANG[b], Feng NING[b], Fengmei CHEN [a,1]

[a] School of Intelligent Manufacturing, Nanning University, Nanning, China
[b] School of Physics and Electronics, Nanning Normal University, Nanning, China
ORCiD ID: Fengmei CHEN https://orcid.org/0009-0002-4777-4508

Abstract. Wrong pen grip posture accounts for a very large proportion of pen grip posture in adults. In order to scientifically explore the problem of wrong pen grip posture in adults, this paper takes a certain number of college students as the research object and investigates their pen grip posture. Then, the paper points out several typical wrong pen grip postures and makes a mechanical analysis of the correct pen grip posture. In addition, considering the relatively weak finger strength of most children, the paper focuses on analysing the causes of wrong pen grip postures in adults from the root, and discusses the possible effects of wrong pen grip postures in various aspects. Finally, these analyses are used to raise awareness of the pen grip posture and help educators to change the traditional educational approach in pen grip posture.

Keywords. Mechanical analysis; Pen grip; Causes; Effects

1. Introduction

Wrong Pen Grip Posture is a common problem among adults and accounts for a significant proportion of the population. In order to explore this problem in depth, this paper selected *500* observation samples of male and female college students from all over the country, and counted their pen-holding postures when they hold pens and write. The results show that male students accounted for *42.3%* of male students' pen-holding errors, and female students accounted for *61.3%* of female students' pen-holding errors. Together, they accounted for *51.8 %* of the total number of boys and girls. The ratio of error rate between boys and girls was about *7:10*. In addition, most of the students with wrong pen grip posture tilted the paper severely during writing, accompanied by incorrect body postures such as excessive bending of the back, eyes too close to the desktop, and the body leaning close to the edge of the desktop. Therefore, the problem of pen grip posture should be paid attention to and studied.

After searching the literature, it was found that there have been studies related to the problem of pen grip posture. These studies mainly started from different stages, including the early childhood stage and the primary and secondary school stage. Gregory S B and Jiang Junli's study, addressing the early childhood stage, showed the impact of developing a correct pen grip posture on young children's writing ability and healthy

---

[1] Corresponding Author: Fengmei CHEN, E-mail: C16677041143@163.com.

development [1-2]. For the primary school phase, a study by Graham, S et al. analysed the current situation of pen grip posture among primary school students and proposed corresponding countermeasures [3-7]. In addition, Zhao Baojun investigated the problem of pen grip posture from the overall stage of primary and secondary school and found that the error rate of pen grip posture at this stage was as high as *73%*, and revealed the irreversible effects of poor pen grip posture on primary and secondary school students' academics and their physical and mental health [8]. However, these studies lacked convincing causal analyses, did not provide in-depth traceability of the wrong pen grip posture, and did not analyse the pen grip posture from a mechanical perspective.

Therefore, this paper will focus on two aspects, firstly to survey the pen grip posture, then to conduct a mechanical analysis, based on the results obtained to trace back and identify the causes, as well as to explore the adverse effects of wrong pen grip posture. The scientific significance of this study is to provide a better understanding of the causes of incorrect pen grip posture and to draw attention to the early stages of children's pen grip and writing, so as to effectively reduce the proportion of people with incorrect pen grip posture. At the same time, this study can also help to change the traditional educational methods and management modes of educators and parents.

2. Correct and Wrong Pen Grip Posture

2.1. Correct Basic Pen Grip Posture

Through a review and analysis of the literature [9-10], the basic correct pen grip posture was identified as shown in Figure 1.

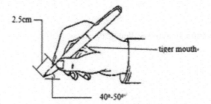

Figure 1. Correct posture of holding a pen

(1) Sitting in an upright position. First, the head should be erect and naturally relaxed forward, with the eyes about *30 cm - 40 cm* from the writing desk. Keep your shoulders flat and slightly tilted forward, with your chest about the size of your own fist from the desk, your left hand pressing the paper and your right hand holding the pen at a certain distance, and your whole body naturally relaxed.

(2) The pen is placed between the tips of the thumb, index finger, and middle finger, with the index finger positioned a little lower than the thumb and the pen tip at a distance of *2.33 cm* to *2.67 cm* from the tip of the finger. The writing paper is held at an angle of approximately *40* to *50* degrees to the barrel of the pen, with the knuckles slightly bent.

2.2. Typical Wrong Pen Grip Posture

The wrong pen grip posture can actually be broken down into *12* types, but there are four typical ones [11]. The first is the index finger over the thumb (Buried Type). As shown in Figure 2(*a*), this is one of the more typical wrong pen grip postures where the thumb is hidden behind the index finger. The second type is the thumb button index finger (Horizontal hitch Type). The second type is thumb over forefinger (horizontal hitch type). This type of pen grip posture is mostly seen in girls, writing too hard, slow and easily fatigued, as in Figure 2(*b*). The third type is the thumb clasping both the middle finger and the index finger. This type of pen grip posture involves holding the ring finger against the barrel of the pen, with the middle finger, index finger and thumb holding the pen at the same time, as in Figure 2(*c*). The fourth type is thumb bending (Twisted Type). This type of pen grip posture involves twisting the thumb and holding the index finger against the barrel of the pen, as in Figure 2(*d*).

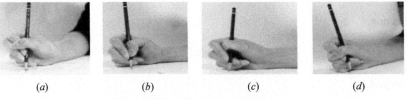

(a)   (b)   (c)   (d)

Figure 2. Typical wrong pen grip posture

Typical types of errors in pen grip posture are usually shown as fisting, where the fingers are closed towards the palm of the hand to approximate the shape of a clenched fist. Three of the common errors are to carry the pen by placing the thumb directly across the index finger and pressing against it, as shown in Figures 2(*a*), (*b*), and (*c*). Another more common error is for the tip of the thumb and the tip of the index finger to be in only slight contact and for both to be at roughly the same height, as shown in Figure 2(*d*). A typical wrong pen grip posture is also characterized by an angle between the pen barrel and the paper surface greater than *45°*, and in some cases as high as *80°* or close to *90°*.

To investigate the causes of adolescents' incorrect pen grip posture, it is first necessary to analyze the mechanics of pen grip posture.

3. Mechanical Analysis of the Pen Grip Posture

Grip mainly by the thumb, middle finger, forefinger and tiger's mouth in four places of the force clamping stable pen, while relying on these places, especially the thumb, middle finger and forefinger on the pen positive pressure on the surface of the pen to produce downward push (downward pressure) friction, and the paper surface of the pen upward force N balance, such as Figure 3 and Figure 4, Figure 3 is the lateral view of the pen, Figure 4 is the longitudinal view of the pen grip.

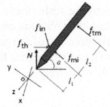
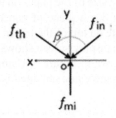

Figure 3. Lateral view of correct writing grip   **Figure 4.** Longitudinal view of correct writing grip

Viewing along the longitudinal direction of the pen shaft, i.e., the z direction, according to Figure 3, the thumb and forefinger are separated by a certain angle to act on the pen shaft, so that the pen shaft is balanced in the x direction. Let f_{th} be the positive pressure of the thumb on the pen barrel, f_{in} be the positive pressure of the index finger on the pen barrel, f_{mi} be the positive pressure of the back of the middle finger on the pen barrel, f_{tm} be the positive pressure of the palm of the hand tiger's mouth on the pen barrel, and N be the upward pressure of the paper on the pen barrel. μ be the friction coefficient of the skin of the hand and the pen barrel.

According to the diagram of forces in Figure 4, the angle between the thumb, index finger and middle finger in the direction of the force on the barrel of the pen when viewed in the direction of the barrel is roughly $\beta = 120°$. Thus, from Figures 3 and 4 and with reference to the coordinates o-xzy the following relationship is established:

x Direction:

$$(f_{th} - f_{in}) \sin(\beta/2) = 0 \tag{1}$$

y Direction:

$$f_{tm} + f_{mi} + N\cos\alpha - (f_{th} + f_{in})\cos(\beta/2) = 0 \tag{2}$$

z Direction:

$$\mu(f_{tm} + f_{mi} + f_{th} + f_{in}) = N\sin\alpha \tag{3}$$

Using the point of contact between the middle finger and the pen as the pivot point, derive the moment around the x-direction:

$$l_1 N\cos\alpha - l_2 f_{tm} = 0 \tag{4}$$

$$f_{th} = f_{in} = \frac{N}{3}\left(\frac{1}{\mu}\sin\alpha + \cos\alpha\right) \tag{5}$$

$$f_{tm} = \frac{l_1}{l_2}N\cos\alpha \tag{6}$$

$$f_{mi} = \frac{N}{\mu}\sin\alpha - \frac{2N}{3}\left(\frac{1}{\mu}\sin\alpha + \cos\alpha\right) + \frac{l_1}{l_2}N\cos\alpha \tag{7}$$

It is worth pointing out that the size of the positive pressure of the pen on the paper is equal to the size of the paper on the pen's support force N. The method of measurement is as follows: lay a piece of paper on top of the flat electronic scale, use a sharpened pencil to write on top of the paper, and the handwriting should be obvious, and then it is clear that the display screen shows the value of the positive pressure of the paper by the pencil, as shown in Figure 5. Using this method of multiple measurements, the average positive pressure value obtained is 0.1 ± 0.02 Kg, taking $N = 0.1$ Kg.

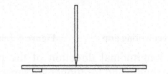

Figure 5. Writing with a pen on paper on a flat weighing surface

The coefficient of friction μ between the pen and the hand can be measured in this way: in the plane of the electronic scale on the surface of a layer of lubricating oil, and then flat put an ordinary pencil, with a finger on top of the pencil held down by the pencil rod, the end of the pencil with a spring loaded force gauge traction. At this time, slowly reduce the finger pressure on the pen until the pencil will appear to slide, record the spring force gauge readings and electronic scale readings, before and after the ratio of the two that is the coefficient of friction μ. The actual results of the measurement for the $\mu = 0.2 \pm 0.03$, take $\mu = 0.2$.

The average inclination of the pen shaft when held correctly is taken as $\alpha = 45°$. The points of force between the pen shaft and the fingers and the palm of the hand at the tiger mouth and the direction of the force are shown in Figure 4. From (1), (2) (3) and (4) and substituting the previously known data, it can be concluded respectively that

Positive pressure of the index finger on the pen: $f_{in} = 0.14\ Kg$;

Positive pressure of the thumb finger on the pen: $f_{th} = 0.14\ Kg$;

Positive pressure of the tiger mouth on the pen: $f_{tm} = 0.035\ Kg$;

Positive pressure of the middle finger on the pen: $f_{mi} = 0.1\ Kg$;

For the wrong pen grip posture, the angle between the pencil and the paper is greater than $45°$, and by setting $\alpha = 90°$, then it follows that

Positive pressure of the index finger on the pen: $f_{in} = 0.17\ Kg$

Positive pressure of the thumb finger on the pen: $f_{th} = 0.17\ Kg$

Positive pressure of the tiger mouth on the pen: $f_{tm} = 0\ Kg$

Positive pressure of the middle finger on the pen: $f_{mi} = 0.17\ Kg$

The results of the mechanical analyses regarding the pen grip posture show that the force f_{in} of the index finger acting on the pen is equal to the force f_{th} of the thumb acting on the pen and increases with the increase of the angle α between the pen and the paper; similarly, the force f_{mi} of the middle finger acting on the pen also increases with the increase of the angle α between the pen and the paper. For using the correct pen grip posture, the force points of the thumb and index finger received the greatest force and amounted to $0.14\ Kg$, while the middle finger, which is used for the middle and back of the finger, received more force than the tip of the thumb and the tip of the middle finger when using the incorrect pen grip posture, amounting to $0.17\ Kg$.

4. Causes and Effects of Wrong Pen Grip Posture

In order to gain a more objective understanding of the causes and effects of incorrect pen grip posture, an awareness survey of pen grip posture was conducted using a sample of college students from two universities. There are two reasons for choosing college students as the target: firstly, college students are the representatives of the cultural and intellectual groups in our country, and their pen grip posture is representative to a certain extent; secondly, pen grip posture is a habit developed from childhood, and may be difficult to be changed once it has been formed and adhered to for a long period of time, so the survey on them is equivalent to the survey on the pen grip posture of the youngest children. As education is somewhat uniform, the sample is from all over the country, which is a good representation. The survey covered the age group when they started to write, their judgement on the correctness of pen grip posture, and whether pen grip posture has any effect on their physical development. A total of 300 questionnaires were distributed to the two universities, including 150 questionnaires each for male and female students. All questionnaires were completed independently by the students and returned on the spot. The results of the survey are shown in Tables 1-5:

Table 1. Age group of starting to write

	6-7 years	5-6 years	4-5 years	3-4 years
Percentage of male student (%)	27.33	25.33	20.00	27.33
Percentage of female students (%)	24.67	28.00	19.33	28.00

Table 2. Subjective judgment of whether one's pen grip is correct or not

	Correct pen grip	Incorrect pen grip	Don't know if the pen grip is correct
Percentage of male student (%)	52.00	14.00	34.00
Percentage of female students (%)	42.67	29.33	28.00

Table 3. Perception of the relationship between pen grip and visual acuity

	Thought to be related to myopia	Not thought to be related to myopia	Don't know if it's related to myopia
Percentage of male student (%)	36.00	48.67	15.33
Percentage of female students (%)	34.67	49.33	16.00

Table 4. Perceptions of pen grip and writing quality

	Consider that the relevant	Considered irrelevant	Don't know if it's relevant
Percentage of male student (%)	72.00	18.67	9.33
Percentage of female students (%)	74.00	18.00	8.00

Table 5. Perceptions of pen grip and physical health

	Considered not to affect t	Considered to affect	Don't know if it will affect
Percentage of male student (%)	26.33	44.67	30.00
Percentage of female students (%)	26.00	38.67	35.33

4.1. Causes of Wrong Pen Grip Posture

At present, the phenomenon of early education is common which causes a larger percentage of the number of people with wrong pen grip posture. From Table 1, it can be seen that *27.33 %* of boys and *28 %* of girls in the age group of *3-4* years have started writing, indicating that about *1/3* of the young children have already started writing at the request of their parents. Combined with the results of the previous mechanical analyses on the correct pen grip posture, it is clear that the magnitude of the force at all the force points is the largest for the thumb and index finger, which amounts to *0.14 Kg*.

However, physiologically, the muscles of the fingers of young children in this period are not yet fully developed and the strength of the front ends of the fingers is weak. For a significant number of children, it is difficult for the tips of their fingers to withstand a force of *0.14 Kg* for a long period of time. Teachers usually ask children of this age to use pencils, which require more downward pressure than water-based pens for legible writing. If teachers or parents require children to write legibly and for long periods of time, then in order to obtain sufficient positive pressure on the pen, children with low finger strength will have to adopt a fisted pen grip posture that leads the fingers into the palm of the hand, which consists of carrying the pen with the thumb directly across the forefinger, pressing it against the forefinger, as shown in Figure 2, because only in this way will there be enough force to grip the pen. At this point, the power point has shifted from the front of the thumb and the front of the index finger to the middle or even the back of the thumb and index finger. Obviously, the middle or back of the finger is much stronger than the front of the finger. Girls are much weaker than boys when it comes to finger strength comparisons, so there will be more girls using the wrong pen grip posture.

In Table 2, *52.00 %* of the male students and *42.67 %* of the female students believed that their pen grip posture was correct, *14.00 %* of the male students and *29.33 %* of the female students believed that their pen grip posture was incorrect, and *34.00 %* of the male students and *28.00 %* of the female students did not know whether their pen grip posture was correct or not. It was also found in conjunction with the visit that the students who thought their pen grip posture was incorrect had almost all of their actual pen grip postures wrong, while most of the ones who did not know whether their pen grip posture was correct actually had the wrong grip posture as well. These two figures add up to *48.00 %* for boys and *57.33%* for girls. The data in this table confirms that more girls currently have the wrong pen grip posture.

The child is unable to write legibly and maintain a correct pen grip posture at the same time, so he or she has to adopt a wrong pen grip posture. Despite being detected by teachers and parents and their best endeavours to discourage the child from doing so, the child still insists on the wrong posture, so teachers and parents mostly choose to tolerate it in the end. Many teachers and parents have incorrect pen grip posture themselves and do not pay attention to their children's mistakes or otherwise. In addition, many parents place more emphasis on their children's academic tasks than on their pen grip posture. This incorrect pen grip posture eventually becomes habitual and difficult to correct, leading to the above observations and statistical results on the pen grip posture of college students. When these children grow up, it is very difficult to change their pen grip posture, even though many of them realise that it is incorrect and has a negative effect on their writing and posture. It is very difficult to change the pen grip posture because it has been adapted for a long time and changing it will make them feel very uncomfortable and unnatural, and they will feel that they have to exert more effort and produce worse writing. Therefore, this kind of change is almost never successful. So only those children who are strong enough to hold the pen correctly from the time they start learning to write, and who know the right and wrong pen grip posture and have been instructed in it by their teachers and parents, will have a correct pen grip posture and will keep it.

4.2. Effects of Wrong Pen Grip Posture

Writing is a thinking activity that involves the co-ordinated development of vision and movement. For children who are just beginning to learn to write, the co-ordination between vision and movement is emerging. However, for children in kindergarten and the early grades of primary schools, their bones have considerable softness and flexibility. If our writing training starts at a stage where the ossification process has not yet been completed, in the long run, this may lead to the development of a wrong pen grip posture, which in turn may lead to problems such as sloping shoulders, tilting of the head, nearsightedness, and hunchbacked Ness.

For example, if people use the wrong pen grip posture, they may not be able to see the tip of the pen when they sit upright and have to write with their head tilted. This can lead to such phenomena as sitting in a crooked position, bending over and slouching the shoulders, having the eyes too close to the writing paper, and writing with the workbook placed diagonally, which can lead to problems such as spinal dysplasia, excessive neck fatigue, difference in the height of the left and right shoulders and arms, hunching of the back, crooked necks, myopia, and strabismus. In addition, a wrong pen grip posture where the thumb and forefinger are crossed or the thumb and forefinger do not touch may lead to a higher incidence of myopia. When writing with the thumb and index finger crossed, the eye's view is blocked by the fingers, and it is natural to write with the head lowered or tilted, shortening the distance between the book and the eyes, which increases the rate of myopia and deepens the degree of myopia in the long run [12]. In addition, cervical spine problems may occur due to excessive head-down writing. As the amount of homework increases, many students have cervical spine problems partly due to incorrect writing postures.

Also, for example, pen grip posture is not correct, long-term writing time is too long, do not get used to the rest, then the thumb, index finger and middle finger three fingers have been taut, fatigue and pain. For a long time, the middle finger will be more painful or long callus, or even joint deformation. Also, the standard posture is to be straight back, long straight back, no proper rest, it will naturally bend the spine, which for years and years the spine deformation.

In Table 3, *36.00 %* of boys and *34.67 %* of girls believe that pen grip posture is related to myopia and *48.67 %* of boys and *49.33 %* of girls believe that pen grip posture is not related to myopia. On this issue, both boys' and girls' perceptions are very close, with one-third believing that it is related and one-half believing that it is not. There are many causes of myopia and wrong pen grip posture is one of the causes. In Table 4, *44.67 %* of boys and *38.67 %*t of girls believe that pen grip posture is related to good health, *26.33 %* of boys and *26.00 %* of girls believe that pen grip posture is not related to good health, and *30.00 %* of boys and *35.33 %* of girls are not sure whether pen grip posture is related to good health. In these three categories, the difference between the percentages of boys and girls is not very great. Overall, more thought it was relevant than those who thought it was not. These data are the result of students' personal experience and better illustrate that wrong pen grip posture has an effect on physical health.

Also, requiring children to write too early can cause them to feel burdened by writing, which can lead to boredom, loss of interest in learning, and loss of patience in practising a correct pen grip. Again, children who maintain a posture for too long without proper rest will change their posture, not paying attention to their posture for a long time, not knowing that they need to pay attention to it, and after adapting to it, they gradually convert to an incorrect pen grip posture or even an incorrect sitting posture.

In addition to that, wrong pen grip posture will not be able to write a standard font, the font is too big or too small, the whole body of writing is not easy, and the font is not correct or beautiful [13]. Table 5 shows that *72.00%* of boys and *74.00%* of girls think that pen grip posture is related to the quality of writing, which is very close to each other, and most of them think it is related. At the same time, according to the above analysis of the forces on the correct pen grip posture, it can be known that the correct pen grip posture can carry the pen freely, the writing speed can be flexible, fast or slow, while the wrong pen grip posture affects the speed of carrying the pen [14].

5. Conclusion

This paper firstly reveals that wrong pen grip posture is prevalent among college students, especially women account for a higher percentage, through a survey of college students' pen grip posture. In order to investigate the causes of this problem, a mechanical analysis of the correct pen grip posture was carried out, which showed that the index finger and thumb were subjected to the greatest pressure and that this increased as the angle between the pen and the paper increased. Combined with the tolerance of children's fingers, it is understood why many children adopt the wrong pen grip posture. In addition, this paper emphasises the adverse effects of wrong pen grip posture on health and quality of writing and it is urged to pay attention to this issue.

In future research, the problem of pen grip posture can be explored in multiple domains, including different age groups and geographic regions, to reveal its differences and associations. In addition, the issue of pen grip posture can also be incorporated into the scope of educational measurement, using specialised measurement tools to quantify the magnitude of forces at various force points when children and adults hold a pen, and to explore the optimal age at which children begin to practise writing as well as the length of time that children of different ages can continue to write with a correct pen grip posture. These findings will provide valuable references for educators and researchers, and will help to promote the further development of research related to pen grip posture.

References

[1] Gregory S B, Karl S R, Sophia L P. Task constraints on preschool children's grip configurations during drawing[J]. Developmental Psychobiology, 2007, 49(2): 216-225.

[2] Jiang Junli. Cultivation strategy of correct pen grip posture of early childhood--Taking the example of early childhood in large class[J]. Jiangsu Early Childhood Education, 2015(02): 82-84. (in Chinese)

[3] Graham, S., Harris, K. R., Mason, L., Fink-Chorizema, B., Moran, S. & Saddler, B. How do primary grade teachers teach handwriting[J]. A national survey. Reading and Writing, 2008, 21, 49-69.

[4] Koziatek, S. M. & Powell, N. J. Pencil grips, legibility, and speed of fourth-graders' writing in cursive[J]. American Journal of Occupational Therapy, 2003, 57(3), 284-288.

[5] Chwellnus, H., Carnahan, H., Kushki, A., Polatajko, H., Missiuna, C., Chau, T. Effect of pencil grasp on the speed and legibility of handwriting after a 10-minute copy task in Grade 4 children[J]. Australian Occupational Therapy Journal, 2012(59): 180-187.

[6] Huang Jinqi. Analysis and Countermeasures on the Present Situation of pen grip posture and sitting posture of primary school students[J]. Western quality education, 2017, 3(20): 227-228. (in Chinese)

[7] Tian Feng. Analysis and countermeasures on the current situation of pen grip posture and sitting posture of primary school students[J]. New Wisdom, 2020(23): 95-96. (in Chinese)

[8] Zhao Baojun. Investigation and research on pen grip posture of primary and secondary school students[J]. Modern Education Science, 2014(12): 147-148. (in Chinese)

[9] Ann-Sofie, S. Pencil Grip: A descriptive model and four empirical studies[M]. Abo Akademi University Press, 2003.

[10] Tang Shujie. Teachers should pay attention to correcting students' pen holding method and writing posture[J]. Research on Educational Practice, 2005, 06: 57-58. (in Chinese)

[11] Schneck, Henderson. Descriptive analysis of the developmental progression of grip position for pencil and crayon control on nondysfunctional children[J]. The American Journal of Occupational Therapy, 1990, 44(10): 893-900.

[12] Wu Yuxiang. A preliminary study on the association between grip strength and pen grip posture and its correlation with myopia in school children[D]. NanChang University, NanChang, 2023. (in Chinese)

[13] Graham, Struck. Dimensions of good and poor handwriting legibility in first and second graders: motor programs, visual-spatial arrangement, and letter formation parameter setting[J]. Development Neuropsychology, 2006, 29(1): 43-60.

[14] Janet, Fatima. Assessment of handwriting speed and factors influencing written output of university students in examinations[J]. Australian Occupational Therapy Journal, 2003, 50: 148-157.

Artificial Intelligence, Medical Engineering and Education
Z.B. Hu et al. (Eds.)
© 2024 The Authors.
This article is published online with Open Access by IOS Press and distributed under the terms
of the Creative Commons Attribution Non-Commercial License 4.0 (CC BY-NC 4.0).
doi:10.3233/ATDE231379

Impact of the Liberalization of Fertility Policy on the Female Labor Market Under Different Educational Backgrounds: Empirical Analysis Based on CFPS Data

Hao WU, Ying GAO[1]
School of Business, Sichuan University, Chengdu, China
1291556974@qq.com

Abstract. Fertility policy is an important public policy to promote population structure optimization and economic and social development in China. Based on CFPS data from 2016, 2018 and 2020, this paper evaluates the impact of universal two-child policy and three-child policy on female labor market in different educational backgrounds by using the method of differential and differential analysis. The research shows that the liberalization of the policy will reduce the employment rate of female labor. Under the policy, the older labor force and the lower education will suffer more discrimination in employment. In addition, compared with highly educated women, women with low education have a higher willingness to have multiple children, indicating that the liberalization of the birth policy has a more significant impact on the employment of women with low education. In contrast, the phenomenon of low fertility level and fertility rate in highly educated families may further rise, and further aggravate the imbalance of fertility rate in China. The research in this paper provides empirical evidence for evaluating the impact of the implementation of the fertility policy on the female labor market.

Keywords. Fertility policy; Educational background; Female workforce; Employment discrimination

1. Introduction

Since 2000, the proportion of population over 65 years old in the total population has reached 7% of the international standard of aging, indicating that China has officially entered aging society. In this context, from 2013 to 2021, The Chinese government has introduced the universal two-child policy and the three-child policy [1].

The relaxation of fertility policy may increase the natural attachment cost of female labor force, as employers take into consideration the potential cost of female labor force in terms of childbirth. This undoubtedly further increases the possibility of gender discrimination in the workplace against female labor force. As the main subjects of childbirth, a proportion of female labor force with lower education levels may choose to

---

[1] Corresponding Author: Ying GAO, E-mail: 1291556974@qq.com.

have multiple births and leave the labor market due to lower opportunity costs of childbirth. On the other hand, female labor force with higher education backgrounds always holds important positions in companies, and in order to ensure the stability of their career development, they may have a lower willingness to have multiple births. Based on this, this study wants to explore whether the relaxation of the fertility policy further exacerbates gender discrimination against female labor force, and whether education level plays a moderating role in the impact of fertility policy on female labor force participation rate.

2. Literature Review and Hypothetical Inference

2.1 Fertility Policy and Female Labor Employment

The discussion about the impact of fertility policy on female labor market can be traced back to the study of labor market. As early as 1976, Becker theoretically demonstrated the correlation between wages and working hours in his book Economic Analysis of Human Behavior [2], which was subsequently empirically tested by more articles [3,4]. At the same time, some scholars tried to study the influencing factors of labor supply or labor participation rate, and found that the number of children, social policies, spouse income and so on are all part of it, and these topics are still popular today [5-8]. Zhang used the labor market supply and demand model to empirically test that under different GDP growth conditions, the "universal two-child" policy can significantly improve China's labor supply and demand relationship and supply structure [9]. When the degree of population aging is relatively serious, the "universal two-child" policy will also increase the total output and working hours. As the main decision-maker of having a second child, the supply of female labor force has gradually received research attention. However, different from the total social labor supply, research shows that the two-child policy may reduce women's labor supply through aggravating family responsibilities and employer discrimination, and the increase in the number of children will also significantly reduce the labor supply, time input and wage level of urban married women [10,11]. Based on the changes in the internal structure of population development, China needs to optimize its fertility policy to alleviate aging. Compared with men, women, as the main body of childbearing, will be the first to take a hit on their employment under the background of fertility policy liberalization. Based on this, we propose that:

H1: The liberalization of fertility policy has a negative impact on the female labor participation rate

2.2 Educational Background and Female Labor Force Employment

A number of studies on the influencing factors of fertility intention show that factors such as the educational background of both parents, family resources, and the gender of the child have a significant impact on the family's intention to have a second or third child [12].Mandal et al. analyzed the fertility intention of Shanghai registered couples who have had a second child from the micro-cost-utility perspective and concluded that families with higher education and income, rich family resources, and a girl as their first child are more willing to have a second child, which coincides with the influencing factors of fertility intention [13]. The research shows that the liberalization of the fertility policy may reduce the labor supply of women through increasing family responsibilities and employer discrimination, and the increase in the number of children will also significantly reduce the labor supply, time input and wage level of urban married women [14]. At the same time, the positive promoting effect of education level on labor supply has been proved for many times [15]. This study believes Highly educated women may be less willing to have multiple children in order to maintain career stability. Women with lower levels of education are more likely to choose to leave the labor market because of their lower childbearing costs. Based on this, we propose that:

H2a: The liberalization of the fertility policy has no significant negative effect on the labor force participation rate of women with high educational background.
H2b: The liberalization of the fertility policy has a significant negative impact on the labor force participation rate of women with low educational background.

2.3 Employment Discrimination and Female Labor Employment

Influenced by the traditional idea that women take the lead in the home and men take the lead in the outside, women are generally believed to devote themselves to taking care of the family. For women's career, if the interruption of childbearing career is too long, they may lose their pre-childbearing career status and lead to downward occupational mobility. Employers are often more willing to recruit male employees under the same conditions when recruiting. This is objectively due to the fact that enterprises bear the maternity insurance for women, and the recruitment of female employees under the same conditions will increase the employment cost of enterprises. The liberalization of the fertility policy has worsened the employment environment for women. Women will spend more time at home than before, and employers will no doubt shun women even more. Therefore, although the employer does not make gender discrimination clauses contrary to the relevant policy on the surface, it actually reduces the possibility of recruiting female employees by raising the entry threshold for women. [16] It can be found that in this social environment, even if women are willing to give up childbearing, they may not be treated fairly in the workplace. Because the high career entry threshold makes women lose the same career development opportunities as men in the beginning. Based on this, this paper proposes:

H3: The liberalization of the fertility policy has a positive impact on the employment discrimination of female labor force.

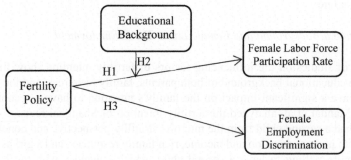

Figure 1. Research Model

3.   Data Sample and Model

3.1 Data Sample

The sample data in this paper are from the China Household Tracking Survey Project (CFPS) implemented by the China Social Science Survey Center of Peking University, and the relevant data of three periods in 2016, 2018 and 2020 are selected. Table 1 shows the descriptive statistics of each variable.

From the descriptive statistics, the mean value of the current working status is 0.757, indicating that 75.7% of the people in the sample are currently employed. The mean for gender is 0.481, indicating that 48.1% of people in the sample are women. The age of the sample women is concentrated between 20 and 45 years old, accounting for 44.85% of the total sample. The mean of the highest academic qualifications of the individuals in the sample is 2.66.

Table 1. Descriptive statistics

	N	Mean	Std. Dev.	min	Median	max
employ	40171	757.	429.	0	1	1
finc	40171	54604.23	55329.19	542	40000	300000
post	40171	663.	473.	0	1	1
gender	40171	481.	.5	0	0	1
postgender	40171	319.	466.	0	0	1
age	40171	31.90	14.82	20	32	45
kids	40171	1.39	1.01	0	1	6
marry	40171	907.	291.	0	1	1
selfdegree	40171	2.66	1.40	0	3	8
degree	40171	125.	331.	0	0	1

3.2 Model Design and Variable Description

In this paper, a difference-difference (DID) model is established to analyze the impact of the fertility liberalization policy on the female labor market. The following model is used to study the matched samples:

$$Employ = \beta_0 + \beta_1 postgender + \beta_2 post + \beta_3 gender + \beta_3 control + \varepsilon \qquad (1)$$

Employ in model (1) is the explained variable, representing the current working status, where 1 is employed and 0 is unemployed; postgender is the cross term of post and gender, and post is the policy dummy variable, which is 0 before and 1 after the birth policy is released; gender was used to control the treatment group and the control group, where 1 was the treatment group and 0 was the control group.

The difference in salary and income of the same job can reflect the discrimination of employers. Refer to the study by Dong [17], use salary and income to measure the degree of discrimination, and the following regression model is established:

$$\text{lnfinc} = \beta_0 + \beta_1 \text{postgender} + \beta_2 \text{post} + \beta_3 \text{gender} + \beta_4 \text{control} + \varepsilon \qquad (2)$$

In model (2), lnfinc is the explained variable, representing salary income; postgender is the cross term of post and gender, and post is the policy dummy variable, which is 0 before the implementation of the "universal two-child policy" and 1 after the implementation. gender was used to control treatment group and control group, where 1 was treatment group and 0 was control group; control is the control variable. See Table 3-2 for the specific Settings of the variables.

Table 2. Variable description table

Variable Symbols	Variable description
employ	Current employment status, with 1 being employed and 0 being unemployed
lnfinc	Lnfinc 2 Take the logarithm of an individual's annual income
fincome1	Annual income
postgender	post's interaction with gender
post	Policy dummy variable, 0 before the implementation of the "universal two-child" policy and 1 after implementation
gender	1 for women and 0 for men
age	Sample age
kids	Number of existing children
marry	Individual marital status, married as 1, unmarried as 0
selfdegree	Individual's highest degree, with a maximum of 8 and a minimum of 1
degree	A person's highest degree is 1 if it is greater than 4, and 0 if it is less

4.   Data Analysis

4.1 The Regression Results of the Influence of Policy Liberalization on Female Employment

M1 is the regression result of employ as explained variable, adding gender, age, marry and kids. The results show that gender and employ are significantly negatively correlated at the level of 1% with a correlation coefficient of -0.164, indicating that the employment rate of females is lower than that of males. M2 is the regression result estimated by using the differential differential model. Specifically, post and the cross-multiplication term between post and gender are added to M1. The result shows that gender coefficient is negative, indicating that the employment rate of female labor force has decreased after the implementation of the policy, which is lower than that of male labor force. H1 is supported.

Table 3. Regression results of the impact of birth policy on female employment

	M1	M2
	employ	employ
postgender		-0.019 **
post		-0.013 **
gender	-0.164 ***	-0.176 ***
age	-0.004 ***	-0.004 ***
kids	0.036 ***	0.036 ***
marry	0.182 ***	0.181 ***
selfdegree	-0.005 ***	-0.005 ***
cons	0.793 ***	0.799 ***
N	40171	40171
adj. R^2	0.096	0.096

t-value in parentheses; * $p < 0.1$,** $p < 0.05$,*** $p < 0.01$

4.2 Test Results of the Influence of Educational Background on Female Labor Market

In order to study the heterogeneity of education level, this paper mainly divides educational background into two groups, with college background as the critical point, which is divided into samples of college education and above and samples of college education and below. Then, the heterogeneity of education level of the two groups was analyzed respectively. The regression results are shown in Table4. M3 is the regression result of the highly educated population. The data show that the coefficient of postgender is positive and the correlation coefficient is 0.080, indicating that the liberalization of the birth policy has no negative impact on the labor participation of highly educated women. M4 is the regression result of people with low education background. The data shows that the coefficient of postgender is significantly negative and the correlation coefficient is -0.017, indicating that the liberalization of the fertility policy will have a negative effect on the employment of women with low education background. As analyzed above, the higher the education background, the higher the value brought to the enterprise. Therefore, women with lower education background are not valued by enterprises in the job market, plus the potential employment costs brought by having multiple children. Therefore, the liberalization of the fertility policy will make it more difficult for these women with lower education background to find employment. H2a and H2b are supported.

4.3. The Impact of Employment Discrimination on Female Labor Market

Table 5 shows the regression results estimated for model (2). M5 is based on lnfinc as the explained variable and the regression results of gender, age, marry and kids are added. The results show that gender and fincome1 are significantly negatively correlated at the level of 1% and the correlation coefficient is -0.132, indicating that women's income in the labor market is significantly lower than that of men. M6 is a regression result obtained by adding post and the cross-multiplicative term between post and gender on the basis of M5. The result shows that the coefficient of postgender is significantly negatively correlated at the level of 1% and the correlation coefficient is -0.061, indicating that the liberalization of the fertility policy has a greater impact on women and women suffer more serious employment discrimination.H3 is supported.

Table 4. Group test of female labor market and educational background

	M3 employ	M4 employ
postgender	0.080 *	-0.017***
post	-0.059 ***	0.019 ***
gender	-0.061 ***	-0.186 ***
age	-0.002 ***	-0.004 ***
kids	-0.053 ***	0.051 ***
marry	0.149 ***	0.189 ***
selfdegree	-0.073 ***	-0.015 ***
_cons	1.249 ***	0.774 ***
N	5040	35131
adj. R^2	0.155	0.130

t-value in parentheses; * p < 0.1, ** p < 0.05, *** p < 0.01

Table 5. The impact of employment discrimination on female labor market

	M5 lnfinc	M6 lnfinc
postgender		-0.061**
post		0.310***
gender	-0.132***	-0.090***
age	-0.013***	-0.013***
kids	0.077***	0.076***
marry	0.183***	0.184***
selfdegree	0.198***	0.198***
_cons	9.755***	9.738***
N	30407	30407
adj. R^2	0.209	0.209

t-value in parentheses; * p < 0.1, ** p < 0.05,*** p < 0.01

References

[1]   Chang J., Huang C., Is the efficiency wage efficient when workers decide on the working time? [J]. Journal of Economics, 2002,77(3): 267-281.
[2]   Becker. Economic analysis of human behavior [M]. Shanghai: Shanghai People's Publishing House,2015: 93-112.
[3]   Siv S G, 1996.Women's labor force transitions in connection with childbirth: a panel data comparison between Germany, Sweden and Great Britain. Journal of Population Economics, Vol.9, No. 3 (Aug. 1996): 223 -246.
[4]   Aly Y H, Quisi , I.A. Determinants of women labor force participation in Kuwait : a logit analyses, The Middle East Business and Economic Review, 1996, 8(2): 1-9:132-138.
[5]   Chan Wengtong,Cheang Chonin. Navigating the demographic shift: an examination of China's new fertility policy and its implications [J]. Frontiers in Political Science,2023,5(5): 35-41.

[6]   Yang X Y, Wan X, Li R. Examining the Influence of fertility policy adjustments on gender equality in China during period of exceptionally slow population growth. [J]. China CDC weekly,2023,5(27): 9-16.

[7]   Wang J J, Yu X H. Birth policy changes and the sustainability of social medical insurance funds: implications for green growth[J]. Economic Change and Restructuring,2023,56(4): 32-43.

[8]   Ma'rifah A R, Khasanah U, Hartanti R D, Khasanah N N. Embracing the new two-child policy era: challenge and countermeasures of early care in China[J]. Education 3-13,2023,51(7): 68-76.

[9]   Mandal B, Wu W J. Examining the effects of a two-child policy in rural India[J]. Journal of Population Research,2019,40(3): 48-62.

[10] Cui M Y, Jiang T T, Liu J F. Research on the influencing factors of female teachers' fertility intention under the "three-child" policy based on grounded theory[J]. Social Security and Administration Management,2023,4(5): 109-121.

[11] Ning N, Tang J F, Huang Y Z, et, al. Fertility intention to have a third child in China following the three-child policy: a cross-sectional study[J]. International Journal of Environmental Research and Public Health,2022,19(22): 33-42.

[12] Ma'rifah A R, Khasanah U H, Khasanah N N. Embracing the new two-child policy era: challenge and countermeasures of early care and education in China[J]. Education 3-13,2023,51(7): 88-96.

[13] Mandal B, Wu W J. Examining the effects of a two-child policy in rural India[J]. Journal of Population Research,2023,40(3): 67-73.

[14] Wang W, Yang J H, Wu K, et, al. The influence of two-child policy on the birth and consumption of two-child families: An investigation based on CFPS data [J]. Journal of Economics and Economics, 2019,46(12): 79-93. (in Chinese).

[15] Zhao Q. The impact of two-child policy on female labor supply: from the perspective of life cycle theory model [J].   Labor Security World,2016(32): 7-8. (in Chinese).

[16] Zhang P. Impact of universal two-child policy on labor supply and demand in China [J]. Statistics and Information Forum,2019,34(04): 51-57 (in Chinese).

[17] Dong Y. Research on gender difference between employment opportunities and wage income [D]. Northeast Normal University,2018: 55-67 (in Chinese).

Artificial Intelligence, Medical Engineering and Education
Z.B. Hu et al. (Eds.)
© *2024 The Authors.*
This article is published online with Open Access by IOS Press and distributed under the terms
of the Creative Commons Attribution Non-Commercial License 4.0 (CC BY-NC 4.0).
doi:10.3233/ATDE231380

Exploration of the Formation of Logistics Professional Cluster Using Dual Outcome-Oriented Integration with Industrial Cluster

Yanfang PAN, Liwei LI, Dalong LIU, Mengqi ZHU[1]
Transportation College of Nanning University, Guangxi, China

Abstract. The innovative driving force of the new round of technological revolution and industrial transformation requires the logistics industry to break through process innovation, technological innovation, and model innovation. As a multi-disciplinary interdisciplinary and integrated logistics engineering major, it will inevitably move towards the development path of professional group construction and industrial group integration. This article takes the development of logistics engineering as the goal, analyzes the difficulties and contradictions in the development of professional talents, and through the construction of a dual core professional group application mechanism based on the value chain and the construction of a "government administration school enterprise" collaborative education platform system based on the integration of professional groups with industrial groups, identifies various factors that affect the dual composition result orientation, and provides reference and reference for professional construction.

Keywords. Logistics engineering major; Achievement oriented; Professional group construction; Industrial cluster construction.

1. Introduction

The logistics industry has become a pillar industry of a country [1]. Although China's logistics industry started late, it has developed rapidly, with indicators such as logistics infrastructure network, logistics enterprise operation entities, and total logistics volume entering the forefront of the world. The development of the logistics industry has provided strong support for China to become the world's second largest economy and the largest trading country [2,3]. The total amount of social logistics in 2022 exceeded 340 trillion yuan, an increase of about 3.6% year-on-year; The total revenue of the logistics industry reached 12 trillion yuan, an increase of about 5% year-on-year. The national railway completed 3.9 billion tons of cargo shipments throughout the year, a year-on-year increase of 4.7%, the highest growth rate in nearly three years; The scale of the cold chain logistics market exceeded 490 billion yuan throughout the year, an increase of about 7.2% year-on-year; The cumulative volume of express delivery business has reached 110.58 billion pieces, a net increase of 2.28 billion pieces compared to the

---

[1] Corresponding Author: Mengqi ZHU, E-mail: 281340537@qq.com.

previous year. The total number of enterprises in the cross-border e-commerce logistics industry showed a slow upward trend from 2017 to 2020, with an annual growth rate higher than the GDP growth rate. Especially since the outbreak of the epidemic, the demand for cross-border e-commerce has surged, driving the growth rate of cross-border e-commerce logistics enterprises to a new peak, reaching 11.82%. The development of the logistics industry is in the ascendant [4].

With the vigorous rise of the logistics industry in various fields in recent years, the prominent supply-demand contradiction of logistics talents has become the main factor affecting the rapid development of logistics majors in Chinese universities [5-8]. To solve this problem, the education community has conducted extensive research. Promote ideological and political education in the curriculum and cultivate talents with both morality and talent [9,10]. Strengthen cooperation between schools and enterprises, adopt collaborative education methods, and cultivate specialized talents capable of logistics work [11-13]. Promoting the integration of professional groups and industrial zones can better achieve collaborative education [14-16]. The complementary advantages between various schools and the establishment of virtual teaching and research rooms nationwide have been proven to be a very effective attempt [17-20]. The construction of the curriculum system has also achieved outstanding results, playing a prominent role in the cultivation of logistics professionals [21-23].

2. Outstanding Contradiction Between Supply and Demand of Logistics Talents

The contradiction between supply and demand of logistics talents has slowed down the speed of industry development. The main problems are reflected in the following aspects.

(1) The mismatch between talent supply and demand is not high, making it difficult to meet the requirements of the modern logistics industry.

The modern logistics industry, as the third source of profit for cross industry and multi-industry integration, has become a new industry that closely combines knowledge intensive, and technology intensive industries based on information technology and high-tech. It is a new composite industry that is compatible and coexisting across industries and departments. This endows the logistics engineering major with a unique nature as an emerging comprehensive edge science. Since the establishment of the undergraduate program in Logistics Engineering in 2001, there have been 138 universities in China that have established undergraduate programs in Logistics Engineering. However, the training of logistics engineering professionals still cannot keep up with the changes of the times and cannot meet the needs of the rapidly developing economic industry. The main reasons are concentrated in two aspects: the mismatch between students' willingness to work and the supply of enterprises, and the mismatch between students' ability level and job requirements. This urgently requires the logistics engineering major to align with the industry, keep up with the pace of industrial development, timely understand market dynamics and the needs of industries and enterprises, and optimize professional talent cultivation in a timely manner. The construction and development of the Industrial College will undoubtedly create a favorable external environment for the development of logistics engineering majors. Nanning University has included the development and construction of the New Energy Vehicle Industry College and the Digital Economy Industry College in the school's 14th Five Year Plan, further promoting the integration and development of logistics engineering majors with industry clusters.

(2) The degree of cooperation and integration between schools and enterprises is not high enough, and the grasp of the era's requirements for innovative development of industrial clusters is not accurate enough

In 2020, the national government proposed to "enhance the modernization level of the industrial chain supply chain", "develop strategic emerging industries", "coordinate infrastructure construction", and "accelerate digital development", promote the development of advanced manufacturing clusters, promote the deep integration of modern service industries with advanced manufacturing and modern agriculture, and accelerate the digitization of service industries. More and more enterprise logistics and logistics companies are transforming logistics into an empowering and value-added entry point, elevating it to an ecological industry chain that can provide comprehensive solutions for the entire process. The logistics industry has ushered in intelligent upgrading and innovative integration development. The "dual core drive" strategy of deepening the development of the Beibu Gulf Economic Zone and the Xijiang Economic Belt in Guangxi's regional development strategy, as well as the construction of the Western Land Sea New Passage, the major project of the Pinglu Canal, the construction of the Free Trade Pilot Zone, RCEP, and the integration into the Guangdong Hong Kong Bay Area, have brought new development opportunities to the logistics industry in Guangxi. Over the years, the logistics engineering major has achieved certain results by integrating industry and education, constructing professional talent cultivation characteristics and course systems, exploring course projects and teaching cases. However, most of the school enterprise cooperation units are concentrated in e-commerce, logistics, and express delivery enterprises, with a single model and less obvious effects. With the upgrading of the industry, the upgrading and replacement of intelligent warehousing, intelligent sorting, and intelligent distribution gradually elevate the job demand to a higher level and put forward different requirements for professional knowledge system and quality. In order to seek development, majors must deepen into industries and fields, strengthen the integration and development of professional groups with industrial groups, and provide systematic, innovative and breakthrough full process logistics service solutions and supply chain solutions for industries and enterprises.

(3) The degree of sharing among professional groups is not strong, and information exchange between different majors and colleges is not smooth, lacking internal communication mechanisms.

Professional groups are often composed of one or several similar related majors and their professional directions and can complete their basic practical teaching in the same training system, with good sharing. The core concept of professional groups is also the sharing concept. However, in the actual operation process, there are often difficulties in sharing and exchanging information among various majors or directions within the group, as well as lack of communication between basic courses and teaching teams. This has brought significant obstacles to the co construction of professional groups, limited the effective implementation of professional group teaching activities, and prevented the advantages of professional group teacher teams from being fully utilized. The sharing rate of training bases and equipment is also at a relatively low level.

3. Industry to Enterprise Integration Based on Dual Composition Fruit Orientation

To achieve good collaborative education, the following ideas have been designed for the integration of logistics engineering majors with industries and enterprises.

(1) Establish a dual core core professional group application mechanism based on the value chain

Combining the professional characteristics and advantages of the School of Transportation, integrating digital economy and business management majors to form a professional chain based on the enterprise value chain. Based on the correlation between majors, a dual core professional group with transportation and new energy vehicle engineering as the core majors and logistics engineering and automotive service engineering as the backbone majors is constructed, highlighting the integration, sharing, and intersection of professional groups, Establish a professional group operation and interaction mechanism. Construct a professional chain structure based on the value chain, as shown in Figure 1.

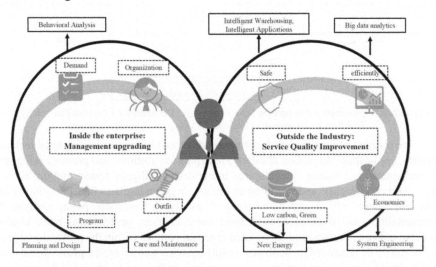

Figure 1. Operating mechanism of dual core professional groups based on value chain

(2) Building a talent training system for the "government administration school enterprise" collaborative education platform based on the integration of professional groups and industrial clusters

Targeting the transportation and logistics industry cluster in Guangxi Zhuang Autonomous Region, collaborating with industry associations and leading enterprises, integrating campus laboratory resources, Guangxi China ASEAN International Joint Key Laboratory of Comprehensive Transportation, and relying on the cooperation foundation established between enterprises and schools, conducting sufficient research activities, establishing a collaborative education mechanism of "government administration school enterprise" linkage, and collaborating to develop and revise logistics engineering talent training plans and curriculum standards, Collaborate to form a mixed practice teaching team, extract and design real engineering problems from industry enterprises as teaching cases and teaching projects, plan and organize the participation of teachers and students in project research, design, development, implementation, operation, and summary activities, and strive to build a talent cultivation model of "industry education integration, engineering learning integration, and knowledge and action integration", as presented in Figure 2.

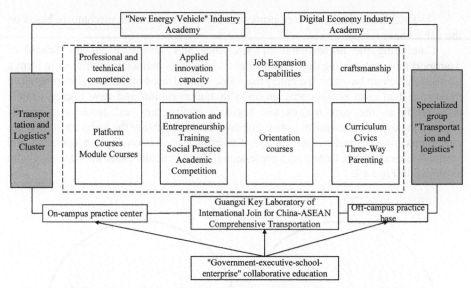

Figure 2. A "Government Administration School Enterprise" Collaborative Education Platform System Based on the Integration of Professional Groups with Industrial Groups

The training of logistics engineering majors should focus on professional technical abilities, application innovation abilities, job expansion abilities, and promoting the spirit of craftsmanship. Taking "developing integrated intelligent transportation services (passenger and freight)" and "building an intelligent green logistics transportation system (low cost, high efficiency, new energy)" as the intersection point, analyze the commonalities and differences in subject basic courses, professional basic courses, professional core courses, and centralized practical courses within the professional group, and based on the knowledge, skill, and quality systems trained by the professional group talents, Build a professional group curriculum system that can be shared at the grassroots level, integrated at the middle level, and mutually selected at the senior level, namely a "platform + module + direction" curriculum system.

4. Factor Analysis of Logistics Professional Group Docking with Industrial Group Based on TOPSIS Method

Constructing a talent cultivation model of "integration of industry and education, integration of engineering and learning, and integration of knowledge and practice" can effectively achieve the integration of logistics majors and industrial clusters and achieve the development of professional group construction. To verify the effectiveness of the "government administration school enterprise" coordinated education platform, the following analysis was conducted on its influencing factors using TOPSIS.

Firstly, the logistics experts determine the evaluation indicators for the plan, as shown in Table 1.

Table 1. Scheme Evaluation Indicators

Serial number	Evaluating indicator
1	Teaching operation system
2	On campus teacher team on the platform
3	Platform off campus teacher team
4	Teaching evaluation
5	On campus teaching resources
6	Off campus business resources
7	Student source situation
8	Course Settings

The evaluation of A's original talent training plan and the plan based on the platform is based on various evaluation indicators, as shown in Table 2.

Table 2. Scoring of various indicators

Serial number	Evaluating indicator	Original talent training plan	Platform solution
1	Student source situation	84	92
2	Course Settings	82	91
3	On campus teaching resources	81	94
4	Off campus business resources	81	95
5	On campus teacher team on the platform	85	90
6	Platform off campus teacher team	84	92
7	Teaching operation system	92	85
8	Teaching evaluation	79	91

Data source: Compiled based on the author's actual investigation.

Next, the forward normalization results of the evaluation indicators are described in Table 3.

Table 3. Positive normalization of indicators

No.	Evaluating indicator	Original talent training plan	Platform solution	Indicator type
1	Student source situation	84	92	Extremely large
2	Course Settings	82	91	Extremely large
3	On campus teaching resources	81	94	Extremely large
4	Off campus business resources	81	95	Extremely large
5	On campus teacher team on the platform	85	90	Extremely large
6	Platform off campus teacher team	84	92	Extremely large
7	Teaching operation system	0	7	Extremely large
8	Teaching evaluation	79	91	Extremely large

Data source: Compiled based on the author's actual investigation.

Using formula $Y_{ij} = \dfrac{r_{ij}}{\sqrt{\sum_{i=1}^{m} r_{ij}^2}}$ to process the data for the forward normalization of indicator scores to obtain a standardized matrix:

$$Y = \left(r_{ij}\right)_{3\times 8} \tag{1}$$

The calculation results are shown in Table 4.

Table 4. Standardization of indicators

No.	Evaluating indicator	Original talent training plan	Platform solution
1	Evaluating indicator	0.547	0.599
2	Student source situation	0.537	0.596
3	Course Settings	0.518	0.602
4	On campus teaching resources	0.520	0.610
5	Off campus business resources	0.551	0.584
6	On campus teacher team on the platform	0.547	0.599
7	Platform off campus teacher team	0	0.614
8	Teaching operation system	0.525	0.605

Data source: Compiled based on the author's actual investigation.

The score matrix Y, which has undergone forward and standardized processing, all data are extremely large and ideal optimal and worst solutions are extracted from it.

Firstly, take out the smallest number in each column to form the ideal worst solution vector:

$$Y^- = [0.547,\ 0.537,\ 0.518,\ 0.520,\ 0.551,\ 0.547,\ 0,\ 0.525]$$

Similarly, the ideal optimal solution vector is the largest number in each column:

$$Y^+ = [0.599,\ 0.596,\ 0.608,\ 0.610,\ 0.596,\ 0.599,\ 0.789,\ 0.605]$$

Apply formula $d_i^+ = \sqrt{\sum_{j=1}^{m} \left(y_j^+ - y_{ij}\right)^2}$ and $d_i^- = \sqrt{\sum_{j=1}^{m} \left(y_j^- - y_{ij}\right)^2}$ separately to calculate the distance between the optimal solution and the worst solution, and then use $C_i = \frac{d_i^-}{d_i^+ + d_i^-}$ to count the distance score and obtain the ranking table of advantages and disadvantages as revealed in Table 5.

Table 5. Evaluation Results

	Original talent training plan	Platform solution
d_i^+	0.810	0.176
d_i^-	0	0.639
C_i	0	0.784
Sort of advantages and disadvantage	2	1

Data source: Compiled based on the author's actual investigation.

$$0 \leq C_i \leq 1,$$

To judge the distance between solution and optimal solution, when d_i^+ smaller, the greater the comprehensive score C_i.

Similarly, the distance between the solution and the worst solution d_i^-, the smaller the comprehensive score Ci.

Sorting according to the comprehensive score can result in the optimized plan one being better than the original plan. The establishment of the platform is helpful for the cultivation of professional talents and the construction of course systems.

5. Conclusion

To truly achieve educational transformation and promote disciplinary construction and professional development, it is necessary to fully leverage the advantages of logistics and achieve dual driving forces of interdisciplinary and enterprise oriented approaches. This requires adjustments to teaching concepts, methods, content, and evaluation to better apply emerging technologies to promote education and teaching, driven by solving practical logistics problems and centered around real enterprise applications, Seize the good opportunity of the construction of the Industrial College, adapt to the future development trend of digital and intelligent logistics, and promote the construction of the "government school business enterprise" collaborative education platform and the construction of logistics virtual teaching and research rooms.

Establish a dual core professional cluster application mechanism based on the value chain, establish a "government administration school enterprise" collaborative education platform talent training system based on the integration of professional clusters with industrial clusters, and use TOPSIS to systematically analyze and evaluate its influencing factors. The above research provides useful exploration for building logistics professional clusters on the basis of dual result guidance and industrial cluster integration and provides reference and reference for the construction of related majors.

Acknowledgement

This paper has got strong support from the Guangxi Higher Education Undergraduate Teaching Reform Engineering Project "Research and Application of Logistics Engineering Major Integration Professional Group Construction under the Background of Industrial College" (2023JGA392) and the Nanning University Virtual Teaching and Research Office Project "Regional Logistics and Digital Intelligent Logistics Virtual Teaching and Research Office" (2023XNJYS01).

References

[1] Moross A. Key development strategies need implementation in logistics industry[J]. Creamer Media s Engineering News & Mining Weekly, 2022, (4): 42.

[2] Fu H., Li H., Fu W. Research on optimization of Anyang logistics industry development[J]. International Journal of Social Science and Education Research, 2020, 3(4): 69-76.

[3] Liu M. Research on the development status, problems and countermeasures of the logistics industry in Guizhou Province[J]. Modern Economy, 2020, 11(3): 632-644.

[4] Nand A., Sohal A., Fridman I, et al. An exploratory study of organizational and industry drivers for the implementation of emerging technologies in logistics[J]. Industrial Management & Data Systems, 2023, 123(5): 1418-1439.

[5] Mccrea B. Logistics labor: solving the talent gap[J]. Logistics Management, 2021, (6): 60.

[6] Han Q., Q. Research on current situation, problems and countermeasures of marine logistics talent training in the postepidemic era[J]. Meteorological and Environmental Research: English Version, 2021, 012(002): 30-33.

[7] Mann H. Cultivating supply chain talent[J]. Inbound Logistics, 2021, (12): 41.

[8] Wren A. Tackling the talent gap from the inside out[J]. Inbound Logistics, 2019, 39(4): 38-38.

[9] Yu Xiaomo. Exploration of the ideological, political, and innovative training system for logistics engineering talents facing China ASEAN[J]. China Logistics and Procurement, 2023, (16): 116-117 (in Chinese).

[10] Zhang Lingmin, Kong Weida. Exploring the practical path of integrating "curriculum ideology and politics" into logistics engineering teaching in the new era[J]. Logistics Technology, 2023, 46(14): 170-172 (in Chinese).

[11] Jiang W., Guofeng Z., Shuyang W. Teaching reform path of architecture specialty under the collaborative education of "production, teaching and research" and its application effect[J]. Landscape Research: English Version, 2021, 13(5): 3.

[12] Ma J. Analysis of the collaborative education system of local universities under the fundamentals of "Emerging Engineering Education" construction[J]. Contemporary Education Research, 2021, 5(5): 5.

[13] Zine Benotmane, Ghalem Belalem, Abdelkader Neki, "A Cost Measurement System of Logistics Process", International Journal of Information Engineering and Electronic Business, Vol.10, No.5, pp. 23-29, 2018.

[14] Liao Xianqiong. The logic and path of building design professional group construction based on the green and low carbon industrial chain[J]. Journal of Taiyuan City Vocational and Technical College, 2023, (09): 12-15 (in Chinese).

[15] Jia Haiyan, Liu Xiaomin. Research on the reform of professional group talent training mode based on modular teaching - taking the professional group of building steel structure technology as an example[J]. Journal of Changjiang Engineering Vocational and Technical College, 2023, 40 (03): 40-43 (in Chinese).

[16] Luo Yao, Tan Qibing. A study on the value co creation path and evaluation of professional groups matched to industrial groups[J]. Occupational Technology, 2023, 22 (11): 56-63 (in Chinese).

[17] Liu Hui, Feng Xiumeng. Exploring the construction path of a new organizational system for virtual teaching and research offices in the era of "Intelligence+"[J]. Chinese University Teaching, 2023, (08): 82-91 (in Chinese).

[18] Li Ming, Liu Yonghua, Ma Mingxiao, Sun Li. Research on the construction of virtual teaching and research rooms in universities under the background of academic community[J]. Health Vocational Education, 2023, 41 (15): 3-6 (in Chinese).

[19] Cheng Yinghui. Construction of integrated teaching mode based on virtual teaching and research room[J]. Science and Education Guide, 2023, (20): 36-38

[20] Nyme Ahmed, Dip Nandi, A. G. M. Zaman, "Analyzing Student Evaluations of Teaching in a Completely Online Environment", International Journal of Modern Education and Computer Science, Vol.14, No.6, pp. 13-24, 2022.

[21] Han Bing, Wang Liwei. Construction of computer professional group curriculum system based on "school enterprise management"[J]. Communication and Information Technology, 2023, (05): 112-114 (in Chinese).

[22] Li Qiaojun, Wang Wei, Zhu Qi. Research and practice on the modular curriculum system of "four positions and four capabilities" in the electronic communication professional group under the background of industry education integration[J]. Journal of Anhui Electronic Information Vocational and Technical College, 2023, 22 (03): 61-64 (in Chinese).

[23] Kong Jili, Liu Jia. Exploration of the construction of graduate professional courses under the background of ideological and political curriculum - taking the course of "Logistics System Engineering" as an example[J]. Logistics Engineering and Management, 2023, 45(09): 192-197+183 (in Chinese).

Artificial Intelligence, Medical Engineering and Education 669
Z.B. Hu et al. (Eds.)
doi:10.3233/ATDE231381

The Talent Selection and Training Mode in the Metallographic Skills Competition for Material Specialty

Qian CAO, Yu MAO, Xingwen WU, Hongyan WEN, Peng WEI, Hu YANG, Qilai ZHOU, Xian ZENG[1]

a School of Materials Science and Engineering, Wuhan University of Technology, Wuhan, China

ORCiD ID: Qian CAO https://orcid.org/0000-0003-2983-9283

Abstract. The Metallographic Skills Competition is a significant scientific and technological event for university students majoring in materials, aiming to cultivate talents with outstanding comprehensive competencies. This paper delves into the deficiencies that arise in the selection and training of talents when holding the competition at Wuhan University of Technology (WHUT). Reforms and practices were implemented at multiple levels, including competition organization, training methods and evaluation systems to address these deficiencies. In the process of practice, it was found that the Metallographic Skills Competition holds broad appeal among materials students. The overall evaluation of the reformed cultivation process was high, with about 87.4% of the students considering the overall arrangement of the competition as reasonable and satisfactory. Regarding competence development, more than 84% of the students believed that their professional competency, hands-on ability, self-learning ability, communication skills and experimental literacy improved through participation in the Metallographic Skills Competition.

Keywords. Metallographic Skills Competition; Talent selection; Training mode; Competency.

1. Introduction

In today's highly competitive and rapidly changing globalized society, the cultivation of outstanding talents has become a top priority for nations and educational institutions [1-3]. The nurturing of talent not only impacts individual success but also relates to a country's competitiveness and the sustainable development of society [4]. With the continuous development of science and technology, the requirements for the comprehensive competencies of talents are gradually increasing. University graduates should not only master solid professional knowledge, but also possess autonomous learning abilities, practical skills, innovation, and creative capabilities [5-9]. Subject competitions, as the second classroom for college students, are particularly important in cultivating comprehensive talents. They not only provide students with a platform to develop critical thinking, problem-solving skills, communication skills, hands-on ability, and innovative awareness, but also provide them with opportunities to showcase their

---
[1] Corresponding Author: Xian ZENG, E-mail: zengxian9925@163.com.

talents and professional expertise [10-14]. These competitions contribute to the professional growth and personal development of students and, at the same time, play a positive role in advancing progress and innovation of society.

The National Metallographic Skills Competition, as an integral part of the college discipline competitions, is a significant event for university students majoring in materials science. In the rapidly evolving field of materials science and engineering, in order to meet the continuous progress of engineering technology and the heightened demands of enterprises for talents, comprehensive competition platforms such as the National Metallographic Skills Competition are urgently needed. It serves not merely as a competition, but also as a way of education and training. It combines theoretical knowledge related to metallic materials with practical skills, nurturing students not only in theoretical knowledge, but also in practical skills, self-learning ability, professional literacy and other aspects, ultimately promoting the all-round development of students [15-18]. The National Metallographic Skills Competition is held annually and has been conducted 12 times to date. The competition mainly assesses students' skills such as metallographic preparation and microstructure observation within specified time limits. In 2019, the competition entered the national ranking of discipline competitions of Chinese universities and attracted participation from over 500 universities across the country in 2023.

At present, the National Metallographic Skills Competition adopts a three-tier competition system of "university level competition-provincial level competition-national level competition" [15]. Participants in the national competition must qualify through the provincial competition, and provincial competitors are selected from the university competition. Since 2016, the university-level Metallographic Skills Competition at WHUT has been conducted as part of the "Material Culture Festival" activity. It is aimed to exercise, cultivate, and improve the professional ability, practical skills, and other competencies of students in material specialty through the training and competition process, and to further select outstanding comprehensive talents for the provincial and national competition.

This paper deeply studies the deficiencies in the organization and training process of the university-level competition of WHUT in recent years. In response to these deficiencies, a new talent selection and training mode for the university-level metallographic skills competition is established and put into practice. Subsequently, an effectiveness analysis of the reformed talent selection and training mode is carried out through analyzing the scale of student participation and conducting questionnaire surveys.

2. Deficiencies in the Current Metallographic Skills Competition

The Metallographic Skills Competition is an important part of WHUT's undergraduate capacity development system, and has been successfully held 8 times since 2016. Given the professional nature of the competition, previously, it was only open to about 70 juniors majoring in metal materials, and participation was compulsory for them. These students had gained a certain understanding of metallographic preparation through theoretical and experimental courses such as the basics of materials science and metallographic preparation technology, etc., in their sophomore year. Before the competition, instructors arranged 1-2 weeks of free practice time for students to practice in the professional laboratories so that students could become proficient in sample preparation methods and equipment usage. During the competition, participants worked on given samples such as 45 steels, 20 steel, ductile iron, etc., and conducted sample preparation and observation within 30 minutes. After the competition, expert judges scored the samples and the on-site performance of the participants based on the standards of the National Metallographic Skills Competition (as shown in Table 1). Ultimately, instructors selected several participants for the provincial competition based on the scores of the competition.

Table 1. Evaluation standards of the National Metallographic Skills Competition

No.	Scoring items	Requirements
1	Metallographic image quality (80points)	Correctness and clarity of microstructures (40 points)
		Scratches (20 points)
		Fake images (20 points)
2	Macroscopic quality (10 points)	Sample surface quality (10 points)
3	On-site performance (10 points)	Normativity of on-site performance (10 points)

However, in years of practice, it was found that training students according to the above-mentioned competition organization, talent selection and training mode had the following shortcomings:

1) The reach and benefit of the competition were limited. There are 9 professional directions, including metal materials, inorganic non-metallic materials, and polymers, materials physics, materials chemistry, etc. spread across 18 classes in the School of Materials Science and Technology. If only students from 2 classes in the metal direction participate in the Metallographic Skills Competition, students in other majors will miss out on the opportunity for capacity development through the competition, and meanwhile lose the opportunity to compete on higher platforms and exercise themselves.

2) The adoption of the compulsory competition mode might lead to a passive learning state for most students, resulting in a lack of interest in the competition. The enthusiasm of students in their daily training and the competition was not high, and there was a lack of healthy competition among them, which results in inadequate development of their abilities.

3) Relying solely on final competition scores as a measure of students' overall abilities lacked rigor. Final scores may reflect students' professional competency, hands-on abilities, and self-learning skills to some extent, but throughout the training and competition process, other abilities such as communication skills and experimental literacy, are also cultivated. These abilities are primarily demonstrated through students' daily performance rather than competition scores. Additionally, students' professional skills, hands-on abilities, and self-learning abilities can also be reflected in their daily practice. Therefore, consideration should be given to the assessment of students' daily performance during training and a comprehensive evaluation of students' individual competencies based on both daily performance and competition scores is needed for talent selection.

3. A New Mode for Talent Selection and Training in the Metallographic Skills Competition

In view of the above deficiencies, this paper carries out various reforms in the organization, talent training, selection, and evaluation mode of the competition.

3.1. Organization and Registration

In the process of organizing student participation in the competition, some significant improvements have been implemented. Firstly, the original compulsory participation policy is changed to voluntary registration. Then, the scope of participation is expanded. The eligibility for participation extends to 9 professional directions, and the grade requirements for participation are relaxed. This change allows sophomore and junior students to voluntarily choose to participate based on their interests, enabling more students with different professional backgrounds to join and experience the competition. This diversified and voluntary approach can encourage greater motivation and initiative among students. Students from different professional backgrounds communicate together, fostering a culture of viewing problems from multiple perspectives. This may help broaden their knowledge and encourages students to delve deeper into learning and explore new areas of knowledge. While expanding the reach of the competition, it also creates a healthy competitive atmosphere and inspires stronger enthusiasm for students in the study of material science.

3.2. Talent Training

As the scale of the competition expands, the talent training method also needs to be reformed accordingly (see Figure 1). Since the competition is open to all students within the School of Materials Science and Engineering, there may exist a knowledge gap for students in majors such as polymer materials, composite materials, new energy materials, etc. Students in these majors may have limited background in the field of metallography. At the same time, due to the scattered distribution of students' majors and grades, their course schedules may vary, making it challenging to coordinate classroom teaching. Therefore, an online training session has been added before the offline practice began, adopting a blended learning approach. During the first week of the activity, instructors use online teaching tools such as Tencent Classroom to conduct online lectures for students. The content of these lectures includes fundamental of metallographic preparation, metallographic structure analysis, preparation methods of competition samples, competition process, scoring standards, and competition guidelines, etc.

When the online training ends, students move on to the offline training session. During this offline training period, the undergraduate teaching laboratory of metallographic preparation will be open to students for 2-3 weeks. This allows students to enter the laboratory, familiarize themselves with the entire process of metallographic preparation, and become proficient in using the relevant equipment. Due to limitations in experimental equipment and space, offline practice operates on an appointment basis. Students are grouped in advance, and schedule appointments with teachers. Throughout this process, teachers record the student's performance, including tracking the frequency and duration of offline training, communication with teachers or discussions among students, the normative and safe use of equipment, etc. In addition, during the whole training process, students can also use resources from their own or other universities for self-study of the basic knowledge of metallography through platforms such as Chinese University MOOC, SPOC, and Superstar Study Pass, etc. [19-20].

After the offline training, all participants compete in groups, and the on-site performance and prepared samples are evaluated by expert judges in accordance with the standards of National Metallographic Skills Competition.

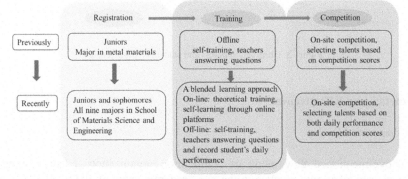

Figure 1. The metallographic skills competition training flow chart of WHUT

3.3. Talent Evaluation

During the whole training process, students' professional competency, hands-on ability, self-learning ability, communication skills and experimental literacy have been exercised and demonstrated. Therefore, it would be inadequate to evaluate students' ability and select talents based on the final competition results alone. In order to examine students' overall competencies more effectively and comprehensively, the daily performance score of students is added when grading of students. The frequency and duration of students' practice, communication with teachers, communication among students, normative and safe use of equipment, post-experiment cleanliness and organization are taken as observation points, examining students' self-learning ability, communication skills and experimental literacy, as shown in Figure 2. After the on-site competition, instructors summarize daily performance scores and competition scores of the participants, and determine final scores with 70% of the competition scores and 30% of the daily performance, as shown in Table 2. These final scores determine which participants advance to higher-level competitions, allowing for a more comprehensive assessment and evaluation of students' abilities than just using competition performance as a selection method.

Table 2. Evaluation form of students' daily and competition performances

Stude nt's name	Observation points of daily performance					Observation points of competition performance	Final score （30% daily performance +70% competition performance ）
	Frequency and duration of practice (10 points)	Communi cation with teachers (5 points)	Communi cation among students (5 points)	Normative and safe use of equipment (5 points)	Post-experiment cleanliness and organization (5 points)	On-site competition score (100 points)	On-site competition performance ）

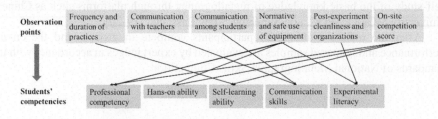

Figure 2. Observation points and students' competencies

4. Practice and Effectiveness

4.1. Competition Scales

The above-mentioned new mode of competition organization, talent training and selection were taken into practice in the two academic years of 2022 and 2023. As the competition expanded to all majors in the School of Materials Science and engineering for sophomores and juniors, the number of student registrations was highly increased annually, from 70 in 2021 to 156 in 2022, and further to 194 in 2023. The increase in the number of participants indicates more intense competition, which could stimulate participants' competitiveness and motivation, driving them to continuously improve. Figure 3 illustrates the students' registrations for the year 2023. From the figure, it could be observed that, at the grade level, there was a small difference in the number of registrations between sophomores and juniors, with juniors' registrations (54%) slightly higher than sophomores' (46%). At the major level, regardless of the grade, students from all nine majors participated, with the most participants coming from three majors: metal materials, inorganic non-metallic materials, and material forming and control engineering, accounting for more than half of the total registrations.

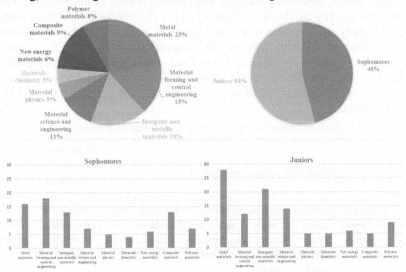

Figure 3. Grade and major distribution of participants in 2023

Based on the data above, the Metallographic Skills Competition has a wide appeal among sophomore and junior students. And it is feasible to implement the competition across all majors in the School of Materials Science and Engineering to select outstanding professionals for provincial and national competitions. By expanding the participating grades and major directions, more students could be attracted to engage in this competition, and foster the improvement of their professional competency, hands-on ability, self-learning ability, communication skills and experimental literacy. Additionally, more participants also signify intensified competition, which is advantageous for talent selection.

4.2. Effectiveness Analysis

After the end of the 2023 university-level competition, a questionnaire survey was conducted among the participants to assess the cultivation process and effectiveness of the Metallographic Skills competition. The cultivation process for the Metallographic Skills Competition encompassed organization, training, and competition. A four-level rating scale was employed, including reasonable, mostly reasonable, partly reasonable, and unreasonable. The results of the questionnaire survey are presented in Table 3.

As can be seen from Table 3, students had a high overall evaluation of the competition, with 87.4% of the students believing that the overall arrangement of the competition is reasonable. Specifically, in terms of organization, on-site competition, and scoring processes, students expressed relatively high satisfaction. However, the evaluation of training process decreased slightly, especially the offline training process. After the questionnaire survey, through discussions with students, it was found that the main reason for the relatively lower evaluation of offline training was the limited availability of laboratory space and equipment setups, which restricted the number of students that could be accommodated in the laboratory during each training. This resulted in some students not being able to practice adequately, ultimately leading to their competition performance falling short of their expected level. Furthermore, due to the heavy course load of sophomore students, some of them suggested extending the duration of offline training.

Table 3. Assessment of the cultivation process of the metallographic competition

Items	Reasonable (%)	Mostly reasonable (%)	Partly reasonable (%)	Unreasonable (%)
Organization	84.8	6.3	5.8	3.1
On-line training	78.0	9.9	6.3	5.8
Off-line training	71.7	15.7	9.4	3.1
On-site competition	91.6	6.3	1.0	1.0
Scoring	89.5	5.8	2.6	2.1
Overall	87.4	6.8	5.2	0.5

The evaluation results of the student competence development effectiveness are shown in Table 4. It can be seen from the table, over 84% of the students believed that their professional ability, hands-on ability, self-learning ability, communication ability and experimental literacy improved through the Metallographic Skills Competition.

More than half of the students indicated that significant improvements in their professional competency, hands-on ability, self-learning ability, and experimental literacy. Notably, the highest improvement was observed in hands-on abilities, with 82.2% reporting significant enhancement. In contrast, the number of students who reported significant improvement in communication skills was the lowest at 34.0%, suggesting a relative weakness in fostering communication skills, which may be attributed to the nature that the Metallographic Skills competition itself is a skills competition. In summary, the Metallographic Skills Competition could effectively cultivate students' professional competency, hands-on ability, self-learning ability, communication skills, and experimental literacy, ultimately promoting the enhancement of their overall competencies.

Table 4. Assessment of student competency development effectiveness

Items	Significantly improved（%）	Improved （%）	Slightly improved （%）	Not improved （%）
Professional competency	53.9	26.7	13.1	6.3
Hands-on ability	82.2	9.9	6.8	1.0
Self-learning ability	55.5	30.9	11.5	2.1
Communication skills	34.0	25.7	24.6	15.7
Experimental literacy	61.8	22.5	14.7	1.6

5. Conclusion

This paper deeply analyzes the deficiencies occurred during previous talent training and selection of the Metallographic Skills Competition at WHUT, and carries out reforms and practices in various aspects including competition organization, training methods and evaluation system. During the implementation of these reforms, it was found that the metallographic competition was highly popular among materials students. Expanding the range of participating majors and grade levels could effectively enhance the reach and benefits of the competition. Students generally spoke highly of the reformed metallographic competition cultivation process, with 87.4% of students believing that the overall arrangement of the competition is reasonable. In terms of competency development, over 84% of students believed that through the metallographic competition, their professional competency, hands-on ability, self-learning ability, communication skills, and experimental literacy improved. In summary, the reforms and practices discussed in this paper have a significant effect on students' competency development, which is conducive to better cultivating material professionals with excellent comprehensive ability, and has certain reference significance for the development of competitions in other disciplines.

Acknowledgment

This work has been supported by the teaching reform and research project of Wuhan University of Technology (Grant No. W2022064 and W2022061).

References

[1] Yuan Qin, Meng Wang, Mei Li. Research on the training of interdisciplinary-based intelligent manufacturing talents[J]. Journal of Contemporary Educational Research, 2023, 6(2): 10-15.

[2] Gao Fei, Zheng Zhiqiang, Weng Zhi, et al. Exploration of robot oriented talent training mode for emerging engineering education[J]. Chinese Studies, 2022, 11(2): 59-67.

[3] Liu Shuang, Chen Peng. Research on cultivation of ethnic minorities IT talents in nationalities universities[J]. International Journal of Modern Education and Computer Science, 2014, 6(2): 33-40.

[4] Xiong Tangfei, Zhang Jianjun, Huang Huiyan. Entrepreneurship education for training the talent in China: exploring the influencing factors and their effects[J]. High Voltage Engineering, 2023, 15: 11664.

[5] Chen Hui, Li Zhanming, Li Wei, et al. Discussion on teaching pattern of cultivating engineering application talent of automation specialty [J]. International Journal of Education and Management Engineering, 2012, 2(11): 30-34.

[6] Jiang Qiongqin, Jin Tian, Chen Haiyu, et al. Research on cultivating undergraduates in the computer science based on students[J]. International Journal of Engineering and Manufacturing, 2020, 10(6): 32-39.

[7] Wang Xianchao, Wang Hao, Wang Xianchuan, et al. Research and practice of "Five-in-One" talent training mode for computer specialties under the background of Emerging Engineering Education (3E) [J]. Springer, Cham, 2022, 98: 750-755.

[8] An Hengjie, Xu Yuanyuan. Cultivation of entrepreneurial talents through virtual entrepreneurship practice in higher education institutions[J]. Frontiers in Psychology, 2021, 12: 690692.

[9] Fang Wei. Exploration of application oriented talent training mode of material science in colleges and universities[J]. MATEC Web of Conferences, 2017, 100:4043.

[10] Yin Honglei, Lv Zhengfang. The research of university librarians participating in the guidance of university students' discipline competition[J]. SHS Web of Conferences, 2023, 171: 02032.

[11] Sui Jinxue, Hua Zhen, Zhu Hilin, et al. Training mechanism of engineering education and innovation talent based on courses-competitions combination[J]. Nanotechnology for Environmental Engineering, 2022, 7(3): 833-871.

[12] Li Xiang, He Jinhuan, Li Fengling, et al. Research on teaching mode of biochemistry curriculum based on internet plus discipline competition[J]. International Journal of Electrical Engineering& Education, 2021.

[13] You Jiaxun, Huang Bin, Guo Chuangxin, et al. Exploration and practice of college students' discipline competition based on engineering practice courses[J]. Advances in Education, 2022, 12(1): 303-307(in Chinese).

[14] He Meiling, Pan Gongyu, Wu Xiaohui. Research and practice on the cultivation of innovative talents in transportation based on discipline competition[J]. International Journal of Social Science and Education Research, 2022, 5(5): 110-115.

[15] Ye Xu, Li Xian, Yao Yaping, et al. Exploration and practice of operational mode of university students' science and technology activity based on multidisciplinary integration[J]. Guangdong Chemical Industry,2019, 46(2): 214-215(in Chinese).

[16] Huang Peng, Sun Jianlin, Mao Jinghong, et al. Combining point and surface, integrating virtuality and reality: improving the comprehensive quality of college students by Metallographic Skill Competition[J]. Research And Exploration In Laboratory, 2022, 41 (2): 151-154(in Chinese).

[17] Guo Qianying, Chen Shenglan, Long Lixia, et al. Exploring on experiment teaching reform for undergraduates based on metallographic skills competition[J]. Laboratory Science, 2021, 24(4):122-125(in Chinese).

[18] Liang Xiaoping, Zhang ZhiJia, Zhang Guifang, et al. Research of skill competition on practice teaching reform of specialty foundation course in the construction of double first-class university specialty[J]. Education Teaching Forum, 2019, 15: 168-169(in Chinese).

[19] Salah Al Khafaji, Sriram. B, "A Concept Review on MOOCs Research Findings – A Qualitative Approach", International Journal of Education and Management Engineering, Vol.13, No.4, pp. 19-25, 2023.

[20] Li Nan, Zhang Yong, "Improvement and Practice of Secondary School Geography Teachers' Informatization Teaching Ability Based on the Perspective of MOOCs", International Journal of Education and Management Engineering, Vol.12, No.1, pp. 11-18, 2022.

Artificial Intelligence, Medical Engineering and Education
Z.B. Hu et al. (Eds.)
© 2024 The Authors.

doi:10.3233/ATDE231382

Research and Practice of Online and Offline Hybrid First-Class Courses Construction--Taking Logistics System Engineering Course Teaching as an Example

Lu CAO[a,1], Xinhe WANG[b]

a Wuhan Technology and Business University, Wuhan, China
b College of Foreign Chinese, Xiangtan University, Xiangtan, China

Abstract. Logistics system engineering is a core course for undergraduate students majoring in logistics management. In order to cultivate all-round logistics management scientific talents, on the basis of building a scientific and reasonable logistics system engineering course content, online and offline hybrid teaching, research and practice are carried out. This paper mainly discusses the background of the course, the problems that need to be solved, the hybrid teaching design of online and offline, the reform of teaching methods, the teaching practice and the design of assessment schemes, in order to improve the teaching quality and effect of logistics system engineering courses.

Keywords. Online and offline Hybrid; Teaching practice; TCO didactics.

1. Introduction

In order to promote the connotative development of higher education and strengthen the construction of a strong country in higher education, the Ministry of Education issued the "Double Ten Thousand Plan" in 2019, which launched the construction of first-class undergraduate courses at the national and provincial levels. In 2020, the first batch of national-level first-class courses was born, and the hybrid first-class courses online and offline were one of the five first-class courses. The importance of blended teaching mode in the current construction of higher education is so prominent, in order to strengthen the connotative development of higher education, it is particularly important to study how to improve the quality of online and offline hybrid courses. In 2018, Wu Yan, director of the Department of Higher Education of the Ministry of Education, pointed out that five types of gold courses should be created around the "once of both sexes": offline "gold courses", online "gold courses", online and offline hybrid "gold courses", virtual simulation "gold courses" and social practice "Golden Lesson". "Golden course" is another name for first-class undergraduate courses. As a hot topic of current teaching reform, online and offline blended teaching has been widely used and explored. The

---

[1] Corresponding Author: Lu CAO, E-mail: cathy6699@126.com.

advancement and deepening of the reform of higher education have made online and offline blended teaching a carrier for promoting the construction of first-class courses and innovating talent training mechanisms.

At present, the hybrid teaching model based on offline and online is also becoming a widely used teaching mode in colleges and universities at all levels in China. For example, the exploration and practice of online and offline hybrid programming first-class courses [1], the evaluation and research of online and offline hybrid course construction [2], the research and practice of online and offline hybrid first-class undergraduate course construction-taking marine biology course teaching as an example [3], the research and practice of online and offline hybrid first-class course construction-taking the "Web front-end development technology" course as an example [4], the connotation, construction goals and construction strategies of online and offline hybrid first-class undergraduate courses [5], research on the application of the blended BOPPPS based on an online and offline mixed teaching model in the course of fermentation engineering in applied universities [6], practice and exploration of online and offline "hybrid" teaching mode in the course of "chorus and conduction" [7], online and offline hybrid teaching mode of piano education under the background of big data and internet of things [8], effectiveness of offline and online learning during COVID-19 pandemic [9]. All these literatures have certain reference significance for improving the quality of teaching.

1.1. Logistics System Engineering Course Construction Process

Initial stage of the course (2010 year-2017 year): Since the establishment of the logistics management major in 2010, it has been opened as a core course of the major, focusing on offline teaching, and teaching is carried out through the method of "listening, practicing, doing, and examining".

Reform and optimization stage (2018 year-2020 year): In March 2018, the national online excellent open course of "Logistics System Engineering" was introduced to explore the reform of online and offline blended teaching, which has continued to this day. It has successively been approved for the reform of smart teaching in schools and the ideological and political reform of the curriculum. In 2020, the "four-in-one" online and offline hybrid teaching model of "independent online learning + discussion-based classroom communication + inquiry-based experimental design + follow-up tutoring innovation" led by ideology and politics was completed and operated smoothly.

Continuous improvement stage (2021year-present): further strengthen the integration of ideological and political elements, update online and offline teaching resources, deepen independent inquiry-based learning, carry out diversified multi-dimensional assessment and evaluation, and explore the teaching reform of "integration of lessons and competitions"; In 2021, the curriculum was further approved as a school-level "results-oriented" course teaching reform project to continuously improve the effectiveness of talent training. In 2023, Hubei Province applied for a provincial-level hybrid online and offline first-class undergraduate course.

1.2. Key Issues to be Addressed in Curriculum and Pedagogical Reform

First, the course teaching resources are limited, how to concentrate online and offline high-quality resources into course teaching [10]?

Second, classroom teaching time is limited, how to make full use of the time before and after class, comprehensively control the teaching process, and achieve close connection between online and offline?

Third, the comprehensive ability training is insufficient, how to get close to the industry practice to promote the transformation of knowledge learning to thinking level, ideological and political literacy, and ability quality?

2. Hybrid Teaching Design of Logistics System Engineering

The overall teaching design adopts the "four-in-one" hybrid teaching mode of "independent online learning + discussion-based classroom communication + inquiry-based experimental design + follow-up tutoring innovation" to realize the "three-dimensional combination" of online and offline, before, during and after class, and knowledge ability and quality training. This is shown in Fig. 1:

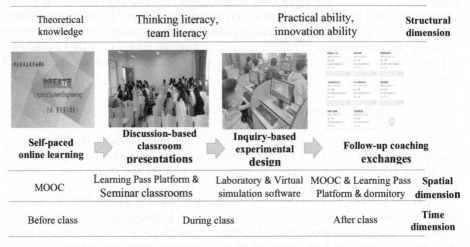

| Theoretical knowledge | Thinking literacy, team literacy | Practical ability, innovation ability | **Structural dimension** |

| **Self-paced online learning** | **Discussion-based classroom presentations** | **Inquiry-based experimental design** | **Follow-up coaching exchanges** |

| MOOC | Learning Pass Platform & Seminar classrooms | Laboratory & Virtual simulation software | MOOC & Learning Pass Platform & dormitory | **Spatial dimension** |

| Before class | During class | After class | **Time dimension** |

Figure 1. Hybrid teaching design of logistics system engineering

Online, apply the national high-quality online course teaching resources, select the corresponding content based on the application-oriented talent training positioning and the objectives of this course, organize students to conduct online independent learning, and lay a theoretical foundation.

Offline, using the "learning platform + seminar classroom + laboratory + virtual simulation software", based on the talent training orientation of logistics majors in our school, we focus on introducing cases of e-commerce logistics and international logistics industry, organize students to carry out practical and inquiry-based learning, cultivate students' systematic thinking, professional ability and teamwork ability, and solve the problem of students' lack of comprehensive ability.

After class, through the "Learning Platform + MOOC Network", follow-up tutoring and mutual evaluation of practical homework are carried out, and combined with subject competitions, students are guided to complete the design of logistics system schemes, promote the generation of practical innovation ability, and solve the problem of limited teaching hours of courses.

The online and offline teaching progress of each chapter of the teaching content is well matched, and the "independent learning-seminar speech-project experiment-innovative plan" are interconnected and progressive, and the "latter link" is used to test and supervise the learning effect of the "previous link", supplemented by MOOC and the learning platform for real-time interaction between teachers and students, solving the problems that students' independent learning process is not easy to control and the connection between online and offline teaching is not tight.

3. Reform of Teaching Methods

Based on "teaching-led and learning-oriented", the TCO teaching method of "task-driven +cooperative learning +outcomes-based" is adopted to improve students' comprehensive ability.

Task-driven (T): clarify the learning purpose and tasks to students, provide MOOC learning resources and case resources, give full play to students' subjectivity, take task solving as the main line, and design the entire teaching process [11].

Cooperative learning (C): In the learning process, create conditions for students' cooperative learning, including: online interaction, student-student mutual assessment, offline group discussion and presentation, team completion of experimental design, participation in discipline competitions [12].

Results-oriented (O): Evaluate the learning effect guided by the achievement of goals, evaluate the achievement of knowledge goals according to online tests and participation topics, evaluate the achievement of students' ability goals according to offline seminars, case reports, experimental reports, design plans and competition results, and achieve value goals throughout the entire learning process. This is shown in Fig. 2:

Figure 2. TCO teaching method

4. Hybrid Online and Offline Teaching Practice

4.1. Teaching Case

The course consists of 2 credits and 32 hours. Taking ability training as the main line and combining online and offline, the course teaching is divided into three teaching modules:

online learning (10 hours), classroom discussion (12 hours) and experimental design (10 hours).

Table 1. Course content design arrangement

Chapter content	Before class （10 Hours）	During class （12 Hours Discuss teaching+10 Hours Experimental teaching）		After class
	Lead with questions Students learn independently online	Student-oriented Conduct in-person classroom discussions and experimental design		Monitor student learning based on mobile platforms
Logistics system engineering overview	MOOC course Chapter 1 （2）	Class discussions （2）	Discuss understanding the knowledge structure of logistics systems engineering Combined with fresh food logistics cases, the application of Hall three-dimensional structure methodology is discussed	Case study report
Logistics Systems Engineering Methodology	MOOC Course Chapter 2 （1）			
Logistics system analysis	MOOC Course Chapter 3 （1）	Class discussions （2） Design of experiments （2）	Use brainstorming, 5W2H method analyze the case of Sinotrans' international development, form an optimization plan	Case study report Design of experiments
Logistics system forecasting	MOOC Course Chapter 4 （1）	Class discussions （2） Design of experiments （2）	The Delphi method was used to forecast the development of Sinotrans green logistics, form a predictive scenario	Case study report Design of experiments
Modeling logistics systems	MOOC Chapter 5 （1）	Design of experiments （2）	Use simulation software, modeling and simulation of logistics centers	Design of experiments
Logistics system simulation	MOOC Chapter 6 （1）			
Logistics system planning	MOOC Course Chapter 7 （1）	Class discussions （2） Design of experiments （4）	Combined with the case of logistics hub construction, the discussion was carried out, use simulation software for logistics hub area planning and layout design	Case study report Design of experiments
Logistics system evaluation	MOOC Course Chapter 8 （1）	Class discussions （2）	Use systematic review methods, Conduct contract logistics development analysis and evaluation	Case study report
Logistics system decisions	MOOC Course Chapter 9 （1）	Class discussions （2）	Apply a systematic approach to decision-making, discuss the development of emergency logistics under the normalization of the epidemic	Case study report

The content of each chapter is taught according to the teaching requirements in accordance with the process of "online self-study-classroom discussion- experimental design" (some chapters are combined for comprehensive discussion and experiments). This is shown in Table 1.

Take the analysis of logistics system in Chapter 3 as an example (shown in Fig. 3): before class, clarify the key learning content and requirements of MOOC knowledge points, release logistics cases and thinking problems for Sinotrans' international development; In online courses, students arrange time to study chapters independently, focusing on understanding the principles, elements, methods, ideas and basic contents of logistics system analysis; In the offline discussion class, interactive questions were exchanged in the form of interactive questions around the theoretical knowledge involved in the case, to test the effect of students' self-learning, to help students clearly grasp the ideas and methods of this case analysis, and then conduct group discussions and report the results of case analysis; In the offline experimental course, according to the results of case analysis, the virtual simulation software was used to simulate and optimize the international operation of Sinotrans to form an optimization plan. After the chapter teaching, the teacher will test the learning effectiveness of the chapter by organizing MOOC chapter quizzes, reviewing the case analysis reports and experimental design plans submitted on the learning pass.

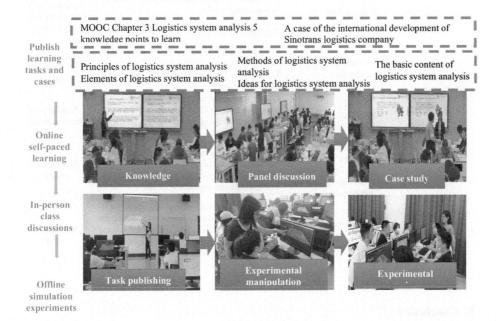

Figure 3. Teaching case

4.2. Course Assessment and Evaluation Plan

The final grade of this course consists of two parts: process assessment and result assessment. Among them, the process assessment score accounts for 60%, and the result assessment (offline final paper) accounts for 30%. The process assessment includes the assessment of the online learning process and the offline learning process, accounting for 30% each, and the specific assessment standards are shown in the following Table 2.

Table 2. Course assessment and evaluation plan

Form of assessment	proportion	Assessment content	Percentage	Assessment points	Evaluation subject
Online process assessment	30%	Online video learning	30%	1. Assess students' online video learning progress 2.The student's single-day study time and continuous cumulative learning days are assessed	MOOC platform
		Online chapter test, homework	30%	1. Assess students' mastery of online theoretical knowledge 2.Subjective assignments require peer assessment, motivate each other to learn	MOOC platform & student
		Online final exams	30%	1. To assess students' mastery of the theoretical knowledge of logistics system engineering, the ability to translate theoretical knowledge into application, Case study capabilities 2. Subjective questions are evaluated by students, Introduce peer evaluation	MOOC & Learning Pass Platform
		Online learning interaction	10%	1. Measure students' activity in participating in topic discussions 2. Assess the quality of students' answers to questions	MOOC & Learning Pass Platform
Offline process assessment	30%	Experimental projects	30%	1. Evaluate students' operation process and experimental results 2. Assess students' reflection and summary of experimental projects	Experimental software and teachers
		Classroom interaction	10%	1. Measure the number of times students participate in class activities 2. Assess the accuracy of students' answers to questions in class	Learning platform and teachers
		Panel discussion debriefing	20%	1. Assess students' teamwork skills and communication skills 2. Assess students' ability to analyze problems and innovate	Teachers and team members
		Case studies, design solutions and mutual evaluations	40%	1. Assess students' ability to transfer and apply theoretical knowledge 2. Assess students' ability to think logically in data analysis and logistics systems	Teachers and students
Results-based assessment	40%	Final paper Discipline competitions		Introduce real cases of logistics enterprises, apply the theoretical knowledge and methods learned in the course, carry out logistics plan planning and design, at the same time, the design scheme can participate in the logistics discipline competition, assess students' practical ability and innovation ability	Teachers and judges

5. Conclusion

The hybrid teaching practice of logistics system engineering courses adopts the TCO teaching method of "task-driven + cooperative learning + outcome-oriented" to achieve teaching-led and learning-oriented and improve students' comprehensive ability.

The student body is fully reflected. The combination of "independent learning + flipped classroom + project practice" forms a "student-centered" teaching and learning. Reasonably arrange online and offline tasks, absolutely do not teach those who can learn by themselves, test students' learning effects with effectiveness, and improve teaching accuracy [13]. Emphasize student participation, so that students can continuously improve their abilities through independent analysis, team discussion, and practical verification.

The course resources are rich and high-quality. The combination of "national high-quality online courses + mobile online resources + practical cases + virtual imitation software" has rich and high-quality teaching resources. The person in charge of the online national quality course is the team member of this course, and the quality and use of online resources are guaranteed. The self-compiled textbook of the course is a national planning textbook, with rich supporting videos, texts, and case resources. Virtual simulation software resources can meet the needs of students' seminars and experimental design.

Teaching time and space are effectively expanded. Which makes full use of information technology such as MOOCs, learning passes, virtual imitation software platforms, etc. And we adopt the "four-in-one" hybrid teaching mode of "independent online learning + discussion-based classroom communication + inquiry-based experimental design + follow-up tutoring innovation", which realizes the combination of online and offline in space, the combination of time before and after class, and the combination of knowledge and ability quality in talent training.

Acknowledgment

This project is supported by university-level first-class experimental course—Smart warehouse management experiments (S2023KC04)

References

[1] ZHAO Yuqin, YANG Dengqi, YANG Haichao. Exploration and practice of first-class courses of online and offline hybrid programming[J]. Computer Education, 2022(06): 163-169(in Chinese).

[2] Ran Meicheng. Research on the evaluation of online and offline hybrid course construction[D]. Dalian University of Technology, 2022 (in Chinese).

[3] AN Xinlong, DU Xin, LI Xuemei. Research and practice of online and offline hybrid first-class undergraduate course construction: a case study of marine biology course teaching[J]. Journal of Higher Education, 2022, 8(19): 5-8 (in Chinese).

[4] GAO Guangyin, CU Jiuliang, CHENG Yan, et al. Research and practice of online and offline hybrid first-class course construction: Taking "Web front-end development technology" course as an example[J]. Computer Age, 2022, (04): 77-79 (in Chinese).

[5] YANG Xiaohong, ZHENG Xin, TIAN Chunyu. The connotation, construction goals and construction strategies of online and offline hybrid first-class undergraduate courses[J]. Modern Education Technology, 2021, 31(09): 104-111 (in Chinese).

[6] Siqiang L, Quanlan L, Shuang G, et al. Research on the application of the blended BOPPPS based on an online and offline mixed teaching model in the course of fermentation engineering in applied universities. [J]. Biochemistry and Molecular Biology Education: A Bimonthly Publication of the International Union of Biochemistry and Molecular Biology, 2023, 51(3): 244-253.

[7] Han L. Practice and exploration of online and offline "hybrid" teaching mode in the course of "Chorus and Conduction"[J]. Computer Informatization and Mechanical System, 2023, 6(6): 110-114.

[8] Yue Y. Online and offline hybrid teaching mode of piano education under the background of big data and Internet of Things[J]. Journal of Computational Methods in Sciences and Engineering, 2023, 23(2): 715-724.

[9] M. Najib and A. Mursidi. Effectiveness of offline and online learning during COVID-19 pandemic: Two-factor analysis of variant approach in S-1 Students of FKIP University PGRI Banyuwangi, Indonesia[J]. Linguistics and Culture Review, 2022, 6: 1-11.

[10] K. Kashinath, R. L. N. Raju. An Empirical Research on the Effectiveness online and Offline Classes of English Language Learning based on Student's Perception in Telangana Schools [J]. International Journal of Modern Education and Computer Science, 2023, 15(2): 40-53.

[11] Blessing Dominic-Ugwu, Ogwueleka Francisca Nonyelum. The Assessment of Multimedia Technology in the Teaching of Mathematics in Secondary Schools in Abuja-Nigeria[J]. International Journal of Modern Education and Computer Science, 2019, 11(6): 8-18.

[12] Sahar A. El_Rahman, Sahar S. Shabanah. Course and Student Management System Based on ABET Computing Criteria [J]. International Journal of Information Engineering and Electronic Business, 2016, 8(3): 1-10.

[13] N. Rachmah. Effectiveness of online vs offline classes for EFL classroom: a study case in a higher education[J]. Journal of English Teaching, Applied Linguistics and Literatures (JETALL), 2020, 3: 19-26.

Artificial Intelligence, Medical Engineering and Education
Z.B. Hu et al. (Eds.)
© 2024 The Authors.
This article is published online with Open Access by IOS Press and distributed under the terms
of the Creative Commons Attribution Non-Commercial License 4.0 (CC BY-NC 4.0).
doi:10.3233/ATDE231383

The Establishing of Practice Teaching System for Intelligent Manufacturing Engineering Major on Application-Oriented Universities

Shiquan ZHOU [a,b], Jiajun YANG [a,b], Wenhui LI [a], Lei JIN [c], Hongwen LIU[d, 1]

[a] *Electromechanical Engineering Department, Wuhua college, Wuhan China;*
[b] *College of Mech. Sci. and Eng., Huazhong Uni. of Sci. and Techn., Wuhan China;*
[c] *Wuhan Gaode Information Industry Company Limited, Wuhan China;*
[d] *College of Mechanical Engineering, Ezhou Vocational University, Ezhou China*

Abstract. Driven by China's strategy of strength manufacturing country, the production mode of Chinese enterprises will change from traditional mechanical and electrical mode to digitizing, networking and intelligent production mode. Therefore, the intelligent manufacturing engineering major grows as a new major under that background. It has become the key to the construction of this major how to build a practical teaching system suitable for the intelligent manufacturing engineering major. Through cooperation with companies such as Huazhong CNC and Gaode Information, the application-oriented universities such as Wenhua college and Ezhou Vocational University have established a practical teaching system: Centered around intelligent manufacturing production lines, taking equipment of production line as the main line, focus on semi physical simulation platforms and digital twin virtual simulation platforms, taking vocational technical level certificates as the guide, taking digital design and programming as the foundation, and strengthened network data collection and communication control. Under the guidance of the practical teaching system, an intelligent manufacturing practical teaching platforms have been built. Which will be laid a solid practical teaching foundation for the construction of intelligent manufacturing engineering majors.

Key words. Strength manufacturing country; The production mode; The new engineering major; Intelligent manufacturing engineering; Engineering practice; Teaching system

1. Introduction

China's strategy of becoming a manufacturing strength country focuses on intelligent manufacturing as its main direction [1]. Intelligent manufacturing should have the characteristics of "using intelligent factories as the carrier, taking intelligence of key manufacturing processes as the core, with end-to-end data flow as the foundation, and taking network interconnection as the support".

The overall goal of intelligent manufacturing is the sustainable development goal

---

[1] Corresponding Author: Hongwen LIU, E-mail: 726389802@qq.com.

of "high-quality, efficient, low consumption, green, and safe", which undoubtedly reflects the value of China's industrial development in the future. The "Made in China 2025" and manufacturing power strategy prioritize intelligent manufacturing as their main focus, and it is pointed out that industrialization should be fully realized by 2035. From the perspective of the development path of intelligent manufacturing in China, most enterprises need to complete digitizing transformation within the next 5 years, some enterprises can realize digitizing and networking transformation, while intelligence may only appear in a few enterprises. It will be another 10 years before most enterprises can achieve digitizing and networking transformation and upgrading, and some enterprises may achieve digitizing, networking, and intelligent production and operation. Therefore, the demand for intelligent manufacturing professionals in enterprises has increased significantly in recent years. The Ministry of Education has timely launched a new engineering construction plan, and various universities have actively applied for new engineering majors while transforming old majors. Since 2018, there have been 212 new intelligent manufacturing engineering majors added in nationwide. Various universities from 985 and Double First Class, 211 to application-oriented universities have majors in intelligent manufacturing engineering. However, due to the fact that intelligent manufacturing itself is a new production and operation model that integrates multiple disciplines and fields, different university types have different positioning for talent cultivation. Some research-oriented universities aim to cultivate future industry leaders [2], so they choose to target the latest technologies that may develop in the future as their teaching objectives. As a local application-oriented university, the goal should be to cultivate intelligent manufacturing professionals who meet the urgent needs of real enterprises. In order to achieve such a goal positioning, in addition to the curriculum system, it is necessary to have a practical teaching system and practical platform that reflects the reality of intelligent manufacturing. However, due to the large number of universities in China and the ongoing construction of education mechanisms for enterprise participation, relying solely on enterprises cannot meet the requirements of intelligent manufacturing practical teaching. Instead, we can only build an intelligent manufacturing practical teaching platform on campus to serve China's manufacturing power strategy and cultivate application-oriented talents with unique characteristics in intelligent manufacturing for the new round of technological revolution and industrial transformation. The new industrial form must be adapted to the new engineering practice teaching system.

However, it is a question worth in-depth consideration what kind of practical teaching system can be suitable for the teaching needs of intelligent manufacturing engineering majors in local application–oriented universities.

2. Construction of Practical Teaching System for Intelligent Manufacturing Engineering major

2.1. The relationship between production mode and practical teaching system

Traditional factories are mostly based on equipment to construct workshops such as turning, milling, machining centers, grinding, electric discharge machining, laser processing, casting, forging, stamping, welding, heat treatment, 3D printing, assembly, etc. Some factories are also based on product to establish flow production lines and workshops, as well as component to build final assembly lines and workshops. Under this model, most internship factories and engineering training centers in Chinese universities have constructed internship types or training rooms according to this model. The equipment and line are isolated and disconnected islands of information. Although some CNC machine tools are connected to computers, they are only for the convenience of programming and transmission, and cannot achieve network control, making networking manufacturing is impossible. Therefore, the traditional engineering practice teaching system is consistent with the architecture of traditional factories and adapts to the traditional production mode. But in the upcoming era of intelligent manufacturing, this traditional production mode has become outdated. Of course, it is not ruled out that a few private and small and micro enterprises still use traditional manufacturing models for production. However, as intelligent manufacturing engineering major, it is necessary to cultivate applied talents for modern enterprises. With the transformation and upgrading of enterprises, so far, most large enterprises in China are undergoing digitizing, networking, and intelligent transformation and upgrading, and it is expected to basically achieve digitizing manufacturing by 2025; By 2035, digitizing and networking manufacturing will be basically achieved; Modern high-tech enterprises are also constantly emerging, intelligent manufacturing factories is the main feature of these enterprises. From a system perspective, an intelligent manufacturing factory is composed of the following levels (as shown in Fig. 1):

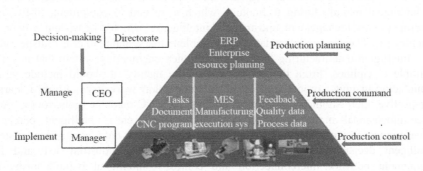

Figure 1. Vertical structure of intelligent manufacturing factory

The first level is the equipment and perception, production control layer; The second level is the SCADA data collection and monitoring layer, which is located between the equipment layer and the production command layer; The third level is the production command layer, which distributes files through MES (Manufacturing Execution System), commands the operation of manufacturing equipment, and uploads relevant production process data; The fourth level is the ERP (Enterprises Resource Planning) layer. From a vertical perspective, from the underlying electromechanical equipment, processing equipment, perception, measurement and control systems, as well as monitoring systems, to the production execution system, these vertical data need to be seamlessly integrated to form a vertical integrated system. The MES software system located on the third level and the SCADA software system located on the second level are the core industrial software for digitizing and networking manufacturing.

In intelligent manufacturing, manufacturing is fundamental, and cloud computing, big data, and the Internet of Things (IoT) are the means of implementation. They realize collaboration among subsystems such as design, logistics, production operation, scheduling, and testing, and persistently establish various production resource databases (technology, parts, products, processes, reliability, and suppliers) for the factory.

Intelligent manufacturing requires the integration and interconnection of networks at all levels to break the disconnect between the original business processes and process control processes, so that the control systems distributed in various production and manufacturing links are no longer information islands. Information exchange requires to run through from the bottom implementation level to the management and decision-making levels. In an intelligent manufacturing factory, all manufacturing links (elements), such as product design, process design, tooling design and manufacturing, parts processing and assembly, detection and data collection, data analysis and optimization, are digitizing and networking (structured). The software systems required in all links are integrated in the same digitizing and networking platform, so that the entire manufacturing process (as a whole) is completely driven (functional) by a single model, avoiding confusion in monitoring and managing the production process of work-in-process products [3].

Obviously, the new manufacturing model calls for a new engineering practice teaching system.

For the intelligent manufacturing practical teaching system, it should include the relevant elements of the production system in intelligent manufacturing factory, such as the elements of the intelligent manufacturing production line and workshop; It should also include a learning system based on intelligent manufacturing factories, which includes establishing software, hardware, and simulation systems for in-depth learning of intelligent manufacturing technology which is related to equipment, instruments, control systems, management, and artificial intelligence, which is consistent with on-site teaching [4]. The two are interrelated and complementary, and neither is indispensable.

Intelligent manufacturing factory is a complex engineering system that integrates multiple disciplines. From the perspective of the factory, it should include various manufacturing units, production lines, and production workshops; From a learning perspective, there should be intelligent equipment (CNC machine tools, robots, AGV, three-dimensional material warehouses, 3D printers, etc.), intelligent perception (measurement equipment and instruments, sensors and data acquisition systems, intelligent decision-making and optimization systems), industrial IoT and PLC (equipment network interconnection and control - intelligent manufacturing unit systems, logistics and warehousing systems), Intelligent manufacturing virtual simulation (virtual intelligent manufacturing production operation, virtual design of intelligent manufacturing systems, virtual operation of intelligent equipment, virtual design of products and manufacturing processes) and other operation training platforms [5]. If all the content involved in intelligent manufacturing is to be included in the practical teaching system of intelligent manufacturing, it will be a very large system, which is unrealistic and unnecessary for a school. Each school can establish a distinctive intelligent manufacturing practical teaching system for students based on its own disciplinary and technological advantages, as well as industry background.

2.2. Construction of practical teaching system for intelligent manufacturing major in local application-oriented universities

By analyzing the disciplinary and technological advantages of applied universities, as well as the trend of students' employment after graduation, and following the training orientation of facing Hubei and embracing Optics Valley, as well as the school's characteristics in mechanical and electrical control, Wenhua college and Ezhou vocational university have collaborated with enterprises such as Huazhong CNC and Gaode Information to build the practical teaching system of "one core, one main line, two platforms, and two certificates" , which takes digital design and programming as basement, strengthens networked data collection and communication control.

One core: taking the intelligent manufacturing production line as the core. Because an intelligent manufacturing factory is usually composed of one or more intelligent manufacturing production lines, the production line already has most of the elements of an intelligent manufacturing system. Therefore, as long as the intelligent manufacturing production line is run, it is necessary to understand the relevant knowledge and technology of the intelligent manufacturing system (IMS). That means the practice of operation production line is the important supply of IMS theories, and provides support and foundation for the theories [6].

One main line: Putting production line equipment as the main line. In the intelligent manufacturing production line, there are various intelligent manufacturing equipment, such as CNC machine tools, industrial robots, three-dimensional silos and AGV cars, laser processing equipment, 3D printing equipment, etc. While the production line is running, it will be unmanned, and students will no longer be able to learn and operate relevant equipment in the line. Therefore, practical teaching of relevant equipment is an important link in deeply understanding the work of the production line.

Two platforms: taking semi physical simulation platforms and digital twin virtual simulation platforms as key point. Equipment can only achieve understanding, operation, and maintenance of individual elements, but for the work process of a unit or line, it includes communication between equipment, mutual relationships among works, and control of work processes. These cannot be directly implemented by operating production lines and units, as the cost is too high; It cannot be achieved by operating individual equipment. In this way, through semi physical simulation and digital twin virtual simulation platforms, students can achieve digital design of the production process of a unit or a production line, system IoT communication and control, system PLC programming, MES operation and integrated debugging under low-cost conditions. So, the semi physical simulation platform and digital twin virtual simulation platform are the key to whether the intelligent manufacturing practical teaching can have connotation. The entire product cycle for the intelligent manufacturing includes product conceive, product and process design, manufacturing implement and production operate, which is the CDIO concepts [7] which is approved by engineering education in worldwide.

Two certificates: Guided by the vocational skill level certificate for integrated application of intelligent manufacturing systems and the vocational skill level certificate for operation and maintenance of intelligent manufacturing systems. These two certificates are vocational qualification certificates issued by China Ministry of Education that combine the needs of modern enterprise intelligent manufacturing positions and work fields [8-9]. By guiding students to learn the knowledge, operate equipment, and practice skills required in the certificates, students can obtain corresponding level certificates before graduation, which will provide career planning for them to quickly enter intelligent manufacturing positions after graduation.

After the construction of the above practical teaching system, the goal of efficient, high-quality, and low-cost manufacturing is achieved through the combination of virtual and real, using virtual to promote real, so as to realize digitizing and networking manufacture. Enable students to understand the connotation of intelligent manufacturing systems through practical teaching, learn relevant technologies and operational skills in intelligent manufacturing, and provide authentic and reliable guidance for their career planning.

3. Construction of Software and Hardware Platforms Based on The Practical Teaching System

To ensure that the practical teaching system can be implemented in practical teaching, it is necessary to have a suitable practical teaching platform, practical teaching courses and textbooks, as well as corresponding guidance books and a high-level team of practical teaching teachers. A suitable practical teaching platform is the prerequisite and foundation. But it is impossible for schools to build such a practical teaching platform entirely, as the teaching staff and engineering capabilities of schools cannot meet the requirements for designing, installing, and debugging an intelligent manufacturing production line. The establishment of a school enterprise cooperative education model is required with leading intelligent manufacturing enterprises, in this way, an intelligent manufacturing practical teaching platform can be established through the responsibility of the enterprise.

Through analysis, companies such as Huazhong CNC and Gaode Information Industry were selected to establish a cooperative education mechanism with the school, as they participated in the construction of China's intelligent manufacturing demonstration factory, their ability is represented that intelligent manufacturing factories are built by using Chinese equipment, systems, and industrial software. Therefore, it can better reflect the spirit of Chinese creation and inspire students' sense of national pride and patriotic enthusiasm.

In order to build an intelligent manufacturing practice teaching platform with high quality and low cost, Huazhong CNC is responsible for designing, installing, and debugging an intelligent manufacturing production line. The production line includes a three-dimensional material warehouse with a port machine, an AGV car for material delivery, two intelligent manufacturing processing units, and a laser marking unit. The entire line is operated and commanded by the MES system, material management and information tracking are carried out through RFID, and communication and network control are carried out through PLC and the IoT. It can achieve digitizing design, manufacturing, and control; networking communication, data collection and visualization, and on-site management of production operations; and meet the requirements of digitizing and networking teaching [10].

A modern manufacturing equipment practical teaching platform had been built, which includes nearly 80 sets of equipment used in production lines, including CNC lathes, CNC milling, machining centers, and five axis machining machines, industrial robots, laser marking machines, 3D printers, etc. It can achieve practical teaching such as digitizing process design, CNC programming, teaching programming and offline programming, machine operation and maintenance. Enable students to hands-on operate the equipment that appears on the production line, and further understand the role, functions, and operational skills of various equipment on the production line.

Collaborating with Gaode Information, 6 sets of intelligent manufacturing unit semi physical simulation platforms had been built, including physical robot controllers, CNC machine tool control panels, RFID+five color light three-dimensional silos, MES systems, and PLC control systems; and virtual execution mechanisms such as industrial robots, CNC lathes, machining centers, and three-dimensional silos. In this way, students can run and debug an intelligent manufacturing unit, including designing product production processes, compiling CNC machining programs, robot loading and unloading programming, CNC machine tool processing operations and debugging, robot loading and unloading point teaching and programming debugging, RFID material information reading and writing and management, MES order and production scheduling management, PLC communication and programmable logic control, human-machine interface operation, production operation and management, etc. Due to the virtual nature of the actuator, even in the event of misoperation, there will be no equipment damage or personnel safety issues. At the same time, all operations are the same as real physical operations, so there is a strong sense of operation experience. And it can be achieved that the teaching objectives of digitizing design and manufacturing, networking communication, and control.

A digital twin intelligent manufacturing virtual debugging platform is built by collaborating with Gaode Information. This platform consists of industrial robot digital twin virtual debugging software, intelligent manufacturing production line digital twin virtual debugging software, industrial robot disassembly and assembly virtual simulation software, and intelligent manufacturing production line virtual simulation software. Students can independently learn the structure and composition, installation, maintenance, and debugging of robots in computers and local area networks; and study composition, function, and role of intelligent manufacturing production lines. Students can independently design industrial robot workstations, install and build workstation scenarios, debug workstation software and hardware, and operate and maintain workstations; They can also independently design production lines, conduct layout and lectotype design, install and debug software and hardware, digitizing design process flow and manufacturing programming, IoT communication connection, material distribution and management, MES order management, automatic scheduling, order production, production line operation and management. These tasks are impossible for students to do on physical production lines, once there are problems, the entire production line will be shut down, making it impossible to complete the teaching tasks on the production line. Virtual debugging software can allow students to make mistakes and learn from setbacks [11]. Therefore, only by effectively utilizing the role of digital twin virtual debugging software can the teaching of intelligent manufacturing systems truly be implemented.

Two vocational skill level certificates of intelligent manufacturing system integration, and operation & maintenance are introduced. These two certificates are jointly developed by enterprises such as Huazhong CNC and universities, and are approved by the China Ministry of Education to implement vocational qualification certificates in universities across the country [12]. The intelligent manufacturing system integration certificate is mainly aimed at installation, debugging, integrated design, functional development, production optimization and trial operation, and other work areas; The operation & maintenance certificate of intelligent manufacturing system is mainly aimed at production process documents and operation preparation, operation and production, maintenance and upkeep, process planning and programming, trial operation, production operation management, production operation optimization, upgrading and health management, and other work areas. The former is for intelligent manufacturing system integration enterprises, while the latter is for product intelligent manufacturing production enterprises. Students can choose corresponding practical and theoretical courses based on their career plans, and then obtain corresponding vocational qualification certificates through practical exams conducted by certification agencies, which will provide support for their future job choices.

4. Discussion and Analysis

The practice teaching system has become the practice levels of talent nurturing mode in Fig. 2. It combines with the curriculum system to realize the talent nurturing objective. This mode has been applied in the teaching of intelligent manufacture major students in grades 2020 to 2022, the students consider they can design CNC program by operating CNC machine tools, robot teaching program by operating robot; and then can design PLC program and connect IoT by operating semi physical platform of intelligent manufacture unit, be able to design the layout of the production line and debug the line by operating digital twin virtual simulation software. Next step, they will be operating the real intelligent manufacturing production line during the 3-4 grades. The teachers of this major also said that teaching effectiveness is increased by using the practice teaching system and platform, the theory can be collaborated with the practice of operating physical and virtual equipment, unit and production line.

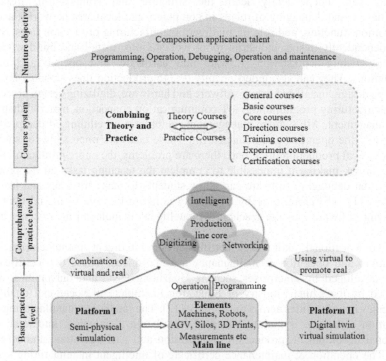

Figure 2. Talent nurturing mode of intelligent manufacturing major

The questionnaire results show that the more the students take part in the new practice teaching system, the deeper they understand to principle and technology of intelligent manufacturing (IM). In the Table 1, the old practice teaching system (PTS) was used for 2020 grade students entirely, the old PTS did not include platform I and II , as well as production line, just had CNC machine tools. The students got the knowledges of IM from the theory curriculum. Therefore, the students just can understand 50% principle and technology of IM. For the 2021 grade students, the 50% old PTS and 50% new PTS were used to their practice teaching. Because of the application of new PTS, the understanding for the IM is increased to 80%. The new PTS was used for the 2022 grade students completely, the students can understand the principle and technology of IM almost completely. It is proved that the established PTS promote the degree of achievement for talent nurture objective.

Table 1. The questionnaire results for intelligent manufacturing understand

Students grades	Old PTS (%)	New PTS (%)	IM understand (%)
2020	100	0	50
2021	50	50	80
2022	0	100	99

5. Conclusion

Due to the fact that the Intelligent Manufacturing major is a newly established engineering major in recent years, there is no experience to draw on. The practical teaching system for intelligent manufacturing engineering majors still needs to be continuously improved, and the construction of corresponding practical teaching platforms also needs to be continuously upgraded. However, having only a practical teaching system and corresponding practical teaching platforms is not enough. It is also necessary to build a practical course system, develop practical course textbooks and guidance books that meet the needs of the course system, and carry out training for practical teaching faculty. The integration of industry and education can solve the shortcomings of universities in terms of technology, teacher level, and other aspects. Therefore, universities should further cooperate with relevant high-tech enterprises, develop intelligent manufacturing teaching equipment, teaching software, and systems, further improve and enrich the teaching content of engineering practice and innovation courses, explore teaching content, and continuously improve teaching quality.

Acknowledgment

This project is supported by the first-class undergraduate specialty construction project in Hubei Province (J09007802) and the teaching quality and teaching reform project of Wenhua University (J09007014); Scientific Research Project of Hubei Vocational Education Association (Project No.: ZJGB2020085).

References

[1]   Research Project Group on Manufacturing Strong Country Strategy. Research on manufacturing strong country strategy. Special volume on intelligent manufacturing[M]. Beijing: China Industrial and Information Technology Publishing Group, Electronic Industry Press, 2015 (in Chinese).

[2]   Zhou Shiquan, Chen Jihong, Xiong Dazhu et al. Establishment of curriculum system of engineering practice based on intelligent manufacturing[J]. Laboratory Science. 2022, 25 (1): 35-38. (in Chinese).

[3]   Du Baorui, Wang Bo, Zhao Lu et al. Basic characteristics and framework system of aviation intelligent factories[J], Aviation Manufacturing Technology, 2015, (8): 26-31.

[4]   Guo Ning. Construction and implementation of innovation computer network practical teaching system [J]. I. J. Education and Management Engineering, 2011, (2): 30-35.

[5]   Zhou Shiquan, Chen Ze, Chen Wene. Exploration of engineering practice teaching model on research-oriented university with the advantage of engineering [C]. The Proceedings of 12th ICMIT, 2018, (10): 347-357.

[6]   Liu Jianbina, Yang Zhiyun. Exploration and practice of SE-CDIO educational pattern[J]. International Journal of Education and Management Engineering, 2012, (3): 51-56.

[7]   Crawley E F, Malmqvist J, Östlund S and Brodeur D. Rethinking engineering education: The CDIO approach[M]. Springer, 2007:10-20.

[8]   Özgen K. The effect of project-based cooperative studio studies on the basic electronics skills of students' cooperative learning and their attitudes [J]. International Journal of Modern Education and Computer Science, 2018, (5): 1-8.

[9]   Jamilurahman Faizi, Mohammad Sarosh Umar. A conceptual framework for software engineering education: project based learning approach integrated with industrial collaboration[J]. International Journal of Education and Management Engineering, 2021, (5): 46-53.

[10] Luis Emilio Alvarez-Dionisi, Mitali Mittra, Rosbelia Balza. Teaching artificial intelligence and robotics to undergraduate systems engineering students [J]. International Journal of Modern Education and Computer Science, 2019, (7): 54-63.

[11] Kong Yinan, Xie Yimin. Professional courses for computer engineering education [J]. International Journal of Modern Education and Computer Science, 2010, (1): 1-8.

[12] Tang Yizhi. Improve the 1+X certificate system to enhance the adaptability of vocational education [J]. China Vocational and Technical Education, 2021, (12): 109-113 (in Chinese).

Artificial Intelligence, Medical Engineering and Education
Z.B. Hu et al. (Eds.)
© *2024 The Authors.*
This article is published online with Open Access by IOS Press and distributed under the terms
of the Creative Commons Attribution Non-Commercial License 4.0 (CC BY-NC 4.0).
doi:10.3233/ATDE231384

The Derivation and Physical Meaning of Wave Function on College Physics Course Ideological and Political Integration

Fanbin TANG[1], Fengmei CHEN

Intelligent Manufacturing College of Nanning University, Nanning, China

Abstract. Many aspects of college physics teaching can be combined with moral education. The article integrates ideological and political elements into the teaching of college physics courses from four aspects, which can stimulate students' spirit of exploration and innovation, improve students' scientific literacy, cultivate students' scientific attitude of seeking truth from facts and establish a dialectical materialist world view. Take the derivation of wave function as an example, guide students to analyze from the perspective of dialectical materialism methodology, analyze the essence of wave from the micro level, and finally get the wave function. At the same time, from the physical meaning of wave function, students should be guided not to be tempted by foreign objects and adhere to their own hearts. Help them establish a correct outlook on life, values and world outlook. Then various educational elements are cleverly integrated into the teaching content to enhance the effect of education.

Keywords. College Physics Course; Ideology and Politics; Teaching Reform

1. Introduction

Physics is a natural science that studies the basic structure, basic forms of motion, interaction and transformation of matter. Its basic theory permeates all fields of natural science, applies to all aspects of production technology, and is the basis of other natural science and engineering technology. In the process of human pursuit of truth and exploration of the unknown world, physics shows a series of scientific world outlook and methodology, which has a profound impact on human's basic understanding of the material world, human thinking mode and social life. It is the cornerstone of human civilization development and plays an important role in the training of scientific quality of talents. College physics course is a public basic course of science and engineering for non-physics majors, which is characterized by long teaching hours and wide benefits. Moral education can be approached from basic concepts, theorems and laws in physics, physicists and history of physics, etc. All these have laid a solid foundation for the organic integration of physics and ideological and political elements [1-4]. As a method, ideology and politics can effectively improve the quality of classroom teaching, better complete the teaching objectives of the curriculum, and improve students' interest in learning.

In recent years, the research on curriculum in China's education circles has been

---

[1] Corresponding Author: Fanbin TANG, E-mail: tangfanbin@126.com.

quite hot, and teachers in various colleges and universities have achieved phased teaching results in different levels, directions and dimensions. For how to build high-quality online courses, their teaching team put forward a series of countermeasures and measures to improve the quality of course construction and teaching, and pointed out that the long-term construction, maintenance and service of high-quality websites also play a key role [5]. The implementation of undergraduate tutorial system can realize the combination of college teaching and moral education, make teaching according to students' aptitude and achieve the purpose of personalized training [6]. Through perfecting the college physics curriculum system, reforming the curriculum objectives, taking the selection of ideological and political elements and the elaboration of cases as the starting point for curriculum reform, a new path of reform is explored [7].

Many teachers have given their different views on the ideological and political teaching research of college physics course. Integrated the space frontier technology into the whole teaching link, reformed the traditional teaching methods and teaching contents, then achieved good results [8]. Introduced the way to integrate moral education into course under the background of   "new engineering" and put forward her own thoughts on how to effectively carry out the teaching [9]. Put forward that the education category of course is outlook on life, values and world outlook, and the education goal is to seek truth, perfection and aestheticism, according to which the ideological and political elements of course are classified [10]. Taking electric field strength as an example, fully exploring moral education elements can give full play to the main channel function of classroom education, so as to realize the unity of knowledge education and quality education [11]. Takes thin film interference as an example to introduce the craftsman spirit through the application of thin film interference, enable students to appreciate the beauty of physical phenomena, the beauty of physical theory description and the beauty of theoretical structure [12]. Took circular motion as an example and explained the transition from circular motion to general curved motion on China's high-speed railway, so that students could understand the laws and characteristics of circular motion [13]. These studies provide new ideas for other teachers' curriculum construction.

2. Ideology and Politics Elements

In recent years, the physics teaching and research department of the university has carried out the experimental work of curriculum ideology and politics in the teaching of college physics courses and set up a teaching team. Through excavating various educational elements, they are cleverly integrated into the curriculum, so that students can shape correct outlook on life, values and world outlook in the process of learning knowledge. The course adheres to the fundamental task of cultivating morality and educating people, takes "environment educating people and making things silent" as the basic idea of course, and integrates the cultivation and practice of socialist core values into the whole process of teaching. The integration of various educational elements into curriculum teaching can be carried out from the following four aspects:

1) Patriotic education should be conducted to help students build the "four self-confidence" of socialism with Chinese characteristics, namely, confidence in the road, theory, system and culture.

2) Dialectical materialism education should be carried out so that students can master the scientific thinking method of Marxist philosophical principles. In the course

of explaining knowledge points, combined with the derivation of physical formula laws, students are guided to analyze and think about problems from the perspective of dialectical materialism.

3) Educate students on the core values of socialism and train successors of the socialist cause. To solve the fundamental problems of who to train, how to train, and for whom to train.

4) Conduct moral education. Moral education is an important part of course teaching, which cultivates students' correct outlook on life, values and world outlook.

3. Teaching Method

Classroom is the main channel to implement teaching. To achieve the effect of ideological and political education, the choice of teaching methods is the key. Make full use of a variety of teaching means to educate and edify students, help students correct learning attitude, establish a correct outlook on life, values and world outlook.

1) Using the online network platform, students can preview before class and review after class, and also expand extracurricular knowledge. Online learning platforms not only support classroom teaching activities, but also provide support for students to carry out mobile learning anytime and anywhere in the extra-curricular environment. Teachers set up online resources applicable to the school on the learning channel, push relevant learning materials before class, and push exercises and summaries after class to consolidate what they have learned in every class, realize the closed loop of course teaching, improve their self-learning ability and cultivate their self-management ability.

Moocs are a large-scale online learning platform, reviews some major research since 2010 and summarizes the findings. Currently, the number of students joining and completing the courses through online is significantly increased which showed that the learners' intention on getting the knowledge in the area of specialization has increased [14]. In addition, in the course teaching process, the course team will introduce some cutting-edge developments and topics into the teaching process to promote students to understand the connection between basic knowledge and frontier and enhance their interest in exploring frontier. Examples include gravitational wave detection, CCD technology, topological superconductivity, spin flow, and so on [15-18].

2) PBL teaching method combined with group discussion. PBL teaching mode is also known as problem-based learning [19-21]. By presetting problem situations containing teaching content, students cooperate and discuss in groups to solve problems together, thus achieving the purpose of learning. Compared with the traditional teaching mode, PBL teaching mode can more effectively stimulate students' learning interest, improve independent learning ability, cultivate teamwork consciousness, exercise scientific thinking and research and problem-solving ability. For example: What is the working principle of the Beidou positioning and navigation system? Speak in groups. This can stimulate students' interest in learning, improve students' scientific literacy, and at the same time, students can also experience the spirit of self-reliance and hard work of scientists.

3) Expository method. Teachers start from the most basic explanation, leading to ideological and political education, the perfect combination of knowledge transfer and value guidance [22, 23]. While helping students master the method of law application, it enables students to enhance the "four self-confidence", form a scientific world outlook

and methodology, grasp the physical thought and method, and finally play the teaching effect of "environment educating people and wetting things silently" [24].

4. Take the Derivation and Physical Meaning of Wave Function as an Example

4.1. Course Introduction Stage

The textbook used is "Physics" (7th edition), edited by Ma Wenwei, and the chapter is the wave function of 10-2 plane simple harmonics, which is the content after vibration, and students have a certain "wave" learning foundation. Push questions online before class, cooperate and discuss in groups as follows:

Question 1: If the mass point does simple harmonic vibration and satisfies the equation of motion $x = A\cos(\omega t + \varphi)$, what happens when put a vibration source into a medium? As shown in Fig.1.

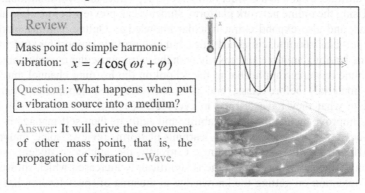

Figure 1. Review and introduce new content

Question 2: The wave source O does simple harmonic vibration, drives other points to move, what motion laws do the other mass points satisfy? How to find the equation of motion? As shown in Fig.2.

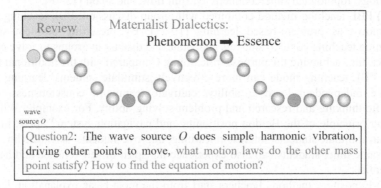

Figure 2. The nature of the wave phenomenon

4.2. Course Implementation Stage

1) Summarize the answers of each group, give the correct answers, and cause students to think.

For question 1, students will quickly find the answer. The wave source that vibrates in the medium will form a wave. The answer can be intuitively obtained from the production and propagation of water waves in the picture.

For question 2, it is suggested that students should use the methodology of dialectical materialism to find the essence of things from phenomena. Phenomena are the external relations and surface characteristics of things, essence is the internal relations between the fundamental nature of things and their constituent elements, essence is the basis of phenomena, and phenomenon is the expression of essence. The vibration of the source in the water can be seen to form a water wave and spread out, so what is the essence?

Through the explanation of question 2, it analyzes the methodology of dialectical materialism and looks at the essence of things from the micro level. Matter is made up of atoms and molecules, and the medium is considered to be made up of particles of the same size. Select a propagation direction for analysis, the vibration source does simple harmonic vibration in the equilibrium position, and the vibration of the vibration source will drive the movement of the surrounding mass points, because only the force of the vibration source medium, so the motion law is the same as the vibration source, that is, each mass point is in simple harmonic vibration, and the movement law of the vibration source is the same. But the starting states of each mass point are different. In order to find the vibration of all the mass points at any time, that is, the motion equation satisfied by each mass point, the concept of wave function is derived.

2) Definition of planar simple harmonic wave function and derivation of expression.

The wave surface is the simple harmonic of the plane, and the displacement of any particle in the medium (coordinate x) relative to its equilibrium position (coordinate y) changes with time, $y(x, t)$ is called the wave function of the simple harmonic of the plane. Each mass point is treated idealized, using the methodology of primary contradiction and secondary contradiction in contradiction theory, and each mass point is treated as that is only affected by neighboring particles in the direction of wave line, but not by other particles. Students are also required to pay attention to two aspects: first, what is the motion law of simple harmonic vibration; Second, what is the relationship between the particle on the wave line and the vibration source, can be analyzed from the perspective of phase difference or time difference. Students can easily analyze that the mass point on the wave line is also doing simple harmonic vibration, and the relationship with the vibration source is one phase behind in phase, or some time behind in time.

In order to derive the wave function for planar simple harmonics. First, discuss the simple harmonics propagating along the positive direction of the Ox axis, the source O is doing simple harmonic vibration, satisfying the vibration equation $y_o = A\cos(\omega t + \varphi_0)$.

Assuming that the medium is uniform and non-absorbing, then the amplitude of each mass point remains unchanged. In order to find the displacement of all the mass points at any time, arbitrary mass point P in the positive direction of the Ox axis, its distance from mass point O is x, and when the vibration propagates from mass point O to mass point P, mass point P will repeat the vibration of mass point O with the same amplitude and frequency. From the perspective of time, the time it takes for the vibration to propagate from mass point O to mass point P is Δt ($\Delta t = x/u$, u is the wave speed), in other words, the vibration of mass point P at time t is the motion of mass point O at time $(t-\Delta t)$. Therefore, the displacement of mass point P at time t is: $y_p = A\cos[\omega(t-\frac{x}{u})+\varphi_0]$.

Since mass point P is arbitrary, the above formula is applicable to all mass point, and the above formula is called the wave function of plane simple harmonics. Derivation process is shown in Fig.3.

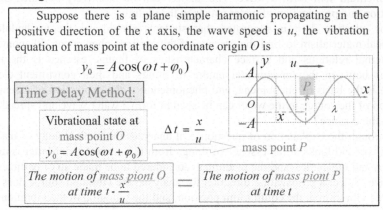

Figure 3. Wave function derivation process

If the wave propagates in the negative direction of the x-axis, then the vibration at mass point P starts some time before mass point O, so the wave function is: $y_p = A\cos[\omega(t+\frac{x}{u})+\varphi_0]$. To emphasize the origin and selection conditions of the plus and minus sign before Δt in the wave function, Let the students deduce the wave function from the phase difference, and judge whether the expression obtained is the same as the expression derived from the time difference, so as to arouse students' thinking.

3) The physical meaning of wave function.

From the above derivation, the expression of the wave function is obtained as: $y_p = A\cos[\omega(t\mp\frac{x}{u})+\varphi_0]$, from the physical meaning of the wave function to understand the propagation of vibration - wave. When x is constant, y is only a function of time t, and this equation represents the vibration equation of mass point x. When t is constant, y is only a function of position x, this equation represents the displacement of each mass point in the direction of wave propagation at time t, which is called the waveform diagram at time t. When both x and t are changing, the equation represents the displacement of each mass point at different times, that is, the waveform at different times, reflecting the propagation of the wave.

4.3. Summary Stage of The Course

1) From phenomenon to essence. The essence of the wave is that each mass point keeps doing simple harmonic vibration in the equilibrium position. Gradually learn to analyze problems with the methodology of dialectical materialism and look at the essence of things from the micro level. The scientific worldview and methodology demonstrated by physics are powerful tools for human beings to understand nature and nature, and embody scientific thinking methods for finding, analyzing and solving problems.

2) Stick to your heart and don't go with the flow. Each particle will not propagate forward with the wave, only sticking to its own position to glow and heat, and finally achieve the wave propagation. In the face of various temptations in today's society, we need to adhere to our heart, not to be affected by external conditions, not to be dominated by desire, and strive to be a pure and noble person.

3) Thinking: The wave function was derived from the perspective of time delay in class, and the wave function was derived from the perspective of backward phase after class, and the results derived from the two methods were compared.

5. Conclusion

Taking the derivation and physical meaning of wave function as an example, this paper shows how to integrate multiple educational elements into classroom teaching with various teaching methods. Introduce the topic from the generation of water wave phenomenon and guide the movement law of simple harmonic vibration learned in the previous chapter, so that students can think about its physical nature. From the Angle of materialist dialectics, we idealized the analysis and processing of the research object. Combined with the characteristics of wave propagation, derived from the time delay, the wave function of plane simple harmonics is finally obtained. Finally, the physical meaning of the wave function is analyzed, and students are warned to adhere to the self and not follow the crowd. In the teaching process, the initiative of students can be effectively mobilized, so that students can participate in teaching activities.

Compared with traditional teaching methods, it has the following three advantages: First, this teaching method can arouse students' thinking online in advance, and help students summarize and improve after class, cultivate good learning habits, and indirectly carry out moral education. Secondly, materialist dialectics is introduced in the teaching process. In the process of deriving the wave function, the idealized conditions of the research object are processed for many times, and the problems are analyzed in combination with materialist dialectics, so that students can master the use of Marxist methodology in the process of learning knowledge. Finally, starting from the physical meaning of wave function, it calls on students not to be confused by foreign things and insist on being themselves. In short, in the whole process of teaching cleverly interspersed a variety of educational elements, so that ideological and political and curriculum perfect integration, to achieve a very good teaching effect. The four aspects of ideological and political elements summarized in this paper can also be applied to other courses and provide a new idea for the construction of other courses.

Acknowledgment

This paper is supported by the fourth batch of "Curriculum Ideology and Politics" demonstration course construction project of Nanning University, No.2022SZSFK11.

References

[1]   Cajori. A history of physics in its elementary branches[M]. New York: Lyon Press, 2008.

[2]   UNESCO. Rethinking education: Towards a global common goods? [M]. Paris: UNESCO Publishing, 2015.

[3]   Darwell B W, Gilding B H. Non-inverse-square force-distance law for long thin magnets-revisited[J]. Dental Materials, 2012, 28: 42-49.

[4]   Neyenhuis B, Christensen D. Testing nonclassical theories of lectromagnetism with ion interferometry[J]. Phys. Rev. Lett. 2007,99(20): 200401.

[5]   Guan Denggao. Material physics & chemistry quality network curriculum construction and teaching practice[J], International Journal of Education and Management Engineering, 2012, 2(5): 24-30.

[6]   Ma Fu. Exploration and practice on reformation mode of undergraduate tutorial system in faculty of computer science[J]. International Journal of Education and Management Engineering, 2012, 2(4): 54-58.

[7]   Gao Xiuying. Reform and practice of ideological and political education in college physics course[J]. International Conference on Data Science, Networking and Education. 2022, 35: 54-57.

[8]   Chen Jiangyong. Curriculum reform on university physics integrated aerospace feature and curriculum ideology and politics education under the background of new engineering education[J]. Physical Bulletin, 2023, 2: 15-18 (in Chinese).

[9]   Cao Haixia. Practice and exploration on curriculum ideology and politics integrating into university physics under the background of "new engineering"[J]. Physical Bulletin, 2020, 12: 9-12(in Chinese).

[10]   Wu Wangjie. Seek truth, perfection and beauty-thinking and practice of ideological and political in college physics courses[J]. Physics and Engineering, 2021, 31: 109-113 (in Chinese).

[11]   Xie Zhenping. Research on teaching practice of "ideological and political course" in major college physics-taking electric field strength as an example. 6th International Conference on Social Science and Higher Education. 2020, 505-510.

[12]   Duan Xiuzhi. Study on the curriculum ideological and political education in the course of college physics: taking film interference as an example[J]. Education and Teaching Forum, 2021, 41: 161-164(in Chinese).

[13]   Zhang Xiaole. Ideological and political research on the course of circular motion in college physics[J]. Physics and Engineering, 2021, 31: 114-118 (in Chinese).

[14]   Salah Al Khafaji, Sriram. B. A concept review on MOOCs research findings-a qualitative approach. International Journal of Education and Management Engineering, 2023, 13(4): 19-25.

[15]   Abbott B P. LIGO scientific collaboration and virgo collaboration, observation of gravitational waves from a binary black hole merge[J]. Phys. Rev. Lett. 2016, 116: 061102.

[16]   Smith G E. Nobel lecture: The invention and early history of the CCD[J]. Rev. Mon. Phys, 2010, 82: 2307-2312.

[17]   Li C. Selective equal spin and reev reflection at ortex core center in magnetic semiconductor /superconductor heterostructure[J]. Scitific Reports, 2018, 8: 7853.

[18]   Noel P. Non-volatile electric control of spin-charge conversion in a SrTiO3 Rashbasystem[J]. Nature, 2020, 580: 483-486.

[19]   David A. Making the case: Professional education for the world of practice[J]. Harvard Magazine, 2003, 58: 9-10.

[20]   Kowalski T J. Case studies of educational administration[M]. New York: Longman, 1991.

[21]   Zhang Chunli. Research on the application of PBL teaching mode in college physics teaching mode [J]. Education and Teaching Forum, 2017, 30: 185-186 (in Chinese).

[22]   Suzan Bandar Al-mutairi, M. Rizwan Jameel Qureshi, "A Novel framework for Strategic Alliance of Knowledge Management Systems", International Journal of Modern Education and Computer Science, vol.6, no.4, pp.38-45, 2014.

[23]   Wan Ting, "Study on the Scientific Research Group Management of Chinese High Technology Enterprises from the Perspective of Knowledge Transfer", International Journal of Education and Management Engineering, vol.2, no.3, pp.57-63, 2012.

[24]   Hu Yu, Zhang Ming, "The Discussion of Teaching Effection about Combination of Architectural Graphing and CAD", International Journal of Education and Management Engineering, vol.2, no.10, pp.30-33, 2012.

Artificial Intelligence, Medical Engineering and Education
Z.B. Hu et al. (Eds.)
© 2024 The Authors.
This article is published online with Open Access by IOS Press and distributed under the terms
of the Creative Commons Attribution Non-Commercial License 4.0 (CC BY-NC 4.0).
doi:10.3233/ATDE231385

The Dilemma and Countermeasures of the Transformation of Scientific and Technological Achievements in Higher Vocational Colleges

Naizhao YU [a], Zhenpeng QIN [b, 1], Xuefei PANG [c]

[a] *Guangxi Open University, Nanning, China*
[b] *Nanning University, Nanning, China*
[c] *Nanning 39 middle School, Nanning, China*

Abstract. As an important component of colleges and universities, the transformation of scientific and technological achievements into teaching is the key to cultivating independent, innovative, high-quality and skilled personnel. Starting from the three aspects of transforming of scientific-technological achievements into teaching, the paper constructs the logical main line of it in higher vocational education, sorts out the dilemma and puts forward the solution, which has a positive impact on promoting the deep integration of science and education in vocational education.

Keywords. Science-education integration, Transformation of scientific and technological achievements into teaching, Higher vocational school

1. Introduction

At present, with the iterative update of science and technology, the traditional university major construction, curriculum, teaching projects and other educational elements are constantly being innovated. The reform of the education mode of integrating science and education in vocational education, represented by the science-technology integration with professional construction, curriculum setting and teaching projects, has become a hot topic in academic circles.

"Science" and "teaching" can be traced back to the 19th century, proposed by the German educator Humboldt, who put forward the concept of "combining scientific research and teaching"[1]. Only when scientific-technological achievements are combined with the needs, and complete the research, development, and application, can we truly realize the value of innovation [2]. The report of the 20th National Congress of the Communist Party of China proposed the direction and path of comprehensive education reform of promoting the vocational education integration, and optimizing the type positioning of vocational education, indicating the way out of the science- education integration for promoting the transformation of scientific-technological achievements

---

[1] Corresponding Author: Zhenpeng QIN, E-mail: 229146126@qq.com.

into teaching [3]. It is the new connotation and requirement of the concept of "combining scientific research and teaching" under the background of science-education integration. However, vocational education has long been out of touch with modern industrial technological innovation [4], there is a contradiction between the scientific knowledge production system of higher vocational scientific research and the demand for high-tech innovation and subversive technological innovation of enterprises [5], which often ignores the scientific research basis and characteristics of vocational education [6], resulting in the separation of production, university and research. Therefore, in order to complete the transformation reform of scientific and technological achievements into teaching in higher vocational colleges, it is necessary to reexamine the logical relationship in the development of the transformation reform of scientific and technological achievements into teaching, clarify the key problems such as "reform logic" and "reform dilemma" in the transformation reform of scientific and technological achievements into teaching. This paper will start from the logical main line of the transformation of scientific-technological achievements into teaching, sort out the dilemma of promoting the transformation of scientific and technological achievements into teaching, and put forward the solution of scientific and technological achievements into teaching for reference.

2. The Logical Main Line of The Transformation of Scientific and Technological Achievements into Teaching in Higher Vocational Colleges

The transformation of scientific and technological achievements into teaching in higher vocational colleges includes three aspects. The first is the main body of transformation, that is, higher vocational colleges; The second is the scientific and technological achievements, namely the transformation content; The third is teaching transformation, that is, transformation path. According to the essence of three aspects from "who to transform", "what to transform" and "how to transform", we can sort out the logic main line of scientific and technological achievements transformation.

2.1. Who to Transform: Explore the Main Body of Transformation of Scientific and Technological Achievements into Teaching

Before we explore the main body of the transformation from scientific - technological results into teaching in higher vocational, first of all, we need to understand its operation. In order to grasp the convesion of scientific-technological achievements in higher vocational colleges better, which is based on the macro policy of the government, we explore its main direction and analyse data, compiled by the Department of Science, Technology and Information Technology of the Ministry of Education of the People's Republic of China in the past five years, from 2017 to 2021.Technology transfer in China's colleges and universities mainly flows to enterprises, and the number of enterprise technology transfer contracts shows an increasing trend year by year, as shown in Table 1 [7-11].

Table 1. Technology transfer in Chinese colleges and universities from 2017 to 2021

Number of contracts	In 2017	In 2018	In 2019	In 2020	In 2021
Total	697	851	1034	1858	2783
State-owned enterprises	51	79	40	39	62
Foreign-funded enterprises	3	1	2	0	4
Private enterprises	561	730	928	1757	2541
Others	82	41	64	62	176
Subtotal of enterprise contracts	615	810	970	1796	2607

What can we learn the table that before the theory of science and education integration was proposed in the report of the 20th Party Congress in 2022, the scientific-technological achievements transformation in higher vocational schools was mainly tilted to enterprises, and the main body included the government, higher vocational colleges and enterprises, which formed a trinity of transformation subjects of scientific and technological achievements, and had the ability to control the transformation flow of scientific and technological achievements in higher vocational schools.

2.2. What to Transform: Explore the Content of Transforming Scientific and Technological Achievements into Teaching

According to the data compiled by the Department of Science, Technology and Information Technology of the Ministry of Education of the People's Republic of China, higher vocational science and technology achievements mainly include scientific and technological works, papers, project results, patents, software works, integrated circuit design, new animals and plants, new drugs, etc., which are summarized as cutting-edge theory, scientific research methods, cutting-edge science and technology.

1) Advanced science and technology theory. Technological achievements often represent the latest development and academic frontier, which are transformed into teaching and integrated into classroom teaching content, which can help students understand the latest trends of scientific-technological and disciplinary development. For example, introducing quantum mechanics theory into university physics teaching can stimulate students' learning interest in physics, which has a great effect on improving their scientific literacy and innovative thinking.

2) Cutting-edge scientific research methods. Advanced scientific research methods and experimental technologies are often adopted. These methods and technologies include the latest scientific research achievements and progress in the discipline. By learning these methods and technologies, students can cultivate their innovative thinking and problem-solving ability, and stimulate their creativity and innovation ability. Make them meet the future social development needs of talents. For example, data analysis, model building, simulation and other scientific research methods can be converted into experimental methods and research methods in the teaching process to help students master advanced scientific research methods and technologies.

3) Cutting-edge science- technology and achievements. The role of cutting-edge science-technology in teaching is diverse and far-reaching, and there are many technological means with educational value in scientific-technological achievements, and provide students and teachers with richer and more efficient teaching resources and

means.First of all, it has changed the way of for students. For example, the application of virtual reality (VR) and augmented reality (AR) technology enables students to learn in a virtual environment, enhances the experience and perception of learning content, and improves the fun and efficiency of learning. Secondly, cutting-edge technology also makes teaching more personalized. The application of artificial intelligence (AI) technology can provide personalized teaching programs, so as to meet different students' learning needs and improve teaching effects. In addition, cutting-edge technology has also promoted the innovation of education, mobile Internet and other technologies, so that educational institutions can better manage and analyze teaching data, so as to provide a basis for teaching reform.

2.3. How to Transform: Explore the Path of Transforming Scientific and Technological Achievements into Teaching

According to the basic elements of higher vocational education, such as professional construction, curriculum and teaching projects, the transformation of scientific-technological achievements into teaching needs to start from many aspects, such as majors, courses and projects, and realize the deep integration of scientific-technological achievements and existing educational resources, so as to cultivate high-quality and skilled talents to adapt to social development.

1) Scientific-technological achievements integrate professional development construction. As a type of education directly facing the professional world, the professional setting of vocational education must be replaced in accordance with the development trend of science and technology and market demand [12]. The deep integration of technological achievements and professional development construction can form a new interdisciplinary discipline or profession, make the profession at the forefront of social development, and promote the cultivation of innovative talents. For example, the combination of artificial intelligence and computer science can form an artificial intelligence major, the combination of mechanical engineering and biomedical engineering can form a medical device engineering major, etc., these new disciplines or new majors make students master the latest scientific-technological achievements, innovation and entrepreneurship, and have strong social adaptability.

2) Scientific-technological achievements integrate professional curriculum. The integration of scientific-technological achievements into the professional curriculum can update and optimize the course content, so that the teaching content is at the forefront of the development of the subject. For example, adding the content of scientific-technological achievements, such as artificial intelligence and big data, to the computer science course can enable students to learn the basic theoretical knowledge while being exposed to the latest scientific-technological progress, so that students have a deeper understanding of the frontier scientific-technological achievements of the discipline.

3) Scientific-technological achievements integration course teaching project. The application of scientific-technological achievements in actual classroom teaching projects can enable students to learn and master cutting-edge knowledge and skills in practice and enhance students' innovative thinking and ability. For example, the introduction of 3D printing technology in mechanical engineering allows students to design and print mechanical parts with specific functions, and the introduction of artificial intelligence technology in computer science allows students to design and develop intelligent algorithms to solve practical problems. When students complete these

teaching practice projects, their innovative thinking and innovative practice ability can be greatly improved.

Based on the above views, the logical main line model design for the transformation of scientific and technological achievements into teaching in higher vocational colleges is shown in Figure 1. The government, higher vocational colleges and enterprises constitute the main body of transformation, which integrating science and technology with majors, science and technology with courses, science and technology with projects, and transforming cutting-edge theories, scientific research methods and cutting-edge technologies.

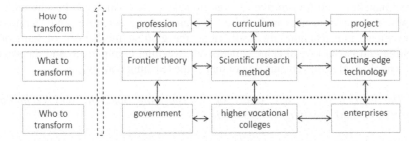

Figure 1. The logical main line model design for the transformation of scientific and technological achievements into teaching in higher vocational colleges

3. The Dilemma of Promoting the Transformation of Higher Vocational Science and Technology Achievements into Teaching

The above logical main line model is designed according to the three aspects of the transformation of scientific and technological achievements into teaching in higher vocational colleges, but it still lacks the feasibility and influence factor analysis. In order to complete the transformation of scientific and technological achievements into teaching, it is necessary to explore the contradictory relationship between the feasibility of transformation and the influencing factors and sort out the difficulties while promoting. The feasibility and influencing factors of the transformation from scientific and technological achievements to teaching (scientific and technological achievements) and terminal (education and teaching) are sorted out as following.

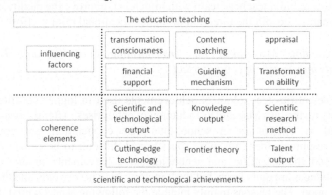

Figure 2. The corresponding elements and influencing factors of the transformation of scientific and technological achievements into teaching in higher vocational colleges

As shown in Figure 2, there are many compatible elements between scientific and technological achievements and education and teaching, including scientific research methods and talent output, cutting-edge theory and knowledge output, and cutting-edge science and technology and science and technology output. Based on this, we can believe that scientific and technological achievements are intrinsically related to education and teaching, and there is no essential conflict in the transformation of scientific and technological achievements into teaching. However, there are also many influencing factors in the transformation of scientific and technological achievements into teaching, including financial support, guidance mechanism, transformation ability, evaluation, content matching and transformation consciousness, etc., which can be summarized as follows: the consciousness and ability of transforming scientific and technological achievements into teaching are insufficient, the guiding mechanism of transforming scientific and technological achievements into teaching is imperfect, and the scientific and technological achievements do not match the teaching content.

3.1. The Consciousness and Ability of Transforming Scientific and Technological Achievements into Teaching Are Insufficient

Most of the higher vocational colleges in our country are prepared by secondary vocational schools (technical schools) upgrading or holding continuing education adult colleges, it makes the lack of solid foundation and high cultural atmosphere. In recent years, the scientific research team has developed in stages and has formed a certain scale. However, the current scientific research paradigm is generally unable to get rid of the mode of ordinary colleges and universities, ignoring its own characteristics and reality, resulting in the separation of production, education and research [13], the consciousness is not strong, and teachers' ability, development and application is insufficient. Scientific research should mainly focus on teaching, research, the application of related technical fields, applied research and practical activities. However, at present, scientific research is to complete the qualification of professional titles and the task of scientific research evaluation, Scientific research achievements mainly include papers, award-winning results, monographs, teaching materials, patents and project materials, etc. [14]. Due to the existing scientific research mode, the limited research, development ability of teachers, the scientific-technological achievements are mainly biased towards the conclusion of topic and the accumulation of achievements, and few of them have real use value. How to build teachers' team with high level, improve the quality, and promote the transformation are still the direction of higher vocational reform efforts at this stage.

3.2. The Guiding Mechanism for Transforming Scientific and Technological Achievements into Teaching is not Perfect

At present, scientific- technological achievements used in higher vocational teaching generally rely on the purchase and introduction of enterprises. After the resources, which are invested by enterprises in school-enterprise cooperation, are converted into educational resources, there are more specific and difficult to be converted into other uses [15]. and the scientific and technological achievements produced by higher vocational colleges are quite large, but the transformation is very rare, and the application effect is not good. The reasons mainly include the following aspects: First, the direction lacks overall guidance, and the positioning of research and development is not accurate, resulting in the application value is not high, which neither meets the market demand nor is suitable for conversion into teaching resources; Second, the transformation mechanism is not perfect. The existing transformation mechanism is generally aimed at market transformation, and there is no relevant policy mechanism for the transformation to university's teaching. Third, higher vocational colleges lack the cultural atmosphere of science-education integration, from the management to the front-line, teachers are unwilling to break the existing teaching methods, and lack the spirit and motivation of education reform and innovation. Therefore, the primary task is to establish a perfect guiding mechanism.

3.3. Scientific and Technological Achievements Do Not Match the Teaching Content

The phenomenon of mismatch between scientific-technological achievements and teaching content is often encountered, which involves various factors like teachers, teaching materials and scientific and technological achievements themselves. First, it has relatively high-tech quality and professional level. Some teachers lack sufficient scientific-technological knowledge, resulting in the inability to effectively integrate scientific-technological achievements into teaching. Second, textbook construction requires strong foundation and comprehensiveness, as well as high professional degree and complexity [16]. At present, the teaching material writing team is teachers, who are unable to integrate cutting-edge knowledge of science-technology into textbook construction due to their limited ability.Third, scientific- technological achievements are complicated, and they often require certain professional knowledge to understand and apply. Some scientific-technological achievements involve very professional fields with high technical content, which may be beyond the reach of traditional teaching, and not all scientific-technological achievements are suitable for introduction into teaching. Fourth, scientific- technological achievements tend to be applied in practice, while some educational contents pay more attention to theory, which may lead to the difficulty of integrating scientific-technological outcomes into theoretical teaching contents. Therefore, how to improve the matching degree between scientific-technological achievements and teaching content is important.

4. The Breakthrough of the Transformation of Scientific and technological Achievements into Teaching in Higher Vocational Colleges

Mr. Pan Maoyuan, the founder of China's higher education discipline, pointed out that returning to the fundamentals of universities requires returning to the fundamentals of training talents and balancing the relationship between teaching and scientific research [17].Based on this, we can believe that it ultimately needs to be implemented in teaching, that is, in teachers, teaching materials and teaching methods, as shown in Figure 3. And the path to implementation, we can seek solutions from three aspects. We can establish the evaluation system for the transformation of scientific and technological achievements into teaching, improving the policy and financial support for the transformation of scientific and technological achievements into teaching, and improving the integration of scientific and technological achievements with teachers, textbooks and teaching methods.

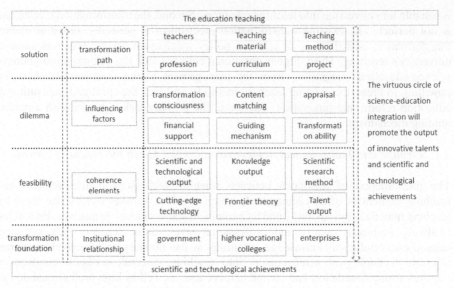

Figure 3. Logical framework model of the transformation of scientific and technological achievements into teaching

4.1. Establish an Evaluation System for Transforming Scientific and Technological Achievements into Teaching

The construction of evaluation system for the transformation of scientific-technological achievements into teaching needs to be considered and comprehensively evaluated from many aspects, including the followings. First, it is necessary to clarify its objectives and positioning, such as improving teaching quality, promoting scientific-technological development, enhancing teachers' scientific-technological research and development ability, and enhancing students' scientific-technological thinking and innovation ability, which are the core elements that need to be considered in constructing the evaluation system. Second, according to the goal, the workflow of the transformation is defined, including the source of scientific-technological achievements, transformation methods, time arrangements, expected results, etc. Third, evaluation indicators should be set up scientifically according to the transformation objectives, positioning and working process. When formulating evaluation indicators, it is necessary to ensure the operability and objectivity of evaluation indicators, and comprehensively consider various factors, such as feedback of students. Fourth, we should implement it, and its effect is evaluated, and the teaching effect data are collected as the basis for adjusting and improving the evaluation indicators.

4.2. We Will Improve Policies and Financial Support for Transforming Scientific and Technological Achievements into Teaching

It needs the joint efforts and support of government, universities, enterprises and all sectors of society to form a concerted and efficient policy force with the same goals, and promote the effective transformation of scientific and technological achievements into teaching. First of all, the government should improve the relevant laws and regulations, policy frameworks and regulatory mechanisms, attract enterprises and institutions to participate in the transformation through various policy means such as tax reduction, increase research and development subsidies, intellectual property protection, and establish an evaluation mechanism and reward mechanism for the scientific-technological achievements transformation, including further streamlining administration and delegating power, streamlining procedures and expanding the independent examination and approval power of universities and colleges. Secondly, the government and universities can set up special funds and attract social capital to participate in the transformation of scientific- technological achievements, the government and schools should also promote the construction of platforms and the development of investment funds, explore a variety of financing models. Finally, universities can cooperate with enterprises to provide practical opportunities for students and improve the quality and effect of teaching.

4.3. Improvement of the Integration of Scientific and Technological Achievements with Teachers, Teaching Materials and Teaching Methods

The core problem is how to improve the scientific-technological achievements integration with teachers, teaching materials and teaching methods.We can start from the aspects of teacher ability improvement training, the development of teaching materials and the innovation of teaching methods. First of all, in terms of teacher ability improvement training, the cultivation and construction of teacher team is a process of continuous "slip" between disciplines and disciplines [18]. The training focuses on the improvement of teachers' scientific-technological literacy and professional comprehensive ability. To encourage them to better integrate scientific-technological research and development into their professional growth; For example, special training, seminars and symposia can be organized to let teachers understand the latest trends and development trends in the frontier of disciplines, learn how to apply scientific-technological achievements in teaching, and improve their teaching level and comprehensive practical ability. Secondly, teaching materials are important carriers for the transformation of scientific -technological achievements into teaching materials. To complete the integration-transformation of scientific and technological achievements into teaching materials, we should adhere to the "docking of teaching materials' content and professional standards" [19], screen scientific-technological achievements and related scientific and technological research methods that match the professional courses, and convert these scientific-technological achievements and scientific-technological research methods into teaching materials' content and teaching resources. The content of teaching materials and scientific-technological achievements are closely integrated to improve the practicability and foresight of teaching materials and teaching resources. For example, organizing professional teachers and researchers to co-write teaching materials and work together to integrate scientific and technological achievements into teaching materials and teaching resources. Finally, as an educational means, science and technology have the value of promoting the innovation of teaching methods, improving teaching efficiency and enhancing teaching interaction [20]. To complete the integration of scientific-technological achievements and teaching methods, we can combine scientific and technological means and tools, actively explore, and innovate teaching methods, and carry out diversified teaching activities, stimulate students' learning interest and enthusiasm, help students master scientific thinking methods and establish scientific world outlook and values. For example, modern teaching means such as virtual reality technology [21, 22] and multimedia technology [23, 24] can be used to transform scientific - technological achievements into visual and interactive teaching resources [25], so as to make teaching activities more vivid, and interesting, enhance students' learning interest and enthusiasm, and thus improve teaching efficiency and quality.

5. Conclusion

In the context of science-education integration, this study builds a logical framework model for the transformation of scientific and technological achievements into teaching based on its essentials, sorts out the institutional relationship, appropriate elements and influencing factors in the transformation of scientific and technological achievements into teaching, and proposes the transformation path to adapt to the requirements of production-education integration and science-education integration, and optimization of the type orientation of vocational education for higher vocational education. The later work will aim at the expansion of logical framework model, the improvement of transformation mechanism and the construction of transformation platform.

Acknowledgment

This project is supported by general project of Guangxi Vocational Education Teaching Reform Research and Practice of Three Education reform in Higher Vocational Education Based on of Science-Education Integration in 2023 (GXGZJG2023B074); Research on the Design and Implementation of Management System for the Transformation of Scientific and Technological Achievements in 2021 (2021KY1925); General project of Vocational Education and Teaching Reform Research in Guangxi in 2020: Research on the Dual Model of Education and Skill Upgrading of New professional Farmers under the Strategy of Rural Revitalization (GXGZJG2020B042).

References

[1] Meng Fanhua, Wang Sidi. Promoting the integration of science and educations: new horizons, new fields, new tracks [J]. Vocational and technical education, 2022, 43(33): 30-34.

[2] Xi Jinping. Speech at the 17th Academician Conference of the Chinese Academy of Sciences and the 12th Academician Conference of the Chinese Academy of Engineering[N]. the People's Daily, 2014-06-10(002).

[3] Xi Jinping. Holding high the great banner of socialism with Chinese characteristics and striving together to build a modern socialist country in an all-round way-report at the 20th National Congress of the Communist Party of China (October 16, 2022) [J]. Party building research, 2022, (11): 2-33.

[4] Bai Yuting, Li Zhongguo. Science-education integration in vocational education: why and what to do[J]. Vocational and technical education, 2023, 44(14): 6-11.

[5] Zhao Zhe. Construction of a long-term mechanism of collaborative innovation between universities and enterprises: from the perspective of university knowledge production[J]. Journal of national academy of education administration, 2023, 301(01): 80-87.

[6] Hua Dongfang. On the logic, dilemma and paths of scientific research governance in vocational colleges from the perspective of science-education integration[J]. Vocational and technical education, 2023, 44(10): 31-36.

[7] Department of Science and Technology of the Ministry of Education of the People's Republic of China. Compilation of Science and Technology Statistics of Colleges and universities in 2018[M]. Beijing: Higher Education Press, 2020, 08 (in Chinese).

[8] Department of Science and Technology of the Ministry of Education of the People's Republic of China. Compilation of Science and Technology Statistics of Colleges and universities in 2019[M]. Beijing: Higher Education Press, 2020, 08 (in Chinese).

[9] Department of Science and Technology of the Ministry of Education of the People's Republic of China. Compilation of Science and Technology Statistics of Colleges and universities in 2020[M]. Beijing: Higher Education Press, 2021, 06 (in Chinese).

[10] Department of Science, Technology, and Information of the Ministry of Education of the People's Republic of China. Compilation of Science and Technology Statistics of Institutions of higher Learning in 2021[M]. Beijing: Higher Education Press, 2022, 04 (in Chinese).

[11] Department of Science, Technology, and Information of the Ministry of Education of the People's Republic of China. Compilation of Science and Technology Statistics of Institutions of higher Learning in 2022[M]. Beijing: Higher Education Press, 2023, 07 (in Chinese).

[12] Zhang Siqi, Kuang Ying. New Positioning, characteristics, and promotion strategy of the science-education integration in vocational education[J]. Vocational Education Forum, 2023, 38(05): 5-12.

[13] Hao Tiancong. Research on innovation of scientific research paradigm in higher vocational colleges under the background of science-education integration[J]. China Vocational and Technical Education, 2023, 838(06): 11-16 (in Chinese).

[14] Zhu Xiaofeng. Study on the mechanism translating research achievement into teaching resources and evaluation system in higher vocational schools[J]. Vocational and Technical Education, 2013, 34(23): 78-81.

[15] Guo Yu, Gong Youkui, Wang Zuopeng. The Attribute, dilemma and path analysis of higher vocational industrialcollege from the perspective of knowledge production mode[J]. Education and Vocational, 2023, 1033(09): 71-74.

[16] Jin Zuxu, Zeng Shaowei. Logical relationship, internal mechanism and practical direction of the reform of "three teachings"based on the synergy of school-enterprise dual subject[J]. Adult Education, 2023, 43(05): 62-68 (in Chinese).

[17] Pan Maoyuan. Back to the basics of the university[J]. Tsinghua Journal of Education, 2015, 36(04): 1-2.

[18] Liu Xiaotong, Liu Shibin. The logic shift of and realization approaches to training top-notch innovative talents from perspective of knowledge production mode transformation[J]. Heilongjiang Researches on Higher Education, 2023, 41(05): 20-26 (in Chinese).

[19] Xu Lan, He Meli, Yi Xiqiong. Practical approach of the reform of three aspects to promote high-quality development of higher vocational education in the digital age[J]. Adult Education, 2023, 43(02): 60-66 (in Chinese).

[20] Zeng Lingqi. A new paradigm for the development of vocational education from the perspective of science-education integration[J]. Vocational and Technical Education, 2023, 44(13): 12-18.

[21] Nimesh Yadav, Aryan Sinha, "Augmented Reality and its Science", International Journal of Education and Management Engineering, 2022, 12(6): 33-44.

[22] Asif A. Laghari, Awais K. Jumani, Kamlesh Kumar, M. Ameen Chhajro, "Systematic Analysis of Virtual Reality & Augmented Reality", International Journal of Information Engineering and Electronic Business, 2021, 13(1): 6-43.

[23] Blessing Dominic-Ugwu, Ogwueleka Francisca Nonyelum, "The Assessment of Multimedia Technology in the Teaching of Mathematics in Secondary Schools in Abuja-Nigeria", International Journal of Modern Education and Computer Science, 2019, 11(6): 8-18.

[24] Chengxun Bei, Jianxin Peng, "Application of Network and Multimedia Technology in University Physical Experiment Teaching", International Journal of Education and Management Engineering, 2012, 2(1): 42-46.

[25] H. Vignesh Ramamoorthy, P. J.Balakumaran, H. Karthikeyani, "An Interactive Teaching – Learning Tool for Underprivileged Children in Rural Schools", International Journal of Modern Education and Computer Science, 2013, 5(7): 27-33.

Artificial Intelligence, Medical Engineering and Education
Z.B. Hu et al. (Eds.)
© *2024 The Authors.*
This article is published online with Open Access by IOS Press and distributed under the terms
of the Creative Commons Attribution Non-Commercial License 4.0 (CC BY-NC 4.0).
doi:10.3233/ATDE231386

Intelligent Upgrading and Transformation of Multimedia Classrooms in Universities Under the Smart Teaching Environment

Lu REN[a], Yuan LI [b,1]

[a] *The Network Information Center, Wuhan University of Technology, Wuhan, China*
[b] *Planning and Discipline Office, Wuhan University of Technology, Wuhan, China*

Abstract. In the context of classroom revolution promoting the transformation of smart teaching environment, to solve the problems of small number of classrooms, few seats, complex equipment operation, and high management difficulty in existing smart classrooms. Based on the concept of intelligent teaching, new technologies such as high-speed networks and intelligent cloud boxes are applied to conduct practical research on the intelligent upgrading and transformation of ordinary multimedia classrooms in universities. On the base of not changing the original equipment, tables, and chairs in the classroom, utilizing the existing teaching resources of the school, adding intelligent teaching functions such as multi-channel projection, multi windows, and live streaming. Since the outbreak of the epidemic, the information technology capabilities of teachers and students and the transformation of teaching methods have greatly improved, promoting the process of intelligent classroom upgrading and transformation, and laying a good foundation for the transformation of more advanced smart classrooms.

Keywords. Smart teaching; Smart teaching environment; Multimedia classrooms; Intelligentization

1. Introduction

Smart teaching has attracted attention and been promoted in various countries around the world [1,2]. It not only requires a change in people's understanding and concepts, but also requires the support of various software and hardware [3-5]. As the main place for teachers and students to teach, the functions and conditions of the classroom have been constantly changing. With the development of information technology, teaching and learning methods have been innovated, and classrooms no longer only have basic requirements for students to see and hear clearly. Many new teaching processes need to be carried out in the classroom [6-9]. In the era of intelligence, the demand for smart teaching is constantly increasing, and building a perfect smart teaching environment as much as possible is also the direction explored by relevant practitioners [10,11]. In recent years, various universities have experienced large-scale and high-cost investment in the construction of "smart classrooms", but the results have been unsatisfactory. Especially in the past three years, driven by the epidemic, the

---

[1] Corresponding Author: Yuan LI, Email: zcyjy@whut.edu.cn

information technology capabilities of teachers and students have been improved, and teaching methods have been constantly changing [12-14]. The use of information technology continues to promote the intelligence and simplification of the teaching process, and the venues and types of smart teaching environment construction are also constantly innovating, enriching, and popularizing [15-17].

As a new, intelligent, and modern teaching system, smart classrooms are an important component of the deeper development of smart campuses. Compared with traditional multimedia classrooms, they are significantly different in terms of characteristics, design ideas, and system composition [18-19].

Smart classrooms are student-centered, enabling interactive teaching methods and sharing of educational resources. The management of classroom teaching is fully intelligent. Most smart classrooms adopt the design concept of multi-dimensional space, changing the traditional spatial layout and better meeting teaching requirements.

As a new, intelligent, and modern teaching system, smart classrooms are based on emerging network information technologies such as cloud computing and the Internet of Things, making classroom teaching more intelligent [20-25].

2. Smart Teaching and Its Environmental Construction

2.1. Interpretation of the Concept of Smart Teaching

The understanding of the concept of smart teaching mostly focuses on the effectiveness of information technology in teaching or is limited to teaching that occurs in the classroom In the era of "Internet plus", the purpose of teaching informatization is to make informatization serve teaching. The role of information technology in teaching is auxiliary rather than leading. In today's context where everyone can learn and everything can be learned, teaching does not just happen in the classroom. Therefore, "smart teaching" can be defined as a new teaching mode before, in and out of class by introducing the "Internet plus + intelligence" technology into the curriculum. Through the overall design of teaching activities, connecting the classroom and improving classroom effectiveness; Use "Internet plus intelligent technology" to collect the data of the whole teaching process, analyze big data, and finally produce the results of optimizing learning behavior.

The smart teaching environment is a place for conducting smart teaching, which includes both physical classroom spaces and virtual spaces such as teaching platforms and teaching big data analysis platforms. There is a relationship between them that is interconnected and integrated with each other. Figure 1 is a summary of the construction architecture of a smart teaching environment based on the definition of smart teaching mentioned above, combined with the weights of each application and its application teaching time period. This model graph can be used to guide the construction of intelligent teaching environments in physical space.

At present, existing research on smart teaching environments mainly elaborates on the composition of smart teaching environments from a theoretical perspective, but there is almost no research on physically connecting these components to form an implementable solution from the perspective of practical construction and application.

2.2. Ordinary Multimedia Classroom

Ordinary multimedia classrooms are the most typical and numerous types of classrooms constructed in universities at present. Its basic components include a central control, desktop computer, projector, screen, power amplifier, and audio system. With the development of information technology, the main composition of such classrooms has remained unchanged, but the equipment performance has been continuously improved, such as the improvement of projector display brightness, the addition of central control functions, and the upgrading of control methods. The characteristics of this type of classroom are low construction cost, short construction period, wide professional coverage, large capacity for students, and simple management and maintenance. However, traditional teaching methods are commonly used in this type of classroom.

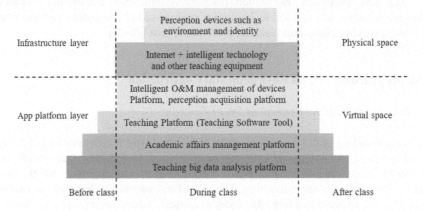

Figure 1. Architecture of Smart Teaching Environment Construction

2.3. Basic Ideas for Intelligent Transformation of Multimedia Classrooms

On the base of not changing the original structure of ordinary multimedia classroom equipment, some intelligent modules with reasonable cost are added, relevant equipment interfaces are expanded, and the existing platform resources of the school are utilized to achieve centralized and flexible scheduling of various teaching resources and centralized access to teaching data. The transformation effect is to empower ordinary multimedia classrooms, increase channels for teacher-student teaching interaction, increase multi scene teaching methods in multimedia classrooms, and facilitate the collection of data throughout the entire teaching process.

3. Current Research Status of Multimedia Classrooms

In the Superstar Discovery System, two keywords of multimedia and classroom were input, with a limit of 2013-2022. A total of 6768 journals were retrieved, including 323 important ones. After screening the 323 journals, 148 were closely related to the construction, management, and application of multimedia classrooms in universities. Through Figure 2, the research enthusiasm for multimedia classrooms is decreasing year by year, indicating a low level of academic research in terms of the number of important entries. Classifying the research content of 148 selected journals, the research and practice of software and hardware in multimedia classrooms remains a key focus of research.

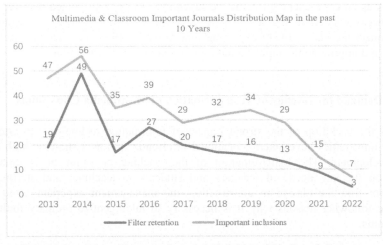

Figure 2. Trend chart of important journals included in multimedia and classrooms

Statistical analysis was conducted on the research content of 148 important indexed journals, which were mainly divided into three categories: multimedia classroom software and hardware construction, subject and information technology teaching application, and classroom management.

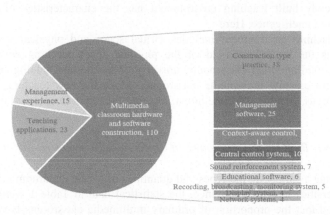

Figure 3. Proportion of research on important journals included in multimedia classrooms in universities

Based on the previous data analysis, Figure 3 can be obtained. Among the 110 studies on the software and hardware construction of multimedia classrooms, a total of 36 were focused on individual systems in the classroom, such as display systems, central control systems, and sound reinforcement systems, accounting for a relatively small proportion and concentrated in 2015 and before. The practical research on the overall construction type of classrooms has been on the rise since 2016, with the goal of exploring a new teaching environment under the background of deep integration of information technology and education. Typically, the rise and construction wave of the concept of smart classrooms. However, by 2020, the research on the construction of teaching environments for smart classroom types has significantly decreased, with more focus on core teaching interactive functions The concept guided research on the full process collection and analysis of teaching data has increased. Construction practitioners are also actively exploring innovative practices in teaching venues and modes, and improving the input-output ratio of classroom construction.

4. The Demand for Intelligent Transformation of Multimedia Classrooms

Against the backdrop of the strong impact of information technology on education, various universities have taken educational informatization as a strategic high ground for development. The transformation of the teaching environment is imperative. Based on the key needs of teachers and students in teaching, and starting from long-term frontline classroom construction and management experience, the author lists the following reasons why it is necessary to intelligentize ordinary multimedia classrooms.

4.1. Classroom Revolution Promotes the Transformation of Smart Teaching Environment

Reform is the fundamental driving force for the development of education. The "Education Informatization 2.0 Action Plan" proposed in 2018 clearly points out the tasks and requirements of building a smart learning support environment and accelerating the construction of an intelligent teaching support environment.

The newly built teaching environment has the characteristics of universality, flexibility, and intelligence. Here

The teaching environment includes virtual space and physical space, and the classroom is the main battlefield of the physical space teaching environment. In addition to building smart classrooms, universities should also intelligently empower and transform existing multimedia classrooms. Make the new teaching environment more ubiquitous, flexible, and intelligent, meeting the requirements outlined in the 2.0 action plan.

4.2. The Newly Built Smart Classrooms in Universities Have not Yet Met the Demand

By conducting a survey on the types and quantities of public classroom construction in seven universities in Hubei Province, the statistical data in Table 1 were obtained. It can be found that the proportion of ordinary multimedia classrooms is very high, far exceeding the capacity of smart classrooms, and is the main part of the teaching venue. During the interview, it was learned that the relatively high construction cost and limited construction funds of smart classrooms have led to a slowdown in the construction process of smart classrooms. Teachers are very eager to use smart classrooms in their hearts, but the number is limited and appointments cannot be made. Those teachers who have used smart classrooms have reported that the technological span is too large, leading to unfamiliarity in operation, and the transformation of teaching methods requires a process of adaptation. The result is that teachers and students have transformed smart classrooms into advanced multimedia classrooms; Constrained by technological operations, classroom efficiency is obviously reduced.

Considering both cost and effectiveness, it is a practical, compromise, and effective approach to intelligently transform ordinary multimedia classrooms that are currently widely used.

Table 1. Statistics of Survey Results on the Construction and Management of Public Classrooms in Seven Universities

Type of the University	985 Universities		211 Universities		Undergraduate		higher voca-tional
University	A	B	C	D	E	F	G
Number of Multimedia classrooms	520	322	491	172	299	80	350
Number of smart classrooms	77	116	74	77	5	0	4
Number of students	59,8 00	56,000	59,8 00	29,000	20,700	20,000	21,000
Number of classroom management staff	38	3	38	2	3	3	3

4.3. The Use Effect of Existing Smart Classrooms is not Ideal

After investigating the usage of smart classrooms in the seven universities mentioned above, the following drawbacks were found:

(1) High construction cost;

(2) The design scheme of the product provider fails to fully meet the school's usage requirements, and the resource utilization rate is not high;

(3) Various teaching and recording platforms have existed in the form of data silos and cannot be integrated into teaching big data;

(4) The operation is complex and visually pleasing, but in reality it is only a continuation of ordinary multimedia classrooms;

(5) The effectiveness of using smart classrooms is highly correlated with the subjective initiative of teachers;

(6) The number of smart classrooms in various schools is generally insufficient, large class teaching is still the norm, and the progress of teaching reform is slow.

4.4. Increased Difficulty in Managing Smart Classrooms

Smart classrooms not only require high information technology skills from teachers, but also put forward high requirements for the management methods and personnel abilities of the classroom operation and maintenance department. The number of management personnel has increased, and the cost of equipment maintenance and repair has also increased. The management and training of various teaching software have also become a new focus.

4.5. Public Classrooms Need to Meet Various Usage Needs

Transforming a multimedia classroom into a smart classroom requires changing fixed tables and chairs into movable ones, resulting in a significant reduction in the number of seats in the classroom and potentially reducing the number of standardized exam rooms. For schools that often undertake various exams in the examination center, the transformation of public multimedia classrooms not only affects teaching, but also affects the development of other activities such as exams and competitions.

4.6. Epidemic Prevention and Control Promote Classroom Renovation, New Demands Provide New Ideas for Classroom Renovation

The epidemic in 2020 forced countless teachers and students to switch from offline teaching to online teaching. The transformation of teaching models has led to a significant improvement in the information technology capabilities of teachers and students, invisibly accelerating the pace of classroom revolution, promoting the transformation of the teaching environment, and providing new ideas and driving forces for classroom transformation.

4.7. 5G Empowers Classrooms to Achieve Optimal Results in Intelligent Transformation

In the 5G era, achieve full connectivity between people and things, and create an ecosystem of cross industry integration. For the field of education, whether it is the construction of smart classrooms or the intelligent transformation of classrooms, the essence is interconnectivity, breaking data silos, rapid data transmission and feedback processing. 5G entering the campus is an inevitable and necessary trend, which provides strong support for the popularization of smart teaching environments and a good user experience.

5. Specific Implementation Path for Intelligent Transformation of Ordinary Multimedia Classrooms

This article takes the intelligent transformation of multimedia classrooms at W University as an example to explore the construction ideas and practical achievements. After feeling the importance and urgency of the transformation task, the teaching environment construction department of W University formed a professional team, formulated relevant work plans, and gradually implemented the intelligent transformation and use of multimedia classrooms.

5.1. Multi Party Collaboration and Transformation Emerged as the Times Require

Education informatization has moved from 1.0 to 2.0, and practitioners and researchers have gradually realized that the plans and ideas for education informatization construction should not be determined by a certain department or product supplier of the school, but should be based on the actual needs and humanized experience of the school and teachers and students, truly meeting teaching needs.

After extensive research in the early stage and clarifying the pain points and difficulties in classroom construction, the teaching environment construction department of W University took the lead in proposing the idea of intelligent transformation of ordinary multimedia classrooms. In the implementation process, not only are relevant classroom construction and management technical talents equipped, but also TPACK vanguard revolutionary teachers are selected based on the characteristics of the discipline in conjunction with the school's Teacher Development Center. These teachers are used as information construction teacher experts, and based on existing school teaching policies and requirements, they participate in the early stage of information construction demand discussions, off campus research, scheme argumentation, later project acceptance, use training, and other processes, Figure 4 shows the workflow diagram of intelligent transformation.

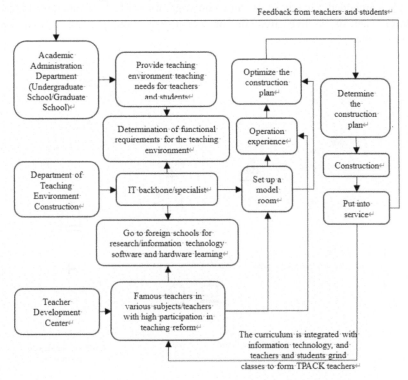

Figure 4. Workflow for Intelligent Transformation of Ordinary Multimedia Classrooms

5.2. Clarify Requirements and Continuously Clarify Transformation Plans

The transformation has only one purpose, which is to fully tap the potential of existing classroom software and hardware under the premise of limited funding. The specific main functional requirements include achieving interconnectivity between classrooms and achieving 1+N one-way and two-way interactive classrooms; Including functions such as group discussion, group interaction, and multi-channel screen projection, providing technical support for the mixed teaching reform of small and large classes; Implement remote course inspection; Easy for teachers to operate and staff to maintain and manage; Compatible with multiple brand devices.

In the topology diagram of the intelligent transformation equipment connection in Figure 5, the original ordinary multimedia classroom equipment still exists and still serves as the main service for classroom teaching. In terms of hardware, only the intelligent cloud box module will be added, and then relevant circuit adjustments and connections will be made. From a software perspective, add an interface window to achieve scheduling, display, and teaching assistance functions: equivalent to a bridge, it can concentrate various applications (such as W University's existing teaching platforms such as Superstar, Youmuke, YuClassroom, Tencent Conference, Office, and other teaching tool software, as well as teacher and student projection screens) in one interface for multi window display. During the teaching process, this window does not generate any teaching data, and the data is still mainly based on the teaching platform used by teachers and students, truly achieving soft and hard separation. At the same time, the embedded window tools can compensate for the lack of functions in teaching platforms such as no live streaming or screen projection, playing a good teaching assistance effect.

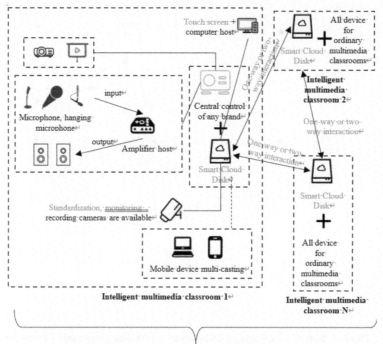

Figure 5. Topology diagram of intelligent transformation equipment connection in ordinary multimedia classrooms

    In the process of formulating and demonstrating the classroom renovation plan, TPACK pioneer teachers were invited to conduct on-site practical operations. The teachers all reported that the operation was simple and practical, especially the experience of using multi window and projection functions was good. After the classroom renovation, 30 classrooms in the two campuses of W University were successfully guaranteed to receive the same class of new student enrollment education during the epidemic period.

5.3. Optimization of Details to Enhance the User Experience for Teachers and Students

To enhance the user experience of teachers and students, it is recommended to optimize from the following details. (1) Change the teacher's computer display screen to a touch screen. Due to the need for multi window scheduling, after changing to a touch screen, the teacher can freely drag and move the content to be displayed, providing a better experience; (2) The tilt angle of the touch screen and the bracket that carries the touch screen must be selected in accordance with the humanized usage habits of teachers, and the stability of the bracket must be ensured. When selecting the type, the focus should be on the material and fatigue testing frequency; (3) Network security: For live streaming or classroom interaction needs, classroom computers must have a running speed of 100 megabytes or above to obtain a good user experience; (4) Only by increasing the training of teachers and forming usage habits can we improve the input-output ratio of construction.

6. Conclusion

The smart teaching environment has never been composed solely of software and hardware, with a focus on breaking data silos, connecting multiple applications, and constructing the collection and analysis of teaching data throughout the entire process. At the same time, it should also be designed and constructed based on the needs of teachers and students, course nature, teaching mode, and other factors. The intelligent transformation of classrooms in W School has achieved results and gained experience in promotion, laying the foundation for teachers and students to use a high-quality information-based teaching environment.

After preliminary intelligent empowerment of ordinary multimedia classroom equipment, the next construction idea is to explore and practice the fixed desks and chairs in ordinary multimedia classrooms, which can meet the switching between group discussions in physical space and normalized teaching modes; And how to intelligently transform the old smart classroom. Intended to play a better role in achieving talent cultivation goals under the new situation.

Acknowledgment

This study received support from two funds: (1) Hubei Province Teaching Research Project " Improving the Teaching Academic Ability of New Engineering Teachers under the Background of First-Class Engineering Construction" (2021107); (2) Wuhan University of Technology Independent Innovation Research Fund Project (No. 2020IVB071)

References

[1]　Wang X., Zhang J., Liu W. The value orientation of teaching reform in the era of smart education[J]. Overview of Educational Theory (English), 2021, (2): 47-52.
[2]　Ilic-Kosanovic T, Ili D, Bulaji S ,et al. New Methodology of Teaching a Smart City Concept: A Case Study[J]. International Journal of Engineering Education, 2021, 37(1): 204.
[3]　Cheng Min. Construction of smart classrooms in an information environment[J]. Modern Education Technology, 2016, (02): 101-107 (in Chinese).
[4]　An Ning, Niu Aifang, Qi Ruihong, Jia Yagang. Exploration and reflection on the construction of smart classrooms in universities[J]. Experimental Technology and Management, 2017 (5): 247-251 (in Chinese).

[5]   Liu Chen, Li Guodong, Zhang Zhe, et al. Construction and research of smart classrooms in universities: Taking Xi'an Jiaotong University as an example[J]. Modern Education Technology, 2018, (10): 70-75 (in Chinese).

[6]   Cai Y. Y. Research and application of smart classroom in surgical practice teaching[J]. Contemporary Education Research, 2022, 6(7): 54-61.

[7]   Bruning M. Flex-STEx. An insight into the development of a flexible smart textiles experience kit for teaching engineering students in an innovative way[J]. Advances in Science and Technology, 2022, 113: 217 - 222.

[8]   Alyousify A. L., Mstafa R. J. AR-assisted children book for smart teaching and learning of turkish alphabets[J]. Virtual Reality & Intelligent Hardware, 2022, 4(3): 263-277.

[9]   Pingxiao W. Research on the English teaching and autonomous learning based on multimedia platform and smart classroom system[J]. International Journal of Smart Home, 2016, 10(9): 373-384.

[10] Wanjiang H., Zhuoyan H., Yifan T., et al. Practice exploration of blended teaching based on smart classroom[J]. Computer Education, 2022(12): 60-67 (in Chinese).

[11] JI Hong, Wangye, Yanzhiming. Analysis on the teaching model of smart classroom in the pre-construction of economics course in Xinjiang Agricultural University[J]. Foreign Language Version: Education Science, 2022, (1): 105-110.

[12] Fati W. U., Hao T., Shurui G. Smart education form under digital transformation in education: key features and generating ways[J]. Frontiers of Education in China, 2023, 18(1): 19-27 (in Chinese).

[13] Cai M. Research on postgraduate classroom construction framework from the perspective of smart education[J]. Contemporary Education Research, 2023, 7(3): 35-42.

[14] Qin H. The Fusion and Construction Strategy of Smart Sports and Traditional Sports Teaching Mode in College and Universities[J]. Overview of Educational Theory (English), 2021, 004(003): 46-50.

[15] He G. Schema interaction visual teaching based on smart classroom environment in art course[J]. International Journal of Emerging Technologies in Learning (iJET), 2020, 15(17): 252.

[16] Terzieva V., Ilchev S., Todorova K. The role of internet of things in smart education[J]. IFAC-PapersOnLine, 2022, 55(11): 108-113.

[17] Domermuth D. Creating a smart classroom[J]. Tech Directions, 2005, 64: 21-22.

[18] Suo Y., Miyata N., Morikawa H., et al. Open smart classroom: extensible and scalable learning system in smart space using web service technology[J]. IEEE Transactions on Knowledge & Data Engineering, 2009, 21(6): 814-828.

[19] Yang Zongkai. Promoting the deep integration of information technology and education[J]. Chinese Journal of Education, 2016, (11): 1 (in Chinese).

[20] Liu Zhiwen, Qian Zhen. Research on the design and application of "quasi smart" classrooms in the "Internet plus" Era[J]. Modern Educational Technology, 2019, (12): 68-74 (in Chinese).

[21] Wu Di, Wang Jun, Wang Meiqian et al. Analysis of the evolution and trends of classroom teaching environment from the perspective of technological development[J]. Open Education Research, 2022 (5): 49-54 (in Chinese).

[22] Long S., Zhao X. Smart teaching mode based on particle swarm image recognition and human-computer interaction deep learning[J]. Journal of Intelligent and Fuzzy Systems, 2020, 39(4): 5699-5711.

[23] Umang Dhuri, Nilakshi Jain. "Teaching Assessment Tool: Using AI and Secure Techniques", International Journal of Education and Management Engineering, Vol.10, No.3, pp.12-21, 2020.

[24] Salako E. Adekunle, Adewale Olumide S., Boyinbode Olutayo K., " Appraisal on Perceived Multimedia Technologies as Modern Pedagogical Tools for Strategic Improvement on Teaching and Learning", International Journal of Modern Education and Computer Science, Vol.11, No.8, pp. 15-26, 2019.

[25] Ramachandra Rao. Kurada, Karteeka Pavan. Kanadam, "A Novel Evolutionary Automatic Data Clustering Algorithm using Teaching-Learning-Based Optimization", International Journal of Intelligent Systems and Applications, Vol.10, No.5, pp.61-70, 2018.

Artificial Intelligence, Medical Engineering and Education
Z.B. Hu et al. (Eds.)
© 2024 The Authors.
doi:10.3233/ATDE231387

Exploration and Practice of Road Engineering Course Teaching Innovation Based on IOPM

Jie SHANG[a], Ting JIANG[b,1], Ahmad Nazrul Hakimi Ibrahim[c], Yanzhi PANG[a]

[a] *Department of Traffic and Transportation, College of Traffic and Transportation,*
Nanning University, Nanning, 530000, China
[b] *China-ASEAN Institute of Statistics, Guangxi University of Finance and Economics,*
Nanning, 530000, China
[c] *Department of Civil Engineering, Faculty of Engineering and Built Environment,*
University Kebangsaan Malaysia, Bangi, 43600, Malaysia

Abstract. In response to the problems in talent cultivation and curriculum teaching, this paper analyzes the pain points in the current situation of curriculum teaching - traditional "teaching" and traditional "learning" teaching, including textbook writing, teaching objectives, teaching organization, and teaching evaluation; An analysis was conducted on students' learning methods, motivation, and goals. We have proposed a breakthrough in traditional innovative concepts and ideas, as well as an implementation path - IOPM, which is guided by ideological education, output-based education, project-based learning, and a multi-dimensional evaluation index system. The application of the IOPM model in teaching practice has verified the feasibility and promotion value of this teaching innovation path. Reflected on the weak points in teaching innovation practice and proposed prospects for continuously promoting teaching innovation.

Keywords. course teaching; Teaching innovation; Teaching pain points; Teaching evaluation

1. Introduction

Talent cultivation means future development and hope for every country [1]. Using a small incision in curriculum reform to drive and solve the major problems of talent cultivation models, and achieving strong breakthroughs in higher education reform, innovation, and development, is a requirement put forward by the Higher Education Department of the Ministry of Education of the People's Republic of China in the key work points for the education industry in 2023 [2]. Since the famous psychologist Carl Rogers first proposed the teaching concept of "student-centered" in the middle of the last century, this concept has been recognized by educators and various curriculum reform practices have been carried out around it [3-5].

Improving the curriculum system, promoting curriculum reform, and carrying out innovative practices in teaching methods, teaching methods, and assessment methods have received high attention from the education community [6-8]. Strengthening the

---

[1] Corresponding Author: Ting JIANG, E-mail: 2158655849@qq.com.

construction of course groups and building virtual teaching and research rooms has also been proven to be very effective methods by many universities' teaching practices [9-12]. Implementing the integration of industry and education, through cooperation between schools and enterprises, creates more opportunities for talent cultivation, and various schools have made tremendous efforts to this end [13-16]. Vigorously promoting the "classroom revolution", eliminating "water courses", creating "gold courses", putting students at the center, and effectively improving the quality of students' learning are requirements put forward by the Ministry of Education for schools, and have also become conscious actions of school staff [17-20]. The improvement of education level and the rapid progress of outstanding talents are just around the corner.

2. Analysis of The Current Situation and Breakthrough Ideas Under the Principle of H-I-C

2.1. Current Situation of Curriculum Teaching - Obstacles to Achieving " H-I-C "

High-order, Innovation, and Challenge, which are abbreviated as H-I-C, and regarded as the standard for the construction of the "Golden Course" [21, 22].

High order refers to the organic integration of knowledge, abilities, and qualities, cultivating students' comprehensive abilities and advanced thinking. Innovation refers to the cutting-edge and contemporary nature of course content. Challenge refers to the degree to which a course must have a certain level of difficulty to stimulate students' vitality and potential. 'H-I-C' is the standard for 'Golden Class'. The traditional teaching mode has hindered the achievement of H-I-C.

(1) Traditional "teaching"

From the perspective of "teaching", "tradition" is mainly reflected in the following aspects:

1) Textbook writing: Most textbooks have similar structures, with a focus on explaining standard clauses, deducing and explaining principles, but not on guiding the application of knowledge systems [23];

2) Teaching objectives: Teachers spend a lot of classroom time helping students achieve general goals such as explaining concepts and principles while teaching, neglecting or having no time to challenge higher order goals;

3) Teaching organization: When teachers teach, they focus on the teacher and focus on teaching methods, lacking innovation. Not motivating students to actively explore and challenge;

4) Teaching evaluation: The evaluation of students is only based on the final exam scores, and the weight of process assessment results is low, without paying attention to students' evaluation of teachers.

(1) Traditional 'learning'

From the perspective of students, the main issues are:

1) Student learning methods: Some students overly rely on traditional classroom teaching with teacher explanations, neglecting pre class knowledge reserves and post class consolidation and improvement.

2) Students' learning motivation: Some students' learning motivation comes from the pressure of exams, rather than from the endogenous motivation generated by the improvement of their own understanding.

3) Students' learning goals: Some students, in their studies, are afraid of challenges, dare not innovate, do not engage in exploratory learning, and do not pursue the achievement of high-level goals.

2.2. "Breaking" and "Establishing" in the Teaching Revolution

There is a saying called 'never break, never stand'. The same is true for education. It is necessary to analyze the obstacles in the process of career progress to overcome them, clear the way forward, and make development and progress smoother. Based on the previous analysis of the problems from different perspectives of teachers and students, we can identify the underlying reasons and propose targeted solutions.

Taking the compulsory course "*Basic Theory and Technology of Road Engineering*" for transportation majors as an example, this paper evaluates the achievement of teaching objectives and provides feedback on the effectiveness from the perspectives of course ideological and political guidance, ability and achievement orientation, project-based learning methods, and the construction of a multi-dimensional evaluation index system.

3. Conception and Practice of Teaching Innovation

The teaching innovation [24-27] of the course adopts IOPM as the implementation path. Guided by ideological education in the curriculum, using moral education to stimulate students' endogenous motivation and drive the improvement of professional knowledge and skills. Design a teaching framework based on output-based education and ability. Starting from Project Based Learning, deconstructing, and reconstructing teaching content, designing and implementing teaching. Using a multi-dimensional evaluation index system as the starting point, evaluate the achievement of teaching objectives and provide feedback on the effectiveness.

3.1 "Ideological Education" is Taken as the Leading

Breaking through the tradition of students' learning motivation, by refining and sorting out the ideological and political elements of the course, identifying the connection points between ideological and political elements and teaching content, constructing a course ideological and political case library and a course ideological and political element mapping table, building a course ideological and political teaching implementation system, and integrating ideological and political elements into teaching design, as shown in Table 1. Using the achievements of moral education to stimulate students' internal motivation for learning is reflected in promoting the improvement of professional knowledge and skills in action.

Based on the above concepts and ideas, a mapping table for the ideological and political elements of the curriculum has been designed, as shown in Table 1.

Table 1. Mapping of ideological and political elements in the course

Course section	Teaching unit	Moral education elements
Design Basis	Introduction to General Theory	Macro: By analyzing the development process of road engineering in the world and China, we showcase the tremendous achievements of road engineering in China, enhance students' sense of pride and professional identity, and enhance patriotism and four confidences.
	Project 1 Road Plan and Vertical Section Design	Mid view: Establishing a scientific development concept and enhancing professional identity. Micro level: rigorous and pragmatic scientific attitude, love for hometown, serve Guangxi, and contribute to the construction of hometown.
Construction and maintenance knowledge	Project 1: Design of subgrade and pavement	Macro: patriotism and international perspective. Mid range: Innovation awareness and professionalism. Micro level: proactive learning, hardworking, proactive innovation, and pursuit of excellence
	Project 2: Discussion on Construction Technology of Roadbed and Pavement	Mid view: Team collaboration Micro level: rigorous and pragmatic work attitude
	Project 3: Maintenance and Management of Roadbed and Pavement	Macro: National pride Mid view: Scientific development concept, closely integrating personal career planning with national development and construction Micro level: High sense of responsibility, hardworking, and craftsman spirit of loving, protecting, and maintaining roads
Design Skills	Project 1: Practical Operation of Road Horizontal, Vertical, and Cross Section Design	Macro: Four Confidences Micro level: fearless of difficulties, pioneering and innovative qualities, and a spirit of craftsmanship that strives for excellence

3.2. Output-Based Education is Taken as the Leading

Breaking through the tradition of teaching objectives and learning methods. Distinguish between general learning objectives and higher-order objectives, emphasize the " H-I-C " of the curriculum, and design a teaching framework. A generative teaching model that emphasizes students as the main body of knowledge construction, with a student-centered approach. Using an information-based teaching platform as the medium, a blended teaching approach of "on the front line+off the middle line+off the line" is adopted. Students achieve general goals through learning on the front line, while off the line learning approaches high-level goals according to different levels of ability. After class, online learning completes the achievement, consolidation, and evaluation of high-level goals.

3.3 Project-Based Learning (PBL) is Taken as the Orientation

Breaking through the tradition of textbook writing and teaching organization. According to the scenario requirements of PBL, the course content is deconstructed and restructured into three project scenarios based on the characteristics of the entire life cycle of road engineering, as shown in Table 1. Systematize the course content based on usage functions. In the implementation of teaching, teaching activities based on POPPS and flipped classrooms are organized, using teaching methods such as discussion and smart ambassadors, emphasizing student-centered participatory and experiential learning. Enable students to learn by doing and learn by doing and gain true feelings through learning and doing. While the level of knowledge and ability has improved, it has also achieved the goals of ideological and political education.

3.4. A Multi-Dimensional Evaluation Index System is Taken as a Foothold

3.4.1. Evaluation Index System for Students' Achievement of H-I-C

Breaking through the tradition of teaching evaluation, is has been customized a multi-dimensional process evaluation index system for students, including online, in class, and after class, to reflect the achievement of learning objectives objectively and truthfully in three aspects, as shown in Table 2.

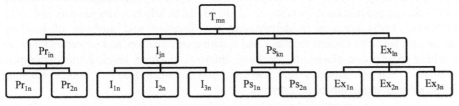

Figure 1. Evaluation index system for achieving H-I-C

Table 2. Evaluation Index System and Weight Assignment of "H-I-C"

Evaluation Indicators	Description	Weight (%)
T_{mn}	Evaluation Results	
Pr_{in}	Pre-class Evaluation	
Pr_{1n}	Preview Video Watching Progress	10
Pr_{2n}	Pre-class Test Scores	10
I_{jn}	In-class Evaluation	
I_{1n}	Attendance	5
$I2n$	Mutual Evaluation Among Students	20
$I3n$	Projects Participation	15
$Pskn$	Post-class Evaluation	
$Ps1n$	Post-class Test Scores	10
$Ps2n$	Teacher's Evaluation of the Projects	30
$Exln$	Extra Scores	
$Ex1n$	Participation in Research Projects	0-5
$Ex2n$	Awarded Prizes Related to the Course	1-5
$Ex3n$	Publication of Papers and Patents	1-5

The parameters involved in the table 2 have the following values:

$i=1，2；j=1, 2, 3；k=1, 2, 3；m=Pr, I, Ps；n=1, 2, 3.$

$$\sum Pr_{in}=20 \tag{1}$$

$$\sum I_{jn}=40 \tag{2}$$

$$\sum Ps_{kn}=40 \tag{3}$$

$$\sum T_{mn}\leq100 \tag{4}$$

3.4.2. Teacher Teaching Evaluation

In addition to evaluating students, combined with the use of Mid term Student Feedback (MSF) consulting services. Counselors conduct classroom observation, collect student feedback, and provide corresponding teaching advice to help teachers identify and solve problems. Assist teachers in determining the direction and methods of teaching adjustment based on student feedback and teaching consultation, and implement them in teaching to improve classroom teaching, improve teaching level, achieve two-way evaluation between students and teachers, and facilitate teachers' timely teaching reflection and improvement adjustments.

4. Analysis of Teaching Innovation Achievements

4.1. Analysis of Course Assessment Quality

The teaching reform practice takes 2018 students as the control group, 2019 and 2020 students as the control group, with the average score as the observation point. Through the implementation of teaching reform, the average scores of students in both 2019 and 2020 levels have significantly improved, as presented in Figure 2.

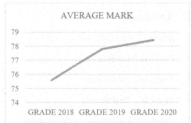

Figure 2. Growth chart of average score of final overall evaluation of road engineering theory and technology from 2018 to 2019

4.2. Student Feedback

The final student evaluation results showed that most students reported that the learning of the course was highly challenging and participatory, and the process was very difficult.

After class, they spent a lot of time, but when they saw their achievements, they felt very fulfilled. I feel like a true designer and construction technician, realizing that the work is not easy and cannot be a bit careless or casual. Feel your own shortcomings and spend more time learning to make up for them in the future.

4.3 Promotion Value

The curriculum emphasizes the output of abilities and achievements, with a student-centered approach and emphasis on students' autonomous knowledge construction, closely linked to the ideological and political aspects of the curriculum. The innovative concepts, ideas, and implementation paths of this course have been promoted to courses such as "Engineering Surveying" and "Traffic Investigation and Analysis", and initial results have been achieved. These courses have successively been approved by the school level curriculum construction project. The methods of course content reconstruction, course organization, and academic evaluation are all universal and applicable to many courses, with strong promotion value.

5. Conclusion

The objectives of this course possess a certain level of sophistication, innovation, and challenge. The teaching content has been restructured in a project-based manner, with a certain depth and breadth, seamlessly connecting with job positions, making students feel more engaged. During the implementation process, the curriculum design emphasizes participatory and experiential learning, cultivates students' autonomous learning and collaborative communication abilities, stimulates their innovative thinking, and embodies the idea of cultivating morality and cultivating people, as well as the educational and teaching philosophy of "student-centered and output oriented". The content and methods of assessment and evaluation are relatively innovative, strengthening the process assessment and the evaluation of achieving high-level goals and ideological and political goals. This course has been taught to three students and has been continuously improved and enhanced in teaching practice.

However, the starting point of online learning and evaluation before and after class is to appropriately increase students' burden and achieve the goal of high order. The quality of its completion directly affects the effectiveness of classroom teaching. However, the formation of students' endogenous learning motivation requires a certain amount of time. When students' endogenous learning motivation is still insufficient and their awareness of extracurricular learning is poor, it is necessary to add certain external measures to ensure the effectiveness of extracurricular online learning to achieve good complementarity between online, offline, and in class and out of class. In this regard, more extensive exploration should be carried out.

The development of information technology is advancing rapidly, and the research results in education and teaching are also changing day by day. Teaching work should also keep up with the trend of the times, carry out continuous reform and innovation. Teaching innovation work has a heavy and long way to go and requires continuous exploration and practice by educators.

Acknowledgment

This project is supported by Key Projects of 14th Five-Year Plan of Guangxi Education Science for Private Higher Education in 2022—Research on Optimizing the Evaluation System of Civics Teaching in Private Colleges and Universities (2022ZJY3163); and The First Batch of High-level Teaching Team Cultivation Program of Nanning College (2021JXTDPY04).

References

[1]   Eliseev A L. Formation of personnel training system for the sphere of state youth policy in the late xx-early xxi centuries[J]. Journal of Public and Municipal Administration, 2020, 9(1):110-118.

[2]   Department of Higher Education of the Ministry of Education of the People's Republic of China Key Points for the Work of the Higher Education Department of the Ministry of Education in 2023 [DB/OL] http://www.moe.gov.cn/s78/A08/tongzhi/202303/t20230329_1053339.html.

[3]   Zhang Xiaoqi, Zhong Mengyuan, Feng Yinghao. Construction and practice of "one main and two wings" teaching system for mechanical majors based on OBE concept[J]. Journal of Changchun Normal University, 2022, 41(6): 134-138.

[4]   Zhao Cunyou, Chen Guojing, Xu Peng. Design of practical teaching system for mechanical majors based on OBE concept[J]. Heilongjiang Education (Theory and Practice), 2022, (4): 84-86.

[5]   Xu Xuelin. Construction of a practical teaching system for mechanical majors based on OBE concept[J]. Internal Combustion Engines and Parts, 2021, (2): 236-237.

[6]   Han Bing, Wang Liwei. Construction of computer professional group curriculum system based on "School Enterprise Management"[J]. Communication and Information Technology, 2023, (05): 112-114 (in Chinese).

[7]   Liu Li, Yi Lilan, Rao Libing, etc. Exploring the implementation path of promoting the "classroom teaching revolution" in applied local undergraduate colleges[J]. Journal of Higher Education, 2022, 8 (35): 148-151, 155 (in Chinese).

[8]   Liu Fang, Yao Li, Liu Bin, etc. Research on graduate classroom teaching strategies from the perspective of constructivism[J]. Journal of Higher Education Research, 2020, 43 (04): 103-106 (in Chinese).

[9]   Jia Haiyan, Liu Xiaomin. Research on the reform of professional group talent training mode based on modular teaching - taking the professional group of building steel structure technology as an example[J]. Journal of Changjiang Engineering Vocational and Technical College, 2023, 40 (03): 40-43 (in Chinese).

[10] Luo Yao and Tan Qibing. A study on the value co creation path and evaluation of professional groups matched to industrial groups[J]. Occupational Technology, 2023, 22 (11): 56-63 (in Chinese).

[11] Liu Hui, Feng Xiumeng. Exploring the construction path of a new organizational system for virtual teaching and research offices in the era of "intelligence+"[J]. Chinese University Teaching, 2023, (08): 82-91 (in Chinese).

[12] Li Ming, Liu Yonghua, Ma Mingxiao, Sun Li. Research on the construction of virtual teaching and research rooms in universities under the background of academic community[J]. Health Vocational Education, 2023, 41 (15): 3-6 (in Chinese).

[13] Li Qiaojun, Wang Wei, Zhu Qi. Research and practice on the modular curriculum system of "four positions and four capabilities" in the electronic communication professional group under the background of industry education integration[J]. Journal of Anhui Electronic Information Vocational and Technical College, 2023, 22 (03): 61-64 (in Chinese).

[14] Jiang W., Guofeng Z, Shuyang W. Teaching reform path of architecture specialty under the collaborative education of "production, teaching and research" and its application effect[J]. Landscape Research: English Version, 2021, 13(5): 3.

[15] Ma J. Analysis of the collaborative education system of local universities under the fundamentals of "Emerging Engineering Education"construction[J]. Contemporary Education Research, 2021, 5(5): 5.

[16] Zhang Yanyan, Huang Na, Guo Rui. Research on the practical teaching system of logistics engineering in applied universities - based on the integration of industry and education[J]. Logistics Engineering and Management, 2023, 45 (07): 196-200 (in Chinese).

[17] Wu Yan. Building China's "Golden Course"[J]. Chinese University Teaching, 2018, (12): 4-9 (in Chinese).

[18] Wu Yan. Bravely standing at the forefront and empowering the future - Leading the transformation of higher education with the construction of Emerging Engineering Education disciplines[J]. Higher Engineering Education Research, 2020, (02): 1-5 (in Chinese).

[19] Inkeri Rissanen, Elina Kuusisto, Eija Hanhimäki, et al. The implications of teachers' implicit theories for moral education: A case study from Finland[J]. Journal of Moral Education, 2018, 47(1): 63-77.

[20] Megan Barnard, Emma Whitt, Stephanie McDonald. Learning objectives and their effects on learning and assessment preparation: insights from an undergraduate psychology course[J]. Assessment & Evaluation in Higher Education, 2021, 46(5): 673-684.

[21] Coulter Robert W. S., Onufer Lindsay. Using student-led discussions and snapshot lectures to stimulate active learning and accountability: a mixed methods study on teaching an implementation science course[J]. Pedagogy in Health Promotion, 2022, 8(1): 30-40.

[22] Jöran Petersson,Judy Sayers,Paul Andrews. Two methods for quantifying similarity between textbooks with respect to content distribution[J]. International Journal of Research & Method in Education, 2023, 46(2): 161-174.

[23] Godwin Gyimah. Effectiveness of group investigation versus lecture-based instruction on students' concept mastery and transfer in social studies[J]. Journal of Social Studies Research, 2023, 47(1): 29-39.

[24] Nyme Ahmed, Dip Nandi, A. G. M. Zaman, "Analyzing Student Evaluations of Teaching in a Completely Online Environment", International Journal of Modern Education and Computer Science, Vol.14, No.6, pp. 13-24, 2022.

[25] Li Nan, Zhang Yong, "Improvement and Practice of Secondary School Geography Teachers' Informatization Teaching Ability Based on the Perspective of MOOCs", International Journal of Education and Management Engineering, Vol.12, No.1, pp. 11-18, 2022.

[26] Ievgeniia Kuzminykh, Maryna Yevdokymenko, Oleksandra Yeremenko, Oleksandr Lemeshko, " Increasing Teacher Competence in Cybersecurity Using the EU Security Frameworks", International Journal of Modern Education and Computer Science, Vol.13, No.6, pp. 60-68, 2021.

[27] Umang Dhuri, Nilakshi Jain. "Teaching Assessment Tool: Using AI and Secure Techniques", International Journal of Education and Management Engineering, Vol.10, No.3, pp.12-21, 2020.

Artificial Intelligence, Medical Engineering and Education
Z.B. Hu et al. (Eds.)
© *2024 The Authors.*
This article is published online with Open Access by IOS Press and distributed under the terms
of the Creative Commons Attribution Non-Commercial License 4.0 (CC BY-NC 4.0).
doi:10.3233/ATDE231388

Methodological Aspects of Teachers' Work in the Electronic Information Educational Environment

Nataliya Mutovkina[a,1], Andrey Gusarov[b] and Shiliang Ding[c]

[a] *Department of Management and Social Communications, Tver State Technical University, Tver, 170012, Russia*
[b] *Department of Information Technologies, Tver State Technical University, Tver, 170012, Russia*
[c] *Shanghai Yucai High School, Shanghai, China*

ORCiD ID: Nataliya Mutovkina https://orcid.org/0000-0003-0137-4189
ORCiD ID: Andrey Gusarov https://orcid.org/0009-0009-2087-2467

Abstract. Currently, it is becoming more and more relevant not just the use of information technologies in the educational process, but the conduct of the educational process in a specially designed electronic information educational environment. As practice shows, not all teachers use such a practice for conducting the educational process. Many teachers still prefer to teach classes according to the traditional classroom system. And there are good reasons for this. This article discusses the method of activating the interest and motivation of teachers for the use of electronic information educational environment in their professional activities. The method is to organize and conducting a refresher course "The work of a teacher in the electronic information environment of an educational organization of higher education". The article provides a brief review of the structure and content of this course, an analysis of the effectiveness of the course based on a survey of students who have completed training. According to the results of the study, measures aimed at activating the interest of teachers in using electronic information educational environment are proposed. The study was conducted at Tver State Technical University. The practical significance of the research is to gain experience in the development and implementation of training courses on the use of electronic information educational environment in the educational process. The authors determined the optimal structure of the course, the content and conducted a statistical assessment of its effectiveness. The effectiveness of the course was determined based on the calculation of the proportion of listeners who, after completing the course, practice remote technologies in their teaching activities, in particular, work in an electronic information educational environment. The scientific novelty is the application of the author's method for developing the course and its application as a special tool for activating the demand for distance learning technologies.

Keywords. Electronic information educational environment (EIEE), educational organization, university, educational process, professional development

---

[1] Corresponding Author: Nataliya Mutovkina, letter-boxNM@yandex.ru.

1. Introduction

Universal digitalization has not spared the education sector. There are more and more publications in international databases on relevance, effectiveness and the need for the development and application of an electronic information environment in educational organizations. In most publications, the electronic information educational environment (EIEE) is considered an effective tool for organizing the educational process [1–3]. Indeed, the use of EIEE gives many advantages to both the teacher and the student in comparison with traditional classroom teaching. But there is a certain system of conditions for the use of EIEE. If at least one of these conditions is not met, then it is no longer possible to talk about the effectiveness of EIEE. In particular, an important condition for the effective use of EIEE is to provide university teachers with a methodological complex and instructions for working with the system, training teachers to work in EIEE. The training is organized as a refresher course for university teachers.

The aim of this study is to analyze the effectiveness of the electronic information educational environment and the possibilities of activating the interest of teachers in working in this environment. The practical significance of the research lies in the development of recommendations for the further development of the course "The work of a teacher in the electronic information environment of an educational organization of higher education" as an effective tool to increase the demand of teachers for the use of distance technologies in the educational process.

One of the most important tasks of the study is to assess the qualitative characteristics of the organization of the advanced training course for the work of teachers in the university's EIEE from the perspective of teachers working in different departments in different areas of student training. The initial information resulted from a survey of listeners of twelve streams for the period from 2017 to 2022. Statistical methods of information processing, namely calculation of variation and dynamics indicators, were chosen as research methods.

2. Methodology

The research includes a review of the literature on digital technologies in educational organizations and the use of EIEE; analysis of the features and working conditions in EIEE; analysis and evaluation of the effectiveness of the teacher training course for working in EIEE as a tool to increase the demand for the electronic environment.

2.1. Literature Review

The last decade of higher professional education can be characterized as a period of mass development and introduction of distance technologies into the educational process. The popularity of this topic continues to gain momentum. So, in articles [4–11] and others, the authors consider the advantages and disadvantages of distance learning. And, despite the obvious shortcomings, many scientists are confident that the future belongs to distance learning technologies [5, 8, 10].

One tool for implementing distance learning technologies is the EIEE of the university [7, 12–14]. The following definition is given in the Regulation on the electronic information and educational environment of TvSTU: The electronic information and educational environment is an information system, which is a set of electronic information and educational resources, information and telecommunication technologies and tools that ensure the development of educational programs [15].

2.2. Features and Conditions of Work in EIEE

For teachers to work in the EIEE, certain conditions must be met. In particular, teachers should be provided with a comfortable workplace equipped with modern computer equipment with unlimited access to the Internet. The time spent by teachers on working with EIEE should be considered in their individual annual work plan, along with the classroom load. In addition, in the individual work plan of the teacher, it is necessary to consider the time to study methodological materials for work in the EIEE.

Employees of a special department of the university dealing with the issues of informatization of educational (and not only) activities should be responsible for the smooth functioning of the EIEE (in the "24 to 7" mode).

An important condition for the effective use of EIEE is an unobtrusive demonstration to the teaching staff of the positive aspects of working in EIEE, such advantages of EIEE over the classroom form of conducting classes as: saving time (for example, in one academic hour through EIEE, it is possible to provide students with 20-50% more educational material than in the classroom), the possibility of instant transfer to students tasks and educational materials, automation of checking the level of knowledge of students and much more [16].

Such a demonstration is quite possible through the advanced training course "The work of a teacher in the electronic information environment of an educational organization of higher education", the content and effectiveness of which are discussed below.

2.3. Working Program of the Course

The working program of the course is developed by leading teachers and approved by the rector of the university. The program is available for review to all listeners registered on the course via a URL link or in the EIEE personal account. For example, the course program "Work of a teacher in the electronic information environment of an educational organization of higher education", developed at TvSTU, can be viewed here: http://cdokp.tstu.tver.ru/site.center/eltraining.aspx.

The working program of the course comprises the following sections:

- General characteristics of the program
- The content of the program
- Organizational and pedagogical conditions for implementing the program
- Evaluation of the quality of the program development
- The compilers of the program
- The list of registration of changes in the work program

The advanced training course fully complies with the work program and the Regulations on the EIEE of TvSTU [15]. Such accordance is a necessary condition for recruiting listeners for the course.

2.4. Course Structure

Classes on the course "The work of a teacher in the electronic information environment of an educational organization of higher education" are held with the teaching staff of the university twice a year. The group of listeners is from 20 to 30 people. The list of listeners is approved each time by the rector's Order "On the organization of training of scientific and pedagogical staff of the University". Some listeners sign up for the course again after successfully completing it for the first time. This is because of the periodic updating and addition of the structure and information content of the course, as well as the increasing relevance of the development of electronic courses of academic disciplines. By the developed electronic educational course posted in the EIEE, the teacher can manage the process of formation of knowledge, skills and competencies laid down in the work program of the discipline. The course page contains all the information about the program, the timing of mastering individual topics, ways to present learning outcomes through completing tasks and attaching results to the system at the time set by the teacher, records and accumulation of rating ratings of each student are kept [6].

The course involves the coordination of individual learning trajectories, considering the main work of listeners, and is available to listeners at the link: https://elearning.tstu.tver.ru/enrol/index.php?id=1122. Listeners enrolled in the course can easily get acquainted with its content. Figure 1 shows the main page of the course, where all its key elements are located.

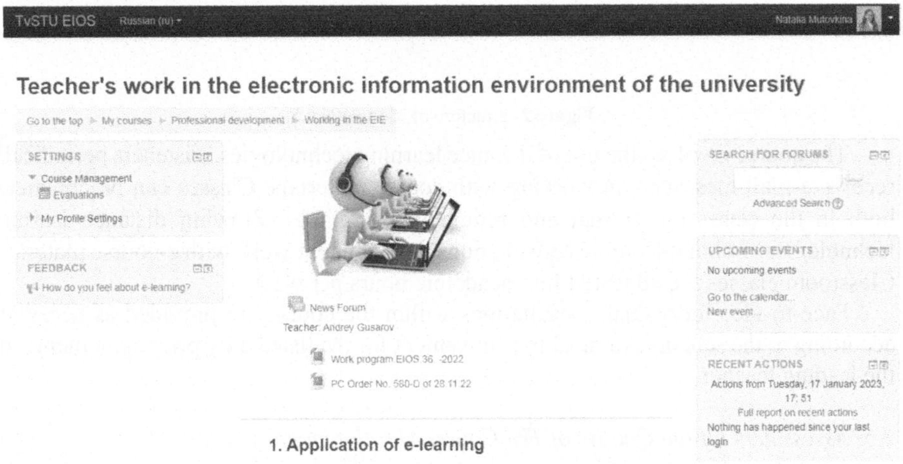

Figure 1. The main page of the course.

The course comprises eight modules. Each module has training materials, assignments, and a discussion section. Presentation files and text files in formats are presented as educational materials .docx and .pdf, video recordings of webinars, regulatory documents (for example, the Regulation on TvSTU EIEE), links to library resources, methodological recommendations, and instructions for completing tasks.

In the "Tasks" sections, depending on the topic and content of the module, from one to five tasks are presented. In the "Discussion" section, listeners discuss the topics of the module, impressions of the course, and the effectiveness of classes.

An example of the structure of one module is shown in Figure 2.

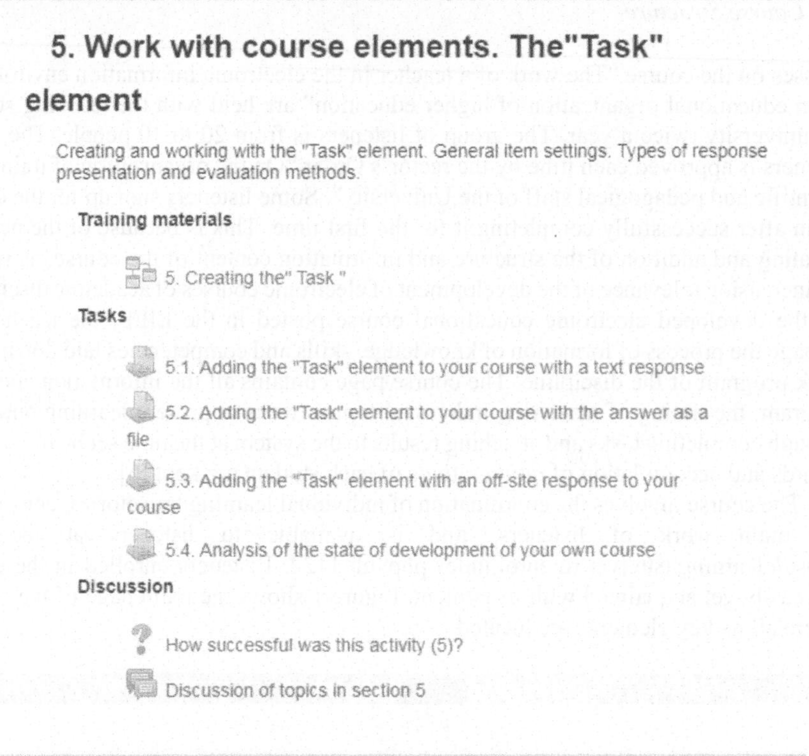

5. Work with course elements. The"Task" element

Creating and working with the "Task" element. General item settings. Types of response presentation and evaluation methods.

Training materials

  📑 5. Creating the" Task "

Tasks

  📄 5.1. Adding the "Task" element to your course with a text response

  📄 5.2. Adding the "Task" element to your course with the answer as a file

  📄 5.3. Adding the "Task" element with an off-site response to your course

  📄 5.4. Analysis of the state of development of your own course

Discussion

  ❓ How successful was this activity (5)?

  💬 Discussion of topics in section 5

Figure 2. Structure of Module No. 5.

The course involves the use of distance learning technologies. Listeners periodically receive e-mail messages on working with course materials. Classes can be conducted both in the classroom format and remotely, using the following distance learning technologies: webinars, online consultations, independent work with e-course materials. Classroom classes are allocated four academic hours per week.

Face-to-face individual consultations within the course are provided as necessary according to the schedule or at a time convenient for the listener by prior agreement with the leading teacher.

2.5. Assessment Of the Quality of The Course Development

To successfully complete the course and get a certificate of advanced training, it is necessary to complete 60–100% of all tasks and tests from modules No. 1–8. Reports on the completion of tasks should be uploaded to the page of the corresponding task in the "Tasks" section for each module. Reports can be generated as a file or simply as text written in the field (Figure 3).

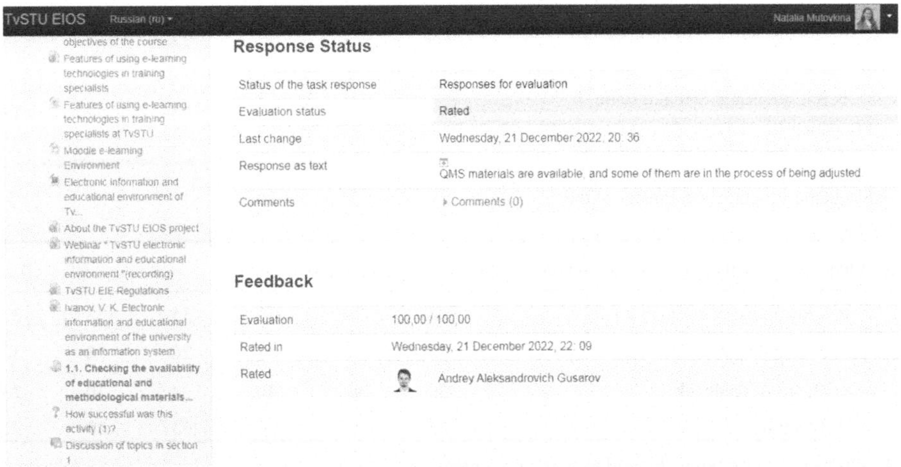

Figure 3. Report and evaluation of one of the tasks.

The lead teacher reviews the answers and gives a score in points from 0 to 100.

According to the results of the course, the average grade is determined as an arithmetic simple average. If this score exceeds 60 points, it is considered that the listener has successfully completed the training and can be issued a certificate of advanced training.

3. Analysis of the Effectiveness of the Course at Tver State Technical University

3.1. Listeners' Attitude to the Course

It is extremely important for developers and teachers of advanced training courses to have feedback, as listeners may express their own opinion about a particular course. The course developers and teachers should promptly respond to the listeners' assessments in order to improve the course and increase its informativeness.

Survey applies to the listeners of the course "The work of a teacher in the electronic information environment of an educational organization of higher education" to identify their attitude to this course. The questions and answers of the respondents are shown in Table 1.

Table 1. Survey results in a relation of listeners to the course, % of the total annual number of listeners

Questions and answers	2017	2018	2019	2020	2021	2022
1. Did the course "Work of a teacher in the electronic information environment of an educational organization of higher education" help you develop electronic courses?						
a. Yes, absolutely	65	68	73	74	71	76
b. I was counting on better help	20	18	18	17	21	18
c. No, it didn't help	15	14	9	9	8	6
2. Do you think it is necessary to improve the course "The work of a teacher in the electronic information environment of an educational organization of higher education"?						

a. No, but some changes are possible in the future	70	72	66	65	69	77
b. It is advisable to make some improvements	21	20	24	25	22	18
c. Yes, it is necessary to completely redesign the structure and content of the course	9	8	10	10	9	5

3. Which components of the course do you consider necessary to improve first?

a. Educational materials	28	30	33	35	38	37
b. Practical tasks	35	32	30	26	28	32
c. Means of feedback	30	42	40	34	30	23
d. Test tasks	33	35	30	33	25	21

4. Was there enough time allocated to study the course?

a. There is enough time	48	50	55	54	58	61
b. It is necessary to allocate more time to study the course	52	50	45	46	42	39
b.1. More for 2 – 6 academic hours	25	26	25	23	20	20
b.2. More for 6 – 12 academic hours	27	24	20	23	22	19

Most of the assessments received show a positive attitude of the trainees about this advanced training course. In order to get a holistic view of the listeners' perception of this course, statistical indicators such as the average value, indicators of variation, and dynamics were calculated (Figure 4).

As seen in Figure 4, the number of listeners adhering to answer a) has increased over the period under review.

Answer options	Average value	Mean square deviation	Coefficient of variation	Average absolute increase	Average growth rate
1a	71,2	3,7	5,2%	2,2	103,2%
1b	18,7	1,4	7,4%	-0,4	97,9%
1c	10,2	3,2	31,8%	-1,8	83,3%
2a	69,8	4,0	5,7%	1,4	101,9%
2b	21,7	2,4	10,9%	-0,6	97,0%
2c	8,5	1,7	20,1%	-0,8	88,9%
3a	33,5	3,6	10,7%	1,8	105,7%
3b	30,5	2,9	9,6%	-0,6	98,2%
3c	33,2	6,4	19,4%	-1,4	94,8%
3d	29,5	5,0	16,8%	-2,4	91,4%
4a	54,3	4,4	8,1%	2,6	104,9%
4b	45,7	4,4	9,7%	-2,6	94,4%
4b.1	23,2	2,4	10,4%	-1	95,6%
4b.2	22,5	2,6	11,7%	-1,6	93,2%

Figure 4. Statistical estimates of the responses of the course participants.

3.2. Teachers' Plans for the Use of EIEE

The attitude of teachers to EIEE and plans for its application were also reflected in the results of the survey. This survey was conducted on the same sample set as the first study. The results of the survey are presented in Table 2.

Table 2. The results of a survey of teachers regarding the prospects for the use of EIEE, % of the total annual number of trainees of the advanced training course

Questions and answers	2017	2018	2019	2020	2021	2022
1. How do you assess the prospects of distance learning with the help of EIEE?						
a. EIEE is an excellent tool for organizing the educational process	30	32	38	40	39	38
b. EIEE is effective only as an additional learning tool	40	39	42	40	41	43
c. EIEE cannot be considered as an effective tool for learning	30	29	20	20	20	19
2. Do you plan to use EIEE in your future professional activity?						
a. Yes, constantly	15	18	23	22	25	25
b. From time to time	30	34	35	33	40	42
c. No, I'm not planning to	55	48	42	45	35	33
3. Has your teaching load changed when using EIEE?						
a. The load has decreased	5	7	4	4	6	7
b. The load has not changed	50	48	49	50	55	53
c. The load has increased	45	45	47	46	39	40
4. Do you think the use of EIEE can be considered as a necessary condition for the competitiveness of an educational organization?						
a. Yes, absolutely	70	75	75	74	74	77
b. Yes, but only when teaching individual courses	15	20	18	17	17	16
c. No, this is not a prerequisite	15	5	7	9	9	7

Answer b) prevails on the first question, answer a) is in second place in popularity. This situation is explained by the insufficient provision of teachers with software and hardware. All digitalization should be provided by teachers themselves at their own expense. In addition, the work of a teacher in EIEE does not replace the mandatory classroom classes prescribed in the individual work plan, so the answer options b) and c) to the second question received the largest number of votes. Many teachers use EIEE only to exchange educational information with students. Here, when answering the third question, answer b) was selected. An increase in the workload was also announced by many respondents. Most teachers believe that the functioning of EIEE at the university is a necessary condition for the competitiveness of an educational organization.

4. Summary And Conclusion

It is possible to change teachers' opinions regarding the use of EIEE in the educational process for the better. To do this, it is necessary to radically revise the organization of the educational process and the terms of the employment contract between the teacher and the university.

- Teachers should be given the right to choose the form of conducting classes with students: classroom (traditional format) or remotely.
- When teachers choose a remote form of classes through the university's EIEE, it is necessary to provide each teacher with a computer device with uninterrupted mobile access to the Internet.
- Establish periodic cash payments to teachers who develop and apply their own electronic courses of academic disciplines. The payment must be made once for the development of the course and then monthly for the use of the course in the educational process.

The proposed measures will increase the interest of teachers in using EIEE, which will contribute to the active digitalization of higher education. The intensification of teachers' interest in working in the EIEE logically entails an increase in the demand for the advanced training course "Teacher's work in the electronic information environment of an educational organization of higher education". Therefore, this course can be considered with confidence as an effective tool for preparing teachers to work in the university's EIEE.

References

[1]   Dushyanthi U. Vidanagama, "Acceptance of E-Learning among Undergraduates of Computing Degrees in Sri Lanka", International Journal of Modern Education and Computer Science, Vol.8, No.4, pp.25-32, 2016.
[2]   Nechaeva OA. Implementation of competence approach in the conditions of the electronic information and educational environment. Modern Problems of Science and Education. 2020; 4: 76-83, doi: 10.17513/spno.30079.
[3]   Mirjana Kocaleva, Igor Stojanovic, Zoran Zdravev, "Model of e-Learning Acceptance and Use for Teaching Staff in Higher Education Institutions", International Journal of Modern Education and Computer Science, vol.7, no.4, pp.23-31, 2015.
[4]   Mirjana Kocaleva, Igor Stojanovic, Zoran Zdravev, "Model of e-Learning Acceptance and Use for Teaching Staff in Higher Education Institutions", International Journal of Modern Education and Computer Science, vol.7, no.4, pp.23-31, 2015.
[5]   Faiz MMT Marikar, Neranjaka Jayarathne, "Effectiveness of MOODLE in Education System in Sri Lankan University", International Journal of Modern Education and Computer Science, Vol.8, No.2, pp.54-58, 2016.
[6]   Tulchinsky GL. Digital transformation of education: challenges to higher education. Philosophical Sciences; 2017; 6: 121-136, URL: https://www.phisci.info/jour/article/view/371?locale=en.
[7]   Bhupesh Rawat, Sanjay K. Dwivedi, "An Architecture for Recommendation of Courses in E-learning System", International Journal of Information Technology and Computer Science, Vol.9, No.4, pp.39-47, 2017.
[8]   Krutova IA, Krutova OV. University digital transformation: hazards and prospects. Modern High Technologies. 2021; 2: 170-174, doi: 10.17513/snt.38513.
[9]   Zamostyanova TV, Kruchinskaya MV. Distance learning and electronic information educational environment in the assessment of teachers and students of the Kalashnikov Izhevsk state technical university. In the collection: Problems and Trends in the Development of the Socio-Cultural Cpace of Russia: History and Modernity. Materials of the VIII International Scientific and Practical Conference. Bryansk, 2021. 202-209. URL: https://elibrary.ru/item.asp?id=47277706&ysclid=lns2sbb6vu302456597.

[10] Yakovleva AA. Transformation of higher education in the digital economy. Management Accounting. 2022; 1-2: 342-348, doi: https://doi.org/10.25806/uu1-22022342-348.

[11] Rakovskii OV. Distance learning: advantages and disadvantages. In the book: Regional Informatics (RI-2022). Jubilee XVIII St. Petersburg International Conference. Conference materials. St. Petersburg, 2022; 344-345, URL: http://www.spoisu.ru/conf/ri2022/materials?ysclid=lns39cc4g1905856161.

[12] Zahraa F. Muhsen, Adi Maaita, Ashraf Odah, Ayman Nsour, "Moodle and e-learning Tools", International Journal of Modern Education and Computer Science, vol.5, no.6, pp.1-8, 2013.

[13] Golitsyna I. Educational process in electronic information-educational environment. Procedia – Social and Behavioral Sciences. 2017 Feb; 237, 939-944, doi: http://dx.doi.org/10.1016/j.sbspro.2017.02.132

[14] Dobudko TV, Malova NV, Pugach OI. Heterogeneous electronic information and educational environment of the university is a problem or an opportunity? Samara Journal of Science. 2020; 9(4): 290-295, doi: 10.17816/snv202094304.

[15] Regulations on the electronic information and educational environment of TvSTU. Approved by the rector on 28.06.2017. Tver: TvSTU. 2017; URL: http://cdokp.tstu.tver.ru/site.services/download.aspx?act=1&dbid=marcmain&did=121878

[16] Popova OI. Transformation of higher education in the conditions of the digital economy. Management Issues. 2018; 5(54): 158-160, doi: 10.22394/2304-3369-2018-5-158-160.

Artificial Intelligence, Medical Engineering and Education
Z.B. Hu et al. (Eds.)
© *2024 The Authors.*
This article is published online with Open Access by IOS Press and distributed under the terms
of the Creative Commons Attribution Non-Commercial License 4.0 (CC BY-NC 4.0).
doi:10.3233/ATDE231389

Developing the English Language Communicative Competence of Future Teachers by Means of Mobile Apps

Anatolii PAHSKO[a] and Iryna PINCHUK[b,1]

[a] *Department of theoretical cybernetics, Taras Shevchenko National University of Kyiv, Kyiv, 01601, Ukraine*

[b] *Educational and Scientific Institute of Pedagogy and Psychology, Oleksandr Dovzhenko Hlukhiv National Pedagogical University, Hlukhiv, 41400, Ukraine*

ORCiD ID:
Anatolii PAHSKO https://orcid.org/0000-0001-6944-8477
Iryna PINCHUK https://orcid.org/0000-0002-1376-3977

Abstract. The integration of Ukraine into the world community requires perfect mastery of English not only from citizens, but also from intending professionals. So, English proficiency becomes an important ability and additional educational skill of the future foreign language teachers. The article deals with using the mobile applications as the means of pre-service teachers' English language communicative competence developing. At first, the main professionally oriented mobile applications for studying English and their advantages were identified. Then criteria and levels of assessing students' English proficiency were defined. Four main language skills (listening, reading, writing, speaking) were chosen as the basic criteria and four levels (high, sufficient, average, low) of assessing undergraduates' English language communicative competence were determined. During the implementing stage of pedagogical experiment, the respondents of experimental group used mentioned mobile apps with the aim of improving English. The comparison of the experimental and control groups took place at the ascertainment, and later at the control stages of the experiment with the help of mathematical statistics methods. The effectiveness of using mobile applications in order to improve English language skills during the educational process at the pedagogical faculty at the university has been proved.

Keywords. English language communicative competence, mobile applications, future teachers, educational process at the pedagogical faculty.

1. Introduction

Today, Ukraine is undergoing changes in the modern conceptual foundations of the national education system. The process of national education integration into the world educational space takes place regardless of the difficult contemporary circumstances in Ukraine. The need to update the educational sector of Ukraine is due to its insufficient compliance with modern demands of society, requirements of intercultural communication, and challenges of linguistic globalization phenomena.

---

[1] Corresponding Author: Iryna Pinchuk, pinchuk@gnpu.edu.ua.

The modernization of an intending teacher training process involves increasing the requirements for their professional level in order to implement the New State Education Standard, which involves the formation of undergraduates' English language competence at the level of B2 English proficiency [1].

To reform the educational sector, there is a need to prepare highly qualified educators for modern school, who can act active in contemporary conditions, to participate in productive professionally oriented international communication. Taking into account the above mentioned, the issue of improving English language communicative competence of prospective teachers in the process of study at higher education establishments is significant. Consequently, the purpose of the article is to study the influence of mobile apps to developing undergraduate students' English competence in the conditions of Ukrainian higher education.

Most part of Ukrainian higher education establishments work in a distance or mixed format today. Nowadays ICT using is especially important for the educational process implementation in higher education establishments in our country. During modern changes, the digital means usage is intended to the opportunities that influence professional becoming of contemporary teachers. Using such means productively allows undergraduates to be ready to the educational communication.

Modern requirements for graduates' professional skills are only growing because they should be competitive to find a job in the contemporary labor market. Accordingly, as part of the individual work planned by the curriculum of the course "English for professional purposes", students should be offered a number of tasks involving the use of mobile applications. Using the professionally oriented mobile applications aimed at improving their level of English proficiency during educational process at the university can facilitate improving English speaking skills. The analysis of scientific literature, interviews, and questionnaires were used as a means of research.

2. Literature Review

There is a considerable amount of scientific literature on developing pre-service teachers' English language communicative competence. The results of the analysis of state documents make it possible to determine that implementing English at higher education institutions of Ukraine take place in accordance with the document: "Methodical recommendations for ensuring quality study, teaching and use of the English language in higher education institutions of Ukraine" [2]. The above mentioned "Methodical recommendations" provided guidelines to the managers and English teachers of higher education establishments in Ukraine regarding the implementation tasks of modern foreign language education, national aims for improving the teaching, learning and use of the English language in higher education. In addition, it is noted about the support of international parterres and the need to participate in international projects. The document lays down the maximum potential of its application in the post-war period of the country's recovery.

Various approaches have been proposed to solve the issue of developing English speaking communicative competence. In particular, Ukrainian scientists I. Lytovchenko et al [3] draw our attention to the interactive English learning methods and techniques as the most productive education means that give the opportunity to build effective cooperation between all the educational process participants. O. Liubashenko and Z. Kornieva [4] outline several reasons for dialogic interactive speaking skills assessment of technical English to tertiary school students. In our previous works [5, 6] we trace the advances in intending primary school teachers' English communicative competence development by methods of mathematical statistic. S. Nykyporets and others [7] in the investigation show that communicative competence development of non-linguistic universities students is effective by means of mind maps. Another group of scientists [8] outline the ways of undergraduates' intercultural communicative competence developing, and propose recommendations for its building. T. Yeremenko et al [9] describe the learning scheme of intending teachers' questioning abilities formation, motivating them to the future professional activity. The researches show the possibility to improve undergraduates' communication skills and actualizing them during the theoretical-practical course, and teaching practice. I. Zadorozhna and O. Datskiv suggest to use positive psychology recommendations to teach the English language in distance challenging environment. [10]. The issue of implementing mobile applications in university educational process with the aim of improving English speaking skills has received much attention in the last five years. More recent evidence reveals that foreign language communicative competence of non-philology majors students can be developed by means of mobile applications [11], with the help of robotics usage [12].

Research results show that it is not only Ukrainian scientists, but also foreign researchers study the problem of using mobile applications for developing English proficiency. Foreign scientists have addressed the issue of implementing mobile applications for improving English language communicative competence of university students. I. Ari et al [13] describe the process of implementing Duolingo mobile application with the aim of improving students' English vocabulary. D. Assanova and A. Prlepessova [14] prove the importance of educational mobile apps in learning English for non-linguistic specialties. A. Basal et al [15] demonstrate the effectiveness of mobile applications in English vocabulary teaching. K. Beatty [16] describes the practical aspects of mobile language learning process. M. Bernacki et al [17] show the advantages of mobile technology in education, advances in understanding and measuring the role of mobile technology. Q. Fu and G. Hwang [18] define the directions in collaborative English learning through mobile technology usage. Y. Hsu and Y. Ching [19] share their experiences of designing the mobile app for teaching educators and using it in an online graduate course. D. Huynh et al [20] present the game assessment of English learning platform Duolingo. S. Rohani and others [21] develop a bilingual electronic English dictionary app and prove its effectiveness.

The study of Ukrainian scientists [22] research both the structure of communicative competence, and the system of its building while teaching English in higher education institutions to the students of economics. Md. Biplob Hosen [23] in his work focuses on analyzing the facts that influence the students' perception about telecommunication service quality on online education during the pandemic situation. The research of W. Yasya [24] aims to prove the influence of ICT for communicative competence improving and social changes in a rural area in Indonesia.

3.   Aim

The analysis of above-mentioned works shows that different aspects of English proficiency developing by means of mobile application have been studied quite thoroughly. However, implementing the professionally oriented mobile applications in the educational process with the aim of building pre-service teachers' English language communicative competence may need further research.

Therefore, the aim of this paper is to research the problem of future teachers' English language communicative competence development by means of mobile applications. To achieve the purpose of the research, we should implement some objectives, the solution of which will ensure the realization of the result. The objectives are: 1) to identify the main professionally oriented mobile applications for improving the English communicative competence of future teachers and describe their advantages; 2) to assess the level of intending teachers' English language communicative competence; 3) to check the effectiveness of using mobile apps to improve English language skills during the educational process at the pedagogical faculty at the university.

4. Results

Table 1. Professionally oriented pedagogical mobile applications for studying English

App	Advantages
"ELT Training" by Oxford University Press	This app offers English language training for English language teachers. It provides interactive activities, videos, and audio content to improve teachers' language skills. It also offers modules on language teaching methodology and classroom management.
"Teach English!" by British Council	This app is designed for non-native English-speaking teachers who want to improve their English proficiency. It offers a range of interactive activities, including listening, speaking, reading, and writing exercises. It focuses on practical English language skills necessary for effective classroom teaching.
"TEFL Training" by TESOL International Association	This app provides resources and training for teachers of English as a foreign language (TEFL). It offers grammar lessons, vocabulary exercises, and pronunciation practice. It also includes lesson planning tips, teaching techniques, and professional development materials.
"Teacher's Assistant Pro: Track Student Behavior" by Thomas Suarez	Although not solely focused on English language training, this app is designed to assist teachers in managing classrooms and tracking student behaviour. It includes features for recording attendance, managing grades, and tracking student performance. It can be useful for English teachers looking for a comprehensive tool to enhance their teaching practices.

The purpose of the research and experimental work was to study the effectiveness of using mobile applications in the process of intending teachers' professional training.

The use of mobile apps help to students of pedagogical specialties to solve the problems related to the English teaching methods . Among the most using educational applications for learning foreign languages are: Lingualeo, Duolingo, Babbel, Rosetta Stone, Memrise, Easy Ten, Pussle English, Polyglot, etc. The most of them are designed to everyday communication. However, our aim was to analyze the apps that aimed at developing professionally oriented English-speaking communicative competence of undergraduates at higher educational institutions.

There are professionally oriented mobile apps available for training teachers' English. These apps are designed to provide targeted language training and resources specifically for educators. So, we study and describe the features of the most popular apps that can be useful in studying English by intending specialists of pedagogical professions (see in the table 1). Based on the analysis of scientific and educational sources, we consider it expedient in the process of evaluating to take into account the following levels of English language communicative competence formation of intending teachers: high, sufficient, average, low (table 2).

Table 2. The levels of English language communicative competence formation

The author's title	British title	The name in accordance with the pan-European recommendations on language education
High	Upper-Intermediate / Advanced	B 2 / C1
Sufficient	Intermediate	B 1
Average	Pre-Intermediate	A 2
Low	Basic / Elementary	A 1

In the process of organizing the experimental work, the complexity and multicomponent nature of the process of English language communicative competence building were taken into account. So, we chose the language skills (listening, reading, writing, speaking) as the basic criteria of assessing undergraduates' English proficiency.

In accordance with the aim and logic of the experiment, the stages of its implementation were defined and substantiated: ascertaining, implementing and control. Certain tasks, corresponding forms and methods of organization characterized each of them. During the ascertainment stage of the experiment, the number of students who possess certain levels according to the main criteria was determined with the aim of finding out the current state of English language proficiency at the pedagogical faculty (table 3).

Table 3. The results of ascertainment stage of the experiment

Criteria	Levels			
	High	Sufficient	Medium	Low
Reading	7,97	48,55	37,68	5,80
Listening	16,67	41,30	39,13	2,90
Speaking	13,04	31,16	55,07	0,73
Writing	6,52	33,33	51,45	8,70

The result of the ascertainment stage (fig.1) shows that contemporary undergraduates have the highest level of English listening, at the same time they have the lowest level of English speaking. The majority of students possess English proficiency at sufficient or medium levels.

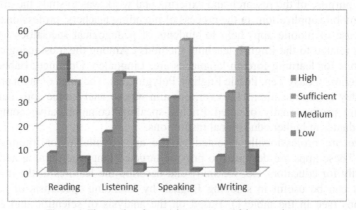

Figure 1. The results of ascertainment stage of the experiment.

The process of developing English language communicative competence requires a certain foundation that enables the achievement of the B2 level of foreign language proficiency as a necessary condition for admission to the master's program. During the analysis of the experimental results, it was concluded that successful mastery of all the language skills in English on professional vocabulary contributes to better English communication. During the implementing stage of the experiment, students used one or more of the mentioned mobile applications as an aid for completing tasks of individual work from the course "English for professional purposes".

In order to ensure the reliability of the obtained data, competent experts of the same qualification (everybody has PhD in Pedagogics and has C1 level of English) from the lectures participated. Compliance with the requirement of probability was aimed at equalizing the basic conditions for conducting a pedagogical experiment in the real conditions of the educational process.

The comparison of the experimental (EG) and control (CG) groups took place at the ascertainment, and later at the control stages of the experiment with the help of mathematical statistics methods. The determination of the results of the integral evaluation by experts of the levels of undergraduates' English proficiency were analysed in order to establish the coincidence or differences in the characteristics of the studied groups by comparing the distributions of the experimental and control groups at the beginning of the ascertaining and at the end of control experiment stages.

5. Methods

Table 4. Dynamics of the English proficiency levels of the respondents in the experimental and control groups during the experiment

Levels Groups	High %	Persons	Sufficient %	Persons	Average %	Persons	Low %	Persons
EG at the research beginning	14.06	9	25.00	16	39.06	25	21.88	14
EG at the end of the research	21.88	14	39.06	25	28.13	18	10.93	7
CG at the research beginning	12.90	8	25.81	16	42.32	25	20.97	13
CG at the end of the research	14.52	9	27.42	17	38.71	24	19.35	12

To realize the aim of the study, such methods were used: theoretical: analysis of pedagogical, psychological, methodical literature; empirical: observation of the educational process, questionnaires, interviews; statistical; graphic. In order to prove the reliability of the obtained results of the experimental research, statistical methods of data processing of the pedagogical experiment were used.

Fundamentals of statistical hypothesis testing. Consider two aggregates. The probability of occurrence of event A in the first set is p_1, and in the second – p_2. It is necessary to check the hypothesis $H_0 : p_1 = p_2$ with the alternative $H_1 : p_1 \neq p_2$. Let n_1 experiments were conducted in the first aggregates in which the event occurred m_1 times, and n_2 experiments were conducted in the second aggregates in which the event occurred m_2 times. Estimates of the unknown probabilities p_1 and p_2 will be the corresponding relative frequencies $\dfrac{m_1}{n_1}$ and $\dfrac{m_2}{n_2}$.

Let's consider the difference $\dfrac{m_1}{n_1} - \dfrac{m_2}{n_2}$.

We have $E\left(\dfrac{m_1}{n_1}\right) = p_1, \ E\left(\dfrac{m_2}{n_2}\right) = p_2$ (1),

$$Var\left(\dfrac{m_1}{n_1} - \dfrac{m_2}{n_2}\right) = \dfrac{p_1(1-p_1)}{n_1} + \dfrac{p_2(1-p_2)}{n_2} \qquad (2).$$

If the main hypothesis $p_1 = p_2 = p$, is correct, then we can assume that (n_1+n_2) observations were made, in which the event occurred $(m_1 + m_2)$ times.

We will use a criterion

$$Z = \dfrac{\dfrac{m_1}{n_1} - \dfrac{m_2}{n_2}}{\sqrt{\left(\dfrac{m_1+m_2}{n_1+n_2}\right)\left(1 - \dfrac{m_1+m_2}{n_1+n_2}\right)\left(\dfrac{1}{n_1} + \dfrac{1}{n_2}\right)}} \qquad (3)$$

to test the hypothesis.

The quantity Z is asymptotically normal with parameters 0 and 1. Therefore, the level of significance α can be found from the condition.

$$P\{|Z| < z_\alpha\} \approx 2\Phi_0(z_\alpha) = 1 - \alpha \qquad (4).$$

According to the results of observations, we find the observed value of the criterion z_s. If $z_s < z_\alpha$, then the hypothesis is accepted, otherwise it is rejected.

According to the assessments of independent experts, recommendations for the assignment of educational qualifications are possible for the undergraduates who possess English proficiency at first three levels, and the assignment of professional qualifications is recommended only for the students who have high and sufficient levels of English language communicative competence.

Table 5. Dynamics of the English proficiency levels of the respondents in the experimental and control groups for professional qualification

Levels Groups	High and sufficient levels		Average and low levels	
	%	Persons	%	Persons
EG at the research beginning	39.07	25	60.93	39
EG at the end of the research	60.93	39	39.07	25
CG at the research beginning	38.71	24	61.29	38
CG at the end of the research	41.93	26	58.07	36

Table 4 for professional qualifications can be converted to Table 5.

For the experimental and control groups at the beginning of the experiment, the value of z is the criterion $z_s = 0.04 < z_\alpha = 1.96$. The hypothesis of equality of probabilities for both groups is accepted.

For the control group at the beginning and at the end of the experiment, the value of z is the criterion $z_s = 0.366 < z_\alpha = 1.96$. The hypothesis of equality of probabilities for the control group at the beginning and at the end of the experiment is accepted.

For the experimental and control groups at the end of the experiment, the value of z is the criterion $z_s = 2.134 > z_\alpha = 1.96$. The hypothesis of equal probabilities for both groups is rejected.

For the experimental group at the beginning and at the end of the experiment, the value of z is the criterion $z_s = 2.475 > z_\alpha = 1.96$. The hypothesis of equality of probabilities for the experimental group at the beginning and at the end of the experiment is rejected.

6. Discussion

Conducting user testing and gathering feedback from teachers is very important part of the research for improving the development process and ensure the app meets their needs and preferences. The survey of pre-service teachers made it possible to determine key considerations and features that are important in the app: user-friendly clean and intuitive interface; comprehensive library of teaching resources, incorporating opportunities for teachers to practice speaking through dialogues, role-plays, and voice recording features; integrating gamification elements; tracking progress and providing performance feedback; implementing synchronization features to update progress and content when the app reconnects to the internet; providing a calendar or scheduling feature to help teachers manage their teaching activities effectively.

It's important to note the most of university staff embrace mobile technologies as an important tools for improving quality of education. Over time, their benefits become more apparent and educators' attitudes evolve. Our paper proves the effectiveness of mobile technologies usage. The issue of using mobile application became especially important nowadays. The works of L. Gorbatiuk et al (2019) and S. Rohani et al (2019), revealed that incorporating mobile apps has valuable influence on quality of education. The results of our article confirms with the previous results (I. Ari et al, (2020), D. Assanova & A. Prlepessova (2020), M. Bernacki et al. (2020)) and proves that mobile means implementation has both positive and negative influence on educational process, and a balanced approach is recommended for effective English learning. The article is in good agreement with O. Kyrpychenko et al (2021) Zadorozhna et al (2023) works. The evidence we found points to the mobile apps as an effective means of English learning.

Considering all the advantages, we can note that using mobile apps for learning English is significant means nowadays. Nevertheless, mobile apps can be used as a perfect additional means for language learning. Mobile applications are not able to substitute full-fledged communication and interaction with live people. We believe, apps usage should combine with other learning methods, such as real-life communication with native speakers, engaging in student mobility and exchange programs, conversation clubs, classes with a teacher.

7. Conclusion

The research has led us to conclude about the significance of using mobile apps for learning English. They can be a valuable tool to enhance the English language skills of undergraduates in higher education institutions.

According to the aim of the paper, we realized some objectives:

1) We have outlined the main professionally oriented mobile apps for improving English proficiency of future teachers : "ELT Training" by Oxford University Press,

"Teach English!" by British Council, "TEFL Training" by TESOL International Association and "Teacher's Assistant Pro: Track Student Behavior" by Thomas Suarez.

2) The levels of intending teachers' English language communicative competence were assessed according to the language skills at the beginning and the end of the pedagogical experiment. University students can enhance their communication abilities by different means, one of the most effective of which is mobile apps for studying professional English. By addressing the challenges in improving communicative competence, pedagogical establishments can better train their undergraduates for the complexities of the teacher profession.

3) The effectiveness of using mobile applications for improving professionally oriented English learning at the pedagogical faculty has been proved. The levels of pre-service teachers' English language communicative competence have increased after the learning English by means of professionally oriented mobile applications.

We see the prospects for further research in the study of the peculiarities of the impact of artificial intelligence usage to the communicative competence development in the course of university studying English.

References

[1] The Standard of Higher Education in Specialty 013 Primary education in the field of knowledge 01 Education / Pedagogy for the first (bachelor) level of higher education, approved by Order No. 357 of the Ministry of Education and Science of Ukraine dated 03/23/2021. [S] https://mon.gov.ua/storage/app/media/vishcha-osvita/zatverdzeni%20standarty/2021/07/28/013-Pochatk.osvita-bakalavr.28.07.pdf (in Ukrainian).

[2] The Draft of the Order "Methodical recommendations on ensuring quality study, teaching and use of the English language in higher education institutions of Ukraine" dated March 28, 2023. [S]. URL: https://mon.gov.ua/ua/news/mon-proponuye-do-gromadskogo-obgovorennya-proyekt-nakazu-metodichni-rekomendaciyi-shodo-zabezpechennya-yakisnogo-vivchennya-vikladannya-ta-vikoristannya-anglijskoyi-movi-u-zakladah-vishoyi-osviti-ukrayini (in Ukrainian).

[3] Lytovchenko I., Ogienko O., Sbrueva A., Sotska H. Teaching English for Specific Purposes to Adult Learners at University: Methods that Work [J]. Advanced Education, 2018, 10: 69-75. URL: https://doi.org/10.20535/2410-8286.149741. (in English).

[4] Liubashenko O., Kornieva Z. Dialogic Interactive Speaking Skills Assessment in the Experiential Teaching of Technical English to Tertiary School Students [J]. Advanced Education, 2019, 6(13): 18–25. URL: https://doi.org/10.20535/2410-8286.156228.

[5] Pashko A. O., Pinchuk I. O. Intellectual Methods of Estimation of Intending Primary School Teachers' Foreign Language Communicative Competence [J]. IEEE International Conference on Advanced Trends in Information Theory (ATIT). Kyiv, Ukraine, 2019. 439–444.

[6] Pashko A., Pinchuk I. Methods of Classifying Foreign Language Communicative Competence Using the Example of Intending Primary School Teachers [J]. In: Babichev S., Lytvynenko V., Wójcik W., Vyshemyrskaya S. (eds) Lecture Notes in Computational Intelligence and Decision Making. ISDMCI. Advances in Intelligent Systems and Computing, 2020, 1246. Springer, Cham. URL: https://ieeexplore.ieee.org/document/9030429.

[7] Nykyporets S., Hadaichuk N., Medvedieva S. Communicative Competence Formation among Students of Non-Linguistic Universities with the Help of Mind Maps in Foreign Language Lessons [J]. GRAIL OF SCIENCE, 2021, 2-3: 412-417.

[8] Mykytenko N., Fedorchuk M., Ivasyuta O., Hrynya N., Kotlovskyi A. Intercultural Communicative Competence Development in Journalism Students [J]. Advanced Education, 2022, 9(20): 121–131. https://doi.org/10.20535/2410-8286.261521.

[9] Yeremenko T., Lukyanchenko I., Demchuk A. Development of Prospective EFL Teachers' Questioning Skills in Classroom Discourse: Interdisciplinary Approach [J]. Advanced Education, 2022, 9(21): 22–39. https://doi.org/10.20535/2410-8286.254730.

[10] Zadorozhna I., Datskiv O. Motivation of Pre-Service English Teachers to Learn English as a Foreign Language in Challenging Circumstances [J]. Advanced Education, 2022, 9(21): 86–99. https://doi.org/10.20535/2410-8286.261715.

[11] Gorbatiuk L. V., Kravchenko N. V., Alekseeva H. M., Rozumna T. S. Mobile applications as means of forming foreign language lexical competence of students of non-philology majors [J]. Information technologies and teaching aids. 2019, 74, 6: 150-164. http://dx.doi.org/10.33407/itlt.v74i6.2529 [in Ukrainian].

[12] Rakhmanina M., Pinchuk I., Vyshnyk O., Tryfonova O., Koycheva T., Sydorko V., Ilienko O. The Usage of Robotics as an Element of STEM Education in the Educational Process [J]. International journal of computer science and network security. 2022, 22 (5): 645-651. https://doi.org/10.22937/IJCSNS.2022.22.5.90.

[13] Ari I., Wilson A., Sutrisno. The Implementation of Duolingo Mobile Application in English Vocabulary, Learning [J]. Journal of English Language Teaching. 2020, 5(01): 8-14. DOI: http://dx.doi.org/10.30998/scope.v5i1.6568.

[14] Assanova D. N., Prlepessova A. B. The role of educational mobile apps in learning English (non-linguistic specialties) [J]. Bulletin of Karaganda University. Series "Pedagogy". 2020, 2(98): 121–125. http://dx.doi.org/10.31489/2020Ped2/121-125.

[15] Basal A., Yilmaz S., Tanriverdi A., Sari L. Effectiveness of mobile applications in vocabulary teaching [J]. Contemporary Educational Technology, 2016, 7(1): 47–59. URL: https://files.eric.ed.gov/fulltext/EJ1105763.pdf.

[16] Beatty K. Mobile language learning: the world in our hands [J]. Anaheim University. 2015, 17. URL: https://www.anaheim.edu/schools-and-institutes/graduate-school-of-education/diploma-in-tesol/243-%20about/faculty-and-staff/tesol-faculty/886-ken-beatty-phd-ken-beatty-phd.

[17] Bernacki M. L., Greene J. A., Crompton H. Mobile technology, learning, and achievement: advances in understanding and measuring the role of mobile technology in education [J]. Contemporary Educational Psychology, 2020, 60. https://doi.org/10.1016/J.CEDPSYCH.2019.101827.

[18] Fu Q.-K., & Hwang G.-J. Trends in mobile technology-supported collaborative learning: A systematic review of journal publications from 2007 to 2016 [J]. Computers & Education, 2018, 119: 129-143. https://doi.org/10.1016/j.compedu.2018.01.004.

[19] Hsu Y.C., Ching Y.H. Mobile App Design for Teaching and Learning Educators, Experiences in an Online Graduate Course [J]. The International Review of Research in Open and Distributed Learning, 2013, 14(4): 117–139. Athabasca University Press. URL: https://www.learntechlib.org/p/148190/.

[20] Huynh D., Zuo L., Lida H. An assessment of game elements in language-learning platform Duolingo [C]. 2018 4th International Conference on Computer and Information Sciences (ICCOINS), 2018, 1–4. http://dx.doi.org/10.1109/ICCOINS.2018.8510568.

[21] Rohani S., Suyono, A. Developing an Android-based bilingual e-glossary application of English for Specific Purposes (ESP) [J]. English Language Teaching Educational Journal. 2021, 4(3): 225-234. http://dx.doi.org/10.12928/eltej.v4i3.5209.

[22] Kyrpychenko O., Pushchyna I., Kichuk Ya., Shevchenko N., Luchaninova O., Koval V., Communicative Competence Development in Teaching Professional Discourse in Educational Establishments. [J] International Journal of Modern Education and Computer Science, 2021, vol.13, No.4, 16-27.

[23] Hosen B. Impact of Telecommunication Service Quality in Bangladesh on Online Education during Covid-19 [J]. International Journal of Modern Education and Computer Science, 2022, vol.14, No.6, 65-75.

[24] Yasya W. Rural Empowerment through Education: Case Study of a Learning Community Telecentre in Indonesia [J]. International Journal of Modern Education and Computer Science, 2020, vol.12, No.4, 12-26.

[25] Zadorozhna O., Bodnar O., Benkovska N., Korshevniuk T., Biliavska T. Peculiarities of Forming Communicative Competence in Students of Nonphilological Specialties. [J]. Ad Alta Journal of Interdisciplinary Research, 13 (2), XXXVI, 27 – 33.

Artificial Intelligence, Medical Engineering and Education
Z.B. Hu et al. (Eds.)
© 2024 The Authors.
This article is published online with Open Access by IOS Press and distributed under the terms
of the Creative Commons Attribution Non-Commercial License 4.0 (CC BY-NC 4.0).
doi:10.3233/ATDE231390

The Influence of High-Level Discipline Competition on the Cultivation of Innovative and Entrepreneurial Talents in Colleges and Universities-A Case Study of W University in Wuhan

Xiangxing YAN[a], Xinchen XUE[b], Jiangbiao WANG[c], Yang YIN[d,1]

[a] *Personnel Department, Wuhan University of Technology, Wuhan, China*
[b] *School of Safety Science and Emergency Management, Wuhan University of Technology, Wuhan, China*
[c] *School of Information Engineering, Wuhan University of Technology, Wuhan, China*
[d] *Committee of the Communist Youth League, Wuhan University of Technology, Wuhan, China*

Abstract. This paper is based on a sample study of students in Wuhan W University which describes the basic situation of high-level academic competitions on the cultivation of innovative and entrepreneurial talents in the university. It also analyzes the influence of high-level academic competitions on the cultivation of innovative and entrepreneurial talents and the internal connection among the dimensions in the evaluation system of innovative and entrepreneurial talents through structural equation modeling. The entropy power method was used to analyze the degree of emphasis and concern on the cultivation of innovative and entrepreneurial talents in different dimensions of high-level academic competitions, and to reveal the influence of high-level academic competitions on the cultivation of innovative and entrepreneurial skills, to provide a theoretical basis for the construction of competition-oriented innovative and entrepreneurial talents cultivation system.

Keywords. Academic competition; Innovative and entrepreneurial talents; Structural equation; Entropy method analysis.

1. Introduction

The 20th National Congress of the Communist Party of China pointed out that we should accelerate the building of an innovative country and cultivate large quantities of world-class scientists and technologists, strategically important in their fields, alongside scientific and technological leaders, young talents in science and technology, and high-level innovation teams. As the main training ground for innovative and entrepreneurial talents, the mission and task of innovation and entrepreneurship education in colleges and universities are particularly prominent [1,2]. Although the

---

[1] Corresponding Author: Yang YIN, E-mail: yy88whut@whut.edu.cn

total number of university graduates has reached a record high year after year, it still cannot meet the demand of society for innovative and entrepreneurial talents. Innovation and entrepreneurship education should develop together with entrepreneurs.

In the new century, higher education has placed higher demands on the innovative and entrepreneurial abilities of university student groups. As an essential platform to carry university students' practice, exercise, and test their innovation and entrepreneurship, high-level academic competitions have also ushered in a new stage of development. In particular, and with the implementation and release of several rankings for the cultivation of innovative talents and academic competitions in universities, academic competitions in universities are highly valued by universities and are gradually occupying an important place in the academic career of university students. High-level subject competitions highlight the importance of students' practical solutions to theoretical problems and are an essential measure for the scientific evaluation of students' academic achievement in universities. Different from the general function of regular teaching in colleges and universities, the subject competition of college students plays a vital role in optimizing talents and improving the quality of skills. Therefore, the cultivation of innovative and entrepreneurial talents through high-level university competitions has become an essential path for the cultivation of innovative and entrepreneurial talents in universities.

The effectiveness and effect of high-level academic competitions on the cultivation of innovative and entrepreneurial talents in universities have been a hot topic of research in the education sector. Some scholars have pointed out that college students' discipline competitions are rich in content, diverse in organizational forms and comprehensive, which is a crucial part of scientific research education in colleges and universities. It is also a useful method and a powerful medium to improve college students' innovative spirit, creativity, and teamwork consciousness. However, some scholars have questioned the cultivation of innovative talents through the current high-level disciplinary competitions [3-5]. Qiguang Zhang pointed out that there are problems such as form over substance, unreasonable design, and unclear educational objectives for university students, questioning the effectiveness of disciplinary competitions [6]. A study has proposed a talent training system that "sets goals, integrates frameworks, designs methods and establishes systems" by incorporating the intellectual property system into the training of innovative and entrepreneurial talents [7]. Some scholars have explored the model of innovation and entrepreneurship ability of applied undergraduate engineering talents [8]. The eight disciplinary approach is the appropriate method to improve the nine future-oriented skills of engineering students was proved by Subramaniam Murugan et al. to develop outstanding innovators [9]. Therefore, how properly constructing a competition-oriented innovation and entrepreneurship talent cultivation system is necessary for innovation and entrepreneurship education in universities.

2.   Study Design and Methodology

The cultivation of innovative and entrepreneurial talents for college students is aimed at enhancing students' knowledge, ability, literacy and belief in innovation and entrepreneurship [10-11]. To achieve this effect, in addition to professional academic training, it is more critical to make outstanding students stand out by means of high-level academic competitions, and ultimately achieve the goal of common progress and talent by virtue of the demonstration role of leading the backward with the advanced.

To clarify the impact of the current high-level discipline competition on the cultivation of innovative and entrepreneurial talents. By constructing a structural equation model, this paper analyzes the impact of high-level discipline competitions on the cultivation of innovative and entrepreneurial talents and the internal connection between the dimensions of the innovation and entrepreneurial talent evaluation system; through the analysis of the entropy weight method, to understand the impact of high-level discipline competitions on innovation and entrepreneurship in colleges and universities at different stages emphasis on different dimensions of talent training; revealing the impact of high-level discipline competitions on the cultivation of innovative and entrepreneurial talents, and providing a theoretical basis for building a competition-oriented innovative and entrepreneurial talent training system.

2.1.   Study Design

This paper creates an evaluation system for innovative and entrepreneurial talents based on four dimensions: knowledge, ability, literacy and beliefs, and uses structural equation modelling for analysis and modelling. The explicit and latent variables were identified according to the research questions and the pathways were mapped according to the relationships between the variables as is shown in Fig. 1:

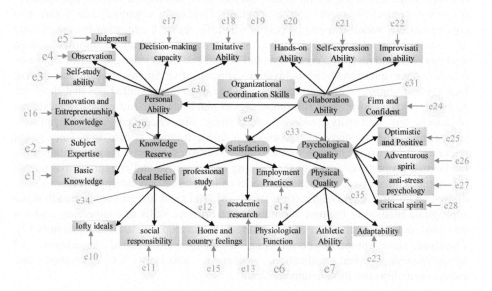

Figure 1. Structural equation model path diagram

In the research model constructed in this paper, the given potential independent variables are knowledge reserve, personal ability, collaboration ability, physical quality, psychological quality, ideal belief and satisfaction. The correspondence between latent variables and observed variables is shown in the following Table 1:

Table 1. Latent variables and their corresponding observed variables

Latent Variables	Observed Variables
Knowledge Reserve	Basic Knowledge Subject Expertise Innovation and Entrepreneurship Knowledge
Personal Ability	Self-study ability Observation Judgment Decision-making capacity Imitative Ability
Collaboration Ability	Organizational Coordination Skills Hands-on Ability Self-expression ability Improvisation ability
Physical Quality	Physiological Function Athletic Ability Adaptability
Psychological Quality	Firm and Confident Optimistic and Positive Adventurous spirit anti-stress psychology critical spirit
Ideal Belief	lofty ideals social responsibility Home and country feelings
Satisfaction	professional study academic research Employment Practices

2.2. Research Methods

(1) The structural equation model is a comprehensive statistical method mainly based on the analysis of the covariance matrix of variables to describe the relationship between variables, and its essence is the extension of general linear models. This paper applies the structural equation model to the field of policy effect evaluation and uses SEM to conduct "counterfactual" inference, hoping to provide a new and more effective policy evaluation method.

(2) The entropy weight method belongs to the objective weighting method. Determining the objective weight according to the level of index variability is the fundamental idea. The lower the information entropy of an index, the greater the variation in the index value, and the more information it provides, the greater the role it can play in the overall assessment and the greater its weight. On the contrary, the higher the information entropy of an indicator, the lower the degree of variation in the value of the indicator, the less information it provides, the smaller its role in the overall assessment and the lower its weight.

3. Samples and Data Sources

This paper takes the students at W University in Wuhan as the survey object, adopts quota sampling and simple random sampling. A combination of online and offline questionnaires was used to collect data. 800 questionnaires were distributed, and 721 valid questionnaires were recovered. The effective rate of the questionnaire was 90.125%. Among them, the proportion of male students was 54.93% and female students was 45.07%, which basically conformed to the gender characteristics of students in W colleges. Among the respondents, 70.2% of the students had participated in high-level discipline competitions, and 29.8% of the students had no experience in participating in these competitions. Among the high-level competitions with a high participation rate of respondents, from the highest to lowest participation rates were "Challenge cup" National College Student Curricular Academic Science and Technology Works Competition, ACM-ICPC International Collegiate Programming Contest, China Undergraduate Mathematical Contest Modeling, China "Internet+" College Student Innovation and Entrepreneurship Competition and "Challenge Cup" National College Student Business Plan Competition, all in the Ministry of Education In the list of academic competitions.

4. Empirical Analysis

4.1. Reliability Tests

Reliability pertains to the degree of consistency or stability of measurement outcomes and primarily represents the reliability coefficient amidst the outcomes of repeated measurements of the same group of subjects at different times. The results of the reliability test for the current latent variable are shown in Table 2:

Table 2. Latent Variable Reliability Test Results

Latent Variables	Number of Variables	Cronbach's Alpha
Knowledge Reserve	3	0.935
Personal Ability	5	0.950
Collaboration Ability	4	0.792
Physical Quality	3	0.827
Psychological Quality	5	0.788
Ideal Belief	3	0.926
Satisfaction	3	0.834

The alpha coefficient for each latent variable exceeds 0.7, signifying significant reliability and rendering it fit for inclusion in the model path map.

4.2. Interpretation and Analysis of Structural Equation Modeling Results

4.2.1. Relationship between Latent Variables

Analyzing the results of the structural equation model, we understand the relationship between the dimensions of the evaluation system of innovative and entrepreneurial talents and the satisfaction of talent cultivation under the influence of disciplinary competitions. Among them, according to the importance of the path coefficients, the path coefficient between "physical quality" and "satisfaction" is not remarkable in the set potential variable relationship, which means the initial assumption is accepted: there is no strong correlation between physical quality and satisfaction with the talents cultivation, which means that the direct influence of physical quality on satisfaction with the talents cultivation in the context of disciplinary competitions is small. In contrast, the path coefficients between the other latent variables are all noteworthy, showing that the assumption holds, and a causal relationship exists between the latent variables [12].

The regression coefficient between the knowledge reserve factor and the satisfaction factor is 0.763. This implies that a one percent increase in the factor of knowledge reserve due to disciplinary competition results in an increase in the satisfaction factor by 0.763 percentage points. It is evident that the knowledge reserve of talents has a strong positive influence on the satisfaction of talent training.

The regression coefficient between the personal ability factor and the satisfaction factor is 0.931, demonstrating that an increase of one percentage point in the personal ability factor under the influence of disciplinary competitions is linked to a 0.931 percentage point increase in the satisfaction factor. It is obvious that the personal ability of talent has an extremely strong positive influence on the satisfaction of talent training.

The regression coefficient between the collaborative ability factor and the satisfaction factor is 0.560, which implies that a one percentage point increase in the collaborative ability factor is accompanied by a 0.560 percentage point increase in the satisfaction factor under the influence of disciplinary competition. It is clear that the collaborative ability of talents has a positive influence on the satisfaction of talent training.

The regression coefficient between the psychological quality factor and the satisfaction factor was 0.634, meaning that when the psychological quality factor increased by one percentage point under the influence of disciplinary competition, the satisfaction factor increased by 0.634 percentage points. It is obvious that the psychological quality of talents has a strong positive influence on the satisfaction of talent training.

The regression coefficient between the ideal belief factor and the satisfaction factor was 0.872, which shows that under the influence of disciplinary competition, the ideal belief factor increased by one percentage point and the satisfaction factor increased by 0.872 percentage points. It can be seen that the ideal belief of talent has an extremely strong positive influence on the satisfaction of talent training.

4.2.2. Relationship between Latent and Observed Variables

In addition to analyzing the relationship between latent variables, we can also explore the correlation between latent and observed variables in the satisfaction model of innovation and entrepreneurial talent training, to investigate the observed variables that have a significant correlation with latent variables.

The regression coefficient of the observed variable on the latent variable represents the degree of influence of the observed variable on the latent variable. Among the knowledge reserve factors, the regression coefficients of basic general knowledge, subject specialized knowledge and innovation and entrepreneurship knowledge were 0.32, 0.85 and 0.83 respectively. It shows that knowledge reserves such as basic general knowledge, disciplinary professional knowledge and innovation and entrepreneurship knowledge all influence the satisfaction of training innovative and entrepreneurial talents, among which disciplinary professional knowledge and innovation and entrepreneurship knowledge are the dominant factors, and training innovative and entrepreneurial talents should focus on these two types of knowledge consciously.

The regression coefficients of self-learning ability, observation ability, imitation ability, judgment ability and decision-making ability in the personal ability factor are 0.95, 0.92, 0.73, 0.65 and 0.43 respectively, indicating that self-learning ability and observation ability are the vital personal ability factors for satisfaction with the cultivation of innovative and entrepreneurial talents in the context of disciplinary competitions.

In the collaborative ability factor, the regression coefficients of practical and hands-on ability, organizational and coordination ability, self-expression ability and improvisation ability are 0.86, 0.73, 0.56 and 0.26 respectively, indicating that innovative and entrepreneurial talents in the context of disciplinary competitions should focus on improving their practical and hands-on ability.

Among the physical quality factors, the regression coefficients for physiological function, athletic ability and adaptability are 0.65, 0.58, and 0.37 respectively, indicating that physiological function is the main influence on physical quality.

Among the psychological factors, the regression coefficients of optimistic and positive, firm and confident, adventurous spirit, critical spirit and stress anti-stress psychology were 0.69, 0.64, 0.58, 0.43 and 0.38 respectively, indicating that optimistic and positive, firm and confident are the most important psychological factors for innovative and entrepreneurial talents.

Among the ideals and beliefs factors, the regression coefficients of 0.77, 0.75 and 0.65 for lofty ideals, social responsibility and home and country feelings respectively have a relatively average impact.

4.3. Entropy Weight Method--the Emphasis of Different Stages of High-level Disciplinary Competitions on Different Dimensions of Innovative and Entrepreneurial Talent Development

4.3.1. Test Method and Process of Entropy Weight Method

In this paper, the entropy weight method is used to calculate the weighting of the preparation phase, the incubation phase and the competition phase for the promotion dimension, as well as to calculate the weighting of the promotion of the different dimensions at a given stage. Through the analysis of entropy weight method, we can know how the ability to focus on training in different stages has changed, so as to refine what kind of ability has been trained in what work. The first comparison of the share of facilitation for dimensions at a given stage is shown in the following Table 3:

Table 3. Horizontal Comparison Dimension Weight

	Knowledge Reserve	Personal Ability	Collaboration Ability	Physical Quality	Psychological Quality	Ideal Belief
Preparation Phase	0.32	0.38	0.12	0.03	0.07	0.08
Incubation Phase	0.16	0.28	0.36	0.06	0.02	0.12
Competition Phase	0.07	0.04	0.52	0.04	0.22	0.11

A visual stacked bar chart is drawn from the table data, as shown in Fig. 2:

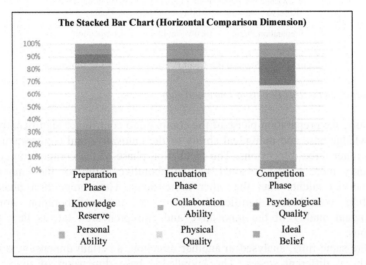

Figure 2. The Stacked Bar Chart (Horizontal Comparison Dimension)

Accordingly, we compare longitudinally the share of promotion weights for a dimension at different stages, as shown in Table 4:

Table 4. Vertical Comparison Dimension Weight

	Knowledge Reserve	Personal Ability	Collaboration Ability	Physical Quality	Psychological Quality	Ideal Belief
Preparation Phase	0.72	0.44	0.42	0.32	0.07	0.37
Incubation Phase	0.12	0.24	0.14	0.3	0.11	0.32
Competition Phase	0.16	0.32	0.44	0.38	0.82	0.31

A visual stacked bar chart is drawn from the table data, as shown in Fig. 3:

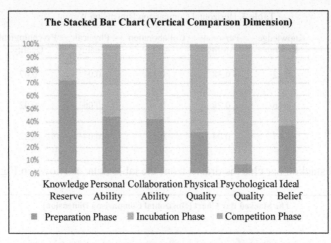

Figure 3. The Stacked Bar Chart (Vertical Comparison Dimension)

4.3.2. Analysis on the Test Results of Entropy Weight Method

Specifically, the preparation phase of the competition contributes significantly more to the knowledge base and individual ability of the innovative and entrepreneurial talent than the other three dimensions. The incubation phase of the competition contributes significantly more to the personal and collaborative ability of the innovative and entrepreneurial talents than the other dimensions. The competition phase of the competition contributes significantly more to the collaboration ability and psychological quality of the innovative and entrepreneurial talents than the other dimensions.

At the same time, analysed in another direction, a certain dimension is improved differently at different stages. The knowledge base dimension of innovative and entrepreneurial talents improves almost exclusively in the preparation phase of the competition. Individual ability is improved at all stages of the competition, with a relatively high degree of improvement in the preparation stage. Collaborative ability is mainly improved in the preparation and competition stages of the competition, and both contribute to collaborative ability to an approximately equal degree. Psychological literacy is improved almost exclusively in the competition phase of the competition. The physical literacy and idealistic belief dimensions remained low at all stages. This is in line with the results shown by the structural equation model.

4.4. Empirical Investigation and Analysis Conclusion

4.4.1. Differential Impact of High-level Disciplinary Competitions on Different Dimensions of Innovation and Entrepreneurship Training in Universities

Based on the entropy weighting method to calculate the weight of academic competitions on the dimensions of innovative and entrepreneurial talent cultivation, we acknowledge that high-level academic competitions have a profound positive influence on the fostering of innovative and entrepreneurial talent in universities. In particular, the four dimensions of the evaluation system of innovative and entrepreneurial talents, namely knowledge reserve, individual and collaborative ability, and psychological quality, have a significant contribution, while the contribution to the dimensions of physical quality and ideal beliefs is weaker. Among the four dimensions that have been significantly improved, it is worth pointing out that the promotion effect on personal ability is the most obvious.

In addition, when analyzing the results of the structural equation model, the regression coefficients of the observed variables on the latent variables represent the degree of influence of the observed variables on the latent variables. In the knowledge reserve factor, the regression coefficients of subject expertise and innovation and entrepreneurship knowledge are similar, while the regression coefficients of basic general knowledge are too small; in the personal ability factor, the regression coefficients from high to low are self-learning ability, observation ability, imitation ability, judgment ability and decision-making ability; in the collaboration ability factor, the regression coefficients from high to low are practical and hands-on ability, organization and coordination ability, self-expression ability, and The regression coefficients of the physical fitness factor are, from high to low, physiological function, athletic ability and adaptability; the regression coefficients of the psychological factor are, from high to low, optimistic and positive, firm and confident, adventurous spirit, critical spirit and anti-stress psychology; the regression coefficients of the ideals and beliefs factor are, from high to low, lofty ideals, social responsibility and home and country feelings.

4.4.2. The Impact of Different Stages of High-level Disciplinary Competitions on the Various Dimensions of the Evaluation System of Innovative and Entrepreneurial Talents in Universities has its own Focus

Using the entropy weighting method, the weight of the impact of each stage of the competition on each dimension of the innovation and entrepreneurship talent evaluation system and the weight of the degree of improvement each dimension receives at different stages are calculated.

The analysis showed that the preparation phase of the competition promoted the knowledge base and personal ability of the innovative and entrepreneurial talents significantly more than other dimensions; the incubation phase of the competition promoted the personal ability and collaboration ability of the innovative and entrepreneurial talents significantly more than other dimensions; the competition phase of the competition promoted the collaboration ability and psychological literacy of the innovative and entrepreneurial talents significantly more than other dimensions.

At the same time, from another perspective, the knowledge reserve dimension of the innovation and entrepreneurship talents was improved almost exclusively in the preparation phase of the competition; the personal ability dimension was improved in all phases of the competition, with a relatively high degree of improvement in the preparation phase; the collaboration ability dimension was improved mainly in the preparation and competition phases of the competition, and the degree of promotion of collaboration ability by both was almost equal; the psychological quality dimension was improved almost exclusively in the competition phase of the competition; the physical quality dimension and the ideal belief dimension remained low in all phases, which is consistent with the results shown by the structural equation model.

5. Conclusion

5.1. For Schools

5.1.1. Improve the Construction of Curriculum System Related to Subject Competition

Subject competitions have a strong role in promoting knowledge reserve, individual ability, collaborative ability and psychological quality in the evaluation system of innovative and entrepreneurial talents. Schools should set up supporting courses for subject competitions, use subject competitions as a guide to optimize students' knowledge structure, exercise students' comprehensive innovative and entrepreneurial ability, and play an important role in subject competitions in promoting knowledge reserve, individual ability and collaborative ability.

5.1.2. Strengthen the Education on the Ideals and Beliefs of Innovative and Entrepreneurial Talents

The structural equation model shows that ideal beliefs are an important factor influencing satisfaction with innovation and entrepreneurship education. However, according to the results of the entropy weighting method analysis, the level of influence of disciplinary competitions on ideal beliefs at this stage is low, and the competition-oriented education for innovative and entrepreneurial talents is missing the important link of ideal beliefs education. Academic competitions should be combined with other cultivation measures to achieve complementary advantages.

5.2. For Students

5.2.1. A Proper Attitude to the Competition, with Competence Development as the Starting Point

The low level of influence of the current academic competitions on ideals and beliefs is not only due to the problems of the construction of academic competitions, but also due to the utilitarian attitude of university students towards competitions, who are accustomed to taking the prize gain as the main reward for participating in academic competitions, while neglecting the more important aspect of academic competitions -- the cultivation of abilities. University students should correct their attitude towards academic competitions and innovation and entrepreneurship education, integrate their personal ideals into the cause of the country and the nation, and contribute to the development of the motherland.

5.2.2. Targeted Competency Training with Your Own Reality

Grasp the multi-dimensional contribution of disciplinary competitions to the evaluation system of innovative and entrepreneurial talents, and find your own ability positioning. Actively engage in disciplinary competitions to improve their own competency structure and build on their strengths and avert their weaknesses. Strive to develop into outstanding innovative and entrepreneurial talents.

References

[1]   Wang Xin. Influencing factors and connotation optimization of innovation and entrepreneurship education in colleges and universities from the perspective of maker culture[J]. Ideological and Theoretical Education, 2021, (02): 106-111 (in Chinese).

[2]   Shi Li, Li Jizhen. Innovation and entrepreneurship education in colleges and universities: connotation, dilemma and path optimization[J]. Heilongjiang Higher Education Research, 2021, 39(02): 100-104 (in Chinese).

[3]   Zhang Jing, Liu Xiangyun, Liu Manlu, Xiong Kaifeng. Exploration of innovative talent training methods based on discipline competition under the background of "Internet+"[J]. Wireless Internet Technology, 2021, 18(16): 164-166 (in Chinese).

[4]   Bai Xue, Wang Jing. Exploration on the ways of college students' discipline competition and innovative talents Cultivation[J]. Invention and Innovation (Vocational Education), 2021, (03): 163+165 (in Chinese).

[5]   Mao Na. The construction of innovative talents training and teaching system based on subject competition[J]. Encyclopedia Knowledge, 2021, (06): 69-70 (in Chinese).

[6]   Zhang Qiguang. The construction and realization path of college entrepreneurship education system in the era of "Internet +"[J]. Journal of Southwest Normal University (Natural Science Edition), 2020, 45(12): 148-153 (in Chinese).

[7]   Liu Yang, Yan Xin, Shiwei Xiao. Assessment of intellectual property-driven innovation and entrepreneurial development using fuzzy analytical method[J]. Journal of Intelligent & Fuzzy Systems, 2021: 1-10.

[8]   Li Gao, Man Cui, Si Chen, Fenghua Wu, Jingyao Yi. Research and exploration on the cultivation of innovative and entrepreneurial ability of applied-oriented undergraduate talents under the background of new engineering[J]. Creative Education Studies,2022, 10(1): 86-90.

[9]   Subramaniam Murugan, Noordin Muhammad Khair, Suppramaniam Murugan, et al. Eight discipline methodology in internship program to improve future proof talents among graduate engineers[J]. Talent Development & Excellence,2020, 12: 1623-1634.

[10] Shen Yunci. The construction of innovation and entrepreneurship education support system in local universities-based on the perspective of industry-university-research collaboration in the whole chain[J]. Science and Technology in Chinese Universities, 2020, (12): 72-76 (in Chinese).

[11] Liu Ya, Xu Zhen, Yang Lei. Reform and exploration of innovative and entrepreneurial talent training in local universities[J]. Heilongjiang Education (Higher Education Research and Evaluation), 2020, (12): 91-92 (in Chinese).

[12] Wang Chenchen. Exploration on curriculum system construction of social work specialty based on dual-system talent cultivation mode[J]. Education Science (English Version), 2022, (1):148-154.

Artificial Intelligence, Medical Engineering and Education
Z.B. Hu et al. (Eds.)
© 2024 The Authors.
This article is published online with Open Access by IOS Press and distributed under the terms
of the Creative Commons Attribution Non-Commercial License 4.0 (CC BY-NC 4.0).
doi:10.3233/ATDE231391

Quality Evaluation of Innovation and Entrepreneurship Education in Colleges and Universities Based on CIPP Model and AHP

Xiaoshi CHEN, Jixu ZHU[1]
Guangzhou City University of Technology, Guangzhou, China
ORCiD ID: Xiaoshi CHEN https://orcid.org/0009-0009-8704-878X

Abstract. Assessing the quality of education related to innovation and entrepreneurship in higher education institutions facilitates the identification and analysis of issues that arise during the process of developing these skills, as well as the advancement of the effectiveness of this process. Based on the CIPP model introduction, this paper attempts to build an index system from four perspectives: context evaluation, input evaluation, process evaluation and product evaluation. The analytic hierarchy process (AHP) is then used to determine the index weights, producing three primary and six subsidiary indicators that have a major influence on how well innovation and entrepreneurship education are taught at colleges and universities, among other things. Lastly, based on these viewpoints, enhancement strategies for the teaching of innovation and entrepreneurship in colleges and universities are suggested. To serve as a guide for enhancing the standard of entrepreneurship and innovation education in colleges and institutions.

Keywords. Innovation and entrepreneurship education; quality evaluation; CIPP; AHP

1. Introduction

Innovation and entrepreneurship education should undoubtedly be incorporated into the overall talent development process, according to the State Council's "Implementation Opinions on Deepening Innovation and Entrepreneurship Education Reform in Higher Education Institutions" (GUOBANFA [2015] No. 36) [1]. Higher education institutions not only have the function of creating a series of systems of knowledge but also can cultivate a group of innovative and entrepreneurial talents through the innovation and entrepreneurship education system, in order to continuously improve the innovation economy driving force. Evaluation is the process of evaluating objective objects based on predetermined standards and assigning values based on how well the object satisfies the subject's demands. Values and evaluation objectives form the cornerstone of innovation and entrepreneurship education. These are evaluated through the application of realistic and scientific methodologies in order to gather data and offer feedback for the advancement of innovation and entrepreneurship education as well as to continuously

---

[1] Corresponding Author: Jixu ZHU, E-mail: zhujixu@gcu.edu.cn

raise the bar for decision-making procedures and innovation and entrepreneurship education. Colleges and universities should strive to develop and enhance entrepreneurial consciousness, innovation spirit, and innovation and entrepreneurship as the ultimate aim of implementing innovation and entrepreneurship education evaluation. To that purpose, we must utilize indicators of the operation state of innovation and entrepreneurship education in colleges and universities, among other things, to assess the development and effectiveness of innovation and entrepreneurship education in each college and university. As a result, it provides management with information and comments on how to improve teaching methodologies, the environment in which innovation and entrepreneurship are taught, and the education of innovation and entrepreneurship [2-3].

Numerous studies have investigated the problems plaguing innovation and entrepreneurship education in China. Chen (2020) revealed that teachers lacked the experience and training required for entrepreneurship [1]. Xia (2021) argued that excessive theoretical teaching failed to provide students with practical skills [4]. Although these studies identify important issues, a comprehensive and systematic evaluation of the overall quality of entrepreneurship education programs is still lacking. To fill this gap, this paper introduces the CIPP evaluation model as an effective framework for assessing the context, inputs, processes, and outputs of innovation and entrepreneurship education in higher education. The CIPP model was originally proposed by Stufflebeam (1971) and has been widely used in educational program evaluation (Wei et al., 2019; Pang, 2021) [5-6]. However, there are relatively few studies using CIPP to evaluate the quality of entrepreneurship education. This study uses the CIPP model to create a more complete and objective evaluation system as well as a reliable evaluation tool to assist the ongoing improvement of innovation and entrepreneurship education in China's universities.

2. Overview of CIPP Model and AHP

2.1. CIPP Model

The CIPP model is a management-oriented model developed by Daniel L. Stufflebeam, a well-known American educational evaluator, based on the breakthrough of Tyler's behavioural goal-oriented mode [6]. There are four components to the CIPP model: first, Context Evaluation (CE), which is to determine the educational goals based on the needs of the evaluated target, to determine whether the educational goals reflect these needs, and thus to discover the differences with the actual results; second, Input Evaluation ((IE) is the evaluation of the conditions and resources needed to achieve the goals based on contextual evaluation, and the evaluation of the feasibility and usefulness of the educational program is its essence; third, Process Evaluation (PE) is the evaluation that monitors and checks the actual operation of the program, identifies problems, and provides effective feedback to decision makers; fourth, Product Evaluation (PE) is the evaluation that provides effective feedback to decision makers through the evaluation of the educational program. Product assessment (PE) is the process of gathering data pertaining to the outcomes in order to assess the true degree of the goals accomplished. A major advancement in the history of educational evaluation is the application of the CIPP model to the quality assessment of innovation and entrepreneurship education in colleges and universities. This shifts the focus from evaluation for the sake of proof to improvement, from goal, result, and proof to decision, process, and improvement [7].

2.2. Analytic Hierarchy Process （AHP）

Early in the 1970s, University of Pittsburgh operations researcher Professor Satie proposed the analytic hierarchy process (AHP). This approach to methodical, hierarchical, qualitative, and quantitative analysis breaks the problem into a number of distinct objectives, which are then further broken down into a number of contributing factors. Depending on the complexity of the problem to be solved, the differentiation level can also be divided into several different levels. In order to link the problem to be solved to the influence weights of the various bottom-level influencing factors on the overall objective, the weights of the influencing factors in the various levels are determined using the fuzzy quantification method of qualitative indicators for the various influencing factors on the upper-level objectives [8]. AHP is a simple and efficient method for calculating indicator weights, which decomposes the elements to be decided into three levels: objective, criterion, and plan, and makes the final decision by fuzzy quantification of qualitative indicator information into simple and clear results of mathematical operations [9].

The Analytic Hierarchy Process (AHP) involves the division of the decision problem into a hierarchical structure consisting of the general objective, sub-objectives at each level, evaluation criteria, and specific alternative solutions. The prioritization of elements within each level is determined using the method of solving the judgment matrix's eigenvectors, which establishes the relative importance of each element in relation to the preceding level. Finally, the method of weighing and summing the final weights of each alternative solution with respect to the general objective is employed to identify the optimal choice [10].

3. Selection and Model Construction of Quality Evaluation Indexes of Innovation and Entrepreneurship Education in Universities Based on CIPP Model and AHP

Starting from the real-life insights of the CIPP education evaluation model, the evaluation indicators are designed around the school's actual situation and from four evaluation levels.

(1) Context Evaluation. The "C" in the CIPP model is Context Evaluation, which is a diagnostic evaluation of the implementation plan of innovation and entrepreneurship education in colleges and universities, and evaluates whether the goals set by the plan are indeed feasible. The focus of this evaluation is to clarify the basic information of the evaluated object, that is, the environmental foundation, and to evaluate whether all the conditions required for the implementation of the program are available and what deficiencies need to be adjusted and improved. The evaluation indexes mainly include top-level design, Safeguard mechanism and cultivation program, etc [11].

(2) Input Evaluation. Input evaluation, which comes after background evaluation, is represented by the letter "I" in the CIPP model. Focusing on whether the program is fully and successfully employed once the goals and concepts of innovation and entrepreneurship education are clearly defined, as well as whether the teachers and

financial inputs required for its implementation are comprehensive and sufficient. The evaluation indexes mainly include faculty input and funding. The evaluation indexes mainly include Faculty input and funding input [12].

(3) Process Evaluation. The "P" in the CIPP model is Process Evaluation, which is used to supervise and give feedback to the implementation of innovation and entrepreneurship education in colleges and universities. The main purpose is to correct and adjust the implementation process, improve and optimize the implementation process, formative evaluation and provide services for the implementation decision. The evaluation indexes mainly include teaching management, practice platform and Innovative entrepreneurial projects [13].

(4) Product Evaluation. The "P" in the CIPP model, also known as product evaluation, refers to the evaluation of the performance results associated with innovation and entrepreneurship education inside higher education institutions. In order to assess the efficacy of innovation and entrepreneurship education inside higher education institutions, an extensive dataset will be gathered encompassing a diverse array of individuals participating in the program. The data will then be analyzed to see if the adoption of innovation and entrepreneurship education accomplishes the desired goals or has other societal advantages. The primary assessment indices comprise student, enterprise, and school levels, among others [14]. Combining the above index elements into one, the evaluation system is shown in Table 1.

Table 1. Quality evaluation index system of university innovation and entrepreneurship education based on CIPP model

First-level indicators B	Second-level indicators C	Indicator Description
Context Evaluation B1	Top-level design C1	Integrating innovation and entrepreneurship education into the overall framework of the school's talent training program
		The concept and objectives are very clear
		Develop an implementation strategy to further the reform of entrepreneurship and innovation education
	Safeguard mechanism C2	Implementing "a handful of projects" and a "school system"
		Develop corresponding rules and regulations for innovation and entrepreneurship education
		Incentive mechanism and assessment methods for innovation and entrepreneurship education work
	Cultivation Program C3	Innovation and entrepreneurship education for all students
		Develop a relatively complete program to develop innovative and entrepreneurial capabilities
		Organic integration of professional education and innovation and entrepreneurship education
		Basic courses on innovation and entrepreneurship education included in the compulsory courses
Input Evaluation B2	Faculty input C4	Input from full-time and part-time innovation and entrepreneurship teachers
	Funding input C5	Innovation and Entrepreneurship Education Funding

(continued)

Table 1. *(continued)*

First-level indicators B	Second-level indicators C	Indicator Description
Input Evaluation B2	Funding input C5	Number of grants for innovative and entrepreneurial projects
Process Evaluation B3	Teaching Management C6	Number of innovative and entrepreneurial courses offered
		Establish a cumulative conversion system for innovation and entrepreneurship education credits
		Course Teaching Mode
	Practice Platform C7	Fixed on-campus innovation and entrepreneurship experiment and practice place
		Off-campus Innovation and Entrepreneurship Education Practice Base
		Using social resources to support the construction of innovation and entrepreneurship education practice platform
		Open the on-campus experimental practice platform to students
	Innovative entrepreneurial projects C8	Number of SRP Program
		Number of participants in the SRP Program
Product Evaluation B4	Student Level C9	Creative thinking and entrepreneurial awareness of students
		Student Innovation and Entrepreneurship Competition Awards
		Student Entrepreneurship Rate
	Corporate level C10	Enterprise evaluation of employment talent quality
		Partner companies promote the transformation of results
		Enterprise mentor, enterprise innovation and entrepreneurship base, enterprise funding input
	School level C11	teaching benefits teachers as well as students
		Social benefits (entrepreneurial alumni satisfaction, employer satisfaction, social reputation)
		ransformation of scientific research results of innovation and entrepreneurship education and application of innovation and entrepreneurship projects

Source: created by the author.

Based on the evaluation index system presented in Table 1, the assessment of high innovation and entrepreneurship education is established as the primary objective layer. This is further supported by four first-level indicators (B1-B4) serving as the criterion layer, and a comprehensive set of 11 indicators in the plan layer (C1-C11). Consequently, an evaluation system for assessing the quality of innovation and entrepreneurship education in higher education institutions is constructed. The evaluation hierarchy model is developed using the meta-decision yaahp software [2]. As seen in Figure 1.

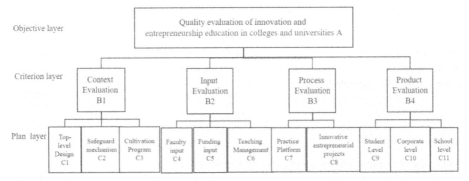

Fig.1. Hierarchical model for evaluating the quality of innovation and entrepreneurship education in higher education

Source: created by the author.

4. Analysis of the Process and Results of Quality Evaluation of University Innovation and Entrepreneurship Education Based on CIPP Model and AHP

4.1. Analysis of the Evaluation Process

Fourteen experts in the field of innovation and entrepreneurship education, who possess experience in overseeing or supporting such initiatives in colleges and universities, and possess knowledge about the overall landscape, achievements, and challenges in innovation and entrepreneurship education in higher education institutions, were requested to assess a questionnaire. The purpose of this assessment was to ascertain the relative importance of various evaluation criteria for determining the quality of innovation and entrepreneurship education in colleges and universities. A judgment matrix was then created, and a consistency test was carried out. The expert group consists of the head of the University Youth League Committee, the head of the Academic Affairs Department, the head of the Career Guidance Center of the Student Affairs Department, the head of the College of Innovation and Entrepreneurship Education (also known as the School of Entrepreneurship Education or Entrepreneurship College), as well as full-time teachers actively engaged in innovation and entrepreneurship education, along with other university leaders.

(1) Construction of judgment matrix model

The relative importance of the factors in Table 1 is judged as follows: citing the numbers 1-9 and their reciprocals as the scale, if the factor Bi is equally important as the factor *Bj* under objective A, assign a value of 1 to *Bi* and *Bj*; if you think Bi is more important than *Bj*, assign a value of 3 to Bi and 1/3 to *Bj*; if Bi is significantly more important than *Bj*, assign a value of 5 to Bi and 1/5 to *Bj*. If *Bi* is absolutely more important than *Bj*, *B*i is assigned a value of 9 and *Bj* is assigned a value of *1/9*, and if it is in the middle of the above two adjacent judgments, the scale value can be 2 or 4 or 6 or 8, and if Bi is not more important than *Bj*, the corresponding value of the above is the inverse of 1 [15].

(2) Hierarchical single ranking and its consistency test

Based on the judgment matrix, hierarchical single ranking determines the weights corresponding to the factors connected with this level in relation to the elements of the previous level. It serves as the foundation for grading each factor's significance at this level in relation to the one before it. The consistency index, or C.I., of the matrix must be determined in order to assess its consistency. It is defined as follows: (Note: The matrix's order is indicated by n).

$$C.I. = \frac{\lambda max - n}{n - 1} \tag{1}$$

where the maximum characteristic root of the matrix:

$$\lambda max = \frac{\sum (AWi)}{nWi} \tag{2}$$

In addition, Thomas L. Saaty proposed to use the average stochastic consistency index R.I. to correct the C.I. R.I. is a constant and the average stochastic consistency index of 1-9 matrix is shown in Table 2.

Table 2. Average random consistency index of the matrix

Number of steps	1	2	3	4	5	6	7	8	9
R.I.	0.00	0.00	0.58	0.90	1.12	1.24	1.32	1.41	1.45

Source: created by the author.

R.I. is merely formal for the order 1 and order 2 judgment matrix. We define the judgment matrix as follows: the judgment matrices of order 1 and order 2 are always the same. In cases when the matrix order exceeds 2, the random consistency ratio (C.R.) of the judgment matrix, denoted as the ratio of the consistency index (C.I.) to the average random consistency index (R.I.) of the same order, becomes applicable. When the consistency ratio (C.R.) is less than 0.1, the judgment matrix demonstrates an acceptable level of consistency. However, if the C.R. exceeds this threshold, it indicates that adjustments or modifications are necessary [16].

After combining the scoring results of 14 experts, the original comprehensive data were obtained, and the relative weights of each factor were calculated, and the judgment matrix and calculation results are shown in the table 3-7.

Table 3. Target layer Judgment matrix and weights

A1	B1	B2	B3	B4	Wi	
B1	1	4	4	5	0.5741	
B2	1/4	1	3	2	0.2124	C.R.= 0.06721 λmax =4.1815
B3	1/4	1/3	1	2	0.1227	
B4	1/5	1/2	1/2	1	0.0908	

Source: created by the author.

Table 4. Context evaluation B2 judgment matrix and weights

B1	C1	C2	C3	
C1	1	5	3	C.R.= 0.0332 λmax =3.0385
C2	1/5	1	1/3	
C3	1/3	3	1	

Source: created by the author.

Table 5. Input Evaluation B2 judgment matrix and weights

B2	C4	C5	Wi	
C4	1	5	0.8333	C.R.= 0.0000
C5	1/5	1	0.1667	λmax =2.0000

Source: created by the author.

Table 6. Process Evaluation B3 judgment matrix and weights

B3	C6	C7	C8	Wi	
C6	1	1/4	4	0.1818	C.R.= 0.0000
C87	4	1	8	0.7272	λmax =3.0000
C8	1/2	1/8	1	0.0910	

Source: created by the author.

Table 7. Product Evaluation B4 judgment matrix and weights

B4	C9	C10	C11	Wi	
C9	1	3	5	0.6370	C.R.= 0.0332
C10	1/3	1	3	0.2583	λmax =3.0385
C11	1/5	1/3	1	0.1047	

Source: created by the author.

From the above judgment matrix and weights, we can get that C.R. is less than 0.1. Therefore, all judgment matrices pass the consistency test and prove that the results are reliable.

4.2 Analysis of Evaluation Results

Based on the relative weights of the factors in Tables 3 to 7 above, the synthetic weights were calculated, and the total ranking consistency ratio C.R. of each level was less than 0.1 after accounting with YaAHP software, so this evaluation result is acceptable.

Table 8. Evaluation index weights of innovation and entrepreneurship education quality in colleges and universities

First-level indicators B	Weights	Second-level indicators C	Weights
Context Evaluation B1	0.5741	Top-level design C1	0.3636
		Safeguard mechanism C2	0.0610
		Cultivation Program C3	0.1496
Input Evaluation B2	0.2124	Faculty input C4	0.1770
Input Evaluation B2	0.2124	Funding input C5	0.0354
Process Evaluation B3	0.1227	Teaching Management C6	0.0223
		Practice Platform C7	0.0892
		Innovative entrepreneurial projects C8	0.0111
Product Evaluation B4	0.0908	Student Level C9	0.0578
		Corporate level C10	0.0234
		School level C11	0.0095

Source: created by the author.

From Table 8, we can see that there are 3 first-level indicators, 6 second-level indicators, etc. that have a greater impact on the quality evaluation of innovation and entrepreneurship education at colleges and universities. The three first-level indicators such as B1 Context Evaluation, B2 input evaluation and B3 process evaluation have greater weights in the criterion level; outcome evaluation B4 has a lagging influence due to the evaluation of outcome performance and social benefits of innovation and entrepreneurship education, and CIPP evaluation shifts the purpose of evaluation from for proof to for improvement, from goal, result and proof to decision, process and improvement, so Product Evaluation B4 The weights are lower. Sorted according to the results of the weight of the program level, the secondary indicators with greater weight are six secondary indicators: C1 top-level design, C2 Safeguard mechanism, C3 Cultivation Program, C4 faculty input, C7 practice platform, and C9 student level.

5. Conclusion and Suggestions

The four CIPP model levels served as the basis for the formulation of the quality evaluation indexes in this study, which employed AHP to assess the caliber of collegiate innovation and entrepreneurship instruction. The quality evaluation system of college innovation and entrepreneurship education based on "CIPP+AHP" was established, adhering to the principles of combining process results, teaching practice evaluation, and objective subjective evaluation. It comprises 11 second-level indicators, such as top-level design, and four first-level indicators, such as context evaluation, input evaluation, process evaluation, and product evaluation of college innovation and entrepreneurship education. The scientificity and rationality of this evaluation index system are empirically analyzed and verified. According to the empirical results, the context evaluation is given the highest weight at the criterion level, suggesting that the school is superior in terms of its promotion of innovation and entrepreneurship in education policies and the quality of its well-established management department. However, Product evaluation has the lowest score, followed by process evaluation and input evaluation. It is clear that there is still room for further improvement in terms of funding input, teaching management, and innovation and entrepreneurship programs. At the plan level, the top-level design has the highest weight, followed by faculty input. Universities should expand the reform of innovation and entrepreneurial education, boost teacher involvement, and incorporate these subjects into the talent development programs of schools. However, the lowest weight is given to the school level in the evaluation of results, which suggests that during the implementation process, schools should concentrate on social benefits and bolstering the transformation of scientific research findings of innovation and entrepreneurship education. The following recommendations are offered in an effort to raise the standard of innovation and entrepreneurship education provided in schools:

(1) Strengthen the leadership mechanism and improve the top-level design

Universities should place a high value on teaching college students about innovation and entrepreneurship, bolster their leadership structures, put the "handful project" into action, and create a collaborative mechanism for this purpose that is overseen by the Academic Affairs Office and coordinated by the Department of Discipline and Science and Technology, the Finance Office, the Personnel Office, the Student Work Office, and other departments.

(2) Establishing rules and regulations and building a perfect guarantee system

Designing an optimal operational framework to facilitate the educational endeavours of college students in the domains of innovation and entrepreneurship necessitates the establishment of a dedicated task force. This specialized working group should be entrusted with the responsibility of orchestrating the provision of office facilities, ensuring an adequate allocation of personnel, and securing the requisite financial resources by including the funding for this initiative into the university's annual budget. Furthermore, it is recommended to motivate each unit to generate financial resources for the purpose of fostering innovation and entrepreneurship by employing diverse strategies. The creation of relevant rules and regulations has been undertaken to facilitate the effective support of institutionalization, specialization, and distinctive growth in the field of innovation and entrepreneurship education.

(3) Create "four fusions" and build a high-quality talent cultivation system

Universities should take a socially conscious approach to their work, incorporating the "four fusions" of thinking and creation, specialization and creation, industry and creation, and discipline as a guide. They should also review their talent training programs, provide courses on innovation and entrepreneurship, pay attention to the development of their faculty, enhance their teaching management and research capabilities, and foster the development of applied innovation and entrepreneurship talents. We will offer compulsory courses on innovation and entrepreneurship for all students, create a practical teaching system that integrates professional and innovation and entrepreneurship; develop an innovative practice section, where each student should obtain corresponding credits, build an innovative credit conversion system, open up the first and second classes, and effectively integrate the innovation and entrepreneurship curriculum and practice system.

(4) Establishing a part-time and full-time teaching team

Interdisciplinary teaching of "innovation and entrepreneurship" ought to be a core responsibility of all university faculty. They should also support full-time teachers who offer entrepreneurship education and coaching, and they should introduce management approaches for all kinds of part-time professionals and technicians. In order to foster an environment conducive to innovation and entrepreneurship, it is recommended that colleges and universities consider the inclusion of part-time instructors specializing in these areas. Additionally, efforts should be made to improve teacher preparation, allocate specific funding for training initiatives, and encourage young educators to engage in entrepreneurship training. Furthermore, the implementation of teaching reforms focused on innovation and entrepreneurship, as well as the establishment of partnerships with businesses for job placements, can contribute to the formation of a well-rounded innovation and entrepreneurship team. This team should ideally consist of both full-time and part-time staff members, operating within a well-structured organizational framework. A suitable structure and a mix of full-time and part-time teachers will make up the faculty.

(5) Focus on the construction of campus innovation and entrepreneurship culture

Universities should carry out diversified forms of innovation and entrepreneurship practice activities, raise the overall caliber of their student body, integrate innovation and entrepreneurship education into campus cultural activities, club activities and social practice, and focus on cultivating market awareness, entrepreneurship, innovation ability and social responsibility necessary for employment competition. We will actively build a system of "college-level-school-level-provincial-level-national" innovation and entrepreneurship competitions to enhance the competitiveness of the school.

Acknowledgement

This paper is supported by the Project of "Key Research Base of Humanities and Social Sciences in Universities of Guangdong Province: Research Base for Digital Transformation of Manufacturing Enterprises" (2023WZJD012).

References

[1]   Chen W W, Chen H, Long N. Quality evaluation of entrepreneurship education in universities in Wuling Mountain area based on CIPP model[J]. Modern Business Industry, 2020, 41(34): 25-28 (in Chinese).

[2]   Fan X, Tian S, Lu Z, et al. Quality evaluation of entrepreneurship education in higher education based on CIPP model and AHP-FCE methods[J]. Frontiers in Psychology, 2022, 13(1): 1-12.

[3]   Rocha, A. C., Silva, M., & Duarte, C. How is sexuality education for adolescents evaluated? A systematic review based on the Context, Input, Process and Product (CIPP) model[J]. Sex Education, 2022, 22(2), 198-216.

[4]   Xia L B. Problems and path analysis of the construction of innovative entrepreneurship education faculty in higher education institutions[J]. Modern vocational education, 2021, 1(47): 128-129 (in Chinese).

[5]   Wei X, Liu X, Sha J. How does the entrepreneurship education influence the students' innovation? Testing on the multiple mediation model[J]. Frontiers in psychology, 2019, 10: 1-10.

[6]   Pang Fangqi. Research on quality evaluation of innovation and entrepreneurship education in applied colleges and universities[J]. Innovation and Entrepreneurship Theory and Practice, 2021, 4(12): 86-88 (in Chinese).

[7]   Basaran M, Dursun B, Gur Dortok H D, et al. Evaluation of preschool education program according to CIPP model[J]. Pedagogical Research, 2021, 6(2): 1-13.

[8]   Li N. A fuzzy evaluation model of college English teaching quality based on analytic hierarchy process[J]. International Journal of Emerging Technologies in Learning (iJET), 2021, 16(2): 17-30.

[9]   Kou L, Chen J Y. Quality evaluation of innovation and entrepreneurship education based on CIPP model and AHP-FCE[J]. Innovation and Entrepreneurship Theory Research and Practice, 2022, 5(10): 177-181+189 (in Chinese).

[10]   Niu B, Liu Q, Chen Y. Research on the university innovation and entrepreneurship education comprehensive evaluation based on AHP method[J]. International Journal of Information and Education Technology, 2019, 9(9): 623-628.

[11]   Sopha, S., & Nanni, A. The cipp model: Applications in language program evaluation[J]. Journal of Asia TEFL, 2019, 16(4), 1360-1367.

[12]   Kaushal V, Najafi M, Sattler M, et al. Review of literature on chemical emissions and worker exposures associated with cured-in-place pipe (CIPP) installation[J]. Pipelines 2019, 2019: 565-573.

[13]   Rocha A C, Silva M, Duarte C. How is sexuality education for adolescents evaluated? A systematic review based on the Context, Input, Process and Product (CIPP) model[J]. Sex Education, 2022, 22(2): 198-216.

[14]   Turmuzi M, Ratnaya I G, Al Idrus S W, et al. Literature review: evaluasi keterlaksanaan kurikulum 2013 menggunakan model evaluasi cipp (context, input, process, dan product) [J]. Jurnal Basicedu, 2022, 6(4): 7220-7232.

[15]   Chen Z, Zhao Y, Yuan L, et al. Index-based biclique percolation communities search on bipartite graphs[C]//2023 IEEE 39th International Conference on Data Engineering (ICDE). IEEE, 2023: 2699-2712.

[16]   Stein, D., & Michael, R. Determinants affecting the decision of German dentists to set-up an office: a multi-criteria evaluation[J]. SCENTIA International Economic Review, 2022, 1(2), 215-241.

Artificial Intelligence, Medical Engineering and Education
Z.B. Hu et al. (Eds.)
doi:10.3233/ATDE231392

Reform of Ideological and Political Education in Asphalt and Asphalt Mixture Experimental Course

Wen XU[a,1], Sheng XU[a], Linbo ZHANG[a], Jian TONG[a]

a School of Transportation and Logistics Engineering, Wuhan University of Technology
Wuhan, China

ORCiD ID: Wen XU https://orcid.org/0000-0003-0136-4204

Abstract. In order to promote the deep integration of ideological and political courses and professional course teaching and cultivate high-quality applied engineering and technical talents with comprehensive development, the research is conducted from the perspective of asphalt and asphalt mixture experimental courses. Based on the characteristics of the course and the combination of professional knowledge points, the educational goals of ideological and political education in the course are determined. Through multiple aspects of ideological integration: deeply explore ideological elements, optimize teaching content containing ideological elements, deepen the design of the teaching process of ideological education, and innovate teaching models and methods. This paper summarizes and analyzes the practice and thinking in teaching reform, which has great significance in promoting students' patriotic awareness, improving learning motivation, and clarifying the direction of efforts. It also provides reference for the reform and construction of ideological education in university courses.

Keywords. Asphalt and asphalt mixture testing; Course ideology and politics; Teaching method; Teaching reform.

1. Introduction

General Secretary Xi Jinping points out that he foundation of establishing a university lies in cultivating morality and cultivating talents. Comprehensively promoting the ideological construction of courses is a strategic measure to implement the fundamental task of cultivating morality and cultivating talents. Colleges and universities should effectively improve their political stance and ideological awareness, fully leverage the role of the teaching staff as the "main force", Course construction as the "main battlefield", and classroom teaching as the "main channel", and integrate values into knowledge transmission and ability cultivation, so that various courses and ideological courses run in the same direction, forming a synergistic effect, and constructing a pattern of educating people from all aspects throughout the entire process [1, 2].

Asphalt and asphalt mixture testing is a professional basic course for students majoring in transportation engineering, mainly studying the composition, performance testing, and application of asphalt pavement materials [3, 4]. By mastering the technical

---

[1] Corresponding Author: Wen XU, E-mail: wenxu@whut.edu.cn.

characteristics, indicators, and evaluation methods of asphalt pavement materials, practical engineering problems can be solved, while also laying the foundation for the subsequent study of relevant professional courses. Asphalt and asphalt mixture testing is not only a necessary basic knowledge for learning professional courses, but also an applied technology [5,6].

Through the reform of the ideological integration experimental Course, it helps students establish a correct outlook on life and values [7]. This paper mainly integrates ideological elements such as national responsibility, craftsmanship spirit, patriotism, legal awareness, and cultural confidence into the experimental teaching of asphalt and asphalt mixture, so that students can understand the importance of road engineering in national infrastructure construction, as well as China's independent research and development strength and achievements in road engineering technology. In the context of new engineering, high-level applied talents should not only possess strong professional skills and the ability to solve complex problems, but also firmly hold a political stance in order to adapt to the new situation.

2. Course Construction Objectives

The fundamental issue of education is to cultivate what kind of people, how to cultivate them, and for whom to cultivate them. The fundamental standard for testing all work in universities is to cultivate virtue and cultivate effectiveness [8]. The construction of ideological education in the Course aims to integrate values into knowledge impartation and ability cultivation, helping students shape correct worldviews, outlooks on life, and values. This is an essential part of talent cultivation and an essential content. The objectives of this course construction mainly include the following two aspects.

2.1 Course objectives

Combining the transformation, transformation, and upgrading of the transportation major in the context of new engineering, we aim to enhance professional vitality, keep up with industry development, and cultivate a group of outstanding scientific and technological talents with innovative and entrepreneurial abilities and high quality in road engineering.

Enrich teaching resources: Through resource construction and the combination of virtual and real methods, stimulate students' interest in learning, help them deeply understand the basic characteristics and requirements of mix design, and establish intuitive and perceptual understanding from the whole to the parts of the experiment, improving students' understanding ability of basic professional knowledge.

Enhance innovative practical ability: By reproducing experimental scenarios and studying the impact of multiple parameters on experimental results, promote students' exploratory and autonomous learning, and improve their comprehensive professional practical ability.

2.2 Goals of educating people

Integrating the education of Marxist standpoint, viewpoint, and method with the cultivation of scientific spirit in curriculum teaching to improve students' ability to correctly understand, analyze, and solve problems. Integrate the relevant content of ideological education into the asphalt and asphalt mixture experimental course, express the purpose of ideological education through subject integration, and achieve the goal of "curriculum education" through value guidance. Integrate learning and thinking, unify knowledge and action, and enhance students' innovative spirit of exploration and practical ability to solve problems. At the same time, it subtly allows students to receive the influence of mainstream values, strengthens students' engineering ethics education, cultivates students' spirit of striving for excellence as a great craftsman, and inspires students' patriotism and mission responsibility in serving the country through technology.

3. Course Construction Plan

How to coordinate the relationship between professional training and ideological guidance? General Secretary Xi Jinping pointed out at the National Conference on Ideological and Political Work in Universities that various courses should go hand in hand with ideological theory courses to form a synergistic effect [9]. Considering the relationship between the above courses and ideological education, based on the same direction and synergy, a teaching concept of mutual integration and promotion between courses and ideological education has been established, that is, to explore and integrate ideological elements in professional courses to achieve the goal of ideological construction; The combination of ideological elements with the basic laws of professional knowledge promotes professional teaching and better achieves professional knowledge goals. On this basis, a curriculum ideological teaching model has been formed as shown in Figure 1.

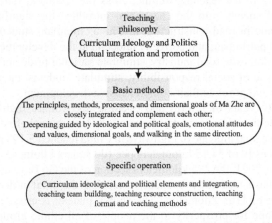

Figure 1. The teaching model of "curriculum" and "ideological and political" integrating and promoting each other

4. Key Points of Ideological and Political Education in the Course

4.1. Integration of Ideological and Political Elements in the Course

The basic methods of ideological education in the curriculum are determined as follows: at the rational level, the curriculum knowledge is closely combined with the principles of Marxist philosophy, complementing each other; At the emotional level, guided by ideological goals, the unified goal of emotional attitude and values is clarified, and we work together in the same direction. The logical relationship is shown in Figure 2.

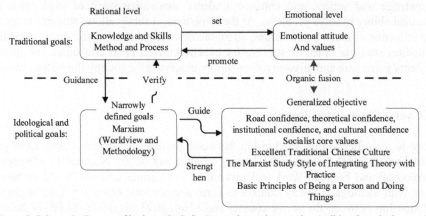

Figure 2. Schematic diagram of basic methods for integrating and promoting traditional curriculum goals and ideological and political goals

The exploration of ideological factors in the teaching content of asphalt and asphalt mixture experiment course mainly involves the following aspects.

1) The Great Country Project Inspires National Pride and Responsibility

In the teaching of asphalt and asphalt mixture experimental courses, teachers need to use the disciplinary thinking of ideological theory education to organize the teaching content. According to the teaching outline, cross the textbook, introduce the positive energy content of society into the classroom, introduce the significant progress and breakthroughs made in road construction in China, stimulate students' sense of social responsibility and patriotism, and correctly understand the development level of various disciplines in the domestic road industry, stimulate national pride and sense of concern, stimulate their sense of social responsibility, stimulate students' interest in the field of civil engineering, and promote their comprehensive development.

In the past 40 years of reform and opening up, China's highway infrastructure construction has achieved leapfrog development. To become rich, first build roads. As of the end of 2020, the total mileage of highways in China reached 5.198 million kilometers, with a highway density of 54.15 kilometers per 100 square kilometers.

On August 21, 2021, the 295 kilometers section of the G6 Beijing Tibet Expressway from Naqu to Lhasa was fully opened, increasing the total mileage of high-grade highways in Tibet to 1105 kilometers. The snowy plateau is crisscrossed by heavenly roads, bringing hope for prosperity to the people of all ethnic groups. On August 23, 2021, the Tianshan Shengli Tunnel on the Xinjiang Wuwei Expressway successfully crossed the largest and most dangerous fault zone in the project and entered the construction "fast lane". After completion, it will become the world's longest highway tunnel [10]. Figure 3 lists engineering projects related to asphalt mixture courses.

(a) Mountain asphalt pavement

(b) Hong Kong-Zhuhai-Macao Bridge Deck Pavement

Figure 3. Major Country Projects Related to Curriculum

2) Promote the spirit of craftsmanship and uphold the professional spirit of loyalty to duty and tenacious struggle

Interpret and guide students to learn the revolutionary spirit of perseverance, self-improvement, and dedication demonstrated by road engineering builders. Professional teachers will introduce advanced figures full of positive energy and a sense of the times into the classroom, such as Chen Gangyi, a Tibetan aid cadre who is loyal to his duties and still leads the project team to overcome the harsh natural environment despite suffering from cancer. Cao Guanghui, the "model of the highway director" who passed away at an early age due to accumulated labor and illness. Xu Zhenchao, who possesses noble sentiments, innovative spirit, and professional spirit, made a glorious sacrifice for rescuing flooded highways and was awarded the title of "Model of the Director of Transportation" by the Ministry of Transportation, including Zhao Jiafu.

The Sichuan Tibet Highway and the Qinghai Tibet Highway have harsh geographical and climatic environments, and many sections are prone to geological disasters. Sudden disasters such as landslides and mudslides are frequent, and the construction and maintenance techniques are complex. They are known as the most dangerous highways in the world. In order to promote the development of the southwest frontier and national unity and progress, in 1950, with the revolutionary heroism belief of "one is not afraid of hardship, and the other is not afraid of death", 110000 Tibetan and Han military people used pickaxes, shovel, hammers, and steel chisels to "break through mountains and build bridges when facing water", crossed 14 mountains, including Erlang Mountain and Queer Mountain, and crossed Minjiang River, Dadu River, Lancang River, and other major rivers; Through 8 major fault zones, spanning countless permafrost areas, swamp areas, earthquake areas, gravel collapse areas, primitive forests, and large glaciers -3000 martyrs sacrificed their lives on the plateau [11].

3) Learn The Spirit Of Liberating The Mind, Daring To Innovate, And Being The First

In the 1980s, the construction of highways in China, such as Shenda, Beijing Tianjin Tang, and Shanghai Jia, was under exploration. The builders adhered to the spirit of "being brave in innovation and daring to be the first" and continuously made breakthroughs in technology, making China's highway construction one of the world's major powers in just 30 years.

The Shenda Expressway is the first long-distance expressway designed and constructed independently in China. Except for a small number of imported key equipment, all equipment and materials are made of domestic products. The construction began in June 1984, when there were no technical standards or practical experience for highways in China. Since 1979, the project team has invited the United States and Japan multiple times for highway related technical exchanges, and sent technical personnel to developed countries to investigate and learn technology. While translating and learning relevant national technical standards, we have also formulated technical standards that are suitable for the actual situation in China. During the construction process, the construction personnel adhere to a scientific attitude and strictly manage, improve the system, and improve the management level. The successful completion of the Shenda Expressway reflects the spirit of road engineering builders in liberating their minds, actively innovating, and daring to make breakthroughs.

4) Using Marxist Leninist Ideology to Cultivate Students' Awareness of Seeking Truth from Facts and Their Ability to Analyze and Solve Problems

Buildings such as roads and bridges are exposed to the natural world for a long time and often suffer from the alternating effects of sunlight, rainwater, and environmental temperature. These natural factors have a significant impact on the performance of materials. Therefore, the dialectical relationship between internal and external factors, inevitability, and contingency in Marxist philosophical principles is introduced to guide students to analyze the influencing factors of material properties from both internal and external factors, and understand the inevitability and contingency of materials possessing this engineering characteristic. Taking the performance and influencing factors of asphalt materials as an example, asphalt materials are subject to environmental temperature, traffic loads, sunlight exposure, and the influence of rainwater. Good asphalt material performance should include good high-temperature stability, strong low-temperature crack resistance, and strong adhesion to stone under the action of rainwater. Therefore, when analyzing its performance, the first step is to analyze it from the internal factors, which depend on the basic component composition and elemental composition of the asphalt material. From the perspective of external factors, it depends on the impact of traffic load, environmental temperature, as well as the influence of sunlight and rainwater. Through the analysis of this example, students can be guided to flexibly apply the principles of Marxist philosophy to analyze and solve problems in their daily life, work, and study in Rizhao. In general, it is necessary to dialectically view the problems encountered in learning, life, and work, establish a correct worldview and outlook on life, and have important practical significance for students' own growth and character shaping.

5) Taking experimental courses as the starting point, integrating elements of legal and regulatory education

Based on material experiments and engineering practices, it is important for students to adhere to the principle of seeking truth from facts when writing experimental reports, and to ensure the authenticity of experimental data. In future work, experimental data often has legal validity and even arbitration, which determines the acceptance results of the construction process and construction quality. The importance of this is self-evident. Therefore, students must always remember and abide by national laws and corresponding rules and regulations, as well as various national regulations and norms. They should be responsible for the experimental testing reports issued, ensure the seriousness of the experimental data, and not engage in favoritism and fraud.

6) Establish the concept of "cultural highway", advocate for humanistic integration, and enhance students' humanistic literacy and cultural confidence

Since the Silk Road over 2000 years ago, roads have not only served as entities responsible for transportation functions, but also as cultural symbols that connect different ethnic civilizations and cooperate and exchange. With the rapid development of China's highway industry, highways have evolved from their initial functions of transportation, greening, and soil and water conservation to integrating elements such as culture, art, science, landscaping, ecology, aesthetics, etc., organically integrating highways with the humanities, history, and natural landscapes along the line. This not only provides infrastructure with transportation functions, but also becomes a carrier that embodies harmonious natural beauty, imbued with cultural connotations, and humanistic colors, Enable pedestrians to perceive the local natural scenery and appreciate the local culture during their journey [12]. Figure 4 shows cases of different cultural highways.

(a) Hemao Highway Culture

(b) The Most Beautiful Rural Highway in Shaanxi: Anlan Road

Figure 4. The Case of "Cultural Highway"

7) Establishing the concept of "environmentally friendly highways"

In response to the negative impact of highway construction on the natural environment, China's highway industry is accelerating the promotion of new environmental protection concepts, proposing the new concept of "no damage is the best protection, maximum protection of the ecological environment in design, minimum damage and maximum restoration of the ecological environment in construction". In the design, it is necessary to fully consider the terrain and topography, save land resources as much as possible, and avoid environmentally sensitive areas such as natural reserves, drinking water source protection areas, scenic spots, geological parks, and residential areas as much as possible; During construction, use temporary land as required to effectively control environmental pollution.

China has achieved a series of scientific research results in the field of energy conservation and emission reduction in highway engineering. Jilin Heda Expressway effectively utilizes the tunnel waste generated during highway construction, not only as a material for roadbed filling and pavement base, but also developed molding equipment to process tunnel waste into concrete components for use in concrete retaining walls and ecological waste. Not only does it reduce the occupation of land resources by tunnel waste, but it also protects the ecological environment and land resources along the highway.

(a) Electric melting ice and snow road surface

(b) Waste tires, rubber, asphalt pavement

Figure 5. Environmental friendly road construction

In addition, waste tire rubber asphalt pavement materials [13], old cement concrete pavement recycling technology, warm mix asphalt technology, and environmentally friendly ice melting and snow melting technology [14] have all been promoted and applied in engineering, achieving good results in resource conservation and environmental protection, as shown in Figure 5.

4. Teaching Resources and Methods

Closely integrating the teaching reform objectives and teaching content design of the course, fully adopting various teaching methods, highlighting the cultivation of students' knowledge acquisition, ability improvement, and quality improvement. Table 1 summarizes the specific content of teaching resource construction and teaching methods.

Table 1. Construction of Teaching Resources and Teaching Methods

Serial Number	Teaching method	Teaching materials	Ideological points	Teaching resources
1		Special report website	The Great Country Project Inspires National Pride	Micro video
2	Online and offline blended teaching; Group learning, compete between groups to obtain scores, and conduct assessments	Special report Record data	Promote the spirit of craftsmanship	Micro videos
3		Special report website	Learn the spirit of liberating the mind, daring to innovate, and being the first	Role Model Story
4		Record data	Integrating elements of rule of law and regulatory education	Cases
5		Scientific research achievements	Establish the concept of "cultural highway", advocate for humanistic integration	Social practice
6		Scientific research achievements	Establishing the concept of "environmentally friendly highways"	Scientific research paper

5. Conclusion

The ideological and political construction of courses is an important component of the moral education function of courses, and it is the specific implementation of the fundamental task of cultivating morality and cultivating people.

1) This article explores and practices the ideological teaching reform of asphalt and asphalt mixture courses, integrating the scientific spirit of national confidence, craftsmanship, seeking truth and practicality, and energy conservation and environmental protection into the curriculum system through case studies. While studying professional courses, it cultivates students' political thinking and moral qualities.

2) Integrating ideological education into the teaching of professional courses, making teaching diverse and three-dimensional, and promoting students' patriotic awareness, improving learning motivation, and clarifying the direction of efforts, are of great significance. At the same time, lay a solid foundation for students to adapt to social needs after graduation, and achieve the teaching goal of cultivating morality and talent.

Acknowledgment

This project is supported by The National Innovation and Entrepreneurship Training Program for College Students (S202310497187), and Demonstration Course Project of

"Curriculum Ideological and Political Education" for Graduate Students (YS2021007).

References

[1] Wang Leifeng, Liu Weiwei. Problems and Countermeasures of Sharing Ideas of the Effectiveness of Ideological and Political Course Teaching in Colleges and Universities from the Perspective of Creative Education[J]. Journal Of Testing and Evaluation, 2023, 51(1): 55-63.

[2] Liu Wei et al. An Image Impulsive Noise Denoising Method Based on Salp Swarm Algorithm[J]. International Journal of Education and Management Engineering, 2020, 10(1): 43.

[3] Hassaan Muhammad. A Comparative Study between Cloud Energy Consumption Measuring Simulators[J]. International Journal of Education and Management Engineering, 2020, 10(2): 20.

[4] Liu Jiacheng, Chau Gavin, Su Pianpain. An efficient method for ideological and political education quality evaluation of colleges and universities with 2-tuple linguistic neutrosophic sets[J]. Journal of Intelligent & Fuzzy Systems, 2023, 44(4): 1-13.

[5] Dongdong Zhang et al. Reform of Electrical Engineering Undergraduate Teaching and the Curriculum System in the Context of the Energy Internet[J]. Sustainability, 2023, 15(5280): 5280.

[6] Xiaoqing He et al. Deep Learning-Based Teaching Strategies of Ideological and Political Courses Under the Background of Educational Psychology[J]. Frontiers in psychology, 2021, 12: 731166.

[7] Yue Xu, Tian'e Chen. The Design of Personalized Learning Resource Recommendation System for Ideological and Political Courses[J]. International Journal of Reliability, Quality and Safety Engineering, 2023, 30(1): 2250020.

[8] Wu Anchun, Jiang Chaohui et al. Implement the fundamental task of cultivating morality and talent— General Secretary Xi Jinping 's Important Essays on Education: Part 10 of Learning Research[J]. Educational Research, 2022, 43(10): 4-13 (in Chinese).

[9] Qu Zhi. Xi Jinping's important discussion on the construction of ideological and political theory courses[D]. Xinyang Normal University, 2022 (in Chinese).

[10] Salah Al Khafaji, Sriram. B. A Concept Review on MOOCs Research Findings – A Qualitative Approach[J]. International Journal of Education and Management Engineering, 2023, 13(4): 19-25.

[11] Kang Xinping. On the historical role and great significance of the construction of the Sichuan Tibet and Qinghai Tibet highways[J]. Tibetan Studies, 2022, (01): 49-57 (in Chinese).

[12] Zhihua Yang et al. Landscape planning and design of tourist highway service area under the background of all-for-one tourism system[J]. IOP Conference Series: Earth and Environmental Science, 2019, 304(3): 032092.

[13] Carpani Carlo, Bocci Edoardo et al. Evaluation of the rheological and performance behaviour of bitumen modified with compounds including crumb rubber from waste tires[J]. Construction and Building Materials,2022, 361: 129679.

[14] Yiqiu Tan et al. Investigation on preparation and properties of carbon fiber graphite tailings conductive asphalt mixture: A new approach of graphite tailings application[J]. Construction and Building Materials,2023, 402: 133057.

Artificial Intelligence, Medical Engineering and Education
Z.B. Hu et al. (Eds.)
© 2024 The Authors.
This article is published online with Open Access by IOS Press and distributed under the terms
of the Creative Commons Attribution Non-Commercial License 4.0 (CC BY-NC 4.0).
doi:10.3233/ATDE231393

The Influence of Educational Expectations on Academic Performance and Education Expenditures: A Mediation Analysis

Jing ZUO[a], Lin SU[b], Tongyao HUANG[c1]

[a] *Nanning University, Nanning, Guangxi*
[b] *Guangxi University of Finance and Economics, Guangxi, China*
[c] *Guangxi University of Foreign Language, Nanning, Guangxi*

ORCiD ID: Jing ZUO https://orcid.org/0000-0002-9118-1040
ORCiD ID: Lin SU https://orcid.org/0009-0003-8051-7770
ORCiD ID: Tongyao HUANG https://orcid.org/0000-0001-5053-6944

Abstract. Scholars have shown interest in education expectations, education expenditures, and academic achievement. However, there is limited research investigating how parents' educational expectations influence their children's academic performance through the mediating role of educational expenditures. Based on the 2020 China Family Panel Studies (CFPS) data, this study employs logistic regression analysis, path analysis, and mediation analysis to uncover the following findings: parents' educational expectations positively impact both objective and subjective academic performance of children; education expenditures positively influence objective academic performance but negatively influence subjective academic performance; education expenditures play a partial mediating role in the relationship between educational expectations and academic performance.

Keywords. Educational expectations, Education expenditures, Academic performance

1. Introduction

Education is widely regarded as a key factor for individual and societal success in modern society. Among them, educational expectations, education expenditures, and academic performance are three crucial components of educational success. Educational expectations reflect the aspirations of individuals and families for future educational outcomes, driving students to strive for learning and their future [1]. Education expenditures refer to the financial investment in children's education by parents, representing the practical actions to achieve educational goals [2]. And academic performance typically refers to students' performance and grades in school, including their performance in various subjects, completion of assignments, and attitudes towards learning [3]. It is an important indicator for evaluating whether students have achieved their expected goals in the educational process [4]. The interrelationships among these three components are of great significance for educators, scholars, and decision-makers.

---

[1] Corresponding Author: Tongyao HUANG, tongyaohuanghty@163.com

Many researchers have conducted studies on the relationship between educational expectations and academic performance. According to the previous studies, this relationship may exhibit various patterns and influence mechanisms. Firstly, scholars like Benner conducted research on high school students and found that the expectations of parents and mathematics teachers have a significant impact on students' academic performance, especially in terms of mathematics grades, overall grades, and post-high school educational attainment. High parents' expectations can amplify the positive impact of high expectations from mathematics teachers on students [5]. Similarly, studies have also found that during secondary school, expectations and efforts are key factors in predicting academic success [6]. Expectations have a certain explanatory power for the variability in academic performance [7]. However, Dochow and Neumeyer questioned this relationship. In their panel data study of German junior high school students, they found that after adjusting for students' fixed effects, expectations have only a weak correlation with students' academic performance and ability. Additionally, the study found that students with stable high expectations and low expectations actually have similar grades by the end of junior high school. These results suggest that expectations may not be the key factor for academic achievement [8]. In contrast to the first two studies, Bui's research focused on whether expectations and academic performance mutually influence each other, and the research results showed a reciprocal causal relationship between expectations and academic performance [9]. From these studies, we can also see that the relationship between educational expectations and academic performance is complex. While some studies support a significant positive impact of expectations on academic performance, others suggest that this influence may not be as strong as we might imagine. Therefore, it is crucial for educators and decision-makers to understand and balance these different research perspectives.

Education expenditure is an important dimension for understanding family financial priorities, societal values, and future expectations. It is also a focus of researchers' attention. Many studies have found clear urban biases in education expenditure, indicating that urban families are more likely to allocate a higher proportion of their income to education [10,11]. Additionally, family characteristics and income levels influence education expenditures. For example, in urban China, mothers with a high school diploma or bachelor's degree tend to allocate more funds for their children's education [2]. A higher family income level also leads to higher education expenditures [12], with parent's expectations playing a vital role as well. Research has found a direct relationship between parents' expectations for their children and the amount they are willing to invest in education [13], especially the mothers' educational expectations [14]. In summary, education expenditures are influenced by various factors including family and region, providing empirical support for this study's exploration of the mediating role of education expenditures between educational expectations and academic performance.

Many scholars have also investigated whether education expenditure affects academic performance. Some studies suggest that education expenditures contribute to improving academic performance. Kang's research found that a 10% increase in education expenditure can improve students' test scores by 0.56 percentile points [15]. This expenditure also extends to tutoring. Dongre's study on students in Grades 1 to 8 found that private tutoring has a positive and significant impact on learning outcomes [16]. In South Korea, a 10% increase in students' tutoring expenditures can lead to an increase in average test scores by 0.33 to 0.72 percentage points [17]. However, there are also many researchers who hold opposing views, arguing that the impact of family education expenditure on children's test scores is not significant [18]. Kushebayev

(2022) discovered that despite increased government spending on education, student academic performance continues to decline, indicating a lack of strong statistical relationship between expenditure and achievement [19]. Overall, scholars' opinions are not unified, and further research on the relationship between these two factors is needed.

While past studies have provided valuable insights into the relationship between educational expectations, education expenditures, and academic performance, the complexity of these relationships still requires further investigation. Additionally, the specific mechanisms of how education expenditures mediate between educational expectations and academic performance remain unclear. Therefore, this study aims to explore the relationship between educational expectations and academic performance, and investigate the mediating mechanism of education expenditures. It is hoped that through this research, educators and policymakers can gain a deeper and more comprehensive understanding, thus helping them formulate and implement education strategies more effectively. Based on existing literature and theories, this study proposes the following hypotheses:

H1: There is a positive correlation between educational expectations and academic performance.

H2: Education expenditures mediate the relationship between educational expectations and academic performance.

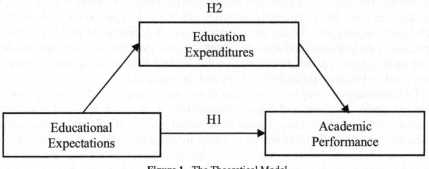

Figure 1. The Theoretical Model

2. Research Methodology

2.1. Sampling

The data for this study was derived from the "China Family Panel Studies (CFPS) 2020" conducted by the Institute of Social Science Survey (ISSS), Peking University. This nationwide, large-scale comprehensive social survey project covers 25 provinces, municipalities, and autonomous regions, ensuring the representativeness and comprehensiveness of the data. Within the CFPS survey, there are four main types of questionnaires: Household Member Questionnaire, Household Economy Questionnaire, Individual Self-Respondent Questionnaire, and Parent Proxy Questionnaire for Children (targeting youths aged 0-15). This study focuses on the parent proxy questionnaires for the year 2020, identifying youths attending primary school and higher education levels. After removing missing values for dependent variables, independent variables, and control variables, the final effective sample size amounted to 3,643 individuals.

2.2. Variable

2.2.1 Dependent Variable

Academic performance serves as the dependent variable in this study, describing children's academic performance through two main aspects: objective performance and subjective performance. Objective performance is measured by the average scores of children's Chinese and mathematics courses. Subjective performance is assessed using a scale that measures the children's level of study effort, homework checks, and frequency of engaging in leisure activities only after homework.

2.2.2 Independent Variable

The independent variable of the study is parents' educational expectations, measured by the scale that inquire about the level of education parents hope their children will achieve. The parents' educational expectations are then converted into years of education, with categories such as "No Formal Education", "Primary School", "Junior High School", "Senior High School/Vocational School/Technical Secondary School", "Junior College", "Bachelor's Degree", "Master's Degree", and "Doctoral Degree" transformed into values of 0, 6, 9, 12, 15, 16, 20, and 24.

2.2.3 Mediating Variable

The mediating variable is education expenditures, where the total educational expenses over the past 12 months from the scale are regarded as education expenditures.

2.2.4 Control Variables

The study includes the following control variables: gender (male, female), educational stage (primary school, junior high school, senior high school), attendance in tutoring classes (yes, no), and parents' involvement in children's education (explained through items in the scale that inquire about parents' involvement in children's education and management).

The descriptive statistics for the relevant variables are presented in Table 1.

Table 1. The Descriptive Statistics

Variable	Type	Mean (Categorical)		Frequency	Percentage (Standard Deviation)
Age	Continuous	10.85		-	-
Education Expenditure (Thousand Yuan Per Year)	Continuous	0.51		-	-
Gender (student)	Nominal		Female=0	1687	46.31
			Male=1	1956	53.69
Educational Stage	Nominal		Primary School=1	2656	72.91
			Junior High School=2	939	25.78
			Senior High School / Vocational School / Technical Secondary School=3	48	1.32
Chinese Grade	Ordinal	2.81	Marginal Pass=1	301	8.26
			Pass=2	1178	32.34
			Merit=3	1060	29.10
			Distinction=4	1104	30.30

Continued Table 1.

Variable	Type		Mean (Categorical)	Frequency	Percentage (Standard Deviation)
Math Grade	Ordinal	2.85	Marginal Pass=1	410	11.25
			Pass=2	990	27.18
			Merit=3	997	27.37
			Distinction=4	1246	34.20
Subjective Academic Performance	Ordinal	3.57	Strongly Disagree=1	19	0.50
			Disagree=2	392	10.80
			Neither Agree nor Disagree =3	1116	30.60
			Agree=4	1801	49.40
			Strongly Agree =5	315	8.60
Expected Level of Education	Continuous	16.04	Primary School=6	5	0.14
			Junior High School=9	51	1.40
			Senior High School=12	450	12.35
			Junior College =15	157	4.31
			Bachelor's Degree =16	2540	69.72
			Master's Degree=20	249	6.84
			Doctoral Degree=24	191	5.24

3. Statistical Analysis

3.1. Primary Factors Affecting Academic Performance

The primary factors influencing academic performance were analyzed using the multiple logistic regression method. The dependent variables were objective academic performance and subjective academic performance, while the independent variables included parents' educational expectations, education expenditures, and control variables. The control variables encompassed gender, educational stage, participation in tutoring classes, and parental involvement in education.

As indicated in Table 2, while controlling for other independent variables, on average, for each unit increase in educational expectations, the expected increase in objective academic performance was 0.067 units ($P<0.001$), and the expected increase in subjective academic performance was 0.025 units ($P<0.001$). Conversely, with control variables and educational expectations held constant, for each unit increase in education expenditures, the expected increase in objective academic performance was 0.062 units ($P<0.001$), while the expected decrease in subjective academic performance was 0.06 units ($P<0.001$). Overall, it can be inferred that both educational expectations and education expenditures significantly influence academic performance, albeit with both positive and negative effects. However, their overall impact remains relatively moderate.

Table 2. Primary Factors Affecting Academic Performance

	Objective Academic Performance			Subjective Academic Performance		
	Model 1	Model 2	Model 3	Model 1	Model 2	Model3
	β(S.E.)	β(S.E.)	β(S.E.)	β(S.E.)	β(S.E.)	β(S.E.)
(Constant)	2.78*** (0.076)	1.726*** (0.111)	1.734*** (0.111)	3.74*** (0.071)	3.349*** (0.106)	3.342*** (0.105)
Educational Stage (Reference Group=Primary School)						
Junior High School	-0.399*** (0.034)	-0.407*** (0.033)	-0.422*** (0.033)	-0.017 (0.031)	-0.02 (0.031)	-0.006 (0.031)
Senior High School	-0.36** (0.127)	-0.393** (0.125)	-0.442*** (0.125)	-0.057 (0.118)	-0.069 (0.118)	-0.021 (0.118)
Attendance in Tutoring Classes (Reference Group=No)	0.338*** (0.033)	0.287*** (0.033)	0.237*** (0.035)	-0.132*** (0.031)	-0.151*** (0.031)	-0.103** (0.033)
Gender (Reference Group=Female)	-0.117*** (0.029)	-0.128*** (0.028)	-0.131*** (0.028)	-0.172*** (0.027)	-0.176*** (0.027)	-0.173*** (0.027)
Parents' Involvement in Children's Education	0.039 (0.021)	0.04 (0.021)	0.041 (0.02)	-0.011 (0.02)	-0.011 (0.019)	-0.012 (0.019)
Educational Expectations		0.067*** (0.005)	0.065*** (0.005)		0.025*** (0.005)	0.026*** (0.005)
Education Expenditures			0.062*** (0.015)			-0.06*** (0.015)

Note: The values represent unstandardized coefficient β values, () indicates standard error, * P < 0.05; ** P < 0.01; *** P < 0.001.

3.2. Path Analysis

Path analysis and mediation analysis were conducted by Mplus.

3.2.1 The Impact of Educational Expectations on Education Expenditures

Educational expectations influence education expenditures significantly and positively, with an estimated value of 0.041, a standard error of 0.005, a t-value of 7.815, and p < 0.001. This implies that for each unit increase in educational expectations, education expenditures are expected to increase by 0.041 units. Refer to Table 3 for the results.

Table 3. Path Analysis of the Impact of Educational Expectations on Education Expenditures

Variable	Estimate	S.E.	Est./S.E.	P-Value
Educational Expectations on Education Expenditures	0.041	0.005	7.815	<0.001

3.2.2 The Impact of Educational Expectations on Academic Performance

Educational expectations significantly and positively influence both objective and subjective academic performance. For objective academic performance, the estimated value is 0.068, the standard error is 0.006, the t-value is 11.628, and p < 0.001. For subjective academic performance, the estimated value is 0.024, the standard error is 0.005, the t-value is 4.606, and p < 0.001. Refer to Table 4 for the results.

Table 4. Path Analysis of the Impact of Educational Expectations on Academic Performance

Variable	Estimate	S.E.	Est./S.E.	P-Value
Educational Expectations on Objective Academic Performance	0.068	0.006	11.628	<0.001
Educational Expectations on Subjective Academic Performance	0.024	0.005	4.606	<0.001

3.2.3 The Impact of Education Expenditures on Academic Performance

Education expenditures significantly and positively influence objective academic performance, with an estimated value of 0.075, a standard error of 0.016, a t-value of 4.704, and p < 0.001. However, for subjective academic performance, education expenditures have a negative impact, with an estimated value of -0.077, a standard error of 0.018, a t-value of -4.267, and p < 0.001. Refer to Table 5 for the results.

Table 5. Path Analysis of the Impact of Educational Expectations on Academic Performance

Variable	Estimate	S.E.	Est./S.E.	P-Value
Education Expenditures on Objective Academic Performance	0.075	0.016	4.704	<0.001
Education Expenditures on Subjective Academic Performance	-0.077	0.018	-4.267	<0.001

3.2.4 Mediation Analysis

The Bootstrap method (with 5,000 resampling iterations) in Mplus was utilized to explore how educational expectations mediate the relationship between education expenditures and academic performance.

As presented in the data in Table 6, the indirect effect of educational expectations on objective academic performance is 0.003 (p < 0.001), signifying a significant mediating effect through education expenditures. Similarly, the indirect effect of educational expectations on subjective academic performance is -0.003 (p < 0.001), indicating a significant mediating effect through education expenditures. Furthermore, the confidence intervals for the indirect effects provided by Mplus do not include 0, indicating that the effects are significant.

Table 6. Mediation Analysis

Variable	Estimate	S.E.	Est./S.E.	P-Value
Educational Expectations on Objective Academic Performance	0.003	0.001	4.124	<0.001
Educational Expectations on Subjective Academic Performance	-0.003	0.001	-3.751	<0.001

4. Discussion

Our findings reveal the intricate relationship between educational expectations, education expenditures, and academic performance. Firstly, parents' expectations for their children's education are positively correlated with higher education expenditures. This may imply that parents are more willing to invest more in their children's education to meet their expectations. This aligns with previous studies which have also found that parents' expectations and family education expenditures have a positive impact on students' academic performance [5]. However, when it comes to academic performance, the situation becomes more complex. While education expenditures have a positive effect on objective academic performance, they have a negative impact on subjective academic performance. This is a novel finding in our study. Possible reasons for these findings include the following: Firstly, as education expenditures increase, students may feel greater pressure as they are aware of the significant financial investment and expectations their parents have made for their education. This pressure may lead to a fear of or avoidance towards study, thereby affecting their subjective academic performance. Secondly, when parents invest a substantial amount of money in their children's education, students may feel that they "must" achieve good grades rather than "want" to. This external drive may weaken students' internal motivation, leading to a loss of interest and enthusiasm in learning. Further research is needed to explore the underlying mechanisms and causality.

Although this study utilized a large-scale dataset, it is limited to specific regions in China and may not fully represent the entire country or other cultural contexts. The data used in this study is based on child respondent surveys, which may introduce response biases or errors. Additionally, the data used in this study is cross-sectional, thus causal relationships cannot be determined. Future research may consider using longitudinal data to further investigate the relationships between these variables.

5. Conclusion

This study reveals the relationship between parents' educational expectations, family education expenditures, and students' academic performance. We have three findings. Firstly, parents' educational expectations are positively correlated with family education expenditures. Secondly, education expenditures have a positive impact on students' objective academic performance. Lastly, for students' subjective academic performance, the influence of education expenditures is negative.

These findings hold significant implications for education policy makers and school administrators. Particularly, when considering how to effectively allocate educational resources and how to balance expectations for students with their mental health. Additionally, parents can also gain insight that excessive education expenditures may not always be beneficial for students, especially from the students' subjective perspectives.

This study provides new insights into the relationship between educational expectations, education expenditures, and academic performance. By delving into the interactions between these variables, we not only confirm previous research findings but also reveal new dynamics, especially regarding how education expenditures impact students' subjective academic performance. Furthermore, this study emphasizes the need to balance academic outcomes with students' mental health when considering education expenditures. This can provide a reference for future research and practical applications.

Acknowledgment

This project is supported by Project of Guangxi Higher Education Undergraduate Teaching Reform (2022JGA394), Projects of Guangxi University of Foreign Language (2023XJ38).

References

[1] SEGINER R, VERMULST A D. Family environment, educational aspirations, and academic achievement in two cultural settings[J]. Journal of Cross-Cultural Psychology, 2002, 33(6): 540-558.

[2] QIAN J X, SMYTH R. Educational expenditure in urban China: income effects, family characteristics and the demand for domestic and overseas education[J]. Applied Economics, 2011, 43(24): 3379-3394.

[3] Aderonke B. Sakpere, Ayomiposi G. Oluwadebi, Oluwatoyin H. Ajilore, Lauretta E. Malaka, The Impact of COVID-19 on the Academic Performance of Students: A Psychosocial Study Using Association and Regression Model, International Journal of Education and Management Engineering (IJEME), 2021, 11(5):32-45.

[4] Neeta Sharma, Shanmuganathan Appukutti, Umang Garg, Jayati Mukherjee, Sneha Mishra, "Analysis of Student's Academic Performance based on their Time Spent on Extra-Curricular Activities using Machine Learning Techniques", International Journal of Modern Education and Computer Science (IJMECS), 2023, 15(1):46-57.

[5] BENNER A D, FERNANDEZ C C, HOU Y, et al. Parent and teacher educational expectations and adolescents' academic performance: Mechanisms of influence[J]. Journal of community psychology, 2021, 49(7): 2679-2703.

[6] SCHOON I, NG-KNIGHT T. Co-development of educational expectations and effort: Their antecedents and role as predictors of academic success[J]. Research in Human Development, 2017, 14(2): 161-176.

[7] Liu K S, Cheng Y Y, Chen Y L, Et Al. Longitudinal Effects of Educational Expectations and Achievement Attributions on Adolescents' Academic Achievements[J]. Adolescence, 2009, 44(176).

[8] DOCHOW S, NEUMEYER S. An investigation of the causal effect of educational expectations on school performance. Behavioral consequences, time-stable confounding, or reciprocal causality?[J/OL]. Research in Social Stratification and Mobility, 2021, 71: 100579. https://doi.org/10.1016/j.rssm.2020.100579.

[9] BUI K. Educational Expectations and Academic Achievement among Middle and High School Students[J/OL]. Education 3-13, 2007[2023-08-16]. https://www.semanticscholar.org/paper/Educational-Expectations-and-Academic-Achievement-Bui/cf29f5a4f5d8c293f6b3ae4af4407d8d74daa17f.

[10] EBAIDALLA E M. Determinants of household education expenditure in Sudan[C]Economic research forum. Working paper. 2017.

[11] EBAIDALLA E M. Understanding household education expenditure in Sudan: do poor and rural households spend less on education?[J]. African Journal of economic review, 2018, 6(1): 160-178.

[12] BAYAR A A, YANIK İLHAN B. Determinants of household education expenditures: Do poor spend less on education?[J]. Topics in Middle Eastern and North African Economies, 2016, 18.

[13] HAO L, YEUNG W J J. Parental spending on school-age children: Structural stratification and parental expectation[J]. Demography, 2015, 52(3): 835-860.

[14] NA Y M, YOON J H. The effect of the mother's educational aspirations and the household's characteristics on private educational expenditures[J]. Korean Journal of Human Ecology, 2011, 20(6): 1199-1212.

[15] KANG C. Does money matter? The effect of private educational expenditures on academic performance[J]. National University of Singapore. Department of Economics Working Paper, 2007, 704.

[16] DONGRE A, TEWARY V. Impact of private tutoring on learning levels[J]. Economic and Political Weekly, 2015: 72-80.

[17] RYU D, KANG C. Do Private Tutoring Expenditures Raise Academic Performance? Evidence from Middle School Students in S outh K orea[J]. Asian Economic Journal, 2013, 27(1): 59-83.

[18] EINSTEIN A , B, PODOLSKY, ROSEN N. Impact of household educational expenditures on the test scores of children[J]. Economics Bulletin, 2013, 33(2): 1177-1184.

[19] Kushebayev, Z., & Nygymetov, G S. The Impact of State Expenditure on Education and on Student Academic Achievement. Economics: the strategy and practice, 2022, 17(4):201-211.

Artificial Intelligence, Medical Engineering and Education
Z.B. Hu et al. (Eds.)
© 2024 The Authors.
This article is published online with Open Access by IOS Press and distributed under the terms
of the Creative Commons Attribution Non-Commercial License 4.0 (CC BY-NC 4.0).
doi:10.3233/ATDE231394

Intelligent Manufacturing Major Construction Based on the Integration of Production and Education

Yang GAO, Chenxi LIN, Zhihui PAN, Wenhui LI[1]

Mechanical and Electrical Engineering Department, Wenhua College, Wuhan, China

Abstract. Intelligent manufacturing is an integrated concept that covers multiple disciplines, including automation, information technology, mechanical engineering, artificial intelligence, etc. This interdisciplinary nature means that colleges and universities need to promote cooperation between different disciplines. Interdisciplinary professional teaching has high requirements for institution and teachers, while enterprises are users of intelligent manufacturing, and their production lines naturally have interdisciplinary characteristics. There is a huge demand for engineers in intelligent manufacturing. It is very meaningful to build a teaching system for intelligent manufacturing major through cooperation between education and production. However, there are many shortcomings in the current production-education integration. Therefore, education institutions need to innovate training models to improve students' practical ability and innovation spirit, while the government should strengthen supporting policies to enhance the enthusiasm of both education and production.

Keywords. Intelligent manufacturing; Major Construction; Integration of Production and Education

1. Introduction

Intelligent manufacturing is a new manufacturing model that integrates information technology, Internet of Things, big data, artificial intelligence, and other technologies. It achieves automated, digitalized and intelligent production through highly integrated production processes, equipment and systems, greatly improving production efficiency and flexibility. The goal of intelligent manufacturing is to build an adaptive and self-learning production system to adapt to constantly changing market demands while improving production efficiency and product quality [1-4].

Intelligent manufacturing is a global trend, and governments around the world are actively promoting the development of intelligent manufacturing. The German government has invested a lot of funds and resources to support the development of relevant enterprises and research institutions [5]. The U.S. government has proposed the "Advanced Manufacturing" plan, which aims to revitalize the U.S. manufacturing industry through technological innovation and digital transformation. The plan includes policies and measures to strengthen research and development and talent cultivation, promote digital transformation, encourage innovation and entrepreneurship, etc [6]. The

---

[1] Corresponding Author: Li Wenhui, E-mail: 247900235@qq.com.

Chinese government has proposed the "Made in China 2025" plan, which aims to promote the transformation and upgrading of the manufacturing industry through digitalization, intelligence, and green technology. The plan includes policies and measures to strengthen technological innovation, build intelligent manufacturing demonstration bases, and promote the application of intelligent manufacturing[7]. The future of intelligent manufacturing requires a large number of professional talents, and the demand for and cultivation of talents also pose new challenges.

At present, the talent cultivation system in the field of intelligent manufacturing has the following deficiencies [8-10]:

One, curriculum offering is not comprehensive enough: Intelligent manufacturing is a cross-disciplinary field that requires knowledge in mechanical engineering, information technology, automation, and other aspects. However, many universities currently have deficiencies in the course offerings related to intelligent manufacturing majors, lacking systematization and comprehensiveness, making it difficult to cultivate compound talents that meet the needs of enterprises.

Two, practical teaching is insufficient: The technology in the intelligent manufacturing field is updated rapidly, and practical teaching is an important part of talent cultivation. However, many universities currently have insufficient practical teaching conditions and insufficient cooperation with enterprises, which makes it difficult for students to gain practical experience and innovation experience, making it difficult to adapt to enterprise needs.

Three, lack of comprehensive talent cultivation: Intelligent manufacturing requires compound talents with multidisciplinary knowledge. However, many universities currently lack comprehensiveness in talent cultivation in the field of intelligent manufacturing, making it difficult for students to integrate multiple disciplines of knowledge together, limiting their development potential.

In view of the deficiencies in the above talent cultivation, it is necessary to adopt the cooperation between schools and enterprises to build a professional practical teaching system that can manufacture. Through cooperation between schools and enterprises, they can jointly develop talent training programs, carry out practical teaching, and share resources to improve the pertinence and practicality of talent training. At the same time, school-enterprise cooperation can also promote technological innovation and product upgrading of enterprises, and enhance their competitiveness and development potential.

2. Current Situation of Enterprise Intelligent Manufacturing and Talent Demand

In the current era of Industry 4.0, intelligent manufacturing has become the mainstream trend of manufacturing development. Intelligent manufacturing refers to the continuous integration of advanced technologies such as information technology, the Internet of Things, big data, and artificial intelligence, and the transformation of traditional manufacturing processes into a new digital, automated, and intelligent manufacturing model shown in Figure 1. The emergence of this model has greatly improved the efficiency and quality of manufacturing, while also posed new challenges and demanded for talent cultivation in universities [11-15].

Highly Information-based: Enterprise intelligent manufacturing systems center on information technology [16,17], utilizing digital technology and big data analysis to collect [18-20], transmit, process, and store various information in the production process for full information management.

Automation and Intelligence: With advanced robotics technology, automation equipment, and artificial intelligence, enterprise intelligent manufacturing systems can achieve automated and intelligent production, significantly improving production efficiency and reducing labor costs.

2.1. Characteristics of Enterprise Intelligent Manufacturing System

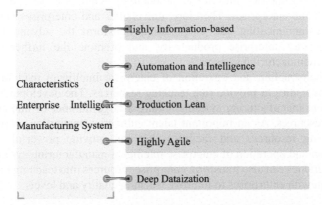

Figure 1. Characteristics of Enterprise Intelligent Manufacturing System

Production Lean: Through digital simulation technology, enterprise intelligent manufacturing systems can predict and address potential issues before production, optimize production processes, and reduce waste to achieve lean production.

Highly Agile: Enterprise intelligent manufacturing systems can quickly adjust production mode according to market demand to meet personalized customized needs and enhance enterprise market response capabilities.

Deep Dataization: Through technologies such as the Internet of Things and sensors, enterprise intelligent manufacturing systems can achieve data interaction between devices and data collection during the production process, providing more reliable data support for enterprise decision-making.

In summary, high information, automation and intelligence, lean manufacturing, high agility, and deep digitization have close logical relationships in intelligent production lines. Only by fully understanding and mastering these aspects can we better apply and develop intelligent production line technology to achieve high-efficiency and high-quality production.

2.2. Cooperation Demand of Enterprise Intelligent Manufacturing System for Universities

The construction and operation of enterprise intelligent manufacturing systems require a large number of talent support. Intelligent manufacturing involves multiple disciplines, such as mechanical engineering, information technology, automation, and other fields, so enterprises need interdisciplinary talents that have a grasp of multiple professional knowledge and skills, as well as innovative thinking and problem-solving capabilities. However, the current talent cultivation mode in universities often focuses too much on the imparting of knowledge in a single discipline, lacks the cultivation of cross-disciplinary comprehensive qualities, and is difficult to meet the talent needs of enterprise intelligent manufacturing systems.

The construction and operation of enterprise intelligent manufacturing systems require universities to provide strong technical support. The development and operation of intelligent manufacturing systems involve the use of various advanced technologies, such as big data analysis, artificial intelligence, the Internet of Things, and other fields. These technologies have been deeply studied and developed in universities, and many teachers and students also possess corresponding technical abilities. However, transforming technology into actual productivity requires close cooperation between universities and enterprises. Therefore, universities and enterprises need to strengthen technical communication and cooperation, transform the advanced technology of universities into enterprise productivity, and promote the further development of intelligent manufacturing systems.

The construction and operation of enterprise intelligent manufacturing systems require universities to provide rich teaching resources. The development and operation of intelligent manufacturing systems require a large number of human, material, and financial resources. As an important talent cultivation institution, universities possess rich teaching resources and facilities that can provide powerful support for the construction and operation of enterprise intelligent manufacturing systems. At the same time, universities can also transform enterprise resources into teaching resources through cooperation with enterprises to improve teaching quality and levels

3. Principles for the Construction of Intelligent Manufacturing Professional Courses Based on School-enterprise Cooperation

The construction of the intelligent manufacturing system curriculum is to cultivate professional talents with intelligent manufacturing technology, improve the technological level and market competitiveness of enterprises, and promote the sustainable development of the national economy. The construction of the intelligent manufacturing major curriculum system based on school-enterprise cooperation should follow the following principles:

Principles	**Enterprise demand-oriented**
	Cross-disciplinary integration
	Emphasis on practical teaching
	International perspective
	Student-centered
	Innovation spirit and innovation ability
	Professional ethics and social responsibility consciousness

Figure 2. Principles for the construction of intelligent manufacturing

3.1. Enterprise Demand-oriented

Intelligent manufacturing is a rapidly developing and constantly innovating field, and the demand for talents in enterprises is also constantly changing. Therefore, the intelligent manufacturing professional curriculum system based on school-enterprise cooperation should be enterprise demand-oriented, deeply understand the requirements for talents' knowledge, skills, and qualities of enterprises, and adjust course offerings and teaching content in a timely manner according to changes in demand. Through cooperation with enterprises, universities can more accurately grasp the direction and goal of talent cultivation, and improve the pertinence and practicality of talent cultivation.

3.2. Cross-disciplinary Integration

Intelligent manufacturing involves multiple disciplines such as mechanical engineering, information technology, automation, and other fields. Therefore, the intelligent manufacturing professional curriculum system based on school-enterprise cooperation should focus on cross-disciplinary integration. Through the intersection and fusion of multiple disciplines, students can grasp more comprehensive knowledge and skills, cultivate their comprehensive quality and innovation ability. In terms of course settings, the restriction of traditional single discipline can be broken to strengthen the connection and linkage between different disciplines, and encourage students to conduct interdisciplinary studies and research.

3.3. Emphasis on Practical Teaching

Intelligent manufacturing is a highly technical and practical field. Therefore, the intelligent manufacturing professional curriculum system based on school-enterprise cooperation should focus on practical teaching. Through cooperation with enterprises, universities can introduce advanced production equipment and teaching resources to build a practical teaching base, providing students with real production environments and opportunities for operation. At the same time, universities can also jointly develop practical teaching courses and textbooks with enterprises to make practical teaching closer to the actual needs of enterprises.

3.4. International Perspective

Intelligent manufacturing is a global field, so the intelligent manufacturing professional curriculum system based on school-enterprise cooperation should have an international perspective. Universities should actively introduce advanced intelligent manufacturing technologies and teaching concepts from foreign countries, carry out cooperative exchanges with internationally renowned enterprises and universities, and expand students' international vision and competitiveness. At the same time, universities should also pay attention to cultivating students' cross-cultural communication and cooperation abilities to provide more opportunities for their future development on the international stage.

3.5. Student-centered

The construction of the intelligent manufacturing professional curriculum system based on school-enterprise cooperation should be student-centered, paying attention to students' individual differences and ability training. In course settings and teaching processes, students' interests, learning characteristics, and career planning should be fully considered to enable students to choose and customize their own learning paths and develop their specialties and potential. At the same time, universities should also pay attention to cultivating students' autonomous learning and lifelong learning habits to lay a foundation for their future sustainable development.

3.6. Innovation Spirit and Innovation ability

Intelligent manufacturing is constantly developing and changing, requiring practitioners to possess innovative spirit and innovation ability. Therefore, the intelligent manufacturing professional curriculum system based on school-enterprise cooperation should pay attention to cultivating students' innovative spirit and innovation ability. In teaching processes, students should be encouraged to identify problems, propose problems, solve problems, cultivate their critical thinking ability and innovative thinking ability. At the same time, universities should also cooperate with enterprises to carry out scientific research projects and innovative practices to provide students with platforms and opportunities for innovative practice, cultivating their innovative abilities and innovative consciousness.

3.7. Professional Ethics and Social Responsibility Consciousness

As future professionals in the field of intelligent manufacturing, practitioners in this field should possess noble professional ethics and social responsibility consciousness. Therefore, the intelligent manufacturing professional curriculum system based on school-enterprise cooperation should pay attention to cultivating students' professional ethics and social responsibility consciousness. In teaching processes, attention should be paid to cultivating students' professional ethics such as honesty, dedication, responsibility awareness, and strengthening cooperation with enterprises to enable students to deeply understand corporate social responsibility and industry norms, cultivating their sense of social responsibility and industry norms awareness.

The relationship of the contents (Figure 2) as following: The internal logical relationship among these principles is interrelated and mutually reinforcing. The demand-oriented approach is the foundation. Only by understanding the actual needs of enterprises can we cultivate talents that meet their needs. Interdisciplinary integration is the means, and only by realizing the cross-integration of multiple disciplines can we cultivate compound talents. Emphasis on practical teaching is the core, and only by focusing on practical teaching can we cultivate students' practical and innovative abilities. The perspective of internationalization is to expand, and only with an international vision can we cultivate talents with international competitiveness. Student-centeredness is fundamental, and only by paying attention to students' individual needs can we cultivate talents with individual characteristics. Innovative spirit and ability are the driving force, and only by focusing on cultivating students' innovative spirit and ability can we cultivate talents with innovative consciousness and ability. Professional ethics and social responsibility awareness are guarantees. Only by focusing on cultivating students' professional ethics and social responsibility awareness can we cultivate talents with noble morality and social responsibility.

4. Exploration of the Model of Cooperation Between Production and Education

There is a huge space for both schools and enterprises to cooperate in intelligent manufacturing. Here are some possible cooperation models (Fig 3) discussing:

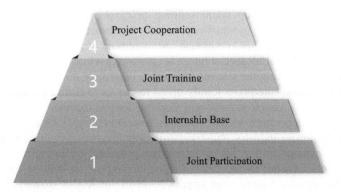

Figure 3. Exploration models

Joint Participation Model: Colleges and enterprises can jointly develop practical teaching plans, including cooperation in practical teaching content, teaching methods, practical teaching time, etc. Through the joint participation of colleges and enterprises in the development of practical teaching plans, practical teaching can be more in line with the actual needs of enterprises and closer to the development trends of the industry. At the same time, enterprises can integrate their accumulated experience and knowledge in production practices into practical teaching, making practical teaching content richer and more useful. Colleges and related enterprises establish cooperative relationships to jointly develop practical teaching plans and carry out practical teaching activities together. Colleges and enterprises can jointly carry out practical teaching activities, including experiments, internships, course design, graduation design, etc. Through the joint participation of colleges and enterprises in the development of practical teaching activities, students can have a deeper understanding of the production practices of enterprises and the application of technology, enhancing students' practical abilities and innovative spirit. At the same time, enterprises can provide internship opportunities and on-site practical experience for students, providing more opportunities and platforms for their future career development. Under this model, colleges and enterprises can jointly invest resources, share risks, and cultivate talents.

Internship Base Model: Colleges cooperate with enterprises to use the enterprise as an internship base, providing students with internship opportunities and on-site practical experience. Of course, the internship base must meet the basic requirements of practical teaching, completing practical teaching plans, practical teaching content, practical teaching management, etc. The internship base should also provide students with appropriate positions, enabling them to participate in the production practices of enterprises, mastering practical skills and management experience knowledge. The internship base should also provide students with necessary guidance and training, including safety operation procedures, quality awareness training, etc., ensuring students' practical effects and safety. The internship base should establish standardized internship management systems, including internship plans, internship assessments, internship safety management regulations, ensuring the quality and effectiveness of internships.

Joint Training Model: Joint training is an important cooperation mode in intelligent manufacturing practical teaching. Through joint training, colleges and enterprises can jointly participate in talent cultivation processes, jointly develop training programs, course settings, and teaching content to make talent cultivation more in line with enterprise and market needs, improving talent cultivation quality. Colleges and enterprises jointly develop talent training programs based on enterprise needs for directional training. After graduation, students can directly enter the enterprise to work. Colleges and enterprises cooperate to combine internships with employment opportunities so that students can intern at enterprises while receiving enterprise training and assessments during the internship process, ultimately remaining in the enterprise to work. Colleges and enterprises jointly invest resources to build a college, jointly develop training programs, course settings and teaching content together.

Project Cooperation Model: Aiming at various technological development needs faced by enterprise industry transformation upgrades, colleges, and enterprises jointly research, develop, and solve problems to promote technological innovation and achievements transformation. Promoting technological innovation and achievements transformation can enhance the overall level of intelligent manufacturing field and cultivate students' innovative abilities. Colleges and enterprises jointly participate in industrial technology innovation alliances to jointly research, develop, and solve problems to promote industrial technology innovation andachievements transformation. Colleges and enterprises can complement each other and learn from each other to achieve industry-academia-research integration and technological innovation, improving the quality of applied talents cultivation.

5. Intelligent Manufacturing Professional Construction Needs Policy Support in School-enterprise Cooperation

As an enterprise engaged in production and operation, talent cultivation is not its main function. Therefore, the successful implementation of school-enterprise cooperation requires schools and governments to introduce relevant policies.

5.1. Policies Needed for Universities to Enhance Support to Improve Students' Practical Abilities and Innovative Spirit

Currently, most school-enterprise collaborations still remain at a relatively shallow level, such as internships and course design, which although provide some help in applying knowledge learned to practice, cannot meet the higher requirements of intelligent manufacturing practical teaching with a single cooperation model. Although these forms of collaboration have their own value, they are not sufficient to cultivate students' comprehensive abilities and innovative spirit. Both universities and governments need to introduce a series of policies as soon as possible to provide support.

As an important base for talent cultivation, universities need to continuously enhance their support policies (Figure 4) to improve students' practical abilities and innovative spirit:

- Strengthening the Construction of Practical Teaching Bases

Universities should actively cooperate with enterprises to build practical teaching bases, providing students with places and opportunities for internships and practical training. Practical teaching bases should simulate the real production environment of enterprises as much as possible, allowing students to be exposed to actual production equipment and manufacturing processes, improving the effectiveness of practical teaching. In addition, universities should increase investment in practical teaching bases, constantly updating equipment and technology to meet the latest needs of the intelligent manufacturing field.

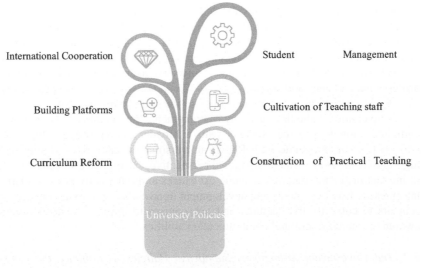

Figure 4. Universities support policies

- Strengthening the Cultivation of Teaching Staff

Excellent teachers play a crucial role in improving students' practical abilities and innovative spirit. Therefore, universities should strengthen the cultivation of teachers to improve their professional quality and practical abilities. Universities can organize teachers to participate in various training courses, academic conferences and seminars to improve their professional level. At the same time, universities can also encourage teachers to participate in enterprise technology research and development and project cooperation to improve their practical experience and practical teaching abilities.

- Perfecting Student Management Mechanisms

Universities should establish sound student management mechanisms to ensure the smooth development of school-enterprise cooperation projects and students' comprehensive development. Universities should formulate clear student management regulations, specifying students' rights and obligations, and establish a comprehensive assessment mechanism to evaluate students' performance. In addition, universities should establish smooth communication channels to timely understand students' needs and problems, and take effective measures to solve students' difficulties and concerns, creating a good study and living environment for students.

- Promoting Curriculum Reform

Universities should actively promote curriculum reform, combining practical teaching with theoretical teaching to improve students' comprehensive abilities and competitiveness. Universities can organize experts and enterprise representatives to jointly participate in course design, developing course content and teaching plans based on the actual needs of enterprises and technological development trends. At the same time, universities can also adopt advanced teaching methods such as project-based teaching methods and case teaching methods, stimulating students' learning interest and motivation, improving their autonomous learning ability and practical application ability.

- Building Innovation and Entrepreneurship Platforms

Universities should build innovation and entrepreneurship platforms for students to encourage them to carry out innovation and entrepreneurship activities, improving their innovative awareness and entrepreneurial abilities. Universities can offer innovation and entrepreneurship courses to cultivate students' innovative thinking and entrepreneurial awareness; can organize innovation and entrepreneurship competitions to stimulate students' enthusiasm for innovation and entrepreneurship; can establish innovation and entrepreneurship parks to provide students with opportunities for entrepreneurial practice; also can invite entrepreneurs, investors, etc. to serve as mentors, providing students with professional guidance and support.

  • Strengthening International Cooperation and Communication

Universities should actively strengthen international cooperation and communication to provide students with a broader vision and development space. Universities can cooperate with foreign universities or enterprises to jointly cultivate high-quality talents with an international perspective; can organize students to participate in international conferences, academic exchanges and other activities to understand the latest research achievements and development trends; also, can invite foreign experts or scholars to come to give lectures or teach courses to improve students' international awareness and cross-cultural communication abilities.

5.2. The Government Strengthens Supportive Policies to Enhance the Cooperation Enthusiasm of Both Schools and Enterprises

The forms of policy support (Figure 5) are diverse, including financial subsidies, tax preferences, talent introduction and training, etc., specifically manifested as:

Financial subsidies: The government provides financial support to enterprises, universities, and training institutions by establishing special funds and providing financial subsidies. For example, giving financial subsidies to enterprises participating in school-enterprise cooperation and supporting universities' practical teaching bases with funds.

Tax preferences: The government provides tax preference policies to eligible enterprises, universities, and training institutions to reduce their operating costs and promote their development. For example, giving tax exemptions or preferential tax treatment to enterprises participating in school-enterprise cooperation and applying preferential tax treatment to universities' practical teaching bases.

Talent introduction and training: The government attracts high-level talents to come to China to engage in research and development work in the field of intelligent manufacturing by formulating various preferential policies. At the same time, it encourages universities and enterprises to jointly cultivate talents to improve the quality and quantity of talent training.

Industrial guidance: The government encourages the development and upgrading of the intelligent manufacturing industry by formulating industrial development plans and guidance policies. For example, encouraging enterprises to increase investment in intelligent manufacturing technology and equipment, improving production efficiency and product quality.

Service support: The government provides various service supports for enterprises and universities, including financing support, intellectual property protection, information consultation, etc. For example, establishing a technology and finance service platform to provide financing support for enterprises; strengthening intellectual property protection to safeguard the legitimate rights and interests of innovative achievements; establishing an information consultation service system to provide timely and accurate information support for enterprises and universities.

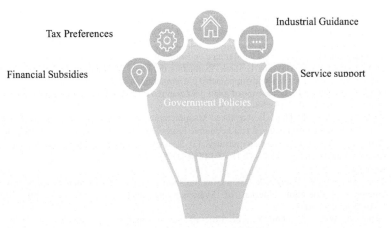

Talent Introduction and Training

Tax Preferences

Industrial Guidance

Financial Subsidies

Service support

Government Policies

Figure 5. Government support policies

6. Conclusion and Outlook

With the rapid development of the global economy, intelligent manufacturing has become an important development direction for manufacturing. As an important way to cultivate intelligent manufacturing professionals, school-enterprise cooperation has received increasing attention. This article discusses the problems, cooperation models, and policy support needed for the construction of intelligent manufacturing majors based on school-enterprise cooperation from multiple perspectives. The construction of intelligent manufacturing majors based on school-enterprise cooperation is an important way to cultivate high-quality and highly skilled talents. Schools and enterprises should actively explore diversified cooperation models and substantive cooperation content, strengthen policy guidance, and support, and jointly promote the development and progress of intelligent manufacturing majors. In the future development, the intelligent manufacturing major will face more opportunities and challenges. The cooperation between schools and enterprises should continue to deepen the content and broaden the fields of cooperation, making positive contributions to promoting the transformation and upgrading of China's manufacturing industry and the sustainable development of the economy.

Acknowledgment

This research is supported by the electrical engineering and automation construction project, mechanical engineering and automation professional construction project of the first-class undergraduate professional construction site in Hubei Province, as well as the teaching quality and teaching reform project of Wenhua College (j0900741220, j0900741802, j0900741004, j0900741014).

References

[1] Hovanski Y, Russell B, Rydalch J. C. Implementing Smart manufacturing: lessons learned and challenges ahead[J]. Journal of Manufacturing Systems, 2019, (47): 48-60.

[2] G. J. Cheng, L. T. Liu, X. J. Qiang. Industry 4.0 development and application of intelligent manufacturing[J]. International Conference on Information System & Artificial Intelligence 2016.

[3] A. Ayman, J John, K Maysam, E Tarek. Evaluating the impact of smart manufacturing on productivity and quality: a multiple case study approach[J]. Automation World, 2017, (53): 20-27.

[4] [4] Qi Y. D., Xu K. G. The essence of intelligent manufacturing[J]. Journal of Beijing Normal University (Natural Science), 2022, (3): 93-103.

[5] [5] Jia G L, Chu S S. The U.S. Advanced Manufacturing Initiatives From the Perspective of Industrial Policy[J]. Research on Financial and Economic Issues, 2019, (7): 38−48. doi: 10.1002/polq.12659

[6] Zhang Q S Meng J Y German Industry 4.0 Strategy and Its Enlightenment to China's Financial Development[J]. 2021, （4):83-87. Doi:10.1504/IJTPM.2021.114308.

[7] www.gov.cn, 2015.

[8] Zhang M, Qiang W, Wang X X. Addressing the Shortcomings of Smart Manufacturing through School-Enterprise Cooperation. Journal of Manufacturing Systems, 2023, (44), pp. 200-215. doi: 10.1093/jiplp/jpad062.

[9] Zhang Q, Wang Z, Zhou Y. The Role of School-Enterprise Cooperation in Promoting Smart Manufacturing Capabilities. IEEE Transactions on Automation Science and Engineering, 2023, (20), pp. 645-656. doi: 10.1017/S1431927612001651.

[10] Wang H, Hu W. Reinforcing the Role of School-Enterprise Cooperation in Smart Manufacturing. IEEE Transactions on Automation Science and Engineering, 2021, (19), pp. 999-1008. doi: 10.1093/jiplp/jpad062.

[11] Li X, Wang Z. Current status and development trends of intelligent production line technology. Journal of Manufacturing Systems, 2020, (46), pp. 42-51. doi: 10.13272/j.issn.1671-251x.17921.

[12] Zhang Y, Liu J, Wang H. Smart manufacturing line technology: state-of-the-art and future challenges. Robotics and Computer-Integrated Manufacturing, 2021, (59), pp.1-10. doi: 10.1093/jiplp/jpab104.

[13] Wang J, Li Q, Zhang L. The role of intelligent production lines in sustainable manufacturing: A review. Journal of Cleaner Production, 2022, (239), pp.1-10. doi: 10.3390/su13126689.

[14] Liu W, Li M. Design and implementation of an intelligent manufacturing line based on industrial internet of things. Journal of Manufacturing Systems, 2023, (58), pp.1-10. doi: 10.1109/TMC.2023.3246176

[15] Liang Z, Wu J, Cheng Y. Transition from lean production line to intelligent production line: A case study. Journal of Industrial Engineering and Management, 2023, (3), pp.1-8.doi: 10.1080/00207543.2023.2207956.

[16] Mowafak Hassan Abdul-Hussin, " Modelling Manufacturing System Controller-based Siphon Petri Nets ", International Journal of Wireless and Microwave Technologies, Vol.10, No.3, pp. 17-31, 2020.

[17] Alovsat G. Aliyev, "Development of Models of Manufacturing Processes of Innovative Products at Different Levels of Management", International Journal of Information Technology and Computer Science, Vol.11, No.5, pp.23-29, 2019.

[18] Asma Omri, Mohamed Nazih Omri, "Towards an Efficient Big Data Indexing Approach under an Uncertain Environment", International Journal of Intelligent Systems and Applications, Vol.14, No.2, pp.1-13, 2022.

[19] Swagata Paul, Sajal Saha, Radha Tamal Goswami, "Detection of Unknown Insider Attack on Components of Big Data System: A Smart System Application for Big Data Cluster", International Journal of Computer Network and Information Security, Vol.14, No.5, pp.47-59, 2022.

[20] Chandra Mohan Bhuma, Ramanjaneyulu Kongara, "A Novel Technique for Image Retrieval based on Concatenated Features Extracted from Big Dataset Pre-Trained CNNs", International Journal of Image, Graphics and Signal Processing, Vol.15, No.2, pp. 1-12, 2023.

Artificial Intelligence, Medical Engineering and Education
Z.B. Hu et al. (Eds.)
doi:10.3233/ATDE231395

Work Family Conflict and Job Satisfaction of Middle School Teachers: A Test Based on a Dual Mediation Model

Shuaifeng GUAN, Huadong SHEN[1]

School of Law Humanities and Sociology, Wuhan University of Technology, Wuhan, China.

Abstract. Whether the relationship between work and family is harmonious is closely related to personal development, and the conflict between work and family will lead to personal dissatisfaction with work. This paper reveals the mediating effects of occupational identity and occupational stress on work-family conflict and job satisfaction. The results show that: (1) Work-family conflict is negatively correlated with job satisfaction. (2) Occupational identity plays a mediating role in the impact of work-family conflict on individual occupational health development. (3) The influence of occupational stress mediating family conflict on individual occupational health development. The results of the study are helpful for individuals to recognize the important role of harmonious work-family relationships on their occupational health development, and are an important reference for relieving psychological stress arising from work and adjusting personal attitudes toward family and work.

Keywords. Family conflict; Job satisfaction; Occupational identity; Occupational stress.

1. Introduction

The mental health of teachers has been the subject of much attention and discussion among experts and scholars in society and academia. Teachers are not only the "pillars" of schools and the "leaders" of students, but also the parents of their own children, the partners of their loved ones, and the children of their parents. Therefore, it is especially important for teachers to manage the relationship between work and family. Resource conservation theory suggests that resources are of extraordinary value to individuals, and that individuals engage in a range of behaviors to acquire and preserve values that are beneficial to them, and when their resources are threatened, individuals respond by trying to protect and maintain those resources that are important to them [1]. When secondary school teachers devote most of their energy to their work, their families and homes are neglected, and if their work does not meet their family's needs, teachers' satisfaction with their job's decreases. When middle school teachers devote their energy and time to their families, they have less time and energy to devote to their jobs, and their ability to do

---

[1] Corresponding Author: Huadong SHEN, shd@whut.edu.cn

their work is not improved, and their job satisfaction decreases. In addition, group identity theory, which states that group members will take the group's goals and behavioral norms as their pursuits, and the degree of their accomplishment determines the cohesiveness of the members within the group which in turn affects their satisfaction with their group [2], the professional identity of middle school teachers can be explained to a high degree. The higher the professional identity of middle school teachers, the more satisfied they are with the job. [3]. In contrast, when teachers' work and family conflict, teachers' sense of belief may be affected as a result, leading to changes in professional identity. Therefore, it is assumed that professional identity is strongly linked between work-family conflict and job satisfaction. Stress theory suggests that group stress occurs when external influences do not align with individual intentions, which will lead to conflicts and contradictions. Aneshensel's research suggests that social status and social support are key components of social stress [4]. Occupational stress arises when teachers' social status and social support do not meet their personal intentions. Teachers' self-determination and occupational stress directly affect job satisfaction [5]. In turn, when teachers' work and family cannot be reconciled, stress arises as a result. Therefore, we assume that occupational stress can closely link work family conflict and job satisfaction

In summary, exploring the mechanisms of work-family conflict on job satisfaction among secondary school teachers has greater research significance for secondary school teacher training and school teaching. Related studies have more often explored the link between the two individually, however, few previous studies have focused on the relationship between occupational identity and occupational stress. Therefore, in order to study the impact of work-family conflict on middle school teachers' job satisfaction, this paper sets the mediating variables as occupational identity and occupational stress, and analyzes their effects on this basis. In this paper, a questionnaire was designed on the basis of theoretical research. The questionnaire was divided into four dimensions, and SPSS26.0 was used to analyze the correlation among the indicators of work-family conflict, job satisfaction, occupational identity and occupational stress to test the mediating role of the four dimensions, To study whether work-family conflict has an impact on job satisfaction, and to explore the mediating role of vocational identity and occupational stress in the relationship between work-family conflict and job satisfaction of middle school teachers. The rest of the paper will cover the following in detail: The second part will review the references and hypotheses; The third part will describe the research design of this paper; The fourth part gives the empirical results on the basis of the empirical research. The fifth part discusses the empirical results obtained above. The sixth part introduces the conclusion and management enlightenment of this paper to the reader.

2. Literature Review and Research Hypothesis

2.1. Work-family Conflict and Job Satisfaction

In recent years, many domestic and foreign experts and scholars have conducted research on the relationship between work-family conflict and job satisfaction. The studies have covered a variety of occupations and fields, including supervisors, managers, R&D personnel, and general employees in the corporate sector, and early childhood teachers, elementary and secondary school teachers, and college teachers in the educational sector. In the field of enterprises, on the one hand, there is a significant negative impact relationship between work-family conflicts and job satisfaction among middle-level professional managers. On the other hand, the support of senior leaders has a certain moderating effect on the impact of work-family conflicts on job satisfaction among these employees [6]. The people who develop a company's products, the solid force that leads the company's innovation, are more susceptible to work-family conflict, and for them, the impact of group work-family conflict on job satisfaction is also negative [7]. Another group of scholars conducted research on the relevant behaviors of employees in real estate agency companies. After comparing and analyzing the relationship between work family conflict and employee job satisfaction in this field, they obtained the same results as the previous study: the two different dimensions of work family conflict - work influenced family conflict (WIF) and family influenced work conflict (FIW) - both have a negative impact on employee job satisfaction. [8]. In addition, studies conducted with knowledge-based employees and employees of manufacturing companies as research subjects yielded the same findings [9-11]. The same research also happened in the field of education, where scholars analyzed the different salary requests of teachers at different career stages, and came to basically the same conclusion after summing-up. Some scholars have used the theory of resource conservation and found that the work-family conflict of junior middle school teachers will have a significant negative impact on their job satisfaction [12], other scholars conducted field investigations on over 200 primary and secondary school teachers in Shandong Province, and based on the analysis results, concluded that there is a negative correlation between work family conflict and the professional happiness of primary and secondary school teachers [13]. In addition, using resource conservation theory and social exchange theory to study primary and secondary school teachers, we can also get basically the same conclusion: the work-family conflict between primary and secondary school teachers will greatly reduce their job satisfaction, and further directly increase the turnover tendency of teachers [14]. Some scholars even combined with the Covid-19 epidemic, arguing that the Covid-19 epidemic has made the conflict between work and family more intense and the conflict has led to a decrease in job satisfaction [15-16]. Therefore, this study sets middle school teachers as the research object and assumes that work family conflicts among middle school teachers have a significant negative impact on job satisfaction.

Hypothesis H1: Work-family conflict has a negative impact on the job satisfaction of middle school teachers

2.2. The Role of Professional Identity

The concept of occupational identity was first proposed by psychologist Erikson's theory of "self-identity". According to Aryee & Tan, occupational identity is an important factor influencing job satisfaction and is closely related to job achievement, length of time in the job and turnover rate [18]. When occupational identity is strong, individuals' sense of belonging to their own jobs will be enhanced and individuals' job satisfaction will increase, and when occupational identity is weak, individuals do not get useful information for themselves at work and individuals' job satisfaction will decrease [19]. Experts have conducted different studies on several groups based on this. In the field of health care, professional identity is not only an important factor influencing job satisfaction of nurses in the post-anesthesia care unit [20]. It can also improve physician assistant job satisfaction through organizational commitment [21]. Especially in the new crown epidemic, physicians and nurses rushed to the front line to guard the people, it is because their professional identity still allowed them to hold job satisfaction [22]. Other scholars believe that social workers' job satisfaction can be improved only when their professional identity is increased. [23], and improving social workers' professional identity is an effective way to improve social workers' happiness [24]. I In the field of education, a good school environment can enhance teachers' sense of identification with their profession, thereby changing the dilemma of low job satisfaction among primary and secondary school teachers [25], and in rural areas, longer working hours, larger class sizes, and lower incomes contribute to the current situation of low job satisfaction among these teachers [26]. Teacher burnout is a common problem in Chinese society today [27], and improving teachers' professional identity is likely to increase their job satisfaction. In addition, studies by other scholars have proved that there is also a significant correlation between preschool teachers' work-family conflict and professional identity [28]. Teachers' passion and love for work can, to a certain extent, enable them to avoid the adverse emotions of work-family conflict [29]. Low occupational identity variables such as autonomy belief, service belief and professional competence will also change employees' job satisfaction [30]. This suggests that there is some correlation between middle school teachers and their work-family conflict, professional identity and job satisfaction. Based on the above research, the following hypotheses are proposed in this study:

Hypothesis *H2*: Work-family conflict is negatively related to the development of professional identity among secondary school teachers.

Hypothesis *H3*: Job satisfaction of secondary school teachers is positively related to the generation of professional identity.

Hypothesis *H4*: Professional identity mediates the effect of work-family conflict on job satisfaction among secondary school teachers.

2.3. The Role of Occupational Stress

Occupational stress is a type of psychological stress, which is usually caused by unmet needs, and if an individual's physical, energy and emotions are not met, occupational stress will result. Secondary school teachers are faced with a series of problems such as complicated and trivial work tasks, and the heavy workload inevitably leads to neglect of family, and conflicts between work and family needs will generate stress in teachers' psychology, and teachers with low psychological capital will feel a strong sense of pressure at this time [31]. Some studies have shown that work-family conflict in secondary school teachers leads to job insecurity, which in turn leads to burnout [32-33] and occupational stress. Thus, occupational stress can arise at any time when work-family conflict arises. For people at work, occupational stress can bring various disadvantages to their lives and work, and scholars have conducted studies on people in different occupations and found that: The work stress of disaster safety management personnel will lead to the decline of job satisfaction [34], which leads to the increase of turnover rate. Occupational stress of psychiatric nurses is negatively correlated with their life satisfaction [35], and occupational stress of preschool teachers also directly affects their job satisfaction [36]. To sum up, there is a strong correlation between work-family conflict, occupational stress and job satisfaction. Therefore, the following hypothesis is proposed in this study:

Hypothesis *H5*: Work-family conflict is positively related to the generation of occupational stress among secondary school teachers.

Hypothesis *H6*: Job satisfaction of secondary school teachers is positively related to the generation of occupational stress

Hypothesis *H7*: Occupational stress mediates the effect of work-family conflict on job satisfaction among secondary school teachers.

The research framework of this paper is shown in Figure 1 below:

Figure 1 Research framework

3. Objects and Methods

324 primary and secondary school teachers in Wuhan voluntarily participated in the questionnaire survey, and after eliminating invalid responses (response time less than 30 seconds, repeated selection of the same option), 302 remained, with an efficiency rate of 92.1%. The respondents covered teachers of all ages and educational levels. Among them, 110 (36.42%) were male and 192 (63.58%) were female; 102 (33.77%) were less than 30 years old, 113 (37.42%) were between 30 and 40 years old, 87 (28.81%) were over 40 years old, 198 (65.56%) possess a master's and doctoral degree, and 104 (34.44%) had a bachelor's degree.

This study modified the classic maturity scale developed by related scholars [37-40] to form the scale for this study. The internal consistency alpha coefficient for these scales all exceeded 0.800. In this study, SPSS 26.0 software was used to classify, test, screen and analyze the data. Analytical methods such as reliability analysis, validated factor analysis with discriminant validity, correlation analysis, and validation of mediating effects using stratified regression and Sobel testing were used.

4. Research Results

4.1. Reliability and Validity Tests

After testing, the reliability coefficient value of the questionnaire is 0.67, greater than 0.6, and the Cronbach alpha coefficients of all four-dimensional variables are greater than 0.8, indicating the existence of High-quality research data reliability. The KMO value is 0.87, the KMO value is greater than 0.8, and the p-value is 0.000, both of which are less than 0.05, indicating that the validity of the data in this study is good. In addition, in order to test the discriminant validity of key variables such as "work family conflict", "job satisfaction", "occupational identity", and "occupational stress", this study constructed a basic model to examine the impact of work family conflict on job satisfaction through occupational identity, while work family conflict points to job satisfaction. The key variables were analyzed using confirmatory factor analysis (CFA). The fitting indices of the three models are all good, with RMSEA less than 0.10, and CFI, NNFI, TLI, and IFI indices all above 0.90. This indicates that the measurement has good discriminant validity.

4.2. Correlations of the Variables

This paper uses correlation analysis to study the interaction between work-family conflict and job satisfaction, occupational identity and occupational stress.

Table 1 shows the results of correlation analysis. Work-family conflict is negatively correlated with job satisfaction (r=-0.57, p<0.01), and work-family conflict is negatively correlated with the generation of professional identity (r=-0.52, p<0.01). There was a significant positive correlation between work-family conflict and occupational stress (r=0.59, p<0.01). The results showed that hypothesis H1, H2, H3, H5 and H6 were all valid.

Table 1. Means, variances and correlations among the main variables (N=164)

	Average value	Standard deviation	1	2	3	4
1. Work-family conflict	3.434	0.879	0.736			
2. Professional identity	3.816	0.997	-0.516**	0.833		
3.Occupational pressure	3.922	0.793	0.594**	-0.354**	0.75	
4. Job satisfaction	3.437	0.967	-0.569**	0.582**	-0.558**	0.767

4.3. Hypothesis Testing

This question uses hierarchical regression and Sobel test methods to test hypotheses. In Table 2, a linear regression analysis with work-family and job satisfaction as the dependent variables shows that the squared value of the model r is 0.324, which means that the work-family conflict variable can explain 32.4% of the change in job satisfaction. Perform an F-test on the model, and the model can pass the F-test (F=36.877, p<0.05), indicating that work family conflict has a strong impact on satisfaction. Therefore, this article sets the model equation as: work satisfaction=5.587-0.626 * work family conflict. The final specific analysis shows that: The regression coefficient of work-family conflict is -0.626, which is very significant (t=-6.073, p=0.000<0.01), and the negative effect of work conflict on job satisfaction is significant. For model 2: After adding a new variable, occupational identity, to model 1, F-value changes significantly (p<0.05), indicating that the addition of occupational identity variable can improve the explanatory ability of the model. In addition, the R-squared value increased from 0.324 to 0.437, which means that the occupational identity variable explains 11.3% of job satisfaction. Specifically, the regression coefficient of occupational identity is 0.381, which is significant at 1%

confidence level (t=3.910, p=0.000<0.01). The results show that occupational identity has a significant positive correlation with job satisfaction.

For Model 4, after adding occupational stress to Model 3, the change in f-value was significant (p<0.05), indicating that adding stress has explanatory significance for the model. In addition, the square value of r increased from 0.324 to 0.399, indicating that the explanatory strength of occupational stress on job satisfaction is 7.5%. Among them, the regression coefficient value of occupational stress is -0.414, which is significant (t=-3.073, p=0.003<0.01), indicating a significant negative relationship between occupational stress and job satisfaction.

In order to further test the significance of the mediating effect, this article uses the Sobel test (see Table 3) to test the significance of the mediating effect of occupational identity and occupational stress between work family conflict and job satisfaction. The results showed that occupational identity had a significant mediating effect between work family conflict and job satisfaction (95CI: -0.450-0.029, Z=-3.516), and occupational stress had a significant mediating effect between work family conflict and job satisfaction (95CI: -0.450-0.029, Z=-3.424). Therefore, the data further supports assumptions H4 and H7.

Table 2. Intermediary effects analysis (hierarchical regression)

	Job satisfaction		Job satisfaction	
	Model 1	Model 2	Model 3	Model 4
Independent variable				
Work-family conflict	-0.626**	-0.403**	-0.626**	-0.404**
Intermediate variables				
Professional Identity		0.381**		
Occupational Stress				-0.414**
Sample size	302	302	302	302
R 2	0.324	0.437	0.324	0.399
Adjustment R 2	0.315	0.422	0.315	0.383
F Value □	F (1, 77) = 36.877, p=0.000	F (2,76) = 29.507, p=0.000	F (1,77) = 36.877, p=0.000	F (2,76) =25.180, p=0.000
△R 2	0.324	0.113	0.324	0.075
△F value □	F (1, 77) = 36.877, p= 0.000	F (1,76) =15.292, p=0.000	F (1,77) =36.877, p=0.000	F (1,76) =9.441, p=0.003

Note: n = 302; ** $p < 0.01$, * $p < 0.05$

Table 3. Mediating effects between work-family conflict and job satisfaction (Sobel)

Paths	β(normalized)	Total effect	95% CI
Work-family conflict → Career identity → Job satisfaction: F=29.51, R2=0.44			
Direct effect	-0.21		-0.450 ~ 0.029
Indirect effects	-0.21		-0.321 ~ -0.083
Total effect		-0.63	
Work-family conflict → occupational stress → job satisfaction: F = 25.18, R2 = 0.40			
Direct effect	-0.21		-0.450 ~ 0.029
Indirect effects	-0.20		-0.323 ~ -0.088
Total effect		-0.63	

5. Discussion

5.1. Work-Family Conflict on Job Satisfaction

Research shows that in the group of secondary school teachers, the correlation between work-family conflict and job satisfaction is strong. This conclusion is basically the same as the results obtained by other scholars using different methods. [13-16]. For secondary school teachers, the limited energy in a day inevitably results in a situation where family and work cannot be combined. When the time and energy that should be spent on family is distracted from work, family will be neglected, and if this happens in the long run, it will inevitably cause conflicts with family members, and the occurrence of conflicts will hinder the smooth progress of work and affect job performance, and at this time, the job satisfaction of secondary school teachers will decrease [12]. In today's society, life is fast-paced, and middle-aged people are faced with the current situation of having an old family and a young family, and inevitably, when their work ability does not match their work results, teachers will inevitably feel a sense of loss and discrepancy, and under this circumstance, if the salary treatment is difficult to meet their expected requirement value, teachers will have doubts about their work and seriously affect their job satisfaction [13]. The above research proves that the work family conflict of middle school teachers is closely related to job satisfaction, and shows a significant negative correlation.

5.2. The Mediating Role of Professional Identity

The mediating effect shows that the work-family conflict of middle school teachers can indirectly predict their job satisfaction by influencing their professional identity first. First, work-family conflict among middle school teachers directly predicts job satisfaction, which process is significant. Second, the likelihood of work-family conflict is significantly reduced when secondary school teachers are not "coerced" by material things, and their time and energy can be well allocated to work and family. With the support of family, encouragement from colleagues, well-behaved students, and a good salary, secondary school teachers will have stronger sense of professional identity. A higher sense of professional identity will reap the envy of others, have an absolute advantage in downward social comparisons, and satisfy their own psychological needs, and in the long run, teachers' satisfaction with their jobs will then skyrocket [29-30]. It can be seen that professional identity can play a mediating role in the process of work-family conflicts affecting the job satisfaction of middle school teachers.

5.3. The Mediating Role of Occupational Stress

For secondary school teachers, work-family conflict can indirectly alter their level of job satisfaction by influencing occupational stress. There are many reasons for middle school teachers to have family conflicts, besides their own reasons, also be due to the interference of other factors, such as malicious competition among colleagues, rebelliousness of students, impersonal parents of students, etc. [32]. Occupational stress occurs when stress arises when it is difficult to do well with work. Stress can lead to the generation of anxiety, when teachers will lose their enthusiasm which have appeared when they first joined the profession, their enthusiasm for their work is reduced, their motivation is weakened, and then they become bored with their work, which seriously affects teachers' satisfaction with their work [36]. It can be seen that occupational stress, as a mediating variable, plays a role in the process of work-family conflicts affecting the job satisfaction of middle school teachers.

6. Research Conclusion and Outlook

6.1. Research Findings

This paper conducted a questionnaire survey to collect extensive data. After data analysis, this study studied the relationship among the four relevant variables of middle school teachers' work-family conflict, job satisfaction, professional identity and occupational stress and found that: (1) Secondary school teachers' job satisfaction is reduced when work and family conflict. Secondary school teachers have a limited amount of time and energy in the day, and job satisfaction decreases when time spent at work takes away from time spent caring for family members. (2) Professional identity plays an intermediary role in the effect of work-family conflict on the job satisfaction of middle school teachers. When there is a conflict between teachers' work and family, the job satisfaction of teachers with a high degree of professional identity will not decline rapidly, and will always remain in a reasonable range. (3) Occupational stress plays a mediating role in the influence of work-family conflict on the job satisfaction of middle school teachers. When teachers' work and family conflicts arise and teachers do not have time and energy to take care of the big picture, their job satisfaction decreases if teachers' occupational stress is high and they have internal doubts about the nature of their work.

6.2. Management Insights

(1) The government should play a leading role by introducing policies to improve the treatment of secondary school teachers and listen to the needs of young teachers, improve their living conditions, and increase their professional identity and job satisfaction. (2) Teacher groups should rationalize the time they spend on work and family, make sure they have a flexible time each day, and use the flexible time to improve the dilemma when family and work time conflict. (3) Schools should carry out a series of activities to relieve teachers' stress and enhance satisfaction and professional identity. More activities such as sunshine sports activities and teacher reunion activities should be held, and teachers should be encouraged to bring their families to the activities to improve their family's recognition of the teaching profession and promote the integration of family and work. In addition, schools should set up teacher counselors on campus, where teachers can ask for free consultation to detect psychological problems and intervene for treatment in a timely manner.

6.3. Research Shortcomings and Outlook

The conclusions obtained in this study can provide some insights for teachers in balancing work family relationships, but there are still many shortcomings in this study. Considering the overall research content of this article, combined with real life and the latest research progress, this paper proposes the following perspectives: (1) Conflict between work and family can affect teachers' job satisfaction and also their life satisfaction. Therefore, in addition to exploring job satisfaction, we can also add relevant content about life satisfaction, analyze job satisfaction and life satisfaction together to increase the hierarchy of the study and improve the integrity of the study. (2) As a special group of secondary school teachers, the conflicts between work and family are divided into various kinds, such as time conflicts, material conflicts, interpersonal conflicts, etc. Therefore, in the study, the study can be divided into dimensions to refine this study, so that the research content is more detailed and the applicable research objects are broader. (3) This study is a cross-sectional study, and the scope of the study is locked on a specific group of teachers, so the study is targeted and not applicable to the study of the influence of work-family conflict on job satisfaction in other occupations, and the subjects are somewhat one-sided, and the data derived from the questionnaire based on the tested population may not reflect the attitudes of other occupations. Therefore, how to expand the reflection of a specific group to other groups in other fields, so that the study can meet the needs of multiple groups in multiple fields, deserves more in-depth research in the future.

Reference

[1]   Hobfoll, S.E., Halbesleben, J., Neveu, J.P., & Westman, M. Conservation of resources in the organizational context: The reality of resources and their consequences[J]. Annual Review of Organizational Psychology and Organizational Behavior, 2018, 5(1): 103-128.

[2]   [2]   Liu, C. Q., Sun, S. J. Emotion and efficacy: theoretical and practical perspectives on group identity in collective action[J]. Journal of Southwest University for Nationalities (Humanities and Social Sciences Edition), 2016, 37(08): 183-190.

[3]   [3] Xu, L. Y., Li, X. W, et al. Relationship between professional identity, career satisfaction, value of competence and growth, and job burnout: A cross-sectional study of primary and secondary school teachers in China[J]. Psychology in the Schools.2022, 60(4): 1234-1248.

[4]   Aneshensel, C. S., Social stress: theory and research [J]. Annual Review of Sociology, 1992, 18: 15-38.

[5]   Hu, G., Zhu., Y. J., Wang, Y. Analysis of factors influencing the quality of life of early childhood teachers--constructive relationship between teachers' self-determination, occupational stress and job satisfaction[J]. Educational Theory and Practice, 2018, 38(26): 43-45.

[6]   Li, X. Y., Gao, J. A study on the relationship between work-family conflict, supervisor support feeling and job satisfaction--an empirical analysis based on middle-level professional managers[J]. Science and Technology Management, 2011, 32(02): 163-170.

[7]   Wang, L. J., Shen, Lei. Work-family conflict and job satisfaction of R&D personnel - the moderating effect of psychological capital[J]. Technology Economics and Management Research, 2015, 230(09): 63-67.

[8]   Qi, Y. L. A study on the relationship between work-family conflict and employees' job satisfaction: the moderating role of employees' mental toughness[J]. Theory and Reform, 2015, 201(01): 112-115.

[9]   Gao, Z. H., Zhao, C. Why is it so difficult to work-family balance? An exploration based on work-family boundary theory[J]. Journal of Psychology, 2014, 46(04): 552-568.

[10] Liu, Y. X., Zhang, J. W., Peng, K. P. Psychological mechanisms of idle behavior in the perspective of work-family conflict: the role of job satisfaction and self-determination tendencies[J]. Psychological and Behavioral Research, 2013, 11(05): 671-678.

[11] Li, X. S. The effect of work-family conflict on job satisfaction of knowledge workers - an analysis of the effect based on psychological ownership[J]. Modern Management Science, 2012, 233(08): 99-101.

[12] Li, X., Lin, X. Y., &Tian, F. Playing Roles in Work and Family: Effects of Work/Family Conflicts on Job and Life Satisfaction Among Junior High School Teachers[J]. Frontiers In Psychology, 2021.

[13] Zhou, M. M., Wang, D. W., et al. The Effect of Work-Family Conflict on Occupational Well-Being Among Primary and Secondary School Teachers: The Mediating Role of Psychological Capital[J]. Frontiers in Public Health, 2021, 9.

[14] Li, X. Y., Chen, X. R., Gao, D. D. Influence of Work-Family Conflict on Turnover Intention of Primary and Secondary School Teachers: Serial Mediating Role of Psychological Contract and Job Satisfaction[J]. Frontiers in Psychiatry.2022, 13: 869344.

[15] Hong, X.M., Liu, Q. Q., Zhang, M. Z. Dual Stressors and Female Pre-school Teachers' Job Satisfaction During the COVID-19: The Mediation of Work-Family Conflict[J]. Frontiers in Psychiatry. 2021, 12: 691498.

[16] Karakose, T., Yirci, R., Papadakis, S. Exploring the Interrelationship between COVID-19 Phobia, Work-Family Conflict, Family-WorkConflict, and Life Satisfaction among School Administrators for Advancing Sustainable Management[J]. Sustainability.2021, 13(15).

[17] Fan, Y. P. From the study of historical contribution to the study of professional identity--a new perspective on the study of journalistic historical figures[J]. International Journalism, 2009, (08): 101-104.

[18] Aryee, S., Tan, K. Antecedents and outcomes of career commitment[J]. Journal of Vocational Behavior, 1992, 40: 288-305.

[19] Mi, Y. C., Sunny K. A Study on the Perception of Youth Worker on Professional Identity and Job Satisfaction[J].2015, 17(4): 239-262.

[20] Yoo J B, Won J. Impact of Job Stress, Organizational Culture and Professional Identity on Job Satisfaction of Post-anesthesia Care Unit Nurses[J]. Journal of The Korean Data Analysis Society. 2018, 20(6): 3211-3225.

[21] Yoo, S., Kim, M. S., Park H S. Mediating Effect of Organizational Commitment in the Relationship between Professional Identity and Job Satisfaction[J]. Journal of Health Informatics and Statistics, 2019, 44(4): 339-348.

[22] Hanum, A. L., Hu, Q. L., et al. Professional identity, job satisfaction, and intention to stay among clinical nurses during the prolonged COVID-19 pandemic: a mediation analysis[J]. Japan Journal of Nursing Science.2022.

[23] Ahn, Tae-Sook. Effects of Professional Identity of Social Workers on Job Satisfaction and Organizational Commitment: Focused on Mediated Effect of Working Environment [J]. The Journal of the Korea Contents Association.2020, 20 (10), 554-565.

[24] Yu, Y. J. Effect of Professional Identity on the Happiness of Social Workers: Focused on JobSatisfaction Mediated Effect. Journal of the Korean society for Wellness, 2020, 15(1), 357-366.

[25] Han, X. Q., Xu, Q., Xiao, J. H. The Influence of School Atmosphere on Chinese Teachers' Job Satisfaction: The Chain Mediating Effect of Psychological Capital and Professional Identity[J]. BEHAVIORAL SCIENCES.2023, 13(1).

[26] Tang, Y. P. It's not only Work and Pay: The Moderation Role of Teachers' Professional Identity on their Job Satisfaction in Rural China[J]. Applied Research in Quality of Life, 2020, 15(4): 971-990.

[27] Xu, L. Y., Li, X. W., et al. Relationship between professional identity, career satisfaction, value of competence and growth, and job burnout: A cross-sectional study of primary and secondary school teachers in China[J]. Psychology in the Schools.2023, 60(4): 1234-1248.

[28] Huang, M., Chen, L., Guo L. P., et al. The relationship between work-family conflict and early childhood teachers' intention to leave: The serial mediating role of professional identity and burnout[J]. Psychological and Behavioral Research, 2021, 19(05): 679-686.

[29] Houlfort, N., Philippe, F.L., et al. A Comprehensive Understanding of the Relationships Between Passion for Work and Work-Family Conflict and the Consequences for Psychological Distress[J]. International Journal of Stress Management.2018, 25(4): 313-329.

[30] Song, H. S., Hwang, M. H. The Effect of Work-Family Conflict on Occupational Identity and Job Satisfaction - Focused on Hotel employee-[J]. Tourism Research.2013, 38 (2): 167-186.

[31] Burkc, I., Simunovic, M., Balaz, B. Work-family conflicts and teacher commitment during the COVID-19 pandemic: a moderated mediation analysis of emotional exhaustion and psychological capital[J]. Educational Psychology.2022.

[32] Richter, A., Naswall, K Naswall, K., et al. Job insecurity and work-family conflict in teachers in Sweden: Examining their relations with longitudinal cross-lagged modeling [J]. Psych Journal.2015, 4(2): 98-111.

[33] Simaes, C., Rodrigues, J., et al. Work-family conflicts, cognitive appraisal, and burnout: Testing the mediation effect with structural equation modelling[J]. British Journal of Educational Psychology.2021, 91(4).

[34] young, koo joo., O-Young, Kwon. A Study on the Factors that Affect Disaster Safety Management Officials' Job and Organizational Perceptions and Stress Management[J]. The Journal of Convergence Society and Public Policy.2022, 16(3): 161-201.

[35] Hu, G., Zhu, Y. J., Wang, Y. Analysis of factors influencing the quality of life of early childhood teachers--constructive relationships among teachers' self-determination, occupational stress and job satisfaction[J]. Educational Theory and Practice, 2018, 38(26): 43-45.

[36] Xu, F., Sun, H. The mediating and moderating role of positive thinking between occupational stress and life satisfaction in psychiatric nurses[J]. China Nursing Management, 2018, 18(09): 1213-1217.

[37] Zhang, F. The impact of work-family conflict on work and life satisfaction among secondary school teachers [D]. Huazhong Normal University, 2020.

[38] Dong, Patrick., Wu, M. C. The relationship between professional identity and job satisfaction of counselors in general universities [J]. Psychological Science, 2010, 33(1): 241-243.

[39] Zhou, K. A study of secondary school physical education teachers' professional identity [D]. Henan University, 2010.

[40] Xu, F. M., Shen, W. L., Zhu Congshu, A study of teachers' occupational stress and coping strategies [D]. Primary and Secondary School Management, 2002(10): 15-16.

Artificial Intelligence, Medical Engineering and Education
Z.B. Hu et al. (Eds.)
doi:10.3233/ATDE231396

Six-Link Teaching Methods for Improving the Creative Practical Ability -Taking "Mechanical Principle" as an Example

Wenhui LI, Chaoying MENG, Xun LIAN, Qin HE, Min KONG, Yang GAO[1]
Department of Mechanical and Electrical Engineering, Wenhua College, Wuhan,
China
ORCiD ID: Wenhui LI https://orcid.org/0009-0005-4891-8069

Abstract. In the construction of "Emerging Engineering Education" and "First-Class Course", "Mechanical Principle" is oriented to the requirements of talent training, the application of innovative thinking and creative practical ability in teaching. Firstly, the teaching system of "Mechanical Principle" is reconstructed. Secondly, based on TRIZ Theory in teaching methods is improved in the "Teaching, Learning, Practice, Creation, Research, Competition" six links. Thirdly, closed-loop process evaluation is adopted in teaching evaluation to reflect the situation of teachers and students. The effect of teaching reform shows that teacher evaluation, student achievement, student work and the achievement of curriculum objectives have been improved after the curriculum improvement. Especially in the second classroom, such as subject competition, innovation, entrepreneurship. The students' innovative practical ability is effectively improved.

Keywords. Teaching methods, Teaching system, Teaching evaluation, Creative practical ability, Mechanical principle.

1. Introduction

"Mechanical Principle" is an important basic course of engineering specialty, which plays an important role in achieving the goal of talent training, especially in cultivating students' ability of innovative design of mechanism [1]. It's hard to link professional knowledge with practical life and engineering practice. Based on the guiding principles of "First-Class Course" construction, it should focus on improving students' innovative comprehensive practical ability, reconstructing the course teaching system and improving teaching methods, so as to break the silence of the course [2].

Liu Xiaoyong et al. improved students' innovative design ability through the teaching reform of "Mechanical Principle" [3]. Wang Bo et al. adopted measures to strengthen the cultivation of students' innovative ability, such as subject competition projects, visiting exhibitions, participating in innovative experimental projects, and enriching curriculum design projects [4]. Yu Jingjun et al. introduced innovative design ideas into the teaching content, teaching methods and practical links in the teaching process of "Mechanical Principle", in order to cultivate students' innovative ability [5].

Teaching students innovative thinking method is an important way to improve

---

[1] Corresponding Author: Yang GAO, Email: 267083084@qq.com.

students' innovative ability and institutional innovative design ability. The innovative thinking method of TRIZ theory is introduced, such as 40 invention principles and morphological matrix method in TRIZ [6]. Adopt innovative thinking methods to deal with problems in mechanism design and establish innovative design schemes.

The course group promotes the integration of theoretical teaching, experimental teaching and curriculum design, and reforms "Mechanical Principle" from the teaching system, teaching methods and teaching evaluation.

2. Based on TRIZ Theory in the Teaching of "Mechanical Principle"

By teaching the innovative thinking methods on TRIZ theory, the students' innovative design ability is improved. In TRIZ theory, the ideal degree of the system is proportional to the sum of useful functions and inversely proportional to the sum of harmful functions [7]. It is defined as:

$$I = \frac{\sum U_F}{\sum H_F + \sum C} \qquad (1)$$

I is the ideal degree of the system. $\sum U_F$ is the sum of useful functions. $\sum H_F$ is the sum of harmful functions. $\sum C$ is the sum of costs.

According to the formula, the ideal final result of the problem is a system with infinitely large useful functions, infinitely small harmful functions and infinitely small costs. The final ideal solution method is used to solve the problem of mechanism innovation design. As shown in Figure 1. Firstly, establish the ideal solution of the problem. Secondly, find the obstacles to achieve the ideal solution. Thirdly, find ways to overcome the obstacles. Fourthly, eliminate obstacles. Finally establish a solution.

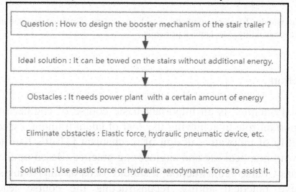

Figure 1. An example of the final ideal solution.

3. Reconstruct the Teaching System of Course "Mechanical Principle"

Guided by the curriculum objectives, the course of "Mechanical Principle" adheres to the fundamental task of cultivating people by virtue, implements OBE education concept, strengthens the innovative thinking in practice, integrates ideological and political education, professional education, innovation, and entrepreneurship education, and constructs a new teaching system of "Mechanical Principle" [8-10], as shown in Figure 2. Through the course learning and application, students can stimulate the spirit of innovation, form three types of student's curriculum designs: classroom works, course design innovation works and subject competition works, realize the organic combination of imparting the knowledge, training the ability and shaping the value.

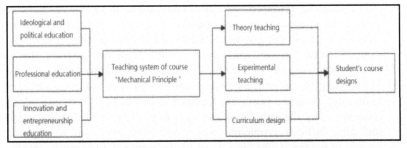

Figure 2. Teaching system of "Mechanical Principle".

The theory teaching of "Mechanical Principle" takes mechanism design as the main line, mechanism analysis as the design service, and students' ability of mechanical system scheme design as the goal. They are composed of four parts: mechanism structure, mechanism kinematics, mechanism dynamics and mechanical system scheme design. They are carried out step by step [11]. The composition principle and structure analysis are composed of linkage mechanism, cam mechanism, gear mechanism, gear train mechanism, intermittent motion mechanism and other mechanisms. Various mechanisms have different functions, types, characteristics, motion principles and design methods. Mechanism dynamics explains the basic concepts and theories of mechanical efficiency, self-locking, balance and machine operation. The design of mechanical system scheme can cultivate students' design ability of the whole machine.

The experimental teaching of "Mechanical Principle" includes the conventional experimental items such as the mapping of the mechanism and the assembly of the mechanism. Use the high-quality virtual experiment resources in the national virtual simulation experiment teaching course sharing platform to enrich the teaching content, carry out experimental rehearsals, help students master the corresponding knowledge points and improve the quality of experimental teaching.

The course design of "Mechanical Principle" adopts traditional questions or optional competition questions. Focus on the general process of product design and manufacture. Introduce modern design methods such as computer aided design. Combine scientific and technological innovation activities, such as mechanical innovation design competition, engineering training competition. During the course of completing, students carry out targeted learning. They take the initiative to communicate with each other, when they encounter problems. If there are problems that cannot be solved, they will take the initiative to consult teachers. The teacher needs to guide, observe, consult and evaluate the implementation. The reformed teaching puts forward higher requirements for teachers' professional ability and knowledge.

4. Improve the Teaching Method

The teaching spiral promotion is based on the six links of "Teaching, Learning, Practicing, Creating, Researching and Competing" based on repetition, feedback, promotion and constantly summarizes the teaching experience in the implementation process. Through course learning and application, students can find problems and solve problems. It's important to have innovative consciousness, innovative ability and collaborative innovation [12].

- 1) Teaching. In a limited time to clarify the core knowledge points. Use the online teaching resources of First-Class Course to enrich students' learning content. Introduce enterprise engineering projects into the classroom to enhance students' professional cognition. Based on project guidance, teachers guide students from passive listening to active thinking, actively discuss and communicate, increase students' participation, and improve teaching quality.

- 2) Learning. Based on the iterative learning process, students can learn small knowledge points, repeat, and feedback continuously, forming a closed-loop process. Using the rain classroom, establish a learning feedback mechanism, including difficult problems, homework correction, unit testing and other aspects of feedback. Teachers focus on the common problems to answer.

- 3) Practice. In the study of theoretical knowledge and project-driven teaching, teachers can give students some major assignments to consolidate. For example, the design and manufacture of a model can be completed in groups. It can be printed in 3D, such as the rack-and-gear and linkage mechanism, the manipulator of opening and closing mechanism, as shown in Figure 3. Corrugated board, wood board and acrylic board can also be used to make models, as shown in Figure 4.

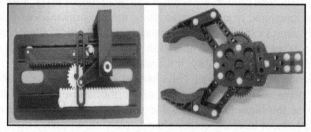

Figure 3. The application of 3D printing in the course of "Mechanical Principle".

Figure 4. The application of wood board in the course of "Mechanical Principle".

- 4) Creating. Teachers can transform the teaching and scientific research results of the course group into students' innovative practice guidance. Design some production models with practice to improve the challenge of the course. As shown in Figure 3, bionic mechanical horse, and bionic butterfly. When the model can realize its function, students gain a sense of achievement and professional pride and stimulate students' desire for knowledge.

- 5) Researching. The school carries out the special subject of scientific research service teaching. Students participate in the teacher's project. Cultivate innovative design talents to meet the needs of society, industry and enterprises. Understand the knowledge and skills that enterprises really need. Students should be familiar with the product design and manufacturing process. Comprehensively improve the professional quality of students.

- 6) Competing. Organize students to participate in class, college, school competitions. Select excellent works to participate in provincial and national mechanical innovation design competitions, college students' engineering training competitions, etc. As shown in Figure 5. Cultivate students' teamwork, innovative literacy and comprehensive practical ability.

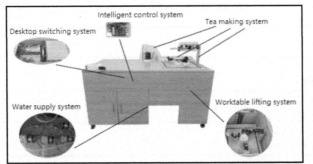

Figure 5. Intelligent tea table for national college students' mechanical innovation design competition.

5. Improve Teaching Evaluation

Teaching adopts closed-loop process evaluation to reflect the situation of teaching and learning, as shown in Figure 6. According to the evaluation of teachers, students' achievements, students' works and students' satisfaction with teaching, the degree of achievement of curriculum objectives is analyzed. Continuous improvement is carried out to optimize the curriculum system, teaching methods and curriculum objectives, so as to improve the teaching quality [13-14].

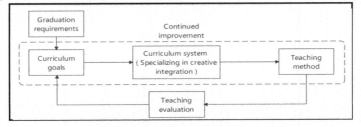

Figure 6. Closed-loop teaching evaluation process.

Teacher evaluation adopts the teaching evaluation method of peer teachers, supervisory teachers, leading cadres and students' evaluation. The students' performance is evaluated by the combination of formative evaluation and result evaluation. Students master the method of using TRIZ theory to analyze and solve innovative design problems. The corresponding relationship between learning content and learning objectives, as shown in Table 1. Let H, M and L denote the strong, medium, and weak relations respectively. Reduce the proportion of final exam scores. Pay more attention to students' learning process. Adjust the proportion of rain classroom unit test, usual classroom performance and classroom assignments. Give relatively objective comprehensive results of the course. To a certain extent, it reflects students' knowledge mastery and innovative comprehensive ability. If teaching evaluation reaches excellent, the teacher wins the teaching quality award.

Table 1. The relationship between learning content and learning objectives based on TRIZ theory

Learning content	Learning goal			
	Familiar with design process	Understand TRIZ theory	Apply TRIZ theory to innovative design.	Cultivate students' ability of engineering quality, innovative thinking and so on
Demand analysis	H	L	M	H
Analyze technology conflicts	M	H	H	M
Find the right principle of invention	L	H	H	M
Analyze the application of the principle of invention	L	H	H	M
Give the scheme design	L	M	M	M

6. Implementation Effectiveness

Through the joint efforts of teachers and students, the curriculum reform has been continuously promoted. Students have received comprehensive training. The average value of students' comprehensive course scores increases year by year, as shown in Figure 7. It tends to be consistent with the achievement of course objectives. From the feedback from the course design, students know how to proceed with the design of mechanical products.

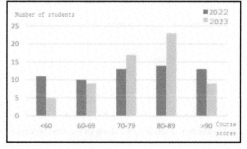

Figure 7. Students' comprehensive course scores distribution chart.

The course experience of the student for specific design objects, purposeful access to information and experience their knowledge acquisition by themselves. Innovative design and handmade ability have been effectively exercised. The submitted works have a sense of achievement.

The enthusiasm of students to participate in competitions has been continuously improved.The number of participating projects has increased. In recent years, the teachers have guided students to participate in the college students' mechanical innovation design competition. They have won one item for national second prize, three items for provincial first prize, three items for provincial second prize and two items for provincial third prize. It can be seen that the students' innovative comprehensive practical ability has been greatly improved.

7. Conclusion

The innovative thinking method of TRIZ theory is applied to the teaching reform of "Mechanical Principle" and improve students' innovative practical ability.

- 1) The teaching system of "Mechanical Principle" is reconstructed, which takes design as the main line, mechanism kinematics and dynamics as the support, and the innovative design scheme of mechanical system as the goal.
- 2) Innovative education is integrated into the six links and various teaching methods of "Teaching, Learning, Practicing, Creating, Researching and Competing".
- 3) The achievement of teachers' evaluation, students' performance, students' works and curriculum objectives are improved.

Design ability plays an important role, but there is a lack of various systematic innovative thinking methods. At the same time, it is also necessary to further explore and establish more application cases.

Acknowledgment

This research is supported by the mechanical engineering and automation professional construction project of the first-class undergraduate professional construction site in Hubei Province(J09007802), as well as provincial First-Class Course "Mechanical Principle" and the teaching quality and teaching reform project of Wenhua College (J09007004/J09007014).

References

[1] Gao Haining, Hongdan Shen, Yinling Wang. Diversified teaching mode reform of mechanical principle and design based on Internet Plus[J]. Lethaia, 2020, 9: 225.

[2] Gao Jian. Reform of database course in police colleges based on working process[J]. International Journal of Modern Education and Computer Science, 2017, 9(2): 41-46.

[3] Liu Xiaoyong, Li Rongli, Yang Huixiang, et al. Research on the reform of mechanical principle based on OBE concept under the background of Emerging Engineering Education[J]. Mechanical design, 2020(A2): 23-26 (in Chinese).

[4] Wang Bo, Pang Jun, Ning Yi, et al. 'Mechanical Principle' teaching reform and practice under the background of Emerging Engineering Education - taking Chuzhou University as an example[J]. Journal of Chuzhou University, 2022, 24(2):117-121, 126 (in Chinese).

[5] Yu Jingjun, Guo Weidong, Zhao Hongzhe. Relying on the course of mechanical principle, cultivate high-order thinking ability[J]. Mechanical design, 2023, 40(3): 155-160 (in Chinese).

[6] Zhang Xiaoli, Yang Yunfeng, Yan Yong. Research on the evaluation index system of college students' innovation and entrepreneurship ability based on AHP/QFD/TRIZ theory[J]. Mechanical Design and Manufacturing Engineering, 2023, Vol.52 (5): 127-134 (in Chinese).

[7] Nyme Ahmed, Dip Nandi, A. G. M. Zaman. Analyzing student evaluations of teaching in a completely online environment[J]. International Journal of Modern Education and Computer Science, 2022, 14(6): 13-24.

[8] Li Nan, Zhang Yong. Improvement and practice of secondary school geography teachers' informatization teaching ability based on the perspective of MOOC[J]. International Journal of Education and Management Engineering, 2022, 12(1): 11-18.

[9] Armando Roman Flores, Enrique Cuan Urquizo, Ricardo Ramirez Mendoza, et al. Design of interactive learning cyber physical tools for mechanical design engineering courses[J]. IEEE Global Engineering Education, 2020, 2:17-24.

[10] ChukwuNonso Nwokoye, Ikechukwu Umeh, Njideka Mbeledogu," GeoNaija: Enhancing the Teaching and Learning of Geography through Mobile Applications", International Journal of Education and Management Engineering, 2019, 9(6):11-24.

[11] Arshia Khan, Janna Madden. Active learning: a new assessment model that boost confidence and learning while reducing test anxiety[J]. International Journal of Modern Education and Computer Science, 2018, 10(12): 1-9.

[12] Jiangling Fan, Junyan Fan, Zhiqing Cheng. Discussion on teaching method reform of mechanical principle course at Private Colleges[C]. In: Tan, J. (eds) Advances in Mechanical Design. Springer, Singapore, Mechanisms and Machine Science, 2021, 2315–2325.

[13] Yang Yong, Jiang Jingliang, Jin Xia, et al. Design and Development of computer aided teaching software for mechanical principle course[C]. Proceedings of the 2016 International Conference on Modern Management, Education Technology, and Social Science. Atlantis Press, 2017, 182-185.

[14] Kashinath, R. L. N. Raju. An empirical research on the effectiveness online and offline classes of English language learning based on student's perception in Telangana Schools[J]. International Journal of Modern Education and Computer Science, 2023, 15(2): 40-53.

Artificial Intelligence, Medical Engineering and Education
Z.B. Hu et al. (Eds.)
doi:10.3233/ATDE231397

The Application of OBE Teaching Mode in the Innovation of Management Accounting Curriculum

Jing LI[1]

Management School, Guangzhou City University of Technology, Guangzhou, China
ORCiD ID: Jing LI https: //orcid.org/0009-0008-2679-9857

Abstract. With the popularization of internet technology, new opportunities are provided for OBE (Outcome Based Education) teaching reform. Based on the analysis of the characteristics of the management accounting course, combined with prolonged teaching experience and in-depth interviews with students, in view of four dimensions and eighteen output points to cultivate Culture, Thinking, Knowledge and Practical of students, carries out PBL oriented teaching content reconstruction, exploring teaching design based on internet, expands multi-dimensional teaching evaluation models, and combines the subtle influence of ideological design, integrating continuous curriculum innovation reform, to achieve the goal of multi-point resonance and all-round interactive teaching.

Keywords. Teaching innovation; Management accounting; Outcome Based Education.

1. Introduction

The management accounting course is a comprehensive and interdisciplinary course. It can be characterized by integrating multiple disciplines, formulas, decisions, and knowledge points [1].

Before the teaching reform, students feedbacked the following learning obstacles: in terms of learning content, chapter knowledge is distributed and sorted according to the theoretical system, but in students' learning way, it appears out-breaking and jumping knowledge, and the content between certain chapters seems to be unrelated. From the perspective of class schedule, students are struggling to grasp the lesson schedule within the teaching plan. In terms of learning difficulty, due to many formulas, methods, application scenarios, and dispersion, the learning difficulty is high. In terms of evaluation and assessment, the daily performance results are not transparent enough, and feedback cannot be tracked in real-time.

2. Four Dimensional Teaching Objective System

In the continuous improvement of teaching process, based on the student-centered and

---

[1] Corresponding Author: Jing LI, E-mail: lijing@gcu.edu.cn.

OBE teaching guide, a goal system based on four dimensions and eighteen output points has been formed. The dimension of knowledge leads students to understand basic concepts, familiarize themselves with basic principles, understand cutting-edge trends, and build a knowledge system. In terms of practical dimension, students need to master simulation experiments, observation records, theoretical calculations, decision- making, and predicting & budgeting abilities. The dimension of thinking inspires students to form logical speculation, exploratory analysis, judgment and selection, inductive summary, and deductive reasoning abilities. Culture dimensions cultivates students' social responsibility, scientific attitude, legal awareness, and professional ethics [2]. As shown in Figure 1.

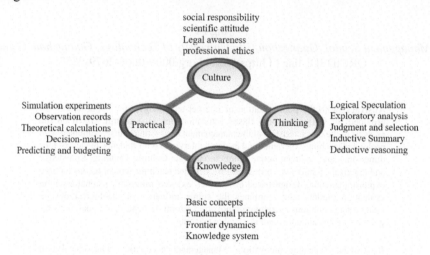

Figure 1. Four-dimensional teaching objectives system diagram for management accounting

3. PBL Oriented Curriculum Content Reconstruction

Makers have introduced entrepreneurial concepts, which can stimulate students' interest in self-directed learning and illuminate their theoretical and practical innovation. Under the PBL (Problem Based Learning) concept, the course focuses on the practical operation of 'Maker' scenario cases and carries out a combination of theory and practice teaching. Not only can it conform to the laws of learning, but also arouses students' curiosity, generates the psychological needs of "I want to learn", encourages students to persist in exploration, independent thinking, critical thinking, cultivates students' ability to learn independently and lifelong, to cooperate and communicate with others [3]. As a result, the course has carried out a problem-oriented restructuring of teaching content, and the comparison is as follows.

Before the restructuring of the teaching content, it was basically taught according to the traditional academic classification, divided into three parts: fundamentals, decision-making accounting, and control accounting. The basic part of management accounting includes introduction, cost behavior and variable cost method, and cost volume profit analysis. The decision-making accounting part includes business forecasting, production and operation decision-making, inventory planning and turnover control, and investment decision-making. The control accounting part includes standard cost management, activity-based cost calculation and management, budget management, performance evaluation, and management accounting reports. Its main drawbacks are observed: Firstly, some foundations are introduced after application, and knowledge points appeared scattered and numerous, lacking coherence. For example, business forecasting is rigidly intertwined between cost-volume-profit analysis and business decision-making, separating it from the closely related budget management. It also scattered the contribution margin analysis method among the fundamentals and business decision-making, and applys mechanically traditional theoretical classifications, breaking away from student learning patterns and their thinking relevance [4]. Secondly, the traditional manual calculation model is no longer suitable for the needs of social production, and management accounting can also use information platforms to improve the efficiency of prediction, decision-making, budgeting, analysis, assessment, and evaluation [5]. Once again, the teaching content of management accounting overlaps with that of financial management [6]. Finally, the course content also lacks humanistic warmth.

After the restructuring of the course content, a continuous teaching concept is adopted, with the scenario throughout the course as the main theme, supported by management accounting automatic integration platform, guiding students to apply what they have learned, integrating knowledge and action, and stimulating students' enthusiasm and potential for autonomous learning.

The organization of course content is based on the relevance of students' learning perspectives, rather than the relevance of knowledge systems. The content with strong relevance during learning is explained together, while others are taught as the final thematic presentation. The arrangement of teaching sequence is based on the independence and difficulty level of the knowledge points during students' learning, rather than just the systematic nature of knowledge points. For teaching content with strong independence, it is also taught in the form of special topics at the end of terms. By explaining the various business decisions based on method types rather than decision types, nearly ten segmented business decisions are classified into three methods: contribution margin analysis, differences analysis, and cost indifference point method [7] Specifically, the contribution margin analysis method is applicated on how to make decisions on which products to produce and how to carry out product portfolio decisions; Turn to the difference analysis method, it discusses further processing decisions, special order pricing decisions, the deficiency decisions, and self-made or outsourced decisions as application scenarios to explain; After introducing both vital methods, we will then introduce the cost indifference method, using self-made or outsourced decision-making and production process decision-making as application scenarios.

The course content adds EXCEL models based on VBA functions, practical teaching content includes cost behavior analysis functions and models, sales forecasting functions and models, breakeven and profit models, EOQ models, comprehensive budget simulation tables, standard cost management practices, and activity-based costing model drills [8]. From the perspective of facilitating learning for students, it redistributes teaching content overlapping with financial management course. It adds professional ethics and legal education and integrating 'Guidelines for the Application of Management Accounting', blends professional ethics into theoretical teaching and practical guidance [9].

4. One Class, One Segment

Taking a segment of class as an example, follow the route of BOPPPS (Bridge-in, Objective, Pre-assessment, Participatory Learning, Post-assessment, Summary) teaching method [10]. Firstly, establish a structured online knowledge system in advance, so that students can learn based on mobile learning terminals or MOOC platforms on computers. The teaching courseware is divided into teacher version and student version, and the student version is sent to students for preview in advance. In the preview navigation, students can watch task videos and guide animations in advance, arousing their interest and giving them an understanding of the teaching objectives for the next class. At the beginning of a class, after a brief review of the previous lessons, warm up the classroom with cases, stories, news, questions or videos. And then, restate the intellectual and technical goals, while the emotional goals are imparted silently using subtle methods.

To further grasp the learning situation and facilitate adjustment of learning depth and progress, online classroom quizzes, flipped classroom reports, and online random questions are conducted for pre-assessment [11]. Then, a series of heuristic participatory teaching methods such as maker practice and model exercises will be used. After completing the teaching of key knowledge points, immediately conduct classroom debate and quizzes race online. At the end of the course, summarize with mind maps and concept charts, and assign extracurricular synchronous online exercises and group training simulation exercises. Synchronize online practice with timely auto-correction can be statistically analyzed by the platform, where teachers can weigh students' theoretical knowledge and provide targeted centralized and decentralized tutoring. Students can also check their progress in their usual grades at any time for motivation. The group training simulation exercise aims to stimulate students' initiative. The teacher organizes various groups of students to discuss the practical issues of management accounting in enterprises and public institutions, guiding them to brainstorm and continuously reflect. At the same time, as a catalyst, teachers create a flexible environment in offline classrooms that encourages individuals and groups to constantly question and reflect, generating both individuals and groups to grow. In this process, students exchange their opinions and reflections on the problem with each other, and express implicit cognition clearly through explicit concepts and language such as conversation or dialogue, achieving the entire process of knowledge condensation, absorption, and creation [12].

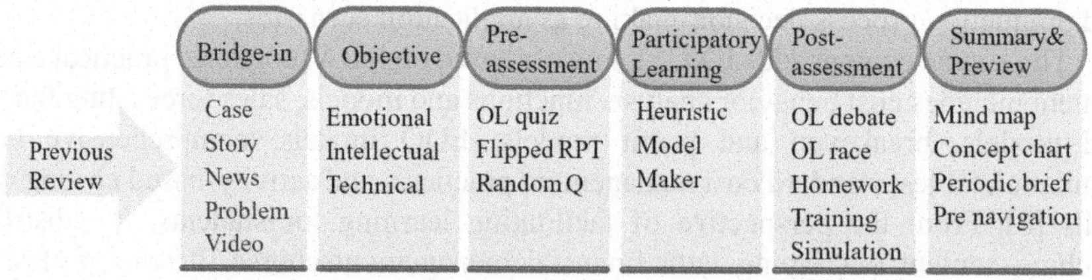

	Bridge-in	Objective	Pre-assessment	Participatory Learning	Post-assessment	Summary& Preview
Previous Review	Case Story News Problem Video	Emotional Intellectual Technical	OL quiz Flipped RPT Random Q	Heuristic Model Maker	OL debate OL race Homework Training Simulation	Mind map Concept chart Periodic brief Pre navigation

Figure 2. Core of management accounting classroom teaching design

5. Multidimensional Teaching Evaluation Mode

From the evaluation mode of "knowledge + skills" to a multidimensional evaluation mode, a comprehensive evaluation is conducted based on knowledge goals, skill goals, and ability goals, combined with the conventional homework of "one lesson, one practice" on online platforms, as well as the level of positivity, learning methods, thinking patterns, personality traits, team spirit, and leadership exhibited by students in situational cases. The specific assessment of the course adopts a combination of process assessment and final closed-book examination, emphasizing the unity of process assessment and final assessment. The final score is evaluated using diversified indicators, including pre class preparation, attendance, classroom performance, post class evaluation, case analysis, unit tests, student mutual evaluation, teacher evaluation, and final exams. By combining online and offline methods, evaluate students' knowledge acquisition and comprehensive abilities.

The multi-dimensional evaluation mode includes:

1) Online personal terminal attendance (5%): check-in with GPS location in site, and online use of dynamic QR codes and during the pandemic [13-15].

2) Course Participation (15%): Weighted synthesis of online flipped classroom learning task completion and offline classroom performance. Flipped classroom learning online task is automatically graded by the platform. Offline participation level of courses is rated by the teacher based on students' classroom performance.

3) Scenario Case Grouping Activity (30%): Group activities revolves around the only scenario theme that runs through the course. It is completed by a spontaneously formed group of students with strong interests. By on-site research, literature search, team collaboration, entrepreneurship projects, ultimately reports are produced and evaluated. The scores are weighted by three core dimensions of intra group, inter group, and teacher overall evaluations, which are based on twelve benchmarks.

Table 1. Scenario case group activity evaluation scale

Dimensions	Items	Score
Behavior and Temperament	Good cultivation and tolerant attitude	
	Teamwork spirit and self-reflection ability	
	Oral expression and communication skills	
	Leadership temperament and influence	
Diligent cultivation	In site investigation data and records	
	Literature retrieval ability and data organization ability	
	The depth and breadth of problem speculation	
	Frequency and quality of speeches	
Report presentation	Structure and logicality	
	Visualization, fluency and readability	
	Calculation accuracy and application of information tools	
	Report feasibility and expected benefits	

As shown in Table 1, three core dimensions refer to behavior and temperament, diligent cultivation, and report presentation. Twelve benchmarks are good cultivation and tolerant attitude, teamwork spirit and self-reflection ability, oral expression and communication skills, leadership temperament and influence belonging to the first dimension; In site investigation data and records, Literature retrieval ability and data organization ability, the depth and breadth of problem Speculation, and the frequency and quality of speeches belonging to the dimension of diligent cultivation; The structure and logicality, visualization, fluency and readability, calculation accuracy and application of information tools, report feasibility and expected benefits of the report presentation dimension.

In addition, continuous teacher evaluations should also be conducted, striving to be realistic, objective, fair, and positive, in order to encourage students to accept, which provide continuous, frequent, and timely feedback to students. Students should be encouraged to actively participate and further transform knowledge into abilities.

4) In-class exercises and online assignments (20%): Course assignments are mainly completed online. Online course assignments are mainly assessed based on each chapter, divided into after-school assignments and in class quizzes.

5) Final evaluation (30%): Based on the separation of examination and teaching, final exam questions are randomly selected from the question bank into two or more sets of A and B. The academic affairs office randomly selects either for assessment, or the ratio of the test questions to the question bank should be less than one-fifth [16].

6. Curriculum Culture Construction

The materials for the culture of management accounting courses can be combined with story cases, legal events, disciplinary development history, professional anniversaries, philosophy, professional ethics, and famous quotes. Curriculum cultural design just like firewood, which can ignite the enthusiasm of teachers and students, provide emotional warmth into teaching, cultivate students' confidence in traditional culture, understand society, and inherit disciplinary spirit.

The cultural design of the curriculum should strive to be subtle, from the collusion of course and policies and regulations, to the closing motto of each class. It is committed to cultivating students' overall awareness, thinking from a global perspective, and forming trustworthy and confidential professional ethics, and permeating positive energy in the curriculum. For example:

1) The study of sunk costs and out-of-pocket cost inspires students to establish a forward-looking mindset, to pursue new life, and not dwell on past failures or setbacks. Instead, they should use future goals to guide their current life and achieve positive progress.

2) The study of business decision-making help students realizes that there are thousands of paths in life, and each decision will produce different results. We have chosen one of the branches to gain related benefits, while taking risks at the same level. We must be perseverant, judgmental, adventurous, and to achieve our goals.

3) Business forecasting and comprehensive budgeting stem from the philosophical idea of 'planning before action', which requires students in management schools to understand that preparedness ensures success, and unpreparedness spells failure. Only if mastering scientific methods, studying the development laws of things, and deducing and practicing the laws, can we further achieve the goal of strategizing and winning thousands of miles away [17].

7. Conclusion

Through the course innovation, the teaching sequence of content has been restructured, with the addition of maker cases as the principal line, and the introduction of information technology models instead of manual calculation models, implicitly infiltrating ideological and political elements. four-dimensional deep fusion is adopted to achieve the goal of multi-point resonance and all-round interactive learning. From the perspective of evaluation, the process evaluation based on the real-time feedback mode of informatization should be implemented throughout the entire teaching.

Acknowledgment

The research is funded by Key Research Base of Humanities and Social Sciences in Universities of Guangdong Province: Research Base for Digital Transformation of Manufacturing Enterprises, (2023WZJD012).

References

[1]   Pauline Weetman. Financial and management accounting: An introduction (6th edition) [M]. London: Pearson, 2013: 435-710.
[2]   Jacobs, Monica. Teaching-learning dynamics: A participative approach for OBE[M]. London: Heinemann, 2004: 1-18.
[3]   Zhang J, Zhu X, Cheng J, et al. Teaching practice of accounting based on jigsaw teaching combined with PBL teaching method[J]. International Journal of New Developments in Education, 2022,4.0(8.0).
[4]   Sun Maozhu, Zhi Xiaoqiang, Dai Lu. Management accounting[M]. Beijing: Renmin University of China Press, 2020: 1-323 (in Chinese).
[5]   Stephan Leitner. Information quality and management accounting: A simulation analysis of biases in costing systems[M]. Berlin: Springer, 2012: 15-28.
[6]   Jin Xin, Wang Huacheng, Liu Junyan. Financial management (9th edition) [M]. Beijing: Renmin University of China Press, 2021: 24-67 (in Chinese).
[7]   Jack Gray, Don RIcketts. Cost accounting: A managerial emphasis[M]. New York: McGraw-Hill Book Company, 1982: 391-452.
[8]   Ali Peyvandi, Nancy Hongola. Managerial accounting using EXCEL 97[M]. New York: McGraw-Hill Book Company, 2000: 19-76.
[9]   Institute of Management Accountants. Wiley CMAexcel learning system exam review 2020, Part2: Strategic financial management[M]. New York: John Wiley & Sons, Incorporated, 2020: 469-508.
[10] Li Q, Chen W, Shi L. Design and practice of "Data Structure" teaching class based on BOPPPS model[C]. IEEE 2016 8th International Conference on Information Technology in Medicine and Education (ITME). Fuzhou, China: IEEE, 2017.DOI: 10.1109/ITME.2016.0120.
[11] Julee B. Waldrop, Melody A. Bowdon. Best practices for flipping the college classroom[M]. London&New York: Routledge, 2016: 131-145.
[12] Lawson, Raef A. Management accounting case book[M]. New York: John Wiley & Sons, Incorporated, 2020.
[13] Satar Habib Mnaathr, "Design Remote Monitoring System for Patients at Real-Time based on Internet of Things (IoT)", International Journal of Engineering and Manufacturing, Vol.13, No.5, pp. 1-10, 2023.
[14] Jyoti Rathi, Surender Kumar Grewal, "Aesthetic QR: Approaches for Beautified, Fast Decoding, and Secured QR Codes ", International Journal of Information Engineering and Electronic Business, Vol.14, No.3, pp. 10-18, 2022.
[15] Md. Motaleb Hossen Manik, "A Novel Approach in Determining Areas to Lockdown during a Pandemic: COVID-19 as a Case Study", International Journal of Information Engineering and Electronic Business, Vol.15, No.2, pp. 30-37, 2023.
[16] Thomas J.Tobin, B.Jean Mandernach, Ann H.Taylor. Evaluating online teaching: Implementing best practices[M]. San Francisco, CA: Jossey-Bass, 2015: 73-246.
[17] Dai Sheng, Cui Gaowei. The Book of Rites[M]. Shen Yang: Liaoning Education Press, 1997:168-175.

Artificial Intelligence, Medical Engineering and Education
Z.B. Hu et al. (Eds.)
© 2024 The Authors.
This article is published online with Open Access by IOS Press and distributed under the terms
of the Creative Commons Attribution Non-Commercial License 4.0 (CC BY-NC 4.0).
doi:10.3233/ATDE231398

Training Mode of Applied Talents in Environmental Design Based on OBE Concept – Taking Public Space Design as an Example

Peng XIAO, Yu HUANG[1]
School of Art and Design, Nanning University, Nanning, China

Abstract. Centering on the environmental design major under the concept of OBE, this paper studies the teaching reform of public space design course, the core course of the major. In the process of implementation, it closely focuses on the orientation of new liberal arts construction and the training needs of applied talents. It reshapes the teaching objectives of this course from three dimensions of knowledge exploration, ability training and value shaping, and implements the teaching concept of "one core, two tracks and three dimensions" throughout the process. It constructs a teaching content system of "knowledge + ideology and politics + art + engineering", closely links the teaching mode with three rings of "pre-class exploration, in-class guidance and after-class extension", and integrates multiple information technologies, combining online and offline, virtual reality and classroom construction. We create a good learning atmosphere and cultivate students' interest in learning through various forms such as practice speaking, student speaking and student evaluation, teacher guiding student performance. Deepen the reform of training applied talents for environmental design majors.

Keywords. OBE concept; public space design; applied talents

1. Introduction

OBE stands for results-oriented, student-centered, continuous improvement. Educators must have a clear idea of the abilities and levels that students should achieve when they graduate, and then seek to design the appropriate educational structure to ensure that students achieve these expectations. This has become the fundamental follow of the current college education reform [1]. In 2021, the Notice of the China Engineering Education Professional Certification Association on the release of the list of majors that have passed the Engineering Education Certification by the Higher Education Teaching Evaluation Center of the Ministry of Education wrote that "all colleges and universities are requested to implement the concept of "student-centered, output-oriented and continuous improvement", firmly carry out first-class professional construction, and deeply promote the "quality revolution" of higher education. We will promote high-quality development of higher education." The OBE concept has significant guiding significance in promoting the teaching reform of environmental design education in

---

[1] Corresponding Author: Yu HUANG, E-mail: 47428727@qq.com.

universities and improving the training quality.

2. Course Introduction

2.1. Course Overview

The public space design course is the core course of the environmental design major, and it is a crucial part of cultivating students' professional ethics and innovation ability. Its reasonable teaching arrangement is key to improving students' knowledge structure and improving students' skills and qualities [2].

This course is a required course for environmental design majors in the third year of undergraduate studies. It covers general design theories, such as introduction to design, three major components, interior design principles, 3Dmax assisted design, hand-drawn scheme design, ergonomics, etc. In addition, it also involves multi-disciplinary content such as construction technology, construction standards, and design psychology. Through the study of this course, students are required to use the basic requirements and basic design principles of public space design, jointly design creation and market orientation, to design public space design works that meet the functional needs, are full of personality, and have aesthetic value, and design and make relevant drawings to express the design works. The construction of the curriculum system, will stimulate students' consciousness of design innovation, form public space design achievements with excellent historical and cultural visual symbols, and reconstruct regional culture, national culture, and traditional culture in innovative ways to increase cultural identity [3, 4].

2.2. Course Content

With the development of technology, the post ability is constantly changing, so the teaching content is also changing. The course content is carried out in the way and process of work, and the work process is restructured in a systematic way to create a curriculum truly based on knowledge application, shown in Figure 1.

3. Learning Situation Analysis

In Figure 2, the course serves as a link between the past and the future for undergraduates majoring in environmental design. The course is for junior undergraduate students majoring in environmental design. It undertakes basic design courses such as 3Dmax assisted design, hand-drawn scheme design, and ergonomics in the early stage, lays the foundation for exhibition design, function, and space, cultural and creative space design courses, and even has an important impact on graduation design. Due to the continuous development of society, the industry, industry, and technology are also constantly updated and changed [5]. Therefore, the main and difficult points in the design of this course are that the design space should be able to meet the new spatial functional requirements and conform to the audience's behaviors and preferences [6].

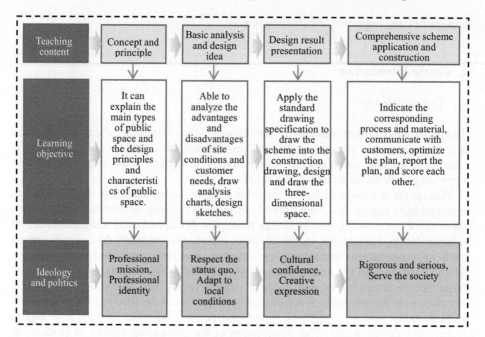

Figure 1. Schematic diagram of course teaching content system

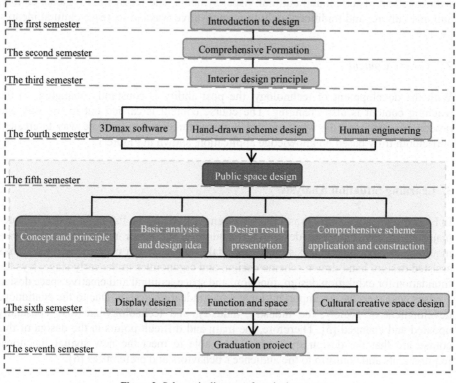

Figure 2. Schematic diagram of curriculum system

This course is offered in the first semester of junior year, so the advantages are as follows: students have a certain reserve of basic design knowledge, and have a certain ability for hand-drawing and software drawing; Unfavorable learning situation: Students' theoretical knowledge is relatively independent and unsystematic, and their performance in the comprehensive practice of the project is weak, which is reflected in the specific practice process that they do not know how to apply the content learned in the early stage to "solve" the corresponding problems, As a result, their abilities do not match the needs of employers[7].

In this period, students are nervous and confused about graduation design and internship, so they have strong learning motivation and interest. However, their preference for art aesthetics is stronger than their preference for engineering, which is not conducive to future internships and work.

4. Curriculum Construction of Application-oriented Talent Training Program Based on OBE

4.1. Course Objectives

Through visiting and investigating universities, enterprises, and industry associations, we can understand their demand for talents' ability and quality combine the school's application-oriented educational philosophy, and determine new talent training goals.

Table 1. The supporting relationship between course objectives and graduation requirements

Serial number	Course objective	Graduation requirements target points	Secondary index point
1	Objective 1. To enable students to master the basic knowledge of interpublic design; Follow and apply the requirements and principles of public space design.	Graduation Requirement 1- Design knowledge	Indicator 1.4. Familiar with environmental design engineering skills.
2	Goal 2. Be able to design a reasonable plan according to the actual project.	Graduation Requirement 2- Problem analysis Graduation Requirement 3- Design solutions Graduation Requirement4- Research	Indicator 2.2. Research, judgment and analysis of specific design problems; Indicator 3.1. Propose solutions to environmental design problems; Indicator 4. Have professional knowledge of theories and skills in the field and be able to use scientific methods to conduct basic research on complex professional problems.
3	Goal 3. Draw the corresponding construction drawings and renderings.	Graduation Requirement 5- Use of modern tools	Indicator 5.2. Use of modern information tools.
4	Goal 4. Through the project-oriented training of public space courses, students will gradually develop their ability of design project manage-ment, design team cooperation and design work communication.	Graduation Requirements 9- Individual and team Graduation Requirement 11- Project Management	Indicator 9.1: Able to independently complete the work assigned by the team; Indicator 9.2: Initiative to work with other members; Indicator 11.2: Have some technical management and economic analysis ability to find reasonable/acceptable solutions.

According to the training goals and the principles of "measurable", "supporting" and "covering", Thirteen graduation requirements were formulated, and the graduation requirement is decomposed into a graduation requirement index point that can be implemented and evaluated [8]. Each index point is supported by a course, and according to the principle of "one-to-one correspondence", the course goal of "Public Space Design" is determined by the index point of graduation requirements [9].

4.2. Teaching mode

Based on the curriculum construction of OBE's applied talents training program, the teaching model of "one core, two tracks and three dimensions" has been formed, with the training of applied innovative talents for environmental design majors as the core, and dual-track teaching and three-dimensional learning platform for enterprises and schools. Through the teaching form of jointly designing teaching content, jointly building a double-qualified team, jointly developing course resource database, and jointly conducting assessment and evaluation, students can truly learn in real projects, do real work in real environments, and truly create in real workflows on the three-dimensional learning platform of online + offline, virtual + actual, classroom + site. So as to cultivate innovative talents with the comprehensive ability of environmental design application.

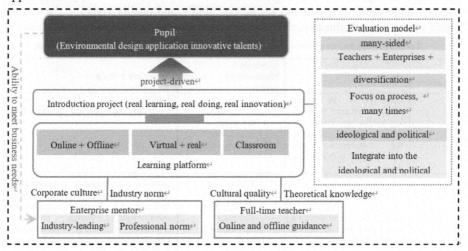

Figure 3. "One core, two tracks, three platform" teaching mode

4.3. Concrete Implementation

Considering the relative connection between profession and industry, classroom and post, curriculum and work process, based on the results-oriented, the public space design course reshapes the course objectives, reconstructs teaching content, innovates teaching mode, enriches teaching activities, resets teaching methods, and resets assessment and evaluation.

Build in-depth production-teaching integration courses [10]. Based on the three characteristics of strong comprehensiveness, strong application, and strong combination with humanity, the in-depth production and education integration mechanism is implemented to promote the industry demand to better integrate into the whole process of talent training. In the course, real projects of enterprises are used as teaching cases and practical projects, and their working processes are completely simulated, so that students can get in touch with the working methods, requirements, and processes of the industry in advance so that the cultivated students majoring in environmental design can seamlessly meet the needs of the society. Through the follow-up and completion of the overall process of the project, the comprehensive ability of students can be improved to meet their professional needs. Course practice projects are selected for the renovation of abandoned factory buildings in Nanning City, local enterprise office space design, and striving to achieve a full range of services.

To promote the effectiveness of talent training in the way of specialized innovation and integration. By "promoting teaching by competition, learning by competition, reform by competition, integration of competition lessons, and combination of competition training", students can not only complete professional knowledge learning tasks, but also deeply polish design projects to participate in professional competitions designated by the Ministry of Education, so that students can gain a sense of achievement in a positive learning experience, and cultivate students' creative ability in the actual competition. According to the reformed assessment method, students' ability to comprehensively apply knowledge to solve practical problems should be examined. Guide students to make use of various new media platforms such as Tiktok, Kuaishou, and XiaoHongshu, which are currently popular across the country, to publicize and promote design, and to integrate professional cross-disciplines, so as to better promote the integration of mass innovation ability and professional skills. In order to create a high-level, innovative, challenging degree of gold course.

Promote the improvement of digital empowerment teaching quality [11]. The course adopts Super Star learning platform, Dingding and Rain classroom, which carries out pre-class task release, interactive teaching in class, homework collection, correction, and learning materials, online course release, online independent learning, and participatory interactive teaching activities [12]. In the part of lesson preparation and course design practice, ChatGLM (GPT artificial intelligence robot) and Wenxin large model are introduced to infer and improve ideas, and the function of digital teaching tools is deeply integrated with teaching activities [13, 14]. In the design process, CAD, 3Ds max, SketchUp, Enscape, sheencity Mars, and other software are used for modeling and rendering, so as to make the design scheme more realistic and realize technology-enhanced learning [15, 16]. In the presentation of teaching cases and design schemes, AR+VR is adopted to transform two-dimensional static pictures into three-dimensional dynamic scenes, and reshape the relationship between the elements of "human-space-art".

We will deeply carry out ideological and political reforms in the curriculum. The ideological and political elements are integrated into the teaching concept, curriculum system, teaching design, teaching content, and the reform path of practical teaching. The whole course, the whole stage, and the full range of the course are permeated with people's cultural points, so that there are thoughts and politics everywhere, and things are moistened silently, so as to cultivate students' craftsman spirit, improve students' humanistic quality, and enhance students' cultural confidence [17].

The establishment of multi-party, multiple, ideological, and political assessment points of the evaluation model [18]. Teaching evaluation has changed from the original single evaluation mode to the current multi-party evaluation of teachers, students, and enterprises, and the original result-oriented evaluation has been changed to process-oriented evaluation, and cultural, ideological, and political elements have been incorporated into the evaluation system.

5. Conclusion

Through the student-oriented and results-oriented OBE model, the teaching mode of "one-core, dual-track and three-dimensional" is practiced in the course of "Public Space Design", which promotes the in-depth cooperation between schools and enterprises, constantly improves the teaching mode of production, university and research, improves students' theoretical level and practical ability and thus increases the employment rate. And guide students to consciously inherit and carry forward the excellent traditional Chinese culture, and strengthen cultural self-confidence. We will improve teachers' ability in scientific research, improve the teaching model for production, study, and research, and strengthen schools' ability to serve society and local economies. Through curriculum reform and practice, in recent years, students' curriculum design works and participation in professional competitions designated by the Ministry of Education have gained a lot. Enterprises are highly satisfied with our professional students, and the design works of the faculty team have won several national awards in the industry. These achievements will continue to help the training of students.

Acknowledgment

This Project of Research and Practice on The Path of Ideological and Political Integration in The Curriculum of Environmental Design Major Under the Background of " Professional Integration with Innovation and Entrepreneurship" in Nanning University (2021XJJG21).

References

[1]   Zheng W, Wen S, Lian B, et al. Research on a Sustainable Teaching Model Based on the OBE Concept and the TSEM Framework[J]. Sustainability, 2023, 15(7): 5656.

[2]   Carmona M. Principles for public space design, planning to do better[J]. Urban Design International, 2019, 24: 47-59. Sui J, Hua Z, Zhu H, et al. Training mechanism of engineering education and innovation talent based on courses-competitions combination[J]. Nanotechnology for Environmental Engineering, 2022, 7(3): 833-841.

[3]   Mao MAO, Chunbao H. Application of Leizu Culture to Interior Design[J]. Journal of Landscape Research, 2017, 9(3): 33.

[4]   Wang X. RETRACTED: The practice teaching of regional cultural expression in rural landscape planning and design under the background of urban–rural integration[J]. The International Journal of Electrical Engineering and Education, 2021. https://doi.org/10.1177/0020720920984308

[5]   Harris A, Jones M, Crick T. Curriculum leadership: a critical contributor to school and system improvement[J]. School Leadership & Management, 2020, 40(1): 1-4.

[6]   Sangshetti J N, Deshpande M, Zaheer Z, et al. Quality by design approach: Regulatory need[J]. Arabian Journal of chemistry, 2017, 10: S3412-S3425.

[7]   Nicolaescu S S, Kifor C V. Teaching methodology for Design for Six Sigma and Quality techniques–an approach that combines theory and practice[C]//Balkan Region Conference on Engineering and Business Education. 2017, 2(1): 328-336.

[8]   Li J, Zhang F, Ye J, et al. A Neutrosophic Evaluation Method of Engineering Certification Teaching Effect Based on Improved Entropy Optimization Model and Its Application in Student Clustering[J]. Neutrosophic Sets and Systems, 2023, 55: 1-12.

[9]   Wang J, Wang X, Weng Z, et al. Implementation Path Exploration of Innovation and Entrepreneurship Education Reform under the Background of "New Engineering" [J]. Advances in Applied Sociology, 2022, 12(4): 102-111.

[10] Chu H. Research on a New Mode of Integration of Production and Education for Applied Undergraduates [J]. economic and social development, 2022, 4(16): 68-72.

[11] Esteve-Mon F, Llopis-Nebot M, Viñoles-Cosentino V, et al. Digital teaching competence of university teachers: levels and teaching typologies[J]. International Journal of Emerging Technologies in Learning (iJET), 2022, 17(13): 200-216.

[12] Biswas R A, Nandi S. Teaching in virtual classroom: Challenges and opportunities[J]. International Journal of Engineering Applied Sciences and Technology, 2020, 5(1): 334-337.

[13] Sabbir Hossain, Rahman Sharar, Md. Ibrahim Bahadur, Abu Sufian, Rashidul Hasan Nabil, "MediBERT: A Medical Chatbot Built Using KeyBERT, BioBERT and GPT-2", International Journal of Intelligent Systems and Applications, Vol.15, No.4, pp.53-69, 2023.

[14] Jiancai Wang,Hua Liang, "Discussion on Domestic Universities Construction of Digital Teaching Platform", International Journal of Education and Management Engineering, vol.2, no.6, pp.1-6, 2012.

[15] Najat Messaoudi, Ghizlane Moukhliss, Jaafar K. Naciri, Bahloul Bensassi, "Machine Learning Algorithms for Quantifying the Role of Prerequisites in University Success", International Journal of Modern Education and Computer Science, Vol.14, No.6, pp. 1-12, 2022.

[16] Neeta Sharma, Shanmuganathan Appukutti, Umang Garg, Jayati Mukherjee, Sneha Mishra, "Analysis of Student's Academic Performance based on their Time Spent on Extra-Curricular Activities using Machine Learning Techniques", International Journal of Modern Education and Computer Science, Vol.15, No.1, pp. 46-57, 2023.

[17] Liu X, Xiantong Z, Starkey H. Ideological and political education in Chinese Universities: structures and practices[J]. Asia Pacific Journal of Education, 2023, 43(2): 586-598.

[18] Uttl B, White C A, Gonzalez D W. Meta-analysis of faculty's teaching effectiveness: Student evaluation of teaching ratings and student learning are not related[J]. Studies in Educational Evaluation, 2017, 54: 22-42.

Artificial Intelligence, Medical Engineering and Education
Z.B. Hu et al. (Eds.)
© *2024 The Authors.*
This article is published online with Open Access by IOS Press and distributed under the terms
of the Creative Commons Attribution Non-Commercial License 4.0 (CC BY-NC 4.0).
doi:10.3233/ATDE231399

Course Questionnaire Design and Teaching Reform Based on CDIO Concept -Taking Management Accounting as an Example

Yiming WANG[a,1], Luxia YI[b]

aGuangzhou City University of Technology, Guangzhou, China
bGuangzhou Industry and Commerce College, Guangzhou, China
ORCiD ID: Yiming Wang https://orcid.org/0009-0000-0931-8128

Abstract. In the course of management accounting, the active application of innovative education concept is helpful to cultivate students' good professional ability and core literacy. This paper introduces the CDIO teaching concept to reconstruct the teaching process of management accounting course, from goal setting to three-level ability outline design, and designs a questionnaire for the implementation effect of teaching reform. According to the feedback data, the results are analyzed, and the teaching optimization countermeasures of management accounting course are put forward, hoping to take this opportunity to improve the teaching level of the course and the core literacy of students' management accounting professional skills, and provide reference for other course teaching reforms.

Keywords. CDIO concept; Management accounting; Teaching questionnaire design; Curriculum reform

1. Introduction

At present, information technology is changing with each passing day, and the wave of big data, intelligence and cloud computing is unstoppable, which will inevitably lead to the "butterfly effect" in various fields of economy and society, as well as the accounting industry. The proposal of CDIO (Conceive-Design-Implement-Operate) engineering education concept provides a reference for cultivating talents with such abilities. CDIO is the latest reform achievement of international modern engineering education proposed by several world-renowned universities headed by Massachusetts Institute of Technology after years of exploration and practice. It consists of four links: Conceive, Design, Implement and Operate. Under the background of the times, the teaching reform of management accounting course and the training of management accounting talents in undergraduate colleges and universities are further put on the agenda.

From the relevant literature, Cheng Ping and Wang Junjian pointed out that under the background of "Internet + accounting" financial intelligence, the CDIO concept has important reference value for the cultivation of compound MPAcc talents [1]. Li Nana integrates the CDIO innovation project of engineering education, that is, the teaching

---

[1] Corresponding Author: Yiming WANG, E-mail: 849162395@qq.com; wangym@gcu.edu.cn

concepts of Conceive, Design, Implement and Operate, into the teaching of management accounting courses [2]. Zhan jiang analyzed the problems existing in the management accounting course of applied undergraduate colleges from the perspective of CDIO, and put forward suggestions for improving the effectiveness of management accounting course by referring to the CDIO concept [3]. Lei Zhen analyzed how to realize the mixed teaching mode of management accounting course in colleges and universities under the environment of rapid development of information technology [4]. Nikoomaram H. et al.evaluated Tehran listed companies based on decision support and business intelligence [5]. M. Alles pointed out that accounting personnel can collect, analyze, manage and report useful information for enterprise decision-making in the big data environment [6]. Elbashir et al. pointed out that the system characteristics based on business intelligence verified the relationship between accounting performance and management performance [7]. G. Schryen argues that BI investments include BI-related software, hardware, infrastructure, human resources, and management capacity investments [8]. Weber uses data mining technology to assist accounting information construction in government financial management, and believes that data mining is a powerful tool for computer-aided audit [9]. The research literature of scholars at home and abroad provides the theoretical basis for this topic.

2. Course Questionnaire Design and Result Analysis Based on CDIO Concept

CDIO (Conceive, Design, Implement and Operate) is the latest achievement of international engineering education reform in recent years. It takes the life cycle of product, process, or system as the main line, so that students can learn in an active, practical, and organic way. To obtain including practical ability, personal scientific and technological knowledge, lifelong learning ability, communication, and team work ability. It covers 1 vision, 1 outline and 12 standards. This theory is applied to the practice and exploration of management accounting and its related courses. The goal is to achieve two-way improvement between teachers and students in the teaching process. Based on the CDIO education concept, teachers can adjust the teaching ideas and directions in time, improve the quality of the course, and cultivate the talents needed by the society in combination with the background of the times. On the other hand, in the process of active learning, students can find the opportunity of the times, constantly enrich and improve the content they have learned, connect the links between courses, cultivate innovative spirit and practical ability, and make learning useful.

2.1. Reconstruction of the Curriculum Outline System

The teaching goal based on CDIO theory is expressed by the CDIO outline. When the CDIO theory formulates the ability training goal, the first-level outline is highly general and does not need to be screened and designed. The second and third syllabuses need to be screened, designed and supplemented in combination with different professional situations. According to the characteristics of accounting major and the training plan of management accounting talents, teachers perfect the syllabus suitable for the characteristics of management accounting course under the guidance of CDIO first-level syllabus theory, which is taken as the teaching goal. The quantitative analysis of the teaching effect relies on the CDIO syllabus to examine the degree of improvement of students' abilities before and after learning, which is used as the criterion for judging whether the teaching objectives are achieved and the basis for improving the teaching process in the future.

The first level outline includes technical knowledge and reasoning ability, personal professional ability and quality, teamwork and communication ability, enterprise and social environment CDIO. Among them, the second-level outline under technical knowledge and reasoning ability includes basic scientific knowledge, core basic knowledge and advanced basic knowledge. The corresponding third-level outline is to understand accounting information system, master management accounting theory and method, forecast, budget, decision-making, evaluation and model creation. The second-level syllabus under personal professional ability and quality includes reasoning and problem solving, exploring knowledge in experiments, systematic thinking, personal skills and attitudes, professional skills and morality. The corresponding third-level syllabuses are qualitative and quantitative analysis, decision-making methods and suggestions, creation of models or analysis of case demonstrations, global thinking, strategic height, creative and critical thinking, lifelong learning, management accounting certificates, rigorous professional behavior and professional ethics. The second-level syllabus under teamwork and communication includes teamwork, communication, and foreign language communication. The corresponding third-level syllabuses are the ability to form a team and run coordination team members, exchange ideas and cases, and Certified Public Accountants English. The two-level outline under the enterprise and social environment CDIO includes external and social environment, enterprise and business environment, conception and management accounting system, design and implementation operation. The corresponding three-level outline is the role and responsibility of management accountants, values, development concept and global view, understanding different corporate cultures, strategic modeling or using software to ensure that goals may be achieved, design plans or projects, design implementation plans, pre-event and post-event management, feedback and optimization, plan or project improvement and evolution, management and reflection.

2.2. Questionnaire on the Realization Degree of Ability Goal Based on CDIO Outline

Based on the management accounting curriculum outline of CDIO ability outline, this questionnaire adopts the answer form of five levels of scores (from 1 to 5), that is, each question can fill in scores 1, 2, 3, 4 and 5 according to its own situation, among which the scores "1 = poor, 2 = general, 3 = medium, 4 = good, 5 = excellent". Please select the corresponding score and fill the score in the back space.

Q1: Changes in the basic knowledge of management accounting before and after learning? Before () After ()

Q2: Changes in management accounting reasoning ability and problem solving ability before and after learning? Before () After ()

Q3: What are the changes of systematic thinking, global strategic thinking and logical thinking ability before and after learning? Before () After ()

Q4: Changes in management accounting professional skills and professional ethics before and after learning? Before () After ()

Q5: Changes in self-learning, team learning and communication skills before and after learning ? Before () After ()

Q6: Changes in the vocabulary of management accounting before and after learning ? Before () After ()

Q7: Changes in external cognitive ability of enterprises and society before and after learning ? Before () After ()

Q8: Before and after the study of management accounting case design and implementation of the ability to change the situation ? Before () After ()

Q9: Changes in project prediction, budget, decision-making, control, assessment and evaluation capabilities before and after learning ? Before () After ()

Q10: Please self-evaluate your learning attitude and learning effect. The beginning of the semester () the end of the semester ()

The effect of the curriculum implementation was investigated, and the degree of realization of the ability goals required by the CDIO outline was evaluated. According to the statistical calculation of 225 student questionnaires, the average score of each question before and after learning is summarized as follows :

Table 1. Scoring table of the realization degree of teaching objectives under CDIO syllabus

Question	Q1	Q2	Q3	Q4	Q5	Q6	Q7	Q8	Q9	Q10
Before learning	1.36	1.56	1.72	2.02	2.02	1.48	1.69	1.65	1.64	2.49
After learning	3.54	3.51	3.57	3.76	3.61	2.85	3.51	3.45	3.55	3.79
Amplitude	2.18	1.95	1.85	1.74	1.59	1.37	1.82	1.80	1.91	1.3

According to the average score increase from high to low order is $Q1 > Q2 > Q9 > Q3 > Q7 > Q8 > Q4 > Q5 > Q6 > Q10$. It can be seen that the most significant improvement before and after learning is the basic knowledge and skills of management accounting. Since the first semester of sophomore year is the first semester of sophomore year, students are exposed to the field of management accounting for the first time. Compared with other skills improvement, basic knowledge and skills occupy the primary position, which also reflects the characteristics of the accounting professional course from the side. The theory and technology are strong. It is necessary to lay a solid foundation for the professional foundation first, and then to improve the ability of teamwork, communication, strategic planning and other aspects. From the perspective of average ranking, compared with the CDIO outline, the degree of realization of the ability goal basically conforms to the order of the first-level outline, which are technical knowledge and reasoning ability, personal professional ability and quality, teamwork and communication ability, and C-D-I-O in the enterprise and social environment. Each ability has different degrees of improvement before and after learning.However, it should be noted that the final ranking is the 10 th question, that is, self-evaluation of their learning attitude and learning effect. The average score of this question has the smallest change, indicating that although students have learned something in the learning process, they have improved their corresponding ability. However, students still have some doubts about their learning attitude and their learning effect. It may be due to modesty and conservative self-evaluation. It may also be that students do not go all out in the learning process and think that their learning attitude needs to be improved. Or the task assigned by the teacher is not well completed, resulting in a slightly worse learning effect. This needs to attract the attention of teachers. In the subsequent teaching process, we should pay attention to guiding and mobilizing students' autonomous learning ability, and diversify the evaluation of learning effect. From the overall perspective of the questionnaire, the ability goals of the CDIO outline have been improved to varying degrees [10].

2.3. Teaching Evaluation Questionnaire Based on CDIO 12 Standards

Teaching evaluation refers to the evaluation methods and standards that are unique to various teaching modes to complete teaching tasks and achieve teaching objectives. Due to the different teaching tasks and teaching purposes to be completed by different teaching modes, the procedures and conditions used are different, and the methods and standards of evaluation are also different. The CDIO reform adopts 12 standards to describe the professional training that meets the requirements. These CDIO standards describe in detail the outstanding characteristics of a major that meets the requirements of CDIO, which can be used as a framework for teaching reform and evaluation, setting up benchmarks and goals for implementing CDIO, and formulating continuous improvement. In other words, the 12 standards of CDIO can be used as the evaluation criteria for teaching based on CDIO theory.

12 Standards of CDIO: (1) Basic environment; (2)Learning objectives; (3) Integrated teaching; (4)Course introduction; (5)Design and implementation experience; (6) Practice place; (7)Comprehensive learning experience; (8)Active learning; (9) Teachers' professional ability; (10)Teachers' teaching ability; (11)Learning assessment; (12) Professional assessment. According to the main indicators and core requirements of the 12 standards of CDIO, it can be summarized into five categories: environmental site standards, curriculum setting standards, student ability standards, teacher ability standards, and professional evaluation standards. Among them, standards 1 and 6 examine the training concept and site environment; standard 2-5 examines the curriculum and content; standards 7, 8, 11 examine students' learning and ability assessment; standard 9-10 examines teachers' ability; standard 12 is an overall professional assessment.

The questionnaire evaluates teaching from two dimensions: objective and subjective. The first is the objective dimension, that is, using the 12 standard setting problems of CDIO to evaluate the teaching mode. The second is the subjective dimension, including students' self-evaluation and teacher evaluation. The specific evaluation indicators of teaching evaluation are shown in table 2.

Table 2. 12 standard teaching evaluation index system classification of CDIO

Dimension	Standard	Code Abbreviation	Classification
Objective Evaluation	standard1、6; standard2、3、4、5; standard7、8、11; standard9、10; standard12;	OE1 OE2 OE3 OE4 OE5	Investigate the concept and environmental site; examine the curriculum and content; examine students ' learning and ability assessment; examine teachers ' ability; professional overall assessment ;
Subjective Evaluation	Students ' self-evaluation; evaluation of teachers;	SE1 SE2	Learning effects, learning gains, etc.; teaching theory, method, effect, etc.;

It should be pointed out that teaching evaluation is only a means to guide and promote teaching. Through teaching evaluation, we can know where there are still deficiencies in the teaching process that need to be improved.

Objective dimension evaluation standard OE1, OE2, OE3, OE4, OE5, evaluation coefficient using 5 scale, from low to high in turn is 'very disagree', 'compare disagree', 'general', 'compare agree', 'very agree', detailed description see table 3 objective dimension teaching evaluation score.

Table 3. Objective dimension teaching evaluation 5 level system

Score values	Corresponding name	Explanation
1	very disagree	There is no content in the standard (no gain or no conditions)
2	compare disagree	There is very little content in the standard (little harvest, to be taken seriously and strengthened).
3	general	The content in the standard has a certain proportion (with certain gains).
4	compare agree	It is close to the height of the standard requirements, attaches great importance to the content of the standard requirements and reflects a lot in the content (better effect or greater gain).
5	very agree	Completely in accordance with the content of the standard to design the corresponding content and process (the effect is very good or harvest).

The questionnaire question setting is shown in Table 4.

Table 4. Objective dimension teaching evaluation questionnaire design

Code	Question(corresponding to 12 CDIO standards)	Option Description and Scores
OE1	Q1: I think it is necessary to introduce the CDIO conception-design-implementation-operation teaching concept into the management accounting course. (Standard1) Q2: Letting students write management accounting cases can reflect the concept of curriculum conception-design-implementation-operation. (Standard1) Q3: There is a laboratory or financial software created by the EXCEL model of management accounting cases. (Standard6) Q4: Multimedia classrooms and laboratory places are convenient for course learning and communication. (Standard6)	1, very disagree; 2, compare disagree; 3, general; 4. Comparatively agree; 5. Agree very much;
OE2	Q5: The curriculum outline and learning objectives of management accounting are clear and complete. (Standard2) Q6: accounting principles, microeconomics, management accounting, financial management, CMA, reflecting the curriculum relevance and knowledge system integration teaching plan. (Standard3) Q7: Management accounting courses stimulate interest in learning in the field of management accounting. (Standard4) Q8: Let students write and publish course academic papers and cases, and create EXCEL model can improve students' participation in and out of class, and enhance students' ability to conceive, design, implement and operate the project. (Standard5)	1, very disagree; 2, compare disagree; 3, general; 4. Comparatively agree; 5. Agree very much;
OE3	Q9: The management accounting course improves the comprehensive learning experience and helps to integrate the subject learning with the CMA practice certificate. (Standard7) Q10: In the process of learning the course of management accounting, I have the ability to learn actively and ask my peers and teachers for learning experience, so as to improve my ability to think and solve problems. (Standard8) Q11: I successfully passed the management accounting course examination. (Standard11) Q12: In the process of learning, management accounting brings me global thinking and strategic height. My professional knowledge, professional quality, communication ability and team cooperation ability have been improved. (Standard11)	1, very disagree; 2, compare disagree; 3, general; 4. Comparatively agree; 5. Agree very much;
OE4	Q13: The change of teachers ' teaching concept and knowledge level will improve their own teaching ability and level.	1, very disagree; 2, compare disagree;

Table 4. Objective dimension teaching evaluation questionnaire design (continued)

Code	Question (corresponding to 12 CDIO standards)	Option Description and Scores
OE4	(Standard9) Q14: Teachers pay attention to introducing the new trends of subject development to students, especially the connection between new and old professional knowledge, which will improve students ' learning satisfaction. (Standard9) Q15: Teachers use a variety of teaching methods, including blackboard writing, multimedia, network, etc., which will affect students ' learning results. (Standard10) Q16 : Teachers ' teaching content and teaching methods reflect the concept design and implementation operation. (Standard10)	3, general; 4. Comparatively agree; 5. Agree very much;
OE5	Q17: Teaching evaluation has feedback to teachers, students and other stakeholders, and continuous improvement. (Standard12) Q18: CDIO concept has a positive effect on the construction of accounting specialty. (Standard12)	1, very disagree; 2, compare disagree; 3, general; 4. Comparatively agree; 5. Agree very much;

The teaching evaluation of the subjective dimension is divided into self-evaluation and evaluation of teachers, which is a text topic, as shown in Table 5.

Table 5. Subjective dimension teaching evaluation

Code	Question
SE1	Please make a brief self-evaluation of the learning effect and learning gains.
SE2	Please make a brief evaluation of teachers.

According to the calculation statistics, the average scores of the questionnaire from question 1 to question 18 are *3.92, 3.52, 3.99, 4.25, 4.08, 4.26, 3.96, 3.82, 4.22, 3.84, 4.05, 3.94, 4.27, 4.32, 4.29, 4.28, 4.15, 4.13*, respectively. Most of the questions scored between 4-5 points, indicating that students think that the teaching process and teaching effect are close to the height of the 12 standard requirements of CDIO, and attach great importance to the content of the standard requirements and reflect a lot in the content (better effect or greater harvest). The results of the summary score table are as follows:

Table 6. CDIO12 standard classification score results summary table

12 Standards	Code abbreviation	correspondence problem	Average
standard1、6;	OE1	Q1-Q4	3.92
standard2、3、4、5;	OE2	Q5-Q8	4.03
standard7、8、11;	OE3	Q9-Q12	4.01
standard9、10;	OE4	Q13-Q16	4.29
standard12;	OE5	Q17-Q18	4.14

From the perspective of classification score, the highest score is to examine the relevant indicators of teachers ' ability, indicating that teachers ' teaching concept, professional skills, teaching design and so on play an important role in the whole teaching process. The lower score is the concept and environmental site related indicators, indicating that students have some gains, but the cognition of CDIO concept needs to be further improved, and the related software equipped in multimedia classrooms and laboratory sites needs to be improved and improved. In the process of asking students to write cases, create models and write papers, some students only participate in some links because of their limited ability. This is also the place that needs to be considered and improved in the future teaching reform process. How to let more students participate and stick to it, and truly realize the application of learning [11].

The teaching evaluation of the subjective dimension is divided into self-evaluation and evaluation of teachers. Most students have gained a lot from the teaching reform process of management accounting under the guidance of CDIO concept, and have a deeper understanding and mastery of knowledge and skills. There are also some students whose knowledge is not solid and the learning process is difficult. These students should be the object of teachers' attention, analyze their difficulties, specify appropriate learning tasks for them, and further improve their ability to conceive, design, implement and operate at their ability level. Students are satisfied with the teacher 's teaching process, and also put forward relevant suggestions, such as suggesting that teachers slow down, reduce the difficulty of some knowledge points, and add more interesting cases [12].

3. Continue to Optimize the Curriculum Teaching Reform Measures

3.1. Improve the Professional Curriculum System.

The establishment of management accounting courses requires pre-courses as the basis, such as accounting principles, accounting information systems, macro and micro economics; the follow-up courses include the course of certified management accountant in the United States and case analysis of management accounting. The professional quality of management accountants needs to be supported by a perfect vertical curriculum system, and the framework of teaching reform and evaluation of the curriculum system of management accountants should be constructed under the guidance of 12 standards of CDIO [13].

3.2. Further Optimize the Curriculum Design Process

According to the CDIO ability outline, this teaching reform cultivates students' ability to conceive, design, implement and operate management accounting knowledge and skills through the three processes of 'research and writing cases-creating EXCEL model-publishing papers'. Through the above questionnaire feedback analysis, for some students whose basic knowledge is not strong, have learning difficulties, and cannot keep up with the progress, the process design is optimized, and the theoretical knowledge support link is added to upgrade the three major processes into four major processes, namely, research and writing cases-theoretical knowledge support-creating EXCEL model-publishing papers. After the group survey case, the teacher conducts targeted counseling for students with weak theoretical knowledge according to the data collected by each group and the first draft of the case, and adopts the intra-group support policy, and the members in the group are responsible for answering questions in different modules of the student. Teachers and students work together to integrate curriculum theory into practical cases, cultivate students' autonomous learning ability, practical operation ability and communication ability, and cultivate students' good teamwork ability and innovative ability, so as to lay a foundation for the subsequent process of creating EXCEL model-publishing papers.In the whole teaching process, teachers should play a macro-coordinated role, guide students to think, analyze and judge various problems, and continue to improve the ability to conceive, design, implement and operate the curriculum section, curriculum content, teaching methods and teaching materials.

3.3. Diversification of Assessment

As shown above, according to the 12 standards of CDIO, it can be used as the evaluation standard of CDIO concept teaching. At the same time, other methods can be used to evaluate students' learning process performance and teachers' teaching performance, and a relatively effective evaluation system can be established. For example, the CIPP model can be used to evaluate the background, input, process and results of teachers and students. Its purpose is to highlight the value of process evaluation and strive to measure the evaluation content as a whole through dynamic evaluation methods. It can provide sufficient feedback information for teachers' teaching in time, help teachers find out the shortcomings of teaching, and diagnose and improve the teaching implementation plan. At the same time, it takes into account the two evaluation subjects of teachers and students and emphasizes the dynamic feedback of the process of "teaching" and "learning".

4. Conclusion and Prospect

The curriculum reform has realized the two-way improvement of teachers' ability and students' ability. Based on the CDIO education concept, teachers can adjust the teaching ideas and directions in time, improve the quality of the course, and cultivate the talents needed by the society in combination with the background of the times. On the other hand, in the process of active learning, students can find the opportunity of the times, constantly enrich and improve the content they have learned, connect the links between courses, cultivate innovative spirit and practical ability, and make learning useful [14].

4.1. Teachers Implement the CDIO Concept from the Teaching Dimension.

First, (Conceive) the ability goal of management accounting course. Strengthen cognition, increase the degree of attention, and first realize the transformation from the low level to the high level from the cognitive level. The goal of management accounting course is not only to enable students to master technology and methods to make predictions, budgets, and decisions for enterprises, but also to enable students to conform to the trend of the times and use intelligent technologies such as computers to create management accounting models to facilitate efficient enterprise decision-making.

Second, (Design) management accounting talent ability training mode. In the context of the intelligent era, the cultivation of management accounting talents focuses on cultivating students' ability to use management accounting theories and methods, and to process data, so as to cultivate students into high-end financial management and decision-making personnel and become a "T" type talent with vertical professional depth and horizontal knowledge breadth.

Third, (Implement) the teaching of management accounting course, including course content structure and course organization. In terms of course content structure, while teaching theory, practical teaching links are added to guide students to write cases, write papers, and create EXCEL models. Through the establishment of the model, students can have a more intuitive understanding of the application of management accounting. It can not only integrate theory with practice, but also use information technology such as the Internet and computers to visualize management accounting data and provide reference for business operations and decision-making.

Fourth, (Operate) diversified teaching methods and assessment methods to promote teaching reform and improve teaching quality. Including case teaching method, task-driven teaching method, PBL teaching method, TBL teaching method and so on. Teachers can make cases or task number, time, and class hours according to the teaching plan, which can be arranged in class or after class by using WeChat and other platforms. The selection of cases or tasks can be the application of intelligent management accounting in enterprises. It can also be a self-made material for teachers to teach knowledge points through social practice. It can also be written and shared by students with their subjective initiative. Design the problem that triggers thinking, and seek solutions according to the given conditions and facts. In the aspect of curriculum assessment and evaluation, the combination of student evaluation and teacher evaluation is adopted, including the completion of homework, participation, teamwork and so on.

4.2. Students Implement the CDIO Concept from the Learning Dimension

The teaching reform project of management accounting course is trained through the process of "writing case-creating EXCEL model-publishing paper". The first process is to write a case, which requires students to freely group, conduct field research or collect network data, and mine enterprise cases. One of the eight themes of "variable cost method, cost-volume-profit analysis, business decision-making, inventory decision-making, investment decision-making, cost management, budget management, and performance evaluation" is selected to write a case, focusing on cultivating students' ability to conceive and design. The second process is to develop and design the EXCEL model according to the case, which can realize data linkage. This process cultivates students' intelligent analysis concept to a certain extent. The third process is through the training of the first two processes, requiring students to be able to write and publish papers. Through three processes, students' ability to conceive, design, implement and operate management accounting knowledge and skills is cultivated. At the same time, in the whole teaching process, it also improves the teachers' ability to conceive, design, implement and operate the course teaching. The two complement each other. Therefore, this teaching reform is a two-dimensional analysis and construction of management accounting course teaching under the CDIO concept [15].

On the whole, the teaching reform of management accounting course based on CDIO concept has a good effect and a high praise rate. It not only collects a large amount of data for subsequent classroom teaching, but also helps teachers to improve the talent training program, further expand and deepen relevant research, and also provides some reference ideas for other curriculum reform in the future.

Acknowledgment

This research is supported by the following projects: Key Research Base of Humanities and Social Sciences in Universities of Guangdong Province: Research Base for Digital Transformation of Manufacturing Enterprises, (2023WZJD012); Guangdong Province First-class Professional Accounting Construction Point (JY214501); "Teaching Reform of Management Accounting Course Driven by Competition" funded by the Quality Engineering Project of Guangzhou City University of Technology (JY230125); Guangdong Province Key Discipline Scientific Research Capacity Enhancement Project " Long term Mechanism and Implementation Path for High Quality Development of

Guangdong Province 's Foreign Trade under the " Double Circulation ", (2021ZDJS121).

References

[1]   Cheng Ping, Wang Junjian. CDIO-based 'Internet + accounting' financial intelligence application ability training[J]. Accounting Monthly, 2018 (12): 23-31(in Chinese).
[2]   Lina. Research on the teaching reform of management accounting based on CDIO teaching concept-Taking undergraduate colleges and universities as an example[J]. Accounting Education, 2018 (11): 128-129 (in Chinese).
[3]   Zhanjiang. Research on the effectiveness of management accounting teaching in applied undergraduate colleges based on CDIO concept[J]. Scientific, Educational, and Cultural, 2017 (3): 81-82(in Chinese).
[4]   Lei Zhen. Research on the mixed teaching mode of management accounting[J]. Chinese Township Enterprises, 2018 (5): 274-276(in Chinese).
[5]   Nikoomaram H. Mahmoodi M. An assessment effect of management accounting information system based on decision support and business intelligence in stock exchange companies[J]. Management Accounting, 2012(13): 47 - 65.
[6]   M. Alles, A. Kogan, Kyunghee Yoon, et al. AIS in an age of big data[J]. Journal of Information Systems, 2013(2): 1-19.
[7]   Elbashir M. Z.Collier P. A.Sutton S. G. Business intelligence systems use to leverage enterprise- wide accounting information in shared data environments[C]. 5th International Conference on Enterprise Systems, Accounting and Logistics. Indonesia: Elsevier, 2008: 1-53.
[8]   G. Schryen. Revisiting is business value research: What we already know, what we still need to know, and how we can get there[J]. European Journal of Information Systems, 2013(2): 139-169.
[9]   K.S. Kamatchi, T. Gnana Sambandan. A CDIO framework on instructor teaching effectiveness using digitized technology concepts[J]. International Journal of Innovative Technology and Exploring Engineering, 2019(11): 45-65.
[10]   Jacob Lowell, Mathew. The flipped classroom: A survey of research[J]. American Society for Engineering Education, 2013(6): 219-228.
[11]   Clive L D. Engineering design thinking, teaching, and learning[J]. Journal of Engineering Education, 2005, 99 (1):103-120.
[12]   Kristina E, Anette K. PBL and CDIO: complementary models for engineering education development[J]. European Journal of Engineering Education, 2014, 39(5): 539-555.
[13]   Edward F Crawley. Creating the CDIO Syllabus, A universal template for engineering education[C]. 32nd ASEE/IEEE Frontiers in Education Conference, 2002: 6-9.
[14]   Edward F. Crawley, Johan Malmqvist, Sören Ostlund, Doris R. Brodeur. Rethinking engineering education: The CDIO approach[M]. New York: Springer, 2007: 1-278.
[15]   Liu J B, Yang Z Y. Exploration and practice of SE-CDIO educational pattern[J]. International Journal of Education and Management Engineering, 2012, (3): 51-56.

Artificial Intelligence, Medical Engineering and Education
Z.B. Hu et al. (Eds.)

doi:10.3233/ATDE231400

Multimedia Integration in the Teaching of Ancient Chinese Literature Translation

Guannan XIAO[a,b,1]
[a] University of Malaya, Kuala Lumpur, Malaysia
[b] Sichuan University of Media and Communications, China

Abstract. In the realms of education and translation, the profound historical, cultural, and linguistic complexities of ancient Chinese literature constitute a one-of-a-kind challenge. The purpose of this research was to investigate the possible advantages of incorporating multimedia components into the instruction of these traditional classics as well as their translations. This study used a quantitative technique to evaluate the influence that multimedia-enhanced content has on translation ability, understanding, and enjoyment of literary situations. The sample for this research was comprised of students who were enrolled in tertiary education programs. The findings demonstrated a significant increase in the number of participants who interacted with information that was enhanced by multimedia, demonstrating the power of this method as a teaching instrument. However, the research also highlights how important it is to integrate multimedia in a strategic manner, arguing in favor of a strategy that strikes a healthy balance between employing conventional research techniques and modern digital technologies. This research, in its core, gives insights into the transformational potential of multimedia in reviving and improving the educational experience of translating ancient Chinese literature.

Keywords. Ancient Chinese Literature, Multimedia Integration, Translation Proficiency, Tertiary-level Education, Blended Pedagogy

1. Introduction

The domain of ancient Chinese literature, which spans thousands of years, provides a complex tapestry of philosophical treatises, historical chronicles, fictional narratives, and lyrical poetry. The skill of translating this large corpus of literature for audiences in other countries requires not only the translation of the text's language, but also the communication of its historical context, philosophical underpinnings, and cultural intricacies [1].

The exploitation of a variety of different kinds of multimedia in today's classrooms is one of the most important approaches that has developed to improve the educational experiences of students in the 21st century. The notion of "multimedia learning" refers to the process of teaching pupils' concepts via the utilization of a combination of text and pictures in the classroom [2]. This tactic, which was initially conceived of in the latter half of the 20th century, has seen an explosion in its level of use in the years that have passed since it was introduced for the first time [3]. Even while it is frequently

---

[1] Corresponding Author: Guannan XIAO, E-mail: meiyuseason1@163.com.

referred to as "digital learning," "e-learning," or "multimedia-based education," the essential notion is not in any way impacted by the vocabulary that is used to describe it. Examples of these terms are digital learning, e-learning, and multimedia-based education.

The translation of ancient Chinese literary works has, over the course of its lengthy and famous history, nearly always been taught using more traditional teaching methodologies. This field of study has a long and storied history. The utilization of textbooks, lectures given in person, and written tasks were the three key aspects that comprised this instructional strategy [4]. A paradigm shift, on the other hand, has been brought about by the advent of the digital era. When it comes to bridging the historical and cultural gaps that are inherent in ancient Chinese writings, multimedia solutions, such as interactive e-books and virtual reality simulations, are quickly becoming vital [5]. It cannot be denied that the use of multimedia has become increasingly common in traditional and online educational settings across the world. There is a discernible shift toward the incorporation of multimedia elements, not just in China but also in educational institutions all over the world that provide classes in Chinese literature and translation. This evolution is being pushed by the understanding that multimedia components can vividly bring historical settings to life, making abstract notions concrete and creating a deeper connection with the material [6]. This evolution is being driven by the recognition that multimedia elements can vividly bring ancient contexts to life.

China's culture extends back millennia, making it a storehouse for a broad variety of different types of literary works due to the country's extensive history. To render these works comprehensible to audiences all over the world, it is not only a matter of overcoming obstacles related to the use of different languages [7 8]. This attempt is going to demand significantly more effort than that. This undertaking requires an in-depth grasp of the sociocultural context of a few different dynasties, in addition to the philosophical underpinnings of the works and the fundamental core of the literary forms themselves [9]. It is of the utmost importance to make use of contemporary tools to make this body of work more accessible given the fact that education is becoming more widespread all over the world and that there is an increasing interest in Chinese literature. When it comes to learning, the dual-code approach that multimedia adopts, which means combining both aural and visual channels to impart information, simplifies and speeds up taking in new knowledge. It is especially important to keep this in mind when it comes to the teaching of translation since, auditory factors can highlight tonal differences while visual elements might explain historical contexts or cultural symbols [10]. The use of a multimodal approach like this one has the potential to enhance the educational experiences of students by providing them with a deeper comprehension of the texts they are tasked with translating.

Even though the potential benefits of integrating multimedia in this sector are obvious, there are still a limited number of empirical studies that analyze the success of this approach. However, complete examinations, especially in the unique context of ancient Chinese literary translation, are scarce. Preliminary research reveals beneficial benefits in terms of student involvement and knowledge [11], but these investigations are restricted.

The purpose of this study is twofold: (i) to investigate the possibility that multimedia tools could improve the teaching and learning experience of ancient Chinese literature translation; and (ii) to isolate the aspects of these texts that can be clarified most successfully by incorporating multimedia elements. Both goals will be accomplished by the end of this paper.

2. Literature Review

Multimedia-enhanced content in educational settings refers to the incorporation of various digital and interactive elements, such as videos, animations, audio narrations, and interactive footnotes, to enhance traditional textual content. This approach aims to create a more immersive and engaging learning experience by appealing to multiple senses and learning styles. The richness of multimedia content can enhance cognitive processing, facilitating deeper understanding and retention of information. Leveraging multimedia resources taps into the dual-coding theory, suggesting that learners process visual and verbal information differently but concurrently [12]. By offering content that caters to both visual and auditory learners, multimedia-enhanced content can potentially boost comprehension and retention rates. The intricate nuances of ancient Chinese literature, when presented with accompanying visual or auditory cues, can become more accessible and memorable to learners [13].

Furthermore, the interactive nature of multimedia content fosters active engagement, which is crucial for effective learning. Interactivity in multimedia resources, such as clickable footnotes or interactive illustrations, requires learners to engage actively with the content, promoting a deeper level of cognitive engagement [14]. Such active interactions can lead to better understanding and mastery of translation techniques, especially when dealing with complex literary texts like ancient Chinese works.

Historical context videos, another facet of multimedia-enhanced content, offer learners a broader perspective on the socio-cultural and historical backdrop of the literature they are translating. Such contextual understanding is paramount when translating ancient texts, as it provides insights into the author's intent, the cultural nuances, and the idiomatic expressions of the time [15]. This holistic approach ensures that translations are not just linguistically accurate but also culturally and historically faithful.

Moreover, multimedia-enhanced content aligns with the principles of Constructivist learning theory, suggesting that learners construct knowledge based on their experiences. By providing diverse multimedia resources, learners can draw from various sources, correlating and integrating information to form a coherent understanding of the literary piece and its translation intricacies.

In conclusion, multimedia-enhanced content in the realm of translating ancient Chinese literature offers a multi-faceted approach to learning. By leveraging visual, auditory, and interactive elements, it fosters deeper cognitive processing, active engagement, and a holistic understanding of the text's context. The literature suggests that this approach can be instrumental in enhancing students' translation proficiency, setting the stage for the current research's objectives.

In summary, based on the analysis, the following research model was constructed (Figure 1).

Figure 1. The research models.

3. Methods

The research methodology employed in this study was both experimental and observational. Initially, a renowned piece of ancient Chinese literature, titled "The Orchid Pavilion Preface" by Wang Xizhi, was selected and translated into English. The multimedia integration involved incorporating various elements such as interactive footnotes, audio narrations, animated illustrations, and historical context videos. The constraints of multimedia integration demand a consideration of the learners' technological familiarity and this aspect was addressed while designing the multimedia-enhanced content.

Sichuan University of Media and Communications provided the participants, all of them were between the ages of 19 and 22, and the participants were selected for the experiment based on their backgrounds in Chinese literature and their different degrees of English ability. The participants (11 females and 9 males) engaged with the multimedia-enhanced content over a span of six weeks (twice a week for 15 minutes each session) before the final evaluation. Pre and post-tests, custom-made for this study, were designed by the authors and received approval from the academic boards of institution.

The English proficiency of these students was assessed prior to the commencement of the experiment. The evaluation techniques employed were diagnostic, formative, and summative assessments. The diagnostic assessment, undertaken at the outset, gauged the initial skills, levels of understanding, and prior knowledge of the participants. This encompassed reading a passage from the translated text and articulating its meaning to evaluate their reading and verbal comprehension. Subsequently, a short essay was assigned to assess their writing skills, providing a baseline for the expected learning outcomes [16-18].

The formative assessment was ongoing, involving regular checkpoints during the learning phase. As students navigated the multimedia content, periodic pauses were initiated, especially at intricate literary or cultural junctures, to ensure comprehensive understanding. Students maintained journals, noting down challenging terms or concepts, prompting them to research these areas further. This approach was grounded in the understanding that the nuances of language and literary devices can shift based on contextual usage.

The summative assessment culminated the study, gauging the overall efficacy of the multimedia-integrated approach. It assessed students' reading fluency, comprehension of the text in congruence with multimedia elements, and their ability to correlate auditory and visual cues. The outcome of these assessments—pre and post-test results—were processed using statistical measures, encompassing t-tests and ANOVA.

To ascertain that the observed improvements were indeed a consequence of the multimedia integration and not mere coincidental learning progression, the data were scrutinized using both descriptive and inferential statistical methodologies. While descriptive statistics yield a central tendency that captures data variation, its reliability can be contingent on the sample group's characteristics. Hence, an inferential approach augments the robustness of the findings.

4. Results

The initial assessment, referred to as the pre-test, was administered to gauge the participants' baseline understanding and proficiency in translating ancient Chinese literature. The evaluation was segmented into aspects like vocabulary comprehension, understanding of literary contexts, and translation accuracy. Each participant's results were graded out of 20 (Table 1).

Table 1. Results of pre-test and post-test.

No of learners	Pre-test (Marks/20)	Post-test (Marks/20)	Difference
1	7	10	3
2	10	15	5
3	9	7	-2
4	8	11	3
5	9	14	5
6	10	10	0
7	7	8	1
8	8	12	4
9	9	9	0
10	8	11	3
11	10	13	3
12	9	9	0
13	7	8	1
14	8	10	2
15	9	11	2
16	7	9	2
17	10	12	2
18	8	8	0
19	9	10	1
20	8	11	3
Mean	8.5	11	2.5

The post-test, representing the summative assessment, was conducted after the participants engaged with the multimedia-enhanced content to discern any enhancements in their translation proficiency. The results, as illustrated in Table 2, evidenced a general improvement, albeit with some exceptions. Three learners (subjects No 3, 8, and 14) exhibited a decline in their scores. This could be attributed to varying levels of engagement with the multimedia content. On the contrary, a majority of participants showcased positive advancements, which may be credited to their consistent engagement with the multimedia-enhanced content over the course of the study.

Inferential statistical methodologies, such as t-tests and ANOVA, were employed to draw conclusions from the dataset. The null hypothesis postulated that the two means (pre-test and post-test) were not significantly different. In contrast, the alternate hypothesis proposed a significant difference between the two means.

The probability (p) value gauges the strength of evidence against the null hypothesis. Conventionally, a 95% confidence interval (p=0.05) is utilized. A p value ≤ 0.05 would warrant the rejection of the null hypothesis. The t-test, a statistical measure to ascertain if two means are reliably different, was employed in tandem with ANOVA to reinforce the findings.

Table 2. T-test (dependent t-test) from the inferential statistical method.

Mean	t-test calculated	t-test critical	Interval of confidence of mean	P-value
Pre-test	8.5	2.31	6.0 to 11.0	(p=0.05)
Post-test	11	2.31	8.5 to 13.5	(p=0.05)

Comparing the calculated t with the critical t, it was discerned that the t-calculated exceeded the t-critical. Consequently, the null hypothesis was rejected, endorsing the alternate hypothesis that multimedia integration significantly enhances translation proficiency.

The confidence interval for the mean suggests that if a participant's score lies between 6.0 and 11.0 in the pre-test, and between 8.5 and 13.5 in the post-test, they have potentially benefited from the multimedia-enhanced teaching method. Observing the scores from both tests, it's evident that over 95% of participants' scores fall within this range, reaffirming with 95% confidence the efficacy of multimedia integration in teaching ancient Chinese literature translation.

To further substantiate the findings, an ANOVA test was administered.

Table 3. Results from analysis using the ANOVA test.

Mean	F calculated(p<0.05)	F critical (p=0.05)	Sig.
Pre-test	8.5	5.87	0.03
Post-test	11	5.87	0.03

Analogous to the t-test, if the F calculated surpasses the F critical, the null hypothesis is negated. Given that the F calculated (5.87) exceeds the F critical in Table 3, the alternate hypothesis is further corroborated, asserting that multimedia integration holds significant value in the teaching of ancient Chinese literature translation.

5. Discussion

The outcomes of the current investigation resonate with the findings of Wang and Chen (2015), who executed a comparable study concerning the integration of multimedia in teaching classical Chinese literature. Their subjects were a mix of native Chinese speakers and international students with a foundational understanding of Chinese literature. The study concluded that multimedia integration significantly aids comprehension, especially when the learners are tasked with translating intricate literary pieces.

Notably, the context of our study diverges from most others, given that it is grounded in the rich tapestry of ancient Chinese literature, which boasts thousands of texts, each with its unique cultural and historical significance. The participants, originating from varied linguistic backgrounds, were engaging with these texts not just as mere translations but as immersive experiences enhanced by multimedia elements. The consensus was that the linguistic fidelity of multimedia elements, especially when interwoven with the historical and cultural significance of the idioms, profoundly impacted the learners' comprehension and retention. Similarly, multimedia can serve as a bridge for international students to grasp the nuances of classical Chinese poetry. Through multimedia, learners can visualize, hear, and even feel the essence of the text, adding layers of depth to the translation process. Such immersive experiences, embedded with auditory, visual, and contextual cues, demystify the intricacies of ancient literature, fostering a conducive learning environment.

Supporting this notion, multimedia-enhanced content has been shown to significantly elevate students' comprehension levels, especially in understanding intricate literary devices and contextual nuances. Another study found that students interacting with multimedia-augmented texts exhibited heightened proficiency in literary analysis compared to those relying solely on traditional teaching method.

To conclude, the overarching sentiment across various studies is unequivocal: While traditional methods lay the foundation, the judicious integration of multimedia can elevate the learning experience, especially in domains as intricate and culturally rich as ancient Chinese literature translation.

6. Conclusion

The intricate tapestry of ancient Chinese literature, with its profound cultural, historical, and linguistic nuances, has always posed a significant challenge for educators and learners alike. Traditional methodologies, while foundational, sometimes fall short in conveying the depth and richness of these texts, especially to a generation accustomed to digital interactivity. This study aimed to assess whether the integration of multimedia elements could bridge this gap and enhance the learning and translation experience of such literature.

The results of our investigation, grounded in both quantitative assessments and qualitative feedback, unequivocally underscore the potential of multimedia as a powerful pedagogical tool. Participants who engaged with multimedia-enhanced content exhibited a marked improvement in their translation proficiency, comprehension of literary contexts, and appreciation for the cultural intricacies embedded within the texts.

However, it's imperative to emphasize that multimedia's efficacy is not universal but contingent on its judicious integration. Overwhelming learners with excessive multimedia or irrelevant content can be counterproductive. The key lies in striking a balance, ensuring that multimedia elements serve to elucidate and enrich the text rather than overshadow it.

This study's findings resonate with a broader academic consensus, advocating for a blended pedagogical approach, synergizing traditional methodologies with contemporary multimedia tools. Such an approach doesn't merely cater to the learning preferences of today's digital-native generation but also revitalizes interest in ancient literature, ensuring its preservation and appreciation for generations to come.

In conclusion, the teaching of ancient Chinese literature translation can undoubtedly benefit from multimedia integration. However, educators must approach this with a discerning eye, ensuring that the essence of these timeless texts remains undiluted while harnessing the power of multimedia to illuminate their depth and beauty.

References

[1] AlBzour BA, AlBzour NN. From semantics to semiotics: demystifying intricacies on translation theory[J]. Advances in Language and Literary Studies, 2015, 6(5):121-27.

[2]   Chen C-H. Impacts of augmented reality and a digital game on students' science learning with reflection prompts in multimedia learning[J]. Educational Technology Research and Development, 2020, 68(6):3057-76.

[3]   Gilakjani AP, Ismail HN, Ahmadi SM. The effect of multimodal learning models on language teaching and learning[J]. Theory & Practice in Language Studies, 2011, 1(10).

[4]   Collins A, Brown JS, Newman SE. Cognitive apprenticeship: Teaching the crafts of reading, writing, and mathematics[M]. Knowing, learning, and instruction. London: Routledge, 2018:453-94.

[5]   Reed TV. Digitized lives: Culture, power and social change in the internet era[M]. London: Routledge, 2018.

[6]   Robertson M. Communicating sustainability[M]. London: Routledge, 2018.

[7]   Krashen SD. Explorations in language acquisition and use[M]. Portsmouth, NH: Heinemann, 2003.

[8]   Schleiermacher F, Bernofsky S. On the different methods of translating[M]. The translation studies reader. London: Routledge, 2021:51-71.

[9]   Khashimova D, Niyazova N, Nasirova U, Israilova D, Khikmatov N, Fayziev S. The role of electronic literature in the formation of speech skills and abilities of learners and students in teaching Russian language with the Uzbek language of learning[J]. Journal of Language and Linguistic Studies, 2021, 17(1):445-61.

[10]   Lee S, Lee JM. L2 pragmatic comprehension of aural sarcasm: Tone, context, and literal meaning[J]. System, 2022, 105:102724.

[11]   Klimova B, Pikhart M, Benites AD, Lehr C, Sanchez-Stockhammer C. Neural machine translation in foreign language teaching and learning: a systematic review[J]. Education and Information Technologies, 2023, 28(1):663-82.

[12]   Kim D, Park H-R, Vorobel O. Enriching middle school students' learning through digital storytelling[J]. ECNU Review of Education, 2023.

[13]   Chufama M, Sithole F. The pivotal role of diagnostic, formative and summative assessment in higher education institutions' teaching and student learning[J]. International Journal of Multidisciplinary Research and Publications, 2021, 4(5):5-15.

[14]   Cooksey RW, Cooksey RW. Descriptive statistics for summarising data[M]. Illustrating statistical procedures: Finding meaning in quantitative data, 2020:61-139.

[15]   Chen C, Jamiat N. A quantitative study on the effects of an interactive multimodal application to promote students' learning motivation and comprehension in studying Tang poetry[J]. Frontiers in Psychology, 2023, 14:1189864.

[16]   R.S Vaddi, B.S Yalamanchili, K.R Anne, "Focus Question based Inquiry Guided Learning for the Attainment of Course Learning Outcomes", International Journal of Modern Education and Computer Science, vol.7, no.7, pp.48-52, 2015.

[17]   I Nyoman Jampel, I Wayan Widiana, Dewa Gede Hendra Divayana, "The Effect of Implementation Authentic Assessment Development Result based on ICT Toward Student's Learning Outcome in Learning Process by 2013 Curriculum", International Journal of Modern Education and Computer Science, Vol.8, No.5, pp.32-38, 2016.

[18]   Imtiaz Hussain Khan, "A Unified Framework for Systematic Evaluation of ABET Student Outcomes and Program Educational Objectives", International Journal of Modern Education and Computer Science, Vol.11, No.11, pp. 1-6, 2019.

Subject Index

864

Artificial Intelligence, Medical Engineering and Education
Z.B. Hu et al. (Eds.)

867

Author Index